ALSO BY LOU CANNON

Ronnie and Jesse: A Political Odyssey

The McCloskey Challenge

Reporting: An Inside View

Reagan

Lou Cannon

PRESIDENT REAGAN

The Role of a Lifetime

Simon & Schuster

New York   London   Toronto   Sydney   Tokyo   Singapore

Simon & Schuster
Simon & Schuster Building
Rockefeller Center
1230 Avenue of the Americas
New York, New York 10020

Designed by Levavi & Levavi
Picture Research by Natalie Goldstein

Manufactured in the United States of America

10   9   8   7   6   5   4   3   2   1

Library of Congress Cataloging-in-Publication Data
Cannon, Lou.
   President Reagan: the role of a lifetime/Lou Cannon.
      p.   cm.
   Includes bibliographical references.
   1. Reagan, Ronald.   2. United States—Politics and government—1981–
1989.   I. Title.
E877.C35   1991
973.92—dc20   81-8980
                                                                            CIP

ISBN 0-671-54294-X

To Mary, with love and appreciation

CONTENTS

Contents

THE ROLES OF RONALD REAGAN

Ronald Reagan and Nancy Reagan are all smiles during a final campaign stop in Manchester, New Hampshire, on February 26, 1980. Reagan's victory that day launched him on the road to the presidency.

President Reagan, confident of reelection, receives an athletic jacket after a speech in Tri-City Airport in Saginaw, Michigan, on November 2, 1984, four days before his landslide victory over Walter Mondale.

THE POLITICIAN

THE COMFORTER

Nancy Reagan wipes away tears while President Reagan prays during a ceremony at Camp Lejeune, North Carolina, on November 4, 1983. The ceremony honored U.S. servicemen killed in the Beirut suicide bombing and during the invasion of Grenada.

President Reagan prepares to assure the nation that "we will never forget" the seven Americans who perished aboard the space shuttle *Challenger* on January 28, 1986.

THE STATESMAN

President Reagan and Soviet leader Mikhail Gorbachev shake hands at the end of their first summit in Geneva on November 21, 1985. The two then signed a pledge to reduce the nuclear arsenals of the two superpowers.

British Prime Minister Margaret Thatcher is welcomed by her friend President Reagan to the White House on February 26, 1981. This was the beginning of the most enduring personal alliance of the Reagan years.

The 40th anniversary of D-Day was commemorated in a ceremony on Utah Beach in Normandy on June 6, 1984. From left are Prime Minister Pierre Trudeau of Canada, Queen Beatrix I of the Netherlands, King Olav V of Norway, King Baudouin I of Belgium, President François Mitterrand of France, Queen Elizabeth II of Britain, Grand Duke Jean of Luxembourg and President Reagan.

THE GREAT COMMUNICATOR

President Reagan surprises the nation with an appeal for an anti-missile defense system, subsequently known as the Strategic Defense Initiative or "Star Wars," on March 23, 1983. While many scientists scoffed at SDI, it won widespread public support.

Reagan was less persuasive as a communicator when he did not have a script. Here, he fends off questions from reporters on defense spending after signing the annual Economic Report on February 5, 1985, in the Oval Office of the White House.

THE HERO

Recuperating after the January, 1981, assassination attempt, Reagan reviews a photo of the White House staff posing on the steps of the Executive Building.

"Ronnie," as she called him, was always a hero to Nancy Reagan. This picture was taken on January 29, 1984. Reagan had just announced he would seek a second term, which the first lady had initially opposed.

PHOTO CREDITS:

Jean Louis Atlan/Sygma—2, 9, 11
Owen Franklin/Sygma—6
Ledru/Sygma—7
Ray Lustig/*The Washington Post*—3, 8
Michel Phillippot/Sygma—5
Sygma—10
UPI/Bettmann—1, 4

ACKNOWLEDGMENTS

Many people made this book possible. My greatest debt is to my wife, Mary Shinkwin Cannon, to whom this book is dedicated. She did most of the research, prepared the chapter notes and bibliography and served throughout as editor, critic and friend. It is an understatement to say that this book could never have been written without her.

Nor would it have been written without the encouragement of my editors at *The Washington Post*, who were most patient and understanding when the completion of this project took a year longer than originally intended. These editors, all of them also authors, are Benjamin Bradlee, Leonard Downie and Robert Kaiser.

I owe a debt of gratitude to my editor at Simon and Schuster, Alice Mayhew, who believed in this book from the beginning, made many constructive suggestions during the course of editing it and was generous in seeing that I had the resources to complete it. And I am also in the debt of my agent, Kristine Dahl, who was always encouraging when encouragement was most necessary, and her helpful assistant, Gordon Kato. I also appreciate the efforts made by George Hodgman, Sophie Sorkin, and others at Simon and Schuster in this book's behalf.

Six friends of considerable professional accomplishment read the book in manuscript, providing pertinent opinions and detecting errors. Three are colleagues at *The Washington Post:* the nonpareil political correspondent David S. Broder; my former editor on the national staff, Peter Silberman; and longtime State Department correspondent Don

Oberdorfer, who made valuable suggestions for the chapters dealing with foreign policy. The other readers were the inimitable writer and scholar William Lee Miller of the University of Virginia, who provided useful criticisms of every chapter; Bill Plante, who covered the Reagan administration for CBS News and shared his insights; and my eldest son, Carl Cannon, national political correspondent for Knight-Ridder Newspapers. Much of the research for the sections of the book dealing with AIDS and poverty during the Reagan years was Carl's work.

Gwen Rubinstein, formerly of OMB Watch, did much of the early research on this book with skill and competence. Her research on adult children of alcoholics was of particular value. Gwen was also principally responsible for the organization of 1,800 files on the Reagan presidency. That these files were in existence was primarily due to the work of my friend James Schwartz of *The Washington Post,* who kept them updated for many years. Michelle Hall, during her years as a researcher for *The Post's* national staff, made many contributions. Mary Drake transcribed my taped interviews with unusual diligence and competence.

I truly appreciate the cooperation of Ronald Reagan, both for this book and my earlier biographies. While in the midst of working on his own memoirs, he took time in his usual cheerful fashion to grant three interviews. My thanks also to Nancy Reagan for her insightful interviews.

Many longtime friends and advisers of Reagan were helpful, among them Stuart Spencer, Michael Deaver, Edwin Meese, Paul Laxalt, Richard Wirthlin, A. C. Lyles, the late William French Smith and the late Bill Roberts. William F. Buckley shared his political and personal insights about the Reagans with typical generosity. The same is true of columnist George Will, whose observations were especially useful.

All of Reagan's four White House chiefs of staff—James Baker, Donald Regan, Howard Baker and Kenneth Duberstein—provided valuable interviews. So did Reagan national security advisers Richard Allen, William Clark, Robert (Bud) McFarlane, Frank Carlucci and Colin Powell. Reagan's other national security adviser, John Poindexter, declined to be interviewed after he left the administration, but I have drawn upon two useful interviews that I conducted with Poindexter during his White House years.

Many former members of Reagan's staff and cabinet gave enlightening interviews. I am particularly thankful to Reagan's secretaries of state, Al Haig and George Shultz, and his secretaries of defense, Caspar Weinberger and Frank Carlucci. John Tower, Brent Scowcroft and

Edmund Muskie, the members of the President's Special Review Board that investigated the Iran-contra affair, were highly cooperative. So was the board's chief of staff, Rhett Dawson. I especially appreciate White House special counsellor David Abshire, whose careful records were beneficial in my reconstruction of events during the period of the Tower Board's inquiry.

President Bush took time from his busy schedule to discuss his role during the Reagan years. I appreciate it. Many other officials in the Reagan administration who gave useful interviews for this book are listed alphabetically below. I want to particularly thank Kenneth Adelman, Richard Darman, David Gergen and Richard Perle for their assistance.

Landon Parvin, a speechwriter for both Ronald and Nancy Reagan, shared his candid observations and encouraged me when I was discouraged. I also appreciate the help given by other former White House speechwriters, especially Anthony Dolan, Peggy Noonan and Bently Elliott.

My colleagues at *The Post* provided information and moral support. I am especially grateful for the help of David Hoffman, my colleague in covering the White House during many of the Reagan years. David shared his notes, interviews and informed opinions and guided me in the use of the computer system on which this book was written. Another colleague, the esteemed financial writer John M. Berry, read and corrected the chapter dealing with Reagan's economic policy. Joe Pichirallo helped with the Iran-contra chapters. Bob Woodward was of assistance on many matters and a consistent source of encouragement. Others at *The Post* who helped include Stuart Auerbach, Bruce Brown, Ann Devroy, Helen Dewar, Karen DeYoung, Tom Edsall, Judith Havemann, Gwen Ifill, Jerry Knight, Ruth Marcus, Joanne Omang, Walter Pincus, Donnie Radcliffe, Megan Rosenfeld and George Wilson. I am indebted to Jennifer Belton, Kathy Foley, Harris Worchell and Kim Klein of *The Post*'s library staff and to the staff of the News Systems of *The Washington Post.* Jay Mathews, chief of the Los Angeles bureau, was supportive and most patient in waiting for me to complete the book and join the bureau.

Many who work for other publications also assisted. Strobe Talbott of *Time,* an authority on arms control issues, shared his expertise. William Safire of *The New York Times* helped on various details in his usual good-humored way. Doyle McManus of the *Los Angeles Times,* co-author of *Landslide,* assisted in tracking down the elusive casualty statistics of the Central American conflict. Others who helped include George Condon of Copley Newspapers, Gene Gibbons of Reuters, Albert Hunt of *The Wall Street Journal, Time* librarian Anne Moffett, Jeremiah O'Leary of *The Washington Times,* Martin Salditch of *The Riverside Press–Enterprise,* Barrett Seaman of *Time* and columnists Charles Krauthammer and Ed Yoder. Robert Schmidt, a longtime Sacramento correspondent for *The Long Beach Independent–Press Telegram,* was kind enough to send me his Reagan files.

I appreciate the cooperation of the Gridiron Club and particularly of three members: Charles McDowell of the *Richmond Times-Dispatch,* James McCartney of Knight-Ridder Newspapers and Warren Weaver of *The New York Times.*

Howard Gardner of Harvard University, author of *Frames of Mind: The Theory of Multiple Intelligences,* contributed a useful interview on the nature of Reagan's intelligence, or, as he would say, "intelligences." He also read Chapter 8, where this subject is examined.

National archivist Don Wilson guided me in the right direction on different occasions. Misty Church, who assisted Reagan in the research for his memoirs, tracked down hard-to-find anecdotes and quotations. Kathy Osborne, Reagan's personal secretary, checked her records at my request on several occasions. Aaron Breitbart of the Simon Wiesenthal Center in Los Angeles put me on the track of Nazi death camp films essential to an important story in this book.

Martin Anderson, author of the important book *Revolution,* and his wife, Annelise Anderson, former Reagan administration officials now based at the Hoover Institution at Stanford University, shared information and observations. Access to Reagan material in the Hoover files was provided by Charles Palm and Pruda Lood. Tom Henriksen made it possible for me to spend a week at Hoover in productive research. W. Glenn Campbell contributed a useful interview based on his long association with Reagan. Rita Ricardo-Campbell and Brenda McClean, among others at the Hoover Institution, also helped.

I appreciate the assistance of David Johnson and Steve Kosiak at the Center of Defense Information, Nancy Katz of the presidential libraries office at the National Archives and Diana Hart of Ford's Theatre.

All biographers are in the debt of other biographies and historians. Books that were particularly useful in addition to Anderson's *Revolution* were *Gambling with History* by Laurence Barrett, *Banana Diplomacy* by Roy Gutman, *Reaganomics* by William Niskanen and *Secrets of the Temple* by my friend and former editor William Greider, now of

Rolling Stone. I have drawn upon my two earlier biographies of Reagan and appreciate the help of those who performed the research and otherwise assisted in those books, especially the research of Tom Kizzia on the James Watt years at the Department of the Interior.

My personal thanks to Garry Wills, author of *Reagan's America,* for generously sharing Reagan material that came his way, his understanding of Reagan's role on screen and off and his many words of encouragement. He never failed to respond to a call for assistance. The same can be said of Terry Eastland, a Justice Department official during the Reagan administration and author of a useful book soon to be published on the Reagan and Bush presidencies. Eastland's manuscript and his comments were of particular help for the sections on ethics and on the courts in the final chapter of this book.

William Quandt and Geoffrey Kemp, National Security Council staff specialists on the Middle East in the Carter and Reagan administrations, respectively, were of special help on the Lebanon chapter.

I also wish to thank Elliott Abrams, Edward Anhalt, Rich Armitage, Kevin Baine, Letitia Baldrige, Michael Ball, Will Ball, Michael Barone, Marybel Batjer, Gary Bauer, Viktor Belenko, Steve Bell, Mark Belnick, James Billington, John Block, Ronald Boster, Arnold Burns, Joe Canzeri, Robert Carleson, Lynne Cheney, Richard Cheney, Jud Clark, Elaine Crispen, Arthur Culvahouse, Lloyd Cutler, Mitch Daniels, Patti Davis, Fred De Cordova, Pete Domenici, Robert Donovan, Bruce Drake, Stuart Eizenstat, Bert Ely, Jane Erkenbach, Fritz Ermarth, Frank Fahrenkopf, Linda Faulkner, Fred Fielding, Marlin Fitzwater, Michael Fix, Gail Fossler, Richard Fox, Craig Fuller, Stephen Jay Gould, Robin Gradison, Willis Gradison, Katharine Graham, Ed Gray, Alan Greenspan, Richard Helms, Anne Higgins, Jacqueline Hill, Dan Howard, Mary Hoyt, William Hyland, Fred Iklé, Jim Jones, Kenneth Khachigian, James J. Kilpatrick, Robert Kimmitt, Al Kingon, Jeane Kirkpatrick, Jim Kuhn, Robert Lindsey, Frank Mankiewicz, John (Tex) Reagan McCrary, Rodney McDaniel, John McMorris, Richard Neustadt, Lyn Nofziger, Robert Oakley, M. B. Oglesby, Bob Orben, John Pike, Neil Reagan, Kathy Reid, Nancy Reynolds, Peter Rodman, Buddy Roemer, John F. W. Rogers, Ed Rollins, Donald Rumsfeld, Fred Ryan, Henry Salvatori, William Seidman, Ann Shinkwin, Robert Sims, William Sittman, Karna Small, Karen South, Larry Speakes, Duncan Spencer, Stanley Sporkin, George Steffes, George Stevens, Robert Strauss, Kent Taylor, Howard Teicher, Edward Teller, Dennis Thomas, Helen Thomas, John Tuck, Margaret Tutwiler, Jack Valenti, John Vessey,

Peter Wallison, Paul Wassmansdorf, James Watkins, Mark Weinberg, Kirk West, Charles Wick, Tom Winter, Paul Wolfowitz and many members of the White House staff.

To all of these people, my deepest thanks. Any mistakes, errors or infelicities of expression in this book are my fault and responsibility. The credit deserves to be shared with all who helped.

PREFACE

My first encounter with Ronald Reagan occurred late in the autumn of 1965 when he visited Sacramento during a trip around the state to drum up interest in his candidacy for governor. Reagan gave a short speech, answered a few questions from a curious audience and stayed afterward to chat with reporters, many of whom remembered him as the host of *General Electric Theater* or *Death Valley Days*. A former Democrat who had become a Republican, Reagan was then a supposedly washed-up actor who was in the process of changing careers. On October 27, 1964, he had stirred conservatives out of their socks with a rousing nationally televised speech in behalf of Republican presidential candidate Barry Goldwater. But Goldwater had been demolished by Lyndon Johnson in the election the following week, and Reagan in 1965 bore a "Goldwater Republican" label. The Democrats were so unimpressed by Reagan that many of them were rooting for him to win the Republican nomination, certain that he would be defeated by Democratic Governor Pat Brown.

Reagan made a good impression on his audience in Sacramento. He readily confessed that he knew little about government but suggested that his lack of experience would give him the advantage of taking a fresh look at California's problems. He answered questions sensibly and without a hint of guile. He was as pleasant in response to skeptical questioners as he was to friendly ones. He fascinated me. What I noticed most was that everyone seemed to like him, the reporters included.

When my editor at the *San Jose Mercury–News* asked me afterward what I thought of Reagan, I said that I couldn't understand why anyone would want to run against such a self-assured and friendly man. And I still don't fully understand why the Democrats regarded Reagan as such an easy mark. Subsequently, he defeated Brown by nearly a million votes, which was no small feat. Although he bore the scars of two-term incumbency, Pat Brown was a capable politician who had routed Richard Nixon in the gubernatorial race four years earlier. How had Reagan done it? And why was it, after his victory, that he so totally dominated the California political landscape? On one level he seemed the "citizen-politician" he claimed to be, almost completely ignorant of even civics-book information about how bills were passed or how an administration functioned. But on another level, he seemed the most consummate and effective politician I had ever met.

The late Carey McWilliams once told me that the essential motive of his books—and he wrote great books about California, farm workers, racial prejudice, anti-Semitism and other issues—was to explain to himself phenomena that he did not fully understand. That was my original reason for writing about Reagan. My first book, *Ronnie and Jesse: A Political Odyssey,* published in 1969, was a dual biography of Reagan and the remarkable politician Jesse Unruh, who revolutionized the California state legislature and lost to Reagan in the gubernatorial election of 1970. A subsequent biography, *Reagan,* published in 1982, was an account of Reagan's early years, his rise to the presidency and his first year in the White House.

This is the third and last book in what became an unintended trilogy on Ronald Reagan. Its focus is on his performance in the presidency. But since Reagan is among the most personal of our chief executives, it is impossible to make sense of his presidency without also examining his life. This I have tried to do, drawing upon scores of interviews with Reagan during the past quarter century, including three for this book, and hundreds of interviews with his former aides, advisers, friends, scholars and critics. I have also relied upon my reporting for more than a thousand articles and columns written as senior White House correspondent for *The Washington Post* during the Reagan presidency.

In the presidency, as in the governorship, Reagan seemed such a simple and straightforward man that it was often said of him that "what you saw was what you got." After he had been president for a while, however, the prevailing view in Washington became that what the people most often saw was the work of his staff, his cabinet, his political advisers or his wife. This low opinion of Reagan deprived him of credit for some of his accomplishments but also spared him the blame for his shortcomings. And it helped Reagan remain an elusive figure, for all his popularity. This book is an effort to penetrate the illusion of the Reagan presidency and to write about him as he truly was.

Lou Cannon

Summerland, California
November 5, 1990

BACK
TO THE FUTURE

One of his magics is looking to the future.

GEORGE SHULTZ,
February 13, 1989[1]

He had always prided himself on knowing how to make an exit, and when the end came, on a day of sun and shadows he called bittersweet, Ronald Reagan understood exactly how to leave the stage. An aide, thinking about it later, would say that Reagan had made fifty-three movies and that being on a movie set was like being cooped up in the White House with your crew all those years. Reagan was ready for the freedom of California and a new role. But some members of his staff were not quite ready and Reagan, recognizing this, tried not to seem overly cheerful during the scenes leading up to his exit. He was mindful that he was president until the curtain fell at noon.

It was 9:50 A.M. on January 20, 1989, when Reagan slipped into the Oval Office for a last look at the room that had been his grandest set. The walls were bare. Gone were the resplendent color photos of his presidency and a bronze saddle that had given the Oval Office a western look. Gone, too, was the barrel chair he had brought with him from California for his Oval Office desk. In its place was a worn chair that had been wheeled in from somewhere when the office was swept clean of personal mementos the preceding afternoon after Reagan finished his last appointment with speechwriter Landon Parvin and departed to the White House family quarters. Reagan looked at the chair, cocking his head as he often did when something was out of place. He walked over to the desk, where he had always worked in coat and tie as a gesture of respect for the presidency, and tried out the chair. The desktop was bare except for a telephone. Tucked in a drawer inside the desk was a note of encouragement he had written the day before for George Bush on stationery emblazoned with the slogan "Don't let the turkeys get you down." * Reagan picked up the phone and asked the White House operator to place a call to Sue Piland, the oldest daughter of his former longtime aide Lyn Nofziger. It was a terrible time for the Nofzigers. Sue Piland was dying of cancer and her father had been sentenced to a prison term for illegal lobbying after he left the White House.† The operator could not reach the daughter in the hospital and Reagan had her call the Nofziger residence, where Lyn's wife Bonnie answered the phone. Turning his back to the aides and the Secret Service agents who had accompanied him into the Oval Office, Reagan cradled the phone and sought to comfort her. It was the last telephone call of his presidency. A White House photographer took a picture of Reagan making the call, and his personal secretary Kathy Osborne later sent it to the Nofzigers.

Meanwhile, Reagan's personal assistant Jim Kuhn had been busy at the second phone in the room, which was tucked away on a wooden stand that fit under an end table near the fireplace. Kuhn, preoccupied with the logistics of the final day, knew he would be with Reagan on the flight west and was not sentimental about leaving the Oval Office. He dreaded the leave-taking in California, but he had other things on his mind this morning. Following a daily routine, Kuhn used the other Oval Office telephone to call Vice President Bush and Chief of Staff Kenneth Duberstein to inform them that "Rawhide," as Reagan was known in the code of the Secret Service, was in his office. Bush was gone forever from the vice president's office, but Duberstein joined Reagan from his office two doors down the hall as he was completing the Nofziger call. With him came Reagan's sixth and most popular

---

* The note said, "Dear George, You'll have moments when you want to use this particular stationery. Well, go to it. George, I treasure the memories we share and wish you all the very best. You'll be in my prayers. God bless you and Barbara. I'll miss our Thursday lunches. Ron."

† Nofziger's conviction was overturned on June 27, 1989, by a federal appeals court on a 2-1 vote. The court majority said that the prosecution had "offered no evidence" showing that Nofziger was aware that his lobbying activities had violated the law.

national security adviser, Lieutenant General Colin L. Powell, who had hitched a ride to the White House with Duberstein that morning after his official car and driver were taken from him. Duberstein was struck by the bareness of the room, from which all signs of Reagan had been removed. He did his business quickly, standing in front of the desk and talking distinctly and loudly to the president even though Reagan was wearing his hearing aids. White House chiefs of staff in the Reagan administration were expected to know the daily script, and Duberstein made a point of being meticulously prepared. He ran through the scenes of the day, telling Reagan what he needed to know about the inauguration ceremony, the departure and his arrival speech at Los Angeles International Airport. He also gave Reagan a rundown on last-minute phone calls, including his conversation with Senator Orrin Hatch of Utah, a conservative who had written Reagan urging him to pardon Oliver North.

Reagan listened to Duberstein without comment, which was often his reaction to even his highest-ranking aides. He had thought of pardoning Nofziger and former key aide Michael K. Deaver, who had been convicted of perjury after an investigation into his lobbying activities. The former aides had made it easy on him by making it known that they considered themselves innocent and not candidates for pardons. Nofziger even said publicly that he would refuse one if it was offered. Reagan also had considered pardoning North, whom he had once called a "national hero," and he especially wanted to pardon former national security adviser Robert C. (Bud) McFarlane, a tragic figure of the Iran-contra affair who had in a moment of despair tried to take his own life and subsequently pleaded guilty to a misdemeanor charge of lying to Congress. "I really want to do something for Bud" was the way Reagan had put it even before the decision came to him.[2] But those closest to Reagan—his wife Nancy, Duberstein and longtime political adviser Stuart K. Spencer—opposed all pardons for former aides on grounds they would blemish his presidency. Reagan had heeded the recommendations, despite misgivings about doing nothing for McFarlane. He had no desire to reopen the question on this final day.

What Reagan wanted was to get on with the last act. He reached into his coat pocket and removed a deceptively plain white laminated card that had the power to summon hell on earth. When properly inserted into the black leather "football" carried by the president's military aide, the white card authorized the launching of nuclear missiles. Reagan had carried the card with him for eight years and said early on that he looked forward to the day when it would not be needed by an American president. Reagan did not think he needed it now, on the last day of a presidency that had begun in bitter U.S.-Soviet hostility and ended in the warm glow of what Reagan called "a new era" in superpower relations. In the final hours of his presidency, in the White House where he and Soviet leader Mikhail Gorbachev had signed the first treaty eliminating a class of nuclear weapons, the white card seemed an anachronism of a darker era and Reagan wanted to get rid of it. "Who do I give *this* to?" Reagan said quizzically. "You can't get rid of it yet," said Powell, who told him that the card would be taken from him after Bush was sworn in. Reagan shrugged and put the card back in his pocket. He looked at Powell, an artillery officer and the first black to serve as national security adviser. Like Reagan, Powell had a commanding presence and a sense of history. In his final briefing he said simply, "The world is quiet today, Mr. President."[3]

It was quiet now in the Oval Office, too. Kuhn glanced at his watch. Reagan had spent a half hour in the Oval Office. Kathy Osborne and the other aides, who had been joined by White House press secretary Marlin Fitzwater, were fighting memories and tears. "It was strange to think he was never going to walk in the office as president again," Osborne thought.[4] Reagan was composed. He waited for the news photographers who had been summoned to take pictures of the leave-taking, but wanted pictures of themselves with the president before they did their business. That was fine with Reagan, who valued pictures and treated photographers with respect. He posed with the photographers, taking his time and joking with them, and then posed for them as he gave a last sweeping look at the bare Oval Office. "It looks like they got everything," he said. It was 10:30 A.M. and Reagan had spent forty minutes in the Oval Office. Without saying more, he turned and walked out into the colonnade beside the Rose Garden.

The leave-taking proved more difficult for Nancy Reagan than for her husband. Nancy Reagan was a trouper, too, and also recognized the value of a graceful exit, but she liked Washington and loved being first lady. On August 15, 1988, at the Republican convention that nominated Bush, she had told luncheon guests who came to honor her that there were times to enter, times to stay, times to depart. "We've had a wonderful run," she had said. "But the time has come for the Bushes to step into the political leading roles and for the Reagans to step into the wings."[5] When the time actually came, however, she could not bear to go. "Don't say anything nice about me," she warned her staff.[6] She knew she would cry if anyone complimented her, and when, respecting her wishes, no one did, she cried anyway.

She was not alone. After the inaugural ceremony the Reagans and Bushes walked together down the steps of the East Front of the Capitol and across a red carpet stretching thirty yards to a Marine helicopter. Reagan turned and saluted his successor. "I was trying to keep the tears from flooding down my cheeks," Bush said later, knowing that he had not fully succeeded. "After eight years of friendship, it's pretty tough." [7] The new president's campaign manager and secretary of state, James A. Baker III, who had served Reagan for eight years as chief of staff and treasury secretary, made no attempt to hide his feelings. Standing to one side with his wife Susan, the usually reserved Baker wept openly as Ronald Reagan climbed into the helicopter and disappeared from view.[8]

But Reagan was not somber. He had thought about the departure scene beforehand, as he always did about big performances, seeing himself as he would be seen by others, and he was ready to leave. As the helicopter dodged clouds and soared high above the monuments of Washington before heading to Andrews Air Force Base and the last, long flight to California, Reagan played the role of the great comforter, giving solace to his wife as she struggled to control her emotions. When the chopper banked over the White House for a final look, he turned to her and said, in a voice that an aide thought was filled with great tenderness, "There's our little bungalow down there." [9] Nancy Reagan smiled at him with tears running down her cheeks.

Much had been done to change that "little bungalow" in the 2,923 days of the Reagan presidency. Drawing on the budgets of four federal agencies, the administration spent at least $44.6 million to renovate and improve the White House complex [10] in a busy program of reconstruction and repairs not seen in Washington since the presidency of Harry S Truman. The exact figure was kept secret, and reporters piecing together the information from government documents suspected that the actual cost was higher. The subject was sensitive to the Reagans. In addition to the public funds, Nancy Reagan had raised more than $1 million in private donations to remodel and redecorate the White House living quarters.[11] Many who had seen the White House before the remodeling thought the renovation was long overdue, but Nancy Reagan had paid a political price for it and for the high style of the Reagan presidency. Even before the inauguration, she came under fire from those accustomed to the less lavish tone of the Carter presidency.

"Spare us from four years of bombardment concerning the 'elegance' of Nancy Reagan," declared a letter to *Time* magazine protesting a Hugh Sidey column a month before Reagan took office. "Most of us cannot identify with it." [12]

But many did identify with the economic changes that took place in the nation during the Reagan years. In 1980, the year Reagan defeated President Jimmy Carter with the battle cry, "Are you better off today than you were four years ago?" the prime interest rate averaged 15.26 percent, inflation 12.5 percent and civilian unemployment 7.1 percent. For the final year of the Reagan presidency, the comparable figures were 9.32 percent, 4.4 percent and 5.5 percent. [13] The gross national product had nearly doubled [14] and per capita disposable income, highest for whites but higher, too, for blacks and Hispanics, had increased from $9,722 to $11,326. [15] The stock market, recovering from the 1987 crash, continued to soar. The Dow Jones industrial averages stood at 2235.36 on the day Reagan left office, up from 950.68 when he was first inaugurated. Reagan delighted in such statistics, though his recitation of them was sometimes flawed by exaggeration of the interest and inflation rates during the Carter years. He delighted, too, in polls showing that most Americans considered themselves better off as a result of the Reagan presidency. [16]

In his final meeting in the Oval Office the day before his departure, Reagan spoke with quiet pride of his administration's record in maintaining "peace through strength," reducing taxes, lowering inflation, creating jobs and "getting government out of the way of the people." It was Reagan's favorite speech, delivered this time for the benefit of Landon Parvin, who was in the White House to help smooth out the Reagan post-presidential script for his return to California. "The policies that we've set have brought about this prosperity," Reagan said to Parvin, who had heard the message many times before. "Government isn't the answer." [17]

Of all Reagan's core convictions, this statement resonated most clearly throughout his public career. "I have always talked generally on one subject—the growth of government," Reagan told me in 1968, [18] in the second of his eight years as governor of California, a comment as accurate on the last day of his presidency as it was then. But his talk had not been matched by comparable deeds. The steady growth of government that began in 1933 during Franklin D. Roosevelt's New Deal had continued unabated during the Reagan presidency, mocking the claims of both those who favored and those who feared a "Reagan revolution." Reagan had not expected this to happen. In the main economic speech of his 1980 campaign, delivered to the International Business Council in Chicago on September 9, 1980, Reagan had promised to "move boldly, decisively and quickly to control the runaway growth of federal spending, to remove the tax disincentives that are throttling the economy, and to reform the regulatory web that is smothering it." Summing up what he saw as the goals of his presidency, he said, "We must balance the budget, reduce tax rates and restore our defenses."

As candidate and as president, Reagan refused to acknowledge any contradiction in these goals or recognize that he had achieved the last two of them at the expense of the first. The national debt, $908.5 billion when Reagan gave his Chicago speech, had nearly tripled to $2.684.4 trillion by the time he left office.[19] The trade deficit, the difference between what Americans spend for foreign goods and what foreigners spend for American exports, had increased more than fourfold, to $137.3 billion.[20] Foreign investment had also quadrupled, to more than $60 billion.[21] The United States of America, once the world's great creditor nation, had become a debtor on Reagan's watch. Reagan, a free-trader since college days when he was an ardent admirer of FDR, welcomed the foreign investment and was sanguine about the trade imbalance. But he refused to accept any responsibility for the budget deficit, which some economists saw as his most enduring domestic legacy. When the question was put to him, Reagan brushed aside the fact that he had never once submitted a budget proposing the revenues to pay for the programs he thought necessary, and blamed Congress for the deficit. His friend, the conservative writer George F. Will, calculated that the middle six budgets of the administration had produced deficits totaling $1.1 trillion and that Reagan proposed thirteen-fourteenths of that total.[22] Congress had added a relatively insignificant $90 billion to the deficit, or $15 billion a year. "Americans are conservative," Will had said presciently at the onset of the administration. "What they want to conserve is the New Deal."

Nevertheless, the deficit was beginning to take hold as a political issue when Reagan left town. Most Americans more or less shared Reagan's passionate conviction that new taxes were unnecessary, but they also were vaguely uneasy that the prosperity of the Reagan years had been purchased at the expense of their children and grandchildren. "He's been a good-time Charlie," complained history professor Walt Rostow of the University of Texas. "Nothing bad's going to happen on my watch. Screw the future."[23] Reagan pollster Richard B. Wirthlin found that nearly one in five Americans cited the budget deficit as the issue on which they were least happy with Reagan's performance, putting it just behind the Iran-contra affair as a negative of the Reagan presidency. Democratic pollster Peter Hart, taking a national poll after the 1988 election, discovered that the deficit overwhelmed every other issue as a matter of public concern.[24] But the pollsters also recognized that relatively few Americans were willing to make personal sacrifices to bring the deficit under control. Sacrifice was out of fashion during the Reagan years. Reagan had never asked Americans to sacrifice to make things right, even though he had predicted in the Chicago speech that his program would "require the most dedicated and concerted peacetime action ever taken by the American people for their country."

What Reagan *had* asked Americans to do was to "dream heroic dreams"[25] and discard what he considered the corrosive pessimism of the Carter years. In accepting the presidential nomination at the Republican National Convention in Detroit on July 17, 1980, and throughout his presidency Reagan scoffed at the notion "that the United States has had its day in the sun; that our nation has passed its zenith." Reagan believed that America's best days lay ahead. "The American people, the most generous on earth, who created the highest standard of living, are not going to accept the notion that we can only make a better world for others by moving backwards ourselves," he said in his acceptance speech.

Reagan's message proved attractive to young voters, who gave him overwhelming majorities in both 1980 and 1984. It was also appealing to businessmen and entrepreneurs, who welcomed the relaxation of myriad government regulations intended to protect the health and safety of American consumers and to guarantee economic competition. One of the central tenets of Reaganism was that these regulations, though well intended, had hobbled American enterprise. Reagan did his best to get rid of them. While he fell short of his goal, the Reagan package of lower taxes, deregulation and unrelenting optimism had succeeded in spurring economic initiative. New businesses proliferated. Corporations were encouraged to expand and to take over other corporations. "The Reagan years have witnessed one of the greatest waves of mergers, takeovers, and corporate restructurings in history, with the tally standing at more than 25,000 deals worth $2 trillion and still rising," concluded one business writer near the end of the Reagan presidency.[26] In 1980 there were 4,414 individual tax returns filed with the Internal Revenue Service listing adjusted gross income of more than a million dollars. By 1987, in the heyday of "Reaganomics," there were 34,944 such returns.[27]

Critics of the new prosperity managed to remain unimpressed by the longest sustained economic recovery since World War II and the steady advance of American living standards. They viewed the Reagan years as an enshrinement of American avarice, epitomized by the "greed is healthy" speech of convicted Wall Street financier Ivan Boesky. Throughout most of the Reagan presidency the complaints of these critics were drowned out by the clamor of the marketplace. But their voices became louder as the end of the decade neared. A poll of 1,001 American workers between the ages of twenty-five and forty-nine, taken by Chivas Regal and released a few weeks before Reagan left office, found that "three-quarters of the working public would like to see a return to a simpler society with less emphasis on material wealth."[28]

Reagan also often talked as if he preferred a simpler society. He was nostalgic about the past, remembering a boyhood in Dixon, Illinois, when "we didn't live on the wrong side of the tracks, but we lived so close to them we could hear the whistle real loud."[29] His economic references were drawn from the Depression days of his youth, a bond he shared with Americans of his generation. He also shared an American enthusiasm for technological gadgets that made life easier and an American proclivity for endorsing progress in the same breath in which he celebrated memories of things past. He was at once old-fashioned and forward-looking, and frequently sounded as if he wanted to go back to the future. But there was no going back. The new prosperity was accompanied by new technologies that changed the lives of many Americans, carrying some of them along into an era of ease and convenience and leaving others hopelessly behind. When Reagan took office, one in six Americans owned a microwave oven[30] and video cassette recorders were a novelty. By the end of his presidency, three out of four Americans owned a microwave[31] and more than six out of ten owned a VCR.[32] During the buying binge of the last six years of the Reagan administration, Americans purchased 105 million color television sets, 88 million cars and light trucks, 63 million VCRs, 62 million microwave ovens, 57 million washers and dryers, 46 million refrigerators and freezers, 31 million cordless phones and 30 million telephone answering machines.[33] They also purchased sports equipment and machines and diet plans that promised shortcuts to body building, weight reduction and healthier living. Reagan saw the buying spree as a sign that the good life had become available to everyone. He hailed the new health consciousness, which was nothing new to him, and continued to do things the old way. Reagan kept his weight down the old-fashioned way, through disciplined eating and daily physical exercise. The elaborate menus at state dinners did not dim his preference for such simple fare as macaroni and cheese. Video cassette recorders abounded in the White House, but Reagan preferred old movies projected on old-fashioned screens that he and his guests watched while eating popcorn. In an age of airplanes and automobiles Reagan spoke wistfully of traveling by train and horseback. Apart from watching movies, his favorite recreations were horseback riding and clearing brush on his California ranch.

Nancy Reagan was fond of saying that her husband had not changed at all in the nearly four decades she had known him. Some Americans thought this a most appealing quality, but the country had changed immensely during this time and even some of Reagan's admirers thought he had not quite kept up with the changes. His adversaries charged that he was insensitive to the needs of those who had not participated in the bounty of Reaganomics. "At his worst, Reagan made the denial of compassion respectable," said New York Governor Mario Cuomo at the end of Reagan's terms.[34] In a nationally televised pre-Christmas interview a month before he left office Reagan dismissed the problem of the homeless by saying that "a large percentage" of them were "retarded" people who had voluntarily left institutions that would have cared for them.[35] Meanwhile, gay and lesbian activists blamed Reagan for a tardy and inadequate response to the epidemic of acquired immune deficiency syndrome. There were only 199 reported cases of AIDS in 1981.[36] Eight years later more than 55,000 persons had died from this new scourge,[37] exceeding the total of U.S. combat deaths in either the Vietnam War or the Korean War.[38] And the AIDS epidemic was spreading steadily.

Reaganomics had also wrought changes. By 1989 the richest two-fifths of families had the highest share of national income (67.8 percent) and the poorest two-fifths the lowest share (15.4 percent) in the forty years the Census Bureau had been compiling such statistics.[39] "In 1987, one out of five American children lived in poverty—a 24 percent increase over 1979—compared to one out of nine adults," a House committee reported.[40] Many of these children were black. While the black middle class had become more prosperous and numerous during the Reagan years, a huge and largely black underclass, alienated and unattended, had become imbedded in the fabric of urban life. Overall, U.S. murder rates declined slightly[41] during the Reagan years and such other measurements of violence as suicides and violent crime remained virtually unchanged.[42] But it was a different story in the inner cities, where murder, drug addiction and inadequate child nutrition in 1988 conspired to lower black life expectancy for the second year in a row.[43] The gleaming monuments and swaths of green over which the Marine helicopter carried the Reagans to Andrews Air Force Base concealed a war zone in the streets of Washington. "It's an indictment of us all," District of Columbia detective Billy Corby told *The Washington Post* on the last day of 1988. "There's easy access to guns. Everybody's got one. You disrespect someone and you're dead."[44] A record 372 homicides were reported in the District in 1988,[45] an 86 percent increase over the 200 murders that occurred in 1980.[46] Sixty percent of the 1988 killings were drug related,[47] a statistic the District did not even bother to keep in the year Reagan was elected president.

The violence and the drug epidemic troubled the Reagans. Despite the scoffers who claimed she was image-making and the doubters who thought it wouldn't do any good, Nancy Reagan had persisted in her "just say no" campaign against drug use. Reagan called her "my secret weapon" in the fight to reduce drug dependency in America. She ran into opposition on all sides, and a group of determined residents in the small community of Lake View Terrace, twenty miles northwest of downtown Los Angeles, ultimately forced her to withdraw plans for an advanced drug treatment center that would have been named in her honor.[48] Her old, unforgiving foe from the White House, onetime chief of staff Donald T. Regan, bluntly concluded that "just say no" hadn't worked.[49] But by the time the Reagans left office, educational efforts to persuade young people of the danger of cocaine and other drugs appeared to be one of the few things that was working in the nation's losing battle with the drug scourge. In 1988, one study found that only 39 percent of high school seniors reported using illicit drugs during the past year, down from 53 percent in 1980.[50] Not everyone accepted this result as valid, but Reagan, as he always did when he found a favorable statistic, quoted it over and over again. His unquenchable optimism had once led him, during the recession of 1981–82, to pick out the only favorable statistic from a series of charts prepared by aides who were trying to change his policies by convincing him that the economy was going to hell in a handbasket. The attempt failed. Neither aides nor critics could succeed in getting Reagan down.

This optimism was not a trivial or peripheral quality. It was the essential ingredient of an approach to life that had carried Reagan from the backwater of Dixon to fame as a sports announcer and then to the stages of Hollywood and of the world. And it was a fundamental component of his idealistic nationalism, expressed best in the phrase he expropriated from Abraham Lincoln that America is "the last best hope of man on earth."[51] Reagan believed in the magic of individual freedom. He believed that the appeal of free markets and personal freedoms ultimately would prove irresistible to all peoples everywhere. He believed in spreading the gospel of freedom. He believed in the attainability of world peace and in the eventual abolition of nuclear weapons. He believed in himself. "Over time, he converted much of the country to his own views and values," wrote David Gergen, who had served as communications director in the Reagan White House and cautioned against measuring the Reagan legacy merely by statistics. "His more important legacy is how much he changed our minds."[52]

This legacy of optimism was especially important to the two million members of the U.S. armed forces, all of whom now were volunteers. Reagan made it a point to heap praise on these men and women, saying that they served for little pay and less respect "on the frontlines of freedom."[53] In his 1980 campaign he had called the Vietnam War "a noble cause,"[54] and he recognized that the U.S. military establishment remained disaffected and disillusioned by the results and domestic unpopularity of that war. Reagan tried to restore national pride in the military "after a time during which it was shamefully fashionable to deride and even condemn service such as yours."[55] The military responded by honoring Reagan. In a ceremony at Andrews Air Force Base eight days before he left office, Reagan received the grateful tributes of the nation's military leaders and said, in a hoarse voice, that serving as commander in chief was "the most sacred, most important task of the presidency."[56]

This view came from the heart. So, too, did the tributes Reagan received from military families whenever Air Force One landed at U.S. air bases throughout the country or abroad. When Reagan's campaign managers wanted to guarantee a favorable crowd during the low points of his presidency, they often held a rally at a military installation or in a community where military families were numerous. But on this last day of his presidency, the crowd of 1,500 at Andrews Air Force Base was somber, as if those who had come to see him off were saddened by the departure of a friend. Nancy Reagan shivered in the cold wind while her husband reviewed an honor guard for the final time. A sign in the crowd read "Air Force One Flies Once More for the Gipper."[57] Reagan waved from the steps of the plane. Bush had been president for little more than an hour when the Reagans left for California.

Despite the sign in the crowd, Air Force One was not Air Force One anymore. That designation is reserved for whatever plane the president is on, and Reagan was no longer president. The specially fitted Boeing 707 that on this day flew westward with the Reagans and a cadre of aides, guests, reporters and Nancy Reagan's hairdresser had been redesignated "Special Air Mission 27000." It was the same plane Reagan had flown throughout his presidency, stripped of its top-secret communications gear and without any military aides on board. Its special mission was to bring the Reagans home. And unlike the Oval Office now in use by Bush, the plane preserved the illusion of the Reagan presidency for an additional five hours. Color photos of the Reagans with world leaders, aides and congressmen decorated the walls of the plane. Air Force stewards served drinks and a lunch of chicken in lemon wine sauce, rice pilaf and broccoli florets.

Throughout his presidency Reagan's news conferences had been carefully controlled, sometimes by himself, more often by zealous aides who feared that the president would reveal ignorance of his own policies or say something the press thought stupid. He almost never talked to reporters on the plane. But the final act of the Reagan presidency was designed for graciousness, and there were no longer any policy options to give away. Soon after he came aboard, Reagan took off his suit coat and donned a blue Air Force jacket with his name on the left pocket. Then he and Nancy, who was warm again and happy that the departure ceremonies were over, began working their way back to the reporters in the cramped rear compartment of the plane, stopping along the way for hugs and handshakes from their friends and aides. The reporters were happy to see them. Several of them had been White House correspondents throughout the presidency and would be reassigned after this last flight, which was also a turning point in their lives. They asked Reagan about his feelings when he turned the reins of government over to George Bush. Reagan told them he had long been ready for the moment when Bush would take the oath of office. "I was prepared and pleased to see him take it," Reagan said.[58] When a reporter remarked that this didn't mean that Reagan had to like it, he replied, "He was the one I would rather see there doing this than anyone else."[59]

Nancy Reagan, who had suffered miserable press relations during the early days of the presidency but had learned to relax among reporters and give genuine answers to their questions, was also ready for this final news conference. When a reporter asked Reagan about the most important accomplishments of his administration, he gave a longish, set-piece answer centering on economic reforms. She answered the same question by simply murmuring, "A peaceful world."[60] And when a reporter observed that she seemed to be battling tears as Bush praised her husband during the inaugural address, Nancy Reagan acknowledged it and said, "I was moved, I was moved."[61] Reagan said he was happy, sad and relieved, all at the same time. A reporter told him that Bush had said the hardest thing he had to do that day was fight back the tears as the Reagans left. "Well, it's a time of tears for a great many people and certainly for us," Reagan said. "I appreciate it if he felt that way."[62]

But the tears were then put aside on SAM 27000. The reporters, no longer helped and burdened by a White House transcription team and a White House press office that drowned them with paper, set to work transcribing the rare airplane interview from their pocket tape recorders, working together and trying to get the quotes straight. Before they finished, the Reagans had called them back to the plane's center cabin to celebrate with bottles of Korbel Natural champagne and a yellow cake inscribed "The Reagan Years 1981–89." Reagan, still hampered by a bandage on his left hand after minor finger surgery, cut the first piece and had trouble balancing the cake and the champagne. He put the champagne down, as he always did if the choice was between an alcoholic beverage and dessert. Then he told stories of the presidency and of Hollywood and war movies. When I asked him if he had any regrets that he had not served in combat during World War II, he replied without embarrassment that he had not given any thought to it. His eyesight was so bad, he said, that he would not have been called up at all had he not been in the reserves. Nancy, who often stood guard over his answers, felt no need to monitor him this day. She sipped champagne and chatted with reporters about her book and her life in Washington. Soon it was time to land.

The Secret Service was taking no chances on this last day of the Reagan presidency. They had almost lost Reagan outside the Washington Hilton on March 30, 1981, and they were determined to bring him safely home to the new Reagan mansion in Bel-Air. Secret Service agent Timothy J. McCarthy, who had been wounded during the assassination attempt, was Nancy Reagan's lead agent aboard this final flight. Security precautions at Los Angeles International Airport were so strict that the Reagans had been brought in at a location designated as "remote terminal ramp" near the southwest corner of the sprawling terminal. The site was far away from the main terminal and the published information about Reagan's arrival was so deliberately sketchy that only seven hundred supporters had found their way to the welcome-home rally organized by the advance office of the Reagan White House staff. All of the welcomers, including the Salvation Army Tournament of Roses band and the University of Southern California marching band, had passed through magnetometers on their way out onto the tarmac.

The ceremony was supposed to be brief. I was on deadline with my story of the flight for *The Washington Post* and had asked Duberstein and Spencer if Reagan planned anything special in his arrival speech. "Don't worry, he isn't going to say anything," Spencer said. Scrawled on the four-by-six cards that Reagan used for nearly every speech were only the names of welcoming dignitaries, the band and a brief note about the joy of coming home. But Reagan by now was almost jubilant. He delighted in the summery, mid-70s weather that contrasted with the chill of Washington. He was stirred by the bands playing "California Here I Come" and the warm greetings of Mayor Tom Bradley, comedian Rich Little, actor Robert Stack and William French Smith, his first attorney general. "You are an example of the true American success story," Stack said to Reagan, a friend of many years. "You changed the course of history." By the time I had filed my story and returned to the platform area, Reagan was still speaking. "He's thrown away the cards, what can I tell you?" Spencer said. The roar of the crowd, which made up in enthusiasm what it lacked in size, had aroused the old actor and confirmed his view that he was back where he belonged. "When you have to stay eight years away from California, you live in a perpetual state of homesickness," he said.[63] He quipped that he had been asked to appear in a remake of his 1951 film *Bedtime for Bonzo,* but said that this time he had been asked to portray the chimpanzee. He promised that he would continue "campaigning out on the mashed-potato circuit for some of the things we didn't get done," including repeal of the Twenty-second Amendment limiting a president to two terms.[64] The crowd responded with the chant "Four more years."

The motorcade that bore the Reagans to Bel-Air was insignificant by presidential standards. Gone were the "wire cars" that carried the wire service correspondents and a pool of reporters. Gone were the television camera cars from which cameramen dangled at personal risk to be in position for the best pictures if anything happened during the motorcade. Gone was the ambulance and the extra limousine in which Secret Service agents rode to fool potential assassins. Gone were the many cars for the local politicians who attach themselves to presidents. What remained was a limousine for the president, a sharply reduced two-car Secret Service detail and two staff cars. Kuhn, remembering the crowds in the streets the day Reagan departed for Washington eight years earlier, was disappointed that the White House staff and the Secret Service had kept the motorcade route a secret. He had wanted a big crowd for the arrival and crowds on the streets, but there was almost no one on the sidewalks of Sepulveda Boulevard as the Reagan motorcade hurtled toward Bel-Air. But at the house some thirty neighbors had gathered and Kuhn remarked, "At least *they* heard about it." [65] The Reagans waved to the neighbors and went inside the house. Reagan's first act of homecoming was to take their dog Rex, who had been cooped up on the plane and in the motorcade for six hours, out in the backyard to relieve himself. "Welcome to the real world," thought Kuhn, [66] but Reagan saw nothing special in it. He was at home.

However, Nancy Reagan was not quite ready to let go. Her world had changed too quickly in six hours, and the friends and trappings of her former life meant too much to her. The Dubersteins and the Kuhns came inside at her urging and she gave Sydney Duberstein and Carole Kuhn a tour of the house while Reagan talked to their husbands. When Secret Service agent McCarthy turned to leave, explaining that the shift was changing and that security for the Reagans had now passed from the Washington office to the Los Angeles office, Nancy Reagan said, "Tim, you can't go." [67] Duberstein tried to make a joke of it, saying that the last presidential act signed by Reagan had transferred McCarthy to Los Angeles. She went along with the gag, smiling through her tears.

Now came the time that Kuhn, who had been so eager to leave the Oval Office that morning, had dreaded throughout the long flight west. He had been worrying how it would be when he said goodbye and was unaccountably nervous in Reagan's presence, the way he had been the first time he met him in 1975 and never since. He just did not know how to say goodbye to the man who would always be his president. He had been brought up not to cry, and he was full of emotion that he could not express. I should be as composed as he is, Kuhn thought, but he was not. He remembered that on the plane Reagan's old friend and strategist Stu Spencer had dealt lightly with the farewells, saying he would see Reagan many times again. Kuhn tried to do the same thing. Reagan then did something that Kuhn had never seen him do before. What Reagan usually did was to speak to everyone in the room as if he were talking to a single audience. He did not do that today, and Kuhn did not know what to make of it. "See you again, Mr. President," Kuhn said. Reagan nodded and, with Nancy standing at his side with tears in her eyes, saw them to the door. He shook hands with each of them. Duberstein was the last to go, and he, too, refused to say goodbye. "See you soon, Mr. President," he said. "We love you, Ken," Reagan said.[68] Then he closed the door and left the judgments to history.

2

A REAGAN PORTRAIT

He's not an easy man, although he seems easy. To everybody he seems very easy, but he is more complex than people think.

NANCY REAGAN,
May 5, 1989[1]

He was the ultimate American success story, or so it seemed, a man for whom the American dream—defined by William Faulkner as "a sanctuary on the earth for individual man"[2]—became a luminous reality. He was of humble origins. His parents were poor and his nomadic boyhood darkly shadowed by his father's alcoholism and frequent unemployment. He worked his way through an obscure, church-affiliated college, where his grades were never more than mediocre. Most of his classmates sought to become ministers or teachers, and his own ambitions to be a sports announcer or an actor seemed hopeless fantasies beyond his training and abilities. When he graduated from Eureka College during the depths of the Depression, he had no prospects of a job.

But the world was one vast opportunity for Ronald Wilson Reagan. He had faith in the future of the country and in his own future, and his unfailing optimism and self-deprecating humor commended him to others. While he formed few close friendships, he was widely popular and people liked to hear him talk. He had a fantastic memory and a knack for explaining things. He succeeded at everything that he tried. At a time when one-fourth of all Americans were out of work, he convinced a radio station manager to hire him for a part-time sports announcing job for which better-qualified applicants had already been rejected. He struggled and eventually became a successful sports announcer. A few years later he casually took a screen test and was offered a movie contract, opening his path to a career that was then the consummate dream of millions of Americans. In Hollywood he became a minor star, distinguished by a cheerful manner, a willingness to cooperate on the set and an ability to memorize a script rapidly. Directors valued his punctuality and discipline.

He was especially popular with women, who responded to his athletic good looks and winning personality. He dated many women, married an actress and had a family. When his wife lost interest in him and divorced him, he married another actress more congenial to his temperament and had another family. Nothing seemed to get him down for long. He became an authority on the film industry and president of the Screen Actors Guild, which he called "probably the best force for constructive good in the motion picture industry of anyone in that industry."[3] He led his fellow actors to victory in their only strike. When his films went out of fashion, he secured a new career on television. And when that career faded, he emerged as spokesman for Barry Goldwater, who would become the most badly beaten presidential candidate in U.S. history, and used the platform and lost cause of that campaign to become a two-term governor of California and two-term president of the United States.

Through it all, Reagan's inner life remained a mystery even to his friends. Ordinary people remarked upon his simplicity and good manners and liked being around him, for he had a knack of making them feel good. When tragedy struck a friend or stranger, he was a consoling force who managed to find the right words of sympathy. But people also observed that he kept his emotional distance, particularly after the collapse of his marriage to Jane Wyman. He rarely inquired about those who went out of his life, even his grown children. When he entered politics, people who left his campaigns and then returned wondered if he had noticed that they were ever gone. Even in early middle age, Reagan frequently forgot the names of aides and colleagues of long standing. He read regularly but often could not recall the title of the book he was reading. But he had a vast hoard of anecdotes, and he remembered childhood incidents and scenes from favorite movies with photographic detail. Sometimes his knowledge of obscure events astonished even his brightest subordinates in Sacramento or Washington. At other times he seemed unable to grasp the essentials of familiar policies or to speak coherently about the simplest matters without consulting the cue cards he carried in the left-hand pocket of his suit coat.

Over time he came to a few settled beliefs and wrote them down in speeches, sprinkled with odd anecdotes. He found his arguments and his anecdotes in *Reader's Digest* and in newspaper stories and rarely questioned their validity. He preached love of country, distrust of government, the glories of economic opportunity, the dangers of regulating business and the wonders of free markets and free trade. He believed in the manifest destiny of the United States of America. He also believed in intuition, psychic phenomena and fate. He was fascinated by the biblical story of Armageddon. He had no use for organized religion, though he said he often prayed. He was modest about his achievements and willing to share the credit with others, but he refused to acknowledge mistakes. When he changed positions on an issue and even when he changed political parties, he insisted that he was being consistent with his past record and that it was others who had changed. He was slow to anger but extremely stubborn. He detested arguments. He trusted everyone who worked for him and considered even mild criticism of the most incompetent subordinate to be a disguised attack on him or his policies. He could be heroic in the face of physical danger, but he shrank from confrontations unless he was on stage. He delighted in the roar of a crowd and could become distracted and listless if kept too long away from audiences. Yet he also had a need to be alone. He liked to write letters in the privacy of his office or at Camp David. He enjoyed building fences, clearing brush, working with his hands and riding quietly on forest trails in the hills of Maryland or across the brown scrubland of his California ranch. He always cleaned his desk before he finished work.

Like most disciplined persons, Reagan was a creature of habit. By the time he came to Washington he had long been accustomed to a daily schedule that told him where he would go and who he would meet and to a script that told him what to say. Reagan appreciated both the schedule and the script, which in the White House were usually sent to him the night before. He followed the schedule scrupulously, crossing off each item as it was completed. In meetings with outsiders he usually stuck to the script that had been scribbled down on his cards, once provoking a furious outburst from House Speaker Thomas P. (Tip) O'Neill, who was angry that Reagan read to him from his notes rather than speaking extemporaneously on subjects they had discussed many times before.[4] But Reagan refused to change his style. He could act decisively when presented with clear options, but he rarely initiated a meeting, a phone call, a proposal or an idea. He thought his staff would tell him anything he ought to know and invested most of his energy and interest in the public performances of the presidency. Though most of his speeches were written by others, many of them still reflected the uncluttered values he had expressed on the banquet circuit for a quarter century. He thought of himself as a man of principle, and he was difficult to push on the issues that mattered most to him. As president, he was at once the most malleable and least movable of men.

Reagan celebrated his seventieth birthday seventeen days after he became president. He was in splendid health but nearsighted and hard of hearing,[5] and he found the acoustics of the Oval Office difficult. He had trouble making out much that was said to him, and his aides learned to raise their voices, speak deliberately and look directly at him when they had something to say. In time he was persuaded to obtain a matched pair of modern hearing aids, which helped in small meetings. But when the conversation came from different directions in a noisy room, he could not follow what was said. As his hearing declined, he became an accomplished lip reader, but he used this skill and paid attention only if a subject interested him. Much of the time it did not. If he became bored during a meeting, he sometimes nodded off. More often, he simply doodled or indicated his lack of interest in the subject matter by telling stories.

Even when he was bored, Reagan loved the surroundings of the White House. He remained cheerful and optimistic, never accepting the notion that the presidency was "a splendid misery"[6] or a lonely burden. He enjoyed being president. He believed in the maxim that it was best to leave an audience laughing and tried to end even the most serious of meetings with a happy story, of which he had a ready store. He remembered intricate anecdotes and told them repeatedly, mimicking dialects and speech mannerisms. He loved to reminisce about the old days, favoring Hollywood stories after he became governor and stories about his governorship after he became president. He rarely met a statistic he didn't like. He remained approachable and considerate in almost all circumstances, but resisted introspection and turned away questions that asked him to reveal himself. "You can get just so far to Ronnie, and then something happens," said Nancy Reagan,[7] who knew him better than anyone and may have been the only person who really knew him at all. People who had worked for him much of their lives suspected that there was something beneath the surface they had never seen, but they did not know what the something was. "Everyone sees what you appear to be, few know who you are and those few dare not oppose the opinion of the many," Machiavelli wrote four centuries ago in an observation that could have been made of Ronald Reagan. He was among the most successful of men, and outwardly one of the happiest. Yet Reagan remained a mystery, even to those who knew him best.

3

THE ACTING
POLITICIAN

*When I was governor and wanted to return a tax surplus
to the people my finance director said, "It's never been
done." And I said, "Well, you've never had an actor up
here before either."*

RONALD REAGAN,
July 10, 1986[1]

What Reagan appeared to be was an actor. He spent the best
years of his life in Hollywood, that real and imaginary world where he
learned his acting craft, honed his skills as a platform speaker, formed
his political ideas and achieved an enduring identity. Hollywood and
its environs were the scenes and sources of his professional triumphs
and defeats, of his marriage, divorce and remarriage and of his transformation into a man of means. His children were born in Southern California, and parents and friends came there from Illinois and Iowa to be
with him. It was in Hollywood that Reagan learned about trade unions,
organized crime, Communists and congressional investigations. The entertainment industry framed his entrance into public life and his departure from it. Asked during his first campaign what kind of governor he
would be, Reagan quipped, "I don't know, I've never played a governor."[2] And when he left the White House twenty-three years later and

came home to California he told Landon Parvin, "Some of my critics over the years have said that I became president because I was an actor who knew how to give a good speech. I suppose that's not too far wrong. Because an actor knows two important things—to be honest in what he's doing and to be in touch with the audience. That's not bad advice for a politician either. My actor's instinct simply told me to speak the truth as I saw it and felt it."³

The last phrase is interesting because what Reagan saw and felt as an actor and a politician frequently did not correspond to the facts. Reagan recognized this and, in a conflict between feelings and facts, usually gave greater weight to his feelings. If an actor did not believe in his part, no one else would believe in it. If a political speaker did not believe in his message, he could not persuade others of its merits. A salesman's version of the same idea—and Reagan had been a powerful salesman for General Electric and the conservative cause—is that a salesman must believe in the worth of his product before he can sell it to others. Since Reagan was convinced that the camera invariably detects insincerity, his adage about speaking the truth as he saw and felt it applied with special force whenever he appeared on television. Reagan always believed what he was saying, even when the message was not strictly factual. He believed in the power of stories, sincerely told. And he was convinced that the actor's truth he had discovered for himself applied in some measure to everyone. This made him sympathetic to others when they also told cherished stories that reflected feelings more than facts.

In 1983 columnist Charles McDowell, an observant journalist, was sitting alongside Reagan at the head table at the annual Gridiron Dinner in Washington and regaled him with a vivid account of the location shooting of *Brother Rat* in Lexington, Virginia.⁴ *Brother Rat*, a 1938 comedy based on the exploits of Virginia Military Institute cadets, is remembered today mainly because it marked the film debut of Eddie Albert and the beginning of the off-screen romance of Reagan and Jane Wyman. But little Lexington is McDowell's hometown, and the filming of *Brother Rat* was the best story of his boyhood. McDowell had been telling the story long before Reagan became a political celebrity, and he told it now, in avid detail, to the president of the United States. Warner Bros. had taken the town over for the filming, confiscating Lexington's only taxicab for a week, which prevented a local housewife from delivering laundry and VMI professors from sneaking away to buy whisky. McDowell went every day to the VMI barracks to watch the filming.

He thrilled to the presence of such movie stars as Wayne Morris and Priscilla Lane. He remembered, as if yesterday, the moment when he walked into McCrum's drugstore and saw his mother and a friend sitting in a booth. Behind them, in another booth, were Ronald Reagan and Eddie Albert. "That just to me captures this marvelous moment in a small boy's life," McDowell told the president.[5]

Reagan listened to the story with delight mingled with some apprehension. He laughed appreciatively at its climax, when McDowell related how he had seen Reagan and Albert together in the drugstore booth. Then he leaned forward and put his hand on the columnist's arm in a fatherly gesture. "I have something serious to tell you," Reagan said. "What's that, Mr. President?" McDowell asked. Reagan confided that he had never in his life been in Lexington because his role in the movie had not required him to go there. "I remember the others coming back from Lexington and telling me what it was like," Reagan said. "But I simply wasn't there."

McDowell was astonished. "Mr. President, how can that be?" he said. "I've known it all my life. I've told it so many times." Reagan asked him how many times he had seen the movie. Five or six, said the crestfallen columnist. "That implanted in your head that I was there," Reagan said gently. "You believed it because you wanted to believe it. There's nothing wrong with that. I do it all the time."[6]

Reagan knew what it was he did, and why it was important to believe in one's best stories. Acting took early hold of him, and never let him go. He had been acting ever since he was a small boy and was thrust willingly into church skits by his mother, Nelle, a religious woman with a flair for the dramatic. Reagan liked the make-believe of the skits better than the sermons at the Christian (Disciples of Christ) churches in Tampico and Dixon. He responded to maternal approval and was comforted by applause. At Dixon High School and Eureka College he participated enthusiastically in school plays, delighting drama teachers because he took direction willingly and quickly memorized parts. And he was a natural on the stage, where, in the words of Garry Wills, he possessed "the movie-star look long before he was a movie star."[7] In his autobiography Reagan rapturously describes his reactions to a famous British antiwar play, Robert Cecil Sherriff's *Journey's End,* when it was performed in Dixon by a traveling company. Reagan emotionally identified with the lead character, a war-weary British captain in what was then called the World War who hides his horror at the slaughter on the western front with a veneer of callousness. "For two and a half hours I was in that dugout on the western front, but in some strange way I was also on stage," Reagan said more than three decades after he saw the play.[8]

His first career as a sports announcer in Iowa deepened his sense of make-believe. He was adept at inventing the word pictures required by radio and particularly skilled at "re-creating" Chicago Cubs baseball games he never saw from terse accounts he received by telegraph from the press box in Wrigley Field. But he wanted to be seen as well as heard. After he passed his Hollywood screen test at the age of twenty-six, he abandoned without qualms his promising radio career. What he always wanted to be was an actor, and he took the first opportunity that came along.

When Reagan moved onto the public stage in the 1960s, he keenly appreciated that his career had given him a head start in politics. He knew how to make a speech and how to deliver a punchline. He knew that it was necessary to look directly into the television camera without bobbing his head, and he knew how to give a concise answer that compressed easily into a fifteen-second sound bite. In California, where politicians with supposedly familiar names found it necessary to mount expensive advertising campaigns to make themselves barely known to a huge and mobile electorate, Reagan enjoyed instant name recognition. He was fifty-five years old in 1966 when he ran for governor of California, and he began his political career as a celebrity. He was accustomed to people of his own generation, many of them women, coming to him after speeches and asking for his autograph. Some of these middle-age fans specifically remembered his performance in *Kings Row* or other films. Others knew him as a television host or vaguely recalled that he had been a likable film performer who seemed much the same in real life. Almost everyone who met him in those days remarked upon his youthful appearance. Reagan had these fans in his corner. And even those who weren't fans accepted him as a genuine celebrity, which counts for something in California.

Politicians, including some in Reagan's camp, were slow to appreciate the magnitude of these advantages. A number of them envied Reagan's widespread name recognition but thought his star quality would quickly fade in the heat of a political campaign. They failed to see that the earnest, affable Reagan was rapidly forming a relationship with potential voters that was an extension of the bond he had forged with movie and television audiences during his long career. On screen and in person Reagan came across as virile and midwestern, expressing patriotic certitudes and old-fashioned values that were somehow softened by his smile. He was tall and handsome, with a commanding bearing, but his manner was self-deprecating and lacking in conceit. He seemed immensely comfortable with being Ronald Reagan, and he had a knack of converting others to his optimism, almost as if he drew upon some private reservoir of self-esteem. People who listened to Reagan tended to feel good about him and better about themselves. His optimism had a special resonance in California, where, as writer Carey McWilliams once put it, "the lights went on all at once, in a blaze, and they have never been dimmed." [9] Reagan was Illinois come to California. He was the wholesome citizen-hero who inhabits our democratic imaginations, an Everyman who was slow to anger but willing to fight for the right and correct wrongdoing when aroused. It was a role in a movie—personified by Reagan's friend Jimmy Stewart in *Mr. Smith Goes to Washington*—in which homespun American virtue prevails over the wily and devious "special interests" that rule the nation's capital. Reagan believed in the role, and he was such a good actor that he did not seem to be an actor at all. He seemed even less a politician. Though his message in 1966 was an only slightly blander version of the conservative sermon he had preached two years earlier for Barry Goldwater, the smile and self-deprecating one-liners softened the ideological edge of his speeches. The Reagan role had been created in Hollywood, out of material he brought with him from the Middle West. It was the role of The Gipper, symbolized by the insouciance of halfback George Gipp when coach Knute Rockne asks Gipp if he can carry the football and Gipp answers, "How far?" It was the role of the real-life Reagan, who believed in happy endings and the American dream. It was a role, but it was also Reagan. And because the role was genuine, or because Reagan believed it to be so, it was thoroughly believable to the California electorate. Reagan playing Reagan, in real life as in the movies, established an enormous presumption of credibility that no ordinary politician could hope to duplicate.

But the impact of Reagan's public impression was lost on the political analysts who attempted to take Reagan's measure at the onset of his candidacy. What they saw, with few exceptions, was the liability of an acting background that imposed a difficult standard of proof on Reagan to demonstrate his qualifications. The conventional political wisdom was that actors were airheads, useful mainly to draw a crowd or add an air of excitement to a campaign. While actors were frequent adornments at political rallies and fund-raising dinners in Southern California, few people in the political community considered them candidate material. They should have known better, at least by the time Reagan ran for governor in 1966. Two years earlier Reagan's friend and fellow actor George Murphy, a Republican, had been elected to the U.S. Senate from California while President Lyndon Johnson was carrying the state by a million votes. Instead of regarding this as a warning signal, politicians of both parties tended to dismiss it as a fluke. To people who had spent their lives in politics, the notion of an actor becoming governor of the nation's most populous state appeared preposterous. But it seemed natural enough to Reagan, who thought he knew the people better than the politicians did.

He also knew how to take direction and how to follow a script, actor's attributes that endeared him to campaign strategists Bill Roberts and Stuart Spencer and to his press secretary, Lyn Nofziger. Reagan assumed that a script would be prepared for him, and his strategists obliged with a political screenplay that might have been called "Citizen-Governor." The purpose of this screenplay was to convert the liability of Reagan's inexperience into an asset. Its premise was that experienced politicians had made such a mess of things they could no longer be trusted to run the government. Reagan was cast as "citizen-politician," a perfect role for an actor who believed that supposedly intractable problems of governance could be solved by courage and common sense. There was an enduring populist streak to Reagan, which he expressed even without benefit of a script. Long before he became a candidate, his speeches were sprinkled with references to the American colonists who took their lives and their government into their own hands. He also invoked the example of that ultimate citizen-politician Cincinnatus, the Roman general and statesman who left his plow in 458 B.C. to lead his nation's besieged troops to victory and then returned to his farm. This tradition of "citizen politics" has deep roots in California, one of the handful of states where the early twentieth-century Progressives actually wrested control of the political system from the major political parties. The Progressives, led in California by Hiram Johnson, detested political parties and did their best to destroy them. They created a tradition of voting for "the man, not the party," a legacy of social reform and an enormous political vacuum that was filled by a chaotic combination of special-interest groups, campaign specialists and newspaper tycoons with private agendas. The vast migrations to California during and after World War II enhanced the antipartisan temperament. The immigrants who sought the good life amidst orange groves and subdivisions demanded a vast array of services from their local governments, but these were without exception nonpartisan. The legislature remained partisan, but few Californians knew the names of their representatives, and even fewer of them cared. Earl Warren, the state's most popular postwar governor, ran for office on the slogan "Leadership—Not Politics" and in 1946 won the nomination of both parties under the unique cross-filing system that had been one of the Progressive movement's quirkier innovations.

Cross-filing was eliminated before Reagan ran for office, but the political culture that produced it remained. The culture made it possible for Reagan and a handful of millionaire friends, dazzled at his ability to inspire people with common wisdom, almost casually to decide that he should become governor. Some of these friends thought that Sacramento was an end in itself, while others perceived it as a way stop on the path to the presidency. All of them thought they could sell Reagan to the people, if not the politicians.

Reagan thought so, too. Like most Californians of his generation, he was an immigrant to the state who had been raised a Democrat and honored the memory of Franklin Roosevelt. After three decades in California he had acclimated to the state's peculiar political culture and was ready to denounce the practice of politics even as he prepared to embark on a political career. Reagan quite naturally spoke in terms of "the people" taking "their destiny into their own hands." He almost never used the words "Republican" or "conservative" in his speeches. He knew that Democrats call their party "the Democratic Party" and dislike the taunt of "Democrat Party" employed by tone-deaf Republicans. Opposition gibes that his ideas were "simplistic" reinforced the citizen-politician theme and Reagan's portrayal of himself as Everyman. "There are simple answers, just not easy ones," [10] he said, expressing an idea that would echo throughout his governorship and his presidency. Reagan also had a ready answer to the charge that his political inexperience made him unqualified for managing a modern state government: "The man who currently has the job has more experience than anybody. That's why I'm running." [11] This characteristic one-liner was Reagan's invention, but it perfectly fit the script composed by his strategists.

The "other fellow" was Edmund G. (Pat) Brown, an amiable, owlish-looking two-term Democratic incumbent governor who had spent his life in politics. Brown was a welfare-state Democrat who believed in the axioms of the New Deal, the Fair Deal and the Great Society. His administration had built freeways and universities and created a gigantic water system to serve arid, populous Southern California with the dammed-up rivers of the north. In 1962 Brown had acquired a national cachet among Democrats by winning a second term against Richard M. Nixon, then trying to rebound from his narrow loss in the 1960 presidential election. But by the time he faced Reagan, Brown had been badly scarred by incestuous political battles and public displays of indecisiveness. A Democratic rival called Brown a "tower of Jell-O," and the label stuck. Nonetheless, Brown thought it inconceivable that voters would exchange an experienced governor for an actor with ties to the "extremist" Goldwater. So convinced was Brown of Reagan's inherent unelectability that his political operatives worked behind the scenes to guarantee Reagan's nomination by smearing his principal opponent in the GOP primary, orthodox Republican and former San Francisco Mayor George Christopher. The effort came to light and tarnished Brown. But even without this embarrassment, Brown suffered from being an experienced politician at a time when experience was suspect. By the time Reagan ran for governor, the tumult of the sixties had a head start on California campuses, where students were among the first to protest in behalf of civil rights and against the Vietnam War. A riot in the black community of Watts had occurred on Brown's watch, at a time when he had the bad fortune to be out of the country. Even when he was around, the old order that Brown epitomized seemed ineffectual in the face of urban riots and campus demonstrations. Perhaps experience was not all it was cracked up to be. Brown, a product of the insular political world of San Francisco and the atypical government community of Sacramento, could not comprehend that the world was changing. He liked to say that he had been solving California's problems while Reagan was making *Bedtime for Bonzo,* a 1951 film in which a chimpanzee plays the title role. The line was good for laughs, but not for Brown's third-term aspirations. Californians, particularly Southern Californians, are not automatically dismissive of movie actors. On balance, they thought more highly of performers than of politicians.

As the walls of Brown's world began to crumble around him, Reagan faced a campaign of derision that drew heavily on the political community's lack of respect for actors. The Democrats had practiced this campaign on George Murphy, who laughed it off. Democrats learned nothing from their loss, rationalizing that their strategy had failed because Murphy's opponent, Pierre Salinger, was a California political outsider with thin credentials. Brown was an insider. And while he was wrong in assuming that voters would automatically reject an actor, he accurately recognized that Reagan was more vulnerable emotionally to an anti-actor campaign than his friend Murphy, who was unabashedly a song-and-dance man without illusions about his theatrical gifts. Reagan never became reconciled to gibes about his acting prowess. While he tried to make light of the slurs on his career, he privately considered such ridicule a form of dirty pool and never forgave Brown for indulging in it. Reagan's managers were content to convince voters that Reagan was something more than an actor following a script. But Reagan wanted to persuade the electorate, particularly younger voters who had never seen his films, that he was a competent actor.

Viewed solely in political terms, the anti-actor strategy was a disaster. Even many Democrats thought it unfair to judge someone by his profession rather than on his merits. The anti-actor strategy cast Reagan in the enviable role of defending both Hollywood and himself, a part he had perfected years earlier in his first forays on the banquet circuit. Reagan's opponents plunged into a swamp from which they never emerged. At the bottom of the swamp was a television spot titled "Man vs. Actor" that featured Brown in a schoolroom telling an integrated class of young children, "I'm running against an actor and you know who shot Lincoln, don'tcha?" [12] All things considered, it was not surprising that Reagan won the 1966 election by nearly a million votes.

But the actor's ego was not assuaged by the landslide victory. Reagan had been stung by the ridicule of his film career, which continued long after he was elected. He acknowledged there was truth to Brown's crack that he had been upstaged by Bonzo the chimpanzee, pointing out that likable animals usually steal the show from human actors. Nonetheless, Reagan had happy memories of his performance in *Bedtime for Bonzo,* an entertaining comedy that had received moderate critical acclaim. Reagan also thought well of many of the fifty-two other movies he made during a film career that began in 1937 and lasted more than a quarter century. Reagan knew that a number of his earliest Warner Bros. movies were B-films that "the studio didn't want good, it wanted them Thursday." [13] He knew that he had never quite achieved the stardom that seemed within his grasp in the early 1940s, when he dropped from public view during World War II while making training films for the Army in nearby Culver City. Perhaps because he never climbed the very top rung of the ladder to movie stardom, he is inclined to exaggerate the importance of his favorite role as the rakish Drake McHugh, who has his legs amputated by a vengeful surgeon in *Kings Row* and wakes up crying, "Where's the rest of me?" But Reagan won plaudits for his performance in this critically acclaimed film, which was released in 1942 after Army reservist Reagan had been called into the service. Prominent critics also praised his deft performances in such postwar romantic comedies as *The Hasty Heart, John Loves Mary* and *The Girl from Jones Beach.* While Reagan's acting range was limited, he held his own on screen with such accomplished performers as Eddie Albert, Humphrey Bogart, Pat O'Brien, Eleanor Parker, Ann Sheridan, Barbara Stanwyck and many more. Usually, he played a variant of what Wills called "the heartwarming role" of Ronald Reagan,[14] in which he would subsequently star as governor and president. His competence as an actor was unquestioned until he went into politics, and *Bonzo* became grist for the anti-actor campaign. And while Reagan learned to spoof some of his own roles, perhaps to keep the hurt from showing, he never accepted the idea that they were fair game for political critics whose real targets were his policies. When I interviewed him late in 1968, a few months after a premature attempt to win the Republican presidential nomination, Reagan was still bridling at what he called "this *New York Times* kind of business of referring to me as a B-picture actor." * Reagan knew that he was a good actor. He told me that when politicians or journalists belittled his film career, "they touch an exposed nerve."[15]

Reagan did not like the belittling, but he invited the depiction of himself as an acting politician. When he was sworn in as the thirty-third governor of California a few minutes after midnight on January 1, 1967, he turned and quipped to his pal Senator George Murphy, "Well, George, here we are back on the late show."[16] Although few in the celebratory and somewhat chilled crowd on the State Capitol steps knew it, Reagan's crack marked a declaration of independence from a restraint he had grudgingly accepted during the campaign and would never abide by again. In the beginning of that campaign Reagan was wary of the reporters assigned to cover him and had attempted to win them over by telling Hollywood stories. Reporters loved the Hollywood yarns and accepted the off-the-record ground rules under which most of them were told. But Lyn Nofziger, Reagan's first and shrewdest political press agent, observed that the candidate's preoccupation with Hollywood tended to reinforce opposition claims that Reagan was "nothing more than an actor." Nofziger talked to Reagan and his campaign managers about it, and the candidate reluctantly agreed to stop talking Hollywood. Reagan told me in 1968 that he had chafed under

---

* I thought Reagan's complaint ironic. Bosley Crowther, the influential film critic of *The New York Times* from 1940 to 1967, frequently praised Reagan's acting.

the restraint but thought it best to follow the guidance of those who knew more about politics than he did.

What Reagan knew about was the movies, and he was pleased to discover in Sacramento that politicians, once he came to know them, seemed to enjoy his Hollywood stories as much as anyone else. What the politicians did not enjoy, and never would, was Reagan's distance from the government over which he now presided. Reagan's bond with the electorate and his experience as an actor would ultimately make it possible for him to mobilize public opinion and translate some of his "simple answers" into useful legislation. But Pat Brown had been right in believing that Reagan was ill prepared to manage a state government with a budget larger than those of all but six nations in the world. As comfortable as he was with himself, Reagan was unfamiliar with the rudiments of political procedure. He did not know how budgets were prepared, how bills were passed or who it was in state government who checked the backgrounds of prospective appointees. While Reagan was a reader, his library was devoid of works on governance. Nor did his Hollywood work habits contribute to rapid acquisition of missing knowledge. Reagan relished the schedule of his moviemaking days, when he would work intensely for a few weeks during the shooting of a film and then take off for an interlude of golf or horseback riding. Reagan was disciplined and capable of mastering an issue when a performance required him to do so. But nothing in his life had prepared him for the everydayness of governance. He had a vision of what he wanted to accomplish in Sacramento, which was to "squeeze, cut and trim" the cost and size of government.[17] But he didn't know what he was supposed to be doing, or how he was supposed to spend his time.

Many of the people Reagan brought to Sacramento with him knew even less about governance than he did. Nofziger thought that all of them, himself included, were "novice amateurs." Looking back on the first two years of Reagan's governorship in 1968, Nofziger observed that Reagan had "materialized out of thin air with no political background, no political cronies and no political machine. He didn't even run his own campaign. His campaign was run by hired people who then walked away and left it. Therefore, when he was elected, the big question was, 'My God, what do we do now?' " [18]

It was a line that would resonate in Sacramento and Washington— and also in Hollywood. A 1972 film, *The Candidate,* set in California and starring Robert Redford, concludes with the newly elected senator turning to his campaign manager and saying, "Marvin, what do we do now?" The film was supposedly inspired by the election to the Senate in 1970 of John Tunney, who resoundingly defeated George Murphy in the same year that Reagan won a second term as governor. But Tunney was a veteran of three terms in the House of Representatives when he won his Senate seat and knew his way around Washington. Reagan, as he had disarmingly put it, had never even played a governor.

Not knowing what to do once he arrived in Sacramento and lacking anyone to teach him, Reagan reverted to doing what he did best: he turned his job into a role. The citizen-politician became a citizen-governor who was proud that he still referred to the government as "them." Citizen-governors exist to defend the people, as Cincinnatus had defended Rome before returning to his plow. Reagan sought to defend Californians from "welfare cheats," foul-mouthed student demonstrators and ivory-tower leaders of the state's entrenched higher-education establishment. Although Reagan remembered his own participation in a student strike at Eureka in a most positive light, he lacked sympathy for the student protesters of the 1960s.[19] He had even less sympathy for highly paid educational bureaucrats who ridiculed his intellectual capacities, most often behind his back, and could not keep order on their campuses. The educational establishment treated the citizen-governor as an unrefined, ultraconservative know-nothing, and a Reagan comment that universities were "subsidizing intellectual curiosity" reinforced the impression.[20] When the citizen-governor tried to reduce the cost of social services and to close down some of the hospital "warehouses" that were then home for the state's large mentally-ill population, he was depicted as the enemy of the people.

Reagan, in fact, was on to something. He had become governor during a time when tranquilizers and other new methods of treatment were encouraging use of community treatment programs in place of huge, inefficient hospitals that were little more than prisons for the mentally ill. While this had the potential for reducing the state budget, it did not quite fit the script of "squeeze, cut and trim." Community treatment would also prove expensive, although this was not then well understood. Certainly, Reagan did not understand it. He liked the idea of shutting down the hospital warehouses, both on humanitarian and fiscal grounds, but he did not know enough to make the case for community treatment. Put another way, he lacked the knowledge to change the script. When the subject arose at a March 15, 1967, meeting of the governor's cabinet, Reagan's participation reflected the limits of his Hollywood experience, not the advantages of having been an actor.

"Do you know how hard it is to mispronounce 'psychiatric' once you know how to pronounce it right?" he said irrelevantly during a key meeting on the mental-hospital budget cuts. "I had to do it in *Kings Row* and at first I couldn't do it. It's like deliberately singing a flat note." [21]

4

THE ACTING
PRESIDENT

And believe me, Bedtime for Bonzo *made more sense
than what they were doing in Washington.*

RONALD REAGAN,
May 25, 1982[1]

Ronald Reagan's cinematic visions and theatrical gifts were better
suited to the grander stage of Washington than to Sacramento. He had
skated through as governor, relying on his charm and negotiating
skills and upon aides who had survived by learning the ways of the
legislature. On balance he was a good governor, though not a great one.
His second term, which ended in 1974, was marked by constructive
welfare, education and tax legislation that owed at least as much to
these no-longer-novice aides and to the Democratic leadership of the
legislature as to his own abilities. But eight years as governor had taught
Reagan that he performed best when he attended to larger visions. Once
he settled in as governor, he became indifferent to the everydayness of
government and unconcerned about his lack of fundamental civics
knowledge. He learned to let others, particularly Edwin Meese III, do
the heavy lifting and to rely upon his directors, as he had done in
Hollywood. Reagan saved himself for the big scenes. By the time he
reached the White House in 1981, after three tries at the presidency,

Reagan felt free to draw upon the themes, examples and anecdotes of his movie days. He had real-life movies in his head and a surer sense of his own role in the production of the Reagan presidency. He knew what he wanted to accomplish, and what he wanted to be. What he wanted to be, and what he became, was an accomplished presidential performer.

Reagan never forgot the gibes about his acting that he endured during his first campaign for public office and periodically throughout his political career. He owed a debt to his acting experience, but he was circumspect about acknowledging it. Not until his final weeks in the White House, when no one any longer cared if he was role-playing, did Reagan publicly discuss the link between his careers as performer and president. ABC's David Brinkley gave him the opportunity a month before he left the White House by asking if he had learned anything as an actor that had been of use to him in the presidency. "There have been times in this office when I've wondered how you could do the job if you hadn't been an actor," Reagan replied.[2] The comment amused Nancy Reagan, who had heard it many times before. And it prompted Reagan's friend George Will to write, "I do not know precisely what he meant, and he probably doesn't either, but he was on to something." What Reagan was on to, in Will's view, was the importance of the "theatrical element" in politics, an awareness, Will said, that Reagan shared with such democratic leaders as Churchill, de Gaulle and Franklin Roosevelt and with such dictators as Hitler, Mussolini and Castro.[3]

While a theatrical element certainly permeated the Reagan presidency, "being an actor" meant more to Reagan than theatrics. Unlike the leaders cited by Will, he had practiced acting as a vocation and allowed it to become his principal mode of behavior. He had learned to play himself on screen, and he had also learned to remain on camera when the shooting stopped. Furthermore, he thought of actors as among the noblest people on earth. In his early days as a banquet speaker he had served as a self-appointed defense committee for the moral standards of the stars, who he thought had been maligned because of the loose lifestyles of a few celebrities. When I asked Reagan three days before he left the White House what he had meant by his answer to Brinkley, he answered me by hitting the button of an old mental cassette filled with his thoughts on the wholesomeness of Hollywood. A passage of this mental tape is a quotation from a column by Irwin S. Cobb, another defender of the filmland faith, who was chiding someone who had accused actors of taking a "childish approach" to life. With a dreamy smile, Reagan recited Cobb for a small group of reporters in the Oval Office who had been expecting to hear about the achievements of his presidency. "He said, if this be true, and if it also be true that when we approach the final curtain that all men must bear in their arms that which they have given in life, the people of show business will march in the procession carrying in their arms the pure pearl of tears, the gold of laughter and the diamonds of stardust they spread on what might otherwise have been a rather dreary world," Reagan said. "And when they reach the final stage door the keeper will say, open, let my children in."[4]

Later, after he had left the White House, I put the Brinkley question to Reagan again. This time he skipped the lyricism and gave a multitude of more specific answers. He said that being an actor had taught him to understand the feelings and motivations of others. He said being an actor had "the practical side" of preparing people to face batteries of cameras and questions from the press. He also claimed that bad reviews and "undeserved criticism" prepared an actor for the rough exchanges of politics, although Reagan could be as thin-skinned and sensitive to criticism as any novice politician. Most important, he said, actors find themselves being called upon to perform on the spot at public gatherings.[5] Reagan, while often dependent on cue cards to discuss the most mundane of issues, was proud of his performances in such moments. He knew what to say when a microphone was thrust at him. Directors could be confident, as television critic Tom Shales observed, that when the camera "cut to reaction shots of Ron and Nancy . . . they'd both be ready with a capital R."[6] Reagan believed, with some insight, that his life as an actor had prepared him for new roles, new challenges and new performances in the world outside Hollywood. "You can't always dictate the stage of life upon which you will perform," he said.[7] But when the spotlight swung to him, Reagan was usually ready.

He also steadily sought new stages. In his moviemaking days Reagan's peers soon recognized that he had interests beyond acting. It showed up in his involvement in the Screen Actors Guild, of which he served as president during six turbulent years. And it showed up, too, in early expeditions into politics for such candidates as Minnesota Democrat Hubert Humphrey, in his first race for the U.S. Senate in 1948, and Los Angeles Mayor Fletcher Bowron, a nonpartisan officeholder supported by liberals and organized labor in 1953. Even on the movie set, Reagan took a broader interest in what went on than most actors. He learned to see things from a director's viewpoint, and he was interested in staging and lighting techniques. "You knew you weren't talking to a bubblehead," said Fred De Cordova, who directed *Bedtime for Bonzo* and was impressed both with Reagan's interest in public affairs and his conduct on the set. "He would make suggestions as many actors do, but what I found with Ronnie is that the suggestions were helpful and not particularly self-serving. He was willing to give up a line not to help himself but to make the scene play better." De Cordova did not see a potential president in "Ronnie," but he believed that Reagan would graduate from the acting ranks to management, perhaps becoming head of a studio or an executive in a talent agency.[8]

Reagan never lost his interest in production, but he kept it in proportion. White House aides who despaired of ever engaging him in a substantive discussion of issues learned they could involve him by discussing the scripts and scenes of the presidency. As on the set of *Bonzo* and other films, Reagan was willing to express ideas that had the potential of improving the script or the production. But he thought of himself as the leading man, not the producer or the director, and he usually counted on his aides and sometimes on his wife to know what was best for him. Reagan thought in terms of performance, and those closest to him approached his presidency as if it were a series of productions casting Reagan in the starring role. The chief impresario of Reagan's first term as president was Michael K. Deaver, a canny public relations man who had been with Reagan since his first campaign. Operating with the understated title of deputy chief of staff, Deaver became the grand producer of the Reagan presidency. He tried to see to it that the script, staging and lighting of each scene provided Reagan an opportunity to give a smashing performance. Every Deaver decision was based on whether it would show Reagan to best advantage. Deaver lacked Hollywood experience, but he had helped produce the Reagan governorship and knew the strengths and limitations of the leading man. And Deaver was also especially adept at dealing with leading lady Nancy Reagan, whom many in the White House considered a better actor than her husband. One of Deaver's tasks was to see that she was happy with her role in the production but didn't make too many changes in the script.

Deaver's attempt to craft each scene of the Reagan presidency proved contagious. Others who observed that he was successful in his work and highly popular with the Reagans because of it copied his methods, sometimes obsessively. Little was left to chance. Reagan was so fond of the phrase "God bless you" that he would have been apt to say it to an atheist, but aides began writing the line into scripts for closing the most trivial of meetings. Since the words were written down for him, Reagan read them instead of remembering them. The scripts usually were written on "half sheets" of heavy bond paper that in the White House substituted for the four-by-six cards Reagan favored in stump speeches.[9] The words were written in oversize type that compensated for Reagan's severe nearsightedness, which in his campaign days had prompted him to switch on most occasions from three-by-five cards to the four-by-six cards. Overuse of the cards and half sheets was bothersome to old friends, who knew that Reagan ad-libbed easily and did not need a piece of paper in his hand to carry on a serious conversation. But his stage managers recognized that Reagan preferred the comfort of the cue cards, and they saw no reason to take chances. "He was an actor and he worked from a script," said Rhett Dawson, the White House chief of operations in the closing years of the Reagan presidency. "If you gave him a script, he would do it."[10]

Over time the cinematic approach became so woven into the fabric of the Reagan presidency that subordinates schooled in economics or statecraft routinely used Hollywood terminology to direct Reagan in his daily tasks. It could be an unsettling practice to those unaccustomed to it. One White House aide recalls that Secretary of State George P. Shultz, huddling with Reagan in the secure vault of the American ambassador's residence in Moscow during the 1988 summit, coached him for his meeting with Soviet leader Mikhail Gorbachev by telling him what to do "in this scene." Shultz proceeded through a series of precise directions in stage terminology, telling Reagan where to stand and what to say. The aide was horrified that the secretary of state would treat the president as a man who "didn't have the intellectual wherewithal to be able to think or act on his own." But Reagan was not offended. He himself saw the meeting with Gorbachev as a significant performance, and he valued the services of a good director.

White House Chief of Staff Kenneth Duberstein, who saw Reagan safely off the stage in the last act of his presidency, also took a benign view of what he called "the performance part of the presidency." Duberstein, who had worked as congressional liaison under White House Chief of Staff James A. Baker III in the first term, shared De Cordova's view that Reagan was an actor with a larger vision of the role in which he was engaged. Assessing what acting meant to Reagan as president, Duberstein said, "Certainly, it's the communication, the ability to communicate, the ability to find the right words in his prepared speeches.

But more times than not, also in his ad libs, to find the right expression or the right anecdote. It is the ability to have people looking at you and you lead comfortably. It is the ability to be assured that sometimes you're playing to a much bigger house than you expected. It is proving yourself each day as an actor, because you have another performance. In the day there are many scenes and you have to get through them. . . . It's welcoming another head of state as another leading actor who is going to share the billing with you, but you know that you always have top billing. It's Reagan graciously sharing top billing. It's how to deal with the bit players in the cameo appearances, and the cameo actors who drift through. It's knowing that there is a final curtain. It's knowing that everything isn't hunky-dory. Sometimes there are tragedies, and you have to do that, too. It's speaking to the families of the Marines who were killed in Lebanon or the families of the soldiers on the USS *Stark*." [11]

Reagan was good at doing all of these things, as even such adversaries as Tip O'Neill acknowledged. But his actor's approach to the presidency required a staff that understood a performer's needs. "You need to have a very strong stage manager-producer-director," said Duberstein, who returned with Howard Baker to the White House in 1987 as part of the production team that sought to salvage the Reagan presidency after the Iran-contra fiasco. "You need to have very good technical men and sound men at all times." When such technical help was lacking, in Duberstein's view, everything "falls apart because the actor-president isn't prepared. He isn't prepared because the people around who are managing, directing, producing are not up to speed and therefore he can't walk into a situation using his years of experience and function effectively." [12]

To those who took a more traditional approach to the presidency, Reagan almost never seemed prepared. He had a handful of bedrock convictions and a knack of charming people of any rank or station. Occasionally, he also demonstrated a useful policy impulse. As we shall see in subsequent chapters, Reagan's perceptions about changes in the Soviet Union and his instincts about how to deal with them outpaced many of his advisers'. But Reagan lacked a technical grasp of any issue, and he was usually bored by briefings. While he valued compromises and had the temperament of a negotiator, he rarely knew enough about the substance of a dispute to be able to understand the sticking points. Most of his aides thought of him as intelligent, but many also considered him intellectually lazy. Reagan wanted, whenever possible, to have the pros and cons of an issue set out in single-page summaries, dubbed "mini-memos" when his then Chief of Staff William P. Clark created them in California. He preferred to have "the boys," as he called the middle-aged and elderly men who were his advisers, settle differences on issues among themselves and bring a consensus recommendation to him for approval. When the boys could not reach a consensus and brought a contentious matter to him for resolution, he asked few questions and often responded to carefully constructed arguments with anecdotes, frequently off the point.

Republican congressional leaders found Reagan uninterested in political strategy, although he was always willing to place a call to a wavering congressman if provided with the script of what he ought to say. What animated Reagan was a public performance. He knew how to edit a script and measure an audience. He also knew that the screenplay of his presidency, however complicated it became on the margins, was rooted in the fundamental themes of lower taxes, deregulation and "peace through strength" that he had expounded in the antigovernment speech he had given in 1964 for Goldwater. The Speech was his bible, and Reagan never tired of giving it. Its themes and Reagan's approach to government were, as his friend William F. Buckley put it, "inherently anti-statist." When a White House discussion even remotely turned to the idea that government was too big or too inefficient, Reagan would participate by drawing examples from the portfolio of antigovernment horror stories he had accumulated during a quarter century of campaigning. But on other issues, especially when the discussion was over his head, Reagan's participation was usually limited to jokes and cinematic illustrations. This is not surprising, as Reagan spent more time at the movies during his presidency than at anything else. He went to Camp David on 183 weekends, usually watching two films on each of these trips. He saw movies in the White House family theater, on television in the family quarters and in the villas and lavish guest quarters accorded presidents when they travel.

On the afternoon before the 1983 economic summit of the world's industrialized democracies in Colonial Williamsburg, White House Chief of Staff James Baker stopped off at Providence Hall, where the Reagans were staying, bringing with him a thick briefing book on the upcoming meetings. Baker, then on his way to a tennis game, had carefully checked through the book to see that it contained everything Reagan needed to know without going into too much detail. He was concerned about Reagan's performance at the summit, which had attracted hundreds of journalists from around the world and been advertised in advance by the White House as an administration triumph. But when Baker returned to Providence Hall the next morning, he found the briefing book unopened on the table where he had deposited it. He knew immediately that Reagan hadn't even glanced at it, and he couldn't believe it. In an hour Reagan would be presiding over the first meeting of the economic summit, the only one held in the United States during his presidency. Uncharacteristically, Baker asked Reagan why he hadn't cracked the briefing book. "Well, Jim, *The Sound of Music* was on last night," Reagan said calmly.

Nevertheless, Reagan's charm and cue cards carried him through the summit without incident. By the third year of his presidency the leaders of the democracies were also growing accustomed to Reagan's anecdotes and to his cheerful sermons about the wonders of the market system and lower taxes. They were awed at what they saw as his hold on the American people. One regular participant in the annual summits said the other leaders would stare at Reagan with rapt attention when he spoke, as if trying to divine the secret of his success. When the leaders took breaks in their meetings for the inevitable "photo opportunities," they clustered around Reagan so they could be photographed with him. In the halcyon days of his presidency Reagan seemed to have no need of briefing books. And even on those occasions when he read them, he was more apt to find solutions in the movies he watched religiously each weekend in the White House or at Camp David.

Sometimes the movies and the briefing books pointed in the same direction. By mid-1983 the U.S. and Soviet governments were beginning to emerge from the mutual acrimony that had prevailed between them since the Soviet invasion of Afghanistan in Christmas week of 1979. Guided by Reagan's impulses and Shultz's diplomacy, the U.S. government was beginning to explore what would ultimately become, after the ascension of Gorbachev, a more optimistic and productive era in U.S.-Soviet relations. But arms control enthusiasts on Capitol Hill were skeptical about Reagan's intentions toward the nation he had called "the evil empire."[13] The administration had been able to persuade a swing group of moderate Democrats to join with Republicans in supporting limited deployment of the MX missile only after Reagan pledged that he would also diligently pursue arms control opportunities. On the first weekend in June 1983, while Democratic support for the MX remained very much in question, Reagan went to Camp David with a briefcase full of option papers on arms control. He made a few personal phone calls, scanned the material in the folders and put them aside. After dinner Reagan was in the mood for a movie, as he usually was on Saturday night. The film that evening was *War Games,* in which Matthew Broderick stars as a teenage computer whiz who accidentally accesses the North American Aerospace Defense Command (NORAD) and almost launches World War III. It was an entertaining antiwar film with a clear message, intoned in the movie by an advanced computer: the only way to win the "game" of thermonuclear war is not to play it.

Two days later Reagan met at the White House with several of the Democratic congressmen who had backed the MX in exchange for the president's arms control commitment. He began the meeting by reading from cue cards tailored to congressional concerns. "I just can't believe that if the Soviets think long and hard about the arms race they won't be interested in getting a sensible agreement," Reagan said. Then he put the cue cards aside and his face lit up. He asked the congressmen if any of them had seen *War Games,* and when no one volunteered an answer launched into an animated account of the plot. The congressmen were fascinated with Reagan's change of mood and his obvious interest in the film. "Don't tell the ending," said one of them. "It was really funny," said Congressman Vic Fazio of California after the meeting. "I was sitting there so worried about throw weight [a measure of a missile's lifting power] and Reagan suddenly asks us if we've seen *War Games.* He was in a very good humor. He said, 'I don't understand these computers very well, but this young man obviously did. He had tied into NORAD!' " Reagan continued with his impromptu review by saying he had found a little bias in the casting of the high school teacher in the movie as "a wimp." Then he turned to Army General John W. Vessey Jr., chairman of the Joint Chiefs of Staff, and said with a smile, "They portrayed the general as this slovenly, mean, unthinking guy." Vessey's face reddened. It was clear to the congressmen that the veteran infantry combat officer did not like being compared by his commander in chief to a celluloid caricature of an unstable military man who couldn't tell a war game from a Soviet nuclear attack.[14]

Reagan at least knew that *War Games* was a film. At other times he related cinematic scenes of heroism as if they were historical events. He also gave historical import to World War II propaganda stories that lodged in his mind as fact. The most famous of these is a story he told on several occasions during the campaigns of 1976 and 1980 and repeated on December 12, 1983, to the annual convention of the Congressional Medal of Honor Society, meeting in New York City. Reagan called it "a thrilling story of heroism," as indeed it was. During the course of a bombing raid over Europe during World War II, a B-17 was hit by antiaircraft fire. The young ball-turret gunner had been severely wounded, and other crew members were unable to get him out of the turret. As the B-17 returned over the English Channel, it began to lose altitude and the commander ordered the men to bail out. "And as the men started to leave the plane, the last one to leave—the boy, understandably, knowing he was left behind to go down with the plane, cried out in terror—the last man to leave the plane saw the commander sit down on the floor," Reagan said. "He took the boy's hand and said, 'Never mind, son, we'll ride it down together.' Congressional Medal of Honor, posthumously awarded."

This report provoked Lars-Erik Nelson, the Washington bureau chief of the *New York Daily News,* to do some checking. He went through the 434 citations of Medal of Honor winners during World War II, found no such award and wrote a column about it.[15] Readers responded to the column, and one of them said that Reagan's story reminded him of a scene in a 1944 movie, *A Wing and a Prayer,* which was set in the South Pacific and starred Dana Andrews. In this scene the pilot of a Navy torpedo bomber with a three-man crew rode the plane down with his wounded radioman after the gunner bailed out. "We'll take this ride together," the pilot said. But another reader was equally certain that Reagan must have found the story in *Reader's Digest,* and Nelson did some more checking on that. It turned out that the magazine had indeed printed a similar story,[16] abridged from an account written by reporter Jack Tait in the *New York Herald Tribune.* Tait's original story was datelined "A Flying Fortress Base, England, Feb. 1, 1944," and was similar to the one Reagan told except that it was another gunner, not the pilot, who went down with the wounded crewman. In Tait's story the last man to jump heard the gunner say, "Take it easy, we'll take this ride together." But Tait was unable to verify the accuracy of the story, which he described as one "circulating at this base that has almost become a legend." This disclaimer was omitted in the abridged *Reader's Digest* account, which was part of a typical package of stories celebrating the World War II heroism of America's fighting men.

Because of the similarities in the wording and the setting, Nelson concluded that Reagan most likely had remembered the *Reader's Digest* account rather than the film. He was offended because Reagan had told a mythical story of heroism to America's most honored heroes, all of whom had impressive and substantiated stories of their own. When Nelson called the White House speechwriting office and asked if anyone bothered to check the accuracy of accounts presented as factual in presidential speeches, he was told by a researcher that it was a story Reagan had told many times before and had brought with him to the White House.[17]

For their part, White House aides could not understand why reporters were making such a fuss about the facts. "If you tell the same story five times, it's true," said White House spokesman Larry Speakes[18] when he was asked about the accuracy of Reagan's story, repeating a rural drollery of his Mississippi boyhood that had become a standard saying among government flacks. Reagan had indeed brought emotional stories of wartime heroism with him to the White House, and his aides thought he had the license to tell them. Long before he spoke to the Medal of Honor winners, the aides had adopted Reagan's own standard of judging stories by their impact rather than their accuracy. The only serious debate within the White House was whether Reagan knew what he was doing when he told a made-up story or whether he had reached a point where he actually could not distinguish films from facts. Many years later Reagan further blurred the issue by acknowledging to reporters that he had seen *A Wing and a Prayer* but also remembered "reading a citation" during his Army days that recommended a medal for a pilot who had ridden his plane down rather than leave a wounded crew member to face death alone. This "citation" may have been the account in *Reader's Digest,* of which Reagan was a faithful reader. But Reagan's comforting comment to Charles McDowell, when the columnist told him a mythical story he believed to be true, suggests that Reagan recognized at some level that he told stories without regard for factual accuracy. After he left the White House, Reagan admitted as much. Discussing the military buildup he had pushed as a top priority, Reagan told Landon Parvin, "Maybe I had seen too many war movies, the heroics of which I sometimes confused with real life, but common sense told me something very essential—you can't have a fighting force without an esprit de corps. So one of my first priorities was to rebuild our military and, just as important, our military's morale."[19] Reagan's stories of heroism were a tool for carrying out this objective. It mattered little to him if the stories he told had been invented by wartime writers and filmmakers or if they had actually occurred.

War movies and the analogies that Reagan took from them would prove to have enormous consequences in his presidency, particularly in

Central America. But peace films such as *War Games* also occupied a crucial compartment in Reagan's emotional arsenal—and would prove even more significant. More than half a century earlier, in a Eureka College production of Edna St. Vincent Millay's antiwar play, *Aria da Capo,* Reagan had portrayed a shepherd who is strangled to death, and he remembered the role in precise detail.[20] In Hollywood he became an avid science-fiction fan, absorbed with a favorite theme of the genre: the invasion from outer space that prompts earthlings to put aside nationalistic quarrels and band together against an alien invader. Reagan liked this idea so much that he tried it out on Gorbachev in their first meeting at Geneva in 1985, saying that he was certain the United States and the Soviet Union would cooperate if Earth were threatened by an invasion from outer space.[21] Reagan's idea was not part of the script, and it startled his advisers. It may also have startled Gorbachev, who did not have at his fingertips the Marxist-Leninist position on the propriety of cooperating with the imperialists against an interplanetary invasion. In any event, Gorbachev changed the subject. Reagan thought this meant he had scored a point, and he proudly repeated what he had said to Gorbachev to a group of Maryland high school students after he returned to the United States.[22] He also repeated it to his advisers, to mixed reactions. Conservative National Security Council staff member Fritz Ermarth, after hearing Reagan deliver a 1987 version of this "romantic fantasy," wrote an angry memo to Colin Powell, then the deputy national security adviser, saying that Earth had in fact been invaded by a devil who forced all the nations of the earth to unite against him. The devil was called Hitler. The memo observed that the great powers had united and defeated him but had not in the process resolved the differences between the United States and the Soviet Union or between democracy and communism.

Powell did not reply to the memo. He knew more than he had ever wanted to know about Reagan's preoccupation with what Powell called "the little green men," and he struggled diligently to keep interplanetary references out of Reagan's speeches. Powell was convinced that Reagan's unique proposal to Gorbachev had been inspired by a 1951 science-fiction film, *The Day the Earth Stood Still,* starring Michael Rennie and Patricia Neal. It was a film with a peace message, one that in a Hollywood still quivering from Red-hunting congressional committees would probably have been permitted only in science fiction. The alien hero of the film, portrayed by Rennie, is an envoy from a benign and highly advanced civilization that has tamed its own violent tendencies by turning peacekeeping duties over to an interplanetary force of robots who are programmed to destroy nations that resort to war. This civilization has been monitoring scientific developments on Earth, with growing alarm. The advanced civilization fears that Earth nations that have penetrated the secrets of the atom will also acquire the means of space travel and carry their weapons and "petty quarrels" into the galaxy. The alien has come to put the planet on notice. His mission is to urge the Earth nations to work together in peace—and to warn them that they will be destroyed by the robotic police force if they do not. For his troubles, the alien is greeted as "a menace from another world" and pursued and eventually killed by U.S. troops. After a miraculous resurrection he gives a departure speech to scientists assembled outside his flying saucer and tells them, "The universe is getting smaller every day. There must be security for all, or no one is secure." The alien then warns the earthlings that they must "join us and live in peace" or be obliterated. "We shall be waiting your decision," he declares before flying away in his saucer. "The decision rests with you."

Reagan's dream of a peaceful, unified planet did not vanish with the departure of this cinematic spaceship. He had been idealistic enough to join the United World Federalists at the end of World War II. He had a horror of nuclear weapons, which he proposed banning altogether in his 1986 meeting with Gorbachev in Reykjavik, and particularly of the reliance of the superpowers on "mutual assured destruction" (MAD) to keep the peace. Reagan also believed in the probability of life on other planets. The fantasy of an interplanetary invasion that would force the nations of the world to cooperate seemed to him a useful and dramatic way of making the point that mankind has a shared interest in world peace.

The president's advisers shared neither Reagan's fantasy nor his belief in the efficacy of the interplanetary analogy. Powell, a conspicuous success in a job where many failed during the Reagan administration, was a distinguished combat officer who was fond of the president and possessed a military man's respect for his commander in chief. He was also among the most moderate, realistic and thoughtful of Reagan's aides. While he would change his stand during the Bush administration, in which he served as chairman of the Joint Chiefs of Staff, Powell during his tenure as national security adviser reinforced Reagan's view that military action in Panama would be resented throughout Latin America. Powell was also one of the few high-ranking administration officials to recognize that the CIA-armed contras lacked much support either in Nicaragua or on Capitol Hill, and he helped engineer the compromise providing "nonlethal aid" to the rebels so that they would neither be wiped out nor cause a wider war on Reagan's watch. But the president's casual references to invasions from outer space made Powell uneasy. He worried that people might think Reagan was really concerned about interplanetary invasions if he kept raising the issue. When the subject came up, Powell would roll his eyes and say to his staff, "Here come the little green men again."

But it was difficult, particularly toward the end of the presidency, to deter Reagan from using favorite stories in a speech. While the president was usually willing to say anything his advisers put in his hands, he liked adding personal touches and dramatic flourishes to important speeches. One of these occasions was Reagan's address to the United Nations General Assembly in 1987, scheduled less than two months before the superpower summit in Washington at which he and Gorbachev would sign the Intermediate Nuclear Forces (INF) treaty. Reagan's speeches to the United Nations were a measure of the distance he had traveled in dealing with the Soviet Union. In 1982, when he gave his first speech to the international body, the United Nations was a forum from which to challenge the Soviets. But in his second term the United Nations became a place for peace speeches, and especially so in this year when Gorbachev was coming to America. When the draft of the 1987 U.N. speech was circulated, Reagan saw another opportunity to draw upon his fantasy of interplanetary invasion. He scribbled out a passage with a version of the story that he had told Gorbachev in Geneva, knowing full well that Powell and Secretary of State Shultz thought the reference naïve. Reagan did not care about that. Maybe there were little green men on other planets and maybe not, but Reagan knew that his story was a transcendent and understandable way of expressing the primacy of world peace and the necessity of cooperation between the superpowers. Powell, who had kept similar passages out of other speeches, realized that the example was important to Reagan and yielded.

"In our obsession with antagonisms of the moment, we often forget how much unites all the members of humanity," Reagan told the U.N. General Assembly on September 21, 1987. "Perhaps we need some outside, universal threat to make us recognize this common bond. I occasionally think how quickly our differences worldwide would vanish if we were facing an alien threat from outside this world. And yet, I ask you, is not an alien force already among us? What could be more alien to the universal aspirations of our peoples than war and the threat of war?"

This was Reagan at his most idealistic, the Reagan who abhorred war and who questioned the foundations of modern deterrence by proposing to the leader of the Soviet Union that all nuclear weapons be abolished. It was the Reagan who proposed "my dream" of an antimissile space shield and who offered to share with the Soviets the technology he believed would make it possible. It was the Reagan who believed, along with the alien in *The Day the Earth Stood Still,* that "there must be security for all or no one will be secure." It was the visionary Reagan, leaving Red Square to proclaim the end of the Cold War and the beginning of a new era in superpower relations.

And it was also the real Reagan, performing as peace president in the role that suited him best. This role dismayed many of his conservative supporters, who preferred his message of freedom to his message of peace. Reagan thought the message was indivisible, and he realized sooner than most of his supporters that the Communist system was on the ropes. Reagan believed that freedom would triumph. He believed in heroism, in the triumph of goodness, in happy endings. He believed in peace through strength, but he also believed in peace.

Most Americans believed in these things, too, and Reagan knew they believed in them. It was not surprising that he drew inspiration and examples from war movies and science-fiction films. Hollywood excels in these, or once did, and Hollywood had been the center of Reagan's life from the time he was twenty-six years old until after he turned fifty. Even when he was gone from Hollywood, Hollywood was never gone from him. He watched movies whenever he could, and the movies were the raw material from which he drew scenes and sustenance. He converted movie material into his own needs. And he remained an actor as well as a moviegoer. He thought of himself as a performer, and he believed that his performances had a purpose. He was an actor, in the White House and out of it. Acting was what he did best.

OFFSTAGE INFLUENCES

Washington needs new men and new ideas. By
your appointments, you can give the country a sense
of excitement, hope and drive to government which
we have not seen since FDR.

RICHARD NIXON,
MEMO TO PRESIDENT-ELECT REAGAN,
November 17, 1980

The diverse supporting cast that accompanied this performing president to center stage was assembled in an unusual manner. Reagan was sixty-nine years old on November 4, 1980, when he was elected the fortieth president of the United States by an electoral landslide. He had bypassed traditional paths to the presidency. Because he had entered public life as a celebrity at the age of fifty-five, Reagan lacked the network of alliances and friendships normally forged by politicians as they scramble up the career ladder. California had been Reagan's home for almost half a century and was the entire source of his political experience. Washington was the strange, faraway seat of "guvment" where Reagan's only significant tie was his friendship with Paul Laxalt of Nevada, a U.S. senator since 1974 and one of the few elected politicians who knew Reagan well enough to call him "Ron." Except for William J. Casey, few other members of the Reagan entourage had any

Washington experience. Most of Reagan's friends were wealthy entrepreneurs who were totally mystified by the ways of Washington. The cadre of aides who had stuck with him since Sacramento—most notably Edwin Meese and Michael Deaver—also knew little about how the world worked in what the president-elect had long described as "the puzzle palaces on the Potomac." But neither Reagan nor his aides seemed troubled by their inexperience nor anxious to rush the presidency by trading California's mild climate for a Washington winter. After the election Reagan vacationed at his mountaintop ranch northwest of Santa Barbara, then flew to Washington on November 17 to meet congressional leaders and members of the Washington establishment. He returned to his home in Pacific Palisades on November 21. Preparations for the advent of the Reagan administration were left to Meese, who directed the transition team and shuttled back and forth between Washington and Los Angeles.

The Reagan campaign of 1980 had been a turbulent experience for Meese, a former deputy prosecuting attorney who had served six years as Reagan's chief of staff in Sacramento. The transition would be trying, too. Meese idolized Reagan, valued his ideas and knew how to give them political shape. He shared Reagan's shining optimism to a remarkable degree, also seeing the world as he would have liked it to be. Outsiders found Meese both agreeable and impenetrable. He claimed to have no agenda other than the success of Ronald Reagan, but he lacked the protective coating that shielded Reagan from his own mistakes. Aides would make excuses for Reagan when he garbled information or presented fantasies as facts, then blame Meese for the candidate's lazy lack of comprehension. Such criticism frustrated Meese. His bland, deceptively affable manner masked an emotional conviction that he was undervalued by colleagues who questioned his political skills and his proclivity for taking on more than he could manage.

Meese's career had been on hold since Reagan left the governorship in 1974. He had served as vice president of an aerospace company, then taught law at the University of California at San Diego. When he rejoined Reagan in 1979, it was with dreams of guiding him to the White House and once more being chief of staff. But the dream quickly turned into a nightmare. Instead of playing the leading role he had anticipated, Meese found himself immersed in a struggle for survival with campaign manager John P. Sears, a brilliant but moody easterner who had directed Reagan's near-miss campaign against Gerald Ford in 1976. Meese and Sears took an instant dislike to each other, perhaps because they shared illusions of indispensability. Sears, who was waging his own rearguard battle with conservatives who thought him insufficiently ideological, had little respect for Reagan's intelligence or work habits. His opinion of the candidate was reflected in a "front-running" strategy that kept Reagan out of range of the national media and out of debates with other candidates. Sears resented what he considered Meese's naïve attempts at political strategy. He poked sarcastic fun at Meese's "bottomless briefcase"[1] into which position papers entered never to emerge. By the time Meese joined the campaign, Sears had already eliminated most of Reagan's cadre of Californians from positions of responsibility. Sears set about to finish the job by attempting to get rid of Meese.

Meese hunkered down, as he had learned to do when under fire in Sacramento, and clung tenaciously to his advisory position in the campaign. He held an unwavering faith in Reagan, and he had seen comets rise and fall around him in California. The Sears comet descended in Iowa on January 21, 1980, when George Bush won a narrow upset victory in the Republican caucuses. Overnight, Sears became the hunted and Meese the hunter. Meese had by now acquired a valuable ally in Laxalt, who believed Reagan was most effective when he abandoned the campaign scripts that had been written for him and followed his own instincts. Laxalt had seen that happen in the North Carolina primary in 1976, and he was confident it could happen again. Laxalt blamed Reagan's defeat in Iowa on the front-running strategy that had avoided an on-the-ground campaign. He knew Reagan well enough to tell him bluntly, "You were sitting on your ass in Iowa."[2]

Reagan listened to Laxalt, who was a vital link with the national conservative movement. He also listened to his wife, who had begun to share Meese's doubts about Sears. Nancy Reagan paid attention to the ledger sheet, and she knew that their wealthy California friends were alarmed by the costs of the campaign, which were bumping up against legal spending limits even before the first primary. The Californians blamed Sears, who was accustomed to the sky's-the-limit spending of the Nixon era, for this profligacy. Sears ignored the alarm bells and concentrated on political strategy. While Reagan was campaigning hard in New Hampshire, Sears effectively maneuvered the other Republican candidates into a debate in Nashua, in which Reagan captured the microphone, and the presidential nomination from George Bush, with a stunning demonstration of onstage presence.* It was a triumph that

---

* Bush was the presumed front-runner after his victory in the Iowa caucuses, and his strategists insisted on a one-on-one debate with Reagan. Sears thought the debate might be necessary, and he had no choice except to accept the ground rules. When Reagan pollster Dick Wirthlin's trackings

came too late for Sears. In the thirty-six days between Reagan's defeat in the Iowa caucuses and his victory in the New Hampshire primary on February 26, 1980, Nancy Reagan had rallied the Californians and the conservatives into an alliance that finished off Sears. Before the results of the New Hampshire primary were known, Reagan called Sears and two other key aides into a hotel room in Manchester and fired them. It was a happy moment for Meese, made even happier that night when Reagan won big in the primary. But Meese was not rewarded with the position of campaign manager. That honor went to William Casey, a wealthy New York attorney with a wartime background in intelligence and a stormy record of government service in the Nixon and Ford administrations. Casey was not well known to the Californians but he had the backing of others who counted with Reagan, including William F. Buckley. What seemed to count especially with Reagan was Casey's reputation for having a way with money and his background as chairman of the Securities and Exchange Commission under Nixon.[4] Casey rescued the campaign from prospective insolvency by firing scores of Washington-based aides who had been brought in by Sears, not even thanking them for their services. But he made a point of cultivating the Californians. Meese took the title of chief of staff, the job he had held in Sacramento and assumed he would be given in Washington. After Reagan was nominated, Casey and Meese set up headquarters in Arlington, Virginia, to run the fall campaign.

But Meese's troubles were just beginning. Neither he nor Casey had any experience in running a national campaign, and they overestimated their candidate at least as much as Sears had underestimated him. Reagan, running loose, displayed his familiar propensity for unverifiable anecdotes and a willingness to say whatever came into his head. What came into his head were happy thoughts about creationism and Taiwan and confusion about the origins of the Ku Klux Klan.* By early Septem-

---

showed that Reagan had pulled ahead of Bush after an earlier multi-candidate debate in Manchester, Sears decided that it was no longer in Reagan's best interests to exclude the other Republican candidates. Sears then invited the four other Republican candidates, who were still campaigning in New Hampshire, to come to Nashua. This attempt to change the ground rules was labeled an "ambush" by the Bush camp and resisted by *Nashua Telegraph* editor Jon Breen, the debate moderator. When Breen instructed that Reagan's microphone be turned off, Reagan emotionally said, "I paid for this microphone, Mr. Green [sic]." Although Breen did not know it, the Reagan camp had made it a point to employ the sound technician, who had no intention of turning off the microphone.[3]

* At a news conference in Dallas, Reagan tried to please a questioner from a religious publication and agreed that creationism should be taught as an alternative theory to Darwinism in the public

ber the candidate's gaffes had become so numerous that reporters on the Reagan plane were hard-pressed to keep track of them, and Democratic strategists were optimistic that the election campaign would be turned into a referendum on Reagan rather than on President Carter. Neither Meese nor anyone else on the Reagan team seemed capable of controlling the candidate. Once again, Nancy Reagan intervened decisively. Ignoring Meese and Casey, she sought help from Stuart Spencer, a onetime favorite strategist who had been blacklisted for leading President Ford's effort to deny Reagan the nomination in 1976. Nancy Reagan was not one to allow old grudges to stand in the way of her husband's election, which she realized Reagan was in danger of blowing. Spencer was flattered to be called in, and willing to help. He had a middle-ground view of Reagan, valuing his uncommon skills as a communicator while also recognizing his capacity for political self-destruction. Spencer flew to Washington to see Reagan. When a reporter asked him what he was doing there, he grinned and said, "I'm here to see old foot-in-the-mouth."[6]

Spencer's irreverence disguised a keen understanding of Reagan. He had worked for him and against him and he understood that Reagan was primarily a performer with a keen sense of how he was playing to his audience. What Spencer realized in his first days on the campaign was that Reagan had a case of the jitters because his performance as presidential nominee was going badly. With Casey and Meese ensconced in Arlington, Spencer and longtime Reagan aide Mike Deaver formed their own team on the campaign plane, LeaderShip 80, where they steadied the candidate by swapping stories with him and smoothing out his schedule. These confidence-building measures proved congenial to Reagan, who settled down and concentrated on his performances. But while Reagan was regaining his sense of direction, a tense rivalry developed offstage between the competing campaign factions. Spencer and Deaver viewed Casey and Meese as self-important ideologues who lacked understanding of practical politics and the tem-

---

schools. On other occasions he made positive references to Taiwan while his running mate George Bush was on a fence-mending mission to the People's Republic of China. The remark that caused the biggest flap occurred on Labor Day, when Jimmy Carter formally opened his fall campaign with a speech in Tuscumbia, Alabama, a center of Ku Klux Klan activity. When Reagan spoke in Detroit that evening, he said, "Now I'm happy to be here while he is opening his campaign down there in the city that gave birth to and is the parent body of the Ku Klux Klan." The crowd gasped. Reagan knew immediately that he had misspoken. "I blew it," he told his aides afterward. "I should never have said what I said."[5]

perament of their candidate. At headquarters Spencer was seen as a hired gun who was indifferent to any policy agenda and Deaver as a sycophant interested in advancing himself with the Reagans. Leader-Ship 80 went its own way, largely ignoring the complicated campaign apparatus that had been created in Arlington. The rival teams managed to work together in uneasy coexistence as Reagan prepared to debate Carter in Cleveland on October 28, but their differences never healed. Spencer and Deaver believed that Meese was too disorganized and unrealistic to function effectively as White House chief of staff, and they knew they would be frozen out if he were given the job. They were determined to deny it to him. The post-debate polls convinced Spencer that the election was as good as won, and that it was time to act. He decided to raise "the Meese question" directly with the Reagans.

Much has been written in the intervening years, some of it by me, about the conspiracy among Spencer, Deaver and that most valuable of allies, Nancy Reagan, to make James Baker the White House chief of staff. The conspiracy existed, all right, and it proved successful. But Reagan was not an unwitting bystander. As Spencer remembers it, he and Deaver were worried that Meese might have the inside track to the job and decided they needed a candidate of their own. Baker, a Texas lawyer with Marine discipline and Princeton polish, fit the bill. Spencer knew Baker from their days on the Ford campaign, and trusted him to be an honest broker with Reagan. Deaver recognized that Baker was an outsider and would need a Californian experienced in Reagan's ways to help him along.

On October 29, the night after the Carter debate, Spencer broached the subject to the Reagans in their suite at the Hyatt Regency Hotel in Dallas. He began by running down a list of possibilities, including Deaver, eliciting a response from Reagan that "Mike should be the number two guy." When Meese's name came up, Reagan was equally emphatic in his reaction. "Ed cannot be chief of staff," he said. "He's not organized." The comment surprised Spencer, who had been pre-pared to make the same point and had anticipated an argument from Reagan. Instead, Spencer simply agreed with the candidate and brought up Baker's name.[7] On the face of it, Baker seemed an unlikely choice. Reagan had known him for only six months, and did not know him well. Most of Baker's political experience had been acquired in oppo-sition to Reagan, first as President Ford's delegate hunter in 1976 and then as Bush's campaign manager in the 1980 primaries. After Bush became the vice presidential nominee, Baker joined the Reagan campaign and conducted the debate negotiations with Carter's strategists. The negotiations had produced the result most desired by the Reagan camp—a single debate late in the campaign under ground rules unfavorable to the incumbent. Still, no president had ever chosen his former adversary's campaign manager as chief of staff. That did not faze Spencer, who knew that Reagan selected people for what he thought they could do for him rather than for what they had done for others. Spencer and his former partner Bill Roberts had learned this back in 1966 when their firm, Spencer-Roberts, was anathema to conservatives for the perceived sin of having managed Nelson Rockefeller's crucial California presidential primary campaign against Barry Goldwater in 1964. Rockefeller narrowly lost, but the winners did not forgive the losers. Reagan had been the exception. He had been told that Spencer-Roberts was the best Republican campaign firm in California, and he hired them to run his gubernatorial campaign. Reagan was exceptional again this evening in Dallas. Instead of expressing skepticism about Baker, he asked Spencer, "Do you think he'd do it?" Spencer knew the answer to that question. On the morning after the election a distraught Meese learned that he would be "counsellor to the president"[8] and that Baker would be chief of staff. Meese was hurt and angry and told Deaver that he could not accept a secondary position. But when his anger subsided, Meese changed his mind. He had fought too hard to remain a member of the team to walk away from Reagan in his moment of victory. Once again, Meese swallowed his pride and went along.

Conservatives who greeted Reagan's election as the triumph of an ideological revolution were dismayed at the Baker selection. It was inconceivable to them that Reagan would want a political pragmatist as his top aide, and they saw the appointment as an ominous sign that Reagan was susceptible to manipulation by business-as-usual Republican politicians. Mainstream Republicans outside the conservative camp jumped to the same conclusion. They thought approvingly that the Baker selection signaled Reagan's willingness to listen to conventional political wisdom. Others who knew Reagan better said cynically that it made no difference to him who directed his movies as long as the atmosphere on the set was congenial and he was free to prepare for his performances. All of these opinions had something to recommend them, but all missed the essential point of the decision. Reagan was indeed susceptible to manipulation, and he was often oblivious to what went on around him as long as a mood of harmony prevailed. But Reagan had seen enough of Baker to recognize that he was disciplined and organized, qualities he himself possessed and that he valued highly in others.

Reagan also had an uncommon appreciation of the strengths and weaknesses of Meese, formed over years of working with him. He appreciated Meese's loyalty, which he would return in full measure when Meese became an embattled attorney general during Reagan's second term. He valued Meese's ability to simplify complicated issues, and he knew that Meese was also able to translate his own ideas into prose and programs. Even Meese's critics described him as Reagan's "conceptualizer," a description that Reagan largely endorsed. But Reagan also believed, as he had told Spencer that night in Dallas, that Meese was "not organized." This evaluation, while not precise, was a useful shorthand for describing someone who accepted so many managerial responsibilities that he found it difficult to discharge any of them. Spencer and Deaver had found that Baker was an easy sale. But Reagan bought the product mainly because he had a keen appreciation of the limits of the principal alternative.

Other appointments did not come as easily. Reagan's victory touched off a transition struggle that his former secretary, Helene von Damm, called "the great job scramble."[9] Campaign manager Casey wanted to be secretary of state. William French Smith, Reagan's longtime attorney, wanted to be attorney general. Smith headed a predominantly California group that included many of Reagan's millionaire "kitchen cabinet" from Sacramento days and was called the Transition Advisory Committee. Meese, starting before the election, had secretly launched a recruiting effort headed by E. Pendleton James, a corporate headhunter who was paid out of leftover campaign funds to find talent for the new administration. Eventually, Reagan was given what he asked for, which was a list of three names for every cabinet post. After his short visit to Washington, Reagan held formal meetings in Los Angeles with the Transition Advisory Committee on November 22 and November 24 and informal meetings at his Pacific Palisades home with Smith, Meese and Deaver. Some decisions were made, but the appointments process dawdled. Reagan did not seem to care. He said he wanted to appoint "the best people" and would take the time needed to do it. He was not a traditional president-elect, and he did not feel the need to do things in a traditional way.

The conventional wisdom that has accumulated in the years since the Reagan transition, much of it based on the accounts of those who were eventually appointed, holds that Reagan's remoteness during this period was a harbinger of his delegative presidency. Perhaps it was, for Reagan was always one to leave the work to others whenever he could. But the more important signal of Reagan's conduct during the transition was of the indirect approach he would bring to presidential decisions, producing an apparent disengagement that distanced him so much from actions and appointments that he appeared not to be responsible if they turned out badly. In reality, Reagan took a lively interest in the appointment of most of the people who would become major actors in the drama of his first term. Smith, Meese and Deaver, whose accounts of the transition differ on many particulars, agree that it was Reagan who wanted a list of multiple recommendations. Reagan truly believed, perhaps naïvely, that the development of such a list was a good way of identifying the "best people" he said he wanted in the cabinet. Since Reagan did not know who all these "best people" might be or whether they were even available, he was willing to have a transition group dominated by his trusted Californians do much of the sifting. But he did not rely solely on the accumulated wisdom of Californians who had never been to Washington. Despite his general skepticism of Washington wisdom, Reagan thought very highly of a Republican politician with whom he had corresponded for many years and whose advice he valued. The politician's name was Richard M. Nixon.

Nixon's influence on key appointments and even some of Reagan's strategic decisions is one of the untold stories of the transition. It has gone untold because the Californians claimed pride of authorship for almost every decision and because Nixon was at the time a political pariah whose advice could not be advertised publicly. But Reagan told Nixon in a post-election telephone conversation that he would welcome any advice he had to give. Nixon, never lacking for an agenda, responded with alacrity. He composed an eleven-page memo that was hand-delivered to Reagan in Washington before he returned to Pacific Palisades on November 21. The memo made an effective case for the political strategy Reagan would follow in his first months in office. It made an even more effective case for the men that Reagan would name as secretary of state, director of central intelligence, attorney general and other positions. And it made the decisive argument against George Shultz, a veteran of the Nixon cabinet whom the former president was determined to keep from landing a high post in the Reagan administration.

Reagan held a complex view of Nixon. While greatly admiring him as a president and politician, Reagan was contemptuous of Nixon's skills as a performer and thought him lacking in manners. These faults were in Reagan's view vastly overshadowed by Nixon's record as a staunch anticommunist and conservative. Reagan was mindful that Nixon was a "self-made man" who had, much like Reagan and his millionaire backers, risen to power from humble origins without the advantages of inherited wealth. A friend of Reagan's told me in 1966 that Reagan admired Nixon for "getting off the floor when he was down," a reference to Nixon's recovery from the political defeats of 1960 and 1962 that were widely presumed to have ended his career.

Nixon's emergence as a national politician coincided with Reagan's conversion from the Democratic political faith of his father to conservative Republicanism. Reagan had supported Helen Gahagan Douglas against Nixon when he was elected to the Senate from California in 1950, but he cast his first Republican vote for the Eisenhower-Nixon ticket in 1952. In 1960, Reagan was a "Democrat for Nixon." He wrote Nixon a letter saying that he had heard "a frightening call to arms" in the acceptance speech of John F. Kennedy at the Democratic National Convention. Reagan said that Kennedy's "idea of the 'challenging new world' is one in which the Federal Govt. will grow bigger and do more and of course spend more." [10] By 1962 Reagan had changed his registration to Republican and campaigned strenuously for Nixon in his unsuccessful attempt to win the California governorship. Reagan subsequently gained firsthand appreciation of Nixon's political skills when Nixon outflanked the abortive Reagan presidential campaign in 1968 by obtaining the endorsement of leading southern conservatives. Despite his disappointment Reagan took time off during a critical period of his governorship to campaign for Nixon that fall. "Reagan thought of Nixon as *the* president," said Deaver,[11] who fought a losing battle to persuade Reagan to distance himself from Nixon and especially from Vice President Spiro T. Agnew as they became engulfed by the scandals that brought them down.

Nonetheless, Governor Reagan had reservations about some of President Nixon's policies. He particularly opposed the Family Assistance Plan, Nixon's progressive proposal for reforming the welfare system, and he served as a rallying point for mobilizing conservative sentiment to defeat it. Reagan also resisted the efforts of the Nixon administration, led by Health, Education and Welfare Secretary Elliot L. Richardson, to pressure California into increasing cost-of-living payments to welfare recipients. Reagan fought HEW in the courts and lost, persuaded Agnew to delay enforcement of a court order that would have cut off federal funds and in March 1971 met with Nixon in San Clemente and worked out a political compromise that was useful to both the president and the governor. While they never announced what they had done, Reagan brought California into compliance with federal regulations and softened his public criticisms of the Family Assistance Plan, and Nixon promised that HEW would not stand in the way of a California pilot program requiring able-bodied welfare recipients to work as a condition of receiving aid. The pilot program had mixed success but established Reagan as the champion of "workfare," which has since become the cornerstone of conservative attempts to reform or limit public welfare assistance.[12]

While Reagan rarely expressed his personal reservations about Nixon, other Republican conservatives were aware of them. According to Barry Goldwater, Nixon rudely snubbed the Reagans at a presidential inaugural ball in 1969,[13] something that did not escape the attention of Nancy Reagan. The view of the Reagan camp in Sacramento was that Nixon, and especially such presumed "liberals" in his administration as Richardson and Robert Finch, were jealous of Reagan's popularity among conservatives and of his grace as a performer. I had a rare personal glimpse of one Nixon-Reagan encounter that demonstrated a prickly aspect of their relationship. On March 14, 1970, I attended a Ridder Publications reception at the Capitol Hilton Hotel in Washington, where my bureau chief, Walter T. Ridder, was being installed as president of the venerable Gridiron Club. Ridder had invited me to be his guest, a courtesy he often extended to new members of his Washington bureau, and placed me in the receiving line alongside Reagan. Nixon arrived, waved his aides away and walked down the receiving line. Reagan warmly greeted him and introduced me by saying, "Hello, Mr. President, this is Lou Cannon, he's just written a book about me." Nixon stopped in his tracks, looking as if he had just been slapped. He glared at me, as if he could not understand why anyone would conceivably write a book about Reagan. Then he glared at Reagan. "Well, I'll *scan* it," Nixon announced, and proceeded down the reception line. Reagan saw that I was shaken by the unexpected ferocity of Nixon's response. He waited until Nixon was out of earshot and said quietly to me, "Well, Lou, he just took care of you—and me."

Three years later I had another personal glimpse of Reagan's dualistic view of Nixon. On April 30, 1973, the unfolding revelations of the Watergate scandal forced Nixon to fire H. R. Haldeman and John Ehrlichman, whom he called "two of the finest public servants it has been my privilege to know." The next day Reagan defended the dismissed aides, saying they "are not criminals at heart." [14] He also continued to defend Nixon as the scandal deepened, declaring in public that Nixon was governing effectively despite Watergate and in private that he was the victim of a "lynch mob" determined to hound him from office. When I talked to Reagan as a reporter for *The Washington Post* in May 1973, shortly after the firings, he expressed firm support for the president. However, in a private conversation afterward he acknowledged discontent with the quality of Nixon's performance in a nationally televised speech announcing the dismissals. Nixon had used the occasion to throw out an ancillary line of defense, suggesting that Watergate was similar to the "excesses" routinely practiced by both parties in presidential campaigns. "Two wrongs do not make a right," he declared. Reagan seemed especially bothered by Nixon's heavy-handed delivery of this sentence. He repeated the words exactly as Nixon had said them, mimicking his voice and giving heavy emphasis to the words "do not." When I asked Reagan what was wrong with this, he replied succinctly, "It's a toss-off line, that's not the way to say it." Reagan then repeated the sentence, as he would have said it, softly and almost as an afterthought. "That's the way to say it," he said.

And yet Reagan stuck with Nixon when it mattered. Even though he had privately disapproved of Nixon's bold stroke in establishing relations with the People's Republic of China, he publicly defended it and accepted Nixon's assignment to explain this great reversal in U.S. diplomacy to Chiang Kai-shek. (Reagan flew to Taiwan on this mission in October 1971 shortly before Henry Kissinger visited Peking to make arrangements for Nixon's visit the following February.) Reagan also stuck with Nixon during the Watergate scandal long after his advisers had concluded that the president was a liar and a lost cause. Not until August 6, 1974, when Nixon's resignation speech was being prepared, did Reagan acknowledge that the president had deceived the country and Congress about the Watergate coverup. Even then, Reagan's demand was not for resignation but for Nixon to go before Congress and explain what had happened. Within three weeks of Nixon's resignation, and before he was pardoned by Ford, Reagan was urging that Nixon not be prosecuted, saying, "The punishment of resignation certainly is more than adequate for the crime." [15]

Perhaps it was this record of support that preserved the Nixon-Reagan relationship over the years. When Reagan challenged President Ford for the Republican nomination in 1976, Nixon called John Sears with friendly advice. "He wasn't supporting Reagan, but he wasn't rooting against him," Sears told journalist Jules Witcover. During the 1980 campaign Nixon again made it a point to keep in touch with Reagan, using his former speechwriter Ken Khachigian as the primary channel. Nick Ruwe, a former Nixon advanceman who was serving as the exiled president's chief of staff, twice flew to Kansas City for secret meetings with Khachigian, who was then writing speeches for Reagan aboard LeaderShip 80. Reagan's advisers solicited Nixon's advice, although it was understood on both sides that anything Nixon said would be kept secret for political reasons. At the time Watergate was a vivid memory and Nixon's personal campaign to rehabilitate himself had barely begun. Nixon's name was poison to the press and much of the public, but not to Reagan. Reagan thought that Nixon knew more about Washington than anyone else on the Republican side, and this view had been strengthened during the campaign. "Nixon uniformly gave excellent advice," recalls Khachigian. "When he was not dealing with his own campaigns, he was an extraordinary analyst." On the weekend before the election, when Reagan's campaign team was nervously waiting out the possibility that Carter would engineer a release of the American hostages in Iran, Spencer had Khachigian place a call to "the Old Man"—as Khachigian usually called Nixon—to obtain his political evaluation of the situation. Nixon reinforced the inclination of the Reagan team to sit tight, operating on the premise that it was too late for a dramatic hostage release to turn the election around.[16]

Nixon's post-election memo, typed single-spaced and initialed "RN," was dated November 17, 1980, and delivered to Reagan at 716 Jackson Place, a government-owned townhouse near the White House where the president-elect stayed on his visit to Washington after the election. The memo began "by observing that Nancy and you have made all Americans proud again by your conduct during and since the election campaign." Nixon said he wanted "absolutely nothing" from Reagan except his success in office, then quickly got down to business. "As you know, I believed before the election that, while foreign policy was to me the most important issue of the campaign, the economic issue was the one which would have the greatest voter impact. Now I am convinced that decisive action on the home front is by far the number one priority. Unless you are able to shape up our home base it will be almost impossible to conduct an effective foreign policy. Consequently, I would suggest that for at least six months you not travel abroad and that you focus the attention of your appointees, the Congress and the people on your battle against inflation. . . . The time to take the heat for possibly unpopular budget cuts is in 1981, not 1982 or 1984." Nixon went on to say that U.S. foreign policy during the first six months of the Reagan administration could be carried out by "experienced people in State and Defense who reflect your views."

This advice to tackle the economy first and shove foreign policy to the back burner squared with Reagan's inclinations and with Reagan pollster Richard Wirthlin's findings that inflation was the number one public concern.[17] Reagan was delighted with the recommendation. Without mentioning Nixon's name, he repeated the opening portion of the memo from memory to a friend and concluded, "If we get the economy in shape, we're going to be able to do a lot of things. If we don't, we're not going to be able to do anything." Gradually, the Reagan inner circle became aware that Nixon's advice had been given and appreciated, although few of them saw the actual memo. One Reagan aide subsequently told me, perhaps a bit cynically, "Nixon is telling us, don't do as he did, do as he says."

Nixon had plenty more to say. The main purpose of his memo was to advance the appointment of his former chief of staff, General Alexander M. Haig Jr., as Reagan's secretary of state. Nixon recognized that his favorite adviser, Henry Kissinger, had no standing with Reagan, and he also realized that Shultz was popular with the Reagan team. After saying that he realized Kissinger was not under consideration, Nixon said that whoever was appointed secretary of state must have "a thorough understanding" of every region in the world. "He must also share your general views with regard to the Soviet threat and foreign policy generally," Nixon wrote. "These requirements pretty much limit those who could be considered. Haig meets them all. He would reassure the Europeans, give pause to the Russians, and in addition, because of over five years as Henry's deputy in the White House and two years at NATO, he has acquired a great deal of experience in dealing with the Chinese, the Japanese, the various factions in the Mideast, the Africans and the Latin Americans. He is intelligent, strong and generally shares your views on foreign policy. Those who oppose him because they think he is 'soft' are either ignorant or stupid. Others who raise the specter that he was somehow involved in Watergate simply don't know the facts. On the contrary, I can vouch from experience that he did an outstanding job helping to keep the wheels of government moving during the time we were under such enormous assault in the Watergate period. He would be personally loyal to you and would not backbite you on or off the record." Nixon said that Haig's "one potential weakness" might be a reluctance to clean house in the State Department because he was "a career man." But Nixon argued that Reagan could circumvent this problem by appointing as Haig's deputy "an administrative type who would come in with a big new broom."

Nixon also helped Haig by warning Reagan not to appoint him as secretary of defense, an advocacy being made within the inner circle by those who did not really want Haig appointed to anything. Since Haig was a military man and the law required the secretary of defense to be a civilian, Congress would have to change the law to enable Reagan to put Haig at the Pentagon. Nixon said Reagan could "probably get" this change but advised against it. He said it would be "a mistake" to name Haig secretary of defense because "you should avoid wherever possible appointing someone who is part of an establishment to clean up an establishment." Nixon's argument on this point suggests he was well informed of the debate within the Transition Advisory Committee, where there were arguments about whether Haig was better suited for State or Defense. This debate had particular pertinence for Caspar W. Weinberger, who had worked for Reagan in California and Nixon in Washington and wanted the appointment as secretary of state. It also was of significance to Shultz, who had served Nixon in multiple capacities, including the cabinet posts of Labor and Treasury, and was on the secretary-of-state list given to Reagan. Nixon, who in 1972 had referred to Shultz as a "candy ass"[18] for his unwillingness to crack down on political opponents, advised Reagan not to hand over State to Shultz. "George Shultz has done a superb job in every government position to which I appointed him," Nixon wrote. "However, I do not believe that he has the depth of understanding of world issues generally and the Soviet Union in particular that is needed for this job."

The Nixon memo arrived at a time when the pendulum had swung away from Haig within the transition advisory group. Haig remembers that former Treasury Secretary William Simon, on the periphery of those influential with Reagan, called him to say that there was sentiment within the kitchen cabinet for making him secretary of defense. Haig wasn't interested. "Bill, it would be wrong for the president and it would be wrong for the country, given my background," he replied. But Haig wanted to be secretary of state, even though he thought the odds were against him. Meese and Deaver, of one mind on this issue, distrusted Haig and did not want him in the cabinet. While Haig appears to have had some support from kitchen cabinet member Justin

Dart,* other members of the Transition Advisory Committee also doubted Haig's loyalty. One of their worries was that Haig was a Nixon man whose appointment would needlessly raise the Watergate issue. But their main concern was that Haig still harbored presidential ambitions. This skepticism persisted even after Reagan had offered Haig the job and he had accepted it. Much to his disgust, Haig was summoned to Washington in December and cross-examined intensely about his ambitions by Laxalt, Meese, Baker, Deaver and Reagan's first national security adviser, Richard V. Allen.[19]

Haig ultimately was appointed because the people in his corner were the ones who mattered most—Ronald Reagan and Richard Nixon. By Haig's own account, he and Reagan had spent less than three hours together at the time of his appointment. Their only private meeting had taken place nearly a year and a half earlier at Reagan's ranch. At the time Haig still fancied himself a potential presidential candidate, and he talked as an equal with Reagan about world affairs and politics while Nancy Reagan discreetly went riding alone. As Haig related the meeting in his memoir *Caveat,* Reagan asked him to "join his team," which he interpreted as an appeal for him to abandon his own putative candidacy. Haig said that it was "inconceivable to me that I could present any threat to Reagan's nomination. But I was not ready to swear fealty to a liege."[20]

What Haig was ready to do, and did, was to tell Reagan that he would not say anything against him or raise any issues of difference beyond the military draft, which Haig favored and Reagan opposed. Reagan was impressed by Haig. After he departed, Reagan called Deaver and recounted the conversation, something he rarely did. Reagan told Deaver that Haig wanted to run for president and that he had urged him to test his support around the country. "Reagan was very smart about that," Deaver said. "It was supportive of Haig, but Reagan knew there wasn't going to be any demand for Haig to run." Reagan concluded the conversation by telling Deaver, "He isn't going to be president, but I'd like to have him in my cabinet."[21]

On matters that were contentious among his advisers, Reagan always preferred to work indirectly. He abhorred personal quarrels of any sort and would go to extreme lengths to avoid them. While projecting an image of decisiveness, he could be resolutely indecisive if his decision

---

* Haig told me that Dart, since deceased, had said to him after he was appointed, "Al, you never would have been a secretary of state but for me." As Haig recalls the conversation, Dart claimed he had convinced a majority of the kitchen cabinet to support him instead of Shultz.

seemed likely to reward one group of advisers at the expense of another. This style could be exasperating to his aides, even Deaver, because Reagan would sometimes nod or say nothing at all if asked to make a contentious decision. At such moments the Great Communicator could be so uncommunicative that aides sought clues to his preferences by trying to read his body language. They did not read him right when they downgraded Haig, a decision that went against Reagan's inclinations and Nixon's fervent recommendation. Reagan told me in a 1981 interview that Haig was his first choice for secretary of state.[22] But he was not the first choice of the Transition Advisory Committee, which gave the president-elect a list of three that ranked Shultz first, followed by Haig and Senator Howard Baker of Tennessee. Prodded by Deaver, Reagan agreed to call Shultz, then at Stanford University. But Reagan did not offer Shultz a position in his cabinet. As Shultz remembers the call, Reagan told him, "I'd love to have you in my administration, but I don't want to impose on you." Shultz had not expected a job offer, and none was made. "Well, I'd like to help you in any way I can, but I like what I'm doing, so proceed your own way," he replied.[23] The next day Reagan telephoned Haig and said he wanted him to be his secretary of state.

Afterward, Deaver would say that Haig won the job because of a "misunderstanding" in the telephone conversation between Reagan and Shultz. As Deaver relates it, Shultz had been told he was on the list for Treasury, a job he had held before and did not want again. Reagan was supposed to offer him the appointment as secretary of state. When Reagan made no mention of it, Shultz assumed he was being asked to become secretary of the treasury and turned him down.[24] There is no doubt that Deaver believes this is what happened, but Shultz's recollections do not support him. Shultz says he did not know he was on the list for anything and that nothing Reagan said to him in their telephone conversation gave him a different impression. Much later, when Haig was gone and Shultz had replaced him, Deaver told Shultz that Reagan had actually wanted him at State in the first place. Shultz, despite a high opinion of Deaver, was skeptical. "If that's what he had in mind, it sure didn't come through to me," Shultz said.[25]

Was the appointment of Haig actually a "misunderstanding"? Did Reagan really forget to identify the job he was offering Shultz? Despite my respect for Deaver's observations on matters relating to Reagan, I do not think the historical evidence supports his opinion. What seems to have happened in this case, as in so many others, is that Reagan did what he wanted to do and found a way to do it without offending his advisers. Some early chroniclers of the Reagan presidency contend that Shultz, the president of Bechtel Corporation, was disqualified in Reagan's mind because he had already chosen Caspar W. Weinberger, the general counsel of this multinational corporation, as secretary of defense. But this was not the sort of consideration that usually deterred Reagan. I find it difficult to dismiss Shultz's impression that Reagan was touching base with him rather than offering him a job. In his calls to other prospective appointees, according to all accounts of which I am aware, Reagan mentioned the specific position he was offering. In cases where he thought there might be resistance, Reagan was also capable of being extraordinarily persuasive, as he was when he offered the chief of staff's job to Baker and was again with Shultz when he called him the day that Haig resigned.* But in his December 1980 telephone call, made from his home in Pacific Palisades, Reagan accepted Shultz's vague statement at face value and then told Deaver that Shultz had "no interest" in returning to Washington. By calling Shultz, Reagan had mollified Deaver, who had early doubts about Haig's stability, and complied with the recommendation of his Transition Advisory Committee. By offering the job to Haig, Reagan had done what he really wanted to do and accepted the advice of Nixon in the bargain.

Additional circumstantial evidence in favor of this conclusion is that Reagan seems to have valued Nixon's other personnel recommendations for major posts, with the conspicuous exception of former Treasury Secretary John B. Connally, who had not troubled to conceal his low opinion of Reagan during the early 1980 Republican primaries. Nixon's memo put in several plugs for Weinberger, who was qualified on paper for a variety of posts. The memo said Bill Casey would do "an excellent job" at the Central Intelligence Agency, which Nixon said needed "an entirely new guard and a complete house cleaning" even more than State and Defense. And Nixon advocated the appointment of Smith, "an outstanding lawyer and a good administrator," as attorney general. Nixon might have guessed that Reagan would reward his old friend and longtime attorney with this appointment. According to the

---

* Baker's wife Susan was distressed when she learned that Reagan wanted him as chief of staff because she knew it meant long days and little time for their family. Reagan, aware of this, came over to her at the end of a news conference in Los Angeles the day after he was elected and said, "Let me tell you something. Your husband's not going to work fourteen hours a day in my White House. I just don't believe in that. I believe in my people spending time with their families." Baker subsequently worked many fourteen-hour days, but his wife was impressed by Reagan's showing of concern. "He won her over then and there," Baker told me later.

separate accounts of Smith and von Damm,[26] the decision was made five days later on November 22 when the Transition Advisory Committee formally recommended Smith after a brief deliberation that occurred while Smith was out of the room. Spencer believes the entire discussion was window dressing. He says that on October 29 in Dallas, the night he broached the appointment of Baker for chief of staff, Reagan told him that he wanted Smith to head the Justice Department.[27]

Casey did not have similar assurances, even though he knew Reagan valued his role in rescuing the campaign from insolvency. In *Veil: The Secret Wars of the CIA 1981–1987,* Bob Woodward recounts that Casey, discouraged and knowing he had been rejected for the coveted post of secretary of state, at one point flew home to Long Island in the belief that he was being left in the cold by the Californians and Nancy Reagan now that they no longer had need of him.[28] But Nancy Reagan was rarely involved in personnel matters outside the White House, and Casey did have the backing of Meese, his colleague from Arlington campaign headquarters. Reagan had not given Meese what he wanted, but he valued his recommendations. The big question about Casey in the transition, as it would later be in the administration, was what to do with him. He was mentioned for several jobs, including secretary of commerce and director of central intelligence. Casey did not want Commerce, and Senator Barry Goldwater was pushing strongly for the appointment of Admiral Bobby Ray Inman as CIA director. Von Damm says that Meese spoke up strongly for putting Casey at CIA, making the same point about the necessity of "cleaning up" the agency that Nixon had made in his memo. Arguing that it was better to put Casey at CIA than at Commerce, Meese said that "Bill could turn the CIA around in two years."[29] Despite the reservations of other Californians, Reagan chose Casey for the CIA post. The announcement mildly surprised Spencer, who had hoped that Casey would be given a lesser job.[30] It did not surprise Casey's booster, Meese, who knew that Reagan appreciated Casey's rescue of the campaign from fiscal insolvency.

Reagan also had his own ideas about Weinberger, who had done even more to rescue the financial condition of California during his governorship than Casey had done to balance the books in the 1980 campaign. Like Spencer-Roberts, Weinberger had survived the original sin of serving on the wrong, or Rockefeller, side in the 1964 California Republican presidential primary. The conservatives who found this unforgivable had kept Weinberger out of Reagan's original cabinet in

Sacramento. When Reagan ran into trouble, Weinberger was brought in to replace an incompetent director of finance and put the novice administration on an even fiscal keel. Weinberger graduated from Sacramento to the Nixon administration, where he served capably in various positions. In his memo to Reagan, Nixon said that Weinberger might agree to become budget director again if the position were upgraded and Weinberger made a member of the National Security Council. Nixon also suggested to Reagan that Weinberger could serve him well in Treasury if Bill Simon did not take the job.

For his part, Weinberger wanted to be secretary of state, with the Pentagon a second choice. Nixon's memo beat the drum for Connally, an "excellent manager," as secretary of defense but it had no resonance with Reagan, who considered Connally a "wheeler-dealer" and a protectionist. Reagan much preferred Weinberger, who was committed to the military buildup he had espoused during the campaign and appeared to have the added plus of being a budget cutter. Jim Baker recalled approvingly that in Weinberger's days as Nixon's budget director he had earned the nickname "Cap the Knife."

When the Transition Advisory Committee began its deliberations, the assumption was that Treasury would be easy to fill. Reagan and most of the Californians wanted Simon, who had held the post during the Nixon and Ford administrations. Nixon liked him, too, saying to Reagan in his memo, "you could not go wrong on Bill Simon." Simon was promptly sounded out for Treasury, but his condition of returning to the post a second time was control of administration economic policy. Reagan was unwilling to give that assurance. At the November 24 meeting of the Transition Advisory Committee the president-elect dropped what he called his "bombshell" among his advisers: Simon had withdrawn his name from consideration.[31] The team's second choice—also boosted by Nixon—was also unavailable. He was Walter Wriston, a New York banker (Citicorp), who set no conditions for the job but was unwilling to make the financial disclosures necessary for confirmation. The job went to the third choice on the list, Donald T. Regan, the head of the Wall Street investment firm of Merrill Lynch, whose name had been brought up by Casey at a time when it seemed certain that Simon would take the job.

Reagan barely knew who Regan was when he called him and asked him to become secretary of treasury. But he knew most of the others that he called, and played a major role in selecting many of them. Richard Schweiker, a loyalist since 1976, let Reagan know through their mutual friend Paul Laxalt that he wanted to be secretary of health and human services. Reagan promptly ordered the appointment, without bothering to consult any adviser or any list. He acted with similar dispatch in appointing Raymond J. Donovan as secretary of labor. Donovan, owner of a New Jersey construction company, had raised prodigious sums for Reagan at a time when financial support was hard to come by in the Northeast. Reagan also acknowledged a debt to Drew Lewis, his point man at the Republican National Committee and a skilled political operative. Lewis' reward was the Department of Transportation. Reagan had been impressed with Jeane J. Kirkpatrick ever since he read her famous article arguing that it was necessary for the United States to distinguish between friendly "authoritarian" regimes and hostile "totalitarian" regimes.[32] He named Kirkpatrick, then still a nominal Democrat, ambassador to the United Nations and gave her cabinet status, a move unpopular with many of his advisers. Reagan also wanted David Stockman, then a congressman from Michigan, as director of the Office of Management and Budget, despite the reservations of some advisers that Stockman was too young and inexperienced for the job. But Stockman had impressed Reagan by effectively impersonating John Anderson and then Jimmy Carter when Reagan prepared for his debates with these adversaries. Performances always counted highly with Reagan, who told Stockman when he appointed him, "Dave, ever since you battered me in those mock debates I've been looking for some way to get even. Now I think I have the answer. I'm going to send you to OMB."[33]

Reagan was uninterested in many of the other cabinet positions, and he was content in some cases to follow the lead of others who were more interested. The secretary of commerce was selected by George Bush, whose choice of outspoken Connecticut businessman Malcolm Baldrige appealed to Reagan largely because Baldrige's hobby was roping cattle at rodeos. He did not know anything beyond that about Baldrige and he knew even less about John Block, an Illinois corn and hog farmer who became secretary of agriculture largely through the efforts of Senator Bob Dole of Kansas. Using Laxalt as his conduit, Dole sent Reagan a map marked with the home states of the cabinet choices. The map made the point that the Midwest was unrepresented in the cabinet, and Block believes this exercise in regional politics gave him the edge over Richard Lyng, who had headed the California Department of Agriculture during the Reagan governorship. At Reagan's invitation, Block flew to Los Angeles and spent two hours at his Pacific

Palisades home chatting with the Reagans, Deaver, Meese and Martin Anderson. Block was impressed with Reagan but realized quickly that neither he nor any of his aides were familiar with the problems of agriculture. Soon after Block returned to his hotel, he received a call from Reagan offering him the job.[34]

Another appointee Reagan had never heard of before his transition advisers came up with the name was Samuel T. Pierce, a New York lawyer and a black man who had served capably as head of the legal division in Treasury during the Nixon administration. Pierce was the recommendation of kitchen cabinet member Alfred Bloomingdale, who took Reagan at his word that he wanted a black in the cabinet.[35] Pierce had a distinguished legal and political résumé and there were murmurings among the transition advisers that he would be an appropriate replacement on the Supreme Court for Justice Thurgood Marshall, the only black ever to serve on the high court, should the opportunity present itself. Pierce was the unanimous recommendation of the Transition Advisory Committee as secretary of housing and urban development.

Reagan had an understanding with Laxalt that he could choose the secretary of the interior, and Laxalt picked Clifford Hansen, a dependable former two-term senator from Wyoming. Hansen, however, was no more willing than Wriston to submit financial disclosure statements, and Laxalt settled for an obscure conservative public-interest attorney named James G. Watt.[36] Another second-choice find of Laxalt's was James Edwards as secretary of energy.[37] A dentist and former governor of South Carolina, Edwards was given the job because he had supported Reagan in 1976 and because the first choice—millionaire Houston oilman Michael Halbouty, another Nixon favorite—also declined to disclose his finances. All of Reagan's substitute appointments would become figures of controversy within the administration, and all eventually would resign under pressure or be fired. But these appointments, except for Watt, did not seem especially significant at the time they were made. Reagan did not care that much who directed the Department of Energy, which he had promised to abolish. He cared even less about the Department of Education, also targeted for extinction, where veteran educator Terrel H. Bell of Utah was installed as head of what Meese had described as a "great bureaucratic joke."[38]

But despite Reagan's lack of interest in what he saw as minor cabinet positions, the overall record of the transition contradicts the conventional wisdom that the president-elect was largely a bystander during the selection of his cabinet. This view of Reagan's role, advanced both by critics and supporters, became a central myth of his presidency and a defense for him when appointments and events went awry. Reagan both began and ended his presidency as a popular leader who essentially pleaded no contest to the accusation that he failed to mind the store. There were certainly occasions, probably far too many occasions, when this accusation had validity because the responsibilities of the president are vast and Reagan focused on a few high-visibility issues of great importance to him. But Reagan was not disengaged during the transition, at least not on the appointments that mattered most to him. The record shows that Reagan accepted advice from many quarters, giving weight to the well-publicized preferences of the Californians and the secret recommendations of Nixon, and that he made his own choices for the positions he considered most important. The supporting cast that surrounded the performing president when he came to Washington was a coalition government in the making, one in which many views and many incompatible temperaments would be expected to blend together. It would be an administration of wide diversity in competence and ideology, with many accomplishments and many failures. But Reagan did not embark on his greatest public performance with a cast that had been assembled by others. As much as any president, he deserves the credit and the blame for what would be done in his name in the puzzle palaces of the Potomac.

6

HEROIC DREAMS

*I have always stated that the nearest thing to eternal life
we'll ever see on this earth is a government program.*

RONALD REAGAN,
April 9, 1986[1]

Reagan arrived in Washington for the first act of his presidency
equipped with a familiar script of his own devising[2] and accompanied
by a production team that was determined to make him a star. The
team included experts in the arts of polling, politics and public relations, most of them secure in their specialties and mindful of Reagan's
reliance on offstage assistance. But it was the script that was compelling,
and it was Reagan who wrote it. While he would become the most
highly managed president in the history of the republic, Reagan did not
depend on his managers for political inspiration. He had found his
ideas for himself, drawing on the resources of his life and the requirements of his performances, and shaped them into a story that would
become the screenplay of his presidency.

Most of the shaping of these ideas had occurred in the 1950s, when
Reagan played host for television's popular *General Electric Theater*
and toured the country giving speeches at GE plants. Reagan's weekly
television appearances kept him visible to an older cinematic audience

from which he was beginning to fade in memory while making him known to a younger generation that had never seen his movies. Reagan often compared General Electric to "the cavalry [riding] to the rescue,"[3] complete with bright lights and a panoply of electrical gadgets for his Pacific Palisades home.

GE's most important contribution to Reagan's political apprenticeship was not built-in appliances but built-in audiences. By his own estimate Reagan spent two of his eight years with General Electric on the road (traveling by train, because he was afraid to fly), visiting all of GE's 135 plants and speaking to 250,000 employees. The script that emerged from this corporate-sponsored odyssey was patriotic, antigovernment, anticommunist and probusiness, and homogenized enough that it could be used before any audience anywhere in the country. It was known as The Speech. While ostensibly and at first genuinely nonpartisan, The Speech was on the cutting edge of the emerging debate between liberals who wanted the federal government to become more activist in reducing social and economic inequities and conservatives who wanted the government to spend less and leave business alone. Reagan could not enter this debate directly because business considerations required his sponsors to maintain a façade of political neutrality. This proved a boon to Reagan, whose speeches were not weighed down by the boilerplate anti–New Deal clichés then fashionable among Republican conservatives. Instead, Reagan constructed his own speech, one that presented essentially controversial ideas as uncontroversial verities and was festooned with Hollywood anecdotes and "human interest stories" clipped from local newspapers or *Reader's Digest*.

General Electric's requirement of nonpartisanship was also psychologically suitable to Reagan, a registered Democrat until the final year of his GE contract, but a Democrat who no longer accepted the central tenets of the national leadership of his party. Ironically, the nonpartisan cast of The Speech eventually made it attractive to those conservatives who recognized that Reagan had a broader reach among Democrats and independents than the usual Republican candidate. Some liberals recognized this as well, and Reagan ultimately became a controversial liability for GE, which dismissed him as host of *General Electric Theater* in 1962. By then, however, Reagan had a personal political following. He gave The Speech in his national political debut for Barry Goldwater in 1964. And while Reagan tinkered with the text and refined some of its rough spots in three subsequent political campaigns of his own, The Speech changed remarkably little during a quarter century when there were many fundamental changes in the United States.

The basic idea of The Speech was that the federal government was too big, too bothersome and too antibusiness. "Government does not solve problems, it subsidizes them,"[4] Reagan was fond of saying, in a one-liner he did not abandon when he became the chief executive of the government. Reagan viewed government as an adversary to be resisted, especially by its leaders. Government by nature was inefficient and centralizing. It stifled individual initiative and restricted profits and was therefore inimical to freedom. "It is time we realized that profit, property and freedom are inseparable," Reagan said. "You cannot have one of them without the others."[5] Reagan was an early reader of *National Review,* the pioneer conservative magazine founded by William F. Buckley in 1955. Long before he was willing to describe himself as a conservative, he was attracted by *National Review*'s anticommunism and its perception that "statism" was advancing the socialist cause within the Western world. He incorporated these insights into The Speech, prompting conservatives to look upon him as a potential political candidate. In 1962 California conservatives urged Reagan to run against moderate U.S. Senator Thomas W. Kuchel in the Republican primary. Reagan, who knew the difference between a cause and a suicide mission, politely turned them down. Instead, he served as campaign chairman for Loyd Wright, an apocalyptic ultraconservative who opposed Kuchel and received only 15 percent of the vote in the primary. The loss did no damage to Reagan, who by then had more speaking requests than he could ever meet.

An essential feature of The Speech was its ridicule of federal income taxes. Taxes were the fuel that propelled government, and its worst feature. "We stand between the taxpayer and the taxspender," Reagan declared when he was inaugurated governor of California.[6] These words were written by Reagan, not a speechwriter, and accurately reflected his outsider's view of government (the "taxspender") and his preoccupation with reducing the revenues that government collected. By the time he became president, Reagan had been exposed to an economic theory that appeared to justify his gut belief that Americans would work harder and produce more if their tax burdens were lightened. "Reagan's arrival in Washington coincided with the arrival of the insight we now know as supply side economics," observed Buckley, his friend and sometimes mentor. "He believed that the encumbrances on government were the causes of the sclerosis of the 1970s."[7]

Reagan was receptive to the "supply side" argument that lower tax rates would spur economic productivity because it squared with his personal experience. Just before Reagan went into the Army in 1941 his agent, Lew Wasserman, had capitalized on the anticipated success of *Kings Row* to negotiate a then-fabulous contract for Reagan—$1 million over a seven-year period. This contract made Reagan a wealthy man in the years after World War II, when marginal income tax rates ranged from 82 to 91 percent. Although Reagan somewhat sardonically referred to himself as "the Errol Flynn of the Bs," his income in 1946 was $169,750, a little less than Flynn's, and the equivalent of $718,300 in 1980 dollars and more than $1 million today. "You could only make four pictures and then you were in the top bracket," Reagan said in the early stages of his presidency as he made the case for lower tax rates to his budget director, David Stockman. "So we all quit working after four pictures and went off to the country."[8]

Stockman accurately concluded from Reagan's frequent repetition of this story that his experience had conditioned him to accept the supply-side dogma that tax cuts were desirable under any economic circumstances—a position Stockman considered foolish. But "taxes" had a deeper and darker significance for Reagan than his young budget director realized. Unlike most of Reagan's stories of Hollywood days, which are usually romanticized and complete with happy endings, his recollection of entering the world of "the big money" is associated with an emotional cluster of unhappy events. While he was reaping the rewards of Wasserman's contract after World War II, Reagan was becoming increasingly disappointed with the light, romantic roles in which Warner Bros. preferred to cast him. Reagan was perfectly suited for these roles, and Garry Wills is probably right in contending that the studio had a sounder perception of Reagan's cinematic appeal than he did.[9] But Reagan was unhappy, nevertheless. And while he was battling the studio for more serious and less romantic roles, his real-life personal romance collapsed. The story told by Reagan is that he came home one day to learn from Jane Wyman that their marriage was over.* Reagan did not contest the divorce, but he was surprised, "miserable"[10] and uncharacteristically resentful of what was happening to him. Wyman was given custody of their two children and Reagan assigned the costs of child support. Despite his huge income, he had a sense that his career

---

* Wyman has consistently refused to comment about her marriage to Reagan. She testified at the divorce proceedings that their interests had diverged because of Reagan's increased activity in the Screen Actors Guild. This satisfied the requirement of "extreme mental cruelty" under the prevailing California divorce statute, without offering any clue as to what had really happened. Wyman herself was intensely active in the guild and helped bring Reagan into the leadership. For more on the impact of the divorce on Reagan's life, see Chapter 11.

was slipping and that his financial future was shaky. Reagan took out some of his negative feelings on the tax system and the Department of Internal Revenue, which he sometimes called "my senior partner." [11] But since he was then a Democrat supportive of the social programs of the Truman administration, he lacked an appropriate political framework for expressing the intensity of his hostility to the progressive income tax. The best he could do was propose a "human depreciation allowance" [12] on the earnings of actors and athletes on grounds that their normal period of productivity was as limited as any oil well. The idea did not catch on, but the cause of lower taxes became a lifelong obsession with Reagan. Over time he would become a wealthy landowner and learn to take immense advantage of tax shelters. But he always remembered the money he had paid in taxes when he was newly rich and unhappy, and he never forgave the government for taking it from him. Late in the first term of his presidency, White House aide Richard Darman explained Reagan's opposition to a proposed tax increase by saying, "The president absolutely loathes and despises taxes."

Reagan's loathing of government stopped at the water's edge of national defense, a view he held as an interventionist New Dealer beginning during World War II and which he carried with him largely unchanged into conservative politics. When Reagan spoke of military spending, abhorrence of government yielded to a powerful set of symbols emanating from the at-home patriotism of World War II. He never considered his 1980 campaign vows to cut the cost of government and to "restore America's defenses" as competing ideas. "Government" was a barrier to individual freedom. Military strength symbolized the power of the nation rather than the authority of government and was the key to cherished national goals. "National defense is not a threat to peace; it is the guarantee of peace with freedom," Reagan often said. [13] This guarantee was so precious that Reagan kept military spending in a separate mental compartment tucked safely away from his bedrock belief that government was inevitably inefficient. He ignored Republicans who told him that the Pentagon was particularly rife with the "waste, fraud and abuse" that Reagan saw everywhere else in government. Richard Nixon made the point bluntly in the portion of his November 17, 1980, memo that guided Reagan away from naming Al Haig as secretary of defense. "The Pentagon should not be a sacred cow," wrote Nixon, who urged Reagan to make a 10 percent across-the-board cut in civilian employment at the Defense Department. "In going after fraud, for example, I could not urge more strongly that the

Defense Department should not be considered off limits," the memo said. Nixon's warning made no impact on Reagan, whose aides had learned during the 1980 campaign that it was impossible to persuade him to put a price tag on the military force he thought necessary to preserve the peace. Reagan refused to do so, saying that the size and shape of the U.S. military force should be determined by the military strength needed to match the Soviet Union rather than the exigencies of the federal budget. Eventually, economists Martin Anderson and Alan Greenspan fashioned their own estimate of defense costs[14] so that Reagan could present a coherent budget proposal in the major economic speech of his campaign. But Reagan did not know or care what numbers his economists had used to construct this mythical budget, and their estimates were never made explicit.

When Reagan became president he did the opposite of what Nixon had urged and what Budget Director David Stockman and Martin Anderson, now his domestic policy adviser, were advocating. Instead of making across-the-board cuts at the Defense Department, Reagan exempted the Pentagon from the strictures on excessive spending imposed on other departments. His faith was in a tripartite creed of reduced government spending, enhanced military defense and substantially lowered tax rates. He did not recognize that the tax rates he favored were insufficient to produce the revenue to pay for the government programs he thought necessary. He saw no necessity of accommodating any one of his beliefs to make the others more plausible.

This trilogy of ideas formed the ideological core of Reaganism. Reagan had draped these beliefs with anecdotes, scribbled them on cards and shaped them into the famous Speech that he had delivered repeatedly at political gatherings, airport rallies, factory gates, fund-raising receptions and banquet dinners. "You have to keep pounding away with your message, year after year, because that's the only way it will sink into the collective consciousness," Reagan told Landon Parvin. "I'm a big believer in stump speeches—speeches you can give over and over again with slight variations. Because if you have something you believe in deeply, it's worth repeating time and again until you achieve it. You also get better at delivering it."[15] Reagan was very good at delivering this speech by 1980. It was the script he worked from when he came to Washington.

For an actor, a script is a means to an end. The end is the performance. Reagan relished his new role as president, but he did not make the mistake of equating his election with the accomplishment of his objectives. For Reagan, the presidency was also a means toward an end. The end was the translation of his dogmas into lower tax rates, a stronger military force and reduced government spending. "Ronnie had a plan," Nancy Reagan put it succinctly,[16] and Reagan's contribution to translating that plan into reality was to use the "bully pulpit" of the presidency to build support for his policies. As Reagan's comments to Parvin indicate, he realized quite clearly that ideas do not easily take root in the "collective consciousness." He also recognized that the presidency had provided him with the best possible platform from which to give his old familiar speech "over and over again." Reagan treasured that platform and tried not to clutter it with minor messages. He believed that his success would be judged by his program and by the quality of his presidential performances.

Samuel Taylor Coleridge, an admirer of George Washington, wrote about the nation's first president after his death, "He had no vain conceit of being himself all; and did those things only which he only could do." Reagan was no Washington, but he had even less conceit and was similarly convinced of the wisdom of doing only those things that could not be done for him by somebody else. The paradox of the Reagan presidency was that it depended totally upon Reagan for its ideological inspiration while he depended totally upon others for all aspects of governance except his core ideas and his powerful performances. In the many arenas of the office where ideology did not apply or the performances had no bearing, Reagan was at a loss. He left to others what he called the "details" of government, a category that included the preparation of a budget, the formulation of foreign policy, the translation of ideas into legislative proposals and the resolution of conflicts among his principal advisers. Those who of necessity accepted these multitudinous responsibilities had a stake in Reagan's success but not necessarily in his agenda. Their concern was that Reagan look right, sound good, stay popular, do well.

Doing well did not necessarily mean doing everything Reagan wanted done, or thought he wanted done. For the stage managers of the Reagan presidency, the popularity of the star was paramount to his success and had to be preserved, even if that sometimes meant changing the script. And Reagan, who was happy in his work and enjoyed being president, often did not know enough about the "details" to recognize the changes. "I think the biggest surprise at first was to find out how little surprise there was in the actual business of being president," Reagan told me after he left office. "After eight years as governor, it's the same kind of routine—scheduling time for the next day that you were going to have and the various meetings and so forth. . . . I was surprised at how unsurprised I was by the job. You just settled into it." [17]

Reagan's comfort with a familiar routine instilled in him a sense of confidence that had been lacking in the first days of his governorship. The confidence was enhanced because he was surrounded not by the "novice amateurs" of early Sacramento days but by a collection of professionals who consulted the accumulated experience of past presidencies in drawing up their political battle plans. At the national level the Republican Party is fundamentally a presidential party. The 1980 Reagan landslide swept the Republicans into unexpected control of the Senate, with consequences that would prove enormously helpful to the new administration, but the GOP was and remains a permanent minority in the House of Representatives. Ever since Nixon's election in 1968, Republicans in Washington have focused their energies and their expertise on the organization and employment of presidential power. When Reagan took office, his inaugural speech was crafted by one of Nixon's ablest speechwriters,[18] his hundred-day plan prepared by a former Nixon communications director,[19] his political tactics formulated by a former strategist for George Bush and Gerald Ford[20] and his paper flow coordinated by a former assistant to Elliot Richardson.[21] Reagan added assets of his own to this team, notably a counsellor who cared about his ideas,[22] a pollster who understood the sources and limits of his political appeal[23] and a deputy chief of staff who was keenly aware of his personal strengths and vulnerabilities.[24] But these were additions to a Republican government-in-waiting already basically in place when Reagan arrived in Washington.

In time this eclectic mix would lose its coherence and fly apart, scattering its particles in a myriad of ideological and personal directions. But Reagan had no premonition of disunity in the heady days before his inauguration and the busy weeks after it. As always, his mind was focused on his performances, especially his inaugural address. What troubled Reagan during this period, he told me later, was a "sense of unreality" about becoming president. While not introspective in the normal meaning of the term, Reagan had a performer's sensitivity for special moments and he was mindful that he lacked the sense of specialness he had anticipated after the election. He had no sense that anything had changed. He had expected that excitement would grip him as he approached inauguration day, but it did not. Instead the feeling, which he described as an absence of special feeling, persisted.

He talked it over with Nancy Reagan before the inauguration, and she could not explain it either. "Both of us kept thinking there was going to come a moment when all of a sudden it hits us, but things kept happening and there you were making a speech, and the crowd, and you still did not have that thing you thought would happen, that moment of awesomeness," Reagan said.[25]

Inauguration day did have a sense of specialness for Ken Khachigian, a graceful speechwriter who had mastered his craft in the Nixon White House. Stu Spencer had brought Khachigian onto the Reagan campaign plane in 1980 because he disliked the time-consuming and frequently contentious process of clearing speeches through the Arlington headquarters. Spencer needed someone who could dash off a punchy speech between campaign stops. Khachigian was suited to this role and quickly earned the confidence of the Reagans and Mike Deaver. After the election they rewarded him with the coveted assignment of drafting the inaugural address. In preparation for this task Khachigian collected memos from many sources and sent them to Reagan. He also read every past presidential inaugural address. "The one thing that struck me about them, regardless of how eloquent or not eloquent they were, was the fact that you could do sort of an historical time line of the United States by reading them," Khachigian said. ". . . The speech sort of told you what was on America's mind every four years."

Khachigian set out to explain what was on the nation's mind in 1980, a year when Americans had been humiliated by the hostage-taking at the U.S. embassy in Tehran and frightened by uncontrolled and seemingly uncontrollable surges in inflation and interest rates. These events had caused a collapse of confidence in President Carter, which Reagan had played to in campaign speeches that climaxed with his famous rhetorical question, "Are you better off today than you were four years ago?" When Khachigian and Deaver went to Reagan's home in Pacific Palisades on December 16, 1980, to discuss the inaugural address, they found Reagan ready to begin where that question left off by assuring Americans that he would work with them to rescue the nation from "economic chaos" and restore international confidence in the United States. "We can do these things," Reagan said.[26]

Reagan had barely browsed through the memos Khachigian had sent him with suggestions for the speech. That did not surprise either Deaver or Khachigian. After Reagan became president, White House officials would assiduously promote the fiction that Reagan read everything that was sent to him, but his closest aides knew better. Reagan read far more than outsiders realized, but he read what he wanted to read. He had his own ideas about the inaugural speech. What Reagan wanted to talk about were the themes that had carried him to the presidency, the unchanging themes of The Speech he had been giving for more than thirty years. Particularly precious to Reagan were the verities of his 1967 inaugural address as governor of California, "a speech I wrote all by my lonesome."[27] The principal verity was that the United States government was of the people, by the people and for the people. "With all the profound wording of the Constitution, perhaps the most meaningful words are the first three, 'We the people,' " Reagan had said in that handwritten speech. "Those of us who have been elected to constitutional office or legislative position are in that three-word phrase. We are of the people, chosen by them to see that no permanent structure of government ever encroaches on freedom or assumes a power beyond that freely granted by the people."

The source of Reagan's inspiration was less the Constitution than the movies. His mind was filled with movie scenes more vivid to him than many actual events, and they were often brought to mind by comments that seemed to have little to do with the scenes themselves. On this day it was Deaver who stirred the Reagan memory bank. "I think there's a hunger among the people for the government to be what they always thought it should be," Deaver said. "For forty years they have been waiting, yearning to be proud again."[28] Listening to this, Khachigian thought that Deaver was playing the courtier but doing so in a way that might inspire Reagan. What it inspired Reagan to recall was a scene from a World War II movie about Bataan in which an actor had said, "We are Americans—what's happening to us?" The Reagan inner circle was used to such cinematic references, but it was the first time Khachigian had heard Reagan explicitly suggest that a movie line become part of his speech. He made a note of it, and resolved to use a version of the line in the speech draft he submitted to the president-elect.[29]

Reagan reviewed the Khachigian draft on January 8, 1981, while flying home from his third and last pre-inaugural visit to Washington. He had met once more with Khachigian before the draft was written, warning him not to be "too harsh" in his references to Carter and again reminding him of passages in his 1967 inaugural speech. Reagan valued Khachigian's work highly, and he would turn to him for speeches in special moments of his presidency. But the inaugural draft seemed too flowery to him, particularly the ending. Khachigian had seen in his mind's eye the imposing vista that would confront Reagan when he stood on the restored west front of the Capitol, facing west toward Washington's celebrated monuments and to Arlington National Cemetery in the Virginia hills beyond. "As God watches over us and guides us in our time of renewal, I shall pray to him for the sustenance given by this moment and this panorama," Khachigian had written. "We have great deeds to do. We shall need all our energies to do them, but do them we will."[30]

Reagan liked the reference to the monuments and the cemetery, but he wanted something that would provide a more personal and dramatic link with the past. He started to edit the speech, which had been typed double-spaced. Then he gave it up, took out a yellow legal pad and began to write another speech, working both from the Khachigian draft and from ideas of his own. What emerged from this four-and-a-half-hour flight would subsequently be described by columnist and former Nixon speechwriter William Safire as "two speeches."[31] The first was "an FDR-style warning of economic peril," with big government rather than big business as the culprit. This came largely from the Khachigian draft, which was in turn heavily indebted to Reagan's basic speech. The second speech was entirely Reagan's own. It was inspired by a letter from a friend about a soldier named Martin Treptow, who had been killed in action in World War I and left behind a diary. On the flyleaf he had written the words "My Pledge" and under it the scribbled words: "America must win this war. Therefore I will work, I will save, I will sacrifice, I will endure, I will fight cheerfully and do my utmost, as if the issue of the whole struggle depended on me alone."[32] These words had an almost cinematic quality to Reagan, although the Treptow story was real. They were words that brought tears to his eyes and that he knew he could use to bring tears to the eyes of his audience. They fit with the movie ending he had suggested to Khachigian at their first meeting. They also fit with the setting, for Reagan thought that Treptow must be buried at Arlington. Reagan wrote the Treptow story on his yellow pad, relating it to the message of his inaugural address. It was the closest he would come in eight years as president to asking Americans to sacrifice for the goals he had set for them. "The crisis we are facing today does not require of us the kind of sacrifice that Martin Treptow and so many thousands of others were called upon to make," Reagan said. "It does require, however, our best effort and our willingness to believe in ourselves and to believe in our capacity to perform great deeds, to believe that together with God's help we can and will resolve the problems which now confront us. And, after all, why shouldn't we believe that? We are Americans."[33]

Three days later Reagan practiced his inaugural address on Khachigian at his Pacific Palisades home. Reagan was dressed casually and in slippers. The living room where they usually met was a clutter of packing boxes, and Reagan searched through the house until he found a room with two unpacked chairs and a desk. He began by praising Khachigian's work and half-apologizing for changing it. He explained to Khachigian that he had to put things in his own words. "How about if I just read it to you?" Reagan said. When he got to the Treptow story, Khachigian's antenna went up. "Where did you get that?" he said. Reagan told him that a friend had written him a letter about Treptow.* "Could you give me that?" Khachigian asked. "We have to check that out." Reagan gave him a wounded look, as if he were asking, "Don't you trust me?" Veterans of the campaign plane were used to that look, which Reagan reserved for aides who questioned stories that often turned out to be apocryphal or drawn from films. Khachigian explained that the inaugural address would receive extraordinary scrutiny, and that any story Reagan used would be checked afterward by the media. He wanted to be certain that the Reagan team had checked it first.[35]

On January 14 the president-elect flew to Washington, where he and Nancy Reagan stayed at Blair House, across the street from the White House, during the week before the inauguration. Khachigian also flew to Washington, where he enlisted the services of Ed Hickey, who had served as Reagan's security chief in Sacramento and would become his military aide in the White House. Together they visited the Pentagon and learned that Martin Treptow had indeed been killed in action in France. From there Khachigian and a Pentagon official, Noel Koch, went to Arlington National Cemetery to search the registry. Treptow was not on it. They found he had been buried not under a white marker at Arlington but beneath a gray granite headstone 1,100 miles away in Bloomer, Wisconsin.

Khachigian returned to Blair House and told Reagan that Treptow was not buried in Arlington. Reagan received the news with equanimity, and said he didn't want to change the story. "Ronald Reagan has a sense of theater that propels him to tell stories in their most theatrically imposing manner," Khachigian said long afterward. "He knew it would

---

* Reagan's records show that the letter-writer who told him about Treptow was Preston Hotchkiss, the chief executive officer of the Bixby Ranch in Saugus, California. Hotchkiss was a supporter of Reagan's and acquainted with a number of his wealthy Southern California financial backers.[34]

break up the story to say that Treptow was buried in Wisconsin." Finally, they settled on a compromise that left Khachigian feeling "half guilty" but was all that Reagan was willing to accept.[36] In the speech Reagan had written on the yellow pad, he had said explicitly that Treptow was buried in Arlington. In the speech he gave, he settled for the implication. "Beyond those monuments to heroism is the Potomac River, and on the far shore the sloping hills of Arlington National Cemetery with its row upon row of simple white markers bearing crosses or Stars of David," Reagan said. "They add up to only a tiny fraction of the price that has been paid for our freedom. . . . Under one such marker lies a young man, Martin Treptow, who left his job in a small town barbershop in 1917 to go to France with the famed Rainbow Division. There, on the western front, he was killed trying to carry a message between battalions under heavy artillery fire."[37]

As Khachigian had predicted, reporters found out within hours of the speech that Treptow was buried not at Arlington but in Bloomer, Wisconsin, where the American Legion post was named after him. Reagan's aides, Khachigian among them, cheerfully admitted the error and took the blame for it. What they did not say was that the mistake had been pointed out to Reagan in advance and that Reagan had decided that the Treptow story was "too theatrically imposing" to blemish it with all the facts. It would prove a portent of his presidency.

7

HALCYON DAYS

How we begin will significantly determine how we govern.

Initial Actions Project report,
January 29, 1981[1]

There was more to Ronald Reagan than his script. He did not know one missile system from another and could not explain the simplest procedures of the federal government, but he understood intuitively that the political success of his presidency would be closely linked to his acceptance in Washington. In this he was the opposite of Jimmy Carter, who knew far more and understood far less. In 1976, after a term and a half of Richard Nixon and a half term of Gerald Ford, Carter had shrewdly exploited the accumulated suspicions of Washington in the wake of Watergate and Vietnam and won election as an outsider. Running against Washington is acceptable political behavior to the Washington community, which stoically endures denunciations of the federal government during election campaigns as a necessary requirement of populist politics. But Carter shocked Washington after he became president by demonstrating that his outsider pose was genuine. He took his campaign rhetoric seriously—indeed, he seemed to take everything most seriously—and freely expressed disdain for the political and social rituals of Washington. Reagan did not repeat this mistake. While he had built his political career on ridicule of Washington, which he once described as "the seat of a buddy system that functions for its own benefit,"[2] Reagan was not one to allow such rhetoric to ruin his evenings or his opportunities. Indeed, he made it clear even before he took office that he intended to be part of the system and share in its rewards. He realized that Washington was a company town, and he had been a company man since his Hollywood days.[3] Since the company business in Washington is politics, Reagan acted the politician and sought out the pooh-bahs of the federal city. His natural charm and self-effacing cheerfulness appealed to a community that Carter had refused to court and that tends to distrust either somberness or aloofness in its politicians. Two weeks after his election the Reagans played host to fifty Washington power brokers at a candlelight dinner at the prestigious F Street Club. "When you come to town, there's a tendency as an officeholder to act as if you're a detached servant," Reagan told them. "Well, I decided it was time to serve notice that we're new residents."[4]

Both by inclination and by calculation the Reagans behaved like social butterflies in the eleven weeks between election and inauguration. She liked parties and wanted to make a social impression. He had an almost boyish faith in the disarming power of his personality and recognized the need to reassure prominent members of the Washington community that they would not be attacked in their beds by militant apostles of "the Reagan revolution." This was an easy reassurance for Reagan to give. He liked to say that even adversaries realized after meeting him that "he didn't have horns," a phrase he would one day use to describe what he thought was Mikhail Gorbachev's impression of him after their first meeting. During the interregnum Reagan made three trips to Washington, a travel strategy that emphasized his celebrity status and the determination of his courtship while also demonstrating that he retained his roots in California. The F Street Club dinner, where the guest list was carefully drawn from a cross-section of Washington's most influential politicians, businessmen, lawyers, lobbyists, religious leaders, educators and patrons of the arts, set the tone for a presidency in which White House invitations became valued status symbols. Nancy Reagan had made it known that the Reagans wanted to meet the movers and shakers in Washington, and they in turn competed for the honor of having the Reagans as their guests. Before he was inaugurated, Reagan had been guest of honor at dinners held by columnist George Will, The Washington Post Company chairman Katharine Graham and Senate Majority Leader Howard H. Baker. He also met privately with President Carter, was briefed by Carter's CIA director Stansfield Turner, paid a well-publicized courtesy call on House Speaker Tip O'Neill, lunched separately with Republican and Democratic senators, flew to New York to meet with Cardinal Terence Cooke and with three black leaders who had supported his campaign, presided at a formal meeting of his new cabinet at the State Department and attended a black-tie dinner at the Corcoran Gallery of Art, also in honor of Senator Baker. On the off chance that anyone in Washington was dense enough to miss the meaning of all this activity, a Reagan aide spelled out its purpose under ground rules of anonymity that would become an administration trademark. "We want to avoid Jimmy Carter's fatal mistake," the aide told *Washington Post* reporter Elisabeth Bumiller. "He never met the power brokers in this city. He never had any real friends here. Governor Reagan not only wants to know them, but he needs to get this place working again." [5]

Reagan himself was generous to Carter in his public comments, even though he did not care for him, as demonstrated by his admonishment to Khachigian to avoid harsh references to Carter in the inaugural address.* The disciplines of Reagan's life had taught him to separate ideology from individuals, beginning with the childhood training in his mother's church that Christians should "hate the sin but love the sinner." Hollywood and Sacramento had reinforced this teaching in nonreligious ways, and Reagan had become accomplished in the art of dealing gracefully with defeated adversaries. In any case there was no need to run down Carter, who was then taking his lumps in almost every media assessment. When *Time* magazine chose Reagan as its "man of the year" for 1980, the cover story observed that Carter was "bitterly resented" by Americans for shrinking their high hopes "down to the size of a presidency characterized by small people, small talk and small matters. He [Carter] made Americans feel two things they are not used to feeling, and will not abide. He made them feel puny and he made them feel insecure." But until the moment he left the Oval

---

* Reagan's dislike of Carter can be traced to a speech Carter gave on September 16, 1980, at the Ebenezer Baptist Church in Atlanta, where he strongly implied that Reagan was a racist. Subsequently, at an October 6 fund-raising dinner in Chicago, Carter said, "You'll determine whether or not this America will be unified or, if I lose this election, whether Americans might be separated, black from white, Jew from Christian, North from South, rural from urban." Reagan was always sensitive to any insinuations that he was bigoted or intolerant.

Office, Carter struggled valiantly to free the American hostages held in Iranian captivity, stirring sympathy in Reagan. Deaver recalls that Reagan took him aside before his inaugural address and said, "I have a feeling they are going to get the hostages back. If it happens, even during my address, I want you to tell me. Slip me a note. Interrupt me. Because if it happens, I want you to bring Carter up to the platform. I think it is outrageous that they are treating this president this way."[6]

Reagan's respectful treatment of Carter also reflected a political calculus. Throughout the transition, Carter made it a point to keep Reagan and his aides closely informed on the progress of the negotiations to free the Americans held hostage in Iran. In contrast, Reagan aides kept the Carter camp in the dark about what the new administration might do to free the hostages if they were still held captive after Reagan took office. Both strategies were deliberate. Carter was concerned that Reagan might not abide by the complicated agreement his administration was negotiating through third parties to free the hostages. He wanted to make certain that Reagan wouldn't be able to say later that he didn't know what was involved in the deal. Reagan, in turn, wanted to preserve his freedom of action in case the negotiations failed. His aides intentionally took what Lloyd Cutler, Carter's White House counsel, described as a "standoffish" position, one that may have made a useful impression on Iran. According to Cutler, chief U.S. negotiator Warren Christopher warned the Iranian government through an Algerian intermediary that Reagan might be unwilling to approve an arrangement that freed the hostages in return for the release of frozen Iranian assets. This was exactly the message that the Reagan team hoped Carter would send to Iran. As Meese put it in 1981, the signal from the incoming administration to Iran was "Don't expect a better deal from Reagan." Meese and regional affairs specialist Paul Wolfowitz, who were monitoring the hostage negotiations for the Reagan camp, believed that conveyance of this message by Christopher would worry the Iranians and speed up the negotiations. Some Carter aides believed that Reagan wanted the honor of freeing the hostages, but the Reagan team was more concerned with political running room than political credit. Reagan aides, especially Meese and Baker, realized that release of the hostages while Carter was still president would free Reagan from an immense burden at the onset of his presidency and allow him to focus his energies on the economy. While Carter and Reagan were highly suspicious of each other, the dictates of patriotism and politics inescapably led them to the identical conclusion that it was best for the hostages to be returned on Carter's watch.*

Reagan spent an hour alone with Carter in the Oval Office on November 20, the fourth day of his first trip to Washington after the election. The meeting, the only extended conversation the two men would ever have, revealed their contrasting approaches to the presidency and, to some degree, cast light on their strengths and limitations. By Carter's account he briefed Reagan on "fifteen or twenty subjects," including the situations in China, Afghanistan, South Korea, Western Europe, Poland and Nicaragua. He also discussed the highly sensitive issue of management of U.S. nuclear forces "in time of attack on our nation" and described the top-secret agreements the United States had with other nations. He then talked about cruise missiles, the Stealth (B-2) aircraft and the B-1 bomber. "Then I listed some of the advantages to our country of honoring the terms of SALT II, pending its ratification, and of maintaining a strong nonproliferation policy," Carter said in his memoirs.[8] He proceeded from there to review the hostage situation and followed this up with separate presentations on foreign-aid legislation, the budget and the freeze on hiring federal employees.

Reagan declined Carter's offer of a writing pad and took no notes. But he did ask for a copy of the three-by-five card on which Carter had made a list of the subjects he wanted to cover, and Carter directed his secretary to make a duplicate of it for the president-elect. Reagan's only substantive comment during this monologue occurred after the president thanked him for sending a message to South Korean President Chun Doo Hwan asking him to spare the life of opposition leader Kim Dae Jung. As Carter remembers it, this prompted Reagan to express enthusiastically "his envy of the authority that Korean President Park Chung Hee had exercised during a time of campus unrest, when he had closed the universities and drafted the demonstrators."[9]

In his memoirs Carter made no attempt to conceal his contempt for Reagan's apparently indifferent response to this lengthy briefing. "He had been with me almost an hour and it had been a pleasant visit, but I

---

* Cutler, Meese and Wolfowitz offer similar accounts about the activities of the Carter and Reagan camps on the hostage issue during the transition period, when the incoming and outgoing administrations were essentially cooperative. Before the election Reagan and his aides feared that Carter would spring an "October surprise" by freeing the hostages at a politically opportune moment. The Reagan camp tried to turn this suspicion to its advantage by spreading the idea that Carter was motivated more by political concerns than by a desire to free the hostages. After Reagan became president, according to Al Haig, he seriously considered repudiating the deal that had freed the hostages but eventually decided to honor it, as Haig had recommended.[7]

was not sure how much we had accomplished," Carter wrote.[10] Privately, he derided Reagan in more caustic terms. Stuart Eizenstat, Carter's chief domestic policy adviser, remembers Carter saying that Reagan had "displayed utterly no interest"[11] in the issues he had reviewed.

Reagan, however, was quite pleased with the briefing and unaware that Carter thought he had been tried and found wanting. He had been comforted to learn that Carter, at least on this occasion, realized the value of storing information on three-by-five cards. In a meeting with his aides at 716 Jackson Place, Reagan held forth for twenty minutes on what had transpired in the Oval Office, using the three-by-five card Carter had copied for him as a reference. Reagan once possessed a powerful memory that his brother Neil had described as "a photographic mind." He had focused intensely on Carter's briefing, even though he made no pretense of understanding many of the policy issues that had been reviewed. But Reagan remembered much of what Carter had told him, or at least gave this impression to his aides. "He was very pleased at how helpful Carter had been," said Meese many years after the event. "I was quite impressed with what a grasp he had of the points Carter made."[12] Meese, of course, was usually impressed by Reagan. But Deaver, less easily amazed, formed a similar opinion. Reagan's problem was not an inability to grasp what Carter had been telling him but a lack of curiosity about anything he deemed irrelevant to his immediate agenda. Carter's interests were so broad that he often seemed to lack focus, even in private conversation. Reagan's range was narrow, but his agenda was compelling. He wanted to get on with the business of cutting domestic government spending, reducing income taxes and building up the military. All other policies seemed to him beside the point.

Reagan had reasons for his economic focus beyond his own predilections. On December 11, the day Reagan announced eight members of his cabinet and went to dinner at Katharine Graham's, a banner headline above the masthead of *The Washington Post* announced that the prime interest rate had reached 20 percent. "I hope and assume we're close to the top," said David Rockefeller,[13] chairman of the board of Chase Manhattan Bank, the first institution to increase its prime lending rate above 19 percent. But the interest rate soared again later in the month, topping out at 21.5 percent, more than nine points above its pre-1980 peak of 12 percent in 1974. Interest rates had been on a roller coaster throughout the year, as the Federal Reserve Board first slowed the growth of the money supply in an effort to hold down inflation, then raised it to avoid a recession. Despite the board's efforts, inflation rose 13 percent in 1980 after increasing 13.3 percent the year before. Economists were gloomy. "It is a sad fact that the basic inflation rate is no lower now than it was before the [1980] recession started," said Arthur F. Burns, former chairman of the Federal Reserve. "The recession accomplished nothing." [14]

The crisis echoed within the Reagan camp in the deliberately apocalyptic warnings of David Stockman. Nearly a month before he was named head of the Office of Management and Budget in early December, Stockman had at the instigation of Congressman Jack Kemp of New York prepared a report for Reagan called "Avoiding an Economic Dunkirk" that forecast dislocations in the credit and capital markets, a 1981 recession, soaring budget deficits and the collapse of monetary policy. The "Dunkirk memo" was summarized for the president-elect at a November meeting in Los Angeles, where it had the effect of reinforcing Nixon's advice and Reagan's own impulse to focus on the economy and let other issues take care of themselves. "This review contains an inescapable warning," the Dunkirk memo declared. "Things could go very badly during the first year, resulting in incalculable erosion of GOP momentum, unity and public confidence. If bold policies are not swiftly, deftly and courageously implemented in the first six months, Washington will quickly become engulfed in political disorder commensurate with the surrounding economic disarray. A golden opportunity for permanent conservative policy revision and political realignment could be thoroughly dissipated before the Reagan administration is even up to speed."

The prospect of economic collapse alarmed Reagan political advisers, even though few of them shared Stockman's understanding of the budget or his sense of ideological urgency. "No American president since Franklin D. Roosevelt has inherited a more difficult economic situation," warned the final report of the Initial Actions Project,[15] a political guide to action prepared for Reagan by pollster-strategist Richard B. Wirthlin with the help of his associate, the late Richard Beal, and David Gergen. This fifty-five-page report, known as "the black book" during the transition, was not formally completed until January 29, 1981, but its essential points were outlined for Reagan in a draft version presented to him at Blair House in mid-December. James Baker, who liked to keep discussions short and to the point, summed up the goals of the new administration by declaring, "We ought to have three goals, and all three of them are economic recovery." [16]

Reagan was undaunted by the economic crisis, which his compulsive optimism led him to view as an auspicious opportunity. This attitude was reinforced by Wirthlin, whose optimism often equaled Reagan's. While the Initial Actions Project report was sprinkled with references to the ominous economic signals and the fragility of the Reagan political coalition, its message was essentially hopeful. "While Americans demand a great deal from a president, they are willing to entrust him with considerable authority to lead," the report declared. It urged Reagan to establish his credibility with "simple, straightforward and understandable" explanations of economic policy. "The first fundamental economic objective of the Reagan presidency must be to restore a sense of stability and confidence, to demonstrate that there is a steady hand at the helm," the report stated.[17] "The second fundamental economic objective of the Reagan presidency must be to convey a sense of hope, that there is a light at the end of the tunnel."[18]

Wirthlin's report appealed to Reagan because it defined his objectives in ways compatible with his conception of the presidency. Reagan's enduring model for presidential performance in times of economic crisis was his first political hero, Franklin D. Roosevelt. The relief programs of the New Deal had provided jobs for his father and brother in 1933,[19] earning from Reagan an emotional loyalty that transcended all subsequent philosophical mutations. The first year of FDR's presidency was also the year in which Reagan began his radio career as a part-time sports announcer in Davenport, Iowa, and became attuned to the rhetorical requirements of radio, which demanded a more conversational approach to political oratory than was customary in the florid stump speeches of the day. Neil Reagan once told me that Reagan had memorized Roosevelt's entire inaugural address of March 4, 1933, with its famous peroration, "My firm belief is that the only thing we have to fear is fear itself." Whether or not Reagan actually accomplished this feat, there is no doubt that he could recite many of Roosevelt's lines by heart and that he was deeply influenced by both the tone and content of FDR's radio speeches. Roosevelt delivered eight of these "fireside chats" during the first two years of his presidency, and they became the model for the weekly radio speeches that helped Reagan stay in the limelight when he was out of office and in touch with the American people after he became president.

Reagan never hesitated to acknowledge his debt to Roosevelt, and it was often said by liberals and conservatives alike that he used FDR's techniques in an attempt to undo what FDR had done. This widely held view largely misses the point of what Roosevelt and Reagan set out to accomplish at the onset of their presidencies. While both men came to office armed with specific policy proposals, they recognized that the decisive aspect of presidential leadership was inspirational rather than programmatic. This meant that cherished policies and promises had to be set aside if they interfered with the overarching goal of restoring national confidence. Roosevelt's commitment to restoration of confidence, particularly during the early days of the New Deal, infuriated radicals who saw the Depression as an opportunity to make fundamental changes in the shattered capitalist society. Two generations later Reagan disenchanted conservatives by his seeming indifference to the "revolution" that bore his name.

Lamenting the failure of "the Reagan revolution" after he left the administration, Stockman reluctantly concluded that Reagan was an insufficiently ideological "consensus politician" who lacked the stomach for a serious assault on the New Deal. "He had a sense of ultimate values and a feel for long-term directions, but he had no blueprint for radical governance," Stockman wrote. "He had no concrete program to dislocate and traumatize the here-and-now of American society."[20] To the contrary, Reagan thought that the nation was already traumatized by the shocks of the 1960s and the "malaise" of the Carter years.* His goal was a restoration of national stability, not dislocation. Reagan had no fixed plan for accomplishing this restoration beyond his dogma that taxes should be reduced and military power enhanced, but he was convinced that it was the president's responsibility to lead the way in restoring a sense of hope and national pride. Roosevelt and Reagan were much alike in this expansive conception of the president's role and in their trial-and-error approach to governance. Reagan, following Roosevelt's lead in 1932, campaigned in 1980 by rashly promising a "balanced budget" and huge reductions in federal spending as a cure for the nation's economic ills. Once in office, Reagan also concluded that a promise based on economic purism was superseded by the immediate needs of the nation. Neither Roosevelt nor Reagan ever submitted a balanced budget, or worried about the price that future generations would have to pay for the measures they pursued to induce

---

* Carter never actually used the word "malaise" in the nationally televised speech he gave on July 15, 1979, that became known in the political community as "the malaise speech." But his contention that Americans were suffering from "a crisis of confidence . . . that strikes at the very heart and soul and spirit of our national will" expressed a view of American attitudes that Reagan repeatedly challenged during the 1980 campaign. "I find no national malaise," Reagan said. "I find nothing wrong with the American people." For a more extended account of Reagan's use of this theme, see pages 301–304 in my book *Reagan*.

economic recovery. Both presidents blamed circumstances (the Depression in Roosevelt's case, runaway inflation and interest rates in Reagan's) and international crises for abandoning a balanced budget commitment that neither of them probably should have made in the first place.

But both presidents succeeded—Roosevelt under admittedly far more dire domestic conditions—in instilling renewed public confidence in a nation that seemed to have lost its way. "In 1933, it was an image of fatherly purpose which reassured and unified a panicky nation," wrote Arthur M. Schlesinger, Jr. about FDR.[21] And in 1981, it was Reagan's projected image of leadership that made Americans feel better about themselves. To this end the Initial Actions Project report quoted presidential historian Thomas Cronin: "The president must be the nation's personal and moral leader; by symbolizing the past and future greatness of America and radiating inspirational confidence, a president can pull a nation together, while directing its people toward the fulfillment of the American dream."[22] These words were music to Reagan's ears. "[The president] must convey in simple, uncluttered ways a sense of direction that will provide hope for Americans who want, above all else, a strong leader to lead," the report concluded.[23] Reagan was well suited for that role.

Reagan's situation in 1981 resembled Roosevelt's in 1933 in two other important ways. Like Roosevelt, he came to office as leader of a political coalition that was united in its longing for economic recovery and national renewal but divided on many points of policy. And like FDR, Reagan had a performer's advantage of following what the audience perceived to be a weak act. This was widely recognized by the disparate elements of the Reagan coalition, and especially the stage managers in the White House, who were determined to learn from Carter's mistakes. One of these mistakes had been the structure of the Carter transition four years earlier. As the *National Journal*'s Dick Kirschten put it, "In 1976, Carter established separate campaign and transition staffs, and the members of both groups fell into open rivalry and ill feeling when the time came to vie for choice jobs in the incoming administration."[24] In contrast, Reagan's pre-election planning was conducted by key members of the campaign hierarchy, and Reagan reached relatively quick decisions on the composition of his cabinet. Reagan's emphasis on restoring economic confidence, buttressed by the arguments in Wirthlin's "black book," gave the transition a central focus. And even such subsequent Meese critics as Deaver and Gergen agree that he functioned effectively during the transition period. Overall, the transition was a stylistic and political triumph for Reagan. It was blemished only by a profligacy that proved a portent of the way the Reagan administration would balance its books.*

Outside the administration, some of the "New Right" conservatives complained from the beginning that Reagan gave too little attention to such "social issues" as abortion and school prayer. Inside, Reagan and his team agreed unanimously that economic issues held priority and also concluded that attempting too much was likely to result in accomplishing too little. Again, Carter was the guide. "We went back and collected the clips and columns after one hundred days of the Carter administration," said Gergen. "And the main theme that came through was that Carter had engaged in a flurry of activity. There had been a blizzard of proposals that had gone to the Hill, but there was no clear theme to his presidency. One person said in a column that he seemed to believe in everything and stand for nothing."[25] In hindsight this view was supported by principal figures in the Carter administration, some of whom cautioned their replacements to follow a different course than the one they had taken in 1977. "We had made a serious mistake in overloading the circuits the first year," said Stuart Eizenstat. "They needed a focus. They clearly learned from our mistakes."[26]

Even without Carter's example, Reagan would doubtless have emphasized the economic items that had been so long the staple of his script. But the Carter experience was a powerful reminder to the new president's White House team of the dangers of diffusion. Reagan benefited enormously from the readiness of his advisers to learn the political lessons of the recent past. He also benefited from the discipline and useful division of labor among his principal trio of aides—Baker, Deaver and Meese. While the members of this troika would in time become famous for their feuds, they cooperated willingly during most of Reagan's first and most productive year in office. Baker was the key. While in some ways as much a private person as Reagan, he was also a visible and accessible politician steeped in the disciplines of the law, the Marine Corps and a string of unsuccessful but skillfully managed political campaigns. When he came to the White House as chief of staff, he barely knew Reagan, whom he had seriously underestimated as

---

* The presidential transition was the most expensive in history. Congress appropriated $2 million; the Reagan transition spent $1,745,000 of this amount. According to the General Accounting Office, another $1,131,865 was raised and spent in private contributions, making the total cost of the transition $2,876,865.

tial candidate. Baker's closest tie within the Reagan adminis-
....~ was to his old friend and fellow Texan George Bush, now the
vice president, who had also underestimated Reagan and was mystified
by his political success. Baker's polished manner concealed a restless
ambition that had led him into a quixotic campaign to become attorney
general of Texas and a pungent candor he occasionally shared with
friends about the deficiencies of some of Reagan's most prominent
cabinet members. Usually, however, both the ambition and the candor
were guarded by an innate caution that prompted Baker to avoid dubious battles. His observant assistant Margaret Tutwiler* called him
"Mr. Cautious," and the caution was reinforced by the initial fragility
of his relationship with Reagan. But Baker was unsurpassed at compensating for his own vulnerabilities. Against the advice of Spencer, who
foresaw that division of authority within the White House would inevitably lead to internecine conflict, Baker went to Meese after the election
and offered to share the responsibilities that normally would have been
entrusted entirely to the White House chief of staff. Meese, while still
resentful at being passed over for the job he had assumed was his, was
mollified by the title of counsellor to the president with cabinet rank
and the ostensible responsibility of "conceptualizing" administration
policy. Baker then struck a vital alliance with Deaver that endured for
the four years they were in the White House together. Others in the
entourage were envious of Deaver's rapport with the Reagans but
tended to view him as a glorified luggage-carrier and public relations
man whose main utility was to prevent the first lady from interfering
with their work. Baker, however, recognized that Deaver had a cool
analytical side and had applied it to understanding the Reagans. He
turned over the schedule to Deaver and depended upon him for daily
assessments of the mood, capacities and preferences of the first family.
He relied almost totally upon Deaver's advice before embarking on any
venture that required participation of the president.

The way that Baker worked was to find people with whom he could
establish an alliance and then rely on them completely to do what they
did best. For economic policy advice he depended upon Stockman,
who possessed a breathtaking command of the budget, and even more
on Richard Darman, a brainy workaholic and former colleague at the

---

* Tutwiler served as Baker's eyes and ears in the White House and in the press corps, where she was
widely respected for her truthfulness and had many friends. Baker valued her willingness to make
candid assessments that were often at odds with the conventional and largely male wisdom prevailing in the White House.

Commerce Department who shared with Baker the advantage of being independently rich enough to walk away from any job he didn't like. It says much about Baker's reliances that he took the risk of installing Darman in a key White House position. Darman was suspect to the right wing of the Reagan coalition because he was a protégé of Elliot Richardson, a Republican who was anathema to movement conservatives and also to Reagan when he was governor of California. Nixonians have long memories, especially for their enemies. They remembered that Darman had supported Attorney General Richardson's refusal to fire Watergate special prosecutor Archibald Cox and walked out with Richardson, whose resignation touched off the "Saturday night massacre" of October 20, 1973. And even Republicans who were neither necessarily Nixonian nor conservative suspected that Darman was too liberal for a Reagan administration. *Time* magazine's Laurence Barrett concluded in his book on the early Reagan years that Darman's "dirty little secret was that he believed in government, including the federal government."[27] But this was no secret to Baker, who was also a government man. Baker knew just enough about the federal government to realize that Darman knew more about the way it worked than he did. He also realized that Darman, who had a reputation for abrasiveness, was of far more use as an insider than as a visible symbol of the Reagan administration. Baker took the knocks for putting Darman on the staff and assigned him the important tasks of coordinating the paper flow to Reagan and chairing the Legislative Strategy Group. The LSG was an informal committee that lacked official standing and was relatively unknown outside the White House. But it became the White House command center in the Reagan administration's dealings with Congress.

For Baker, nothing mattered more than these dealings. He had watched as Gerald Ford, with all his hard-won understanding of the House, was chewed up by a veto strategy that stamped Ford as a man of principle but damaged his reputation for leadership. Baker saw that Carter had ruined his chances for a successful presidency by remaining an outsider after he occupied the White House and by repeatedly displaying his contempt for congressional wisdom and congressional prerogatives. Baker set out to win Congress over. He prided himself on being a political "realist"—a word he much preferred to the media label "pragmatist"—and recognized that the great gift of the 1980 electoral landslide was the Republican capture of the Senate. One of his first tasks was to forge a firm partnership with Senator Howard H. Baker Jr. of Tennessee, who was grateful that Reagan's political coattails in western and southern Senate races had made it possible for him to become Senate majority leader. Howard Baker was a bottomless store of knowledge on the vanities, divisions, strengths and weaknesses of the Senate, and he recognized that it was in his interest to share his lore with James Baker.

For knowledge of the House, James Baker depended upon his experienced chief congressional lobbyist, Max Friedersdorf, and his young assistant Kenneth Duberstein. At the time, Duberstein was unknown to the public and the Reagans, but he had bipartisan friendships in the House and knew that Democratic Party loyalty was shaky in southern constituencies where Reagan had done well. This squared with Baker's knowledge of the political situation in his home state of Texas, which Reagan had carried by 600,000 votes while Democrats were winning nineteen of twenty-four congressional districts. The "Boll Weevil" Democratic congressmen in Texas and other states of the old Confederacy worried that voters back home might replace them if they undercut Reagan, but they wanted assurances they would not be betrayed by the White House if they gave the president their support. Baker, who cared little about ideology and everything about results, blandly told them that Reagan would not campaign against them in 1982 if they supported his budget and tax cuts. The idea was instantly accepted by Reagan, despite its unpopularity with Republican professionals who viewed the 1980 election as a sign that the South was ripe for political realignment. Although Reagan was promising to stay out of precisely those congressional districts that Republicans appeared to have the best chance of winning in 1982, Baker's view was that legislative success would best serve both the Reagan and the Republican cause in the long run. His concern was immediate victories rather than future realignments. This was Reagan's concern, too. Conservative sniping from outside the White House at the "pragmatism" of Baker, Darman and Deaver had little impact on the president because Reagan at the time shared the political realism of his aides. He had placed a high premium on success throughout his various careers, and he often complained that some of his erstwhile conservative supporters wanted to go "off the cliff with all flags flying." That was rarely Reagan's way. He told me after he was elected in 1980 that the most enduring lesson of his governorship for his presidency was the realization that he could work successfully with the legislature.[28] During the first hundred days of his presidency, Reagan held sixty-nine meetings with 467 members of Congress, prompting some of them to say that they had seen more of Reagan in four months than they had of Carter in four years.

In the cold Washington winter of 1981, James Baker worked sixteen-hour days courting Congress and cultivating the media. He never left his White House office without returning every phone call that had been made to him that day by a member of Congress, however obscure. He devoted several hours of every week explaining the administration's goals, motives, strategy and tactics to White House reporters for the networks, news magazines, wire services and major newspapers, advancing himself with this accessibility but advancing Reagan even more. Baker was truthful with reporters, which won them over, and he held their interest by discreetly sharing his political insights with selected members of the White House press corps. His political experience had taught him to trust reporters, up to a point, and the value of establishing a working relationship with them in advance of crises. Baker had an especially keen sense of the ephemeral nature of politics, expressed in Washington by the aphorism that twenty-four hours is a long time in the life of a politician. He knew that even popular presidents can be overtaken by events they cannot control. Because Reagan's fast start had created a high expectation of performance, Baker expressed a sense of urgency about bringing the Reagan budget and tax bills to a vote while the president was still popular with the public, the press and the Washington community. In Baker's view anything that extended the honeymoon was helpful, and he and Deaver even were able to see the near-tragedy of the attempt on Reagan's life as a political opportunity. Reagan was seriously wounded in this assassination attempt outside the Washington Hilton on March 30, 1981, in which his popular press secretary, James S. Brady, was permanently injured. But the president rattled off one-liners in the face of death and emerged from the ordeal as a hero. As soon as it became clear that Reagan would survive, Baker began planning a strategy to take advantage of the surge of public sympathy for the seventy-year-old president. Less than a month after the shooting, while the old performer was still recovering from the wound that nearly killed him, Baker and Deaver easily persuaded Reagan to address a joint session of Congress on behalf of his economic recovery program.

Even before the shooting, the Reagan presidency in its early days possessed an aura of invincibility. Jubilant Republican congressmen overlooked Reagan's disturbing habit of consulting his cue cards when he talked to them about familiar issues and treated the president as a sort of superman who had restored their party to greatness. "At the beginning there was an almost universally positive view of the man and his program," recalls Congressman Willis Gradison of Ohio, a moderate Republican who had served in the government since the Eisenhower administration. "He had not only defeated an incumbent Democratic president but brought in a Republican Senate and a working majority in the House. There was a sense of euphoria that at first translated into almost automatic support." [29]

Democrats were less euphoric, but many of them also were charmed by Reagan and, at least in the case of the Boll Weevils, feared the political consequences of opposing him. Even House Speaker Tip O'Neill, who had rashly warned Reagan during the transition that Washington was the "big leagues" where the quality of political performance transcended Sacramento, was touched by the Reagan magic. After the Democratic majority had suffered two devastating budget defeats at the hands of the Republican–Boll Weevil coalition, O'Neill returned to Boston and was asked by a constituent what was happening to him. "I'm getting the shit whaled out of me," O'Neill replied succinctly. [30] The Speaker believed from beginning to end that Reagan was lazy and lacking in compassion, but he also quickly recognized that he had seriously underestimated Reagan's reach with the public. Late in 1981, after suffering further defeats, it was O'Neill who gave the most telling assessment of the reasons for Reagan's success. "People like him as an individual, and he handles the media better than anybody since Franklin Roosevelt, even Jack Kennedy," O'Neill said. "There's just something about the guy that people like. They want him to be a success. They're rooting for him, and of course, they're rooting for him because we haven't had any presidential successes for years—Kennedy killed, Johnson with Vietnam, Nixon with Watergate, Ford, Carter and all the rest." [31]

It is not clear whether Reagan realized that he had history on his side. But he did understand, without needing to consult Wirthlin's polls or his cue cards, that he possessed a special "something" that transcended the appeal of ordinary politicians. "Reagan's solutions to problems were always the same as the guy in the bar," said Stu Spencer, [32] who had worked for Reagan and against him and never ceased to marvel at his naturalness. One of the keys to understanding Reagan is to recognize that he was highly aware that he possessed this talent, which he believed had been honed by his life's experience as a performer. When a radio reporter asked Reagan on election eve what it was that Americans saw in him, he replied, "Would you laugh if I told you that I think, maybe, they see themselves and that I'm one of them? I've never been able to detach myself or think that I, somehow, am apart from them." [33] There was an element of innocence to this answer—and an element of artifice. Reagan genuinely liked people, but he also practiced hard to do those things that people liked. "I don't think you can be a performer without liking people," he said after he had left the White House. "You like the audience. You want to please the audience." [34]

Reagan tried to please the audience in myriad ways during these early energetic days of his presidency. His formal speeches were deliberately dramatic, conveying a sense that the nation had reached an economic crossroads. "We've come to a turning point," he said on the eve of his seventieth birthday. "We're threatened with an economic calamity of tremendous proportions, and the old business-as-usual treatment can't save us." [35] At the same time he promised a new direction he also sought to reassure Americans, to the private despair of Stockman and other apostles of "the Reagan revolution," that Social Security and other cherished New Deal social programs would be spared the budget ax. Neither Reagan nor the American majority saw these assurances as contradictory. Most Americans believed the federal budget could and should be cut but opposed reductions in the programs from which they directly benefited. While his policies would prove enormously beneficial to the wealthy, Reagan saw himself as the tribune of ordinary working-class and middle-class Americans who were skeptical about the efficacy of government while taking for granted that government would see to many of their needs. Long after he became president Reagan still referred to the federal government in the third person, reversing the modern practice under which presidents take credit for anything done by others in their name. Reagan was perfectly willing to credit others, a practice that seemed generous but also made others appear responsible for policies he had advocated and approved. The principal recipient of this double-edged credit in the first months of the Reagan administration was Stockman, whose denunciations of pork-barrel programs dominated the nightly news and framed the debate on the budget. Though Reagan's campaign speeches had been crammed with purported examples of government waste, he cheerfully confessed ignorance of the details of the proposed budget cuts neatly compiled by Stockman in a 145-page black binder. When a reporter during a photo session late in January asked the president whether he would soon have ready an expected executive order on cost-cutting, Stockman started nodding vigorously, and Reagan said, "I have a smiling fellow at the end of the table who tells me we do." [36] And at a cabinet meeting on February 13, the Friday before Reagan's budget proposals were formally presented to Congress, the president turned to Stockman and said, "We won't leave you out there alone, Dave. We'll all come to the hanging." [37]

As always, Reagan's pride of authorship was reserved for his performances, especially the nationally televised speeches that became the basic mode of public communication during his presidency. On February 18 he unveiled his "program for economic recovery" in a speech to a joint session of Congress in which he paraphrased Abraham Lincoln and the peroration of his own 1964 speech for Goldwater by asking Congress to join in "restoring the promise that is offered to every citizen by this, the last best hope of man on Earth." The program called for cutting $41.4 billion from the Carter budget and making mild to fatal reductions in eighty-three federal programs. Without dwelling on many of the proposed specific cuts, Reagan said that "waste and fraud in the federal government" was "an unrelenting national scandal, a scandal we're bound and determined to do something about." He also restated his commitment to a 30 percent income tax reduction over three years, called for an increase in defense spending, pledged to maintain Social Security and promised to exempt the "social safety net of programs" that benefit "the poverty-stricken, the disabled, the elderly, all those with true need" from any budget cuts. A year earlier Republican (and later independent) presidential candidate John Anderson had succinctly described how Reagan could accomplish all this while simultaneously balancing the budget. "You do it with mirrors," Anderson had said.[38] But Congress was in no mood to challenge the popular and newly installed president. Reagan's speech was repeatedly interrupted by applause that accurately anticipated public reaction. A *Washington Post*–ABC news poll taken during a two-day period after the speech showed 2-1 support for the Reagan economic program. Reagan, who never needed polls to tell him when he had made a hit with his audience, was jubilant the next day as he departed for the first of many holidays he would spend at his California ranch during his presidency. When a reporter asked him aboard Air Force One how he felt about the speech, the president replied, "You're always in good spirits when you figure you got by without losing your place or forgetting your lines." [39]

Reagan, in these early months, experienced the happiness of a seasoned actor who succeeds beyond expectation in the leading role. The orderly pace of the White House routine suited him, and his dream of restoring a sense of national purpose by reducing the size of the federal government seemed to be coming true. Reagan was reminded not of his difficult early days in Sacramento but of the heyday during his second term as governor, when the Democratic-controlled legislature had co-operated in the passage of useful welfare reform and tax relief measures. Reagan really did believe that Washington was Sacramento on a grand scale, and this view was reinforced by the Californians in the White House, who sometimes lapsed and called him "governor." Lyn Nofziger did this on one occasion and quickly apologized, but his apology was waved off by Reagan, who said, "Maybe we should set a day aside each week to call me governor, so we'll remember where we came from." [40] The president and his aides were on top of the world. "Sometimes I have to pinch myself to see if this is real," Deaver said one day to Reagan. The president looked up at him and smiled. "So do I," he said. [41]

KIDDING
ON THE SQUARE

*It's true hard work never killed anybody, but I figure
why take the chance?*

RONALD REAGAN,
March 28, 1987[1]

Reagan's sense of humor was a key to his character. He was the
resident humorist and gag writer in a White House where nearly everything else was done for him while he engaged in governance by anecdote. While adversaries interpreted his heavy reliance on anecdotes as
a telltale reflection of a deficient intellect, Reagan treasured humorous
stories and knew that his willingness to poke fun at himself was a vital
component of his popularity. A sense of humor was essential to the role
Reagan had created for himself in Hollywood and politics and, in humorist Bob Orben's phrase, the basis for the "balance of goodwill"[2]
upon which he drew in time of trouble.

Reagan came to this role quite naturally. His father, Jack Reagan, had
a gift for storytelling, common among Irish-Americans and useful for
any salesman. And his mother, Nelle, nurtured Reagan's interest in
dramatics, for which he had a natural flair. Reagan's appreciation for
anecdotes was further honed in Hollywood, where the self-deprecating
jokes that form an essential characteristic of Jewish humor were deeply

embedded in the film culture. One of Hollywood's most valued ceremonies is the "roast," an entertainment at which celebrities are feted
with an exchange of personal insults that concludes in sentimental tribute to the guest of honor. Reagan was an adept participant in such
events, and he was pleased to learn in Sacramento that the roast also
prospers in politics, perhaps because of the respite such events provide
from the ferocity of daily political combat. As president, Reagan exploited his mastery of this art form, fully matching Washington reporter
Owen Ullmann's description of him as "the Johnny Carson of national
politics, the Joker-in-Chief of the United States."[3] Reagan quipped,
kidded and bantered in nearly every White House meeting, charming
visitors and aides alike. Early in his presidency Reagan met in the Oval
Office with his wife, Mike Deaver and John F. W. Rogers, the young
White House administrative officer. Rogers had been brought into the
Oval Office this particular morning to discuss the decorations and the
furniture, a subject in which Reagan had no interest. When Deaver and
Nancy Reagan went into a side room to continue the discussion, Rogers
was left alone with the president for the first time in his life. He was
nervous, not knowing what to say, and Reagan picked up the slack. "I
guess they're going to go and figure out what we're supposed to do,"
said Reagan, as if Rogers shared with him the predicament of having
others decide his affairs. Rogers still did not know what to say, and
Reagan tried again. Glancing at the Oval Office wall, he pointed to a
famous portrait of George Washington in which the father of our country has a hand thrust inside his coat in Napoleonic pose. "What do you
think he's doing with his hand?" Reagan asked. Rogers had no idea. "I
bet he's in there scratching himself," Reagan said. Rogers, disarmed,
laughed heartily with the president.[4] Reagan had put him completely at
ease.

This was Reagan's way. During his eight years in the White House
he won the allegiance of subordinates and secretaries with endless ban-
ter and little jokes that reassured them and made them feel part of a
great enterprise. These quips and patter enabled Reagan to keep his
emotional distance from his entourage while also giving the White
House rank and file a sense of belonging. Anecdotes were Reagan's
fundamental form of communication. He used his stock stories and
improvised one-liners to break the ice, entertain aides, pass the time,
practice for performances, amuse audiences, deflate adversaries and fill
awkward gaps at meetings when the discussion bored him or drifted
beyond his depth. Reagan needed the approval conveyed by laughter

and engaged in a constant quest for stories that would enhance his repertoire. Members of the inner circle who in other administrations might have contested over policy responded to Reagan's need for stories by competing among themselves to find anecdotes that pleased the president. This competition was even more intense among cabinet members who wanted to become part of the inner circle. Some cabinet members, notably Treasury Secretary Donald Regan, quickly learned that they stood a better chance of gaining Reagan's attention with an anecdote than with an argument and used Reaganesque stories to ingratiate themselves. Others, notably Secretary of State Alexander Haig, never understood this and failed to form the easy relationship with Reagan that was necessary for political survival.

Though Reagan liked stories for their own sake, there was usually a purpose to his patter. In his years on the banquet circuit he had learned that stories tend to soften up audiences and make them more receptive to the speaker's message. "He often used humor as a bonding device to put an audience at ease," says Bob Orben. "The essence of presidential humor is to eliminate the huge psychological gap of awe that exists between a president and his audience. Reagan used humor to put his audiences on the same level. In doing so, he built up a tremendous store of goodwill."[5] E. B. White once wrote that Americans "cherish the ideal of the 'sense' of humor and at the same time are highly suspicious of anything that is non-serious."[6] It is doubtful if Reagan had read E. B. White, but he shared the understanding that humor was too important to be strictly a laughing matter. He insisted on anecdotes in his speeches and provided them himself when speechwriters failed to do so. If he did not like the anecdotes that were sent to him, he substituted stories of his own. Economist Alan Greenspan formed the view that Reagan was "psychologically a professional comedian, a professional raconteur"[7] who had accumulated a vast store of anecdotes that he used to express his fundamental ideas and his attitude toward life. Greenspan considered Reagan's grasp of economic issues to be unsophisticated and often superficial, but he also recognized that Reagan could convey the import of an idea through an anecdote and that he possessed a comic talent for puncturing economic portentousness with deft one-liners. ("You know economists; they're the sort of people who see something works in practice and wonder if it would work in theory."[8] And: "If all the economists in the world were laid end to end, they still wouldn't reach a conclusion."[9]) While it was Greenspan and Martin Anderson who had in 1980 constructed the budget plan that gave Reagan's economic proposal a semblance of credibility, it was Reagan who had devised the formulation that roused the public: "A recession is when your neighbor loses his job. A depression is when you lose yours. And recovery is when Jimmy Carter loses his." [10]

Reagan occasionally yielded to puns, a form of humor in which Lyn Nofziger excelled, to make a point. When, as governor, he acceded to the appeal of a tiny Indian tribe and blocked construction of a high dam that would have violated an ancient treaty by flooding sacred burial grounds, Reagan said, "We've broken too damn many treaties." [11] He liked jokes that made fun of government, Communists, ministers, movie producers and himself. He also liked trick answers. (Attempting to cheer up a downcast aide on a helicopter flight over Washington's monuments, Reagan asked her, "How many are dead in Arlington Cemetery?" She was baffled, and he said, "They all are.") [12] Reagan also favored long-remembered one-liners of such vintage that younger people who heard them wrongly assumed them to be original. ("Honey, I forgot to duck," he said to Nancy Reagan after he was shot, recycling a quip attributed to Jack Dempsey when he lost the heavyweight boxing title to Gene Tunney in 1926.) Many of the one-liners in Reagan's mental card file were scraps of film dialogue that popped out at unexpected but often appropriate occasions. (The most famous of these, or at least the most effective, was Reagan's line when he seized the microphone and routed George Bush in their celebrated 1980 debate in Nashua, New Hampshire. "I paid for this microphone, Mr. Green," [13] said Reagan, winning the audience while he mangled the name of the moderator, Jon Breen. But Spencer Tracy had said it first, in the 1948 film *State of the Union:* "Don't you shut me off! I'm paying for this broadcast.")

Reagan related the story of his life in anecdotes. As Nofziger once put it, Reagan was always nostalgic for "the job he did before the job he was in." [14] When Reagan was an actor he told stories about his days as a sports announcer. When he became governor, he told acting stories. And when he became president, he told stories, both real and invented, about his days in Sacramento. [15] Reagan also told dialect jokes in stage-Irish to evoke his father's Irish Catholic heritage, populist jokes to emphasize his humble origins ("I was born in a small town in the Midwest, and I was in poverty before the rich folks got hold of it") and Russian jokes to remind conservatives of his anticommunist credentials at a time he was promoting a fundamental change in U.S.-Soviet relationships. Often, his stories were tailored to specific audiences. Recognizing that people laugh readily at good-humored jokes about their vocations, he relished telling anti-economist jokes to economists, anti-lawyer jokes to attorneys and anti-clerical jokes to ministers. These stories were so carefully chosen that some of Reagan's listeners adopted them as their own, as Greenspan did with a joke that became a standard anecdote in his own speeches. (Brezhnev is watching the annual May Day parade of Soviet military might from the Kremlin wall. Amid the tanks and nuclear missiles and rows of soldiers is a truck containing a collection of unkempt civilians. An aide apologizes to Brezhnev for their presence, saying he doesn't know what they are doing in the parade. "Calm down, comrade," Brezhnev says. "Those are my economists, an integral part of the military might of the Soviet Union. I put them in the parade. You have no idea how much damage they can do.") [16] White House Counsel A. B. Culvahouse similarly appreciated Reagan's stories about lawyers. (A pope and a lawyer arrive at St. Peter's gate simultaneously. The pope is assigned a modest condominium in a courtyard while the lawyer is given a splendid Tudor mansion overlooking a golf course. "How can this be?" the lawyer asks St. Peter. "The father of Christendom merits only a nice condominium and I have been given this magnificent mansion." St. Peter replies, "Well, we have thirty-nine popes here, but you're the first lawyer.") [17] Reagan used variations of this story, depending on the audience. Sometimes it was politicians who were the rarity in heaven.

Reagan's most frequent target was Reagan. No president since Lincoln was as self-effacing, and no president in the history of the republic was as effective at self-ridicule. In public and in private Reagan regularly poked fun at his age, his work habits, his movies, his ideology, his vanities, his memory lapses, his supposed domination by his wife and even the widely held view that he was unintelligent. Reagan was aware that many of his critics thought him a modest man with much to be modest about. But he also realized that he could upstage his adversaries by beating them to the punch. When he was informed during the 1980 campaign that some of his opponents intended to make a point of his age by sending him greetings on his sixty-ninth birthday, Reagan started using Jack Benny jokes about his birthday, which he called "the thirtieth anniversary of his thirty-ninth birthday." (Debating Republican rivals in Chicago, Reagan said that wage and price controls had been a failure since they were first instituted by the Roman emperor Diocletian and added, "I'm one of the few persons old enough to remember that.") [18]

This tactic diffused the age issue so effectively that such jokes became a permanent part of the Reagan repertoire, sometimes combined with references to other presumed disabilities. ("You know, that brings me to a story—almost everything does. Maybe I've told this story to you before, but then you'll just have to hear it again, because life not only begins at forty but so does lumbago and the tendency to tell the same story over and over again.")[19] Reagan could do this because he was personally secure enough to make himself the butt of his humor. He once explained to me in some detail how his friend Jack Benny had used self-ridicule as the foundation of his comedy, emphasizing that it was Benny's self-security that made his art possible.[20] In Reagan's view this freed him to portray a character (stingy, self-centered) that was the opposite of the real Jack Benny. Reagan most often played himself, but it seemed to me that he was saying something about himself as well as Benny. Reagan could poke fun at his ignorance because he considered himself abundantly blessed with common sense. He could laugh at himself because he knew he had a serious purpose. He was not afraid to say what came into his head. When a wire service reporter asked him to autograph an old studio picture showing Reagan with the chimpanzee Bonzo, he happily obliged. The inscription read "I'm the one with the watch."[21]

Poet Marianne Moore might have had Reagan in mind when she penned her famous observation that "humor saves a few steps, it saves years."[22] Not even the most devout of Reagan admirers considered him a hard worker, and even aides who thought he put in enough hours in the Oval Office regarded him as intellectually lazy. Reagan believed that he worked quite diligently at those things that mattered most to him. He thought that the Hollywood pattern of working intensively in spurts was quite sensible. Reagan wasn't kidding in the slightest when he told television interviewer Charlie Rose during the 1980 campaign, "Show me an executive who works long, overtime hours, and I'll show you a bad executive."[23] But Reagan recognized the comic value of his reputation as a nine-to-five president who napped the day away, and he deflated his critics by outdoing them in jokes about his work habits. (Autographing a photo of a sleeping Marlin Fitzwater that had been taken on Air Force One, Reagan wrote, "Hey, Marlin, we're only supposed to do this in cabinet meetings.") Reagan knew that humor must touch the heart, and that it must not spare the humorist or his frailties in the process. In this sense, humor was Reagan's ultimate self-defense and his ultimate weapon. It was also a way of reaching him. His more attentive advisers knew that Reagan found it extremely difficult to acknowledge mistakes, inconsistencies or policy failures in formal discussions, but could be made to face them if he needed an anecdote to impress an audience. ("I'm not worried about the deficit; it's big enough to take care of itself," he said at the 1984 Gridiron Dinner.) This ability would prove a saving grace late in his presidency when Reagan's public credibility was shattered by the Iran-contra affair, and those who cared most deeply about him were trying to make him face the unpleasant truth that he had traded U.S. arms for American hostages.

Reagan's skill at self-deprecation also reassured Americans that his head had not been turned by the presidency. By telling jokes about himself, said columnist Mark Shields, Reagan conveyed an "egalitarian message" that was appreciated by the public. "He's saying, 'Even though I'm up here, I'm not so important. I still want your approval and acceptance.' "[24] Reagan accomplished this by kidding on the square, with stories that cut close to the bone. ("Let me tell you a story," he would say, if someone complimented him on the way he looked or the relaxed manner in which he bore the burdens of the presidency. "There were two psychiatrists, one young and one old, with offices across the hall from each other. Every morning they'd meet in the elevator, fresh and dapper, but by day's end, when they met leaving the building, the young psychiatrist was disheveled and exhausted while the older man looked as neat and rested as he had when he arrived. One evening the young psychiatrist could stand it no longer. He said to the older man, 'I don't understand it. You look so fresh all the time. I hear these terrible stories from my patients every day. How do you put up with it? What's your secret?' The older man looked at the young psychiatrist and said, 'I don't listen.' ")[25]

Reagan's joke file included many off-color stories that he shared with his closest aides at morning staff meetings or the old members of his California kitchen cabinet at their increasingly infrequent gatherings. His generation eschewed such jokes in mixed company, an etiquette Reagan violated only in times of unusual stress. He also told a range of stories for private consumption that were less politically palatable than his public witticisms, although not necessarily less humorous. When an aide asked him during his first term what he would do if Senator Edward M. Kennedy became a presidential candidate again, Reagan winked and said, "I guess I'd just have to point out that I used to be a lifeguard." In 1988, he told the annual Alfalfa Club Dinner, "The other night I had a dream that Gary Hart was president, and he was meeting with Margaret Thatcher. Mrs. Thatcher told him, 'I want your hands off Nicaragua, your hands off Afghanistan and your hands off my knee.' "[26] The joke was a hit with the good old boys of the Alfalfa Club, a Washington organization of the important and self-important that holds an annual dinner without the perceived impediments of women guests or reporters of either gender. And Reagan also won a hearty laugh from his Irish-American rival, House Speaker Tip O'Neill, during hard bargaining with him over the budget in 1982. (A doctor asked a simple Irish washerwoman for a specimen to conduct a laboratory test. The washerwoman, not wishing to confess her ignorance, returned home and went next door to ask a neighbor the meaning of the doctor's request. She came back bruised and disheveled. When her husband asked what had happened, she said, "I asked her what a specimen was, and she told me to go pee in a bottle. So I said, 'Go shit in your hat' and the fight was on.")

Reagan often told elaborate jokes in an exaggerated dialect that he fondly believed to be Irish, one of them a long-winded story about an Irishman who collects a large insurance settlement after an auto accident by pretending that his injuries have put him in a wheelchair for life. When representatives of the insurance company warn him that he will be pursued by them the rest of his life until they establish the fallacy of his claims, he responds by telling them that they will be following him to the Catholic religious shrine of Lourdes and "there you're going to see the greatest miracle you've ever seen in your life."[27] Reporters groaned after they had heard this story for the umpteenth time, but most of Reagan's audiences seemed to like the tale, fake dialect and all.

Reagan did less well during the 1980 New Hampshire primary when he unwisely told a different sort of ethnic joke to aides within the earshot of national reporters who were covering the campaign. ("How do you tell who the Polish fellow is at a cock fight? He's the one with the duck. How do you tell who the Italian is at the cock fight? He's the one who bets on the duck. How do you know the Mafia was there? The duck wins.")[28] When the account of this joke was published, it caused consternation in the Reagan camp and prompted Ed Meese to make a Reaganesque quip: "There goes Connecticut,"[29] in reference to the prominent political participation of Italian-Americans in that state. But Reagan realized, then and always until the Iran-contra affair, that he could best the media in a contest of credibility. When the supporter of another candidate asked Reagan about this joke following a Republican debate in Manchester, Reagan said he had been "stiffed" by the press and calmly lied on national television, claiming he had told the story as an example of jokes that politicians shouldn't tell.[30] Reagan got away with it, in part because the joke was relatively innocuous and in part because the national press is unpopular with conservative New Hampshire voters. These voters, especially Italian-American voters, might have been less amused by some of the ethnic stories Reagan told his kitchen cabinet and others whom he trusted to keep their mouths shut. One of these jokes, which Reagan began telling in his days as governor of California, concerned a fellow who was prejudiced against Italians. Walking down the street with a friend one day, he encountered an Italian organ-grinder with a monkey and threw five dollars in the monkey's hat. The friend was aghast. "You've been telling me for years how much you hated Italians, and here you do that," he said. Replied the man who was prejudiced against Italians, "Well, they're so cute when they're little."[31]

Reagan was the butt of jokes as well as a master raconteur. Long before he became president, he was notorious for gaffes and oddball statistics.* The most outlandish of these tended to be flights of fancy that were loosely based on stories or statistics he had taken from *Human Events, Reader's Digest* or the local newspaper and lodged in his mental card file. Reagan was sort of an equal opportunity reader, who tended to believe that anything he saw in print was true, particularly if it reinforced his point of view. He had a powerful but indiscriminate memory that rarely distinguished between the actual and the apocryphal. He also had an eye for topical stories and startling statistics that could be used to spruce up his basic speech and make it more relevant to his audiences. All of this had worked well for him in the General Electric days when he was of necessity his own researcher, but his methodology proved insufficient for the more exacting standards applied to presidential candidates. During the six-year interregnum between the end of his governorship and the beginning of his presidency, Reagan often stirred up a storm by drawing upon information in his mental card file that turned out to be unverifiable or demonstrably inaccurate. In the 1980 campaign he claimed that "the finest oil geolo-

---

* During the Reagan presidency I called these "Reaganisms" and ended my weekly column in *The Washington Post* with a "Reaganism of the Week." White House aides, some of whom offered their own contributions to this feature, told me that Reagan regularly read the "Reaganism," though not always the column.

gists" had told him that the United States had more oil reserves than Saudi Arabia, an absurdity that Mark Shields spoofed as reflective of Reagan's belief that there is "more oil under second base at Yankee Stadium"[32] than in the Middle East. Reagan attracted even more attention with his discovery that trees and other vegetation were primarily responsible for air pollution and with his wildly incorrect "suspicion" that the Mount St. Helens volcano had released more sulfur dioxide into the atmosphere "than has been released in the last ten years of automobile driving."*

Reagan's campaign aides despaired at his misstatements but found it difficult to keep up with them because they often had no clue to Reagan's sources. As Martin Anderson blithely explained to a *New York Times* reporter, one problem was that Reagan used "hundreds of stories for examples" in his campaign speeches. "Ninety-nine times out of a hundred, things checked out, but sometimes the source was wrong."[33] And sometimes Reagan was wrong, too. Experienced damage-control experts on the Reagan team, of whom Anderson was one of the best, recognized that the candidate's mind sometimes wandered during briefings, particularly those that bordered on the technical. The talent most valued in a briefer by the Reagan inner circle was the ability to explain complicated issues in everyday language. The best briefers were those who could make their points through anecdotes.

After Reagan became shielded by the presidency, the problem of protecting him from unwanted questions became marginally easier, while the consequences of potential misstatements increased. It was a constant worry for the aides, particularly Deaver, who knew that Reagan's natural friendliness prompted him to answer questions even when he didn't know the answers. Deaver was inventive at devising rules to protect Reagan from random questioning, but reporters quickly learned that the president would often respond to shouted questions even when his aides would have preferred him to keep silent. And Reagan liked to make news. When Ed Meese urged him during a preparatory session for an early news conference to "be dull, Mr. President," Reagan responded honestly, "Being dull is very hard for me."[34]

Being dull was rarely Reagan's problem. He was consistently colorful

---

* Mount St. Helens at the peak of activity produced 2,000 tons of sulfur dioxide daily, compared to 81,000 tons of sulfur dioxide then produced each day by automobiles. As for the trees, Reagan apparently confused nitrous oxide, emitted by plants, with nitrogen dioxide, which is emitted by smokestacks. No other mistaken belief of Reagan's in the 1980 campaign was as widely ridiculed. When he spoke at Claremont College in California, students tacked a sign to a tree: "Chop Me Down Before I Kill Again."

even when his comprehension failed, and he was unable to resist playing to whatever audience he had at hand. When his cabinet members were wrangling in 1981 over the best way to dispose of a prodigious government store of surplus butter, Reagan brought the meeting to a tumultuous conclusion by declaring, "Four hundred and seventy-eight million pounds of butter! Does anyone know where we can find 478 million pounds of popcorn?"[35] But when everyone had stopped laughing they realized they were no closer to finding a politically acceptable solution to the butter disposal problem than when the meeting began.

And this was typically the case when a decision required Reagan's participation. Reagan sometimes used humor to avoid facing issues he ought to have faced, particularly the reality that it was impossible to increase military spending, reduce taxes and balance the budget simultaneously. His biggest problem was that he didn't know enough about public policy to participate fully in his presidency—and often didn't realize how much he didn't know. Reagan's legal advisers learned that he knew little about the law, his national security advisers found that he was devoid of knowledge on the capabilities of most U.S. and Soviet weapons systems and his economists discovered that he was poorly informed on economics, even though he sometimes reminded them that he had majored in economics and sociology at Eureka College. Sometimes his ignorance became evident in public. At a December 17, 1981, news conference, Reagan was asked his view of an affirmative action agreement between an aerospace company and a labor union to train minorities and move them up in the work force. "I can't see any fault with that," Reagan said. "I'm for that." But his administration wasn't in favor of affirmative action, then or ever, even when management and labor agreed on its desirability. At the insistence of Attorney General William French Smith, the White House press office several days later issued a statement saying that the Justice Department was seeking to overturn in court the very agreement with which Reagan found no fault.

The gaps in Reagan's knowledge were compounded by gaps in his memory. Reagan remembered stories, statistics, movies and dramatic events. He could memorize almost anything that was given to him on paper, even though he often mentally erased the material immediately after delivering it. But he had an exceptionally faulty memory for names, possibly the consequence of living so long in an actor's world where casts, scripts and scenes changed constantly. Reagan called Environmental Protection Agency administrator William D. Ruckelshaus "Don" at one important meeting. He shocked National Security Adviser Robert (Bud) McFarlane months after his appointment by entirely forgetting his name. Such private lapses were injurious to the egos of some administration officials but did no larger damage. In contrast, Housing and Urban Development Secretary Sam Pierce, the only Reagan cabinet member to serve a full two terms, never quite recovered from the embarrassment of being addressed by the president as "Mr. Mayor" at a June 12, 1981, visit of a dozen mayors to the White House. This was a revealing lapse. Reagan's failure to recognize his HUD secretary after both of them had been six months on the job accurately reflected the president's almost total lack of interest in HUD, which he never visited during his eight years in office. Some of Reagan's other lapses appeared simply to have been the product of absentmindedness. During a picture-taking session with Liberian leader Samuel K. Doe, Reagan referred to this military ruler as "Chairman Moe." Doe's views of the incident were not recorded. Neither was the reaction of Singapore's Lee Kuan Yew when Reagan greeted him at the White House south portico by saying, "It gives me great pleasure to welcome Prime Minister Lee Kuan Yew and Mrs. Lee to Singapore." [36]

All politicians and performers make fluffs, of course, and Reagan was better than most of them at shrugging off his gaffes and goofs and proceeding with the business at hand. He often had much to shrug away. White House transcripts of presidential speeches were dotted with asterisks informing reporters that Reagan had meant to say "Mayor Bradley" instead of "Mayor Bartlett" [37] or "1981" instead of "1941." Some of these mistakes were simple reading errors. Reagan, who has been badly nearsighted since childhood, often misread his texts unless he was wearing glasses or using a TelePrompTer. [38] But he also often did not pay attention to what he was saying. At a Republican fund-raiser he said, "Now we're trying to get unemployment to go up, and I think we are going to succeed." [39] Launching a campaign for welfare reform he declared, "Even though there may be some misguided critics of what we're trying to do, I think we're on the wrong path." [40] He told the Washington bureau of the *Dallas Morning News* that he had not read even the summary of his Treasury Department's tax reform proposal "because my mind is too filled with the budget." [41] He told a group of business leaders that "nuclear war would be the greatest tragedy, I think, ever experienced by mankind in the history of mankind." [42] He sent a group of high-school student ambassadors off to Europe after telling them, "And yes, it's all right to have an affinity for what was the mother country for all of us, because if a man takes a wife unto himself, he doesn't stop loving his mother because of that. But at the same time, we're all Americans." [43]

These locutions and an array of dubious assertions ("There has never been a war between two free countries") [44] tended to ratify the widely held Washington view that Reagan's intellect fell considerably below rocket-scientist standards. The conventional estimate of Reagan's intellectual capabilities was summed up by Clark Clifford at a fashionable Georgetown party, where he described the president as "an amiable dunce." [45] The phrase stuck, and the opinion it expressed was not limited to Democrats or Reagan's critics in the media.

The portrait of Reagan that most often emerges from the memoirs written by departed and often disaffected members of his administration is of a president who was long on decency and determination and short on intellect. David Stockman's portrayal of Reagan in action is particularly searing. When the budget director explained to Reagan that members of his cabinet were planning payroll reductions that would save only a half-billion dollars at a time when the projected budget deficit ranged between $111 billion and $185 billion, Reagan treated this bad news as if Stockman had delivered a glowing progress report. "That's just what's going to happen when the management efforts of our people take hold," [46] Reagan said, appearing to miss the point entirely. "Somehow, he had drawn the exact opposite conclusion from what I had just told him about how little the cabinet was willing to cut from the payroll," recalled Stockman despairingly. [47] Similar difficulties were encountered by Dick Cheney and other members of the Republican congressional leadership when they tried to engage Reagan in substantive discussion of weapons systems or arms control. Reagan would listen, but respond to the congressmen from the "talking points" written on his cards. Eventually, the congressional leaders gave up and conducted their policy discussions with Reagan's ever-changing cast of national security advisers or other members of the White House staff.

Even some of Reagan's friends and supporters on the right had their doubts about his intellectual candlepower. Richard Perle, the brainy resident nemesis of arms control at the Pentagon, thought that Reagan consistently engaged in "intellectual delegation of authority." [48] Columnist George Will, who probably saw more of Reagan at close quarters during his presidency than any other conservative intellectual outside the administration, wondered how anyone so uninformed could reach the top of the American political system. Reagan's substitution of anecdotes for analysis particularly annoyed Will, who is highly analytical. At a reception preceding a White House dinner just before he left the presidency, Reagan startled Will and William F. Buckley by saying, "Well, you know, Bill, is it possible that we conservatives are the real liberals and the liberals are the real conservatives?"[49] Will thought the remark a "terribly banal . . . Durango, Colorado, Rotary thought." Buckley, also unimpressed but more inclined to accept Reagan on his own terms, murmured something affable. Will, offended by what seemed to him an empty comment, did not. "I knew you were a liberal all along," he said to the president, and walked off.[50]

Nonetheless, Will and others who knew Reagan personally or who dealt with him over a long period of time usually concluded that he was smarter, maybe much smarter, than he seemed on the surface. While Reagan was sometimes stunningly ignorant about matters on which he was expected to be well informed, those with the most exposure to him reject out of hand the view that he is a "dunce." Some of them also believe that Reagan's amiability was overstated. Martin Anderson, an intellectual economist and writer, decided that Reagan was bright, decisive and tough-minded—but basically uncaring about the human feelings of those around him, "a warmly ruthless man."[51] His wife, Annelise Anderson, also an economist and writer, served as one of Stockman's principal deputies and attended numerous meetings with Reagan in the early days of the presidency. She was impressed with Reagan's decisiveness and intellectual grasp and reached the conclusion that Reagan was underrated intellectually because he always dealt in "specific concrete experience" rather than the abstractions preferred by academics.[52] Pollster Richard Wirthlin, who also has an academic background, thought Reagan "extremely gifted and extremely bright in picking up oral briefings."[53] Wirthlin was convinced that Reagan was so highly focused on the three or four things he wanted to accomplish —"relations with the Soviets, the economy, federalism"—that he deliberately excluded almost everything else except his performances from his mental radar screen. This view was expressed to me repeatedly with only minor variations by a number of persons who dealt with Reagan at close range in the White House, including Deaver, Meese, Ken Duberstein, Paul Laxalt, Howard Baker, David Gergen, Colin Powell, Paul Wolfowitz and the Andersons. These up-close observers believed that Reagan usually operated on the basis of sound instincts and common sense.

While a number of those closest to Reagan were put off, at least initially, by his extreme passivity, they also were impressed by his ability to focus on his core objectives. George Shultz, often considered the most accomplished member of the Reagan cabinet, thought that the "substantive achievements" of the administration, in particular the improvement in U.S.-Soviet relations, were in large part a product of Reagan's highly focused approach to governance. "I think he manages to get the essence of the problems pretty well," Shultz said. "And often times the people who are immersed in the detail sort of lose the essence."[54] It was in the essences that Reagan excelled. "He understood the ambient circumstances, which required a high degree of intelligence and knowledge," said Buckley, who was a friend to Reagan and took him seriously. "He knew, for instance, that people were afraid of inflation. He had an innate capacity to know what things people were worried about."[55] Buckley's observation is an elegant version of what Stu Spencer saw as the "Joe Sixpack" in Reagan. This was the quality that set Reagan apart from other politicians and refutes the description of "amiable dunce."

But the nature of Reagan's intellect remains a puzzlement. Annelise Anderson came to the conclusion that he was "super bright," and observed that in discussions he often rejected the conventional wisdom, "a characteristic of extremely intelligent and creative people."[56] Robert Kaiser of *The Washington Post,* a liberal journalist with expertise in Soviet affairs and the arcane discipline of arms control, notes that Reagan particularly scorned the conventional wisdom of "the nuclear priesthood." He was not terrified at holding in his hands the power to unleash thousands of nuclear weapons because he understood better than his predecessors that the superpowers would never use these weapons, Kaiser believes.[57]

Reagan's ideas and ideology had been forged in the crucible of experience. He had, in Annelise Anderson's phrase, "fought very hard for the knowledge and understanding"[58] he had acquired, and he did not surrender his positions easily. The mask of amiability concealed a stubbornness that was at once the wonder and despair of those who worked for him. Stockman, Baker, Darman and Commerce Secretary Malcolm Baldrige ran into a stone wall when they tried at different times to make the deficit-reduction case for higher taxes. So, later on, did Buckley, Will and other conservatives when they opposed the Intermediate Nuclear Forces (INF) treaty and tried to convince Reagan that Soviet leader Mikhail Gorbachev was not to be trusted. On things that mattered to him, the passive president could also be unyielding.

He could also be curious, despite his widespread reputation as the least curious of men. Again, the question is more complicated than it seems at first glance. Reagan was certainly uncurious about most aspects of public policy. He never peeked to find out what was going on below the surface of the government of which he was the chief executive. While he often fumed over "leaks" about the feuds and policy struggles within his official family, he rarely sought to locate the sources of these stories, even when they were obvious to almost everyone else in Washington. And he was so quiet at White House briefings that his aides sometimes wondered if he had been paying attention. But Reagan sometimes expressed curiosity about subjects far from the beaten track of the presidency. During a luncheon at *The Washington Star* in August 1981, when the discussion had turned to mistranslations of the dialogue in Hollywood westerns when the subtitles were in French or Italian, Reagan suddenly asked, "Where did we get the English language? Where did English come from?" There was an awkward pause while the editors attempted to calculate the intent of the question. Finally, an answer came from Ed Yoder, a Rhodes scholar and Pulitzer Prize–winning editorial page writer, who explained to Reagan that English was "a blend of Anglo-Saxon and Norman French that began to develop in the eleventh century . . . and reached a recognizable modern form in Chaucer's time." Reagan thanked Yoder, who was struck by Reagan's lack of embarrassment at asking a question that it would have been inconceivable for other presidents to ask.[59]

On another occasion Reagan turned to George Will and asked, "What makes the Blue Ridge Mountains blue?" Will didn't have the foggiest notion of the answer, but he never forgot the question. He, too, was struck by Reagan's lack of concern about displaying ignorance and he became convinced over time that Reagan possessed an "eclectic curiosity" about matters that lay outside the boundaries of his settled views. "On the first nine levels Reagan is the least interesting of men," Will said. "But if you postulate a tenth level, then he's suddenly fascinating."[60]

I share that fascination. I have interviewed Reagan at least forty times over the past two decades and have been with him in informal or social settings on about the same number of occasions. I have watched him give hundreds of speeches and perform at scores of news conferences and other question-and-answer sessions. (News conferences became a rarity during the Reagan presidency but were held on a near-weekly basis during much of Reagan's first term as governor.) The overall impression of this experience is contradictory. Reagan was usually highly effective with a script and often ineffective without one. But the most passionate and effective political speeches of his life came in the 1976 North Carolina primary when he discarded his script and spoke from the heart about the issues that mattered most to him. In many of his presidential news conferences he groped for words and sometimes lost his train of thought. But when he was challenged sharply by a reporter or a political opponent in a debate he could display the same fire and eloquence he had shown in Nashua. Most of Reagan's formal interviews were disappointments, at least from a journalist's point of view, because he so frequently resorted to familiar formulas or oft-told anecdotes when asked to analyze an issue or explain the details of his position. This did not necessarily bespeak a lack of intelligence; on the contrary, Reagan often demonstrated considerable skill in evading politically troublesome questions he did not wish to answer. When speaking informally or off the record, he was less evasive but not always more comprehensible. He was apt to lapse into incoherence when even slightly tired, almost as if the mental cassettes in his mind could not be pushed into a "play" position. At other times he was insightful, particularly when explaining the craft of performance or offering consolation to someone who had suffered a personal loss. It was clear to me that he was not a dunce, amiable or otherwise. But it was difficult to understand how his mind worked.

What fascinated me most were the lengths Reagan would go to demonstrate that his present opinions were consistent with past views, even when they obviously were not, and his tenacity at defending policy positions with whatever argument came to mind. For instance, Reagan had long used Lenin as the measure of Marxist morality and often quoted some of the more cold-blooded declarations by the founder of the Soviet state to show that Communists would stop at nothing to achieve their goal of world domination. Answering a question from Sam Donaldson about the Kremlin's motives at the first news conference of his presidency, Reagan said about the Soviets that "the only morality they recognize is what will further their cause, meaning they reserve unto themselves the right to commit any crime, to lie, to cheat."[61] The answer ratified the worst fears of the Soviet leadership about Reagan and prompted a furious denunciation of the new president in the Soviet press, which compared him to Hitler. When I asked Reagan about his answer at a subsequent interview, he replied blandly that he was only quoting Lenin. But by the end of his presidency, when Reagan was defending his view that Mikhail Gorbachev was "a different kind of

Soviet leader" against conservative criticism, he had another Lenin in mind. One difference in Gorbachev, the president told me without any sense of irony, was that "he is the first leader that has come along who has gone back before Stalin and that he is trying to do what Lenin was teaching." [62] Reagan went on in this vein, praising Lenin and Gorbachev as if they were new-age capitalists. He seemed to have no memory whatsoever of the lying, cheating Lenin whose quotations had been a staple of his speeches on the conservative banquet circuit. This new Lenin drove conservatives up the wall, without resolving my perplexities about Reagan's intelligence. I reached the conclusion that Reagan was wonderful about Jack Benny and worthless on the subject of Lenin. He was intelligent about some matters some of the time.

And so, it seems, are all of us, or almost all of us. The riddle of Reagan's intelligence for a long time seemed insoluble. When I asked people who knew Reagan well and were willing to honestly discuss the issue of his intelligence, I found they were often equally frustrated in trying to understand what made him tick. "People say he is a simpleton, which isn't right, and when they realize he isn't they're apt to go to the other end of the spectrum and compare him to Socrates, which doesn't work either," said William Buckley. [63]

For the more thoughtful members of the inner circle, Reagan's intelligence was an enigma. If offered the protection of anonymity, friends and family members could cite contradictory examples of Reagan's "brilliance" or "ignorance" but found it difficult to construct a theory that would account for his varying modes of intellectual behavior. Then I came across the work of Howard Gardner, a Harvard psychologist who has pioneered in developing a theory of "multiple intelligences." Gardner's work, which has gained grudging acceptance in the scientific community, challenges the conventional belief that "intelligence" is a general capacity possessed to greater or lesser extent by every human being. In place of a single intelligence that can be measured by a standardized "intelligence test," Gardner postulates seven specific intelligences with distinctive characteristics.* In Gardner's categorization Reagan ranks high in a form of intelligence he calls "interpersonal," high in "bodily-kinesthetic intelligence," high in an aspect of "language intelligence" and low in the "logical-mathematical intelligence" at which lawyers and professors usually excel. Reagan is not the least

* The seven intelligences are linguistic, musical, logical-mathematical, spatial, bodily-kinesthetic and two forms of personal intelligence. See Howard Gardner, *Frames of Mind: The Theory of Multiple Intelligences,* published by Basic Books.

lawyerlike. "Reagan's good with language, but not logically," Gardner observes. "He makes sense of the world narratively. Scientists can be deductive and understand logic but often can't tell stories. Stories are not necessarily logical." Gardner believes that the combination of intelligences exhibited by Reagan is unusual for a president, but not necessarily for an actor. "Actors find it easier to mimic than to understand," says Gardner. "They are kids who often have difficulty with the usual school stuff, but they can parrot things back and get reinforcement from others. Many people in acting are not happy with who they are. What sets Reagan apart is that he is extraordinarily happy with himself —and with the role of Reagan." [64]

Gardner's analysis of the way Reagan functions intellectually produced in me the sense of discovery that a scientist or a detective must feel when a gigantic mystery abruptly becomes comprehensible. I have spent a quarter of a century tracking Reagan and was said to know him well. What I knew was that he understood all manner of things that suggested powers of analysis without possessing any visible analytical ability. The mistake that I and others made was in trying to fit Reagan into a preconception of the way an "intelligent politician" behaves. This made no sense, for anyone who has spent any amount of time with Reagan knows he is unlike other politicians. I knew he was intelligent, but in his own terms. It was only when Gardner's theory helped me throw the mold away that I could say what I had always seen.

Others who have struggled even longer to explain Reagan think this theory of his intelligence makes sense. "That's exactly right," said Stuart Spencer, who understands Reagan as well as anyone I know. "Exactly. I'm always asked to explain him, and I talk about him as intelligent but not intelligent in the way politicians are intelligent. This explains him." [65] Spencer had been telling me for more than two decades that the ability Gardner describes as "interpersonal intelligence" was Reagan's strong suit. It was what Spencer had in mind when he warned me, many years ago, never to underestimate Reagan's abilities. Former White House chief of staff Ken Duberstein also believes that Gardner's analysis is valid. Duberstein had often told me that Reagan was more intelligent than he seemed to the politicians who watched him read from four-by-six cards.

If Reagan is viewed as an intelligent person whose combination of intelligences is unusual in a president, a number of apparent mysteries of his behavior become soluble. Take the mimicry and the memory, for instance. When I interviewed Neil Reagan, then sixty, while writing my first book about his brother in 1968, he told me that the young Ronald Reagan had "a photographic mind." Neil recalled that one of Ronald Reagan's professors at Eureka College (probably economics professor Archibald Gray) had complained that he "never opened a book" but always knew the answers at examination time. He then explained the way that his brother did his studying: "He would take a book the night before the test and in about a quick hour he would thumb through it and [mentally] photograph those pages and write a good test."[66] This ability freed Ronald Reagan for activities he enjoyed more than studying, and it stood him in good stead in Hollywood, where he earned the reputation as a quick study who rapidly memorized his lines.

But Reagan's ability to mentally "photograph" and store textual material proved a mixed blessing in public life. As Gardner puts it, people lacking Reagan's phenomenal skill of memorization learn to translate or "recode" the information they receive into a language of their own in order to remember it. "A good linguistic memory can collide with analytic facility because if you remember something perfectly, there is no need to re-code it, thereby making it your own," Gardner observed.[67] Over time, the advantage of Reagan's superior memory gave way to the disadvantage of his deficient analytic skills. These were not skills he could have acquired when he was elected president at the age of sixty-nine, even if he had perceived their necessity. But their absence perpetuated the view that Reagan was an intellectual lightweight or, alternatively, intellectually lazy. "He was a highly intelligent man who, when confronted with big workloads and easy workloads, would always pick the easy workloads," said Richard Allen, Reagan's first national security adviser.[68] In the Reagan White House, this was a prevalent view.

What also became prevalent, for those who understood Reagan, was the practice of briefing him with narratives and anecdotes that played to the strength of his memory rather than the weakness of his analysis. Without ever constructing a theory of Reagan's intelligence, the aides who were most effective in communicating with him learned empirically the wisdom of Annelise Anderson's observation that Reagan always thought in concrete examples rather than abstractions. One of the earliest learners was Martin Anderson, who gradually came to believe that Reagan used anecdotes and experience to construct a coherent idea of the way the world works and what he wanted to accomplish. "He never sat down, at least to my knowledge, in the campaign or the administration and said, 'Now here is my grand design, what I want to do and all the theory,' " Anderson said. "And yet, if you stepped back and added up all the specific things he said and looked at them, it formed a grand design. In other words, he did it by inference rather than deduction. It's a different way of thinking."[69]

This different way caused repeated problems for Reagan at news conferences, where the demand was for information rather than anecdotes. Ed Meese has observed that Reagan's mistakes at news conferences often were the result of an unsuccessful attempt at literal repetition of technical material from a meeting or briefing paper. When Reagan groped for words, as he frequently did, he was actually trying to reconstruct visually what he had read or heard, much as he had done when taking tests at Eureka. Sometimes he misremembered vital details of the information he had tried to memorize, in effect producing an out-of-focus picture from his photographic mind. At other times he recalled exactly what had been said to him and repeated it in answer to a question on a related but slightly different subject, producing an answer that was off the point. Meese, who worried more about this problem than he acknowledged publicly, was usually an effective briefer of Reagan because he understood the way his mind functioned. "When I briefed Reagan, I wanted him to remember the substance," Meese said. "There were really two modes with him. When he had a script he felt compelled to use it, probably because of his acting background. When he grasped a subject, he was able to deal with it on his own. But when he was briefed technically, he often felt compelled to repeat what he had been told." When I pressed Meese to tell me exactly what he did to prepare the president for a news conference, he replied, "I tried to talk with him rather than give him a lawyer's brief."[70]

Greenspan's remark that Reagan was "psychologically a professional comedian" is also a valuable key to understanding him. What first made me think that Reagan was intelligent was his sense of humor, readily evident in his early political career when he wrote his own material and obscured in the White House by the armada of speechwriters that surrounds any president. In the old days Reagan wrote his own one-liners ("Their signs said, make love, not war, but they didn't look like they could do either"),[71] and he could also be spontaneously humorous. At one tense situation on the University of California's Santa Cruz campus during his governorship, when Reagan's limousine was slowly proceeding through a group of hostile demonstrators, a bearded youth stuck his face up to the car, yelling, "We are the future." Reagan borrowed a piece of paper from an aide and scribbled a message that he held up to the car window. It said, "I'll sell my bonds."[72]

Reagan also understood, both consciously and intuitively, that humor was a wonderful tool for deflating political opponents and sidetracking their most significant assertions. During the rehearsal for Reagan's 1980 debate with independent candidate John B. Anderson, Stockman imitated Anderson's grim assessment of Reagan's environmental policies. "Well, John, sounds like I better get a gas mask," [73] Reagan responded. This remark never made it off the cutting-room floor, but Reagan's most famous line in his 1980 campaign debate with Carter was the product of a similar process. By this time, Stockman was impersonating Carter. During one rehearsal he hammered away at Reagan on the nuclear proliferation issue. Reagan was ineffective in response. In a critique afterward, aides pressed Reagan to sharpen the content of his answer while Reagan mused about his rhetorical ineffectiveness. Commenting on the reply he had delivered in rehearsal, Reagan said, "I was about ready to say, 'There you go again.' I may save it for the debate." [74] And he did, rescuing an otherwise deficient reply to Carter's claim that Reagan "began his political career campaigning against Medicare" by saying, "There you go again." The response was funny, irrelevant—and thoroughly authentic. It did not answer Carter's point, but it revealed a functioning intellect. What was on display that October night in Cleveland, as in the Carter and Reagan presidencies, were different types of intelligence.

Ultimately, Reagan's sense of humor provided a measure of the man. The people recognized this quickly, and his wiser adversaries learned it over time. Paying tribute to Reagan at the 1988 Gridiron Dinner, New York Governor Mario Cuomo quoted John F. Kennedy's observation that "there are only three things in life that are real—God, human folly, and laughter—and since the first two are beyond our comprehension, we must do what we can with the third." Cuomo went on to compare the two presidents, saying that Kennedy's gift of laughter was one of the reasons that Americans loved him and "it's one of the reasons that we Americans love and respect another man of gentle humor, our president, Ronald Reagan." [75]

Reagan treasured that tribute. When he was riding high, his stories and one-liners delighted audiences and heartened all who heard the sound of his voice. When he was down, his self-deprecating stories helped him overcome his own fears and uncertainties and sent a message to the nation that all would ultimately be well. "Please tell me you're all Republicans," [76] he said to the doctors who were preparing him for surgery after he was shot on March 30, 1981. Reagan was deeply frightened at the time and doing his best to laugh in the face of the

Great Fear. That night, in the recovery room at George Washington Hospital, with tubes in his throat that prevented him from speaking, Reagan signaled for a notepad. "All in all, I'd rather be in Philadelphia," [77] he wrote, paraphrasing comedian W. C. Fields. In his greatest personal crisis, and all others, Reagan's sense of humor proved his saving grace.

9

HAIL TO THE CHIEF

*I've seen all those photographs that have been printed in
various articles of someone slouched looking out the
Oval Office windows and then beside it the quote about
[the presidency being] the loneliest [job] and so forth.
I have to tell you, I enjoyed it. I didn't feel that way
about it.*

RONALD REAGAN,
May 5, 1989[1]

The presidency proved both the best and worst of offices for
Ronald Reagan. His amiable temperament and passive fatalism spared
him the private terrors that beset presidents in the nuclear age and
inoculated him against the maladies provoked by the exercise of unaccustomed power. "Power is poison," wrote Henry Adams three quarters of a century ago, in words that echoed through the age of Vietnam
and Watergate. "Its effect on Presidents [has] been always tragic,
chiefly as an almost insane excitement at first, and a worse reaction
afterwards; but also because no mind is so well balanced as to bear the
strain of seizing unlimited force without habit or knowledge of it."[2]*

---
* Adams had Theodore Roosevelt in mind. "Roosevelt enjoyed a singularly direct nature and honest
intent, but he lived naturally in restless agitation that would have worn out most tempers in a

Reagan was not afflicted with such excitement, as he had learned to his own surprise on inauguration day. His perspectives were unaltered by the presidency, perhaps because he did not need high office to impart a sense of self-esteem. If anything, Reagan's sense of well-being was excessive, and it was enhanced by the congenial schedule devised for him by Deaver and Nancy Reagan. As the first lady well knew, Reagan was a creature of habit who required at least eight hours of sleep and rest breaks during the day to perform effectively. He was capable at any age of productive bursts of energy, as he had shown in critical stretches of his political campaigns, but he could become irritable and snappish when subjected to a relentless daily grind. A lenient schedule was a necessity for Reagan, although he was usually too obliging and passive to insist upon it. Reagan had never cared for actors who made trouble on the set, and he regarded the events on his daily schedule as stage directions he was obligated to obey. Throughout the campaign Nancy Reagan had struggled with Deaver, Spencer and campaign headquarters in Arlington to prevent "overscheduling" of Reagan, who would observe his seventieth birthday seventeen days after he took the oath of office. She had lost many of these battles, since the exigencies of presidential campaigns make few allowances for age or the protectiveness of spouses. But it was a different story in the controlled, hothouse atmosphere of the White House, as the Reagans had accurately anticipated. Reagan may have been the one president in the history of the republic who saw his election as a chance to get some rest. When he grumbled shortly before the election that he was being roused too early to campaign, Stu Spencer told him cheerfully, "You better get used to it, Governor. When you're president, that fellow from the National Security Council will be there to brief you at seven thirty every morning." Reagan was not impressed. "Well," he said, with a characteristic pause, "he's going to have a helluva long wait."[4] And a long wait it would have been, except that Reagan's national security advisers, whatever their other deficiencies, knew better than to arrive early at the Oval Office. The typical NSC briefing for Reagan began at 9:30 A.M. and was over before 10:00.

As an institution, the American presidency is remarkably flexible in accommodating varying modes of behavior. Each occupant of the White House shapes the presidency to his own needs and is in turn

---

month, and his first year of Presidency showed chronic excitement that made a friend tremble," Adams wrote.[3]

shaped by the many-sided requirements of this unique office. But Reagan was an actor, accustomed to many roles, and he was fully shaped when he reached the White House. He loved being president and respected the traditions of the office, but he was neither awed by his new role nor bowed by the burdens of office. He wanted to do what he had always done—make speeches, delight his aides with anecdotes, write letters, work out every day in the small gym adjacent to his living quarters and, in general, take more time for himself than most presidents would have considered possible. While recuperating after the assassination attempt, Reagan said he preferred working in the White House residence rather than the Oval Office because he could make telephone calls to members of Congress "without bothering to get dressed."[5] When he wasn't making calls or spending time with Nancy, he watched television or read. His reading tastes ran to adventure novels and autobiographies, rather than briefing papers. He wrote each evening in his diary, filling five red leather-bound books during the eight years of his presidency. And he took time while walking from the residence to the Oval Office to feed the squirrels. Power was not "poison" for Reagan, who remained serenely undistorted by the presidency.

Reagan's easy approach to the duties and responsibilities of his office was to a large measure reflected in the White House daily schedule, especially the real schedule that was tucked into the president's packet of homework each evening, rather than the edited and sometimes fake version of this document that was distributed to the media the following morning. The real schedule shows that Reagan typically arrived at the Oval Office after nine and returned to the residence by half past five, often earlier if his presence was required at an evening social event. Usually, he took Wednesday afternoons off. On Fridays, he often left in midafternoon for Camp David. Except in times of crisis, and sometimes even then, his schedule allowed him at least two or three hours during the day for "personal staff time," a phrase that on the 1980 campaign plane had been considered a euphemism for "nap time." Meese laughed when I told him the campaign joke that Reagan's best-known movie had been reissued under the title "Staff Time for Bonzo."

After Reagan was elected, however, his relaxed work habits were less a laughing matter, and White House aides periodically waged an unconvincing campaign to portray the president as a workaholic. The effort did not fool anyone, in part because Reagan himself rarely participated in it. He understood from beginning to end that presidents would not be judged by how often they punched a time clock. On his many trips to his California ranch, where he spent 345 days of his presidency, he refused to use the euphemism "working vacation" favored by so many of his predecessors on their holidays. When a newsmagazine commissioned a piece on "a day in the life of the president," one of those perennial banes of journalism, the running joke in the White House press room was that the phony schedule constructed in anticipation of this article was really a month in the life of the president. This wisecrack got back to Reagan, who thought it funny. He also took it well when Deaver, to the despair of the first lady and Meese, acknowledged that Reagan sometimes nodded off during meetings of the cabinet.[6]

The truth was that Reagan found it almost impossible to lie down and nap during the day, which was one of the reasons he sometimes fell fast asleep at meetings. He most frequently used his "staff time" to exchange stories with aides or to write personal replies to letters selected for him by his chief of correspondence, Anne Higgins, an enthusiastic conservative who had performed the same function for Richard Nixon. "I hope you do for him what you did for me," Nixon said when he called Higgins to congratulate her during the first week of the Reagan presidency. "Make sure he hears from the general public and that he gets a chance to answer them."[7] This advice suited Reagan, who had been carrying on a brisk private correspondence since his Hollywood days. One of Reagan's axioms, before and after he became president, was that correspondence kept him in touch with the American people. The letters he received were carefully chosen by Higgins to spare him an overload of bad news and, since Higgins was an ardent anti-abortionist, the sentiments of citizens who believed that abortion was a matter of individual choice. Both Higgins and Deaver considered Reagan a sucker for hard-luck stories and tried to limit the number of letters he received from people undergoing hardships, to which the president would often respond with advice and a small personal check. Some aides were appalled that a president who dealt lightly with critical memoranda devoted so much time answering the letters of persons he had never met. But the aides, knowing it would have been unavailing, never registered their complaints with Reagan. The president liked fan mail, and he was so scrupulous about answering the letters given to him that he often took them along with him to Camp David on the weekends.

Reagan was not interested in changing his ways, and he was not puffed up with the presidency. Often, he held the reins of power so lightly that he did not appear to hold them at all. He kept busy, without taxing himself. And he was a happy president, pleased with his script, his cue cards and his supporting cast. For Reagan, the job that Thomas Jefferson had called "a splendid misery" turned into a splendid routine. It was in this sense that the presidency was the worst possible job for Reagan, although he did not know it. He was so self-secure and set in his ways that he refused to allow the presidency to challenge him, as it inherently had the capacity to do. As most Americans suspected, Reagan was unchanged by the office. It was at once his most appealing quality and his greatest defect as president.

"No one can examine the character of the American presidency without being impressed by its many-sidedness," British historian Harold J. Laski wrote in his famous study *The American Presidency*. "The range of the President's functions is enormous. He is ceremonial head of the state. He is a vital source of legislative suggestion. He is the final source of all executive decision. He is the authoritative exponent of the nation's foreign policy. To combine all these with the continuous need to be at once the representative man of the nation and the leader of his political party is clearly a call upon the energies of a single man unsurpassed by the exigencies of any other political office in the world."[8]

Other students of the presidency have discovered other functions. George Reedy, for instance, held that "the President, for all practical purposes, is the United States. He affords the only means through which we can act as a nation and the only consciously creative governmental force."[9] Reagan was suited to the presidency in this sense, for he embodied the historical hopes and aspirations of the nation. Bud McFarlane, the third of his national security advisers, has suggested that it would be possible to derive a coefficient of national values by relating Reagan's characteristics to the significant elements of American history. "It would," he said, "tote up to be a very positive expression of what appeals to Americans, what they think is good."[10]

The functions of the presidency on Laski's list most descriptive of Reagan were "representative man of the nation" and "ceremonial head of the state." He was better suited to leading the nation than commanding its government. And for all his easy informality, he sometimes displayed royalist tendencies, at least in the stylistic sense observed of earlier presidencies by the noted Washington journalist Peter Lisagor: "In the American personality somewhere there must be a royal itch, a kind of an imperial itch."[11] Reagan had an almost monarchical appreciation of patriotic ceremony and tradition. His stylistic model was first and always Franklin D. Roosevelt, the patrician with the common touch who had given form and shape to what became "the imperial presidency." When the office was so defined by Arthur M. Schlesinger Jr. in his 1973 book, *The Imperial Presidency,* the excesses of Vietnam and Watergate were prompting second thoughts about an office which the press and public had long viewed with awe and reverence. On August 9, 1974, the day Nixon left office, President Ford ordered the Marine guards removed from the front of the West Wing in symbolic diminution of the power of the presidency. The diminished presidency subsequently enjoyed a vogue in Washington, encouraged by the studied informality of Nixon's successors and the celebration of this symbolism by the national media. Much was made, too much, of the unremarkable discovery that President Ford toasted his own English muffins for breakfast. Even more was made of President Carter's walk down Pennsylvania Avenue on inauguration day and his habit of wearing sweaters in the Oval Office. Reagan, despite his view that he was always "one of the people" and inseparable from them, suspected that such calculated displays of ordinariness detracted from the dignity and purpose of the presidency. He knew, without anyone telling him, that Americans expect their presidents to be bigger than they are without being too big for their britches. Since he was a celebrity before he became a politician, Reagan accepted this as entirely natural. He invariably charmed people in personal meetings with his egalitarianism and by acting surprised, as Ken Adelman put it, if he was treated as "someone special." [12] But his approach to the institution of the presidency was consciously respectful, reflected in Reagan's refusal to take his coat off whenever he worked in the Oval Office. This attitude rubbed off on Reagan's White House team, which carefully set about to restore the symbolism of the traditional presidency.

One of the principal engineers of this restoration was John F. W. Rogers, the young White House administrative officer who had been so surprised when Reagan joked with him about the picture of George Washington. Rogers was a student of the presidency and a collector of presidential memorabilia whose attention to detail had commended him to Jim Baker and Deaver during the transition. He was also caught up in the anti-Carter mood of the new team and believed that Reagan's predecessor had "basically debased the presidency in a number of ways" by bringing his anti-Washington sentiment intact into the White House and behaving as if "the presidency was nothing exalted." [13] Rogers set about undoing what he believed that Carter had done, in the process also restoring symbols that had been swept away by Gerald Ford. It was Ford, for instance, who had for a time replaced the playing of "Hail to the Chief" with the "Michigan Fight Song," a stirring march that had the added value of reminding voters that Ford had been an All-America football player at the University of Michigan. Under Carter, the military bands often played "Jubilation," by Sir Arthur Bliss, when the president arrived. For Reagan, the band always played "Hail to the Chief."

Rogers also restored the prestige of the Herald Trumpeters, a branch of the United States Army band that had been created during the Eisenhower administration and relegated to the shadows during the Ford and Carter years. Sergeant First Class Dennis Edelbrock, a member of the Herald Trumpeters, responded to this restoration with "A Salute to a New Beginning," an uplifting air that was dedicated to Reagan and often played at presidential ceremonies. And Rogers helped change the lyrics of the institutional presidency, as well as the music. He redesigned the bunting used on presidential platforms, arranged for Reagan to review the troops at arrival ceremonies and saw to it that Oval Office visitors received cufflinks decorated with the presidential seal. This attention to behind-the-scenes detail was encouraged and sometimes insisted upon by the principal producers of the Reagan show, most notably Deaver and Nancy Reagan. "These things didn't just happen," said Rogers. "You didn't have people coming to work in blue jeans one day under Carter and then dressing in suits and ties the next day." [14] In the Reagan White House at the beginning of the first term, much attention was paid to appearances. The changes were welcomed by Reagan, who was keenly attuned to the ceremonial side of the presidency and performed splendidly as chief of state.

Serving as head of government was less congenial to the Reagan temperament. He was certainly, in Laski's phrase, a "vital source of legislative suggestion," particularly in the first two years of his presidency when his litany of reduced government, lower taxes and increased military spending set the congressional agenda, but he was at best a diffident participant in many of the meetings at which he was required to preside. When McFarlane, then Haig's deputy, observed Reagan in action for the first time in mid-1981 during a discussion of budget revisions, he thought the president resembled "a king . . . who had assembled his subalterns to listen to what they had to say and to preside, sort of." [15] Similar metaphors were used to describe Reagan by Martin Anderson, who compared him to an "ancient king," and by

David Stockman, who thought the president resembled a "ceremonial monarch."

But Reagan was more an actor than a king. On one occasion Haig returned from a cabinet meeting complaining to McFarlane that Reagan hadn't understood anything that had been said to him about U.S. intermediate nuclear weapons in Europe. The secretary of state was particularly perturbed that Reagan didn't seem to understand that a U.S. proposal to remove all of these weapons—later advanced by Reagan as "the zero option" that would become the basis for the 1987 INF treaty —would have an unsettling effect on NATO allies. When Haig tried to make this point to him, he told McFarlane, the president expressed a vague conviction that everything would somehow turn out for the best. The combination of optimism and lack of comprehension distressed the secretary of state, who was often easily distressed. After listening to Haig's summary of the cabinet discussion McFarlane said, "It sounds to me as if he was [saying], 'Write me a happy ending.' " Haig, frustrated from the first day of the presidency about his inability to get through to Reagan, thought about it a moment. "I guess that's right," he said.[16]

The habits of the Army died hard for General Haig, who had retired as supreme commander of NATO in 1979 after thirty-one years of service. The president's easy delegation of authority to people Haig thought of as lackeys bothered him, and he was bothered even more when the president allowed Meese to run the cabinet meetings. "What really began to worry me was that he was being manipulated by the shell around him," Haig said. "And because enough questions were not asked on key issues and enough debate was not held on key issues, I [was worried] that he could be terribly misled."[17] Stockman was also perturbed by the bland confidence of the president's entourage, but he was exasperated even more by Reagan's inclination to wave away obstacles with generalities. "We're here to do whatever it takes," Reagan was apt to say when his budget director was prodding him to make difficult decisions. The phrase was one of Reagan's favorites and, in Stockman's view, his most meaningless. The budget director called it Reagan's "mantra."[18]

What Reagan was actually trying to do was focus on issues that had never crossed his mental horizon before he entered the White House. One of the ways he did this was to take issues that were presented to him and try to make them fit the experiences of Hollywood or Sacramento. Sometimes this worked. More often it induced bizarre results, such as Reagan's comparison of Soviet leaders to Hollywood producers with whom he had negotiated as head of the Screen Actors Guild. Reagan's insistence on analogy made his intelligence suspect to many of his cabinet officers. But even cabinet officers who did not think Reagan very bright thought he often made up in decisiveness what he lacked in intelligence. Haig, who could not resist comparing Reagan to Nixon, observed that Reagan had the ability to make decisions readily without second-guessing himself, even though he did not always understand the full consequences of what he had decided. Reagan followed the Nixon practice of rarely making a decision at a cabinet meeting, but the resemblance ended there. "[Nixon] would sit in anguish for hours over a decision before it was made," Haig said. "I never sensed that with Reagan. He was the most graceful and easy decision-maker I've ever seen." [19]

Other observers of Reagan, including Dick Darman and Bill Clark, thought the president was proficient at reading the "body language" of participants in a meeting. Reagan tried to calculate the importance of what was being said to him in part by the way people behaved when they were saying it, sometimes coming to conclusions that surprised his aides. The truth was that Reagan had difficulty following many discussions. In the early months of his presidency he was overwhelmed by issues for which he had no appropriate frame of reference, and he was also hard of hearing, a handicap his actor's skills sometimes concealed. Reagan was adept at appearing interested even when he was not. He typically responded to a briefing or a presentation with little nods of his head or an occasional quip, and cabinet members sometimes did not recognize that he had not heard everything that was being said to him. The aides who saw the president every day in the White House or had served under him in California knew better, and they worked at getting Reagan's attention. Clark, chief of staff in Sacramento during a critical period of Reagan's governorship, made it a point to maintain eye contact when speaking to him and used his voice for emphasis, avoiding the monotone that was his normal conversational speaking level. Clark also coached his allies in the administration—especially CIA Director William Casey, who was inclined to mumble—on the most effective way to make their presentations to the president. "I'd think back and urge them not to overwhelm him with different issues," Clark said. And he gave this additional advice to colleagues and subordinates: "If you think there are particular points that you really want to score, you're going to have to dress them up a little bit, tie them to a metaphor [or]

an analogy and put a little sex appeal in it. Plus raise your voice. . . .
And that would register with him [Reagan] to the point that he would
embellish it, it would sound natural. No cards. I didn't use those damn
cards."[20]

Clark's advice reflected knowledge born of experience in dealing
with Reagan. He realized that Reagan's intelligence functioned differently from his own, or for that matter, differently from others he knew
in public life. All the lawyers who knew Reagan well—Clark, Meese,
Darman, Caspar Weinberger, William French Smith—realized that
Reagan took a different intellectual approach than they did. All of these
lawyers also recognized that they could reach Reagan if they were willing to tune into his mental wavelength. The problem was that Reagan's
reliance on metaphor and analogy for understanding made him vulnerable to arguments that were short on facts and long on theatrical gim-
micks. The Californians who had long experience with Reagan were
particularly skilled at reaching him in this way, as Stockman discovered
to his dismay at a crucial September 9, 1981, meeting where his carefully drawn case for the necessity of making deficit-reducing cuts in the
defense budget was overwhelmed by a multicolor graphics display prepared by the Pentagon at Weinberger's direction. "One of the real eye
stoppers was a chart showing an overlay of a Soviet tank factory on top
of a map of Washington, D.C.," Stockman recalled. "It covered the
whole Mall, from the Capitol to the Lincoln Memorial and then some.
The arsenal of Marxist-Leninism was larger than the heart of the Capitol of the free world! Great pitch—only I wasn't proposing to cut a
single tank out of his budget."[21]

In his book *The Triumph of Politics,* Stockman repeatedly scorns
Weinberger's use of graphics and cartoons. "It was so intellectually
disreputable, so demeaning, that I could hardly bring myself to believe
that a Harvard-educated cabinet officer could have brought this to the
President of the United States," Stockman wrote about one such effort.
"Did he think the White House was on Sesame Street?"[22] But Stockman, also a Harvard-educated cabinet officer, himself resorted to trick
approaches in his campaign to persuade Reagan of the necessity for
deeper budget cuts. Stockman's prize gimmick was the multiple-choice
"SAT test," so called by insiders because of its resemblance to a college
board examination. During preparation of the 1983–84 fiscal year budget, late in 1982, Stockman presented Reagan with sheets of paper
showing three spending levels for each of fifty budget items.[23] Reagan
was asked to check a box showing the level of spending he preferred.

One level of spending in each budget category provided no cuts in services, another level called for a moderate reduction in the rate of spending increases, and the third level provided for Draconian cuts in vital programs.* Not surprisingly, Reagan chose the middle level in almost every case. When Stockman totted up Reagan's "score" on this test, he had, in the budget director's view, "flunked the exam." By the figures Stockman was using at the time, Reagan's budget choices added up to a deficit of $800 billion.

Was the "SAT test" an honest and reasonable way of trying to make Reagan face the budgetary crisis? Annelise Anderson, who served as one of Stockman's associate directors and who was, like him, imbued with the fervor of "the Reagan revolution," has her doubts. She believes that the test, rather than measuring Reagan's deficiencies in dealing with the budget, was a setup that inevitably led the president to a mid-range course that in most cases was, not coincidentally, favored by Reagan's pragmatic advisers and often by Stockman himself. She compares Reagan's test responses to the way someone might reply to a solicitor for the United Fund who offered a prospective donor the choice of giving nothing, making a reasonable contribution or turning over all his assets to charity. "There is really only one answer to this question," she said. "I remember Stockman saying that there is really only one choice here, and it would be irresponsible for the Republican Party to propose more drastic cuts."[24] That is also what Reagan remembers. Commenting on Stockman's retrospective accusations that he had been unwilling to make the hard choices during his first two years in office, Reagan observed to Ken Duberstein near the end of his presidency that he recalled Stockman saying to him that "there was no point in sending up budget items that would be DOA [dead on arrival]."[25] While Reagan's memory on points of policy was hardly his strong suit, the accounts of his political advisers and of Annelise Anderson bear him out on this point. In addition to being the administration's budget wizard, Stockman was the only member of the White House team with congressional experience. Reagan and the White House staff often looked to him not only for numbers but for guidance as to what was

* For example, Stockman's three budget levels for law enforcement called, at one extreme, for an increase of 14 percent in "real program growth" and the construction of seven new prisons. This was the increase requested by Attorney General William French Smith and designated level one on Stockman's chart. At the other extreme (level three), program growth was reduced by 5 percent and all new prisons eliminated. Reagan understandably chose level two, which provided for program growth of nearly 6 percent and construction of three prisons. "Real program growth" is budget growth adjusted for inflation.

politically achievable, especially in the House of Representatives. "I think it's extremely unfair of Stockman to claim as he does in his book that the president was unwilling to accept the difficult cuts when he was specifically advised by the nature of this document against accepting them,"[26] Anderson said. In fact, Stockman knew that the drastic level-three cuts were unattainable in Congress. Early in 1983 he gave the "SAT test" to seven conservative Republican congressmen, most of them former colleagues, in a closed room in the Capitol. On most issues the congressmen also flunked the exam. When Stockman scored their tests, he found that their spending preferences produced a budget deficit as large or larger than the one provided by the Reagan budget.[27] Whatever Professor Stockman was trying to accomplish through his SAT test, it was clear that the pupils who mattered most were uninterested in revolutionary lessons.

But it is not enough for Reagan to say in retrospect that he was willing to do more than he was asked to do. As we shall see in Chapter 12, both Reagan and Stockman (as well as Chief of Staff James Baker) did less than the Senate asked of them early in the presidency, when balancing the budget still seemed within the administration's grasp. Whatever Reagan might have been willing to do, his vulnerability to such devices as Stockman's SAT test, as well as to Weinberger's graphics and cartoons, demonstrated a fragile grasp of the material he needed in order to make responsible decisions. President Ford, in contrast, had briefed the press on the budget in 1975 without notes, duplicating a feat once performed by President Truman. Ford and Truman, of course, were products of Congress, not of Hollywood. They naturally knew far more than Reagan would ever know about the budget, though they were no match for him in expressing the passions of the nation as chief of state. But after all allowances are made for Reagan's reliance on advisers who misled him, he did not know enough. He should have made more of an effort to master the content of both the budget and his briefing papers. His inability to understand the budget was particularly glaring because he had the experience, which he often cited as evidence of his qualification for the presidency, of serving eight years as governor of California, a state with a budget exceeded in size only by the budgets of the United States and five other nations in the world. Instead of boning up on what he did not know, Reagan's consistent inclination was to fall back on the store of anecdotes and information he had acquired on the banquet circuit. His White House advisers, Darman in particular and also Meese and Clark, tried to supply him with material to fill his knowledge gaps, but they were swimming upstream. For one thing, the advisers were under steady pressure from Nancy Reagan to compress the homework the president took with him each evening to the residence. And while Reagan often read the material his advisers sent home with him, the briefing books could not compete effectively with the movies, television programs and adventure novels that were the president's preferred evening fare. When Reagan watched *The Sound of Music* in Williamsburg rather than reading the economic summit briefing book Jim Baker had prepared for him, he was following the pattern of his presidency.

The Californians in the White House had the advantage of familiarity with Reagan's work habits. As Reagan's chief of staff in Sacramento, Bill Clark had devised the "mini-memo," a television-age model of brevity that reduced the analysis, arguments and recommendations on a given issue to a single page. The mini-memo was designed to play to Reagan's strengths and dodge his weaknesses. He was good at making decisions, which the mini-memos encouraged, and poor at doing his homework. The mini-memos accepted as an axiom Reagan's celebrated view that the answers to problems of government are simple, just not easy. While they were successful in removing a clutter of minor issues from Reagan's desk, they failed to steer him through the shoals of complexities that did not yield easily to ideological solutions.

In Washington the mini-memo approach ran aground, although a number of the president's men tried approximations of this approach in their efforts to meet the requirement of limiting Reagan's homework. Compressing the discussion on issues became a necessity during Reagan's recuperation from the wounds suffered in the March 30, 1981, assassination attempt. His working hours were strictly limited by doctors' orders and the insistence of the first lady, and even his national security briefings had to be delivered to him in written form. Some aides came to believe that the assassination attempt had an unfortunate impact on the inner life of the Reagan presidency, even though its immediate political impact was beneficial. In human terms, Reagan's behavior in the aftermath of the shooting was exemplary. His grace under pressure won the admiration of the nation and smoothed the path of his programs in Congress. His rapid recovery testified to his vital spirit and the advantages of clean living, and the incident encouraged him to become even more disciplined about physical exercise than he had been before the shooting. But Reagan's wounds also took him out of commission for several weeks during what could have been a critical learning period of his presidency and reduced the flow of briefing papers to a trickle. Worse, Reagan's political success in the months after the shooting reinforced the view of the Californians that Reagan could operate in Washington without changing his ways. It would have been difficult to force a change in any event, but Reagan had demonstrated during his second term in Sacramento that he was capable of dirtying his hands and becoming directly involved in the political process when such participation was necessary for achievement of his objectives.* No such reason was apparent to him in Washington, nor was any presented to him by his aides. Reagan was so popular and so politically successful during the six months following the shooting that he had absolutely no motivation to alter his approach. His aides, blinded by the glare of early success, behaved as if Reagan were invulnerable. They saw no reason why he could not govern as successfully by anecdote in Washington as he had in Sacramento.

When Bill Clark became Reagan's second national security adviser at the beginning of 1982, he found that the president knew next to nothing about what was going on in many corners of the globe. Clark, who had quit the California Supreme Court to become Reagan's troubleshooter at the State Department in 1981, was aghast. Clark himself had come to Washington so unknowledgeable about fundamental foreign policy issues that *Newsweek*'s account of his confirmation hearings was headed "A Truly Open Mind." [28] But Clark had learned a lot in his year at the State Department, and he realized from his first day at the White House that the gaps in the president's knowledge were potentially dangerous ones that needed to be filled. His technique for doing this demonstrated an understanding of Reagan's mental processes and work habits that was unmatched in the White House. Clark knew that the president responded to visual aids and reasoned that he would be most receptive of all to films. So he took Reagan to the movies. Clark obtained Defense Department movies on "the Soviet threat," the problems in the Middle East and other issues and showed them to Reagan in the White House theater. Enlisting Bill Casey's cooperation on his project to educate Reagan through the medium he knew best, Clark asked the CIA to provide a "profile movie documentary" on world leaders Reagan was scheduled to meet. "And the agency started pro-

---

* The outstanding example of this was Governor Reagan's series of negotiations with Democratic Assembly Speaker Bob Moretti in 1971. The result was a welfare reform bill that established significant safeguards against welfare fraud while also increasing the grants of the poorest recipients. A detailed account of this episode is given in my book *Reagan*, pages 176–184.

ducing some great stuff that was enjoyable for all of us," Clark said. "[It was] far more interesting to see a movie on Mrs. [Indira] Gandhi covering her life than sitting down with the usual tome the agency would produce. And that would spark questions from the president that I could fire back to the agency. I knew from Sacramento days that he liked celluloid. After all, it was his profession." [29]

Clark's unusual approach to educating Reagan provoked much hilarity among more sophisticated White House advisers. It nonetheless made good sense. Reagan was receptive to the sensory impressions of films, and he was apt to retain what he saw and heard on the screen. He might have been better served if he had been shown some of these films earlier. At a June 16, 1981, news conference six months before Clark arrived at the White House, Reagan gave a deplorable performance whenever the questions turned to foreign policy, even about events then in the news. Nine days earlier Israeli jets had bombed and destroyed a French-made nuclear reactor in Iraq on grounds this was necessary to prevent Iraqi development of a nuclear bomb. It was obvious that questions would be asked about this incident, but the president was not ready for them when they came. Asked his reaction to Israel's refusal to sign the Nuclear Non-Proliferation Treaty and submit to inspections by the International Atomic Energy Agency, Reagan said: "Well, I haven't given very much thought to that particular question there, the subject about them not signing the treaty, or, on the other hand, how many countries do we know that have signed it that very possibly are going ahead with nuclear weapons. It's, again, something that doesn't lend itself to verification." After saying that it was difficult for him "to envision Israel as being a threat to its neighbors," Reagan concluded his answer by saying, "I'll have to think about the question you asked."

He had an even more difficult time tracking the question when asked if he shared the view that a conventional U.S.-Soviet war in Europe would inevitably become a nuclear conflict. "Well, it's a frightening possibility, and history bears it out," Reagan responded. "If we want to look for one little bit of optimism anyplace, the only time that I can recall in history that a weapon possessed by both sides was never used was in World War II—the use of poison gas. And possibly it was because the weapon was available to both sides. But the weapons are there, and they do extend to the battlefield use as well—the tactical weapons as well as the strategic." Later in the news conference Reagan described surface-to-air missiles that the Syrians had installed in Lebanon as "offensive" weapons. This statement produced the first official correction from the White House press office, one that compounded Reagan's ignorance with a gratuitous falsehood. Instead of simply acknowledging that Reagan had erred, an option that held even less appeal to the president's men than to the president, the announcement said that Reagan had meant to say "defensive" weapons.

While neither the press nor the president realized it at the time, this news conference was a decisive event in the Reagan presidency. Reagan came to office open to the idea of frequent news conferences. He had faced the press on a weekly basis for a long stretch in Sacramento, and he had been reasonably accessible as a presidential candidate. He liked most reporters because he liked nearly everyone, and many of the reporters also liked him. Reagan's competitive streak had served him well at his Sacramento news conferences, where he started shakily and gradually rose to the challenge of becoming better informed on state issues. Lyn Nofziger, his communications director during the early years of the governorship, recognized that the news conferences were a useful learning experience, and his view was shared in large measure by Clark and Meese. Reagan also seems to have accepted Nofziger's evaluation of the use of frequent news conferences, as best I can judge from comments he made to me during an interview in 1968. Because Reagan had done so well with the media, many of his advisers assumed that he would make himself available at least for monthly news conferences during his presidency. And it started out that way, with Reagan conducting two relatively successful news conferences during his first seven weeks in office before Press Secretary James S. Brady was shot and Larry Speakes became the de facto spokesman. During the weeks of his recuperation from the shooting, however, Reagan was barely briefed on foreign affairs, and the White House preparation of him for the June 16 news conference was exceptionally casual. By then Reagan was riding the crest of public and congressional approval, and the administration's budget and tax bills were marching merrily through Congress. Baker and Darman were focusing on legislative strategy, and no one paid attention to the problems that were likely to beset the Great Communicator when he arrived unrehearsed for a performance.

The June 16 news conference was a potent reminder of the dangers of turning Reagan loose without a script. William Safire, the most notably independent conservative columnist during the Reagan years, explained afterward in his column what had happened: "The President has been skimping on his preparation, neglecting the black book, relying instead on oral give-and-take with his aides for a couple of hours before press conferences. He thinks he can wing it. Some member of the inner circle with a great sense of security should tell him this is how a democracy tests its leader's range of comprehension, and that he has been flunking the test." Safire did not consider Reagan to be stupid. On the contrary, Reagan's conduct in debate had demonstrated that he had "the mental capacity to absorb briefings and to think on his feet. All it takes is a change in priority of his time and a lot of hard studying." [30] Reagan, however, was unwilling to do such studying, and his aides had no interest in changing his priorities. Except for Meese, who knew how to prepare Reagan and remembered the progress he had made when faced with the discipline of regular news conferences in Sacramento, White House aides concluded that news conferences were not worth the trouble they caused. Instead of accepting Safire's useful advice and doing with Reagan what Nofziger had done with him in Sacramento, the White House team opted to shield the president from the press. Deaver and Baker were the architects of this overprotection, but they had no shortage of accomplices. Reagan did not hold another news conference until October 1, by which time so many events had intervened that it was impossible for anyone to brief him adequately. He staggered through, further reinforcing the staff view that news conferences were ordeals rather than opportunities. The big loser was Reagan, who was deprived of the learning experience that had served him well in Sacramento, where the news conferences proved exceptionally valuable because they exposed him to questions that helped him gauge the public mood. Without them, he was more dependent than ever on his aides, which was better for them than it was for Reagan.

Perhaps Reagan sensed this, even though he never did anything about it. Different aides told me over the years that Reagan occasionally asked them when he would be holding his next news conference. I was always skeptical about such statements, and remain so today, for it was not Reagan's normal habit to inquire about his White House schedule. But he never balked at holding a news conference when it was proposed to him, and it is almost certain that he would have held far more of them if his aides had been less shaken by his early performances, especially on June 16. Once the White House staff decided that news conferences were events to avoid, the die was cast. His aides could always find handy excuses for not holding a news conference, which even for the most skilled of presidents requires many hours of intense preparation. Reagan left his preparation and his schedule to his White House producers.

Late in 1982, Reagan was asked at a picture-taking session if he would be going to visit the Vietnam Veterans Memorial. "I can't tell until somebody tells me," he replied factually. "I never know where I'm going."[31] And when he went to a news conference, Reagan often did not know what to do when he got there. The fault was his, but he had help.

Two days before the assassination attempt, in the best one-liner of the 1981 Gridiron Dinner, Reagan had quipped that "sometimes our right hand doesn't know what our far-right hand is doing."[32] It was funny, and had the added value of being accurate. By then, slightly more than two months into the presidency, the honeymoon harmony on the White House staff was beginning to fray. The factions on the staff, and their supporters in Congress and the Republican community outside Washington, were battling each other on matters of substance and strategy. Within the White House the scramble was on for proximity to the presidential throne. More often than not, these battles were portrayed as ideological conflicts between "conservatives" who were true to the principles of "the Reagan revolution" on one side and "pragmatists" or "moderates" on the other. This was a wildly oversimplified version of the conflict, as we shall see in later chapters, and it overlooked the reality that all of the high-ranking White House aides, with the possible exception of Darman, qualified as "conservative" in the normal meaning of the term. The principal fault lines within the inner circle were regional and personal. The non-Californians—Baker, Bush, Darman and Gergen—held a low opinion of Reagan's intellect and thought that he and they were better off if the press saw little of the president in unscripted settings. The Californians—Meese, Clark and Martin Anderson—tended to the other extreme and believed that Reagan did best when left unsmothered by advisers. Deaver was in the middle. He needed constantly to take account of Nancy Reagan's protective impulses and was often at odds personally with Meese, the president's principal booster. Meese exaggerated Reagan's abilities as much as Darman and Stockman underrated them. In conversations with reporters, and sometimes even with White House aides, he was given to rhapsodic appraisals of Reagan that bordered on unintended parody. "The president has made a remarkable start," Meese said less than two weeks after the disastrous June 16 news conference. "He probably is as well or better acquainted with what's going on in the government than any other president at this time in his term."[33]

Unfortunately for his own reputation, Meese did not recognize that such fatuous declarations raised questions about his own judgment without advancing Reagan's cause. They were unnecessary, because no one doubted Meese's loyalty, and they obscured Meese's useful insights into Reagan. At a practical level Meese understood from experience that Reagan had an actor's intelligence, even though he lacked a theory to explain it. In their personal discussions he avoided lawyer's language and made ample use of stories and anecdotes. But Meese could never bring himself to acknowledge even the slightest of Reagan's imperfections. It cost Meese dearly in credibility, both in the White House and outside it.* The cabinet officers who struggled with Reagan to make him understand the realities of the deficit or the defense budget were infuriated by Meese's bland unwillingness to help them. By refusing to acknowledge that Reagan needed to be educated rather than exalted, Meese inevitably allowed moments crucial to the president's understanding to slip away from him. Stockman and Haig were most affected because they had no independent relationship with Reagan and did not know how to get through to him. At a critical November 1982 meeting where Stockman thought that one of his graphics displays had brought Reagan near the point of understanding the pernicious effects of a long-term budget deficit, Meese interjected with what Stockman called his "usual solution" at such moments. "We'll have to go back to the drawing board over Thanksgiving and then we'll see where we are in December after the cabinet comes in with their ideas for new budget savings," Meese said.[34] This was a sad misrepresentation of reality. The cabinet had not volunteered any budget cuts, and many cabinet officers had sought substantial increases for their departments. Meese knew this, but he lacked the will or capacity to prod Reagan into a reexamination that might have rescued his budget before the deficit became unmanageable. His title was White House counsellor, but he functioned as a cheerleader for the president.

Weinberger was as sycophantic as Meese, with even more devastating results. He had performed brilliantly as state finance director under Reagan in California, where governors enjoy the policy advantage of the line-item veto. Reagan used it frequently, and most of the line items were identified by Weinberger. As budget director for President Nixon,

---

* Meese had a particular credibility problem with reporters. On one occasion a reporter who knew Meese from his California days was interviewing him and became frustrated with Meese's gushy descriptions of Reagan. The reporter suggested that they continue the interview under ground rules of anonymity. Meese agreed, indicating that would enable him to say what he really thought. In response to the first question under the new ground rules, Meese said, "On background, I want to say that the president is really doing a wonderful job."

who also thought well of him, Weinberger had added to his reputation for fiscal prudence. Baker and Stockman were initially optimistic that "Cap the Knife" would demonstrate his budget-cutting skills at the Pentagon, and Reagan never allowed any evidence to the contrary to convince him otherwise. "I can assure you that Cap is going to do a lot of trimming over there in Defense to make sure the American taxpayer is getting more bang for the buck," Reagan told local officials on March 2, 1981, using a slogan of the Eisenhower presidency. "I've even heard that there was a sigh of relief in several other departments when it was learned that Cap the Knife was going to Defense and not to those other departments."

Reagan's assumption that Weinberger was a penny-pincher by nature was understandable, given his own experience with him in Sacramento. It was also mistaken. He was instead the ultimate advocate—a shrewd, articulate and extremely stubborn lawyer—who used his legal skills to champion whatever client he represented at the moment. As head of what was then the Department of Health, Education and Welfare, Weinberger had been an ardent advocate of social services. He had been a cost-cutter as Nixon's budget director. And as Reagan's secretary of defense, he became a promoter of hang-the-cost military spending. This inevitably put him on a collision course with Stockman, who was struggling to maintain the mirage of a balanced budget. While Stockman had an unmatched command of budget intricacies, he was Weinberger's inferior in the craft of bureaucratic maneuver. Weinberger was then sixty-four years old and had acquired a crafty knowledge of how to work the government bureaucracy for whatever purposes he had in mind. Stockman was only thirty-four, and he was not competing on a level playing field. During the campaign Reagan had presented his promises to balance the budget, cut taxes and increase military spending as of equal value, but he had also said that the U.S. military budget should be determined by the dimension of the Soviet military threat. Weinberger recognized that the practical effect of this statement was that Reagan gave precedence to restoration of the balance of military power between the United States and the Soviet Union. Whether an actual imbalance existed was, and remains, a matter of dispute. But there was no doubt in Reagan's mind about it, and he reflected the conventional wisdom at the time. Former Defense Secretary James R. Schlesinger, whose views Reagan respected, estimated that by 1981 the Soviets were outspending the United States by 85 percent on weapons procurement.[35] Stansfield Turner, CIA director under Carter, declared that "in the last several years all of the best studies have shown that the balance of strategic nuclear capabilities has been tipping in favor of the Soviet Union."[36] In 1981 a consensus rare in American peacetime history favored huge increases in military spending. Even after the economic downturn caused the president's popularity to slide near the end of the year, public opinion surveys continued to show heavy support for the Reagan defense buildup. Reagan and Weinberger took advantage of this opportunity to improve the readiness of U.S. conventional military forces with new weapons, equipment, ships and planes. But the public's source of concern, as well as the CIA's, was the Soviet accumulation of strategic nuclear missiles that could strike U.S. targets at the touch of a button and cause unimaginable death and destruction. In dealing with this issue, as with the budget, Reagan again lacked the expertise necessary for independent decision-making. And once again, he was also damaged by reliance on advisers who patronized him with analogies and graphics at the cost of facts.

The first key strategic decision of the Reagan administration was waged over deployment of the MX intercontinental ballistic missile, a gigantic and highly accurate long-distance weapon that is armed with ten nuclear warheads. It is examined here as a case study that shows Reagan's limitations on issues where he needed not an actor's understanding of the public presidency but a command of strategic knowledge and technical detail. The curious struggle over the MX also demonstrates the perils of partisan stereotypes. The stereotypes in question on this issue depicted Reagan as a sword-rattler whose belligerence toward the Soviets risked international conflict and Carter as a weak president who had allowed the United States to become dangerously vulnerable to Soviet attack. Neither stereotype was accurate. Carter had inherited the MX from the Ford administration and originally thought of it as a dubious weapon. He rescinded MX funding early in 1977 but reversed himself in November of that year after his respected Pentagon weapons expert, William J. Perry, informed him that the Soviets had staged a breakthrough in missile guidance. Perry and Defense Secretary Harold Brown believed that the Soviets could outfit existing nuclear missiles with the new guidance system and obtain the capability of destroying the entire arsenal of 1,000 U.S. Minutemen land-based nuclear missiles in a single surprise attack. Perry's discovery was the origin of the so-called window of vulnerability that Reagan made so much of in the 1980 campaign. He did not acknowledge or did not know that Carter had tried energetically to close this "window."

U.S. strategic doctrine in the nuclear age is based on a land-sea-air "triad" of nuclear options. The triad gives the United States the ability to strike the Soviet mainland with land-based intercontinental ballistic missiles (ICBMs), submarine-launched ballistic missiles (SLBMs) and nuclear bombs carried by aircraft. But the bomber fleet was aging in 1981, and SLBMs are less accurate than ICBMs. If the U.S. land-based missiles became sitting ducks that could easily be destroyed in their underground silos, a "window of vulnerability" would exist until the United States could develop a new land-based missile that would be protected either by its mobility or by some form of hardened shield. The Pentagon considered more than a dozen alternatives for preserving the land-based leg of the triad. Carter carefully worked his way through the proposals, none of which he found particularly appealing. He settled on a plan known as "MX/MPS" for "Missile Experimental/Multiple Protective Shelters" that called for building two hundred MX missiles and shuttling them back and forth among 4,600 shelters in the Nevada and Utah desert.* "The basing scheme is key to MX's contribution to deterrence, for it is the basing scheme that determines the degree of survivability or vulnerability," Brown wrote in his final report to Congress.[37] Originally, the Carter administration's plan called for the MX missile launchers to be deployed in "racetrack" loops that would make them easily verifiable under the pending strategic arms limitation treaty known as SALT II. After Carter withdrew this treaty in 1979 in the face of bipartisan Senate opposition and the Soviet invasion of Afghanistan, his administration abandoned the "racetrack" idea in favor of a "linear" system that would cost less money and use less land. "I see no virtue in the closed-loop system," Brown told a Senate subcommittee on May 6, 1980. "If you wish to say the racetrack is dead, go ahead." The senators understood what Brown was saying, but the word never reached Reagan. He had been told earlier by campaign defense adviser William Van Cleave that it would be a mistake for the United States to spend billions of dollars on shelters that would conceal the MX missiles and then inform the Soviets of the location of the shelters. This argument stuck in Reagan's mind even after it was no longer applicable. For Reagan, the words "MX" and "racetrack" were indelibly linked.

---

* Carter essentially made a negative decision. He disliked the MX basing plan that he approved but thought it superior to the alternatives. A senior Pentagon official who was no fan of Carter's said approvingly of him, "Carter was a slave to logic." No one that I know ever made that accusation of Reagan.

What was linked for Weinberger was the association of MX/MPS with the vanquished Carter administration. Weinberger realized that the president wanted nothing to do with a weapons system associated with Jimmy Carter. As a lifelong Republican politician, Weinberger also realized that MX/MPS was bad Republican politics. Deployment of the system in the Nevada and Utah desert was under fire from an unusual coalition that included environmentalists and the Church of Jesus Christ of Latter-day Saints (Mormon). Seventy percent of Utah's population is Mormon. The state's two senators were Mormons and Republicans. Worst of all, MX/MPS would be partially deployed in Nevada, where it was opposed by Republican Senator Paul Laxalt, the president's only close friend in Congress. All of this counted heavily with Weinberger, who knew far more about Reagan and the political situation than he did about nuclear weaponry. When Seymour Zeiberg, who had been Perry's top assistant, briefed Weinberger in February 1981 he was appalled by the technical ignorance of the questions put to him.[38] Zeiberg soon left the Pentagon, and Weinberger never afterward wanted to hear from MX proponents, however well informed. His reaction virtually shut out the Air Force, the lead agency in past MX studies and an advocate of MX/MPS, from the decision-making process. After consulting with Meese, Weinberger came up with the kind of solution Meese always liked—appointment of an expert panel to study alternatives. But the defense secretary conveyed his misgivings about MX/MPS to the chairman of the panel, Nobel-winning physicist Charles Townes, and the Pentagon started exploring other actions long before the panel returned with its recommendations. Weinberger's personal favorite, an air-mobile MX missile, had been tried and found wanting in both the Ford and Carter administrations. Carter had rejected the plan for converting C-5A transports into MX missile carriers because Air Force tests had found many deficiencies in it, one of them being that the wings of the planes were likely to fall off if the missiles were actually fired. Weinberger toyed with a substitute for this idea, dubbed "Big Bird" after the character in *Sesame Street,* but the scheme died of its own impracticality because it would have required development of a fleet of new, fuel-efficient, large-winged planes.

Despite Weinberger's maneuvering to reject the proposal he had concluded in advance that Reagan did not want, the Carter idea of basing MX in deceptive shelters had support within the administration. Bill Casey, for one, liked the idea. So did United Nations Ambassador Jeane Kirkpatrick, who frequently displayed an independence that annoyed her fellow cabinet members and angered the White House staff. Haig, who distrusted Weinberger from the outset, pointed out to Reagan that the European allies had agreed to accept 572 American medium-range nuclear missiles and said the allies might balk at carrying out the agreement if the United States was unwilling to replace its vulnerable missiles with the MX. Stockman, who was busy fighting the battle of the budget, was worried that Weinberger's alternatives would wind up costing even more money than MX/MPS. But none of these officials was guiding U.S. policy on the MX. Neither was Reagan, who had turned over the decision to Weinberger. The defense secretary, confident he was doing what Reagan wanted done, ignored Haig and struck up a Sacramento-style alliance with Meese that protected his White House flank. Meese knew next to nothing about the MX, but he shared Weinberger's feeling that it was undesirable for Reagan to embrace a program so strongly identified with Carter. He was also comfortable with Weinberger, who had skillfully performed as Reagan's surrogate on budget matters in Sacramento. On July 30, 1981, Meese told the Washington bureau of the *Los Angeles Times* that MX/MPS was "a bad idea." Emulating his president, Meese knew so little about the substance of the issue he was discussing that he did not even get the nomenclature right. In the interview he called "MPS" the "multiple positioning system."

The Townes panel, meanwhile, had done its work honestly despite pressure from Weinberger to reach the conclusion that Weinberger wanted it to reach. When Townes met with Weinberger late in June and told him that the panel was leaning to MX/MPS, the defense secretary urged him to go back and have his committee reconsider the air-mobile idea. But the idea had neither merit nor support among the diverse group of experts represented on the committee. When the Townes Committee issued its final report in late July, Weinberger kept it secret because it did not support his own preconceptions. The committee waffled in its opening section, making an obvious observation that no land-based system was survivable if an adversary committed enough missiles to destroying it. In its conclusion, however, the panel came out firmly for the MX. It proposed a compromise basing plan to put one hundred MX missiles in as many new shelters, with the option of adding additional shelters at a later date.

Even this vastly scaled down proposal did not appeal to Weinberger, who was interested in the Townes Committee report only to the extent he could use it to derail MX/MPS. What he wanted was something that could not be said to resemble the solution that had been advocated by President Carter. When expert opinion in the military services and Congress rose up against the air-mobile idea, Weinberger explored still another option that had been discredited by Pentagon studies—the idea of converting the D-5 Trident II missile that was being developed for use in submarines into a "common missile" that could also be installed in silos on land.

Reagan was on a month-long vacation in California while all this was going on, and pressure was building on Capitol Hill for an MX decision. On August 21, Senate Armed Services Committee chairman John G. Tower of Texas and William L. Dickinson of Alabama, the ranking Republican on the House Armed Services Committee, made the case for MX/MPS to Reagan and Weinberger in the president's top-floor suite of the Century Plaza Hotel in Los Angeles. They, too, used graphs and charts in an effort to rescue MX/MPS with a presentation that Reagan would find comprehensible. Tower left the meeting thinking that MX/MPS—rechristened and with some minor changes that could have enabled Reagan to label it his own program—had a chance.[39] But it was too late. Dickinson came away from the meeting with "the distinct impression that one or both [Weinberger and Reagan] were against MPS and they were studying to look for alternatives. Reagan had a deep-seated bias, and Weinberger was affected by Reagan's feelings."[40]

Dickinson was right. While Weinberger claimed in 1981 to be impartial, he acknowledged in an interview with me in 1989 that he had always been against MX/MPS. "I didn't like it," he said. "I was totally against the MPS system."[41] The basis for his opposition appears to have been almost entirely political rather than strategic. In the 1989 interview Weinberger advanced as fact the erroneous opinion that Carter had not explored other alternatives before proposing MX/MPS. Along with Reagan, Weinberger had forgotten, if he ever knew, that Carter had abandoned the "racetrack" idea more than eight months before Reagan took office. And like Meese, Weinberger could not get the nomenclature straight, calling MPS the "multiple protective system." All Weinberger really knew in 1989 was that he had been against MX/MPS and that Reagan was against it as well. But in 1981, with pressure mounting for a decision, Weinberger had also needed to be for something, and he and Pentagon research chief Richard DeLauer came up with a unique idea that mocked Reagan's campaign pledge to close the "window of vulnerability." They decided that the MX would be produced but the ultimate basing decision postponed for several years. While the basing mode was being decided, a small number of MX missiles (originally thirty-six) would be deployed in existing Minuteman or Titan silos. These silos were supposed to be "superhardened" for protection, even though existing research did not support the idea that any hardening could protect them from Soviet attack. The proposal astonished military planners and was opposed by the Joint Chiefs of Staff. But it had a virtue that overwhelmed its technological deficiencies: it had not been proposed by Jimmy Carter.

What Weinberger did next starkly revealed the limitations of the decision-making process in an administration led by a president who was susceptible more to analogies and visual aids than to arguments. The defense secretary, after touching base with Meese, took his make-shift plan to Reagan at a meeting in the second-floor sitting room of the White House living quarters on the afternoon of September 28, 1981. Reagan, who had just returned from a speaking trip to New Orleans, was tired. Weinberger was brief, and clever. He used what Meese called "the weak recommendation" of the Townes Committee against itself, pointing out that the panel had said that no missile was survivable. The defense secretary did not bother to tell Reagan that the Pentagon had estimated that 9,200 one-megaton Soviet missiles would be required to destroy MX/MPS and that only two hundred missiles would be needed to take out the Weinberger option. Haig, already battle-weary from his many fights with the White House staff and Weinberger, much preferred the Townes proposal to the Weinberger plan. But he did not fight for his preference in this meeting, in part because he was relieved that Weinberger at least had agreed to a land-based missile that could be cited as evidence of American good faith in prodding the allies to accept U.S. missiles in Europe. The others in the room—Baker, Deaver, Richard Allen and Vice President Bush—deferred to Weinberger, who did not waste his time in argument. Instead, he whipped out a four-panel cartoon drawn by Mike Keefe of *The Denver Post.* In the cartoon Uncle Sam plays a shell game with a Russian who distantly resembles Soviet leader Leonid Brezhnev, inviting him to guess which shell contains the MX missile. Instead of guessing, the Russian takes out a hammer and destroys all the shells. Reagan chuckled, and approved the Weinberger plan.

The president could not, however, explain what he had done or why he had done it. This became painfully apparent four days later when Reagan showed up in the East Room of the White House to announce the decision, which was presented as part of a larger plan to "modernize" U.S. forces by building one hundred B-1 bombers "as soon as possible" and by expanding the nuclear submarine program. Reagan started out by reading a Weinberger-drafted statement that misrepresented the process leading to the decision and once more claimed that "a window of vulnerability is opening" that would jeopardize "our hopes for peace and freedom." After reading the statement, Reagan announced he would answer a few questions and then turn the podium over to Weinberger "for all the technical matters." But Reagan couldn't deal with even the nontechnical matters. When a reporter asked the president why he favored putting the MX missiles in vulnerable silos if there was in fact a "window of vulnerability," Reagan said haltingly, "I don't know but what maybe you haven't gotten into the area that I'm going to turn over to the secretary of defense." The president staggered through three more questions to which he also didn't know the answers, with Weinberger standing slightly behind him and vainly trying to coach him sotto voce. Finally Reagan said, to derisive laughter from the press corps, "I think that my few minutes are up and I'm going to turn that question over to Cap." It was a sorry performance that reminded me of a time early in Reagan's governorship when a Sacramento reporter asked him what was in his legislative program. The novice governor did not have a clue. Turning plaintively to aides who were attending the news conference, he said, "I could take some coaching from the sidelines if anyone can recall my legislative program." [42] Aides piped up and told Reagan some of the items in "his" program. By the time Reagan announced the MX decision some fourteen years later, even coaching couldn't help.

Whatever the merits of MX/MPS, it is doubtful if any strategic determination in the nuclear age had been made by a president as casually and with as little consideration of the consequences as Reagan's MX decision. Reagan's decision made almost no sense in either strategic or economic terms, as almost everyone who has examined it agrees. It was, as Reagan administration arms control chief Ken Adelman later described it, "the worst of all possible solutions." [43] The goal of nuclear deterrence is to prevent war by insuring that sufficient nuclear forces will survive an attack to destroy the rival superpower. The MX, at least as deployed by the Reagan administration, retreated from that goal. Because the multiple-warhead MX is much more destructive and accurate than the Minuteman, it is a far more worrisome weapon to the Soviets. But because the MX was housed in vulnerable Minuteman silos it also became, in the conservative Adelman's words, "a most inviting target."[44] The Weinberger-Reagan basing mode for the missile also made the MX a hair-trigger weapon. In any nuclear conflict, a president would face a temptation to launch the MX force immediately since he would know that the missiles could not survive a Soviet attack.

The MX decision did not go down well in Congress, where it was distrusted by those who wanted to make the MX less vulnerable and those who wanted no MX at all. Proponents of MX/MPS thought the Reagan administration was spending a lot for a little, and subsequent events proved them right. Reluctantly, after much maneuvering, Congress accepted the recommendations of the Scowcroft Commission, headed by the once and future national security adviser Brent Scowcroft, to deploy fifty MX missiles. When Reagan left office, nearly $15 billion had been spent to construct these missiles and put them in the Minuteman silos and another $8.5 billion was needed to complete the deployment. By this time the Weinberger-Reagan solution had been so totally discredited that President Bush and his secretary of defense, Richard Cheney, faced a new debate on MX basing at a time when defense spending was no longer popular and the Reagan budget deficit was forcing cutbacks at the Pentagon. Bush was left with the decision of whether to move the MX missiles out of the silos and put them on railroad cars (a system known as Rail Garrison and favored by Cheney), build a new mobile missile or try to do some of both. The issue remains unresolved at this writing, although funds for converting the MX to the Rail Garrison system were included in the first Bush budget. If this is accomplished, the cost of deploying fifty MX missiles in railroad cars a decade after Reagan was first elected will top $30 billion. Had Reagan simply accepted the Townes Committee report, he would have been able to deploy twice as many missiles for far less money. And he would have been able to deploy two hundred MX missiles if he had been willing to go along with the Carter plan at a time when Reagan was popular, the deficit was small and there was public support for a military buildup.

What happened in the MX debate is instructive because it is representative of much of the decision-making process in the Reagan presidency. If the window of vulnerability truly existed, Reagan had thrown it wide open. Congress was unable to close it because it is the president and only the president who is, in Laski's phrase, "the final source of all executive decision." This does not mean that a president needs a scientific background to make strategic or technical decisions. With the exception of Carter, no president since Herbert Hoover has been an engineer. But in order to wisely exercise their constitutional function as executive decision-makers, presidents need a process that will allow them to consult a wide range of expert opinion, and they also need to know the questions they should ask. Reagan had no idea of the questions, let alone the answers, and the uninformed subordinates to whom he delegated responsibility in the MX matter were focused on trying to accommodate his preconceptions. Since Weinberger and Meese believed that Reagan wanted to reject MX/MPS out of hand, rejection became a self-fulfilling prophecy. Seen either in military or economic terms, the nation paid a high price for a president who skimped on preparation, avoided complexities and news conferences and depended far too heavily on anecdotes, charts, graphics and cartoons.

10

PASSIVE PRESIDENT

He assigns to everybody else his own makeup.

NANCY REAGAN,
May 5, 1989 [1]

Ronald Reagan was humanly accessible to people who had never met him and impenetrable to those who tried to know him well. "He is a genuinely nice man," said Lyn Nofziger, an observant member of the Reagan cast. "But there's kind of a barrier between him and the rest of the world, a film you can't get through. You can't get inside of him." [2] This friendly barrier kept out everyone but Nancy Reagan, and sometimes even her. It surrounded him like a force field, protecting his star quality and shielding him from the consequences of actions that might have ruined ordinary politicians. The barrier also shielded Reagan from the risks of close relationships with his children and his most devoted aides. He seemed to have no need of closeness nor any understanding of how desperately it was sometimes desired by those around him. His aides were of two minds on this point. Some thought that Reagan was oblivious to the needs of others. Others believed he knew their needs but opted to protect himself to compensate for some childhood hurt. Whatever they thought, the barrier made Reagan a magnet as well as a mystery. He was a friendly leader with few friends, but he attracted people to him who wanted to see beyond the barrier yet never could.

Up close or far away, Reagan made a striking first impression. Frank Fahrenkopf, the Republican national chairman during the Reagan presidency, thought this was because Reagan knew "how to carry himself"[3] and how to smile. Author Tom Clancy, meeting Reagan in the White House, found him strong and robust—"the guy has a handshake like a lumberjack"—with "very active, bright eyes."[4] Years after they met Reagan, aides often remembered with considerable precision the circumstances of their first encounter. What most often stuck with them, as Jim Kuhn put it, was that the real-life Reagan was the same "friendly, genuine person" he had portrayed in movies and on television. "And when I stuck my hand out just to say hello, not only did he shake my hand, but he stopped and looked at me in the eyes and asked me how I was doing," said Kuhn. "I thought, 'Gee, he really is the way he appeared to be on TV.'"[5] Kuhn was just out of college when he met Reagan at a 1975 speech in Cleveland. But older and more sophisticated people reacted similarly, finding Reagan special because he did not behave as if he were a celebrity. "He doesn't treat himself like a statue of himself," Jeane Kirkpatrick said after meeting him in 1979.[6]

In workaday matters, Reagan also displayed a natural humility that aides in general and women in particular found becoming. "He is a normal person," said Margaret Tutwiler, who as Baker's deputy saw the president frequently. "He fills the screen, but he's not intimidating, argumentative, overwhelming, full of braggadocio. He's larger than life, but he doesn't have the qualities that go with a bigger-than-life person."[7] Speechwriter Peggy Noonan said that Reagan "acts as if he's lucky to be with you."[8] Anne Higgins, chief of correspondence in the Reagan White House, remembers that he asked her at the beginning of his presidency if the secretaries would prefer to have him write his letters or dictate them. "Mr. President, it's not a question of which would be easier for us," she replied. "Which do you prefer?" He never told her. Higgins was left to figure out for herself that Reagan preferred to write letters in longhand in the privacy of his office and then give them to her to have them typed.[9]

Reagan's aides became accustomed to figuring out things for themselves, for he managed by indirection when he managed at all. Aides who had worked for more directive presidents found this disconcerting. "He made no demands, and gave almost no instructions," said Martin Anderson, a veteran of the Nixon administration. Anderson thought Reagan's management style odd but rationalized that it was "a small thing, an eccentricity that was dwarfed by his multiple, stunning qualities." [10] And yet Anderson was bothered more by this "small thing" than he let on in his useful book *Revolution,* or maybe even more than he realized. It was Anderson who told me that when he returned to the campaign in 1980 after a long absence during the Sears interregnum, he was not quite sure if Reagan realized he had ever been away. [11] Others less self-secure than Anderson or less convinced of Reagan's greatness were bothered even more by the way their leader distanced himself from people and events. "He is on one level the easiest person to work for, always or usually genial, pleasant, disciplined, in control of himself, but if anyone relies on Reagan for emotional support, he's making a big mistake," said George Steffes, who played a key role in some of Reagan's early political victories as director of the governor's legislative affairs office in Sacramento. "I was close to him, closer than most people," said Steffes. "He remembered my name when I worked for him, which is more than he did for most people. And I was willing to talk to him bluntly, not reverentially, which he seemed to like. But he is removed from people in some central way, and people who depend upon him or who care about him are hurt by that." By the time Steffes departed the governor's office to become a lobbyist, he had lost his illusions about Reagan. He knew he would never hear from Reagan after he had left, and he said this to Mike Deaver, adding, "And once you're gone, he'll never call you." [12] The words proved prophetic.

Some observers reached the conclusion, as CBS White House correspondent Bill Plante expressed it, that Reagan's remoteness was central to his success. [13] By keeping his emotional distance from the lives and struggles of his subordinates, Reagan was less affected by what happened to them than were presidents with closer relationships. The rise and fall of Al Haig and of David Stockman were independent dramas in which the president seemed more bystander than accomplice. It did not matter all that much to him who was in the supporting cast. Actors came and went in Washington, as they had done in Hollywood and Sacramento, without altering his purposes or changing his conception of himself. Reagan remained serene in the center of his universe, awaiting his next performance.

While his distancing of himself from others may have been useful or even necessary for Reagan, it took a heavy toll among the entourage. Principal members of the Reagan team were misled by his manner or misled themselves into an expectation of friendship. They competed to be Reagan's favorite person. "Here he was, enormously successful in things that he had done, very confident, comfortable with himself, and a very likable man," said White House aide Robert Sims. "And he had these other people who were mature adults, most of them successful in their own rights—the Shultzes, the Weinbergers, the Bill Clarks—who had done things on their own and been successful, but Reagan was always up there at a level above these advisers and they all seemed to want to get his favor." [14] Reagan did not consciously play these subordinates off against one another, as Franklin Roosevelt might have done. Instead, he bestowed approval in a general sense on all "the fellas" or "the boys," as he was wont to describe his inner circle, while withholding his approval from any one of them in particular. He was not, as Martin Anderson observed with understatement, "overly thoughtful to those who worked for him" and he "rarely acknowledged what they had done for him." [15] Dick Allen, a foreign policy adviser through two campaigns and national security adviser during the first year of the presidency, remembers only one occasion when Reagan ever thanked him.*

The more self-confident members of the entourage, or those who had grown accustomed to Reagan's ways in Sacramento, accepted his detachment as a necessary hazard of White House employment. Others could not bear the burden of working for a pleasant but essentially unreachable president with whom they could establish no personal relationship. Many of Reagan's ablest subordinates drifted away from the White House or out of government in the midst of his presidency, depriving him of valuable experience and expertise. Some of them avenged themselves, or tried to explain the peculiarity of working for a man with whom they had no personal connection, by writing memoirs of their experiences. The "kiss-and-tell books" they produced revealed presidential lapses and deficiencies that in most administrations would have been disclosed only after a chief executive was dead or at least long out of office. While Reagan was still in the White House, dismissed or disenchanted former members of his cabinet and staff produced ten memoirs that reflect the frustrations of those who made the mistake of trying to breach the personal barrier. The authors were Martin Ander-

---

* In the transition period between his election and inauguration Reagan faced a sensitive situation in Korea, where the military-ruled government headed by former General Chun Doo Hwan had imprisoned dissident leader Kim Dae Jung and was threatening to execute him. President Carter publicly warned that U.S.-Korean relations would suffer if this sentence was carried out, and Reagan used Allen to send a similar private message. Chun spared Kim as the price of a February 2, 1981, visit to the White House, where, as Allen relates it, "Chun made known his pledge to stay in office for one seven-year term." [16] Reagan was appreciative of Allen's guidance in averting what could have been his first foreign policy crisis and told him so.

son, Terrel Bell, Anne Burford, Michael Deaver, Alexander Haig, Donald Regan, Larry Speakes, David Stockman, Helene von Damm and James Watt.* While some of these books are vengeful and all are in some respect self-serving, they offer a fairly consistent portrayal of presidential detachment and of a chaotic administration led by an enigmatic monarch who reigned rather than ruled. With the partial exception of Michael Deaver's *Behind the Scenes,* the memoirs find Reagan a puzzlement. Where they differ is less in their description of Reagan than in the talisman the authors use to explain presidential behavior of which they do not approve or cannot understand. Stockman blames Reagan's unquenchable optimism and political pragmatism for his refusal to face economic reality. Donald Regan faults Nancy Reagan's reliance on an astrologer rather than himself or the president for Reagan's difficulty in regaining public favor after the Iran-contra disclosures. Ted Bell blames "movement conservatives" in general and Meese, "the keeper of the radical right dogma," [17] in particular for Reagan's antipathy to the Department of Education. Haig blames his demise on a Machiavellian White House staff.

Whoever they blame or say they blame, the memoirists show little sense of loyalty to Reagan, and find even less loyalty in him. David Gergen, who held important White House posts under Nixon and Reagan, believes that Nixon's aides often cared more for him, even after he betrayed them, than Reagan's aides did for their president. "I felt that somehow subconsciously a lot of people had the feeling that loyalty ran up to Reagan, but it didn't run down to you," said Gergen, who did not write a memoir. "He didn't make you feel needed. He made you feel like you were working there for a cause or for the success of the presidency, but not enough for him. People left and didn't hear from him, and there was no real sense of connection. I think they felt hurt by it, and vented some of their frustrations in their books." [18]

Reagan's detachment from his own administration was particularly evident when scandal struck. His aides were often expert at "cutting our losses," as they euphemistically described forced resignations of administration officials who had become embarrassments, but Reagan detested confrontations, particularly over personnel. In 1983 the White

---

* These ten books contained 3,314 pages and sold for a total retail price of $191.50. All of them except Watt's more or less fit the "kick-and-tell" description given them by Ken Adelman in a post-presidential memoir that did some kicking of its own. Other memoirs that offered glimpses of Reagan from specialized vantage points within the administration were written by Constantine Menges, William Niskanen and Clyde Prestowitz. A list of these memoirs is included in the bibliography of this book.

House staff prodded Anne Gorsuch Burford to resign as administrator of the Environmental Protection Agency after widely publicized charges that her agency had been tolerant of polluters and hampered by conflicts of interest in cleaning up the nation's hazardous waste sites. Burford resisted, and Jim Baker and White House cabinet secretary Craig Fuller realized that a phone call from the president would be required for her to get the message. Reagan agreed to call. Reading from the script his aides had prepared for him, he told Burford that "a wonderful compromise" had been worked out in a dispute between the administration and a House committee that was trying to force her to testify. Since the "wonderful compromise" would have left Burford facing a likely criminal contempt citation without any representation from the Justice Department, she bluntly told the president that it was "the worst agreement possible" for her. Reagan's response was at first "a stunned silence," eventually followed by a statement that he had been pleased by what his aides had told him about the agreement. "It struck me then —as it would later on—that Mr. Reagan seems at a loss when the response to his first statement or question is unexpected," Burford wrote in retrospect. ". . . It does seem he has great difficulty in dealing with an unscripted response."[19]

This difficulty was compounded in the second term when Don Regan took on his own shoulders the responsibility of dismissing aides he thought no longer served the best interests of the president. One of these was Bently Elliott, a conservative speechwriter who had worked in the White House since 1981 and headed the speechwriting section since 1983. Regan, who commonly equated dissent with disloyalty, thought that Elliott was too outspoken in staff meetings and decided to fire him. He relayed this decision to Elliott through White House communications director Patrick J. Buchanan. Elliott, who was viewed by all except the Regan clique as intensely loyal both to the president and "the Reagan revolution," was shattered by the decision but understood after six years in the White House that Reagan was probably unaware of it. Elliott decided to make him aware. At a farewell picture-taking ceremony Elliott said boldly, with his wife and children standing nearby, "Mr. President, it's a great honor to work for you. I'm not leaving on my own accord."[20] As Elliott later described the scene to his friend and fellow speechwriter Peggy Noonan, the president physically recoiled from the information and did not respond.* Noonan was

* This is Noonan's recollection from Elliott's account soon after the event. Three years later Elliott told me that Reagan had said in response to his statement, "I didn't know that." Whatever Reagan

shocked. She thought the episode cruel treatment of a decent man who had served Reagan with loyalty and skill.[21] But it was typical conduct for Reagan, who was bothered even more by claims on his personal allegiance than he was by "unscripted responses." Loyalty rarely ran downward in the Reagan administration and even more rarely extended to middle-level assistants. Most White House aides liked the president and valued his accomplishments. But as George Steffes had learned in Sacramento, they could never depend upon him for emotional support.

It was a different story when Reagan was called upon or called upon himself to console the bereaved. He had developed a habit, while answering fan mail by phone or letter in Hollywood, of reaching out to strangers who had suffered a personal loss, and he was so adept at it that aides referred to him as the Great Comforter. Frequently, Reagan would telephone family members of servicemen or peace officers who had been killed in the line of duty. On one occasion Deaver entered the Oval Office when Reagan was consoling the daughter of an FBI agent who had been killed in a plane crash and was so moved by what the president was saying that he was embarrassed to be there.[22] I have personal experience of Reagan's skill in such moments. He called me at home after my mother died in 1983. Her death seemed merciful, for she had been ill a long time, but I was surprised how little I had been prepared for it. When I said as much to Reagan, he responded, "You are never prepared for the death of your mother," then proceeded to tell me his feelings when his own mother had died under similar circumstances. I was consoled and overcome. In such moments he did not need a script.

Reagan also performed as a comforter in his correspondence and in Oval Office conversations, to the wonder and delight of Anne Higgins. At times she brought him children who had survived severe handicaps, citing them as examples of the inhumanity of abortion. More often she delivered letters, to many of which Reagan insisted on responding with a personal message. In one case he sent a midwestern mother who had described her young son's diligence in school a personal check of "over $100"[23] to start his college fund. Her banker advised her not to cash it, saying that it would one day be worth far more than its face value.

---

said or didn't say, there is no doubt that it was Don Regan and not the president who dismissed Elliott. At the time of his dismissal one of Regan's aides bragged to me, under ground rules of anonymity, that Elliott was being fired because he was troublesome. Elliott says he was told by Buchanan that "the chief [meaning Donald Regan] doesn't want you here anymore."

Higgins learned of this and told Reagan. The president then called the woman and told her to cash the check, saying that he had arranged with his accountant for it to be sent back to her. Reagan enjoyed these involvements in the lives of ordinary people. His optimism was infectious, perhaps because he truly believed that life's problems would turn out well, as they nearly always had for him. Rexford Tugwell's description of Franklin Roosevelt as "a man with fewer doubts than anyone I had ever known"[24] is also a perfect description of Reagan. His optimism was unquenchable. He never ceased believing in the eventual vindication of his economic policies, when Stockman and nearly everyone else in the White House had given up on them. He was certain that the Soviets would return to the bargaining table in Geneva after they walked out on November 23, 1983. Reagan's favorite story, at least until Stockman parodied it in *The Triumph of Politics,* was of two little boys, one a dour pessimist and the other an extreme optimist, who were taken by their parents to a psychiatrist. The parents wanted to encourage the pessimistic son and to make the optimistic boy more conscious of the obstacles of life. To accomplish this, the pessimist was placed in a room with shiny toys and the optimist in a room containing horse manure. When the parents returned, the pessimistic child was crying. He had refused to play with the toys out of fear that he would break them. The parents found the optimistic child happily shoveling through the manure. He told them, "With this much manure around, I know there's a pony in here someplace."[25]

Reagan was always the boy who sought the pony, the child who believed that success was there for the finding and that it would surely come his way. Hollywood producer A. C. Lyles, a friend for more than fifty years, thinks Reagan possesses "the most optimistic viewpoint I have ever known in my life." Reagan always believed that the next day, or the next moment, would be better. If the weather became stormy on location during the making of a film, it was Reagan who would cheer up the director. "He'd say, 'Don't worry. It's going to clear up any time. You see that little light in the east over there. It's going to clear up,' " Lyles recalled. "The bottle, as he said, is always half full, never half empty. And he doesn't think in negative thoughts. He thinks in positive thoughts as a general rule, and he sees the best in everybody."[26]

For those who dealt with Reagan episodically or saw him chiefly in social situations, his optimism and good manners more than compensated for any vagueness or impenetrability. Richard Helms was charmed by Reagan's insistence on violating presidential custom and having guests precede him to dinner and by the little devices he used to conceal his difficulty in remembering names. "He would say, 'Oh, it's so nice to see you this evening' or 'welcome' or 'sit down and have a drink' or whatever the case might be," said Helms. "But since he wasn't using any names, you didn't particularly notice that he didn't use yours."[27] In conversation Reagan reminded Barry Goldwater of John F. Kennedy. "Both Kennedy and Reagan could walk in a room and not know their rear end from a hot rock," wrote Goldwater. "They wouldn't say a word for five minutes. Then, slowly, each would join the conversation in a way that made you believe they knew what they were talking about. I watched both do it at various times and came away amazed."[28] Caspar Weinberger thought Reagan was underrated by "serious people" in Washington because they were "totally unused to a president who is light-hearted, serene, secure within himself, a happy man who wants to have all the people in the room that he's meeting with happy, too, and wants to have his countrymen happy and serene."[29]

And yet the Reagan White House was often not a happy place, and the atmosphere was rarely serene. Aides appreciated the evenness of Reagan's temperament and valued his honesty. ("I found him without guile," said Arthur B. Culvahouse, who took over as White House counsel in the critical period after the Iran-contra revelations.)[30] But they operated under the pressure imposed by inexperience and the constant strain of trying to protect Reagan from his own credulity. "Whenever somebody told him something, he assumed they were telling the truth," said Martin Anderson. "He wasn't suspicious. I don't think he could conceive of people deliberately deceiving him or lying to him, and he figured if someone told him something, it was true. And if he read it, in the newspaper or in an article, and it sounded reasonable, he accepted it as true."[31] This was what Nancy Reagan meant when she said that her husband "assigns to everyone his own makeup." It mattered little to Reagan whether the newspaper was *The New York Times* or the Washington right-wing weekly *Human Events.** And it

---

* Reagan liked to clip stories from *Human Events,* and aides waged a long and losing battle to keep the publication out of his hands. On the campaign plane Deaver sometimes hid it from him, and Stu Spencer kidded Reagan by saying that if he made mistakes in his speech they wouldn't let him have his next copy. After Reagan became president he sometimes complained that he couldn't clip a story out of *Human Events* without ruining another story on the reverse side. According to one source, this led Dick Darman to jocularly suggest that Reagan be given two subscriptions. During his tenure as White House chief of staff, Ken Duberstein dealt with the problem by reading *Human Events* articles that Reagan clipped and returning them to the president with memos that corrected any perceived misstatements.

mattered even less if the someone who told him something was a qualified expert, a political aide or a casual visitor to the Oval Office. Reagan was apt to accept as valid any story, statistic or policy recommendation that squared with his prejudices. He was often an easy mark for subordinates trying to promote their own agendas, especially when the agendas were disguised in Reaganesque phrases. It was Reagan's indiscriminate trustingness, more than anything else, that prompted the White House triumvirate of James Baker, Mike Deaver and Ed Meese to decide that one of them should always be present when Reagan held a meeting. Their successors reached similar conclusions. Over time, the phrase "Let Reagan be Reagan" became a mantra for conservatives outside the administration who feared the president was being turned from his natural ideological course by pragmatic White House aides. Within the White House, however, pragmatists and conservatives alike viewed the protection of Reagan as an operational question rather than an ideological one. Except when he was isolated on his mountaintop ranch or in bed for the night, Reagan's aides were constantly on alert for fear that the president would say whatever came into his head or make decisions based on whatever he was told by the official who saw him last. These aides, particularly the Californians, liked Reagan but had no confidence in him. They saw their task as protecting the Reagan presidency from the clear and present danger of Ronald Reagan.

Whether Reagan needed as much protection as his aides believed remains an open question. What was indisputable was that he required advisers who were honest brokers and who saw to it that he received a full range of policy options. Reagan, unbelievably passive when not on stage, never tried to obtain these options on his own. One White House staff member who dealt frequently with the president told me that Reagan did not react to 95 percent of the material that was brought to him. Most of the president's rare responses occurred when a comment tripped what Colin Powell called a "built-in transistor," [32] by which he meant a remark that touched a central Reagan theme or stirred a cinematic memory. Unless this happened, Reagan operated confidently on the assumption that he was being told what he needed to know. "The consequence of this unusual trait is that Reagan is very dependent upon his personal advisers," wrote Martin Anderson. "Because he does not actively and constantly search out and demand things, he must rely on what is or is not brought to him." [33] While Reagan suffered from the delusion that he was "a hands-on president," [34] he recognized the essential elements of his management style. "I think what I was following was exactly what is considered good management policy out in the world of business and industry," Reagan told me. "And that is that you get the people that you believe in and that can do the things that need doing. The decisions about policy are mine, and I make them."[35]

This approach worked reasonably well for Reagan on domestic issues during his first term, largely because his 1980 campaign agenda of lower tax rates, increased military spending and cutbacks in domestic programs had framed the terms of the political debate. It worked less well in foreign affairs, where Reagan had impulses (anticommunism, free trade, a desire for a more peaceful world) rather than policies. The limits of Reagan's management style became more fully evident in the second term, when his detachment encouraged Chief of Staff Donald Regan to function as a surrogate president and the National Security Council staff to serve as a secret government. "Surround yourself with the best people you can find, delegate authority and don't interfere as long as the policy you've decided upon is being carried out," Reagan said in an ill-timed interview with *Fortune* less than two months before the disclosure of the Iran arms deal.[36] Reagan wrongly believed that the establishment of policy, both foreign and domestic, could be totally separated from its execution. He thought he had done everything he was supposed to do when he set broad policy outlines in meetings with his policy advisers. And he was encouraged in this fallacy by a commitment to "cabinet government," an idea that has beguiled nearly every modern president in his struggle to manage what governmental scholar Bradley H. Patterson Jr. has called "the vast plurality" of the executive branch.[37] Reagan came to office after declaiming for decades about the need to bring the federal government under control and make it the servant rather than the master of the people. He believed he could accomplish this by taking people of like mind and putting them in control of departments and agencies, then assembling them to make decisions. Despite his one-liners at the expense of bureaucrats, Reagan never really appreciated either the skill or the tenacity of the permanent government. He did not realize that cabinet secretaries, however conservative or strong-minded, often are captured by the bureaucracies they are supposed to manage, as Weinberger ultimately would be at the Pentagon. "Cabinet members are vice presidents in charge of spending, and as such they are the natural enemies of the president," said Charles G. Dawes, the first director of the Bureau of the Budget.[38] Reagan thought that bureaucracy was the enemy. He did not know that this enemy was lurking in the cabinet, within the palace gates.

Reagan's devotion to the grail of cabinet government was kindled during his governorship in Sacramento, where he met weekly with his agency and department heads. In theory, these meetings were instruments of decision-making. In practice, they were more often convenient forums for keeping "citizen-governor" Reagan roughly familiar with issues and for ratifying decisions that had been made before the cabinet assembled. At the beginning of his governorship in 1967, Reagan's office was directed by a strongman chief of staff named Phil Battaglia, who often acted on his own. Battaglia was succeeded by Bill Clark and then by Ed Meese, both of whom behaved collegially but preferred to make big decisions in small, informal meetings. This was a necessity in Sacramento, and even more so in Washington. Cabinet members tend to posture or say what is expected of them when formally convened. They are far more inclined to say what is on their minds in a small group or in a private session with the president than in a cabinet meeting. Reagan introduced an added note of unreality in formal cabinet sessions by occasionally lecturing against the advocacy of policy on purely political grounds. "We've come here to do what's right, not what's political," Reagan would say. The practical effect of this high-minded but impractical sentiment was to force genuine political discussion out of the cabinet meetings and into other arenas.

Nonetheless, Reagan hugely enjoyed the spectacle of cabinet meetings, even if he did not always stay awake at them.* The idea of governance-by-cabinet squared with Reagan's notion that government was analogous to a corporation in which the governor or president served as chairman of the board. Both in Sacramento and in Washington, Reagan encouraged department heads to speak out, even on subjects on which they lacked expertise. This egalitarian innovation added spice to the cabinet sessions while diminishing their already limited utility. Meese, recognizing that full cabinet meetings were apt to be little more than show-and-tell sessions, created five (later six) subgroups called cabinet councils. Reagan was the nominal chairman of each council, which functioned in specific policy areas and often met without the

---

* Deaver made an on-the-record acknowledgment of Reagan's proclivity for napping in cabinet sessions when he told NBC's Chris Wallace on August 13, 1984, that it had "more to do with what's going on in the meeting than what time of day it was." He added, "These meetings are sometimes boring, and I doze off, too." For disclosing this open secret, Deaver was roundly criticized by Nancy Reagan and Ed Meese, among others. But many White House officials had said the same under ground rules that did not permit them to be quoted. In *Trading Places,* Clyde V. Prestowitz Jr., then the Commerce Department's counselor for Japan affairs, relates how Reagan "appeared to doze off" during a presentation on the need for modernizing American industries.[39]

president under the chairmanship of a president pro tem. Martin Anderson makes the point that the cabinet councils met in the White House, which "was a powerful reminder to every member of the cabinet that it was the president's business he was about, not theirs or the department's constituents."[40]

But the cabinet councils were irrelevant to much of the decision-making process, which was concentrated in the hands of the White House staff. At the beginning this meant the triumvirate of Meese, Baker and Deaver. Meese was supposed to be the heavy hitter in this batting order. He knew more than Deaver, and he had a firm relationship with Reagan that Baker lacked. On paper he also had an organizational advantage, since both the domestic policy staff and the NSC staff reported to him. But Meese was typically spread too thin, and he was overly fond of tables of organization that described the world as he wanted it to be rather than the way it was. "Every single day Ed Meese was in that White House he lost power or gave up power," observed Ed Rollins, the White House political director from 1981–85. "Every single day Jim Baker was in that White House he accumulated power —or Dick Darman accumulated power."[41] Baker formed an enduring alliance with Deaver that overcame the thinness of his personal relationship with the Reagans. He worked closely with the Republican Senate leadership headed by Howard Baker and with Senator Paul Laxalt to develop White House initiatives and respond to congressional proposals. This made the Legislative Strategy Group, headed by Darman, a more significant policy instrument than any of the cabinet councils beloved by Meese and Martin Anderson. Meese did not fully understand this, but others saw what was happening and resented it. "Decisions would get made in the cabinet councils and unmade by the Baker team," said Robert Carleson, a conservative Californian who chaired the Cabinet Council on Human Resources.[42] This was because Baker, Deaver and Darman understood, as Reagan and Meese did not, that establishment of policy cannot be separated from its execution.

The modern presidency created by Franklin Roosevelt is of necessity a centralizing force. No president can manage the "vast plurality" described by Bradley Patterson through the cabinet, and most presidents followed the FDR example of relying on a small group of trusted personal advisers clustered around them in the White House. President Eisenhower held 236 cabinet meetings during his eight years in office but often followed the course advocated by Chief of Staff Sherman Adams. President Carter followed the lead of his White House staff late in 1979 in a mass firing of four cabinet secretaries that damaged him politically. And Reagan, because of his credulity and knowledge gaps, was more at the mercy of his staff than either Eisenhower or Carter. This did not mean that he was merely a pawn, as it often seemed to outsiders. Both in private and in public, the whole of Reagan's performance was often greater than the sum of its parts. He could be effective in small settings that enabled him to draw upon his life's experience and his "interpersonal intelligence." Aides thought him adept at reading body language even when he did not follow the details of a presentation. While Reagan tried to stuff everything he heard or read into the view of the world he had brought with him to Washington, he appreciated the value of compromise and negotiation. "He also liked to see the people around him work towards an acceptable compromise," said White House cabinet secretary Craig Fuller. "Both words are important. Acceptable in a sense that it met his criteria, narrow as they might be. Compromise in that nobody got exactly what they wanted, but nobody lost." [43]

Reagan did not fit the neat ideological stereotype that was presented in alternative forms by movement conservatives and liberal activists. He was an American original, both in form and substance. His views on some issues—free trade, for instance, and U.S. support of Israel—had changed little from his liberal Democratic days. He was as hostile as ever to the income tax, although his old views now wore the new clothing of supply-side economics. And on nearly all issues, Reagan was simultaneously an ideologue and a pragmatist. He complained to aides that true believers on the Republican right such as Senator Jesse Helms preferred to "go off the cliff with all flags flying" rather than take half a loaf and come back for more, as Reagan believed liberals had been doing since the days of the New Deal.

Reagan liked victories. Nancy Reagan believed that competitiveness was a key to his nature and that it undercut the argument that he was truly passive.* This was an overstatement, but one with a large grain of accuracy. It was often said, by me and many others, that Reagan presented minor victories and sometimes even defeats as major accomplishments. What was less often said but was also true was that Reagan adopted this tactic not to fool the people but to convince himself that whatever compromise he was considering was ideologically permissible. He was enough of a true believer to demand consistency in himself, a

* "He is a very competitive man," Nancy Reagan said, when I asked her about Reagan's passivity. "And he can't be passive and be competitive." [44]

trait that encouraged aides to invent arguments designed to persuade him that proposals in conflict with his advocacies actually advanced them. Thus, the Tax Equity and Fiscal Responsibility Act of 1982, a tax increase by any other name, became "tax reform" in order to satisfy Reagan's self-imposed requirement of consistency. He accepted such transparent rationalizations because the competitive side of his nature demanded political victories, particularly in the early years of his presidency. This desire to prevail even at the expense of his program served as a check on ideology, and his more pragmatic aides took advantage of this tendency whenever they could. Aides learned to read the signs. When Reagan was at his most ideological, he would remind those around him of how they had come to Washington to make a revolution. When he was in a compromising mood, he was apt to reminisce about negotiating contracts with producers on behalf of the Screen Actors Guild, an indirect but effective way of reminding hard-liners of the value of compromise. Usually, when push came to shove, Reagan was more concerned with outcomes than with accolades. This was fortunate for his presidency, even if often damaging to his personal reputation.

It is an axiom of White House public relations practice to credit a president for victories and to blame surrogates for defeats. Almost exactly the opposite practice prevailed during long stretches of the Reagan administration, where aides could and did exaggerate their own roles at the president's expense. Staff members told stories about presidential lapses that would have invited instant dismissal in other administrations. It was freely said, for instance, that Nancy Reagan yelled "Cut!" every night when the president returned to the residence, as a film director would do when a scene is finished. Reagan tolerated such gibes and also tolerated stories that gave Baker and Darman and later Regan the credit for the administration's legislative accomplishments. A sign on Reagan's desk in the Oval Office proclaimed, "There is no limit to what a man can do or where he can go if he doesn't mind who gets the credit." [45] This is the antithesis of Washington political wisdom, but Reagan believed it. He did not consider himself a politician, and he really didn't mind who got the credit.

What Reagan did mind was being pushed in a direction he did not want to go. His passivity concealed a stubborn streak that did not yield easily to the demands of staff or spouse. This was especially true when a member of the Reagan team was under fire on questions of judgment or ethics from a White House official, the Democrats, the media or a combination of the three. Whatever his deficiency in providing emotional support for aides who sought his friendship, Reagan was steadfast in defending subordinates who in other administrations would have been discarded as damaged goods. Haig was persona non grata with the White House staff for more than a year before Reagan would even listen to demands for his resignation. Reagan retained David Stockman after the budget director had publicly exposed the administration's economic estimates as a shell game. He rejected pressure from James Baker to fire Labor Secretary Raymond Donovan after Donovan became the target of a criminal investigation. He refused to replace Weinberger as defense secretary, a change keenly desired by key congressional Republicans who resented his intransigence on budgetary matters, and which White House officials told me was urged by Nancy Reagan after the 1984 election. He stuck by Don Regan for more than two months in the trough of his presidency when his wife, the Republican congressional leadership and his most trusted political advisers were telling him that Regan had to go. He stuck by Meese to the end. When he got his back up, Reagan's stubbornness often overcame his common sense or the findings of Dick Wirthlin's polls. Those who understood this trait, as Meese did, were able to exploit it for their own purposes at Reagan's expense while steadfastly proclaiming their loyalty to the president. When a change needed to be made, his aides often found it impossible to go through Reagan. Instead, they learned how to go around him.

Richard Allen, the conservative national security adviser brought into the White House by Meese, was the first significant victim of a White House staff conspiracy. Deaver was the principal architect of his downfall, made easier by Allen's lone-wolf approach to a job in which collegiality is an essential asset and by a widespread perception that Allen was in over his head. Whatever Allen's defects, he was a scapegoat for the larger deficiencies reflective of Reagan's detachment and lack of interest in foreign policy. Allen's demise became a paradigm for the way in which aides who enjoyed Reagan's trust and confidence compensated for the president's passivity by orchestrating competing forces capable of driving out an offending official. No one was ever fired in a straightforward way by Reagan, and no one in the higher ranks departed because of policy differences. Intense frustration, personality conflict, suspicions of scandal and an inability to penetrate the management maze in which the president declined to be a participant were the principal agents of turnover within the Reagan administration. All were involved in the downfall of Dick Allen.

Reagan came into office carrying the mental baggage of cabinet government and committed to downgrading the role of the national
security adviser, a goal in which he succeeded beyond his wildest
expectations. He believed, and had been encouraged in this view by
Allen, that Henry Kissinger under Nixon and Zbigniew Brzezinski
under Carter had exercised authority as national security advisers that
was properly vested in the secretary of state. Reagan did not understand
that even when the secretary of state takes the lead role, as Kissinger
had done after replacing William Rogers at State during the Nixon
administration, a president needs a well-informed foreign policy adviser
at his side who can sort out the conflicting recommendations that come
to him from State, the Pentagon and the Central Intelligence Agency.
A case can be made that no one in the upper ranks of the White House
understood this. The trio of Baker, Deaver and Meese had neither
experience nor expertise in foreign policy. In addition, they were committed with Reagan to an ambitious domestic agenda that shoved foreign policy to the back burner. As we have seen, this strategy was
encouraged by Nixon at the onset of the presidency and it was broadly
supported by the Republican congressional leadership. The return of
the American hostages from Iran soon after Reagan's inauguration relieved the administration from popular pressure to pursue an activist
foreign policy. Reagan was distanced from the foreign policy process,
which was made even more remote by Meese's system of having the
national security adviser report to him, rather than to the president. As
a result, Reagan often received his daily national security briefing in
writing through Meese rather than orally from Allen, a dubious practice
that became standard operating procedure during Reagan's recuperation from the wounds inflicted on him by would-be assassin John W.
Hinckley. For Reagan, his national security adviser was both out of
sight and out of mind.

If a president is unwilling to pursue foreign policy, foreign policy will
pursue him. Western European allies, committed to the deployment of
U.S. nuclear missiles on their soil, were waiting for signals from a
president who had been stereotyped abroad as an uncertain cross between a cowboy and an actor. So were U.S. adversaries, especially the
Soviet Union and the People's Republic of China. So was the Middle
East, where friends and foes alike were confused by the conflicting
comments from Haig, who was pro-Israel, and Weinberger, who was
not. President Carter had promised Saudi Arabia the sale of advanced
radar surveillance aircraft known by the acronym AWACS (Airborne

Warning and Control System aircraft) that could detect other planes at a range of up to 350 miles. Reagan inherited the decision and Israel's opposition to it, which the Israeli lobby expressed with its usual effectiveness in Congress. Paul Laxalt and former Senator Jacob Javits warned the White House of rising congressional discontent, and Allen was put in charge of pushing the embattled proposal through Congress. Haig and Weinberger, mutually supportive of AWACS despite their many disagreements, believed that Allen was disorganized and ineffective in this role.* So did James Baker, who placed a high premium on political effectiveness. Deaver dismissed Allen as a dependent, right-wing ally of Meese. This alliance, however, proved of little benefit to Allen, who came to think of Meese as a "400-pound obstacle."[46] Much of Allen's time was spent vainly trying to shove decision documents and position papers through the funnel-like management system that Meese had created to spare Reagan from decision-making. The system did not work. All of Martin Anderson's domestic policy proposals and all of Allen's foreign policy recommendations emptied out on Meese's desk, and too many of them stayed there. At one point in Allen's year-long tenure, fourteen separate papers requiring presidential decisions were blocked by the Meese bottleneck.[47] Neither Allen nor Haig could pry them loose. Deaver, while knowing little about the policy implications of AWACS or other foreign policy issues, had long experience with Meese's management practices. He and Baker talked it over but concluded they could not safely move against Meese. What they decided to do instead was pry the foreign policy portfolio away from the overextended White House counsellor. This meant getting rid of Allen and replacing him with someone who had an independent relationship with Reagan and was acceptable to him. At the State Department, sitting at Haig's right hand, they had a willing candidate in the person of Bill Clark.

Clark, a tall and deceptively soft-spoken conservative, had played a consultative role in the putsch that replaced John Sears with William Casey during the 1980 campaign. As a justice on the California Supreme Court, where Reagan had placed him in 1973, Clark was barred from an overt role in the campaign. While Clark liked the idea of being part of the Reagan team in Washington, he was initially reluctant to give up

---

* Complaints from the two cabinet secretaries and from Capitol Hill led to removal of Allen as administration point man in the AWACS lobbying effort. A scaled-down version of the sale was approved on October 29, 1981, in the Senate after skillful maneuvering by Senate Majority Leader Howard Baker and personal lobbying by the president.

his seat on a court closely (and bitterly) divided between liberals and conservatives. Clark knew that Democratic Governor Edmund G. (Jerry) Brown was likely to replace him with a liberal, tipping the court's ideological balance. However, this consideration became moot after the death of one justice and the resignation of another gave Brown two appointments and the court's liberals a clear majority. Clark then began exploring possible assignments in the new administration. Meese and Deaver told him he could be useful to Reagan at the State Department, keeping an eye on Al Haig. Late in the transition Allen broached the idea to Haig, who seized upon it. Since Haig was even more worried about the White House staff than the staff was about him, he liked the idea of having Clark on his team. Haig thought he needed an interpreter, "a guy who can speak Californian." [48] Despite Clark's lack of foreign policy experience, Haig chose him as deputy secretary of state. And during the first year of the Reagan presidency, as Haig fought and feuded with the White House and with Weinberger, it seemed the wisest of choices. Clark shielded Haig from White House sniping and gave him useful advice on how to deal with a president who seemed consistently uncomfortable in the realm of foreign policy. Reagan also quickly became uncomfortable with his volatile secretary of state, who was always making demands upon him that he could not meet. It was far easier for both Reagan and Haig to deal through Clark, who made no demands and rarely raised his voice. Haig complained that the White House staff would not let him talk to the president. Clark, in contrast, could pick up the telephone and get through directly to the Oval Office.

From Deaver's point of view, Clark's personal relationship with the president qualified him as an ideal replacement for Allen. Deaver did not want any strangers wandering into the Oval Office, and he knew Reagan would be more amenable to a change in national security advisers with a known quantity from California. Laurence Barrett has traced the conspiracy between Deaver and Clark to the weekend of July 11–12, 1981, when the two Californians and their wives visited Helene von Damm at her home at Beach Haven Crest on the New Jersey shore. [49] Clark was a friend of von Damm, who had worked as his secretary in Sacramento before becoming personal secretary for Reagan. At the time, von Damm was White House chief of personnel and well aware of the complaints about Allen and the Meese bottleneck. In the discussions that weekend Clark said he was willing to become national security adviser but only if he had direct access to the president. There the matter stood, while Deaver tried to figure out a way to get around Meese.

Then on August 19, with Reagan in Los Angeles, two U.S. Navy F-14 fighters flying sixty miles from the Libyan coastline were attacked by two Soviet-made Libyan jets. The F-14s returned the fire and downed the Libyan planes. The incident occurred at 10:20 P.M. California time, while the Reagans were having a party for their son Michael in the presidential suite of the Century Plaza Hotel. Deaver was vacationing in New England and Baker was in Texas. Meese was in charge. He learned from Allen of the downing of the Libyan planes at 11:04 P.M., by which time the Reagans had retired for the evening. Meese immediately notified Vice President Bush and other members of the National Security Council, but he unaccountably did not tell Reagan what had happened until 4:24 A.M. the following day. Reagan listened to the news approvingly, then went back to sleep.[50] He subsequently said Meese had acted appropriately because no presidential decision had been required.[51] But Nancy Reagan was furious about the delay in notifying her husband. So were Baker and Deaver, who realized the public relations imperative of demonstrating that Reagan had his hand on the presidential throttle. The Libyan incident publicly exposed the fragility of Meese's judgment in crisis situations and subjected Reagan to a barrage of media ridicule. Describing Reagan's vacation as if it were a summer-camp outing, humorist Art Buchwald wrote, "We had a lot of fun. I cut brush, cleared out trees, hiked with my best girl Nancy, and shot down two Libyan planes. I was sleeping when we shot them down and my best friend Ed Meese didn't wake me up in time. But it was fun hearing about it."[52] Baker and Deaver resolved to take the foreign policy portfolio out of Meese's hands.

Deaver was in charge of the schedule. When Reagan returned to Washington in September, Deaver arranged a series of meetings in which Haig, Weinberger, Bill Casey and Paul Laxalt were given an opportunity to discuss the national security process with the president. All agreed, for different reasons, that Allen should be replaced by a new national security adviser who would have independent access to Reagan. I was told at the time by White House and State Department sources that Reagan expressed interest in replacing Allen with Jeane Kirkpatrick and tried out the idea on several subordinates. This idea produced rare agreement between Haig and Deaver, who shared the view that Kirkpatrick was opinionated and potentially troublesome. Reagan dropped the idea, which would surface again later in the administration.

Clark at the time had no comparable adversaries within the inner circle or the cabinet. Reagan's only concern about naming him was the sensible one of whether he could be spared at State. Deaver's answer to the president when he asked this question was that Clark had established a working relationship with Haig and would be a useful go-between for him in the White House. Essentially, he was making the opposite of Haig's argument that Clark could "speak Californian," arguing that it was Clark who could speak the sometimes mysterious tongue of the secretary of state. Reagan was persuaded. Clark went on vacation to Antigua, fully expecting to become national security adviser on his return.

Instead, one of Haig's periodic bursts of temper delayed the change. The proximate cause was an unpublished column by Jack Anderson, who had written that "the secretary of state reportedly has one foot on a banana peel and could skid right out of the Cabinet before summer."[53] White House communications director David Gergen was queried by Anderson for this column and correctly suspected that his boss Jim Baker would be suspected of being the source. Gergen, fueling a fire he was trying to douse, called Haig to tip him off about the prospective column and to deny Baker's involvement. Haig blew up. He took his case to the press, telling reporters that a "guerrilla campaign" was being waged against him by the White House and leaving the impression that Allen was the head guerrilla. Haig also telephoned Reagan, who for once took the call and tried to reassure his angry secretary of state that he was not being pushed out of the administration. Armed with this presidential vote of confidence, Haig called Anderson and denied the report. Reagan also telephoned the columnist with a similar denial.

The effect of the furor was to make the unpublished Anderson column a far bigger story than it could possibly have been if published and ignored. Belatedly recognizing this, the White House staff tried to make amends by staging a presidential show of strength. Reagan called Haig and Allen into his office on November 5, 1981, and ordered them to stop feuding. The event was a sham, concocted with the media in mind. Gergen told reporters that "the meeting was called at the president's initiative."[54] What he did not tell them, and may not have known, was that Reagan had been urged to demonstrate this "initiative" by several of his advisers, including Deaver and Allen. Gergen and deputy press secretary Larry Speakes depicted Reagan as a firm chief executive who was acting decisively to end administration infighting and establish control over foreign policy. Reagan's inner circle knew, however, that he had been roused from his habitual passivity at the direction of others.

Allen, meanwhile, had more troubles. On January 21, the day after the inauguration, he had intercepted a $1,000 gratuity paid to Nancy Reagan by the Japanese magazine *Shufo no Tomo* (The Housewife's Friend) in exchange for an interview. It was paid in $100 bills enclosed in an envelope. Allen promptly gave the envelope to a secretary, who deposited it in a White House safe. He then forgot about it, a carelessness that his critics claimed was illustrative of the way he operated. When the envelope was discovered in mid-September, Meese called the Justice Department and the FBI to ask for an inquiry. Nancy Reagan complained that Meese was being more protective of Allen than of the president, although it is difficult to see what else Meese should have done. The investigation became public on November 14, producing an embarrassing round of stories. Allen soon departed on leave to mount a legal defense, never to return to the White House. Though the investigation cleared Allen of any wrongdoing, his absence allowed Deaver to seal the deal for Clark. Deaver also took the opportunity to remind Reagan of Meese's management deficiencies, underscoring an argument the president had grown accustomed to hearing from Nancy Reagan. Reagan went off to his annual post-Christmas holiday in Palm Springs, where one of his longtime California associates told me that the president hoped Meese would stick to being a counsellor instead of trying to function as a rival White House chief of staff. But Reagan, perhaps in gratitude for past services, never gave a public hint of his private disappointment in Meese. Instead, as Meese put it, he was allowed "to get on top of the situation" by taking false credit with reporters for recommending an upgrading in the status of the national security adviser—a proposal he had long opposed.[55]

On January 1, 1982, in Palm Springs, Reagan signed a memorandum making Clark his national security adviser and specifying that he would have direct access to the president and administrative control of the National Security Council staff. The president waited until he returned to the White House three days later to announce the changeover. Allen was rewarded with a letter in which Reagan expressed his "confidence, trust and admiration for your personal integrity and your exemplary services to the Nation." The letter was drafted by Ed Meese.

It took the White House staff longer to remove Haig, whose fall was from a greater height. On paper and in person Haig was an imposing figure, both warrior and diplomat. He was a West Pointer who had obtained a master's degree in international relations from Georgetown. He had served as supreme commander of NATO forces and as an aide to Henry Kissinger. As White House chief of staff in the last difficult days of the Nixon presidency, Haig was familiar with the agony of political decision-making under crisis conditions. He also knew from experience how harmful a fragmented foreign policy process could be for any president, and he had raised this issue when Reagan called and asked him to be his secretary of state. As Haig recalls it, Reagan told him: "Al, you will be my foreign policy principal. You will be my spokesman. And you will be the integrator of foreign policy in my administration."[56] Haig's account of this conversation squares perfectly with what Reagan and Allen were then saying about the role the secretary of state would play in the new administration.

But Haig, who liked to call himself Reagan's "vicar," never gained the trust of the men around Reagan nor understood how important that trust was for his success. On December 3, 1980, eight days before Reagan called him, Haig attended a dinner at the Madison Hotel for newly elected Jamaican Prime Minister Edward Seaga, who was in Washington to celebrate his victory over a leftist candidate and appeal for U.S. financial aid. Before dinner, Haig was summoned by Senator Laxalt to a room in the hotel, where Meese, Baker and Allen questioned him about his political intentions. Meese opened the meeting by asking Haig if he wanted to be president of the United States, a question Haig thought "ludicrous" and naïve.[57] "The last thing I would ever do, if that were my intentions, would be to be secretary of state because he's got to be the president's shock absorber and scapegoat, and he's expendable," said Haig, who then lectured his interrogators on the fate of such former secretaries of state as Dean Acheson, Dean Rusk and Cyrus Vance.[58] The meeting was an omen of mutual mistrust. On inauguration day, still dressed in formal clothes, Haig went to the White House to present Reagan with a National Security Decision Directive (known to all forevermore as NSDD 1) that gave the State Department sweeping control over the national security process. Meese invited Haig into his office, where the new secretary of state had once worked round-the-clock for Kissinger, and took the document. With Baker and Deaver alongside, Meese subjected NSDD 1 to a "dogged critique" and said it needed to be cleared with the secretary of defense, the CIA director and the national security adviser before it could be signed.[59] Haig thought that Meese was acting presumptuously, wielding authority he did not properly possess. The White House staff triumvirate had a different view. As one of them told me later, Haig was pushing the president "before he even had a chance to change his clothes."

It is difficult to understand why Haig, either at the time or retrospectively, was so totally devoid of insight into Reagan's style of governance. Reagan had a widely advertised track record in Sacramento of dealing with his cabinet through his staff. Meese and Deaver, the two aides initially most troublesome to Haig, went back fifteen years with Reagan and were known to speak for him. Cabinet officers with less of a personal relationship with Reagan than Haig were aware of the president's delegative proclivities, and most of them quickly formed alliances with one or more of the White House staff triumvirate. Yet Haig professes even to this day to be baffled by the extent of White House staff influence in the Reagan presidency. With the assistance of writer Charles McCarry, Haig expressed his bewilderment in *Caveat:* "To me, the White House was as mysterious as a ghost ship; you heard the creak of the rigging and the groan of the timbers and sometimes even glimpsed the crew on deck. But which of the crew had the helm? Was it Meese, was it Baker, was it someone else? It was impossible to know for sure." [60] This passage conceals the depth of Haig's feelings, and his customary manner of expressing them. As Haig put it to me more typically in discussing the infighting, "Do you think I gave a shit about guerrilla warfare with a bunch of second-rate hambones in the White House? For Christ sake. I've lived through more guerrilla warfare in my lifetime than anybody I know." [61]

White House aides resented Haig's contempt for them, but more was at work in Haig's descent than personal hostility and a battle over turf. In the early months of 1981, when the White House staff was focusing on the administration's ambitious economic game plan, Haig wanted to lay down a "marker" against the Soviet Union and Cuba in the Western Hemisphere. He sought in particular to make El Salvador, where Communist rebels were active, a test case of administration willingness to resist hemispheric subversion. Since Reagan was staunchly anticommunist, Haig expected support from the president on this initiative. Reagan, who had promised repeatedly during the 1980 campaign that there would be "no more betrayal of friends by the United States," was supportive, but he had a greater sense of urgency about his economic program than about any item on the foreign policy agenda. While Reagan was willing to increase U.S. military aid to the El Salvadoran government and send a handful of military advisers to aid the anti-guerrilla campaign, he didn't want to talk about it. Haig found this difficult to understand. When I told Haig seven years after his resignation that even his former boss Richard Nixon had recommended that

Reagan expend his initial energies on economic policy, Haig shook his head and said he thought such a suggestion would have been "uncharacteristic" of Nixon, "who in my experiences with him was totally preoccupied with foreign policy and genuinely believed that foreign policy was the main burden of a successful president."[62]

Reagan was, in fact, so highly focused on the economic agenda to the exclusion of foreign policy that he approved a three-week delay in a State Department "white paper" aimed at documenting the flow of military weapons from Communist countries to the El Salvadoran rebels. When the document was finally issued on February 23, coinciding with disclosures that the United States was increasing aid to El Salvador and sending fifty-five military advisers, it confirmed the fears of the president and his staff that foreign policy distracted from the economic agenda. Television coverage shifted from Stockman to Haig, who proclaimed the administration's determination to resist "Cuban adventurism." But it was Haig's adventurism that worried the White House staff. Fearing that the El Salvador issue would undo the congressional bipartisanship he was trying to cultivate in support of the president's economic program, Baker called up Haig and urged him to limit his television appearances.[63]

Haig proved even more troublesome in private meetings than on television. As Deaver tells it, Haig responded at one meeting to a comment that Cuba was the source of subversion in Central America by saying, "Give me the word and I'll make that island a fucking parking lot."[64] By his own admission, Deaver rarely paid much attention to foreign policy discussions, but he was frightened by Haig.[65] Leaving the room, Deaver turned to Clark, then Haig's deputy, and said, "Good God, I cannot believe that I'm in the room with the president of the United States and the secretary of state's talking about bombing Cuba." Clark replied that it was done for effect. "Well, it certainly had a good effect on me," Deaver replied. "It scared the shit out of me." Later, Deaver would say that Haig's remark also "scared the shit out of Ronald Reagan."[66]

For Baker and Meese, Haig was a political impediment and an annoyance. For Deaver, after this incident, the secretary of state seemed a danger to Reagan and the world. Deaver was closer to Reagan than other White House aides and more conscious of his shortcomings. He believed strongly that Reagan had a dark side to his nature that could be roused by fervent anticommunism. Haig's little speech about making a "parking lot" of Cuba, whether or not delivered for effect, echoed the sentiments Reagan had expressed in one of his jingoistic moods after President Johnson ordered bombing raids of North Vietnam and committed U.S. troops to the Vietnam War. "We should declare war on Vietnam," Reagan had said in October 1965. "We could pave the whole country and put parking stripes on it and still be home by Christmas."[67] Deaver did not share these sentiments. While conservative in the normal meaning of the term on economic issues, he was far less interventionist or reflexively anticommunist than any other member of the Reagan team. He took Reagan's campaign vow of "no more Vietnams" to mean that the United States should avoid getting bogged down in jungle wars, and he from time to time reminded Reagan and other staff members that public support was lacking for U.S. intervention in Central America. By the second term, long after Haig was gone, Deaver reached the conclusion that administration support for the Nicaraguan contras was dragging the United States into a "bottomless pit" in Central America.[68] The contras did not yet exist on the memorable day when Haig talked about attacking Cuba. But Deaver resolved from this time forward never to allow Haig to see Reagan alone, and Haig never did until the end.

Haig lasted eighteen months as secretary of state, battling with his peers and the "hambones" on the White House staff over policies, perquisites and real and imagined slights. The worst of these slights, from Haig's point of view, occurred on March 24, 1981, when Reagan put Vice President Bush in charge of the administration's Crisis Management Team (later rechristened the Special Situations Group). Haig was distraught, believing that the president had violated his pledge to make him the "integrator" of foreign policy. He told Clark that the president had "lied to him," and talked of resigning.[69] Clark warned Haig of the dangers of threatening to resign and calmed him down. But Haig did not stay calm. He fought with Allen, who might have been his ally, and contributed to the national security adviser's isolation. He fought with United Nations Ambassador Jeane Kirkpatrick, who sometimes sought to circumvent the State Department.* And he fought repeatedly with the White House staff.

---

* One of Haig's most bizarre performances occurred after Kirkpatrick steered a compromise resolution through the U.N. Security Council that deplored the June 7, 1981, Israeli bombing of an Iraqi nuclear reactor but headed off sanctions against Israel. Haig was in China at the time. On a New Zealand stopover on the return trip, he belittled Kirkpatrick and took credit for the resolution. Reagan was told of this by his aides, called Kirkpatrick to congratulate her and complained that Haig kept "straying off the reservation."[70] When Haig returned, he blamed the White House staff for the controversy. Responding to a Japanese diplomat who said politely that Haig had been

Haig's squabbles with others in the administration might have made little public impression except for his performance on national television during the tense hours after Reagan was shot by John Hinckley on March 30, 1981. Vice President Bush was flying back from Texas, not knowing if Reagan would survive. Baker and Meese were at George Washington Hospital, where the president was undergoing surgery for removal of a bullet that had lodged within an inch of his heart, missing the vital aorta by the same distance. Haig was sitting at a long table in the White House Situation Room, in the basement of the west wing, arguing inconclusively with Weinberger about the alert status of U.S. military forces. Other aides and cabinet members who had gathered in the room were watching network coverage on an oversize television set perched over Haig's head. At 3:41 P.M., soon after Reagan was wheeled into the operating room, Haig remarked, to no one in particular, "The helm is right here in this chair." At 4:10 P.M., Larry Speakes entered the White House briefing room and began fending off questions from reporters. He had already conducted a briefing at the hospital, and he was unaware that Haig and the others were clustered in the Situation Room. Speakes had been given no guidance on how the government would operate while Reagan was out of commission, and he refrained from guessing. When a reporter asked whether Bush would become "acting president" if Reagan was under anesthesia, Speakes replied, "I cannot answer that question at this time." That was upsetting to Haig, who turned to Allen and said, "We've got to get him off." Before most people in the room knew what was happening, Haig was racing up a narrow stairway to the briefing room with Allen in his wake. Allen thought Haig was ready to collapse.[72] Back in the Situation Room, White House counsel Fred F. Fielding, who had been sitting across from Haig, looked over and saw that he was no longer in the room. Then he looked up at the television and saw that Haig had replaced Speakes at the podium in the briefing room. The secretary of state was out of breath and struggling to control his emotions. But he was also armed with information that Speakes lacked. Despite his emotional state, Haig was conducting an exemplary briefing until a reporter asked him who was making the decisions for the government while Reagan was on the operating table. "Constitutionally, gentlemen, you have the president, the vice president and the secretary of state in that order,

---

going all over the world "like a swallow," Haig said, "I've been going around the world like a swallow to avoid buckshot from the White House."[71]

and should the president decide he wants to transfer the helm, he will do so," Haig replied in a quavery voice. "He has not done that. As of now, I am in control here, in the White House pending return of the vice president, and in close touch with him. If something came up, I would check with him, of course." [73]

The printed words do not begin to convey the frenetic impression made by Haig at this moment. Except for his muddled explanation of the presidential succession—the speaker of the House and the president pro tem of the Senate are actually in the line of succession before the secretary of state—Haig had accurately described the situation as he knew it, in what was certainly an honest attempt to reassure the nation and keep the media informed.[74] And Haig was technically the staff member in charge at the White House in the absence of Bush and Baker. The problem was that Haig's frenzied demeanor alarmed people instead of reassuring them. To those who watched him in the briefing room, the Situation Room and on television sets across the nation Haig seemed badly out of control rather than in control. He never recovered from this performance. "I'm in control here" became a stock Washington wisecrack for use in situations when no one was in control. In a mercurial moment in the briefing room, Haig had given the nation an inner glimpse of the man who had frightened Deaver by offering to obliterate Cuba.

For all this, Reagan did not readily abandon Haig. The passive president may not always have known the identity of his speechwriters, but he stuck by members of his cabinet who came under fire. Reagan realized that Haig, despite his outbursts, was both well informed and well-meaning. "Al hasn't steered me wrong yet," he told an aide during one of Haig's periodic battles with the White House staff.[75] As long as he was Haig's deputy at the State Department, Clark reinforced this view. But after he replaced Allen, Clark stopped being Haig's interpreter at the White House and gradually became his adversary. This opposition proved crucial. Clark sided with Kirkpatrick when Haig tried to have her fired for supporting Argentina in the Falklands dispute while Haig was attempting to head off an Argentine-British war. Reagan backed Haig's efforts to avert the war and he stuck with his British ally Margaret Thatcher when war came, but he also refused to fire Kirkpatrick and upbraided Haig for trying to bring her to heel.[76] That should have been a signal to Haig that his days were numbered. Instead, Haig made a last desperate effort to seize control of administration foreign policy.

Early in June of 1982, Reagan made his first trip as president to

Western Europe. It was a troubled journey that revealed much about Reagan's ignorance of the allies and even more about Haig's ignorance of Reagan's ways. The trip coincided with several foreign policy crises. Israel was invading Lebanon. The U.N. Security Council was debating a resolution on sanctions against Britain over the Falklands War. And Reagan, with the support of Clark and other conservatives, was trying to dissuade the allies from going through with their agreement to help construct a $10 billion Soviet pipeline that would bring natural gas from Siberia to Western Europe and provide Moscow with badly needed hard currency. Until this trip Reagan had largely remained out of the range of Haig's rages, in part because Deaver had made good on his vow never to leave the two of them in a room together. But Reagan saw much of Haig on this long journey, and he did not like what he saw. Reagan, as Bud McFarlane would later put it, expected good manners from his secretary of state, and he was appalled at Haig's repeated displays of temper over what seemed to the president to be minor matters of protocol.[77] Haig did not like his accommodations on Air Force One, where he was placed by Deaver in the third compartment instead of the second one directly behind the president's quarters.

It was on this trip that Clark and Haig also came to a parting of the ways. Their conflict had policy overtones, but was at bottom a struggle over presidential prerogatives. On the policy side, Haig had a strong case. While Clark subsequently blamed him for ostensibly giving the "green light" to the Israeli invasion that occurred in the early days of this trip, Haig had been warning for months about Israeli fury at acts of terrorism by the Palestine Liberation Organization in Galilee. On May 21, 1982, Haig had proposed a three-point diplomatic initiative intended to avert the war but proved unable, in his words, "to drive the message through the incoherent NSC system."[78] On June 2, the day after the presidential party arrived in Versailles for the annual economic summit of industrialized nations, the Israeli ambassador to Great Britain was shot and seriously wounded by Arab terrorists. Israel responded by bombing an empty sports stadium in Beirut, blowing up an ammunition dump behind the grandstand. The PLO retaliated by bombing towns in Galilee. On June 6, the concluding day of the economic summit, Israel launched a full-scale invasion of Lebanon. Haig briefed reporters regularly during this period, inaccurately predicting that Israel would halt its invasion after securing a buffer zone in Lebanon that would protect its citizens from random shelling. The briefings certainly gave me and others who attended them the impression that Haig was an apologist for the Israeli invasion. We did not know then that he had also tried to prevent the war.

Similarly, Haig sought to head off conflict on the troublesome pipeline issue. While resolutely anti-Soviet, Haig also realized that the allies were determined to go through with the deal for economic reasons. He sought a compromise under which the United States would acquiesce to the pipeline in return for an agreement of allied consultation on future technology transfers. Despite his bluster, Haig was at heart a realist who valued allied unity far more than the quixotic goal of halting the pipeline. Reagan was naïvely convinced that he could talk the allies out of an economic decision they had already made by warning them of the danger of depending on the Soviet Union. Instead of realizing that it was the president who was intransigent, Haig chose to believe that the policy he opposed was being foisted on the president by Clark and the "hambones" on the White House staff.

But it was his personality more than his policy advocacies that kept getting Haig in trouble. After his complaints about his accommodations on Air Force One, Haig again made a fuss when he was not assigned to the president's helicopter on a flight from Heathrow Airport in London to Windsor Castle, where the presidential party spent two nights as guests of the queen. At a luncheon at 10 Downing Street, Haig misunderstood the arrangements and stood in the receiving line, leaving only when Margaret Thatcher whispered to him that he was not supposed to be there. Nancy Reagan thought that Haig was making a fool of himself and trying to make a fool of her husband.

At Windsor Castle, Haig and Clark tangled again, this time over a U.N. Security Council resolution that sought to impose sanctions on Israel because of the Lebanon invasion. There was no policy difference on this issue. Reagan, as well as Clark and Kirkpatrick, opposed the sanctions, and Haig knew it. But Clark insisted that the decision was Reagan's to make and that Haig should give the president his recommendations rather than acting on his own. Haig and Clark wound up in a shouting match that marked the end of any accommodation of the secretary of state. Haig backed down, but too late. On the trip home, Haig's adversaries on the White House staff began to talk openly among themselves on how he could be ousted.

The presidential party returned to Washington on June 11, a Friday. Reagan was exhausted and left immediately for Camp David. While he was resting up over the weekend, Haig and Clark plunged into another battle, this time over the instructions that should be given to Philip

Habib, a U.S. special envoy who was shuttling among Middle Eastern capitals trying to work out an agreement that would end the Israeli siege of Beirut and get foreign forces out of Lebanon. Again, the dispute was over presidential prerogatives rather than policy. The Special Situations Group, in which all departments were represented, had agreed to the wording of the instructions, which were largely drafted by Haig. The Pentagon had reservations about some minor details, which Clark thought could be resolved at a National Security Council meeting on Monday. He did not want to disturb Reagan at Camp David but sent him a Datafax of the proposed instructions. Haig insisted that the instructions couldn't wait. He telephoned Reagan at Camp David on Sunday and "detected a note of puzzlement in his relaxed and amiable voice" when he asked about the instructions to Habib. Instead of realizing, as those who knew Reagan better would have, that the president simply had not read the instructions, Haig concluded that Clark had not even sent them to Camp David.[79] Haig then sent them to Habib himself, without bothering to wait for the NSC meeting.

This was too much for Reagan. On Monday, June 14, he called Haig into his office and asked him what he would do if one of his subordinate military officers acted on his own. "I'd fire him, Mr. President," Haig said.[80] They were now close to the inevitable resignation, but Reagan did not press the issue. "No, no, I didn't mean that," Haig recalled the president as saying. "But this mustn't happen again. We just can't have a situation where you send messages on your own that are a matter for my decision," Reagan said. Haig heard the president out, then issued a warning of his own. "I simply can no longer operate in this atmosphere," he said. Haig told Reagan that unless the president was willing to "make the necessary changes to restore unity and coherence to his foreign policy, then it would be in the country's interest to have another secretary of state." Haig suggested he depart after the November midterm elections, so that his resignation would not become an issue in the campaign.[81]

Haig had resigned, although he did not seem to know it. A White House aide, relating what had happened under ground rules of anonymity, told me after this meeting that Reagan was "shaken" by the encounter and realized that Haig was no longer a member of the team. To Clark and Deaver that meant that the only question was the timing of the resignation and the selection of a replacement. But Reagan thought it would look bad for him to fire Haig, and he seems to have realized that the secretary of state had reached the point where he was likely to fire himself. While Reagan never said this directly, as far as I can determine, he stopped trying to pacify Haig after the June 14 meeting and instead took a deliberate action that was certain to provoke him. On Friday, June 18, while Haig was conferring in New York with Soviet Foreign Minister Andrei Gromyko, the National Security Council made its decision on the pipeline issue. The so-called hard option, favored by Clark and Weinberger, penalized European firms and American subsidiaries that cooperated with the Soviets in construction of the pipeline. The State Department, represented at the NSC meeting by Undersecretary Lawrence Eagleburger, supported a softer alternative that avoided sanctions in favor of negotiations with the allies to prevent future technology transfers. As Haig related it, "Clark placed only the strongest option paper before Reagan, who uncharacteristically approved it on the spot."[82] Haig would have been even more disturbed if he had known what had occurred before the meeting when Clark's deputy, Bud McFarlane, briefed the president on both options. McFarlane knew from experience that Reagan wanted a quick summary of the issues. While the president was rarely interested in details, he prided himself on being fair-minded and sensitive to the opinions of his cabinet officers. That was not the case this day. Brushing aside the merits of the arguments, Reagan pointedly asked McFarlane where Haig stood on the options. When McFarlane told him, Reagan "couldn't wait" to do the opposite of what Haig wanted.[83] "It seemed to me one of the very few times when the president really asserted himself for reasons other than what he thought about policy," McFarlane said afterward.[84]

The White House staff compounded the injury by the insult, as Haig saw it, of informing the press about Reagan's decision before either the allies or the Soviets were notified through diplomatic channels. On June 19, Gromyko angrily confronted Haig. Either Haig had misled him, Gromyko said, or he did not speak for the Reagan administration. "Mr. Foreign Minister, I'm afraid it is the latter," Haig said.[85] But the secretary of state was still not ready to leave. He pressed Clark for another meeting with the president to resolve the issues he had raised in their June 14 session. Clark told him the president would see him on Thursday, June 24. In advance of that meeting McFarlane discussed the matter with Haig's assistant, Sherwood D. (Woody) Goldberg. Unlike their principals, McFarlane and Goldberg had continued to work together to resolve points of friction between the secretary of state and the White House staff. Goldberg talked not of resignation but of "a clearing of the air," leaving McFarlane with the impression that Haig's talk of resignation was a stratagem to force Clark and the White House staff to heel. McFarlane warned Goldberg that there was now so much "animus" on both sides that he "couldn't be sure of the outcome." Clark then dropped into McFarlane's office, on his way to see Reagan before Haig arrived. Knowing that McFarlane respected Haig's abilities, Clark asked him if he thought the president should accept his resignation. McFarlane, convinced that there was now an "enormous gap" that could not be bridged, told Clark that he thought Reagan should.[86]

Reagan and Haig now held their last meeting together, alone in the Oval Office. As Haig recalls the meeting, he presented Reagan with a "bill of particulars" prepared by his staff describing the record of what he saw as interference in his conduct of foreign affairs. He also gave Reagan a second memorandum detailing his differences with Clark and Kirkpatrick during the Falklands crisis. Haig has described these documents, which have never been released, as "forthright."[87] Aides told me that they directly accused Clark of undermining his authority, relating an account of how the national security adviser had dealt with a Saudi official through a back channel and allegedly undermined Habib's mission in the Middle East. After the meeting, Reagan told Clark and Deaver that Haig also had shown him a letter of resignation. He repeated this assertion to Laurence Barrett a month later, saying that the letter was in an envelope and that Haig showed it to him, but "kept it in his hand."[88] Haig did not mention this letter in *Caveat,* enabling him to make the point that Reagan accepted a letter of resignation he had never submitted. This is technically accurate, but gives a misimpression. Haig had made it clear he was leaving unless Reagan reduced Clark's authority, which he knew the president had no intention of doing. As far as Reagan was concerned, Haig had twice resigned and the only open question was whether to accept the resignation immediately or wait until after the election. Reagan's aides believe he acted immediately because he did not want several more months of disharmony and confrontations. "This has been a heavy load," Reagan wrote in his diary.[89] He was happy to be rid of his troublesome secretary of state and would say in looking back on Haig's service, "He didn't even want me as the president to be involved in setting foreign policy—he regarded it as his turf."[90]

On Friday morning, June 25, Reagan told Clark to track down George Shultz. Clark had been keeping close track of the whereabouts of Shultz, who was then in London, waiting for the moment of Reagan's decision. Even though a pro forma list had been prepared of four potential replacements, Clark knew that Reagan's interest was limited to Shultz.* When Clark's call came, Shultz was attending a business meeting for the Bechtel Corporation, of which he was president. A secretary sent Shultz a note telling him there was a message from "George Clark," a miswriting of "Judge Clark." [91] Shultz did not know any George Clark and ignored the message. Soon, another message came from the White House asking Shultz to go to the American embassy, where he could talk with the president on a secure telephone line. Shultz went. Reagan told him that Haig had resigned but that the resignation had not been announced.

"I would like you to be secretary of state," Reagan said.

"Mr. President, are you asking me just to accept this job over the telephone?" Shultz asked.

"Yes, it would help a lot because we don't want to have a period when there isn't anybody—when there's a lot of speculation about who's going to be secretary of state and so on," Reagan replied. "That's a bad thing. We want to be able to announce the new secretary when we announce the old secretary has left."

"Okay," Shultz said. [92]

Reagan then told Shultz not to mention his appointment until he had announced the change in Washington. [93] At 3:04 P.M. the president came to the White House briefing room, and in a 156-word announcement said he was accepting Haig's resignation "with great regret" and replacing him with Shultz. He refused to answer the shouted questions of reporters and departed immediately by helicopter for Camp David.

Five days later, at a news conference in the East Room, I reminded the president that he had criticized President Ford in 1976 for refusing to explain why he had fired Defense Secretary James Schlesinger. "Lou, if I thought that there was something involved in this that the American people needed to know with regard to their own welfare, then I would be frank with the American people and tell them," Reagan replied. He had no intention of discussing the confusion and acrimony that had led to the frustration of foreign policy and the forced resignation of his vicar. He did not know that the troubles with Haig were a harbinger of greater troubles to come.

---

* Well before the European trip, Deaver and Clark had brought Shultz to the White House to brief Reagan on international economic policy. Reagan thought Shultz's calm, professorial manner a refreshing contrast to Haig's excitability, which was exactly the point that Deaver and Clark wanted to make. The other names on the list of prospective replacements for Haig were Weinberger, Senate Majority Leader Howard Baker and Senator Henry M. Jackson, a Democrat who had once been high on President Nixon's list for the same job. Reagan said simply that he wanted Shultz.

11

THE LONER

A great inner migration has occurred in that man.

GEORGE WILL,
January 31, 1989[1]

The Al Haig affair aroused Reagan from his habitual passivity and engaged him in the conduct of the presidency. He was not easily so aroused. While physically courageous, Reagan was apt to retreat within himself when confronted by situations that demanded emotional engagement. Haig did not recognize it, but he had evoked an unusual response from Reagan, who rarely asked for anyone's resignation, whether it was submitted to him or not. Reagan was an inner-directed man whose experience had taught him the perils of personal confrontation. He brimmed with optimism but did not readily confide in others, except for his mother and his second wife. Reagan had learned hard boyhood lessons of emotional survival and built on this knowledge to gain the secrets of success in the outside world. Though life and Hollywood had cast him as best friend, Reagan remained a loner. He depended upon others for management and stage direction, but kept the managers outside the boundaries of his personal world. Ronald Wilson Reagan believed in God, his luck, his mother, Nancy Reagan and the United States of America. His trust was in himself.

In his autobiography *Where's the Rest of Me?*, Reagan both confronts and romanticizes his nomadic boyhood in small-town Illinois, where he was born in Tampico on February 6, 1911. His father, John Edward (Jack) Reagan, an Irish-American shoe salesman who moved from town to town in Illinois before settling in Dixon, was an alcoholic. When he was eleven years old, Reagan came home to find his father lying on his back on the front porch "drunk, dead to the world."[2] More than a half century later, Reagan could vividly recall recoiling at the sight. Jack Reagan's arms were spread out "as if he were crucified—as indeed he was, his hair soaked with melting snow, snoring as he breathed." No one else was there to help the boy. "I wanted to let myself in the house and go to bed and pretend he wasn't there," said Reagan. Instead, he grabbed his tall, muscular father by the overcoat and wrestled him into the house and to his bed. Years later, when Reagan was in college, his father arrived home "with a severe list to port." Knowing that Jack had taken the car, Reagan went out "and found it right where it had proved too much for him—sitting in the middle of the street with the door open and the motor running."[3]

The stories Reagan told had a purpose. His autobiography, dictated to Richard G. Hubler in 1964 and published the following year when Reagan was preparing to run for governor of California, was his attempt to demonstrate the continuity of a life he believed had prepared him for public service. By the standards of political memoirs, he was unusually frank, so much so that his adversaries thought the book would prove an embarrassment.[4] But Reagan also wanted to demonstrate the moral purpose of his actions. He makes no secret of his abhorrence of Jack Reagan's drinking, but calls the act of dragging his drunken father from the porch "that first moment of accepting responsibility."[5] He would continue to exercise that sense of responsibility throughout his father's life, and he attempts to portray Jack Reagan favorably in the autobiography. Reagan describes a charming but rather weak man who failed to realize the potential of his life because of alcoholism. He remembers his father as "a restless man, burning with ambition to succeed," an effective salesman and "the best raconteur I ever heard, especially when it came to the smoking-car sort of stories"[6] that were not to be told in mixed company. Politically, Jack Reagan was "a sentimental Democrat who believed fervently in the rights of the working-man."[7] He was also a Roman Catholic at a time when anti-Catholic prejudice flourished in America, and a fierce foe of intolerance. As the autobiography tells it, their father refused to allow Ronald and his older brother, Neil, to see the film *The Birth of a Nation* because it glorified the Ku Klux Klan. If true, this must have been a story told within the family, since Ronald Reagan was only four years old when the movie was released. His father also told the boys that he had once slept in his car rather than take lodging in a hotel where the registration clerk had boasted that Jews were not allowed.

Reagan was skilled at softening hard memories with happy stories. His description of his boyhood as "one of those rare Huck Finn–Tom Sawyer idylls"[8] follows a passage describing the near-fatal influenza illness of his beloved mother, Nelle Reagan, and precedes a sentence relating how children sometimes drowned in the swift waters of the canals near Tampico. Reagan's boyhood does not seem to have been that much of an idyll. And while his portrayal of his father is drawn to show much light among the shadows, the recollections of Jack Reagan's drunkenness are infinitely more dramatic and convincing than the collection of anecdotes the son selects to display the father's virtues. In my experience, Reagan never talked about his father unless obligated to do so. When I interviewed him in 1968 and asked him to tell me about his parents, he responded with a longish speech about the sterling qualities of his mother. He said nothing about his father until the question was put to him again. I did not find this surprising, for children of alcoholics have difficulty understanding or accepting the conduct of an alcoholic parent.* Jack Reagan, by Ronald Reagan's account, engaged in "week-long benders."[9] Even Neil (Moon) Reagan, who is far less inclined than his brother to rose-colored recall, finds discussion of his father's drinking bouts uncomfortable. "Sometimes I'd be asked, 'Does your dad drink?' and I'd say, 'Hell, yes.' What else would I say? There were times when he didn't open the screen door, he just walked through it," Neil said.[10]

The consequences of Jack Reagan's drinking dogged the sons long after they left home. It seems to have bothered Ronald more than Neil, who was two years and seven months older and, as Neil put it, had "a rougher finish" than his brother.[11] From Des Moines, where he had achieved professional success as a sports announcer for radio station WHO, Ronald Reagan in the mid-1930s sent a letter to his father trying to trick him into abandoning alcohol. "I told him I had the same problem, and I thought it might help him that he could set an example for me," Reagan told me.[12] It was a well-meant lie. Ronald Reagan has

* My father, Jack Cannon, was also an alcoholic and a second-generation Irish-American.

never had a drinking problem, and he remembers feeling that he had done "something kind of dishonest" in telling this false story to his father.[13]

Reagan's poignant account of this incident is the only time I ever heard him acknowledge a lie. He must have had a desperate feeling about his father's drinking to write such a letter and to remember it so feelingly more than a half century later. As a salesman who believes in his product or as a performer who knows his lines, Reagan is quite willing to depart from the truth for purposes of dramatization. Usually, however, he succeeds as salesman or performer by first convincing himself that whatever he is saying is true. He finds it painful to lie knowingly, and the conscious falsehoods he tells are both rare and significant. Reagan felt uneasy about sending the letter to his father, and he did not follow up on it. Conceivably, this attempt to engage his father in dealing with his drinking by telling him they had a mutual problem was inspired by his mother, who frequently visited Ronald Reagan in Des Moines. In any event, it was unavailing. Jack Reagan continued to drink heavily until the last two weeks of his life.* He did not reply to the letter his son had sent him, and Ronald Reagan never knew if his father had believed him.

Years later, when *Knute Rockne—All-American* premiered at Notre Dame in 1940, Reagan's mother interceded with her son on Jack's behalf. Jack had never seen a Notre Dame team play, he'd never been to South Bend, and "he thought Pat O'Brien was the greatest man since Al Smith."[15] Including his parents on the Warner Bros. railroad junket from Los Angeles to South Bend was a simple thing for Reagan to arrange, but he relates in his autobiography that he "felt a chilling fear that made me hesitate."[16] The fear was justified. Reagan took his parents along, and his father promptly went out drinking with O'Brien. Reagan remained apprehensive throughout the trip, even though he gives the story a typically happy ending. His father and O'Brien became fast friends. Jack Reagan, his son tells us, "had the most wonderful time of his life."[17] Less than a year later, he died of a heart attack at the age of fifty-eight.

It has long been understood that children of alcoholics suffer terrors

* Ronald Reagan told me this story, from an account given him by his mother: Jack and Nelle Reagan were discussing "what everything might have been like" if he had not been an alcoholic. Jack said he wasn't going to drink anymore. Nelle reminded him that he had made such promises in the past. Jack replied, "You've never seen me do this before" and took from hiding "a jug" he had concealed from his wife and poured it down the sink. "And two weeks later he was dead," Reagan said.[14]

and frustrations they find difficult to confront or to describe to others. Popular psychology in the 1980s has expanded this perception by focusing on the continuing impact of this childhood experience in adult life. "Children of alcoholics had to survive essentially alone, because that is the nature of the disease," observes one well-known work on the subject. "It is an isolating, separating and lonely disease." [18] These are comments of Herbert L. Gravitz and Julie D. Bowden in *Recovery: A Guide for Adult Children of Alcoholics.* In another popular book, *Adult Children of Alcoholics,* Janet Geringer Woititz finds that these adults keep feelings to themselves, lie when it would be as easy to tell the truth, frequently seek approval and affirmation, overreact to situations over which they have no control and have difficulty with intimate relationships. They also consider themselves different from other people, which to a degree they actually are. Frequently, they judge themselves harshly. And some of these adults become adept, as Reagan certainly was, at reading emotional storm signals. "They learn to be so sensitive and perceptive to what is happening that they can walk into a room, and without even consciously realizing it, figure out just what the level of tension is, who is fighting with whom, and whether it is safe or dangerous," write Gravitz and Bowden. [19]

This literature offers valuable insights into the behavior of adult children of alcoholics, but its generalizations should be applied with caution to any particular individual, including Ronald Reagan. Most such books are directed at helping adult children of alcoholics who have not, as the psychologists put it, "recovered" from their childhood experiences. Relatively few studies have focused on the experiences of successful children of alcoholics, of whom Reagan is an outstanding example. One exception is a study of "resilient children of alcoholics" by Emmy E. Werner of the Department of Applied Behavioral Sciences at the University of California at Davis. [20] She found that children who overcame the adversity of their upbringing to live successful, well-adjusted lives possess common characteristics, including a temperament that elicits "positive attention from [their] primary caretakers." [21] These resilient children display at least average intelligence and adequate reading and writing skills. They also hold an "achievement orientation," [22] a responsible, caring attitude, a positive self-image, "a more internal locus of control" [23] and a belief in the importance of self-help. These resilient offspring differ from other children of alcoholics in having a mother ("primary caretaker") who lavishes attention on them during infancy, in having no other births in their family during the first two years of life that might divert such attention and in an absence of conflict between the parents during this period. We cannot from this historical distance ascertain the extent of parental conflict in the Reagan household during Ronald's infancy. Neil Reagan's testimony is that Nelle Reagan kept her sons "pretty well protected" from the impact of Jack's drinking, but she also made both boys and certainly her husband highly aware of her abhorrence of alcoholic beverages in any form. The other characteristics listed by Werner provide a recognizable description of Ronald Reagan. He was his mother's pride, and similar to her in temperament. Neil has observed on several occasions that he took after his father and Ronald after his mother. Nelle Reagan had permitted Neil to be baptized in the Roman Catholic faith of his father but enrolled Ronald in her Christian Church (Disciples of Christ). According to both boys, she practiced the preachings of her church by caring for prisoners and the needy. Her moralizing little speeches seemed to have impressed her younger son, who modeled his own first speeches after them. And her teachings also made an imprint. Ronald Reagan became his brother's keeper, cajoling him into quitting work and entering Eureka College and then finding him a job at radio station WOC in Davenport, Iowa, in the midst of the Depression. He also looked after his parents. Many adult children flee from alcoholic parents, never to return, but Ronald Reagan sent for his parents soon after he arrived in California. He tried to understand what had happened to his father. When I interviewed Reagan for this book, he called alcoholism "the Irish curse" and offered both ethnic and medical explanations for the illness that had afflicted Jack Reagan.*

Ronald Reagan is unambiguous about his mother. He credits her for wisdom and courage and especially for imparting to her sons a sympathetic understanding of their father's condition. "My mother told us— my brother and I when we were both just kids and she knew that we would be exposed to this and see it—that we must not turn against our father . . . that this was a sickness he could not help," Reagan told me.[26] It was an enlightened attitude. "It's incredible that in that day and age

---

* Reagan said in one interview with me that "there's a controversy over whether alcoholism is triggered by a sugar shortage in the person's system or whether it's triggered by something psychological." He also said, "Irish[-Americans] are the most prone to alcoholism of any other people, except the Indians. And the Indians, we found, could not handle it."[24] When Reagan has discussed his father's alcoholism in interviews, he has often stressed the "sugar theory" and remarked on his father's fondness for desserts. However, according to an authority on the subject, foods with a high sugar content increase an alcoholic's depression, irritability and tension and intensify his desire for a drink to relieve these symptoms.[25]

she understood that, and that may be a very important factor in his [Ronald Reagan's] ability to function well and not feel that he has to take the blame," says Roberta Meyer, a specialist in the impact of alcoholism on families.[27] But Nelle's equanimity was countered by a hostility to alcoholic beverages that reflected the stern views of the Disciples of Christ. As Garry Wills put it, the Disciples were "the driest of the dries."[28] Carry Nation was a Disciple. Disciples were active in the campaign for the ill-fated Eighteenth [Prohibition] Amendment, which was ratified three weeks before Ronald Reagan's eighth birthday in 1919. Nelle Reagan rejoiced in the new law. Wills has discovered that she wrote a play for the Christian Church in Dixon in which the drunkard's daughter says, "I love you, Daddy, except when you have that old bottle."[29]

Ronald Reagan's young life was centered on his mother. He worked after school at the Christian Church and acted in church skits at his mother's behest. He says his mother was the "dean of dramatic recitals for the countryside" and a "frustrated actress."[30] To his father's amazement, she taught him to read at the age of five by reading books every night to the boys, "following each word with a finger, while we watched over her shoulder."[31] She also imparted her faith in human goodness, perhaps the foundation of the credulity Reagan would display as politician and president. "Nelle never saw anything evil in another human being, and Ronnie is the same way," says Nancy Reagan. "Sometimes it infuriates me, but that's how he is."[32] Maureen Reagan, who adored her grandmother, said of her, "She had the gift of making you believe that you could change the world."[33] One of Nelle Reagan's favorite sayings—it is a central tenet of the Christian faith stressed by the Disciples—was that God has a reason for everything that happens in this world. Reagan accepted this teaching literally. He told Nancy Reagan that meeting her after his divorce from Jane Wyman demonstrated the goodness of God's plan.[34] When he learned, on a 1975 flight to Omaha, that another passenger was making the trip because her father had been stricken by a heart attack, Reagan passed her a note expressing his sorrow at what had happened. "I've always believed in a divine plan and that God has such a plan for each one of us," Reagan wrote. "We find it hard to understand at times, but we must trust in His infinite wisdom and mercy. I'll say a prayer, too."[35] Both the reaching out and the fatalism are characteristic. Whatever happens, says Nancy Reagan, her husband comforts himself with the thought that "if it's to be, it will be."[36]

Nancy Reagan believes that her husband's inwardness is partly a byproduct of his itinerant boyhood. "I think it's a combination of the childhood and never feeling any roots anywhere and never having an old friend for a long, long time, plus the fact that he was affected by the first marriage," she said to me.[37] Given the record of his family's wanderings, it would have been almost impossible for the young Ronald Reagan to form deep boyhood friendships. Jack Reagan was by inclination and experience a salesman, always on the go. His alcoholism, which at times made it hard for him to hold a job, inevitably contributed to his wanderlust. The Reagans moved from Tampico to Chicago when Ronald Reagan was three years old. They moved to Galesburg when he was four, Monmouth when he was seven, back to Tampico when he was eight and to Dixon when he was nine. In Dixon, the Reagans moved five times. Neil Reagan says that the boyhood home that has been restored and opened to the public in Dixon is "the wrong one for Ronald's principal memories of the town."[38] Ronald Reagan may have needed to live within himself because he had had so many temporary homes. Neil Reagan remembers his younger brother as "a sort of quiet boy, not one you would expect would wind up as an actor or a politician, even," who played alone for hours with lead soldiers. "I always sort of ran with gangs," Neil said to me in 1968. "He didn't."[39] In Galesburg, the child Ronald found an "enormous collection of birds' eggs and butterflies" in the attic of the house his family had rented.[40] In Dixon, he wandered along the Rock River, imagining that he lived the life of a trapper. But he withdrew from a scheme of Neil's to sell poultry and rabbits for meat because he had helped raise the rabbits and did not want to kill them.

Reagan read constantly and drew passably. For a time he dreamed of becoming a cartoonist, and the quality of the doodles he drew of cowboys and football players when he was presiding over meetings of his presidential cabinet suggests he might have done well. The doodles are more the product of imagination than of observation: Reagan is severely myopic, and he describes in his autobiography how he "shouted with delight" when he tried on his mother's glasses at the age of nine and "suddenly saw a glorious, sharply defined world jump into focus."[41] As a boy, Reagan fed his imagination with adventure stories and tales of improbable success. A favorite book was a now-forgotten novel called *That Printer of Udell's,* by Harold Bell Wright, in which the hero works by day as a printer, attends night school and marries a beautiful socialite, whom he saves from a life of prostitution. Reagan also loved the

improbable novels of Edgar Rice Burroughs, preferring the more obscure science-fiction exploits of a Martian warlord named John Carter
to the popular Tarzan books. He has read science fiction throughout
his life and is a fan of science-fiction films. Patti Davis describes her
father as fascinated with stories about unidentified flying objects and
the possibility of life on other worlds.[42] The second sentence of her
autobiographical novel *Home Front* compares the "madness" of a presidential inauguration day to "a fifties movie in which flying saucers
descend on the metropolis." Perhaps she, too, had been subjected to
The Day the Earth Stood Still. As we have seen, Reagan's fascination
with such possibilities emerged in conversation with Mikhail Gorbachev when he suggested that the United States and the Soviet Union
would band together if threatened with an interplanetary invasion. Reagan's thoughts turn readily to outer space. His proposal to build an
impenetrable "space shield" that would defend Americans from nuclear
missiles has tangled roots that will be examined more fully in Chapter
13, but the idea arose in Reagan's imagination. Reagan is also an avid
supporter of manned spaceflight. When David Stockman sought on
fiscal grounds to limit NASA to unmanned space probes, Reagan was
resistant, saying that the public's imagination had been captured by the
manned space program.[43] Reagan understood this because spaceflight
appealed to his own imagination. He had been reading about imagined
worlds long before President John F. Kennedy launched the program
that put men in space and on the moon. And he may have found it easy
to conceive of life on other worlds because he lived in an imaginative
world of his own.

We know now that Ronald Reagan clung hard to his boyhood dreams
of glory, including the seemingly unattainable ambition of becoming an
actor. His brother and his boyhood contemporaries did not know that.
They thought of him as something of a "momma's boy," and Neil has
said that his brother hung out with "sissies" rather than with his crowd
at the pool hall.[44] Ronald Reagan's early infatuation with football may
have been in part an attempt to win the approval of his brother's
rougher crowd. Boys in those days were supposed to excel in team
games, and Ronald Reagan's extreme nearsightedness disqualified him
from baseball as it would in adult life from military combat. He was
short and slight of build when he entered Dixon's Northside High
School in 1924 at the age of thirteen and a year behind his classmates
in physical maturity because he had skipped a grade during one of the
family's many moves. He wore thick, horn-rimmed glasses that he de-

tested. But on the lightweight football team, limited to boys weighing less than 135 pounds, he displayed pluck and persistence that overcame his lack of skill and size. He was made captain of the lightweight team and promoted to the varsity in his junior year. In his senior year Reagan gained thirty pounds and shot up to a height of nearly six feet. At 165 pounds, he was both the best and the lightest tackle on the 1928 Dixon High team, which lost seven games and won only two. He played in the shadow of his older brother, who had graduated two years earlier after starring on an undefeated Dixon team.

In his autobiography Reagan ranks football with dramatics and politics as a ruling passion in his life. "The rough reality of disorganized play had gradually invaded my dream world," [45] he says of the pickup games of his boyhood, leaving him with bruises and a feeling of happiness. Long after he dictated these words, Reagan celebrated football as a healthy alternative to warfare that satisfies a human need for combat and permits "a kind of clean hatred." [46] But despite football's role as a rite of passage to manhood and his first career as sports announcer, the game held no enduring interest for Reagan. He far preferred the more solitary sports of swimming, golf and horseback riding, and he only occasionally attended football games after moving to California. He even gave up reading the sports pages. In Sacramento he told me that instead of watching football on television he preferred old movies or such spy thrillers as *Mission Impossible.*

Reagan had no need to demonstrate manliness through a pretended interest in organized sports. Unlike the physically awkward Richard Nixon, who barely made his high school football team, President Reagan never telephoned a professional football coach to describe a favorite play or timed his travel schedule so that he could watch the Washington Redskins on television. Even his boyhood years are defined more sharply by his starring role as the sole lifeguard at Lowell Park than by his supportive one as a lineman on the Dixon High and Eureka College football teams. Lowell Park is on a dangerous section of the Rock River three miles north of Dixon. In six summers as a lifeguard there from 1927 through 1932, Reagan rescued seventy-seven people from drowning. The *Dixon Daily Telegraph* reported in a page-one story on August 3, 1928, that seventeen-year-old Ronald Reagan had pulled a drowning man to safety in the darkness after another rescue attempt had failed. Garry Wills has documented both the rough accuracy of the rescue count and the arduous routine of Ronald Reagan's workdays in these summers, which he began each morning by picking up a 300-

pound block of ice at the icehouse and breaking it into three 100-pound blocks. Sometimes, on hot days, he would double or triple the ice order. Wills found that Reagan worked at least twelve hours a day, seven days a week. Reagan accepted these hours cheerfully.[47]

He was modest about his rescue efforts and devoted only four paragraphs of his autobiography to his youthful career as a lifeguard. But he liked being a lifeguard, a job perfectly suited to his personality. Lifeguards are solitary objects of adoration who intervene in moments of crisis and perform heroic acts without becoming involved in the lives of those they rescue. Reagan was a handsome youth, and one of the most enduring pictures of him shows him as a twenty-year-old at Lowell Park, with the words LIFE GUARD emblazoned across the chest of his tank-top suit. After Reagan became famous a legend arose that he had come to the rescue of pretty girls who were in no danger of drowning. Reagan says this is a myth. He told me in 1981, "I never got my suit wet unless there was a need for it."[48] I believed him, but had a feeling that he rather liked the legend. His only complaint about his lifeguard service, recorded in his autobiography and repeated many times to me and other biographers, was that people rarely thanked him or rewarded him when he saved their lives.

Money was much on Reagan's mind in his latter years as a lifeguard, for his family was poor, the Depression was at hand and he was saving the dollars he earned at Lowell Park for his college education. When his parents moved to an apartment near Southside High School, Reagan remained at Northside, which today might be described as an upscale school. Neil attended Southside, where the boys congregated at the pool hall after school and more often than not found work in town after graduation, often at the Borden condensed-milk plant or the Grand Detour Plow Company. Northsiders gathered at an ice cream parlor and talked of going to college. Ronald Reagan was student body president of Northside in his senior year. His plan, which he carried out, was to attend Eureka College with his high school sweetheart Margaret Cleaver, the daughter of a Disciples of Christ minister. In these years Reagan often sought career advice from older men who were more successful than his father. One of these was Margaret's father, Ben Cleaver. Another was a Kansas City businessman named Sid Altschuler, whose daughters Reagan had taught to swim at Lowell Park. Altschuler offered to help give Reagan a start. Reagan, always reluctant to confide his dreams, could not bring himself to tell Altschuler that he wanted to be an actor, because this seemed too improbable an ambition. Instead, he asked him about getting into radio. Altschuler had no broadcasting connections, but he advised Reagan to take any job at any radio station, no matter how insignificant, just to get a start.[49] Reagan valued that advice. He had been taught by his mother that hard work would be rewarded, and he believed in himself. His great expectations were expressed in the caption beneath his senior picture in the Dixon High School yearbook: "Life is just one grand, sweet song, so start the music." The caption was written by Reagan and expressed his sentiments, even though his early life had been neither grand nor sweet. He had no known close male friends, but he was a happy person who knew how to make a good impression. He had learned much from the moralistic exhortations of his mother, and much from his role as a lifeguard at Lowell Park. "Lifeguarding provides one of the best vantage points in the world to learn about people," Reagan wrote in his autobiography.[50] He was the lifeguard, the lonely figure on the beach who worked hard, watched others and responded in time of crisis. He had no cause to doubt what he could do.

Retrospectively, it is easy to underrate Reagan's role in his achievements by saying that he was in the right places at the right times, or that he was blessed with good luck. As keen an observer as Stuart Spencer believes that "the Reagan luck" was a vital ingredient of his success. Others have depicted Reagan as the agent of impersonal ideological or social forces, especially the tidal wave of social conservatism that swept over suburbia in the sixties in reaction to protests for civil rights and against the Vietnam War. Some still consider Reagan a tool of his millionaire kitchen cabinet, which he has mostly outlived, or of the conservative movement. Some have attributed his success to Nancy Reagan, who was blamed by liberals in the sixties for Reagan's conversion to conservatism and by conservatives in the eighties for his conversion to détente. What all the theories share in common is a tremendous underestimation of Ronald Reagan. His genial demeanor and genuine modesty shielded a hard, self-protective core that contained both a gyroscope for maintaining balance and a compass pointing toward success.

Most of those who dealt with Reagan in public life saw the soft surface instead of the hard core, and underrated him. Before he became a "Teflon president" who seemed unaccountable for failure, he was an underestimated president who was given no credit for success. I argue elsewhere in this book that the "Teflon" view that nothing stuck to Reagan does not withstand close scrutiny.* Reagan was not immune to

---

* The phrase is the coinage of Congresswoman Patricia Schroeder, a Democrat from Colorado.

the laws of political gravity. His ratings would fall when times were bad or when he was out of touch with the public mood, as they do for other presidents. But there is a small kernel of truth in the rather large grain of Teflon theory. The truth is that the American people understood that he was "one of them," as Reagan said on the eve of the 1980 election, and extended to him the forgiveness they expected for themselves. Reagan had climbed the ladder of success from the lower rungs, demonstrating a combination of persistence and humility rare among either politicians or actors. While skeptics might say that Reagan was a modest man with much to be modest about, he understood the democratic calculus. Reagan knew, and there was an element of calculation in his knowledge, that the public appreciates humility in its political servants. Anticipating in his autobiography the self-deprecating jokes he would one day tell about his presidential work habits, Reagan quotes a construction foreman on a summer job as telling his father, "This kid of yours can get less dirt on a shovel than any human being that's human."[51] He says nothing at all about the long hours he put in at Lowell Park.

What distinguished Reagan in his long climb to the presidency was perseverance toward his goals. For all his amiability, he could be highly manipulative in pursuing these goals, a trait often found among adult children of alcoholics. When Reagan wanted to ride horses in Des Moines, he talked his way into the 14th Cavalry Regiment and faked an eye test to win a reserve Army commission. When he decided to get into the movies, he arranged a screen test in Hollywood through a girlfriend and took the test on a trip paid for by radio station WHO when he was supposedly covering the spring training of the Chicago Cubs baseball team. When he subsequently met with agent Bill Meiklejohn, Reagan said, "I decided a little lying in a good cause wouldn't hurt, so the Eureka Dramatic Club became a professional stock company."[52] This set the pattern for his climb through Hollywood. By the end of his film career the ambitious Reagan was working as a client and employee of Music Corporation of America and as a producer on *General Electric Theater* at the same time he was negotiating on labor's behalf with MCA as president of the Screen Actors Guild. Reagan saw no conflict in this arrangement, though others did. He also saw no conflict in giving MCA, represented by his former agent Lew Wasserman, a blanket and secret waiver that violated the long-standing practice of allowing actors to retain agents who were also movie producers —in effect serving as spokesmen for both sides. An intricate Justice

Department investigation of this deal provided an early forum for the forgetfulness that Reagan would later display as president. Though dark hints were made about the nature of Reagan's relationship with MCA, nothing was ever proven against him. Wills concluded simply that Reagan "was always prepared to think the best of his own bosses."[53] He displayed an attitude conducive to success.

"Mr. Norm is my alias," Reagan wrote in a *Photoplay* article in 1942, describing his supposed averageness to his fans in an article that appeared after he had been called into military service as a reservist. "Mr. Ambitious" might have been a better description. Although Reagan steadfastly insists to this day that he entered politics reluctantly, those who were present at this particular creation remember it differently. For Stu Spencer, a vital sign of Reagan's ambition was his ready acceptance of airplane travel as a candidate despite a long and deep-seated fear of flying.[54]* Another sign was Reagan's willingness to play the party unifier. Reagan realized after the Goldwater debacle of 1964 that conservative and moderate Republicans needed to be reconciled if he were to have a chance of becoming governor of California in 1966. Subsequently, as we have seen, Reagan stoutly defended Richard Nixon even in the eye of the Watergate storm. But once Gerald Ford had replaced Nixon, Reagan bad-mouthed the new president at every opportunity. Party loyalty counted little to Reagan when it stood in the path of presidential ambition, as Ford failed to realize when he was deluding himself in 1975 that he could dissuade Reagan from seeking the Republican presidential nomination. "I never knew what he was really thinking behind that winning smile," Ford wrote later.[55] Those who knew Reagan understood that he was thinking about becoming president, even if it meant elbowing Ford aside.

Reagan almost did it. He came so close to winning that he established himself as the Republican nominee-in-waiting after Ford lost narrowly to Jimmy Carter in the 1976 election. What is now largely forgotten is that Ford, armed with Spencer's insights into Reagan's vulnerabilities, nearly succeeded in driving Reagan from the race early and in all probability ending his political career.[56] Ford put Reagan on the defensive in the opening New Hampshire primary and won a narrow victory. The

* Reagan's fear of flying can be traced to a choppy flight to Catalina in 1937. This was the same trip west on which Reagan took his screen test. He returned to Des Moines by train and did not fly again for nearly thirty years. At Reagan's insistence, his contract with General Electric stipulated that he would travel by train. In 1968, two years into his governorship, Reagan acknowledged to me during a campaign flight to the South that he still disliked flying but realized he had no alternative.

New Hampshire result snowballed, as it often does. Approaching the North Carolina primary on March 23, 1976, Reagan had lost five straight primaries. His campaign was virtually broke, and his principal aides were engaged in backdoor negotiations for Reagan's withdrawal. Reagan, however, was not ready to withdraw. He brushed aside public opinion polls that saw him as a slipping candidate, threw away his cue cards and rallied conservatives to his banner with a furious attack on the Panama Canal treaties and Secretary of State Henry Kissinger's policy of détente. Paul Laxalt, sticking with Reagan in what then appeared to be his end game, thought it was Reagan's finest hour. "He told me to get rid of the damn [cue] cards, and he was beautiful for a full week there," Laxalt recalls. "He was a spontaneous candidate, and it's the only time I've ever seen Ronald Reagan spontaneous."[57] But most of the national journalists assigned to the campaign overlooked the signals of spontaneity. They suspected they were watching the final act in the Reagan political drama and peppered him with questions about when he would withdraw. I was one of those correspondents. Reagan became angry about our coverage, and then defiant. When I asked him in a campaign plane interview when he was going to get out of the race, his jaw tightened and he said, "You, too, Lou?" Then he looked directly at me and said firmly, "I'm *not* going to quit."

Reagan's stubbornness and determination emerged in such crucial moments, providing a glimpse of the steel beneath the placid exterior. Usually, however, the ambition was concealed by Reagan's amiable disposition. Bursts of anger were uncommon, and they rarely lasted long. His younger son, Ron, said his father became "really mad" at him only once or twice and added, "I don't think I've ever seen him yell."[58] Reagan's peers in Dixon and Des Moines did not know him well, but they considered him a cheerful sort and easy to be around. He was also resourceful. Reagan arrived at Eureka College in the autumn of 1928, bringing with him a steamer trunk and $400 accumulated from his Lowell Park savings. He had been accepted in advance as a pledge by the Tau Kappa Epsilon ("Teke") fraternity, and quickly negotiated an athletic scholarship which paid half of his $180-a-year tuition and board. It was the maximum scholarship allowed by the underendowed Disciples of Christ college, which Reagan has described as "perpetually broke." He earned the rest of his room charges first by washing dishes at the fraternity and then by doing the same chores at the girls' dormitory, which Reagan called "the best job I ever had."

Reagan formed a love-at-first-sight relationship with Eureka that has never ended. He returned to the college frequently after graduation, served on its board of trustees and spoke at the dedication of the library and of the physical education center named for himself and his brother. I have never seen Reagan more joyous than he was on the night of October 17, 1980, when he returned to Eureka in the midst of the presidential campaign for a pep rally that had little to do with politics. Reagan's memories of Eureka are of football, girls and dramatics, and he relived them all at a celebration where he lit the bonfire outside the gym and joined with the students in a full-throated chorus of the school song. "Everything good that has happened to me—everything—started here on this campus," Reagan said.[59] As often happened on such sentimental occasions, there were tears in his eyes.

The past was always present for Ronald Reagan, who took the fragments of his life that mattered most to him and fashioned them into powerful stories of personal experience. Paul Laxalt thought Reagan's memory was "frighteningly" retentive. "You can tell him something just idly, tell him a joke, and he'll store it. It's like sticking it on a chip. And God only knows when it will surface."[60] When Reagan told real or imagined stories of the past, they possessed a visual immediacy we now associate with instant replays. When he auditioned for his first radio job at the age of twenty-one, he described play by play from memory the fourth quarter of a football game that Eureka had lost. Typically, however, Reagan gave the game a happy ending, and Eureka won a victory in the auditioning studio that it had been unable to achieve on the football field. Reagan was hired by station WOC in Davenport as a part-time sports announcer of University of Iowa football games. Within four months WOC had been incorporated into WHO in Des Moines and sports announcer "Dutch Reagan"[61] was a regional celebrity well launched on the path of greater goals.

Des Moines was a valuable way stop for Reagan. He capitalized on his young fame by launching his speaking career, lecturing on the virtues of temperance and clean living to youth groups and civic associations. The Prohibition amendment was repealed on December 5, 1933, a little more than six months after Reagan arrived in Des Moines. Reagan and his friends—many of them fellow Tekes from nearby Drake College—frequented Cy's Moonlight Inn in the west end of town where the near beer in Prohibition days was sometimes spiked with alcohol. His acquaintances of this period remember Reagan as being more interested in the girls than the spiked beer, but he was not an abstainer. This suggests that Reagan, in his balanced way, had come to terms with his father's alcoholism even if he could not dissuade Jack from drinking. Some adult children of alcoholics become alcoholics themselves, while others react to the experience by never allowing liquor into their lives. Reagan followed a middle course. He would occasionally sip wine or beer or a "screwdriver" made of vodka and orange juice, which he had been told was good for his kidneys.[62] But he did not drink much, and he became accomplished at conveying the impression that he was imbibing heartily when he was hardly drinking at all. At a Florida fundraising reception in the heady days after his New Hampshire primary victory in 1980, Reagan joined in several celebratory champagne toasts. A Republican acquaintance commented that Reagan was having a good time. He was, but he didn't need the assistance of champagne. As we left, I glanced at his glass and saw that it was more than half full.

Reagan remained a lifeguard in Des Moines even when he was no longer paid to rescue people. While swimming at Camp Dodge, he saved a girl from drowning. And he also learned to rescue people with his wits. One Sunday evening in the early autumn of 1933, a few months after Reagan arrived in Des Moines, a nursing student at Broadlawns General Hospital named Melba Lohmann returned from her home in Sheffield, Iowa, by bus. She decided to walk to the hospital. When she was half a block away, a man thrust an object into her back and demanded her purse and suitcase. She offered him the purse, which contained only three dollars. But the man grabbed both her purse and suitcase. Then she heard a voice coming from the window of a second-floor apartment above her. "Leave her alone, or I'll shoot you right between the shoulders," said Ronald Reagan.[63] The would-be robber dropped the purse and suitcase and fled. Reagan came downstairs in robe and pajamas and walked Lohmann to the hospital, where she told the story to her supervisors. Reagan apparently saw nothing unusual in his feat. He did not brag about what he had done or stay in touch with Lohmann. But in an interview in the February 1984 issue of the pro-gun magazine *Sports Afield,* Reagan said it was lucky that he had a gun in his possession that night. His campaign staff found Melba Lohmann, now Melba King, and brought her together with the president when he made a trip to Iowa. Reagan, meeting her for the first time since the incident, told her that the gun he pointed at the robber "was empty; I didn't have any cartridges."[64] Wills has questioned whether he even had a gun. Bill Boyarsky, who related the incident in his 1967 book on Reagan, said Reagan had three guns, none loaded.[65] Whether he had no guns or one or three, Reagan was well armed with imagination, bravery and a willingness to become involved in a situation where his own life could have been at risk. He was not passive in such moments.

The imagination was especially significant. Even before he became an actor, Reagan blurred the distinction between reality and imagination when it suited his convenience. His specialty at WHO was "re-creation" of Chicago Cubs baseball games, which actually meant describing them from a play-by-play account he received by telegraph while the game was in progress. Since the telegraphic report told only whether the batter had made a hit or an out, the announcer was required to invent all the details and color of a game he could not see. Reagan's most oft-told story of his radio days is of the time the telegraph broke down and he kept the broadcast going by having the batter repeatedly foul off pitches until the telegraph was repaired. Reagan was proud of his skill at "re-creation." It must have been easy for him to make the small but crucial slide into inventing stories of his own life and telling them as if they were real. Perhaps he had already learned to do this in childhood. One of the imaginary stories he liked to tell emphasized the virtues of truth-telling. Harking back to his days on the Dixon High School football team, Reagan would say, "I'll never forget one game with Mendota," and then tell a story about acknowledging an infraction of the rules that the referee had not detected. The penalty cost Dixon the game. Reagan would never forget this game because he had invented it. By the time I first heard the story in the late sixties, the hero was anonymous and the game was no longer set in Dixon. The player who called a penalty on himself had become a player who admitted dropping a forward pass that the referee had called a touchdown. The story should have been suspicious on its face, but I did not realize what Reagan had done until on one trip he lapsed into the old Mendota version of the tale and made himself the hero. The story was a fake in all its versions, although Reagan had probably long ago convinced himself of its verity.[66]

But the public expected such make-believe from Reagan and rarely reacted harshly to him when it was exposed. Perhaps people recognized that he was genuinely modest and capable of real-life heroism. As a human being, Reagan was certainly no fake. But in his performances, he consistently demonstrated a willingness to substitute dramatic fiction for prosaic fact when it served a moralizing purpose or enabled him to rationalize a policy. This permitted him to ignore his speechwriter and bury Martin Treptow in Arlington National Cemetery instead of in Wisconsin where he knew the remains of the real-life Treptow were interred. It enabled the imaginary pilot of the B-17 to ride his plane down to death and glory with his wounded gunner. And it encouraged Reagan, as we shall see, to accept a false but dramatically satisfying account of how the U.S. armed forces were racially integrated and to offer a mythic explanation of U.S. involvement in Lebanon.

Reagan was twenty-six years old when he left Des Moines in 1937. He was a popular local celebrity and already an accomplished public speaker. He had money in his pocket and hope in his heart. In 1936 he had bought his first new car, a Nash convertible that he had admired in the company showroom in Des Moines. "The young women thought he looked handsome in it—beige car, brown hair, brown tweed, brown pipe," wrote Myron S. Waldman.[67] Reagan drove the car to Hollywood. He also brought with him to California a midwesternness of speech and outlook—even a preference for plain food—that time would not erode. And he did not feel himself a stranger in Southern California, which was then something of a midwestern outpost. A former Iowan, Frank Merriam, was governor of the state. A novel of the period, Darwin Teilhet's *Journey to the West,* called its Southern California section "The Iowa Coast." Carey McWilliams tells us that there were so many Iowa immigrants in the state that a popular joke was that California should be renamed "Caliowa."[68] State societies flourished, binding together newcomers in nostalgic celebrations at mammoth annual picnics. The state societies of Iowa and Illinois were especially prominent. Illinois was the largest source of immigrants to California for the three decades from 1910 to 1940. It must sometimes have seemed to Reagan that the world he had known in Dixon and Des Moines had moved with him to California.

And, in a sense, he brought his own world with him. He sent for his parents in September 1937, three months after he moved to California and well before the renewal of the six-month stock contract he had been given at Warner's. His brother soon followed. So did three of his "Teke" friends from Des Moines, who had decided one night at Cy's Moonlight Inn that they also wanted to partake of the good life of Southern California. Reagan kept in touch with his fans back in Des Moines by writing his impressions of filmmaking in a series for the *Des Moines Sunday Register* that began on June 13, 1937, and continued through October 28, after his first film had been released. In this movie, *Love Is on the Air,* Reagan played the part of a small-town radio announcer who uncovers corruption. The announcer is wide-eyed, cheerful and moralistic, which is simply to say that Reagan was cast as himself. From beginning to end, it was his most effective role.

Reagan was surrounded in Hollywood by people who knew him or knew of him from the Midwest. One of his principal boosters was gossip columnist Louella Parsons, who also hailed from Dixon. Parsons and her chief rival, Hedda Hopper, were powerful forces in the movie industry whose words of praise could signal the presence of a rising star. Reagan was a Parsons protégé. So was Jane Wyman, then a pert blonde who was trying to escape typecasting in chorus-girl roles. Reagan and Wyman met during the filming of his ninth movie, *Brother Rat,* in 1938. Parsons took both of them along on a nine-week "stars of tomorrow" vaudeville tour in 1939, where the Reagan-Wyman romance blossomed, with Wyman taking the lead. Parsons announced their engagement in her column. She also gave the wedding reception after Reagan and Wyman were married on January 26, 1940. The young couple moved into a Beverly Hills apartment where Wyman had lived before the marriage. A daughter, Maureen Elizabeth, was born on January 4, 1941, Wyman's twenty-seventh birthday.

Even though it was Wyman's second marriage (she had briefly been married to apparel manufacturer Myron Futterman), the Reagan family was made to order for the Hollywood publicity mills. Hollywood had been promoting wholesomeness ever since a series of morals scandals rocked what was then called the "movie colony" after World War I. A production code and a censor's office relentlessly policed the themes, messages and morals of every movie. A morals clause was a standard part of an actor's contract. Leading ladies (and sometimes leading men) were, in Wills' phrase, more often "chastity symbols"[69] than sex symbols. Studios and fan magazines proclaimed Hollywood's propriety, offscreen and on. This seemed perfectly natural to Reagan, the moralizer from Dixon and Des Moines. Hollywood wholesomeness would become a favorite topic for him in the defensive years after his divorce, a theme he buttressed with such Reaganesque statistics as the high rate of church attendance in Hollywood.

There was much to support Reagan's view of Hollywood, where films in those days reflected the traditional American middle-class family values that Reagan embodied and proclaimed. On-screen, Reagan was a pleasant second man. Offscreen, he spent his time in athletic outings with friends and family. "He wasn't a night club kid," said Robert Taylor. "When I first met him, he was vitally interested in athletics and keeping himself in great condition."[70] Reagan was also a company man who after his marriage to Wyman submitted without a murmur of protest to the exploitation of his private life required by the promotion of Hollywood wholesomeness. The headline of a release from the Warner Bros. publicity department on June 2, 1941, catches the tone: "THE HOPEFUL REAGANS. They Are Looking Forward to More of Everything Good—Including Children." The release quotes Reagan as saying, "The Reagans' home life is probably just like yours, or yours, or yours. We do the same foolish things that other couples do, have the same scraps, about as much fun, typical problems and the most wonderful baby in the world."

Despite this cozy promotional portrait, Reagan remained a loner. Screenwriter Edward Anhalt remembers that Reagan "didn't have close friends" in their days together during World War II in the First Motion Picture Unit of the Army Air Corps at Culver City. "The group in the Motion Picture Unit were jocks or intellectuals," Anhalt recalls. "He had no sympathy from the intellectuals. The jocks didn't like him because he wasn't vulgar. He didn't drink or chase girls. His main quality was his optimism. You get a feeling that everything is going to be all right from him." [71] It was a portrait that could accurately have been drawn of Reagan in Dixon or Eureka or Des Moines. And it was his ability to project the feeling that "everything is going to be all right" that would be his most distinctive quality as president.

In his early days, Reagan's extraordinary optimism had enabled him to cope with the dark spells caused by Jack Reagan's drinking. Later, it permitted him to forge ahead relentlessly, changing courses, careers and ideology in his climb to the presidency. But there was another side to the coin. Reagan counted so much on his attitude to see him through that he was apt to be stopped in his tracks when confronted with an emotional hurdle that optimism could not scale. When this happened, Reagan denied reality and withdrew inside himself, leaving the decisions of his life to others until he could construct a rationalization that enabled him to function. This is what happened when Ronald Reagan was told by Jane Wyman that their marriage was over, when Governor Reagan was informed that one of his most trusted aides was head of a "homosexual ring" and when President Reagan lost public credibility after disclosure of the arms-for-hostages deal with Iran. Reagan's course in every one of these circumstances was denial. As governor, he let the trusted aide resign on a pretext and lied to the press about what he had done. [72] As president, he persuaded himself in defiance of all the facts and his own diary entries that he had never traded arms for hostages.

Other presidents have also rationalized to cover their misjudgments —it can be argued that Franklin Roosevelt denied the nature of Stalinism, that Lyndon Johnson denied the realities of Vietnam, that Richard

Nixon denied the extent of his complicity in Watergate. But Reagan's capacity for self-denial in personal matters was extraordinary. He had been raised to believe that marriage, even a difficult marriage like that of his parents, lasts forever. When Wyman told him that their marriage was over, Reagan moved out but denied the reality of what had happened. Thirty years later, he was still evading it. In an interview after the 1980 election, Reagan was asked if he had changed the image of the presidency by becoming the first divorced man to hold the office. "No," he replied. "Adlai Stevenson had been divorced, and I don't think that is why he wasn't elected. I've never talked about this, but it's true: I *was* divorced in the sense that the decision was made by someone else." [73]

Reagan was thirty-seven years old when he and Wyman separated early in 1948. Maureen was seven years old and her brother, Michael Edward, adopted by Reagan and Wyman soon after his birth in March 1945, was only three. What little has been disclosed about the reasons for the breakup, beyond Wyman's courtroom explanation that "there was nothing in common between us, nothing to sustain our marriage," has been provided by Reagan, usually filtered second-hand through the children or Nancy Reagan. We do know that the year preceding the separation had been exceptionally trying both for Reagan and Wyman. On June 26, 1947, she gave birth to a baby girl who was four months premature and died the following day. Reagan was not present when this happened. He was fighting for his life at Cedars of Lebanon Hospital with viral pneumonia, from which he was four months recovering. And his film career was nearly as shaky as his health. He had not fulfilled the promise that Warner Bros. had seen in him and that he had glimpsed in himself when the 1942 film *Kings Row* was released after he had been called into the Army. The contract negotiated by his agent Lew Wasserman on the basis of *Kings Row* had made him wealthy, but Reagan was battling Warner's for hefty dramatic roles that the studio believed were over his head. Reagan competently played the lead in two 1947 films—*That Hagen Girl* and *The Voice of the Turtle*. He would make seventeen more movies from 1949 through 1955, a transition period in which he remarried and formed the association with General Electric that proved the path to his political career. But there were no Reagan films in 1948, the year Wyman won an Academy Award for her role as a deaf mute in *Johnny Belinda*. Long freed from the worry of being left in the chorus line, Wyman had by now surpassed Reagan in their mutual craft and was growing as an actress. She attended the

Academy Award ceremony where she received her Oscar in the company of Lew Ayres, who played her sympathetic doctor in the film. Reagan went alone.

As always, Reagan tried to face adversity with a quip. He told columnist Hedda Hopper, "I think I'll name *Johnny Belinda* as the co-respondent."[74] But Reagan was actually despondent. He had been surprised by the breakup and was unprepared for it. According to Nancy Reagan, in an account undoubtedly based on what Reagan told her, he had arrived home one afternoon and was told to "get out" by Wyman.[75] "That's pretty hard to take, particularly if you're the kind of person Ronnie is," Nancy Reagan said. "Ronnie is not a sophisticated fellow. It was very hard."[76] Nancy, of course, did not know Reagan then, but her retrospective view is sustained by contemporary recollections. Actress Patricia Neal said that Reagan "cried" at a party soon after the separation was announced, "and it was sad because he didn't want a divorce."[77] A close friend of the Reagan-Wyman family told me that after the divorce Reagan was "despondent in a way I have never seen, because he usually was such a happy, optimistic man." Reagan told me he was "miserable"[78] at the time, and he became uncharacteristically contentious. He went public with his demands for better roles from Jack Warner. In one particularly bitter interview in 1950, he even threatened to quit the movie business and go back to being a sports announcer.[79]

According to his own recollections, Reagan recovered his customary equilibrium in 1951 after he began seeing Nancy Davis, whom he married on March 4, 1952.* But he would remain forever guarded about his first marriage, bearing scars that recalled the wound. "You can get just so far to Ronnie, and then something happens," said Nancy Reagan in 1989.[80] "It took him a long time, I think, to feel that he could really trust me."[81] He would never completely share that trust with his children of either marriage. Ron Reagan, the younger child of the Reagan-Davis marriage, said in 1986 that he enjoyed a "friendly and loving" relationship with his father, but added that "you almost get the sense that he gets a little bit antsy if you try and get too close and too personal and too father-and-sonny." His speculation was that Ronald Reagan behaved the way he did because "he didn't really have a role model himself for a father. So what fathering he did, he had to come by on his own."[82]

---

* Their daughter, Patricia Ann Reagan, was born seven and one-half months later on October 22, 1952. She uses the name "Patti Davis" professionally. Ronald Prescott (Ron) Reagan was born on May 28, 1958.

Reagan's children are unanimous in testifying to their father's difficulty in dealing with closeness. Maureen Reagan, who was seven when the Reagan-Wyman marriage dissolved, wrote despairingly in her memoir about the inability of either of her parents to "go below the surface" and explain what had happened.[83] Michael Reagan, in a candid and courageous book called *Michael Reagan: On the Outside Looking In,* says his father was often "completely oblivious" to others. When Reagan attended Michael's high school graduation from an Arizona boarding school, he literally did not recognize him in his cap and gown and said, "My name is Ronald Reagan. What's yours?"[84] Patti Davis said to me about her father, "I never knew who he was, I could never get through to him."[85] Ron Reagan said, "I know him as well as anybody, outside my mother. But still, you know, there is something that he holds back. You get just so far, and then the curtain drops, and you don't go any farther."[86]

Despite Reagan's remoteness, his children have attested to their love for him and prized the rare times they were alone with their father. All of the children except Patti have repeatedly demonstrated their loyalty by campaigning for him. Michael Reagan said he was "the only adult male I ever trusted."[87] The children felt that their father cared for them, but he was not a person in whom they could confide. Maureen Reagan endured a physically abusive and terrifying first marriage to a policeman without ever telling her father about it.[88] She did not tell her father that she was being beaten and harassed, even though she was carrying on a lively correspondence with him at the time about his political ambitions.* Michael Reagan was burdened by the even more oppressive trauma of a boyhood molestation by a camp counselor. He was unable to tell his parents until 1987, when he confided it to a sympathetic Nancy Reagan while his father "gazed into the distance."[90] Patti Davis was unable to tell her father much of anything—and unable to listen to anything he told her. As an adult, she met a man who had been a childhood friend and was struck when he said to her that "he never knew where her father came from." The friend meant this in a physical sense, saying that Ronald Reagan would suddenly materialize as a presence among the children, who never knew whether he had walked in from outside or from a room within the house. "It was like he came in

---

* In 1962, while working as a secretary in Washington, Maureen Reagan wrote a letter to her father expressing concern over the liberal direction of the country and encouraging him to run for governor of California. He wrote her back, saying, "Well, if we're talking about what I could do, Mermie, I could be president."[89] As far as I have been able to determine, this is the first expression from Reagan, even in jest, of presidential ambition. "Mermie" or "Merm" was Maureen's family nickname.

smoke and disappeared in smoke," she said.[91] Years later in the White House, speechwriter Peggy Noonan would observe, "I never remember hearing his footsteps."[92]

Nancy Reagan, far more emotionally open than her husband, has never fully solved the riddle of what she described to me as "the strange mixture with Ronnie."[93] In her book, *My Turn,* she said of him: "Although he loves people, he often seems remote, and he doesn't let anybody get too close. There's a wall around him. He lets me come closer than anyone else, but there are times when even I feel that barrier."[94] This is a remarkable statement, for no one else is likely to surmount the wall. The popular impression is that the Reagans are so close that they drive everyone else out, even the children. That may be unfair to Nancy Reagan. Her presence gives others an excuse for not being able to get beyond a barrier that was built long before she came into his life. She did not build it, and she cannot take it down.

If she cannot always get beyond the barrier, Nancy Reagan understands better than anyone else the elements of its construction. She realizes that the emotional wall Ronald Reagan built around him was shaped by his reaction to his father's alcoholism, by the hurt and isolation he felt after the collapse of his first marriage and by the wanderings of the Reagan family through small-town Illinois where the young Ronald learned the art of living without friends. Nancy Reagan gives more weight to the nomadic nature of her husband's early existence than others do. Perhaps she understands its importance because of her own childhood dislocation after she was abandoned by her natural father. Whatever the source of her understanding, she senses a rootlessness in Ronald Reagan that is oddly at variance with his sense of continuity and place. It may be that in this respect Reagan resembles his father, who was a wanderer, more than he does his mother. For even when he is at rest, Reagan projects what Landon Parvin calls a "sense of movement."[95]

There is a solitary quality about this movement, even when Reagan is surrounded by adoring crowds and others who have come along for the ride. "I think Hollywood essentially makes those people loners," said Paul Laxalt, the politician who knew Reagan best. "They get so egocentric. The whole world centers upon their lives. That makes you a loner."[96] Reagan has called Southern California home for more than half a century. Instead of drifting from town to town as his father had done, Reagan moved from picture to picture, changing best friends and directors along the way. But Reagan already lived in a world of illusion when he arrived in Hollywood. "He who would bring home the wealth of the Indies must carry the wealth of the Indies with him," it has been said,[97] and Reagan arrived in California bearing the treasures and burdens of his boyhood experiences. He used his optimistic imagination to transform his difficult childhood into an "idyll." He used it to broadcast word pictures of games he never saw. Later, he would invent an America that never was and share with his fellow citizens a bright, shining vision of our nation's greatness founded on an imagined version of the past. The vision would be accepted because of its power and because of Reagan's belief in it. But it was not a vision that thrives on close encounters.

"He was carried by an idea," said Parvin. "He was passive, but he was carried so much by that idea that it transcended his passivity. He just held on to the idea."[98]

"He's a loner," said Laxalt. "He's a loner even in his relationship with his God. And the same way, unfortunately, with his kids."[99]

"He can give his heart to the country, but he just finds it difficult to hug his own children," said Michael Reagan.[100]

Ronald Reagan could give only what was inside of him. He had his own purposes, and his indirect ways of accomplishing them. Even in the presidency, he remained unknown and unknowable. He was a child of Dixon, of light and darkness, of lifting his father to safety in the storm, of a broken marriage and of a nurturing one. He was the child of America, a land where anything is possible. Even in old age, he clung to youthful dreams. He was the lifeguard on the shore.

12

STAYING
THE COURSE

They don't call it Reaganomics anymore.

RONALD REAGAN,
IN MANY SPEECHES

The first two Novembers of his presidency were unkind months
for Ronald Reagan and the interval between them cruel and costly for
the Americans who had accepted his invitation to dream "heroic
dreams." In November 1981 the shaky underpinnings of Reagan's economic assumptions were disclosed by publication in *The Atlantic* of
William Greider's "The Education of David Stockman." A year later
the Democrats gained twenty-six House seats in the midterm elections,
giving House Speaker Tip O'Neill sufficient Democratic regulars to
overcome the coalition of Republicans and "Boll Weevil" Democrats
who had given the Reagan administration a working majority. In the
year between these two events, the U.S. economy recorded its worst
decline since the Depression. By November 1982 more than 9 million
Americans were officially unemployed, a statistic that would rise to
11,534,000 by January.[1] Grim as they were, these statistics understated
actual unemployment. Between 2 and 3 million Americans had been
out of work so long they were not actively seeking jobs and therefore
were not officially counted in the army of the unemployed. Many other
Americans, perhaps as many as 10 million, had been forced by factory

shutdowns or relocations to take service or pickup jobs at lower pay. With the job losses came business failures—17,000 of them in 1981 alone, the second-highest figure since the Depression year of 1933.[2] By the end of 1982, the nation's steelmakers were operating at only 35 percent capacity.[3] In January 1983, 20,000 people lined up in 20-degree weather to apply for 200 jobs at an auto-frame factory in Milwaukee.[4]

Reagan, whose jaunty optimism rekindled memories of Franklin Roosevelt, was compared in these hard times to Herbert Hoover instead. Arriving at a Minneapolis political fund-raiser in February 1982, Reagan was greeted by a banner proclaiming "Welcome President Hoover." In June, organizers for the homeless pitched a ramshackle "tent city" in the shadow of the White House and conducted similar encampments in fourteen other cities. The tent cities were called "Reagan ranches" and were intended to evoke memories of the Depression shantytowns known as "Hoovervilles." The White House dismissed the protest as a publicity stunt, but disillusionment with Reagan's leadership was evident in the public opinion polls. Reagan's approval ratings, stratospheric after the assassination attempt and high throughout the spring and early summer of 1981, tumbled with the economy. When the nation edged into recession in midsummer, Reagan's approval rating stood at 60 percent. It fell to 49 percent by year's end and continued dropping. By the end of 1982, only 41 percent of Americans said they approved of Reagan's governance, a substantially lower rating than his four elected predecessors had received after two years in the White House.[5] When the economy went to hell in a handbasket, "Teflon" did not apply.

Within the White House gates and in the offices of the Republican National Committee on Capitol Hill, strategists who in the springtime of 1981 had excitedly envisioned a Republican congressional majority began to wonder if they could hold the White House in 1984. Particularly alarming to pollster Richard Wirthlin was Reagan's rapid decline of support among blue-collar families. Nancy Reagan was dejected. She was more attentive to the message of the polls than was her husband, and she confided to friends that he might decide not to seek a second term.* But Ronald Reagan did not take counsel of the fears and apprehensions of his wife and aides. The comparisons to Hoover notwithstanding, Franklin Roosevelt remained Reagan's model. Like FDR, Reagan believed that public confidence was a key to economic restoration. When confidence ebbed as the recession deepened, he did what

---

* The concerns of Nancy Reagan led me to believe that Reagan was unlikely to seek a second term, a mistaken judgment that I rashly issued as a prediction in the concluding pages of *Reagan*.

Roosevelt would have done (in fact, had done): he blamed the nation's troubles on his predecessor. He also accused the media of delaying the recovery with negative stories. Reagan was not negative. He saw himself as a leader who would unshackle an economy that he thought was capable of miracles. "Here we were, a country bursting with economic promise, and yet our political leadership had gone out of its way to frustrate America's natural economic strength," he would say in looking back upon these days. "It made no sense. My attitude had always been —let the people flourish."[6]

That comment explains Reagan's mind-set, if not his economic program. Reagan believed he had been elected because of his reliance on the American people, and he was determined to lead them out of the wilderness of misguided overreliance on government. This role suited him. Reagan could not explain his economic program to the satisfaction of his economists and budget director, but he had an abiding faith in the genius of the marketplace. And he was stubborn in his optimism. For a year and a half he steadfastly resisted pressure from Republican senators, including his friend Paul Laxalt, for a tax increase that would ease budget deficits. When he finally yielded in the late summer of 1982 to an inevitable tax increase that restored one-third of the reductions he had pushed through Congress a year earlier, he persuaded himself that he had merely agreed to "tax reform" that closed loopholes in the original bill.

Reagan could convince himself of nearly anything, but the key to his conduct was not semantic self-deception but an unshakable conviction that everything would turn out well. Throughout the 1981–82 recession, he displayed the persistence that had characterized him since Dixon. His aides found him cheerful. Shrugging off the polls and the worries of his wife, Reagan told anyone who would listen to him that better days were coming. "Stay the course" became the Republican political slogan in 1982, but it was more than a slogan for Reagan. He was convinced that the outcome of his policies would be a prosperous America.

"Reaganomics," like "the Reagan revolution," would come to have many definitions, some unrelated to Reagan's original purposes. For some, it was a code word for the supply-side doctrine that lower taxes and added incentives would increase productivity. More often, it was a term of derogation—an echo of the word "Nixonomics."[7] In 1982 the liberal economist Robert Lekachman gave the phrase currency by using it as the subtitle of a polemic, *Greed Is Not Enough: Reaganomics,* whose point of view was expressed in its opening sentence: "Ronald Reagan must be the nicest president who ever destroyed a union, tried to cut school lunch milk rations from six to four ounces, and compelled families in need of public help to first dispose of household goods in excess of $1,000." This line of argument was usually summarized by the phrase that Reagan was attempting to "balance the budget on the backs of the poor," although he never seriously attempted to balance the budget at all.

In time, Reagan recognized that a balanced budget (promised also by FDR in 1932 and by Jimmy Carter in 1976) was beyond his reach and described his campaign pledge as a "personal dream."[8] His economists came to this conclusion long before he did. The promise of a "balanced budget" is omitted from the document that stands as the basic blueprint of Reaganomics, the 281-page message submitted by the White House to Congress on February 18, 1981, and publicly issued under the title *America's New Beginning: A Program for Economic Recovery*. This document defines what history has come to know as Reaganomics. It proposed:

—A budget reform plan to cut the rate of growth in federal spending.
—A series of proposals to reduce personal income tax rates by 10 percent a year over three years and to create jobs by accelerating depreciation for business investment in plant and equipment.
—A far-reaching program of regulatory relief.
—And, in cooperation with the Federal Reserve Board, a new commitment to a monetary policy that will restore a stable currency and healthy financial markets.

Broadly speaking, the program reflected Reagan's advocacies of a quarter century. It called for reductions across the board in the size and scope of government and for shrinking the government's revenue base. This reduction of the federal role was the unifying element of Reaganomics, which otherwise reflected the competing priorities of the Reagan political coalition. "The Reagan economic program, like the Reagan constituency, reflected a range of views on economic policies," observed William A. Niskanen, a member of the Council of Economic Advisers from 1981 to 1985. "For the traditional Republicans a lower growth in federal spending was a necessary complement of any reduction in taxes. . . . For the new 'supply-siders,' a reduction in tax rates was necessary to induce the economic growth that would permit a lower growth in federal spending."⁹* The traditionalists included most of the senior Republican senators and administration officials who had served in prior Republican administrations, such as Martin Anderson. Many of the younger Republicans in the House, epitomized by Jack Kemp of New York, adhered to the supply-side view that massive reductions in taxes and government regulation would unleash pent-up entrepreneurial energies and produce an economic boom.

The conviction that the size of the economic pie must be increased, not simply sliced differently, was fundamental to supply-side doctrine. For Kemp and others who sought to convert traditionally Democratic blue-collar voters to Republicanism, this was a more appealing message than orthodox "trickle-down" economics that cast Republicans as defenders of wealth and privilege.[10] The bibles of this new economic gospel were Jude Wanniski's *The Way the World Works,* published in 1978, and George Gilder's *Wealth and Poverty,* published in 1981. The fundamental supply-side nostrum was the 30 percent tax cut first proposed by Kemp and Senator William Roth of Delaware in 1977. But supply-side economics was an encompassing theory that looked beyond Kemp-Roth to a world stripped of the tax preferences, subsidies and economic regulations that the supply-siders believed were strangling capitalism. Supply-siders believed that these reforms would produce unprecedented economic growth in which even government would share. While tax rates would be reduced, the increased productivity would generate so much new wealth that government revenues would actually increase. The evidence for this proposition was skimpy, resting chiefly on the disputed outcome of a far more limited tax cut during the Kennedy administration. The supply-siders, however, thought the validity of their economic doctrine self-evident. Many of them expressed their convictions with an evangelical fervor more appropriate for a religious crusade than an economics discussion. Traditional economists and orthodox politicians soon learned that the supply-siders, with occasional exceptions, were impervious to argument. They believed in their economic gospel passionately, and matters of faith are not subject to empirical disproof.

The supply-side faith was briefly shared by Stockman, a man of

---

* Niskanen's 1988 book *Reaganomics: An Insider's Account of the Policies and the People* is a definitive and notably objective account of administration economic policies. It ranks with Martin Anderson's *Revolution* for its insights into Reagan's economic views. The observations of Niskanen and Anderson quoted in this chapter are drawn both from their books and from my interviews with them.

restless intellect and swiftly changing visions. Raised on a farm in Michigan as an orthodox Republican conservative, Stockman had turned to radicalism at Michigan State, where he became a fervent opponent of the Vietnam War and a campus critic of the established social order. His pilgrim's progress carried him to Harvard Divinity School, which sheltered him with a draft deferment and introduced him to moral philosophy. At Harvard, Stockman found himself offended by the "nihilistic radicalism" he saw everywhere around him and reverted to his familial conservatism.[11] He also changed his major to the social sciences. (One thing he did not do, he boasted to me and other reporters as late as 1981, was take a course in economics.) Stockman had many mentors. He wangled a job as live-in babysitter for Daniel Patrick Moynihan, then the resident Democrat in the Nixon White House, and used his Moynihan connection to land a spot in a Harvard seminar taught by David S. Broder. Impressed with his work, Broder introduced Stockman to another Harvard visitor, Congressman John Anderson of Illinois. Anderson was looking for a bright young man to help define Republican policy and hired Stockman. Before long, Stockman was the Republican Conference's research director and an invaluable aide to House Republicans hungry for something tastier than the stodgy gruel of partisan denunciation. Stockman gave it to them. He had a knack for putting deft and insightful budgetary analysis into a political context. And he also had a talent for self-promotion. In the spring 1975 issue of *The Public Interest,* Stockman attracted favorable attention from conservative intellectuals with an article titled "The Social Pork Barrel" that vigorously challenged the congressional budget process. It was Stockman's contention that special interest groups and their advocates within the bureaucracy had combined with "conservative duplicity and liberal ideology" to reduce Congress to a weak buffer group. "With revenues fully committed for years in advance, the federal budget process, potentially the basic forum for serious policy choices, has been reduced to a mere annual ritual of accounts juggling," he wrote.

Stockman ran for Congress in 1976, violating an unwritten taboo that is supposed to prohibit congressional aides from opposing members of their party. His prospective opponent was a veteran congressman made vulnerable by his diehard support for Richard Nixon two years earlier. When Stockman announced, the congressman withdrew and Stockman was elected easily from the Michigan district in which he had been raised. Already influential, he distinguished himself by breaking with his fellow Michigan Republicans and opposing legislation to bail out the then-failing Chrysler Corporation. "I had the impression that he had swung over completely to the free-market economy as almost an article of religious faith," John Anderson said later. "He left me completely as soon as he was elected to Congress. He left me completely even though I had gone up to his district to help him raise money and to campaign." [12] As budget director, Stockman would soon leave the supply-siders as well, although they had no inkling of that in the heady false dawn of the Reagan revolution. His goal was dismantling the welfare state, not financing it.

Reagan largely ignored the debate that raged in his camp between supply-siders and traditional Republicans. He favored both tax reductions and spending cuts and saw no need to choose between them. Kemp-Roth touched the Reagan nerve that had been exposed when his acting income was taxed at the high marginal rates prevailing in the late 1940s, and he had endorsed the tax reduction bill in 1978 before it became official Republican policy. But Reagan did not abandon Republican fiscal orthodoxy when he accepted supply-side insights. He wanted to have his cake and eat it too. Reagan's central objective since his General Electric days had been to reduce the role of government. He simply assumed that this goal was compatible with supply-side objectives.

To say that Reagan stood apart from this central quarrel in his camp is not to say he was irrelevant to it. Reagan had a sense of the direction in which he wanted his economic program to go, even if he did not have a road map for getting there. "He didn't have an analytic grasp, but he had damn good convictions" is the way that Niskanen put it. "Often, economic advisers are fighting a president's convictions, and that wasn't the case with Reagan. [But] Reagan is not an analytic person. He was bored with argument, and he made it clear he was bored with argument. He wanted to hear the conclusions and check to see if they agreed with his priors [prior convictions]." [13] Reagan had formed these convictions over a long period of time. Martin Anderson claims that Reagan had "read and studied the writings of some of the best economists in the world, including the giants of the free market economy—Ludwig von Mises, Friedrich Hayek and Milton Friedman—and he spoke and wrote on the economy, going through the rigorous mental discipline of explaining his thoughts to others." [14] This is an exaggeration. Unlike Stockman, who gave Reagan almost no credit for his own program, Anderson often went to the opposite extreme and attributed to Reagan a greater grasp of issues than he had.

In fact, Anderson was the free-market economist most often consulted by Reagan in the 1976 and 1980 presidential campaigns and during the critical period after his election. When the tensions between the supply-siders and the traditionalists became particularly acute in September 1980, it was Anderson and Alan Greenspan who took the conflicting arguments and wove them together in a political version of a seamless web. Reagan relied on a variety of economists, but he was more inclined to read journalistic summaries of the arguments made by the "giants of the free market economy" than to consult the original texts. He learned best from oral briefings, and Anderson saw to it that he was regularly exposed to influential economists, including Friedman, Murray Weidenbaum and the supply-sider Arthur Laffer. George Shultz, then president of Bechtel and a part-time economics professor at Stanford, recalls that Governor Reagan asked him to lunch in Sacramento in 1974 and "really pressed me on how the federal government worked, how the budget worked, what the process was, and what the problems were . . . and so on." Shultz went away from the meeting convinced that Reagan was interested in being president, not simply being elected president. "He [was] interested in how you do it once you're elected," Shultz said. "So many people want an office of some kind, but they don't really think about what they're going to do when they get in it." [15]

Reagan's combination of strong convictions, a sense of direction and lack of analytic grasp was not unique in the presidency. The president he most resembled in this respect was Franklin Roosevelt, who once exasperated his "brains-truster" (later "brain-truster") Raymond Moley by taking two incompatible drafts of a major tariff speech and saying to him, "Weave the two together." [16] Reagan may not have known as much about economics as Roosevelt (whose own advisers, including Moley, did not think he knew very much), but he was similarly interested in results rather than economic tidiness. Stockman, even more contemptuous of Reagan's intellect than Moley was of FDR's, thought that the president brushed aside his arguments about the nature and magnitude of the deficit because he could not follow them. It would be more accurate to say that Reagan, like Roosevelt, was far more interested in economic recovery than he was concerned about the deficits that would be the by-products of his policies. The quarrel between supply-siders and traditionalists completely bored him. Reagan wanted both tax cuts and spending reductions. He believed that he would get more of each if he did not choose between competing policies.

On the spending side, he did not get that much. Indeed, he did not really ask for much. For all the furor they created, the first-term Reagan budgets were mild manifestos devoid of revolutionary purpose. They did not seek to "rebuild the foundation of our society" (the task Reagan set for himself and Congress in a nationally televised speech of February 5, 1981) or even to accomplish the "sharp reduction in the spending growth trend" called for in the Economic Recovery Plan. Reagan wanted to reorder budget priorities, but he had no intention of dismantling the New Deal. He made this point in passing in another nationally televised speech on February 18, the day he submitted his economic plan to Congress. "It's important to note that we're only reducing the rate of increase in taxing and spending," Reagan said, but it was not much noted.

As matters turned out, even the reduction of the rate of increase was modest. Throughout the Reagan first term, real spending (spending adjusted for inflation) increased at a rate of 3.7 percent annually, less than the 5 percent annual increase of the Carter years but hardly revolutionary. Looking back on it, Niskanen would say that the initial Reagan economic program "represented a rather cautious evolution of a number of policy changes initiated in the 1970s."[17] But such incremental evaluations were drowned out by the rhetoric of the Reagan revolution. Even though the president's words in his February 18 speech were carefully chosen, his enthusiasm for what he was doing soon led him to make extravagant claims. When my *Washington Post* colleague Lee Lescaze and I asked Reagan on March 27 for a scorecard on his first two months in office, he declared that "the main accomplishment has been that our economic program, which calls for the greatest attempt of savings in the history of the nation plus a complete tax plan, is . . . moving before the Congress right now."

Tip O'Neill's view of this "greatest attempt of savings in the history of the nation" was equally sweeping. He said, "We're not going to let them tear asunder programs we've built over the years."[18] The eighteen members of the Congressional Black Caucus called a press conference to accuse the administration of planning to make the poor "hungrier, colder and sicker."[19] Jerry Wurf, president of the American Federation of State, County and Municipal Employees, said, "What we are seeing is the beginning of an administration that will do two things—reward the rich and screw the poor."[20]

The rhetoric was inflated because the battleground was limited. Most of the programs targeted for severe reduction or elimination by the first

Reagan budget were "discretionary spending" products of Lyndon Johnson's Great Society rather than the bedrock social programs of the New Deal. Some of the reduced programs, such as child nutrition and subsidies for mass transit, or the ones entirely eliminated, such as public service jobs provided by the Comprehensive Employment Training Act, were extremely important to the constituents of the Congressional Black Caucus, among others. But the emotions expended over these programs obscured the reality that most of the budget was untouchable, either as a matter of law or as a matter of policy. Nearly half the federal budget is spent on "entitlement" programs such as Social Security, Medicare and unemployment compensation that provide guaranteed benefits for anyone eligible to receive them. The benefits are determined by formulas written into law and made generous over the years by Congress. If, to use the example of William Greider,[21] the entire ($700 billion, in fiscal 1982) federal budget was seen as a single dollar, 48 cents of it was spent on Social Security, pension and welfare benefits and money paid out to doctors and hospitals who provided care for the elderly and the poor. Another 25 cents went to military spending, and Reagan was committed to increase it. Another 10 cents went for interest on the national debt. This left 17 cents of the federal dollar, some of which was soon exempted from reduction. Anxious to defuse Democratic charges that his budget plan was an assault on the poor, Reagan ruled out cuts in two Social Security programs and any substantial reduction in five others: Medicare, veterans benefits, school lunches, Head Start and summer youth jobs. Stockman said these programs, taken together, formed a "social safety net" that protected the "truly needy." This preemptive political strike made the budget easier to defend but impossible to balance. By March 17, 1982, Stockman was accurately complaining that "administration policies and political decisions have progressively insulated 90 percent of the fiscal equation from consideration."

Social Security was the most tempting and politically risky factor in this equation. As the largest domestic program, it met the vital test of Willie Sutton, who said he robbed banks because that's where the money is. Social Security entitlements, however, were guarded more zealously than any bank by a growing army of the elderly and their political battalions in Congress. And Social Security was also the most enduring domestic legacy of the New Deal. It had been created in 1935 as a retirement system that would be financed by taxes on employers and workers, an alternative that had been selected after the Roosevelt administration had rejected a proposal that would straightforwardly have required the federal government to pay a share of the cost. FDR took a long view of history. The principal reason that he rejected direct government financing of Social Security was because of estimates showing that this plan would cost the government estimated annual costs of $1.4 billion by 1980. "It is almost dishonest to build up an accumulated deficit for the Congress of the United States to meet in 1980," Roosevelt said. "We can't do that. We can't sell the United States short in 1980 any more than in 1935." [22]

Because of its financing mechanism, Social Security from the beginning imposed a disproportionately high tax burden on young and lower-paid wage earners and provided retired workers with far more benefits from the system than they had put into it. The first Social Security check, of $22.54, was issued in 1940 to Ida Fuller of Brattleboro, Vermont, who had paid a total of $22 in Social Security taxes. By the time she drew her last check in 1974, shortly after her 100th birthday, she had collected $20,944 in Social Security payments. [23] Small wonder that even orthodox conservative economists such as Niskanen considered Social Security to be an "intergenerational Ponzi game." [24] Stockman and other conservative intellectuals also described Social Security as a pyramid scheme. As *Time* magazine put it when the Social Security debate was raging in 1982, "The aged have been misled for two generations into believing that Social Security payments constitute no more than a return to them of the payroll taxes they have paid during their working years. This is dramatically untrue. The average retired person today can expect to collect lifetime benefits five times as great as the total taxes that he or she once paid, plus interest." [25]

Congress was principally to blame for this inequity. Between 1950 and 1972 Congress raised Social Security benefits or extended eligibility eleven times—six times in an election year. The most significant change occurred in 1972 when House Ways and Means Committee chairman Wilbur Mills of Arkansas was making an abortive bid to win the Democratic presidential nomination. He sponsored and Congress passed a bill raising Social Security benefits by 20 percent and indexing the benefits so that recipients received a raise whenever the Consumer Price Index (CPI) increased by 3 percent. Many economists disparaged the use of the CPI for this purpose because it was disproportionately influenced by housing and mortgage interest costs, and few seniors buy houses. Once embedded in the system, however, these cost-of-living increases became nearly as sacrosanct as Social Security itself. By the time Reagan came to office, Social Security accounted for 21 percent of the total budget. It continued to grow by nearly 3 percent a year during Reagan's first term.

Social Security was always more tar baby than Teflon for Reagan. He told me when he was governor of California that Barry Goldwater's 1964 campaign had demonstrated that Republicans could not safely discuss the issue, but Reagan could not stop talking about it. I have no doubt that he shared the view that Social Security was in fact a Ponzi scheme. Reagan was particularly intrigued with the idea of a voluntary Social Security plan that would have allowed workers to make their own investments. This idea, which had widespread currency among conservatives in the 1960s, would have undermined the system by depriving Social Security of the contributions of millions of the nation's highest-paid workers. Reagan had raised the idea in his October 27, 1964, speech for Barry Goldwater and returned to it periodically in unguarded public moments over the years. On February 8, 1976, he said that Social Security "could have made a provision for those who could do better on their own" and suggested that such recipients be allowed to leave the program upon showing that "they had made provisions for their own non-earning years."[26] This declaration sent shudders through the ranks of Reagan's political advisers, who knew his true feelings about Social Security. When Stu Spencer joined the Ford campaign in 1976, he attempted to exploit Reagan's vulnerability on the issue by suggesting that Reagan's proposal to transfer $90 billion in federal programs to the states would jeopardize Social Security financing. This strategy damaged Reagan, particularly in the Florida primary, even though Social Security was not one of the programs he proposed to transfer to the states. The issue continued to have a residual impact among elderly voters four years later, according to Wirthlin's polls. When Spencer joined the 1980 campaign, he advised Reagan to reaffirm his support for Social Security if the subject arose and warned him otherwise to avoid the issue. This was hard for Reagan to do. While walking down a hotel corridor in Jacksonville, Reagan responded to a woman who asked his past views on Social Security by declaring, "I said that since it is billed as an insurance program, that certainly a person who paid into it should have the right to choose his beneficiary."[27]

After Reagan became president he showed a White House aide an article from *Human Events* that described Social Security as a dismal failure. But Reagan was now surrounded by advisers, especially White

House Chief of Staff James Baker, who shared Spencer's fears about the negative political potential of the issue. As Stockman put it, Baker "thought of Social Security as Ronald Reagan's Achilles heel and was determined to keep the president as far away from it as possible."[28] When the White House less than two months into Reagan's presidency was handed a congressional initiative that would have braked the growth of Social Security and significantly reduced the budget deficit, Baker saw the proposal as a pitfall rather than an opportunity.

The White House response to this congressional initiative provides a case study as revealing of Reagan's budgetary misconceptions as the MX decision was of his misunderstanding of the "window of vulnerability." Both cases suggest that a president must do more than focus on public performance while leaving the homework to others. And both cases show that the president, for all his talk about working with Republicans in Congress, was willing to ignore knowledgeable and influential senators and congressmen of his own party if their advice conflicted with the pet theories of the cabinet or the White House palace guard.

The Social Security proposal that might have rescued the administration from itself came from Senator Pete V. Domenici of New Mexico, a thoughtful Republican from a state that most often sends Democrats to the Senate. The unexpected Republican capture of the Senate in 1980 had made him chairman of the Senate Budget Committee. Domenici was an economic traditionalist who believed in budget-balancing and was unconvinced by the supply-side claim that massive tax cuts would ignite the economy and produce budget surpluses. Like many other senators of both parties, Domenici understood that entitlement programs were out of control and threatened the nation's fiscal stability. He wanted budget reform, not a revolution. Domenici's budget staff, headed by trusted associate Stephen E. Bell, had done its own economic analysis, providing the senator with a view of future budgets that did not match the White House happy talk. Domenici believed that the tax cut would shrink government revenues and that Stockman's proposed economies, many of which he supported, would be insufficient to avert major budget deficits. He thought Reagan should take advantage of his political honeymoon to make difficult decisions that would be impossible later on.

Domenici's concerns about the deficit were shared by conservative Democrats on the Budget Committee, notably Senator Ernest F. (Fritz) Hollings. The white-maned South Carolinian had advocated a slowdown in automatic cost-of-living allowances (COLAs) while Carter was in the White House, and he continued his advocacy after Reagan was elected. Hollings and Domenici were friends and had discussed the issue many times. In February 1981, Hollings informed Domenici that he was prepared to support a freeze in Social Security COLAs and other federal pension programs. This was not news. What interested Domenici was that Hollings also told him that at least four other Democrats on the Budget Committee were prepared to vote for a freeze or severe reduction in the COLAs. Since Domenici knew he could count on eleven of twelve Republican votes on the committee (everyone except Dan Quayle of Indiana) for such a proposal, this meant he had the makings of a bipartisan deal. Domenici even had a political rationale for his plan, which he believed could be honestly presented as a measure necessary to preserve the fiscal integrity of a Social Security system then in shaky financial condition. The chairman had everything he needed except the crucial element of White House support.

This support was not forthcoming. After Senate Majority Leader Howard Baker informed Jim Baker of the impending Budget Committee proposal, the chief of staff and Stockman conspired to prevent Reagan from accepting it. Jim Baker, as Stockman put it, "went into a red alert." [29] Based on my conversations at the time with Jim Baker and other White House officials, I believe he was motivated by his campaign-inherited view that Social Security was an untouchable issue for Reagan. Stockman's motivations were more devious. He had identified $74 billion in immediate savings that were meticulously spelled out in the budget and another $44 billion of "unidentified savings" to be made later. Howard Baker sardonically said that the unidentified savings should be noted in the budget with a "magic asterisk," [30] a phrase that later became shorthand for the creative economies of OMB.

But Stockman knew all along where he intended to find the $44 billion. His secret plan was to take it from Social Security after Congress had approved the $74 billion in budget cuts. [31] It was a politically naïve idea, as Domenici (or either of the Bakers) would have told Stockman if he had been forthright enough to have shared it. Privately, however, Stockman was nearly as contemptuous of Domenici as he was of the president. He clandestinely promoted a *Wall Street Journal* editorial, headed "John Maynard Domenici," that disparaged Domenici as an advocate of Keynesian economic policies. [32] When I interviewed Stockman late in 1981, he concealed his disdain for Domenici because he was then dependent upon him for some additional budget reductions that the administration was trying to push through the Senate. Later, however, Stockman unfairly disparaged Domenici as a "Hooverite," saying that the Senator believed that "budget expenditures needed to be drastically reduced and the budget balanced quickly."[33] This would have been a fair summary of Reagan's own campaign promise on the budget. But Stockman, caught up in dreams of revolution, ignored the fact that the Domenici-Hollings initiative had the potential for producing much larger savings than his own budget proposals. Instead of evaluating the initiative objectively, Stockman rationalized that the senators were proposing entitlement cuts merely to avoid other reductions that were crucial to his idea of crippling the welfare state. "They wanted those entitlements cut so they could preserve their energy projects, soil conservation grants, EDA projects, highway funds and education aid," Stockman wrote in *The Triumph of Politics*. "Those were the mother's milk on which Republican politicians—self-professed conservatives as well as moderates—lived no less profitably than their Democratic colleagues."[34] The point is arguable, but the arithmetic is deficient. It was runaway entitlement costs far more than the pet congressional projects Stockman hated that stood between Reagan and his goal of a balanced budget. Reagan didn't know this, and Stockman didn't tell him. Offhandedly, he rejected an opportunity that could have averted a significant proportion of the deficits that became the Reagan administration's principal albatross.

Stockman, however, did not have to convince Reagan to reject the initiative. Fearing a political fallout and not realizing that Stockman planned a riskier later assault on Social Security, Jim Baker already had mobilized the White House staff and turned Reagan against the deal. This was the heyday of the White House troika. Baker, Meese and Deaver had their differences, but they were in agreement about the risks to Reagan of embracing any plan that could be interpreted as a proposal to reduce Social Security. The troika's argument to Reagan was that he would be reneging on his campaign promise if he agreed even to a prospective reduction in Social Security benefits. All of Reagan's political aides knew that an argument that he would be going back on his word was nearly always persuasive to the president. The members of the troika were not versed in economics. Judging from my frequent conversations with troika members in those days, I think it is fair to say that none of them had focused on the prospect that the Reagan budget was likely to produce significant deficits. Baker, prodded by Dick Darman, would come to realize that the depth and breadth of the tax cut was a mistake, but he did not know this in March 1981.

And when Reagan journeyed to the Hill to meet with Republican senators on March 17, he had been primed by Baker to resist the Domenici proposal.

Reagan met the senators at 9:30 A.M. in Howard Baker's office in Room S-230 of the Capitol. A fire burned briskly in the fireplace. Howard Baker was flanked by the Senate leadership and members of the Budget Committee known at the White House as the "College of Cardinals." Baker, as always, sat with his back to a window that overlooked the Mall, with the light streaming in behind him. He did this, it was said in the Senate, that he might see his visitors better than they could see him. On this day Howard Baker saw a confident president, with Jim Baker and Stockman on either side. Howard Baker already had been informed of Reagan's reaction to the Budget Committee proposal, but he had made the point to Jim Baker that the other senators needed to hear it from the president himself. Reagan opened the meeting with an Irish joke, then said he had heard that the committee had a proposal from the Democrats that would cut Social Security.

"Well, you know I made a commitment during the campaign not to cut Social Security, and I think anything I do to go back on that commitment is going to cause me a real problem," Reagan said. "I don't want to go back on my word." [35]

"Let's talk about this commitment for a while," Domenici replied. "You made a commitment not to cut Social Security. We don't propose to cut Social Security. Not a single benefit that's now being received will be cut, and not a single person eligible will be denied access." [36]

Domenici then explained that he had eleven Republican votes and five Democratic votes, more than two-thirds of the twenty-two-member Budget Committee, for a proposal that would change the basis of future cost-of-living increases and save $10 billion in the immediate budget and $25 billion by the fifth year. The actual savings, however, would be larger because the senators proposed to apply it to all COLAs.

Reagan was taken aback at this explanation, but Jim Baker was not.

"Now wait a minute, but isn't it true that if you didn't act these folks would get this kind of increase?" Jim Baker said. "So compared to what they would expect to get there will be a cut from their expectations." [37]

"That's true," Domenici said. "But if you want to apply that to everything else, then we can't cut anything. We're not going to be able to cut anything in this budget if that's the kind of analysis you want to use. That's the current services analysis and that's what the Democrats have always done to measure cuts. Why should we be like them?" [38]

Domenici then warned the president and his advisers not to use a different standard for measuring entitlements than they were using for defense spending or the tax cut. But the exercise was, as Stephen Bell subsequently put it, like "pissing up a rope. Jim Baker had already made his mind up, Stockman had made his mind up. . . . And the president just simply was not focused on this subject in any kind of broad way."[39] The Republican senators were not willing to desert their president this early in his term, and Reagan knew it.

"Well, you know, I really do think you boys ought to stick with me on this one," Reagan said. "And, Pete, I want you to tell Fritz you can't go with him."[40]

Other senators—William Armstrong of Colorado, Slade Gorton of Washington, Rudy Boschwitz of Minnesota and John Tower of Texas —jumped into the discussion, reinforcing Domenici's arguments. Armstrong made the strongest case.

"We're not talking about a cut," Armstrong said. "We have a unique bipartisan opportunity. It will save more money than almost any other single action we can take over the next four or five years, and we really hope you'll reconsider this advice to us, Mr. President."[41]

But Reagan would not reconsider, and Howard Baker said that Republicans would go along with him. "Mr. President, we hear you loud and clear,"[42] Baker said. The meeting broke up. In a Budget Committee session that afternoon on the markup of the budget reconciliation bill, Domenici summarized his exchange with Reagan for the benefit of the Democrats. Hollings was sympathetic to Domenici, but said he wanted to pursue a reduction in COLAs anyway. He had little support for it. Few of the Budget Committee Democrats were willing to climb out onto a shaky political limb and try to brake Social Security costs without Republican help. Even if they had been willing, they did not have the votes. Republicans, many of whom credited Reagan for GOP control of the Senate, were simply unwilling to go against the president. Even the senators most skeptical about the wisdom of cutting taxes—and Domenici was high on this list—were reluctant to undercut Reagan. On the Budget Committee only a defiant Armstrong ignored the president's appeal and supported a COLA cut. But the senators were not happy that the president had spurned their gift of a built-in budget reduction. They would not offer it to him again.

Nor would Republican senators offer aid and comfort to Stockman, who still needed to find the $44 billion in savings that had been defined by the magic asterisk. Actually, Stockman wanted far more from Social Security than the savings needed to meet his budgetary goals. In 1981

Stockman thought of himself as a revolutionary and of Social Security as "closet socialism."[43] He wanted to eliminate various welfare programs that had been grafted onto the Social Security tree and to reduce drastically the benefits for early retirement. The issue was already under consideration in Congress, spurred by the realization that the basic old age, survivors and disability (OASDI) program would run out of money within a few years. A House Ways and Means subcommittee chaired by Democrat J. J. (Jake) Pickle of Texas favored a modest stretch-out of the age at which retirees received full Social Security benefits. Health and Human Services Secretary Richard Schweiker wanted to solve the short-term fiscal problems of Social Security by bringing in government and nonprofit workers who had their own retirement systems. As Stockman told me in 1981, these ideas held no appeal to him because they offered no immediate budget savings.[44] Stockman's radical alternative was a plan that would have saved $110 billion by tightening up on disability payments and reducing some of the benefits of wage-indexing. He might have obtained bipartisan support for some of these ideas, but his proposal contained a booby trap for workers who retired at age sixty-two instead of sixty-five. Existing law imposed a 20 percent penalty on these early retirees. The fine print of the Stockman plan, never explained to Reagan, changed this to a 55 percent penalty. Stockman enlisted Martin Anderson's support for the idea and eventually lined up Schweiker behind it as well. Neither Anderson nor Schweiker focused on the political impact of these changes. Stockman circulated the plan to the White House staff on May 9, a Saturday, but its implications were not widely understood. This was no accident. As Stockman boasted afterward, his option paper was "written in perfectly incomprehensible Social Security Administration format and jargon which obscured almost everything" and accompanied by "a cover memo which explained almost nothing."[45] On May 11 he took the proposal to the president.

Making a case by cartoon, as Weinberger had done to scuttle MX/MPS, is intellectually dubious. But Reagan at least could understand cartoons, and he had been exposed, if belatedly, to arguments from those who disagreed with Weinberger. Stockman gave Reagan less of a choice. The president's attention span was extremely short in the weeks after the assassination attempt, and Stockman's proposal had been deliberately written to make it incomprehensible. Niskanen said the one-hour presentation left Reagan with "his eyes glazed by technical detail and no alternative but to accept or reject the package."[46] Stockman made a strong theoretical argument for phasing out early retirement, observing that it had not originally been part of Social Security. Afterward, Stockman would say it was this point "that carried the day."[47] Reagan, picking up on Stockman's argument, said, "I've been warning since 1964 that Social Security was heading for bankruptcy and this is one of the reasons why."[48] He was right, but Reagan did not realize, and Stockman did not tell him, that the proposal he was being asked to approve had an immediate and Draconian impact on those Social Security recipients who had been planning early retirement for years and were counting on the benefits that had been promised them. A more politically palatable version of this plan had been circulating within the administration for weeks. It called for a 5 percent increase in the penalty for early retirement, an idea that had some support on Capitol Hill but did not provide the savings Stockman thought he needed. So Stockman latched onto this proposal in a cabinet council meeting and converted the moderate reduction in benefits into the extremist proposal he took to the president. Stockman's version of the plan would have taken effect on January 1, 1982, cutting the monthly retirement check for an early retiree from $469 to $310. Most of the early retirees had been counting on their Social Security income, and many of them had already notified employers that they intended to retire. Had the proposal been presented to Reagan in these terms, the political outcry such a plan was certain to provoke would have been apparent to the president and his political advisers. But neither Stockman nor anyone else mentioned the effective date of the proposal. Anderson supported Stockman, addressing the ideology of the proposal rather than its practical impact. "You'll be the first president in history to honestly and permanently fix Social Security," Anderson said to Reagan. "No one else has had the courage to do it."[49] Reagan took the unusual action of approving the Stockman option on the spot.

For one of the few times in his White House service, Dick Darman was taken completely by surprise. He had hastily skimmed the Stockman option before the meeting, and had not spoken during the discussion. Without fully understanding what was going on, he suspected that the jargon of the document concealed a politically dubious proposal. Darman, the acknowledged brain-trust of the Baker team, had been relaxed about it because he knew that Reagan rarely made decisions on the spot. The usual practice with sensitive issues was for Reagan to take them under consideration. This gave the White House staff a chance to analyze any proposals that were on the table and take political soundings. If a pending proposal was deemed politically risky, Baker and Darman, operating through the troika or the Legislative Strategy Group, usually found a way to derail it. On this day, however, Reagan had short-circuited the usual process by making a decision on the spot. That left Baker and Darman with the responsibility of marketing the Social Security plan, which they quickly decided to do without a White House label. At a Legislative Strategy Group meeting convened two hours after Reagan's decision, Baker decreed that the Social Security plan would henceforth be known as "Dick Schweiker's plan," and be announced the next day by Schweiker at Health and Human Services rather than the White House. Schweiker and Stockman protested, to no avail. Although Baker and Darman lacked authority to overturn a presidential decision, they had complete control over its presentation. Meese, away on a speaking trip, was out of the picture. Schweiker didn't like it, but he dutifully announced the proposal the next day at HHS.

But it was the decision, not the location of its announcement, that turned out to matter. A banner headline in the May 13 editions of *The Washington Post* proclaimed, "Reagan Proposes 10% Cut in Social Security Costs." In a page-one analysis, the newspaper's senior political correspondent, David Broder, wrote: "Reagan did what no previous American president has ever dared to—urge Congress to take a major slice from the most cherished and widely supported benefits program on the books."[50] Congress was not about to do that. Senate Republicans were infuriated and demoralized, while Democrats in both houses were delighted with the opportunity the administration had handed them. Tip O'Neill, rebounding from the passage of the Reagan budget bill over his opposition on May 7, called the proposal "despicable." Senate Finance Committee chairman Bob Dole immediately warned the White House that Republicans would not support the plan. Jeered by the Democrats, who were amazed that Reagan had given them such an easy opportunity, the Senate Republicans took the lead in scuttling the proposal, which was voted down unanimously on May 20. Niskanen, reviewing the works of Reaganomics many years later, would accurately call the Social Security package "the major domestic policy mistake of the Reagan administration—an extraordinary political misjudgment by Stockman and Schweiker, both of whom had served in Congress through 1980."[51]

Reagan recovered politically from this calamity, but he would never again mount a major assault against the basic premises of the federal budget. After the twin fiascoes of March 17 and May 12, the administration was reduced to tinkering at the margins with entitlements rather than seeking Reagan's promised "sharp reduction in the spending growth trend." Republicans were thrown on the defensive in the 1982 midterm election campaign, where the administration assault on Social Security became the dominant theme of Democratic political commercials. Reagan was driven into reactive, face-saving bipartisanship. On December 16, 1981, he latched onto a proposal originally made by Senator Armstrong and named a bipartisan commission headed by Alan Greenspan to deal with the continuing Social Security fiscal crisis. The members were appointed by the president, Tip O'Neill and Howard Baker. White House input to the deliberations of the National Commission on Social Security Reform was controlled by Darman and Jim Baker, who worked closely with Greenspan and heeded the political constraints that Stockman had ignored.

After the 1982 elections Greenspan engineered a delicate compromise that averted a Social Security crisis without resolving the system's long-term structural problems. The compromise boosted payroll taxes for employers and employees in two stages, gradually raised the retirement age from sixty-five to sixty-seven by the year 2027, taxed the benefits of high-income recipients for the first time and delayed payment of the annual Social Security COLA by six months.* These and other changes produced savings of about $165 billion, supposedly sufficient to salvage the Social Security system until the turn of the century. Long-term problems of Social Security solvency were pushed into the future, as they have been since the system's creation. Reagan, however, believed he had faced up to these problems and solved them. On April 20, 1983, an unseasonably cold and windy day, Reagan signed the new Social Security amendments into law in a ceremony on the South Lawn. "This bill demonstrates for all time our nation's ironclad commitment to Social Security," Reagan said. Tip O'Neill, speaking after Reagan, said, "This is a happy day for America."

It would have been a happier day for Reagan had he accepted the Domenici-Hollings initiative when it was offered two years earlier. The potential impact of this lost opportunity is demonstrated by the fiscal effect of the 1983 amendment that delayed Social Security COLAs for six months. This provision alone produced savings of $12 billion in the next three fiscal years and continued to provide budget savings into

---

* House Rules Committee chairman Claude Pepper of Florida, champion of the elderly and a member of the commission, blocked attempts to increase the penalty for early retirement. Instead, the benefits paid to early retirees were reduced from 80 percent of full benefits to 75 percent in 2009 and to 70 percent in 2027.

perpetuity. Domenici had wanted in 1981 to freeze or reduce COLAs for a full year, at a time when inflation rates were far higher and the savings potential much greater. Halting or severely restricting Social Security cost-of-living increases in 1981 (for the fiscal 1982 budget) would have lowered the base from which future increases were computed, produced significantly lower deficits and changed the entire budget calculus. But Reagan did not know in 1981 that the calculus needed changing. He was deceived by wildly inaccurate economic forecasts, by his natural optimism and by a reliance on supply-side dogma that did not in fact describe the way the world worked. Later, Reagan's apologists would say that he was also deceived by Stockman, as if the budget director knew all along what would happen. But Stockman's true deception was of himself. He was, to paraphrase Niskanen, brilliant rather than wise, and his budgetary insights were undermined by a contempt for politics rare among those who have served in Congress. Strange as it seems in retrospect, Stockman did not recognize that the pork barrel politics against which he inveighed rested on a solid foundation of public support. He lacked his friend George Will's understanding that the conservatism of Americans expressed itself in a desire to conserve the New Deal. Consequently, Stockman overestimated the potential of "the Reagan revolution," as he recognized by the time he wrote *The Triumph of Politics* in 1986. By then, he was also self-critical of his easy acceptance of economic forecasts that had allowed him to believe that he could quickly remake the world. "We were not headed toward a brave new world, as I had thought in February," Stockman wrote. " . . . Where we were headed was toward a fiscal catastrophe." [52] By then, Stockman was able to compare the rosy assumptions of the original Reagan economic plan, which projected a budget surplus of $28 billion by 1986, to the actual results of $1.193 *trillion* in accumulated deficits over the five-year period. The deficits had forced a cutback in Reagan's vaunted defense buildup and required a series of disguised tax increases that raised $80 billion a year by 1986. The tax increases were necessary because the original Reagan budget proposed to lower tax collections to 16.9 percent of GNP, while built-in government spending amounted to 24 percent of GNP. "In early November 1981 the political and economic facts of life said that the Reagan Revolution was plunging into the drink," Stockman wrote. "But it was still not too late to have changed the course. We were only one month into the plan then, not sixty months and countless irreversible decisions later, as we are today." [53]

It would have been even easier to change the course before the

Reagan ship left port on its destination to unparalleled deficits. This destination may have been a mystery to the crew, but it was apparent to many on Capitol Hill and the business community who watched the embarkation. Eleven days before the economic program was introduced, financial writer John M. Berry reported in *The Washington Post* that "the Reagan administration will soon publish a highly optimistic economic forecast predicting recession for the middle of this year but rapid recovery and a declining rate of inflation in 1982."[54] The headline on this story used the phrase "rosy scenario" that Stockman would subsequently adopt as his own description for the overoptimistic fiscal assumptions of the Reagan budget. At the time, however, the "rosy scenario" that the headline described ("rosy forecast," in the story's words) was viewed by Stockman as a public relations problem rather than a valid economics critique. Stockman knew that the Reagan economic program required a perception of credibility to induce Congress to climb aboard, and a forecast that combined soaring real growth with sharply declining inflation described an unlikely combination of events. As Stockman later explained it, this forecast was the product of an unlikely compromise between conflicting economic doctrines. It combined the estimates of monetarists such as Treasury Undersecretary Beryl Sprinkel, who was intent on restricting the money supply to reduce inflation, with the estimates of supply-siders such as Treasury's Paul Craig Roberts and Norm Ture, who were preoccupied with economic growth. The monetarists wanted the forecast to show the lowest possible figures for "money GNP"—a measurement of real growth in the gross national product plus inflation. The supply-siders wanted the highest possible figures for the real growth they believed the tax cuts would create. No one wanted a high inflation figure. The consequent forecast of high growth and low inflation expressed, as Stockman put it, "a world close to the [supply-side] ideal of inflationless, capitalist growth."[55]

The forecast troubled Murray Weidenbaum, the usually easy-going chairman of the Council of Economic Advisers. Weidenbaum, described by Stockman as "a first-rate free market economist,"[56] was not a supply-sider, and he was unwilling to risk his professional reputation on a forecast he thought lacked credibility. Weidenbaum was unusually blunt for an economist. Stockman said he "had one virtue extremely uncommon among his breed: he spoke in short, English sentences."[57] This virtue reflected an intellectual honesty that would make Weidenbaum a short-timer in the councils of the Reagan ad-

ministration.* On February 7, 1981, the day of Berry's story, Weidenbaum told Stockman that he would not accept a forecast that showed
inflation, then at an annual rate of 11.7 percent, falling to 6.5 percent
in 1982 and to 3 percent by 1984.[58] Later that day he forced the issue
by telling Stockman that he would appeal directly to the president
unless the forecast was revised to contain a higher inflation number.
Stockman relented. Weidenbaum supplied a new and higher prediction
of inflation. When others on the administration team asked him where
it came from, Weidenbaum reportedly slapped his stomach and announced that its source was his "visceral computer."[59] Whatever the
source, the economic forecast that was ultimately issued projected a 7.7
percent inflation rate in 1982 and retained the estimate of 5.2 percent
economic growth. Stockman programmed the OMB computers accordingly. This combination of estimates enabled the administration to project what Stockman subsequently called a "mountain of money GNP
[and] phantom tax revenues"[60] leading to a balanced budget by
1984.

But the forecast was a fantasy. At the time it was issued, the Federal
Reserve had already embarked on a campaign to reduce inflation by
contracting the money supply. Instead of growing by 5.2 percent in
1982, the U.S. economy shrunk by 1.5 percent. And while the supply-
siders, of whom Stockman was then one, were surprised by this result,
many economists and businessmen were not. Late in February, economist Otto Eckstein, who had served on President Johnson's Council of
Economic Advisers, said of the 1982 budget, "With only a little additional bad luck, the government could experience a deficit of $100
billion."[61] (The actual 1982 deficit was $113 billion.) DuPont chairman
Irving Shapiro said at the same time, "I have a lot of trouble with this
new economic religion. No businessman would run his business on the
basis of an untested thesis."[62]

In his mea culpa memoir Stockman would put the blame on himself
and his fellow supply-siders for the resulting deficits, saying that Reagan, Treasury Secretary Donald T. Regan and the senior White House
staff "were almost entirely innocent and uninformed."[63] But innocence
is an inadequate defense to economic negligence of the magnitude practiced by the Reagan administration. The deficit catastrophe was not a

---

* Weidenbaum resigned on July 23, 1982. The announcement of his resignation was due to be made
the following day, but Reagan inadvertently announced it on a trip to St. Louis, saying afterward
that he had "goofed" in mentioning it. On August 6, Martin Feldstein was named as Weidenbaum's replacement.

natural disaster that came whistling out of the blue. The Senate Republican leadership was suspicious of the impact of Reagan's tax cuts, and warnings similar to those sounded by Eckstein and Shapiro came almost daily from the business community after the president had announced his economic program. Reagan chose to ignore these warnings, many of them from administration supporters, and to adopt the happy ending or "rosy scenario" as his own. While Stockman's manipulative zeal contributed to the deficit disaster, the policies that produced it were conceived and advocated by the president. Reagan had campaigned for the tax cut and the defense buildup. He had promised to preserve Social Security, the guiding impulse behind his rejection of the Domenici-Hollings initiative. While Reagan was initially hesitant on foreign affairs, he always knew his mind on economic issues. He never questioned the wisdom of simultaneously trying to reduce taxes, increase military spending and balance the budget. His ideological commitment and his traits of optimism and stubbornness would have led him to pursue these incompatible objectives regardless of the identity of his budget director. Long after it had become apparent to such reliable conservatives as Paul Laxalt that tax increases were necessary, Reagan continued to resist them.

Stockman has been disproportionately blamed for the failure of "the Reagan revolution" in part because he tried to take too much credit for creating it. He deserves both less credit and less blame than he gives himself, a point that has been made gently by Niskanen and more bluntly by Martin Anderson. Stockman was a master of illusion. His encyclopedic knowledge of the budget and his intellectual nimbleness enabled him to dominate the congressional discourse in the early months of the presidency and distract attention from the smoke-and-mirrors assumptions of the Reagan economic program. His restless energy and revolutionary fervor inspired a talented staff that tried to emulate his workaholic habit of working fifteen to eighteen hours a day, seven days a week. Ascetic and driven, Stockman was then a young man of relatively modest means in a cabinet dominated by aging millionaires. He was a rallying point for youthful conservatives in and out of the administration and an inviting target for those who lacked the stomach for a frontal assault on Ronald Reagan. "When attacking the president personally was dicey, Stockman served easily as a surrogate Scrooge as he sought to economize on the school lunch program, unemployment benefits and the stipends of welfare mothers," wrote Laurence Barrett. "Cartoonists portrayed him as cold, bloodless. They caricatured his thin face as a mask of indifference, his shaggy graying hair as a thick helmet."[64]

It was always my impression that Stockman rather welcomed these caricatures, which established him as the point man of the Reagan revolution. He was inclined to displays of intellectual exhibitionism, especially in congressional testimony where he indulged himself with fanciful assaults on pork barrel programs and dazzling displays of knowledge about arcane aspects of the budget. Stockman disdained the sleek cars, fancy offices, rings of government bodyguards and other perquisites that delighted more conventional members of the cabinet. He ate plainly, drank hardly at all and dressed in blue jeans whenever he could get away with it. In person, he was friendly, polite and often self-deprecating, although he could be devastating to journalists who failed to do their homework. "When I said something dumb about productivity, he rolled his eyes heavenward and indicated that productivity is a complex subject that I should leave to the adults," his friend George Will recalled. "He says such things agreeably, like a Gatling gun that has studied with Dale Carnegie."[65] I lacked Will's instant access to Stockman but saw him often enough to appreciate this quality. Usually, Stockman was able to show off his knowledge without being overbearing. The role in which he had cast himself was resident genius of the Reagan administration. What he seemed to want, more than influence and power, was for others to think of him as the smartest man in town.

And Stockman was indeed a bright star in the administration's murky firmament. Even his critics acknowledged that his initial budget reduction package had been prepared with exceptional skill and attention to detail. Within the limited arena in which he was allowed to operate, Stockman discovered genuine economies and translated some of them into worthwhile budget reductions. He might have accomplished much more than he did if Reagan had ever supported him in his budget battles with Weinberger or if Jim Baker had realized that the Domenici-Hollings initiative offered a unique political opportunity to brake the runaway costs of Social Security and other entitlements. On the other hand, both Weinberger and Baker justifiably believed that they were responding to imperatives (boosting military spending in Weinberger's case and preserving Social Security in Baker's) that had been proclaimed by Reagan in his campaign. They did not invent the policies they defended, although Weinberger may have been, in the old phrase, more Catholic than the Pope in advancing Pentagon priorities. But it was Reagan, more of a New Dealer than he knew, who always wanted government to provide more services than he was willing to finance from current revenues. Over time, the president would change budget directors and chiefs of staff and, finally, defense secretaries. No matter who held these positions, Reagan never once came close to submitting a budget to Congress that provided the revenues to pay for the government programs he thought necessary. The deficit was not a Stockman Deficit or a Weinberger Deficit or a Baker Deficit. It was a Reagan Deficit, bequeathed to future generations.

Stockman recognized the myths of Reaganomics more quickly than his colleagues because he knew more about the budget than they did. Since he also possessed a greater sense of revolutionary mission, he was more deeply disillusioned. Although his memoir is contradictory on this score, Stockman seems to have had intimations of catastrophe on June 25, 1981, when the House passed the second budget-cutting bill, known as Gramm-Latta II. Reagan and his staff were at this time riding high. Ensconced in his skyroom suite at the Century Plaza Hotel in Los Angeles, the president had telephoned twenty-nine congressmen, mostly "Boll Weevil" Democrats, urging them to vote for a key procedural motion that brought the budget cuts to the floor as a single package. Reagan's telephone pitch, written for him by Baker, was a simple one. The message was close to the parody of the irrepressible Art Buchwald in which the president tells a mythical Congressman Lighter: "I would like you to break from your party and the Democratic leadership, and vote your conscience by passing my budget recommendations without reading them."[66] The House did. The key parliamentary motion passed by seven votes and the bill by six.

Reagan had been prepared to denounce the Democratic majority of the House in a speech that day to the California Taxpayers Association in Los Angeles. But the House voted out Gramm-Latta II shortly before the speech, and Reagan kept his audience waiting as his aides reworked it. Instead of denouncing the House, Reagan praised the thirty-one "courageous" Democrats who had joined with the Republicans to pass Gramm-Latta II. "It means that for the first time in many years, we have the opportunity to forge a new coalition in this country—a coalition built upon people from all parties and from every background who will work together for the good of the nation," Reagan said. "It means, in fact, that we can have a new beginning in America, a new beginning toward economic progress for all of our people." I put this claim in the lead of my story from Los Angeles, saying, "Reagan looked forward to a 'new coalition' dedicated to further reductions in the size and scope of government."[67] Actually, Reagan was looking forward to a weekend of riding on his ranch, to which he departed soon after his speech.

Stockman, back on the front lines in Washington, would say later that my story "captured well the false euphoria that the White House concocted from its unknowing defeat."[68] This is disingenuous, since Stockman was at the time expressing a similar euphoria, even though he had begun to have private doubts. Stockman knew that the second budget-cutting bill had made only $16 billion in actual cuts, although more than twice that amount was promised in future reductions. The administration needed more than $250 billion in spending cuts to realize Reagan's goal of a balanced budget by 1984. Stockman understood that too much of the budget had been walled off politically to make reductions of this scale even a remote possibility. Reagan, riding with his wife in the remote splendor of his mountaintop ranch, thought he had won a famous victory.

Afterward, Stockman would say that the California experience on which Reagan prided himself had made it difficult for him (and Meese) to understand the federal budget process, in which the spending decisions made in 1981 would vitally affect the budgetary outcomes of 1984. In California, as in many other states, the law requires the state budget to be balanced annually. This makes each annual budget battle an independent struggle and each spending bill a self-contained document. As late as May 1981, Reagan was still predicting that the budget would be balanced in 1984, and he clung to this view as administration victories multiplied throughout the summer. On July 27 he made a nationally televised speech for the tax reduction bill that was full of happy talk about the nation's economic prospects and the change of attitudes in Washington, "where something very exciting has been happening." On July 29, Congress passed the bill, and Reagan predicted that the nation would be "seeing some signs" of prosperity by the end of the year.*

What the nation actually saw, when July economic indicators became

---

* The tax bill, proposed as a 30 percent income tax reduction over three years, was passed as a 25 percent cut, with the first 5 percent reduction beginning on October 1, 1981. Ten percent cuts were made on July 1 of 1982 and 1983. As the tax bill emerged from Congress, it was a Christmas tree laden with added gifts that had little to do with any economic theory except greed. The oil industry and the savings and loan business, heavy financial contributors to congressional campaigns, were particular beneficiaries of this largesse. The administration acquiesced to the changes on political grounds. One congressionally induced change favored by Reagan had particular significance: tax rates were indexed so that government revenues no longer rose automatically with inflation.

available a few days later, were signs that the economy had slipped into a recession. Stockman's growing pessimism had by now penetrated the sanctuary of the White House staff, and Baker and Darman realized that the combined impact of the tax cut, increased military spending and recession pointed to mammoth deficits. Reagan would resist these insights until the fall. "I think there's a slight recession and I hope a short recession," Reagan told reporters on October 18. "I think everyone agrees on that." [69] Five days later, the national debt went over the trillion-dollar mark. On October 23, Treasury Secretary Regan said that a balanced budget in 1984 was "not probable." And on November 6, a date when unemployment figures reached a six-year high, Reagan finally redefined his objective of a balanced budget as "a goal." When he was asked by a reporter at a South Lawn ceremony what year he would balance the budget, Reagan replied, "I'll answer that further down the road." [70]

Stockman celebrated his thirty-fifth birthday on November 10, 1981, the day Senator Gary Hart of Colorado obtained an advance copy of *The Atlantic* and read into the *Congressional Record* the text of William Greider's "The Education of David Stockman." It was a bombshell. Greider, who had known Stockman since he was a congressional aide, was then assistant managing editor for national news at *The Washington Post*. He was intellectually curious, politically liberal and highly knowledgeable about the budget. The supply-side revolution fascinated him, although he realized (as Stockman did not) that the pork barrel programs so popular on Capitol Hill had strong constituencies back home. In December 1980, Greider had proposed to Stockman that they meet regularly to discuss the progress of the revolution with the understanding that nothing would be published "until after the season's political battles were over and our program had become legislation." [71] Stockman agreed. He respected Greider, wanted a sounding board outside the inner circle and was captivated by the prospects of proselytizing an editor of *The Post*. "My intellectual impulse was to try to penetrate the citadel of establishment opinion makers—and those opinion makers hung out, so to speak, in the pages of *The Washington Post*," Stockman wrote. "They were the modern secularists I was trying to convert." [72] *

---

* Greider was then my editor at *The Washington Post*, and I understand why Stockman valued him as a sounding board. He was known at *The Post* as a man of ideas who was keenly interested in social and economic policy. During the 1980 campaign he prodded me to explain Reagan's background and ideas, at one point commissioning a Reagan mini-biography that he saw to it appeared for four consecutive days on page one of *The Washington Post*.

Over the next ten months Stockman described the changing fortunes of the Reagan revolution to Greider at eighteen tape-recorded Saturday breakfast conversations. These became the basis for *The Atlantic* essay, which described Stockman's passage from optimism to disillusionment. While the article was written in an empathetic and philosophical tone, Stockman's admissions were devastating. He acknowledged that he had changed the OMB computers to reflect the optimistic economic projections that he did not fully share. He also acknowledged the flimsy basis of supply-side doctrine. "The whole thing is premised on faith," Stockman explained. "On a belief about the way the world works." More damaging still was Stockman's candor about the "internal mysteries" of the budget process of which he was supposed to be a master. "None of us really understands what's going on with all these numbers," he confessed. Most damaging of all, Stockman admitted that the grand theory of supply-siders was really a cover for the older, largely discredited idea of "trickle-down"—the view that tax cuts for corporations and the wealthy produce beneficial effects on the lower rungs of the economic ladder. The Kemp-Roth bill, in Stockman's colorful phrase, was really a "Trojan horse" intended principally to reduce the top tax rate from 70 to 50 percent. "It's kind of hard to sell 'trickle-down,' so the supply-side formula was the only way to get a tax policy that was really 'trickle-down,' " Stockman said. "Supply-side is 'trickle-down' theory." [73]

For an administration dedicated to the politics of illusion, the article came as a heavy blow. Supply-side citadels such as *The Wall Street Journal* demanded Stockman's dismissal. So did some Republican congressmen who anticipated that Stockman's indiscretions would be draped around their necks in the next election. At the White House the article provoked an unusual alliance between the then-feuding Ed Meese and Mike Deaver, both of whom wanted to fire Stockman. They were motivated in the main by the public relations problem Stockman had caused the Reagan presidency, but neither of them especially liked the budget director, who had never made a serious attempt to conceal his disdain for their abilities. Deaver was also reflecting Nancy Reagan's view that Stockman had damaged her husband.

Jim Baker, however, stuck with Stockman. Many within the White House believed that he did so at the insistence of Darman, who was an ally and friend of Stockman and knew it would be difficult to find an adequate replacement. But Baker needed no prodding to come to Stockman's defense. The chief of staff believed that enemies of his enemies were his friends, and he shared Stockman's foes among the more extreme supply-siders at Treasury and on Capitol Hill. Baker had been George Bush's campaign manager in 1980 when Bush described the supply-side theory as "voodoo economics," and he shared the vice president's skepticism about the supply-side vision of a painless prosperity. Though not particularly well versed in economics, Baker suspected that there was something screwy about the idea that massive tax cuts would increase government revenues. Later, he would privately express regrets that the deficits had "gotten away" from the administration and wished he had paid more attention to the consequences of the tax cuts. In many respects his doubts mirrored Stockman's, although he refrained from the budget director's colorful metaphors. When *The Atlantic* story broke, Baker was furious with Stockman not for talking to Greider but for the naïveté of permitting himself to be quoted. Baker himself held many candid conversations with reporters, but he protected himself with ground rules that guaranteed his anonymity.

There was another side to Baker that he tried to keep from showing. Outwardly, he was hard-boiled and well organized. He loved political competition and longed for others to think him a master of the game. But he was not always the political mastermind he fancied himself to be. While he had few superiors in the craft of maneuver, his innate caution discouraged him from taking bold, strategic risks. If he had been a football quarterback, sportswriters might have said of him that he was dependable but rarely tried to make the big play. Baker's caution had prevented him from grasping the opportunity presented by the Domenici-Hollings initiative. In 1984, it would prompt him to wage an almost issueless reelection campaign for Reagan and Bush. But in human relationships, Baker was more caring than he thought it prudent to reveal. His first wife had died of cancer, and the memory of it haunted him even though he remarried and had another family.[74] During one of the busiest periods of the presidency Baker made out-of-town trips on weekends to visit a terminally ill friend. His loyalty to his friends was matched by a kindness and compassion to subordinates who were suffering through life's crises. Like Reagan, he found it extremely difficult to fire anyone. Baker, however, concealed his softheartedness, which conflicted with the political image he had created for himself. In that respect the wealthy and patrician Baker much resembled Stu Spencer, his streetwise ally from the other side of the tracks. Spencer, also outwardly hard-bitten and privately kindhearted, reached out to friends in trouble but rationalized his actions as good politics. This is what Baker did when Stockman's job was on the line. While

Baker advanced political arguments for forgiving Stockman, other members of the White House team believed that he simply liked and respected the budget director and did not want to lose him. ("Baker admired his brains and thought he was gutsy," said David Gergen.)[75] And Baker was able to prevail, despite the demands for Stockman's scalp from other members of the troika and Nancy Reagan, because he understood that Reagan shared his feelings. The troika in those days did the high-level hiring and firing in the White House. Since all its members knew of Reagan's desire for consensus, the troika normally recommended appointments or asked for resignations only when there was unanimity among the members. In effect, any member of the troika had a veto, and this was particularly true on recommendations for resignation. Reagan accepted resignations only when his advisers were unanimous. He was always relieved if there was an alternative to dismissal.

The alternative in this case was a supposed "woodshedding" of Stockman, a staff-concocted scenario that was as much a charade as the supposed dressing-down that Reagan had administered to Al Haig and Richard Allen a week earlier. Deaver helped Baker with the script preparation after it was clear Reagan would retain Stockman. The only "woodshedding" that occurred was when Baker met privately with the budget director, subjecting him to what Stockman later called "a verbal thrashing." After telling Stockman that everyone else wanted him fired, Baker looked at him coldly and said, "You're going to have lunch with the president. The menu is humble pie. You're going to eat every last mother-f'ing spoonful of it. You're going to be the most contrite son-ofabitch the world has ever seen." [76] The lunch, soup and tuna salad, was on November 12, 1981, a week to the day after the fake dressing-down of Allen and Haig. Stockman told the president his life story, offered him his resignation and apologized for the harm he had caused him. Reagan comforted him, telling him he had read the entire article in *The Atlantic* and saying he recognized that the quotes from it then being circulated in the media had been taken out of context. "I wish you hadn't said them," Reagan told him. "But you're a victim of sabotage by the press." [77] Reagan asked Stockman to stay. In the White House briefing room, deputy press secretary Larry Speakes issued a statement in Reagan's name in which the president "expressed particular dismay at the possible suggestion that his administration—or any members of his administration—might seek to mislead the American public."

Like other presidents before and after him, Reagan was apt to blame the media rather than himself or his subordinates when administration deceptions came to light. In Reagan's eyes, Stockman's mistake was not changing the OMB computers to reflect economic assumptions in which he did not believe but confiding this to Greider. Reagan himself would never have made such a confession, for he always persuaded himself that he had done the right thing. Reagan was convinced of the essential merits of his economic program, and he believed that the media was undermining it. As the recession deepened, the White House mounted a public relations campaign against "unfairness," by which Deaver, Speakes and Gergen meant not the impact of the Reagan budget cuts but the media portrayal of the human misery they supposedly caused. Television was, in Gergen's phrase, "the preoccupying medium." [78] Stories about the increasingly desperate plight of the poor and unemployed were commonplace in newspapers and newsmagazines, but Reagan and his aides knew that the most enduring public perceptions were shaped by television. Each evening, often in his pajamas, Reagan watched the evening network news shows with Nancy Reagan in the comfort of the White House residence. Back in the working White House, Gergen and Speakes monitored the network news on triple-screen television sets in their offices that permitted simultaneous monitoring of the three networks. (In the second term, Cable News Network also would become a fixture in the White House.) Baker and Deaver had television sets in their offices. For harried White House officials who often worked long into the night, the network news hour was often a time to pause and share perceptions. "Business didn't quite stop, but if we were in Baker's office, we'd turn on the television to see what was on the news, sometimes keeping the sound down low until something came on we wanted to see," said Gergen. "It was a reality check." [79]

And the reality that was reflected on television screens in the early months of 1982 was sobering. On April 21, CBS aired *People Like Us,* a documentary narrated by Bill Moyers that emotionally presented four accounts of hardship and destitution. An Ohio man with cerebral palsy had been dropped from the Social Security rolls. A Hispanic woman in New Jersey, cut from welfare and Medicaid rolls, could not afford preventive cancer surgery for her thirteen-year-old son. A Wisconsin mother who had been caring for her comatose daughter at home was forced by new Medicaid regulations to move her to an institution, at far greater cost to the government. A Milwaukee church that provided food for the downtrodden was overwhelmed by increasing requests for aid.

"These are people who slipped through the safety net and are falling away," Moyers said in his introduction. "In the great outcry about spending, some helpless people are getting hurt."

This powerful documentary became a rallying point for Reagan's critics and a principal target of the White House. Gergen said it "hit below the belt" and issued a point-by-point rebuttal, disputing the factual accuracy of some points and denying that the incidents Moyers depicted were the result of Reagan administration policies. *Washington Post* television critic Tom Shales, dazzled by the documentary, compared its potential impact to the 1979 NBC program of Roger Mudd's that he believed had dashed Senator Edward M. Kennedy's campaign for the Democratic presidential nomination. Nine days before the Moyers documentary, Reagan had returned from an Easter vacation in Barbados at the luxurious home of Claudette Colbert. "The president splashes about in the lap of luxury while Americans go hungry," Shales wrote. "Even the people on this program, victims of Reaganomics all, are reluctant to say a word against him, but the program leaves one feeling that a very fragile bubble is just about to burst."[80] This view of the program's impact, if not its accuracy, was shared in the White House. "The issue had been building prior to the Moyers special," Gergen said many years later. "He crystallized it and made it a much more devastating case against the administration. While he made some valid points, it was a one-sided show."[81]

One-sided or not, *People Like Us* set a tone for television coverage of economic issues and raised awareness that people were slipping through the vaunted Reagan-Stockman "safety net." It was not only Reagan who thought this emphasis was unfair. Writing about the "unintended political consequences" of such coverage, *Time* asked rhetorically early in 1983, "Which story more truly reveals the state of the economy and the performance of Reaganomics: the drop in inflation from 12.4% in 1980 . . . to about 5% in 1982, a change that is often conveyed flatly and numerically? Or the simultaneous rise in unemployment from 7.4% to 10.8%, a development that lends itself to anecdotes and dramatic interviews with the jobless?"[82]

Reagan, the master of anecdotes, took the stories of hardship personally. "He didn't see himself as heartless or lacking in compassion," Gergen said. "If you call him a racist or say he is anti-poor, he has a hard time dealing with it. She [Nancy Reagan] did, too."[83] When Reagan was asked, in an exceptionally sympathetic interview with reporters from *The Daily Oklahoman* on March 16, 1982, whether his "rightful image as a compassionate, kind, generous man could be eroded" by television coverage of the recession, he replied, "I think there's not only a possibility. I think they've done a pretty good job of it. I'm Scrooge to a lot of people, and if they only knew it, I'm the softest touch they've had for a long time."

He was, however, a soft touch with many grievances. When the deferential *Oklahoman* reporters asked him if foreign policy "leaks" to *The Washington Post* were damaging, Reagan said they were, and used the question to present his litany of complaints about television's economic coverage: "In a time of recession like this, there's a great deal of psychology in economics. And you can't turn on evening news without seeing that they're going to interview someone else who's lost his job, or they're outside the factory that has laid off workers and so forth— the constant downbeat that can contribute psychologically to slowing down a new recovery that is in the offing." This was happening, Reagan said, because the networks were engaged in a ratings battle that made them "more concerned with entertainment than delivering the evening news. It's an entertainment medium, and they're looking for what's eyecatching and spectacular. . . . Is it news that some fellow out in South Succotash someplace has just been laid off, that he should be interviewed nationwide?"

At the time it seemed ironic to those of us in the White House press corps that Reagan, the virtuoso of symbolism, should complain that television coverage was symbolically discrediting his economic program. Few days went by without a gaudy "photo opportunity" with a desirable backdrop in an attempt, often successful, to show off the president favorably on the nightly news. What was of more significance than Reagan's unseemly complaint that television also relied on symbolism was his conviction that the economy would improve if the news media preached hopefulness rather than "doom and gloom." He was quite sincere in this belief, which was widely shared in the White House. Meese said at one point that what happened to the economy was 50 percent psychological. Treasury Secretary Regan predicted in February 1982 that the economy would come "roaring back like a lion" in the springtime.[84] The day of Reagan's interview with *The Daily Oklahoman,* Gergen told me he expected a recovery in the second quarter of 1982. Whether these aides were simply parroting what they said to each other or reflecting Reagan's optimism, I never knew.

What had become apparent by this point was that the most important economic influence in the government was not the White House or the

Treasury Department but the Federal Reserve Board, a mile away on Constitution Avenue. Neither Reagan nor the networks were the custodians of American economic confidence, then at a particularly low ebb. The man of the hour (he graced the cover of *Time* on March 8, 1982, and had become a household name to Americans) was Paul Adolph Volcker, the implacable chairman of the Federal Reserve Board. At six foot seven and one-half inches, he was a half foot taller than Reagan, and many thought that the Fed's monetary policies also towered over the eclectic economic program of the Reagan administration. As the recession persisted, it became clear both in the White House and on Capitol Hill that it was Volcker who held the key to the success or failure of Reaganomics.

Volcker, who had served as Treasury undersecretary for monetary affairs in the Nixon administration, was the fifty-one-year-old chairman of the New York Federal Reserve Bank when Jimmy Carter made him chairman of the Fed in 1979, at a time when the annual inflation rate was 13 percent and climbing out of sight. The appointment was a victory for Wall Street, which viewed Volcker as a determined foe of inflation with the toughness to resist political pressures from the White House. In his confirmation hearings Volcker described himself as a "pragmatic monetarist," a term that Niskanen noted tartly "is often used by those who believe that money is important but lack a clear sense of what should be done about it." [85] What Volcker basically did about it, through a series of technical measures, was to change (on October 6, 1979) the historic Fed procedure of controlling interest rates to one of controlling the money supply. He believed the new procedures gave the Fed a better handle on controlling inflation, which Volcker regarded as Public Enemy No. 1. His experiment would continue through most of the first two years of the Reagan administration, with consequences that are still being debated among economists.

The Constitution grants Congress the power to coin money and regulate its value. In 1913 Congress delegated this authority to the Federal Reserve System. "Over its history," in Niskanen's words, "the Federal Reserve Board, rather like the Supreme Court, has developed an aura, influence and independence that go far beyond the intentions of its creators." [86] The Fed's inner workings are deliberately shrouded in mystery and transcripts of its proceedings no longer published. Its chairman is routinely viewed as second in power only to the president of the United States, and this was especially true during the critical economic period of Volcker's reign. The Fed is supposed to see to it that the economy has sufficient money and credit to carry on its business and grow. Too little money and the price of borrowing it (interest) rises, and the economy contracts. Too much money results in inflation. Such, at least, is the theory. In practice, the measurement of money supplies is arcane and difficult, and Volcker and the six governors of the Fed were often accused by their critics of mismeasuring it. By 1982 the economy had contracted so much that the interest-sensitive housing industry was working at its lowest pace since 1946. Automobile sales had fallen to a twenty-year low, and manufacturers and farmers were crying for relief. The cover of the January-February 1982 issue of *Tennessee Professional Builder* consisted of a wanted poster of Volcker and the other Fed governors, charging them with "premeditated and cold-blooded murder of millions of small businesses" and "kidnaping (and holding for ransom) the American dream of home ownership."[87] By then, Don Regan was openly attacking Volcker for holding back economic recovery. The supply-siders wanted his scalp even more than they wanted Stockman's. Jack Kemp called for Volcker's resignation and made common cause with Democrats who threatened legislation that would force the Fed to lower interest rates.

Reagan, however, was firmly on Volcker's side, even though this was not widely understood outside the White House. Three days after his inauguration, Reagan had startled the Secret Service by walking out the front door of the White House and down Pennsylvania Avenue to the Treasury Building, where he lunched with Volcker. Aides who attended the lunch would never forget it. Reagan was barely seated before he said to the chairman, "I was wondering if you could help with a question that's often put to me. I've had several letters from people who raise the question of why we need any Federal Reserve at all. They seem to feel that it is the Fed that causes much of our monetary problems and that we would be better off if we abolished it. Why do we need the Federal Reserve?"[88]

Martin Anderson, sitting directly across from Volcker, observed that "his face muscles went slack and his lower jaw literally sagged a half-inch or so as his mouth fell open. For several seconds he just looked at Reagan, stunned and speechless. It is a good thing Volcker had not had time to light one of his long cigars because he might have swallowed it."[89] Long afterward, Anderson told me that he believes Reagan's question was inspired by the theories of iconoclastic conservatives who have argued in favor of a self-regulating system in which currency would be issued by private banks. Reagan made no pretense to expertise on the subject, though he had been exposed to the theories in letters from friends and stories in right-wing publications. He also had no concern about advertising his ignorance. Reagan asked the question about the purpose of the Fed as innocently and naturally as he had asked Ed Yoder about the origins of the English language or said to George Will, "What makes the Blue Ridge mountains blue?"

Volcker, however, recovered quickly from his surprise, and gave a good account of himself. Acknowledging that others held the same concerns Reagan had expressed, Volcker said, "I think you can make a very strong case that the Federal Reserve has operated well and has been very important to the stability of our economy."[90] He then lectured Reagan briefly on the Fed's role in regulating the money supply. His answer apparently satisfied the president, who never raised the question again.

Over the next two years Volcker met periodically with Reagan, always at the White House. Anderson, who attended all the meetings before he left the administration in 1982, said Volcker did most of the talking, speaking directly to the president and illustrating his points with charts and graphs. "Reagan never asked him to either ease or tighten the money supply," Anderson said. "I think Volcker very much appreciated the lack of direct pressure. Given that Volcker was a Democrat appointed by President Carter, a surprising amount of goodwill seemed to develop between the two."[91] In part this may have been because Reagan was willing to allow Volcker more running room than Carter had given him. The Carter White House had pressured Volcker to adopt credit controls, which the Fed did in March 1980. Gross national product dropped at a 9 percent annual rate in the second quarter of 1980, the steepest decline in modern history. The Fed backed away from credit controls in June, and the last six months of the year witnessed one of the biggest surges in the money supply in history. "Carter whipsawed Volcker," said Niskanen. "Reagan didn't understand monetary policy any better than Carter did, but he gave Volcker more leeway."[92]

This is a judgment shared by politicians in the Reagan White House who made no pretense of understanding monetary policy at all. Deaver, who had the keenest sense of Reagan's personal likes and dislikes, said that Reagan appreciated Volcker and thought he was doing the best he could.[93] White House officials treated Volcker with respect. The Fed chairman had asked for a White House pass so that he would not have to produce his driver's license at the White House gates. The request was bureaucratically denied by John F. W. Rogers, who informed Volcker that each pass required security investigations that cost the government $3,000. Volcker was offended, and wrote a short, angry letter to Martin Anderson saying, "I didn't know you distrusted my security that much!" Anderson complained to Meese and Baker about the snub, and Volcker was promptly issued a special White House pass along with an apology.[94]

The judgment of those close to Reagan in this period is that he found Volcker a kindred soul. They were certainly alike in the trait of stubbornness. Reagan was convinced in the depth of the recession that his own policies were sound, and Volcker believed that the Fed was following the course necessary to throttle the menace of inflation. Volcker's campaign appealed to the Nelle Reagan in the president—to the moralistic streak that says everything happens for a purpose and that people must pay for past misdeeds. "We were Calvinists in a way," said Niskanen. "The feeling was that good things don't all come in a package, that you have to have a little pain."[95] None of this "pain," of course, was suffered by the well-heeled members of the Reagan entourage, and very little of it by the even wealthier big bankers who were Volcker's principal constituency. But Volcker's strict views appealed to Reagan's fundamentalist conviction that America would have to pay a price for a half century of living beyond its means. "The purgatory view of inflation was out of sight, but not out of mind," said Stockman. "It was never articulated in public, but privately the president was tolerant of the circumstances. It fulfilled the old Ronald Reagan's expectations of what would happen when you shifted from Keynesian liberalism to a sound policy. The president would say to us: 'We've been on a binge for thirty years. This is the price you have to pay.' "[96]

For Reagan, as for other adult children of alcoholics, the word "binge" has a special meaning. He thought of the government programs of the Great Society as a terrible drinking spree from which the nation was suffering a monumental hangover. It was the message he had once proclaimed on the conservative banquet circuit, before he had sipped the elixir of supply-side economics. Reagan did not realize that the supply-side tax cut he had so enthusiastically endorsed would prevent the deficit-addicted economy from sobering up. Even though his policies were abetting creation of the greatest deficits in American history, Reagan believed that deficits were inherently evil.

While Stockman was right in observing that Reagan held a "purgatory view of inflation," he was wrong in saying that the president did not express these views publicly. Once Reagan realized that the United States was indeed gripped by a recession, he used the word "binge" nine times in public appearances to describe the economic situation, beginning with a lunch at the New York City Partnership on January 14, 1982, where he said, "Yes, we're in a recession. Our administration is cleanup crew for those who went on a non-stop binge and left the tab for us to pick up. The recession hurts. It causes pain. But we'll work our way out of it." By now, Reagan had forgotten that the economy had surged in 1981 before sliding into the recession. He blamed the entire recession on Jimmy Carter and the spending proclivities of past Democratic Congresses and became ever more enamored of this theme—and of the metaphors of alcoholism—as the 1982 elections approached. "The decisions made by Americans next Tuesday and throughout this decade will determine whether we stay the course and maintain our national renewal, or whether we stagger off on one more economic binge—a binge that we and our children would have to pay for, and we'd pay for it with another pounding hangover," Reagan declared at a Republican rally in Great Falls, Montana, on October 28, 1982.

One thing Reagan never did was blame himself for the recession. He rarely blamed the Fed, either, although others in the White House were prone to occasional Fed-bashing. Some of the criticism of the Fed came from Jim Baker, who was enough of a Texan to have his reservations about Wall Street. As the administration's political point man, Baker was also the recipient of constant complaints about Volcker's tight-money policies from western and southern Republicans, including Howard Baker and Paul Laxalt. With an eye to the midterm elections, Howard Baker told Republican congressional strategists late in 1981, "Volcker's got his foot on our neck, and we've got to make him take it off." [97]

Inflation plummeted rapidly in 1981, dropping to an annual rate of 5 percent by the end of the year. But interest rates, after a mild slide, rose again. The real interest rate, as measured by short-term Treasury bills, rose from 5 percent in the second quarter of the year to 5.5 percent in the third quarter to 8.2 percent in the final quarter. Until mid-October, banks kept their basic loan rate at 19 percent. The reason for the persistence of high rates was both a source of mystery and a matter of dispute. The Treasury blamed the volatility of the money supply, which the Fed had reduced beyond initial administration guidelines. The Fed and many economists blamed the deficit, which they said was sopping up a disproportionate share of investment capital. Others pointed to the 1981 tax law, which increased real interest rates by increasing the post-tax return on new investment. Still others said that Volcker and the Fed were deliberately keeping interest rates unreasonably high. Niskanen came to the view that Volcker was trying to accomplish with monetary policy what Caspar Weinberger was doing with military spending—gaining as much of his objective as possible before he was stopped. "My judgment is that Volcker believed that the consensus for monetary restraint was temporary and that the American political system would not tolerate the slow, steady reduction in money growth recommended by the initial Reagan guidance," Niskanen concluded in 1988. "He may have wanted to reduce inflation as rapidly as possible, despite the temporary adverse effects on the economy and the destruction of the consensus for sustained restraint."[98]

The confusion over what was actually happening worked to Volcker's advantage in the White House. "Reagan's attitude was that Volcker was a very sound professional, doing his best not to submarine the economy," said Martin Anderson. "Everyone thinks the Fed is supposed to know what to do, but the truth is that the Fed's information is kind of fuzzy. Our feeling was that it was wrong to lean on the Fed, that it might cause them to do something dumb."[99] Whenever he was faced with conflicting recommendations, which was often, Reagan tended to follow his instinct and support the Fed. He wavered only when Regan and Stockman, who normally could not stand each other, teamed up at a January 1982 economic briefing to express concern about the Fed's inconsistency in controlling the money supply. For reasons no one seemed to understand, the money supply had increased in November, surged higher in December and continued to grow during the early weeks of the new year. Following this briefing, Reagan was asked at a January 19 news conference about the reasons for declining capital investment. "I think there's a little caution at work and perhaps part of it is waiting to see what the Federal Reserve system is doing, because there's been an upsurge, for example, in the money supply just recently, which sends, I think, the wrong signal to the money markets," he said. "In other words, they want to be more sure that interest rates and inflation are going to continue coming down as they have been." When a reporter followed up by asking Reagan if he agreed with calls for Volcker's resignation, the president said he couldn't respond to the question "because the Federal Reserve System is autonomous."

It is worth noting that this rare presidential criticism of Volcker occurred because Reagan thought the Fed was tightening interest rates too little rather than too much. When the Fed in February 1982 took actions that resulted in tightening of the money supply, Volcker then came under fire from Treasury Secretary Regan and Capitol Hill for purportedly slamming the brakes on the economy. Reagan, however, was prepared to defend monetary austerity, despite Jim Baker's worries that Volcker was making hash of Republican political prospects in the midterm elections. On February 15, 1982, Reagan met again with Volcker at the White House and was reassured by the Fed chairman that he would hold the line on the money supply. Three days later, at another news conference, Reagan gave Volcker a resounding vote of confidence and endorsed the Fed's 1982 money growth targets. "The administration and the Federal Reserve can help bring inflation and interest rates down faster by working together than by working at cross purposes," Reagan said. "This administration will always support the political independence of the Federal Reserve Board."

Reagan stuck with Volcker in the hard months of the recession ahead, and he reappointed him chairman of the Fed in 1983 despite the reservations of Jim Baker and the opposition of Don Regan. But Volcker did not stick with the controversial experiment of targeting the money supply. Although interest rates declined and the stock market soared in the summer of 1982, the economy remained weak and Capitol Hill clamored for a relaxation of money controls as the midterm elections approached. But it was financial developments at home and abroad, not political criticism, that forced Volcker to relent. In July the Federal Deposit Insurance Corporation closed down Penn Square Bank in Oklahoma City, seizing its assets and sending shock waves through the banking community. This event coincided with the debt crisis in Mexico, which had been battered by the long stretch of high interest rates. If Mexico defaulted on its loans, most of which were held by the big U.S. banks that were Volcker's principal constituency, other debt-ridden nations in the hemisphere were sure to follow. This in turn threatened a world depression on the pattern of 1929, when the Federal Reserve tightened the money supply at the very time it should have been easing it.

"It was getting to the point where we had to ease, regardless," Volcker would say later. "I became particularly antsy about the economy. Clearly, those earlier expectations that the economy would recover were wrong. I'd gotten fairly pessimistic. The strains in the financial system and the LDC [less-developed countries] debt, all these things were pushing us. So I jumped when the opening came."[100] The Fed began pumping money into the system. In October, the Fed also abandoned its three-year monetarist experiment of trying to target the money supply.

Retrospectively, Reagan's support of Volcker seems sounder politically than most Republican politicians and administration officials—including Jim Baker and Don Regan—perceived it to be at the time. Since Republicans held on to the Senate in 1982, the loss of 26 House seats proved an acceptable price for a policy that paid Reagan rich political dividends in 1984. A case can be made that Reagan intended the policy or at least accepted it as inevitable. Although he had obligatorily opposed recession as a cure for inflation during the 1980 election campaign, he shared Volcker's fundamental view that it was necessary economic medicine. As Stu Spencer has often observed, Reagan had a knack for divining the popular will even when he could not articulate it, and there was strong support in the land for harsh measures to remedy inflation, even among those who were being hurt by the cure. Reagan believed that Americans were paying for what he had called the "failed policies of the past." He also believed, as he always did, that there would be a happy ending to the script. But Reagan was not temperamentally suited to darkling roles, and the austere figure of Paul Volcker was a useful surrogate for those who wanted to blame someone other than the president. "One was shadowy and remote, an ominous figure; the other, bright and cheerful," wrote William Greider. "Paul Volcker was the stern father who admonished and prophesied, uttering mysterious incantations of numbers. Ronald Reagan was the generous king who inspired hope, whose rhetoric evoked streaks of sunshine across the darkened sky. Together, they promised redemption—if only the faithful flock would first accept the penitential sacrifice."[101]

Reagan's own popularity would reach its first-term low point of 35 percent in January 1983, a time when confidence in the administration's (and Volcker's) policies was even lower. Less than 20 percent of Americans thought that the economy was improving.[102] Reagan, however, was the most hopeful member of this minority. On February 5, in his weekly Saturday radio speech, he claimed that his economic recovery program was working even while joking that "Reaganomics" was not the name he would have chosen for it. ("It sounds like a fad diet or an aerobic exercise," he said.) On February 9, in a meeting with editorial-page writers in the White House, Reagan claimed that "all the signs we're now seeing point toward an economic recovery."[103] On March

25, during a question-and-answer session with high school students at the White House, Reagan said his critics had named his program "Reaganomics" when they didn't think it was working and added, "I'm wondering what they're going to call it now that it is working." [104] By April 29, at a fund-raising dinner for Senator John Tower in Houston, with the recovery in full bloom, Reagan gave the one-liner the twist he would use throughout his presidency: "They aren't calling it Reaganomics anymore."

Later in his presidency, after Reagan had become a remote and disengaged monarch, first-term aides would recall the grim months of recession as if they were a golden age. They would remember Reagan scoffing at his critics and the polls and defiantly proclaiming that he would "stay the course" with his economic program. "The greatest show of his leadership was then," said speechwriter Bently Elliott. "He had the courage to accept the criticism. After that, he notched down a little bit." [105]

Even before the president "notched down," however, it was evident that the course he pursued with such determination had produced results that contradicted his expectations. Both the achievements and the failures of Reaganomics were monumental. Defying periodic predictions of economic downturn, the recovery that began in 1983 continued through Reagan's second term and carried over into the Bush administration, providing by far the longest peacetime expansion in United States history. Eighteen million new jobs were created. The annual inflation rate, which averaged 12.5 percent in the final year of the Carter presidency, averaged 4.4 percent in 1988. Meanwhile, the unemployment rate had been reduced from 7.1 percent to 5.5 percent and the prime interest rate cut nearly six points to 9.32 percent. "On the surface," as John M. Berry observed late in 1988, "these achievements suggest that the administration's policies of fostering private entrepreneurship, reducing the size of government and cutting tax rates have wrought a significant change in the American economy." [106]

But there was a price for this prosperity. The nation's private wealth grew only 8 percent in the six years after the end of the recession. "In a comparable five-year period between 1975 and 1980, so often derided by Reagan as an inflation-prone, unproductive era, the nation's real private wealth increased 31 percent—almost four times as much," Berry noted. [107] Meanwhile, the national debt grew robustly. It nearly tripled, to $2.684.4 trillion, while the trade deficit more than quadrupled, to $137.3 billion. The size of the deficits was in part attributable to the tax cuts and the military buildup, but it also reflected deficient White House political decisions in rejecting the COLA freeze in 1981 and, even more significantly, a Senate budget compromise in 1985. The combination of reduced taxes and high interest rates attracted a flood of foreign investment to the United States, boosting the value of the dollar and making it difficult for American manufacturers to compete with foreign goods, either at home or abroad. Some basic American industries were driven to their knees by these policies, while others learned to compete more efficiently. The mammoth budget deficits did not produce the widely predicted consequences of crowding out private investment and raising interest rates. Instead, they crowded out exports of American goods while imports crowded into the United States.

Eventually, under pressure from U.S. allies and with Jim Baker pushing for new policies at Treasury in the second term, the value of the dollar declined. But the United States had by then become a debtor nation for the first time since 1914. Americans were left at the mercy of foreign investors who financed the trade deficit with loans and purchases of U.S. stocks, bonds, land, factories and buildings. The consequences of this development extended far beyond the economy. "People simply do not view their debtors in the same light as they do their creditors," observed political economist Benjamin M. Friedman. "It is no accident that America emerged as a world power simultaneously with our transition from a debtor nation, dependent on foreign capital for our initial industrialization, to a creditor supplying investment capital to the rest of the world. The same happened to Spain in the sixteenth century, and in Britain in the nineteenth." [108]

Reagan's great experiment with supply-side tax cuts also did not produce the results its enthusiasts anticipated. Tax incentives failed to spur personal savings, which averaged 5.4 percent of after-tax income in the 1980s after averaging 8 percent in the 1970s. While the tax cuts at first produced a mild gain in taxable income, much of it transferred from tax shelters, the long-term impact of the cuts reduced federal revenues. It is hard to see how it could have been otherwise. "There was never an empirical basis for the assertion that a general reduction in tax rates would increase revenues, and no administration economist or revenue projection ever supported that irresponsible claim," said Niskanen. [109] Yet Reagan acted as if he believed that this "irresponsible claim" was valid. He never sought the taxes needed to finance the military buildup, and he never really tackled the basic budgetary issues, despite Stockman's prodigious assault on discretionary spending in

1981. To a large degree Reagan was taken in by his own rhetoric, expressed in the superficial notion that federal spending could be significantly reduced by eliminating "waste, fraud, extravagance and abuse."

Nonetheless, the tax policy of the Reagan era had a profound impact on the economies of the United States and other Western industrialized nations, much of it arguably beneficial. When Reagan took office, marginal tax rates (the rate at which the last dollar of income is taxed) stood at 70 percent. When he left, thanks to the 1981 tax bill and the 1986 tax reform measure that broadened the base and eliminated many special tax preferences, the marginal rate had been more than cut in half, to 33 percent. In the view of such economists as Niskanen and Greenspan, this created a ripple effect of lower taxes and economic activity in other industrialized nations. "You just can't have tax rates differing substantially across advanced countries because you would have a flight both of capital and brains," Niskanen contends.[110] Moving money out of tax shelters may also have increased public confidence in a tax system that was widely viewed by nearly all segments of society as unfair. Although the evidence is far from conclusive, some economists believe that the lower tax rates have discouraged tax cheating in the United States and other industrialized nations. Certainly, the lower rates that now prevail provide less incentive for shielding or concealing income.

The most notable economic accomplishment of the Reagan years was the long-term reduction of inflation. Reagan recognized that inflation, as Senator Domenici put it, is "the big no-no in the pursuit of economic prosperity."[111] Despite the misgivings about Volcker's policies within the White House staff and the cabinet, Reagan stuck by the Fed chairman when it counted. Inflation initially was reduced by harsh methods, principally the extreme tightening of the money supply and the traditional remedy of high unemployment, and many small businesses and small farms went under in the process. But the inflation rate stayed low after the money supply increased and the jobless rate fell. A principal reason was the policies of the Federal Reserve, which squeezed the economy again in 1985 when the dollar peaked and inflation expectations rose. Normally, the dollar's fall would have increased the prices of imported goods, but many foreign manufacturers elected to keep prices low and maintain their share of the U.S. market at the expense of profit margins. This decision in turn influenced rebounding U.S. industries to hold the line on prices and on wage increases, often with union cooperation, to meet the foreign competition. And a world oil glut drove energy prices down in 1986, also contributing to the decline of inflation rates.

The long period of low inflation had a stabilizing effect in the United States and was of enormous political benefit to Reagan, whose approval ratings soared in 1983 and remained relatively high for most of the four-year period between the end of the recession and the disclosure of the Iran arms sale. When Alan Greenspan replaced Volcker as chairman of the Federal Reserve Board in 1987, he continued to make restraint of inflation his top priority, without resorting to the Draconian tactics employed by Volcker. The Fed restricted interest rates in 1987 until the stock market crash in October and again in 1988, although it did not return to the Volcker experiment of attempting to control inflation by tightening the money supply. "Policymakers now understand that maintaining a constant growth of the money supply does not ensure the economy's health and may even imperil it," concluded economist Alan S. Blinder in 1989.[112] But the Reagan-Volcker legacy of treating inflation as Public Enemy No. 1 has lingered into the Bush administration and may well prove the most enduring and popular of Reagan's conflicting economic legacies.

Policymakers disagree on the long-term impact of the budget and trade deficits that were one of the principal legacies of Reaganomics. Interest payments on the national debt consumed 15 percent of the budget in the first year of the Bush administration, compared to 10 percent during Jimmy Carter's last year in office. The ultimate impact of the continuing deficit will depend in large measure upon whether the Bush administration and Congress are willing and able to reduce it, either through tax increases, budget cuts or some combination of the two. No such willingness to make hard choices was apparent either at the White House or on Capitol Hill during the first year and a half of the Bush presidency. And even if willingness had existed, the opportunity for deficit reduction was impaired by the vast costs of the savings-and-loan bailout. The savings-and-loan collapse, examined briefly in the concluding chapter of this book, was a true bipartisan calamity reflective of the Reagan administration's passion for deregulation and a congressional thirst for campaign contributions. The costs of the S&L bailout, widely estimated at at least $500 billion by the late summer of 1990, more than offset the prospects of defense savings and deficit reduction resulting from the collapse of the Soviet empire and the decline of the Soviet military threat. And what remained of any promised "peace dividend" was swallowed up in the sands of Saudi Arabia by the U.S. military buildup in the Middle East following Iraq's invasion and absorption of oil-rich Kuwait in August 1990.

The economic policies promulgated on Reagan's watch largely reflected his personal priorities. While he chose to identify with the positive aspects of these policies and put the blame on others for what went wrong, he helped shape the global economic agenda of the 1980s both for better and for worse. He was a most effective salesman for the tax reductions that Greenspan, Niskanen and many other free-market economists believe strengthened the global economy and fed the longing for a better life in Eastern Europe. Reagan understood and often said that economic recovery and lower tax rates in the United States would spur similar developments in the industrialized democracies and demonstrate the economic bankruptcy of the "command economies" of the Soviet Union and other communist states. He viewed capitalism as a cornucopia from which material abundance inevitably overflowed, and he believed that Western economic success would promote a longing for change in Eastern Europe and even in the Soviet Union. Mikhail Gorbachev and more visionary Soviets deserve the principal credit for recognizing that their experiment had failed, but they were also spurred by the contrast between their ruined economy and the prosperity of the West. Reagan played a large role in promoting this prosperity, even while leaving future generations to pay the bill for it.

While Reagan viewed himself as an untrammeled advocate of free-market policies, his actions reflected a more conflicted economic perspective. He was a guns-and-butter president, favoring both a military buildup and continuation of the welfare state created by the New Deal. His actions said he valued the economic stimulus provided by lower tax rates more than he did the pay-as-you-go Republican traditionalism of balanced budgets, or at least budgets that stabilized the federal deficit. His actions also showed that Reagan realized the corrosive dangers of inflation and that he was willing, at the temporary cost of his own popularity, to stay the course with Paul Volcker through the worst U.S. economic crisis in fifty years. These actions spoke louder than all of Reagan's words.

13

FOCUS OF EVIL

*I told him [Gorbachev] that there was a very unique
situation. I said, "Here are the two of us in a room and
probably the only two people in the world who could
start World War III. And we're also the only two
people, perhaps, in the world that could prevent World
War III."*

RONALD REAGAN,
February 10, 1989[1]

At the beginning of his presidency Ronald Reagan responded to
a question about Soviet intentions by denouncing the inherent immorality of Marxism-Leninism. By the final year of his two terms in the White
House, Reagan thought of Mikhail Gorbachev as a friend and praised
the Soviet leader for "trying to do what Lenin was teaching"[2] by encouraging a limited amount of private production in the Soviet Union.
The distance between these assessments was greater than the 4,876
miles from Washington to Moscow that Reagan traveled in 1988 for a
summit in which he proclaimed a "new era" in U.S.-Soviet relations.
This new era was supposedly based entirely on an alteration of Soviet
attitudes, which did indeed change markedly under Gorbachev. But
Reagan also changed, even though he did not recognize any ideological

odyssey. His voyage from the past into the future is not easy to retrace. What we know about his inner journey is that it was guided often by the compass of convictions. Reagan believed staunchly in the power of freedom. He abhorred communism. He was convinced that Communist systems were antithetical to the will of God and the highest aspirations of humanity, and he did not believe that the Soviets could compete successfully in any marketplace. Reagan started from the premise that Soviet leaders respected strength. He believed, and accurately forecast, that the Soviets would respond to a U.S. military buildup by proposing to reduce the strategic arsenals of both sides. He was convinced of his ability to engage Soviet leaders, like the Hollywood producers to whom he compared them, in productive negotiations. He was also horrified by the prospect of nuclear war. Reagan was convinced that American technology could produce an invulnerable space shield that would protect the civilian population from nuclear annihilation. He believed all this before he and the world ever heard of Gorbachev. Some of Reagan's beliefs were as extravagant as the science fiction that was occasionally their inspiration, but he had a sense of the world as it would be and as it might be, not merely of the way it was. Reagan wanted a world without nuclear weapons, and a world without walls and iron curtains. He was, in this respect, a man for the age.

At the onset of his presidency, few opinion-makers viewed Reagan as a visionary. Liberals were disturbed by his anticommunist rhetoric. Conservatives were delighted that at last the United States had a president who would proclaim from the White House podium what they long had been saying from the sidelines. The scene of this first act was Reagan's initial presidential press conference. The setting was Room 450 of the Old Executive Office Building. The time was 4:00 P.M. on January 29, 1981. Reagan was on center stage. Sam Donaldson asked the new president if he believed that the Kremlin was still "bent on world domination that might lead to a continuation of the Cold War" or whether "under other circumstances détente is possible." Reagan replied,

> Well, so far détente's been a one-way street that the Soviet Union has used to pursue its own aims. I don't have to think of an answer as to what I think their intentions are; they have repeated it. I know of no leader of the Soviet Union since the revolution, and including the present leadership, that has not more than once repeated in the various Communist congresses they hold their determination that

their goal must be the promotion of world revolution and a one-world Socialist or Communist state, whichever word you want to use.

Now, as long as they do that and as long as they, at the same time, have openly and publicly declared that the only morality they recognize is what will further their cause, meaning they reserve unto themselves the right to commit any crime, to lie, to cheat, in order to attain that, and that is moral, not immoral, and we operate on a different set of standards. I think when you do business with them, even at a détente, you keep that in mind.

This answer had the virtue of accuracy. Vladimir Lenin, the founder of the Soviet state, had said in 1920: "We repudiate all morality that proceeds from supernatural ideas or ideas that are outside class conceptions. Morality is entirely subordinate to the interests of class war. Everything is moral that is necessary for the annihilation of the old exploiting social order and for uniting the proletariat."[3] Leonid Brezhnev, four years older than Reagan and the leader of the Soviet Union for two decades when Reagan began his presidency, had said in 1968: "Our party has always warned that in the ideological field, there can be no peaceful coexistence, just as there can be no class peace between the proletariat and the bourgeoisie."[4]

Not everyone thought it wise for Reagan to launch his presidency with blunt reminders of Marxist-Leninist objectives. *The Washington Post,* while acknowledging that the Soviet record supported Reagan's assertion, warned editorially that "a good-vs.-evil approach risks missing what legitimate opportunities for honorable accommodation there may be."[5] The Soviet news agency Tass said that Reagan's comments were "deliberate distortions" of Soviet policy. The assumption among liberals and conservatives alike was that Reagan had embarked on a premeditated campaign of anticommunism. Edward Luttwak, a conservative military expert, wrote that the "U.S. is now speaking to the Russians in the same way the Russians have been speaking to the U.S."[6] But Reagan, who had been making such statements for more than thirty years, professed not to understand what the fuss was about. He told aides he had simply repeated the words of Soviet leaders.[7]

Reagan's comment that he didn't "have to think" about his response to Donaldson's question was especially revealing. He had answered reflexively, expressing views acquired in Hollywood during the turbulent period after World War II when world communism was a monolithic force centered in Moscow and the wartime U.S.-Soviet alliance had turned into the Cold War. As Soviet forces consolidated control over Eastern Europe, anticommunism became the ruling political passion in the United States and Soviet spying the principal national security concern. Communists and suspected sympathizers were rooted out of positions of influence in government, labor unions, political organizations, educational institutions and the entertainment industry.

Hollywood, always sensitive to changes in the public mood, was particularly vulnerable to anticommunist anxiety. The movie colony had been a center of radical ferment since the Depression, and charges of "Communist influence" were frequent weapons as rival labor unions struggled to organize the film industry. While these charges were often made recklessly, they were not totally baseless. The Communist Party of the United States (CPUSA) accorded a high priority to Hollywood, then the citadel of American mass culture, during the two decades that Reagan made his principal living as a movie actor. A romantic interest in the ideals of communism flourished in the hothouse atmosphere of Hollywood long after Stalin's purge trials of the mid-1930s had disillusioned American liberals in the East. The Communists, intent on winning liberal adherents, tolerated deviations from party policy that would have been impermissible almost anywhere else. This enhanced their influence in Hollywood, especially during the heyday of the "Popular Front" from 1935 to the signing of the Hitler-Stalin pact in 1939, and again during the wartime U.S.-Soviet alliance. Some of Hollywood's most talented screenwriters made no secret of their Communist affiliations, and one of the most reliable histories of the period estimates that 25 to 30 percent of the Screen Writers Guild members "most regularly employed" were members of the Communist Party by the middle of World War II.[8]

But the party had been largely discredited in Hollywood by 1946, when Reagan joined two organizations that had been heavily infiltrated by Communists. This was largely the doing of Stalin, whose repressive policies within the Soviet empire required obedient, lockstep Communist organizations in the West. On Stalin's orders the moderate U.S. Communist leader, Earl Browder, was replaced in 1945 with a hard-line Stalinist. A year later Browder and his followers were expelled from the party, and "Browderism" became a mortal Marxist sin. This purge reduced the Communist Party to a skeletal pro-Soviet force at the very time it was becoming a principal target of investigation by the FBI and Congress.

As far as I have been able to ascertain from discussions with Reagan and those who knew him in this period, he knew almost nothing about the Soviet Union and was totally ignorant of the history of Communist activity in Hollywood when he joined the American Veterans Committee (AVC) and became a board member of the Hollywood Independent Citizens Committee of the Arts, Sciences and Professions (HICCASP). He did not last long in the AVC, which the Communists quickly reduced to a negligible political force. As he described it in his autobiography, Reagan was at the time "a near-hopeless hemophiliac liberal"[9] who bled for causes and joined supposedly liberal organizations without bothering to find out who was minding the store. It would not have taken much research to learn that Communists were a force in HICCASP, which began as a broad coalition of leftists and liberals supporting Franklin Roosevelt's fourth-term candidacy in 1944 and ended as a narrow Communist-controlled group that became the forerunner of the Independent Progressive Party, which nominated Henry Wallace for president in 1948. The truth was that Reagan didn't care that much about who was running the organization. His brother Neil, an anticommunist conservative of long standing, had warned him repeatedly about the dangers of the Red menace, but Ronald Reagan argued with him whenever he mentioned the word "Communist."[10]

Later, Reagan would say that he was "unusually naïve" during this period,[11] and his actions support this assessment. It took him a year and a half of encounters with Communists and other leftists in HICCASP before he quit the organization. Eventually, when the executive committee of HICCASP refused to support a resolution repudiating communism, Reagan resigned along with James Roosevelt, Dore Schary and Olivia de Havilland. He had also become disenchanted with the Communists for their role in a 1946 Hollywood jurisdictional strike centering on the issue of which labor unions should have control of movie set construction. The historical record of this complex strike suggests that it was provoked by the movie producers, who saw an opportunity to take advantage of labor union rivalry to eliminate jobs and exercise greater control over production.

Reagan became president of the Screen Actors Guild midway through the strike, chosen by the board of the union to complete the term of actor Robert Montgomery, who had to resign because he became a producer. The Screen Actors Guild proclaimed neutrality in the strike, but was actually supportive of the producers. Reagan defended his conduct in a lengthy account of the strike in *Where's the Rest of Me?* He believed that the strike was the work of Communists, then a widely held view that has not stood the test of historical inquiry.* In his own eyes, Reagan was an innocent who cared about his country and turned against the Communists because they were betraying it and ruining the happy world of Hollywood in the process. He saw himself as a good guy standing up to evil, the role he was most often called on to perform in his movies.

Reagan played out this role in 1947 when the House Un-American Activities Committee (HUAC) launched an investigation of Communist influence in the movie industry. Although the Communists were by then an isolated political force in Hollywood, investigating them had become big political box office. The declared purpose of the inquiry was to determine if "Communist propaganda" had been injected into Hollywood films, but HUAC's real interest was in identifying and branding those with whom it disagreed as Communist sympathizers. The committee used FBI files and the secret testimony of informants to ruin the livelihoods of people who were accused of no crime. Friendly witnesses, many of them as hostile to the New Deal as they were to communism, were allowed to settle personal and political scores with leftists and liberals. Unfriendly witnesses who refused to cooperate with the investigation by naming names of Communists in the film industry were cited for contempt and imprisoned.

Aside from the militantly conservative Motion Picture Alliance for the Preservation of American Ideals (MPA), few people in Hollywood had much use for HUAC. Even after Reagan became convinced that the Communists were agents of a foreign power and cooperated with the FBI, he called the congressional investigators "a pretty venal bunch." [12] But the studios were afraid that films and stars suspected of a Red taint faced a public boycott. This fear undermined any determination to resist the anticommunist inquisition and eventually resulted in Hollywood's capitulation to HUAC's demands that the film community rid itself of real or suspected Communists.

Reagan, viewed by the Right as too liberal and by the Left as too lightheaded, managed to walk a middle ground during the initial investigation. Testifying before HUAC in 1947 as president of the Screen Actors Guild, he denounced communism but contended it could be

---

* The origins of the strike are examined by Garry Wills in *Reagan's America*, pp. 231–40. Wills rejects Reagan's account. As for HICCASP, the most detailed study of Hollywood politics of this period, *The Inquisition in Hollywood: Politics in the Film Community, 1930–1960*, concluded (p. 238) that Reagan "hardly contributed" to the efforts to rescue the organization from Communist militancy.

contained by democratic measures. "I detest, I abhor their philosophy, but I detest more than that their tactics, which are those of a fifth column, and are dishonest, but at the same time I never as a citizen want to see our country become urged, by either fear or resentment of this group, that we ever compromise with any of our democratic principles through that fear or resentment," Reagan said. "I still think that democracy can do it." [13] Reagan viewed his own testimony as exemplary, and even one of his more persistent critics agreed that he made "a fine statement of civil-libertarian principles on the stand." [14]

But Reagan's subsequent role was more ambiguous. Even though the Screen Actors Guild assisted actors who were targets of the unofficial vigilante blacklists that sprang up in Hollywood in the wake of the investigations, Reagan and the union went along with the studios in denying employment to actors who had refused to cooperate with HUAC. Reagan denied that a blacklist of Communists existed but said the studios had the right to consider an actor's outside activities or reputation, since these could affect the public acceptance of a film.

Reagan emerged from the Hollywood investigations without visible scars. The middle road had worked for him, and he was not outwardly obsessive about his anticommunism. As the events receded into the past, their importance increased to Reagan, who made of his experience a morality tale in which he was a hero as well as wholesome innocent. His favorite citation was the testimony of actor Sterling Hayden, who told HUAC in 1951 that Communists in the Screen Actors Guild had been thwarted by a "one-man battalion" named Ronald Reagan. [15] Throughout the late 1940s and early 1950s, Reagan continued to support liberal causes and Democratic candidates. His 1948 speeches for President Truman and other Democrats emphasized such economic issues as "Republican inflation" more than anticommunism. In 1950 Reagan also backed the candidacy of liberal Democrat Helen Gahagan Douglas, who was defeated by Richard Nixon in the U.S. Senate race in California after a tawdry, Red-baiting campaign. As late as 1952, in the recollection of Frank Mankiewicz, the Los Angeles County Democratic Central Committee declined to endorse Reagan as a prospective Democratic candidate for an open House seat because he was considered "too liberal." Mankiewicz, a liberal member of the central committee, believes that Reagan would have run if he had received the party endorsement. [16]

Despite outward appearances, it is possible that Reagan's involvement with the Hollywood investigations left wounds that never fully healed. His growing awareness of Communist activity coincided with an unhappy cluster of events that strained his customary optimism. When Reagan testified before the House Un-American Activities Committee in October 1947, he had barely recovered from a prolonged siege of viral pneumonia, and it was soon afterward that Jane Wyman told him that their marriage was finished. He was also struggling with Warner Bros. for better movie roles, and he seems, at least retrospectively, to have developed the conspiratorial view that Communists were partially responsible for the decline of his film career.

As Reagan saw it, the real blacklist victims were those who had taken an uncompromising stand against communism. He told me in 1968 that he had been declared virtually unemployable by unnamed producers who were "afraid of being on the outs" with their associates if they cast him in a movie. "There is no question my career suffered from anticommunism," Reagan said.[17] He felt personally victimized by his brief encounter with Communists, much as he did during this same period by the burdens imposed on him by what was then a steeply progressive federal income tax. Interviewing the usually amiable Reagan in 1980, Laurence Barrett was struck by the "cold fury" he displayed when recalling his run-ins with film colony Communists. "And I discovered it firsthand—the cynicism, the brutality, the complete lack of morality in their positions, and the cold-bloodedness of their attempt, at any cost, to gain control of that industry," Reagan said.[18] Firsthand discoveries are the ones that matter to Reagan. When he expressed his view of Communist morality at his first presidential news conference, he believed he was talking from experience.

For Reagan, however, experience also meant religious and extrasensory encounters. "A mystical feeling about oneself comes easily to performers in the spotlight, cheered by so many people,"[19] observed Garry Wills, and Reagan had a strong sense of communion with worlds unseen. The origins of this outlook may have been the early and intense religious training he received from his mother, who was also something of a mystic. Whatever its origins, Reagan believed in spiritual visitations. At his father's funeral, feeling "desolate and empty," he heard Jack Reagan saying to him, "I'm okay and where I am it's very nice. Please don't be unhappy."[20] The desolation vanished. Reagan was convinced that the experience was entirely genuine and not a product of his imagination.

Reagan had a strange experience while he was governor that would affect his views of nuclear war as profoundly as his Hollywood encounters with Communists would influence his attitude toward the Soviet Union. In 1970, singer Pat Boone brought evangelical ministers Harald Bredesen and George Otis to visit the Reagans at their residence in Sacramento. They prayed together, with the prayer led by Otis, a radio evangelist who operated the High Adventure Ministries in Southern California. During the prayer Otis was seized by what he took to be a visitation of the Holy Spirit. The tone and message of his prayer changed, and he prophesied that Reagan would become president. A participant in the meeting who was clasping Reagan's hand felt "a bolt of electricity" run through it. Otis's own hand was shaking uncontrollably at the time. When he subsequently learned that Reagan's hand also had been shaking, he regarded it as an authentication of the prophecy.[21] Reagan also accepted the prophecy as valid.

The visit of the evangelical ministers to Sacramento stirred Reagan's interest in Armageddon, the dramatic biblical account of the world's final battle. The story appealed to Reagan's adventurous imagination and met his requirement of a happy ending. As Reagan understood the story, Russia would be defeated by an acclaimed leader of the West who would be revealed as the Antichrist. He, too, would fall, and Jesus Christ would triumph in the creation of "a new heaven and a new earth." Reagan's earliest known expression of interest in the Armageddon story occurred in 1968 when his pastor, Donn Moomaw of the Bel-Air Presbyterian Church, and Billy Graham visited him in the hospital, where he was recuperating from minor surgery. They talked about biblical prophecies, and Graham told Reagan that West German Chancellor Konrad Adenauer had predicted that the "next great event of world history" would be the second coming of Jesus Christ.[22] This intrigued Reagan, who is far more curious about biblical portents than about governmental processes. He quotes Scripture, remembers Bible stories from his childhood days in the Christian Church and regards Christ as his personal savior and as a hero of history. (Reagan told television interviewer David Frost in 1968 that Jesus Christ was the historical figure he most admired.) When Otis and Bredesen visited him, Reagan discoursed on modern historical events that seem to have fulfilled biblical prophecies. Reagan was especially fascinated by the founding of the state of Israel in 1948, an event crucial to those who accept the intricate story of Armageddon as a literal forecast of the end of the world.* In 1971, at a banquet for California Senate president pro

* Reagan may have been influenced by *The Late Great Planet Earth*, a popular, speculative work on Armageddon by Hal Lindsey that was published in 1970. Lindsey calls Israel "the fuse of Arma-

tem James Mills, Reagan startled the biblically knowledgeable Mills by telling him, over the cherries jubilee, that the end of the world was nigh. "For the first time ever, everything is in place for the battle of Armageddon and the second coming of Christ," Reagan said.[23] One of the portents, he said, was that Libya had become Communist. In 1980, in an interview on Jim Bakker's PTL television network, Reagan said, "We may be the generation that sees Armageddon."[24]

Reagan is hooked on Armageddon. He told me in 1989 that the omens include "strange weather things," including such natural disasters as earthquakes. Speaking as if he were describing a movie scene, he related a terrifying episode in the Armageddon story where an invading army from the Orient, 200-million strong, is destroyed by a plague. Reagan believes that the "plague" was a prophecy of nuclear war, where "the eyes are burned from the head and the hair falls from the body and so forth."[25] He believes this passage specifically foretold Hiroshima. As he vividly related the story, I understood why campaign strategist Stu Spencer had worried that the media would focus on Reagan's fascination with Armageddon. "Why do they spend so much time in the media worrying about horoscopes and astrologers and its connection to government?" Spencer said. "It seems to me Armageddon has much more depth and meaning. It's rooted in the Bible [and could be related to] international relations, nuclear war. Nobody ever pursued Armageddon."[26]

The issue was, in fact, briefly and inconclusively pursued during the 1984 presidential campaign after Reagan confided his view that Armageddon might well be nigh to Thomas Dine, director of the American-Israel Public Affairs Committee.[27] Marvin Kalb raised it at the second debate between Reagan and Democratic presidential candidate Walter F. Mondale on October 21, 1984, asking Reagan if there was a relationship between his Armageddon beliefs and U.S. planning for nuclear war. Reagan acknowledged having had "philosophical discussions" on the issue but said that "no one knows" if "Armageddon is a thousand years away or the day after tomorrow. So, I have never seriously warned and said we must plan according to Armageddon." That answer did

geddon." The capture of old Jerusalem by the Israelis in 1967 made theoretically possible the reconstruction of the Temple destroyed in A.D. 70 at its original site on the Dome of the Rock. According to some, the Antichrist will make his headquarters in the Temple prior to the second coming of Christ. Reagan apparently accepts this version of the Armageddon story, for he mentioned the significance of the Dome of the Rock to me in a May 5, 1989, interview. A mosque now exists on the site, which is a holy place for Muslims as well as Jews.

not satisfy a group of liberal Christian and Jewish leaders, who warned that Reagan's foreign policy might be unduly influenced by "a theology of nuclear Armageddon."[28] But Armageddon did not catch on as a political issue. The Mondale campaign let it drop in favor of a confusing advertising campaign against the Strategic Defense Initiative (SDI, or "Star Wars") that had no discernible impact. While public opinion polls showed many misgivings about other aspects of Reagan's foreign policy, a majority of Americans accepted the sincerity of Reagan's repeated assertion that "a nuclear war can never be won, and must never be fought." And they were right to do so. The Armageddon story did not reconcile Reagan to nuclear war. He regarded the biblical prophecy as a useful warning, much as if a long-range weather forecast had foretold an impending hurricane. Since Armageddon was coming, Reagan thought it prudent to protect people from its consequences.

Robert (Bud) McFarlane, who played a significant role in the formulation of SDI, was convinced that Reagan's interest in antimissile defense was the product of his interest in Armageddon. "From the time he adopted the Armageddon thesis, he saw it as a nuclear catastrophe," said McFarlane, who as Reagan's national security adviser became highly familiar with his discourse on Armageddon. "Well, what do you do about that? Reagan's answer was that you build a tent or a bubble and protect your country."[29] This was a remarkable and illogical display of optimism, even for Reagan. He believed Armageddon was inevitable and, despite his reply to Kalb, probably imminent. But he also believed that even preordained catastrophes could be averted or at least mitigated. "This was one of the intellectual contradictions in Reagan's thinking," said McFarlane. "He sees himself as a romantic, heroic figure who believes in the power of a hero to overcome even Armageddon. I think it may come from Hollywood. Wherever it came from, he believes that the power of a person and an idea could change the outcome of something even as terrible as Armageddon. This was the greatest challenge of all. . . . He didn't see himself as God, but he saw himself as a heroic figure on earth."[30]

In responding to the challenge of Armageddon, Reagan's imagination held sway. He saw it as his mission to protect Americans from the risk of nuclear annihilation. He regarded nuclear weapons in Russian hands as particularly dangerous, and this conviction would be the underlying basis of his readiness at Reykjavik to sign an agreement with Gorbachev that would abolish all U.S. and Soviet nuclear weapons. Reagan was guided both by extraordinary vision and by remarkable ignorance. He was suspicious of the traditional attempt to regulate the pace of the arms race with accords and treaties that encouraged the two superpowers to improve the quality of their offensive nuclear weapons and to increase the size of their nuclear arsenals. Unlike the traditionalists, Reagan was convinced that it was necessary to reduce the numbers of nuclear weapons on both sides and eventually to get rid of them. This seemed commonsensical to Reagan, as well as morally imperative. "He would say to me that nuclear weapons are inherently evil," said Frank Carlucci, the fifth of Reagan's national security advisers. Carlucci vainly pled the traditional case for nuclear deterrence, saying that nuclear weapons had kept the peace for forty years. He did not convince Reagan, who responded to the argument by telling Carlucci about Armageddon.[31]

But Reagan did not know enough about nuclear weapons systems to formulate a policy to accomplish his objectives. He was susceptible to manipulation by advisers who shared his militant anticommunism but not his distaste for nuclear deterrence and who wanted neither arms reduction nor arms control. We have already seen how Reagan's ignorance contributed to his dubious decision (in reality, Caspar Weinberger's decision) to deploy the MX missile in vulnerable silos. Early in 1983, when Brent Scowcroft was chairman of a commission that was one of the consequences of this decision, he was amazed to learn that Reagan did not realize that the principal Soviet nuclear threat to the United States was posed by mammoth land-based intercontinental ballistic missiles. When Reagan was asked during an interview with *Time* why such elemental information had escaped him, he replied, "I never heard anyone of our negotiators or any of our military people or anyone else bring up that particular point."[32] Doubtless this was true. Reagan had declaimed so often during the 1980 campaign about the purported U.S. "window of vulnerability" to a surprise Soviet attack that even advisers who held a low opinion of his intellect could reasonably have expected him to know that it would be ICBMs that would be coming through that window. But it was never safe to assume that Reagan was informed, unless the material was before him on cue cards. In October 1983 the president astonished a group of congressmen as much as he had startled Scowcroft by telling them that bombers and submarines did not carry nuclear missiles.[33] Such essential factual information was not readily stored in Reagan's mental computer, which was crammed with the collected myths, memories, stories and perceptions of his long life. When Reagan received new information, he mentally scanned the stored files much as if he had hit the "search" key of the computer. If the new information touched what Colin Powell called a "transistor," Reagan responded to what he was being told with one of his old stories. If it didn't, he would wait, usually saying nothing, until something that was said to him struck one of his mental buttons.

Over time, skilled subordinates learned how to manipulate Reagan by framing their advocacies to activate the response they wanted to produce. White House Chief of Staff James Baker and Mike Deaver, who were themselves skilled in this technique, guarded against the overturning of supposedly settled presidential decisions by trying to prevent cabinet officers from seeing Reagan alone. William Clark's independent access to Reagan during the twenty-one months he served as national security adviser worried Baker and Deaver, as it did Nancy Reagan, because they thought he appealed to the president's darker instincts. In short, the combination of Reagan's credulity and analytical deficiencies made him exceptionally vulnerable, despite his strong convictions. It is no accident that the Reagan administration took a confrontational approach to the Soviet Union when Al Haig was secretary of state and Clark the national security adviser and became more accommodating after George Shultz replaced Haig and McFarlane succeeded Clark.

But it can also be argued that the appointments of Shultz and Mc-Farlane were as much the result of events as the cause of them. Reagan's vision of nuclear apocalypse and his deeply rooted conviction that the weapons that could cause this hell on earth should be abolished would ultimately prove more powerful than his anticommunism, perhaps because Reagan did indeed, as McFarlane observed, see himself as a "heroic figure." It is the peacemakers and those who reduce the risks of war who are the heroes of the nuclear age. Long before the first atomic bomb was dropped, Reagan had portrayed a cinematic hero (Secret Service agent Brass Bancroft in the 1940 movie *Murder in the Air*) who stops a spy from stealing a death ray known as the "Inertia Projector" that can bring down distant enemy airplanes. After he was discharged from the Army Air Corps in 1945, Reagan joined the United World Federalists, a utopian organization dedicated to the creation of a single, peaceful nation of Earth. A utopian renunciation of atomic weapons was also the dream of the alien hero in *The Day the Earth Stood Still*. Perhaps, as Colin Powell believed, this antiwar, science-fiction film was a source of inspiration for Reagan's idea of sharing SDI technology with the Soviets. Such sharing of sophisticated technology seemed silly to politicians of every description, from Richard Perle to Walter Mondale, but Reagan meant it. He was appalled by the vengeful doctrine of "mutual assured destruction" (MAD) in which the United States and the Soviet Union keep the peace by holding civilian populations hostage. Reagan wanted to replace MAD with what he called "mutual assured survival." He saw antimissile defense as essential to a free and peaceful world, and he delighted in any story that perpetuated this vision.

After Reagan left the White House, I learned from a mutual friend that he had while president read the 1985 potboiler *Air Force One Is Haunted*, in which a decent but rather muddled president rescues the United States from a militant Soviet challenge, a crippled economy and a scheming national security adviser by following the advice of the friendly ghost of Franklin Roosevelt. The dénouement, arguably of less scientific plausibility than the spectral appearance of FDR aboard the presidential aircraft, occurs when 390 antimissile satellites are simultaneously deployed in a defense system known as Umbrella that is tested by a barrage of several hundred dummy missiles fired from nuclear submarines. The Soviets, faced with a technological miracle that could thwart even Armageddon, renounce war and turn to peaceful economic development. To Reagan, it was an appealing fantasy that touched the right transistors and concluded in the essential happy ending.

Reagan has been a reader since childhood, and he often read books that had no practical bearing on his presidency. According to Nancy Reagan, he usually read himself to sleep at night. His mental cassettes were crammed with odd scraps of information and obscure insights that he had acquired from his reading and committed to memory. In a 1942 *Photoplay* article written in the style of his early speeches, Reagan said that his favorite books were *"Turnabout* by Thorne Smith, *Babbitt, The Adventures of Tom Sawyer* and the works of Pearl Buck, H. G. Wells, Damon Runyon and Erich Remarque."[34] In his politically reformative years during the 1960s Reagan read Barry Goldwater's *The Conscience of a Conservative* and Whittaker Chambers' *Witness,* the seminal work of American anticommunism. While Reagan was resistant to the inner despair that pervaded the life of Whittaker Chambers, he could quote from memory the famous passage where Chambers watches his sleeping daughter and decides that he can no longer be an atheist. He was impressed that Chambers had abandoned his belief in communism while still believing that the forces of Marxism-Leninism would prevail.

One reason that outsiders underestimated the extent of Reagan's reading was that he often forgot the titles of books, even books he quoted. He also seemed to have a reader's conceit that books were secret, personal treasures: he never cared, as far as I could tell, if anyone else knew that he was a reader. Nancy Reagan and some of his advisers did care, for they realized that the portrayal of Reagan as an intellectual lightweight was encouraged by the repeated reports that he never read. But the advisers also worried that acknowledging Reagan's interest in such books as *Air Force One Is Haunted* would raise other and perhaps more troubling questions in the press. As a result, they largely limited themselves to the daunting task of trying to convince reporters that Reagan read his briefing papers. Often, he did not. He would pore over material that interested him, but he frequently skipped over supposedly required reading in favor of popular fiction. Reagan read the entertaining anti-Soviet novel *Red Storm Rising* by Tom Clancy in preparation for the Reykjavik summit on the pretext that much of it is set in Iceland. Somewhat more plausibly, he read Suzanne Massie's *Land of the Firebird: The Beauty of Old Russia* to give himself a feel for Russian traditions in advance of the Moscow summit.

Reagan also read numerous accounts written by or about Communist defectors, among them *MiG Pilot* by John Barron. This is the story of Soviet aviator Viktor Belenko, who in November 1976 defected to the West by flying his advanced MiG-25 fighter to Japan while on a routine training flight. Despite pangs of cultural dislocation, Belenko settled in the United States, where he at first could not believe that the well-stocked stores and supermarkets he was shown in the Virginia suburbs of the District of Columbia were accessible to ordinary Americans. Belenko's story appealed to Reagan, perhaps because it resembled so much his own imaginings about the way Russians would react to a firsthand glimpse of life in the United States. Reagan invited Belenko to the White House to hear his impressions.[35] He liked talking to heroes, and to authors of books he had read. Clancy and Massie were among the several authors invited to the White House for chats with the president.

No one doubted Reagan's anticommunism or his interest in accounts of Soviet travails. His periodic flights of fancy about ridding the world of nuclear weapons were taken less seriously. In his bid to attract conservative support during his 1976 campaign against President Ford, Reagan had assailed "Dr. Kissinger" (never Nixon) and emphasized the dangers of détente. When he ran for president in 1980, he took a different tack. The argument he made against the unratified Strategic Arms Limitation Treaty (SALT II) signed by Carter and Brezhnev was that it was "fatally flawed" because it permitted the superpowers to increase their nuclear arsenals rather than reduce them. This line of reasoning suited Reagan's political purpose of softening his hard-line public image, and reporters tended to dismiss his genuine objection to SALT II as a ploy conceived by his strategists to change the Reagan image. But the argument was Reagan's own. In a dramatic concession speech to the Republican National Convention in 1976, Reagan told the delegates that they faced the dual challenge of preserving individual freedom and keeping the world safe from nuclear destruction. "We live in a world in which the great powers have poised and aimed at each other horrible missiles of destruction that can, in a matter of minutes, arrive in each other's country and destroy virtually the civilized world we live in," Reagan said, in a speech that many took to be his curtain call. At a time when the emotions of the delegates were focused on the political struggle that had just ended in the nomination of President Ford, Reagan did not speak of himself or of his party. Instead, he addressed the issue that mattered most to him, speaking from his heart and without notes or cue cards. It was a clue of what was to come.

This clue did not lead us anywhere, however, because most of us in the journalistic community did not realize then that there was a mystery to solve. By 1980, Reagan was a familiar figure on the national political stage. There seemed nothing enigmatic about him. He was stereotyped as a likable and decent man who was lacking in intellectual candle-power. Most reporters focused on the maneuvers of Reagan's strategists rather than on Reagan's inner goals. Often, the strategists were also focused on themselves. They respected Reagan's performing skills and paid little attention to his larger purposes. This attitude was com-pounded when Reagan reached the White House; many of his advisers viewed his dreamy imaginings and original ideas as irrelevant to his presidency. "We were always dazzled by the success of his approach and never quite willing to trust it," said one of Reagan's foreign policy advisers.

Reagan's approach posed a special problem for Martin Anderson, one of the few intellectuals in his entourage. Reagan intrigued and puzzled Anderson, who came to believe that Reagan's economic ideas added up to a comprehensive theory even though they were not pre-sented in an analytical fashion. Reagan's approach to U.S.-Soviet rela-tions presented a similar problem. Anderson wrote down what Reagan had said and thought and used it to construct his own theory of what it was that Reagan believed. In *Revolution* he reduced Reagan's views to six "basic premises" that, he thought, were the basis of "a grand strategy, never fully articulated, that [Reagan] relentlessly pursued." [36] The premises, listed here in the order given them by Anderson, were:

A belief that a U.S.-Soviet nuclear war would have devastating consequences for both sides.

A commitment to the reduction of nuclear arms instead of a limitation of their increase or a freeze at current levels.

A moral revulsion to the "doctrine of mutually assured destruction (MAD) that had been our national nuclear weapons defense policy for some twenty years."

A belief that the Soviet Union was "an implacable foe" and the center of "an evil empire."

A belief "that the productive power of the United States economy was vastly superior to the Soviet economy, that if we began a drive to upgrade the power and scope of our military forces, the Soviets would not be able to keep pace."

A skepticism about arms control treaties, based on a book that argued that nations kept their treaty agreements only when it suits their interests to do so.

The book that became Reagan's bible on treaties was *The Treaty Trap: A History of the Performance of Political Treaties by the United States and European Nations,* written in 1969 by Laurence W. Beilenson, a friend of Reagan's who had once been the attorney for the Screen Actors Guild. The underlying premise of Beilenson's book is evenhanded: he observes that the United States follows the same standards of self-interest as other nations in deciding whether to adhere to treaties it has signed. But the book provided theoretical undergirding for the conservative argument that it was dangerous to engage in "treaty reliance" when dealing with the Soviet Union, and Reagan used it for this purpose. In a speech at West Point on May 17, 1981, where he referred to the Soviets as an "evil force," Reagan said that *The Treaty Trap* "makes plain that no nation that placed its faith in parchment or paper, while at the same time it gave up its protective hardware, ever lasted long enough to write many pages in history." *The Treaty Trap* was the source of Reagan's view that any arms accord with the Soviets must provide for thorough verification. "Trust but verify" became Reagan's motto, and he repeated it so often that Gorbachev would hold his hands over his ears when he heard it.

Reagan's negative assessment of Soviet economic capability was also significant. For all his worries about the "window of vulnerability," he understood better than many conservatives that the Soviet Union was not ten feet tall. The prevailing conservative view of the Soviets in 1980 was dualistic and contradictory. While maintaining that a Communist system was incapable of competing successfully with capitalism, conservatives also contended that the Soviet Union could and would commit overwhelming economic resources to its military machine and the Marxist-Leninist goal of world subjugation. Reagan yielded to no one in his mistrust of Soviet intentions, as he had demonstrated at his first presidential news conference. But he understood better than many of the experts that Soviet economic backwardness would inevitably afflict Soviet military capability.

As a result, Reagan was sanguine about the prospects of stepped-up arms competition with the Soviet Union. He told reporters and editors of *The Washington Post* on June 18, 1980, that it "would be of great benefit to the United States if we started a buildup." Lyn Nofziger, present at this luncheon interview, visibly tensed when his candidate openly advocated an arms race, but Reagan knew what he was saying and had no qualms about it. "I think there's every indication and every reason to believe that the Soviet Union cannot increase its production of arms," Reagan said. "Right now we're hearing of strikes and labor disputes because people aren't getting enough to eat. They've diverted so much to military [spending] that they can't provide for the consumer needs. So as far as an arms race is concerned, there's one going on right now, but there's only one side racing."[37] In Reagan's view, a U.S. buildup would inevitably prompt the Soviets to seek negotiations to reduce nuclear weapons. Martin Anderson said Reagan often made the same point to his advisers.

Once in office, Reagan was in no hurry to rush into arms discussions with the Soviets. He believed that the United States would have more leverage with the Soviets once Congress had actually approved the military budget increases he had been advocating throughout the campaign. This point was seized upon by Haig and Richard Allen, who believed that in the interim the new administration should put the Soviet Union in its place. Veteran Soviet Ambassador Anatoly Dobrynin received a cool reception from Allen during the transition when he sought to explore the new administration's willingness to preserve SALT II. He received an even colder one from Haig a few days after Reagan took office. Haig revoked the privilege extended by Henry Kissinger during the Nixon administration, and continued during the

Ford and Carter presidencies, of allowing the Soviet ambassador to enter the State Department through its underground garage, a practice that reflected the special nature of the superpower relationship. Dobrynin's chauffeured limousine was turned away when the driver tried to pull into the garage, and Haig made sure that reporters were told of the incident. The new administration seemed to be sending a bristling message to the world that there would be no more U.S. coddling of the Soviets.

But Reagan was not actually as hostile to a U.S.-Soviet dialogue as his rhetoric and the studied slights of his foreign policy team made it appear. Reporters in these early weeks of the presidency were told at briefings conducted under the usual ground rules of anonymity (and in the usual jargon) that Reagan wanted to "lay down a marker" in his dealings with the Soviet Union. Reagan nonetheless was more willing than Haig, Allen and Defense Secretary Weinberger to offer gestures of accommodation to the Soviet Union. The president sought, for instance, at a February 4, 1981, cabinet meeting to redeem a campaign pledge and lift the grain embargo that Carter had imposed on the Soviet Union after the invasion of Afghanistan. Haig dissuaded Reagan temporarily, on grounds that this would give the Soviets the concession they wanted most without getting anything in return. But on April 24, 1981, Reagan formally lifted the embargo at the urging of Agriculture Secretary John Block.* On the same day, Reagan sent a handwritten letter to Soviet leader Leonid Brezhnev that he had begun writing while convalescing in the White House from the wounds he had received in the assassination attempt.

Reagan's letter is of special interest because it is one of the few foreign policy documents composed by Reagan in the early years of his presidency without the assistance of speechwriters or formal position papers from his various departments. Reagan says in his memoirs that Haig was "reluctant" to have him draft it.[39] But Reagan wrote it anyway and, attired in bathrobe and pajamas, passed around the draft at a meeting in the White House family quarters on Monday, April 13, that was attended by Haig, Allen, Weinberger, Vice President Bush, James Baker and Mike Deaver. On April 16, at another meeting with the same cast, Allen returned a version of the letter to Reagan that had been rewritten at the State Department into what Deaver described as "typical bureaucratese."[40] Reagan disliked the reworking but said, "Well, I

---

* Block, who had urged in January that the blockade be lifted, said that Ed Meese was helpful in persuading Reagan. "Meese was concerned with the president keeping his promises," Block told me.[38]

guess you fellows know best. You're the experts." Deaver interrupted, saying to Reagan that he had been elected president and that the State Department and National Security Council had been "screwing up for a quarter of a century." [41] "If you think that's a letter that ought to be sent to Brezhnev, don't let anybody change it," Deaver said. "Why don't you just send it?" [42]

Reagan agreed, and the letter was sent as he wrote it despite Haig's view that it naïvely undercut the administration's militant strategy in dealing with the Soviets. The State Department version was also sent, but it was Reagan's handwritten message that attested to his willingness to enter into a dialogue with those who he had said reserved "the right to commit any crime, to lie, to cheat" in order to attain world domination. In the opening passage, Reagan recalled meeting Brezhnev when he had visited President Nixon at San Clemente in 1973:

> Mr. President: When we met, I asked you if you were aware that the hopes and aspirations of millions of people throughout the world were dependent on the decisions that would be reached in those meetings. You took my hand in both of yours and assured me that you were aware of that and that you were dedicated with all your heart and mind to fulfilling those hopes and dreams.
>
> The people of the world still share that hope. Indeed, the peoples of the world, despite differences in racial and ethnic origin, have very much in common. They want the dignity of having some control over their individual destiny. They want to work at the craft or trade of their own choosing and to be fairly rewarded. They want to raise their families in peace without harming anyone or suffering harm themselves. Government exists for their convenience, not the other way around. If they are incapable, as some would have us believe, of self-government, then where among them do we find people who are capable of governing others?
>
> Is it possible that we have permitted ideology, political and economic philosophies, and governmental policies to keep us from considering the very real, everyday problems of peoples? Will the average Soviet family be better off or even aware that the Soviet Union has imposed a government of its own choice on the people of Afghanistan? Is life better for the people of Cuba because the Cuban military dictate who shall govern the people of Angola? [43]

This was vintage Reagan. The letter's message was similar in tone and content to the one Reagan had delivered regularly in radio speeches in the interval between his governorship and presidency. It continued in the same moralistic tone. When World War II ended, Reagan observed, the United States was "the only undamaged industrial power in the world" and was the sole power in possession of "the ultimate weapon, the nuclear weapon, with the unquestioned ability to deliver it anywhere in the world. If we had sought world domination then, who could have opposed us?" Instead of seeking such domination, we had "used our power and wealth to rebuild the war-ravished economies of the world, including those of the nations who had been our enemies." Reagan averred that America remained committed to these goals. "It is in this spirit, in the spirit of helping the people of both our nations, that I have lifted the grain embargo," he concluded. "Perhaps this decision will contribute to creating the circumstances which will lead to the meaningful and constructive dialogue which will assist us in fulfilling our joint obligation to find lasting peace."[44]

In later years, when he was fending off a mixture of conservative criticism and liberal praise for the supposed transformation in his attitude toward the Soviet Union, Reagan would cite this letter as evidence of his consistency in promoting favorable U.S.-Soviet relations. Late in 1985, while preparing for the first of his five meetings with Gorbachev, Reagan said he had always been willing to negotiate with Soviet leaders and would have done so earlier in his presidency except that they "kept dying on me."[45] This formulation was a source of amusement within the White House, where one aide told me with tongue in cheek that it showed the accuracy of Reagan's view that the Communists "would stop at nothing" in their attempts to frustrate him. But there was something to Reagan's perception, despite his curious way of expressing it. The Soviet Union was entering a critical transition period when Reagan took office. Brezhnev, slightly more than four years older than Reagan, was in declining health and, in the words of one Moscow observer, "his physical frailties were aggravated by the rapid degeneration of his mental faculties."[46] Brezhnev died on November 10, 1982, and was succeeded by Yuri Andropov, who also soon became ill. He died on February 9, 1984. Andropov was succeeded by Konstantin Chernenko, a caretaker for the Soviet old guard, who died on March 10, 1985. It is unlikely that any American president would have made much headway in U.S.-Soviet relations during this period.

And it is also unlikely that Reagan could have dealt successfully with any Soviet leader early in his presidency. Reagan was a capable letter writer, but he had no plan for translating his commitment to "meaningful and constructive dialogue" with the Soviet Union into a policy. His administration was torn by fundamental conflicts of strategy and personality that could be settled only by the exercise of presidential authority. But Reagan was unable or unwilling to resolve these conflicts, and he did not realize how much of a negative impact they had upon U.S. allies who were looking to Washington for guidance. His foreign policy was indeed in the hands of "the experts"—and they were divided among themselves on how to proceed with the Soviets. None of the experts shared Reagan's vision of a world free of nuclear weapons, and some of them believed it was a dangerous vision. Haig told me many years later that Reagan had wanted to write a letter to Brezhnev that went beyond the advocacies in the letter he actually sent to the Soviet leader.

"Very early on, at Camp David, he handcrafted a letter to Mr. Brezhnev which he gave to me the following Monday morning," Haig said. "[When I read it] I found myself astonished at his attitude when I measured it against the backdrop of what he was saying publicly, and what was attributed to him as a classic cold warrior." [47] According to Haig, this particular letter "talked about a world without nuclear weapons, it talked about disarmament"—the very points Reagan would raise with Gorbachev at Reykjavik. "It reflected a demeanor that if only those two men could sit down as rational human beings, the problems of the world would be behind us." Haig said he dissuaded Reagan from sending this letter. He considered such an approach "naïve" in view of Soviet support for "wars of national liberation in Afghanistan, Central America [and] Kampuchea," and he believed that a letter expressing Reagan's genuine views on nuclear weapons would be "perhaps confusing to the Soviet leaders." [48] No doubt it would have been, since U.S. policy was (and is) grounded in nuclear deterrence. This traditional view, as expressed by Haig, is that nuclear weaponry is "the greatest guarantor of peace and stability." Reagan, in contrast, thought that nuclear weapons were inherently evil and should be abolished. His conviction made him vulnerable to unrealistic proposals that sounded as if they would accomplish his ultimate aim of reducing nuclear arsenals.

Reagan's distaste for deterrence was well known to Caspar Weinberger, who had listened carefully to the Armageddon lecture. The secretary of defense was as militantly anticommunist as Reagan and far more willing than the president to confront the Soviet Union. He shared neither Reagan's antinuclear vision nor the commitment of Nixon traditionalists to détente and superpower summitry. Weinberger also had wanted to be secretary of state in the Reagan cabinet, and both Haig and George Shultz complained that he frequently acted as if he were in charge of foreign policy rather than the Pentagon. And in the first term, on an issue of great concern to the Western alliance, it was the Pentagon rather than the State Department that wound up defining the Reagan administration's position.

At stake was the prospective deployment in Western Europe of new U.S. medium-range nuclear missiles, the slow-flying ground-launched cruise missiles (GLCMs or "Glicums") and the swift-moving Pershing II ballistic missiles. This deployment had arisen out of NATO concerns, voiced especially by West German Chancellor Helmut Schmidt, that Western Europe was menaced by a new, medium-range nuclear missile, the SS-20, that the Soviets were rapidly deploying throughout Eastern Europe. Responding to this concern, President Carter had agreed in 1979 to deploy 572 U.S. missiles in Western Europe while simultaneously undertaking negotiations with the Soviets to produce a balance of these intermediate-range missile forces. This was known as the "two-track decision." But negotiations had stalled, and progress on either track seemed questionable by the time Reagan took office. Peace activists on both sides of the Atlantic believed that U.S. deployment would intensify the arms race, and they soon mounted a campaign against it, which blossomed into the "nuclear freeze" movement. Western Europeans of many persuasions worried that the U.S. missiles would make their nations nuclear targets in the event of a U.S.-Soviet conflict. Conservatives within the Reagan administration feared that negotiations aimed at balancing deployment of intermediate-range missiles would simply provide a forum for the Soviets to mobilize European public opinion against U.S. deployment while leaving the SS-20s in place. Some conservatives also questioned if deployment of the Pershings and cruise missiles was worth the political and economic cost.

But Reagan, encouraged by the State Department and the NATO allies, committed his administration to pursue the two-track solution at a meeting with British Prime Minister Margaret Thatcher early in February. Weinberger was not keen about the two-track approach, but he knew that Reagan would never back away from such a commitment once having made it. Instead of trying to undo the decision, Weinberger devoted his considerable energies to devising a U.S. proposal he believed the Soviets would never accept.

Weinberger's principal asset in this mission was Assistant Secretary of Defense Richard Perle, a capable neoconservative who had learned the art of fighting rear-guard battles against arms control under his mentor, Democratic Senator Henry M. Jackson of Washington state. As Strobe Talbott observed, "Perle ended up having more impact on policy in arms control than any other official in the U.S. government, an achievement that was all the more remarkable in that he held a third-echelon job." [49] This achievement was possible in part because of Perle's formidable intellect and knowledge of arms control issues and in part because Weinberger zealously backed him at the White House. The option put forth by Perle in the intermediate-range missile negotiations was carefully calculated to appeal to Reagan's desire to reduce the total number of nuclear weapons rather than simply limiting their deployment. It was called the "zero option" because it advocated the removal of all Soviet SS-20s, in Asia as well as Europe, in return for U.S. agreement to cancel deployment of the cruise missiles and Pershing IIs. No one, least of all Perle and Weinberger, thought the Soviets would ever accept a deal that required them to remove actual missiles in return for U.S. agreement not to deploy weapons that were still on the production lines. But they were right in thinking that this approach would appeal to Reagan. The State Department advocated a negotiating position known as "zero plus" that would have permitted both sides to keep small numbers of missiles. Reagan much preferred the Pentagon plan. On November 12, 1981, Reagan called in Weinberger and Haig and informed them that he had decided to go with the zero option, which, many turns and twists later, would become the basis for the INF treaty of 1987.

One detail of this decision reveals Weinberger's understanding of Reagan's method of operation and Perle's skill in devising stratagems to take advantage of it. Weinberger knew that Reagan disliked coming down firmly on behalf of one of his principal subordinates at the expense of another. He therefore saw to it that the option paper presented by the Pentagon on the zero option provided for the illusion of a compromise. This was possible because the State Department opposed not only the zero option itself but the Pentagon's definition of "zero," which included some shorter-range nuclear weapons systems. The latter issue was of minor importance to Perle and Weinberger, and they used it to give Reagan an opportunity to split the difference between his secretaries of state and defense. "That was quite a deliberate strategy," said Perle. "We both made sure that the paper that went to the president divided the issue into two parts, and we let the NSC staff know that we could live with a defeat on part two. As it happens, in one of the ironies of that particular decision, Gorbachev later gave us part two." [50]

Of such maneuvers was foreign policy made in the Reagan administration, particularly in the first term. Reagan had clear convictions and improbable dreams, but he never mastered the nuclear calculus or the details of complicated issues. When Reagan brought in Haig and Weinberger to tell them of his decision on the zero option, he began the meeting by telling a typical anecdote, this one involving a long-ago performance by Paul Muni when he played an idealistic union leader in a play performed by Lower Manhattan's Yiddish Theater. The script called for the second act to close with Muni telling an overbearing employer, "I will give them *nothing*." Instead, he declared, "I will give them *everything*." The audience applauded, but the players had to write a new opening for the third act during intermission. [51]

The anecdote lacked relevance to the zero-option decision. It was probably triggered by the talk of the missile negotiations with the Soviet Union, which often reminded Reagan of when he was negotiating with producers on behalf of the Screen Actors Guild. This was one of Reagan's most easily accessible mental transistors. He had a consistent need in any substantive discussion to come up with stories that gave him a sense of continuity between Washington and Hollywood. John Naisbitt, the author of *Megatrends,* told me after a lunch with Reagan that the president had responded to every point he made with an anecdote, "about half of them right on point and the other half having no relevance whatsoever." (When I mentioned this to Stu Spencer, he said, "That's about it. He bats about .500.") [52]

Like his anecdotes, Reagan's intuitive decisions were almost always reactive. He rarely solicited policy options during his eight years in office. In fact, he so rarely made inquiries of his staff about anything that the exceptions were always notable. As far as I have been able to determine in scores of interviews, Reagan never once asked his national security advisers about the progress of arms control negotiations or other foreign policy initiatives. The closest he ever came to this, and it is an important exception, was inquiring about the feasibility of missile defense. On other aspects of nuclear diplomacy, Reagan was content to be a performer rather than a policymaker. He gave speeches when required to do so by events or the exigencies of his schedule, and he acted on the premise that his advisers would tell him anything he needed to know. They did not always meet this standard, in part because they sometimes assumed that Reagan knew more than he did.

On May 9, 1982, for instance, Reagan gave a speech at Eureka College that was highly promoted by the White House public relations team as an expression of the president's eagerness for a reduction in the strategic nuclear arsenals of the superpowers. Its central feature was a proposal to reduce U.S. and Soviet ballistic missiles by one-third. The Soviets dismissed this offer as one-sided, and most U.S. deterrence traditionalists agreed with them. Reagan thought the criticism reflected the prejudices of the arms-control community, notably its commitment to the doctrine of mutually assured destruction. These prejudices were real enough, but there was a more fundamental problem with the Reagan proposal. Instead of being the evenhanded starting point for a serious negotiation that Reagan believed it to be, the U.S. proposal called for cutting the land-based ICBMs of the two superpowers by equal proportions. This meant that far greater reductions in strategic arsenals would be required of the Soviets than of the United States, because the Soviet strategic force was concentrated in land-based ICBMs while the U.S. force was dispersed among the land, sea and air triad. Since Reagan did not propose comparable reductions in U.S. planes that carried nuclear bombs or in submarine-launched nuclear missiles, his plan was viewed by the Soviets as a rather crude effort to extend (or establish) U.S. nuclear superiority. Reagan did not understand that the Soviet objections had a basis in fact. As Scowcroft would learn to his surprise nearly a year later, Reagan simply did not know that the Soviet strategic force was heavily concentrated in land-based missiles.

Ignorance has consequences. Reagan's lack of knowledge, or even interest, in the substance and processes of foreign policy and arms control gave an enormous advantage to those who made the last presentation to the president on any contested issue. Officials plotted among themselves for this opportunity. Those who favored a policy position that failed to win the president's imprimatur often persuaded themselves that the outcome would have been different if they had managed to engage Reagan's attention or have a final word with him. It was not easy to do either. Until the run-up to his first meeting with Gorbachev late in 1985, Reagan was far more interested in economic recovery and cutting taxes than in any aspect of foreign policy. He devoted his energies to speeches, personal correspondence and ceremonial appearances. He was closely guarded by his wife and staff. Even cabinet officers with influence often had difficulty seeing Reagan alone. Vice President Bush was an exception, but he was reluctant to be the bearer of bad tidings or indeed of any message that might even faintly damage his own standing with the president. Bush was nonetheless firmly in the camp of the "pragmatists" or "realists" within the administration. On issues of superpower diplomacy and arms control these pragmatists did constant battle with the "conservatives" or "Reaganauts," whom they called "hard-liners" or "crazies." The conservatives were equally unflattering to their opponents, often describing them as "accommodationists" and occasionally as "one-worlders," an odd scrap of opprobrium left over from the struggles between internationalists and isolationists before World War II. These labels lacked relevance beyond the byzantine confines of the Reagan court. All the contestants for the heart and mind of Ronald Reagan were political conservatives in the usual meaning of the term. All were staunchly anti-Soviet and pro-capitalist, and favored the military buildup that Reagan considered the essential precondition of successful diplomacy. Where the two camps differed, as McFarlane expressed it, was on the purpose of the buildup. "I thought that realism had to be one of the pillars of the new U.S.-Soviet relationship—realism and strength," McFarlane said. "But I also felt that an arms buildup that gave us nothing except peace in our time was irresponsible. You had to convert this ephemeral event [the buildup] into treaties, agreements and rules of the road that would last after Reagan."[53]

In the second term McFarlane would become a controversial and tragic figure in the administration's ill-starred adventurism in Iran and Nicaragua. But his belief that something should come of the U.S. investment in military spending helped steer Reagan away from the shoals of confrontation during the ebb tide of U.S.-Soviet relations in the first term. On issues of U.S.-Soviet diplomacy McFarlane was a member of the pragmatist team of which George Shultz became the undisputed captain. The players on Shultz's side who mattered most in the critical period from his appointment in mid-1982 until the end of the first term were McFarlane, Deaver, James Baker, Bush and Nancy Reagan. Arrayed against them were Weinberger, Clark, Casey and Jeane Kirkpatrick. Ed Meese was the principal ally of the conservatives on the White House staff, but his influence on foreign policy dwindled in the latter half of the first term. Both groups had allies in Congress, although the Republican congressional leadership tilted toward the pragmatists. Within the bureaucracy the pragmatists were strongest at the State Department and weakest in the National Security Council staff and the Arms Control and Disarmament Agency, where director Kenneth Adelman was an outspoken conservative. Within the White House the speechwriting department was a conservative enclave.

None of this was quite as tidy as it sounds. The members of both camps had tactical differences among themselves, and competing priorities. Neither Shultz nor Weinberger paid much attention to Central America, for instance, except when forced to do so by events. McFarlane tended to side with the conservatives on Nicaragua while remaining staunchly pragmatic on arms control issues. The U.S.-Soviet relationship was the touchstone issue where the battle lines were most clearly drawn. The conservatives believed that the Soviets responded only to military power. The pragmatists distinguished between "strength" and "peace through strength." Their watchword, as McFarlane expressed it, was "realism," which meant cashing in on the Reagan buildup and the Reagan rhetoric by driving hard bargains with the Soviets at the negotiating table.

Reagan fueled the policy disagreement within his administration by blurring distinctions between the contradictory advocacies that came across his desk. This was partly a product of his knowledge gaps, but it also reflected an inner conflict between ideological and practical impulses. Reagan was simultaneously a conservative and a pragmatist. He agreed with the conservatives that even Republican presidents had tended to be too accommodationist in their dealings with the Soviet Union. But he was also committed to reducing the nuclear arsenals of the superpowers, and this goal required negotiations with the Soviets. Reagan was abundantly endowed with common sense. He knew without Shultz or McFarlane telling him that the U.S. military buildup would not last forever. While he claimed never to act out of political considerations, Reagan recognized that he needed something to show for the buildup. This recognition gradually led him into the pragmatists' camp, and was reflected in the tiresome analogy comparing Soviet leaders to movie producers, which seemed ludicrous to conservatives and pragmatists alike. But such comparisons pushed Reagan in the direction of diplomacy. Reagan's desire for an "acceptable compromise," as Craig Fuller had described it, gave the pragmatists an inherent advantage and helped to undermine the influence of conservatives who viewed the military buildup as an end in itself. Shultz recognized this. He also recognized that Reagan, despite his knowledge gaps, had "pretty good instincts for how to conduct something, and . . . a lot of staying power."[54] What Reagan lacked was not a sense of direction but a foreign policy. As Don Oberdorfer of *The Washington Post* expressed it, "Reagan brought with him to Washington no blueprints for conduct of foreign policy, and he created an administration with fewer experi-

enced officials in top-level foreign policy posts than any in recent decades."[55] Haig's effort to supply a blueprint had failed, largely because
he lacked the trust of rival architects and eventually of Reagan. Shultz
realized that it was necessary to involve Reagan in the construction
process. He also came to realize that Reagan's seemingly irrelevant
anecdotes were tools that the president used to comprehend the world.
"He often reduced his thinking to a joke," Shultz said. "That doesn't
mean it didn't have a heavy element to it."[56]

But it was never easy for Reagan to proceed from anecdotes to analysis. He was not overcome by his ideological impulses, but he was
hampered by them, and he was hampered even more by an unattainable
desire for harmony between the rival factions within his administration.
Reagan strove to please all the principal players on his team, even when
their objectives were incompatible. "The president didn't want to come
down so clearly on one side that the other side would be deeply and
profoundly disappointed," said Richard Perle.[57] In this respect, Reagan's desire for "acceptable compromise" was a drawback. He had
learned as a child the art of pleasing others, and he had been known in
Hollywood as an agreeable actor who readily accepted changes in the
script or shooting schedule. As president, he tried to please his cabinet
officers by blending contradictory advocacies into a compromise solution in which there were no winners or losers.

This proclivity for splitting the difference would produce disastrous
results in Lebanon and Central America, and it provided obstacles to
coherent diplomacy in every region. Perle once said to me only partially
in jest that the administration's arms control initiatives were formed by
taking the worst parts of conflicting policy option papers, including his
own, and fashioning them into a single, incoherent proposal. Such
proposals deepened Soviet suspicions of Reagan's motivations and often
prompted counterproposals that were designed more for propaganda
purposes than for negotiation. This, in turn, tended to confirm Reagan's
view that the Soviets were uninterested in realistic negotiations. This
circular exchange was on balance helpful to the conservatives within
the administration, since their goal was the negative one of fending off
constructive U.S.-Soviet discussions that might ripen into arms control
agreements. Shultz and the pragmatists had the more demanding task
of trying to fashion options that would pass muster with the conservatives, win the acceptance of the president and then be taken seriously
by the Soviets. In the trench warfare within the administration, the
conservatives held the advantage of defensive positions. They needed

only stalemate to achieve their goals, and it was easy to create a stale-mate as long as Reagan's condition for signing off on a specific proposal was agreement among his principal advisers. It took Shultz many battles and much maneuvering to break through the lines of interior defense constructed by Weinberger, Clark and Casey.

Shultz has the tenacity and temperament for protracted conflict. "Knowing that he is a Marine who has a [Princeton] tiger tattooed on his butt tells you more about him than any State Department biogra-phy," observed a friend who had worked with him. The biography was also impressive. Shultz had emerged from turf struggles in the Nixon administration, the University of Chicago, Stanford and the Bechtel Corporation with a reputation for integrity and effectiveness. His bland and Buddha-like demeanor and somewhat professorial manner con-cealed a smoldering temperament that occasionally erupted in volcanic outbursts and a probing intellect that he devoted to understanding Ronald Reagan. Mike Deaver was his ally in this task. Many of the conservatives and even some of the pragmatists dismissed Deaver as a glorified valet or as a scheduling obstacle to be overcome. Shultz knew better. He respected Deaver's intelligence ("Mike is very analytical," Shultz told me),[58] and he knew that Deaver was an unerring guide to Reagan's moods and to the favor of the first lady, whom Shultz also cultivated. It was no accident that Shultz was virtually the only high administration official who escaped the wrath of Nancy Reagan in her book, *My Turn*. Shultz, also the beneficiary of a long and happy mar-riage, took it for granted that wives influence their husbands. He paid close attention to his own standing with Reagan, recognizing that Haig had been undone by the absence of a strong relationship with the president. Deaver saw to it that Shultz had the personal access to Rea-gan that Haig had never been able to obtain. Nearly every week when they were both in Washington, Shultz came over to the White House for a private lunch with the president that often lasted for two hours. Afterward, he would drop by Deaver's office to chat. "How are things going?" Deaver would ask. "You tell me," Shultz would say. Deaver, while beset by his own insecurities, recognized that even the worldly Shultz needed reassuring feedback of the kind Reagan almost never gave even his most trusted subordinates. "You're doing fine," Deaver would say typically. "The president thinks you're terrific. Nancy thinks you're terrific. We all think you're terrific."[59]

Deaver's sentiments were widely shared in the White House. Chief of Staff James Baker and Vice President Bush, who often worked in concert, believed that Weinberger and Clark brought out the worst in Reagan and welcomed Shultz as a counterforce. Meese, who trusted Clark and Weinberger, had become wearied by Haig's histrionics and much preferred Shultz's more subdued style. So, at first, did Clark, but the honeymoon between the new secretary of state and the national security adviser was brief. While he respected Shultz, Clark had no use for the State Department bureaucracy and he quickly leaped to the conclusion that Shultz had become its captive.

Shultz and Weinberger never had a honeymoon. They were natural rivals, burdened by ancient animosities and a competing view of U.S.-Soviet relations. Weinberger worried that a premature return to the days of détente would undermine public support for the military buildup. He brushed aside arguments that Congress would be more willing to keep the buildup going if he slowed it down or if spending on new weapons systems was coupled to a strategy of U.S.-Soviet negotiation. Weinberger thought that Congress was unrealistic in its constant demand for "a settlement, a consensus, a compromise, an agreement" on defense spending. He was a student of Winston Churchill, and he saw parallels between Churchill's unheeded warnings about the Nazi military buildup in the 1930s and his own dire forecasts of Soviet military superiority. On the wall behind Weinberger's desk in the Pentagon was a framed quotation from Churchill: "Never give in, never give in, never, never, never, never; in nothing great or small, large or petty, never give in." Weinberger's critics questioned the value of never giving in as a motto in the nuclear age, but the Churchill quotation typified the secretary of defense's attitude toward compromise. Weinberger believed that it was the Soviets who were dealing from strength, and he did not want to bargain with them. This attitude would have put Weinberger on a collision course with any secretary of state who sought, as Shultz did, to practice traditional superpower diplomacy. "I felt all along that we should push very hard to engage the Soviet Union," Shultz said.[60]

Events did not conspire to make Shultz's task an easy one. Secretaries of state cannot choose the events that pop up on the world's radar screens, and the United States was preoccupied with the Israeli invasion of Lebanon when Shultz became secretary of state. On July 6, 1982, while Shultz was still awaiting confirmation, Reagan agreed "in principle to contribute a small contingent" of U.S. troops as part of a multinational force for "temporary peacekeeping" in Beirut. Of that, more in the next two chapters. Suffice it here to say that the Middle East preoccupied Shultz until September 1, when Reagan delivered a significant speech, largely crafted at the State Department, calling for limited self-government for the Palestinians living on the West Bank of the Jordan and in Gaza.

Even after he turned his attention to U.S.-Soviet relations, Shultz proceeded slowly. Late in September he held exploratory talks in New York with Soviet Foreign Minister Andrei Gromyko, but made little progress. Brezhnev was dying, and U.S.-Soviet relations were tense and unproductive. Reagan was in a confrontational mood. When arms control negotiator Paul Nitze, about to leave for a new round of INF talks in Geneva, warned Reagan at a National Security Council meeting in mid-September that the Soviets would find the U.S. position unacceptable, the president replied, "Well, Paul, you just tell the Soviets that you're working for one tough son of a bitch." [61] When Brezhnev died in November, Shultz suggested to Reagan that he attend the funeral and meet Yuri Andropov. No one seconded the motion. Deaver, who usually favored anything Shultz proposed, thought it would be tasteless to use Brezhnev's funeral as the occasion for an unofficial mini-summit. Reagan was even less impressed with the idea. He was not ready for superpower summitry of any sort, and he always avoided funerals whenever he could. The president sent Shultz and Bush to represent him in Moscow.

Shultz kept trying. He sensed that the change in Moscow had provided an opportunity to probe for openings in the towering wall of suspicion that then existed between the Reagan administration and the Kremlin. Encouraged by Deaver, he also realized that Reagan wanted to improve the superpower relationship, despite his occasional confrontational remarks. Within a few weeks of Andropov's ascension to leadership, Shultz and Reagan held a meeting in which the secretary of state asked Reagan for authority to explore opportunities across the gamut of U.S.-Soviet relationships. Reagan gave him the green light,[62] and Shultz launched what he called a "work program" with Soviet Ambassador Dobrynin, systematically reviewing U.S.-Soviet differences.

The first payoff on these discussions was a meeting between Dobrynin and Reagan at the White House on February 15, 1983, that at the time was shrouded in mystery. Dobrynin had that day gone to the State Department to hold his regularly scheduled meeting with Shultz, who had given him no advance warning that he was to see the president. After they had talked awhile, Shultz bundled the Soviet ambassador into his limousine, which proceeded from the underground garage at the State Department to the White House, where it entered unobserved through the East Gate. Dobrynin was then taken to the family quarters for a private chat with Reagan that was not announced to the media. It was a shrewd stroke. Shultz recognized that personal encounters with Soviet officials would produce more pragmatic responses from the president than abstract discussions of U.S.-Soviet issues. Dobrynin, then the dean of the Washington diplomatic corps and a gregarious storyteller, was the ideal Soviet official for engaging Reagan.

Later, conservatives who sought to discredit Shultz would use this meeting as a symbol of what they saw as the secretary of state's overeagerness for U.S.-Soviet accommodation. Helene von Damm, a friend of Bill Clark's, wrote that Clark was "fit to be tied" when he learned that Shultz had "sneaked" Dobrynin into the White House.[63] There is no doubt that Clark, consistently distrustful of the Soviets, was bothered by the portents of the Reagan-Dobrynin meeting. And there is also no doubt, as both Shultz and Clark agree, that the secretary of state informed the national security adviser of the meeting in advance. Mindful of the suspicions among conservatives of what he was doing, Shultz made it a point to call Clark and tell him what was afoot. Clark thanked him and blamed Deaver and the first lady, rather than the secretary of state, for a meeting he thought unwise. "Mike and Nancy were anxious for an outbreak of world peace," said Clark. "They thought that by getting Dobrynin into the East Wing, peace would prevail."[64]

Peace did not break out at the Reagan-Dobrynin meeting, but it did provide the crucial opening that Shultz had been seeking. Reagan was at the time concerned with the plight of five members of a Pentecostal family who had rushed past Soviet policemen on June 27, 1978, and taken refuge in the U.S. embassy in Moscow, where they had lived ever since. Understanding the predicament of the Pentecostals required no mastery of arms control arcania. As Reagan saw it, the Soviets were simply denying freedom to an innocent family that wanted to practice its religion without harassment from the state. He made this point bluntly and with passion to Dobrynin. After the meeting, Shultz followed up by pushing hard for the freedom of the Pentecostals. It was a ticklish negotiation, because the Soviets were wary of establishing a precedent that would encourage other Soviet citizens to seek refuge in Western embassies, and the Pentecostals were reluctant to accept a Soviet promise of safe conduct. When the promise finally came, Shultz staked his reputation on it. On June 26, 1983, the five Pentecostals were allowed to leave the embassy and emigrate with ten other members of their family to Israel. "That was an act of faith," said Shultz, and it proved justified. "I had dealt with the Soviets in the Nixon administration and felt that on carefully defined things, even then, if they said they would do something they would do it," he said.[65]

Shultz's diplomatic efforts yielded other results. Completing an initiative that had been launched and largely worked out by Haig, he arranged on August 17, 1982, for acceptance of a joint U.S.-China communiqué that limited U.S. arms sales to Taiwan in exchange for a vague pledge by the Chinese government to strive for "peaceful unification of the Motherland." (Reagan was under the inaccurate impression that China had pledged never to take Taiwan by force and phoned Dan Rather to complain after the CBS anchorman had described the communiqué as an example of "reversed policy.")[66] The communiqué was sharply criticized by some of the administration's most conservative supporters, with William Safire calling it Reagan's "greatest foreign policy blunder."[67] These conservatives were dismayed again in November, when Shultz succeeded where Haig had failed and persuaded Reagan to lift U.S. sanctions imposed five months earlier on participation by the European allies in a Soviet natural gas pipeline. And in March 1983, Shultz convinced Reagan to back away temporarily from his insistence on the "zero option" and offer a revised agreement that would "substantially reduce" the number of Pershing II and cruise missiles the United States intended to deploy in Europe if the Soviets would agree to scrap some of their already installed SS-20 missiles. Much to the relief of conservatives committed to the zero option, Gromyko described the U.S. proposal as "absurd" and the Soviets rejected it.

Shultz also tried to lay the basis for a summit meeting between Reagan and Andropov. Weinberger and Clark reacted coolly to a State Department memo proposing a summit, and Reagan, while intrigued by the idea, did not attempt to resolve the differences among his advisers. Instead, he straddled them, telling Helen Thomas of United Press International on May 19 that prospects for a summit were dim in 1983 but "likely" in 1984.[68] The issue quickly became moot. Stories about Andropov's poor health began to circulate in Eastern European circles near the end of June, when leaders of the Warsaw Pact nations met in Moscow. Shultz reacted philosophically, knowing there was no point in pushing for a summit with a Soviet leader whose health was questionable. In his dealings with Reagan and the Soviets, Shultz resembled a long-distance runner who realized the importance of conserving his energy for the final lap. He believed that a Reagan-Andropov summit was a missed opportunity, but he also believed that such opportunities would come again.

Shultz needed that long-distance perspective to carry him through the first eighteen months of his tenure, one of the chilliest periods in U.S.-Soviet relations since the onset of the Cold War. This period included the final months of the Brezhnev era and most of Andropov's brief reign. Cracks were beginning to show in the façade of Soviet empire, particularly in Poland, where the then-outlawed Solidarity union was organizing strikes and protests. Battle lines were being drawn between the Reagan administration and Congress on a range of foreign policy issues, and the first serious resistance emerged to the military buildup. Reagan's domestic popularity, low during the recession, began to climb again in 1983, but not with the Soviet leadership. The Soviets had hoped Reagan would prove "another Nixon" who valued détente and traditional arms control.[69] "For a long time the Russians simply ignored President Reagan's challenge, as if it could be wished away," observed Moscow correspondent Dusko Doder.[70] But by the end of the Brezhnev era, Reagan could no longer be ignored. In a speech to Soviet generals and Defense Ministry officials on October 28, 1982, two weeks before his death, Brezhnev accused the United States of pursuing a foreign policy of "adventurism, rudeness and undisguised egoism" that threatened "to push the world into the flames of nuclear war."

Reagan viewed these denunciations as confirmation of his view that freedom and democracy were everywhere on the march, even within the boundaries of the Soviet empire. In a prophetic address to British members of Parliament at the Palace of Westminster on June 8, 1982, he said that the Soviet Union, "the home of Marxist-Leninism," was gripped by a "great revolutionary crisis." Reagan accurately saw Poland, which was then under martial law but "magnificently unreconciled to repression," as the pivot of that crisis. He expressed optimism about the outcome in Poland—indeed, he was optimistic that a "global campaign for freedom" would ultimately prevail. "It is the Soviet Union that runs against the tide of human history by denying human freedom and human dignity to its citizens," Reagan said. "It also is in deep economic difficulty. The rate of growth in the national product has been steadily declining since the fifties and is less than half of what it was then. The dimensions of this failure are astounding. A country which employs one-fifth of its population in agriculture is unable to feed its own people. . . . Overcentralized, with little or no incentives, year after year the Soviet system pours its best resources into the making of instruments of destruction. The constant shrinkage of economic growth combined with the growth of military production is putting a heavy strain on the Soviet people. What we see here is a political structure that no longer corresponds to its economic base, a society where productive forces are hampered by political ones."

The Westminster speech expressed more cogently than any other address of his presidency Reagan's belief that the forces of freedom would triumph over communism. Some of its passages were predictive of the events that would occur in Eastern Europe seven and one-half years later when he was no longer in the White House. Reagan forecast that there would be "repeated explosions against repression" in Eastern Europe and warned that "the Soviet Union itself is not immune to this reality." In a paraphrase of a famous Marxist line, he said that "the march of freedom and democracy . . . will leave Marxism-Leninism on the ash-heap of history as it has left other tyrannies which stifle the freedom and muzzle the self-expression of the people." He called upon the West to encourage this process by assisting democratic institutions behind the Iron Curtain—"the system of a free press, unions, political parties, universities, which allows a people to choose their own way to develop their own culture, to reconcile their own differences through peaceful means." And he concluded by saying, "Let us now begin a major effort to secure the best—a crusade for freedom that will engage the faith and fortitude of the next generation. For the sake of peace and justice, let us move toward a world in which all people are at last free to determine their own destiny."

Reagan's speech, liberally studded with quotations from Winston Churchill, struck a patriotic chord in Britain, then engaged in that leftover struggle of empire known as the Falklands War. The audience in the royal gallery at Westminster cheered when Reagan said that the British troops in the Falklands "fight for a cause—for the belief that armed aggression must not be allowed to succeed, and the people must participate in the decisions of government . . . under the rule of law." Much of the British press focused on Reagan's unequivocal support for Britain rather than his larger message. *The Times* of London, reflecting the views of the Thatcher government, was an exception. It led with Reagan's prediction that Marxism-Leninism would be deposited on the "ash-heap of history" and a quotation from Thatcher describing the address as a "triumph."

American commentary was more inclined to dismiss Reagan's view of the precarious condition of the Soviet empire as wishful thinking. *The Philadelphia Enquirer* pointed to the contradiction between Reagan's policies and his words, noting that he had lifted the grain embargo at the same time he was pressing U.S. allies against Moscow trade credits and participation in the natural gas pipeline. *The New York Times* scorned the speech as an appeal for "flower power" and said that "curiously missing from his plan was any formula for using Western economic strength to promote political accommodation."[71]

The formula was missing because the internally divided Reagan administration did not agree with its allies on how to use this economic strength. Less than three weeks before the Westminster speech, Reagan had signed a secret National Security Decision Directive (NSDD 32) calling for various efforts, including economic measures, to "neutralize efforts of the USSR to increase its influence." But the European allies, notwithstanding the Polish situation, favored increased commerce with the Soviet empire. Reagan pressed his case at the economic summit in Versailles the week before the Westminster speech but could not win even Thatcher's support for the forlorn crusade against the natural gas pipeline. The allies simply had no interest in isolating the Soviet Union economically, and all references to this objective were wisely deleted from the Westminster speech, which on the whole merited Thatcher's glowing description of it. Reagan always regarded that speech as one of his best, perhaps because of the value he attached to plainly stating his views of communism. "In retrospect," he said in 1989, "I am amazed that our national leaders had not philosophically and intellectually taken on the principles of Marxist-Leninism. We were always too worried we would offend the Soviets if we struck at anything so basic. Well, so what? Marxist-Leninist thought is an empty cupboard. Everyone knew it by the 1980s, but no one was saying it."[72]

Reagan's best speeches are composed of such verities, and the Westminster speech stands the test of time as the most farsighted and encompassing of Reagan's anticommunist messages. But it was the narrower and more moralistic speech he delivered on March 8, 1983, to the National Association of Evangelicals, meeting in convention in Orlando, Florida, that came to epitomize Reagan's view of the Soviet Union. This is the speech in which he described the Soviet Union as "the focus of evil in the modern world." Its most enduring phrase was part of a passage that had the practical political objective of urging the evangelical ministers to oppose a nuclear freeze:

So in your discussions of the nuclear freeze proposals, I urge you to beware the temptation of pride—the temptation of blithely declaring yourself above it all and label both sides equally at fault, to ignore the facts of history and the aggressive impulses of an evil empire, to simply call the arms race a giant misunderstanding and thereby remove yourself from the struggle between right and wrong and good and evil.

White House speechwriter Anthony Dolan, a former Pulitzer Prize–winning reporter who was a protégé of William F. Buckley and a friend of William Casey, was the lead writer for the Westminster and Orlando speeches. Dolan was, like Buckley, a devotee of Whittaker Chambers. The White House pragmatists considered him a wild man who was far to the right of Reagan. But the two speeches, which were edited by Reagan, faithfully reflected in tone and content the president's long-held view of the immorality of communism. Reagan's message had been much the same when Dolan was a toddler and Reagan was writing his own speeches on three-by-five cards. Nonetheless, pragmatists blamed Dolan for the stridency of the "evil empire" speech, while conservatives gave him excessive credit for this provocative formulation of Reagan's views. David Gergen, a pragmatist with oversight responsibility for the speechwriters, recalled that he was disturbed by "outrageous statements" in the draft of the Orlando speech and worked with McFarlane to tone down the final product.[73] Dolan's recollection is that most of the changes made in the speech draft involved passages relating to abortion and that Reagan himself actually "toughened" the references to the Soviet Union.[74] McFarlane, who does not remember the specific changes, says he was "marginally indifferent" to the speech, which he accurately described as "of a piece with Reagan's disdain for Commies."[75] McFarlane believed, then and now, that the speech served a useful purpose. "Realism had to be one of the pillars of the new relationship," he said. "We had to say that we had no illusions about Marxists."[76]

By the time of the Orlando speech, the Soviets had lost whatever illusions they might have had about dealing with Reagan. When the president on March 23 gave a bristling speech in behalf of the U.S. defense buildup and unveiled the Strategic Defense Initiative, Andropov accused Reagan of "attempting to disarm the Soviet Union in the face of the U.S. nuclear threat" and said his strategic proposals were "irresponsible" and "insane." By September 28, Andropov was accusing Reagan of risking actual war in his ideological struggle against the Soviet Union. "To turn the battle of ideas into military confrontation would be too costly for the whole of mankind," Andropov said. "But those who are blinded by anticommunism are evidently incapable of grasping this. Starting with the bogey of a Soviet military threat, they have now proclaimed a crusade against socialism as a social system. Attempts are made to persuade people that in general there is no room for socialism in the world." [77]

Andropov's statement reflected the extreme tension that existed in U.S.-Soviet relations during the last half of 1983. The situation had gone beyond words. On September 1, 1983, a Korean Air Lines jumbo jet with 269 people aboard, including sixty-one U.S. citizens, wandered into Soviet airspace and was shot down by a Soviet fighter. Reagan denounced the action as a "crime against humanity." A war scare developed in the United States and Europe, where French President François Mitterrand warned that the situation was comparable in seriousness to the Cuban missile crisis of 1962. And it would have been serious even without KAL 007. On November 22, after a two-day debate, the West German Bundestag approved by a vote of 286–226 the deployment of U.S. Pershing II and cruise missiles. The following day the Soviets broke off the INF talks in Geneva amidst denunciations on both sides aimed at European public opinion. By then the Soviet press was comparing Reagan to Adolf Hitler, and even Reagan was becoming wary of further ideological exchanges. In separate year-end interviews with *Time* and *Newsweek,* the president said he would no longer use the words "focus of evil" to describe the Soviet Union. *Time* chose Reagan and Andropov as their "men of the year," featuring them on the magazine cover standing grimly back to back. Reagan was in fact on the verge of adopting the more conciliatory approach to the Soviets that would be a distinguishing feature of his second term in office, but it was not publicly evident at the time. "This has been a foreign policy without a guiding star," said William Hyland, editor of *Foreign Affairs* and a respected official in former Republican administrations. "It has been the most ideological administration of U.S. foreign relations I've seen and the least conceptual, in terms of a clear vision of what the world ought to be like and what we should do to get there." [78]

Reagan did, in fact, have a vision of what he wanted the world to be like. It was the vision expressed in the Westminster speech: the Berlin Wall torn down, pluralism and human rights in the Soviet Union, free elections in Poland and in every Communist country in the world.

Above all, it was a vision of a world safe from the threat of nuclear Armageddon that he had referred to in the Westminster speech as "predictions of doomsday." But Reagan's "guiding star" was a dream, not a foreign policy. It was a dream embodied in the Strategic Defense Initiative, which would become better known to the world by its critics' label "Star Wars."

The dream was the product of Reagan's imagination, perhaps of Brass Bancroft and the Inertia Projector and *The Day the Earth Stood Still,* and certainly of the vivid prophecy of Armageddon that Reagan accepted as a valid forecast of the nuclear age. But it was also the product of reality. On July 31, 1979, Reagan toured the headquarters of the North American Aerospace Defense Command (NORAD) at Cheyenne Mountain in Colorado. After viewing this network of radar detectors designed to warn the United States of a surprise attack, Reagan asked Air Force General James Hill what could be done if the Soviets fired a missile at an American city. Nothing, Hill told him. He said NORAD would track the incoming missile, enabling it to warn city officials that it was on its way ten or fifteen minutes before it hit. "That's all we can do," he said. "We can't stop it." According to Martin Anderson, who was with him, Reagan couldn't believe that the United States had no defense against Soviet missiles. "We have spent all that money and have all that equipment, and there is nothing we can do to prevent a nuclear missile from hitting us," Reagan said to Anderson on their flight home to Los Angeles.[79]

Polls showed subsequently that many ordinary Americans shared Reagan's mistaken assumption that the United States could protect itself from nuclear attack. This is not surprising, since few people wish to dwell on nuclear extinction. But it is surprising that Reagan was so surprised. Reagan was at the time already a proponent of antimissile defense. At the invitation of famous nuclear physicist Edward Teller, Reagan in 1967 attended a briefing on defensive technologies at the Lawrence Livermore National Laboratory in Livermore, California. Teller's recollection is that Reagan, then the new governor of California, asked "good and fundamental questions,"[80] which presumably would have included a question about whether the United States possessed an antimissile defense of any kind. Reagan did not express either support or opposition to missile defense at this time, according to Teller, but it is certainly conceivable that this briefing planted in his mind the seeds of an alternative to the doctrine of mutual assured destruction. By the time Reagan ran against President Ford in 1976, three years before his

NORAD visit, he was using an analogy that he repeated to me in a 1989 interview: "It's like you and me sitting here in a discussion where we were each pointing a loaded gun at each other and if you say anything wrong or I say anything wrong, we're going to pull the trigger. And I just thought this was ridiculous—mutual assured destruction. It really was a mad policy." [81]

Missile defense was one of the few issues beyond his economic program that actively engaged Reagan once he was in the White House. One measure of his interest is that he claims, most uncharacteristically, full credit for the idea. "SDI was my idea," [82] says Reagan, and so it was. But it took many midwives to bring about its birth. Anderson was one of them. In August 1979, a few weeks after the NORAD visit, he wrote a memorandum calling for development of a "Protective Missile System" in which he said that the idea of a population defense "is probably fundamentally far more appealing to the American people than the questionable satisfaction of knowing that those who initiated an attack against us were also blown away." [83] The idea, however, was fundamentally unappealing to Reagan's campaign strategists, who feared that any talk of missiles would simply scare people. Reagan said nothing about missile defense, even though the Republican Party had for the first time gone on record as favoring it. The platform adopted at the 1980 national convention in Detroit declared: "We reject the mutual-assured-destruction (MAD) strategy of the Carter administration which limits the President to a Hobson's choice between mutual suicide and surrender." A platform plank called for "vigorous research and development of an effective anti-ballistic missiles system, such as is already at hand in the Soviet Union, as well as more modern ABM technologies." After the election Anderson met with Ed Meese, Richard Allen and Reagan's science adviser, George Keyworth, and formed what Anderson called "a small informal group on strategic missile defense . . . within the White House." [84] This group was joined at a September 14, 1981, meeting in Meese's office by Teller and two advisers with military expertise, Karl Bendetsen and General Daniel Graham, former head of the Defense Intelligence Agency. Graham was probably the nation's best-known proponent of a missile defense system. He headed an organization called High Frontier, which promoted a space-based missile defense. The group met again on October 12 and then with Reagan on January 8, 1982, at a meeting that Anderson regarded as a "critical turning point" for SDI. [85] Bill Clark had by then replaced Allen as national security adviser. Also attending the meeting was a trio of conservative Reagan fund-raisers who were attracted by the idea of missile defense: Jaquelin Hume, William Wilson of California (the president's representative to the Vatican) and Colorado brewer Joseph Coors. The meeting lasted an hour. Reagan asked questions about the feasibility and cost of missile defense but, as usual, did not commit himself. "It was clear from his demeanor that he was convinced it could be done," Anderson said.[86]

Reagan was always easily convinced that American ingenuity could overcome technological obstacles of great magnitude. He had been an ideal spokesman for General Electric, where the motto was "Progress Is Our Most Important Product," in part because he accepted the inevitability of scientific progress as an article of faith. Reagan's belief in the unlimited capacity of American inventiveness was reflected in an anecdote he told about the days when as governor of California he met a group of students who complained that Reagan's generation was out of touch with reality. "You didn't grow up in an era of space travel, of jet travel, of cybernetics, computers figuring in seconds what it used to take men years to figure out," a student said to him. "It's true . . . we didn't grow up, my generation, with those things," Reagan replied. "We invented them." Reagan liked to tell this story to groups of seniors, but he also related it on February 7, 1983, at a White House ceremony commemorating the bicentennial year of air and space flight. In this speech, six weeks before the announcement of the Strategic Defense Initiative, he also said, "God gave angels wings. He gave mankind dreams. And with His help, there's no limit to what can be accomplished."

Reagan had no fixed view, as he readily acknowledges, of the form or shape that the new missile defense system should take. He knew only that he wanted a non-nuclear system.* Whether the system was space-based or ground-based or whether it used lasers or other technology was a matter for the scientists to decide. What Reagan wanted, he said, was "a defensive screen that could intercept those missiles when they came out of the silos."[87] No such screen existed, outside of science fiction. But this was no barrier for Reagan, who thought the system was just waiting to be invented and was urgently required on moral grounds.

---

* Teller for a long time believed that the most promising technology on which to build a defense system was the nuclear-pumped X-ray laser, which would require setting off nuclear explosions in space. On January 17, 1990, Teller told me that Reagan never liked the idea of using nuclear explosions and that "he had a better idea than I did." Teller said he now favors the kinetic-energy system known as "brilliant pebbles."

The recognition that the only response the United States could make to a Soviet nuclear attack was to incinerate millions of innocent civilians seemed to him truly appalling—as it must also seem to many ordinary citizens who dwell upon the premise of deterrence. As Kenneth Adelman expressed it, "How ironic it is that liberals, who pride themselves on their moral motives, advocate such a bloodcurdling approach, namely that all is well as long as we can launch enough missiles to kill a hundred million or so Soviets." [88]

But it was not only "liberals" or, as the 1980 Republican platform put it, "the Carter administration" that accepted this premise. The 1972 Anti-Ballistic Missile (ABM) treaty had been signed, sealed and delivered in 1972 by President Nixon, who was less of a dreamer than Reagan and who reached a very different conclusion about the wisdom of a defense that would shield Americans from incoming missiles. "Although every instinct motivates me to provide the American people with complete protection against a major nuclear attack, it is not now within our power to do so," Nixon said soon after coming into office. "And it might look to an opponent like the prelude to an offensive strategy threatening the nuclear deterrent." [89] These two points would become core arguments of SDI's opponents, who argue that it is scientifically impossible to construct a leakproof shield against incoming missiles that would protect civilians, and who also contend that the Soviets would view the attempt to develop such a system as an aggressive act.

Variants of these arguments had been heard before. In 1968, President Johnson had announced a controversial program called Sentinel to protect Americans from the threat of prospective Chinese nuclear attacks in the 1970s. Nixon had followed this up in 1969 with a program known as Safeguard to protect U.S. missile silos from Soviet missiles. These systems depended on huge phased-array radars to detect the incoming missiles, which then would be intercepted and destroyed by rocket-fired U.S. missiles. Both systems were questioned, as SDI would be, on grounds that the defensive systems would be more expensive than the offensive measures necessary to overcome them. By the time Reagan came to office, a combination of scientific problems, economic costs and political objections had led the United States to abandon even the most rudimentary of missile defense systems. Although the ABM treaty allowed each side to build a limited defensive system with up to one hundred interceptors, the United States had lost interest in missile defense during the Nixon and Ford years. The Soviets built the one system allowed them by the treaty around Moscow (and also constructed a radar system at Krasnoyarsk, which they acknowledged during the Bush administration was a violation of the ABM treaty). The United States put one Safeguard system into operation near Grand Forks, North Dakota, in 1975 but deactivated it a few months later because of its high cost and limited military value. This was a decision made not by Democratic liberals or the Carter administration but by orthodox Republican believers in deterrence during the Ford administration.

Reagan was not orthodox. "He was a romantic, a radical, a nuclear abolitionist," avers *Time*'s Strobe Talbott, an advocate of traditional deterrence.[90] But despite Reagan's ardor for an alternative, the prospects of any kind of U.S. missile defense system seemed remote in 1982. Anderson's informal White House group lacked the background and the Pentagon support necessary to fashion a strategic defense proposal. Soon after the January 1982 meeting he regarded as critical for the success of SDI, Anderson left the administration and returned to the Hoover Institution at Stanford. The White House working group broke up, and the Reagan administration's efforts were focused on obtaining funding for the MX. Had this effort, related in Chapter 9, not been bungled, it is doubtful if the Strategic Defense Initiative would have ever come into being. But bungled it was. After Congress refused to accept Weinberger's discredited option of an air-launched MX missile, the administration proposed an even more fanciful substitute known as "Dense Pack." This basing option would have clustered one hundred MX missiles in hardened silos near Cheyenne, Wyoming, on the land of a farmer who, Richard Cheney, then the state's congressman, told me, was the only person in America who wanted the MX on his property. But Dense Pack depended for its success on a dubious hypothesis known as "fratricide," in which the incoming enemy missiles aimed at the closely clustered MX silos were supposed to blow each other up instead of destroying their targets. Congress wouldn't buy it. On December 8, 1982, the House responded to this option by handing the Reagan administration its first major defense policy defeat. By a vote of 245-176, the House dropped all money for production of the MX missile from the budget and set in motion the events that created SDI.

McFarlane, then deputy national security adviser under Clark, was the principal creator. Clark's expertise was in his understanding of Reagan. On weapons systems and much else he relied without apology on the expertise of McFarlane, a decorated Marine officer who had served two combat tours in Vietnam, worked for Henry Kissinger and been a congressional aide to Senator John Tower of Texas. McFarlane was disturbed at the plight of the orphan MX. He believed that Reagan had awakened Americans to the need for restoring the nation's military defenses, then failed to climb through the window of opportunity he had created. The MX fiasco particularly bothered McFarlane. He blamed Weinberger for frittering away precious time with questionable basing options that lacked credibility. "These pendulum swings [toward defense spending] don't last forever," McFarlane said. "And we had blown it badly."[91]

After the Dense Pack defeat McFarlane talked to Senators Sam Nunn of Georgia and William Cohen of Maine in an effort to save the MX. As McFarlane recalls it, Cohen said to him: "You and I can sit down and figure out a decent MX basing scheme, and Jimmy Carter did, for that matter. But that isn't the point. Anything that is brought up here by Cap Weinberger next spring is going to fail."[92] Cohen's advice to McFarlane was to find outside experts who had the credibility with Congress that Weinberger lacked. McFarlane took the idea back to Clark, who had quietly been doing some checking of his own about Weinberger's standing in Congress. While widely regarded as a naïf who knew even less than Reagan about foreign policy, Clark could be an effective backdoor politician. He realized that McFarlane's assessment of Weinberger's low standing on Capitol Hill was accurate. Though he was an ally of Weinberger on most issues, Clark approved the recommendation to name a commission of outside experts to rescue the MX, and The President's Commission on Strategic Forces was formed. Reagan accepted McFarlane's suggestion to name Brent Scowcroft, who had served as President Ford's national security adviser, as the chairman.*

While the Scowcroft Commission did its work, McFarlane and the Joint Chiefs of Staff took a fresh look at strategic defense. Despite Reagan's interest in the issue and the ruminations of the Anderson group in 1981, nothing had been done for a year to bring strategic defense closer to reality. Reagan was not passive about this issue, as he

---

* The Scowcroft Commission report, issued on April 6, 1983, recommended prompt deployment of one hundred MX missiles in Minuteman silos and became the basis for eventual approval of limited production of the MX. But the report, written largely by Washington attorney R. James Woolsey, also contended that "greater flexibility in the long run" would result from replacing the MX with a small, mobile, single-warhead missile known as Midgetman. The MX vs. Midgetman debate was never resolved in the Reagan administration and remained an open question near the end of President Bush's second year in office.

was about so many others, but he lacked the scientific background and military support necessary to launch a serious strategic defensive effort. McFarlane stepped in to fill this void.

McFarlane was not and never would be a nuclear abolitionist. He accepted the logic of deterrence, and he believed that the stability that effective deterrence requires was in jeopardy. As McFarlane saw it, the strategic competition between the superpowers was being conducted under conditions favorable to the Soviets. Operating without the restraints of a Congress or public opinion, the Soviets were building ever more powerful intercontinental ballistic missiles and attaching multiple warheads (MIRVs) to them. U.S. nuclear weaponry was sophisticated and diverse, but the power ("throw weight") and number of the Soviet ICBMs compensated for U.S. advantages. McFarlane believed that development of a large-scale U.S. ballistic missile defense might change the equation, forcing the Soviets to compete with American technology in the development of highly sophisticated technologies that required extraordinarily powerful computers and complex software that could distinguish between real missile warheads and decoys. The prospective obstacles and costs of such competition in multiple technologies were staggering. Advocates of strategic defense generally agreed that it would be most desirable to destroy Soviet ICBMs in their "boost" phase, which lasts from the time the missile is launched until after it has left the atmosphere and released the "bus" that would carry its devastating warheads to their targets. But even missile defense enthusiasts did not agree among themselves on which technologies held the most promise of meeting this objective.

Missile defense meant research into space-based chemical lasers, ground-based lasers with space-based mirrors, nuclear-pumped X-ray lasers, space-based particle beams and space-based kinetic-energy weapons such as "smart rocks" (later "brilliant pebbles") and microwave generators. The overwhelming opinion in the U.S. scientific and military communities was that the Soviets could not hope to compete successfully with the United States in research, development and deployment of a defensive system based on one or more of these arcane technologies. This was the attraction of SDI and also the reason that so many traditionalists found it frightening. The traditionalists believed that the Soviets could not afford to stand idly by while the United States developed a system that would make a dead letter of the ABM treaty and provide the United States with a significant military advantage. They foresaw that the Soviets would respond to the challenge by a massive increase in the production and deployment of multiple-warhead ICBMs, offensive strategic weapons that would have the capacity to overwhelm any defensive system. For the traditionalists, strategic defense meant the end of arms control and its replacement by, in Strobe Talbott's words, "unceasing competition without stability."[93]

McFarlane shared the premises of traditional deterrence, but they led him to a contrarian conclusion. He reasoned that a serious U.S. effort to develop a ballistic missile defense system, whether or not it could actually protect civilians, would scare the Soviets because of the possibility that it would lead to U.S. technological breakthroughs. Any defensive system is also potentially an offensive system, as the Soviets never tired of pointing out in their campaign against SDI. McFarlane believed that the Soviets genuinely feared "space strike weapons," as they called them, and that this fear could be converted into a political bargaining chip by the Reagan administration. "The idea of SDI, that is, [of] providing a shield for Americans against nuclear attack, was Ronald Reagan's idea absolutely," McFarlane said. "The idea—a different idea—to use high technology in the form of SDI to leverage Russian behavior, to reduce nuclear weapons, was my idea."[94]

As McFarlane saw it, the United States would launch a gigantic ballistic missile defense research program with great fanfare. Elimination of this program long before it reached the deployment stage would become a central Soviet objective, as indeed it quickly did. The United States would then offer to scrap the system—or in Reagan's actual proposal, share the technology with the Soviets—in return for Soviet agreement to reduce its ICBM force by such magnitudes that a defensive system would be unneeded. What the United States would actually be doing was trading away a research proposal of dubious scientific feasibility for massive reductions of offensive nuclear weapons that had already been produced and deployed. This concept, privately referred to by McFarlane as "The Sting" and later as "The Grand Compromise," was a bold and imaginative political idea. It was, however, McFarlane's idea. He never shared his strategy with Reagan, and he did not realize until too late the firmness of Reagan's commitment to strategic defense as an end in itself.

For Reagan, strategic defense was the ultimate answer to Armageddon, not a ploy to force the Soviets to the bargaining table. Reagan truly wanted reductions in nuclear arms, but he did not want to give up strategic defense to get them. It was a crucial difference that did not appear all that important to McFarlane in 1983, when neither a defensive system nor an arms agreement was on the horizon. McFarlane rationalized that he and Reagan really had the same objectives. As McFarlane saw it, the threat of SDI would lead the Soviets to accept such vast reductions in nuclear arms that the president would agree that a defensive system was unnecessary. "I was wrong on that, but that was what I reasoned," McFarlane said.[95]

Developing a strategic defensive system for any reason required an advocate on the Joint Chiefs of Staff, and McFarlane found one in the person of Admiral James D. Watkins, chief of naval operations. Watkins, a nuclear engineer with moral qualms about the arms race, shared McFarlane's concern that the administration was being ground down in the congressional debate over an appropriate MX basing system, and also shared some of Reagan's repugnance for the doctrine of mutual assured destruction. The Roman Catholic bishops had at the time issued a pastoral letter condemning nuclear arms and the doctrine of deterrence. Watkins, a committed Catholic, thought the letter an "outrage" because it "mentioned nothing about the Soviets, as if somehow we had developed these weapons solely for our own amusement."[96] But as he wrestled with the issue in discussions with other Catholics and at a conference he convened at the Naval War College, Watkins began to have doubts about absolute reliance on deterrence to the exclusion of any other alternatives. "It [the moral issue] was important in that the American people thought mutual assured destruction morally distasteful—and it was a political loser," Watkins said subsequently.[97]

Soon after the Dense Pack defeat, Watkins confided his views to fellow admiral John Poindexter, then serving as Clark's military assistant. Poindexter passed them on to McFarlane. As Watkins saw it at the time, the future of the MX, and the continued effectiveness of deterrence to keep the peace, was in doubt. Watkins wanted to offset the Soviet advantage in land-based ICBMs, and he believed that missile defense offered the promise of doing this. As Watkins told his staff, "The genius of this country is to take a new technological concept (which the Soviets may well have in their minds, as we do) and build it —field it—which they can't do. So why don't we use our applied technological genius to achieve our deterrent instead of sticking with an offensive land-based rocket exchange which they will win every time? They have bigger rockets, they can lift more stuff into space, and they have no political obstacles in basing their missiles. We shouldn't continue to play a game like that."[98]

As McFarlane remembers it, he suggested to Watkins that the chiefs discuss a ballistic missile defense option with Reagan as part of their review of strategic issues when they met with the president at their regular quarterly meeting on February 11, 1983. Watkins, already heading in the same direction, agreed. What Watkins did not know was that the other chiefs, equally alarmed by the defeat of Dense Pack, were receptive to a new approach. This was particularly true of Air Force General Charles Gabriel, whose technical analysis was highly respected by his colleagues, and also of Army General John Vessey, the plainspoken soldier who was then chairman of the Joint Chiefs of Staff. Vessey, who said subsequently that he had "spent a lot of time keeping BMD [ballistic missile defense] alive in the Army," also shared a combination of moral and military qualms about deterrence.[99] "Relying totally on the idea that you would destroy the other side is not moral, and it's not very logical," Vessey said. "It leaves you with two unacceptable alternatives. Not only do you wipe out the population of the Soviet Union, but you have a fair chance of wiping out your population as well."[100]

The chiefs plunged ahead, with Watkins leading the way. On January 20, 1983, Watkins lunched with Teller and heard the physicist explain a plan called "Excalibur," which would destroy ICBMs in their boost phase by using "pop-up" nuclear-driven X-ray lasers. Watkins didn't favor Excalibur. He realized that any defensive system that employed nuclear devices presented significant political obstacles. Like the president, Watkins favored space defense against ICBMs by non-nuclear means, although he did not believe that a U.S. strategic defense plan should be based upon any single concept. Nonetheless, Watkins was impressed with Teller, who conveyed a "vibrant, intense feeling about the projected state of technology."[101] Watkins directed that several of Teller's points be incorporated into a "white paper" he was preparing as the basis for briefing Reagan. This ten-page paper, largely drafted by a naval captain named Linton Brooks, was presented by Watkins to the other chiefs on February 2 at a meeting that became a rehearsal for the briefing of the president. Watkins did not foresee the popularity of his position when the meeting began. He had expected to present the case for strategic defense to Reagan unilaterally, and said he was "flabbergasted" when Gabriel proposed that the chiefs adopt Watkins' view as their own. Gabriel's motion passed unanimously, and Vessey agreed to include the Watkins paper as part of his presentation to Reagan the following week.[102]

The qualified enthusiasm of the Joint Chiefs of Staff for strategic defense was not shared by Caspar Weinberger. While the secretary of defense would quickly transform himself into a cheerleader for the Strategic Defense Initiative once Reagan had announced the plan, Weinberger's statement to me that he "always" supported the program is contradicted by the recollections of others who attended the February 11 meeting. Watkins and Vessey recall that Weinberger opposed the endorsement by the chiefs of U.S. investment in ballistic missile defense and politely said so when the chiefs presented their report to the president. "I don't agree with the chiefs, but you should hear them out" is the way Watkins recalls Weinberger bringing up the issue at the meeting.[103] Vessey then presented the report, which focused on the precarious state of the land-sea-air triad in the wake of repeated congressional rejections of a basing system for the MX. As naval historian Frederick H. Hartmann has observed, strategic defense "was not the centerpiece of the briefing" as far as the chiefs were concerned. "It was only a part of a comprehensive brief on all aspects of the strategic dilemma," Hartmann wrote. "The chiefs were not saying they were ready to make defense the primary strategic response, let alone fund it on any substantial scale."[104] The last section of Vessey's presentation was a slightly modified version of the Watkins paper on strategic defense. It called ballistic missile defense a "middle ground" between the "dangerous extremes of (a) threatening a preemptive strike or (b) passively absorbing a Soviet first strike." The paper also said that defense was "more moral and therefore more palatable to the American people."[105]

While this was a striking departure from anything the chiefs had said to the president on the subject in the past, Vessey's presentation and Watkins' comments on it at the meeting stopped far short of Reagan's subsequent claim that technology could devise a space shield that would protect American civilians from nuclear missiles. "We never believed in the umbrella," Watkins said. "What we said is that if you could confuse the Soviets [with a defensive system that would stop some of the missiles] there would never be a first strike."[106] But Watkins presented the issue more dramatically to Reagan, and McFarlane, who knew what was coming, picked up the cue.

"You know, Mr. President, I think that the time has come where we ought to [take] another look at defensive technologies," Watkins said. "And it seems to me that it's possibly within reach that we could develop systems that would defeat a missile attack."[107]

"Wait a minute, Jim," said McFarlane, who was sitting in for Clark at the meeting. "Are you telling me that you think it's possible that we might be able to develop defensive systems that would prevent ICBMs from reaching our country?" [108] (According to Hartmann's version, McFarlane said, "Stop! Mr. President, do you understand how important a statement that is?") [109]

Reagan did realize it. Turning to Gabriel, Vessey and the other chiefs, he said, "What about you fellows? What do you think about what Jim just said?" [110]

One by one, the chiefs agreed that Watkins was right. Their response delighted Reagan, who had not known until this meeting that the chiefs had an entirely different opinion than Weinberger about the value of ballistic missile defense. "Let's go back and look at this and get ready to push it hard," he said. [111] Many years later Reagan would recall that the chiefs had said to him at a subsequent meeting, "We have gone into what you proposed and, yes, we do believe that with the technology of today there can be such a [defensive] screen." [112]

Reagan overstates the case the chiefs actually made to him. None of them believed that the "technology of today" made possible a population defense. He also has forgotten that he had already unveiled the Strategic Defense Initiative by the time of this subsequent meeting, which occurred on April 4 at the White House. The truth is that Reagan liked the idea so much that he couldn't wait. This was immediately realized by Bill Clark, who was briefed by McFarlane on the February 11 meeting. Clark knew little about the technological feasibility of strategic defense, but he knew Reagan. Clark also realized that the proposal was certain to encounter powerful opposition from traditionalists in Congress and within the administration. He believed that Reagan should grasp the political initiative with a dramatic announcement of the program. Poindexter would say later that the chiefs "didn't realize how fast we intended to move once they were generally in favor of it." [113] And move fast they did. The prime mover was Reagan. "He wanted it," said Watkins. "When you have five military leaders saying the same thing, he had to grab hold of it. He hadn't done it before because no military leader had said anything to him except, 'What's the next basing mode?' " [114]

There was nothing passive about the usually passive president's approach to strategic defense in the weeks after the briefing. McFarlane wanted to hold the announcement until the Scowcroft Commission had reported. He believed at the time—a view he now says was "naïve"— that Reagan could have invited House Speaker Tip O'Neill to the White House and made strategic defense a bipartisan initiative. "Reagan wanted it out as soon as possible," McFarlane recalls. "He was so swept away by his ability to stand up and announce a program that would defend Americans from nuclear war [that] he couldn't wait."[115] When Clark told Reagan that the White House had already requested network time so that Reagan could make a nationally televised speech on the defense budget on March 23, the president said, "Let's do it."[116] On March 19, McFarlane drafted a surprise ending for this speech that quickly became known within the core group of missile defense advocates as "MX Plus." "We didn't tell anyone else what we were doing," Poindexter said. "The chiefs didn't know. Defense didn't know. State didn't know. After we developed the insert, we talked to the president about it. And he agreed; that's what he wanted to do."[117]

Watkins was one of the first to receive a copy of "MX Plus." On March 20, the day after it was written, he went to Andrews Air Force Base, where Vessey was preparing to leave on a foreign trip, to discuss it with the chairman of the Joint Chiefs. "The speech caught us all by surprise," Vessey said. He had expected after the February 11 meeting that Reagan's response to the chiefs' report would initiate "orderly reexamination of allocation of resources to put more emphasis on defense."[118] Vessey had "reservations about the timing" and wondered where the money would come from to pay for the new initiative. But it was also clear to him that his commander in chief was determined to make the speech, and that was enough for him.

Vessey had more warning than Shultz and Weinberger, who learned about the speech only at the last minute. This was a deliberate strategy by Clark, who knew that Weinberger opposed the plan and suspected that Shultz would, as well. (According to Strobe Talbott, Shultz thought the idea was "lunacy.")[119] But Clark's biggest worry was that the bureaucracies at State and the Pentagon or the pragmatists at the White House would leak "MX Plus" to the media and expose the Strategic Defense Initiative to criticism in advance of the announcement. If that happened, said Clark, SDI "would never be born."[120] In the days leading up to the speech, Clark had become an uncritical booster of SDI. "We needed the initiative," he said long afterward. "And I still love the cartoon of Joe Sixpack in front of his six o'clock news and his wife goes into the kitchen and she says, 'Well, if it's so expensive, and if it doesn't work, why are the Soviets so concerned about it?' "[121]

The argument that there must be something good in any proposal that was opposed by the Soviets would become a central feature of the conservative case for SDI. But most conservatives were as astonished as the pragmatists on the White House staff by the surprise ending to

Reagan's March 23 speech. Weinberger, who was in Portugal, asked for a twenty-four-hour delay so he could inform U.S. allies but was turned down on grounds that the network time for the speech was already scheduled. No one bothered to inform White House spokesman Larry Speakes. The White House press office had geared up to defend Reagan's case for increasing the defense budget and had almost no information to provide reporters about the reasons or rationale for Reagan's new initiative. Surprise was what Reagan and Clark had wanted, and surprise was what they got. Reagan began his speech with a routine warning that Congress had trimmed the defense budget "to the limits of safety." After appealing for continued public support for the buildup and for Soviet cooperation in "stabilizing the nuclear balance" through mutual arms reductions, he attacked the premise of deterrence. Depending on the threat of mutual nuclear annihilation to keep the peace, Reagan said, was "a sad commentary on the human condition":

> Wouldn't it be better to save lives than to avenge them? Are we not capable of demonstrating our peaceful intentions by applying all our abilities and our ingenuity to achieving a truly lasting stability? I think we are. Indeed, we must.
>
> After careful consultation with my advisers, including the Joint Chiefs of Staff, I believe there is a way. Let me share with you a vision of the future which offers hope. It is that we embark on a program to counter the awesome Soviet missile threat with measures that are defensive. Let us turn to the very strengths in technology that spawned our great industrial base and that have given us the quality of life we enjoy today.

Reagan acknowledged that he was proposing a "formidable technical task" that "may not be accomplished before the end of this century," but that "current technology has attained a level of sophistication where it's reasonable to begin this effort." He also acknowledged that defensive systems could be combined with offensive ones in pursuit of an aggressive policy. "But with these considerations firmly in mind, I call upon the scientific community in our country, those who gave us nuclear weapons, to turn their great talents now to the cause of mankind and world peace, to give us the means of rendering these nuclear weapons impotent and obsolete." Such an achievement, Reagan concluded, "holds the promise of changing the course of human history."

And so, the Strategic Defense Initiative was born. From obscure beginnings it would grow into a $17 billion program[122] that would dominate strategic arms control debate for the remainder of the 1980s and become a principal bone of contention in the negotiations between the United States and the Soviet Union. More than any other specific program of the administration, SDI was a product of Reagan's imagination and Reagan's priorities. Another president might well have proposed an income tax reduction or a rebuilding of the defense budget, but no other prominent American politician was even talking about construction of a space shield that would protect civilians from a nuclear holocaust. Reagan never appreciated the depth and range of scientific skepticism about the feasibility of his idea. Nor did he realize that McFarlane, who would soon become his national security adviser, favored creating a missile defense system largely because he wanted to bargain it away. Reagan totally believed in the science-fiction solution he had proposed without consultation with his secretary of state or his secretary of defense. The belated caution of the Joint Chiefs did not discourage him. He paid no attention when the Scowcroft Commission declared two weeks after the announcement of SDI that the "applications of current [ballistic missile defense] technology offer no real promise of being able to defend the United States against nuclear attack in this century." Reagan was convinced that American ingenuity could find a way to protect the American people from the nightmare of Armageddon. As he saw it, the Strategic Defense Initiative was a dream come true.

14

FREEDOM FIGHTERS

So, I guess in a way [the Nicaraguan rebels] are counterrevolutionary, and God bless them for being that way. And I guess that makes them contras, and so it makes me a contra, too.

RONALD REAGAN,
March 14, 1986[1]

In reacting to the threat of nuclear holocaust, President Reagan was guided by a futuristic vision. But in responding to almost every other foreign policy challenge, his perspectives were the product of the past. Reagan's mental pictures of the world had been formed when the Nazi storm was gathering in Europe and imperial Japan was on the march in China. He viewed the world through World War II eyes, and he had learned his generation's lesson that unwillingness to prepare for war invites aggression. For Reagan, the word "appeasement" carried connotations of "surrender." He believed that U.S. military strength was the best guarantee of peace. "War will not come again, other young men will not have to die, if we will speak honestly of the dangers that confront us and remain strong enough to meet these dangers," Reagan said at Arlington National Cemetery on Memorial Day, 1982.

But Reagan's picture of a golden, patriotic past was filtered through the dark, distorting lens of Vietnam. California had been on the cutting edge of the peace movement during Reagan's governorship, and the student protests against the Vietnam War had left a lasting impression. While Reagan was never on the side of the students, he also had reservations about the war, or at least the way he thought the war was being waged. He sensed that the divisiveness of Vietnam somehow bound Americans together in shared emotions of frustration and anger. As a political outsider, Reagan was well positioned to exploit this frustration. He bore no responsibility for the decisions that led to American participation in the Vietnam War, and he shared the inveterate conservative skepticism about the wisdom of land wars in Asia. As the protests mounted, Reagan became a spokesman for those who believed the United States was losing the war in Vietnam because Washington lacked the will to win it. This view fit with his all-purpose contention that the federal government was responsible for most of what was wrong in America. In Vietnam, as Reagan saw it, Americans had been the victim of their government. "Let us tell those who fought in that war that we will never again ask young men to fight and possibly die in a war our government is afraid to win," Reagan said repeatedly in a rafter-shaking applause line of his 1976 presidential campaign.[2] Over time he condensed this declaration into a vow of "no more Vietnams," a pledge that appealed to those who thought the war an immoral undertaking as well as those who shared Reagan's opinion that it had been "a noble cause."

"No more Vietnams" was more than political contrivance. Reagan was always his own best audience, and he listened to what he said about Vietnam. As an old-fashioned patriot, Reagan assumed the moral legitimacy of America's cause and celebrated a cinematic vision of national valor. But he was also an intuitive, modern politician who sought to be a successful president. He knew that wars created casualties as well as heroes. He recognized that the Korean War had turned public opinion against President Truman and that the Vietnam War had been responsible for the ruin of President Johnson. Most importantly, he realized that the Vietnam legacy had deprived American presidents of the option of deploying U.S. troops in protracted wars designed to stop the spread of communism. Reagan was willing to sponsor Nicaraguan rebels in what he saw as an effort to rescue a democratic revolution and stop the Communist tide from rushing through Mexico and lapping across the Texas border. He described these rebels and the Afghan guerrillas who were bravely resisting the Soviet occupation of their country as "freedom fighters," a term he was unwilling to apply to the blacks struggling to overthrow the tyranny of a white minority government in South Africa. Reagan believed that it was in the U.S. interest to arm and supply anticommunist guerrillas and to promote their cause in the marketplace of world opinion. But Reagan had mastered the most valuable lesson of Vietnam. He knew that it was realistically impossible for any president to commit U.S. troops to a protracted war that lacked the support of the American people.

This underlying core of realism inhibited Reagan's ideological impulses, much as his aversion to nuclear war eventually helped tone down his oratorical assaults on the Soviet Union. Reagan relished sounding the battle cry of freedom. He rhapsodized about the exploits of the Nicaraguan rebels, whom he described as "the moral equal of our Founding Fathers and the brave men and women of the French Resistance."[3] Later, he would proclaim himself "a freedom fighter" and later still proudly accept the Sandinista description of the rebels as "contras" (from the abbreviation of the Spanish word for "counterrevolutionaries") as a label that also applied to him. But Reagan's realism governed many of his decisions. Early in his presidency, it led him to spurn Al Haig's advice that he should "go to the source" and blockade Cuba to prevent arms from flowing to Nicaragua and to the Marxist rebels in El Salvador. Near the end of his term, it led him to resist the temptation to use U.S. troops to topple strongman Manuel Antonio Noriega, an option that appealed to Assistant Secretary of State Elliott Abrams and would eventually be exercised when George Bush became president. Reagan was more militant in words but less in deeds than Bush. He knew that use of U.S. troops in El Salvador or Panama would inevitably arouse regional hatred against what he repeatedly called "the colossus of the north." *

Reagan's realism checked and balanced his belief that it was imperative for the United States to commit its resources in the worldwide struggle to halt the spread of communism. On the stump he was a

---

* This was a recurrent image of Reagan's. According to Colin Powell, Reagan referred to "the colossus of the north" whenever use of U.S. troops to oust Noriega was discussed. This image also influenced Reagan's attitude to use of U.S. troops in Nicaragua. "Now, some of the people far to the right, they'd have marched in the troops," Reagan told me. "Well, here's what they weren't paying any attention to: [the] image in Latin America of the big colossus of the north sending in the Marines is still so much in their minds that even the friendliest of those nations that want our help in doing the things that we've been doing and helping them have democracies . . . will always add, 'Don't send in the Marines.' In other words, they don't want a return to that thing of the big colossus coming in and taking over."[4]

missionary who sought to spread the gospel of freedom. In the Situation Room he was often a cautious and uncertain leader who was tugged first one way and then another by the conflicting advocacies of competing factions who claimed to speak in the authentic voice of Reaganism. The president himself spoke in many voices and responded to contradictory imperatives. He liked the ring of FDR's famous phrase that the United States should serve as an "arsenal of democracy," while simultaneously accepting the post-Vietnam reality that the United States could no longer play policeman to the world. The realistic voice ultimately prevailed in Central America, but only by the smallest of margins. Weakened by the Iran-contra scandal and determined to leave the stage successfully, Reagan finally recognized in 1988 that the contras were a lost cause. He never said as much in a speech. But after conservatives had made a last-ditch appeal for U.S. military aid to continue the Nicaraguan war, Reagan told his chief of staff, Kenneth Duberstein: "Those sonsofbitches won't be happy until we have 25,000 troops in Managua, and I'm not going to do it."[5]

Reagan did not allow such realism to subvert the purpose of his public performances. More often than not, his standard speeches were set pieces that viewed with alarm, pointed with pride and waved the American flag. On foreign affairs, Reagan and his writers crammed these speeches with gaudy certitudes about democracy and moralistic warnings about the evils of communism that the president delivered with the same earnestness he had displayed as a young sports announcer warning Des Moines civic groups about the dangers of hard liquor, late hours and tobacco. Reagan was largely removed from the unending debate that raged within his administration on the distinctions between speeches and policy or even on whether there was a distinction between speeches and policy. He never confused a speech with a fact-finding expedition. Instead, Reagan recognized the salesman's truth that salesmen sell themselves before they sell their products, and he used his speeches to reaffirm his personal relationship with the American audience. This point was often lost on his bickering disciples who battled among themselves about the purposes and meaning of "the Reagan revolution."

Even though there was nothing selfish about him, Reagan knew that the cause was Ronald Reagan. He sought to restore national self-confidence by transferring his own self-confidence to his countrymen. This was not an easy task. It required Reagan not merely to make Americans feel good about themselves, a frequent and usually disparaging description of his rhetorical purpose, but also for him to focus their grievances on political alternatives. Reagan's confidence had not been ruined by the introspection of the post-Vietnam era or by the national humiliation inflicted on the United States when Americans were held hostage in the U.S. embassy in Tehran during the last painful year of Jimmy Carter's presidency. While Reagan never would be able to translate the yearning of frustrated Americans to "stand tall" into an endorsement of the covert war in Nicaragua or a ratification of the muddled U.S. involvement in Lebanon, his speeches did succeed in reviving national pride and soothing patriotic sensibilities.

Many Americans shared Reagan's innocent conviction that they were the good guys in a world no longer appreciative of goodness. Like British subjects of an earlier generation who mourned the loss of empire, Americans in the 1980s longed for the days when the American flag was an honored emblem and "Yanks" were the envy of the earth. Reagan's speeches stirred dreams of glory. "Some of us are old enough to remember back a few years before World War II when Americans could be anywhere in the world, in a banana republic revolution, in a war, whatever it might be, and all he would have to do is pin a little American flag on his lapel and he could walk through that war and no one would dare lay a finger on him because they knew that the United States would go to the rescue of any of its citizens wherever they might be," Reagan said in New Hampshire during the 1980 campaign. "How we've let that get away from us, I'll never know." [6]

No speechwriter composed this burst of patriotic gush. Reagan was an unabashed sentimentalist whose eyes had moistened at the sight of the American flag long before he learned the trick of an actor's tears. In his mind's eye he still saw the flag-draped streets of his Dixon boyhood, where a long-since demolished arch over Main Street celebrated the deeds of the Americans who had fought and died in Europe for what Reagan had been taught was the cause of lasting peace. Reagan believed in that cause. His speeches lifted the spirits of ordinary Americans, boosted military enlistment rates and roused the conservative faithful. But they also made his decision-making more difficult. Nostalgic reveries would not restore the days of Reagan's lost youth when America was safe between two oceans. Americans abroad who pinned flags in their lapels in the 1980s were apt to become targets of terrorists who were beyond the reach of the U.S. Marines. Reagan knew this, at least offstage. He was neither a war lover nor a demagogue. During crises he tended to be quiet and even-tempered. He understood the paradox of power in the nuclear age, where the logic of survival restrains the strongest nations from using their most militarily effective weapons. He recognized that the Vietnam legacy also limited the terms of U.S. participation in lesser wars, unless, as in the Grenada invasion of 1983, a quick and easy American victory was assured. Despite his longing for bygone days when American soldiers were the world's heroes, Reagan was reluctant to take major military risks. He meant it when he promised "no more Vietnams."

Nonetheless, Reagan's administration became involved in costly and controversial foreign adventures, most notably in Lebanon and Nicaragua. The former was the by-product of what Reagan and George Shultz intended as a constructive diplomatic intervention in the Middle East. The latter derived from Reagan's determination to stop the spread of communism in the hemisphere. But both the Lebanese entanglement and the U.S.-backed contra war were as much the result of Reagan's deficient grasp of governance as of any limitation of diplomacy or ideology. Reagan was not really interested in government. He was contemptuous of the bureaucracy on which he was sometimes overly dependent. He did not understand that a decision made at a meeting of the National Security Council or one of its subgroups required presidential follow-up to avoid being swallowed up, watered down or undone in an institutional, bureaucratic maze of interagency memos and meetings. Often, Reagan did not understand that what he considered a "detail"—such as the specifics of the U.S. Marine deployment in Lebanon—was actually the essence of a difference of opinion within his cabinet. As a result, he frequently believed that he and his advisers had reached agreement when they had really postponed or sidestepped a crucial decision. "It never ceased to amaze me how inconclusive meetings at the highest level were," said Richard Perle. "They were almost never decisive."[7]

This inconclusiveness was compounded by Reagan's distaste for choosing between contradictory options proposed by key cabinet members, especially when Shultz and Weinberger were in conflict. As Donald Regan observed, Reagan did not want to choose between "two good friends, two of his staunchest supporters, two of the more brilliant people in the cabinet, two of the people he relied on."[8] And as Regan also observed, Reagan often did not know which of these two trusted advisers was right in any given situation. But Reagan paid a heavy price for his indecision. By leaving the details to "the fellas," he encouraged Shultz and Weinberger to continue battling for their options through the bureaucratic process even after the president had supposedly reached a decision. Reagan was far more willing to override Shultz and Weinberger when his decisions would disappoint them equally, as he demonstrated when he proposed the Strategic Defense Initiative and later when he approved the sale of U.S. arms to Iran. Reagan was not afraid to go it alone against his cabinet. What he was unwilling to do was side openly with one highly valued cabinet member against another, especially Shultz and Weinberger, old foes who ruffled easily at real or imagined slights. Reagan was sensitive, too sensitive, to their feelings and too desirous of maintaining a façade of harmony. His unwillingness to give offense to either cost him dearly.

The president might have mitigated the perils of his amiable irresolution by using his national security adviser and the NSC staff to resolve the bureaucratic competition that arose from the conflict among his cabinet officers. But Reagan detested "bureaucracy" too much in the abstract to appreciate its importance in the particular. His infatuation with "cabinet government" blinded him to a modern president's need for a strong, loyal, knowledgeable national security adviser who can rise above the inevitable institutional prejudices of his cabinet. Some of his national security advisers had some of these virtues, but none before Frank Carlucci stepped into the job late in 1986 had all of them, and Reagan did not grant any of them the authority they needed to resolve the repeated conflicts between Shultz and Weinberger. Richard Allen, despite his past relationship with Reagan, never achieved the independent status or access to Reagan that he needed. Clark had that access but it cost him dearly, for he did not enjoy the trust of Haig, Shultz, the first lady or the White House staff. McFarlane, who came in as a compromise candidate after Reagan had heeded conservative hostility to James Baker and Shultz's opposition to Jeane Kirkpatrick, was despised by Weinberger and found working with White House Chief of Staff Donald Regan impossible. John Poindexter was originally welcomed by Shultz, Weinberger and Regan alike, in part because he seemed an unthreatening adjutant who would be reluctant to express his own opinions. Poindexter saw his role as "honest broker" but lacked the standing with Reagan to resolve irreconcilable disputes between Shultz and Weinberger. He soon became as frustrated as his predecessors.

Too often, Reagan's national security advisers wielded insufficient influence and excessive power. Their influence on broad policy decisions was limited because of Reagan's deference to his cabinet and to his concept of cabinet government. At the same time, their authority on day-to-day operational decisions was often enormous and unchecked because Reagan provided them with minimal guidance and even less supervision. Reagan did not really know what a national security adviser was supposed to do. What he most often asked his advisers to do was "work things out" by finding a middle ground when none existed between incompatible options advocated by his secretaries of state and defense. Even when a national security adviser was fortunate enough to find such a compromise, he usually lacked the authority to make it stick. In short, it was extraordinarily difficult to be a successful national security adviser to President Reagan. The job ground up Allen in less than a year, drove Clark and McFarlane to despair and out of government, and ruined Poindexter, who was fired and convicted of felonies for his attempts to exercise authority in a presidential vacuum.

All of these national security advisers contributed in different ways to their own demise, but Reagan was the principal source of their frustrations. His national security advisers were ministers without portfolio who worked punishing hours in a monarchical presidency where the king clung merrily to his opinions, believed in happy endings and allowed his policies to make their own way. Allen never knew whether his memos would make it beyond Meese's desk and reach the president. Clark was uncertain in his policy recommendations and enmeshed in political conflicts. McFarlane was enormously insecure about his personal standing with the president. Poindexter was in over his head. Reagan never recognized the personal vulnerabilities of his national security advisers nor realized how much his system put them under strain. At times he didn't even know their identities. "The president doesn't even remember my name," McFarlane once said despairingly after Reagan failed to recognize him at a key meeting on a particularly difficult day. McFarlane was not alone in his despair. A few days before he left the White House to become secretary of the interior, Clark told me that he felt so pressured by his job and White House conflicts that he sometimes was awakened by bad dreams or found it impossible to sleep.

And the policies that came out of this tense process also often resembled a nightmare, particularly in Central America and the Middle East. After the spotlight of the Iran-contra revelations exposed the deficiencies of the process, Reagan was finally forced to hire national security advisers (Carlucci and after him Colin Powell) who had the requisite combination of professional experience and personal access to make the system work. But much that was unrecoverable had been lost by then. On balance, Reagan was a strong man, but an extraordinarily weak manager. He restored public confidence in the presidency without mastering the difficult art of wielding presidential power.

Central America provided the first test of Reagan's managerial skills as president. At the time it was not a test that Reagan, preoccupied with his economic recovery program, particularly sought, even though he had a residual interest in the region. Jeane Kirkpatrick recalls that Reagan steered the discussion to Central America at their first meeting early in 1980 and again at dinner that night at George Will's.

California-based politicians often are more interested than their eastern counterparts in developments that occur south of the Mexican border, and Reagan was no exception. He had begun his 1980 campaign for president by proposing a "North American accord" that would link Canada and Mexico economically to the United States. Reagan's political strategists encouraged such vague talk about hemispheric cooperation, but they did not want him to speak out about Communist penetration in Central America. Their fear was that Reagan would remind voters of how he had revived his lagging 1976 campaign against President Ford with jingoist declarations about U.S. proprietary rights to the Panama Canal. The exploitation of this issue had been largely a matter of political calculation. On the ropes and deeply in debt after losing a series of early primaries to Ford, Reagan had sought an issue that would light a spark among conservatives. Richard Wirthlin's polls told him that this issue was the then-pending "giveaway" of the canal to Panama through two treaties that had been endorsed by five presidents, including Ford. The Panama Canal was also an obsession of ultraconservative Republican Senator Jesse Helms of North Carolina, a state where Reagan was waging a desperate bid to win his first primary. Reagan won the backing of the Helms organization, and the primary, by focusing on the Panama Canal. "We bought it, we paid for it, it's ours, and we're going to keep it," he said repeatedly, usually to flag-waving applause.[9]

But Reagan's interest in the Panama Canal declined after the issue had served its political purpose. This also was a poll-driven decision. Wirthlin's soundings showed that Reagan's position on the Panama Canal, while popular with the conservatives who participate in disproportionately high numbers in Republican primaries, had little appeal to moderate voters. Reagan could not walk away from the issue after having made so much of it, but he noticeably muted his rhetoric in 1977, when the treaties were finally signed by President Jimmy Carter. When William F. Buckley, who supported the treaties, suggested to Reagan that he debate the issue on his television program *Firing Line,* Reagan was reluctant to do so.[10] Eventually, Reagan agreed to the debate but used it to make a larger point that would become his rationale for U.S. intervention in various foreign conflicts, including Lebanon, during his administration. Contending that other nations would view the Panama Canal treaties as a continuation of "our bug-out in Vietnam" and the abandonment of Taiwan, Reagan said of them, "I think that the world would see it as, once again, Uncle Sam putting his tail between his legs and creeping away rather than face trouble."[11]

The Senate ratified the treaties by a single vote in 1978, and Panama quickly faded from the news. In 1979 the focus of Central American attention shifted to Nicaragua, where a Marxist-led coalition named for a Nicaraguan revolutionary hero, Augusto Sandino, overthrew the despised dictatorship of Anastasio Somoza. While the United States had done much to keep Somoza in power, the Carter administration denounced the "inhumane conduct" of the Nicaraguan dictator's regime, blocked loans to his bankrupt government and in June 1979 introduced the resolution in the Organization of American States calling for his "immediate and definitive replacement." When the Sandinista government took over, Carter provided it with $125 million in economic assistance. Conservatives grumbled that the Carter administration was helping Cuba and the Soviet Union to establish a beachhead on the American mainland, and Helms and his allies inserted a plank into the 1980 Republican platform promising to "support the efforts of the Nicaraguan people to establish a free and independent government." Nonetheless, the issue commanded little attention from Americans preoccupied with economic issues and the plight of the Americans held hostage in Iran. But on January 10, 1981, the day before Reagan sat down in his half-empty house in Pacific Palisades to discuss his inaugural address with speechwriter Ken Khachigian, Marxist guerrillas launched what they called their "final offensive" against the pro-American government in El Salvador. The Sandinistas supported the guerrillas. The bloody guerrilla uprising, while far from a final offensive, ended the efforts of Robert D. White, the U.S. ambassador to El Salvador, to work out a negotiated settlement between the government and the guerrillas. In his last week in office Carter suspended U.S. economic aid to Nicaragua and sent $10 million in arms and equipment as well as nineteen U.S. military advisers to El Salvador. On the day before Reagan's inauguration the U.S. Army attaché in San Salvador received word that the Pentagon was planning to send in U.S. military personnel to train Salvadoran forces.

Events in Central America thus engaged the new president before he was ready to engage events. While Reagan's administration would in time be amply stocked with firebrands willing to promote armed conflict in the region, the president's initial inclinations were cautious. At his first two National Security Council meetings Reagan listened almost without comment when Al Haig argued that the new administration should make El Salvador, an impoverished Massachusetts-size nation of 3.5 million people, a test case of its determination to resist Soviet and Cuban imperialism. "Mr. President, this is one you can win," Haig said.[12] But the White House staff saw Central America as a political loser, and the findings of Wirthlin's polls reinforced the gut inclinations of James Baker, Mike Deaver and Ed Meese that there was little to gain and much to lose if the Reagan administration risked commitment of any significant number of U.S. military advisers in El Salvador. Meese, who soon became a hero to conservatives, was as unenthusiastic as his more moderate colleagues about the value of Central American adventures. He shared Baker's view that giving emphasis to El Salvador could undercut bipartisan support for Reagan's economic program. When all members of the trio worked in tandem, as they did through most of 1981, their strategy usually prevailed. Reagan, who did not need much convincing, accepted the recommendation of Meese and Baker to delay for three weeks a State Department "white paper" purporting to document the chain of Soviet-Cuban-Nicaraguan support for the Salvadoran guerrillas. The paper was not issued until February 23, five days after Reagan unveiled his economic recovery plan on national television. Reagan did approve additional military supplies for the Salvadoran government, then headed by the centrist José Napoleón Duarte, and cautiously increased the number of U.S. military advisers to fifty-five. Even this small deployment touched off a furor in Congress and the media, ratifying the fears of the White House staff that Central America was an unneeded diversion.

During the first six months of his administration Reagan remained mindful of Richard Nixon's warning that foreign policy events would distract from his efforts to engineer an economic recovery. While he was ready and willing to assist the Duarte government and denounce the leftist guerrillas who sought to overthrow it, he at first downplayed the significance of the U.S. commitment to El Salvador. In his first newspaper interview as president—with *The Washington Post* on March 27—Reagan emphasized that the U.S. military advisers were "in garrison, simply training recruits." He called the Salvadoran rebels "terrorists" and said they were part of a "revolution being exported to the Americas, to Central America and further south, and we're going to be of help to this [Salvadoran] government."[13] Reagan castigated the Soviets and Cubans in this interview but made no mention of Nicaragua. He criticized the Sandinistas publicly only once during 1981, telling Walter Cronkite in a March 3 interview that the administration was "watching very carefully" to see if Nicaragua was sending arms to El Salvador. His formulation was cautious, if somewhat confusing. Reagan said that the administration was "informing Nicaragua of the part that they have played in this, using diplomacy to see that a country decides they're not going to allow themselves to be used anymore." But Haig and CIA Director William Casey had ideas about Nicaragua that went far beyond diplomacy.

Haig was the first to move. He wanted to draw an anticommunist line in the Central American dust, and El Salvador provided an ideal opportunity. In the spring of 1981, Haig told his counselor McFarlane, "You get a band of brothers from CIA, Defense and the White House and you put together a strategy for toppling Castro. And in the process we're going to eliminate this lodgement in Nicaragua from the mainland."[14] McFarlane assembled a team that included Nestor Sanchez, then Casey's deputy for Latin America; Francis (Bing) West, the assistant secretary of defense for international security affairs; and General Paul Gorman, an assistant to the Joint Chiefs of Staff, who later headed the U.S. Southern Command in Panama. This "band of brothers" quickly concluded that Haig's strategy was "not a sensible thing to try," either militarily or politically. When McFarlane told this to Haig, the secretary of state chewed him out at a staff meeting. "This is just trash, limp-wristed, traditional cookie-pushing bullshit," Haig said.[15] He ordered McFarlane to try again. The group ultimately produced an eight-point paper, foreshadowing the Kissinger Commission report issued four years later, advocating military aid and economic development assistance to friendly nations in Central America. Haig thought the proposal worthless and declined to forward it to the White House.[16]

As often happened, Reagan administration policy quickly retreated to the lowest common denominator of agreement—in this case continued assistance for the Duarte government in El Salvador. It was a limited policy, and it met with limited success. The Salvadoran rebels were beaten back militarily with heavy losses but remained a disruptive force to the nation's crippled economy. El Salvador's rightist military forces became restive. When leftists boycotted the March 28, 1982, Salvadoran elections, the rightists won a majority in the Constituent Assembly and the following month elected the notorious Roberto d'Aubuisson as their president. D'Aubuisson was an inspiration to El Salvador's infamous death squads, and U.S. officials claimed he was linked to the unsolved 1980 murder of Roman Catholic Bishop Oscar Arnulfo Romero. The death squads, never fully under control in the best of circumstances, became even busier.

Haig's scheme to squeeze Nicaragua and the Salvadoran rebels by blockading Cuba was a motion that died for lack of a second. "It was a plan that might best and most fairly be described as folly," said National Security Adviser Richard Allen, summarizing the prevailing view.[17] And it was also a plan that set a curious and recurring pattern for the Reagan administration in which military solutions that arose at the State Department were resisted by uniformed officers and the civilian leadership at the Pentagon. In this case, the Joint Chiefs of Staff contended that the immense resources required for an effective naval and aerial blockade of Cuba would weaken U.S. forces in the Persian Gulf and other regions where they were more vitally needed. The chiefs also believed that the blockade itself was of dubious military value. Their opinion was fully supported by Weinberger, who thought that blockading Cuba or gradually escalating the U.S. military presence in Central America were harebrained ideas. It is doubtful if Reagan would have risked a blockade in any event, considering how strongly he and the White House staff felt about giving priority to the economic recovery program. But with Weinberger and the chiefs opposed to the plan, the Haig proposal did not really get a serious hearing from the president. It was the first of many policy frustrations suffered by Haig, and he took the rejection hard. In an observation that foreshadowed subsequent complaints of Shultz and McFarlane about Pentagon reluctance to support diplomatic initiatives with military force, Haig told Laurence Barrett, "We build the highest defense capability in the history of this country. . . . We skew our whole budgetary problem because policy making is not being done properly and the right questions are not being asked. While we're doing this, we refuse, philosophically and compulsively, ever to apply these resources to back up American diplomacy."[18]

The military resistance to blockading Cuba and later to deploying

Marines in Lebanon and invading Panama was primarily the application of lessons learned in Vietnam. In the 1960s U.S. military professionals had lagged behind the politicians in understanding the extent of public hostility to this unpopular war. In the 1980s, when the politicians had mostly moved on to other matters, the living memory of Vietnam obsessed the officer corps and influenced almost every military recommendation. This is not surprising. Beyond its toll in casualties, the Vietnam War had cost the professional military the public standing and much of the high morale it had won in World War II and retained throughout the Korean conflict.

The Korean War was also unpopular—more unpopular among blue-collar voters even than the Vietnam War, according to some surveys—but it had ended in a stalemate. After Korea, it was relatively easy for professional military men to rationalize that the outcome would have been different if General Douglas MacArthur had foreseen China's entry into the war or if President Truman had not imposed restraints upon the U.S. military response. The Vietnam War had ended in ignominious defeat, and the military rationalization for its reasons was more complicated. While many soldiers were bitter about the way the war had been portrayed at home by politicians and the media, the Vietnam War also profoundly politicized the military establishment. Vietnam encouraged leaders of the services, especially U.S. Army officers, to resist combat commitments that lacked popular support. The services were further encouraged to take a political role by the budgetary consequences of Vietnam, which produced a relative decline in military spending and crucial shortages of equipment and spare parts. Not until President Carter's final year in office did defense spending as a proportion of the federal budget resume an upward spiral, and the Joint Chiefs remained sensitive about shortages and supply problems well into the Reagan era.

Weinberger, despite his fondness for quoting Winston Churchill, was even more cautious than the chiefs. A profile described Weinberger in the early Reagan years as "a soft-spoken and courtly Renaissance man who speaks only of hardline anticommunism; an Anglophile whose comments lock him in combat with the allies of Europe; an ambitious man with a zest for diplomatic mission but no taste for diplomatic nuance; an Episcopalian who has a Jewish surname, Arabist instincts and a special fondness for Saudi Arabia." [19] Within the administration, Weinberger was also a figure of unrivaled tenacity. Despite a childhood spinal injury that made him seem shorter than his actual five foot nine inches, he had enlisted in the Army during World War II, won a Bronze Star as an infantry officer in the South Pacific and served for four years on General MacArthur's staff. He often quipped that he had been six feet tall when he became secretary of defense but had been worn down by the pressures of the job.

In fact, it was Weinberger who most often wore his adversaries down.[20] Weinberger had been appalled at the backlash against the military after Vietnam and what he saw as shabby treatment accorded veterans of that conflict. He had reflected extensively on the appropriate uses of military power by a democracy and concluded that it was particularly dangerous for the United States to allow itself to be drawn gradually into conflict by political commitments. "You can't fight Congress and public opinion and an enemy at the same time," he said. "That's why Vietnam was the crime of the century."[21]

As Weinberger saw it, the "gradualist, incremental approach" employed by the United States in Vietnam "almost always means the use of insufficient force."[22] After Lebanon, Weinberger devised what he called "six major tests to be applied when we are weighing the use of U.S. combat forces abroad."[23] As Weinberger saw it, combat forces should be committed to action only on matters vital to the interests of the United States and its allies, only when there was "reasonable assurance" that the commitment would have public support and only as a "last resort." * Long before he put forth these formal criteria in 1984, Weinberger opposed committing U.S. combat troops in pursuit of diplomatic and political objectives in Central America and the Middle East. He viewed the Reagan military buildup as a means of preserving peace, not conducting war. In this, his thinking resembled the president's, but he was even more averse than Reagan to military risks. Weinberger opposed the blockade of Cuba, the commitment of U.S. forces to combat duty in Central America and the second, fatal deployment of U.S. Marines to Lebanon. He supported only those military actions that offered a reasonable prospect of immediate success in behalf of a strictly defined objective—the invasion of Grenada, the air strike in Libya and the deployment of naval power in the Persian Gulf. While his intransi-

---

* Weinberger outlined his "six major tests" in a speech to the National Press Club on November 28, 1984. His other conditions were that U.S. troops should be committed only with a clear intention of winning, only when there were clearly defined political and military objectives and only with the understanding that "the relationship between our objectives and the forces we have committed . . . must be continually reassessed and readjusted if necessary." Weinberger believed that the second deployment of U.S. Marines in Lebanon—examined in the next chapter—failed to meet these tests.

gence on military budget issues undermined his effectiveness in Congress, Weinberger was an influential voice within administration councils through most of his tenure at the Pentagon. More often than not, it was a voice that spoke on behalf of military restraint.

The reluctance of Reagan's warriors to wage war had an unintended consequence. Since nuclear war could neither be won nor fought and since conventional warfare required an improbable consensus, covert action was the only remaining military alternative for opposing the advance of Soviet-style regimes in the Third World. Reagan did not understand the full consequences of such conflict. He knew little about covert action and had a hard time understanding why his political advisers wanted him to keep silent about U.S. assistance to nationalist groups that he saw as the forces of freedom. These advisers recognized that Reagan naïvely failed to understand that the public was likely to react negatively to a presidential admission that the United States was arming a guerrilla force in Central America. They worried that Reagan would inadvertently (and honestly) acknowledge the U.S. role if a question were put to him about it. They had a basis for their concern, as we shall shortly see, and it was one of the reasons that the White House staff sought to limit Reagan's exposure to the media.

Reagan did not understand that covert action has a different set of dynamics than conventional war. One of these dynamics is obsessive secrecy. To finance the contra war in Nicaragua, the U.S. government turned to Saudi Arabia and other foreign countries, a practice that was subsequently outlawed by the second Boland Amendment passed by Congress on October 11, 1984. But legal or illegal, this fund-raising was conducted without the knowledge or approval of Congress and the American people. Whether such approval could ever have been obtained—or whether the Saudis would have contributed the money if anyone had known that they were doing it—is problematical. But because the Central American war was conducted under covert rules, the debate that Weinberger believed was necessary for development of a public consensus never really took place. This enabled opponents of any sort of U.S. intervention in Central America to implant the suspicion that contra aid would inevitably lead to direct U.S. involvement in a Vietnam-style war. Reagan was never able to overcome this suspicion because he could not reveal that the contra war was being partially funded by foreign countries. Since he was not in a position of being able to tell the full truth about the product he was attempting to sell to the American people, he became an ineffective salesman.

The secrecy surrounding the contra war also channeled some of the most important decisions about the conduct of that war into the dark corridors of the CIA and the National Security Council staff. Until the wholesale changes made by Frank Carlucci after the Iran-contra disclosures, key NSC staff positions were often occupied by self-important advocates of covert action who were contemptuous of congressional opposition and American public opinion. These NSC aides believed, along with Casey, that the resources of the West should be mobilized to fight Communists with their own methods. One of the most forceful of these polemicists was Constantine Menges, who served for two years as Casey's national intelligence officer for Latin American affairs until the old-boy CIA professionals tired of his lectures and Casey shipped him to the NSC. A few weeks before Clark left the NSC in October 1983 to become secretary of the interior, he installed Menges as a special assistant on the NSC staff with responsibility for Latin American affairs. Menges, dubbed "constant menace" by White House and State Department pragmatists, was a principled conservative who believed the United States should suppress right-wing death squads and promote land reform in Central America as vigorously as it fought the Salvadoran rebels and the Sandinistas. He believed that the United States should compete with the Soviets in sponsorship of "national liberation movements" in Third World nations. In a 1968 essay for the Rand Corporation, written at the height of the Vietnam War, Menges had proposed what he called "a bizarre alternative" based on the premise that "Communist regimes are very vulnerable to a democratic, national revolution that is conducted with skill and determination to succeed." [24] This "bizarre alternative" is what Menges and followers believed they could accomplish in Nicaragua.

Another key player in the covert Central American drama was Jeane Kirkpatrick, the U.S. ambassador to the United Nations. She was the only woman in the original Reagan cabinet, the only Democrat (she later switched her registration to Republican) and the only high-ranking administration official to side with Argentina during the Falklands War. Kirkpatrick was a laser-quick neoconservative who had attracted Reagan's favorable attention in the 1980 campaign with an article in *Commentary* called "Dictatorships and Double Standards" in which she argued that the Carter administration had acted against the nation's best interests in abandoning dictators such as the deposed Somoza and the Shah of Iran who were "positively friendly" to the United States. Haig and Shultz considered her a diplomatic menace and almost reflexively resisted her. Bill Clark admired her and frequently praised her to the president. Menges was a natural ally of Kirkpatrick, who also believed that the United States needed to promote democracy and economic development in Central America as well as oppose communism. But Kirkpatrick's most important ally was Casey, a kindred Cold War spirit who would unsuccessfully urge Reagan to make Kirkpatrick his national security adviser.

Casey, a canny multimillionaire corporate lawyer and financial wizard who had served with distinction, but not without controversy, in the Nixon and Ford administrations, was the mystery man of the Reagan presidency. He had survived a plagiarism suit and various congressional investigations into his tangled financial dealings. Neither his allies nor his adversaries had a settled view of Casey, perhaps because he displayed, as Bob Woodward put it, "a hundred different faces to a hundred different worlds."[25] The face he presented to Reagan was that of an affluent and rugged individualist who had learned the complex ways of Washington and Wall Street. Reagan idolized such self-made men and had since boyhood turned to them as role models. As a teenager in Dixon, Reagan had sought out Kansas City businessman Sid Altschuler and asked him for advice on how to make his way in radio. In Hollywood he had admired the Lew Wassermans and Taft Schreibers, entrepreneurs of the entertainment world with a talent for advancing themselves. Holmes Tuttle and most of the other "Friends of Ronald Reagan" who financed his first campaign for governor were also wealthy, self-made men. So was Donald Regan, the cabinet member with whom Reagan felt most comfortable. Casey enjoyed the added asset of Reagan's gratitude for rescuing the 1980 presidential campaign from fiscal insolvency. Reagan's feelings about Casey went a long way in overcoming the reservations about Casey's judgment shared by Nancy Reagan and most members of Reagan's political inner circle except Ed Meese. Casey was too much the Cold Warrior for Stu Spencer and Mike Deaver and too much the eastern establishment Republican for some of Reagan's wealthy California friends. Reagan was mindful of these opinions, which may have been why he never seriously considered giving Casey the coveted portfolio of secretary of state. But in making Casey his director of central intelligence, he had rewarded him with a most important consolation prize.

From Reagan's World War II perspective, Casey was perfectly suited to be DCI. While Reagan was making Air Force training films and sopping up the war stories that he would later relive vicariously, Casey had been serving with the Office of Strategic Services (OSS), the ancestral organization of the CIA. Late in the war Casey had supervised the dropping of spies behind enemy lines in Nazi-occupied Europe, and he had written a book, *The Secret War Against Hitler*, which would be published only posthumously. But Reagan had read this vivid book in manuscript and was impressed with it. He shared Casey's view that American spies are also American heroes. Modern intelligence professionals who obtain their information from the spy satellites and computers known as "national technical means" tend to look upon the OSS period as the bow-and-arrow days of espionage. Reagan made no such invidious distinction. He liked having a hero of the good war in charge of America's spies, and he quickly came to look upon Casey as an authority. "He was the CIA director," said Deaver. "Once someone was cast in any role, Reagan believed him."[26]

Reagan's intimates disagree among themselves about the extent of Casey's influence with the president. Some say that Casey was highly influential, directly with Reagan and indirectly through his ties with Meese, Kirkpatrick, Clark, Regan and Oliver North. Others believe that Casey's influence was exaggerated, partly by the CIA director himself to enhance his standing among professionals at the agency. Deaver, who kept the closest track of comings and goings at the White House, says Reagan and Casey met alone only five or six times from 1981 through 1985. And it is not clear how much passed between them on these occasions since Reagan, normally uncomplaining, sometimes acknowledged that he had difficulty understanding what Casey was saying to him. "He'd give you problems . . . because of his mumbling," Reagan said.[27] Even such a staunch ally as Bill Clark quipped that Casey was so difficult to understand that he was the only CIA director in history who didn't need a scrambler on his telephone.

But Casey's mumbling was not a joke to Reagan, who was so hard of hearing that he often found it necessary to resort to lip-reading even when his hearing aids were turned up. "The only one that I ever saw really speak up to him [Casey] and literally say, 'Straighten up and open your mouth when you speak,' was [U.S. Information Agency Director] Charlie Wick," Reagan said. "But they got along great together, and so he'd stop him and say, 'Damn it, Bill, now come on. Speak plainly to me.'"[28] To make matters worse, Casey could also be difficult to lipread, particularly in meetings. He usually looked down at his notes when making a presentation instead of establishing eye contact with Reagan and speaking distinctly, two requisites for effective communication with the president. During one important NSC meeting, Reagan slipped a plaintive note to Vice President Bush, asking him, "Did you understand anything of that?"

Casey kept a low profile during much of 1981 while the Senate Select Intelligence Committee scrutinized the complicated stock and bond transactions in which he had engaged while in private legal practice. Not until December 1 did the committee decide that "no evidence has been found for concluding that Mr. Casey is unfit to hold office as Director of Central Intelligence." On the same day that Casey received this backhanded endorsement, he obtained Reagan's signature on a presidential finding that authorized the first U.S. commitment of aid to the contras, $19 million that was intended to help Argentina train a 500-man anti-Sandinista military force in Honduras. This finding was the result of informal discussions begun in April between Casey and a Honduran officer named Gustavo Alvarez, who had come to Washington to explore the possibility of obtaining U.S. aid for covert military action against the Sandinistas.[29] Casey made no commitments but in August he dispatched Duane (Dewey) Clarridge, his chief of Latin American operations, on the first of two trips to Honduras to meet with Alvarez and outgoing military president General Policarpo Paz. Encouraged by Alvarez, scattered remnants of the Somoza national guard defeated by the Sandinistas in 1979 were already encamped in Honduras. Alvarez wanted to forge them into a rebel army that could disrupt the Nicaraguan economy and provoke the Sandinistas into a war with Honduras that he hoped would lead to U.S. intervention and overthrow of the Sandinista government.

In the interval between Alvarez's visit to Washington and the first of Clarridge's trips to Honduras, a former colonel in Somoza's national guard named Enrique Bermúdez had actually formed the nucleus of the contra army that Reagan would compare to the American revolutionaries. Aided by anti-Sandinista activists and American adventurers, Bermúdez had obtained Argentine aid to train what was then a sixty-member force largely composed of veterans of the discredited Somoza national guard. Assuring the Hondurans that he spoke for President Reagan, Clarridge said the goal of the U.S. government was free elections in Nicaragua. "We must change the government of Nicaragua to give the Nicaraguan people the chance to democratically elect its own government," he said.[30] Bermúdez summarized the plan by saying, "The Hondurans will provide the territory, the Americans the money and the Argentines the front."[31]

As Roy Gutman observed, Casey responded to the idea of underwriting the contras as if he were "a stock market investor with insider knowledge." [32] * But Casey needed the participation of other investors in the administration before he could go through with the deal. His first sale of contra stock was to Thomas O. Enders, the assistant secretary of state for Latin America and a celebrated foreign service officer who epitomized "the best and the brightest" who in the 1960s had stood for civil rights at home and the Vietnam War abroad. Enders, a Yale-educated scion of a wealthy Republican family from New England, was a formidable figure. At six foot eight he towered over Casey and Reagan. His intellect was equally imposing, and the Californians found him overbearing, furtive and manipulative. Like Casey, Enders had a foot in many camps and the trust of none. He had an unsavory reputation among liberals because of his role in the secret bombing of Cambodia. But when conservatives looked at Enders, they were apt, despite the physical dissimilarity, to see Henry Kissinger. And they were not entirely wrong. Enders possessed a passion for secret diplomacy and a conviction that the United States could impose its terms on smaller powers by combining the promise of economic aid with the threat of military intervention. Though he had no illusions that the contras were likely to become a significant military force, Enders saw them as a useful stick to use in negotiations in which he also dangled the carrots of U.S. nonintervention and economic aid. Together and separately, Enders and Casey gained from Haig a reluctant endorsement of the contra program. They then began peddling contra stock to the Pentagon and to George Bush, whose background as director of the CIA during the Ford administration gave him standing when any issue involving covert action was presented to Reagan. With Enders doing most of the talking, the case for supporting the contra force was made to Reagan at a meeting of the National Security Council on November 16, 1981. As Enders explained it, the contras were a small part of a large program aimed at promoting democracy in El Salvador and staving off further Communist intervention in the region. And they were an alternative to other, more militant options, such as the "empty box" of Cuban interdiction or direct U.S. intervention in Central America. The contras would pressure the Sandinistas to do the right thing. "It [the contra army] will harass the government, waste it," Enders said. [33]

* The most authoritative account of Nicaraguan policy in the Reagan years is Gutman's book *Banana Diplomacy: The Making of American Policy in Nicaragua 1981–1987*, published in 1988. Gutman was then the national security correspondent for *Newsday*. The account of Clarridge's discussion with the Hondurans is drawn from this book.

As was his habit, Reagan did not say much in response to Enders. He approved the plan in principle but at Haig's request withheld a final decision while the secretary of state pursued diplomatic discussions with Cuba. Typically, Haig wanted a bolder plan. But he was unsuccessful in wresting any diplomatic concessions from Cuban Vice President Carlos Rafael Rodríguez at a November 22 meeting in Mexico City, perhaps because the Cubans were aware that Haig was playing a weak hand within the administration. Haig gave a bleak report on the Mexico City meeting to Reagan, setting the stage for approval of the Casey option. On December 1—a cold, rainy Tuesday in Washington where the news was dominated by the reopening of U.S.-Soviet arms talks in Geneva and the signing of a U.S.-Israeli pact calling for "strategic cooperation"—Reagan signed the presidential finding approving covert aid for the Nicaraguan rebels.

Reagan, Bush, Casey, Haig, Weinberger, Meese, Baker and Deaver, all of whom lacked expertise in Central America, attended the National Security Planning Group (NSPG) meeting where this historic decision was made. Normally, a national security adviser would also have been at Reagan's side. On this day he had none, since Allen had taken leave to fight the allegations against him and Clark had not yet been named to replace him. (Allen, ironically, was cleared this same day of charges that he had acted improperly in accepting the gratuity for Nancy Reagan from a Japanese magazine.) Of those attending the meeting, only Casey expressed enthusiasm for the contras, but he made no claims that they could ever be developed into a military force capable of marching into Managua. As Casey viewed the situation, or at least as he explained it to the president, the contras were simply a mechanism for prodding the Sandinistas into more reasonable behavior and for discouraging the delivery of arms to the rebels in El Salvador. which is separated from Nicaragua by a narrow neck of Honduran territory. Others at the meeting were unimpressed with the contras but anxious to restrict more ambitious proposals. Weinberger in particular supported the Casey plan for negative reasons. He had spent most of the year fending off variations of Haig's proposal to "go to the source" in Cuba and viewed covert action by Nicaraguans as infinitely preferable to any plan involving the use of U.S. combat forces.

Baker and Deaver, while distrustful of Casey, were similarly inclined. They thought that military involvement in Central America was a sure-fire political loser. As a Texan, Baker realized that southwestern conservatives had acute concerns about the Sandinistas. He worried that military successes by the Salvadoran rebels would stir a demand among these conservatives for U.S. action against Nicaragua, and that the administration would become "sucked into" a war it did not want. Casey played to these fears by shrewdly presenting the covert aid program not as a U.S. commitment to a new war but as a means of discouraging the Sandinistas from continuing to help their Marxist allies in El Salvador. This argument appealed to Meese. Bush, who often agreed with Baker but rarely opposed any cabinet officer in a large meeting, silently went along.

Haig, the only person in the room with military command experience, had a low opinion of contra military potential and was justifiably skeptical that a Honduras-based guerrilla force would have much impact on the flow of Cuban and Nicaraguan arms to El Salvador. He accepted Casey's plan largely because everything else had been rejected, and he believed that doing something was better than doing nothing. For entirely opposite reasons, Haig's recommendation was the same as Weinberger's. While the secretary of defense was concerned that rejection of the Casey proposal would lead to more ambitious military schemes, Haig was worried that without contra aid there would be no military program at all. A more negative consensus is hard to conceive. The covert aid program that made it possible for the contras to become a fighting force was approved by Reagan because four and possibly five of the seven advisers in attendance (Haig, Weinberger, Baker, Deaver, and probably Bush) thought it less dangerous than an alternative course of action. It was an inauspicious beginning to a covert war that would during the next seven years cost thousands of lives and hundreds of millions of dollars, devastate the shaky Nicaraguan economy, bitterly divide Congress, damage the reputation of the CIA and undermine Reagan's capacity to govern.* None of that was foreseen on that rainy day in December.

What also was not foreseen at this NSPG meeting that launched the

---

* The casualty figures are in dispute. According to Nicaraguan government figures, 29,270 persons were killed (21,097 contras and 8,173 members of the Nicaraguan army and civilians) from 1981 through 1988. Doyle McManus of the *Los Angeles Times,* a respected authority on the war, accepts the Nicaraguan statistics as a valid count of their own casualties, though not necessarily of contra losses. The U.S. government has not provided any comprehensive casualty figures. But since peak estimates of contra strength never exceeded 20,000 and most of the war's battles were of small scale, the Sandinista estimate of contra casualties is almost certainly high. More is known about U.S. costs of the war. Congress approved $306 million in aid to the contras from 1981 through 1988, including $132 million in military aid. At least an additional $48 million was provided the contras from aid generated with U.S. help, including $32 million provided by Saudi Arabia. Pax Americas, an organization opposed to the war, estimated total U.S. costs, including aid supplied through Argentina and Honduras, at more than $433 million.

contra adventure was the difficulty of mustering U.S. public support for a war that could not be explained to the American people because of its covert nature. No one even sought to explain it. The prevailing view among pragmatists and conservatives alike during the early stages of the covert war was that the less said about the contras the better. And this view was compounded because Reagan and the White House staff were more preoccupied with the deepening recession than with any aspect of foreign policy. When Reagan mentioned Central America, it was to promote support for the overt U.S. policy of defeating the Marxist guerrillas in El Salvador rather than the covert policy of assisting the antigovernment guerrillas in Nicaragua. A myth would later arise in conservative circles that Reagan's failure to mobilize public support for the contras was largely the fault of a national media that paid scant attention to the president's speeches in behalf of the "freedom fighters." But there were in fact no such speeches for a year and a half after Reagan approved the first allocation of contra aid. The existence of the covert aid plan was first revealed in a February 14, 1982, story in *The Washington Post*. Another *Post* story on March 9 disclosed that Reagan had approved the plan. Bob Woodward has recounted in *Veil* how Casey went through the motions of trying to suppress the latter story and the reasons that executive editor Ben Bradlee decided to publish it.[34] White House officials at the time were furious with Casey, who they were convinced was the source of the story in *The Post*. Reagan, who often complained about leaks, was sanguine about this one, which led me to believe that he was less reluctant than his staff to tell the truth about what was going on in Central America. At a news conference on February 18, I asked Reagan whether he had "approved of covert activity to destabilize the government of Nicaragua." This was his reply:

> "Well, no, we're supporting them. Oh, wait a minute, wait a minute. I'm sorry. I was thinking El Salvador. . . . Here again, this is something upon which [because of] the national security interest, I will not comment."

Had Reagan simply misheard the question, as he sometimes did at news conferences? I wasn't sure, but I knew from my conversations with White House officials that they were eager to keep media attention away from Nicaragua and were afraid that Reagan might blurt out the truth about the covert aid program. When Reagan spoke to the Organization of American States six days later, he made the case against the Sandinistas, saying that "for almost two years Nicaragua has served as a platform for covert military action," but said nothing about the commitment of U.S. aid he had made to the contras. After his speech he was kept out of range of reporters. Such isolation of Reagan was a frequent tactic employed by Baker, Deaver and Larry Speakes, working in cooperation with the Secret Service, when they feared that a stray comment by the president might reveal or undermine administration strategy. Conversely, the staff made sure Reagan was always available at a "photo opportunity" on occasions when they wanted him to make a point. But the White House communication strategists simply did not want Reagan sounding off about the contras, and the president went along.

For the balance of 1982 and the early months of 1983 Reagan kept his silence on covert aid while the contra force grew from a ragtag band of 500 former members of the Somoza National Guard to a guerrilla army of 7,500. As the contra forces increased in number, the former guardsmen were joined, in the words of a congressional report, by "anti-Somocistas who had supported the revolution but felt betrayed by the Sandinista government and Nicaraguans who had avoided direct involvement in the revolution but opposed the Sandinistas' increasingly anti-democratic regime."[35] The contra forces conducted cross-border raids from the sanctuary of Honduran territory and began some operations on Nicaraguan territory. While these operations were militarily insignificant, they gave the Sandinistas an excuse for keeping Nicaragua on a war footing and suppressing internal dissent. This repression was well under way before the first contra shot was fired, but the raids enabled the government to portray itself as the beleaguered victim of Yankee imperialism.

While Reagan remained silent, the Sandinistas and U.S. congressional opponents of administration policy also mounted an effective public relations campaign in the United States. The contras were thus introduced to the American people by those who opposed their existence rather than by Reagan. While he would later give some twenty television and radio speeches trying to rally support for the Nicaraguan "freedom fighters," Reagan's only use of the term during this crucial period when public opinion was being formed was derisive. As Reagan explained it, the term "freedom fighters" was a euphemism applied by revolutionaries to their terrorist activities. "Very effective worldwide propaganda has tried to convince the world that Communist guerrillas and terrorists were freedom fighters representing and having the support of the people of El Salvador," Reagan said in an April 8, 1982, speech to eastern Caribbean leaders in Barbados denouncing leftist violence in the March 28 Salvadoran elections. This was his first public use of the phrase as president. More than a year later, in an April 27, 1983, nationally televised speech in which he offered a broad-scale defense of U.S. policy in Central America, he was still using the words in the same context. In this speech he said the Salvadoran leftists were "so-called freedom fighters in the hills . . . a small minority who want power for themselves and their backers, not democracy for the people." Small wonder that Richard Wirthlin's polls found repeatedly in later years that most Americans did not know who the "freedom fighters" were or whether the administration was for or against them. The Great Communicator deserves at least some of the responsibility for this confusion by using approvingly for U.S.-backed guerrillas a term he had long used in derogation of guerrillas who opposed U.S.-supported governments.

And Reagan himself was confused in his first reference to "the freedom fighters of Nicaragua," which came in response to a reporter's question on May 4, 1983, the day after the Democratic majority of the House Select Committee on Intelligence had voted to cut off U.S. assistance to the contras. Reagan said this action would set "a very dangerous precedent" because "it literally was taking away the ability of the executive branch to carry out its constitutional responsibilities." [36] But he did not stop there. Unfortunately for Reagan, the issue had arisen during an experimental question-and-answer session with eight selected reporters in the Oval Office. Newspaper reporters had long complained that their only exposure to Reagan other than "photo opportunities" was at infrequent prime-time press conferences where the format favored television and wire service correspondents. The Oval Office session was designed to mollify the print reporters by giving them access to Reagan in a format where television cameras were prohibited. But the White House unwisely had scheduled the question-and-answer session early in the afternoon, a time of day when Reagan was usually most apt to be in need of a nap. On this particular day Reagan was tired to the point of incoherence. He rambled, groped for words, referred to the Salvadoran leftists as "the freedom fighters in El Salvador," then tried to rescue himself by saying, "only I don't call them freedom fighters because they've got freedom and they're fighting for something else. They're fighting for a restraint on freedom." [37]

Reagan's performance dismayed his stage managers, though it did not attract much attention outside of Washington because of the restrictions on television coverage.* And even a good performance may not have helped the contras. By this time, public opinion had solidly congealed in opposition to the administration's Central American policy—a self-fulfilling prophecy of the White House staff that Americans would not support Central American intervention in any form. Reagan did not give a nationally televised speech explaining the case for the contras until May 9, 1984.

The absence of an effective White House communications campaign on behalf of U.S. policy on Nicaragua reflected divisions within the administration about the purpose of this policy and the strategy and tactics necessary to pursue it. Congress contributed to the problems by on-again, off-again support for contra aid and by a post-Vietnam inclination to micro-manage foreign policy. But the essential incoherence was the product of the administration's irresolution. In the five-year interval between Reagan's approval of the first $19 million in covert aid and the discovery that proceeds from the Iran arms sale had been illegally diverted to the contras, hostile factions within the administration competed to carry out contradictory policies in Central America without either direction or interference from the president. The pragmatists, which usually included Secretary of State Shultz, held the limited objective of preventing the Sandinistas from exporting their revolution to other countries in the region. The conservatives, led by Casey, Clark, Kirkpatrick and Menges, wanted the Sandinista government replaced. But even those who were determined to remove what they regarded as a Soviet-Cuban base on the Central American mainland held profound differences about how this should be accomplished. Kirkpatrick and Menges doubted that a Marxist regime would ever share power or allow itself to be voted out of office. Others, including Enders and McFarlane, thought that a combination of political, economic and military pressure might eventually induce the Sandinistas to take the un-Marxist risk of free elections.

Reagan was clear about what he *wasn't* willing to do in Central

---

* Reporters were allowed to listen to the interview in the White House briefing room over an internal communications system. Some reporters laughed at some of Reagan's responses, and I described the president's performance the next day in *The Washington Post* as "rambling and sometimes confusing." Mike Deaver and other White House officials blamed spokesman Larry Speakes for what had happened, since he had favored the new format. Speakes retaliated against the press corps, which he said had been disrespectful of Reagan, by refusing to allow subsequent interviews to be piped into the briefing room. But the format was quickly abandoned anyway, because no one on the staff wanted to take the risk of allowing Reagan to give unscripted answers in an election year.

America. At the February 18, 1982, news conference he had responded to a question about the conditions under which he would consider sending U.S. troops to El Salvador by quipping, "Well, maybe if they dropped a bomb on the White House, I might get mad." And from beginning to end, he took the same view about using U.S. troops in Nicaragua. But Reagan's critics always suspected (or said they suspected) that he was seeking a pretext that would allow him to invade Nicaragua, and his rhetoric fueled these suspicions. His comparison of the contras to the Founding Fathers and to the French Resistance suggests that he viewed the Sandinistas as a colonial or occupying power. These dubious analogies also led logically to the conclusion that Reagan favored following the historical U.S. pattern of sending the Marines into Nicaragua, perhaps comparing them to the French and Poles who had provided military aid to the American colonists in the Revolutionary War or the Allied armies that had liberated France in World War II. "I don't think he [Reagan], in his mind, really had thought his way through to what would be a range of acceptable outcomes," said Rodney McDaniel, executive secretary of the National Security Council staff under John Poindexter.[38]

This lack of clarity encouraged contending policymakers to convince themselves that they were only doing what Reagan really wanted done. McDaniel ultimately decided that Reagan favored a negotiated settlement. He based this conclusion on Reagan's favorable reaction in 1986 to a six-page "scholarly paper" produced by Peter Rodman of the NSC staff that defined the U.S. objective in Nicaragua as a "negotiated settlement." Almost every position paper that went to the president required his signature or initials or a check mark in a box to indicate that he agreed or disagreed with the conclusions or recommendations. Reagan signed this particular paper. While Reagan was sometimes suspected of signing material he had not actually read, McDaniel was convinced that the president had perused this particular document because he had corrected a misspelling and punctuation errors.[39]

Aides often relied on such circumstantial evidence in attempting to ascertain Reagan's motivations. The president rarely discussed his rationale for decisions if he could not summarize his reasoning with an anecdote. Whether this was because Reagan was uneasy with analysis or merely reluctant to give the appearance of siding with one cabinet member against another is hard to know. Despite Reagan's even-tempered affability, the president's men were often baffled about his motives or the true extent of his knowledge. In their own behavior the aides much resembled pre-glasnost Kremlinologists who found important clues in small deviations from routine. Reaganology was largely based on whatever gleanings could be obtained from body language. An almost imperceptible bobbing of Reagan's head was supposed to mean that he was pleased with a point, while a slight tightening of the mouth was considered a sign of disapproval. But on many occasions Reagan did not betray his thoughts by any physical movement, leaving aides to ponder whether or not he had any opinion—or any thought—at all.

Reagan was not always inscrutable. While he rarely expressed himself beyond a quip in large meetings, he sometimes summarized what had been said to him in an NSPG session. He could express himself in a discussion of human situations, such as the plight of the American hostages held in Lebanon. He could also become abruptly attentive if he perceived that the information being conveyed to him was useful for a public performance. But Reagan was often so obviously wearied by extensive analysis, particularly of foreign policy, that aides plunged into arcane material at their peril. If Reagan became sufficiently bored, he simply nodded off, a response that cost any aide luckless enough to induce this reaction the good opinion of his colleagues.

More often, aides dealt with Reagan on what they fancied to be his level, dramatizing or dressing up their presentations with stories intended to be compelling. This practice had its own risks. Sometimes it induced Reagan to reply with an anecdote that steered discussion into generalities and away from the decision the meeting was supposed to produce. Menges accurately observes that it was not in Reagan's "nature to assert himself in pursuit of his own policy."[40] But the roots of the problem ran deeper. Because Reagan's aides were reluctant to press him into making specific decisions, they reinforced his tendency to leave what he called the "details" of policy—really the essence of what was being discussed—to his contending subordinates. As a result, meetings with the president often ended without resolving the vital points of difference. Frequently, the participants in a meeting with the president could not even agree on what had been decided, much less on how the decision should be carried out.

Reagan's decision-making on foreign affairs often consisted of little more than checking a box on a multiple-choice list of options, much as he had done on Stockman's vaunted "SAT test" of budgetary choices. Which box Reagan checked often depended on how the issue was presented to him and on who presented it. As a result, the CIA and later the NSC staff waged guerrilla warfare in Nicaragua, while the State

Department encouraged regional peace efforts to end the conflict. The White House legislative staff sought to build a congressional consensus for contra aid, while Casey, McFarlane and Poindexter concealed information from Congress about the extent and nature of the contra war. Some officials encouraged opposition participation in the Nicaraguan elections, while others dismissed them in advance as fraudulent. Even the most accomplished Reaganologist was hard pressed to explain which of these conflicting actions most truly reflected Reagan's "own policy" and which reflected the contending advocacies of his squabbling subordinates.

Reagan kept himself, as Kirkpatrick observed, removed from the policy battles that raged among his principal advisers.[41] In a sense he was on all sides of the issue, for he supported the contras but also thought it made sense to negotiate with Nicaragua. "The president always felt there should be a negotiating track, but he never linked it to whatever else was going on," said McDaniel.[42] Perhaps Reagan might have made this linkage if he had ever decided to meet with Nicaraguan President Daniel Ortega, as he did with Mikhail Gorbachev, but Reagan ruled out direct U.S.-Nicaraguan negotiations early in his presidency and never relented in this view. Reagan simply had no use for the Sandinistas. Aides told me that his attitudes on Nicaragua were largely based on accounts he had read in the Washington weekly *Human Events*. Mike Deaver had succeeded in keeping this hard-core conservative tabloid out of Reagan's hands during much of the 1980 campaign, but *Human Events* was delivered directly to the White House residence every weekend, eluding the screen on Reagan's reading material constructed by the White House staff. Reagan read it, frequently marking or clipping articles and giving them to his aides. Months before Casey proposed covert U.S. aid for the contras, *Human Events* was grimly depicting Nicaragua's drift to communism and its export of revolution to other nations in the region.

On August 29, 1981, *Human Events* reprinted a speech of José Francisco Cardenal, a businessman who had fled Nicaragua in 1980 "when I realized that the Sandinista policy was to eliminate private enterprise from Nicaragua and to establish a Cuban-style, Marxist-Leninist dictatorship in my country." On March 20, 1982, *Human Events* devoted its front page to an unsigned editorial headlined "The Sandinista Government *Should* Be Overthrown." The editorial said that while "Nicaragua is not yet Cuba . . . if we fail to oust the present rulers fairly quickly, it is bound to become another strong, Soviet-controlled base, complete with a Russian combat brigade." Reagan took such warnings seriously. The White House pragmatists believed he often paid more attention to articles in *Human Events,* particularly at the outset of his administration, than to the information he received in his national security briefings.

Reagan parted company with the editors of *Human Events* in their call for the United States to act "alone, if necessary" to overthrow the Sandinistas. Baker, Deaver and Kirkpatrick, all familiar with Reagan's attitudes in this period, agree that he never even entertained the idea of using U.S. troops to deal with the Sandinistas. Eventually, as his remark to Duberstein quoted earlier in this chapter suggests, Reagan became angry at what he saw as pressure from conservatives outside the administration to use U.S. military force in the region. But *Human Events* did help shape Reagan's understanding of events in Nicaragua, much as the right-wing tracts he read while giving speeches on the banquet circuit provided him with a stark and oversimplified view of world affairs. Reagan did not revel in complexities. He made sense of foreign policy through his long-developed habit of devising dramatic, all-purpose stories with moralistic messages, forceful plots and well-developed heroes and villains. When these stories were memorized and incorporated into Reagan's repertoire, they acquired the power of personal experience and became a barrier to a deeper understanding of the events they were designed to explain. This is where Reagan's skill at rote memorization and his weakness at analysis betrayed him. The more Reagan repeated a story, the more he believed it and the more he resisted information that undermined its premises.

In the second term, as Colin Powell observed, Reagan's habit of sticking to stories that no longer had a factual basis made it difficult for the president to understand the changes that were taking place in the Philippines. Ferdinand Marcos had been a hero to Reagan since World War II, and he found it nearly impossible to adjust to the idea that Marcos had become a corrupt and discredited despot. Reagan did not bring similar baggage to his understanding of events in Nicaragua, but his desire (or need) to reduce complicated events to a simple tale of a revolution betrayed led him to exclude inconvenient history from his story of the Sandinistas. What Reagan discarded in his storytelling was his own awareness that Nicaraguans, and not just the ruling Sandinista regime, had a well-grounded historical basis for their fears of U.S. intervention. The United States has intervened eleven times in Nicaragua since 1853, often at the behest of governments that were trying to subdue revolutionary unrest. U.S. Marines were stationed almost continuously on Nicaraguan soil from 1912 to 1933. This history was well known to Reagan (indeed, it was the basis of the mantra that the United States was viewed in the region as "the colossus of the north"), but it interfered with his message and therefore had no place in it.

As Reagan saw it, the Sandinistas had exploited accumulated grievances against Somoza and attained power with U.S. support. Only when the Sandinistas were firmly in control of the army and the police did they reveal themselves as the puppet villains of the Soviet Union and Cuba. The heroes of Reagan's story were the contras, cast not as a counterrevolutionary army led by officers of the ousted discredited regime but as valiant peasants who were fighting for freedom. According to Peggy Noonan, the famous comparison of the contras to the ragged armies of Continentals who had worn down and eventually defeated a militarily superior British force originated with Reagan, not with the speechwriters.* In Reagan's mind, the description of the contras as "the moral equal of our Founding Fathers" was not an analogy designed to manipulate public opinion but an actual explanation of events. Five days after his confusing question-and-answer session with reporters in the Oval Office, Reagan delivered a polished version of what would become his standard Sandinista story in a prime-time nationally televised speech from the Oval Office on May 9, 1984:

> The Organization of American States, on June 23, 1979, passed a resolution stating that the solution for peace in Nicaragua required that Somoza step down and that free elections be held as soon as possible to establish a truly democratic government that would guarantee peace, freedom, and justice. The Sandinistas then promised the OAS in writing that they would do these things. Well, Somoza left, and the Sandinistas came to power. This was a negotiated settlement, based on power-sharing between Communists and genuine democrats, like the one that some have proposed for El Salvador today. Because of these promises, the previous U.S. administration and other Western governments tried in a hopeful way to encourage Sandinista success.

---

* Noonan told me that the phrase "moral equivalent" was hers, but that the instruction to compare the contras to the Founding Fathers and to the French Resistance originated with Reagan and was relayed to the speechwriting department in a note from White House communications director Patrick J. Buchanan.

It took some time to realize what was actually taking place, that almost from the moment the Sandinistas and their cadre of fifty Cuban covert advisers took power in Managua in July of 1979, the internal repression of democratic groups, trade unions, and civic groups began. Right to dissent was denied. Freedom of the press and freedom of assembly became virtually nonexistent. There was an outright refusal to hold genuine elections, coupled with the continual promise to do so. Their latest promise is for elections by November 1984. In the meantime, there has been an attempt to wipe out an entire culture, the Miskito Indians, thousands of whom have been slaughtered or herded into detention camps, where they have been starved and abused. Their villages, churches and crops have been burned.

The Sandinistas engaged in anti-Semitic acts against the Jewish community, and they persecuted the Catholic Church and publicly humiliated individual priests. When Pope John Paul II visited Nicaragua last year, the Sandinistas organized public demonstrations, hurling insults at him and his message of peace. On this last Good Friday, some 100,000 Catholic faithfuls staged a demonstration of defiance. You may be hearing about that demonstration for the first time right now. It wasn't widely reported. Nicaraguan bishop Pablo Antonio Vega recently said, "We are living with a totalitarian ideology that no one wants in this country"—this country being Nicaragua.

The Sandinista rule is a Communist reign of terror. Many of those who fought alongside the Sandinistas saw their revolution betrayed. They were denied power in the new government. Some were imprisoned, others exiled. Thousands who fought with the Sandinistas have taken up arms against them and are now called the contras. They are freedom fighters.

Later in this speech Reagan linked support of the contras to his belief that the United States had an obligation to aid freedom's friends and resist freedom's enemies. While he had several months earlier forsworn further descriptions of the Soviet Union as "the focus of evil," Reagan had no doubt about the identity of the principal adversary or about the legitimacy of U.S. efforts to fight the Soviets on their own battlegrounds. "If the Soviet Union can aid and abet subversion in our hemisphere, then the United States has a legal right and a moral duty to help resist it," Reagan said. "This is not only in our strategic interest; it is morally right. It would be profoundly immoral to let peace-loving friends depending on our help be overwhelmed by brute force if we have any capacity to prevent it." [43] Reagan viewed U.S. aid to the contras as a continuation of the policy of resistance to Soviet expansionism that the United States had followed since 1947, when President Truman provided military aid to a conservative Greek government then at war with Communist guerrillas who were armed by Yugoslavia, Bulgaria and Albania at the instructions of Moscow. Significantly, Reagan's speech quoted from Truman's address to a joint session of Congress on March 12, 1947: "The free peoples of the world look to us for support in maintaining their freedoms. If we falter . . . we may endanger the peace of the world, and we shall surely endanger the welfare of the nation."

Reagan speechwriter Bently Elliott, who worked on the May 9 speech, said that the use of the Truman quotation was "very deliberate." [44] Although Reagan did not mention it, he was quoting from the speech that signaled the birth of what would be called the Truman Doctrine—the animating U.S. policy of the Cold War. "The collectively written speech [Truman] delivered was certainly the most controversial of his presidency and remains probably the most enduringly controversial speech that has been made by a president in the twentieth century," wrote Truman historian Robert Donovan three years before the Reagan presidency. [45] At the time Truman spoke, the United States was already engaged in trying to halt possible Soviet domination of Europe by Communist parties with ties to the Kremlin. The Truman Doctrine broadened this policy. While it narrowly referred only to the policy of supplying arms to the Greeks and to a Turkish government that was also under heavy pressure from the Soviets, the Truman Doctrine became the recognized standard for U.S. efforts to contain Soviet expansionism. Truman put the case with characteristic straightforwardness: "I believe that it must be the policy of the United States to support free peoples who are resisting attempted subjugation by armed minorities or by outside pressures." [46]

Truman's speech was nationally broadcast on radio. It stirred an immense public and congressional debate and discomforted Republican isolationists, who hated foreign aid almost as much as they detested communism. Secretary of State Dean Acheson felt impelled to assure the Senate Foreign Relations Committee that the aid request would not necessarily set the pattern for future foreign aid requests. [47] Six weeks after Truman's speech, Congress passed the Greek-Turkish aid bill. Despite Acheson's assurances, the Truman Doctrine did in fact set the pattern for the policy that American presidents would pursue until the dismantling of communism in Eastern Europe in the first and second years of the Bush administration. In the thirty-seven-year interval between Truman's speech and the nationally televised address that Reagan made on behalf of the contras, the U.S. commitment to support "free peoples" in their anticommunist struggles had led to direct U.S. military involvement in Korea and Vietnam and to massive U.S. military aid programs to nations free and unfree around the globe.

Reagan's speech was organically related to the Truman Doctrine in its rationale and rhetoric; in most respects the anticommunist policies Reagan espoused were direct descendants of the policies that had been proposed by Truman and accepted by an opposition Congress. But Reagan's call to aid the contras made a vital leap beyond the Truman Doctrine. When the United States had intervened in the hemisphere during the Cold War years against leftist governments in Guatemala and Chile, it had acted covertly, on presidential directives on which Congress had no say. When Reagan requested military aid for El Salvador, he was seeking what Truman sought in 1947: help for an embattled government that was seeking to repel an overthrow by Marxist guerrillas. Reagan won this battle, despite congressional qualms about the Salvadoran death squads. Even in the post-Vietnam era, Congress has found it hard to say no to a president who seeks military aid to prevent a government from being toppled by Communists. But assistance for the Nicaraguan "freedom fighters" pushed the Truman Doctrine to its breaking point. What Reagan did in his May 9 speech was ask Congress to support not a government that was resisting insurrection but armed insurrectionists who sought to overthrow a legitimate government in the name of democracy and anticommunism. The Sandinistas, despite their Marxism and their repression of democratic institutions, were by any definition a legitimate government, internationally recognized, even by the United States. While Reagan's own personal aim may not have been the overthrow of the Managua government by force and violence, this was the declared war aim of the contras. It is testimony to how far the United States was willing to go in the name of anticommunism that Reagan almost won, prevailing on several congressional votes on contra aid and losing others by only a handful of votes. Had Reagan acted earlier and more openly in behalf of the radical idea that it is legitimate to wage guerrilla war against a duly constituted government if that government is Marxist-Leninist, he almost certainly would have won. But the war had been raging covertly for more than

two years when Reagan made his appeal for open support of the guerrillas. And he was seeking to restore a "free people" to power in a
nation which had never known democracy and where the United States
was historically associated with the despotic oligarchy that the Sandinistas had ousted.

Reagan did not call what he was doing the Reagan Doctrine. That
phrase was coined by columnist Charles Krauthammer in a thoughtful
essay in the April 1, 1985, issue of *Time* magazine. Krauthammer took
as his text a passage in the president's February 6, 1985, State of the
Union address in which Reagan declared, "We must not break faith
with those who are risking their lives on every continent from Afghanistan to Nicaragua to defy Soviet-supported aggression and secure rights
that have been ours since birth. . . . Support for freedom fighters is self-
defense." Krauthammer was struck by this passage. In 1983 he had
written a column for the *New Republic* urging the administration to
abandon the pretense that its Nicaraguan policy was based merely on
the desire to halt the flow of arms to the Salvadoran rebels and openly
proclaim an intention to support the contras in the overthrow of the
Sandinista government.[48] "That's why, two years later, I seized on the
State of the Union Speech as the foundation for the 'Reagan Doctrine,' " Krauthammer said. "I hoped that a 'doctrine' enshrining the
legitimacy of overthrowing nasty communist governments would ob-
viate the need for rhetorical ruses . . . and keep the debate—and the
Reagan administration—honest." [49] In his *Time* essay Krauthammer described the Reagan Doctrine as a policy of "democratic militance" that
"proclaims overt and unashamed American support for anti-Commu-
nist revolution" on grounds of "justice, necessity and democratic tradition." [50]

But the administration's "support for freedom fighters" was less consistent than Krauthammer's rationale. While the idea of aiding anti-
Communist insurgencies appealed to Reagan in the abstract, neither he
nor the administration's conservative theorists ever succeeded in for-
mulating a doctrine of assisting them that was broadly applicable.
A case can be made, in fact, that Reagan really did not believe in
the Reagan Doctrine, except in Nicaragua and perhaps in Angola. In
dealing with most other insurgencies, Reagan followed State Department guidance and basically continued policies that were already
in place.

In Mozambique, on the east coast of Africa, the administration provided financial aid to a Marxist dictatorship hard pressed by the mur-

derous resistance of the rightist RENAMO guerrillas. Across Africa on
the west coast, the administration opposed a government of similar
ideology in Angola and supported the anti-Marxist UNITA rebels. But
what was going on in Angola was more than a civil war. The government there was able to stay in power against the UNITA forces of Jonas
Savimbi only with the support of thousands of Cuban troops. Reagan
was barred from aiding Savimbi by a congressional restriction known
as the Clark Amendment that was in place when he took office. Savimbi
turned to South Africa for the military assistance he could not obtain
from the United States. Congress repealed the amendment in August
1985, and the Reagan administration six months later began a program
of $15 million annually in covert aid to Savimbi.

What made a difference in Angola was not this relatively minor
amount of covert aid but the constructive diplomacy practiced by Assistant Secretary of State Chester A. Crocker. After eight years of slowly
escalating warfare, the failure of two Angola offensives designed to
crush the Savimbi forces and a substantial financial drain on the coffers
of South Africa, Angola, Cuba and the Soviet Union, Crocker finally
brokered a political settlement during Reagan's final year in office that
provided for gradual withdrawal of Cuban troops from Angola and the
independence of South African-dominated Namibia.

In Cambodia, the Reagan administration's policy was guided by the
priority, which it shared with Communist China and other nations that
made no pretense of being democracies, of ending the Vietnamese
occupation of that troubled country even at the risk of a restoration to
power of the genocidal and Communist Khmer Rouge. Vietnam finally
did withdraw from Cambodia in the first year of the Bush administration, but the Khmer Rouge risk remains. The Bush administration finally abandoned the policy it had inherited and turned, with the Soviets
and the Chinese, to the hope of a United Nations–brokered solution.
In Cambodia, as in Angola and Mozambique, the dynamics of Reagan
administration policies were guided by multiple imperatives of power
politics in which pure anticommunism was a submerged component.
Taken together or separately, the policies the administration pursued in
these conflicts fell far short of a definable "Reagan Doctrine" that put
democracy as a first priority.

Except for the contras, the only "freedom fighters" in which Reagan
showed much interest were the Afghan *mujahadeen*. And even though
he frequently issued bristling denunciations of Soviet behavior in Afghanistan, Reagan was relatively slow to provide the *mujahadeen* with

the military assistance they sought. Throughout Reagan's first term the *mujahadeen* tried unsuccessfully to obtain U.S. Stinger antiaircraft missiles that could be used against the Soviet helicopter gunships that were then the most devastating weapon of the Afghan war. In his public performances Reagan expressed revulsion at the brutal destruction of Afghan villages and such Soviet practices as the scattering of mines disguised as toys that killed and maimed Afghan children. But Reagan nonetheless initially heeded Pentagon concerns that the Stingers would be captured and copied by the Soviets.

Undersecretary of Defense Fred Iklé, a conservative who strongly backed the *mujahadeen* and the contras, thought that the Pentagon concerns were unjustified. The Army, he said, wanted to hold on to the Stingers "to fight World War III."[51] The CIA bureaucracy also was cautious about supplying advanced weapons to the Afghan rebels. It took pressure from Iklé and Casey on their bureaucracies and bipartisan pressure from Congress, led by Texas Democrat Charles Wilson in the House and New Hampshire Republican Gordon Humphrey in the Senate, to convince Reagan to supply the *mujahadeen* with the Stingers that became so crucial to their cause. And it took the realism of Mikhail Gorbachev, who called Afghanistan a "bleeding wound,"[52] to face the unpopularity of the costly war at home and finally withdraw Soviet troops.

Unlike the contra war, the U.S. commitment to the Afghan rebels was popular with the American people. Americans were not worried that U.S. combat troops would be sent to faraway Afghanistan, and the rebels were romantically portrayed in the U.S. media as valiant underdogs who were securing surprising military victories against the Red Army. The Carter administration had provided $30 million in aid to the rebels, a trickle that would eventually become a torrent of $600 million during the Reagan years. In 1986 Stingers were finally sent to the *mujahadeen,* who used them to good effect against the Soviet helicopter gunships. But the administration's assistance to the *mujahadeen* did not require Reagan Doctrine justification or even Truman Doctrine rationale. Afghanistan was a sovereign nation that had been invaded in the most flagrant act of Soviet expansionism since the early Cold War years. The invasion was opposed and denounced by every Muslim nation and by every democracy in the world save India. Communist China, which saw the Afghan war's destabilization of Pakistan as a threat to its own interests, provided significant military aid to the *mujahadeen.* So did Pakistan and Saudi Arabia, nations hardly motivated by "democratic militance." In imposing a U.S. grain embargo on the Soviets and canceling U.S. participation in the 1980 Olympic Games in Moscow, President Carter had gone farther in reacting to the invasion of Afghanistan than Reagan was willing to go. The frustration of the Soviet occupation in Afghanistan and the subsequent withdrawal of Soviet troops by Gorbachev was one of the seminal events in the Cold War. But it was a product of events and circumstances, not the creation of a new U.S. foreign policy doctrine.

While Krauthammer's term caught on with the media, the meaning of the so-called "Reagan Doctrine" remained a mystery within the Reagan administration. "That was something you people [in the media] talked about; it wasn't a phrase we used inside," said McDaniel, who nonetheless believes that Reagan himself rather liked the term.[53] In any event, it was a phrase, not a policy. Robert McFarlane observed that none of the more than two hundred National Security Decision Directives signed by the president referred to a "Reagan Doctrine." Nor, said McFarlane, did the administration ever develop a comprehensive plan for aiding anticommunist insurgencies or devise a set of standards to determine which insurgencies were deserving of U.S. aid and which were not. "Doctrines are things which come from thoughtful analysis of problems, threats, possible ways of dealing with them and rather comprehensive, intra-governmental work," he said. "Not one nanosecond went into any [analysis] associated with the support of pro-democracy insurgent elements throughout the world. . . . There was never any criteria established by the government."[54] In 1986, the NSC staff belatedly composed a well-written pamphlet, "Freedom, Regional Security and Global Peace," that depicted "Soviet-client states" as "an almost unique threat to peace."[55] However, it did not use the "Reagan Doctrine" phrase, and it avoided becoming specific about what the U.S. government should do to rid the world of these Soviet-client states. McFarlane, no longer in the government, saw the pamphlet as a belated attempt to capitalize on the public debate over a "Reagan Doctrine." It was, he said, "an attempt to make a virtue out of happenstance."[56]

The war in Nicaragua was not a matter of happenstance, nor did it suffer from a shortage of criteria. Instead, too many conflicting criteria were applied by too many people. While Reagan settled into his role as chief salesman for the freedom fighters, his principal subordinates battled one another with a ferocity rarely equaled by the contras in combat. "There was a real lack of mutual respect and a real lack of what I would call disciplined limits at the top in the Reagan administration," said Jeane Kirkpatrick.[57] Casey, Clark, many of the White House speech-writers and Kirkpatrick herself distrusted Shultz, who clashed with them and Weinberger. White House Chief of Staff James Baker and Casey bluntly called each other a liar.* Deaver and Clark were barely on speaking terms. Reagan tried to distance himself from these conflicts but nonetheless found them unnerving. "I learned from watching him that he was discomforted by the feuds and the battles between strong-willed secretaries or the internal battles on the staff," Bush told me after he became president. He said that as vice president he had tried as best he could "to put oil on the troubled waters."[58]

Reagan had learned in childhood from his father's alcoholic eruptions to withdraw at any sign of disharmony. And withdraw he did from "the feuds and the battles" that attended his policy in Nicaragua, functioning even less than usual as a manager. Kirkpatrick observed that everyone who stayed on reasonably good terms with Reagan shared "an understanding that the president hated disharmony and didn't want to hear about it, and he didn't want people telling him about their disagreements or their quarrels or their concerns or coming to him about them—and even enforcing his own decisions if it involved disharmony on the team. He just didn't want to hear about it."[59] Reagan's distaste for disharmony made it difficult for his administration to reach a coherent decision on any issue where profound disagreements existed, as they did persistently on policy in Central America. And it made it even more difficult for anyone to follow through on Reagan's decisions, since he was unwilling to do so himself. "What was missing was follow-through," said Kirkpatrick. "The president would make decisions three, four, five times, and they would never be implemented. . . . What was missing was the president saying, 'Now do it, or do it this way. Cut it out. Don't do that.'" Kirkpatrick came to the conclusion that politics within the Reagan administration was "Shakespearian" rather than "Machiavellian." What she meant was that much of the conflict in-

---

* Although Baker and Casey were often on opposite sides of issues, their hostility had personal roots. Prior to the October 28, 1980, debate between President Carter and Reagan, the Reagan campaign obtained some briefing papers that had been used in Carter's preparation. When this was revealed in June 1983 by Laurence Barrett in *Gambling with History,* it touched off a congressional investigation even though Barrett concluded that the "filched papers" had played a negligible role in the outcome of the debate. A House subcommittee headed by Democrat Donald J. Albosta of Michigan failed to resolve the source of the theft. Baker and Casey accused each other of being responsible and of lying about what had happened in an effort to besmirch each other's reputation.

volved "personal strivings and personal rivalries and personal prefer-
ment" rather than a struggle over policy. "This is what went on
endlessly," Kirkpatrick said. "And Ronald Reagan was the somewhat
remote sort of king who was really absent from these debates. He wasn't
absent in NSPG meetings when he directed discussion or made decisions. He did that. But he was absent from all of this [conflict among
subordinates]. Just absent. Just not there." [60]

The absence of the lead actor was made more critical by the turnover
in the supporting cast. In addition to changing national security advisers
more often than Italy does governments, Reagan ran through four ambassadors to Honduras, three ambassadors to Nicaragua and four special envoys in charge of Central American relations. Four people of
divergent ideologies and political skills served in the key position of
assistant secretary of state for inter-American affairs. All of these assistants had different plans for dealing with the Sandinistas. All became
caught up in the internecine struggles within the administration, and all
were brought down or discredited.

While many of these struggles were driven by personality conflicts or
competing ambitions, they were undergirded by fundamental differences over the U.S. objective in Nicaragua. In the crucial years of 1983
and 1984, as battle lines on Central American policy hardened in Congress, the State Department sought primarily to achieve a negotiated
settlement that would have left the Sandinista government in place in
return for a cutoff of assistance to the Salvadoran rebels. The conservatives, often called "the war party" by their adversaries, wanted the
Sandinista government replaced. They differed among themselves, however, as to whether this objective could be accomplished only by an
outright contra military victory or through free elections brought about
by a combination of pressure from the contras, U.S. economic sanctions
and Nicaragua's regional neighbors. Ultimately, they also differed as to
whether those who sought to help the contras were bound by the
restrictions of federal law.

Pragmatists and conservatives also differed among themselves and
with each other over the emphasis that should be given to Central
America. Some of the more politically minded of Reagan's advisers
simply wanted the issue to go away, particularly in election years. Others wanted the president to take an economic as well as a military
initiative in Central America. On this issue, ideological divisions were
not clear. McFarlane and Kirkpatrick were convinced that military efforts in the region had to be accompanied by vigorous economic devel-

opment and land reform. So was the best-informed military man in the region, Wallace Nutting, the commander in chief of the Southern Command. Advocates of U.S. economic commitment to Central America believed that it was insufficient to oppose communism; they also sought to remove the conditions of poverty and instability under which communism flourishes. They were animated by the thinking that had guided President Truman after World War II, when he had proposed not only the Truman Doctrine of military aid but also the Marshall Plan that restored Europe to economic prosperity.

But Reagan, who had voted for Harry Truman and still admired him, was no Truman. Reagan had the vision to see that more than military aid was needed in Central America, but he lacked the capacity to manage his divided government. While prudent about the use of U.S. forces, his reliance on analogy led him to overestimate the military prowess of the contras. And he suffered, in a curious way, from his strengths as well as his weaknesses. Reagan was far more open-minded than is generally realized. He believed in giving all his principal subordinates a fair hearing. He listened to all the contenders for control of Central American policy, and saw merit in their opposing advocacies. He felt it imperative to arm the contras. He saw the value of bringing other Latin American nations into a negotiating process that would resolve conflicts in the region. He liked the idea of a dramatic U.S. commitment to economic development in Central America. At times he accepted the counsel of those who sought to put Central America on the back burner in the interest of domestic politics. In short, Reagan was on all sides of the foreign policy issue that most deeply divided his administration. Rodney McDaniel had put his finger on the problem when he said that Reagan believed in a "negotiating track" without linking it to anything else. This lack of linkage produced a policy of cacophony and confusion.

Tom Enders was the first in the Reagan administration to pursue the negotiating track, and he became a symbol of its failure. As assistant secretary of state for inter-American affairs, Enders helped midwife the contra aid program and practiced confrontational diplomacy with the Sandinistas. But while the Sandinistas and some Latin American leaders friendly to the United States viewed Enders as too arrogant in manner and too hard-line in approach, he was seen as accommodationist by Clark, Casey and Menges. In El Salvador, Enders wanted a "two-track initiative" that would simultaneously seek a power-sharing agreement with the guerrillas while the U.S. continued to assist the Salvadoran government in its military campaign against the rebels. In Nicaragua, Enders sought an agreement that would halt the flow of arms to the Salvadoran rebels. This was also a "two-track" policy, since U.S. aid to the contras was the leverage that would be used to induce the Sandinistas to cooperate. Enders complicated his problems with lone-wolf diplomacy that deprived him of potential allies on the White House staff. The pragmatists often knew even less about what Enders was up to than Clark did. Lawrence Eagleburger, the undersecretary of state for political affairs, said that Enders made "everyone mad at him because he runs everything out of his hat."[61]

The incident that undid Enders involved a vague mission undertaken by Kirkpatrick to Latin America on February 8–12, 1983. The trip was Clark's brainchild. Frustrated with Enders' secret maneuverings, Clark convinced the president to send Kirkpatrick on a fact-finding mission to Panama, Costa Rica, Honduras, El Salvador and Venezuela. She carried with her an innocuous and friendly letter signed by Reagan that reiterated the U.S. commitment to democracy in the region. The mission irritated Enders and struck many of Clark's critics as naïve. Kirkpatrick had little experience in diplomacy and little advance notice of her assignment. She met with government, opposition, union and business leaders in the nations she visited but avoided, as Roy Gutman observed, "the military establishments [that] are at the heart of power in Latin America."[62] Along the way a U.S. ambassador who was unsympathetic to Enders showed Kirkpatrick a secret "ambassador's eyes only" cable that Enders had sent him just before her visit. As she interpreted its message, the cable instructed the ambassador to ignore both Kirkpatrick and the Reagan letter and await new negotiating instructions from George Shultz, then on a trip to China. Kirkpatrick, who later told me she found an "enormous, almost indescribable unhappiness with Tom Enders" among the leaders she visited, thought the cable was an "incredible" display of arrogance.[63] She sent a memo to the president advocating a regional program of economic development, $60 million in emergency aid to El Salvador and continued support for the contras. She also passed on the Enders cable to Clark and Casey, who used it to convince Reagan that Enders was trying to undercut presidential policy in Central America.

Though Enders clung to his job for another three months and waged other battles with the conservatives, the cable he had sent to the ambassadors destroyed Reagan's confidence in him and insured that he would eventually be replaced. What hurt Enders more than the two-track initiative itself was his way of pursuing it. Reagan did not always follow

Kirkpatrick's counsel, but he usually displayed an almost avuncular protectiveness if anyone tried to attack or embarrass her. An aide who was not especially sympathetic to Kirkpatrick told me after Enders was fired that Reagan was furious about the cable—not because it undercut him personally but because he saw it as an attempt to undermine Kirkpatrick.

The cable and the conservatives' complaints about Enders stirred Reagan into a rare decision to dismiss a principal policymaker. Realizing that Reagan had made up his mind to fire Enders, Shultz did not fight to save his assistant secretary's job. But he was angered at the campaign against him and followed up on the May 25 dismissal of Enders by sending Reagan a memo proposing a "simple and straightforward" process with Shultz in charge. "You will look to me to carry out your policies," Shultz wrote in the memo. "If those policies change, you will tell me. If I am not carrying them out effectively, you will hold me accountable. But we will set up a structure so I can be your sole delegate with regard to carrying out your policies."[64]

It did not work out that way. Various structures were established in an attempt to establish a coherent Central American policy, but no "sole delegate" was ever put in charge. The post of assistant secretary of state for inter-American affairs was filled after a short interlude by Langhorne (Tony) Motley, an Alaskan land developer and Republican fund-raiser. Born in Brazil, Motley spoke fluent Portuguese and had proven a success as the Reagan administration's ambassador to Brazil, where he projected a confident, "can-do" militance that appealed to Clark and Casey. But Motley was less ideological than they believed. Since he began his new assignment with the confidence of Shultz and at least the neutrality of the White House pragmatists, his appointment should have provided the administration with an opportunity to make a fresh start at a time when a negotiated outcome of the Nicaraguan war was still possible. This opportunity was soon consumed by Motley's internal battles with Richard Stone, a former Democratic senator from Florida brought on board by Clark as special Central American envoy. While neither Motley nor Stone had any illusions about the Sandinistas, both were practical politicians who recognized the value of negotiating U.S.-Nicaraguan differences. But both also wanted the distinction of negotiating the agreement that would resolve the Nicaraguan problem, and Motley was far more skilled as a political infighter. As a Stone visit to Nicaragua was pending, Motley used the good offices of Vice President Bush to engineer a trip of his own to Managua, where he told Nicaraguan President Daniel Ortega that Stone was nothing more than "a propaganda front."[65] In February 1984, Stone quit in disgust.* Having disposed of his rival, Motley found himself the target of conservatives who believed he had been captured by the State Department bureaucracy and was too ready to negotiate. After another ten months of infighting, Motley also resigned. He was succeeded in 1985 by Elliott Abrams, a firebrand who was one of the most outspoken champions of the contras.

Within the administration, Shultz's appointment of Abrams was widely seen as a sop by the secretary of state to deflect the hostile fire of administration conservatives while he focused on superpower negotiations. Whether or not this is explicitly accurate, it was clear by the time Abrams assumed his post that the State Department had failed in its efforts to control Nicaraguan policy and keep it primarily on a negotiating track. The year of decision was 1984, when the White House staff was preoccupied with Reagan's reelection campaign. Baker's strategy was to focus on a ratification of the economic recovery ("It's morning again in America") and to keep contentious foreign policy issues out of the campaign as much as possible. This strategy, embraced also by the Republican congressional leadership, helped speed the withdrawal of U.S. forces from Lebanon and encouraged Shultz's efforts to smooth the path of U.S.-Soviet relations. On Central America, this strategy dictated a bipartisan congressional consensus on Salvadoran and Nicaraguan policy.

At the beginning of 1984 it looked as if such a consensus was achievable. The vehicle for building it was the National Bipartisan Commission on Central America headed by Henry Kissinger and referred to by everyone, including Reagan, as the "Kissinger Commission." The idea had been suggested in April 1983 by Democratic Senator Henry M. Jackson, the last great leader of the Cold War liberals, pushed by Clark and Kirkpatrick and embraced by Baker, who was always attracted to proposals that might produce congressional compromises. Kirkpatrick had proposed Kissinger as chairman, and Reagan had readily agreed.[66] On January 11, 1984, eighteen days before Reagan formally announced his candidacy for a second term, the commission issued a 132-page report containing forty-one recommendations, many echoing the ideas that McFarlane had put forth in his rejected 1981 report to Haig and that Kirkpatrick had advocated in her 1983 memo to Reagan.

---

* Stone's resignation was welcomed by Shultz and the White House pragmatists, largely because he had been brought into the government by Clark. But Stone, who had good ties with the contras, was not a stereotypical conservative. He genuinely believed that a negotiated outcome was possible in Nicaragua. On balance, his departure was a setback for the cause of U.S.-Nicaraguan diplomacy.

The twelve-member commission of six Democrats and six Republicans proposed providing $8.4 billion of economic aid to Central America over a five-year period and substantially increasing military aid to El Salvador, then at an annual level of $65 million. It proposed immediate economic aid of $400 million to the region, government loans for private economic development, 10,000 scholarships for higher education and the creation of a Literacy Corps. The commission pleased liberals by saying that Salvadoran military aid should "be made contingent upon demonstrated progress" toward human rights, free elections and the abolition of the death squads. But it pleased conservatives even more by rejecting a power-sharing formula in El Salvador and by accepting Reagan's premise that it was in the national interest to resist the spread of communism in Central America. "The use of Nicaragua as a base for Soviet and Cuban efforts to penetrate the rest of the Central American isthmus, with El Salvador the target of first opportunity, gives the conflict there a major strategic dimension," the commission report declared. "The direct involvement of aggressive external forces makes it a challenge to the system of hemispheric security and, quite specifically, to the security interests of the United States. This is a challenge to which the United States must respond."

The Kissinger Commission report, dedicated to Senator Jackson, who had died suddenly the previous September, is likely to be remembered as one of the great missed opportunities of the Reagan administration. Despite liberal reservations about its strategic arguments, the report briefly enabled the administration to occupy the political high ground in its eight-year running debate with Congress on Central American policy. But, as usual, there was a lack of White House follow-up. Although Reagan said in his weekly radio speech three days after the report was issued that the commission had "rendered an important service to all Americans," he barely mentioned the report in his televised State of the Union speech on January 26, which had a far bigger audience, and he did not mention it at all in two January political speeches. This was because Reagan was then embarked on his reelection campaign, and his political strategists preferred patriotic generalities to the discussion of anything so controversial as Central American policy. Reagan simply read the campaign scripts prepared for him by his managers, while conservatives grumbled and pushed for a nationally televised speech on Central America.

But by the time the president actually gave such a speech on May 9, the administration's Nicaraguan policy had already been irreparably damaged. Four days before the Kissinger Commission report became public in January, mines were laid in Sandino harbor, an operation that would continue into February, accompanied by other mine-layings, sabotage of Sandinista communications and destruction of an arms depot. All this was supposedly the work of anti-Sandinista insurgents. On April 6, however, reporter David Rogers of *The Wall Street Journal* disclosed that the mining of the harbors had been conducted by the CIA. The disclosure produced an international outcry, an angry denunciation of CIA Director Casey by Senator Barry Goldwater and other members of the Senate Intelligence Committee and a "sense of the Senate" resolution condemning the mining that passed 84-12.

The mines were so-called "firecracker" mines, designed primarily to damage and scare off ships rather than destroy them, but they were a clear violation of international law.[67] While Reagan often claimed that his Nicaraguan policy was unpopular because of effective Sandinista "disinformation" campaigns, the illegal harbor mining handed the Sandinistas a propaganda coup far exceeding anything resulting from their own efforts. Even Richard Nixon called the operation "Mickey Mouse."[68] The Sandinistas took their case to the International Court of Justice in the Hague (popularly known as the World Court) and won, though the administration refused in advance to recognize the court's jurisdiction. The mining of the harbors was an example of "force against another state," the court said, and U.S. support of the contras "amounts to an intervention of one state in the internal affairs of the other."[69]

The harbor-mining fiasco ruined the prospects of contra aid in Congress and indirectly gave diplomacy another chance. With the CIA in retreat, Shultz moved to fill the policy vacuum by holding direct talks with Nicaraguan President Ortega. Working through McFarlane but without disclosing his plan to other members of the cabinet, Shultz met privately with Reagan and obtained his approval to make a side trip to Managua on June 1, 1984, after attending the inauguration of President Duarte in El Salvador. The Managua trip was shrouded in secrecy. Casey, Weinberger and Kirkpatrick were briefed by Motley only after the mission had been approved by the president, and other high-ranking officials were not told at all. Shultz later described the meeting with Ortega as "businesslike and civil."[70] It was also unproductive. The secretary of state had reiterated U.S. concerns about the Nicaraguan military buildup and the supplying of arms to the Salvadoran rebels but also had made the point of most concern to Reagan that the Sandinistas had failed "to fulfill their 1979 promises of pluralism, democracy and elections."[71] Ortega replied that Nicaragua's internal affairs were not the business of the United States. After two and one-half hours of discussion Shultz and Ortega could agree only that the two sides should meet again. They agreed to have their representatives continue talks later that month in Manzanillo, Mexico.

But administration conservatives had become as suspicious of Shultz as they were of the Sandinistas. "Everybody was worried," said Kirkpatrick, that Shultz was "about to definitively compromise something, but we weren't quite sure what, in the Manzanillo talks. And since he didn't keep anybody informed, Casey or Cap or anybody, everybody felt free to develop their own fantasies, as in a Rorschach [ink-blot] test."[72] The principal conservative nightmare was that Shultz would agree to "sell out" the contras with a high-sounding negotiated agreement that would be dependent on worthless Sandinista promises. Few of the conservatives even realized that Casey had sold the contra aid program to Reagan as a means of obtaining precisely the kind of negotiated settlement that Shultz was trying to achieve. And even the few conservatives who were aware of this then-unpublished bit of history disregarded it, for the contras had by 1984 become an end in themselves. Loyalty to the contras had become the litmus test for loyalty to "Reagan's policy" among conservatives. "Man, if you weren't hard enough in your support for the contras, you were a commie," said a senior White House official who lacked the requisite enthusiasm. "You had to be hard." Among the conservatives clustered in the White House speechwriting department, according to Ben Elliott, it was freely said that the State Department needed "an American desk."[73] Constantine Menges summed up the conservative perspective in his memoir, *Inside the National Security Council,* in which Shultz is depicted as an ambitious captive of the foreign policy establishment who was "taken in, again and again, by the dominant State Department faction." From Menges' point of view, Shultz took advantage of his envied private access to mislead the president and to undo his policies. Menges claims to have witnessed "seven major episodes where some of President Reagan's closest advisers tried to short-circuit the [national security] process."[74] Most of these incidents involved actions originated by Shultz or his assistant secretaries.

While none of the administration conservatives said as much directly, their comments suggest that they thought of Reagan as a trusting dolt who could easily be manipulated. Their obsessive concern over Reagan's weekly private meetings with Shultz, a normal enough activity in most administrations, reflected a lack of confidence in the president as much as it did in the secretary of state. But the pragmatists viewed Reagan through a mirror image. They were equally convinced that the president could be led down a path that contradicted his enunciated policies, and they were as mistrustful of the conservatives as they were mistrusted by them. The pragmatists worried that the conservatives would plunge Reagan into a war he did not want by exaggerating contra military prowess and portraying a negotiated settlement as a State Department trap. The mirror image of Shultz as villain was Casey, who was believed to have Svengali-like powers. Casey in fact saw Reagan alone far less often than Shultz did, but Baker insisted that Deaver debrief the president any time Casey had been alone with him. "He [Baker] was like a dog with a bone," recalls Deaver. "He would say that the crazies want to get us into war [and that] we cannot get this economic recovery program going if we get involved in a land war in Central America." 75 *

Baker was worried even then that "the crazies" would circumvent the prohibitions Congress had imposed in October 1984 on U.S. aid to the contras. "We cannot do indirectly what we can't do directly," Baker had warned at an NSPG meeting in the summer of 1984. "If Congress says you can't give aid to the contras, you'd better be careful about going out and getting it from third countries." 76 Baker's opposition to secret foreign policy arrangements that circumvented the law reflected a political sensitivity that was rare on matters relating to the contras. He knew that secret dealings to help the contras were unlikely to stay secret and that it would be difficult to defend them once they became public. With Clark no longer national security adviser, Baker had identified Casey as the leader of the forces who appealed to Reagan's "dark side." The conservatives reciprocated in their opinion of Baker, whom they accurately perceived as putting Reagan's reelection campaign well ahead of the fortunes of the contras. It was no accident that Baker would subsequently be excluded by John Poindexter from discussions of the Iran arms deals, even though he remained a member of the National Security Council after he left the White House in 1985 to become secretary of the treasury.†

As it turned out, the suspicions of the pragmatists in the summer and fall of 1984 had considerably more foundation than the worries of the

---

* This perception did not fade with economic recovery. In the heady days after Reagan's landslide reelection, I asked Baker what issue might undo the president in his second term. "Central America," he replied.

† A Reagan administration official told me that Poindexter went to Baker after the Iran-contra

conservatives. Nothing much was going on in the U.S.-Nicaraguan talks at Manzanillo. The two sides could not even agree on an agenda or on the relationship of the negotiations to a separate peace process being conducted by four Latin American nations—Colombia, Mexico, Panama and Venezuela—begun on Contadora Island in January 1983. Although Reagan often said he welcomed this mediation, administration conservatives were contemptuous of Contadora because of Mexican participation in the process. The Mexicans were viewed by the conservatives as closet Sandinistas. "Our friends in the region often referred to the Mexican ambassador in Managua as the tenth commandante," wrote Menges.[77] But while the Manzanillo talks were proceeding toward inauspicious disagreement, the Reagan administration botched a far bigger opportunity.

Ortega had yielded to pressure and called elections for November 4, two days before the U.S. elections. Reports received by the State Department from inside Nicaragua indicated that popular discontent with the Sandinistas, fueled by economic woes and the military draft, was growing. While the conservatives were certain that no Communist government would ever permit itself to be voted out of power, the State Department saw the Nicaraguan election as an opportunity to test Sandinista intentions, at least if a sufficiently strong opposition candidate could be induced to oppose Ortega. Such a candidate was available in the person of Arturo Cruz Sr., the former Sandinista ambassador to the United States who was now living in Washington. Craig Johnstone, the deputy secretary of state for inter-American affairs, encouraged Cruz to become a candidate. McFarlane also was intrigued by the idea of a Cruz candidacy, believing that it would leave the Sandinistas with the unpalatable alternative of either holding free elections or being exposed to the world as a nation that did not permit genuine democracy. The formulation used by Reagan expressed both sides of the equation. "We would wholeheartedly welcome a genuine democratic election in Nicaragua," Reagan said in a Menges-composed passage of a speech to Caribbean heads of state in Columbia, South Carolina, on July 19. "But no person committed to democracy will be taken in by a Soviet-style sham election."

Cruz, who realized he was getting mixed signals from Washington, made a trip to Nicaragua and delivered an anti-Sandinista speech that

---

disclosures had become public and apologized to him for cutting him out of the NSC meetings in which Iran arms sales were discussed. "John, you don't realize what a favor you've done me," Baker replied.

was carried over the government radio network. He made three other political appearances, one of them at a rally in Chinandega where his supporters faced down a Sandinista mob.[78] But in the end, with his candidacy opposed both by the contras and the CIA, Cruz decided not to run. Gutman makes a convincing case in *Banana Diplomacy* that Cruz might actually have won a free election and that he would have received a high percentage of the vote in any case. As it was, a third of the Nicaraguans who went to the polls voted against the Sandinistas even though Ortega had no major opponent. Too late, Cruz decided that he had made a mistake in deciding not to run.[79] It was another missed opportunity for the Reagan administration.

Long before Congress cut off U.S. military aid for the contras, everyone in the White House who cared about the issue recognized that it would be extremely difficult to sustain a covert aid request in a presidential election year. The Democratic House had voted for the first time in 1983 against contra aid, while the Republican Senate had approved an aid package. In early December a Senate-House conference committee had reached a shaky compromise that put a $24 million "cap" on contra funding and prohibited the CIA from using its contingency reserves to make up any shortfall. This action postponed a congressional showdown on contra aid until mid-1984 and promoted an administration search for new sources of funding to keep the contras going. The administration simply lacked the votes in the House, where resurgent Democrats led by House Speaker Tip O'Neill on May 11 fell only four votes short of blocking the administration's measure providing for $500 million in continued military aid to El Salvador.

Even though Reagan's popularity had rebounded with the economy, Richard Wirthlin's highly detailed polling taken for the White House throughout 1984 showed consistently that the administration was potentially vulnerable on its Central American policy. And the administration was actually more vulnerable than Wirthlin knew, because Casey, McFarlane and Oliver North were already engaged in secret efforts to solicit funds from other nations to fight the contra war. In 1987, McFarlane would testify to the joint congressional committees investigating the Iran-contra affair that as early as February or March of 1984 he had considered "the possibility of in effect farming out the whole contra support operation to another country, which would not provide the funding, but give it some direction."

The first country of choice was Israel, which was presumed to have the military expertise needed to wield the inexperienced contra recruits into an effective fighting force. On March 27, without telling Shultz,

McFarlane met with Casey and discussed a plan for approaching other countries for contra aid. Casey liked the idea and sent McFarlane a memo saying, "I am in full agreement that you should explore funding alternatives with Israel and perhaps others."[80] The Israelis turned McFarlane down in April, and Shultz, when he heard about the request from the U.S. ambassador in Tel Aviv, admonished McFarlane against making such solicitations. "We must not get dependent on others," Shultz told him. "We must do it ourselves." But the contras were virtually out of money by May, and O'Neill said triumphantly that the administration's request for another $21 million in contra aid was "dead." McFarlane turned to Prince Bandar, the Saudi ambassador to the United States, telling him that it was nearly "inevitable that the administration would fail" to win congressional approval of additional contra aid. The Saudis are always anxious to please U.S. presidents, and Bandar was responsive to the solicitation. As McFarlane subsequently put it in his testimony, Bandar offered to "provide a contribution of $1 million per month, ostensibly from private funds, that would be devoted to—as a humanitarian gesture—to sustenance of the contras through the end of the year." The payments began arriving in July, assuring the administration that the contras would remain a military presence no matter what Congress did.

How much did Reagan know of what was going on? Enough, certainly, to have stopped what was happening if he had wanted to do it. But Reagan clearly did not want to stop Saudi contributions to the contras any more than he wanted to block Shultz's efforts to find a diplomatic solution to the Nicaraguan problem. According to McFarlane, the president in 1985 directed him to help hold the contras together "body and soul,"[81] an instruction that McFarlane transmitted to Oliver North, then a Marine lieutenant colonel and NSC staff aide who was the administration's principal liaison with the contra forces. Reagan's endorsement of third-country solicitations for the contras has subsequently been overshadowed by the $64 question about whether he approved the 1986 diversion of Iran arms sales proceeds to the contras. But Reagan has never contested McFarlane's assertion that he was informed of the original Saudi contributions. McFarlane testified that he informed Reagan of Bandar's commitment soon after it was made by placing a note card in his daily briefing book and that he was later called in after the daily briefing to "pick up the note card which expressed the president's satisfaction and pleasure that this had occurred."[82] Subsequently, on a February 1985 visit to Washington, Saudi King Fahd told Reagan he was increasing the contra payment to $2 million a month (for a total of $32 million) and was thanked warmly by the president.

The question of the legality of the contributions was discussed at the June 25, 1984, NSPG meeting attended by Reagan, Bush, Shultz, Weinberger, Casey, Meese and McFarlane. Shultz said at this meeting that James Baker had told him that it would be "an impeachable offense" for the U.S. government to act as a conduit for third-country funding. Casey responded that such funding was legal if the third countries contributed directly to the contras. Meese backed Casey but said the matter should be reviewed by Attorney General William French Smith before a decision was made. McFarlane's minutes of this meeting were introduced at the North trial. They quote Bush as saying that he did not see "how anyone could object to the U.S. encouraging third parties to provide help" as long as nothing was given in return for the contributions. But the participants in the meeting anticipated a negative reaction if the solicitations became known. McFarlane, the next-to-last speaker, said, "I certainly hope none of this discussion will be made public in any way." Reagan agreed. "If such a story gets out, we'll all be hanging by our thumbs in front of the White House until we find out who did it." [83]

The next day Attorney General Smith supported the vice president's position. Smith said (according to a memo written by CIA general counsel Stanley Sporkin) "that he saw no legal concern if the United States Government discussed this matter with other nations so long as it was made clear that they would be using their own funds to support the Contras and no U.S. appropriated funds would be used for this purpose." North did not wait for the ruling. His notes show that on June 25, when the issue was still unresolved, he sent a message to contra leader Adolfo Calero saying that funds would be transferred to him in twenty-four hours from a foreign account.

None of this was known to Congress, which was moving toward what was widely believed to be a permanent cutoff of contra aid. No one, least of all Casey, had any doubt that Congress would have barred third-country contributions, and the congressional intelligence committees were not informed of the Saudi contributions while Casey remained at the CIA. But Congress was aware that individual conservatives outside the administration were raising funds for the contras, and the House Democrats sought to bar outside assistance to the contras of any kind. That is what they thought they had done—and what McFarlane also believed they had done—when they passed legislation late in 1984 introduced by Congressman Edward Boland of Massachusetts and known afterward as Boland II. Included as an amendment to an omnibus appropriations bill that Reagan signed into law on October 12, 1984, the amendment barred use of any funds "available to the Central Intelligence Agency, the Department of Defense or any other agency or entity involved in intelligence activities" for the purpose of "supporting, directly or indirectly, military or paramilitary operations in Nicaragua by any nation, group, organization or individual." Boland mistakenly believed that his amendment meant the end of Reagan administration military assistance for the contras.

Reagan responded to Boland II as he so often responded—with a story that reflected his feelings, his Democratic heritage and his unwillingness to accept congressional restriction of his policies. On October 26, during a White House interview with representatives of Scripps-Howard Newspapers, Reagan answered a question from David Brown, the executive editor of the *Commercial Appeal* in Memphis, who related the efforts of a group of southerners to provide private assistance to "stop communism before it gets to our borders." Brown wanted to know how Reagan felt about this effort.

"Well, I have to say it's quite in line with what has been a pretty well-established tradition in our country," Reagan replied. "Nothing was done legally about the formation of a brigade, a Communist brigade of Americans, in the Spanish Civil War. In World War II, we had pilots being recruited to go to the Flying Tigers [in China]. . . . So I don't know. I'm not a lawyer, so I never asked about what is the actual legality of anything of that kind. But at the same time, as I say, it's been a tradition, and Americans have always done this. And I would be inclined to not want to interfere with them."

Brown recognized, even if Reagan didn't, that the examples were a bit wide of the mark. "Weren't the examples that you raised [of] people who went to fight for governments who were fighting other governments' tyranny?" he asked. "In this case we have Americans who are going to Central America to help rebels. . . . Do you see a difference there?"

"Well, as I say, 'I'm not so wise as those lawyer guys,' as Mr. [Robert] Service said in his poem," Reagan said. "I haven't really gotten into that. . . . My own personal reaction to it was it seemed to be a long and honorable tradition. And in a sense, our own interest in Nicaragua has to do with their overt support of guerrillas, themselves, who are trying to overthrow a duly elected government of a neighboring country—El

Salvador. So, now one has raised the issue before of these individual Americans."

Brown continued to press the president. Even if the activity was legal, was it morally justified?

On this question, at least, Reagan had no doubts. "Well, if you get into the moral issue of it," Reagan said, "we were certainly tested with regard to that Spanish Civil War I mentioned because I would say that the individuals that went there were, in the opinion of most Americans, fighting on the wrong side."

An analogy has been defined as a comparison in which the essential similarities outweigh the essential differences. If this definition is applied, Reagan's analogy failed dismally. According to the Gallup poll, Americans (by margins ranging from 2-1 in 1937 to 3-1 in 1938) overwhelmingly supported the Loyalist, democratically elected government of Spain, which was backed by the Soviets in resisting a rebellion led by General Francisco Franco and supported by Nazi Germany and Fascist Italy. The Roosevelt administration, determined to remain neutral, discouraged the participation of Americans in the Abraham Lincoln Brigade. During the Cold War these veterans were labeled "premature antifascists" and placed on the attorney general's list of "subversive organizations."

Reagan himself did not necessarily think the Abraham Lincoln Brigade had been fighting on the wrong side. McFarlane remembers that in private discussions Reagan would often cite approvingly the role of the brigade whenever "we'd dump on him our woes of no money for the contras."[84] As Boland II had made its way through Congress, administration conservatives expressed concern that its restrictions would hamper efforts to help the contras through private donations. Reagan didn't want to hear it. According to McFarlane, he would often reply, "Those guys in the Lincoln Brigade were doing the right thing."[85]

Right or wrong, what Americans had done during the Spanish Civil War really had no relevance to the contras. Reagan, who reasoned by analogy instead of analysis, did not accept that. "His judgments were often formed by simply what he thought [was] the right thing to do, with no more institutional, legal or other framework than that," said McFarlane. "What do I, the heroic figure, believe Americans would want me to do? And he would do it."[86]

Reagan thought that helping the contras in their fight against the Sandinista government was "the right thing to do." He had no interest whatever in the legal restrictions that Congress believed it had imposed on him and on the executive branch by passing Boland II.

15

LOST IN LEBANON

Many Americans are wondering why we must keep our forces in Lebanon. Well, the reason they must stay there until the situation is under control is quite clear: we have vital interests in Lebanon.

RONALD REAGAN,
October 24, 1983[1]

Despite the conflicts that beset Reagan administration policies in Central America, the president and his contentious cabinet at least agreed that U.S. national interests required resisting the spread of Communist influence in the Western Hemisphere. While fears of Soviet influence in the Middle East would also influence Reagan's actions in that region, his administration was never able to agree on a common objective of U.S. policy in Lebanon, much less the means of attaining it. Lebanon is a war-torn ruin of a land the size of Connecticut where rival clans and sectarian forces battle for military and political supremacy. It is, as a U.S. report put it, "a country beset with virtually every unresolved dispute afflicting the peoples of the Middle East."[2] By the time the Reagan administration became militarily involved in Lebanon in 1982, nearly 100,000 persons in this nation of three million people had died in hostilities that began with a violent civil war in 1975.

Because rival barons in Reagan's cabinet could not agree on what the United States hoped to accomplish in the Middle East and because the president was unable to resolve their conflicts, Lebanon also became an arena for trial-and-error U.S. foreign policy initiatives that ended in debacle. If measured in loss of American lives abroad, Lebanon was the greatest disaster of the Reagan presidency. Reagan without hesitation ruled out use of U.S. combat troops in Central America, a region arguably crucial to national security. But he twice deployed troops to Lebanon, on the periphery of U.S. security concerns, in behalf of changing and ill-defined diplomatic goals and in defiance of the recommendations of his military advisers. When the second mission resulted in a terrorist attack on a Marine barracks that claimed more American lives than any engagement in the Vietnam War, Reagan defended his decision by contending that the deployment had been vital to U.S. strategic interests.

The story of the Reagan administration's involvement in Lebanon is a case study of foreign policy calamity. More than any other undertaking, the U.S. involvement in Lebanon demonstrates the naïveté, ignorance and undisciplined internal conflict characteristic of the Reagan presidency. It is also the undertaking most illustrative of Reagan's ability to avoid responsibility for actions that might well have ruined other presidents. Reagan's standing with the American people would be grievously damaged in the final two years of his term by the revelations of the Iran-contra affair. But he almost entirely escaped political damage for what happened in Lebanon, largely because the invasion of Grenada two days after the bombing in Beirut provided Americans with a victory to celebrate as well as deaths to mourn. Nonetheless, the U.S. involvement in Lebanon is significant to any assessment of the Reagan presidency. More than any of his other decisions, Reagan's actions in Lebanon demonstrate his deficiencies when confronted with cabinet conflicts he could not resolve by reliance on his basic script. More than any other policy, Reagan's course of action in Lebanon displays his proclivity for splitting the difference between irreconcilable positions at the sacrifice of clarity—and in this case, of American lives. More than any other crisis, Lebanon illustrates the ambiguity of Reagan's presidential leadership.

For all this, Lebanon was a catastrophe born of good intentions. When he began his presidency, Reagan believed the United States could play a constructive role in the Middle East. He accepted Secretary of State Haig's view that the United States could foster a "strategic consensus" in the region by working with Israel, Egypt and Saudi Arabia to frustrate any Soviet attempts at mischief-making in the region. Like Haig, Reagan operated on the assumption that U.S. interests were linked to those of Israel. An FBI dossier prepared on Reagan after World War II portrays him as an emotional foe of anti-Semitism who denounced persecution of the Jews in radio broadcasts and nearly came to blows at a party with a guest who said that the Jews had profiteered from the war.[3] Reagan believed that Jews deserved a nation of their own, and he rejoiced in 1948 at the creation of the state of Israel. While his views on most other subjects changed during his metamorphosis from liberal Democrat to conservative Republican, Reagan remained staunchly pro-Israel. As a liberal, he felt that U.S. protection of Israel was owed the survivors of the Holocaust. As a conservative, he came to regard Israel as a strategic bulwark against Soviet intervention in the Middle East. "The crucial element determining the success or failure of American policy [in the Middle East] is the fate of Israel," Reagan said in a policy paper issued early in his 1980 campaign. While his assumption that Israel was automatically right would be shaken by its invasion of Lebanon and his personal encounters with Menachem Begin, Reagan did not easily change positions. And even after he came to realize that Israel could be a problem as well as a solution, he proved unable to translate this awareness into a policy that might have spared the United States the trauma of its intervention in Lebanon.

The seeds that led to the bitter harvest in Lebanon were planted in April 1981, when the Syrians bombarded the Christian town of Zahle in the Bekaa Valley. Zahle had been infiltrated by forces loyal to the charismatic Maronite Christian leader Bashir Gemayel, who had close ties to Israel and to the United States.* The Syrians worried that the Israelis would team up with Gemayel's forces and establish a permanent presence in Lebanon menacing Syria. Later that month, the Israelis shot down two Syrian helicopters. The Syrians then deployed Soviet surface-to-air missiles near Zahle, and Reagan named Philip C. Habib as special

---

* The Maronite Christians have lived in the rugged territory of what is now northern Lebanon since followers of St. Maron settled there in the fifth century. They formed a union with the Vatican in the twelfth century, becoming one of the Eastern rite Roman Catholic churches. Pierre Gemayel, Bashir's father, founded the Phalangist Party in 1936, taking its name from the fascist Falange Party headed by Spanish leader Francisco Franco. When Lebanon became independent in 1943, political power was divided among the religious groups according to the 6-5 ratio of Christians to Muslims in the Lebanese population. Long after the Muslims became a majority, the Gemayel clan and the Phalangists sought to perpetuate Christian rule. Bashir Gemayel, the clan's most effective leader, had united various Christian factions in pursuit of this goal.

envoy to the Middle East in an effort to head off a Syrian-Israeli war. A cease-fire was achieved on June 8, but conflict soon resumed between the Palestine Liberation Organization (PLO) forces and Israeli troops in southern Lebanon.

On July 17, Israel conducted a major air raid on Beirut with the declared objective of destroying PLO headquarters. Some three hundred persons were killed and another eight hundred injured in the bombing. It was the first of many actions that would undermine Israel's standing in the court of world public opinion and it distressed Reagan, then in Canada attending his first economic summit of the industrialized democracies. A U.S. shipment of F-16 fighter planes to Israel had already been delayed as a consequence of a June 7 Israeli raid that destroyed a French-made nuclear reactor in Iraq. This earlier raid had not alarmed Reagan, even though the administration formally protested it. White House officials told me at the time that Reagan sympathized with the Israeli view that it was necessary to eliminate Iraq's capability to manufacture atomic weapons. But Reagan had a much more emotional and negative reaction when he watched television footage of bodies being removed from the wreckage of Beirut apartment buildings after the July 17 raid. Television pictures mattered to Reagan, and what he was seeing on television did not square with his fundamental feelings about Israel. Reagan agreed in the wake of the July 17 attack to postpone the F-16 shipments to Israel. He also instructed Habib to arrange a cease-fire between the Israelis and the PLO, which Habib accomplished with help from Saudi Arabia. The cease-fire took effect on July 24. Lebanon virtually vanished from Reagan's mental radar screen until the Israelis launched their invasion on June 6, 1982.

In the interval between the cease-fire and the invasion, Reagan had learned much about Begin that was not to his liking. Near the end of the summer of 1981, White House legislative strategists had taken over direction of lagging efforts to obtain congressional approval of an $8 billion sale of sophisticated AWACS aircraft to Saudi Arabia. Reagan believed this sale would encourage the Saudis to help maintain the cease-fire in Lebanon because Habib, in reporting to him, had called the Saudi role "absolutely invaluable and indispensable for our future efforts."[4] But Israel adamantly opposed the sale and exercised its political clout in the U.S. Senate, where a bipartisan coalition opposed the deal. Begin paid a state visit to Washington on September 9. In his conversations with Haig and Reagan he left the impression that he would oppose the sale but make no attempt to mount a major public campaign against it. Then Begin denounced the AWACS sale in a speech to Congress and in several television interviews.

Again, Reagan was sensitive to what he saw on television. Had Begin left the AWACS sale in the capable hands of the Israeli lobby, Israel might well have succeeded in defeating it. But Begin's tactics galvanized Reagan into an unusual display of political involvement. Encouraged by White House Chief of Staff James Baker, Reagan made the AWACS deal a test of his personal prestige, then sky-high among Republicans. On October 1, 1981, Reagan opened his news conference with a blunt reply to Begin. Reagan said it was his duty to define national security objectives, adding, "It is not the business of other nations to make American foreign policy." On October 7, a day after Anwar Sadat was assassinated by Muslim fanatics in Cairo, Reagan met privately with forty-three Republican senators and put the issue to them in terms of loyalty to their president vs. loyalty to Israel. When Senator Slade Gorton of Washington protested that the Israeli lobby did not control his vote, Reagan responded tartly, "That may be so, Senator, but the world will perceive that they do."[5] On October 28, after further intense lobbying by the president and White House staff, the Senate approved the AWACS sale by a four-vote margin.

U.S.-Israeli relations deteriorated over the next seven months, a period when the administration pursued a Middle East policy that one expert defined as "keeping the lid on."* Though Haig would later be seen as an apologist for the Israeli invasion of Lebanon, he was at the time striving to forestall it. When Begin told Haig at Sadat's funeral that he was planning a move into Lebanon, Haig replied, "If you move, you move alone." But Haig was also sympathetic to Begin, of whom he later wrote: "His entire motive is to preserve the lives of Jews."[6] In addition to his sympathy, Haig had a practical objective. The Israelis were scheduled to complete withdrawal from the Sinai Peninsula by April 26, 1982, under provisions of the Egyptian-Israeli peace treaty engineered by the Carter administration, and Haig was worried that Begin might find an excuse to back out of the commitment. "The administration was afraid that an Israeli invasion of Lebanon before the

* The expert quoted here is William B. Quandt, who headed the Middle East office of the National Security Council from 1977 to 1979. His useful overview, "Reagan's Lebanon Policy: Trial and Error," appeared in the Spring 1984 issue of the *Middle East Journal*. Another expert whose views were consulted in the preparation of this chapter is Geoffrey Kemp, who headed the Near East and South Asian affairs office on the NSC staff from 1981–84. Kemp's thoughtful examination of the Reagan administration experience, "Lessons of Lebanon: A Guideline for Future U.S. Policy," appeared in the Summer 1988 issue of *Middle East Insight*.

end of April would trigger a strong Egyptian reaction against Israel," observed William Quandt. "This, in turn, might be used by the Begin government to justify not returning the last piece of Sinai."[7] Accordingly, Haig urged restraint by the Reagan administration after Begin on December 14 pushed a provocative bill through the Knesset annexing the strategic Golan Heights, which Israel had seized from Syria in their 1967 war. Syria called the move a "declaration of war," and a furious Weinberger called upon Reagan to penalize Israel for the action. "How long do we have to go on bribing Israel?" Weinberger said. "If there is no real cost to the Israelis, we'll never be able to stop any of their actions."[8]

Following his usual practice, Reagan sought a middle ground that would split the difference between his secretaries of state and defense. He was guided less by policy perceptions than by an impulse to keep harmony within his official family. The compromises that resulted from this impulse often produced half-measures that satisfied no one and would in the long run have catastrophic consequences in Lebanon. In this instance, however, Reagan reached what appeared to be a judicious compromise. He agreed with Weinberger that Israel should be penalized, and he agreed with Haig that the penalty should be limited. In response to the annexation the United States postponed a "memorandum of understanding" providing for U.S.-Israeli military cooperation in defending the Middle East from external attack and also canceled export agreements that cost the Israelis some $300 million in arms sales. This relatively mild response did not stop Begin from calling in Samuel Lewis, the U.S. ambassador to Israel, and subjecting him to a tongue-lashing about U.S. military actions in World War II and the Vietnam War that had caused heavy civilian casualties. "Are we a vassal state of yours?" Begin said to Lewis. "Are we a banana republic? . . . You will not frighten us with punishments. He who threatens us will find us deaf to his threats."[9]

As recounted in Chapter 10, Reagan had just begun a busy, ten-day visit to Europe when the Israeli ambassador to Great Britain was shot and wounded on June 2 by Arab terrorists. Israel then destroyed an empty sports stadium in Beirut that was being used as an ammunition dump, and the PLO bombed towns in Galilee, providing Israel with a *casus belli* for the invasion of Lebanon. The Reagan administration had been warned by Begin that Israel might find it necessary to move into Lebanon to protect itself from the PLO, but Reagan was disturbed by the timing of the Israeli action. "Boy, that guy makes it hard for you to be his friend," Reagan said of Begin.[10] From Versailles, where he was attending the economic summit, Reagan sent Begin a note, drafted by Haig, asking Israel not to instigate further hostilities. Instead, the Israeli cabinet approved an invasion plan called Operation Peace in Galilee. Begin informed Reagan and Haig that the purpose of the invasion was to drive the PLO back from the Israeli border "so that all our civilians in the region of Galilee will be set free of the permanent threat to their lives."[11] Haig anticipated that the operation would be over within three or four days.

During this crucial period Reagan was preoccupied with his own performance on the world stage rather than with the grim drama unfolding in Lebanon. It was his first trip outside the Western Hemisphere as president, and he was overscheduled, overextended and overtired. On June 7, the day after the invasion, Reagan nodded off in the Vatican during a televised meeting with the Pope. His sleepiness reflected the demands of an ambitious and unrealistic schedule that had crowded into a single trip the economic summit, the Vatican stopover, a state visit to Britain, the Westminster speech, a NATO meeting in Bonn and various other appearances. Most of Reagan's conversations about the invasion while he was in Europe consisted of hurried consultations with Haig and National Security Adviser William Clark, who were engaged in a running feud over policy and perquisites. Meanwhile, Israeli forces, under the direction of Defense Minister Ariel Sharon, were conducting a war that went far beyond the operation actually approved by the Begin cabinet. In a massive air battle on June 9 that involved more than a hundred warplanes, Israeli jets downed more than twenty Syrian planes and destroyed the Syrian surface-to-air missiles in the Bekaa Valley. The same day, Israeli troops advanced within sight of Beirut. Not until June 10 did Reagan, now in Bonn, send a message to the Israelis urging them to end hostilities. Begin agreed to a cease-fire on June 11, but it lasted only two days. On June 13, in Haig's words, "Israel closed the ring around Beirut," trapping the PLO inside. Syrian forces had been cut off. "To all appearances, the Israelis had cast off restraint entirely," said Haig.[12]

In the two months following the Israeli invasion, violence swept over Lebanon like a summer storm. During one period, late in July, Israeli planes bombed West Beirut for seven consecutive days as American public opinion turned steadily against the Israelis. On June 21, five days before Haig's forced resignation, Begin once more came to the White House. He was by now largely friendless within the high councils of the

Reagan administration, where Bush and Baker had joined Clark and Weinberger in urging the president to take a firm line with the Israeli prime minister. Reagan did. As Haig recalled it, "An expressionless Reagan read off the American position from typed file cards; Begin responded with equal coldness. There was no exchange of pleasantries, no dialogue, no hint of the warm sympathy that had up to now characterized their relationship." [13]

In fact, although he hesitated to criticize the Israeli prime minister publicly, Reagan had been devoid of "warm sympathy" for Begin since the AWACS battle. While remaining supportive of Israel, Reagan was increasingly receptive to the Clark-Weinberger view that Begin and General Sharon had deliberately deceived the U.S. government about Israeli intentions in Lebanon and that Haig had been taken in by the deception. The words Reagan read to Begin at this June 21 meeting in the Oval Office reflected the increased administration suspicion of the Israeli government. They had been typed for the president on four-by-six cards by the NSC staff, and Reagan read them without any anecdotal deviations from the script. He said the invasion of Lebanon had raised serious problems for the United States in the Arab world. He called upon Israel to cease hostilities immediately, as Habib had insisted in his peacemaking efforts in Lebanon. He said also that Israel should engage in renewed discussions on Palestinian autonomy. Begin, who needed no notes to make his points, bridled at the use of the word "invasion." He called the Israeli action a necessary "intervention" to defend its citizens and said Israel would withdraw only after other foreign forces were removed from Lebanon.

The Reagan-Begin impasse continued over lunch in the Cabinet Room, where other aides joined the discussion. Begin became agitated when Weinberger defended the value of arms deals with Saudi Arabia and other "moderate" Arab nations. There was nothing "moderate" about the Saudis, said Begin, observing that they were committed to the elimination of the state of Israel. Reagan replied that the same could have been said about the Egyptians a few years earlier. The luncheon ended without the customary presidential toast, and the brief departure ceremony that followed on the White House south grounds was uncharacteristically stiff and formal. "It's been worthwhile to have Prime Minister Begin at the White House again," Reagan said. "All of us share a common understanding of the need to bring peace and security to the Middle East." Begin spoke after him, using the ceremony as a means of telling the world that the U.S.-Israeli relationship remained unchanged. To the dismay of White House aides, Begin referred to the president as "my friend" and said that he and Reagan had engaged in a "very fruitful discussion." Then Begin repeated what he had said in the Oval Office, denying Israeli responsibility for the invasion. "I have read in some newspapers in this great country that Israel invaded Lebanon," he said. "This is a misnomer. Israel did not invade any country. You do invade a land when you want to conquer it or to annex it or, at least, to conquer part of it. We don't covet even one inch of Lebanese territory."

How little "common understanding" actually existed between the U.S. and Israeli governments became apparent within a few days of Begin's visit. Reagan announced Haig's resignation on the afternoon of June 25. Before dawn that same day the Israelis launched a bombardment of West Beirut, a move that Haig would describe as "a heavy-handed act that nearly shattered the fragile political consensus in Lebanon." [14] For the next eleven days U.S. diplomats struggled to obtain first a cease-fire and then a settlement under which first the PLO and then other foreign forces would withdraw from Lebanese territory. Reagan did not want even to talk about a long-term strategy in Lebanon until Shultz was on the job. Haig was communicating with the White House staff and with Clark through subordinates, and it was difficult to know who was making decisions at any given moment. But Haig functioned as best he could as a lame-duck secretary of state for more than a week, trying to find a formula that all contending parties could accept. His task was complicated by the geographical dispersion of administration officials. Habib was negotiating, sometimes around the clock, in Lebanon. Shultz was winding up his private affairs in California.

At a June 30 news conference Reagan said the United States was committed to a Lebanese government of national unity, security for Israel's northern border and expulsion of the PLO from Lebanon. The next day Reagan flew to Los Angeles, where he denied that the United States had given advance approval of the Lebanon invasion and described Habib as a "hero" who was doing his best to secure a settlement. "He's done a superhuman job," Reagan told a group of reporters. "And he's still there and negotiating. And that's why I don't want to do anything to louse up his act." [15] Reagan then departed by helicopter for his mountaintop ranch northwest of Santa Barbara and Haig withdrew for the July 4 holiday weekend to the Greenbrier, a resort in West Virginia.

During this period, when everyone and no one was in charge, Reagan committed the United States to participating in a multinational peace-keeping force in Lebanon. Habib was its chief proponent. The idea had been discussed inconclusively at the State Department and within the NSC staff prior to the Begin visit. Reagan's military advisers never liked it. The first document signed by General John W. Vessey after he took over as chairman of the Joint Chiefs of Staff was a memo (dated June 19, 1982) in which he urged Weinberger to tell the president that it would "be very unwise for the U.S. to find itself in a position where it had to put its forces between the Israelis and the Arabs." [16] But at the time, the precise mission of a peacekeeping force had not been defined. It was simply an idea that Reagan had approved "in principle," which enabled Haig to explore the proposal secretly with French Foreign Minister Claude Cheysson, who was receptive. Haig was no more eager than Vessey to interpose U.S. forces between the Israelis and the PLO. As Haig saw it, a multinational force should enter West Beirut, to which the Israelis had now cut off supplies of food, fuel and electricity, only after the PLO had been totally withdrawn and the Lebanese govern-ment was in charge of its own capital. The rub was finding a haven outside Lebanon for the PLO, which was as distrusted and feared by most of the Arab nations as it was by Israel. Arab leaders often cheered when the PLO conducted terrorist raids into Israel, but they balked at the prospect of becoming the permanent hosts for Yasir Arafat's forces.

The Arab League was meeting in Tunis, and Haig used the good offices of the Saudis in an attempt to persuade Syrian President Hafez Assad to accept the surrounded PLO forces. Haig made progress, but time was running out on him. The Israelis, determined to destroy the cornered PLO or at least to oust them from Lebanon, had resumed the attack on Beirut. Habib was striving to halt the fighting. U.S. commit-ment to participate in a peacekeeping force that would oversee removal of the PLO from Lebanon would give him leverage in the negotiations with the Israelis. He sent a cable to Washington explaining the situa-tion. "I had to get the PLO out of Lebanon and that was the only way I was going to get them out," Habib said afterward. "They weren't going to walk out under the guns of the Israelis. You're not going to get a multinational force if you're not prepared to put your own troops in." [17] Habib's proposal was relayed to Clark and Shultz in California, who discussed the idea in telephone conversations with Reagan at his ranch. The conversations were brief, but Reagan was impressed with the argument that U.S. commitment to a peacekeeping force would end

the fighting. On the evening of Friday, July 2, he approved U.S. participation in the multinational force. A White House official subsequently
told Herbert Denton of *The Washington Post* that Reagan had agreed
to the U.S. troop commitment because Habib believed the force was
necessary as a "bargaining chip" to resolve an impasse in negotiations.[18]

Reagan's commitment remained a secret until the following Tuesday,
July 6, when stories were leaked to Israeli newspapers in what some
NSC staffers saw as an attempt by Ariel Sharon to kill the plan.[19] Reagan
had returned to Los Angeles that day to give two speeches and meet
with the *Los Angeles Times* editorial board. With reporters clamoring
for an explanation of the Israeli press reports, he opened one of the
speeches by reading an announcement adopted from a passage in Habib's cable. Reagan said he had "agreed in principle to contribute a
small contingent of U.S. personnel, subject to certain conditions" to a
peacekeeping force in Lebanon.[20] The "certain conditions," part of the
deal worked out by Habib, included a request from the Lebanese government for the peacekeeping force, participation in it of at least one
other country and a time limit on the deployment. White House spokesman Larry Speakes predicted that the U.S. deployment would be "com-
paratively brief," probably no more than thirty days.

And so began the Reagan administration's commitment to send
troops to Lebanon, an obligation undertaken with even less debate
about long-term consequences than the decision made the previous
December to finance the Nicaraguan rebels. At least on the contra aid
decision Reagan and his principal advisers had assembled in a room
together to hear Casey's proposal and discuss overall administration
policy in Central America. In contrast, the agreement to deploy U.S.
troops in Lebanon was a tactical decision engineered by a hard-pressed
diplomat who was desperately trying to negotiate a cease-fire before a
weak and divided Lebanese government disintegrated. The decision
was ratified in a brief telephone conversation with Reagan at a time
when the United States was for all practical purposes without a secretary of state. Haig thought Reagan's announcement "ill-conceived," but
his views no longer mattered to the president.[21] On July 5, Shultz telephoned Haig from California to tell him that he was taking over as
acting secretary of state at Reagan's order. Haig insisted on hearing the
message firsthand, and Reagan called him from the ranch to say that
Shultz had spoken with his approval. Reagan remained on vacation until
July 11, when he returned to Washington.

Meanwhile, the U.S. decision was reverberating in world capitals.

The Soviets warned the United States not to send troops to Lebanon. France announced it would participate in the peacekeeping force. In Washington, Reagan's decision was greeted with cautious bipartisan support on Capitol Hill and an editorial in *The Washington Post* which declared that U.S. deployment "is a risky maneuver but one with enormous political potential."[22] The risks were more apparent than the potential to Senate Majority Leader Howard Baker of Tennessee, one of the few Republicans who was from the first opposed to sending U.S. Marines into Lebanon. "I have previously expressed my opposition to the use of American troops in Lebanon, and I've expressed that directly to the president," Baker said.[23]

But the decision had been made, at least in principle, and Weinberger and the chiefs were bound to support it. In the succeeding seven weeks before the first contingent of Marines arrived in Lebanon on August 25, Weinberger and Vessey struggled to define the U.S. mission as narrowly and specifically as possible. Habib meanwhile continued his negotiations. Shultz, who was confirmed by the Senate on July 15 and sworn in by Reagan the following day, devoted his energies to the Middle East proposal that the president would announce with considerable fanfare on September 1. But the Israelis were in no mood to wait. Beginning on July 21, Israeli planes bombed West Beirut for seven consecutive days, causing heavy civilian casualties. The carnage created by these bombings became a principal focus of the nightly news, much to the dismay of the White House staff. Later some would say that White House aides were motivated in their opposition to Begin and Sharon principally by their public relations consciousness. This was a factor, but more than public relations was involved.

The bombing of Beirut was one of those rare events during the Reagan presidency that produced an emotional reaction among White House aides that cut across the usual lines of pragmatist-conservative division. The conservatives in the White House speechwriting department, where Landon Parvin had quietly refused in June to write the welcoming remarks for Begin, were outraged. So was Mike Deaver, who usually stayed out of foreign policy discussions. But almost everyone in the White House wanted Reagan to "do something" about Begin, particularly after August 1, when a precarious Lebanese truce collapsed and Israel mounted its fiercest bombardment of Beirut since the invasion began.

On August 4, Israeli armored units rolled into West Beirut under cover of artillery fire. Reagan sent a sternly phrased message to Begin urging him to observe the truce. In response, Begin issued a statement declaring that Israeli forces would continue their attacks until the PLO had withdrawn from Lebanon. On August 12, Israeli planes bombed West Beirut for eleven consecutive hours. This was too much for Deaver, who told Reagan that he intended to resign, saying, "I can't be a part of this anymore, the bombings, the killing of children. It's wrong. And you're the one person on the face of the earth right now who can stop it. All you have to do is tell Begin you want it stopped."[24]

Reagan had been getting similar signals, expressed more diplomatically, from Shultz and Bill Clark. He had also been bothered by what he had seen on television after the bombings in Beirut. While usually hesitant to express himself personally to a foreign leader, Reagan on this occasion instructed his secretary to place a telephone call to Begin. And he allowed himself to become unusually emotional and angry. Geoffrey Kemp, the Oxford-educated head of the NSC Middle East section, had the responsibility of monitoring the Reagan-Begin conversation. He would remember it as the only time he heard Reagan express his feelings.

"Menachem, this is a holocaust," Reagan said.[25]

"Mr. President, I think I know what a holocaust is," Begin replied, in a voice that Kemp would recall as "dripping with sarcasm."[26] According to Deaver, Reagan continued "in the plainest of language" to tell Begin what he thought about the bombing of Beirut, concluding by saying, "It has gone too far. You must stop it."[27]

Twenty minutes later Begin called back and said he had issued the order to Sharon to stop the bombings. After he had hung up the phone Reagan said to Deaver, "I didn't know I had that kind of power."[28]

Reagan was less successful in resolving the conflicts that soon flared up again within his cabinet. While he had succeeded in speaking bluntly to Begin, he failed to exercise "that kind of power" within his cabinet. Reagan craved harmony and inevitably withdrew from conflicts among his advisers. In this respect he was a classic adult child of an alcoholic who had learned early in life to retreat from discord and unpleasantness. "Outside of his one outburst about Begin, I never heard him say anything," said Geoffrey Kemp. "This is what we couldn't understand. He'd come in with his riding gear on [Reagan often took Wednesday afternoons off to go riding] and not say anything. Not anything. He was John Wayne with his big bulging muscles, and he wouldn't say anything. I never saw him once raise his voice."[29]

Reagan's silence frequently baffled those who watched him operate in the confines of NSPG or National Security Council meetings. He gave few hints about what he felt or thought. Sometimes at the end of a meeting he would tell a joke or anecdote which, in Undersecretary of Defense Fred Iklé's words, "amazingly always had some connection with the meeting." [30] Aides who observed Reagan in these meetings disagreed among themselves on the reason he so rarely participated. Some believed that Reagan simply lacked sufficient knowledge of foreign affairs to join in the discussion, while others thought that he lacked the confidence to express himself. Iklé, among others, believed that Reagan deliberately sought to avoid prejudicing discussions by indicating his own views before everyone had spoken. This may have contributed to Reagan's reticence, although it does not fully explain why he so often kept his own counsel after his advisers had spoken.

Except on those rare occasions when he could resolve a contested issue by reliance on his ideological catechism, which was of little help in Lebanon, Reagan welcomed and needed the frank assessments of his cabinet members. He gave everyone a fair hearing and was unfailingly courteous in his treatment of subordinates. But those most familiar with Reagan's modes of behavior, particularly Deaver and Clark, recognized that he pulled back when members of his cabinet bickered or battled in his presence. He could deal with conflicting options but not with arguments in his presence. Whenever possible, Reagan wanted his national security adviser or his White House staff to produce an acceptable compromise that would end the argument. This trait inevitably invited middle-ground solutions aimed at mending differences, even in circumstances such as Lebanon where the middle ground courted catastrophe.

The Reagan administration's drift into dubious battle in Lebanon cannot be understood without an examination of the persistent conflict between Shultz and Weinberger, which for the better part of six years affected almost every phase of U.S. foreign policy. Those who observed the conflict at close hand differ in their assignment of fault but are nearly unanimous in believing that the struggles between these two powerful cabinet secretaries undermined policy coherence and wore down Reagan. It is natural and inevitable, of course, for secretaries of state and defense and their respective bureaucracies to disagree. Their responsibilities differ and they inevitably have different ways of looking at the world. Properly channeled, the State-Defense rivalry can be beneficial in exposing institutional assumptions and the range of options available to a president. But all presidents need help in sorting out these options. Reagan, who lacked the background or genuine interest in many foreign policy issues, required more assistance than most presidents and received far less. As we have seen, he lacked in his first term a national security adviser who combined knowledge of issues with the authority to broker a decision when Shultz and Weinberger disagreed. These two cabinet officers were stubborn and strong-willed, but they wielded enormous influence in part because there was such weakness at the center. This weakness was not readily apparent to the public because Reagan projected a decisive image of leadership. Those who saw the president at work in the Situation Room often held a different view. What they saw was a president who hated discord but lacked the means of achieving consensus. Too often, issues were discussed in terms of "keeping George happy" or of "finding a formula that Cap could accept." Too often, after decisions were made for any reason, Reagan did not follow through. Too often, Reagan was a performer and presidential leadership an empty shell.

No one, least of all Reagan, intended for this to happen. Reagan truly wanted to end the violence in Lebanon. He also believed that he had taken an important step in achieving cabinet harmony when he agreed to jettison Haig. This mistaken optimism was widely shared inside the administration and in the media, partly on the assumption that Shultz and Weinberger would work well together because they had been colleagues in the Nixon administration and at Bechtel. (Richard Perle recalls saying as much to Frank Carlucci, who told him this theory was "rubbish.")[31] Reagan seems to have had no inkling of the long rivalry between Shultz and Weinberger before they actually began arguing in front of him during cabinet meetings. As it turned out, the conflict between Shultz and Weinberger proved more enduring and certainly as damaging as Haig's frequent skirmishes with Weinberger and the White House staff. Haig was outmaneuvered almost from the start. Shultz and Weinberger were long-distance runners, exceptionally well matched as adversaries and experienced in the competitive ways of Washington. Both were capable, intelligent, opinionated, energetic and turf-conscious. Both had tempers that could unexpectedly erupt when they felt slighted or betrayed. Both recognized that Reagan did not want to give offense to either of them and took advantage of their high standing with the president in different ways. Weinberger's way was to dig in his heels and resist on trivial issues with the same tenacity he exhibited on matters of principle. Shultz, who knew that Reagan did not want to lose a second secretary of state, too readily threatened resignation when he thought himself circumvented.

Neither Shultz nor Weinberger made life easy for Reagan. Weinberger was convinced he knew what Reagan would do if left to his own instincts, and Shultz behaved as if he knew what was best for the president. But the self-indulgent scenes they staged in the president's presence did not bring out the best in Reagan. What Shultz and Weinberger most often did was encourage Reagan's tendency to withdraw. Instead of asking questions that he should have asked at a contentious meeting, Reagan often just wanted the meeting to end. One can hardly blame him, given this disconcerting example of pettiness that has survived in notes made by an administration official:

> SHULTZ: I wanted to give you a military opinion on this matter, Mr. President, but I couldn't get one. The secretary of defense wouldn't let me talk to the Joint Chiefs of Staff.
>
> WEINBERGER: You could come to me for the military opinion. My phone number's in the book.
>
> SHULTZ: I wanted another opinion.
>
> WEINBERGER: You could have called me and asked. As I said, my phone number's listed.[32]

The discussion continued in this vein for several minutes while aides looked away in embarrassment. Ken Adelman, whose account this is, compared the reactions of others in the room to the response in "a double-dating situation if the other couple started fighting about who should take out the garbage."[33] As usual, Reagan listened and said nothing.

Adelman's metaphor is apt. Shultz and Weinberger had been carrying on this way for so long that neither seems to have recognized how disconcerting their behavior was even to those who did not share Reagan's craving for harmony. In this, they indeed resembled an old couple who air ancient grievances in public, oblivious to the impact their feuding has on others. They had been doing this since the Nixon administration, when Shultz was director and Weinberger deputy director of the Office of Management and Budget. Carlucci, the No. 3 man, respected both of his superiors but could not stand their quarreling. During one argument in 1970, Carlucci recalls saying to Shultz and Weinberger in exasperation, "For God's sake, can't you two guys talk sensibly to each other?"[34]

The answer was usually no. "George put it very well to me at one point when he said that he was by nature analytic, and Cap was a position taker," Carlucci said. "Cap was very quick to take positions and George had a professorial background [and] liked to study all sides. Cap was a lawyer. George was not a lawyer. They tended to approach issues from very different perspectives."[35] McFarlane remembers Shultz once telling him of an occasion when Bechtel had been sued. Weinberger was convinced the corporation could win the lawsuit and wanted to fight it. He was dismayed when the president of the corporation told him he didn't want a lawsuit. Colin Powell, who worked for Weinberger and admired and also got on well with Shultz, thought that Shultz was "always looking for a solution."[36] In contrast, he found Weinberger reluctant to back away from any position he had taken, especially on Lebanon. Weinberger's approach, said Powell, was "all sails up, full speed ahead, where is the brick wall—I wish to run into it now, sir."[37]

The conflict was complicated by Weinberger's fascination with foreign policy and by Shultz's willingness to use military force in behalf of diplomatic objectives. The two men naturally wandered onto each other's turf, and Reagan unwittingly may have encouraged this tendency with the little speech he sometimes made instructing cabinet members to express opinions outside the domain of their expertise. After one discussion in which Shultz had expounded at length about the military situation, Reagan turned to Weinberger, who said, "Since the secretary of state has covered all the military aspects, I'm going to deal with foreign policy."[38]

Shultz and his aides were convinced that Weinberger wanted to be secretary of state. Weinberger and his team viewed Shultz as a World War II Marine who spoke out freely on military matters which he knew very little about and did not appreciate the constraints Vietnam had imposed on the use of U.S. forces. Vietnam was a shadow over Lebanon. "Weinberger was a lot like Reagan in that World War II was wonderful, all the soldiers were brave and honorable, all the sisters were virtuous and the American people were singing songs and honorable," said Powell, who was Weinberger's military aide when the Reagan administration launched its Lebanon intervention. "Then Vietnam, yuck, because these six tests had not been met with respect to vital interest, national purpose, people behind us and all of that. He [Weinberger] never wanted to ever preside over anything like a Vietnam involvement by U.S. forces, whereas George saw the U.S. forces as a

flexible tool of diplomacy. Why do we pay for all this stuff if we can
never use it short of World War III? The answer was somewhere [in]
between. Sure, use it if it's sensible and it'll serve a purpose. But Beirut
wasn't sensible and never did serve a purpose. It was goofy from the
beginning." [39]

Powell was a modern U.S. military man, enlightened by the grim
experience of Vietnam. He had a healthy respect for the roles that
Congress and the media performed in the U.S. political system and a
recognition that it was difficult to sustain any foreign military involvement unless it was understood and endorsed by the American people.
Few Americans understood the complexities of Lebanon or liked the
idea of putting American troops at risk there. "Lebanon is a harsh
teacher," wrote William Quandt. "Those who try to ignore its complex
realities, whether Israeli grand strategists, ill-informed optimists sitting
in Washington, or ambitious Lebanese politicians, usually end up paying a high price." [40]

But Reagan's optimism that a U.S. presence in Lebanon could make
a difference was widely shared in the month of achievement that followed his dramatic August 12, 1982, telephone call to Begin that
stopped the bombing of Beirut. Two days later Syria indicated willingness to withdraw its troops and the PLO guerrillas under its command
from Beirut. The following day the Israeli cabinet accepted Habib's
plan for a multinational force (MNF) that would oversee the expulsion
of the PLO from Lebanon. On August 21, 350 French paratroopers
arrived in West Beirut as the first element of this force and the first
PLO fighters left Lebanon. The French were soon joined by an Italian
military contingent. At dawn on August 25, 800 U.S. Marines landed in
Lebanon and were interposed between 30,000 Israeli troops and 15,000
Syrian and Palestinian soldiers. Despite the worries of the Joint Chiefs,
the MNF was welcomed by the people of Beirut, where peace reigned
briefly. The only gunfire during the next several weeks came from PLO
troops firing their weapons into the air. On August 23 the Christian
Phalangist leader Bashir Gemayel was elected president of Lebanon.

By September 1 the Reagan policy seemed a rousing success. The last
of the Syrian and Palestinian troops left West Beirut, enabling the
Lebanese government to take control. On the same day Reagan interrupted a seventeen-day vacation in California to make a nationally televised speech from the studios of KNBC in Burbank announcing the
Middle Eastern plan on which Shultz had labored since his appoint-

ment. Known as the "Reagan Plan," it marked the end of Haig's experiment of "strategic consensus" in the Middle East. The proposal sought to build on the success of the Camp David accords, in which Israel had exchanged captured land for peace with Egypt. The new plan made Jordan the focus. Palestinians would be given autonomy "in association with Jordan," and Israel would be required to return most of the territory captured in the 1967 Israeli-Arab War.

Reagan's speech was greeted warmly by moderate Arab leaders and glumly by Begin despite the president's promise to balance the desire of Palestinians for a homeland with Israeli security needs. King Hussein of Jordan hailed the speech as "the most courageous stand taken by an American administration since 1956," and Egypt's Hosni Mubarak also reacted positively. Reagan seemed to have made a good effort in following up on the promise of the Camp David accords with a proposal that he acknowledged had been delayed because "the conflict in Lebanon preempted our efforts." But the speech, crafted largely by Shultz, made the mistake of assuming that this conflict had been resolved. "The Lebanon war, tragic as it was, has left us with a new opportunity for Middle East peace," Reagan said.

Ten days later, on September 10, the U.S. Marines were evacuated from Lebanon to their ships, despite the misgivings of Shultz and Habib. Weinberger, supported by Vessey and the chiefs, convinced Reagan that the Marines should be withdrawn on grounds they had accomplished their primary mission of evacuating the PLO. Reagan gave no hint of the profound disagreement within his administration when he announced the withdrawal to reporters on the afternoon of September 8 after meeting with Shultz and Habib. Typically, Reagan read from notes that had been prepared for him by the NSC staff, saying that the withdrawal showed he was "keeping our commitment to have them out within thirty days."[41] He declined to answer questions, dashed off to give a speech on the balanced-budget amendment and turned the briefing over to Habib. France and Italy quickly followed the U.S. lead, bringing out their own MNF contingents. Then disaster struck.

On September 14, nine days before he was to assume the presidency of Lebanon, Christian leader Bashir Gemayel was speaking at the local office of his Phalangist Party in East Beirut when a powerful bomb exploded, killing him and destroying the building. On September 15, Israeli troops entered West Beirut in force, violating the agreement under which the PLO had been evacuated. The Israelis claimed they were acting to protect Palestinian civilians from revenge at the hands of Gemayel's militia. Instead, the militia entered the Palestinian refugee camps at Sabra and Shatila and massacred more than 700 people, many of them women, children and babes in arms. The slaughter continued for two days without intervention from the Israelis. The pictures of the victims, some of them mutilated, shocked the world, provoking comparisons to Nazi atrocities and demands for Begin's resignation even from some of Israel's staunchest supporters in the United States. In Connecticut, a middle-aged Jewish attorney who said he had defended Israel "in every way imaginable all my life" arose during a public meeting with a Democratic political candidate to denounce the "genocide" of Sabra and Shatila and demand an end to U.S. aid to Israel.[42] PLO leader Yasir Arafat, in Rome, called upon the MNF to return to Beirut. In the Knesset, Labor Party leader Shimon Peres declared that "this abominable act" had left Israel in "moral ruins." In ruins also was Reagan administration policy in Lebanon.

Reagan spent the weekend of September 18–19 at the White House, closeted in the family quarters and watching in horror the television accounts of Sabra-Shatila while his advisers blamed the Israelis and each other for what had happened. The White House press office issued a brief statement in Reagan's name expressing the president's "outrage and revulsion over the murders." Weinberger was on the defensive. Shultz, Habib and the NSC staff were convinced that premature withdrawal of the Marines had created the conditions for Gemayel's assassination and the killings in the camps. Habib had pledged to Arafat that the United States would guarantee the safety of the Palestinians in West Beirut. "The Italian force was right outside those camps," Habib said. "The Phalange troops would never have moved in there if the MNF had remained."[43] Kemp, who was on vacation that weekend, subsequently pointed out that "it was our allies, the Israelis, who permitted the massacre to happen, and it was our boy Bashir Gemayel's troops that did the killing."[44] The reference to "our boy" was literally true: as Bob Woodward reported in *Veil,* Gemayel was a longtime "asset" that the Central Intelligence Agency had shared with its Israeli counterpart, the Mossad. When Weinberger called on Gemayel in Lebanon a few days before his assassination, Gemayel told him that Lebanon should become "the 51st state."[45]

The chiefs were opposed to the second deployment, as they had been to the first. While Vessey was sickened by the massacres, he contended that Lebanon was "the wrong place" for U.S. troops to be engaged.

Shultz favored sending the Marines back into Lebanon. Howard Teicher, the NSC action officer for the Middle East that weekend with Kemp away on vacation, remembers that "everyone," including Clark, seemed to think that sending the Marines back into Lebanon "was the right thing to do."[46] The "everyone" did not include Weinberger. "A lot of people were saying that if the Marines hadn't been taken out, Gemayel wouldn't have been assassinated," Weinberger recalled. "I thought that was nonsense."[47] But Weinberger had lost Reagan's ear the weekend after Sabra-Shatila. "I think the president was impressed with the argument that [sending the Marines back in] was a way to preserve stability and get his peace plan adopted," Weinberger said.[48]

Reagan announced the formation of what he called a "new multinational force" in a televised speech on September 20, saying that "the scenes that the whole world witnessed this past weekend were among the most heart-rending in the long nightmare of Lebanon's agony. . . . There are actions we can and must take to bring that nightmare to an end." U.S. goals were now "the restoration of a strong and central government" in Lebanon and the removal of all foreign forces. "With the expected cooperation of all parties the multinational force will return to Beirut for a limited period of time," Reagan said. "Its purpose is not to act as a police force, but to make it possible for the lawful authorities of Lebanon to discharge those duties for themselves." The "limited period of time" was expected to be sixty days, which was the figure used by Vessey in his instructions to European commanders who were providing men and materiel for the deployment. "We figured that once we got over our feeling of guilt and a little bit of law and order was established, the Marines would be withdrawn," Vessey said. "I guess that was the fundamental wrong assumption in Lebanon—that things were going to get better."[49]

And things did get better, at first. On September 20, Bashir Gemayel's older brother Amin was unanimously elected president of Lebanon. It was a rare display of unity for a parliament divided along religious lines, but Geoffrey Kemp saw it as "more an act of desperation than resolve."[50] Amin lacked his brother's popularity, and was widely viewed as a weak and inexperienced leader who was heavily dependent on his Christian advisers and the United States. The violence nonetheless subsided in the months after his election. "Because of the traumas of the past six years and the special horrors of the past summer, Lebanese politicians of all confessions seemed prepared to give Amin a chance, at least for a few months or so," said Kemp.[51] The Syrians and the

Israelis also gave Amin a chance, more out of necessity than of choice. Syria's air force had been nearly destroyed. Israel remained militarily strong, but the Sabra-Shatila killings had destroyed the national consensus that had supported the invasion since the announcement of Operation Peace in Galilee.

The Reagan administration was unable to take advantage of this time of opportunity. While violence took a brief holiday in Lebanon, the divided factions within the U.S. government resumed their intramural warfare. Shultz and Habib focused on attempts to obtain an Israeli-Lebanese agreement that they thought would lead to withdrawal of all foreign forces from Lebanon. Weinberger urged U.S. pressure on Israel to make a unilateral withdrawal, using the veiled threat of a denial of U.S. arms. The NSC staff, in a proposal first advanced by Kemp and Teicher and later supported by McFarlane and Clark, called for a more ambitious U.S. policy in which the MNF would have assumed a greatly expanded peacekeeping role in Lebanon. This bold idea was opposed by the Pentagon because it would have required the use of U.S. Army divisions in addition to the Marines. And it was opposed by Habib on grounds that a larger U.S. presence would complicate the negotiations. Politically, this idea was a nonstarter. Although Tip O'Neill provided strong bipartisan support for the Lebanon involvement, congressional skepticism was increasing. But because of fear that violence would flare again if the Marines were withdrawn, Reagan kept them in Lebanon, interposed between the Israeli and Syrian armies in an ill-defined mission. "I suspect that one of the reasons it was hard to win the argument to withdraw them was that everyone said, look what happened when they went out," said Weinberger.[52] In the meantime the Soviet Union resupplied Syrian air defenses and sent the Syrians new surface-to-air missiles to replace the ones destroyed by the Israelis. U.S.-Israeli relations reached a low point that did not improve until early February 1983, when Sharon was dismissed as defense minister as a result of an Israeli commission's investigation of the Sabra-Shatila massacres. He was replaced by Moshe Arens, a popular former ambassador to Washington. But by then, the time of U.S. opportunity in Lebanon had passed.

Violence returned to Lebanon on April 18, 1983, when a delivery van filled with explosives detonated on the grounds of the U.S. embassy on Beirut's waterfront. The midsection of this horseshoe-shaped, eight-story building collapsed, killing sixty-three people, including seventeen Americans. One of the dead was Robert C. Ames, the chief CIA analyst of Middle Eastern affairs, who was convening a meeting of CIA officials when the explosives went off. All eight CIA officials were killed. Ames was highly respected throughout the CIA, and his counsel was valued by Casey and by Shultz. His death cost the Reagan administration— and the Marines in Lebanon—an irreplaceable intelligence resource at the very time that his skills and store of information were most critically needed.

Accurate intelligence is always a precious commodity in the Middle East. It was particularly important during this period because of radical changes in the balance of forces that threatened all Americans, military and civilian, who remained in Lebanon. After the Israeli invasion in 1982, Syrian ruler Hafez Assad had allowed units of the Iranian Revolutionary Guards into the Bekaa Valley, where they established a headquarters in the dusty fortified city of Baalbek. They served as a link to radical factions of Shiites, the most rapidly growing sect in Lebanon and the one most underrepresented in the government. These radical Shiites, especially the faction known as Hezbollah (Party of God), were more of a potential menace to the United States than the expelled PLO, which had been honeycombed with informants for the CIA and Mossad. Hezbollah was relatively invulnerable to penetration by Western intelligence agencies. The destruction of the U.S. embassy was seen in retrospect as a signal that the holy war declared against America by Shiites in Iran four years earlier had been extended to Lebanon. At the time, however, it seemed a more isolated terrorist calamity, one that Shultz vowed would not deter the U.S. effort to obtain a peaceful settlement in Lebanon.

The chief obstacle to such a peaceful settlement was Syria, although neither Habib nor Shultz seemed to recognize the depth or consequences of Syria's opposition. Israeli intelligence had traced the murder of Bashir Gemayel to Syria.[53] And U.S. intelligence intercepts analyzed after the bombing of the embassy showed that Shiite terrorists in Lebanon were directed by the Iranian Foreign Ministry and the Iranian Revolutionary Guards, operating out of Baalbek. Palestinian suspects, one of them an embassy employee, were rounded up by the Lebanese government and a CIA official after the bombing of the embassy. They were tortured into confessions and implicated a Syrian intelligence officer, who had wired the explosives in the delivery van. U.S. intelligence officials thought it unlikely that such an operation could have been launched from Syrian-controlled territory with Syrian participation without the knowledge of Assad or at least of his brother Rifaat, who headed the Syrian intelligence services. But the evidence was circumstantial, and Syria denied any involvement. Neither Reagan nor Shultz made an issue of it.

The Reagan administration did something worse than ignore Syrian-sponsored terrorism. It essentially ignored Syria, which historically claimed hegemony over Lebanon. "Of all the misjudgments made by the Reagan administration concerning Lebanon, those involving Syria were the most consequential," observed Quandt. "Here policy makers seemed to fall victim to their own rhetorical flourishes—Soviet arms had been defeated by American arms, therefore 'radicals' were in disarray and 'moderates' would be emboldened—and to a heavy dose of wishful thinking."[54] Syria had been invited into Lebanon in 1975, with tacit U.S. and Israeli support, to protect Christians who were being killed in the civil war. A settlement in Lebanon was impossible without Syrian concurrence, a point made in White House meetings by Kemp and McFarlane on behalf of the NSC staff, and also by Weinberger. But the NSC staff and the Pentagon approached the issue from opposite directions. McFarlane and Kemp favored an expanded military role in Lebanon, while the Pentagon opposed a U.S. military presence altogether.

These conflicting advocacies strengthened Shultz's hand, for Reagan always preferred to opt for what seemed the middle ground when confronted with complexities that could not be resolved ideologically. Reagan recognized that the Middle East peace plan he had unveiled the previous September had little chance of success as long as Israeli forces remained in Lebanon, a point frequently driven home by Shultz. So it is not surprising that Reagan followed Shultz's lead and focused on Israel to the exclusion of Syria, a nation about which he knew next to nothing. After the bombing of the U.S. embassy, Reagan also embraced Shultz's argument that the United States should not allow itself to be driven out of Lebanon by terrorism. When the bodies of sixteen of the Americans who had been killed in the embassy were returned to Andrews Air Force Base on April 23, Reagan rededicated himself to the Lebanon commitment. "These gallant Americans understood the danger they faced, and yet they went willingly to Beirut," Reagan said. "And the dastardly deed, the act of unparalleled cowardice that took their lives, was an attack on all of us, on our way of life and on the values we hold dear. We would indeed fail them if we let that act deter us from carrying on their mission of brotherhood and peace."

Shultz was soon in the Middle East, completing the negotiations begun by Habib for an accord between Israel and Lebanon that they hoped would result in withdrawal of all foreign forces from Lebanon. The key provision of the agreement required all Israeli troops to pull out within eight to twelve weeks, provided all Syrian forces also left the country. The plan was approved by Gemayel on May 4 and "in principle" by the Israeli Knesset on May 6. Then, and only then, did Shultz go to Damascus, to show the completed accord to President Assad. Speaking through an interpreter, Shultz explained the provisions of the agreement and of "side letters" between Israel and Lebanon in which Begin made it clear that the Israelis would not withdraw unless the Syrians did. Assad told Shultz bluntly that this meant the plan was dead, because he had no intention of withdrawing Syrian troops from Lebanon.[55] Geoffrey Kemp was surprised that Shultz was surprised by Assad's response. The Syrians had made known their objections to the plan. They objected, after being invited into Lebanon in 1975, to being treated as "co-equal" invaders with the Israelis. And they objected to rewarding Israel for its invasion with the strengthening of a Christian government that was unresponsive to the demands of the Muslim majority. "The overwhelming information from intelligence was that the May 17 agreement wouldn't work," said Kemp. "The CIA had it right. Why was Shultz impervious to that?"[56] Kemp's answer to his own question is that Lebanon was really Shultz's first foray into international relations and that it became for him "a brutal learning experience, a baptism by fire."[57] *

Even though the Syrian response had rendered the agreement essentially meaningless, it was signed by Israel and Lebanon on May 17, becoming known thereafter as the May 17 agreement. Weinberger met Shultz in Paris on his return from the Middle East and in a private conversation told him that he thought the agreement was worthless. "George thought [the agreement] was the greatest thing since sliced bread," said Weinberger. "It was nothing, not even an agreement. It gave the Syrians a veto power, and they exercised it. From then on, I argued that the Marines should be brought back to the ships."[59]

But the secretary of defense was not persuasive with the president. Weinberger had frequently waved the flag in behalf of defense spending proposals that David Stockman and the White House staff considered

---

* Shultz says the Syrians were left out of the negotiations because they wanted to be left out of them on grounds that they considered Lebanon part of Syria. He quotes Assad as saying to him, "We don't have an embassy in Lebanon. We never have, because you don't have an embassy in Chicago." This, said Shultz, "was a very revealing kind of comment by Assad."[58]

outrageous. Reagan had always sided with Weinberger in these con-flicts, saying that the United States must do whatever was necessary to maintain national security. Now, with Shultz and later McFarlane mak-ing patriotism the test of the U.S. commitment in Lebanon, Weinberger was on the losing side of the national security argument. "He [Reagan] was being told all this stuff," Weinberger said. "Marines don't cut and run. Americans don't run when the going gets tough. Americans don't pull down the flag. I said, 'Nonsense, they're not doing any good over there,' but these arguments appealed to the president." [60]

As spring wore into summer, Syrian hostility to the May 17 agreement increased. "By July it was clear that without some level of cooperation from Syria there was no hope of reconciling the various conflicts be-tween the Lebanese confessional groups, especially the rivalry between the Druze and the Maronites in the Shuf Mountains," said Kemp. [61] The Druze, a fiercely independent sect that broke off from the main body of Islam during the eleventh century, held the high ground overlooking Beirut. The only force between them and Muslim militias opposed to the Gemayel government in West Beirut was the Israelis.

Shultz returned to Beirut on July 5 in an effort to bolster the Leba-nese government. Amin Gemayel was now viewed as a weak and divi-sive leader. The various Muslim factions had withdrawn their support for him after it became clear that Gemayel was intent on maintaining the domination of the Christian minority in the government. And the more Gemayel depended upon the United States for support, the more the U.S. Marines were seen by the Muslim majority as the soldiers of the enemy. That was not what Shultz had envisioned when the May 17 agreement was signed. He had expected the Lebanese government to grow stronger, with the Lebanese Armed Forces gradually replacing the MNF as the troops that kept order in Beirut. But the Lebanese Army had been virtually destroyed in the 1975 civil war, and U.S. efforts to rebuild it into an effective fighting force were unsuccessful. The divi-sions that plagued the rest of Lebanon also afflicted the Lebanese Army, whose Muslim members were reluctant to take up arms against militias of their own faith. Increasingly, the Israelis found themselves cast in the role of keeping peace among the Druze, the Christian militias and the Lebanese Army, which, as Kemp dryly observed, was "not a role that Israel had in mind when the May 17 agreement with Gemayel was reached." [62] In contrast to the militance that had prevailed a year earlier, Israeli public opinion had turned against the war.

Shultz went from Beirut to Damascus on July 6, once more to confront his nemesis Assad. The Syrian leader was "calm and reasoned in his approach to the U.S. delegation."[63] Syria is not a democracy, and Assad's rule is not based on the consent of the governed. In February 1982 he had brutally suppressed a Muslim fundamentalist revolt in Hama, where an estimated 30,000 people were killed. Assad realized that neither the Israelis nor the United States would accept the casualties necessary to remain a military presence in Lebanon. Late that summer, Syrian Foreign Minister Halim Abdul Khaddam would predict to his Lebanese counterpart, Elie Salam, that the United States would withdraw after it had lost a few Marines.[64]

Reagan was not considering withdrawal. He did not recognize that the Marines were in extreme danger, and he was then under no particular political pressure to bring them home, even though they had been deployed in Lebanon for nearly a year on their ill-defined mission. Lebanon had become such a back-burner issue that the subject had not even been raised at the president's June 28 news conference. On the rare occasions when questions about the Marine role arose at White House or State Department briefings, they were brushed aside with the formula answer that the Marines were participants in a multinational force that was keeping peace and order in Lebanon. And that was how Reagan thought of them. On August 15, en route to a vacation at his Santa Barbara ranch, Reagan told the national convention of the Veterans of Foreign Wars in New Orleans that "whatever progress we've made [in Lebanon] is largely due to our Marines, who along with peacekeeping troops from France and Italy are striving to give Lebanon a chance to pull itself together." On August 23 in Seattle, where he interrupted his vacation to address the American Legion convention, Reagan said that the presence of the MNF "strengthens the resolve of the Lebanese government to assume the tough task of maintaining order."

These statements were boilerplate, routinely crafted by White House speechwriters working from State Department guidance and inserted into speeches that focused on the renewal of American confidence and military prowess. ("As a nation, we've closed the books on a long, dark period of failure and self-doubt and set a new course," Reagan said in Seattle, where he also declared, "Our military forces are back on their feet and standing tall.") In the summer of 1983 Reagan was far less focused on Lebanon than he had been a year earlier when the televised accounts of the bombardment of Beirut had commanded his attention. While optimistic about the eventual outcome, Reagan did not pretend to understand the baffling intricacies of the many-sided Lebanese conflict. On this, he had plenty of company within the administration. Weinberger once counted twenty-six different armed groups in Lebanon. He thought the situation hopeless, and said so. Even Kemp, the Middle East expert at NSC, was finding it difficult to keep up with the conflicting reports that were coming in from the field. "We were all struggling in the dark," he said. "The president had pretty good practical instincts, but there was so much indecision in the administration, so much conflict between State and Defense. The net result of that indecision was chaos." [65]

This indecision and conflict periodically required Reagan to appease disgruntled members of his official family, casting him in a managerial role that he disliked and in which he was rarely successful. The member of the team most out of sorts in the summer of 1983 was Shultz, who suspected Clark of pursuing a separate foreign policy in Central America and the Middle East, sometimes in concert with Weinberger or Bill Casey. Late in July, Shultz read in *The New York Times* that the Pentagon was planning military maneuvers off the coast of Honduras intended to intimidate the Sandinistas. On August 1, *Time* featured Clark on its cover against a background of Central America with bold letters that proclaimed "The Big Stick Approach." Fifteen pages into the story was a sidebar on Shultz headed "Disappearing Act on Foggy Bottom" that included a picture of Shultz with a caption saying, "Too reticent to take control." Two days later I wrote an article in *The Washington Post* describing Clark as "the strong man of President Reagan's many-sided policy in Central America." [66] The message of these stories upset Shultz, who said he was bothered even more when he learned that Clark had in July sent McFarlane on an independent mission to Saudi Arabia, Syria, Israel, Jordan and Egypt.* Shultz called the White House and asked for a meeting with the president. With Clark, Baker and other aides looking on, Shultz told Reagan that he was resigning.

"Mr. President, you don't need a guy like me for secretary of state if that's the way things are going to be done," Shultz said. [67]

"No, I want you to be secretary of state," the president replied. [68]

---

* According to McFarlane, the dates of the trip were July 11–14, 1983. He flew in a Gulfstream jet owned by Prince Bandar, the Saudi ambassador to the United States, who accompanied him on the mission. Some accounts of this trip have said McFarlane went to Lebanon. McFarlane says he did not but that Wadia Haddad, the foreign policy adviser to the Lebanese president, accompanied the party on its mission after boarding on a refueling stop in London.

According to Shultz, Reagan then asked him for suggestions to improve the process. Shultz suggested regular meetings with Reagan, "just us." * Reagan agreed. This account is bluntly disputed by Clark, who said that Shultz already had private access to the president and had been informed of McFarlane's mission in advance. In fact, said Clark, the McFarlane trip was proposed by Shultz. "I didn't want to lose him [McFarlane] at that time," said Clark. "I needed his expertise, and his trip to the Middle East was a loss to me. Of course George knew." [70] The principal purpose of McFarlane's mission was to find out if Syria was still willing to hold discussions with a U.S. negotiator. Philip Habib had been declared persona non grata [PNG] in Syria in the wake of the May 17 agreement. "We wanted to find out if we were PNG'd as a country or whether this applied only to Habib," said McFarlane. [71] As it turned out, Assad spent three and one-half hours talking to McFarlane, much of it a long, rambling monologue by the Syrian leader about the Bermuda Triangle and the influence of supernatural and extraterrestrial forces on human events. [72] But Assad also made it clear that a U.S. envoy would be welcomed in Damascus, as long as it wasn't Habib.

Habib resigned as Middle East envoy without argument, realizing that he could no longer function in the region if Syria found him unacceptable. Clark proposed McFarlane as his replacement, and the idea was promptly endorsed by Shultz. Reagan announced the appointment of McFarlane as special envoy on July 21, the same day he met with Amin Gemayel at the White House and affirmed his support for the government of Lebanon. By the time of Shultz's attempted resignation on August 4, McFarlane and Geoffrey Kemp were back in the Middle East trying to negotiate withdrawal of foreign forces from Lebanon.

The contradictory accounts offered by Shultz and Clark about their communication prior to McFarlane's mission are unresolvable by Reagan's memory or any written record of which I am aware. They are illustrative of the obstacles facing historians of the Reagan presidency and also of the problems faced by a president who was often so detached from foreign policy that he functioned only as an occasional

---

* Shultz says that he soon afterward suggested that these "just us" sessions also include the national security adviser. According to Shultz, he wanted the national security adviser in the meeting because "lots of people in the White House nominated themselves" to serve as his channel to Reagan. Shultz said he thought that "multiple channels" between the president and the secretary of state was a bad idea and that his channel was the national security adviser. [69]

court of last resort. Reagan invested enormous responsibility in his secretaries of state and usually sought to appease them when they became unhappy. But Reagan's detachment provided an opportunity, bordering on an invitation, for the secretary of state's adversaries to circumvent him. Shultz's rivals justified their actions by saying that he often pursued his own policy goals instead of the president's. But it was often unclear, except in the most general of terms, what "Reagan's policy" was in any given situation since his indirect management and frequent silences encouraged all parties to believe that the president was siding with them.

Although Shultz was sufficiently prudent to avoid blaming Reagan for this state of affairs, he considered the foreign policy process a "disgrace."[73] He had also come to share the Baker-Deaver view that Clark was a schemer who encouraged Reagan to take an ideological and sometimes adventuresome approach to foreign policy. For their part, Clark, Weinberger and rank-and-file White House conservatives viewed Shultz as a prima donna who talked a good game about foreign policy processes while actually relying on Deaver and the first lady to get his way with the president. Shultz's adversaries complained that he rarely convened interagency meetings to resolve conflicts and said he took advantage of Reagan's obvious reluctance to risk the uproar that would be caused by the loss of a second secretary of state.

The widely held view that Shultz was a great compromiser and that Weinberger and Clark were militant, uncompromising conservatives had considerable relevance to the arms control debate and some application to Central America. But these stereotypes did not fit the circumstances of Lebanon, the involvement in which American military men were most directly at risk. Weinberger and the chiefs were convinced that Shultz and his diplomats were blind to the dangers of allowing the Marines to remain in the hostile environment of Lebanon. Clark, who was close to Weinberger, was increasingly supportive of the military assessment that the risks required removal of the Marines. According to Weinberger, it was Clark who first proposed the formula that the Marines should be "redeployed" to ships offshore, enabling advocates of a pullout to make a semantic distinction between "withdrawal" and "redeployment" when they presented their case to Reagan. To Shultz, an ex-Marine whose stubbornness was a match for Weinberger's, the chiefs were cautious doves willing to take flight at the first signs of a storm. Shultz wanted the Marines to stay in Lebanon as participants in the MNF, despite Syrian refusal to accept the May 17 agreement. And, in one of those odd alliances that so frequently confused the plot lines of administration policy, McFarlane sided on this crucial issue with the secretary of state against Clark and Weinberger. While Reagan was talking Shultz out of resigning, McFarlane was already in Lebanon attempting to persuade Gemayel and Walid Jumblatt, the leader of the Druze, to allow the Lebanese Army to gradually replace Israeli forces in the Shuf Mountains overlooking Beirut. But by then, the Marines were no longer the peacekeepers that Reagan and Shultz believed them to be. Instead, they had become targets. As Weinberger would later put it, they were "sitting right in the middle of the bull's-eye."[74]

When the Marines had returned to Lebanon late in 1982, they were welcomed by the various Muslim groups, including the Shiites, who had been among the victims of the Sabra-Shatila killings. But in July and August of 1983 the Marines were increasingly viewed as a prop for the Gemayel government. On July 22 the Beirut International Airport was shelled by Druze mortar and artillery fire that wounded three Marines and temporarily closed the airport. The following day Walid Jumblatt announced the formation of a "National Salvation Front" opposed to the May 17 agreement. The Druze, supported by the Syrians, were now fighting both the Christian militia of Gemayel and the Lebanese Army, which was supported by the U.S. government and bolstered by Marine patrols. Meanwhile, the prominent Shiite group known as Amal (an acronym for "Movement of the Disinherited") was battling the Lebanese Army in the Beirut suburbs.

Marines positioned at the airport came under increasing mortar and rocket fire. On August 28 the Marines returned the fire for the first time. The next day two Marines were killed in a mortar attack and Marine artillery silenced a Druze battery in the mountains. On August 31 the Lebanese Army swept through West Beirut, driving out Amal. The Marines were now regarded as the enemy of the people they had come to save. On September 1, Amal leader Nabih Berri said that the Marines had "turned into a fighting force against Muslims in Lebanon."[75] Jumblatt declared in Damascus the same day that "the mere fact that they [the Marines] are providing the Lebanese factional army with logistic support, expertise and training is enough for us to consider them enemies."[76]

The wheel had now come full circle for the Marines and the MNF of which they were the most vital component. The Marines had returned to Lebanon a year earlier because the Israelis were occupying Beirut while their allies, the Christian militia loyal to Gemayel, were killing

Muslims. Now, the Israeli forces were operating under the direction of the realistic Arens instead of the intransigent Sharon. The Israeli people wanted their troops home, and Arens was determined to withdraw them —or at least to move them to safer military positions—by the Jewish New Year in early September. The United States, which in 1982 could not convince the Israelis to leave Lebanon, could not in 1983 persuade them to stay. But the Israeli withdrawal posed a clear danger to the Marines. When Israeli troops pulled back from their strategic positions in the heights overlooking Beirut to a southern defense line behind the Awali River, it was inevitable that the positions they had abandoned would be occupied by the rival militias. Weinberger, the chiefs and the Marine commanders on the ground perceived this danger and expressed their concerns to the White House. Seldom have U.S. policymakers had a more appropriate opportunity to follow the famous advice attributed to Senator George Aiken of Vermont during the Vietnam War: "Declare victory and get out." [77] But Reagan and Shultz were no longer focused on what was happening in Lebanon. Instead, with Reagan still vacationing at his ranch, they were trying to deal with the crisis caused by the Soviet downing of KAL 007 on September 1.

U.S. policy in Lebanon, largely determined in the field by Habib during the critical period a year earlier, now passed during an equally crucial time into the hands of McFarlane and the NSC staff. Like Shultz, he was a former combat Marine who believed in the legitimacy of U.S. military power to accomplish diplomatic objectives. But unlike either Shultz or Habib in the months preceding the May 17 agreement, McFarlane had limited authority to do what he thought needed to be done. Realizing that the situation would become untenable for the Marines after the Israelis withdrew, McFarlane favored the time-honored military solution of taking the high ground. He wanted the Marines to accompany the untried Lebanese Army into the Shuf Mountains and occupy the positions the Israelis were preparing to vacate. He also requested that naval forces off the Lebanese coast be reinforced with the battleship *New Jersey* and its 16-inch guns. The president himself was in awe of the firepower of the *New Jersey,* which was capable of hurling 2,000-pound projectiles ("the size of Volkswagens," Reagan would sometimes say) a distance of more than twenty miles. Weinberger and the chiefs readily agreed to send the battleship to Lebanese waters, where it would arrive on September 26. But the Pentagon rejected McFarlane's request to allow the Marines to help the Lebanese Army occupy the Israeli positions in the mountains, fearing this would simply widen U.S. participation in the war. After the Israelis withdrew on September 4, two more Marines were killed in a barrage of Druze artillery fire. Amidst reports that the Druze and the Christian militiamen were conducting mutual massacres in towns in the Shuf Mountains, the Lebanese Army advanced cautiously into the foothills.

As McFarlane had feared, the 24th Marine Amphibious Unit stationed at the Beirut airport came under constant indirect fire in the wake of the Israeli withdrawal. Colonel Timothy Geraghty, the battalion commander, sent a situation report warning that "the stakes are being raised weekly" and declaring that "our contribution to peace in Lebanon since 22 July stands at four killed and twenty-eight wounded." [78] Within a week of the Israeli pullout a force of 2,500 Druze militiamen, supported by a few hundred Palestinians and Iranian Revolutionary Guards and Syrian artillery, had occupied most of the high ground overlooking the airport. Facing the Druze in the market town of Souk al Garb on a nearby ridge was the 8th Brigade of the Lebanese Army, an inexperienced force of comparable size. On September 10 the Druze force attacked a company of this brigade, killing seven and wounding forty. One of the dead was the company commander, who was hacked to pieces by axes in an incident that U.S. advisers later concluded was intended to terrorize the Lebanese Army. The attack also had a profound impact on McFarlane, who was sequestered with Kemp and other members of his staff at the U.S. ambassador's residence in the Beirut hills, only three miles from the fighting. The ferocity of the attack and the method used to kill the company commander reminded McFarlane of terrorist attacks committed by Communist forces in Vietnam. He was worried about the morale of the remaining companies of the 8th Brigade and about what might happen to the U.S. Marines if the Lebanese were routed. And he was frustrated that the Lebanese Army was undergoing its trial by fire alone, without the assistance of American military power. McFarlane believed that the situation could be saved if the president changed the rules of engagement governing U.S. forces in Lebanon to permit U.S. destroyers offshore to fire their 5-inch guns in support of the Lebanese Army in Souk al Garb.

This was another turning point for the United States in Lebanon. Like Habib a year earlier after the killings in the Sabra and Shatila refugee camps, McFarlane believed that the answer to instability and conflict in Lebanon was the prompt and forceful intervention of the United States. McFarlane dictated a cable—later described as "the-sky-is-falling" cable—to the White House saying that the government of

Lebanon was "threatened with impending takeover by an uncivilized foreign force." He emphasized the savagery of the attack on the Lebanese Army, which he said "included ax fighting and hand-to-hand fighting of a brutality equal to the worst atrocities of Vietnam." Though his account was subsequently disputed, McFarlane maintained in his cable that no Lebanese had participated in the attack on the Lebanese Army brigade, which he said was conducted by "a PLA [Palestine Liberation Army] brigade and Iranian elements."[79] This presentation was calculated to convince Clark, and through him Reagan, that the war in Lebanon was a struggle between Lebanese and outside terrorists who were supported and armed by the Soviets. This was a persuasive if not entirely accurate contention, and McFarlane was able to reinforce it through his direct satellite access to Clark in the Situation Room of the White House. Later, Clark would recall hearing shellfire in the background as McFarlane spoke to him. Clark was impressed with McFarlane's bravery and with his argument.[80] On September 11, a Sunday, Clark and members of the NSC staff debated McFarlane's request in the Situation Room.[81] There were telephone conferences with Shultz and Weinberger. Through the Joint Chiefs, Reagan near the end of the day transmitted an order allowing the use of naval artillery fire and air strikes to support the Lebanese Army. As usual, the chiefs were not enthusiastic. As a concession to the Pentagon, the order said that "nothing in this message shall be construed as changing the mission for the U.S. multinational force."

This order was a contradiction in terms, as Colonel Geraghty realized. In *Best Laid Plans: The Inside Story of America's War Against Terrorism,* David C. Martin and John Walcott quote Mark Gatanas, who was McFarlane's military aide, as saying that the NSC officials had overreacted and that Geraghty held "the most realistic perspective."[82] Geraghty realized that U.S. bombing or shelling of Druze positions would make the Marines full-fledged participants in the Lebanese war. He resisted for a week, using the new authority granted him in the presidential response to McFarlane's cable. The Lebanese Army continued to occupy Souk al Garb, despite McFarlane's warning on September 11 that it might not last the night. But the 8th Brigade was under heavy pressure from the Druze and Palestinian forces. On September 19, Geraghty finally yielded to the entreaties of Lebanese Army commanders and McFarlane and ordered a bombardment of the Souk al Garb ridgeline. The fire restored the shaky morale of the 8th Brigade, which held the town. It also ended any pretense that the Marines remained a neutral, peacekeeping force in Lebanon.

. . .

Here was another moment when the Reagan administration might have declared victory and withdrawn. But instead of trying to extricate the Marines safely from Lebanon, key White House officials once more expended their energies in internecine conflict. The conflict was triggered by news reports about the president's order permitting the Marines to call in artillery fire and aerial bombardment against the Druze positions. The order was first disclosed by NBC correspondent Chris Wallace in the network's nightly news on September 12. The lead story in *The Washington Post* the following morning, appearing under my byline and that of veteran Pentagon correspondent George C. Wilson, said:

> President Reagan has authorized Marines in Beirut to call in air strikes against forces shelling their positions, serving notice on Syria that the United States is ready to escalate its power in Lebanon, White House officials said last night.[83]

This *Post* story quickly became a focus of controversy in the White House post mortem on the "leak" of the presidential order. In part this was because I was known to have good relations with both Baker and Clark, who typically blamed each other for the leak. During this period the inner circle of the White House conducted its Byzantine battles in an atmosphere of what Mike Deaver described as "semi-rampant paranoia."[84] Knowing that Reagan was frustrated by the frequent disclosures of secret decisions in the media, officials routinely sought to curry presidential favor by blaming rivals for any unauthorized disclosures. Leaks riled Reagan, as they have other presidents, but he had a better sense of proportion than many members of his staff. Left to his own devices, Reagan was usually inclined to blow off steam about a "leaked" story he disliked rather than engage in any serious effort to locate the source of the story. He had the good sense not to let the press make life miserable for him, and he quickly moved to the next item of business once he had vented his frustration.

While convinced that the media were innately liberal in their sympathies, Reagan neither nursed grudges nor compiled enemies lists. He was remarkably uninformed, almost innocent, about the way his staff did its business or the way White House reporters gathered information. It never seemed to occur to the president that aides who piously agreed with him when he denounced leaks often worked zealously to plant stories that they believed would further Reagan's objectives or their own. A more sophisticated president might have recognized that the "leak" in this particular instance served the useful purpose of warning Syrian and Druze gunners that they could no longer shell the Marines with impunity. High-ranking military officials who in other circumstances became enraged by leaked accounts of military information on this occasion welcomed the NBC and *Post* reports, as well as a story by Hedrick Smith in *The New York Times* saying that the Marines had been authorized to engage in "aggressive self-defense."[85] They hoped these reports would deter the shelling of the Marines. And the shelling did not resume until September 19, after the U.S. ships off the Lebanese coast laid down their barrage in support of the Lebanese Army. But no one pointed this out to Reagan. Instead, Clark told the president that the *Post* story, by identifying McFarlane as the U.S. official who argued for the change in the rules of engagement, had put McFarlane's life in danger.

Clark's assertion was based on an intelligence warning that McFarlane was the prospective target of an assassination attempt. (Kemp later confirmed the warning but discounted its importance. He said such reports were commonplace in Lebanon.) "I became very angry," Clark said later. "I walked into the Oval Office. . . . I said, 'Mr. President,' and showed him the article. I said, 'This puts not only our policy in peril, but could endanger McFarlane himself. We know that they are looking for him in Lebanon. . . . I want you to consider ordering the attorney general of the United States to investigate this forthwith. We've had several investigations by the bureau [the FBI] on unauthorized disclosures recently that affect your policy, but I think unless you ask Mr. [William French] Smith to take personal charge of this, simply nothing is going to be done. And at least if nothing is accomplished, it will signal among those who were present yesterday, one of whom had to have disclosed this, that we're damn sick and tired of this type of leakage.' "[86]

Ed Meese was in the room with Reagan when Clark delivered his outburst. He seconded Clark's proposal, and Reagan agreed that the matter should be pursued. Clark and Meese then drafted a one-page order in the form of a letter empowering Smith to conduct the investigation and ask for the resignation of whoever was found to have leaked the information. The last line authorized the attorney general to use polygraphs to find the culprit "to the extent allowed by law."

Mike Deaver learned about the investigation when he strolled into the Oval Office on routine business late on the morning of September 14 and found the president meeting with Clark and Meese. Reagan was in the process of signing the letter to Smith. Deaver asked what was going on. He received no reply from Meese and Clark, but Reagan showed Deaver the letter. Deaver went off to tell Baker, delivering the message in a White House car as the two of them rode to lunch at a nearby hotel. Now it was Baker's turn to be furious. The chief of staff had a reputation for adept, anonymous and frequent dealings with reporters. He saw the Clark-Meese maneuver as an attempt by his rivals to point the finger of blame at him or members of his immediate staff. Baker had realized from his earliest days in the White House that he was an inviting target for movement conservatives. Anticipating precisely the kind of situation he now faced, Baker had eighteen months earlier asked and been granted by Reagan the authority to determine when, if ever, polygraph tests would be administered to White House officials. Later, Baker would say that two attorneys—one a former justice of the California Supreme Court and the other a future attorney general—had conspired to have Reagan sign an order that was obviously unconstitutional. Baker's point was that the attorney general had no authority to seek the resignation of the vice president or cabinet officers. But Baker was not in this moment of crisis concerned about constitutional law. He wanted to head off the internal investigation before any damage was done. When Deaver told him what had transpired, Baker ordered the driver to return immediately to the White House. Then, in an uncharacteristic display of boldness, Baker interrupted the president while he was having lunch with Bush and Shultz. Baker was angry but under control. He pointed out that the letter ordering Smith to conduct the investigations contradicted the authority the president had conferred on him as chief of staff. He said the lie detector tests would lead to problems. He told Reagan that he would be displaying a lack of trust in his own team if he allowed the vice president or the secretary of state to be given lie detector tests.

Shultz picked up the cue. If anyone tried to polygraph him, he said, they would only do it once. Bush, who rarely took sides unless he was alone with the president, agreed that the lie detector tests were a bad idea. Reagan was upset by the discord and the renewed hints of resignation by his secretary of state. Only forty days earlier he had talked Shultz out of resigning, and he wanted no more such scenes. "Bill shouldn't have done that," Reagan said, forgetting how much he had been angered by the leak when Clark called his attention to it. The president telephoned Smith on the spot and recalled the letter, saying he wanted to "roundtable" it that afternoon.

A few hours later Reagan assembled his fractious team in the Oval

Office. The cast included Bush, Clark, Baker, Meese, Deaver and Smith. By now, everyone in the room knew that Reagan wanted to back away from the threat of lie detector tests, especially in the face of Shultz's implicit warning of resignation. Clark and Meese nonetheless insisted that it was important to find the source of the leak. Baker said the president would look ridiculous if it became known that he subjected his closest associates to lie detector tests. If the president did not have confidence in his aides, he should ask for their resignations. As for finding out the source of the leak, said Baker, "Go ahead and have the investigation, but don't strap people up." [87] Clark suggested that Baker was objecting because he didn't want to be polygraphed. Baker said that wasn't the issue and offered to take a polygraph in an appropriate circumstance. As an example, he offered to submit to a lie detector test on his dispute with Bill Casey on the then-raging side issue of the supposed pilferage of the Carter briefing papers in 1980.

It was obvious to others in the room that Baker and Clark considered each other the leaker in the Lebanon story. What was also obvious was that Reagan was distressed by the infighting. The president agreed with Meese and Clark that the FBI should investigate the source of the leaks to NBC and *The Washington Post*. But he sided with Baker on the key issue of polygraphs, which he said would not be administered to cabinet members or his immediate aides. Clark was angry with the compromise, even though he viewed Baker's refusal to take a lie detector test as a back-handed admission that he was responsible for the leak. And Clark also believed he had made his point. "In my mind, it was never anticipated that any of us would go onto a damn polygraph," Clark said later. "But I was mad, and I wanted action. And we got it." [88]

This action, such as it was, generated an investigation that was widely resented among the White House aides who were questioned by the FBI. It ended inconclusively months later, with the FBI determining that the order given the Marines had been so widely circulated that it was impossible to know who had been the source of the stories. The action of which Clark was so proud also marked the end of his influence with Reagan on matters of national security. Baker and Deaver had long wanted to rid themselves of Clark, and the polygraph battle had given them new allies. I was told that Shultz used the incident as the basis for privately expressing to the president his reservations about Clark's performance as national security adviser. Bush may have done the same, for he was now convinced that Clark was a divisive influence.

Even more significantly, Clark had cemented the enmity of Nancy

Reagan, who already viewed him as an impediment to her goal of bettering U.S.-Soviet relations. The first lady never forgave aides for making her husband uncomfortable, unless they were doing so at her instigation. She was convinced that Clark was a menace. And she also was persuaded that Clark had been the source of the *Washington Post* story. At least that is what she told Clark, who accurately but unavailingly denied that he had been my source. While Reagan often remained doggedly loyal to aides who had incurred his wife's wrath, Clark was now bereft of White House allies except for Meese. His adversaries sensed he had lost his special standing with the president, a conclusion they reached by observing Reagan's coolness when Clark was in the room. But he did not confide to them what he was thinking, if anything. That was not Reagan's way.

What was on Clark's mind was less of a mystery. I had been impressed with his steadiness and sense of purpose during the seminal crisis of Reagan's governorship, when Clark restored the morale of a shattered staff in the wake of the "homosexual scandal." But he had mastered the dynamics of Reagan's situation in Sacramento, while the foreign policy landscape remained forever strange to him. Long working hours and sleepless nights had also taken a heavy toll, and Clark was now afflicted by self-doubt. I had the impression that, much like his nemesis Mike Deaver, Clark felt insufficiently appreciated. Even though he had instigated the controversy and provided an opportunity for his adversaries, Clark believed he was acting in the president's best interests. He did not see himself as a schemer who appealed to Reagan's dark side. As Clark viewed things, Baker and his deputy Dick Darman were manipulating the president, with the aid and counsel of Deaver and the first lady. In truth, they were all manipulators, Clark included. The sad, shared secret of the Reagan White House was that no one in the presidential entourage had confidence in the judgment or capacities of the president. Often, they took advantage of Reagan's niceness and naïveté to indulge competing concepts of the presidency and advance their own ambitions. Pragmatists and conservatives alike treated Reagan as if he were a child monarch in need of constant protection. They paid homage to him, but gave him no respect.

After the lie detector blowup, Clark began looking for a way to leave the White House. This may have been because he was winning fewer and fewer of his battles, but his desire to leave also reflected a restless streak that made Clark more valuable as troubleshooter than as marathon man. He had stepped in effectively when Reagan needed him in the governor's office, on the California Supreme Court and at the State Department. Now he was ready to step out. Among his adversaries, only Nancy Reagan was perceptive enough to take him at his word. Many years later she observed that Clark was always seeking a position other than the one he held and said that he may not have known what he wanted to do with his life. What Clark most wanted to do in the fall of 1983 was return to his ranch in California without giving the appearance of abandoning the Reagan administration. Many of the conservatives, especially Meese and Weinberger, urged him to stay. While Clark was agonizing, an unexpected opportunity intervened that provided an outlet for his troubleshooting talents. The opportunity-provider was Interior Secretary James G. Watt, foe of liberals and environmentalists and an ardent promoter of private development of public lands. Watt had long been out of favor with Nancy Reagan and the White House pragmatists. Wirthlin's polls showed that Watt was among the least regarded of Reagan's appointments, and Baker believed that Watt would become a major political liability if he remained in the cabinet through the 1984 election. Reagan nonetheless stuck by his embattled interior secretary. At least he stuck by him until Watt self-destructed during a breakfast speech to the U.S. Chamber of Commerce on September 21. Extolling a commission that was reviewing the Interior Department's coal-leasing program, Watt said, "We have every kind of mix you can have. I have a black, I have a woman, two Jews and a cripple. And we have talent."

Even for Watt, this offhand statement was a stunner. Never had a public official offended as many constituencies in so few words. And Watt had also offended people who weren't among his enumerated categories, notably Senator Paul Laxalt of Nevada. Laxalt had been Watt's sponsor and frequent defender. He was also an able and sensible politician who realized immediately that Watt's latest outburst was indefensible. As the administration's point man on political matters dealing with the Department of the Interior, Laxalt knew that the only open question now was who should replace Watt as secretary. Before the week was out, Laxalt was discussing Watt's replacement with the first lady, the White House staff and Senate colleagues. He also spoke realistically to Watt, advising him to resign gracefully and spare both himself and the president further embarrassment.

Laxalt was now back where he had been three years earlier, trying to recruit an acceptably conservative westerner for the cabinet post that matters most in the West. Laxalt tried Clifford Hansen, his first choice in 1981, but the conflict-of-interest issues that had dogged Hansen at the time still existed. Hansen withdrew his name. Several other names were suggested, including two who later became members of the Bush cabinet: Manuel Lujan and Richard Cheney. In Laxalt's view, these were Gerald Ford people and he was looking for a Reaganite. All of a sudden, he had one. The volunteer was Clark, an outdoorsman who looked upon Interior as an attractive alternative to continuing in the national security post or opting for semiretirement in California. Being a troubleshooter for Reagan always appealed to Clark, and there had been a lot of trouble at Interior. On October 9, Clark broached the idea to Reagan, who responded enthusiastically. The proposal also had instant appeal to the first lady, Deaver and Baker. The White House chief of staff referred to Clark's proposal as a "twofer" that would get Clark out of the White House and Watt out of the government. Two weeks after Clark had touched off a bitter power struggle, support for him as secretary of interior was unanimous in the divided corridors of White House power.

This unanimity was a prelude to a failed palace coup that would have significant consequences.[89] Watt stepped down on Sunday, October 9, acknowledging in a letter to Reagan that the president would best be served by "a different type of leadership" at Interior. At the suggestion of Baker and Deaver, Reagan delayed the announcement of Clark's appointment, ostensibly so that a replacement could be found for the national security adviser. This search did not take Baker and Deaver far. Talking it over together and with Dick Darman, they came up with a plan: Baker would replace Clark as national security adviser, Deaver would become White House chief of staff, Darman would move to the NSC as Baker's principal deputy. It was a bold power play that would have given the pragmatists control. Like Clark's maneuverings, it had multiple motivations. Baker was widely seen as a political wizard, but he lacked foreign policy experience. A tour of duty as national security adviser would remedy this gap in his résumé. Darman, who always planned ahead, also was anxious to expand his horizons and authority. Deaver, scorned by the conservatives as little more than a glorified valet ("Lord of the Chamber Pot," in Pat Buchanan's derisive phrase), wanted to demonstrate that he could be more than an adjutant for the Reagans.

But it was not quite as crass as it sounds in this summary. All these aides believed, and not unreasonably, that their scheme would benefit the Reagan presidency. Baker operated from the premise that the key to a president's political success was his ability to "control the agenda." The White House had been remarkably successful at accomplishing this control in domestic affairs during Reagan's first three years in office. Baker believed he could help Reagan gain a similar edge in foreign affairs. The idea was quietly discussed with Bush and Nancy Reagan, both of whom favored it. Shultz, who had close relations with Deaver and good relations with Baker, approved. So did Stuart Spencer, the outside adviser the Reagans most readily consulted in times of crisis. But Clark, Meese and other White House conservatives were deliberately kept in the dark. Baker and Deaver realized that the conservatives would try to block the plan if they were given advance warning. What they wanted was a fait accompli, knowing that Reagan would support the staff changes once he had announced them.

The coup almost succeeded. Reagan announced the appointment of Clark as secretary of interior on October 13, a Thursday. He had agreed with Baker and Deaver that he would announce their appointments the following day. Under Darman's guidance the draft of a press release was prepared and typed by Baker's assistant Margaret Tutwiler. Some reporters, including me, were told to be in the White House briefing room by four o'clock, about the time Reagan would be leaving for Camp David. This was usually a signal that Reagan had an announcement to make, which that day was widely thought to be the appointment of McFarlane as Clark's replacement. But there were no presidential announcements this particular Friday. Reagan had lunch at the White House with Shultz, who knew of the plan. He was then scheduled to attend a one-hour National Security Planning Group meeting in the Situation Room, where he would have announced the staff changes. Then he was expected to return upstairs while the White House press office was notified of the changes, go to the press briefing room and make the announcements and depart for Camp David. Normally, either Baker or Deaver or both of them would have accompanied the president to the NSPG meeting.

On this day, however, Reagan lingered in Deaver's office, talking about what he would say downstairs. Baker and Deaver had decided to stay away from the NSPG meeting, a decision that Deaver later concluded was a mistake. But the bigger mistake of Deaver and Baker may simply have been not getting Reagan to the NSPG meeting on time. Clark is a stickler for punctuality. He had no inkling of what was happening upstairs, but he was presiding for the last time at an NSPG meeting and he wanted to get on with it. At one o'clock, he telephoned upstairs to ask Reagan's whereabouts. When five minutes had passed and the president had not arrived, Clark decided to walk up to the Oval Office and personally escort Reagan to the Situation Room. On the way down, the president almost casually told Clark he had found an appropriate successor at NSC in the person of James Baker. Clark was horrified, but reacted calmly. He asked Reagan who would take over as chief of staff. Deaver, he was told. From Clark's point of view, this was a double disaster. Thinking quickly, he asked Reagan if he would delay making an announcement at the NSPG meeting and talk with him afterward about it.

Clark's request and Reagan's acquiescence to it proved crucial. Once Reagan announced his action at the NSPG meeting, it would have become, in Baker's parlance, "a done deal." It would have been uncharacteristic of Clark or Meese, and even more so of Casey or Weinberger, to have openly opposed a decision in a group meeting once Reagan had announced it. And even if they had been so inclined, they probably would have been inhibited from bluntly denouncing Baker in the presence of Shultz and others in the meeting who were not part of the White House power struggle. Clark knew this, and he passed notes to Weinberger, Meese and Casey asking them to come to his office after the meeting. As soon as it broke up, the four of them assembled with the president in Clark's tiny office next door to the Situation Room. According to the participants and aides who were told about the meeting afterward, all of them objected vehemently to the changes, focusing their attack on Baker but objecting to Deaver as well. One of their principal arguments was that the selection of Baker as national security adviser would send a signal of accommodation to the Soviets. This was a far more potent argument in the fall of 1983, when memories of KAL 007 were still fresh, than it would have been a few months later. Clark and Casey also objected that Baker was a "leaker," saying this would be particularly risky at NSC.

In *The Power Game,* Hedrick Smith quotes Casey as saying of Baker, "He can have my job even though I know he's the biggest leaker in town. He can't go to NSC!"[90] Smith's account of the conservatives' rebellion against the Baker-Deaver appointments differs significantly from my reconstruction on an important point. According to Smith, Reagan said to Clark on the way downstairs to the Situation Room that he had not conferred with Shultz on the appointment of Baker. But I was told that Reagan said in his meeting with the conservatives in Clark's office after the NSPG meeting that he was surprised by their opposition because he had talked the matter over with "the two Georges" (meaning Shultz and Bush) and they had no objections. It seems unlikely that Reagan at his lunch with Shultz would have failed to mention what he intended to do. The secretary of state had offered his resignation on August 4 and hinted at resigning again on September 14 during the lie detector controversy. Reagan was highly sensitive to Shultz's feelings and didn't want to lose him. As subsequent events would demonstrate, he was unwilling to appoint a national security adviser who lacked Shultz's blessing. And the change would have been beneficial to Shultz. Deaver was his friend and ally in the White House court.

Both Deaver and Baker shared Shultz's view that a change for the better in U.S.-Soviet relations was of the highest priority to the Reagan administration. The appointment would have given Shultz an advantage, as Weinberger realized immediately that afternoon in Clark's office. Weinberger was bothered by the "two Georges" comment because Reagan had consulted with Shultz and not with him. But the secretary of defense did not put his objection in personal terms, saying instead that it was important to have "an honest broker" at NSC. Weinberger's idea of an honest broker was Clark, who by now was having second thoughts about his resignation. Clark suggested that perhaps the president would want to send Baker to Interior and leave him in his present job. Reagan scotched this proposal immediately, pointing out that Baker's ownership of Texas oil and gas leases would disqualify him from the Interior post. Reagan's point was well taken. It was surprising, however, to the four conservatives, which suggests how little they knew Baker. In a White House where ethical considerations were too often a matter of individual preference, Baker set high standards. Reagan was aware that sending Baker to Interior would involve a conflict of interest because the chief of staff had made it a point to recuse himself from all White House decisions on energy matters, whether or not they had any impact on his own holdings. Reagan's reply on this point convinced everyone in the room, including Clark, that sending Baker to Interior was not open to further discussion. But Clark and his conservative cabal had prevailed on the main point. Shaken by the ferocity of the opposition to a change he had expected to go smoothly, Reagan agreed to put off his intended announcement in the White House briefing room.

Upstairs in Deaver's office, the organizers of the coup became worried when Reagan did not return on time from the NSPG meeting. Reagan was disciplined about his schedule, and he did not like to delay his departures to Camp David. His failure to return to the Oval Office on schedule obviously meant that something had gone wrong. Deaver anxiously called downstairs to inquire on the president's whereabouts and was told by Clark's secretary Jacque Hill that Reagan was meeting with Clark. Baker and Deaver now feared the worst. When Reagan returned to the Oval Office, he buzzed for Baker and Deaver. "The fellas have a real problem with this," he said. "I want to think about it over the weekend." Baker, disappointed but calm, offered to withdraw and spare the president the decision. "No," said Reagan. "I said I would think about it over the weekend, and I will." According to Smith's account, Deaver "yelled" at Reagan, saying, "You don't have enough confidence in me to make me chief of staff."[91]

As Deaver remembers what happened, he withdrew into the background, as he often does when he is upset, and let Baker do the talking. Deaver recalls retreating to his office, where he ousted aides who had been waiting for him and "let off steam" with Baker. But there is no doubt that he was angry, and that Reagan was aware of it. "I was very emotional," said Deaver. "I was really pissed off. I may have said [to Baker] that this was typical of Reagan and that he really didn't want me as chief of staff."[92] Reagan wrote in his diary that evening that "Jim took it well but Mike was pretty upset."[93]

Deaver was closer to Reagan than any other aide. In the White House and in the media it was often said, without intended irony, that Reagan and Deaver had a "father-son" relationship. What needs to be added to this observation is that Reagan's sons often felt distanced from their father. Deaver had given much of his life to the Reagans. He had abandoned his share of a public relations business he owned with Peter Hannaford when conflict-of-interest questions were raised after he had gone to the White House in 1981. Deaver wanted badly—too badly, as it turned out—to become a rich man, but he wanted even more to be recognized by Reagan as a grownup who could do more than serve as the White House staff's go-between with Nancy Reagan. Deaver felt rejected. He was reminded of a painful scene at the Reagan home in Pacific Palisades on Thanksgiving Day, 1979, when John Sears had attempted to oust Deaver from the presidential campaign by accusing him of overcharging Reagan for his public relations services. Deeply hurt, Deaver had resolved the situation on that occasion by walking out, returning to the campaign only after Sears was fired the following February.[94] "I had a sense of déjà vu," said Deaver. "The entire weekend was like the period of time when Sears was getting rid of me—you couldn't get through, you couldn't find out what was going on."[95]

When Reagan returned from Camp David on Monday, October 17,

he told Baker and Deaver that he had decided against their plan. The president had been hearing from the conservatives by telephone over the weekend. The conservatives were so implacable in their opposition to Baker and Deaver that Reagan feared that some of them might resign if he made the appointments—or so I was later told. Reagan wrote later that he had decided to scrap the change he had agreed to because opposition to Baker and Deaver was so intense that he thought the result of appointing them "would be friction among the cabinet and the White House staff." [96]

The conservative candidate to replace Clark as national security adviser was Jeane Kirkpatrick, the U.N. ambassador. She was totally unacceptable to Shultz. Kirkpatrick said she was informed later, probably by Casey and Clark, that Shultz threatened to quit if she was named to the post.[97] Shultz has denied making such a threat, but Baker and Deaver believe that he might very well have left if Kirkpatrick had been named. Baker was equally opposed to Kirkpatrick, believing that her appointment would perpetuate the ideological infighting. Deaver doubts that Reagan ever seriously considered appointing her. Instead, Reagan followed his pattern of allowing neither faction a total victory. After allowing the conservatives to block the appointment of Baker and Deaver, he permitted the pragmatists to block Kirkpatrick. This left McFarlane, who was everyone's distant second choice, as the compromise candidate. Reagan named him the same day. This, too, followed a familiar pattern. Throughout his presidency Reagan often turned to a deputy who was already on the job to fill a disputed position, a practice that would two years later make John Poindexter his national security adviser. The president didn't know much about McFarlane, though he may have been impressed with reports of his performance close to the front in Lebanon.[98] "I should tell you that I was looking for more than experience in filling this post," Reagan said in announcing the appointment in the White House briefing room. "I also wanted someone of strong principle, someone of keen judgment, and someone who could effectively manage the affairs of the NSC."

Although Reagan did not realize it at the time, he had made one of his most crucial decisions as president, and one that would have disastrous consequences. "My decision not to appoint Jim Baker as national security adviser, I suppose, was a turning point for my administration," Reagan wrote in his memoirs.[99] The president's irresolution had disillusioned the key members of an able staff and guaranteed their departure from the White House. Though they hid their disappointment from the president and continued to work effectively, Baker and Darman decided to leave the White House after the 1984 election. So did Deaver, despite being told by Nancy Reagan that her husband wanted him to become chief of staff "someday." [100] Clark succeeded at Interior, where he washed away much of the bad taste left by Watt. But Clark had burned his bridges at the White House and would never again be a close Reagan adviser. The conservative victory also quickly turned to ashes for Weinberger, as he and McFarlane found each other impossible. Only Casey and Meese were happy with the outcome.

Over time, Reagan would pay a heavy price for failing to recognize that the quality of his own presidential performance required a strong supporting cast. Reagan was a kindly, monarchial president who depended upon his aides for information and otherwise took them for granted. He was forever moving from one performance to another without seeing anything except his script. His aides liked him and were liked by him, but what they noticed most was how little he noticed them. Reagan treated his most valuable aides—which arguably included Clark as well as Baker, Deaver and Darman—as indifferently as he did his children, ignoring their quarrels until a crisis compelled him to intervene. Like an absentminded father, he was an arbiter rather than a participant in the struggles of his entourage. This indifference encouraged personal ambition at the expense of loyalty, for it is difficult for aides to remain truly loyal to a leader who does not value them and cannot distinguish bad work from good. Familiarity with Reagan was productive of affection rather than respect. Aides who dealt with the president occasionally or from a distance were invariably impressed with his gentle manners. Those who worked with him at close quarters over extended periods usually wound up feeling unappreciated or cast aside. It was no accident that every key official in the Reagan White House had departed or changed jobs by 1985. Those who remained through the second term—most notably Baker and Meese—found job satisfaction in the cabinet. Within the White House itself, there were few rewards for success and even fewer penalties for failure. Reagan had known too many aides, and made too few distinctions among them. He too easily cost himself the acquired knowledge of those who served him best.

What Reagan had also done was create the conditions under which a shadow, renegade government engaged in high-risk foreign policy adventures could flourish within the NSC. This would become apparent after the Iran-contra disclosures, when it was widely said in administration circles that the scandal could have been avoided if Clark had stayed at the NSC or if he had not prevented Baker from replacing him. Deaver's continued presence in the White House might also have dissuaded the president from trading U.S. arms for American hostages, for Deaver often saved Reagan from himself. But as Deaver would say, losing Baker was the key.[101] Baker tended to take a long-range view of the political impact of decisions. As a White House official later said of Baker, "He would have realized that the consequences of success of an arms-for-hostages trade with Iran might have been nearly as serious for Reagan as the consequences of failure. And he would have known that it could never have remained a secret." Baker's adversaries shared this view. Although Baker remained a member of the National Security Council after he became treasury secretary, John Poindexter deliberately excluded him from the meetings in which the sale of arms to Iran were discussed. "Baker is supercautious," observed Stuart Spencer. "He is very concerned about what Congress thinks. Iran-contra simply wouldn't have happened if Baker had been the national security adviser." [102]

But it is doubtful if Baker's appointment as national security adviser would have saved the U.S. Marines in Lebanon. Like Shultz and McFarlane, Baker had served in the Marine Corps. He had been outraged by the bombing of Beirut and the Sabra-Shatila massacres and believed that the Marines had been legitimately deployed in Lebanon to save lives and achieve a diplomatic settlement. Baker's political instincts told him that it would be imperative to remove the Marines from Lebanon well before the 1984 election, but he had no sense of urgency about it. On matters of foreign policy Baker tended to rely on Shultz and Bush for guidance, and both of them believed that the Marines were serving a useful purpose in Lebanon. With Clark gone, Weinberger was the only influential member of the administration who continued to advocate withdrawal of the Marines. The secretary of defense was not shy in espousing his views, but he recognized that Reagan was listening to Shultz and especially to McFarlane, who was then on the ground in Lebanon as the president's special envoy in the Middle East.

Reagan also did not want the United States to be forced out of Lebanon by congressional clamor, which became louder each time a Marine was killed by artillery or sniper fire. Congressional opponents of the Lebanon involvement were trying to invoke the 1973 War Powers Resolution, which would have required the president to remove U.S.

forces within ninety days. This law was passed over President Nixon's veto when Congress was incensed about Vietnam and Nixon was weakened by Watergate, and all presidents since then have considered it a usurpation of executive authority. Reagan averted a showdown on war powers with the help of House Speaker Tip O'Neill, who did not want to undermine the position of the Marines while they were under fire. On September 20, a day after U.S. naval artillery shelled Druze positions in the hills above Beirut, Reagan reached a compromise with congressional leaders permitting the Marines to remain in Lebanon for another eighteen months. The time limit had been suggested by O'Neill, whose support guaranteed the resolution's passage in the House. Senate Democrats were opposed to the extended deployment, but Republicans had a majority in the Senate. On September 29 the resolution passed the Senate 54-46 on a vote virtually along party lines. The White House press office nonetheless issued a statement after the vote declaring that "America stands united, we speak with one voice" on Lebanon. But that "one voice" now proclaimed a mission for the Marines that went far beyond peacekeeping. In a radio speech from Camp David on October 8, Reagan linked the Lebanon conflict to the global struggle against communism and asked rhetorically, "Can the United States or the free world stand by and see the Middle East incorporated into the Soviet bloc?" On October 16 a sixth Marine was killed by sniper fire in Lebanon. When Reagan announced McFarlane's appointment the following day, he was asked by a reporter, "Why are we letting our Marines be there [in Lebanon] to get killed every day?"

"Because I think it is vitally important to the security of the United States and the Western world that we do everything we can to further the peace process in the Middle East," the president replied.[103]

The Marines faced more acute danger than sniper fire, and Reagan should have known it. The Hezbollah and other pro-Iranian factions in Lebanon were dedicated to the destruction of Americans. Because of the U.S. role in training the Lebanese Army and the U.S. naval shelling at Souk al Garb, the Marines were viewed by the Druze, the Amal, the Palestinians and their Syrian supporters as a military prop for the despised, minority Christian government of Amin Gemayel. The Israeli troops who had restrained or defeated these Muslim forces were gone. And the Israeli withdrawal had deprived the Marines of the high ground, leaving them pinned down at Beirut International Airport. Because of ongoing airport construction, heavy trucks often remained in the area overnight. The Marines rarely had their weapons loaded.

They were in Lebanon not to fight but to keep the peace by maintaining a "presence."

Later, it would be noted that the risk of terrorist attacks against U.S. forces in Lebanon had been raised by intelligence analysts as early as July 1982, after Reagan had made a commitment of U.S. participation in the MNF but before he actually sent in the Marines. The terrorist threat had been viewed as a clear and present danger by U.S. intelligence agencies after the destruction of the U.S. embassy in April. Between May and October these agencies were flooded with more than one hundred warnings of prospective car-bomb attacks. Few of the threats had materialized, and some of the warnings had not even been passed on to the Defense Department.[104] But the commonplace terrorism in Lebanon had been a frequent topic of discussion at Reagan's national security briefings and NSC meetings. Reagan had often described terrorism as a worldwide threat. What the commission of inquiry (Long Commission) would say retrospectively had been pointed out to Reagan many times before the Marines became the victims of terrorism: "Lebanon [is] an ideal environment for the planning and execution of terrorist operations." Echoing the warning of Weinberger and the Joint Chiefs when Reagan approved the second U.S. deployment to Lebanon, the commission observed that the Marines were "ideal targets."[105]

But in the fall of 1983 Reagan believed that there was cause for hope in Lebanon. His attitude reflected both his natural optimism and the advice being given him by Shultz and McFarlane, who believed that the September show of U.S. force was producing results. On September 23, McFarlane flew from Beirut to Damascus where he informed Assad that the battleship *New Jersey* would soon reach Lebanese waters. On September 25, a day before the *New Jersey* arrived, the warring factions in Lebanon agreed to a cease-fire and negotiations in Geneva. Beirut International Airport was reopened. In the early weeks of October the airport averaged thirty-five flights and 2,400 passengers a day. "We packed our bags and left in early October, and everything was hunky-dory," Kemp said. "There was a lot of optimism in Lebanon after the cease-fire."[106]

This optimism was not shared by the Marines, the Joint Chiefs or the secretary of defense. Weinberger put the issue directly to the president at a National Security Council meeting on October 18, the day after McFarlane's appointment. He noted that the Marines were now viewed as combatants instead of peacekeepers by the Syrians and the various militias opposed to the Gemayel government. He observed that the chiefs unanimously favored removal of the Marines, saying again that they were "sitting on a bull's-eye" when they could be safely "redeployed" to ships offshore. Weinberger contended that such a "redeployment" did not mean abandoning the government of Lebanon. The Marines could always be sent back ashore if needed, and Syrian and Druze positions were in range of the *New Jersey*'s artillery. Weinberger thought he had a strong case, but it attracted little support. In part this was because of the change in national security advisers: Clark had become increasingly skeptical of the Lebanon deployment, while McFarlane stood with Shultz in contending that the continued presence of the Marines was necessary to maintain the cease-fire. And because he had been so recently the special envoy in the Middle East, McFarlane's position was solicited at this meeting by the president. While they would have their share of differences later on, Shultz and McFarlane at this juncture teamed up to make the case for keeping the Marines in Lebanon. Shultz, pointing out what had happened when the Marines had been withdrawn before, said it would be a mistake to bring them out just as U.S. policy was on the verge of success. Weinberger had so little support for his position that he did not even insist on a formal vote. He realized that the president intended to keep the Marines in Lebanon.

Neither the public nor Congress was sufficiently aware that the nation's highest-ranking military men had opposed the policy to which their commander in chief was committed or that Weinberger was urging Reagan to pull out the Marines. In part that was the fault of the chiefs. While consistently opposed to use of the Marines in Lebanon, the chiefs too often expressed their opposition in memos that Reagan probably never read and let Weinberger do their talking. "None of us marched in and told the president that the U.S. is going to face disaster if the Marines didn't withdraw," Vessey said later.[107] Nor did the chiefs make it easy for Republican members of Congress, many of whom had doubts about the Marine deployment, to challenge their popular president. In September, when Congress was debating the resolution to keep the Marines in Lebanon for another year and a half, Chief of Naval Operations James Watkins testified, "It is the opinion of the Joint Chiefs of Staff that withdrawal of the multinational force at this time probably would have a devastating effect and could plunge Lebanon into anarchy."[108]

Later, it would be said bitterly at the Pentagon that Shultz and

McFarlane had misled the president, costing him the last of several opportunities to save the Marines. This was true enough, as far as it went, but the chiefs might have achieved a different result if they had "marched in" and made their case with the same force with which they afterward criticized the secretary of state and the national security adviser. By October 18, when Weinberger made the case for withdrawal at the NSC, it may have been too late. Even if Reagan had decided then to withdraw the Marines to waiting ships, the administration would have been obligated to discuss the pullout with the Gemayel government and with France and Italy, the U.S.'s partners in the MNF. And there was no time left for such discussion.

At 6:22 A.M. on Sunday, October 23, 1983, a smiling young man with a bushy mustache drove a yellow stake-bed Mercedes truck through the public parking lot of the four-story steel and reinforced-concrete headquarters building where 350 members of the 1st Battalion, 8th Marine Regiment, were sleeping. As the official report described it, "The truck drove over the barbed and concertina wire obstacle, passed between two Marine guard posts without being engaged by fire, entered an open gate, passed around one sewer pipe barrier and between two others, flattened the Sergeant of the Guard's sandbagged booth at the building's entrance, penetrated the lobby of the building and detonated while the majority of the occupants slept. The force of the explosion ripped the building from its foundation. The building then imploded upon itself. Almost all the occupants were crushed or trapped inside the wreckage."[109]

Beneath the rubble lay 346 U.S. servicemen, most of them Marines. A thick cloud of dust, pierced only by the cries and screams of the wounded, covered the scene. During the next six and one-half hours the bodies of 234 Marines would be recovered from the wreckage. Another 112 Marines would be pulled out alive, of whom seven would die. Many survivors were permanently injured, among them Lieutenant Colonel Howard Gerlach, the commander of the Battalion Landing Team. Gerlach, who had been wounded in the abdomen in Vietnam, had a broken neck and lost the use of his legs. FBI experts determined that the bomb had exploded with the force of 12,000 pounds of TNT, producing the largest non-nuclear blast on record. And it was not the only bomb that went off in Beirut on this bloody Sunday. Two miles away from the U.S. Marine headquarters, in the heart of West Beirut, another powerful bomb exploded soon after the airport blast. It brought down a nine-story building, killing fifty-eight French paratroopers. Together, the two explosions had claimed more than half as many lives as the total casualties sustained by Israeli forces in their sixteen-month invasion of Lebanon.

It was twenty-two minutes after midnight in the eastern United States when the bomb destroyed the Marine headquarters in Beirut. The Reagans were asleep in the master suite of the six-bedroom Eisenhower Cottage at the Augusta National Golf Club, where the president was spending the weekend at the invitation of Shultz and former New Jersey senator Nicholas F. Brady. The weekend had not gone well. At 2:45 A.M. on Saturday, Shultz had been notified that the Organization of Eastern Caribbean States, a group of six small former British colonies, had requested U.S. military aid to restore "peace and stability" in Grenada. Maurice Bishop, the Marxist prime minister of Grenada, had been held under house arrest for six days and then murdered on October 19 by a renegade faction of his own party. A shoot-on-sight curfew was declared by the military council that now proclaimed itself the government. Even before Bishop was killed, the State Department had convened an interagency group to discuss the possible danger to U.S. citizens. When Bishop was murdered, Reagan put Vice President Bush in charge of a Special Situation Group to discuss contingency plans in Grenada. The group diverted to the Caribbean a Marine battalion and a naval task force led by the carrier *Independence,* which had been headed for Lebanon.

The State Department at first envisioned what an official subsequently called a "nonpermissive evacuation" of U.S. citizens from the island.[110] But the cable from the Caribbean nations was an invitation for an invasion. Shultz, who was staying in another bedroom of the Eisenhower Cottage, discussed it with McFarlane and the two of them then conferred with Bush in Washington. They waited until 5:15 A.M. to awaken Reagan. Shultz and McFarlane briefed Reagan, still in his pajamas, in the lower-level sitting room of the cottage. They told him that anarchy prevailed on the island and that the lives of the 1,000 Americans there could be in jeopardy. Reagan favored an invasion, which he then and afterward described as a rescue of the Americans, most of whom were students at the St. George's School of Medicine. "He was very unequivocal," McFarlane said. "He couldn't wait."[111]

Reagan suggested that the presidential party return immediately to Washington. McFarlane pointed out that the Special Situation Group was already proceeding with invasion plans, and Shultz said that a change in Reagan's schedule might draw attention to the possibility of

U.S. intervention. Reagan decided to remain in Augusta. At 9 A.M. Bush convened a National Security Council meeting in the White House Situation Room. Reagan, Shultz and McFarlane participated in a portion of the meeting on speaker phones. The president spoke for only five minutes. When a White House staff member observed that there could be a "harsh political reaction" to a U.S. invasion of a small island nation, Reagan replied, "I know that. I accept that." [112]

Later, Reagan went golfing with Shultz, Brady and Treasury Secretary Donald Regan. The presidential party had reached the sixteenth fairway by 2:15 P.M., when a bearded gunman wearing a flannel shirt, jeans and a hat with the slogan "Dixie—The Closest Thing to Heaven" crashed his pickup truck through the golf club gate. Wielding a .38-caliber pistol, he confronted seven persons, including White House assistant David Fischer, in the club's pro shop and threatened to kill them unless he could talk to Reagan. Fischer told the gunman, an unemployed pipefitter named Charles Harris, that he would go speak to the president. He found Reagan at the sixteenth green, six hundred yards away from the pro shop, where he had taken refuge in his armored limousine at the insistence of worried Secret Service agents. Reagan tried five or six times without success from the limousine to persuade the gunman to talk to him on the phone. The Secret Service then took the president, who was described as disappointed that he could not finish his golf game, back to the cottage. Two hours later, the gunman freed the hostages and surrendered. The Reagans retired for the night at ten. At 2:27 A.M. Reagan was awakened by a call on his secure telephone line from McFarlane, who was staying in an adjacent guest house. "We've had a terrible attack on the Marines with a substantial loss of life," McFarlane said. "I believe we should get together." McFarlane then called Shultz and the two of them reassembled in the sitting room of the Eisenhower Cottage to tell Reagan what they knew about the calamity in Beirut. [113]

Years later, Reagan would remember it as the "saddest day of my presidency, perhaps the saddest day of my life." [114] "Part of it was my idea—a good part of it," he said, speaking of the decision to send the Marines to Lebanon. [115] For McFarlane, the news was almost unbearable. He had visited the Marines on the ground in Beirut, he knew several of the officers, he had made the case that they should remain in Lebanon. Reagan and Shultz were also in distress. As McFarlane recalled it, the president responded to his report of casualties (then estimated at about two hundred) with "a look of deep grief" and "a long, thoughtful staring at the carpet." [116]

The three men had special reason for their grief. Reagan and Shultz shared with Habib the responsibility for sending the Marines to Lebanon, and they shared with McFarlane the responsibility for keeping them there. Following Shultz's and McFarlane's recommendations, Reagan had repeatedly ignored the warnings of his military advisers that the Marines were an exposed symbol of American presence in Beirut. He had also ignored the deadly harbinger provided by the terrorist attack on the U.S. embassy six months earlier. Like most Americans, Reagan found terrorism a particularly appalling and frustrating form of warfare and had few practical ideas on how the United States should respond to it. He looked upon terrorists as "cowards" and "barbarians" who preyed on the innocent and refused to fight fair. As Reagan saw it, the Marines were as innocent as any civilians, for they had been sent to Lebanon to keep the peace and prevent the Lebanese from killing each other.

On the hour-long plane ride back to Washington, Reagan's anguish turned to anger. He denounced the perpetrators of the bombing and talked of striking back at them, even though it was difficult to know at whom to strike. Reagan had often read letters from Marines in Lebanon and from their families. In his October 9 radio speech he had quoted from a letter written by a Marine corporal in Lebanon to his hometown paper which said that Americans "must be prepared to defend and, if necessary, to die for what we believe in, for the American way of life." Reagan had not known when he read from that letter that so many Marines would die. Now that they had died, he did not want America to surrender to their killers.

Reagan arrived on the south grounds of the White House by helicopter in a driving rain. Normally, he would have been driven from Andrews Air Force Base in such weather, but he was in a hurry to get back to the White House. He clambered down the helicopter steps with Nancy Reagan, holding her hand as they walked to a microphone near the South Portico. Each of the Reagans held an umbrella, while Shultz and McFarlane stood bareheaded behind them in the rain. Reagan spoke without notes. He said there were "no words that can express our sorrow and grief over the loss of those splendid young men and the injury to so many others." Nor, he said, were there words to express his outrage at the "despicable act" that had killed the Marines or the earlier bombing "that took the lives of scores of people at our embassy in that same city, in Beirut." And he concluded: "But I think we should all recognize that these deeds make so evident the bestial nature of those who would assume power if they could have their way and drive us out of that area that we must be more determined than ever that they cannot take over that vital and strategic part of the earth or, for that matter, any other part of the earth." It was Reagan's way of saying that the Marines had died, as he once said of American soldiers in Vietnam, in pursuit of a noble cause. But the cause in Lebanon, unlike Vietnam, had never been supported by the president's generals or by his secretary of defense.

Reagan's heartfelt little speech at the South Portico turned out to be as mistaken as the U.S. military commitment in Lebanon. The terrorist bombing that killed the 241 Marines did, in fact, drive the United States from Lebanon, although it would take three and one-half months for events and advisers to persuade Reagan to agree to the withdrawal plan. The withdrawal was steadfastly opposed by Shultz, who continued to believe that U.S. diplomatic interests required the United States to remain in Lebanon. "We are in Lebanon because the outcome in Lebanon will affect our position in the whole Middle East," Shultz testified to Congress on October 24. "To ask why Lebanon is important is to ask why the whole Middle East is important—because the answer is the same."

Weinberger would never see it that way. He thought that Lebanon was hopeless and that the Marines had no useful purpose there. "I've never seen Cap look as sad as he did after the Marines were killed," said Colin Powell. Recalling the NSC debate of the previous Tuesday, Weinberger told Powell, "I wished I had been more persuasive with the president." [117] Even as the Marines proceeded with the grim business of identifying the dead and notifying their next of kin, Weinberger and the chiefs were arguing the futility of further sacrifices in Lebanon. They staked out their position almost as soon as Reagan, Shultz and McFarlane had taken their seats in the Situation Room on the Sunday morning that the presidential party returned from Augusta. And this time they also told the media and Congress what they were doing. When Republican Senator Dan Evans of Washington left the White House that Sunday, he said the administration was debating whether to put the surviving Marines on ships or give them a more defensible perimeter by expanding the territory they held. [118] "Senior administration officials" anonymously told the press that putting the Marines on the ships was the more likely option.

Putting the Marines on ships, under whatever guise, meant withdrawal. And public opinion might have forced Reagan to take this option immediately if attention had remained focused on Lebanon. Congress was in an uproar. Democratic Senator Ernest F. Hollings of South Carolina said that the Beirut bombing pointed out the "stupidity of the original decision" to put the Marines in Lebanon. "They do not have a mission," Hollings said on NBC's *Today* show. "If they were put there to fight, there are too few. If they were put there to die, there are too many." Editorial reaction was mixed but largely critical. *The Washington Post* said, "For a power with America's responsibilities, it is inconceivable to hand the bombers the victory they sought by pulling the Marines out." [119] But the *New York Daily News* called for a "full, open, honest all-cards-on-the-table debate" over U.S. policy and immediate actions "to reduce the clay-pigeon status of our remaining Marines in Lebanon." [120] *USA Today* said, "Through our tears and anger, many Americans will be asking again the punishing question: Why are our fighting men in Lebanon?" [121] Even more worrisome to White House political strategists than the congressional and editorial reaction was a Richard Wirthlin poll that on Monday showed a precipitous overnight decline in Reagan's approval rating.*

Reagan was rarely a poll-driven president. He took many positions, most notably in supporting the contras and in opposing abortion, where Wirthlin's polls found him out of step with American public opinion. But Reagan's staff, especially James Baker and Mike Deaver and later Donald Regan, paid close attention to the polls. Wirthlin's overnight survey after the bombing in Lebanon was especially helpful because the Grenada invasion complicated the public response to both events. Public opinion supported the action in Grenada, and Reagan's approval ratings remained steady or actually increased in most of the published polls. But the politically minded White House staff had a glimpse, thanks to Wirthlin's pre-invasion poll, of what the reaction would have been without Grenada. While the pre-invasion survey was never made public, it served as a private warning of the consequences of further adventures in Lebanon. The White House staff soon became an active ally of the Pentagon in the campaign to withdraw the Marines.

Despite the dark suspicions of Reagan's critics, most notably Tip O'Neill, the Grenada invasion itself was not influenced by events in Lebanon. O'Neill based his view that "Grenada was really about Leb-

---

* Wirthlin was in the field conducting his monthly survey when the bombing occurred in Beirut. He continued to poll throughout the week. "Most of the polls that came in after Grenada found it difficult to disentangle the two events," Wirthlin said. "Because of when we were polling, we were able to isolate them." [122]

anon" on remarks made by Reagan on Monday evening, October 24, to congressional leaders who were brought to the White House to be told about the invasion decision. A comment by McFarlane triggered one of Reagan's mental cassettes, prompting the president to recount a story in which Filipinos celebrated the liberation of their country in World War II by waving American flags and throwing flowers at American soldiers and Marines who were returning to the United States. "I can see the day, not too many weeks from now, when the Lebanese people will be standing at the shore, waving and cheering our Marines when they depart," Reagan said.[123] O'Neill concluded from this typically Reaganesque performance that the invasion of Grenada was being undertaken to give Americans something to cheer about after the disaster in Lebanon.

The facts tell a different story. The invasion planning—or at least planning for a military evacuation of Americans that would have required an invasion—had been under way since Bishop's execution the previous Wednesday. Reagan had expressed support of the invasion (enthusiastically, according to McFarlane) in Augusta early Saturday morning and again later in the morning when he addressed Bush's planning group in the Situation Room over a speaker phone. When the Saturday meeting broke up at 11:30 A.M. there was a consensus for an invasion of Grenada. Reagan, who was by then on the golf course, was not asked to sign a formal order because Weinberger and Vessey wanted to wait for additional intelligence on the disposition of Cuban forces on the island.

There is no doubt that Reagan was genuinely worried about the plight of the Americans on Grenada, especially the eight hundred students at the St. George's School of Medicine. Considering the violence and anarchy that then prevailed on the island, it is not surprising that Reagan's advisers reached the conclusion that Americans were endangered. The specter of the Iranian hostage crisis haunted the Reagan administration. As Weinberger put it, there was little disagreement over the invasion "because the costs of not doing Grenada were obviously greater than the cost of doing it. We didn't want students held 440 days as hostages."[124]

But Reagan had other reasons to look with favor on the invasion. He was determined to counter Communist influence in the hemisphere, and he possessed what a White House official described to me at the time as "an obsession" about Grenada.[125] As early as February 24, 1982, the president had talked of a "dark future" foreshadowed by "the tightening grip of the totalitarian left in Grenada and Nicaragua." On April 8, 1982, he had visited Barbados and found Caribbean leaders fearful of Grenadian military intentions. Reagan shared their concern that Grenada could become a Communist beachhead. "That country now bears the Soviet and Cuban trademark, which means that it will attempt to spread the virus among its neighbors," he told the Caribbean leaders. In the nationally televised March 23, 1983, speech in which he unveiled the Strategic Defense Initiative, Reagan displayed an aerial photo of a 10,000-foot airport runway that Cuban laborers were constructing in Grenada. Addressing Congress in behalf of contra aid on April 27, Reagan said that this runway, when completed, could be used by Libya and other U.S. foes to deliver arms and supplies to the Sandinista regime.

If anything, the destruction of the Marines in Lebanon may have caused Reagan to hesitate in giving the final go-ahead on the Grenadian operation. A *Time* magazine account reported by the usually well-informed Douglas Brew said that Reagan "momentarily . . . considered abandoning the invasion" after the Beirut bombing out of concern for additional American casualties.[126] The "pain and hurt" showed on Reagan's face throughout the 103-minute NSPG meeting in the Situation Room on Sunday. The meeting recessed at 10:40 A.M., resuming at 4:00 P.M. for another three hours of discussion that began with Lebanon and concluded with Grenada. At one point Reagan tried reading aloud the letter of a father whose son was a Marine in Lebanon and could not get through it. Mike Deaver thought that Reagan was a most "tired and unhappy man." [127]

On Monday, October 24, the president was better rested but not any happier. No coherent government appeared to be functioning on Grenada. Reagan had been told at the Sunday NSPG meeting that the U.S. government had received a written appeal for intervention from the Organization of Eastern Caribbean States, signed by Prime Minister Eugenia Charles of Dominica. This would enable Reagan to say after the invasion, "After receiving a formal request for help, a unanimous request from our neighboring states, I concluded the United States had no choice but to act strongly and decisively." Reagan had also received an urgent appeal for intervention from Governor General Sir Paul Scoon, head of state of Grenada, which remained a member of the British Commonwealth. Scoon's request was kept secret until Grenada was secure because he feared for his life.[128]

Reagan gave preliminary approval to the invasion on Monday afternoon, then signed a formal order authorizing it at 6:55 P.M., shortly before his meeting with the congressional leaders. He then tardily called British Prime Minister Margaret Thatcher, who bluntly told him she was opposed to the invasion. But Reagan had no intention of calling it off, even for his most trusted foreign friend and ally. At 5:36 A.M., 400 Marines from the helicopter carrier *Guam* landed at Pearls Airport on the western shore of Grenada. Thirty-six minutes later, U.S. Army Rangers parachuted onto the uncompleted runway at Point Salines, on the southeastern tip of the 133-square-mile island. They encountered unexpectedly heavy antiaircraft fire and resistance on the ground from Cuban soldiers and members of the labor battalion building the airstrip, some of whom were armed with AK-47s. It took two days of fighting to subdue the outnumbered Cuban forces and evacuate the medical students.

Later, the quality of U.S. intelligence and many other aspects of the invasion would be subjected to a withering critique by Pentagon analysts. But the chiefs and the officers who directed the invasion were jubilant at the time. "We blew them away," declared Vice Admiral Joseph Metcalf III, commander of the American task force in Grenada. It had been what one correspondent called with intended irony "a lovely little war." [129] The killers of Maurice Bishop were captured, and order was restored. An immense cache of arms—enough to provision a force of 10,000 men with automatic rifles, machine guns, rocket launchers, antiaircraft guns, howitzers and cannon—was found, along with armored vehicles and coastal patrol boats.

Casualties in the 5,000-member attacking force numbered 115 wounded and 19 dead, including four Navy Seals who drowned on a reconnaissance mission and an Airborne trooper who blew himself up when he opened the breech of a captured recoilless rifle. Fifty-nine of the 800 Cuban defenders on the island were killed and another 25 wounded. The rest surrendered and were returned to Cuba. Forty-five Grenadians were killed and 337 wounded. The first of the evacuated students from the medical school kissed the tarmac when they arrived in Charleston, South Carolina, thirty hours after the invasion. Wirthlin's polls showed that an overwhelming number of Americans approved of the Grenada operation.

Fortunately for Reagan, the invasion of Grenada would overshadow the disaster in Beirut throughout the 1984 campaign. This was Reagan's doing. The invasion was not a product of events in Lebanon, but the president and his White House staff were shameless and successful in using the easy victory in Grenada to wipe away the stain of the unnecessary disaster in Beirut. Viewed strictly in political terms, Reagan's nationally televised speech of October 27, 1983, was a masterpiece. Weaving together the disconnected tragedies of KAL 007, Beirut and Grenada into a single message of patriotism and anticommunism, Reagan blamed the ills of the world on the Soviet Union and its surrogates. The Korean airliner had been downed by a Soviet plane. The Soviets had wrecked the possibility of peace in Lebanon by arming Syria. The Marxists on Grenada were in cahoots with Cuba and the advance guard of the Soviet attempt to dominate the world:

> The events in Lebanon and Grenada, though oceans apart, are closely related. Not only has Moscow assisted and encouraged the violence in both countries, but it provides direct support through a network of surrogates and terrorists. It is no coincidence that when the thugs tried to wrest control over Grenada, there were thirty Soviet advisers and hundreds of Cuban military and paramilitary forces on the island. . . .
>
> You know, there was a time when our national security was based on a standing army here within our own borders and shore batteries of artillery along our coasts and, of course, a navy to keep the sea-lanes open for the shipping of things necessary to our well-being. The world has changed. Today, our national security can be threatened in faraway places. It's up to all of us to be aware of the strategic importance of such places and to be able to identify them.

The last sentence could serve more readily as an indictment of U.S. policy in Lebanon than a defense of it. None of Reagan's military advisers considered Lebanon to be of "strategic importance." Retrospectively, neither did McFarlane, who came to the conclusion that he should have realized the hopelessness of depending on the Amin Gemayel government and advised Reagan to withdraw the Marines from Lebanon rather than urging him to keep them there. "Ronald Reagan called Lebanon vital to United States national security interests, which, in any context, it is not," McFarlane said. "If Lebanon disappeared, it wouldn't affect the United States' security interests very much." [130]

Reagan, however, would never second-guess himself. He had decided that Lebanon was "vital" to U.S. interests and "vital" it would always remain to him, even after U.S. forces were withdrawn. In an extraordinary triumph of optimism over reality, Reagan convinced himself that the attack on the Marines symbolized the success of U.S. policy in Lebanon. "The multinational force was attacked precisely because it is doing the job it was sent to do in Beirut," Reagan said in his October 27 speech. "It is accomplishing its mission." In a January 16, 1984, interview with *The Washington Post,* Reagan extolled the success of the MNF and waxed lyrical about the U.S. Marines. "We arrived and were well received by the people there," Reagan said. "As a matter of fact, our American Marines in the typical American military fashion pretty soon were organizing helpful things for kids, teaching them to play ball and all the sort of things of this kind in the city. I have mail that indicates that the people felt that finally they had a chance to live relatively normal lives." [131]

After bloody Sunday, normalcy for the surviving Marines in Beirut was underground. The Marines were dispersed in bunkers, moving from post to post in covered trenches and having no contact with the people of Beirut. "They lived like moles," said the U.S. defense attaché. [132] Back in Washington, Weinberger and the chiefs tried to extricate them. They no longer cared how Reagan described the mission as long as he withdrew the Marines. But Reagan resisted, supported once more by his secretary of state. Reagan and Shultz were convinced that withdrawal was the equivalent of surrendering to terrorism. "We must not strip every ounce of meaning and purpose from their courageous sacrifice," Reagan said of the Marines in his October 27 speech.

Republican politicians on Capitol Hill and within the White House took a different view. With few exceptions, they had lined up loyally behind the president on Lebanon, even though Senate Majority Leader Howard Baker had always been skeptical about the merits of intervention. Now, Republican congressmen and White House Chief of Staff James Baker looked at Lebanon and saw Vietnam. The two Bakers knew that Grenada and the president's October 27 speech had bought them time, and they wanted to use it to construct a rationale for withdrawal. The Bakers believed that Lebanon had the potential to become a major Republican political liability in 1984. Though neither of them had rapport with Weinberger, they became de facto allies of the Pentagon in the attempt to maneuver Reagan into withdrawing the Marines. In hindsight, this withdrawal seems inevitable. But in the aftermath of the bombing in Beirut, the Bakers were uncertain if Reagan could be persuaded to redeploy the Marines. As distanced as he was from day-to-day decision-making, Reagan could be stubbornly resistant to changing his position once he had taken a stand. He believed what he had told the nation on television. He did not want to abandon what he called the "successful" U.S. mission in Lebanon.

Four events forced Reagan to face political reality. The first was the failure of a retaliatory mission that was pushed by the State Department and opposed by the Pentagon. The second was the report of the Department of Defense Commission on Beirut, chaired by retired Admiral Robert Long. The third was the reaction of Congress, agitated by changing public opinion during its Christmas recess. And the fourth was the collapse of the Lebanese Army, on which the administration had lavished much equipment, training and false hopes.

Even while still basking in the glow of Grenada, Reagan was determined to retaliate in Lebanon. He discussed retaliation with Stuart Spencer in the White House residence a few days after the bombing. "He was angry and wanted to strike back," Spencer said.[133] Reagan's political advisers, including Baker and Deaver as well as Spencer, were cautious. So was Weinberger, earning the respect of Spencer, who was no Weinberger fan. "I'm not an eye-for-an-eye man," said Weinberger afterward.[134] The secretary of defense had denounced Israeli retaliations that killed civilians, and he now opposed any U.S. action that might have similar results. Reagan agreed on this point; he wanted a strictly military target. The chiefs settled, not without qualms, on the Sheik Abdullah Barracks in Baalbek, headquarters of the Iranian Revolutionary Guards and their Lebanese Shiite allies. Baalbek was protected by Syrian antiaircraft power, and General Vessey warned that U.S. planes could be lost in the attack. His fears were justified. The bombing of Baalbek was conducted on December 4 by twenty-three aircraft from the carriers *Independence* and *Kennedy*. Two A-6 bombers were lost to Syrian antiaircraft fire, and a pilot killed. Lieutenant Robert Goodman, the bombardier of one of the downed planes, was captured by the Syrians and later released. The raid proved a propaganda coup for the Syrians, who lost two gun emplacements and a radar building, which was quickly repaired.

The Long Commission report was completed on December 20 and delivered to Reagan on Friday, December 23. The administration delayed releasing it for another five days, ostensibly so a nonclassified version could be prepared but actually because its findings discomforted both the White House and the Pentagon. Weinberger, who believed the Marines had done their best with an impossible mission, thought the report came down too hard on the Marine commanders in Lebanon, Colonel Timothy Geraghty and Lieutenant Colonel Howard

Gerlach. The report found that they had concentrated too many men in a single building and failed "to take the security measures necessary to preclude the catastrophic loss of life." The report was particularly embarrassing to Marine commandant P. X. Kelley, who had repeatedly expressed confidence in the security measures.

The report was also an embarrassment to the White House, although it steered away from personal criticism of the president. The commission concluded that "as progress toward a diplomatic solution slowed," the administration had relied increasingly on military options without paying "clear recognition" to changing political conditions or the threat of terrorism. "It was contemplated from the outset that [the Marines] would operate in a relatively benign environment," the report said. One of the report's principal recommendations was that Weinberger "continue to urge that the National Security Council undertake a reexamination of alternative means of achieving U.S. objectives in Lebanon . . . [including] a more vigorous and demanding approach to pursuing diplomatic alternatives."[135] In plain language this meant: Get the Marines out of Lebanon.

But as the result of a White House trick, the first press accounts of the report's findings focused almost entirely on the security lapses at Marine headquarters rather than on the commission's comments about the confused and ill-defined nature of the Marine mission. White House officials anonymously leaked the findings about lax security measures to reporters on the day after Christmas, while saying nothing about the implied criticism of Reagan's policy. The next day, moments before he left for his annual post-Christmas vacation in Los Angeles and Palm Springs, Reagan read a statement in the White House briefing room declaring that he had received the report and "reviewed it thoroughly." In his comments Reagan emphasized the report's discussion of "the problem of terrorism" and said that "today's terrorists are better armed and financed, they are more sophisticated, they are possessed by a fanatical intensity that individuals of a democratic society can barely comprehend." For this reason, Reagan said, he did not believe that the Marine commanders on the ground, "men who have already suffered quite enough, should be punished for not fully comprehending the nature of today's terrorist threat. If there is to be blame, it properly rests here in this office and with this president. And I accept responsibility for the bad as well as the good."

In saying that he was accepting responsibility, Reagan was actually evading it. By omitting mention of the Long Commission's criticism of the definition of the Marine mission, he focused attention where he wanted to focus it—on the terrorists in Lebanon and on the Marine officers rather than himself. In sparing the officers from the ordeal of courts-martial, Reagan also spared himself from an airing of the policy that had made the Marines sitting ducks. And White House officials, including Baker and McFarlane, had calculated correctly that later stories about the larger implications of the Long Commission report would never catch up with Reagan's original announcement.

But U.S. voters were beginning to focus on Lebanon. The outburst of national pride and patriotism that had sustained the administration after the invasion of Grenada had subsided, and polls in January 1984 showed that a majority of Americans favored withdrawing the Marines. The returning Congress had heard this message. Democrats pressed resolutions calling for a pullout, while Republicans shared their concern with the White House staff. In the House the effort was led by Tip O'Neill, who was having second thoughts about the wisdom of supporting the extended Marine deployment. When he attended the Super Bowl on January 22, O'Neill said, "everybody came up to me and said, 'Get those Marines out.' "[136] As McFarlane would put it, a presidential election year "does concentrate your mind."[137] Before Christmas, McFarlane had talked about moving the Marines to a safer location in Lebanon—a proposal Weinberger was unwilling to consider. Now, McFarlane was tugged by the rising political tide. "Gently but persistently, Jim [Baker] began to say, 'Bud, what is the light at the end of the tunnel here?' And I had to tell him, 'There really isn't any,' " McFarlane said.[138]

As in Vietnam, the most decisive factor in the U.S. decision to abandon its commitment in Lebanon was the military situation. The Lebanese Army on which McFarlane and Shultz had based their hopes had fallen apart, largely because Gemayel had used it for the factional purpose of preventing the Muslims from having a greater say in the governance of Lebanon. Druze and Shiite leaders called upon Muslim members of the army to lay down their arms. Many did, and some who did not were killed or beaten. Even Shultz was shaken. According to one account, he told a meeting of the National Security Council, "If I ever say send in the Marines again, somebody shoot me."[139] Shultz nonetheless continued to support a U.S. military presence in Lebanon.

Reagan was also a holdout, although a misleading White House chronology issued after the withdrawal made him seem a hypocrite instead. At a White House meeting on February 1, 1984, Weinberger used the

Long Commission recommendation as a basis for again urging the president to withdraw the Marines. His by now familiar argument was that the May 17 agreement was a dead letter, with the Israelis gone from most of Lebanon and the Syrians determined to stay. Shultz was away on a trip to South America and Grenada, and State was represented at the meeting by Undersecretary Lawrence Eagleburger. He said the United States would send the wrong signal by walking away from its agreements. Reagan said almost nothing, and Eagleburger left the meeting believing that the policy had not changed. According to a chronology issued a week later by White House spokesman Larry Speakes, from information supplied to him by NSC assistant John Poindexter, Reagan actually made a decision "in principle" on February 1 to withdraw the Marines. In fact, Reagan was still insisting on February 2 that the Marines would stay in Lebanon. In an interview that day with *The Wall Street Journal,* Reagan said, "If we get out, it also means the end of Lebanon." Albert Hunt, the *Journal*'s Washington bureau chief, opened the questioning on Lebanon by observing that Tip O'Neill had called the Lebanon policy a failure and saying that the House was expected to pass a resolution calling for withdrawal of the Marines. Hunt asked Reagan how he would respond to that.

"Well, I'm going to respond that he may be ready to surrender, but I'm not," Reagan said. "As long as there is a chance for peace, the mission remains the same." [140]

It was an undeserved slur, especially since O'Neill's support three months earlier had made it possible for the administration to gain congressional approval of the resolution authorizing continued deployment of the Marines—a fact Hunt noted before asking his question. But Reagan's combative answer accurately reflected his belief that the United States should not pull out of Lebanon. In his radio speech from Camp David on Saturday, February 4, he was even more forceful, if less personal. "Yes, the situation in Lebanon is difficult, frustrating and dangerous," Reagan said. "But that is no reason to turn our backs and to cut and run. If we do, we'll be sending one signal to terrorists everywhere. They can gain by waging war against innocent people."

Even as Reagan spoke, the Lebanese Army and the Gemayel government were disintegrating. On February 2 the Lebanese Army shot and killed a young Shiite Amal militiaman in retaliation for shooting of two of its soldiers by snipers. Shiite fighters took to the streets and overran two army positions. The army responded with heavy shellfire. On February 4, Nabih Berri, the leader of Amal, called on Muslim members of the government to resign and on Muslim members of the army to lay down their arms. The Gemayel government collapsed on February 5. By February 6, with many of the Shiite members of the army remaining in their barracks, Amal and Druze militiamen had seized most of Beirut.

Reagan left Washington on February 6 for a sentimental journey to Illinois, where he attended a celebration in honor of his seventy-third birthday at Dixon High School. Afterward, he spoke at Eureka College, saying that he had brought an end to "an era of paralyzing self-doubt" when other nations could threaten the United States. "We've changed this," Reagan said to the students and faculty of his alma mater. "We're trying to see to it that American citizens—and it doesn't matter whether they're Navy pilots in the Gulf of Sidra or medical students in Grenada —can no longer be attacked or their lives endangered with impunity."

Americans in Lebanon held a different view. "It was an intolerable situation," said Major Joseph Englehardt, the Army attaché. "With the Lebanese Army gone, you realized just how thin a line a Marine amphibious battalion really is. We were surrounded by hostile militias, and we either had to get serious about defending ourselves or we had to get out. There was no more good to be done."[141]

In Washington, this was also McFarlane's view. "We had to face up to the fact it wasn't working, and we were putting lives at risk," he said.[142] The presidential party by now had proceeded on to Las Vegas, where Reagan was to give two speeches the following morning. The White House press office, set up on the casino level of the Sands Hotel, issued a "statement on the situation in Lebanon" calling on the government of Syria to cease its support of "terrorist attacks on the people of Lebanon" and proclaiming that "The commitment of the United States to the unity, independence and sovereignty of Lebanon remains firm and unwavering." Upstairs, White House Chief of Staff James Baker talked to Vice President Bush, who would be convening an NSPG meeting the following morning. Bush, whom outsiders viewed as a nearly invisible Reagan loyalist, was at the center of things, as he had been in the planning for the Grenada invasion. The vice president agreed with Baker that it was time for the United States, if not to cut and run, at least to cut its losses in Lebanon.

Weinberger, who had never really wanted the Marines in Lebanon, now had the support he had long sought in his campaign to "redeploy" the Marines. The NSPG meeting that would produce this decision convened at 11:00 A.M. on Tuesday, February 7, and proceeded for more than two hours while Reagan was speaking to the National Association of Secondary School Principals and then to a Nevada Republican Party fund-raising luncheon in Las Vegas. He made no mention of Lebanon in either speech. At the NSPG meeting, Weinberger was strongly supported by McFarlane, who had in October agreed with Shultz that the presence of the Marines was indispensable to a political settlement in Lebanon. It was now evident to McFarlane that Amin Gemayel was incapable of making the concessions needed to form a united government of Lebanon, and the national security adviser thought it irresponsible to risk more American casualties in this cause. Bush firmly supported withdrawal. Eagleburger was the only dissenter when the vice president formally put the proposal to the NSPG.

Technically, the decision was still Reagan's to make. Actually, as McFarlane would say afterward, it had been made in the NSPG meeting.[143] After his speech in Las Vegas the president was taken to a holding room in the Herbst-Collins Executive Hangar at McCarran International Airport, where Bush reported to him over a secure phone line. The vice president emphasized that all of Reagan's advisers except Shultz favored the decision, which he presented as a "redeployment," as Weinberger had suggested. The United States would continue to support the government of Lebanon with naval artillery fire and air support. Reagan agreed, ending the U.S. commitment in a phone conversation even briefer than the one in which he had originally authorized Habib to commit the United States to participation in the MNF.

Air Force One departed from Las Vegas en route to the Point Mugu Naval Air Station on the shining coast of California, where a helicopter was waiting to take the president to his ranch. It was now approaching midnight in Lebanon, and Donald Rumsfeld, who had succeeded McFarlane as special envoy to the Middle East, was breaking the bad news to Gemayel in the basement bunker of his bombed-out presidential palace. The Israelis had been informed of the decision.

When Air Force One landed at Point Mugu, copies of a new "statement on the situation in Lebanon" were distributed to the small pool of reporters traveling on the presidential aircraft and simultaneously made available to reporters who had remained at the press room in Las Vegas after being alerted that a new statement on Lebanon would be issued. The statement announced "decisive new steps" that included "naval gunfire and air support against any units firing into greater Beirut from parts of Lebanon controlled by Syria," a promise of accelerated training of the Lebanese Army once the government of Lebanon was able "to reconstitute itself into a broadly based representative government" and a request to Weinberger to submit "a plan for redeployment of the Marines from Beirut Airport to their ships offshore." Reagan did not use the word "withdrawal." The statement said the new measures "will strengthen our ability to do the job we set out to do and to sustain our efforts over the long term."

Reporters were not allowed to come close enough to Reagan to question him, but John Poindexter remained at Point Mugu to answer their questions. Speaking anonymously as "a senior administration official," Poindexter discussed the military situation in Lebanon and said that Weinberger would soon present his plan to Reagan. He too avoided the word "withdrawal" but emphasized that "the immediate fighting in the streets of Beirut is a problem for the government of Lebanon and the Lebanese armed forces to control." This government by now hardly existed, as Poindexter knew, but he could not say that. Instead, he said that "the U.S. has not given up on the government of Lebanon. We still support the government of Lebanon. We think that it is a viable entity." [144]

But that was not the way it looked in Lebanon.

16

AN ACTOR ABROAD

You'd be surprised how much being a good actor pays off.

RONALD REAGAN IN CHINA,
April 30, 1984 [1]

Though he disliked traveling, Ronald Reagan's talents as a performer were suited to the world stage. His writers lavished their finest scripts and his White House impresarios their most elaborate productions on Reagan appearances in London, Normandy, Korea, Moscow and at the Berlin Wall. Reagan, often at his best when the spotlight shone most brightly, responded with sprightly performances. On rare occasions he even performed effectively without a script, drawing upon his life's experience to convey a sense of hope and purpose. Curious university students in Shanghai and Moscow were fascinated with Reagan's autobiographical account of how a small-town boy from Illinois, living in a land where anything is possible, became a movie actor and subsequently president of the United States. Even students handpicked for Marxist-Leninist reliability and armed with anti-American questions were charmed by Reagan's friendly, self-deprecating manner and his homely observations about life. "I should tell you that when you get to be my age you're going to be surprised how much you recall the feelings you had in these days here and . . . how easy it is to understand the young people because of your own having been young once," Reagan said in answering a student's question at Moscow State University in 1988. "You know an awful lot more about being young than you do about being old." *

Reagan also fascinated and often charmed world leaders, even though some of them wondered how a man of his background could become president of the world's most powerful democracy. When they came to know him, they were apt to wonder even more. "You could see it in the faces of the foreign leaders—Mitterrand, Thatcher, even Gorbachev," said a U.S. official who accompanied Reagan in many meetings with foreign leaders. "They didn't pay much attention to what he was saying. Either they had heard it before, or they realized it was just talking points. But Reagan the man, the politician, fascinated them. It was almost as if they were saying, what does this man have that works so well for him? It was like they wanted to bottle it and take it home and use it themselves."[2]

During the first year of his presidency, when he was preoccupied by necessity and choice with his economic program, Reagan ventured no farther abroad than Canada. But he traveled widely in the succeeding seven years, visiting twenty-five nations and the Vatican and attending all of the annual economic summits conducted by the world's seven leading industrialized democracies. Counting multiple visits, including six trips to Mexico and five to Canada, Reagan made forty-four stopovers in foreign countries during his White House years. He took six trips to Europe, three to Asia and one to South America and met Mikhail Gorbachev in Geneva, Reykjavik, Washington, Moscow and New York. He never visited Africa or Australia. A contemplated visit to the Philippines that worried Nancy Reagan was canceled because of security concerns.

In all his travels, Reagan played the role of the quintessentially innocent American. He lowered his voice in the Vatican, gazed in amazement at the size and splendor of Windsor Castle and was dazzled by the marvel of excavated life-size terra-cotta warriors from the Xin dynasty in Xi'an, the cradle of Chinese civilization. ("You had gone through so much of civilization before . . . the Roman Empire even came into being or fell," he said afterward.)[3] He was an actor, cognizant

---

* After the speech Gary Lee of *The Washington Post,* a Russian-speaking correspondent then assigned to Moscow, overheard two women students enthusiastically praising Reagan's remarks. "You can see why he's called the Great Communicator," said one of them.

of the cameras even when the cameras were not rolling, but he was also a quiet patriot whose eyes moistened at the sight of any American soldier's grave in a foreign land. Reagan felt "lucky" to be an American, using the word in the same sense, he once said to me, that the great Joe DiMaggio had used it in the title of his autobiography, *Lucky To Be a Yankee*.[4] His happy acceptance of the good fortune of his nationality showed in his confident walk and gestures and the smiling informality with which he posed with foreign leaders, who alongside him appeared wooden and contrived. On his foreign trips, as in so many of his movie roles, he portrayed the wholesome hometown boy who had made good. Americans abroad cheered at the sight of him, and even those of us in the press corps who relentlessly parodied Reagan's locutions (quoting him, perhaps, as saying to a group of Frenchmen, "Well, we're all Americans") were vaguely reassured by his unassuming Americanness.

On location overseas, as citizen-president of the United States, Reagan was the embodiment of American idealism. Foreigners appreciated his sense of world community and his awareness of the contributions that foreigners had made to the creation and renewal of America. "You have to understand that Americans come from every corner of the world," Reagan said. "I received a letter from a man [who] said you can go to live in France, but you cannot become a Frenchman; you can go to Germany, you cannot become a German—or a Turk, or a Greek or whatever," he said in Moscow and many other places. "But anyone, from any corner of the world, can come to live in America and become an American."[5]

Reagan was a democratic internationalist. He believed that those who did not live in America were equally entitled to the blessings of freedom and material prosperity. History had cast him as an apostle of freedom, and he made the most of the part. He needed no prompting to present Gorbachev with lists of imprisoned dissidents or of others held in the Soviet Union against their will. In China, Reagan quoted from the Declaration of Independence and said, "We believe in the dignity of each man, woman and child. Our entire system is founded on an appreciation of the special genius of each individual, and of his special right to make his own decisions and lead his own life." The Chinese authorities did not want the Chinese people to hear these words, and they censored them from Reagan's speech before it was broadcast on national television. Reagan responded by delivering another speech in defense of democracy at Fudan University in Shanghai. Answering questions from students beforehand, he predicted that freedom and

technology would transform their lives. "I can remember my first automobile ride," he said. "There were no airplanes then, there was no
television, there was no radio, and there was certainly no travel in space.
But . . . in one generation we have gone from horse and buggy to the
moon in a spaceship. And . . . those are the building blocks that you
have with which to go forward from here. And don't be afraid to dream
and make your dreams come true."[6]

Reagan was himself a dreamer, capable of imagining a world without
nuclear weapons or trade barriers. In announcing his presidential candidacy on November 11, 1979, he had proposed a "North American
accord" in which commerce and people would move freely across the
borders of Canada and Mexico. This idea, largely overlooked or dismissed as a campaign gimmick in the United States, rankled nationalist
sensibilities in these neighboring nations. But Reagan was serious in his
proposal. Though he traveled only once outside the North American
continent during the first fifty-seven years of his life, he was neither
insular nor isolationist. California has windows to the world in Asia,
and Reagan thought of the United States as a Pacific power as well as
an Atlantic one. He also had a Californian's consciousness of Mexico
and an actor's appreciation of Canadians, who are well represented in
the film community and on the stage. The dream of a North American
accord would drive the administration in successful pursuit of a U.S.-
Canadian free trade agreement and a future-oriented "framework"
trade agreement with Mexico.

As governor of California, Reagan made four foreign trips at the
behest of President Nixon from 1969 through 1973. Except for the
dirty work of explaining Nixon's shift in China policy to Chiang Kai-
shek on Taiwan, all these trips abroad were ceremonial or "goodwill"
missions to such innocuous events as the opening of the Philippine
Cultural Center in Manila in 1969. Nixon seems to have thought of
Reagan as an ideal representative to rightist allies of the United States
abroad, much as he was a bridge to the conservative movement at home.
On Nixon's behalf Reagan met with Chiang and also with Ferdinand
Marcos in the Philippines, Francisco Franco in Spain and Lee Kuan
Yew in Singapore. He also met a scattering of mainstream world lead-
ers, including British Prime Minister Edward Heath and Japanese
Prime Minister Eisaku Sato. After Nixon, Reagan traveled on his own
to London in 1975 and took two extensive trips to major capitals in

Europe and Asia in 1978 in preparation for his 1980 presidential campaign. This enabled Reagan to deal with questions about his inexperience in world affairs by rattling off a list of all the foreign leaders he had met (usually omitting Franco) in demonstration of his qualifications. As Reagan saw it, these meetings really had taught him much of what he needed to know, for he viewed a president's dealings with foreign leaders as primarily ceremonial.

Reagan had a domestic focus when he came to office and no grand designs of summitry. Despite his internationalist impulses, he privately acknowledged that he found it hard to keep up with the name changes of countries that had come into existence since World War II—not a novel complaint for someone of his generation. But as president, Reagan sometimes had trouble even with nations whose names had not been changed. On December 1, 1982, at a state dinner in Brasília, Reagan raised his wine glass in a toast to Brazilian President João Figueiredo and "the people of Bolivia," a gaffe which he attempted to correct and instead compounded by saying, "That's where I'm going next." Reagan's next stop was actually Colombia, and his faulty toast became big news in that country as well. The double blooper so dismayed the White House press office that it altered the public transcript and quoted Reagan as toasting "the people of Bogotá," the Colombian capital.[7] On Air Force One returning from the five-day trip, which also included stops in Costa Rica and Honduras, Reagan said he had "learned a lot" about Latin America. "I went down to find out from them and their views," he said. "And you'd be surprised, yes, because, you know, they're all individual countries."[8]

My report of Reagan's discovery appeared in *The Washington Post* under the headline "Latin Trip an Eye-Opener for Reagan." It prompted a few angry letters complaining that the president had been portrayed unfairly as an ignoramus. But the more lasting import of Reagan's interview was to convince his staff of the necessity of restricting media access to the president that might detract from the emphasis or "spin" that the White House wanted to place on events. It would be nearly a year and a half before Reagan would again be allowed to express his reactions while returning from a foreign land. I was told that Reagan himself had reacted with some anger to my account of his interview. All he had intended by his observation about "individual countries" was to point out that many Americans, including himself, had too often lumped together Latin American nations as a single entity. "You don't talk that way about Europe," he said. "You recognize the differences between various countries. And the same thing is true here."[9]

Reagan *did* recognize differences in Europe, and he also understood that these differences were reflected in American politics. Reagan's various managers valued his father's Irish heritage and Roman Catholicism, which they regarded as advantageous attributes for a contemporary American politician. Reagan is not and never has been a Catholic, and he knew very little about his father's family background before 1980 when research by Debrett's of London and Hibernian Research of Dublin established that Jack's great-grandfather, Michael O'Regan (as it was then spelled), left County Tipperary during the famine of the 1840s and settled in England.[10] Reagan had not displayed any particular interest in his father's roots before the presidential campaign. He did not visit Ireland on his first and most extended trip abroad—to Britain late in 1949 for the filming of *The Hasty Heart*—or on three later visits to London. His only trip to Ireland had been in 1972, when Dublin was the final stop on a seven-nation goodwill tour he made as Nixon's emissary.

But the idea of a "roots" trip to Ireland in the presidential reelection year of 1984 was highly appealing to Mike Deaver and the political staff, and Reagan was not resistant. The stopover in the Republic of Ireland proved a boon to the souvenir business in the dusty, out-of-the-way village of Ballyporeen, where local merchants imaginatively marketed little packages of dirt purported to be samples of the Reagan family sod. "I can't think of a place on the planet I would rather claim as my roots more than Ballyporeen, County Tipperary," Reagan declared, as the cameras rolled.[11] Later, he would say to Dublin mayor Michael Keating that he was in Ireland "representing more than forty million of our fellow citizens whose roots are here in Ireland."

"Forty million voters?" asked Helen Thomas of United Press International.

"Just forty million good citizens," Reagan replied without batting an eye.[12]

But for all his sturdy show of Irishness, Reagan much preferred to be in London, visiting the queen or, even better, Prime Minister Margaret Thatcher. Reagan was an ardent Anglophile, so much so that his warm feelings for the British survived a nasty London winter where *The Hasty Heart* was filmed on a drafty stage with the actors wearing tropical clothing befitting the movie's Burmese setting. It was widely believed that Reagan's Anglophilia was a product of World War II, when Hollywood was ardently pro-British and Reagan participated in the making of such training films as *The Memphis Belle,* William Wyler's famous movie about the B-17 "Flying Fortress" bomber. But Reagan's admiration for the British may have been formed during his Illinois boyhood rather than in Hollywood. Reagan said in his autobiography that he first realized he wanted to become an actor when he identified with Captain Stanhope, the hero of the British antiwar play *Journey's End,* which a touring London company performed in Dixon. It would be difficult to identify with Stanhope without also identifying with the British.[13]

There is nothing speculative about the origin of Reagan's admiration for Thatcher, whom he first met in 1975 on a trip to London soon after she became the Conservative Party leader. They hit it off immediately, talking for more than an hour about the need for economic reform in Britain and the United States. Reagan was asked that evening at a reception what he thought of Thatcher. He replied that she would make "a magnificent prime minister." His British questioner demurred, saying that it would be unthinkable for a woman to become prime minister. "England had a queen named Victoria once who did rather well," Reagan said. The Englishman replied, "By Jove, I'd forgotten all about that." [14]

Quite possibly this story is apocryphal, since it is unlikely that any Englishman attending an upper-class reception in London would have forgotten about Queen Victoria. But Reagan did indeed sing Thatcher's praises following their first meeting and ever afterward. When Thatcher visited Washington a month after Reagan's inauguration, he praised her effusively despite suggestions from some of his advisers that he maintain a respectful distance from what then seemed a doomed effort to restore fiscal order in Britain. Instead, Reagan said that he and Thatcher believed that "people will stay free when enterprise remains free." In the same ceremony Reagan also paid homage to the Anglo-American alliance, saying that on matters vital to Western security, "there is one element that goes without question: Britain and America will stand side by side." [15] Thatcher responded in kind. The following year, at a luncheon at 10 Downing Street after what Thatcher called Reagan's "magnificent speech" at Westminster, she said to him, "Mr. President, both before and since you took office, I've come to know you as a personal friend who can be relied on in times of danger, who's not going to compromise on the values of the free world, who seeks the reduction of world tensions and the strengthening of world security, who will do everything possible to encourage creative enterprise and initiative." [16]

Such flowery public exchanges persisted throughout Reagan's presidency and afterward and revealed the genuine sentiments of the two leaders. Thatcher and Reagan did not in fact always stand "side by side" on issues. She was more flexible than he in dealing with the pre-Gorbachev Soviet Union and far less flexible in dealing with domestic opposition. The two differed on such important matters as the Soviet natural gas pipeline to Europe, the Strategic Defense Initiative and the U.S. invasion of Grenada. Thatcher was also far more of a fiscal conservative than Reagan: she found the U.S. federal budget deficits alarming, even though she never publicly challenged Reagan's inaccurate explanation that they were entirely the fault of Congress. But Thatcher appreciated Reagan's support during the Falklands War, and the president valued the prime minister more than any other foreign leader, and with good reason. He knew he could always count on her to come to his defense ("like a mother hen," said one White House aide) if he floundered or came under fire at an economic summit or NATO meeting. He also recognized that their fundamental philosophical agreement far outweighed their differences. Both leaders were committed to the triumph of capitalism at a time when other democracies were moving left of center. Each of them seemed less lonely in international affairs because of the presence of the other. "When we attempt an overall survey of President Reagan's term of office, covering events both foreign and domestic, one thing stands out," Thatcher wrote in *National Review* in the final month of Reagan's second term. "It is that he has achieved the most difficult of all political tasks: changing attitudes and perceptions about what is possible. From the strong fortress of his convictions, he set out to enlarge freedom the world over at a time when freedom was in retreat—and he succeeded." [17]

Reagan was particularly appreciative of having Thatcher in his corner during his early ventures onto the world stage, when his inner confidence may not quite have matched his fortress of convictions. His first encounter with world leaders was at a Sunday dinner marking the opening of the seventh economic summit on July 19, 1981, from which all aides were excluded except interpreters. The setting, one of the most picturesque of any of the economic summits, was the Château Montebello in a wooded area of lakes and streams sixty-two miles east of Ottawa. Reagan was meeting the leaders of France, Italy and Japan for the first time. He had met Canadian Prime Minister Pierre Trudeau, who would never be his favorite, on a visit to Canada earlier in the year and had twice met briefly with West German Chancellor Helmut

Schmidt. But Reagan placed his confidence in Thatcher, or so I surmised from a comment he made later to a White House aide that he had really valued "having Maggie on his side" at the dinner.

In preparing for the summit Reagan had expressed to his aides the naïve and appealing idea that the heads of government should take advantage of their face-to-face meeting to talk openly about whatever was on their minds, whether or not it related to the formal agenda of the summit. This was an intuitively useful view of the real value of these meetings, which usually produced platitudinous and technical communiqués largely worked out in advance by the experts, or "sherpas," who planned the meetings. Reagan regarded the communiqué as just another boring detail, which in a sense it was. But his staff was horrified at the thought of Reagan conversationally roaming the world political landscape without a guide or map. They convinced him that it was necessary at the Ottawa summit to reassure the allies of his willingness to reduce high U.S. interest rates and of his desire to improve relations with the Soviet Union. Reagan dutifully took to dinner the talking points his aides had prepared for him, transcribed onto the usual cards. But he was spared by Thatcher from using them. After short speeches by Japanese Prime Minister Zenko Suzuki and French President François Mitterrand, who were also attending their first summit, Thatcher suggested that the evening might go best if they all just had "a free-wheeling discussion." [18]

According to Ed Meese, who was not there but debriefed Reagan afterward, this conversation focused on the political mood of Europe and "the very great sentiment in that area" for arms control negotiations with the Soviet Union.[19] That was not the principal message Reagan took away from the meeting, however. On the return flight from Ottawa two days later, Reagan told Hedrick Smith and me that he had been pleasantly surprised at the critical view of the Soviet Union expressed by Mitterrand. "His resoluteness with regard to the Soviet threat . . . could have sounded like me or anyone else," Reagan said.[20]

Mitterrand has been a long and persistent critic of the Soviet system and it is unlikely, perhaps inconceivable, that any other world leader would have been similarly astonished. But to Reagan, who used the words "socialism" and "communism" interchangeably, the discovery that the Socialist president of France was a staunch anticommunist was a revelation. The only news to come out of the interview was Reagan's comments about Mitterrand, about whom he said he had a "surprisingly" good feeling. Unsurprisingly, he was fulsome in praise of

Thatcher. "There were many times that Margaret Thatcher spoke up and put her finger on the little thing we were trying to resolve or settle, or the wording of something," Reagan said.[21]

What was surprising to me was Reagan's condition. He was exhausted nearly to the point of incoherence throughout much of the interview and could not remember the substance of any subject that had been discussed apart from Mitterrand's expression of anticommunism. He spoke haltingly, as if every word were an effort. I had not seen Reagan at such close range since the assassination attempt nearly four months earlier, and was shocked at his condition. That did not stop me from joining Smith in pressing Reagan, since both of us were soon acutely aware that an interview we had persevered to obtain was not providing much of a story.* Our efforts were in vain. Reagan simply was unable to recall the content of the talks in which he had just participated. When Smith asked him if there were "any light moments" in the summit meetings, the president repeated his old story about the boy who digs happily in manure in hopes of finding a pony. He said he had told this story to Schmidt.

In the midst of the interview, Reagan received a telephone call from Sarah Brady, responding to a call placed to her by the White House operator. When Deaver handed the president the phone, he abruptly brightened as if awakening from a nap and congratulated Sarah Brady and his recuperating press secretary James Brady on their wedding anniversary. Brady, who had watched summit reports on television, told Reagan his Canadian performance was getting good press back home. When the call was completed, Reagan handed the phone back to Deaver and lapsed once more into a state of weary exhaustion. I remember thinking that Reagan was a kindly man who was barely able to perform the duties of his office.

The interview concluded ten minutes later at a signal from Deaver, who did not seem to find the president's condition unusual. This is what happens all the time, I thought. But it was difficult to know this with any certainty, since any seventy-year-old who was recovering from

* It was unusual for *The Washington Post* and *The New York Times* to be doing such an interview together. Smith and I, highly competitive, had been lobbying different White House officials for an exclusive interview with Reagan after the summit. Neither of us knew that the other's request had been granted. We were told shortly before the return flight that our only choice was to do the interview together or not do it at all. At the time I thought this was a White House trick to place substantially the same story in both papers. But the White House had no product to sell on this particular day. Apparently, Reagan's staff had simply decided that the president was too tired to do two interviews.

a gunshot wound might well have been stressed by a trip that had required him to perform at successive nights at dinner. In my story of the interview I noted that "Reagan appeared tired to the point of near-exhaustion" but drew no larger conclusion.[22] Nonetheless, I was bothered by the discrepancy between what I had seen and the description of Reagan's performance in the U.S. media, particularly television. Brady had been right in observing that Reagan's summit performance had received good press in the United States, although this was at least as much the doing of the Canadians as of the White House. As James Reston put it, the Canadians had deliberately isolated the seven leaders "in the most opulent log structure in the world, housed and fed them there, surrounded by security guards—even by divers in the river, presumably to ward off submerged reporters and other terrorists—and then flew them from one safe haven to another in helicopters."[23]

Many of the 1,500 members of the media assigned to the summit did not see the leaders in person until these helicopters brought them to Ottawa for a luncheon and their final meeting on Tuesday, July 21. But the other leaders at least had briefed their accompanying press corps when the summit was over. Reagan was in no condition to conduct a briefing, though no hint of this permeated the glowing assessments of his performance given to reporters by Meese, Larry Speakes and David Gergen. That few of these assessments made their way into print was largely because the summit itself was overshadowed by the story of escalating violence in Lebanon. And television needed pictures, not assessments. These were provided by an array of photo opportunities in which Reagan managed to impress a goodly number of people without saying much of anything. Even Reston took favorable note of Reagan. In a post-summit column he described Reagan as "smiling the most and speaking the least—hard on defending his economic policy at home and even his high interest rates—but conciliatory in a vague way, with a general ease and charm in talking to everybody."[24]

This ease and charm served Reagan as capably as his convictions, enabling him to skate over issues and controversies while resting for his big performances. And his next foreign trip was largely a rest stop. The occasion was the International Meeting on Cooperation and Development, in which twenty-two nations gathered in Cancún, Mexico, on October 21–24, 1981, to discuss the problems of underdeveloped nations. Each of the seven economic summit nations except Italy sent a high-ranking official to the conference, at which China, India and several South American and African nations were also represented. Reagan's speech to the plenary session was a skillful message recalling that the United States had contributed $57 billion to the developing nations during the past decade while also striking an appropriate tone of modesty. ("The U.S. is here to listen and learn," he said.) The meeting was one of the few of Reagan's presidency where he was exposed to pleas for help from such impoverished nations as Bangladesh.

As usual, the process was made as painless as possible for Reagan by the White House staff. The president's hotel suite was converted into an extension of the Oval Office for a series of one-on-one meetings with fourteen world leaders, most of whom Reagan had never met before. He was briefed before each meeting by the appropriate experts, and he dutifully read the requisite policy points from his cards, floundering only when he departed from the prepared script. During a meeting with Indian Prime Minister Indira Gandhi the Indian delegates were pleased when Reagan lauded the "green revolution" that had vastly improved their nation's agricultural yields. But the Indians were also bothered that Reagan did not seem to realize that the Indian government had played an important role in this agricultural revolution, which he depicted as strictly a triumph of capitalism. Later, during a conference session on food production, Reagan was expounding on the accomplishments of free-enterprise farming in the United States, when Tanzanian President Julius Nyerere interrupted and said, "Let me tell you something. U.S. agriculture is the most heavily subsidized in the world."[25]

None of this controversy found its way into the official briefings conducted by U.S. officials for reporters, at which Reagan's meetings with other leaders were uniformly depicted as sessions of sweetness and light. Al Haig misrepresented a meeting between Reagan and Nigerian President Shehu Sagari as displaying a "remarkable convergence of views" on the subject of Namibia, when the two leaders had actually differed over U.S. policies in dealing with South Africa.[26] Overall, however, the conference was less contentious than the U.S. delegation had expected, and the other leaders seemed generally pleased by Reagan's willingness to hear them out. "Reagan won his major gamble in coming to Cancún by emerging without any scars," wrote Lee Lescaze in *The Washington Post.* "On the president's first venture into an arena dominated by the concerns of poor nations, Reagan found much more spirit of cooperation than of controversy."[27]

From a White House public relations point of view, Ottawa and

Cancún were dress rehearsals for Reagan's big European trip of June 3–11, 1982—the troubled odyssey through France, the Vatican, Italy, Britain and West Germany that we encountered earlier in this book. This was the trip on which Reagan unsuccessfully opposed extending credits to the Soviet Union at the economic summit at Versailles, nodded off during a televised meeting with Pope John Paul II, accurately predicted the demise of Marxism-Leninism in his Westminster speech and tried to cope with discord between his protective White House staff and his temperamental secretary of state during the crisis provoked by the Israeli invasion of Lebanon.

Deaver had been planning the trip for nearly a year, working around the fixed dates of the economic summit. He thought in terms of backdrops and photo opportunities and such ceremonial events as Reagan's horseback ride with Queen Elizabeth at Windsor Castle. But Deaver also realized that the trip provided Reagan with an opportunity to demonstrate that he was a man of peace at a time when Europeans were restive about U.S. nuclear arms policy. The White House goals were accurately summarized by *The Wall Street Journal* six days before the trip:

> To convince ordinary European men and women that Mr. Reagan is a sensible and reliable ally rather than the simple-minded, trigger-happy cowboy that many of them still consider him to be; [and] To prove to Americans that whatever troubles the President might be having with the U.S. economy, he can perform successfully and be accepted by his peers as a world statesman.[28]

Reagan's progress toward these objectives was mixed. After the trip I wrote that Reagan had "largely accomplished his major political goal of reassuring the nations he visited that he is not the sort of man who would lead the Western alliance into war" but had also managed "to raise doubts about his capacities and mastery of detail among those who saw him close up."[29] Fortunately for Reagan, the latter category was small. The only Europeans who obtained a firsthand impression of Reagan, except for Queen Elizabeth and the Pope, were the six Western leaders who met with him at Versailles and the additional nine heads of state or government who heard him speak at the NATO summit meeting in Bonn a week later. Reagan was no longer a novelty to the economic summiteers, who showed him less deference on European soil than they had in Canada.

Writing under the heading "Dissareagan," *New York Times* columnist William Safire observed that Reagan's "summit partners treated with cool contempt his call for significant credit restraints to the Soviet bloc."[30] And at the NATO meeting, applause was muffled as Reagan read from his four-by-six cards in platitudinous praise of the alliance and predictable criticism of the Soviets. Canadian Prime Minister Trudeau complained at a briefing afterward that Reagan had engaged in ritual speechmaking rather than discussion.[31] And so he had.

Reagan's meager contributions to the private economic summit and NATO meetings were drawn from his own knowledge and talking points compiled by the NSC staff from administration position papers. His speechwriters and White House producers, aware that Reagan was always more comfortable and convincing when he had the stage to himself, virtually ignored the private meetings and focused their energies on Reagan's public and internationally televised performances. Except for his address at Westminster, the most important of these was a speech to the Bundestag in Bonn, where Reagan's homage to "reasonable strength" was carefully balanced with an expression of U.S. willingness to reduce nuclear arsenals. The speech was widely praised in the West German press. "Remarkable was the understanding President Reagan showed in his speech for public demonstrations of concern about the danger of nuclear war and about the increasing arms arsenals," editorialized *Die Welt,* the leading German conservative newspaper. Reagan's delivery at the Bundestag, as at Westminster, was polished and forceful. He was heckled by two left-wing members of the parliament, one of whom shouted, "What about El Salvador?" Reagan ignored the heckling at first. When it persisted, he said good-humoredly, "Is there an echo in here?" using a line he had employed to put down student protesters in the sixties. The Bundestag broke into laughter and applause.

The hecklers were a tonic to Reagan, who was even more in need of a long nap. He was extremely tired when he spoke to the Bundestag, late in the afternoon of June 9. Nancy Reagan and Deaver were aware that he was exhausted from the rigors of the trip, and his condition would be evident to close observers the following morning when he addressed the NATO Council. But Reagan's stage presence carried him through a closing day that included a five-minute speech to U.S. soldiers and dependents who welcomed him at Tempelhof Airport, a tour of the Berlin Wall and an address to 20,000 Berliners who crowded the grounds of the Charlottenburg Palace. The speeches at Westminster and the Bundestag had been loaded with World War II references, and Reagan was in a World War II mood at Tempelhof, where he told the cheering soldiers that Americans "know that you are their G.I. Joes and Jills and they love you, too." Speaking without a prepared text, Reagan recounted the fictitious story about how a Congressional Medal of Honor was awarded the pilot of a B-17 who went down with his plane rather than abandon his wounded gunner.[32] He contrasted this with the Soviet Union awarding "its highest honor, a gold medal" to a man who "buried a pick-axe in . . . Leon Trotsky's head. They gave their highest honor for murder. We gave our highest honor to a man who had sacrificed his life to comfort a boy who had to die."[33]

Touring the Berlin Wall by car after his speech, Reagan had his limousine stop at Checkpoint Charlie, where he strode over to the white line that separated the U.S. and Soviet zones. When reporters cautioned that he would enter Soviet territory by stepping over the line, Reagan playfully dangled a foot over it but did not put it down. Then he walked along the wall while the cameras rolled. When he returned to his car, a reporter asked what he thought of the wall. "It's as ugly as the idea behind it," Reagan said. Another reporter wanted to know if Reagan thought Berlin would ever again be a united city. "Yes," he said.[34]

This brief exchange was as close as Reagan came to an interview during his ten days in Europe. Deaver knew the dangers of allowing Reagan to give unscripted answers, particularly when he was tired, and no one in the presidential party wanted to chance an interview. Television and radio reporters complained that they couldn't get close enough to Reagan even to shout a question. They were told that he was being kept out of shouting range because of security requirements. This explanation annoyed some members of the Secret Service, who resented the White House using security as an alibi for something that had nothing to do with the president's protection. The "security" alibi was discarded whenever the White House staff thought a photo opportunity could be used to political advantage. Even in the dangerous environment of the Berlin Wall, "security" did not deter Reagan from approaching reporters and saying what he wanted to say.*

---

* Reagan was kept far more isolated than other Western leaders or his White House predecessors. Initially, this reflected Secret Service reaction to the 1981 assassination attempt. The White House staff soon realized, however, that it was more acceptable to say that Reagan was being kept away from reporters for security reasons than to acknowledge that the real reason was that he might give the wrong answer to a question. A Secret Service agent who discussed this with me on condition of anonymity said that security manpower was wasted on the European trip by searching reporters before they entered press rooms or press planes when they would not be in proximity to the

Reporters were openly critical of White House manipulativeness when they returned from Europe. Judy Woodruff, then of NBC, criticized the "misplaced security" that protected the president "from people who were no danger to him."[35] Tom DeFrank of *Newsweek,* who had made fourteen trips abroad with presidents, called Reagan's "far and away the most ineptly organized."[36] But the reporters were less angry than Nancy Reagan, who made it widely known throughout the White House that she considered Deaver responsible for overscheduling Reagan so that he ruined one of the trip's premier photo opportunities by falling asleep during his appearance with the Pope in the papal library on June 7.

None of us then knew of the complications caused in White House scheduling by the first lady's obsessive interest in astrology, and Deaver wasn't in a position to reveal it. In truth, the schedule had been a far too grueling one for Reagan, then seventy-one years old, no matter what the basis of its determination. The Reagans had attended a dinner, an opera and a fireworks display in Versailles with the economic summit participants on the night of June 6 and flown to Rome the next morning. Reagan slept about six hours. His schedule for June 7 included a private meeting with the Pope before their joint appearance. It continued afterward with a brief speech to American seminarians, a luncheon with Italian President Alessandro Pertini, a meeting with Prime Minister Giovanni Spadolini, a flight to London, an arrival ceremony at Heathrow Airport, another arrival ceremony at Windsor Castle and a private dinner with the queen. The public meeting with the Pope had occurred early in the afternoon, the time of day when Reagan was most in need of a nap. Deaver's only defense, unconvincing to the first lady, was that he had pointed out the pitfalls of the schedule to Reagan ahead of time. "I showed him the schedule and said it was going to be very tough," Deaver said. "He signed off on it. Sure, he gets tired. Who doesn't? But in the long run it's going to be seen as a very successful trip."[37]

As a result of the Vatican fiasco, Reagan would never again be overscheduled abroad. If anything, Deaver and his successors went to the other extreme in their efforts to guarantee that Reagan would always

---

president. White House aides defended the practice by saying that someone could put a bomb in a reporter's hand-carried luggage without his knowledge. The agent observed that the hand luggage of White House aides was equally vulnerable but that these aides were not searched before entering the same planes or press rooms.

arrive rested in a foreign land. The presidential party took so long getting to Beijing in 1984 that reporters referred to the trip as the "slow boat to China." As a result of Deaver's precautions, Reagan was a relaxed and effective performer on the three major foreign trips he took during a seven-month period from mid-November 1983 through mid-June 1984, all planned as events in his reelection campaign. Reagan went first to Japan and Korea, then to China and finally to Ireland, Britain and France. The trips demonstrated how an adept White House staff can use the power of the presidency to dominate the domestic political agenda—at least when an accomplished actor plays the role of president. They are examined here, in chronological order.

Japan and Korea
November 9–14, 1983

An additional camera crew accompanied the White House press corps on the first of Reagan's Asian trips. It was provided by the Republican National Committee, already operating on the assumption that Reagan would seek a second term. Reagan had agreed in May, when Japanese Prime Minister Yasuhiro Nakasone visited the White House in advance of the Williamsburg economic summit, to pay a return visit to Japan. The trip also had the diplomatic purpose of reassuring South Korea of U.S. support in the aftermath of the Soviet downing of KAL 007 and the October 9 murder of seventeen Koreans, including four high-ranking government officials, in Rangoon, Burma, by a bomb believed to have been planted at the instigation of North Korea. The Korean visit had been planned in advance of these incidents, but Reagan's political advisers believed that denouncing Soviet conduct on Korean soil would give force to the administration's case. Standing alone, such a message might have seemed too strident. But packaging Japan and Korea together in a single trip enabled the White House to cast Reagan in different roles, as a president who favored both strength and peace.

Scene One was an amiable luncheon in Tokyo on November 10 with Nakasone. Reagan and he had hit it off so well on Nakasone's May 27 visit to the White House and at Williamsburg that reporters referred to their friendly public colloquies as the "Ron and Yasu Show." American reporters often wondered if Nakasone had his own Mike Deaver. Whatever the case, it was soon apparent that the Japanese prime minister, then in political trouble at home, was as adept as Reagan in using a symbolic visit to demonstrate his status on the world stage. In his luncheon toast, Nakasone drew on a metaphor from his White House visit. He compared Reagan to a baseball pitcher and himself to a catcher who together formed "a formidable battery over the Pacific" and were "excellent teammates of the free world." Reagan quipped in response that he sometimes didn't know "who was pitching and who was catching." He then talked for ten minutes about the "deeply held values" shared by the United States and Japan, a scene which played to Nakasone's benefit that evening on Japanese television.

When Japanese viewers turned on their sets the following evening, they were treated to an extended filming of the Reagans visiting their friends, the Nakasones, at their rustic mountain retreat outside Tokyo. After a tea ceremony, the Nakasones helped the Reagans into sleeveless padded jackets, and the two couples were served a six-course Japanese lunch. For the benefit of American reporters, Nakasone's Los Angeles–born niece, Ritsuko Nakata, translated the elaborate calligraphy on the dining room wall: "When a person gets desperate, his actions will reveal his true nature."[38]

Reagan's big scene in Japan was a well-delivered speech to the Diet on November 11 in which he denounced the "folly" of protectionism, called for a "partnership for peace" and declared that "Japanese-American friendship is forever." It was the first speech given by an American president to the Japanese parliament. Reagan was interrupted by applause twenty-five times, most loudly when he said, "I believe there can be only one policy for preserving our precious civilization in this modern age: a nuclear war can never be won and must never be fought. The only value in possessing nuclear weapons is to make sure they can't be used—ever. I know I speak for people everywhere when I say our dream is to see the day when nuclear weapons will be banished from the face of the earth."

Nakasone was buoyed by the visit. After seeing Reagan off at Haneda Airport, he announced that parliamentary elections would be held the following month. Reagan flew on to Seoul, where scores of thousands of Koreans lined the streets to welcome him, many bearing identical banners that said "Welcome Ron and Nancy" and "You love us; we love U.S." In advance of the visit the South Korean government had arrested forty-five prominent dissidents who had written Reagan a letter urging him to draw attention to human rights violations on his visit, as President Carter had done when he met with dissidents in Seoul in 1979. U.S. officials said that Reagan preferred to deal with such issues through "quiet diplomacy." Secretary of State Shultz dismissed the letter, telling reporters they were "overplaying" the denial of civil liberties in South Korea and suggesting that they concern themselves with North Korea instead.[39] That was certainly Reagan's concern.

Armed with rhetoric from conservative White House speechwriter Ben Elliott, Reagan was his old fiery anticommunist self at a state dinner that night hosted by Korean President Chun Doo Hwan. "The murder of 269 innocent people in a defenseless airliner, the very absence here tonight of some of your nation's finest servants, these events have written in blood the stark contrast between those nations that respect human life and those that trample it," Reagan said in his toast to President Chun. "The vicious attack in Rangoon dramatizes the threat your people face. We must stand together to confront this dangerous challenge and to preserve the peace. And this we will do."

On Sunday, November 13, Reagan went to see the threat for himself, visiting Camp Liberty Bell overlooking the Korean Demilitarized Zone [DMZ]. After being driven into the DMZ from Guardpost Collier, six-tenths of a mile from North Korea, a camouflaged Reagan peered through field glasses at a fake town known as Propaganda Village where a 75-foot statue of North Korean leader Kim Il Sung was surrounded by a cluster of building façades. "It looks like a Hollywood back lot, only not as important," Reagan said.[40]

Reagan had reason to be contemptuous of North Korean propaganda, which at the DMZ consisted of ancient loudspeakers blaring martial music and crude pamphlets dropped on the South Korean side by balloons. White House propaganda was more sophisticated. "For Michael K. Deaver," wrote Francis X. Clines of *The New York Times,* ". . . the Asian trip was a triumph of well-chosen events and camera angles built around patriotic tableaux and the Reagan presence. All this was blessed by sunshine when it was most needed, such as the outdoor chapel service at the DMZ, where the robes worn by the choir of Korean orphans were dappled with shadows from the artillery netting that arched overhead as the children sang 'Jesus Loves Me.' "[41] The service was guarded by an armored personnel carrier. When a reporter asked a military policeman why the armored vehicle was there, the MP succinctly replied, "It's there as a backdrop."[42]

This was a day when Reagan was served even by his missteps. When he addressed troops of the 2nd Infantry Division in the mortar bunker area of the camp, he referred to the commanding general who introduced him as "Colonel." The soldiers laughed appreciatively. And they also appreciated a speech that had been calculated to appeal to men who had the lonely duty of patrolling the windswept dividing line between the two Koreas. Reagan thanked the soldiers for serving on "the frontlines of freedom." He said they stood "between the free world and the armed forces of a system that is hostile to everything we believe in as Americans." He said they were appreciated back home. "We know about the cold, windswept nights that leave you aching from head to foot, I'm sure," said Reagan. "We know about having to stay awake and alert on guard duty when you'd rather be at a movie." And he recalled the events of August 18, 1976, when ax-wielding North Korean troops had crossed the DMZ and killed two U.S. Army officers. "Let me state for the record—and I know you feel this way—nothing like that better happen again," Reagan said.

This incident, the last of its kind to involve U.S. soldiers in the DMZ, had occurred more than seven years earlier, when Gerald Ford was president. Three Sundays earlier, on Reagan's watch, 241 Marines had died in the bombing of their headquarters in Beirut. Reagan said the Marines were "peacekeepers in the true sense of the word." And he talked also of Grenada, contrasting the "rescue mission" on that Caribbean nation with the brutal Soviet occupation of Afghanistan. "To call what we did an invasion, as many have, is a slur and misstatement of fact," Reagan said, even though he himself had called the operation an invasion. It didn't matter. Reagan was a hit with the troops. They cheered him when he finished speaking and cheered him again after he dined democratically with them in the enlisted mess, returning one of the two cheeseburgers that had been given him. I was sitting near Reagan's table and noticed that he seemed to be hugely enjoying himself. As we were leaving, a reporter called out, "Strike the set," and Reagan smiled. Later, I wrote that the scene at the camp was "reminiscent of one of those cast-of-thousands films where reporters, White House staff members and soldiers wandered freely from set to set between the various scenes."[43] Reagan was the star of his real-life performance, and all of us had been absorbed into the supporting cast.*

Happiest of all was the Republicans' camera crew, who had been given a choice position to film Reagan's sortie into the DMZ on a hilly

---

* White House officials were so proud of their staging of the DMZ scenes that they inspired me to write a story depicting the day as the filming of a movie called "Frontlines of Freedom" and to describe the Japanese leg of the trip as another film, "Partnership for Peace." A patient editor wisely deleted these excesses, saying that his actions were necessary to keep the story on the front page. He had not reckoned with the headline writer, who wrote over the story, "Reagan's Asian Takes Are in the Can."

outpost where space was so limited that most reporters had to be left in the camp below. But the television networks weren't complaining. Two weeks earlier they had criticized the U.S. military for preventing them from filming the invasion of Grenada. At the DMZ, Deaver had arranged not only for the networks to have the pictures they needed but also for the means of delivering them in time for the evening news. After lunch, when Reagan went off by helicopter to tour Korean Army positions, another Army helicopter airlifted out the precious videotapes of the day's shooting. Newspaper reporters were also able to file before they boarded the buses that took them back to Seoul. The Army had provided a score of telephones from which reporters could direct-dial their home offices from the DMZ over lines so clear it sounded as if they were calling from next door.

Nothing in the trip had been left to chance. Everything had been planned, produced, orchestrated, recorded and flown out. And the White House producers had provided a touching "visual," as Deaver and the television people called them, to complete the trip. Two Korean children in need of open heart surgery were taken by Nancy Reagan aboard Air Force One on the return flight to Washington. When the Reagans returned to the White House by helicopter from Andrews Air Force Base, they walked across the south grounds hand in hand with the youngsters, a seven-year-old girl and a four-year-old boy, to waiting microphones where the president proclaimed his journey a success that was "more than symbolism." That evening, the Reagans and the children were a network visual, exactly as the White House producers had planned. But Mike Deaver was not there to see his handiwork. He had stayed behind and flown on to China, the site of Reagan's next overseas performance.

China
April 26–May 1, 1984

Reagan spent six days in the People's Republic of China, visiting Beijing and Shanghai. He was a week getting there, and he spent another day and a half in Alaska afterward, meeting once more with Pope John Paul II. From the standpoint of White House planning, this trip crowded too closely upon the showcase D-Day anniversary trip to Europe. Deaver had wanted Reagan to make the China trip in 1983. State Department officials, led by Paul Wolfowitz, the assistant secretary for East Asian and Pacific affairs, insisted that the United States would be viewed as needing the U.S.-Sino relationship more than the Chinese if

Reagan went to Beijing before Premier Zhao Ziyang came to Washington. After some diplomatic dickering, it was announced before the Japan–Korea trip that Zhao would visit Washington in January 1984, clearing the way for Reagan to go to China.

The China trip was Reagan's first visit to a Communist country, and the part was more difficult for him than his role had been in Japan and Korea. Reagan had, after all, long been Taiwan's leading political champion in the United States. The government in Beijing was "Red China" or, at best, "mainland China." When he was elected, Reagan still believed that the government that had fled to Taiwan in 1949 was the legitimate government of China. It had taken considerable effort by Haig and later Shultz to persuade Reagan that it was unwise to sell modern fighters and spare parts to Taiwan, an action that the two secretaries of state realized would jeopardize the U.S. relationship with the Beijing government that Richard Nixon and Henry Kissinger had forged in 1972.

Nixon proved influential with Reagan on China. I was told that Nixon had sent Reagan one of his periodic memos, emphasizing the importance of China as a counterweight to the Soviet Union. He also briefed Reagan by telephone before the trip, while Reagan was at his California ranch. Anti-Soviet arguments appealed to Reagan, and he took seriously the political and foreign policy advice given him by Nixon, even though he did not publicize it. Former president Gerald Ford, who had visited China in 1975, also talked to Reagan about the importance of the U.S.-Sino relationship. And the China visit was strongly supported by George Bush, who had served as U.S. representative in China after the 1972 "normalization" of relations and traveled there on Reagan's behalf during the 1980 election campaign.

Nonetheless, Reagan needed to undergo a process of rationalization before he became comfortable with the idea of visiting China. And until he was actually on Chinese soil, rewriting the role that had been defined by Nixon, it wasn't easy. As late as December 2, 1983, in response to a high school student's question about why he was going to China, Reagan said, "Well, President Nixon some years ago opened the door to what was Communist China—still professes to be Communist, although it has undergone many reforms and liberalizations of that kind of rule. But here are around a billion people in the world—capable, energetic people. And it didn't seem right, as he [Nixon] felt at that time, that we should shut the doors, not communicate at all." So far, so good. But when Reagan then tackled what he called the "very delicate problem" of Taiwan, he showed that his basic feelings hadn't changed.

"And we have made it plain, also, that in continuing and trying to build this friendship, relationship, with the People's Republic of China on the mainland, we in no way retreat from our alliance with and our friendship with the Chinese on Taiwan." [44]

The China trip was flanked by "bookend" appearances, as the White House planners called them, in Tacoma, Washington, and Fairbanks, Alaska, where Reagan emphasized the economic advantages of expanded Asian trade. But at the Port of Tacoma, Reagan was nostalgically reminded of the 1940 movie *Tugboat Annie Sails Again,* in which he had played a poor sailor with whom a wealthy socialite (Jane Wyman) fell in love. The film had not done well. Reagan recalled that the cast had been brought into the Tacoma harbor on a yacht for the premiere, "and then that night they saw the movie. And the next morning there we were all alone, out on a curb, trying to flag down a cab." [45]

Such reveries did not disturb Nancy Reagan or Mike Deaver. Their worry was that Reagan might fall asleep in China, a thought that had also crossed the president's mind. When a Weyerhaeuser employee at the Port of Tacoma asked Reagan about his China schedule, he drifted off into a discussion of the international date line and said, "These last several days, every once in awhile I'd stop and think—you know here it is the middle of the afternoon, and what time is it in China? Well, it's the middle of the night. And I've been wondering about when I'm going to find my eyes closing, and it'll be at the wrong time." [46]

This was on April 19, a Thursday. Reagan spent that night and the next two nights at his ranch, followed by two days in Hawaii (where he hammed it up for the cameras by running with a coconut along the beach as if it were a football) and a day in Guam. When he finally arrived in Beijing on the afternoon of April 26, he was physically prepared for a long evening banquet and two days of talks with Deng Xiaoping, Zhao Ziyang and Chinese Communist Party leader Hu Yaobang.

What he was not prepared for was the reaction of the Chinese leaders to speeches which extolled the power of freedom and the magic of the marketplace. Deaver and White House spokesman Larry Speakes had told reporters that the Chinese had agreed to carry Reagan's remarks to a forum in Beijing on April 27 live on Chinese national television. Instead, the Chinese videotaped the speech and deleted passages extolling democratic values and criticizing Soviet behavior. (Among the deletions was a passage saying that the United States drew its power "from two great forces: faith and freedom" and another which said, "Abraham Lincoln defined the heart of democracy when he said, 'No man is good enough to govern another man without that other's consent.'") A Chinese Foreign Ministry spokesman, focusing on the anti-Soviet passages that had been censored, said blandly that it was "inappropriate" for the president to criticize "a third country" while in China.

Reagan responded by reiterating his anti-Soviet views in an interview with Chinese Central Television in Beijing on April 28. Again, the offending remarks were deleted from the television broadcast. The White House put out a statement through Speakes accusing the Chinese of bad faith. On April 30, in the relatively more liberal atmosphere of Shanghai, Reagan again denounced the Soviets and extolled "my own values" of faith in God, free markets, compassion and fairness. This time the speech received lengthy news coverage in the Chinese press and was shown in full on local television but without translation.

I thought that Reagan's persistence in saying what he wanted to say was more impressive than any of the rigged events in the DMZ. "The president says what he thinks," Shultz said. "He's the same man whether he's in Washington, Peking, London or wherever he is."[47] This display of principle overshadowed the policy agreements of the trip, of which much was made at the time. Reagan and Zhao signed a tax agreement designed to encourage private investment in China and a new cultural exchange agreement, both of which had essentially been worked out in advance by the State Department and the Chinese Foreign Ministry. In his eight hours of private meetings with the Chinese leaders, Reagan stuck entirely to the State Department script on Taiwan, and he was surprised by the tactfulness with which the Chinese leaders pressed their claims. Deng referred matter-of-factly to Taiwan as "the knot in our relationship," saying he wanted progress "so that it can be settled after I'm gone."[48] Zhao asked Reagan to cut back arms sales to Taiwan at a faster pace than required by the U.S.-Sino communiqué of 1982. Reagan, who had been braced for an angry lecture, responded simply that he would honor the accord. In talking about Taiwan's future he reiterated the formula response that it was a matter for China and Taiwan to decide peacefully between themselves.

The White House producers of the trip, briefly thrown off stride by the censorship of Reagan's speech, were satisfied by its conclusion. The side trips to Xi'an and the Great Wall and a final day in Shanghai, where hundreds of thousands of Chinese jammed the streets and cheered Reagan, provided useful visuals for the network news and added footage for the Republicans' camera crew. One of these visuals was of Reagan trying his hand at a soldering iron borrowed from a white-smocked worker during a tour of the Shanghai Foxboro Corporation, China's first industrial joint venture with an American partner, the Foxboro Company of Massachusetts. Later, as Reagan inspected a model commune in Shanghai where spotless designated farmers performed their bit parts as adeptly as the president played his lead role, impresario Deaver offered his impressions. "We're going to have our work cut out to top this one in Europe," he said.[49]

Reagan was jubilant. He gave a brief interview to a pool of reporters on Air Force One for the first time since the South American trip a year and a half earlier. "I feel very good about it," Reagan said in summing up his Chinese journey en route to Fairbanks. "I really believe we've reached a new level of understanding." The more Reagan thought about what was going on in China, the more he liked it. By the time he addressed community leaders in Fairbanks on May 1, he was saying the Chinese leaders differed from other Communists in that they "have no expansionist ideas at all." Reagan also had concluded that China was on the road to capitalism. "American concerns can create branches of their own in China, in this so-called Communist China, and they don't have to be in partnership with anyone," Reagan proclaimed enthusiastically as he recounted his visit to Shanghai Foxboro. "And capitalism will be there in these plants."

Reagan stayed overnight in Alaska so he could meet on May 2 at Fairbanks International Airport with the Pope, who was en route to a ten-day tour of Asia. Public and parochial schools had been closed for the day and the president and pontiff took turns addressing a happy and celebrative crowd in which there were many children. Vendors did a brisk business selling T-shirts that proclaimed the meeting as "Great Minds in the Great Land," a slogan parodied by a handful of skeptical demonstrators with T-shirts and posters reading "The Pope Meets the Dope." The White House producers freely if anonymously acknowledged that the meeting was intended to enhance Reagan's appeal with Roman Catholic voters in an election year.[50] "In a violent world, your Holiness, you have been a minister of peace and love," said Reagan. The Pope ended his speech by saying, "God bless America."[51]

Ireland, London and Normandy
June 1–10, 1984

A month later, Reagan was once more an actor abroad. After the blarney of Ballyporeen and an address to the Dáil in Dublin, he flew to London and rested in preparation for his performances in Normandy on June 6, where France, Britain and the United States were commemorating the fortieth anniversary of the Allied invasion of Europe. The economic summit in London that followed these events was beside the point for Deaver, who was focused on putting Reagan at center stage in the high-visibility events in Normandy and finding the French most difficult.

According to the original schedule prepared for June 6, President Mitterrand was to welcome Reagan to Omaha Beach at a French-American ceremony scheduled to begin at 4:00 P.M., or 10:00 A.M. EDT, too late for the morning television shows in the eastern United States. This would have conceded the morning news shows to coverage of the June 5 Democratic presidential primary in California. Deaver wanted Reagan to speak shortly after 7:00 A.M. EDT at Pointe du Hoc, where U.S. Rangers landed on D-Day and where the French had preserved the visual memory of war by leaving gaping bomb craters and rusting barbed wire that had been removed from other beaches in Normandy. The French resisted the schedule change, arguing that Reagan should be welcomed by Mitterrand before he made a speech on French soil. When the advance men were unable to resolve the dispute, Deaver summoned Bernard Palliez-Vernier, France's ambassador to the United States, to the White House and reminded him of how warmly Mitterrand had been received in Washington earlier that year. The ambassador got the message, and Mitterrand personally approved the change in schedule that allowed Reagan star billing at Normandy.

Reagan made the most of his opportunity. He was equipped with a superb speech crafted by White House speechwriter Peggy Noonan and the most visually dramatic site in Normandy from which to deliver it. "Pointe du Hoc is a knife, stood on its edge, pointed into the sea," wrote John Vinocur in *The New York Times*. "It looks lethal, a palisade of boulder and mean rocks where Normandy's green softness has reclaimed nothing."[52] Reagan spoke on the point of this rock, standing in front of a stone memorial to the U.S. Army Rangers who had scaled a 130-foot cliff with grappling hooks and ladders borrowed from the London Fire Department. His audience was the aging veterans who had performed this feat.

The Rangers looked up and saw the enemy soldiers at the edge of the cliffs shooting down at them with machine guns and throwing grenades. And the American Rangers began to climb. They shot rope ladders over the face of these cliffs and began to pull themselves up. When one Ranger fell, another would take his place; when one rope was cut, a Ranger would grab another and begin his climb again. They climbed, shot back and held their footing; soon, one by one, the Rangers pulled themselves over the top—and in seizing the firm land at the top of these cliffs they began to seize back the continent of Europe. Two hundred twenty-five came here. After two days of fighting, only ninety could still bear arms.

Behind me is a memorial that symbolizes the Ranger daggers that were thrust into the top of these cliffs. And before me are the men who put them there. These are the boys of Pointe du Hoc. These are the men who took the cliffs. These are the champions who helped free a continent. These are the heroes who helped end a war.

Many of the Rangers wept when they heard these words, and a number of us in the press corps wept with them. Even the Secret Service agents, trained to watch for danger instead of listening to presidential speeches, did not disguise their feelings. Reagan never broke the mood. His speech paid homage to the other Allied soldiers who had fought and died in France and to the "great losses suffered by the Russian people during World War II: twenty million people perished, a terrible price that testifies to all the world the necessity of avoiding war." Later, he knelt in silent prayer with Nancy Reagan at the Omaha Beach Chapel and toured the Normandy American Cemetery, where a sea of white crosses and Stars of David mark the graves of 9,386 American servicemen. He stopped to lay a bouquet of red and white carnations and blue iris on the grave of Brigadier General Theodore Roosevelt Jr., the son of President Theodore Roosevelt, whose valor had won him the Congressional Medal of Honor and cost him his life. Small French and American flags marked the graves. As the Reagans walked through the cemetery in silence, a gentle breeze wafted in from the English Channel.

Reagan gave another speech that afternoon at the official ceremony at Omaha Beach, scene of the bloodiest fighting on D-Day. Again, he honored the Allied soldiers, quoting General Omar Bradley as saying, "Every man who set foot on Omaha Beach that day was a hero." And he read from a letter sent to him by the daughter of one of these heroes, PFC Peter Zanatta of the 37th Engineer Combat Battalion, who was in the first assault wave at Omaha Beach. Zanatta had survived the assault and promised to return to Normandy after the war to see "the beach, the barricades and the graves." He never did. When he was dying of cancer three decades later, his daughter Lisa Zanatta Henn had promised to return for him and put flowers on the graves. She had done that this day, and Reagan fought back tears when he read from the letter. "Through the words of his loving daughter, who is here with us today, a D-Day veteran has shown us the meaning of this day far better than any president can. It is enough for us to say about Private Zanatta and all the men of honor and courage who fought beside him four decades ago: We will always remember. We will always be proud. We will always be prepared, so we may always be free."

If Normandy was Reagan's best performance abroad, it was because he had graphic remembrances of this war in which he had not fought. At the DMZ in Korea he had been overtly cinematic, enjoying his role and valuing the production. Striding down Utah Beach with Mitterrand, Trudeau and five royal European heads of state in a sprawling international photo opportunity after the speeches, Reagan gave the impression of returning to Normandy.* He belonged as much to the scene as Mitterrand, a former soldier who had escaped from a prisoner-of-war camp after being captured by the Germans. Reagan had spent D-Day at his desk in the First Motion Picture Unit of the Army Air Corps at Culver City. He had been no closer to Normandy than the combat films he had later seen of the landing. "And I would watch as closely as I could, knowing this was real and they were under fire," Reagan told Hugh Sidey of *Time*. "It just used to tear you in two because you'd see the individuals that were hit go down."[53]

Films are real to Reagan. His performance in Normandy recalled the experiences of Captain Reagan—an actor who wore his uniform to work in Culver City, played the lead role in *This Is the Army* and participated in a top-secret project used to train U.S. bombing crews for their destructive raids on Tokyo. As Reagan tells the story, "Our special effects men—Hollywood geniuses in uniform—built a complete miniature of Tokyo"[54] on a sound stage, above which they rigged a crane and camera mount. They then photographed the miniature, showing the targets as they would look from planes flying at different altitudes and speeds under varying weather conditions. Reagan was the narrator, guiding pilots into their targets. His claim in his autobiogra-

---

* The royalty included Queen Elizabeth II of Britain, King Baudouin I of Belgium, King Olav V of Norway, Queen Beatrix I of the Netherlands and Grand Duke Jean of Luxembourg.

phy that the secrecy of this enterprise ranked "with the atom bomb project"[55] is preposterous, but the film was a useful tool for briefing bombing crews in the Pacific. Reagan participated in World War II, as Garry Wills put it, "involved in a war service based on the principled defense of faking things."[56] And Reagan was part of a community that often believed its own propaganda, as evidenced by the construction of air raid shelters in Hollywood studios for use in case of a Japanese attack.

Wills points out that the fan magazines consistently treated Reagan as if he were "off at war," and that Reagan behaved as if he really were.[57] "By the time I got out of the Army Air Corps, all I wanted to do—in common with several million other veterans—was to rest up awhile, make love to my wife, and come up refreshed to a better job in an ideal world," Reagan wrote in his 1965 autobiography.[58] He had spent his nights at home throughout World War II. But because he believed he had been to war, he was able to play his part perfectly in Normandy, where old soldiers wept at his speeches and eighty-eight-year-old retired General Lawton Collins, the "Lightning Joe" who had commanded the U.S. VII Corps that took Utah Beach on D-Day, proudly told reporters that he had voted for Reagan and would vote for him again.[59]

Because films were real to Reagan, he remembered them with the clarity of actual experience. He seemed to be returning to Normandy because he had already been there in his mind. The threat of nuclear war, and the Armageddon he associated with it, was real because Reagan had seen the pictures of what the atomic bomb had done at Hiroshima and Nagasaki. And Reagan, removed from settings where such statements would have damaged him politically, defended the reality of what he had seen on film. As he told Landon Parvin, "Maybe I had seen too many war movies, the heroics of which I sometimes confused with real life."[60]

Reagan would return to Europe in 1985, rekindling darker memories of World War II than he had at Normandy with a speech at the concentration camp at Bergen-Belsen and a wreath-laying ceremony at a West German military cemetery at Bitburg. But before Reagan made this trip he would express other confusions between films and life, the most bizarre of which was his tale of how he had served as a Signal Corps photographer who had filmed the horrors of the Nazi death camps. I did not believe this story on first encounter, which was in the February

10, 1984, issue of *Near East Report,* a weekly pro-Israeli newsletter. Under the headline "Reagan's Real Feelings," the newsletter carried an approving account of an article in *Ma'ariv,* an Israeli newspaper close to the government. The article said that Reagan had told Israeli Prime Minister Yitzhak Shamir, during his November 29, 1983, visit to the White House, that the roots of his concern for Israel could be traced to World War II when he photographed the Nazi death camps. Afterward, Reagan said, he had saved a copy of the death camp films for himself because he believed that the day would come when people would no longer believe that six million Jews had been exterminated. Years later, said the article, Reagan was asked by a member of his own family if such an event had really occurred. "That moment, I thought this is the time for which I saved the film and I showed it to a group of people who couldn't believe their eyes," *Ma'ariv* quoted Reagan as saying. "From then on, I was concerned for the Jewish people."

An editor who had also received the newsletter sent it to me with a quizzical note penned in the margin: "First time I ever heard of this." I was busy with other stories and put the newsletter aside. Then, on February 16, 1984, Nazi-hunter Simon Wiesenthal and Rabbi Marvin Hier called upon Reagan to discuss the dedication of the Simon Wiesenthal Center in Los Angeles. After the meeting Wiesenthal told *Washington Post* reporter Joanne Omang that he was "very, very satisfied" with Reagan's interest in efforts to track down a former Wehrmacht officer believed responsible for the murder of a quarter million Jews who was hiding in Chile. While Omang was writing this story, she asked me when Reagan had photographed the Nazi death camps. "Never," I told her. "He was never out of the country during the war." She then related to me an account from Hier and Wiesenthal that was nearly identical to the story that Reagan had purportedly told Shamir. In the version he told Hier and Wiesenthal, Reagan had shown the films soon after the war to a person who claimed that reports of extermination of the Jews had been exaggerated. "He [Reagan] said he was shocked that there would be a need to do that only a year after the war," Hier said.[61]

I remained journalistically cautious, perhaps overly cautious, even though it seemed unlikely that Shamir and Wiesenthal had reached identical misunderstandings at their separate meetings with Reagan. But all I knew about the Reagan-Shamir conversation had come from a secondhand account of a report in an Israeli newspaper. I let the story sit until Ed Walsh, then *The Washington Post* correspondent in Jerusalem, was able to confirm the accuracy of the *Ma'ariv* report with Dan

Meridor, the Israeli cabinet secretary. Shamir had accepted Reagan's moving story at face value and had related it to the cabinet as evidence of the president's support of Israel. Finally, in mid-March, I sought to confirm this story at the White House, sending the press office into red alert. Bob Sims, the deputy press secretary I had asked to check on the meeting, called me back to deny Reagan had ever claimed to have photographed the death camps. "There's no story here," he said. "The only story here is that *The Post* is out to make the president look bad." This was an unusual comment from Sims, who was known for gentle manners and honesty. Never before had he responded to any inquiry of mine in an accusatory manner. I told him that his answer wasn't good enough and that I needed to know Reagan's personal response to what he was alleged to have said. Pretty soon, I received a call from James Baker, who preferred to talk to reporters on background. Not this time, I said. Baker was a great douser of fires, particularly in an election year. He went to Reagan immediately and called me back, saying that the president had told him he "never left the country" during World War II and "never told anyone that he did." Baker said Reagan had told him he kept a copy of a film on the death camps after he left the service because he remembered that World War I atrocities had been questioned and "didn't want atrocities against the Jewish people to be forgotten." Reagan had told Baker that "a Jewish friend" had questioned him about the accuracy of the death camp reports a year or two later. Reagan had shown him the copy of the film. I put this in a column that concluded with the reservations that I hold today:

> How could Shamir and Wiesenthal, fluent in English and known for their grasp of detail, have misunderstood so completely what Reagan said to them in two different meetings more than two months apart? What Jew would doubt the existence of the Holocaust?
> The story in any of its versions was new to this reporter, who in the course of preparing two biographies and interviewing many persons who knew Reagan during his World War II days, had never heard it. There is no reference to it in any other Reagan biography nor in his autobiography. It is a story no one seems to have heard.[62]

But it was a story Reagan seems to have believed when he was telling it to Shamir and Wiesenthal.* Garry Wills found "an obvious continu-

---

* Reagan subsequently wrote me a letter reiterating the denial he had made through Baker. We never discussed the subject again. My view of the matter, then and now, is that it is quite likely

ity between this tale" and one told by *Modern Screen* in 1942 that described Jane Wyman's loneliness after her husband "went off to join his regiment," as if he had actually gone away to war.[63] This fiction was embedded in their lives. On April 29, 1985, Reagan was asked by a French journalist about a *New York Times* report that some of the SS soldiers who had massacred the 642 inhabitants of the French village of Oradour were buried in the West German cemetery he was about to visit. "Yes, I know all the bad things that happened in that war," Reagan said. "I was in uniform for four years myself."[64]

Reagan did indeed know about the "bad things" that had happened, at least if they had been recorded on film. His version of the death camp story related to me by Baker withdrew only the unsupportable assertion that he had photographed the camps himself. Reagan still maintained that he had been asked by a Jewish friend soon after the war if such a thing as the Holocaust had really happened. He also claimed that he had seen more than the general public because of his access to unedited military films of the death camps. In an April 30, 1981, speech in the East Room of the White House commemorating the victims of the Holocaust (where Reagan said nothing about a Jewish friend or anyone else questioning the events that had taken place), he said that his wartime service had given him access to unedited films that "we edited into a secret report for the General Staff." Reagan told of seeing the first secret film of the death camps in April 1945, a film which "still, I know, must exist in the military . . . and I won't go into the horrible scenes that we saw." He said he was "proud" that nearby townspeople had been ordered to see a liberated camp, "and the horror on their faces was the greatest proof that they had not been conscious of what was happening so near to them."

The "secret film" that Reagan was talking about had, in fact, been shown in American movie theaters in April 1945, the same month it was received in Culver City. The town he is describing is Ohrdruf, in what became East Germany, and the person who ordered the towns-people to see the camps was General Dwight D. Eisenhower, who inspected Ohrdruf on April 12, 1945, a week after it was liberated by

---

Reagan became so emotionally engrossed in the story that he told it from the point of view of the photographer witnessing the scene. Such a defense would not have been acceptable to Baker, who was sensitive to accusations that Reagan could not distinguish film from reality. In trying to discredit my column, White House officials engaged in the questionable tactic of alleging that Shamir and Wiesenthal spoke faulty English and must have misunderstood Reagan. Both men speak with an accent, but their English is fluent.

the 4th Armored Division of the Third Army and a day after the first American soldiers reached Buchenwald, where Simon Wiesenthal was a prisoner. The sights and smells of Ohrdruf made even hardened General George Patton physically ill. Eisenhower promptly cabled Washington and London asking that journalists and members of Congress and Parliament be sent to the camps so that word of what the Nazis had done could be quickly spread. "I felt that the evidence should be immediately placed before the American and British publics in a fashion that would leave no room for cynical doubt," Eisenhower wrote afterward. There were no secret U.S. military films of Ohrdruf or of Buchenwald. Because of Eisenhower's response, the films of what the U.S. Army had found in these camps were showing in American theaters before the end of April 1945. The most compelling and unbearable of these pictures, accompanied by a vivid commentary, were incorporated into the April 1945 Universal short movie *The Nazi Murder Mills*. Many of these pictures also appeared in Paramount and United Artists newsreels. All of them tell the story Reagan told about how the townspeople had been ordered to view the camps.* The story of horror that Reagan remembered as a secret film had been and is available to the world, if the world chooses to remember it.[66]

Reagan spoke at Bergen-Belsen on May 6, 1985, a Nazi concentration camp where 60,000 persons had died, half of them Jews. His speech was in political compensation for his participation the same day in an eight-minute wreath-laying ceremony at the German military cemetery near Bitburg, where forty-nine members of the SS were buried amidst 2,000 German soldiers. "Bitburg" had become a synonym for Reagan's supposed insensitivity to the feelings of Nazism's victims, especially Jews. The circumstances which led to Reagan's participation in the Bitburg ceremony are related in a subsequent chapter. What must be said here is that Reagan was not insensitive to the Holocaust. He shares the views of Jews and many others that the Holocaust must be remembered so that it can never happen again. His imagined accounts of having filmed the liberation of the death camps showed not only his difficulty in distinguishing actual from cinematic experience but the deep impression the Holocaust had made upon him.

But Reagan did not want to return to any of the scenes where this crime of crimes had been committed. He could deal with scenes of

---

* After inspecting Ohrdruf, Eisenhower also ordered all nearby U.S. military units not on the front lines to tour the camp. "We are told that the American soldier does not know what he is fighting for," Eisenhower said. "Now, at least, he will know what he is fighting *against*."[65]

death related to a heroic purpose, as at Normandy, but he was emotionally helpless in the presence of genocide. Deaver and Nancy Reagan knew this about him and had always before sheltered him from suggestions that he should visit a concentration camp on one of his European trips. They had done their best to protect him after the political furor over Bitburg made him agree to the Bergen-Belsen appearance. Ken Khachigian had been brought in from California to write a life-affirming speech. A Roman Catholic priest, a Protestant minister and a rabbi had been asked to participate in the ceremony at Bergen-Belsen as a demonstration of interfaith remembrance. Deaver remembers that Reagan was "ashen" when he told him, on Air Force One en route to Bergen-Belsen, that the rabbi had refused to come in protest of Reagan's participation in the Bitburg ceremony. Reagan was a shaken man as he toured the camp and saw the photographs of the stacks of bodies of the human beings who had died at Bergen-Belsen. A reporter noticed that he kept his arm around Nancy Reagan, "partly to steer her and partly, it appeared, to derive some support from her presence."[67] Somehow, Reagan made it through the camp tour and gave his speech. When I heard it, I thought that if it took Bitburg to see this camp and give this speech, then Bitburg had been worth it. For what Reagan said at Bergen-Belsen meant more than his silent participation in the ceremony at the Bitburg cemetery. "Here lie people—Jews—whose death was inflicted for no reason other than their existence," Reagan said at Bergen-Belsen. He recalled Anne Frank, who had died there three weeks before the camp was liberated by the British. He read from her diary, while Nancy Reagan dabbed at her eyes with a handkerchief.

> Everywhere here are memories—pulling us, touching us, making us understand that they can never be erased. Such memories take us where God intended His children to go—toward learning, toward healing, and, above all, toward redemption. They beckon us through the endless stretches of our heart to the knowing commitment that the life of each individual can change the world and make it better.

> We're all witnesses; we share the glistening hope that rests in every human soul. Hope leads us, if we're prepared to trust it, toward what our President Lincoln called the better angels of our nature. And then, rising above all this cruelty, out of this tragic and nightmarish time, beyond the anguish, the pain, the suffering for all time, we can and must pledge: Never again.

Reagan's moving address at Bergen-Belsen would prove the last great commemorative speech of his presidency. Mikhail Gorbachev had become president of the Soviet Union less than two months earlier, and he would soon become a dominant figure on the world scene. After 1985, the requirements of statecraft and the evolving U.S.-Soviet relationship would restrain the solo showmanship Reagan had displayed in Japan, Korea, China, Ireland and Normandy. Reagan would travel widely in the second term—to economic summits in Tokyo in 1986, Venice in 1987 and Toronto in 1988. He would take side trips to several European nations and Indonesia. But while Reagan wandered down memory lane on many of these occasions, his most stirring speeches looked to the future of the new era in East-West relations rather than to the past.* The performances that mattered most in Reagan's second term were not celebrations of milestones in World War II and the Cold War but shared summits in the spotlight with Gorbachev at Geneva in 1985, Reykjavik in 1986, Washington in 1987 and Moscow in 1988. Though Reagan remained an intriguing figure on the world stage, he was after 1985 overshadowed, if not eclipsed, by Gorbachev.

---

* The exception was a celebratory visit to Grenada on February 20, 1986, where Reagan looked back with pride on the 1983 U.S. invasion and warned of the danger of "Communist tyranny" in Nicaragua. But even on this trip Reagan was more subdued than he had been in the grandiose performances of his first term. When Sam Donaldson asked him how it felt to be on the scene of his "greatest military triumph," Reagan replied, "Sam, I didn't fire a shot."[68]

MORNING AGAIN IN AMERICA

Ours is the land of the free because it is the home of the brave. America's future will always be great because our nation will always be strong. And our nation will be strong because our people will be free. And our people will be free because we will be united, one people under God, with liberty and justice for all.

RONALD REAGAN,
November 4, 1984 [1]

In between the journeys to Normandy and to Bitburg, Ronald Reagan won a second term as president by the largest electoral-vote landslide in U.S. history. He carried 49 states, receiving 525 electoral votes to 10 for Democratic nominee Walter F. Mondale, who carried his home state of Minnesota by less than one percentage point and also won the District of Columbia. Reagan won 59 percent of the popular vote. He gained a majority in every region of the country, in every age group, in cities, towns, suburbs and rural areas and in every occupational category except the unemployed. Sixty-one percent of independents and a quarter of registered Democrats voted for Reagan. He won the votes of 62 percent of the men and 54 percent of the women, even though Mondale set a precedent by choosing Geraldine Ferraro as his running mate. Reagan's showing was an improvement from 1980, when only 47 percent of women had voted for him. A polling analyst concluded that the "gender gap" had damaged Mondale, who "had bigger problems with male voters than Reagan had with females."[2] Reagan had majorities among every ethnic group except Hispanics, where he increased his percentage of the vote from 37 percent to 44 percent. He won a majority among voters earning $10,000 or more a year and a majority among whites earning more than $5,000. Sixty-three percent of all white voters cast their ballots for Reagan—and 73 percent of white Protestants. Fifty-six percent of Catholics voted for Reagan. Mondale won the votes of two out of three Jewish voters and nearly nine out of ten blacks. He became only the second Democratic presidential candidate, after George McGovern in 1972, to lose a majority of the blue-collar vote to his Republican opponent.*

Reagan had coasted through much of the campaign, relying on the glow of the economic recovery and his identification with what Richard Darman had described in a campaign memo as "mythic America." As *Newsweek* put it, Reagan embodied "America as it imagined itself to be —the bearer of the traditional Main Street values of family and neighborhood, of thrift, industry and charity instead of government intervention where self-reliance failed."[3] But Reagan was a candidate of the future as well as of the past. He celebrated a nation in which an ever-expanding economy would make jobs available for everyone who wanted to work and enable all Americans to "share in a dynamic, exciting future." He believed in a world without trade barriers in which the United States would help create a gigantic common market. He envisioned a space shield that would protect Americans from nuclear war as reliably as an umbrella wards off rain. He favored a manned space program, which Mondale had opposed, and looked forward to the day when orbiting space stations would become outposts in the exploration of the universe. "And what we've done and must continue to do is to help push back our newest frontiers in education, high technology, and space," Reagan said in California's Silicon Valley on the day he opened his fall campaign. "America has always been greatest when she dared to be great. I'm convinced we will be leaders in devel-

---

* The survey results cited in this chapter are from ABC exit polls or the *Washington Post*–ABC poll unless otherwise noted. The figure on Reagan's support among white Protestants is from a *New York Times*–CBS poll. ABC reported that Reagan won 56 percent of the vote of all Protestants, including blacks. ABC exit-poll results for most demographic groups were similar to those of a post-election survey conducted by Richard Wirthlin, the principal White House pollster.

oping these frontiers, because the American people would rather reach for the stars than reach for excuses why we shouldn't."[4]

When Reagan talked this way, in cadences that echoed the optimism of his old hero Franklin Roosevelt, he transcended partisan barriers. "He really isn't like a Republican," said Vincent Rakowitz, a retired brewery worker in San Antonio. "He's more like an American, which is what we really need."[5] Rakowitz was sixty-five years old. Reagan's message held even more appeal for young voters, who liked hearing that America's future was as appealing as its past. Young voters had been a Democratic mainstay since the days of the New Deal, but in 1984 three out of every five new voters cast ballots for Reagan. Most of his campaign rallies featured youthful, flag-waving audiences that interrupted his speeches with chants of "U.S.A.! U.S.A.!" in emulation of that summer's patriotic refrain at the Olympic Games in Los Angeles. Because of the boycott of these games by the Soviet Union and most of the nations of Eastern Europe, the 1984 Olympics became a showcase for U.S. athletes and a backdrop for the Reagan campaign.

In May, Reagan greeted the Olympic torchbearer at the White House. In July, he declared in a radio speech that "our young people are running for their country, running for greatness, for achievement, for that moving thing in man that makes him push on to the impossible."[6] Reagan was running, too, campaigning for reelection as the star and leader of America's team. "The American ideal is not just winning; it's going as far as you can go," he declared on the opening day of the Olympics to cheering U.S. athletes and the Republican camera crew that had followed him to the frontlines of Korea and the beaches of Normandy. Reagan had grown accustomed to the cheers. Much of his campaign resembled a long victory lap in which the only task of the triumphant competitor was to jog easily around the stadium, gracefully accepting the tribute of the adoring multitude. Reagan seemed a winner before he ever ran. It was only when the cheering stopped and Reagan came down from the clouds to engage Mondale in the face-to-face combat of the presidential debates that he seemed an ordinary man. In Louisville on October 7, at the first of these encounters, Reagan became so rambling and incoherent in his responses that it seemed for a few fleeting days as if a genuine contest for the presidency had developed. This proved an illusion, like so much else in the presidential campaign of 1984.

· · ·

A majority of Americans strongly backed Reagan's policies in 1984. While it was often said, sometimes in derogation, that Americans "liked" Reagan, his landslide victory was much more than a personality triumph. Two-thirds of the voters surveyed in the ABC exit polls said they liked Reagan personally, but those (about one in every thirteen) who liked him but disapproved of his policies voted for Mondale. Most Americans not only liked Reagan but agreed with what he was saying, at least on the issues most important to them. "One need simply imagine that instead of talking about God, family and country, the President was extolling Zen Buddhism, unilateral disarmament and sexual license," wrote sociologist Amitai Etzioni three days before the Louisville debate. "His rating would of course crash within a week. No matter how great an actor he is, the script is still what matters most to most Americans."[7]

Americans also believed that Reagan was a leader. When voters in the ABC polls were asked why they liked Reagan, many cited his stand on government spending or said he would keep the nation economically prosperous and militarily strong. But 40 percent of these voters—nearly twice the number who cited any specific issue—said that what they liked most was that Reagan was "a strong leader." This ratified the opinion of the Reagan campaign team, which had made "Leadership That's Working" the slogan of the reelection campaign.

The public perception of Reagan's leadership abilities rested in part on his enduring identification with the values of mythic America, a country of the mind in which presidents are necessarily strong leaders. But the perception depended even more on congressional passage of his budget and tax bills in 1981. White House pollster Richard Wirthlin had observed at the time that most Americans, after years of stalemate between Congress and the White House, viewed congressional approval of administration programs as a sign that government was working. Voters consequently gave high leadership marks to Reagan whenever Congress passed portions of his program. "[This 1981] show of leadership was enough by itself to buy Reagan the time he needed," wrote ABC polling director Jeffrey Alderman in a 1984 post-election analysis. "It allowed him to survive the worst recession since World War II with much of the public—at Reagan's urging—blaming the Democrats of the past for the problems of the present. Though ABC/ *Washington Post* polls at the time showed Reagan with an overall approval rating below 50 percent and running behind potential Democratic opponents, the bottom held remarkably firm for Reagan throughout the recession. Unlike Carter, who began losing fellow Democrats when his ratings started to slide as inflation and interest rates rose, Reagan hung onto his core Republican support throughout the recession."[8]

Another source of the public's view of Reagan's leadership ability was his response when 13,000 members of the Professional Air Traffic Controllers Organization (PATCO) walked off their jobs on August 3, 1981. At the urging of PATCO president Robert E. Poli, the union had backed Reagan during the 1980 campaign, at a time when support from organized labor was rare and highly prized. But Reagan did not hesitate in following the advice of Transportation Secretary Drew Lewis to fire the PATCO strikers. "I'm sorry, and I'm sorry for them," Reagan said as he dismissed controllers who had not returned to work in forty-eight hours. "I certainly take no joy out of this."[9] Sorry or not, Reagan's action sent a resonant signal of leadership that would be long remembered. "It struck me as singular," said Donald Rumsfeld, White House chief of staff under President Ford and no Reagan admirer. "You had a president who was new to the office and not taken seriously by a lot of people. It showed a decisiveness and an ease with his instincts. . . . [And] by contrast with his predecessor, it staked out a leadership position that was anti-inflationary."[10] Reagan did not fully realize the importance of his decision at the time, but would later say that his action in the strike was "an important juncture for our new administration. I think it convinced people who might have thought otherwise that I meant what I said."[11]

Reagan's confident decisiveness made a good first impression on the professional politicians who dealt with him early in his presidency. He had the particular gratitude of Republican leaders in the Senate, who knew they owed their committee chairmanships and other positions of power to Reagan's coattails in 1980. And he had the advantage of following Carter, who was liked neither by the Republicans nor the old-line Democratic leadership. Many in Congress were also in awe of Reagan's mastery of television and seeming domination of the media. They were impressed with the vigor of his recovery after the 1981 assassination attempt. Congressmen liked going to the White House, where Reagan usually greeted them cordially and often related off-color anecdotes that they afterward shared with their colleagues. Some of the congressmen even appreciated Reagan's stubbornness. Buddy Roemer, later governor of Louisiana, would remember an incident where he was being lobbied heavily by the administration and the House leadership on a crucial MX vote. Roemer favored the MX but was close to the leadership. After he voted for the MX, Reagan called him to the White House to thank him. Roemer, wanting to have something to show for his vote to his colleagues, made a pitch for the Democratic budget proposal. He got nowhere. "Buddy, you're wrong on this," Reagan said, and proceeded to tell him why he was wrong. Roemer, who had backed the administration on the contras as well as the MX, was impressed. "He's a tough guy," Roemer said.

But the good first impression that Reagan made on the politicians did not last. Reagan at least knew Roemer's name. That set the Louisiana congressman apart from many of his colleagues, who found that Reagan did not seem to recognize them outside the setting of a leadership meeting, and sometimes not even there. Even when Reagan recognized everyone in the room, he rarely knew enough about the substance of an issue to become an avid participant in the discussion. Members of the congressional leadership became adept at concealing their annoyance when Reagan responded to an argument with an anecdote, often an irrelevant story from his Sacramento days. And even the most tolerant and pro-Reagan congressmen in time became bothered by his practice of reading to them from his four-by-six cards instead of responding to them on the issues they had raised.

When the Reagan tax reduction bill was pending in Congress during the summer of 1981, White House legislative liaison Ken Duberstein called House Budget Committee chairman Jim Jones of Oklahoma, a widely respected Democrat, and said the president wanted to talk to him. Jones opposed the Reagan tax bill because of its impact on the budget deficit. He had also opposed Reagan's budget, which he believed inferior to the Democratic alternative prepared by the Budget Committee. But after the Reagan budget passed, Jones promised the president his support on budget reconciliation, the process by which Congress applies the overall budget spending levels to individual programs. When Duberstein called, Jones said he was willing to talk to Reagan about reconciliation but that it would be a waste of time to discuss the tax bill. Fine, said Duberstein, you can just talk about reconciliation.

The next day Jones was brought into the Oval Office, where the president was surrounded by his political and economic advisers. Reagan read to Jones from his four-by-six cards, telling him how glad he was to see him and praising the virtues of his tax bill. Jones exchanged glances with Duberstein, who raised his eyebrows in resignation. There was nothing he could do once Reagan was launched on his cards. Jones waited until the president had finished. "I figured, well, maybe I can be an old fart, too," Jones recalled. Instead of responding to Reagan's pitch on the tax bill, Jones acted as if he hadn't heard a word of what Reagan had said and gave the president a full report on budget reconciliation.[12] Reagan didn't know enough about the subject to respond. Instead, he picked up the cards again and read to Jones some more about the tax bill.

Jones held a balanced view of Reagan. He believed Reagan had "a labor negotiator's sense of timing" and "really did understand the use of semantics, painting pictures with words." He also thought him the least analytical and most ill-informed president he had ever met—and Jones had known presidents going back to Dwight Eisenhower.[13] This last opinion was a prevailing view, although it was rare for any congressman to show Jones's boldness in mimicking Reagan's card-scripted spiel. One congressman who did challenge Reagan was Tip O'Neill, who became so angered by Reagan's performance during a bipartisan leadership meeting on January 28, 1986, that he accused the president of spreading "a bunch of baloney" about unemployment.[14]

Reagan's cue cards on this particular day were crammed with statistics designed to minimize the impact of unemployment, including the irrelevant point that the jobless figure (then about 7 percent) would be lower if members of the armed services were included as members of the work force. But what set O'Neill off was Reagan's assertion that the unemployed could get jobs if they really wanted them. "I'm told about the fellow on welfare who makes phone calls looking for work," O'Neill recalls Reagan as saying. "On the third call they offer him a job, and he hangs up. These people don't want to work."[15] This angered O'Neill. "Don't give me that crap," he said. "The guy in Youngstown, Ohio, who's been laid off at the steel mill and has to make his mortgage payments—don't tell me he doesn't want to work. Those stories may work on your rich friends, but they don't work on the rest of us. I'm sick and tired of your attitude, Mr. President. I thought you would have grown in the five years you've been in office, but you're still repeating those same simplistic explanations."[16]

When Reagan was challenged in this way, his jaw tightened and his eyes flashed. Republican Senator Alan Simpson of Wyoming, recognizing the danger signals, jumped in and gently chided O'Neill, saying that it was not right for him and the president to bicker. O'Neill subsided and said he always had the greatest respect for the presidency. "With the exception of this incumbent," Reagan responded.[17] * The president usually felt comfortable with O'Neill and liked him so much that he would in the last year of his presidency offer him the ambassadorship to Ireland. But Reagan resented any attempt to embarrass him, and he had no intention of abandoning the anecdotes that had worked so well for him. Some of the Republicans who had attended the meeting, however, were privately pleased that O'Neill had spoken up. They too found Reagan's repetition of mindless irrelevancies an irritation, though they had not personally challenged the president. Soon after O'Neill's blowup, I spoke with a Republican member of the leadership who was no particular fan of the House speaker and asked him what he thought. "Off the record?" he responded. Okay, I said. "Off the record, Tip's right," he said. "The president's just out of it too much of the time."

O'Neill and his fellow Democrats failed to make effective political use of their insights into Reagan's inadequacies. When they went after him publicly, they usually wound up saying too little about his ignorance and too much about his supposed lack of compassion for the poor and dispossessed. Reagan was not as insensitive as his anecdotes. He remembered the personal hardships of his parents during the Depression, and he was able to respond understandingly to letters relating individual misfortunes. He genuinely believed that his economic policies had proved a boon to lower-income Americans by protecting them from the ravages of inflation and lowering their tax burdens. Many Democratic politicians did not understand that Reagan could be challenged more effectively if his motives were conceded. Instead of campaigning against the ineffectual, uncomprehending Reagan who read to them from his four-by-six cards, the Democrats campaigned against a caricature of a heartless president who had turned his back on the problems of the poor. The caricature was not convincing to a majority of white Americans. They might have been persuaded that Reagan did not know enough, but it was more difficult to convince them that he did not care.

The Democrats compounded their problems in 1984 by presenting a foreign policy caricature of Reagan little changed from the one rejected by the voters four years earlier. An early 1980 Richard Wirthlin memo

---

* Although some of the participants in this meeting were more than willing to talk about what had happened, the story of the Reagan-O'Neill confrontation was completely overshadowed by the explosion of the space shuttle *Challenger* later in the day. O'Neill said subsequently that he had seen "Reagan at his worst" in the Oval Office and "Reagan at his best" in his nationally televised speech after the *Challenger* tragedy. "It was a trying day for all Americans, and Ronald Reagan spoke to our highest ideals," O'Neill wrote.[18]

had anticipated that President Carter's team would portray Reagan as "dumb, dangerous and a distorter of facts." Refute any one of these propositions, Wirthlin reasoned, and the others would have less credibility. Carter's overstatement made the task easier for the Reagan side. Reagan was not dangerous, and the Democrats were not good learners. In 1984 they made little of Lebanon and much of Reagan's commitment to Star Wars, which the Mondale team described as a refusal to restrain the arms race. Reagan wanted to end the arms race and saw Star Wars as a path to this goal. When Wirthlin tested the Mondale team's Star Wars commercials, he found that they actually helped Reagan.

Reagan's tight little circle of White House advisers and political strategists were always happiest when Mondale's team harped about Star Wars or the president's supposed indifference to the poor. They were most concerned when Reagan's competence became an issue. The incoherent answers which startled those who watched the Louisville debate were not a novelty to James Baker, Mike Deaver, Stu Spencer and Paul Laxalt, let alone to Nancy Reagan. They viewed the conservative plea to "let Reagan be Reagan" as an invitation to catastrophe and, almost without discussion, reached an early command decision that there would be no news conferences during the fall reelection campaign. (Reagan's last formal news conference before the election was on July 24, five days after Mondale was nominated.) The caricature drawn by the inner circle was of a masterful, decisive president, a Reagan who never was. The White House caricature was more convincing than the competing Democratic version, in part because Reagan conveyed an impression of leadership and in part because his handlers were usually more adept at concealing his deficiencies than the Democrats were at exposing them. Still, the White House image-makers were often fearful that Americans would learn too much about the real Reagan and decide that he was not up to the demanding job of serving as the nation's chief executive. That was why they kept Reagan as isolated as possible and resolutely (and untruthfully) denied that he napped or fell asleep in meetings.

A rumor nonetheless developed early in 1984 that Reagan, then seventy-three years old, had grown tired of the presidency and might not serve a full second term. The president himself inadvertently fueled this rumor during an interview with *Family Weekly* magazine when he was asked if Vice President Bush was "ready and able" to assume the duties of the presidency. In response, Reagan lauded Bush, saying he was "probably the best vice president we've ever had" and fully capable of serving as president. But Reagan neglected to say that he had no intention of turning the presidency over to Bush. This inspired ABC correspondent Mike Von Fremd to ask Reagan if he was "absolutely committed to serving all four years" of a second term or if he might instead step down in a year or two "when you're seventy-five or seventy-six years old." Reagan hit this softball question right out of the park at a prime-time news conference. "What the devil would a young fellow like me do if I quit the job?" he replied.[19]

Such rumors persisted not only because of Reagan's age but because he gave the impression that he was one of the few presidents who could walk away from the White House and never miss it. It was a misimpression. While Reagan was not dependent upon the presidency for emotional self-definition, he was highly competitive and possessed a sense of mission. He had felt destined to be president. Once he reached the White House, he felt destined to be president again. Two days after Reagan's inauguration in 1981, George Will called on Reagan and asked if he would be a two-term president. Reagan laughed. "Well, you know I never could have achieved welfare reform in California without a second term," he said.[20] Will decided then and there that Reagan intended to spend eight years in the White House. Mike Deaver reached a similar conclusion early in the first term, even though he knew that Nancy Reagan was afraid of what a second term might bring. Because I knew of her attitude, I rashly predicted in my 1982 biography *Reagan* that he was unlikely to seek reelection. When Deaver read this, he quietly took me aside and told me that he expected Reagan to be a candidate in 1984. Since Deaver knew that Reagan wanted to run again, he assumed that Nancy Reagan would eventually come around to the idea.

Nancy Reagan usually did come around to her husband's way of thinking on the decisions that mattered most to him, even though it was widely believed that it was he who most often yielded when they disagreed. Energetic and direct while he was easygoing and almost placid, she conveyed a sense of forceful ambition that belied her elegant, diminutive appearance. Actor Jimmy Stewart, who was a friend of the Reagans and had campaigned for him, summed up the prevailing view of Nancy's role when he said that Ronald Reagan would have won an Oscar if he had married her sooner. The underlying assumptions of this assessment were that Nancy Reagan was the driving force in the Reagan team and that her ambition was focused on her husband's success. The latter point is undisputed. If Reagan had won an Oscar, it would have been his award and she would have been happy for him. She took pleasure in his accomplishments without taking credit for them. He called her "Mommy," a special compliment from a man who as a child had depended upon his mother for stability and guidance in a world made unstable by his father's alcoholism. One of Reagan's gifts was his ability to attract people who helped him get ahead, and no one since his mother had helped him as much as Nancy Reagan. "Ronnie Reagan had sort of glided through life, and Nancy's role was to protect him," wrote Mike Deaver after he left the White House. "She accepted almost total responsibility for their family and home, and at the same time remained his closest adviser in public life."[21]

They made a good political team. He was a dreamer, preoccupied with ultimate destinations. She was a practical person who worried about what loomed around the next bend in the road. "She's more tactical; he's more strategic," said Stuart Spencer, who was both.[22] Because she understood her husband's limitations and valued his star status, she was sometimes too cautious. She had opposed his debate with President Carter in 1980, fearing that it would not show him to good advantage. Reagan had debated despite her fears, accepting the counsel of Spencer and James Baker that the debate offered opportunities that were worth the risks. Nancy Reagan was glad when it was over. She knew that her husband was vulnerable on many grounds, which is why she always defended him against his critics. But she did not always agree with him and often waged what Deaver called "a quiet campaign" behind the scenes to change his opinions.

The campaign was not quite as quiet as Deaver thought. Although she was as good an actress as he was an actor, she was not equally adept at concealing what she truly thought or felt. Her opinions were widely known throughout the White House, and people always knew where they stood with her, while frequently wondering what Reagan thought about them, or if he did. Ronald Reagan was a striver, but his striving was masked by his courteous, amiable manner and enduring fatalism. Hers was out in the open, all cards on the table, for anyone to see. With a directness unusual either in Hollywood or Washington, Nancy Reagan favored anyone who helped her husband or advanced his career and opposed anyone who stood in his way. She put people off, while he put them at their ease. Because people were almost always comfortable in Reagan's presence, they made excuses for him when he did not perform according to their expectations. They were less comfortable with her because she so often put them on the spot. But he had more to conceal than she did, because his ambition was so much bigger. What Ronald Reagan wanted was not an Oscar but the presidency of the United States. Nancy Reagan did more than anyone to help him get what he wanted.

Despite his frequent protestations that he was not a politician, the world of politics was easier for Reagan than for his wife. He forgot the names of people he had met a dozen times and displayed an absolute disinterest in the mechanics of politics, but he thrived on political performances. She did not care for them, despite her adoration of her husband. When the Reagans went to Sacramento in 1967 after his election as governor, she made little effort to conceal her distaste for politics and politicians. She possessed a Southern Californian's strong dislike of Sacramento, then suffering through a dank winter, and re-fused to live in the old governor's mansion, a Victorian relic on a one-way truck route through town. With a frankness that offended the government community, Nancy Reagan complained that the mansion was a firetrap and unsafe for their eight-year-old son. Reagan accom-modated her by moving to a Tudor-style house with a pool in a pleasant residential area of the city. The cost of this was borne by the millionaire "Friends of Ronald Reagan" who had bankrolled his candidacy. They bought the house for $150,000 and leased it to the Reagans.

Nancy Reagan was happier in these new quarters but still disliked the political life, and liked even less that their home was sometimes picketed by opponents of Reagan's policies. On April 11, 1967, oppo-nents of capital punishment held an all-night vigil outside the house to protest Reagan's refusal to grant clemency to Aaron Mitchell, sentenced to death for the murder of a Sacramento policeman. Reagan talked to Rev. Donn Moomaw about his decision to refuse clemency and later told an associate that it was the worst decision he had to make.[23] But he went off to bed early, while Nancy stayed awake and fumed about the pickets. Mitchell was executed at 10:00 A.M. the following day in San Quentin's gas chamber.*

Ronald Reagan became accustomed to the pickets and demonstrators who marched on the State Capitol in behalf of various causes in the early years of his governorship. Nancy Reagan was always bothered by

---

* This was the only execution carried out in California during Reagan's eight years as governor, a period that overlapped a long, undeclared national moratorium on executions while the U.S. Supreme Court weighed the constitutionality of capital punishment. Reagan granted clemency in the one other capital case that came to him, on the basis of evidence that the condemned man had a history of brain damage. Reagan did not attend either of the clemency hearings, which were conducted by Ed Meese, his legal affairs secretary.

such scenes. Her biggest adjustment, and one she never fully made, was learning to accept the raucous give-and-take of politics. Reagan had been inured to politics by his experiences on the GE trail and the Hollywood custom of exchanging insults at banquets designed to express appreciation of celebrities by "roasting" them. He had been taught to believe that men must show themselves to be good sports, and he easily mastered the art of socializing with politicians who had the same day attacked his policies in the state legislative chambers. She found it difficult to pretend politeness with people who had reproached her husband and even more difficult to accept media criticism of him.

Despite these unpromising beginnings, Nancy Reagan learned much about politics in eight years as wife of the governor of California. In an interview at the 1984 Republican Convention, she would say that politics had changed her while also saying that Reagan had not changed since she married him. It was a shrewd observation about both of them. Despite a manner that some thought snobbish, Nancy Reagan was a better listener than her husband. She also was better than he at distinguishing between those who really cared about him or his policies and those who followed his banner to advance their own interests. Reagan knew where he wanted to go, but she had a better sense of what he needed to do to get there. She had sensible reservations about the wisdom of his abortive and amateurish run for the presidency in 1968. When he tried again in 1976, he started earlier and waged a professional campaign under the direction of John Sears, a respected Washington-based strategist who had been one of Nixon's chief delegate-hunters in the 1968 campaign.

Nancy Reagan had been an ardent advocate of hiring Sears, in large part because she realized that her husband needed to go beyond his California circle to someone who understood the nuts and bolts of national politics and was accomplished in dealing with the eastern media. With Sears directing strategy, Reagan almost succeeded in wresting the nomination from President Ford. Four years later, when Reagan's needs were different and Sears seemed more an impediment than an asset, Nancy Reagan organized the effort to oust him. In getting rid of Sears, she was doing what Reagan wanted done but did not know how to do himself. Reagan loyalist Paul Laxalt believes that the replacement of Sears with William Casey was the decisive action that enabled Reagan to become president.[24]

But Nancy Reagan also soon developed reservations about Casey. When the campaign foundered, she called in Stuart Spencer, of the

Spencer-Roberts team that had managed Reagan's first gubernatorial campaign. Spencer was an apostate to many longtime Reagan loyalists, who would never forgive him for siding with Ford and deflecting the Reagan challenge in 1976. Nancy Reagan didn't care. That was then and this was now. Although Nancy Reagan could be a collector of grievances, she had a habit of putting them aside when they were of no practical use. She had learned that politics is the art of the moment. At the moment she called Spencer, early in September 1980, her husband was a shaky candidate. She knew that Spencer had a gift for steadying him. After Spencer joined the campaign, Reagan quickly righted himself. Nancy Reagan and Spencer became permanent allies. Ever afterward, she would call on him in times of political crisis.

Reagan's desire for a second term was one of these crises, at least for Nancy Reagan. She was worried both *about* Reagan and *for* him. "It was two things," said Spencer. "One, he got shot at. Was this going to happen again? And, secondly, just alone with her, she was all over my case, [asking,] 'No bullshit, can we win this thing again?' And I told her the truth as I saw it."[25] Nancy Reagan may have been intuitively seeking a more negative answer than Spencer gave her, for Washington had lost its charm for her, and she seems to have had a feeling that the second term would not turn out as well as the first. "I yearned for more family time, and more privacy," she wrote in *My Turn*. "I missed my friends and my family, and I missed California. Ronnie had already accomplished so much that maybe it was time to pull down the curtain."[26]

Outwardly, Nancy Reagan seemed enamored of the glamour of being first lady, and she saw to it that her public conduct did not convey her inner doubts. But her friends were well aware that the doubts were there. The first four years had been easier for President Reagan than for his wife. He had treated Washington as if it were simply a bigger Sacramento, while she went through a difficult adjustment that resembled her early days in the California state capital. Nancy Reagan could not refuse to live in the White House, as she had the governor's mansion, but she found the family quarters in the White House run-down and shabby. ("Some of the bedrooms on the third floor hadn't been painted in fifteen or twenty years!" she would write.)[27] As in Sacramento, she turned to wealthy Republican donors, who financed an expensive redecoration of the family quarters and plunged her into a series of lifestyle controversies from which she never successfully emerged. After the redecoration came the acquisition of new White

House china. Before and after the china came the clothes, always a big-ticket item for Nancy Reagan, who exercised daily and maintained a perfect figure. Her inaugural wardrobe alone was estimated at $25,000, and that was just the beginning. Dresses and gowns loaned to Nancy Reagan by famous designers provided an enduring story that lasted beyond the Reagan presidency.* Administration critics used the White House lifestyle as a political symbol of conspicuous consumption during the 1982 midterm elections, which turned out badly for the Republicans. One of the most popular postcards in Washington during this period featured "Queen Nancy" in ermine cape and jeweled crown. There was no comparable well-known postcard of Reagan, perhaps the most monarchical president in the history of the republic. But Reagan had the public image of a cowboy, not a king.

Behind the scenes at the White House, Nancy Reagan played a difficult but necessary role. There she was the bad cop who protected Reagan from his own gullibility. "It's hard to envision Ronnie as being a bad guy," she said. "And he's not. But there are times when somebody has to step in and say or do something. And I've had to do that sometimes—often."[28] She would have done it even more if her husband had permitted, for Nancy Reagan took a dim view of a number of his cabinet appointments—including James Watt, William Casey and Caspar Weinberger. Mike Deaver would say of her that she "used her persuasion with care," backing off when Reagan resisted and returning to the fray when an opportunity presented itself.[29]

Deaver also claimed in his book that "Nancy wins most of the time," but most of the examples he gave contradict the point. "She lobbied the president to soften his line on the Soviet Union; to reduce military spending and not to push Star Wars at the expense of the poor and dispossessed," Deaver wrote. "She favored a diplomatic solution in Nicaragua and opposed his trip to Bitburg."[30] Reagan went to Bitburg, and he relied more on the contras than diplomacy in Nicaragua. He also vastly increased the rate of military spending, which leveled off only when Congress refused to approve the funding requested by the administration. He spent billions on Star Wars and decreased the relative amount of federal spending for the poor. Of the issues cited by Deaver, Nancy Reagan was persuasive only on influencing his approach

---

* According to published accounts, the Internal Revenue Service as late as 1990 was investigating to see if the Reagans owed back taxes for clothing allegedly accepted by Nancy Reagan and not reported as income. She denied, in conversations with me and in her book *My Turn,* that she kept any of the clothing that was loaned to her.

to the Soviets, admittedly a pretty big "only." Her common sense told her that it was "ridiculous"[31] and dangerous for the United States and the Soviet Union to continue on a path of confrontation. But she also says accurately of the more accommodating approach that Reagan took to the Soviets beginning in 1984, "If Ronnie hadn't wanted to do it, he wouldn't have done it."[32]

Nancy Reagan had a better understanding than the entourage, a better understanding even than Deaver or Spencer, of how difficult it was to persuade her husband to oppose his instincts or his ideology. Behind his amiable exterior, Reagan was a stubborn man. He resisted her opposition to Watt until the interior secretary had publicly discredited himself. He resisted her suggestions that Labor Secretary Raymond Donovan be asked to resign until Donovan became the first sitting member of the cabinet in history to be indicted. He resisted her suggestion that he replace Defense Secretary Caspar Weinberger at the beginning of the second term. He even resisted her—and Deaver, Spencer and many prominent Republicans on Capitol Hill—as long as he could before dismissing White House Chief of Staff Donald Regan in the second term. Reagan often did not ask the right questions, or any questions at all, which made it possible to manipulate him or lead him down paths where he did not wish to go. But he did not like to be pushed by anyone, not even Nancy Reagan.

She nonetheless pushed him to speak more softly to the Soviets. When Stu Spencer told her "the truth as I saw it," part of what he said was that Americans remained fearful of Reagan's seeming readiness to risk a U.S.-Soviet confrontation. Later, as the economic recovery gathered momentum and Mondale repeatedly proclaimed his willingness to raise taxes, Spencer had no doubt that pocketbook issues would prove decisive for Reagan. He was less certain about that in 1983. Wirthlin's polls then showed that many Americans who otherwise approved of Reagan were uncomfortable with the hard edges of Reagan's "evil empire" rhetoric. Spencer's gut said the same. Americans wanted a president who would stand up to the Russians but also talk with them, as Wirthlin often said, and Reagan had not yet met with any Soviet leader.

Public concern about Reagan's hard-line anticommunism was a latent fear that flared up in times of international crisis or whenever the president made some careless or confrontational remark about the Soviets. Women were especially fearful of war and desirous of improved U.S.-Soviet relations, and Nancy Reagan was the only woman in the Reagan inner circle. She did not need to be told how women felt about the issue, but she read Wirthlin's polls and listened to Spencer. When she asked Spencer if her husband could win a second term, he replied positively but also noted Reagan's potential vulnerability on his dealings with the Soviets. Nancy Reagan had great respect for Spencer's political judgment, and what he said reinforced her own feelings. Improving U.S.-Soviet relations became Nancy Reagan's special cause. Although few thought of her as a peaceful force, she became a force for peace within the White House.

While helping her husband to become a more palatable candidate, she continued throughout the late summer and fall of 1983 to resist him on a second term. Reagan would say after his formal announcement that she was the only one he had talked to about running again. She was also the only person he had to convince. "For a while we talked about it every night, until it became obvious this was something Ronnie just had to do," she said. "Finally, I said, 'If you feel that strongly, go ahead. You know I'm not crazy about it, but okay.' "[33] It has been suggested to me that this "okay" was given less graciously than she remembers. But given it was, and aides who had been hedging their bets on a second term began telling me shortly after Thanksgiving that Reagan would run again. The White House was then emerging from a particularly difficult time of factional strife played out against a background of international tension. KAL 007 had been shot down on September 1, touching off one of the most acrimonious periods of the Cold War.

Late in October the invasion of Grenada had followed closely on the heels of the catastrophe in Lebanon. Public and congressional clamor for the withdrawal of the Marines was growing. Within the White House, Nancy Reagan and the inner political circle were dispirited. James Baker and Mike Deaver still smarted from the rejection of their attempted palace coup by the conservatives. While the conservatives savored this victory, they were not especially happy either. They shared Nancy Reagan's view that Bud McFarlane, the new national security adviser, was likely to be supportive of Shultz's efforts to improve U.S.-Soviet relations, a development they did not welcome. While the process of change had been untidy and destructive of various egos, the pragmatists were now dominant in the White House. With Clark at Interior and Ed Meese headed for the Justice Department, there was no longer any influential opposition within the White House to the proposition that Reagan should soft-pedal his enmity toward the "evil empire."

Reagan, who was happiest when his aides were in agreement, unresistingly headed off in the direction of dialogue. In an internationally televised speech to Europe on January 16, 1984, he called for "constructive cooperation" between the superpowers and proclaimed that "1984 is a year of opportunities for peace." The speech reflected the policy views of Shultz and McFarlane, both of whom worked on the draft that was sent to the speechwriting department. The president's new approach was encouraged by Nancy Reagan and promoted avidly by Baker, Deaver, Spencer and Dick Darman, then the overseer of the speechwriters. Their consensus view was that the January 16 speech signaled a prospective turn in U.S.-Soviet relations, as indeed it did.

Two weeks after this speech, in a brief nationally televised speech from the Oval Office on January 29, Reagan formally announced that he was seeking reelection. His new direction was reflected in a sentence of the thirteen-paragraph statement in which he said, "By beginning to rebuild our defenses, we have restored credible deterrence and can confidently seek a secure and lasting peace, as well as a reduction in arms." He claimed in another passage that "we're here to lift the weak and build the peace." Reagan made no direct mention of the Soviet Union. The phrase "evil empire" would never publicly pass his lips again, unless he was responding to a question or criticism about why he had used the words in the first place. He was a peace-and-prosperity candidate, as he and his staff and Nancy Reagan wanted him to be. But as is often the case, public awareness of Reagan's new approach lagged behind the changes that were occurring in the administration's foreign policy. On February 9, George Gallup, after noting growing public approval for Reagan's handling of the economy, would say, "At the same time, however, he appears to be increasingly vulnerable on foreign policy issues at a time when Americans' concern over the threat of war has grown to its highest point since the Vietnam War." Gallup's figures showed 49 percent of Americans disapproving and only 38 percent approving of Reagan's overall handling of foreign policy. Reagan's marks were even lower on Central America (28–49 disapproval) and lower still on Lebanon, where 28 percent of voters approved and 59 percent disapproved. But Gallup's findings were based on a survey that had been conducted in mid-January, just before the "year of peace" speech and when U.S. forces were still mired in Lebanon. By the time the Gallup analysis appeared in print, Reagan had already announced the "redeployment" of the Marines who remained in Lebanon.

"Once we pulled the troops out of Lebanon, it was never close again," Ed Rollins said many years later. "We knew the troops were a major, major obstacle."[34] Rollins, one ring removed from the inner circle, believed that it was desirable to speak more softly to the Soviets but absolutely imperative to ease public fears about the possibility of another Vietnam in the Middle East. The actions were actually mutually reinforcing. In calming public doubts about his conduct of U.S.-Soviet relations and allowing the Marines to be "redeployed" at the same time, Reagan had taken a long step toward focusing the campaign away from foreign affairs and onto the issue of economic prosperity. After the withdrawal of the Marines and the proclamation of the "year of peace," the Reagan campaign was free to use foreign policy themes in a celebratory fashion, which is why the Republicans' camera crew had been sent abroad. In *Our Country: The Shaping of America from Roosevelt to Reagan,* political historian Michael Barone would say that the election was over by June 6, when Reagan in his D-Day speech recalled "a moment in history with reverberations greater than any [Democratic] candidate's primary victories."[35]

It is difficult to find a turning point in an election that ends in a 49-state landslide. Some analysts would later say that the election had been decided when Gary Hart pressed Walter Mondale in Iowa and defeated him in New Hampshire, forcing Mondale into a protracted contest to win a nomination that might have stood a better chance if he had been able to achieve it more easily. Others, including presidential campaign historians Jack W. Germond and Jules Witcover, would say that Mondale all but clinched the election for Reagan when he declared in his acceptance speech on July 19, 1984, at the Democratic National Convention, "I mean business. By the end of my first term, I will cut the deficit by two-thirds. Let's tell the truth. Mr. Reagan will raise taxes, and so will I. He won't tell you. I just did." The members of the Reagan campaign team could not believe their ears. "I was in ecstasy," Spencer said. "The political graveyard is full of tax increasers."[36]

I concluded that Reagan had a lock on the election on September 23 after reading my colleague David Broder's account in *The Washington Post* of voter attitudes in Michigan, an economically ravaged state where unemployment was higher than the national average. Broder wrote that the issues of the campaign were "clouded by the euphoria produced by burgeoning economic growth and Reagan's powerful personality."[37] But the passage that caught my eye was an interview Broder had conducted with a young couple in a Grand Rapids shopping mall on the

day Reagan had made a political appearance in the city with hometown
hero Gerald Ford:

> Richard Lewis, 25, had just moved from the Detroit area to look
> for work. In response to standard polling questions used nationally
> by *The Washington Post* and ABC News, he said Reagan "sides with
> the special interests" while Mondale "sides with the average citizen."
> His companion, Michigan State University student Anne Whipple,
> 23, agreed with these judgments and said, in answer to another ques-
> tion, that Mondale "would be more likely to keep the United States
> out of war."
> Lewis disagreed, saying he thinks Reagan "knows what the dangers
> are." But both said Mondale would "do a better job of ensuring that
> government programs and policies are fair to all the people."
> "Reagan likes the rich," Lewis said.
> "That's right," Whipple agreed. "That's where he comes from."
> For whom do they plan to vote in November? Both said Reagan.
> "I like his style," Lewis said. "He's brought the country back
> together." As for Mondale, he said, "I don't see how he can step in
> and keep people together like President Reagan has."
> Whipple said she would like to see Democratic vice-presidential
> nominee Geraldine A. Ferraro "get in there for women's sake," but
> added, "I don't see how she or Mondale could pull people to-
> gether."[38]

This belief that Reagan had "brought the country back together" was
a recurrent refrain in voter interviews conducted during the campaign
by *The Washington Post* and other news organizations and in the elec-
tion-day exit polls. Many voters had felt this way before the campaign
began, and their feelings were reinforced by inspirational television
commercials designed to identify the Reagan presidency with all that
was good in America. The commercial called "Morning Again in America" opened with glimpses of a farmhouse, followed by scenes of a
wedding party and of an elderly man raising the American flag while
young faces watched in adoration. As the flag filled the screen to the
sounds of soft and stirring music an announcer said, "It's morning again
in America. Today, more men and women will go to work than ever
before in our country's history. With interest rates at about half the
record high of 1980, nearly two thousand families today will buy new
homes, more than at any time in the past four years. This afternoon,

sixty-five hundred young men and women will be married, and with inflation at less than half of what it was four years ago, they can look forward with confidence. It's morning again in America. And under the leadership of President Reagan, our country is stronger, and prouder, and better. Why would we ever want to return to where we were less than four short years ago?"

Reagan loved these lyrical commercials, which were called "feel good" ads and were reminiscent of his old General Electric commercials that had inspired consumers to buy the company's light bulbs by making them feel good about America. Reagan had sold himself in these ads, which concluded with the slogan "Progress Is Our Most Important Product." In 1984, the campaign commercials made a similar pitch for the Reagan presidency, and the message was believable because times were good and Reagan had a high degree of what marketing specialists call "product acceptance." He was a salesman, and he valued the work that salesmen did. At the first White House meeting of his campaign advertisers, known as the Tuesday Team, Reagan poked his head in the door and said to them, "Since you're the ones who are selling the soap, I thought you'd like to see the bar."[39] The admen got a kick out of it. They liked working for a president who had enough understanding of their work to think of himself as a product.

Reagan took advertising far more seriously than he ever took himself. Though he skimmed or ignored many a briefing paper, he rarely missed a showing of a new campaign commercial. He was a perfect audience for the feel-good ads, which were aimed at "the slightly upscale voter" who had prospered during the Reagan recovery. The ads made Reagan feel good, too. He was a powerful and sentimental salesman who understood that the magic of his presidency was linked to his ability to embody the values of mythic America. When he saw himself on the screen, he saw America. He wept when he first saw the eighteen-minute film created by the Tuesday Team from news footage and the work of the Republican camera crew. The film, far more powerful than Reagan's second acceptance speech, was the emotional highlight of the Republican National Convention that summer in Dallas. Later, it would be enlarged into a thirty-minute documentary and shown simultaneously on all three networks and leading independent stations in the nation's major markets early in September. Soon afterward, the Reagan campaign started running the "Morning Again in America" commercial and a companion ad, "America Is Back." And soon after these ads came another series of commercials that were specifically designed to rouse the pride and patriotism of viewers who had awakened to the happy American morning. Reagan's favorite was one in which he did the narration against a background of armed services flags. "Four times in my life, America's been at war," he said. "Such a tragic waste of lives. It makes you realize how desperately the world needs a lasting peace. Just across the hall here in the White House is the Roosevelt Room. And often as I meet with my staff, I gaze up at the five service flags, each representing one of the five military services. Draped from each flag are battle streamers signifying every battle campaign fought since the Revolutionary War, each ribbon a remembrance of a time when American men and women spilled their blood into the soil of distant lands. My fondest hope for this presidency is that the people of America give us the continued opportunity to pursue a peace so strong and so lasting that we never again have to add another streamer to those flags."

These ads were the essence of the Reagan reelection campaign. In selling Reagan as if he were indeed a bar of soap or a soft drink, they made Walter Mondale seem irrelevant to what was going on in America. But the ads were credible only because so many Americans felt good about their president and the direction in which he was taking their country. Voters in the ABC exit polls had stronger positive feelings about Reagan than negative ones about Mondale. In this the 1984 election was a reversal of the 1980 election, which had been a negative referendum on Jimmy Carter, capsulized in Reagan's rhetorical question, "Are you better off today than you were four years ago?" Had Reagan been seeking reelection under circumstances where the economy was declining, the issue undoubtedly would have been flung back into Reagan's face by the Democrats, as the Republicans had used Jimmy Carter's "misery index" against him in 1980.* Wirthlin knew this, and he had been asking the "better off" question in his polls long before the campaign began. The "feel-good" commercials would have been laughed off the screen in the depth of the 1982 recession. They had resonance in 1984 because so many Americans thought their lives had improved during Reagan's first four years in the White House. The ABC exit polls on election day discovered that those who answered the "better off" question affirmatively cast their ballots for Reagan. This

---

* The "misery index" was the rate of inflation added to the percentage of unemployment, a gimmick that Carter had invented during his campaign against President Ford in 1976. It became a derisive reference point for Reagan in 1980, when the misery index was far higher than it had been four years earlier.

was not surprising. Nor was it surprising that most of the one-fifth of Americans who said they were worse off than they had been in 1980 voted for Mondale.

It was often said, particularly when Reagan ran into trouble in his second term, that many of his problems were the product of his "issue-less" reelection campaign. The argument was that Reagan, while obtaining a less numerically impressive victory in 1980, had nonetheless gained a mandate because he had campaigned "on the issues" and told voters exactly what he intended to do. In 1984, he was said by many (including me) to have won a landslide without a mandate.

In retrospect, a better argument might be that the 1984 campaign was less a failure of issues than of arithmetic. Although Spencer and White House troubleshooter Dick Darman rummaged around for some new proposals with which to dress up the old rhetoric, they quickly realized that the 1984 campaign was framed by the federal budget deficit as well as by the economic recovery. It was difficult for Reagan to be an "issues candidate" in 1984 because he had failed to carry out his 1980 promise to balance the federal budget or its subsequent variations to reduce the budget deficit. Reagan found it easy to rationalize that this failure was the fault of the "big spenders" in Congress, but his inner circle knew that the administration had never once presented a budget that provided the revenues for the programs Reagan was pledged to keep. The combination of a continuing commitment to low taxes and high military spending made it impossible to pay even for existing programs, let alone new ones. "Stockman, Darman and Baker all realized that the budget numbers didn't add up and that the second term was going to be terrible," said Ed Rollins.[40]

Reagan did not realize this. The budget numbers had never added up, either in 1980 or in 1984, but Reagan had never computed the costs of the progress he was peddling. "We see an America where every day is Independence Day, the Fourth of July," Reagan proclaimed in a concluding round of campaign addresses produced from old speeches literally stored in the computers of his speechwriters. "We want to lower your tax rates, yours and everyone's in this country, so that our economy will be stronger, our families will be stronger and America will be stronger." He was convinced that the morning that had come to America was just the beginning of a glorious new day. "The United States of America was never meant to be a second-rate nation," he said repeatedly. "So, like our Olympic athletes, let's aim for the stars and go for the gold . . . America's best days are yet to come."

· · ·

But there were millions of Americans for whom it was not "morning again in America." Reagan recognized this, although he rarely made the concession in his campaign speeches. He was an apostle of the market-place whose premise had always been that the U.S. economic pie should be enlarged, not that everyone should receive an equal slice. And while the pie had indeed become larger, it had changed less than the size of the pieces. An Urban Institute study concluded in 1984 that average annual income (using 1982 dollars) for American families had risen 3.5 percent during Reagan's first term, or about $700 a year. During this period the typical middle-class family's income rose from $18,857 to $19,034, or only about 1 percent. Meanwhile, the average income of the most affluent one-fifth of Americans had increased from $37,618 to $40,888, or nearly 9 percent. And the average income of the poorest one-fifth of all families had declined, from $6,913 to $6,391, or nearly 8 percent.[41]

The discrepancies among the fortunes of different groups of Americans were even greater when age, gender and race were taken into account. The conservatives who were Reagan's core supporters ideal-ized traditional American families in which the husband worked while the wife took care of the children, but the income of such one-earner families declined slightly during Reagan's first term while the income of two-earner families increased. The income of families headed by some-one sixty-five or older rose 9.5 percent—nearly three times the increase for all families. As a group, the elderly were hurt least by the high unemployment of the 1981–82 recession and helped most by the rapid decrease in inflation. But the income of a typical nonelderly, female-headed family in the middle fifth of income dropped by nearly 5 per-cent. Black families fared badly. "With the exception of the elderly, their real incomes declined both absolutely and relative to the income of whites," the Urban Institute study concluded. Overall, the income of black families fell by 3.7 percent.[42]

And despite the sea of happy children's faces that graced the "feel-good" commercials, poverty exploded in the inner cities of America during the Reagan years, claiming children as its principal victims. By 1984 some 13 million children lived below the poverty line, more than when Lyndon Johnson declared the "war on poverty" in 1965. During this period poverty among children in two-parent families had been cut in half. But these gains were drowned out by the poverty of children born to never-married mothers, a social problem that the Reagan administration neither created nor addressed. Many whites saw the issue as "a black problem," and it was true that a black child in America during the Reagan years was twelve times more likely than a white child to have a never-married mother. But other minority or white children who were the offspring of a never-married mother were just as likely as blacks to be poor. The plight of these children was reflected in statistics of increasing crime, hunger, malnutrition, illiteracy, drug use and homelessness. The Massachusetts Department of Public Health reported in a 1983 study that one in five poor children suffered from stunted growth or was anemic or abnormally underweight because of malnutrition.

The Reagan administration's responsibility for the increasingly difficult plight of the nonelderly poor remains a matter of dispute. The Urban Institute study concluded that discrepancies in income would have increased even if pre-Reagan policies had remained in place but that the redistribution to the rich had been accelerated under Reagan. The study also concluded that the elderly were the only group, other than the wealthiest one-fifth of Americans, to benefit from administration policies. Children suffered from the Reagan prosperity despite David Stockman's contention in 1981 that the administration was "interested in curtailing weak claims rather than weak clients."[43] The principal reason for this suffering was that programs targeted to low-income families, such as Aid to Families with Dependent Children [AFDC], were cut back far more than programs such as Social Security, which serve families irrespective of income. As a result of cuts in such targeted programs—including school lunches and subsidized housing—federal benefit programs for households with incomes of less than $10,000 a year declined nearly 8 percent during the Reagan first term while federal aid for households with more than $40,000 income was almost unchanged. When all was said and done, it was in fact the "weak clients" who had the weakest claims upon the Reagan administration and Congress.

The declining living standards in the inner cities and the poverty of the increasing number of children born to unwed mothers were occasional topics of discussion in the "issues luncheons" held with Reagan on many Mondays in the White House. And Reagan could be affected by individual stories of poverty and hardship drawn to his attention by Deaver or in a letter given him by Anne Higgins. As noted in an earlier chapter, Reagan looked upon these letters as fan mail, sometimes responding to them with notes of encouragement accompanied by a small check. "It never ceased to move him when he heard the figures describing what was happening to inner-city families," said Gary L. Bauer, his domestic policy adviser.[44] This was an overstatement. While Reagan was certainly capable of compassion, he was also, in Deaver's view, "a terrible listener [who] was always thinking of what he was going to say" rather than about what he was hearing.[45] Even Bauer recalls that the solutions Reagan advocated were rather "bloodless" ones that expressed his fundamental mistrust of government. "When he did think about these problems, he tended to convert them into budget arguments or arguments about federalism—you know, that we were too centralized in our welfare programs—instead of thinking about them as larger social problems," Bauer said.[46]

Bauer and his fellow conservatives among the second tier of Reagan policy advisers did relate welfare issues to "larger social problems" but differed radically with those who believed that increased federal assistance would alleviate poverty. In a 1986 report, "The Family: Preserving America's Future," Bauer argued that welfare programs, especially AFDC, created "family fragments, households headed by a mother dependent upon public charity. In that process the easy availability of welfare in all its forms has become a powerful force for destruction of family life through perpetuation of the welfare culture."

Reagan had made welfare fraud a cornerstone of his reelection campaign for governor of California in 1970 and also exploited the issue in his presidential campaigns. He had dealt constructively with welfare issues in his second term as governor, working with Democratic leaders of the legislature to produce legislation that tightened welfare eligibility requirements and increased the grants of the poorest recipients. But he had dealt demagogically with welfare in his 1976 campaign, when he repeatedly told the story of a Chicago woman who "has eighty names, thirty addresses, twelve Social Security cards and is collecting veterans' benefits on four nonexisting deceased husbands. . . . Her tax-free cash income alone is over $150,000."[47] The woman was convicted in 1977 of welfare fraud and perjury for using two aliases to collect twenty-three public aid checks totaling $8,000. To Reagan she was the "Chicago welfare queen," an enduring symbol of welfare fraud. When congressional leaders called upon the president early in 1981 and asked him how he intended to achieve the budget savings he had promised, Reagan told them the story of the "welfare queen."[48] He also repeated the anecdote in meetings with foreign leaders. During his visit to Barbados on April 8, 1982, Reagan met with J. M. G. (Tom) Adams, then prime minister of that Caribbean nation. When the discussion turned to welfare, Deaver recognized the telltale signs. He nudged James Baker and whispered to him, "He's going to tell the story of the Chicago welfare queen next." And sure enough, Reagan did.

The "welfare queen" was a black woman named Linda Taylor. As far as I can determine, Reagan never identified her either by name or race in any of his speeches, although her picture became well known to midwestern television viewers after she was put on trial in 1977. Even before the trial, Taylor's case generated considerable publicity in Illinois, where she became the symbolic embodiment of welfare fraud for legislative conservatives who were trying to reduce welfare costs. Some of Reagan's critics believed that his repeated citation of the "welfare queen" was a subtle appeal to racial prejudice, and this suspicion was reinforced during the 1976 campaign when *The New York Times* reported that Reagan, in a speech to a southern audience, had used a regional term of racial derision in referring to a food stamp recipient as a "young buck."

I do not believe that Reagan was racially prejudiced in the normal meaning of the term. He had been taught by his parents that racial intolerance was abhorrent, and the many people I interviewed who knew him as a young man were unanimous in believing that he absorbed these lessons. In his autobiography Reagan tells how he volunteered to take Eureka College's two black football players into his home in Dixon after they were refused admission at a hotel on one of the team's trips to an Illinois college. The players were welcomed by Reagan's parents, as Reagan had known they would be. One of these players was William Franklin Burghardt, who had played center on the line next to Reagan. The two became friends and corresponded regularly until Burghardt's death in 1981. Burghardt vividly remembered the incident where he and his black teammate had been refused admission to the hotel and supported Reagan's account of what had happened. "I just don't think he [Reagan] was conscious of race at all," Burghardt said in 1981. "If you listened to the Carter debate during the campaign, Reagan said that when he was growing up they didn't know they had a race problem. It was the dumbest thing a grown person could say, but he'd never seen it. I believe that [the hotel incident] was his first experience of that sort."[49]

Racial segregation was at the time routine in many communities in the Middle West. Reagan was opposed to it. He had helped recruit Burghardt to play at Eureka from Greenfield, Illinois, where his grandfather and uncle worked as barbers. Nearly a half century later, when he was governor, Reagan named a black to the state board that licenses and regulates the barber industry in California. When Deaver asked him why he was bothering to do this, since he had so little political support among blacks, Reagan explained that he had once been told by a black that he had been turned away by a white barber who said he didn't know how to cut a black man's hair. "If I put a black man on the barber's board this isn't going to happen," Reagan said. "It's the right thing to do."[50]

But Reagan never supported the use of federal power to provide blacks with the civil rights systematically denied to them by southern states since the end of Reconstruction in the nineteenth century. He opposed the landmark Voting Rights Act of 1965, which was overwhelmingly supported by congressional majorities of both parties. Reagan cited constitutional grounds for his position, but many suspected that his position also involved an element of political calculation. Reagan avidly courted the support of white southerners during the mid-1960s, and he consistently refused during his abortive campaign for the presidency in 1968 to criticize George Wallace's segregationist advocacies. This seemed to me like political pandering, although Reagan always denied any such motive. But Reagan told Laurence Barrett in 1980 that the Voting Rights Act had been "humiliating to the South."[51] While he made political points with white southerners on this issue, Reagan was extremely sensitive to any suggestion that his stands on civil rights issues were politically or racially motivated, and he typically reacted to such criticisms as attacks on his personal integrity.

In discussing racial prejudice Reagan often cited his opposition, as a sports broadcaster, to the long and shameful practice of barring blacks from major league baseball. This last little speech was known to Deaver and the small circle of Reagan staff as "the Jackie Robinson story," after the famous Brooklyn Dodger who in 1947 became the first black to play in the major leagues. Reagan invariably told it when he met privately with any group of blacks. Deaver was not overly fond of the story, which Reagan told to demonstrate his opposition to racism but which also suggested that he had not done much lately for the cause of civil rights. The Jackie Robinson story was omitted from the speech Reagan gave to the convention of the National Association for the Advancement of Colored People in Denver on June 29, 1981, where he received one of the coolest receptions of his presidency. The reaction was partially a reflection of Reagan's snub of the NAACP the year before, when he had turned down an invitation to speak because it would have interfered with his riding vacation. But the NAACP also disliked Reagan's message, which was that government programs had created "a new kind of bondage" for blacks. Nor were the delegates impressed when Reagan related the story of Garfield Langhorn, a black soldier in Vietnam who had posthumously received the Congressional Medal of Honor for saving fellow soldiers by throwing himself on a live grenade. As Reagan told it, Langhorn's last words were "You have to care."

The president was so cut off from the counsel of black Americans that he sometimes did not even realize when he was offending them. One glaring example occurred early in 1982 when Reagan sided with Bob Jones University of Greenville, South Carolina, and the Goldsboro Christian Schools of Goldsboro, North Carolina, in a lawsuit to obtain federal tax exemptions that had been denied them by the Internal Revenue Service. The IRS had long followed a practice of denying tax exemptions to the segregated private schools that proliferated in the South after schools were racially integrated during the 1960s. The IRS policy had been authorized by President Nixon in 1970 and continued by Presidents Ford and Carter. In many cases the schools that lost tax exemptions had been created simply in a transparent attempt to pre-serve segregation, but the IRS net also enmeshed a number of Christian schools in existence long before the civil rights struggles. Many of them were schools such as Bob Jones University, which enrolled a handful of minority students but prohibited interracial dating and marriage. It was on the basis of this discrimination that the IRS had denied the tax exemption for Bob Jones University. The university cited Scripture as the basis for its discriminatory rules, which made the issue one of religious freedom to the religious wing of the New Right.

At the 1980 Republican Convention the New Right succeeded in inserting a plank in the party platform that declared, "We will halt the unconstitutional regulatory vendetta launched by Mr. Carter's IRS com-missioner against independent schools." Citing this plank, Congress-man (now Senator) Trent Lott of Mississippi wrote a letter to Reagan late in 1981 calling attention to the Bob Jones–Goldsboro case, which was then making its way to the Supreme Court. Lott wanted the federal government to change sides, intervening on the side of the Christian schools. When the letter reached the White House, Reagan wrote on it in a place in the margin reserved for comment, "I think we should." An assistant to Ed Meese returned the letter to Lott.[52]

Reagan would later say that the case had never been presented to him as a civil rights issue, which was true. More astonishingly, he did not even know that many of the Christian schools practiced segregation. "Maybe I should have but I didn't," he said on May 10, 1982. "I was getting complaints even before I got here as president . . . that some of the Internal Revenue agents . . . were harassing some schools, even though they were desegregated. . . . I didn't think that this was the place of Treasury agents to be doing this. So I told the Secretary of Treasury that I didn't think that . . . I didn't know that there were a couple of legal cases pending. All I wanted was that these tax collectors stop threatening schools that were obeying the law." [53]

Neither Meese nor Attorney General William French Smith pointed out to Reagan that he was reversing the civil rights policy of three previous administrations without any consultation with blacks or engaging in detailed discussion of the issue with anyone. A subsequent case study of the Bob Jones affair concluded that Smith reached his decision on the basis of an extended legal analysis and without consideration of the political implications. [54] Meese also did not anticipate the political firestorm. He did not tell Baker or Deaver what was happening until two days before the Justice Department announced that it would withdraw from the Bob Jones–Goldsboro lawsuit. Deaver believed Meese was leading Reagan into a political minefield without benefit of mine detectors and decided to intervene. He thought Reagan might reach a different decision if he talked to blacks. Since no black then held a prominent position in the White House, Deaver sought help from Thaddeus Garrett Jr., domestic affairs adviser to Vice President Bush, and Melvin Bradley, a minor official in the Office of Policy Development. Deaver persuaded the president to meet with Garrett and Bradley on January 12, four days after the IRS ruling. Garrett, trained as a Methodist minister, dramatically related to Reagan a sermon he had heard in church two days earlier that had been inspired by the Bob Jones decision. The minister had recounted the parable of the serpent, a story about how a woman saves the life of a wounded snake and is ungratefully bitten in return. "Reagan is that snake!" the preacher had concluded. The congregation had responded with a chorus of amens. [55]

Reagan was impressed with this story—"horrified," as Deaver remembers it—and ready to beat a retreat. "The president," said Bradley, "was visibly hurt by what he read in the newspapers, because he had never supported segregated academies and had fought all his life on the opposite side of the fence. He stressed to us that he had done this because he didn't feel the IRS should go into private schools without legislative authority. He wanted to know if there were any people he should call to reassure, and he was ready to do it right then." [56]

After this meeting, Baker led the way in drafting a new administration policy. Reagan's reconsidered position was that it was morally right to deny the tax exemption to the Christian schools but morally wrong to do so by regulatory fiat. As a compromise, the White House proposed legislation that would have allowed the IRS to deny the tax exemptions, a plan that enraged the New Right without assuaging civil rights advocates, who had counted on the government to support the IRS ruling. The best that can be said about Reagan's performance is that he did not blame his staff for the contradictory signals he was sending, as Deaver urged him to do. When the president was asked at a January 19, 1982, news conference whether he was responsible for the decision "or did your staff put something over on you?" he replied, "The buck stops at my desk. I'm the originator of the whole thing, and I'm not going to deny it wasn't handled as well as it could be."

Later in the news conference he claimed that he had "prevented the IRS from determining national social policy all by itself." This was hardly true, inasmuch as the IRS was following a policy that had been supported by three presidents, two of them Republican, and was then more than a decade old. The White House bill died a quiet death in Congress, where it was opposed by religious groups and deemed unnecessary by civil rights organizations. Eventually, the Supreme Court sided with the civil rights groups. On May 24, 1983, the Court ruled 8-1, in an opinion written by Chief Justice Warren Burger, that the IRS had acted legally in denying tax exemptions to Bob Jones University and the Goldsboro schools. The decision left a bitter taste with the New Right, which blamed Reagan for retreating from a position that Deaver and Baker believe he never would have taken if Meese had flagged the issue for discussion before an announcement was made at the Justice Department. "They got the worst of both worlds," observed Paul Weyrich, a New Right leader who had lobbied in behalf of the tax exemptions. "They came down right on the issue at first, but then they flip-flopped when it created so much controversy, and all they wound up doing was making both sides mad." [57]

Later that year, Reagan outraged blacks with his comments about Martin Luther King, Jr. Reagan had long opposed making King's birthday a national holiday, while also saying that King should be honored for freeing the United States from "the burden of racism." As it became apparent that Congress intended to make King's birthday a holiday, Reagan agreed to sign the bill. The legislation was opposed by Senator Jesse Helms, who called for the opening of FBI records on King that had been sealed by a binding agreement with King's family. At an October 19, 1983, news conference Reagan was asked about Helms's accusation that Martin Luther King had been a Communist sympathizer. "We'll know in about thirty-five years, won't we?" Reagan responded. "No, I don't fault Senator Helms's sincerity with regard to wanting the records opened up. I think that he's motivated by a feeling that if we're going to have a national holiday named for any American, when it's only been named for one American in all our history up until this time, that he feels we should know everything there is to know about an individual." The answer dismayed Reagan's advisers, who had laughed earlier in the day when Reagan gave essentially the same reply at a rehearsal for the news conference. His advisers had thought the remark just another Reagan one-liner, not a serious reply. "I just assumed he'll never say that in a press conference," said White House communications director David Gergen afterward. "I almost lost my dinner over that."[58]

Reagan tried to make amends. He spoke movingly about King's contributions at an observance of his birthday on January 15, 1987, urging American youth "to accept nothing less than making yours a generation free of bigotry, intolerance and discrimination." And he took other symbolic steps to mollify blacks, including the promotion of Melvin Bradley to the position of special assistant to the president with a responsibility to study "the needs and priorities of the minority and disadvantaged communities." When *The Washington Post* reported that a suburban black family had been harassed, Reagan visited the family. He twice visited a black high school in Chicago and paid tribute to black scientists, businessmen and military heroes in a commencement address at Tuskegee University in 1987. But blacks, the most conspicuous dissenters in the "Morning Again" landslide of 1984, never gave Reagan high marks. And the skepticism about Reagan's commitment to civil rights was not limited to blacks alone. Reagan was simply reluctant to use federal authority in the cause of punishing discrimination of any sort. This was demonstrated in his response to a 1984 Supreme Court decision (*Grove City College v. Bell*) that limited antidiscrimination laws only to specific programs that received federal funds, not to the entire institution in which discrimination had occurred. The case involved was one of sex discrimination, but it also had broad implications to laws prohibiting discrimination against minorities, disabled persons and the elderly.

The practical implications of the decision were enormous. As an example, a college that received federal funds for, say, its science department would have to observe antidiscrimination laws in that department as a condition for receiving the money but would be free to discriminate in other departments that were not recipients of federal money. Civil rights groups mounted a struggle to overturn this decision and expand the reach of antibias laws. Reagan took no part in this battle, except to issue a brief statement through the White House press office in 1985 saying that he favored the most limited of the several bills intended to remedy the Supreme Court decision.

A bill that undid *Grove City* and slightly extended the scope of antibias laws finally passed Congress early in 1988. It was known as the Civil Rights Restoration Act. Although Reagan was by now a lame-duck president with no need of cultivating support among either conservatives or civil rights advocates, he vetoed the bill, arguing that it would "vastly and unjustifiably expand the power of the federal government over the decisions and affairs of private organizations, such as churches and synagogues, farms, businesses and state and local governments." This veto message of March 16, 1988, was accompanied by a maneuver that curiously echoed Reagan's unsuccessful face-saving conduct in the Bob Jones affair six years earlier. Along with his veto message Reagan sent to Congress a new bill, "The Civil Rights Protection Act of 1988," which overturned *Grove City* for most institutions but exempted educational institutions "closely identified with religious organizations" from the sexual discrimination provisions. Whether such a proposal could have succeeded in 1985, when Reagan's popularity was high and Republicans controlled the Senate, is doubtful. By 1988 this counterproposal was so belated and such an obvious public relations gimmick that it was not taken seriously even by the White House press office. Congress ignored it. With twenty-one Senate Republicans and fifty-two House Republicans joining solid Democratic majorities, Reagan's veto was promptly overridden and the Civil Rights Restoration Act became the law of the land.

Blacks were not the only Americans who dissented from the proposition that it was Morning Again. Concealed beneath the Reagan landslide were pockets of Democratic strength in older, industrial cities of the East and Middle West and in states originally settled by New England Yankees, which included Oregon, Washington, Iowa and Wisconsin as well as southern New England. While Reagan received more support overall from 1980 supporters of John Anderson than Mondale did, the Democratic nominee seems to have done well with those Anderson voters who, in Mark Shields's phrase, drove Volvos and braked for small animals.

Put another way, Mondale did relatively well among environmentally conscious voters. Fortunately for Reagan, however, the environment was not what political analysts call a "cutting" or determinative issue in 1984. Only 4 percent of the voters in a *Los Angeles Times* poll listed environmental protection as one of the issues most important to them in casting their presidential ballot. Of these voters, three out of four voted for Mondale. Early in the first term, Richard Wirthlin had worried that environmental protection had the potential to become a damaging issue for Reagan in 1984. His concern was shared by Reagan's political advisers in the White House, who took a lead role in forcing Anne Gorsuch Burford to resign as Environmental Protection Agency administrator after an EPA scandal and who were delighted when Interior Secretary James Watt's intemperateness eventually led to his resignation. Whatever potential the environment might have had to become a high-visibility issue in the 1984 campaign faded with the departure of Burford and Watt from the administration. Reagan's political strategists were glad to see them go.

But even when Watt and Burford were under heavy fire, Reagan did not share the fears of his strategists that he would be damaged by environmental issues. Reagan believed he brought a common-sense view to environmental issues that was widely shared by Americans. He always considered himself an "environmentalist," a word he defined so loosely that he applied the term to Watt as well.[59] Left to his own devices, Reagan rarely thought about the environment in political terms. He has as much need for solitude as for a stage, and he has loved the outdoors since his boyhood wanderings among the "woods and mysteries" of rural Illinois. Perhaps the Rock River was an early retreat for Reagan from the alcoholism of his boyhood home. Certainly, he thought of his mountaintop California ranch as a "haven and refuge" (words he often used to describe it) from the cares of the presidency. Whatever his needs or motives, each of Reagan's four ranches has been more isolated than its predecessor.* And the ranches changed Reagan's leisure-time lifestyle from the social activity of team sports and golf,

* In the late 1940s, when he was still married to Jane Wyman, Reagan bought an eight-acre horse ranch in Northridge, in what was then open country but has long since been overrun by Southern

which he played passably well in his thirties, to the more solitary pre-occupations of riding and ranch chores. Reagan was in many ways a frustrated cowboy, who had repeatedly pleaded with Warner Bros. for western roles. He had learned to ride in Des Moines, and it became almost an obsession with him after he purchased his first ranch at Northridge, near Los Angeles, in 1948. Reagan was appalled to learn on his first visit to Camp David as president that Richard Nixon had paved over many of the riding trails.

Reagan's 688-acre ranch in the Santa Ynez Mountains northwest of Santa Barbara was found for him in 1974 by millionaire investment counselor and fellow rider William Wilson, whom Reagan later named U.S. ambassador to the Vatican. The ranch nestles on a mountaintop that, at 2,250 feet, is often bathed in sunlight while fog shrouds the Pacific Ocean below. The view and the remoteness appealed to Reagan at first sight. He named it Rancho del Cielo ("heavenly ranch") and after the end of his second term as governor in 1974 threw himself into clearing trails and brush and remodeling the old one-story adobe house to make it comfortable for Nancy Reagan. Working with a former highway patrolman who had driven Reagan's limousine when he was governor, Reagan knocked out walls, redesigned the kitchen, tore out a screened porch and replaced it with a family room. He removed the corrugated roof, replaced it with old fence boards and covered these with fake tile. He built a fence around the house out of old telephone poles and constructed a patio from rocks he dragged into place, filled with cement and sprayed with water. The ranch was a place where Reagan was not on camera and could be comfortable without a script.

When he proudly showed off Rancho del Cielo in 1976, shortly before he lost the Republican nomination to Gerald Ford, I was re-minded of the famous scene in *Death of a Salesman* where Biff Loman talks about how his dead father had enjoyed building a bathroom and a new porch and putting up the garage. "You know, Charley, there's more of him in that front stoop than in all the sales he ever made," Biff

---

California's suburban sprawl. He sold this ranch in 1951 and bought two parcels of land totaling 290 acres in the Santa Monica Mountains north of Los Angeles for $85,000. Fifteen years later he sold 236 acres of this property to 20th Century Fox, which owned extensive adjoining acreage, for $1,931,000. Reagan used the remaining acreage as a down payment on a ranch in Riverside County which he purchased for $347,000 in 1968 and sold eight years later in a then-undisclosed sale to a friendly land developer for $856,000. Reagan became a millionaire through these land dealings, which are discussed in more detail in *Reagan*, pages 353–56.

says. That was the way it was with Reagan, though he was not finished selling. He never missed a chance to get to the ranch, either as candidate or president, and he spent most of his time there outdoors. Nancy Reagan would keep him company on a morning ride when the weather was nice but she otherwise spent her time inside, usually reading or on the telephone. It was an open secret in the White House that the first lady much preferred Beverly Hills to Rancho del Cielo, but she made a show of liking it for his benefit. And this must at times have been wearying for her.

Reagan managed to spend 345 days of his presidency—nearly a full year—at Rancho del Cielo, which he reached by helicopter from the Point Mugu Naval Air Station near Oxnard. His staff stayed at the Biltmore Hotel in Santa Barbara, connected to him by a secure telephone and sometimes by couriers who made the 30-mile ride from Santa Barbara to Rancho del Cielo, the last six and a half miles of it over a twisting, one-lane road that passes from Refugio State Beach and the Pacific Coast Highway through a brush-covered canyon teeming with wildlife. It was a common complaint of aides that Reagan was "really out of touch" when he was "up on the mountain," as they called the ranch—that he tended to be more ideological and even less interested in briefing papers than usual. Reagan did not dispute this. "When you get in there [at Rancho del Cielo], the world is gone," he said in an interview in 1985.

Reagan made a number of important presidential decisions at the ranch and never apologized for the time he spent there—or, for that matter, at Camp David. He said he preferred the 1,500-square-foot ranch house or the cabins at Camp David to living in the White House, where "you can get a kind of a bird-in-a-gilded-cage feeling." And while he was otherwise supine about his schedule, going wherever his aides instructed him to go within the limits permitted by Nancy Reagan, he took an active interest in planning his trips to Rancho del Cielo and in remaining there as long as possible. When Deaver suggested early in the presidency that he should postpone or shorten a long vacation he had planned at the ranch to avoid media criticism, Reagan engaged in a rare display of temper. "Look, Mike, you can tell me to do a lot of things, but you're not going to tell me when to go to the ranch," Reagan said. "I'm seventy years old and I figure that ranch is going to add some years onto my life, and I'm going to enjoy it." [60] And he did.

This appealing display of cowboy independence was one of the qualities that Americans liked about Reagan. But it was also part of a problem that consistently affected the way Reagan as president dealt with environmental issues. Reagan is a true westerner who typifies a region that throughout its history has been torn by conflicting claims of development and preservation. Westerners always have fancied themselves independent from Washington, which until well into the twentieth century did little to manage or control the expanses of timber, grazing and desert lands under its jurisdiction. But westerners have also always been dependent upon the federal government, which drove out the Indians and the Mexicans, laid the telegraph lines, provided the homesteads, built dams and subsidized water for agricultural development. "The paradox of the West," said former Colorado governor Richard Lamm, "is that people consistently destroy what they come out to seek." [61]

Reagan was an embodiment of that paradox. As a ranch owner, he was a good steward of the land. In an area of steep hillsides, low water pressure and high fire danger (the Refugio fire in the Santa Ynez Mountains burned 80,000 acres in 1955), Reagan cleared away the brush from his homesite but otherwise left the land intact. He was so caring of the wildlife at Rancho del Cielo that he had rattlesnakes near the ranch house trapped and carted away, instead of following the usual ranching practice of simply killing them. But he lacked even elemental understanding of what private developers would do to irreplaceable national treasures. Environmentalists sniffed at the lack of appreciation for natural esthetics evidenced in such famous Reagan remarks as his comment during the 1966 campaign, "You know, a tree is a tree—how many more do you need to look at." In part this was a reflection of Reagan's commitment to the western ethic of development—an outlook widely shared by his pro-business friends. "People seem to think that all redwoods that are not protected through a national park will disappear," Reagan said on one occasion as governor. And on another he commented, "I'll be damned if I take away all this privately owned land for no reason. I owe that much to these people in the counties [where the redwood park was set aside]. I wonder, has anybody ever asked the Sierra Club if they think these trees will grow forever?" [62]

Reagan has a westerner's sense that "forever" is just around the next bend in the river. The West is so vast, beautiful and deceptively rugged that it is difficult for westerners of Reagan's mind-set to believe that the region's fragile ecological system stands at the raw edge of existence. His sense that a land of severe limits is actually limitless was encouraged by the remoteness of life at Rancho del Cielo, where, in the days before he was guarded by the Secret Service, he could ride for miles without seeing another human being. There is so much of the West that Reagan found it difficult to understand how much it is endangered. Once, on a flight over Colorado in 1979, Reagan turned to me and, with a gesture toward the expanse of mountain wilderness below, remarked that the unspoiled land still available in the United States was much more abundant than the environmental movement realized. He seemed not to notice that the plane in which we were flying had taken off through a layer of smog in Los Angeles and was landing through another layer of air pollution in Denver.[63]

Despite the limitations of his outlook, Reagan compiled an environmental record as governor of California that was better than his comments during the campaign would have led anyone to believe. Partly, this was because Congress came to the rescue of the redwoods, creating a Redwoods National Park, whose boundaries were largely determined by liberal Democrat Phil Burton of San Francisco, a city-dweller who lived within walking distance of the U.S. Capitol and would have found life at Rancho del Cielo even less interesting than Nancy Reagan did. And partly it was because Reagan was served in Sacramento by environmentally conscious Resources Director Norman (Ike) Livermore, a Sierra Clubber and rancher who led the fight to save California's dwindling number of wild rivers, and State Parks Director William Penn Mott, who was largely responsible for adding 145,000 acres of land and two underwater Pacific Ocean preserves to the state park system during Reagan's two terms as governor. Livermore had an ally in William Clark, then Reagan's chief of staff in Sacramento. The two of them played on Reagan's antagonism to the federal government to block a high dam proposed by the Army Corps of Engineers at Dos Rios that would have destroyed the middle fork of the Eel River and flooded scenic Round Valley, violating a treaty made long ago with a tiny Indian tribe. Indians in full regalia were brought to the governor's office, where they argued that the Dos Rios dam would be the latest in a long line of broken promises to the Indians by the federal government. It was a clinching argument with Reagan, who shocked California's powerful water establishment and the Corps of Engineers by rejecting the dam.[64]

In the six-year interval between his second term as governor and his first as president, Reagan had no pro-environment advisers and became increasingly dependent on his pro-development friends in business and industry. On the rare occasions that environmental issues were brought to his attention, it was apt to be, as Livermore subsequently observed, by such wealthy western entrepreneurs as Colorado brewer Joseph Coors, "who feel they've been strictured by environmental laws and regulations."[65] Reagan essentially relinquished environmental policy to Coors and his allies, who were represented in the Reagan inner circle by Senator Paul Laxalt of Nevada. Laxalt was not interested in making waves. He wanted a conservative secretary of the interior who would show prudent respect for development interests but also make the compromises necessary to get along with Congress. As noted in Chapter 5, his first choice for Interior—former U.S. senator Clifford Hansen of Wyoming—fit this bill perfectly. But after Hansen turned down the job, Laxalt turned to James Watt, a Denver-based lawyer with Washington experience whose skills were highly prized by Ed Meese.

Watt was a radical who favored virtually unlimited development of public lands. Before his appointment he had served as president of the Mountain States Legal Foundation, a counterforce to public interest law firms that had blocked nuclear plants and high dams and helped save parkland and wild rivers in the intermountain West. The purpose of Mountain States, as defined by Watt, was "to fight in the courts those bureaucrats and no-growth advocates who create a challenge to individual liberty and economic freedoms."[66] As secretary of the interior, Watt deployed the resources of the federal government in this cause. He was contemptuous of such previous Republican interior secretaries as Walter Hickel, a millionaire Alaskan developer whose appointment had been vehemently opposed by the environmental movement but who had turned out to be an effective conservationist before he was fired by President Nixon.

From Watt's point of view, Hickel and his successor, Rogers C. B. Morton, had surrendered to the conservationist impulses of the Interior bureaucracy and the national media. Watt vowed repeatedly that he would not be "Hickelized." He divided people into two categories— "liberals and Americans"—and dismissed the respected Audubon Society, which wanted him fired, as "a chanting mob." Watt even took on the National Wildlife Federation, the most mainstream and conservative of the environmental organizations. He proclaimed his determination to open up wilderness areas and regaled national park concessionaires by telling them about a "tedious" float trip through the Grand Canyon which ended on the fourth day, when "we were praying for helicopters, and they came." The best that can be said about Watt's hostility to the environment is that he never disguised it. "We will mine more, drill more, cut more timber," he said, and he meant it.

Even though Reagan would never have put the anti-environmental case so bluntly, Watt was doing what Reagan wanted done. "I appointed him with the understanding that he was going to do those things that he and I had talked about," Reagan said in defending Watt in 1990. "And he knew when he took the job that he would turn enough people off that pretty soon he would lose any effectiveness that he had if he did the things that we wanted done. . . . And I have to say, if you look back and analyze point by point the things that were done, he was darn good." [67]

Fortunately for the nation, Watt was less effective than Reagan (and many of Watt's critics) remember. His success in opening up public lands to development was limited, not for lack of trying, but because his confrontational approach aroused vigorous opposition. Watt's efforts to turn strip-mining controls back to the states were blocked by Congress, which also expanded the National Park system over his opposition. On these and several other environmental issues, Republicans in Congress deserted the administration en masse at a time when they were giving Reagan nearly unanimous blank-check support on economic issues. Watt, again fortunately for the environment, was his own worst enemy. He moved with such imperious disregard for federal law that several of his oil-leasing decisions were blocked in the courts. He also had a gift for galvanizing the opposition. During Watt's reign the Wilderness Society tripled its fund-raising and the Sierra Club increased its membership by 25 percent. "If there hadn't been a James Watt, we would have had to invent one," said one prominent Sierra Club official in 1981. [68] When the Urban Institute reviewed the record at Interior in 1984, more than a year after Watt's departure, it found that "in spite of all the *Sturm and Drang*" "no truly fundamental change can be claimed to have taken place." [69]

Nor did much fundamental change occur at the Environmental Protection Agency during this period, although this inaction had far more negative environmental consequences. Though the General Accounting Office found that more than 378,000 toxic waste sites required corrective action, EPA put only 850 of these dumps on its priority list and had managed to clean up only six of them, and not very thoroughly, by 1985. [70] The EPA scandals of 1981–82 led to the dismissal of Rita Lavelle, who headed the agency's hazardous waste program. She was convicted in 1983 on charges of perjury and obstruction of justice. On March 9, 1983, the EPA scandals forced the resignation of Burford, a move largely engineered by White House aides James Baker and Craig

Fuller even though Reagan disclaimed any knowledge of White House involvement in her ouster.

William Ruckelshaus, the highly respected first administrator of EPA in the Nixon administration, was brought in to replace Burford. He quickly restored shattered morale by pledging his commitment to EPA's mission and removed or transferred officials whose competence or integrity were in question. Much as Clark would later do at Interior, Ruckelshaus also performed the political mission of calming congressional fears about the direction of the agency and defusing the impact of the environmental issue. But Ruckelshaus made little headway in persuading Reagan to increase federal resources to clean up environmental pollution. Reagan was simply not that aroused by environmental issues, and his staff lost much of its interest once the EPA scandals had disappeared from the front pages and the nightly newscasts. Ruckelshaus became so out of sight and out of mind that Reagan literally did not know who he was. During a key 1984 meeting in which Ruckelshaus urged a major budget commitment to reduce acid rain, the president apparently confused him with Middle East special envoy Donald Rumsfeld. After Reagan had addressed Ruckelshaus as "Don" a second time, James Baker felt compelled to slip the president a note telling him that his EPA administrator was named Bill.

Ruckelshaus was more amused than annoyed by this lapse. But he was dismayed by the president's cavalier dismissal of the importance of acid rain, which has destroyed fish and plant life in thousands of American and Canadian lakes and streams and has endangered the Adirondacks, the greatest remaining U.S. wilderness east of the Mississippi. Acid rain is primarily the product of sulfur and nitrogen oxides emitted by towering smokestacks of smelters and fossil-fueled plants and automobile exhausts. During the 1970s it had become an environmental and a nationalist issue in Canada, which objected to the pollution originating in U.S. smokestacks in the Middle West and deposited in Canadian forests and lakes. President Carter and Canadian Prime Minister Trudeau had in 1980 signed a memorandum of intent to negotiate an international air quality agreement requiring vigorous enforcement of antipollution standards, and Reagan had promised Trudeau during his 1981 visit to Ottawa to honor the agreement.

After three years of much talk and little action by the United States, Ruckelshaus wanted the administration to make a major budget commitment to reducing the causes of acid rain. His proposal was assailed as wasteful government spending by David Stockman and rejected by

Reagan, who questioned the scientific evidence on the causes of acid rain and was reluctant to impose additional restrictions on industry. It proved to be one of Reagan's most significant penny-wise and pound-foolish decisions. By the time President Bush and Congress faced the issue in 1990, many more lakes and streams had perished and the costs to industry and government of facing neglected problems of air pollution had increased.

Ruckelshaus did not make a public fuss about his defeat. He had returned to EPA from industry with some reluctance, but he was a loyal Republican and team player who had no desire to embarrass his party in an election year. Nevertheless, he had also had enough of the Reagan administration. Disgusted by Stockman and disappointed by Reagan's unwillingness to listen to the evidence on acid rain, Ruckelshaus waited until after the election and quietly resigned on November 28, 1984, after serving little more than a year and a half of his second tour of duty at EPA.

Campaigns can be learning experiences for political candidates. Jules Witcover has made a persuasive case that John F. Kennedy was never the same after he campaigned in West Virginia's coal-mine country during the 1960 primary, learning firsthand of the plight of the miners and descending a mining shaft "in his suit that cost more than a miner earned in a week."[71] Witcover thinks it no accident that President Kennedy's first executive order provided an expanded distribution of food to needy families.

Reagan's early campaigns were also rich in learning experiences, if not in liberal lessons. Reagan was a performer, and he learned from his audiences. When he toured General Electric plants in the 1950s, he was struck by the resentment of his business-oriented audiences to regulations imposed by the federal government and he forever afterward saw it as his mission to protect industry from government interference. Late in 1965, when Reagan was appearing at question-and-answer forums in California in preparation for his run for governor, he noted that "this university thing comes up each time I talk."[72] As a result of this interest of his audiences, Reagan made what he called "the mess at Berkeley" a principal theme of his speeches at a time when student demonstrations on the University of California campuses were barely registering as an issue in the voter surveys commissioned by his campaign strategists. Reagan went through a similar learning process after losing the early primaries in his 1976 presidential campaign. Observing that audiences responded enthusiastically whenever he denounced the pending Panama Canal treaties, he made this issue the centerpiece of his comeback campaign that almost won him the nomination.

But Reagan learned nothing from his reelection campaign in 1984, when most of his audiences were as carefully prepackaged as his speeches and he himself more isolated from unscripted reality than he had ever been in Hollywood or Sacramento. Reagan's only contribution to the campaign seems to have been the one-liner "You ain't seen nothin' yet," often used as the tag line in his set-piece campaign speeches. This was a paraphrased borrowing from Al Jolson, who had said "You ain't heard nothin' yet" in the first talking motion picture, *The Jazz Singer,* which captivated the nation in 1927, when Reagan was sixteen years old. Except for this one-liner, Reagan originated nothing in the campaign that produced his lopsided victory. He proposed no new programs and discussed no new ideas. Others developed the themes, invented the slogans, wrote the speeches, created the ads and decided the political strategy.

Reagan took it easy, as he was always apt to do if no one pushed him. And he was almost never pushed in 1984, except when preparing for the presidential debates. After playing the world stage while the Democrats damaged each other in the primaries, Reagan had returned to Washington on June 10 and spent the following six weekends at Camp David. He took an eighteen-day vacation at his ranch in late July and the first two weeks of August. He engaged in only two genuine campaign swings that lasted as long as a week. All that the campaign staff expected from the candidate was a sufficient illusion of activity to generate television coverage and demonstrate that Reagan was not taking the election for granted. This was accomplished by a series of "day trips" that enabled Reagan to visit states within easy Air Force One range of Washington two or three times a week and spend his nights at the White House. The schedule kept Reagan rested and provided the networks and local television stations in major markets with a series of set-piece speeches delivered against carefully chosen backdrops and emphasizing a preselected "theme of the day." From a public relations standpoint this was a refinement on the presidential campaign of 1972, when Richard Nixon had mostly stayed in the White House and avoided troublesome questions about the mysterious burglary known as Watergate while his surrogates discredited George McGovern. Except for the debates, Reagan was as isolated within the gilded cocoon of the presidency as Nixon had been.

Unlike Nixon, Reagan liked people. He would have been perfectly happy to campaign more frequently, address contentious audiences or conduct regular news conferences if his managers had encouraged him in this direction, as they had in past campaigns when it was felt necessary to show that Reagan was vigorous or competent. Reagan really didn't care how he campaigned, as long as he was allowed his ranch time and weekends at Camp David. He was, in Stuart Spencer's view, a nearly perfect candidate who put himself in the hands of his staff and followed whatever schedule they devised for him, usually without complaint. In 1984, Reagan's campaign strategists were convinced by midsummer that he could not be defeated unless he did something to beat himself. They saw many risks and no compensating advantages in allowing the president to wander away from his script. This conviction was reinforced on August 11 when Reagan, then at his ranch, declared during a microphone check for his weekly Saturday radio speech, "My fellow Americans, I am pleased to tell you today that I've signed legislation that will outlaw Russia forever. We begin bombing in five minutes." This was typical of Reagan's clowning when warming up for a performance. But the Soviets made a fuss about it, and Wirthlin's polls showed a slight decrease in Reagan's margin over Mondale and an alarming increase in the percentage of Americans who thought Reagan might get the United States into war. Reagan's aides were reconfirmed in their belief that it was best to keep him as far away as possible from even the friendliest of reporters.

The White House used many tactics to spare Reagan from questions that might require unscripted answers. The crudest and most reliable of these, as David Hoffman of *The Washington Post* observed, was simply to rev up the engines of the Marine helicopter that was taking Reagan to Camp David or a campaign speech so that he could not hear the questions that were being put to him. The most questionable of these tactics was to use the Secret Service for nonsecurity purposes. White House reporters have passes issued to them by the Secret Service after security checks, and they also frequently pass through metal detectors. A pool of reporters accompanied Reagan on Air Force One. Yet Secret Service decisions on when to allow members of this pool or other reporters within the vicinity of the president were frequently determined not by security considerations but by the White House staff's political requirements. The Secret Service parted like the Red Sea on July 26 in Hoboken, New Jersey, to let the pool through at St. Ann's Catholic Church because the staff wanted close-up television footage of

Reagan with Italian-American voters. On August 19, when Reagan's margin over Mondale in Wirthlin's daily tracking polls had dropped to 8 points and the staff was especially sensitive about his bombing-the-Soviets crack, reporters were kept away from the president while he shook hands with strangers at the Missouri State Fairgrounds in Sedalia. When this produced inadequate "visuals," as Mike Deaver called them, photographers were allowed to approach Reagan on August 30 at Goddard Space Flight Center in Greenbelt, Maryland, while reporters were kept away. All of these decisions were based on what Sam Donaldson of ABC, whom Reagan liked, called "political security."[73] Donaldson blamed the White House staff, not the Secret Service agents. "They take their cue from Mike Deaver and Nancy Reagan and the others at the top," he said. "When the staff wants reporters close, they're close. And when the staff doesn't, they're not. They have taken the Rose Garden on the road."[74]

In misusing the Secret Service as a political screen, the White House staff operated on the premise that news organizations would be reluctant to make an issue of anything done in the name of security, particularly to protect a president who had survived a shooting by a would-be assassin. But the White House tactics during the reelection campaign produced some grumbling even among Secret Service agents, one of whom told me privately that the requirements of political security sometimes interfered with the service's mission of protecting the president from physical harm. I wrote a column that recounted the incidents noted in the previous paragraph and asserted that "Reagan's White House managers have co-opted the Secret Service for purposes that have nothing to do with the president's security, reduced reporters to the unwilling role of props and contemptuously treated the president as a communicator in constant need of a keeper."

The column appeared on Labor Day, September 3, when Reagan opened the fall campaign with a rally in Orange County, California. When White House Chief of Staff James Baker read it, he summoned me to his hotel suite. This was unusual. Baker was straightforward, and he normally took critical columns in stride. If he objected to something I had written, he would usually pick up the phone and call me, often registering his complaint in a jocular tone. He was not jocular on this occasion. While acknowledging that Reagan was being kept away from reporters, Baker insisted that the fault was the Secret Service's rather than the staff's. To make his point he had called in the head of the White House Secret Service detail, who nodded dutifully as Baker gave his pitch. I didn't buy it, and said so. "During a period when he is supposedly taking his case to the American people, Reagan is being deliberately isolated by a staff that wants to take no risks," my column had concluded. "How isolated would he be in a second term, when he and his staff would be beyond reach of the voters?"[75]

Although I didn't know it then, even Reagan was beginning to chafe under the restrictions imposed on him by his campaign team. It did not matter to Reagan whether or not he saw reporters, but he found his prepared script too restrictive. Mondale and his surrogates charged repeatedly that Reagan had a "secret plan" for raising taxes after the election or, alternatively, for reducing Social Security and Medicare benefits as a means of cutting the budget deficit. Reagan was offended by these charges and wanted to reply to them, but his strategists insisted he stick to the "Morning Again in America" script. Social Security had been a tar baby for Reagan since 1964, and his campaign strategists did not want the president to become stuck in a dialogue that might remind voters of his past attacks on the system. If the Social Security issue came up, Spencer had advised Reagan in 1980 and again in 1984, the way to deal with it was to promise never to tamper with Social Security and then move on to another topic. Reagan knew this was good political advice, but he was never comfortable with it and even more uncomfortable with the larger strategy of ignoring Mondale altogether. But the strategy was working, which was all that mattered to the campaign staff. Mondale's campaign had started badly and sputtered through September. He had failed to goad Reagan into engaging him. On the day of the Louisville debate, Wirthlin's trackings and the *Washington Post–ABC* poll gave Reagan identical leads of 55-37 percent, with the remaining 8 percent undecided.

Ostensibly, Reagan prepared for his first debate with Mondale much as he had prepared for his debate with Jimmy Carter four years earlier. He held five preparatory debates with the ubiquitous David Stockman, who had skillfully impersonated John Anderson and Carter in 1980, and now was razor-sharp in the role of "Fighting Fritz" Mondale. Better than anyone else in the administration, Stockman understood the shaky underpinnings of the economic recovery. Some of those in the entourage also suspected that he enjoyed the opportunity to show Reagan up. He was so effective in the final rehearsal three days before the Lousiville debate that Reagan lost his temper during an exchange on Social Security and yelled "Shut up!" Stockman continued to pound away. When the session ended, a shaken Reagan shook Stockman's hand and said, "You better send me some flowers because you've been nasty to me." Stockman flushed and said, "Baker made me do it." [76]

Stockman had certainly performed the role he had been instructed to play. Baker and Dick Darman, who served as head coach of the debate team and mastered the arguments for Reagan with his usual thoroughness, had encouraged Stockman's aggressiveness in an attempt to shake what they perceived as Reagan's complacency. At the time of the final rehearsal Reagan had not even cracked his briefing book, even though Darman had complied with Nancy Reagan's imperative not to "overwork" Reagan and had restricted it to twenty-five pages. Reagan always coasted when he could, and he had been encouraged to take it easy ever since he returned from the D-Day trip four months earlier. After months of resolutely isolating Reagan and allowing him no opportunity to respond to any questions about his policies, his staff was now trying to prepare him for a critical performance in a few days. It didn't work. Facing Stockman on the stage in Room 450, as an aide told me later, Reagan suddenly seemed old and frail.

And that is exactly how Reagan appeared to millions of Americans the following Sunday in Louisville. If one read the debate transcript, without seeing the candidates, it would be difficult to understand what the fuss was about. Both candidates overstated their positions and misstated important facts, as they often did in their campaign speeches. Neither had anything really new or particularly startling to say. But the televised confrontations known as presidential debates—hardly "debates" in a traditional sense, since the questions are put to the candidates by outside interlocutors rather than each other—have never been exercises in the in-depth exploration of issues. Beginning with the first debate, between Richard Nixon and John F. Kennedy in 1960, the debates have always been personality contests. "It is interesting that, without exception, all those candidates who are generally thought to have lost their debates—Richard Nixon, Gerald Ford in 1976 and Jimmy Carter in 1980—have believed themselves to have won 'on the facts' and lost on some intangibles of presence and performance," wrote Meg Greenfield in judging Mondale the winner of the Louisville debate. [77]

No one knew this better than Reagan, who had routed George Bush in Nashua with an old Spencer Tracy line and then bested Carter with a rehearsed one-liner of his own devising. Reagan had deliberately made these encounters a test of presence and personality, and he had come out on top. He was four years older in 1984, but a bigger difference is that he was also out of practice. Reagan had tuned up for Nashua by practicing against the Republican field in a debate in Manchester a few days earlier. By the time he debated Carter, Reagan had also survived debates with Republican rivals in Illinois, with Bush in Texas and with independent candidate John Anderson, no slouch in any kind of debate. By the time he faced Carter, debates held no terror for Reagan. Carter, while highly knowledgeable, had not debated anyone since he had faced Ford in 1976, and his rusty performance showed it. The situation was reversed for Reagan in 1984. Mondale had debated his rivals in the Democratic primaries while Reagan was resting or engaging in solo performances on the world stage. Reagan was not ready to debate Mondale in Louisville, and Stu Spencer, who dined with the Reagans in their suite beforehand, would say afterward that Reagan himself realized it.

Mondale was ready. Jack Germond and Jules Witcover have made the useful point that the Democratic nominee, after a year of telling voters that "what you see is what you get" and deploring television gimmickry, discarded this conviction in preparing for the Louisville debate and devised an approach designed to rattle Reagan and expose his deficiencies.[78] He was guided in this endeavor principally by Pat Caddell, who had worked for Gary Hart in the primaries and was distrusted by many in the Mondale inner circle. But Caddell realized that Reagan was not the candidate in 1984 that he had been in 1980, and he wrote Mondale a long memo explaining Reagan's vulnerabilities and how to take advantage of them. Germond and Witcover would call this memo "the essence of political hardball,"[79] which it certainly was, but it displayed more insight into Reagan's weaknesses than any other document of the campaign. "Reagan has been so cocooned that the public may not realize that Reagan is having more difficulty hearing, following arguments, etc., than he did several years ago," the memo said. "If the rumors around are true, there may be more deterioration than anyone suspects. If so, he will be super-scripted by the White House—which makes the surprise strategy even more relevant."[80]

The "surprise strategy" was for Mondale to physically dominate Reagan by pivoting toward him and walking toward him from the podium when he addressed the president. It called for Mondale to combine aggressiveness with occasional expressions of deference to Reagan and his office—sort of the way one might treat a valued uncle who was no longer up to the job. Mondale had too many scruples to do everything that Caddell had advised. He rejected, for instance, a proposal in the memo that he "probe the extent of Reagan's infirmities" by changing his voice level or turning away so that the president could not hear him. But Mondale, despite much pre-debate gush about debating the issues, accepted the essential Caddell strategy of seeking to throw Reagan off his stride. He also accepted Caddell's advice to guard this strategy with a "bodyguard of lies" that successfully deceived the media and the Reagan team into thinking that Mondale would simply be the old "Fighting Fritz" who pounded away at the issues, instead of at the president.

The strategy worked. Mondale carefully mingled praise of Reagan with his attack, giving the impression that he was being fair to the president even while he was saying that he was not up to the job. In his first answer Mondale proclaimed his respect for the presidency and for President Reagan. When he was asked to name the "most outrageous thing" Reagan had said during the debate, he declined and said, "I think the president has done some things to raise the sense of spirit, morale, good feeling in this country, and he's entitled to credit for that." In his closing statement he also thanked Reagan for agreeing to debate. "He didn't have to, and he did, and we all appreciate it," Mondale said. This show of deference helped Mondale score heavily in the fundamental confrontation of the debate, which occurred during a line of questioning on taxes initiated by Fred Barnes of the Baltimore *Sun*. After Mondale had charged that Reagan would find it necessary to raise taxes after the campaign, Reagan had responded with the "There you go again" line that he had used so effectively against Carter. Mondale had been expecting the line, and he pounced on it when it came his turn for rebuttal. Turning and facing Reagan, Mondale said, "Now, Mr. President, you said, 'There you go again,' right?"

"Yes," Reagan said.

"You remember the last time you said that?" asked Mondale.

"Mm-hmmm," said Reagan.

"You said it when President Carter said that you were going to cut Medicare, and you said, 'Oh, no, there you go again, Mr. President.' And what did you do right after the election? You went out and tried to cut $20 billion out of Medicare. And so when you say, 'There you go again,' people remember this, you know," Mondale said.

This was perhaps the least factual passage in the entire Mondale presentation. Reagan had barely touched Medicare in the 1981 budget cuts. He had four years later proposed Medicare restraints on hospitals and doctors that were, as an otherwise pro-Mondale editorial in *The Washington Post* noted, "not all that different from the Carter administration's." But Reagan had been thrown on the defensive, and he looked it. As Mondale delivered his response, he looked directly at the president until Reagan dropped his eyes—something I had never seen Reagan do in any other public encounter.

This confrontation ruined Reagan, who had been off his stride since the opening moments of the debate. He could not seem to get a grip on either his opponent or his own material, and he was additionally undone by his determination to rebut Mondale's charge that he had tried to reduce Social Security benefits. Here, Mondale was on factual grounds, although Reagan seemed to have entirely forgotten the ill-conceived ploy to slash Social Security benefits conceived by Stockman and Richard Schweiker in 1981 and quickly rejected by Congress. The Reagan briefing book had urged the president to respond to this charge by changing the subject and pointing out that the fiscally ailing Social Security system had been rescued by the changes proposed by the bipartisan presidential commission in 1983. Reagan, however, could not restrain himself. After delivering his scripted line early in the debate that he would "never stand for a reduction of Social Security benefits for the people who are now getting them," Reagan returned to the issue three times, twice when it had not even been raised by Mondale. This is Reagan, responding to a question by Diane Sawyer of CBS about "the most outrageous thing" Mondale had said during the debate:

> I'll tell you what I think has been the most outrageous thing in political dialogue, both in this campaign and the one in '82. And that is the continued discussion and claim that somehow I am the villain who is going to pull the Social Security checks out from those people who are dependent on them.
>
> And why I think it is outrageous—first of all, it isn't true. But why it is outrageous is because, for political advantage, every time they do that, they scare millions of senior citizens who are totally dependent on Social Security, have no place else to turn. And they have to live and go to bed at night, thinking, "Is this true? Is someone going to take our check away from us and leave us destitute?" And I don't think that should be a part of political dialogue.

Reagan, of course, had made the issue "part of the political dialogue" in previous campaigns and in his attempt to reduce Social Security benefits in 1981. He had also, with this answer, reinforced the fears of elderly viewers by graphically stating just what it was that scared them about Reagan on this issue. And Reagan compounded his problem with a wandering, statistics-laden closing statement that contained none of the eloquence Americans had come to expect from him. Mondale's closing statement was not particularly dazzling, but he projected an image of crispness and competence on a night when Americans had reason to wonder if their president possessed these qualities.

As soon as he left the stage, Reagan confessed to Spencer that he had flopped. "Reagan always knows when he's done well on stage and when he hasn't," Spencer said later, "and he told me right away that he was terrible."[81] Nor did Reagan improve at a Republican rally after the debate, which fortunately for him came too late for network television. He began by urging the election of the Republican candidate for the U.S. Senate, whom he called "Mitch O'Connell." His name is "McConnell," someone told Reagan, who corrected himself. "McConnell," he said. "McConnell. I must have been thinking of the archbishop. I said O'Connell. McConnell."

Reagan's strategists had remained in the debate hall, participating in the post-debate ritual known as the "spin patrol" in which seconds of the candidates circulate among deadline-pressed reporters and try to persuade them that their man has won a glorious victory. They did better at their work than Reagan had done at his and managed to soften the impact of the coming storm in the first stories of the debate. But they knew that a storm was/coming. James Baker acknowledged to reporters that Reagan had not performed up to expectations, and Richard Wirthlin bluntly told a campaign aide, "It's going to raise the age issue." And so it did, although it took a couple of days. None of the major newspapers really described Reagan's shaky performance on the Monday morning following the debate, although David Broder in *The Washington Post* did compare Mondale's performance to Kennedy's in the 1960 debate against Nixon and said that Mondale "managed to sound and look sharper than his older, better-known and more credentialed opponent."[82] Broder added, however, that Reagan had "remained in command of himself and the situation throughout the evening."[83] That was not the verdict of the focus groups that Wirthlin had put together to watch the debate. Nor was it the view of a focus group *The Washington Post* had assembled in Hanover Park, Illinois, where even Reagan supporters found themselves "troubled by some of the things he said and the sometimes faltering way in which he said them."[84]

But on Tuesday, October 9, *The Wall Street Journal* joined the issue directly with a lead story that was headlined "New Question in Race: Is Oldest U.S. President Now Showing His Age?" Its most telling paragraph (fourth in the story) was a quotation from Eugene Jennings of Michigan State University, who had backed Reagan in 1980. "I am very concerned, as a psychologist, about his inability to think on his feet, the disjointedness of his sentences and his use of the security blanket of redundancy," Jennings said. "I'd be concerned to put him in a corporate presidency. I'd be all the more concerned to put him into the U.S. presidency."[85] The same day in *The Post* I quoted Laxalt and Baker as acknowledging that Reagan's closing statement had been ineffective and Wirthlin as predicting that Reagan's 18-point margin over Mondale was likely to drop to 12 or 13 points by the end of the week.[86] (His margin had actually already dropped to this level in Wirthlin's daily trackings. By the end of the week it was back up to 16 points.) The television networks got into the act slowly but with devastating impact. The clip of Reagan nodding off at the Vatican in 1982 was reshown. So was a clip of Reagan groping for an answer on August 1, 1984, when he had been asked during a photo opportunity at his ranch what the United States could do to bring the Soviet Union to the bargaining table. Reagan went blank for several seconds until Nancy Reagan whispered to him, "Doing everything we can." Reagan smiled and said dutifully, "We're doing everything we can."

In the wake of the debate the White House staff lifted the usual screen of political security just enough to allow Reagan to display a self-confidence he did not feel. Reporters were allowed to question him as he boarded Air Force One for a day of campaigning the morning after the debate. When they asked him to assess the outcome, he said, "I'm smiling, I'm smiling," and gave the thumbs-up sign. But he wasn't smiling very hard. Two days later he complained at a photo session that incumbents were at a disadvantage in presidential debates. "I never realized how easy it was to be on the other side," he said. The more he thought about his performance, the more it troubled him. On October 12 reporters were allowed to put a few questions to Reagan with the helicopter engines turned off as he departed the White House for an Ohio campaign trip. The White House purpose was to enable Reagan to praise the performance of Vice President Bush in his debate with Mondale's running mate Geraldine Ferraro the night before. Reagan handled that assignment easily but floundered when a reporter asked him if he would change his tactics in the next debate against Mondale. "What's that?" he said. The reporter then asked if he would be briefed differently for the second debate. "I just personally will not find it necessary to keep reviewing the things that I already know, which is what I did the last time," Reagan said.

"Are you going to be yourself this time?" the reporter asked.

"What?" said Reagan.

"Are you going to be yourself?" the reporter repeated.

"Well, I thought I was myself the last time except that I kind of flattened out," Reagan said.[87]

Nancy Reagan had spared herself the ordeal of watching the debate rehearsal with Stockman. But she had seen the actual debate and did not need any focus groups, polls or newspaper stories to tell her that it was a disaster for Reagan. "What have you done to my husband?" she asked Deaver. It was more than the question of an anguished wife. Reagan was a star who had performed miserably; she held his directors responsible for his incoherence. She did not overlook his inadequacies, as many believed. She simply assumed that they were also widely known to those who had coached him and that they would have taken them into account in preparing for the debate. Nancy Reagan went on the warpath. She was aware that Reagan's poor performance had made his second debate with Mondale a critical event and she also realized that some public explanation was needed for what had happened in Louisville. She discussed it with Spencer and with Paul Laxalt, who had been uncomfortable with how the Stockman rehearsals were conducted. Laxalt was the only member of the administration's conservative faction on the campaign team, but he and James Baker had been allies since the campaign began and Laxalt valued their relationship. Laxalt's nominee for scapegoat was Dick Darman, the coach of the debate preparation team. The two men did not care for each other. Laxalt, who held pride of place as the resident Reagan loyalist, shared some of the prevalent conservative suspicions about Darman's loyalty. Darman, who had a sharp wit and an acid tongue, viewed Laxalt as intellectually lazy. Privately, he had said that conversations between Laxalt and the president were likely to be "content free." Nancy Reagan was willing to lay the blame on Darman, but she was also angry at Baker, who was, after all, the White House chief of staff. It seemed to her that Baker took credit for her husband's political achievements and so he should bear responsibility when Reagan did poorly. Staff was expendable to Nancy Reagan. Her husband was the star, and he needed her protection.

On October 10, at a Washington news conference conducted in his capacity as the general chairman of the Republican Party, Laxalt laid out the case against the coaches without mentioning any of them by name. Yes, Reagan had done poorly at Louisville. No, it was not really the president's fault. "Yes, he had an off night . . . but it wasn't because of any physical or mental deficiency," Laxalt said. "He was brutalized by a briefing process that didn't make any sense." The problem was that Reagan had engaged in six rehearsals and been loaded down with briefing books. "The man was smothered with numbers," Laxalt said. He acknowledged that Reagan had engaged in much the same preparation process for his 1980 debate against Carter but said it was "totally unfair" to use the same system when Reagan was burdened with the responsibilities of the presidency. Laxalt said he regretted not having interfered in the process, but said that everyone now recognized that it was important to allow "Reagan to be Reagan." Predicting that Reagan would be more aggressive in the second debate, Laxalt said, "We are coming out of the ivory tower and onto the streets."[88]

Baker and Darman, while acutely aware of their own political interests, were in fact loyalists. They had worked their usual sixteen-hour days to prepare Reagan, without much help from either Laxalt or Nancy Reagan and even less help from the loafing candidate who was supposed to be the "Great Communicator." During the first four years they often covered up for Reagan's failings, as a White House staff is supposed to do, and they also accepted the political necessity of holding someone other than the president responsible for the Louisville debacle. But Baker is less of a hard-bitten politician than he pretends to be, and the public scapegoating of the coaches reinforced his feeling that the Reagans, especially the first lady, were "takers" who lacked any real appreciation for what was done for them. Baker was too realistic to complain, and the immediate priority was to restore Reagan's equilibrium so that he would perform satisfactorily in the next debate. But a friend of Baker's told me that this incident was a kind of last straw that hardened his resolve to leave the White House after the election.

Darman, sensitive behind his façade of wit and sarcasm, was also hurt. He blamed Nancy Reagan more than Laxalt for the alibi that the debate coaches had been responsible for Reagan's performance and bitterly told one friend that she was "insane." Baker and Darman were all the more embittered because they shared with Deaver the secret that the timing of the Louisville debate had been determined not by rational political considerations but by Nancy Reagan's consultations with astrologer Joan Quigley, whose charts had convinced her that October 7 was an ideal day for the Reagan-Mondale confrontation.[89] Darman and

Baker also knew that it was nonsense to say that Reagan had been "smothered with numbers." No one had wanted Reagan to spout statistics at Louisville. The briefing book had reduced issues not to numbers but to the one-page "mini-memos" that Reagan had found helpful ever since his days in Sacramento. But Reagan rarely met a statistic he didn't like. He often used numbers as a substitute for thought, particularly when the one-liners would not come to him. His problem at Louisville had been in most respects the opposite of what Laxalt had described. "He wasn't overprepared," said Spencer. "He was just plain lazy in preparing, and he knew it." [90]

Apart from the business about the numbers, however, Nancy Reagan and Laxalt had a point. Reagan had always required practice and a sense of "being up" to perform well. When he conducted weekly news conferences in Sacramento, he had become reasonably adept at them by treating them as regular performances that required both factual preparation and a ready store of one-liners. These skills atrophied rapidly in Washington, less because of Reagan's age than because he did not practice. Similarly, as previously observed, he had been sharpened for his debate with Carter in 1980 because of his practice that year in debates with other candidates. The impressions of those who attended the rehearsals for the 1980 debate and the first 1984 debate is that Stockman played Carter more good-humoredly than he did Mondale. Reagan did not become angry during the 1980 rehearsals; he used them to invent one-liners, including "There you go again."

After Louisville, the campaign team focused on restoring the candidate's self-confidence, always a prerequisite of successful performance for Reagan. The rehearsals for the second debate were cut from five to two. Laxalt and Spencer spent private time with Reagan, telling him how good he was. Richard Nixon wrote him an encouraging letter, saying that Mondale was seen as the winner only because he had done better than expected and pointing out that Reagan would be the underdog in the second debate. Nixon subsequently talked to Reagan by telephone, again encouraging him and telling him he would do better in Kansas City. Since the subject of the second debate was foreign policy, and Nixon was the presumed expert, he also sent a long follow-up memo through Ken Khachigian that Reagan read and found useful. Finally, media consultant Roger Ailes, known as "Dr. Feelgood" to the staff, was brought in to settle Reagan down. Ailes was to reassurance what Nixon was to foreign policy. He had coached candidates in more than forty state elections and had instructed businessmen on how to improve their public speaking. He knew that Reagan needed praise, not criticism, and interrupted the first rehearsal for the Kansas City debate to declare that the president had just given a "terrific answer" to some minor question. He also worked privately with Reagan, telling him that the age issue would probably be raised at the debate because "for the last ten days you've been pounded that you're too old for the job." Reagan thought about this a moment, smiled and said, "I can handle that."[91]

It may seem surprising that anyone with Reagan's onstage experience would need the services of a confidence-building debate coach this late in his career. Reagan's powers, such as they were, had not declined by 1984. While debates were always something of an ordeal for him, his knack for simplifying (and oversimplifying) issues often rescued him, and his sense of humor and stage presence served him well in any encounter. While his knowledge base was shaky, he knew far more about issues and about the world in 1984 than he had known four years earlier. Darman's critics would offer the second-guess complaint that he had overtrained Reagan out of lack of respect for his intelligence, but no one else in the entourage had ever confused Reagan with a rocket scientist. The problem in the first-debate preparation, beyond Reagan's laziness, was that his handlers, including Darman, simply assumed that he would deliver a smashing performance if he mastered the facts. But great performances are not that automatic, even for great performers. Garry Wills has compared the plight of Reagan in the first debate to that of Laurence Olivier, who suffered an unexplained but paralyzing bout of stage fright late in his career. The condition lasted five years and became so serious during performances of *Othello* that Olivier insisted that Frank Finlay, who was playing Iago, remain in the wings where Olivier could always see him. Wills wrote:

> What happened to Reagan in his first debate with Mondale was a bit like the stage fright that hit Laurence Olivier after decades of dramatic success—and Olivier, too, turned to his fellows for some hand holding. He needed his Iago always in sight, even when he was apparently alone on the stage. Reagan needed Nancy in sight—and his team was careful that he knew where to look for her in Kansas City. Paradoxically, because his presidency is based more than any predecessor's on public eloquence, the raised stakes make him most susceptible to hurt on this point, most in need (a wife will commendably believe) of urgent support. The one thing a performer must always deliver is the performance.[92]

In recognizing the actor's truth that it is the performance that is crucial, Nancy Reagan had saved the day, however bruising and unfair her intervention may have been to Baker and Darman. And once Ailes embarked on the task of rebuilding Reagan's confidence, the effort proved contagious within the entourage. Almost everything that was done in the interval between the debates was aimed at making Reagan feel good about himself and ready for his return engagement with Mondale. Khachigian, Reagan's favorite campaign speech writer, composed an attack speech that the president delivered repeatedly during a one-day whistle-stop tour of Ohio from the caboose of the railroad car once used by Harry Truman. Although neither Baker nor Darman cared for attack speeches, this tour helped Reagan get his resentment of Mondale out of his system. In one passage Reagan said that he had become angry with Mondale for distorting his record and thought of saying to him, "You are taxing my patience." But then, said Reagan, "I caught myself. Why should I give him another idea? That's the only tax he hasn't thought of." The crowds loved it and chanted, "Four more years, four more years."

The candidate's relaxed, combative mood was sustained in Kansas City, where Reagan (at the suggestion of Ed Rollins) addressed a pep rally before the debate so he wouldn't sit around worrying beforehand. Before he entered the Music Hall of the Kansas City Convention Center to meet Mondale, Ailes gave Reagan a final pep talk and Jim Baker handed him a note that said, "Chuckle again, and have fun out there." Nancy Reagan smiled at her husband from her front-row seat. And Reagan began the rematch in good spirits, as was apparent to Mondale, who later was quoted by Germond and Witcover as recognizing at first glance a "night and day" difference in Reagan's stage presence between Louisville and Kansas City.[93] Mondale's appearance was also different, although he did not know it. His aides had tried to improve the way he looked on television by placing reflective white paper on the podium, a trick they had used to good effect in Louisville. But in Kansas City, the reflected lighting made Mondale's face appear pasty and accentuated the bags under his eyes.

Taken as a whole, the debate added little to the understanding of Americans about the conduct of U.S. foreign policy. The differences between Reagan and Mondale on U.S. policy in Central America and the Strategic Defense Initiative were well known, although Mondale made a feint at Reagan on SDI from the right by saying he would not share missile defense technology with the Soviets as Reagan had proposed. Mondale was more aggressive and less deferential than he had been in Louisville, more the "Fighting Fritz" that the Reagan team had anticipated in the first debate. He tried to portray Reagan as uninformed about U.S. weapons systems and badgered him about a CIA-sponsored manual that instructed the Nicaraguan contras in terrorist tactics, including assassinations. Reagan promised that any U.S. official found responsible for the manual would be removed, but in the process inaccurately declared that the CIA station chief in Nicaragua (the "man in charge") had edited the controversial pamphlet. There were not supposed to be CIA agents within Nicaragua's borders, and Reagan corrected himself before the debate was over. But it is doubtful if many viewers really knew or cared that much about the disputed manual. A few moments later Reagan worked himself into a small rage in replying to Mondale's accusation that he had once said that submarine missiles could be recalled in flight. (Reagan had actually been trying to say that submarines could be called back before they launched their missiles but had said it so badly that he had created confusion about what he meant.)[94] Reagan chided Mondale for repeating this story, which he said had also been distorted by the press. "But I hope from here on you will no longer be saying that particular thing, which is absolutely false," Reagan said. "How anyone could think that any sane person would believe you could call back a nuclear missile, I think is as ridiculous as the whole concept has been." The audience laughed, and I remember thinking that Reagan was indeed himself again.

Even so, Reagan was barely holding his own against a challenger who had come into the debate knowing he had to score heavily to have any chance of winning the presidency. Then, thirty minutes into the debate, came the only question that really mattered politically that night, on the issue that Ailes had warned about and for which Reagan was waiting. Henry Trewhitt of the Baltimore *Sun* observed that Reagan was the oldest president in U.S. history and noted that some members of his staff had said he was tired after the Louisville debate. "I recall . . . that President Kennedy had to go for days on end with very little sleep during the Cuban missile crisis," Trewhitt said. "Is there any doubt in your mind that you would be able to function in such circumstances?"

Reagan answered him calmly. "Not at all, Mr. Trewhitt, and I want you to know that also I will not make age an issue of this campaign," Reagan said, deadpan. "I am not going to exploit, for political purposes, my opponent's youth and inexperience."

Everyone laughed, including Mondale. But, as David Broder wrote the next day in *The Washington Post,* "It well may have been that the biggest barrier to Reagan's reelection was swept away in that moment."[95]

In all likelihood Reagan would have won the election even if this barrier had not been swept away. He led Mondale by 13 points in Wirthlin's daily trackings on the day before the Kansas City debate and by 11 points on the day of the debate itself. Few of the voters who had been dismayed by Reagan's performance in Louisville had actually switched to Mondale. What Mondale did in the debate was therefore in a sense irrelevant. The only question was whether Reagan still had the wit, presence and capacity to conduct the duties of the presidency. For Reagan, the burden of proof was exceptionally light and he more than met it with his inspired one-liner. Reagan's crack about not making Mondale's age an issue vanquished public doubts about the president's capacity, even though he was rambling somewhat incoherently along the Pacific Coast Highway by debate's end.* But the election was over. By Monday evening, Reagan had moved back into a 17-point lead in Wirthlin's trackings, and he held a lead of 15 points or better throughout the remainder of the campaign.

Despite the size of his landslide, however, the wounds inflicted by Reagan's letdown at Louisville would never fully heal. The inner circle realized that the floundering president whom the public had glimpsed at Louisville was as much the real Reagan as the confident performer at Kansas City. And the inner circle was feeling the strain of carrying a president who depended primarily upon the quality of his performances to demonstrate his leadership. The strain was greatest inside the White House. After the election, Stu Spencer returned to California, as he always did, and Paul Laxalt went back to Capitol Hill to serve a final two years in the Senate. Dick Wirthlin returned to his polling firm, which he had moved from Orange County to the Washington suburbs of northern Virginia during the Reagan years. James Baker, Mike Deaver and Dick Darman were unwilling and perhaps unable to face

---

* Reagan's rambling prevented him from completing his closing statement in the allotted four minutes, with the result that he was politely but firmly cut off by moderator Edwin Newman. Reagan was recounting a story he had related to the Republican National Convention in 1976 about a letter he had written for enclosure in a time capsule scheduled to be opened in Los Angeles in 2076. The letter had caused Reagan to muse about "nuclear weapons of terrible destructive power, aimed at each other, capable of crossing the ocean in a matter of minutes and destroying civilization as we knew it." Reagan said the people who opened the time capsule "will know whether we used the weapons or not." He had intended to finish with a line about how the present generation owes responsibility to the next but never reached this sentence because he interrupted himself to praise Vice President Bush and talk about the "wonderful experience" they had shared in campaigning.

another four years in the White House working for a president who took their existence for granted. Ed Meese, a valuable counsellor despite his blind spots, had already left the White House to become a constant storm center at the Justice Department. Baker went off to Treasury, taking Darman with him. Deaver, afflicted with an alcohol problem he had kept hidden from the Reagans and his colleagues, would also soon leave the White House, depriving Nancy Reagan of her most effective instrument for indirectly influencing her husband.

Although Nancy Reagan did not realize it sufficiently and Ronald Reagan realized it not at all, the landslide of 1984 had left the people who had done the most to help the president during his first four years burned out and disillusioned. Most of them couldn't wait to leave the White House, where it was no longer Morning Again in America.

18

TURNING POINT

But I was to learn that I created some problems when I appointed [Don Regan] to succeed Jim Baker as White House chief of staff.

RONALD REAGAN, diary entry,
January 17, 1986[1]

Donald T. Regan was not among the disillusioned members of the Reagan team. By 1985, the onetime Marine officer and multimillionaire former stockbroker had spent four years as secretary of the treasury doing battle with his enemies within the cabinet and relentlessly cultivating Ronald Reagan's favor. While Regan's involvement in the reelection campaign had been largely limited to surrogate fund-raising speeches, he had not been idle during 1984.

In his State of the Union address to a joint session of Congress on January 25, 1984, the president had announced that he was "asking Secretary Regan for a plan of action to simplify the entire tax code so that all taxpayers, big and small, are treated more fairly." This was a tall order, but it was vastly diminished by the qualifier that Regan would not deliver "specific recommendations" for such a plan until December. The qualifier had been the brainchild of White House Chief of Staff James Baker, who wanted to take tax reform and the questions it would raise about the budget deficits out of the 1984 election campaign. The congressmen who had crowded into the House chambers to hear the president's speech understood the maneuver. Democrats erupted in a gale of cynical laughter in an unusual sign of disrespect for the president. Reagan did not become angry at the response because he did not understand what the laughter was about. He plowed on to the next passage of his speech—a call to build a permanent manned space station—as the laughter persisted. Finally, he noticed it. "I said something funny?" he said with a puzzled look. Since he was totally serious about tax reform, Reagan had not realized that the wording of the announcement would make his commitment seem a political ploy to dodge the issue. But skepticism about the prospects of tax reform was pervasive in 1984, and not only in Washington. Speaking to a business group in Florida the day after the election, Senator Bob Dole waved a blank sheet of paper at his audience and quipped, "I've just obtained a copy of President Reagan's secret tax plan." The businessmen laughed, as Congress had done in January.

Regan, however, did not regard tax reform as a laughing matter. After the State of the Union speech he assembled a team of experts at Treasury, who spent the next 310 days preparing a tax plan intended to accomplish the goals declared by the president in his address. This proposal would become the launch vehicle for the legislation that two years later emerged from Congress as the Tax Reform Act of 1986, arguably the most important domestic accomplishment of Reagan's second term.

The contents of "Treasury I," as Regan's proposal was called, remained closely guarded throughout 1984. Displaying his usual lack of curiosity, Reagan did not inquire about the progress of Regan's work. Others at the White House were also kept largely in the dark, since Regan feared that some member of the staff might leak the plan to the media. But security held, and Regan congratulated himself on his precautions at a November 15 cabinet meeting by reminding the president that the now-completed plan had been kept a secret. He also used the occasion to denounce press leaks by other administration officials, particularly those who worked at the White House. Baker and Richard Darman were used to such thinly veiled criticism, but they were disgusted by Regan's performance. In their view the treasury secretary was an apple-polisher who never missed a chance to play up to Reagan or take digs at other cabinet members. But the president was pleased that the contents of the report, on which he himself would not be briefed for another eleven days, had been closely held. After Regan finished his denunciation of leaks, he started in on another favorite whipping boy, the Federal Reserve. His complaint was the familiar one that the Fed had overly restricted the money supply and supposedly endangered economic recovery.

On November 16, the following morning, Regan opened his copy of *The Washington Post* and found a page-one story written by my colleague David Hoffman that began, "Treasury Secretary Donald T. Regan warned President Reagan and his cabinet yesterday that the economy has been slowing down and suggested that the Federal Reserve may be partly to blame because it has been too restrictive with money and credit, administration sources said." Regan angrily telephoned Baker and accused him of leaking the story. Baker heatedly denied it. Regan told Baker to "fuck yourself and the horse you rode in on," one of his favorite phrases, and hung up.[2] He then impulsively dictated a letter of resignation and sent it to the Oval Office. Reagan correctly interpreted the letter as a reflection of Regan's temper rather than his intent and talked it over with Baker. Both of them assumed that Regan would change his mind once he calmed down, but Baker agreed to go across to Treasury and pacify him just in case. Before he did, Reagan called Regan and told him he was tearing up the letter of resignation. According to Regan, the president told him he was "the only friend I have around here."[3] Regan, always susceptible to presidential flattery, immediately withdrew his resignation.

No one in the White House believed that Regan had the slightest intention of quitting. At the beginning of the second term Regan was one of the few domestic policy officials in the administration who had a product to sell: he believed in the imaginative tax plan the Treasury experts had produced and he wanted to push it into law. Regan also saw the White House as a better power base than Treasury from which to accomplish this goal. Since he was observant as well as temperamental, he recognized that Baker wanted a change of scene. "I was watching from across the street a process in which one Jim Baker gradually became more and more tired, more and more fed up," Regan told me later. "I recognized the symptoms. I had seen it in other executives at Merrill Lynch." When Baker dropped in at Treasury later that morning for a conciliatory chat, he found Regan equally conciliatory. They exchanged apologies and the chat became a lunch in Regan's private dining room and a reflective discussion of the burdens of running the White House.

"You know your problem, Baker?" Regan said. "You're too damn tired. You're fed up. You want out and you don't know how to get out. You're a caged rat and you're biting at everybody."

"You're right, I am tired," Baker said.

"You know what we ought to do?" Regan said. "Swap jobs." *

Baker would sometimes put a pen in his mouth when he talked. As Regan remembers what happened next, Baker responded, "You're kidding," and almost swallowed the pen. But Baker, although he certainly *was* tired, was not quite as wide-eyed at the suggestion as Regan believed. After four years as Reagan's chief of staff, Baker had become a bit of an actor himself. He was weary of playing the role of superservant to a president who focused on personal performances, and he longed for a prominent cabinet post, preferably State, Defense or Justice. State, at the top of the list, was secure under George Shultz. Reagan had also made it clear that he did not intend to replace Caspar Weinberger at Defense, as the Republican leadership in the Senate hoped and as Nancy Reagan had suggested.

That left Justice, which was at best a remote possibility. Attorney General William French Smith had spent the first term living in a Washington hotel. He had resigned early in 1984, anxious to return to his prestigious Los Angeles law firm. Reagan had immediately announced that he intended to replace Smith with White House counsellor Ed Meese. But soon afterward, reports surfaced that Meese had received financial assistance from several people whom he had helped obtain federal jobs. The clamor forced Smith to appoint an independent counsel (the successor to the "special prosecutor" of Watergate days) to investigate the allegations. Meese spent the reelection year in limbo, remaining on the payroll as White House counsellor while taking no role in the campaign. The investigation was concluded in September 1984, with independent counsel Jacob Stein determining that there was no basis upon which to indict Meese, a conclusion that failed to dispel the doubts of critics who believed that a higher standard than absence of criminal behavior should be required to head the Justice Department. As Baker pondered his career course after the election, Meese still faced opposition from Democrats in the Senate, which would not vote to confirm him until February 23, 1985. Ever the realist, Baker had

---

* This account is from an interview with Regan on July 11, 1986. A more refined and less colorful version of this conversation was used by Regan in his book, written more than a year later, and in a 1989 interview with me. Baker has confirmed the substance of Regan's account, though not the specific language.

concluded by the time of Regan's proposal to him that Meese would weather the confirmation storm. Baker also confided that he doubted Reagan would name him attorney general even if Meese didn't make it.

The Treasury Department had not been on Baker's wish list, partly because it seemed a cut below the cabinet posts he coveted and because he had no inkling that Don Regan was also looking for a new assignment. But Regan's blowup and letter of resignation on the morning of November 16 had given Baker a new perspective by the time he sat down for lunch with the treasury secretary. Baker knew that Treasury would be in the thick of the fight on any tax reform bill, which would draw on his political skills. But what interested him most about Regan's proposal was that it gave him a chance to get a foot in the door on foreign policy. Baker's credentials were then entirely domestic—service in the Commerce Department in the Nixon and Ford administrations, a leading role in Ford and Reagan presidential campaigns and four years as White House chief of staff. Baker knew that foreign policy experience was needed to round out this résumé, which was a principal reason that the national security adviser's post had interested him in 1983. Treasury at least dealt with international economic policy, which was a start. Baker had made these initial calculations by the time of his lunch with Regan, and he was not as astonished by the proposal as his host believed. He was, however, intrigued by it. Baker told Regan he wanted to talk it over with his wife, Susan.

Even though I knew nothing of this luncheon, I had realized since the recriminations after the Louisville debate that Baker was looking for the first train out of the White House. When I asked him about his plans the day after the election, he blandly assured me that the president "doesn't want to break up a winning team."[4] This was hardly the scoop of the century, since Reagan was also usually reluctant to break up even a losing team unless goaded into it by his wife and staff. What Baker's comment meant to me was that he had not yet figured out how he could make his break from the White House without causing a fuss. He needed to leave the White House, for reasons that went beyond advancing his career. Part of the problem was certainly that he was "tired," as Regan had observed, but Baker was a workaholic who would continue to work as unrelentingly at Treasury as he ever had at the White House.

The root of the problem was Baker's feeling that he was insufficiently valued by the president. Baker's cool political façade concealed an inner core of ego and emotion that had been repeatedly bruised, first by failure of the coup that would have made him national security adviser and then by the open criticism of Nancy Reagan and Paul Laxalt after Louisville. It was a measure of Baker's disillusionment that he had seriously flirted with the idea of becoming baseball commissioner, when that opportunity seemed open to him, even though he was not much of a baseball fan. "He was sensitive to the fact that, God damn, he put in four years there, he had done a helluva lot and so on, and he felt, as the Reagans do make you feel, that you're never really appreciated," said Dick Darman. "And that bothered him. He's human."[5]

Baker's wife and closest allies quickly embraced Regan's proposal. Susan Baker hoped that the job change would make it possible for her husband to spend more time at home, and she also shared his feeling that he was unappreciated by the Reagans. Darman was instinctively supportive, although he went through a typical analytical routine of making a list of the pluses and minuses of Regan's proposal before proclaiming it a good idea. The others whose advice mattered to Baker —principally his executive assistant Margaret Tutwiler and Mike Deaver—also endorsed the plan. Deaver wanted to leave the White House to become a lobbyist, and he anticipated that the Reagans would try to deter him because of the services he performed for the first lady. Since Reagan and Regan shared a generational camaraderie, Deaver reasoned that the president would be more amenable to his departure if Regan rather than someone else replaced Baker as chief of staff.

Deaver, who had more influence with Nancy Reagan than all the other aides combined, became the middleman who sold the idea to her. She was not crazy about it. Despite her outburst after the Louisville debate, she recognized that Baker and his team had performed effectively. She also perceived that Regan could be blunt and abrasive, although he had never personally offended her. But Deaver made it clear to her that Baker was going to leave, one way or the other, and that the president would need a new chief of staff. Nancy Reagan knew that her husband genuinely liked Regan. She rationalized, as Baker and Darman also did, that Deaver might be persuaded to stay at the White House and he could deal with Regan. Grudgingly, Nancy Reagan accepted the proposal.

By late December, Baker and Regan had agreed on the mechanics of the job switch, which they kept a closely guarded secret. They did not want the story to slip into print until they completed the detail of informing the president, who was as oblivious as ever to the plottings of his staff. "When I heard about it, it sounded all right to me," Reagan told me subsequently.[6] But he did not hear about it for several weeks after Regan and Baker had first discussed the idea. Not until the morning of January 7, 1985, did Baker, Regan and Deaver greet the president in the Oval Office and unveil their plan. "Mr. President, I finally brought you someone your own age to play with," quipped Deaver.[7] Although Regan does not remember this wisecrack, which would have been typical of Deaver, all of the participants in the meeting agree that the discussion that morning was relaxed and brief. Reagan had been alerted in advance by Nancy, with whom he discussed most personnel changes in the White House.

Regan, who did not realize that the first lady was the president's most influential political adviser, noticed only that the president was not surprised. "He seemed equable, relaxed—almost uncurious," Regan later wrote. "This seemed odd under the circumstances."[8] It did not seem odd to either Baker or Deaver, who understood Nancy's role and were accustomed to Reagan's almost total lack of curiosity about White House affairs. Since Nancy Reagan was on board, however reluctantly, they regarded the unusual job swap as, in Baker's familiar phrase, "a done deal." Regan, however, was astonished when the president made no inquiries at all about the proposal. "I did not know what to make of his passivity," Regan stated.[9] He launched into an extensive explanation of the conversations he had held with Baker, and when he had finished, Reagan still had no questions. After less than half an hour of discussion, most of it consumed by Regan's presentation, and without asking either Baker or Regan about their qualifications for the new positions to which they had appointed themselves, the president laconically ratified the plan. For Reagan, it was merely another shift of cast and directors.

And so, with remarkable casualness and virtually no consideration of the consequences, Reagan began his second term by agreeing to break up the team that had been largely responsible for his first-term successes. Although he did not know it, the replacement of Baker by Regan would lead to deactivation of the protective system that had repeatedly put the White House staff on damage-control alert whenever the president had blundered in the first term. Under Regan, the blunders would become more frequent and damage control would be lacking.

I am not certain that Reagan fully realized that James Addison Baker III had performed remarkably as White House chief of staff, although Baker's political skills were acknowledged even by his adversaries. A fellow Texan, big-time Democratic operator Bob Strauss, claimed that Baker was the best chief of staff in White House history, and while

Strauss was Baker's friend, there were many in Washington who agreed with this assessment. Baker was a disciplined and tough-minded politician who was highly respected and well liked by Congress and the media. Because he knew that a politician's word is his bond, Baker was slow to give his word but invariably kept it. While competitive to a fault, he was also cautious and realistic. Though Baker was conservative in his social and economic views, he had no illusions that either his position or his performance as chief of staff had overcome the suspicions about him among the hard-core right. Baker knew that political loyalty is based on first allegiances, and his allegiances had been given to Gerald Ford and George Bush, not Reagan. "I'm in here on a pass," he once told me, and he never forgot it.

In part because he was always worried about the thunder on the right, Baker had forged alliances of convenience with key Reagan conservatives, particularly Laxalt. He had a gift for recognizing his limitations and compensating for them by drawing on the strengths of others. Within the White House, he delegated freely, which gave him a huge advantage in his struggles with the conservative faction headed by Ed Meese and also enabled him to spread the blame when something went wrong. Baker valued results too much to be a one-man band.

Unfortunately for Reagan, the other most accomplished members of the Baker band were leaving the White House at the same time he did. Baker took his brain-truster Darman with him to Treasury. He also took the dedicated Tutwiler, who served as Baker's eyes and ears among the White House press corps, where she was valued for integrity and frank appraisals that spared not even Baker. Deaver, the glue that had bonded the Baker band to Nancy Reagan, would depart in May, leaving a void that Regan would never be able to fill. David Stockman, a wholly owned subsidiary of Baker's since the chief of staff had saved his job, would leave by July, taking with him an irreplaceable understanding of the federal budget process. And Ed Rollins, whose political skills had been honed in the 1984 campaign, would quit in September after his authority and access to the president had been diminished by Regan. While none of these people, including Baker, may have been indispensable, the loss of all of them within a few months proved a heavy blow to the Reagan presidency.

Baker and Darman knew when they left that their departure could prove costly, for they did not underrate their own accomplishments. But they had had enough of the Reagan White House, and they acted in their own best interests rather than the president's. The first failure of Reagan's second term was that he made no effort whatsoever to keep intact the team that had performed so well for him. He did not recognize that his presidency had reached a turning point. In viewing the members of his team as interchangeable, Reagan was reaping the lack of loyalty that his indifference to his supporting cast had produced.

The Reagan presidency had also lost something that even the Baker band did not fully appreciate, which was the benefit to a passive president of a White House staff driven by inner competition. The first-term feuding and jockeying for power between the pragmatist and conservative factions had been an irritant to Reagan. The president viewed any story that did not originate with an official announcement as a "leak," and he was particularly disturbed by the constant flow of stories describing the conflicts within the White House. But these conflicts and the reports of them had been a blessing in disguise to Reagan, forcing him to confront issues that he might otherwise have ignored. By challenging one another and exposing Reagan to conflicting options, Baker, Deaver, Meese and Clark had also challenged their uncurious president. Don Regan did not see this. He knew that Reagan preferred a harmonious environment, and he was determined to end the leaks and the conflicts they reflected. He had not become chief of staff in order to challenge the president. He saw himself as a corporate chief executive officer who would make the tough decisions and permit Reagan to enjoy the harmony he craved. Too many battles in the White House during Regan's tenure would be conducted out of sight of the president. Reagan would not be challenged in his second term until it was too late.

Donald Thomas Regan was an unlikely harmonizer. In origins and style he resembled the manner-born Baker far less than he did the combative California entrepreneurs who had found their voice in Reagan and bankrolled his early campaigns. Like many members of the California kitchen cabinet, Regan was a "self-made man" who had amassed wealth by outworking and outmaneuvering his competitors. Like them, he was also faintly distrustful of those whose inheritance had given them a head start. Regan's roots were in Irish Catholic South Boston. His father, William Francis Regan, was a policeman who was fired by Governor Calvin Coolidge during a Boston police strike when Donald Regan was nine months old. Afterward, Bill Regan made a modest living as a railroad security guard. When Don Regan was ten his only brother, Billy, who was twelve, died of peritonitis, while convalescing from an appendectomy. Billy had been a brilliant student destined for great achievements in the opinion of his parents, who had held him up as an example to his more unruly younger brother. "You're going to have to take Billy's place," his father said to him after the funeral. "From now on you're going to have to be two sons to us." As Regan remembers it, his parents never recovered from the loss.[10] Regan, who can talk about his brother's death as if it happened yesterday, may not have recovered, either.

Don Regan became the surrogate of Billy Regan's imagined destiny, an embodiment of his family's ambitions and a serious student who needed to work hard for his grades. Work hard he did. In 1936 he won a partial scholarship to Harvard, then a rare feat for a South Boston "townie," which he supplemented by caddying, ushering and other jobs. His memory of life at Harvard, in the same class as John F. Kennedy, is almost entirely a memory of work. He graduated fourth in the Class of 1940 and earned a scholarship to Harvard Law School. Instead of becoming a lawyer, Regan volunteered for officer's training and received a commission in the Marines. After service in Iceland he spent thirty-three months in the South Pacific, taking part as an artillery officer in the battles of Guadalcanal, New Georgia, North Solomon, Guam and Okinawa. Because he had married while in the service and was a father of one child with another on the way, Harvard Law School seemed an impractical option when Regan left the Marines in 1946. He felt he needed to make money, and went to work as a trainee for the New York brokerage firm of Merrill Lynch, Pierce, Fenner and Beane.

Regan, feisty and driven, was a natural on Wall Street, where the intricacies of the market were explained to him by a New York University economics professor named Birl Shultz—the father of fellow ex-Marine George Shultz. Years later Regan wrote that he "felt the exhilaration of having made the right choice in life," a feeling he had also had when he married and when he joined the Marines.[11] Regan had found mathematical subjects and all abstractions difficult in college, but he had a gift for practical finance and a decisiveness that served him well on Wall Street. He became a multimillionaire the old-fashioned way: by working hard and adopting innovations that kept him a step ahead of his competitors.

When Regan became head of Merrill Lynch after thirty-four years, he eliminated fixed commissions for brokers and invented the cash management account, a revolutionizing practice that allowed clients to write checks against their brokerage accounts. Merrill Lynch became one of the first Wall Street firms to go public and one of the most aggressive pursuers of small investors. But Regan was more successful than popular. His business adversaries respected his ability but resented his boastfulness. His subordinates were afraid of him. Regan ran Merrill Lynch with an iron hand. Those who failed to meet his exacting standards of performance or disagreed with him were quickly replaced. A former colleague of Regan's told journalist Myra MacPherson at the time he became White House chief of staff that Regan had a "quick, incisive mind," but added, "His weakness is that his ego was so strong he did not pick good subordinates. Or if they were, he broke them. He couldn't stand the competition." Regan had another explanation for why he had been disliked on Wall Street. "Do you know why I'm hated?" he said to MacPherson. "I broke up their cozy little club. Wall Street was a cartel. They proclaimed capitalism—but practiced cartelism. We shouldn't be closet cartelists if we're capitalists." [12]

Reagan thoroughly liked Regan, as he did most salesmen who had made good. They shared a penchant for Irish jokes and locker room humor and a basic conviction that what Regan called "the free American economy" was one of the wonders of the world. They also shared a distrust of financial establishments. Ronald Reagan was simultaneously a populist and a conservative. While he admired overachievers of humble origins who had amassed vast fortunes, he retained a residual midwestern Main Street distrust of Wall Street and the "economic royalists" whom President Roosevelt had denounced in the days of the Depression. Regan, who privately boasted that he had "fuck-you money" [13] that made him independent of Washington political pressures, appealed to both the populist and conservative sides of the president. Reagan was delighted by Regan's stories about how he had succeeded on Wall Street and bested the traditional establishment by practicing capitalism. Like Reagan, Regan expressed his philosophy in direct and easily understood anecdotes drawn from his life experiences. The two men shared common traits of optimism and self-confidence and a common disability of poor hearing. Reagan's hearing had been steadily declining for several years, while Regan was practically deaf in his right ear. While resisting the president's suggestion that he follow his example and wear hearing aids, Regan spoke habitually in a booming voice that others described as "loud" but that made him comprehensible to the president. Regan thus did naturally what members of the first-term team had trained themselves to do in Reagan's presence: speak loudly while looking directly at the president. Reagan and Regan also shared an inner wariness that belied their outward gregariousness. When Myra MacPherson profiled Regan for *The Washington Post* in

1985, she found that those who had worked with him on Wall Street and at Treasury used such phrases as, "No one really knows Don. Not the kind of guy who ever had drinks with the guys after work. A loner. He doesn't have close friends."[14] These could as well have been descriptions of the president.

Reagan and Regan were also alike in defining themselves by their former occupations and disdaining the craft of politics. Even more than Reagan, Regan used the words "politics" and "politician" as terms of opprobrium. Regan's political credentials were much thinner than the president's, and he tried retroactively to emphasize his Republicanism by noting that he had cast his first presidential vote for Wendell Willkie in 1940 (when Reagan, of course, had voted for Roosevelt). But Regan had never been politically active, and some of his former associates on Wall Street did not even know if he was a Democrat or a Republican. His participation in the 1980 campaign had been limited to serving, at Bill Casey's request, as chairman of a fund-raising dinner. As recounted in Chapter 5, Regan had gained his cabinet post by default after William Simon had posed unacceptable conditions for becoming treasury secretary and Walter Wriston had declined. No less than Baker, Regan had entered the administration on a pass. While he had cultivated the president assiduously at cabinet and economic policy meetings, Regan had never spent a moment alone with him when he became the White House chief of staff.

No presidency has ever undergone such a thoroughgoing transformation in management style as Reagan's did under his new chief of staff. Because of Reagan's passivity, his presidency easily assumed the coloration of whoever was running the White House. Baker's and Regan's styles were totally contrasting. Where Baker was collegial, Regan was directive. Where Baker was cautious, Regan was bold. Baker preferred to operate behind the scenes, forging a political consensus and framing it in terms that Reagan could endorse. Regan charged ahead, dismissing arguments he disagreed with as readily as he had dismissed contrary opinions at Merrill Lynch. He liked the limelight and repeatedly drew attention to his personal role. (Baker and Deaver were horrified when Regan instructed that he be introduced as "White House chief of staff" at the president's out-of-town appearances.) Baker and Deaver had been protective of Reagan to a fault, always sensitive to the possibility of self-inflicted wounds. Regan was unmindful of the president's blind spots and exposed him to damaging controversies on Bitburg and South Africa that a more prudent chief of staff would have avoided.

It can be argued that Regan was more open as well as more politically ignorant than the first-term team. The floundering and ill-informed president whom the American people were allowed to glimpse in 1985 was at least as much the real Reagan as the masterful leader depicted in the reelection propaganda of 1984. Regan may not have realized, at least at first, how vulnerable Reagan was when left to his own devices. Because he had spent so little time with Reagan and had seen him mostly in cabinet settings where his participation was largely limited to anecdotes and set speeches, Regan had accepted much of the campaign propaganda at face value. Regan saw it as his task, he said, to "let Reagan be Reagan," an all-purpose phrase that sometimes meant letting the president make a fool of himself. When Regan talked of protecting the president, he meant protecting him from exposure to conflicting options that tended to bring out Reagan's inclination to compromise. While Regan believed that the president was fundamentally a centrist and therefore gave a different meaning to the "let Reagan be Reagan" rubric than the conservatives did, he had no grasp of what was needed to make the center hold. Too often, the president was left to fend for himself while Regan underwent on-the-job training in 1985.

Before we examine some of the disasters that occurred on Regan's White House watch, it is necessary to note that he brought assets to the Reagan presidency as well as liabilities. While the Tax Reform Act of 1986 would not have become law without the effective lobbying of Baker and Darman at Treasury and the congressional leadership of such men as Congressman Dan Rostenkowski and Senator Robert Packwood, the bill might never have been proposed except for Regan. At Treasury, he had displayed a willingness to reduce individual tax rates at the expense of the corporations he had battled on Wall Street. At the White House, Regan became an ardent advocate of sticking with tax reform when the prospects of passage seemed dim. Regan's bull-headedness made him an ineffective negotiator with Congress on this or almost any issue. But he bolstered Reagan's inclination for reform by the useful tactic of quoting the president's own past speeches to him about the necessity of "making the whole system more fair and simple for everyone." Reagan himself had often taken advantage of tax shelters (such as lowering his tax burden by keeping a few head of cattle at Rancho del Cielo), but he had little appreciation of the magnitude of tax avoidance by the wealthy. When Regan delivered the Treasury I tax reform proposal to the president on November 26, 1984, he effectively underscored its objective with a telling anecdote. He asked Reagan how much he had paid in taxes before he became president. Reagan told

him. "Sucker," said Regan. "With the right lawyer and the right accountant and the right tax shelters, you needn't have paid a penny in
taxes even if you made more than a million dollars a year—and it would
have been perfectly legal and proper. The tax system we have now is
designed to make the avoidance of taxes easy for the rich and has the
effect of making it almost impossible for people who work for wages
and salaries to do the same." [15] This point had often been made by such
congressional tax-reform advocates as Senator Bill Bradley and Congressmen Jack Kemp and Richard Gephardt. But it had special force
for Reagan when presented to him in anecdotal form by a member of
his cabinet who was said to be worth more than $30 million. More than
anyone else in Washington, Regan reinforced Reagan's inclination to
stand for tax reform.*

But Regan was ill-suited to serve as any president's chief of staff.
Though many chiefs of staff, including Baker, had been highly ambitious, the job requires a show of self-effacement of which Regan was
incapable. Neither Baker nor Deaver was quite sure why Regan even
wanted the job. There was some truth to Nancy Reagan's gibe that
Regan liked the sound of "chief" but not of "staff," [17] and Regan subsequently acknowledged to me that he was gripped by "Potomac
fever." [18] According to Mike Deaver, Regan said to him after the job
switch was made, "At dinner parties I sit below the salt now. There are
a lot of interesting people there." [19]

But Regan's motivations should not be assigned entirely to his enormous ego. He also believed that he could help the president by institut-
ing what he regarded as good management practices at the White
House. The cacophony of "leaks" from the White House in the first
term genuinely offended Regan's sense of managerial discipline and
order, even though he would be far less successful in controlling them
than he anticipated.† Regan shared Reagan's erroneous view that run-

---

* In *Showdown at Gucci Gulch*, the definitive account of how the Tax Reform Act of 1986 was
enacted, authors Jeffrey H. Birnbaum and Alan S. Murray observe that Regan "sensed the president's passion for lower [tax] rates and was eager to win a prominent place for himself on the
president's agenda." The authors also concluded: "The most important player in tax reform was
Ronald Reagan himself. The president seldom took an active role in the two-year tax debate. . . .
Nevertheless, the conservative president's support for an effort once considered the bastion of
liberals carried tremendous symbolic significance." [16]
† Regan claimed considerable success in shutting down White House leaks, saying in his book that
"at one point I laid down the rule that no member of the senior staff could talk to the press unless
a member of the White House Press Office staff was present. I myself always observed this rule."
I know of at least one occasion where Regan violated it, although that was generally his rule. But
when I challenged his assertion that he had effectively shut down leaks, Regan surprised me by

ning the White House was much like running a corporation and saw himself as the chief executive officer who carried out the company agenda that had been proclaimed by a distant chairman of the board. "He thought he could whip things into shape organizationally and they would have a smooth-sailing ship," a friend of Regan's said to me. "He didn't understand the importance of developing relationships with staff or the media or Congress. He'd never been a staff person. He wanted to have a wonderful relationship with the president."

Regan brought four deficiencies to his new job, any one of which might have been enough to do him in. The first was his ego. The second was his disdain for politics in a job that is surely among the most political in the world. Soon after the job switch was announced, Regan said to me dismissively that he realized that Baker was adept at politics, almost as if he were describing his tennis stroke or some other skill irrelevant to the job. Regan could not understand why Baker took the time to return the telephone calls of rank-and-file congressmen, let alone why he spent so much time with the media. He did not understand that storing political capital in Washington is as important as accumulating financial assets on Wall Street, and he had no reserves to draw upon when crisis struck. Regan's third deficiency, which intersected with the second, was that he had no appreciation for the important political role that Nancy Reagan played in all of her husband's endeavors. This was directly a product of his attitude toward women. "Regan didn't understand how important Nancy was, and what she had to offer," said a close friend of Regan's who was no admirer of the first lady. "Regan was almost incapable of understanding this relationship, which was so different from his own marital relationship or the marital relationships he knew about. He was a victim of his generation. He came from a man's world, and the wives in his world didn't have anything important to say about the business. He looked upon them to entertain, to keep things in order at home and not to embarrass their men. He was able to keep this view at Treasury. He brought in experts, as he did at Merrill Lynch, but he was the boss. Treasury secretaries are treated like kings."

Regan compounded his problem by bringing with him to the White House from Treasury a collection of aides who were unflatteringly dubbed "the Mice," a description they adopted as their own. "The

---

agreeing. "I know it, too, Lou," he said. "I know it now in retrospect. I didn't know it at the time I was writing the book."[20]

Mice" were Regan's fourth deficiency and perhaps his biggest. While they realized they had to be nice to the first lady, they valued her even less than Regan did. Nor did they especially value the president. Regan had drummed into them at Treasury that loyalty to him was the principal virtue, and they never transferred this loyalty to Reagan after they went to the White House. I became aware of this at the end of Regan's long struggle to force Margaret M. Heckler, a former congresswoman from Massachusetts, out of her cabinet post as secretary of health and human services. Regan considered Heckler an administrative disaster and began pressure to oust her in March 1985. According to his subsequent account in *For the Record,* he was acting at the behest of Nancy Reagan, who also had doubts about Heckler's effectiveness and was troubled by news accounts of Heckler's highly publicized divorce. Regan's solution, which Reagan accepted and Heckler resisted, was to make her ambassador to Ireland. Regan had intended to do this quickly, but the action was delayed while Heckler recuperated from an operation. On September 30, 1985, responding to a question whether Heckler was being dumped, the president said inaccurately during a photo opportunity in the Oval Office, "There's never been any thought in my mind of firing Margaret Heckler. I don't know where these stories have come from. They are not true."[21]

But they were true. The next day Reagan appeared in the briefing room with Heckler and rather defensively announced that "Margaret Heckler has agreed to my request that she become the ambassador to Ireland."[22] He denounced the "malicious gossip" that she was being forced out and lied that she could have remained on at HHS if she had wanted to do so. When I asked one of the Mice afterward why Regan had sent the president out into the briefing room and put him in the position where he felt it necessary to lie, I was told, "Regan needed a win."

The Mice had been telling me for months that Heckler was going to be ousted, and I believed them. I doubt that they knew Nancy Reagan was behind it, if she was, because they were never hesitant to criticize her if they could do so anonymously. The Mice were named David Chew, Al Kingon, Tom Dawson and Dennis Thomas. While occasionally candid in their comments about Reagan, they competed with each other in lavish praise of Regan, whose legendary temper they seemed to fear. Peggy Noonan described them in this way:

> They were not as vivid as their boss, and I think that's part of the reason they were there. There were four of them but when people

thought of them they thought, there are three of them. It was one of those funny things, but even when they were thought of en masse there was something diminished about them. There was David, who was in charge of the paper flow; we sometimes called him "Yah Yah Understood," because that's what he said to us on the phone before he ignored what we were saying. There was Al, who dealt with policy and who had the forlorn look of Stan Laurel after Ollie bopped him on the head. There was Tom, who became famous, perhaps unfairly, as the aide charged with finding the joke du jour for Mr. Regan's morning meeting with the president, and Dennis, who would be spoofed in a witty piece in the *New Republic* as "America's Guest," so much did he enjoy being entertained at expensive dinners paid for by the networks and the mainline press.[23]

The Mice did not know the Reagans, and they were incapable of filling the vacuum left by the departure of Darman, Deaver and other members of the Baker band. Regan did not realize that one cannot be a strong White House chief of staff without strong subordinates. By surrounding himself with the Mice, who served as his own protective shield, Regan isolated himself from the accumulated experience of the few midlevel aides who remained at the White House after the first term. Most of them soon left, too. The exception was Larry Speakes, who conducted the daily press briefings and usually served as White House spokesman. Reagan had kept a promise to retain the wounded James Brady as his press secretary, so Speakes held the title of principal deputy press secretary. During the first term Speakes had often been a secondary source of information for White House reporters who had access to Baker, Deaver, Darman and Gergen. But Regan was neither confident nor experienced in dealing with the media, and he found it necessary to rely on Speakes for his dealings with the increasingly restive White House press corps. This was good for Speakes, who welcomed no longer having to compete with other officials as the media's principal official source of information. It was not necessarily good for Regan or the president. While Speakes was more competent than the Mice, he was widely distrusted by the White House press corps. He ratified the worst suspicions about the quality of information in White House briefings when he confessed in his book that he had made up inspiring statements and presented them as the words of Ronald Reagan.[24]

Regan did bring one new aide to the White House who was most definitely not a Mouse. He was Patrick J. Buchanan, a combative former Nixon speech writer who had first gained national attention as a principal author of then–Vice President Spiro Agnew's attacks on the media in 1969. Anxious to appease conservatives who were wondering aloud about the administration's ideological drift, Regan early in February made Buchanan director of communications and gave him jurisdiction over the speechwriting department, the main bastion of conservatism within the White House. As a prolific columnist and conservative celebrity during Reagan's first term, Buchanan had attacked not only such favorite targets as liberals, Democrats and the big media (which he described as the "polemical and publicity arm of American liberalism")[25] but also the White House pragmatists and everyone within the Reagan administration who favored "the grand illusion" of détente with the Soviet Union. Under Reagan, wrote Buchanan in one column, the "continued socialization" of America has "proceeded apace." When Reagan in his turning-point speech of January 16, 1984, proclaimed "a year of opportunities for peace," Buchanan retorted sarcastically that pressure from Europe, the media and the Democrats had "converted Mr. Reagan into a President of the Order for Peaceful Coexistence."[26]

Deaver opposed the hiring of Buchanan in the belief that, as he subsequently put it, "Ronald Reagan does not need anyone to the right of him."[27] While sharing a talent for public relations, Deaver and Buchanan represented the antipodes of the Reagan administration during the three months of 1985 that they served together in the White House. Deaver's loyalty was to Reagan the man, not to the conservative cause or to any ideological creed. His reputation was based not on knowledge of policy matters, on which he had made little effort to inform himself, but on his skills as master producer of White House visuals and photo opportunities. In conservative circles Deaver was regarded as little more than a glorified valet. Buchanan had derided him in a column as "Lord of the Chamberpot." But as we have seen, Deaver also was an advocate behind the scenes. He had threatened to resign over the bombing of Beirut, had encouraged Shultz to promote improved U.S.-Soviet relations and had sought to influence Reagan to take a more enlightened position on civil rights issues.

Buchanan's purpose was the opposite of Deaver's. He barely knew Reagan personally and was far more concerned with advancing conservative causes than the political fortunes of the president. But if Deaver's influence on policy was underrated, so were Buchanan's skills as a publicist and communicator. Buchanan knew how to provoke a confrontation, and he did not let ideology determine his choice of media. When he wanted to draw attention to one of his causes, he invariably chose the op-ed page of *The Washington Post,* where his columns were always welcomed by editorial-page editor Meg Greenfield, instead of *The Washington Times,* where Buchanan's column found a compatible home before he went to the White House and after he left it. Unlike Deaver, Buchanan was well liked by many of his ideological adversaries, including Tom Braden, with whom he had served for years as co-host on a politically focused radio talk show on WRC in Washington. But in describing Buchanan, Braden chose a famous quotation from William Butler Yeats: "The best lack all conviction, while the worst are full of passionate intensity." [28]

While using the appointment of Buchanan to give him some breathing room on the right, Regan also sought to harness his passionate convictions. "I reminded Pat of an old phrase I think most of you will recall of accepting the king's shilling," Regan said when he appointed Buchanan. "And when you accept the king's shilling, you sign aboard." [29] The metaphor was revealing, for Regan was regent in the monarchial Reagan White House, and Buchanan reported to the president through the chief of staff. Buchanan, accustomed to the hierarchical structure of the Nixon White House, accepted Regan's conditions in return for the increased influence he believed he could exercise on administration policy. He was convinced that Reagan had been deflected from the path of true conservatism by Nancy Reagan, Mike Deaver, James Baker and George Shultz, among others. If it was necessary to be loyal to Regan to influence Reagan, Buchanan was willing to do it. He refrained from bad-mouthing Regan, even when he disagreed with him, and he served unhappily as the messenger when Regan insisted on firing speech writer Bently Elliott, a conservative Reagan loyalist whose tactless dismissal was described in Chapter 10. But Buchanan's obeisance gained him neither the access nor the influence he anticipated. He was not allowed to see Reagan alone. And he proved unable to discourage the president's turn toward improved U.S.-Soviet relations, since the "grand illusion" of world peace was shared by Reagan as well as by the first lady and the secretary of state.

Buchanan did have dubious success, however, in disseminating Reagan's tolerant views of the South African government and his hostile ones of the Sandinista government of Nicaragua. White House speeches excusing South Africa's ruthless suppression of anti-apartheid protests that might have been squelched when Dick Darman was overseeing the speech writers easily received Buchanan's imprimatur. And because Buchanan was deeply committed to the contra cause, he played an active role in reinforcing Reagan's perception that the Nicaraguan rebels were "freedom fighters" comparable to the American revolutionaries of 1776. In his political tactics, however, Buchanan remained more a Nixonian than a Reaganite, and he tried to discredit the patriotism of those who opposed aid for the contras. "With the vote on contra aid, the Democratic Party will reveal whether it stands with Ronald Reagan and the resistance—or Daniel Ortega and the communists," Buchanan wrote in a column in *The Washington Post* on March 5, 1986, which warned that the Communists "will be in San Diego" unless they were militarily halted in Central America.[30]

This sort of Red-baiting had been an effective tactic in keeping Congress in line through much of the Vietnam years but had become counterproductive in the 1980s. Democrats were offended by Buchanan's column, which he wrote in his capacity as White House communications director at the same time that White House legislative lobbyists were courting fence-straddling southwestern Democrats in behalf of a new package of $100 million in contra aid. Instead of backing down, the Democratic leadership made opposition to contra aid a test of party loyalty. Two weeks after Buchanan's column, the House voted down the contra aid package. Buchanan had succeeded in drawing attention to himself, but he had proved ineffective in building support for the contras.

But it should also be said that Buchanan was not part of the cabal that undermined democratic processes by waging a secret and undeclared war against the government of Nicaragua. Buchanan wanted Reagan to take his case to the country and try to mobilize public support for the Nicaraguan rebels. This was a path that posed far less peril than the one on which Reagan embarked. Reagan was popular enough to withstand open advocacy of unpopular causes. His presidency would be damaged almost beyond repair not from an honest expression of convictions but by the subterfuge of the Iran arms deal and the deception by which proceeds from the sale of these arms were diverted to the contras in defiance of Congress and the Constitution.

Edward J. Rollins was as outspoken as Buchanan and less loyal to the new White House chief of staff. Rollins, a former amateur prizefighter who had knocked out 154 of 167 opponents, was an exponent of political hardball who had succeeded Lyn Nofziger as head of the White House political office in 1982. In this role he had earned a reputation for candor that delighted the press but consistently landed him in hot water with his superiors. On one occasion Rollins had said that the

White House had obtained the vote of Republican Senator Roger Jepsen of Iowa for the AWACS sale to Saudi Arabia because "we just beat his brains out."[31] On another he had confided to a reporter that the president's daughter Maureen Reagan, then contemplating a race to become a U.S. senator from California, was the worst Senate candidate he had ever seen. Reagan rebuked Rollins (although he didn't, as Rollins noted privately to me, dispute his political assessment), and James Baker intervened to save his job. In 1984 Baker closed down the White House political office and sent Rollins to the Republican National Committee with the title of director of the Reagan-Bush campaign. Baker had promised to bring Rollins back to the White House as political director in 1985, and Regan honored this commitment, much to his later regret. Rollins was far too outspoken for Regan, and their working relationship did not survive the controversy that soon developed over Reagan's unfortunate decision to honor Nazi Germany's war dead.

Reagan's visit to Bitburg was the seminal symbolic disaster of an administration that placed great store in symbolism. In laying a wreath at a German military cemetery that contained the graves of Waffen SS troops, Reagan abandoned the moral high ground of his intense convictions about the Holocaust to satisfy his political relationship with West German Chancellor Helmut Kohl. By his stubborn insistence on going through with this ceremony after its negative implications had been pointed out to him by the world Jewish community, veterans groups, Republican leaders and Nancy Reagan, Reagan inflicted needless political damage on his presidency in the critical opening months of his second term. Bitburg exposed the weakness of Don Regan's premise that the Reagan presidency functioned best if Reagan were left to his own devices. It also provided a test of Regan's damage-control abilities, which he badly flunked.

The Bitburg trip was the unwitting child of Reagan's symbolically most successful journey—his commemorative D-Day visit to Normandy in 1984. Kohl had been dismayed by his exclusion from this ceremony. When he came to the White House on November 30, 1984, Kohl gave what was described to me as a tearful account of how he and French President François Mitterrand had visited the graves of German and French soldiers who had fallen in battle at Verdun in World War I and urged Reagan to participate in a similar ceremony of reconciliation honoring the military dead of World War II. Reagan, appreciative of Kohl for his government's acceptance of U.S. nuclear missiles in 1983 and responsive to his show of emotion, almost offhandedly agreed. He did not know that the Verdun analogy was inapplicable because there are no German military cemeteries in which both U.S. and German soldiers were buried. If Kohl knew this, he did not tell Reagan. Nor did anyone else inform him of this vital fact before the trip was announced the following spring.

Reagan was already scheduled to visit Bonn in 1985, when it was West Germany's turn to host the economic summit. The summit was scheduled for early May, coinciding with the fortieth anniversary of the defeat of Nazi Germany by Allied armies. Kohl proposed that Reagan visit a concentration camp and a cathedral and that they together lay a wreath in a military cemetery. Nancy Reagan, who knew how difficult it was for her husband to perform in any circumstances he found depressing, opposed the concentration camp stop as soon as she heard about it. At a veterans home in Indiana early in the 1980 campaign, Reagan had been overcome at the sight of the ailing and aged veterans who had been assembled to hear him and had literally been unable to complete his speech. Nancy Reagan, seeing him falter, stepped forward and smoothly completed the speech for him, only later expressing her fury at the local politician who had brought them there. She did not want Reagan speaking at a concentration camp.

When *Der Spiegel* reported on January 19, 1985, that Reagan was considering a visit to Dachau, the first lady expressed her misgivings to Deaver and to her husband. By then, as *Der Spiegel* had implied, the West Germans were also having second thoughts about the idea. The White House announced that Reagan would not be visiting a concentration camp. Defending this decision, Reagan said at a news conference, "I feel very strongly . . . that instead of reawakening the memories and so forth and the passions of the time, that maybe we should observe this day as the day when, forty years ago, peace began and friendship." [32] When I commented in a subsequent interview with Reagan that he had often said the Holocaust must not be forgotten and asked him if he was passing up an opportunity to call attention to it, he reiterated that "we should never forget the Holocaust" but observed that the bulk of the German population were "small children or not born yet" when it occurred. "And there's no question about their great feeling of guilt—even though they were not there to participate in it—of what their nation did," he said. "And then to take advantage of that visit, on that occasion, to go there—I just think is contrary to what I believe." [33]

Deaver advanced the trip in February, taking with him to West Germany his designated successor, William Henkel, an experienced advance man who would eventually become the only White House official to remain simultaneously on speaking terms with Regan and Nancy Reagan. Deaver had by now served notice on the Reagans that he was leaving the White House to go into business for himself, and he intended to leave on a high note. On its face, Reagan's 1985 trip to Europe, which also included stopovers in Spain, Portugal and France, seemed less challenging than either the overscheduled 1982 excursion or the theatrical Normandy appearance. Reagan had been overwhelmingly reelected, and Deaver felt freed from the political constraints that had guided the schedules of previous foreign trips. When he inspected the cemetery at Bitburg, he found it picturesque, with snow covering the graves. While Deaver did instruct the deputy U.S. chief of mission at the American embassy to make sure there was "nothing embarrassing here," both Deaver and the embassy accepted the blanket assurances of German chief of protocol Werner von der Schulenberg that "no war criminals" were buried at Bitburg.

But forty-nine SS soldiers were buried there, including SS Staff Sergeant Otto Franz Begel, who had been awarded the German Cross for killing ten American soldiers. Neither Reagan nor Deaver nor anyone else in the White House involved with the president's participation in the Bitburg ceremony realized that many Germans distinguished between the regular SS forces, the most fanatical killers of the Nazi regime, and the Waffen SS, who had been attached to military units. As the Germans saw it, many of the Waffen SS had been forced into military service and were therefore not war criminals. When he was being pressed to cancel his visit to Bitburg, Reagan would adopt as his own the official German explanation that the SS soldiers buried in the cemetery were "young teenagers that were conscripted, forced into military service in the closing days of the Third Reich, when they were short of manpower."[34]

There were teenage German soldiers buried in the Bitburg cemetery, but SS Sergeant Begel was not one of them. His tombstone showed that he was thirty-eight years old when he was killed on January 22, 1945, in the midst of the Battle of the Bulge, the most ferocious fighting in history between German and American soldiers. Bitburg had been the staging area for this battle, the final German offensive on the western front, and one that claimed nearly 70,000 American and 100,000 German casualties. On December 17, 1944, the second day of this offensive, the German First SS Panzer Division overran an American field-artillery battalion in the Belgian town of Malmédy and captured seventy-one U.S. soldiers, who were led with their hands over their heads into a nearby field where they were shot by machine guns and rifles and finished off at close range with pistol shots. While such atrocities were common on the eastern front, this was the greatest massacre of American prisoners in the entire war. Forty-three SS officers were sentenced to death for these crimes after the war, although their sentences were commuted to life imprisonment and eventually short prison terms after Senate protests led by Joseph McCarthy of Wisconsin. Many of the SS soldiers buried in Bitburg had subsequently fallen in the Battle of the Bulge, which raged for six weeks through Belgium and Luxembourg.

Kohl was so anxious for his reconciliation ceremony that the Germans did nothing to alleviate the ignorance of the Americans. Henkel alone seems to have had gnawing worries about what the cemetery would reveal when the snow melted on the graves, and he inquired again about it on a follow-up trip to Germany in March. His concerns were dismissed by American diplomats, one of whom said to him, "What do you think—Josef Mengele is buried there?"[35] There was nothing more that Henkel could do about it. The specific itinerary—including the Bitburg wreath-laying but without a concentration camp stop—was approved in early March after it was signed off on by Reagan, Regan, National Security Adviser Robert McFarlane and Secretary of State George Shultz.

The itinerary was announced on April 11 by Larry Speakes in Santa Barbara, while Reagan was vacationing at his ranch. "Who's buried in Bitburg?" asked Myron Waldman, the White House correspondent for *Newsday*. Speakes did not have a clue. The information that Bitburg was strictly a German military cemetery had been contained in an advance off-the-record report filed by George Skelton of the *Los Angeles Times*, who had accompanied Henkel on the final advance trip in March, but neither the White House press office nor the press had focused on it. Speakes promptly checked, however, and told the reporters what he had found out about the cemetery. He did not know about the graves of the SS soldiers. But even without this information the stories filed that day from Santa Barbara caused a furor. Elie Wiesel, the author who had survived Auschwitz and Buchenwald and won the Nobel Peace Prize for his efforts to keep alive the memory of the Holocaust, could not believe the news. "I know the president," Wiesel said. "I know this is not his sentiment."[36] The American Legion issued a statement saying that "we are terribly disappointed" by the visit.[37]

Ed Rollins was taking a day off painting his cabin in the Virginia hills on the day Speakes announced the itinerary of the German trip. Regan called him and asked, "What do you think of this Bitburg thing?"[38] Rollins wasn't sure, but he stopped painting and began calling Reagan supporters in the Jewish community. They bluntly told him that going to Bitburg would be a disaster and urged that the wreath-laying ceremony be dropped. Soon, Rollins was receiving similar messages from Senate Majority Leader Bob Dole, a severely wounded veteran of World War II, and from Republican Senator Paula Hawkins of Florida, already justifiably worried about her 1986 reelection campaign. Rollins called Regan back and told him the negative reaction he was getting. "Well, goddamn it, this is bigger than just a Jewish issue, this is the president," Regan said.[39] He nonetheless agreed that it was a good idea to bring Jewish leaders to the White House to discuss alternatives to Bitburg.

On the weekend of April 13–14, the news broke that forty-nine SS men were among the 2,000 soldiers buried at Bitburg. White House officials were now besieged. Some of them complained that the press, and particularly Jewish reporters, were blowing up the story in an effort to discredit Reagan. As Pat Buchanan saw it, the liberal media were always seeking an issue upon which they could seize to damage a popular president. He urged resistance, to the Jews and to the media. "Buchanan argued for a harder line, a bigger gesture, a clearer defense of the new Germany and virtually an amnesty for the Third Reich," said Deaver.[40] At the other end of the spectrum was Nancy Reagan, who wanted to end the controversy by cancelling the Bitburg stop.[41] Reagan would not hear of it, saying that he had made a promise to Kohl. His stubbornness usually came to the fore when he was asked to back away from a personal commitment for political reasons. In 1980 his pollster Richard Wirthlin had told him that he would be sending an undesirable signal by attending the Neshoba County Fair in Philadelphia, Mississippi, where three civil rights workers had been murdered with police complicity in 1964. Reagan said something about how his experience had taught him the importance of keeping a booking once it was made and reminded Wirthlin that he had promised Mississippi Republicans he would attend the fair. When Wirthlin persisted, Reagan's neck became red and he threw his briefing papers at the pollster. "Well, I guess, Governor, you're pretty well set on going," Wirthlin said, realizing that the discussion was over.[42] Reagan's response to polls showing public opposition to the Bitburg visit reminded Wirthlin of this incident. Recognizing that Reagan would not back down, Deaver did not even try to talk him out of going to Bitburg. Rather than subtract the cemetery ceremony from the trip, Deaver's solution was to add a concentration camp stop. Nancy Reagan, more flexible than her husband, dropped her earlier objections to a concentration camp event but continued to oppose the Bitburg ceremony. Reagan was willing to speak at a concentration camp, providing this solution was acceptable to Kohl. An "invitation" from the West German leader to add a "suitable site" at a concentration camp to the itinerary was quickly arranged, and Deaver and Henkel flew off to Germany on April 15 to survey Dachau and Bergen-Belsen. The task of controlling the political damage at home was left in Don Regan's hands.

Instead of containing the damage, Regan compounded it. Though he would later tell me that he did not want Reagan to go to Bitburg,[43] Regan was furious at the Jewish community for making a fuss about it and especially annoyed that Wiesel had served notice that a stop at a concentration camp site would not be acceptable as a trade-off for going to Bitburg. After his conversation with Regan the previous Thursday, Rollins had arranged for Wiesel, in his capacity as chairman of the U.S. Holocaust Memorial Council, and five prominent Jewish Republicans who had supported Reagan and contributed to his campaigns to come to the White House for a meeting on Tuesday, April 16, to discuss alternatives to the Bitburg visit. They were told, as Rollins had been and as Speakes had announced at Santa Barbara, that the Bitburg ceremony itself was under review.

The meeting with the Jewish leaders was scheduled for 1:15. A few minutes beforehand Rollins and Buchanan met with Regan in his office to discuss the meeting. As soon as he closed his office door, Regan whipped out a copy of a statement he said Reagan would deliver later that afternoon. In the statement Reagan said he intended his visit to Germany "to commemorate not simply the military victory of forty years ago but the liberation of Europe, the rebirth of German freedom and the reconciliation of our two countries." Reagan would also announce that he was visiting a concentration camp, which had been absent from his original itinerary "because of my mistaken impression that such a visit was outside the official agenda."[44] Rollins was stunned and angry to learn that everything had already been decided. "Well, Don, you've asked me to have these people fly in . . . to give you counsel and advice," he said. "They're going to be pissed. It would be better not to have the goddamned meeting." Regan said, "Well, don't tell them we've made the decision." Rollins replied that he did not intend to "sit there and bullshit them"[45] and that those attending the meeting would quickly figure out that the decision had already been made.

One of the Jews who came to the White House that day was Richard Fox, a Philadelphia developer who headed the National Jewish Coalition, a pro-Reagan Republican group. Fox had served as state chairman of the Reagan campaign in Pennsylvania in 1980. In the 1984 election he had led the national campaign to win Jewish votes for the Reagan-Bush ticket. His first question to Regan was whether a decision had already been made. "No," Regan said.[46] Wiesel made an impassioned plea for Reagan to abandon the Bitburg ceremony, drawing upon the history of the Holocaust and the SS role in it. All of the Jews argued that the decision would be morally and ethically improper. Buchanan, also impassioned, said that it would be difficult for Reagan to change his decision under political pressure unless there was a compelling reason to do so. He told the Jews that they were "Americans first,"[47] as if there was somehow something un-American about opposing the Bitburg ceremony. But what enraged the Jews was not so much what Buchanan said but what they observed he had written over and over again in his notebook: "Succumbing to the pressure of the Jews."[48]

The discussion continued, with Regan siding with Buchanan and Rollins with the Jews. Fox was sitting between Regan and Rollins. Midway through the meeting Rollins quietly slipped to Fox a copy of the president's statement and a White House schedule that showed the visiting Jewish leaders being greeted by the president after the meeting with Regan. Regan observed what Rollins was doing and, as Fox remembers it, "turned purple" with rage. "It became fairly evident that there had been a game in play and we were part of that game, in which Regan figured he would get us to go out on the White House lawn, the president would thank us for working out the problem and allowing him to go to Bitburg and also go to Bergen-Belsen," Fox said.[49] Now it was Fox's turn to become angry. "Come on, let's quit bullshitting each other," he said. "Is the president not going out at two to make this announcement?"[50]

Regan lamely replied that the statement had not been "finalized."[51] The meeting broke up in anger and frustration, and the Jews left the White House without seeing the president or talking to the press. As they were leaving, Reagan was announcing his decision to go to Bitburg at the Old Executive Office Building adjacent to the White House. He was speaking to a conference on religious liberty.

Still, the pressure against the Bitburg visit continued. On April 18, fifty-three U.S. senators announced that they opposed the visit. The same day, Reagan poured fuel on the flaming controversy by declaring in a speech that the SS soldiers buried in the Bitburg cemetery "were victims, just as surely as the victims in the concentration camps."[52] The next day, in an event that had been scheduled long before the Bitburg controversy, Reagan presented the Congressional Gold Medal to Wiesel in the Roosevelt Room of the White House, paying tribute to the victims of the Holocaust and the "spirit of reconciliation" that he said now prevailed in the world. "Memory can fail us, for it can fade as the generations change," Reagan said. "But Elie Wiesel has helped make the memory of the Holocaust eternal by preserving the story of the six million Jews in his works."[53]

Wiesel had debated with himself whether to accept the medal, which he did on the grounds that it had been voted by Congress. He said he was grateful for it and grateful to Reagan for being "a friend of the Jewish people." He said the medal belonged not to him alone but "to all those who remember what SS killers have done to their victims." He observed that April 19 was the anniversary of the Warsaw Ghetto uprising of 1943 and told of how it had been crushed while "the leaders of the free world" did nothing. "You spoke of Jewish children, Mr. President; one million Jewish children perished," Wiesel said. "If I spent my entire life reciting their names, I would die before finishing the task. Mr. President, I have seen children—I have seen them being thrown in the flames alive. Words, they die on my lips." Wiesel said he had "respect and admiration" for Reagan and acknowledged that Reagan had not known that members of the SS were buried at Bitburg when he agreed to the ceremony. "May I, Mr. President, if it's possible at all, implore you to do something else, to find a way, to find another way, another site," Wiesel said. "That place, Mr. President, is not your place. Your place is with the victims of the SS."[54]

Don Regan was angry at Wiesel for making this public plea, so angry that he would afterward misremember and say in his book that Wiesel had promised not to use the ceremony for this purpose.[55] Wiesel had made no such promise, as Regan subsequently acknowledged.[56] Nancy Reagan, despite her continued opposition to the trip, was also angry at Wiesel for embarrassing her husband in public. But the president was both shaken and moved by Wiesel's words, and his vaunted stubbornness was beginning to crack. Reagan was made uncomfortable by any suggestion that he was insensitive to the Holocaust. The newsreels of the death camps he had seen in 1945 were such a vivid part of his memory that he was able to imagine, as we have seen, that he was actually at the site of the concentration camps when they were liberated by the Allied armies. While Reagan was resentful of the media for what he regarded as unfair coverage of his decision to go to Bitburg, he watched the evening news and read the newspapers and had learned that at least some of the SS soldiers buried in Bitburg were not teenagers who had been pressed into military service. He wanted a way out, if a way out could be found.

Whether West German officials also had an intimation that Reagan was wavering, I have been unable to determine. But Kohl made a timely telephone call to Reagan on April 19, once more urging that he keep his commitment to lay the wreath in the Bitburg cemetery and stick with the itinerary that now also included Bergen-Belsen. My contemporary and subsequent interviews with White House officials and political advisers involved in the Bitburg controversy have convinced me that it was this April 19 telephone call rather than the more celebrated and longer telephone conversation between Kohl and Reagan ten days later that proved decisive.

Some of Reagan's advisers, especially his longtime political strategist Stu Spencer, did not want the president to take any calls from the West German chancellor. Spencer, who was later an adversary but then an ally of Regan, knew that Baker and Deaver had screened Reagan's calls during the first term when they thought it was necessary to protect him from making damaging commitments that he would have felt obligated to keep. Spencer himself had used this tactic during Reagan's campaigns. In Spencer's view, Regan should have thrown himself into the breach on April 19 and told Kohl that the president was too upset to come to the phone and that it would be better for them to talk later. That would have created some uncertainty in Bonn and perhaps encouraged Kohl to make a counterproposal of his own. This was not a tactic, however, that Regan would have pursued even if it had occurred to him, for he believed then (although less so later) that the president could and should make his own decisions. It was also a tactic that might not have worked, since Reagan had already given his commitment to Kohl. In any case, it was a tactic that was not tried. Regan allowed Reagan to be Reagan, and the president once again promised Kohl that he would go to Bitburg.

In the week after Wiesel's emotional speech, the White House was buffeted by criticism from quarters that were normally supportive. Bob

Dole, who was sometimes at odds with the White House on domestic budget issues but usually provided unstinting support on foreign policy, said five days after the Wiesel ceremony that it would be a "mistake" for the president to visit Bitburg.[57] The same day, Reagan was criticized in public for the only time during his presidency by his friend Charles Z. Wick, director of the U.S. Information Agency, who said Bitburg would be "a tragedy" that the Soviets would exploit for propaganda purposes.[58] On April 23, Reverend Billy Graham told me that Reagan had asked him if he should go through with the Bitburg ceremony. Graham proposed that he find an alternative site and suggested the idea, which he attributed to NBC's John Chancellor, of substituting a stop at the Konrad Adenauer memorial for the wreath-laying ceremony. "Christians and Jews alike should pray for the president because his motives were peaceful motives," Graham said. "He was trying to be a peacemaker, but I don't think that he and his advisers or Chancellor Kohl thought through the implications."[59]

Harry Truman once said that anyone who needed a friend in Washington should get a dog. Reagan had a dog, and he also had the faithful support of Richard Nixon, who had survived his innumerable crises and was always willing to help a fellow Republican in the White House. Whatever else can be said of him, Nixon was no fair-weather friend. He had helped restore Reagan's shattered confidence after the Louisville debate eight months earlier, and he now called Reagan and told him that his decision not to back away from Bitburg would strengthen U.S.-German relations. Henry Kissinger offered similar advice, also stressing West Germany's importance to the Western alliance. Although Nixon's calls and messages to Reagan were usually kept secret, White House aides were so grateful for any showing of support for Bitburg that they allowed Nixon's position to become known.

But Deaver, Henkel, McFarlane and Nancy Reagan still hoped to find a way out. So, belatedly, did Don Regan, who was frustrated that Bitburg was overshadowing all other actions of the administration. Everyone realized that Reagan would never go back on his promise to Kohl, but the White House staff still held a glimmer of hope that Kohl might relent if a face-saving option could be found. To this end McFarlane sent his counterpart, Kohl's national security adviser Horst Teltschik, a cable saying that Reagan would keep his commitment but that Bitburg was causing Reagan political damage. McFarlane's hope was that Teltschik would come up with an alternative site and persuade Kohl to accept it. But when McFarlane reported this to the president,

Reagan "came down upon me like a ton of bricks" [60] and reiterated that he would keep his commitment to Kohl.

The problem in finding an alternative site to Bitburg was that there were no easy options, since Waffen SS soldiers were also buried in every other German military cemetery surveyed by the advance team. Finally, however, the American embassy found an alternative—Festung Ehrenbreitstein, a shrine to the German dead of both world wars on a bluff near Koblenz. It contained no graves and had often been a site for memorial ceremonies. Henkel was ecstatic. He took the proposal to Regan, Deaver and McFarlane, all of whom endorsed it. So did George Shultz. On April 29, with these officials and Assistant Secretary of State Richard Burt on hand, Reagan agreed to make a final try to change Kohl's mind. A telephone call was placed to the German chancellor. Using notes prepared for him by State Department and National Security Council officials, Reagan talked to Kohl for nineteen minutes and made the case for Festung Ehrenbreitstein. Kohl adamantly refused, saying he would be politically and personally embarrassed by any change in the ceremony and that his government might fall. Kohl's stiff-necked response irritated the U.S. officials who were clustered around Reagan in the Oval Office, but there was nothing they could do about it. Once more, Reagan agreed to go to Bitburg.

The entire Bitburg controversy had been an ordeal for Deaver, straining his relationship with the Reagans and damaging his reputation for public relations wizardry at the very time he was leaving the White House to make his living as a lobbyist. Don Regan rubbed it in by reminding critics disturbed by his own clumsy political handling of the situation that it was Deaver who had chosen the Bitburg site. Deaver was further disappointed by the failure of his efforts at damage control; he could not even find a rabbi who would participate in an interfaith ceremony at Bergen-Belsen. And after Reagan had been stuck with Bitburg, and Deaver with the blame, Deaver's ordeal continued in the form of a bizarre scheduling sideshow with Nancy Reagan and astrologer Joan Quigley over the portents for the West German trip.

Nancy Reagan, frightened and desperate for reassurance after the assassination attempt on her husband's life, had sought out Quigley in April 1981 at the recommendation of family friend Merv Griffin.[61] Her action reflected a superstitious outlook also shared by Reagan, who believed that his presidency had been prophesied by a college teacher known for her psychic abilities. Reagan knocked on wood, threw salt over his shoulder and carried a good-luck penny. At a low point in his acting career he had accepted the only Las Vegas booking of his life after reading the astrological "word of the day" written by a friend, Hollywood astrologer Carroll Righter.[62] But Reagan was more casual about his superstitions than his wife, as he tended to be more casual about nearly everything. By 1985, Nancy Reagan had long become convinced that Quigley's advice had protected her husband from a repetition of the assassination attempt.*

After committing himself to a ceremony honoring Nazi Germany's war dead, Reagan was now allowing an astrologer to determine the timing of his visit to Bitburg and Bergen-Belsen. Reagan paid no attention to this. While well aware of Nancy Reagan's reliance on Quigley, he was oblivious to the problems this dependency caused his schedulers. Regan was unaware at the time of Quigley's role, and it had also been kept a secret from Henkel. The specific schedule for the trip was being drawn up by Henkel, supposedly at Deaver's direction. But it was actually being dictated by Nancy Reagan after consulting with Quigley. Often, Quigley's services were limited to designating favorable and unfavorable days for travel. But because the first lady was so worried about the consequences of Bitburg and Bergen-Belsen, she sought Quigley's advice on the timing of both events. According to Quigley, Nancy Reagan became exasperated when Quigley's charts and Deaver's schedule conflicted and put Deaver on the phone with the astrologer with instructions to him to follow her advice.[64]

Deaver's recollections about the Bitburg scheduling differ somewhat in detail from Quigley's account and are considerably more vivid. He had suffered more than he knew from the strain of concealing Nancy Reagan's astrological obsession, which had often required him to make irrational schedule adjustments that others in the administration, let alone outsiders, found inexplicable. A White House official who served with Deaver believes that he was badly served by his loyalty to Nancy Reagan on all counts. "The astrology business was the worst thing but not the only thing," this official said to me under ground rules of confidentiality. "Mike was the heavy all the time. He had to dump on the old friends. He was the bearer of the bad news. He would have to deal with Maureen and the [other] children and with anyone that Nancy was upset with—Dick Allen, Bill Clark, Helene von Damm. As

---

* "Was astrology one of the reasons?" wrote Nancy Reagan in her memoirs. "I don't *really* believe it was, but I don't *really* believe it wasn't. But I do know this: It didn't hurt, and I'm not sorry I did it."[63] Her reliance on Quigley, who was sent monthly checks of an undisclosed amount by Nancy Reagan for her services, remained a secret until revealed by Don Regan in his 1988 memoirs.

a result, everybody looked on Mike as one royal pain in the ass." This official remembers that people would avoid Deaver when he went across the street to the Old Executive Office Building on business. "They were afraid of him, they thought he was power-crazy. I don't think Mike ever understood that. He paid for it after he was out."

Deaver was a Christian (Episcopalian) who thought that astrology was nonsense but after a while came to regard Quigley as simply another burden of the job. He or his deputy William Sittmann, who also knew about Quigley, would send out survey teams to do advance planning for events, a standard procedure in any White House. But when the teams returned and presented their scheduling proposals, Deaver was required to submit them to the first lady, who then consulted with Quigley. "We were always under constraints anyway because President Reagan needed a lot of rest, as we had learned on the Versailles trip," said the White House official who told me of Deaver's burden. "We would plan these trips to accommodate this need, plus all the other things that had to be taken into account. All of a sudden we'd have to change our schedules at the eleventh hour. We couldn't fly at night, we couldn't fly on a Monday." Deaver dealt privately with these inconveniences by joking to Sittmann or Baker that the schedule had been changed by decree of "Madame Zorba," as he sometimes called Quigley. He also tried to invent rational reasons for the irrational changes in the schedule, explanations that most who heard them found singularly unconvincing. After a while, Deaver stopped trying to explain the changes and refused to answer any questions about them. "I was terrible in the scheduling meetings, absolutely outrageous," Deaver told me much later. "People would come in with perfectly reasonable ideas, and I would say to them, 'That's crazy, are you out of your mind?' I couldn't talk about why we were doing what we were doing, so I insulted people. I'm not proud of it, but that's what I did." [65]

Deaver's behavior, within the White House and with the media, gave him a reputation for arrogance that undoubtedly contributed to his fall. Many in the White House complained about Deaver's high-handedness, and some of these complainers apparently became sources for the unfavorable stories about Deaver after he left the White House. These stories and Deaver's greed and determination to build a big-time lobbying business while Reagan was still in office led to a congressional inquiry into his lobbying activities, the appointment of an independent counsel to investigate charges of influence peddling and Deaver's eventual conviction on perjury charges. In my own dealings with Deaver near the end of his White House service I sometimes found him furtive and troubled, and wondered if he was ill. But I had no clue as to the toll being taken by the first lady's obsession with astrology and Deaver's alcoholism. Like others who had known him as a calmer, happier Mike Deaver in Sacramento, I ascribed his behavior to the poison of White House power and thought his position had gone to his head. Three years after Bitburg, Deaver told me that the difficulty of the deception in which he was engaged had imposed an inner strain that "I probably don't even know about yet."[66] Since then, with much help from his faith, his wife and Alcoholics Anonymous, Deaver has courageously struggled to repair his damaged life. But he was close to cracking at the time of Bitburg.

Deaver had been able to bear the strain in the first term in part because Jim Baker was in on the secret of Nancy Reagan and her astrologer. When his conduct seemed capricious, he knew that Baker would sympathize with him and defend him, as he always did. Baker was grateful to Deaver for sparing him the necessity of dealing with Nancy Reagan. But Deaver had no one in the White House with whom to share his burden in early 1985 except Sittmann, who quit the White House in April before the Bitburg trip. Because of her anguish over Bitburg, Nancy Reagan was even more frantic than usual, and she demanded a series of wrenching, last-minute schedule changes at Quigley's instigation.

First, Nancy Reagan saw to it that the Bitburg ceremony was moved from the morning (German time) to the afternoon. Then, when Deaver informed her of the departure time from Bonn to Bergen-Belsen, she told him to delay the flight by twenty minutes because Quigley thought the scheduled time was a "dangerous" one for Reagan to be airborne. Deaver called Henkel in Bonn and told him to change the time. Henkel asked why, and Deaver told him just to change it. Henkel did. Then Nancy called again, telling Deaver it was necessary to delay the arrival time at Bergen-Belsen by another twenty-five minutes. Deaver told her that she would be inconveniencing about six hundred people. "I'm talking about my husband's life," she said. Deaver once more called Henkel, who was himself becoming crazed by the unexplained last-minute changes, all of which required a complex overhaul in security procedures and clearance with the Germans. Finally, on the final advance trip to Bitburg, Deaver could stand it no more and confided to Henkel the reasons for his seemingly inexplicable instructions. Henkel, who had never understood the reasons for the many changes and had himself been burdened by them, was sympathetic. "Why didn't you tell me?" he said. When Nancy Reagan ordered still another schedule change, Deaver and Henkel conspired to tell her that they had made it, without actually altering the schedule. This was a subterfuge Deaver had used before on minor matters, because Nancy Reagan did not always notice whether the final schedule actually conformed to Quigley's charts. But going through such pretenses was always a burden to Deaver, because there was always a possibility that Nancy Reagan might learn what he had done. "It was a nightmare," he told me.[67]

I have earlier described how Reagan alleviated the ignominy of Bitburg with a moving delivery at Bergen-Belsen of a sensitive speech written for him by Ken Khachigian at Nancy Reagan's bequest. It was a striking example, of which there have been many in Reagan's life, where he was rescued from poor judgment by a successful performance. And Reagan's discomfort was also eased by the participation of ninety-year-old General Matthew Ridgway, who had led the U.S. 82nd Airborne Division in the war against Nazi Germany and who volunteered to lay the wreath with Reagan at the Bitburg cemetery. While Ridgway's participation did not dim the criticism of the president's action, it made the ceremony easier for Reagan to endure.

The Bitburg controversy nonetheless left scars that did not heal. Reagan would never again fully recapture the moral high ground he had sacrificed at Bitburg. Even after the event had become a distant memory, he did not regain the trust within the Jewish community that he had taken for granted in the earlier years of his political career and the first four years of his presidency. Nor was Reagan the only one to bear the scars. Deaver's reputation as master orchestrator was deeply tarnished, and Don Regan had shown himself lacking in the skills of political damage control that had distinguished his predecessor. The relationship of Regan and Rollins was ruined, and Rollins left the White House within a few months. Though Nancy Reagan's original opposition to Bitburg was commendable and her decision to bring in Khachigian to write the Bergen-Belsen speech sound, her irrationality about the scheduling demonstrated to Henkel (and to Regan, when he was told about Quigley's role by Deaver before he left the White House) that the first lady was a force to be avoided rather than consulted.

In any case, Bitburg was more than a logistical disaster arising from Deaver's failure to determine what lay beneath the snow in the cemetery. Basically, the decision to hold the ceremony at all demonstrated a failure of historical understanding by Reagan and Kohl that was compounded by the political selfishness of the West German chancellor and the stubbornness of the American president. On the day after the Bitburg visit was announced, *Die Welt* political editor Christoph Bertram, who was seven years old when the Third Reich collapsed, observed that Germany had been able to become a member of the community of civilized nations after the war not by denying but by accepting its Nazi past:

> The Reagan-Kohl idea of a historic harmony is, therefore, an insult not only to those who suffered and died in the camps. By originally envisioning no more than a visit by the president and the chancellor to the military cemetery of Bitburg, the White House and the chancellery have suggested that May 8, 1945, was just one more of those dates—of which there are so many in European history—when the successes of victors and vanquished commemorate past victories and defeats in that well-known ritual [of] politicians depositing wreaths on the tomb of the unknown soldier, a guard of honor marching slowly up and down to the sounds of patriotic music, the flags flying half-mast. But the mere idea that this could be the way Reagan and Kohl would act . . . demonstrates the shallowness of the original plans. World War II was not just another European war. It was the darkest hour of European civilization. Its end brought to an end the world's most atrocious regime and the world's hitherto most dangerous conflict. It also laid the basis for a democratic West Germany and a united West.

Reagan did not recognize this. He was a master of symbolism, but he did not recognize what it was that May 8, 1945, symbolized. Both he and Kohl, as Bertram said, "simply failed to recognize the significance of the anniversary."[68]

This failure of historical understanding would be fateful for Reagan in his second term. Within two months of Bitburg, Reagan would authorize the first stages of a backdoor deal with Iran that would demonstrate in even greater measure the qualities of inadequate historical understanding, political naïveté and awesome presidential stubbornness that had characterized the Bitburg affair. Bitburg was a catastrophe in its own right. It was also the prelude to the greater catastrophe of the Iran-contra scandal.

19

DARKNESS AT NOON

I agreed to sell TOWs to Iran.

RONALD REAGAN, diary entry,
January 17, 1986[1]

The Bitburg controversy was barely behind Reagan when he plunged into the clandestine foreign policy initiative that would overshadow much of his second term and tarnish the credibility he had nurtured and preserved as actor and politician. Operating first in cooperation with the Israelis and then through a covert U.S. initiative managed by Oliver North, the Reagan administration from the late summer of 1985 to mid-autumn of 1986 supplied antitank and antiaircraft weapons to Iran in violation of its proclaimed policy of withholding weapons from nations that sponsored terrorism and of a specific embargo on arms sales to Iran. Reagan sought by his actions to use Iran's influence to free U.S. hostages in Lebanon, the scene of the most costly foreign policy calamity of his first term. The Iranians were overcharged for the weapons they received, and some of the proceeds from the arms sales were diverted to rebel forces in Nicaragua—the contras, or "freedom fighters," as Reagan called them—in defiance of congressional restrictions specifically designed to prevent such assistance. In combination, the Iran initiative and the diversion of funds to the Nicaraguan rebels became known as "the Iran-contra affair." It is to an examination of these events in the Reagan presidency that this chapter and the next are devoted.

Any contemporary historian must apply certain caveats to an account of the Iran-contra affair. Vital questions remain unresolved, among them the issue of whether Reagan gave approval of the diversion of Iran arms-sales proceeds to the contras. Reagan has consistently denied knowledge of the diversion—a denial he repeated to me for this book and in his memoirs. But such denials can hardly be regarded as conclusive, even by those who believe Reagan is telling the truth as he remembers it. As has often been observed in these pages, Reagan long ago learned to accept as the truth whatever version of events he used to explain things. This habit served him well politically but has proved a barrier to historical reconstruction. Reagan's memory of several key events relating to the arms sales is exceptionally faulty, as he has acknowledged in sworn testimony, public statements and various interviews.

John Poindexter, the fourth of Reagan's six national security advisers, testified before the congressional committees that investigated the Iran-contra affair that he withheld knowledge of the diversion from the president, saying that "the buck stops here with me."[2] But Poindexter's credibility is questionable: he participated with North and McFarlane in constructing a false chronology of Iran-contra events, and he provided much of the information for Reagan's misleading speech to the American people about the Iran initiative on November 13, 1986. Well before he helped construct a false chronology for this speech, Poindexter had demonstrated a willingness to lie whenever he believed such conduct to be in the national interest. As described in Chapter 15, he had also instructed the White House press office to issue a false chronology about the decision-making process of withdrawing U.S. Marines from Lebanon. He had also lied to Larry Speakes, saying in response to a question from the White House spokesman that a report of the imminent invasion of Grenada was "preposterous." Speakes had unwittingly repeated this lie to CBS reporter Bill Plante a few hours before the invasion, at a time when reports of the intended U.S. action were being broadcast throughout the Caribbean by Cuban radio.[3]

Admiral Poindexter believed in protecting the president, and he had the courage of his convictions. Loyalty was widely preached and rarely practiced in the Reagan administration, but Poindexter was consistently loyal to his duty as he saw it. He did not see his duty as requiring him to tell the truth to Congress, the American people or the media, but there was no doubt of his readiness to risk a prison term to protect his former commander in chief—as indeed he did. Poindexter did not testify at his own trial, which ended with his conviction on five felony counts of conspiracy, obstruction of Congress and lying to Congress. He has kept his silence while his conviction is under appeal.

Oliver North has been anything but silent, but his credibility is even more suspect than Poindexter's. Much time was spent by the congressional committees trying to unravel the lies that North had told to Congress, his colleagues and the press. North was convicted on three felony counts of obstructing Congress, destroying documents and accepting an illegal gratuity. The conviction for destroying documents was later reversed because an appellate court determined that the trial judge had erred in his instructions to the jury on the law. The other two convictions were at least temporarily set aside, pending a review of whether jurors had been influenced by North's prior congressional testimony.

North was acquitted of nine other felony charges, including a charge of lying to Congress, apparently because the jury accepted his explanation that he was carrying out a policy he believed to be presidentially approved. In testifying reluctantly as a prosecution witness in Poindexter's trial, North contradicted elements of his congressional testimony. It is difficult in examining the record to know when North was telling the truth and when he was not. In any case, White House records show that he was never alone with Reagan and that there were at least three other persons present on each of the thirty-seven occasions when North and Reagan met. North and Poindexter declined to testify before the Tower Board, which conducted a commendable investigation but lacked subpoena power. Neither the congressional committees that investigated the Iran-contra affair nor independent counsel Lawrence E. Walsh reached a conclusion as to whether Reagan knew about the diversion.*

---

* The "Tower Board," formally the President's Special Review Board and sometimes called the "Tower Commission," was appointed by Reagan on December 1, 1986, to review the Iran arms sales and examine the role of the National Security Council staff. The board was chaired by former Senator John Tower. Its other members were former Secretary of State Edmund Muskie and former (and future) national security adviser Brent Scowcroft. It issued its report on February 26, 1987. The congressional committees consisted of the House Select Committee to Investigate Covert Arms Transactions with Iran and the Senate Select Committee on Secret Military Assistance to Iran and the Nicaraguan Opposition. The two committees held forty days of joint public hearings, reviewed more than 300,000 documents and examined more than 500 witnesses before issuing their report on November 13, 1987. Walsh was appointed on December 19, 1986, and has yet (as of January 1991) to issue a final report. Eight defendants, including North and Poindexter, were convicted or pleaded guilty to various charges arising from Walsh's investigation of the Iran-contra affair.

Historians of the Iran-contra affair may find the documentary evidence as inconclusive as the contradictory statements of the participants, particularly on the subject of the diversion. Although some 14,000 documents have been made public, North destroyed hundreds of other documents in his celebrated "shredding party" after the arms sale was disclosed. Whether any of these documents specifically implicated Reagan is unknown. Nor is it known what might be revealed about Reagan (or President Bush) in the thousands of documents that are inaccessible to historians or the American public because of classification, ostensibly for purposes of national security. Even if these documents eventually become public, they may not resolve the question of what Reagan knew and when he knew it—or of what he knew and no longer remembers. Documents rarely tell the full story of Reagan administration decisions even on matters of lesser controversy, and members of the Tower Board were dismayed by the absence of note-taking or the sketchiness of notes at important meetings relating to the Iran arms sale.[4]

Many questions also remain unanswered about the role of CIA Director William Casey, who died of a brain tumor on May 6, 1987. Casey, who believed strongly that presidents needed to be able to deny knowledge of controversial actions relating to national security, was often reluctant to express himself in large meetings for this reason and preferred to do his business with Reagan on the telephone. Many of the former officials whom I have interviewed about the Iran-contra affair are of the opinion that Casey took secrets about the Iran-contra affair with him to his grave. Others contend, however, that Casey's incapacitation by a brain tumor soon after the scandal was revealed made him a convenient scapegoat for actions that may have been conducted with full knowledge of the president.

If there is much that remains a mystery about the Iran-contra affair, there is also much that is known. That Reagan approved the Iran arms sales is not a matter of dispute. Nor is it disputed that Reagan and other White House officials deliberately concealed knowledge of these sales from Congress, keeping them secret until American hostage David Jacobsen was released on November 2, 1986, and a Lebanese magazine, Al-Shiraa, the next day disclosed the U.S. arms sales and the information that McFarlane had visited Tehran. The initiative provided Iran, then in the midst of a prolonged and bloody war with Iraq, with 2,004 TOW antitank missiles and more than 200 spare parts for ground-launched HAWK antiaircraft missiles. It produced the release of three

American hostages, who were promptly replaced by the kidnapping of three other Americans. The Iran arms sales were channeled through The Enterprise, the covert network of dummy corporations, Swiss bank accounts, aircraft and other resources operated by Richard Secord and Albert Hakim. The Enterprise generated nearly $48 million from sales of the arms and from contributions from private citizens and third countries. It spent nearly $35.8 million on covert operations. At least $3.8 million of the income generated by the arms sales was diverted to the contras, less than the $4.4 million that Secord, Hakim and their associate Thomas Clines kept for themselves in "commissions." The balance of the unspent funds remained in Swiss bank accounts when The Enterprise ceased operations after the November 1986 disclosures.[5]

The complex tapestry of the Iran-contra affair is composed of seven distinct and identifiable strands. The first strand is the diminished sense of political accountability that prevailed after Reagan's landslide reelection gave him a second term at the age of seventy-four (as of February 6, 1985) and made him constitutionally ineligible to succeed himself. The second strand was Reagan's frustration at his inability to mount an effective response to terrorist activities or to rescue Americans held hostage in Lebanon. The third strand was the view of CIA officials and members of the NSC staff that Iran was strategically important and vulnerable to Soviet influence. The fourth was the strategic concern of Israel, which wanted to prevent its old enemy Iraq from winning the Iran-Iraq war. The fifth was the contras, whom Reagan had instructed McFarlane to keep together "body and soul" after Congress withheld military aid to the rebels. The sixth was the opportunity for profit that the initiative presented to arms dealers, including the directors of The Enterprise.

The seventh and connecting strand was the severely reduced political competence of the White House staff. The Iran initiative would have been inconceivable during the first term, when the president was surrounded by politicians who guarded his public approval ratings and by former Californians accustomed to protecting Reagan from himself. But Reagan had almost casually cut himself off from the political moorings that had prevented him from drifting astray during his first four years in office. Gone were Baker, Deaver and Darman, the trio of pragmatists associated with most of his political successes. Gone were Clark and Meese, the two conservatives most loyal to Reagan and most aware of the dangers of allowing him to indulge his predilections. The pragmatists and probably Meese would have recognized the political risk of selling weapons to Iran, knowing Reagan would be likely to forfeit his precious public credibility if he broke his promise and bargained with kidnappers. Clark was highly suspicious of the Israelis and, like Weinberger, tilted to Iraq in the Iran-Iraq conflict. As far as the Iran initiative was concerned, this group had been replaced by Regan, the one-man band as chief of staff, and McFarlane. Both were well intentioned but notably lacking in political judgment. McFarlane, who was close to the Israelis and had long favored a strategic opening to Iran, proposed the arms initiative. Regan, who indulged Reagan rather than protecting him, became its cheerleader. No one thought to warn Reagan, as Stu Spencer believed Baker or Deaver would have done, "Look, we can't do this. Look what we did to Carter on this issue."[6] Spencer and such White House officials as Rollins and his successor, Mitchell Daniels, or even Patrick Buchanan would certainly have seen the political danger, but they were not privy to the initiative. Neither was Nancy Reagan. The evidence that the first lady did not know about the Iran initiative until after the fact, beyond her own statement, is that she did not discuss the issue with Spencer or Deaver, with whom she maintained close relations after he left the White House, or with her astrologer Quigley.

Reagan's own political instincts were dulled by the magnitude of his reelection victory, his isolation in the White House and his concern for the American hostages. But he often responded to good political advice when he was given it, even while claiming that he was not a politician. In dealing with the Iran affair he was bereft of political advisers. George Shultz and Caspar Weinberger did oppose the initiative on policy grounds, and they periodically allowed themselves to be convinced that they had halted it. But they never worked together to stop it, and they lacked the daily access to Reagan enjoyed by Regan and McFarlane. Despite the president's alleged commitment to cabinet government, the Reagan administration was White House–centered. What happened in Reagan's little world within the White House was usually decisive.

Understanding what happened in that White House world in 1985 requires a brief examination of the contentious and ultimately destructive relationship between Regan and McFarlane. At the time Baker and Regan engineered their job swap, McFarlane seemed secure in his role as national security adviser. During the 1984 election year the pragmatists had learned to count on McFarlane as an ally, even though he was considerably more bullish than they were on the prospects of the contras. Nicaragua aside, McFarlane had won the plaudits of the White House staff and the first lady for the importance he attached to improving U.S.-Soviet relations. He had proven helpful, despite his earlier advocacy of an expanded U.S. military role in Lebanon, in the effort to defuse Lebanon as a campaign issue by pulling out the Marines. The pragmatists believed that McFarlane shared their appreciation of the role of Congress and also valued his willingness to stand up to Weinberger, whom the pragmatists found stubborn and unyielding. When Baker left for Treasury, he believed that the national security adviser's post was in good hands.

McFarlane, the son of a three-term New Deal congressman from Texas, was short in stature and shy in demeanor, if not in ambition. To his friend Robert Timberg, a fellow Annapolis graduate and Vietnam veteran who was the White House correspondent for the Baltimore *Sun* during most of the Reagan years, McFarlane resembled "the real-life counterpart of the fictional Victor (Pug) Henry, the naval officer in Herman Wouk's *Winds of War* . . . who just happens to show up for every pivotal event of World War II." [7] McFarlane served almost uninterruptedly in increasingly influential White House positions in the Nixon and Ford administrations from 1971 to 1977, a pivotal period that included the U.S. opening to China, Nixon's resignation, the October 1973 Mideast War and the withdrawal of U.S. forces from Vietnam after the fall of Saigon. Vietnam had been McFarlane's war. On March 8, 1965, he went ashore at Danang in command of an artillery battery with the first Marine combat unit to serve in Vietnam. He volunteered for a second Vietnam tour of duty in 1967, saying subsequently that he was motivated by a strong attachment to the Vietnamese people. "As a Marine in the country, the palpable support from the people was very clear," McFarlane said. "I felt they needed me." [8] McFarlane's combination of military credentials and the master's degree he received in international relations between his two combat tours commended him to Henry Kissinger, who made him his military assistant in the final years of the Nixon administration. After Kissinger left the White House, McFarlane stayed on as executive assistant to Brent Scowcroft, President Ford's national security adviser. He retired from the Marines in 1979 and took refuge on Capitol Hill during the Carter years, working for Senator John Tower on the staff of the Senate Armed Services Committee.

Outwardly, McFarlane was self-effacing, disciplined and deferential. After Bill Clark brought him to the White House as his deputy in 1982, one of the pragmatists described McFarlane as "the perfect No. 2 man —or maybe No. 2 and one-half."[9] This remained the prevailing view long after McFarlane had replaced Clark. In 1985 New Right activist Paul Weyrich said that McFarlane "was created by God to disappear into crowds," and Timberg wrote that McFarlane had accumulated White House influence "under a cover of dullness."[10] But many of those who dealt frequently with McFarlane found him confusing rather than dull. While he could at times be impressively analytical, McFarlane was overly fond of big words and backward sentences. Since he usually spoke in a low monotone, Reagan found it difficult either to hear him or to follow his train of thought. In this last respect, Reagan was not alone. "Whatever the policy was, whether it was arms or locomotives for the Sudan, [McFarlane] was very monotone, he was sort of round-about and curvy," said a Pentagon official who often dealt with him. "It took a while to get to the point. And you weren't quite sure where you were on the journey at any one time and you weren't quite sure when you got to the end ... I found it personally very difficult to follow."[11]

McFarlane himself promoted a self-effacing image, frequently relating the story of how a television producer once told him he had "the most boring face" she had ever seen. But his placid exterior and self-deprecating manner concealed turbulent and complex emotions, a sensitive nature and a desire for accomplishment. His friends valued his mordant wit (he once suggested that White House publicists who wanted to label the MX missile the "Peacemaker" could more accurately call it the "Widowmaker") and his ability to deliver a near-perfect imitation of Henry Kissinger. His enemies, especially Weinberger, came to believe that the Iran initiative was inspired by McFarlane's emulation of Kissinger's 1971 China initiative. This analogy had occurred to McFarlane, although not to him alone. Regan told me that he also found the China comparison appealing and said that Poindexter did as well. In considering the risks of the operation, said Regan, "the answer that we gave ourselves, right or wrong ... [was] if we're successful in this endeavor, it'll be the equivalent of Kissinger in China."[12] Richard Nixon, whose counsel was so valued by Reagan, may have held similar views. According to William Safire, Nixon after the Iran-contra disclosures wrote a long letter to *The Wall Street Journal* under the pseudonym of his assistant, John H. Taylor, in which he empathized with Reagan. "If the Iran initiative had freed all the hostages, toppled Khomeini, or both, we would today be reading about President Reagan's farsighted willingness to buck the anti-Iran political tide," Nixon wrote. "Instead, the initiative failed, and the President is expected to have anticipated the failure and therefore never made the try." [13]

McFarlane was coming into his own as national security adviser when Regan arrived on the White House scene, but he was finding the journey difficult. While his influence had grown steadily throughout 1984, he felt he lacked standing in the Reagan inner circle and sufficient rapport with the president. As McFarlane saw it, Reagan admired and listened only to wealthy, successful, self-made men such as Shultz, Weinberger and Regan. While there was merit to the observation, McFarlane made too much of it. When he raised the point with me over a drink, I observed that Mike Deaver and Ed Meese, neither of them rich, had managed to become highly influential in staff roles. McFarlane, who was disconcerted on the occasion of our meeting because the president had that day forgotten his name during an arms control discussion, despaired of ever having similar influence. Behind his disciplined façade, McFarlane was remarkably lacking in self-confidence for a man of his credentials.

Along with almost everyone else who had served in the Reagan White House, McFarlane also showed the scars of the feuding and infighting that were a constant feature of the Reagan administration. While skilled at bureaucratic management, he lacked the authority or the temperament to referee the interminable quarrels between Shultz and Weinberger. McFarlane's relations with Weinberger had been strained by their policy disagreement over Lebanon and McFarlane's support of congressional demands for an outside commission to investigate Pentagon mismanagement. (Reagan, despite Weinberger's opposition, on June 17, 1985, named David Packard to head such a body.) The secretary of defense also missed working with Bill Clark, whom he had known and liked during Governor Reagan's administration in Sacramento. Weinberger made no effort to conceal his low opinion of McFarlane, and the national security adviser reciprocated.

After the 1984 election, George Shultz had told Reagan at one of their weekly meetings in the White House that he might do better in the second term by choosing between him and Weinberger, since they both held strong and often conflicting views. Reagan put Shultz off, saying he wanted to think about it. McFarlane was present at the meeting. A few weeks later, when he was alone with Reagan on Air Force One returning from California to Washington for the inauguration, McFarlane pressed the president to make a decision. The national security adviser said that the constant disagreements between Shultz and Weinberger were producing a "paralysis" in foreign policy. By his own account, McFarlane went so far as to suggest that Reagan should fire Weinberger, although he phrased his recommendation more neutrally. "I don't speak for George, but he feels you would be better off building your team around Cap alone with George gone or George with Cap gone, but that it can't go on as it is and expect to get anything done," McFarlane said.[14] Reagan said he was aware of the disagreements but didn't want to lose either Shultz or Weinberger. "Make it work," he said.[15]

Even if Reagan had changed defense secretaries, McFarlane would have found the going difficult once Don Regan replaced Baker at the White House. Baker, intuitively aware of McFarlane's emotional frailties, had cultivated him as an ally and treated him with respect. Regan tried to crush him, and McFarlane gave him an opportunity when he awakened the president about 6:00 A.M. on March 25 to tell him that Army Major Arthur D. Nicholson had been shot and killed by a Soviet guard the night before while on a reconnaissance mission in East Germany. Regan did not learn about the incident until the morning staff meeting, and he was furious that he had not been told. Angrily dressing down the national security adviser, Regan told him never to call Reagan again without telling him first. McFarlane, equally angry, stood his ground. If Regan didn't like the way he was doing his job, McFarlane told him, he would quit. Then he walked out of Regan's office. Regan had then been chief of staff for less than two months, and he realized he couldn't afford a McFarlane resignation so early in his tenure. He telephoned McFarlane and apologized.

McFarlane stayed for the time being, but he and Regan coexisted uneasily. Their edgy relationship was damaging to the president, who was always better served when his chief of staff and national security adviser could compensate for his own lack of operational involvement by working together. Baker and McFarlane had shared the burden in 1984, and even smoother working relationships would be achieved by Howard Baker and Frank Carlucci in 1987 and by Kenneth Duberstein and Colin Powell in 1988. But in the critical year of 1985, when the Iran initiative was conceived and put in motion, Regan and McFarlane were barely speaking. McFarlane considered Regan a meddler who knew next to nothing about foreign affairs. Regan, who thought of himself as the White House CEO, resented McFarlane's independence and secretiveness. Neither man ever trusted the other.

McFarlane was thinking boldly in 1985, but his thoughts were inspired by the illusions of the Cold War. He longed for the days when Iran, under the rule of Shah Mohammed Reza Pahlavi, had been a bulwark for U.S. interests in the Middle East. "Iran, because of the great leadership of the Shah, is an island of stability in one of the most troubled areas of the world," President Carter had declared during a 1977 trip to Tehran.[16] That island of stability had been overrun in February 1979 when the Ayatollah Ruhollah Khomeini led an Islamic fundamentalist revolution that ousted the shah. After Iranian militants seized the U.S. embassy in Tehran on November 14, 1979, and took sixty-six Americans hostage, the Carter administration suspended all arms shipments to Iran as part of a general embargo. The embargo remained in effect after the hostages were freed 444 days later at the onset of the Reagan administration.[17] American resentment at the televised scenes of Iranians burning the American flag, taunting the hostages and yelling "Death to the United States" also lingered. (Richard Wirthlin's polls, he told me, showed that Khomeini was as unpopular with Americans as Adolf Hitler.) But McFarlane looked upon Iran as a prize for which the United States and the Soviets were competing. As early as 1981, while he was still Al Haig's deputy at State, McFarlane was advocating reevaluation of U.S. policy toward Iran. He sent a memo to Haig advocating an exploration of ways to end the U.S.-Iran confrontation and "deny the region to the Soviet Union."[18] A version of the memo made its way to the White House, where it then aroused no interest.

Despite the U.S. arms embargo, Iran at first had an adequate supply of weapons with which to fight the war imposed on it by less populous Iraq. The Reagan administration counted forty-one countries that at one time or another had supplied weapons or spare parts to the Khomeini regime. Recovering from early reversals in the war, Iran took the offensive against Iraq. By the spring of 1983 Shultz and Weinberger were worried that a protracted war or an Iranian victory would disrupt the flow of Persian Gulf oil. With the State Department taking the lead, the United States on December 14, 1983, launched Operation Staunch, urging all nations engaged in the arms trade to "stop transferring arms to Iran because of the broader interests of the international community in achieving a negotiated end to the Iran-Iraq war." Operation Staunch was a boon to Iraq, which received a plentiful supply of Soviet weapons. Weinberger particularly welcomed this tilt to Iraq, saying in his memoirs, *Fighting for Peace,* that "the Iranian outrages against our people, beginning in 1979, made it difficult for me to remain neutral in any conflict to which Iran was a party." [19] One of these outrages was the October 23, 1983, bombing of the Marine barracks in Lebanon, supposedly by a radical Shiite group with links to Iran and its ally Syria. McFarlane, then newly installed as Reagan's national security adviser, continued to believe that U.S. strategic interests required a rapprochement with Iran. When I talked to McFarlane in Japan during Reagan's visit there three weeks after the bombing in Lebanon, he told me that the United States would eventually find it worthwhile to improve U.S.-Iran relations.

Instead, the Reagan administration moved in the other direction. On January 13, 1984, Geoffrey Kemp, NSC director for Near East and South Asian affairs, sent McFarlane a memo describing the Khomeini government as a menace and calling for resumption of covert activity against it. On January 20, Shultz designated Iran as a sponsor of international terrorism. Three days later the United States imposed additional export controls on Iran. By the summer of 1984, the losses inflicted by the war and the pressure imposed by Operation Staunch had made Iran desperate for weapons. The CIA was being deluged with requests "from Iranians and Iranian exiles [offering] to provide us with very fancy intelligence, very important internal political insights, if we in return can arrange for the sale of a dozen Bell helicopter gunships or 1,000 TOW missiles or something else that is on the contraband list." [20] On August 21, 1984, McFarlane requested an interagency study of U.S. relations with Iran in anticipation of the death of Khomeini. This study, completed in October, concluded that the United States would be unable to influence significantly the outcome of events in Iran even after Khomeini was no longer on the scene.

McFarlane nonetheless continued to pursue a U.S. modus vivendi with Iran. His single-mindedness in this regard would make him vulnerable to the accusations of his adversaries, especially Weinberger, who charged in his memoirs that McFarlane and others on the NSC staff pursued "their own agenda" and promoted the idea "that the Soviets—but not the United States—could take advantage of any chaos that might develop in Iran." [21] But it is one of the functions of the NSC staff to explore alternatives, and there were many agendas at the NSC. While McFarlane and other members of the NSC staff—principally Howard Teicher and to a lesser extent the late Donald Fortier—indeed favored an Iran initiative, they were hardly the exclusive villains of the Iran initiative that Weinberger made them out to be. The Iran initiative had a more powerful friend in the Reagan court than any NSC aide. William Casey, who carried far more weight with Reagan than Mc-Farlane did, was also pushing hard for a change in U.S. policy in dealing with Iran.

Casey had multiple motivations. He desperately wanted to recover William Buckley, the CIA station chief in Beirut who had been kidnapped on March 16, 1984, by terrorists with links to Iran. Buckley would later die in captivity of medical neglect, but the fear for long after his capture was that he was being tortured to reveal vital secrets, including names of CIA agents in the region. Even more than Mc-Farlane, Casey was consumed by a Cold War vision and longed for the glory days of the U.S.-Iran relationship that had existed under the shah. As a student of history, the CIA director was well informed of the agency's role in toppling the Iranian nationalist Muhammad Mossadegh in 1953 and insuring the supremacy of the shah and U.S. influence in the region. Casey wanted to revive that influence. He believed that the "twin pillars" of U.S. policy toward Iran often cited by Shultz—denying arms to Iran and warning that the United States would respond to Iranian-sponsored terrorist attacks—had outlived their usefulness. On May 17, 1985, he was buttressed in this belief by a memo from Graham Fuller, the CIA intelligence officer for the Near East and South Asia, that took a dim view of existing U.S. policy toward Iran. The five-page memo, titled "Toward a Policy on Iran," warned:

> The US faces a grim situation in developing a new policy toward Iran. Events are moving largely against our interests and we have few palatable alternatives. In bluntest form, the Khomeini regime is faltering and may be moving toward a moment of truth; we will soon see a struggle for succession. The US has almost no cards to play; the USSR has many. Iran has obviously concluded that whether they like Russia and Communism or not, the USSR is the country to come to terms with: the USSR can both hurt and help Iran more than the US can. Our urgent need is to develop a broad spectrum of policy moves designed to give us some leverage in the race for influence in Tehran.

Fuller, while frankly acknowledging that "nobody has any brilliant ideas about how to get us back into Tehran," then proceeded to analyze various proposals to accomplish this objective. He concluded that the best course would be to "have friendly states sell arms that would not affect the strategic balance as a means of showing Tehran that it had alternatives to the Soviet Union." Three days later this idea received Casey's imprimatur in a Special National Intelligence Estimate [SNIE], drafted by Fuller with input from Fortier, which reiterated that the United States could do little to directly influence Iran and added that "European states and other friendly states—including Turkey, Pakistan, China, Japan and even Israel—can provide the next most valuable presence or entree to Iran to help protect Western interests. The degree to which some of these states can fill a military gap for Iran will be a critical measure of the West's ability to blunt Soviet influence."[22]

Fuller had not been preparing his analyses in a vacuum. According to Bob Woodward in Veil, Casey had been urging Fuller for months to come up with ideas for getting the United States back in Iran.[23] And the NSC staff was prodding Fuller as well. A formal request for the SNIE on Iran had been made by McFarlane through Fortier as a result of missions to Europe and Israel by Michael Ledeen, a pro-Israeli historian and former assistant to Haig with connections in the Israeli government. Armed with a letter from Poindexter declaring that he had "the complete confidence of Bud McFarlane and myself," Ledeen traveled to Europe in March 1985.[24] As Ledeen subsequently related it, he met with a high intelligence officer from a European country who told him that "the situation there [in Iran] was more fluid"[25] and that the United States could play a significant role there. Ledeen said the official suggested that the United States talk to the Israelis about it.

When Ledeen related this to McFarlane and proposed going to Israel, even normally pro-Israeli members of the NSC staff were suspicious. Fortier and Teicher advised against using Ledeen, with his known sympathy for the Israelis, as "the primary channel for working the Iran issue with foreign governments." McFarlane ignored this advice. He sent Ledeen to Israel, where he met on May 3 with Prime Minister Shimon Peres and Israeli defense officials. According to Ledeen's account of these meetings, the Israelis were eager to cooperate with the United States in developing a new policy toward Iran and also wanted to supply artillery shells to Iran, if the United States approved. While Ledeen maintained that there was no discussion of the Americans held hostage in Lebanon, an Israeli official subsequently recalled that Ledeen had told him about "offers by various Iranians to help get the hostages released."[26] Ledeen reported his version of the meetings to Fortier, then working with Fuller in preparing the new intelligence estimate on Iran. The outline for an arms-for-hostages deal was taking form.

Ledeen's mission had tied together U.S. and Israeli strategic strands in a way that suggested a mutual interest of the two nations in dealing with Iran. In fact, the interests of the United States and Israel profoundly diverged. U.S. strategic interests, as Shultz recognized in proclaiming Operation Staunch, were to keep the Iran-Iraq war from widening and to insure a continued free flow of oil to the West and Japan from the Persian Gulf. This view, also supported by Weinberger and proclaimed by the president, was official U.S. policy. McFarlane and Casey were trying to supplant it with their unlikely Cold War vision of a world in which fundamentalist Iran would once more become a U.S. strategic barrier against Soviet influence in the region. But Israel, surrounded by a sea of hostile Arab powers, was driven by overriding strategic interests in accommodating Iran, the leading non-Arab power in the region other than Israel itself. These interests transcended Israeli internal differences as well as Iran's transformation into a fundamentalist Muslim state under Khomeini. The Israelis operated on the principle that the enemy of their enemies was their friend. They could accept an Iraq-Iran war that bled both nations, but they understandably feared a victory by Iraq, which had been Israel's enemy in two wars. Israel and Iran had cooperated on defense matters throughout the shah's regime, and Israel's basic strategic view had remained unchanged after the shah's fall despite fervent hostility to Israel.

The Israelis were also concerned with the plight of some 80,000 Iranian Jews, whose safety and freedom to emigrate depended on maintaining a business relationship with Iran. As a result of these multiple concerns, Israel had continued supplying weapons to Iran after Khomeini came to power, although shipments were halted at the objection of the Carter administration after the U.S. embassy was overrun. Some arms shipments resumed after the hostages were released. As Ledeen observed, "Arms have long been the lubricant for good relations between countries" in the Middle East,[27] and the Israelis had need for a lot of lubrication. Sending weapons to Iran made strategic sense for Israel, even if such action was contrary to the interests of the United States.

Ledeen's report and the new CIA intelligence estimate gave McFarlane the opportunity to draft a proposed National Security Decision Directive on June 17, 1985, that would have reversed U.S. policy expressed by Operation Staunch by encouraging other nations to supply arms to Iran. An NSDD is a presidential policy directive. In most administrations such documents, at least on major issues, are the product of intense debate among interested departments and agencies and of discussion with the president. But because Reagan preferred to receive consensus recommendations, most of the discussion about such directives in his presidency was carried on among his cabinet secretaries and national security adviser. As a result, what Reagan often received was a predigested compromise on which there had been little discussion of the issues in his presence. On McFarlane's draft NSDD on Iran, no such compromise was possible. The key passage of McFarlane's proposal called for encouraging "western allies and friends to help Iran meet its important requirements so as to reduce the attractiveness of Soviet assistance and trade offers, while demonstrating the value of correct relations with the West. This includes provision of selected military equipment as determined on a case-by-case basis."

Casey promptly endorsed the draft NSDD, which sent Shultz and Weinberger and their respective bureaucracies into orbit. A memo written to the secretary of state by Peter Rodman, then of Shultz's planning and policy review staff and later a staff member at NSC, argued against the idea and also took issue with the "China analogy" so often used by McFarlane as the rationale for pursuing an opening with the Khomeini regime. Rodman, along with others at State, saw an objective difference between the Nixon-Kissinger opening to China, which had been sought by China during a time of wholesale policy change in that nation's relations with the Soviet Union, and the will-o'-the-wisp of a new strategic relationship with militant Iran. "My view was that you don't go chasing after radical regimes," Rodman said. "There may well have been Iranian moderates, but the way to help them was to show that radical policies wouldn't work. I thought it was strategically crazy to make obsequious overtures to Iran."[28] In his response to the draft NSDD, Shultz said that it "appears to exaggerate current anti-regime sentiment and Soviet advantages over us in gaining influence. Most importantly, its proposal that we permit or encourage a flow of Western arms to Iran is contrary to our interest both in containing Khomeinism and in ending the excesses of this regime. We should not alter this aspect of our policy when groups with ties to Iran are holding U.S. hostages in Lebanon."[29]

Weinberger was equally critical of the proposal and more scornfully dismissive of its premises. He scribbled in the margin of the draft NSDD a comment saying that helping the Khomeini regime would be like "asking Qadaffi over for a cozy lunch."[30] Later, Weinberger issued a formal rebuttal in which he said giving U.S. blessing to Iranian arms deliveries "would be seen as inexplicably inconsistent by those nations whom we have urged to refrain from such sales . . ." In keeping with his pro-Arab position and support of Iraq in its war against Iran, Weinberger added, "It would adversely affect our newly emerging relationship with Iraq."[31]

All of this debate took place out of sight and mind of Reagan, who little more than a month after Bitburg had been plunged into one of the gravest crises of his presidency. On the morning of June 14, 1985, TWA Flight 847 took off from Athens, bound for Rome, with 153 passengers and crew aboard, including 135 Americans. Once aloft, the plane was hijacked by two grenade-wielding Arabs, later identified as Mohammed Ali Hamadi and Hassan Ezzendine. The pilot was forced to fly to Beirut, then to Algiers and back to Beirut again, where the hijackers brutally beat and then shot to death U.S. Navy diver Robert Dean Stethem, whose body was dumped onto the tarmac. After refueling, the plane was flown back to Algiers and then back to Beirut again. Most of the passengers were released either in Beirut or Algiers during this terror-filled odyssey, but when TWA 847 returned on June 16 to Beirut a final time, thirty-nine American passengers and crew members were herded off the plane and held captive in Lebanon, most of them under control of Amal Shiite leader Nabih Berri. The hijacking had become a kidnapping that mocked Reagan's vow of taking swift and effective retribution against terrorism.

While the hijackers were certainly ruthless killers, they were not engaged in a mindless act of terrorism. The hijacking was a residue of the war Israel had waged in Lebanon and of the intervention there by U.S. Marines. Its principal purpose was to force Israel to release more than 700 young Shiites taken captive for "security offenses" during the invasion of Lebanon and held in a prison near Haifa in violation of the Fourth Geneva Convention, which prohibits transferring civilians to the territory of an occupying power. The hijackers had struck at the United States rather than Israel because lax security at international airports made Americans vulnerable targets and because the United States was Israel's principal ally. In their rage at the uncomprehending and terrified passengers aboard TWA 847, the hijackers had shouted the words "Marines" and "New Jersey." Their reference was not to the state, as some of the passengers first believed, but to the battleship that had fired 288 shells from its 16-inch guns into Shiite camps, towns and hillsides as the U.S. Marines were withdrawing from Lebanon in February 1984. Since this barrage and earlier shellings by the *New Jersey* were laid down without the aid of forward spotters, they were inevitably inaccurate. Even the U.S. defense attaché in Beirut had described them as "senseless shelling." [32] And there were other senseless acts for which the United States, fairly or not, was also blamed. When the air controller in charge of the Beirut tower rebuked Hamadi for killing Stethem, the hijacker replied, "Did you forget the Bir al Abed massacre?" [33] This was a reference to an attempt, supposedly at the instigation of the CIA, to murder the militant Shiite leader Sheik Mohammad Hussein Fadlallah. An explosives-laden car sent to do the job had exploded near his suburban Beirut home on March 8, 1985, missing Fadlallah but killing 80 people and wounding more than 200 others.

As usual, Reagan spent the weekend following the hijacking at Camp David. His inclinations were to continue his normal schedule, instead of overreacting to the hijackers, and Regan and McFarlane agreed. Reagan's optimism about outcomes led him to take risks with public opinion when approving secret initiatives, such as aid to the contras or the arms-for-hostages deal. But he was politically surefooted in judging public reaction to events that commanded the attention of television. The hijacking was a media spectacular, and Reagan knew how to react when America was watching. Reagan remembered how Jimmy Carter had been manipulated by the takeover of the Tehran embassy, and he was determined to demonstrate that he would not become a long-distance hostage of the hijackers. "[There] was a conscious determination not to cancel a single meeting," Pat Buchanan told me five days after the hijacking,[34] although Reagan later in the crisis with some misgivings postponed a vacation trip to California. Behind the façade of normalcy, however, Reagan found it difficult to conduct business as usual. The killing of Stethem had angered him, and he identified with the plight of the passengers who remained in captivity. When Reagan returned from Camp David on Sunday afternoon, June 16, he went immediately to the Situation Room in the basement, where he emotionally read a letter signed by thirty-two of the hostages from Flight 847 that said, "We implore you not to take any direct military action on our behalf. Please negotiate our immediate release by convincing the Israelis to release the 700 Lebanese prisoners as requested. Now." [35]

This letter put Reagan on the spot. The only choice that promised any prospect of success was negotiation to free the TWA passengers. The U.S. crisis management team had made plans to storm the plane when it was still in Algiers, but no comparable military solution was available once the passengers had been returned to Beirut. Nor did a military solution seem necessary. Israel had already made it known that it was willing to free the Shiite prisoners, if the United States made the request and the American passengers were freed. Both Shultz and McFarlane counseled patience. McFarlane was particularly cheered by the entrance into the scene of Nabih Berri, whom he had known while serving as U.S. special envoy to Lebanon in 1983. In addition to being the leader of Amal, the largest Shiite group, Berri was a lawyer who had lived in the United States. Once he identified himself as chief custodian of thirty-two of the thirty-nine hostages, Berri had a stake in seeing that they were released unharmed. He saw to it that the hostages were clean-shaven and well fed, and he proved adept in displaying the hostages against comfortable backdrops for the benefit of television and in using the hostages' spokesman, a Texas oilman named Allyn Conwell, to make the case for the Shiite cause. While Larry Speakes accurately described the proceedings as "a media circus," Berri's public orchestration of the hostages also created self-induced pressure to free them.

Ultimately, the Americans were released through a combination of diplomatic pressure that included the intervention of Syrian President Hafez Assad, whom Reagan had phoned and written, and unsubtle suggestions from McFarlane to Berri that he would be held personally responsible if they were harmed. When the hostages were finally released on June 30, Assad and Berri received most of the credit. But they had sought and received important help from an unpublicized ally, particularly in freeing seven of the passengers and crew who had been separated from the main body of hostages because they had government passports or Jewish-sounding names. These hostages were held by more militant Shiites who, like the hijackers themselves, were connected to Hezbollah, the fundamentalist group whose ties were to Iran. While the full details remain unknown, the U.S. intelligence community believes that Assad received an assist from Hashemi Rafsanjani, the speaker of the Iranian parliament, who stopped off in Damascus on his way back from an arms-buying trip in Libya and helped Assad to negotiate the freedom of all the American passengers with leaders of the Iranian-sponsored terrorist network in Lebanon. McFarlane told me cryptically afterward that Iran had been of help, and Casey suggested that Reagan send a message of thanks to Rafsanjani, which he did. By emphasizing Rafsanjani's role in their discussions with the president, Casey and McFarlane were also watering the seeds of their intended Iran initiative.

Public approval for Reagan's handling of the crisis soared in the final days of June, when it became evident that the captive TWA passengers were likely to be released. But the result was really a stunning political success for the hijackers, who had drawn world attention to their cause and succeeded in their principal objective of freeing the Shiites held by Israel. Reagan remained frustrated by his inability to deal effectively with terrorism, a policy failure of which there were many reminders.

During the last weeks of June 1985, international terrorists seemed in command of world events. On June 19, Salvadoran guerrillas attacked a sidewalk café frequented by off-duty U.S. servicemen in San Salvador, killing thirteen persons, including four U.S. Marines. The same day, a bomb went off at the airport in Frankfurt, West Germany, killing three people and wounding forty-two. On June 23, an Air India Boeing 747 crashed into the Atlantic Ocean with 329 persons aboard, the victim of Sikh terrorism. Reagan had no answer to these events except words. He attended a ceremony for the Marine victims of the San Salvador bombing when their coffins were returned to Andrews Air Force Base, pledging that their killers "will not evade justice on earth any more than they can escape the judgment of God," but he took no action in El Salvador. After the Marines were killed, Rollins and Buchanan put aside their differences and jointly urged Reagan to retaliate militarily against terrorism. Their appeal prompted Reagan to ask McFarlane if there were any guerrilla staging areas that could be targeted in El Salvador. Not without large-scale killing of civilians, McFarlane told him.[36] Reagan had already put himself on record against such indiscriminate attacks at a news conference on June 18, the day before the San Salvador bombing, when he said that killing civilians in a strike against terrorists would be "an act of terrorism itself." It would be nearly another year before Reagan would put these scruples aside in the U.S. raid on Libya. For five years of his presidency, Reagan talked tough about terrorism but did virtually nothing in the way of retaliatory action to stop it.

He did, however, continue his effort to show that terrorists and hijackers were not determining the White House schedule. On June 28, as part of the business-as-usual campaign, Reagan flew to Chicago to give two long-scheduled speeches at Bloom High School in Chicago Heights. As an add-on, the White House staff had scheduled a private meeting in the school library between Reagan and family members of the TWA Flight 847 hostages. Some of the family members had been clamoring for a meeting with the president. While the hostages were still held captive on this day, exactly two weeks after the hijacking, it was clear that the diplomatic efforts to free them were making headway.

Under these circumstances, the risks of having the president meet with the families seemed less than the risks of snubbing them. "There was a debate about whether it was a good idea, and basically it was decided as a PR thing," said William Henkel. "We were getting hammered for not meeting with them, so we went ahead."[37]

Throughout 1984, as American hostages accumulated in Lebanon, Baker and Deaver had kept hostage family members away from the president. This was partly to spare him from emotionally trying encounters and partly to prevent him from making unwise commitments. Reagan responded humanly to crises. While he could be loftily (or sleepily) disengaged from consequential policy decisions, he was rarely passive when confronted with a personal situation where he thought he could be of help. Early in the first term, a domestic kidnapper had taken a hostage and threatened to kill him unless he was allowed to speak to the president. To Baker's astonishment, Reagan wanted to talk to the kidnapper. Baker and Meese managed to talk him out of it, but the incident reminded the president's staff how much he needed to be protected from himself. Don Regan, who knew nothing of this incident and did not realize how much Reagan needed protection from his impulses, saw the potential public relations advantage of having Reagan meet the hostage families but not the risks of such a meeting. And the risks became greater when the White House yielded to the demands of Republican House member George O'Brien and allowed the congressman and the relatives of Father Lawrence Jenco to attend the meeting in the school library.

Jenco, from nearby Joliet, was a member of a large and closely knit Catholic family who had been taken hostage on January 8, 1985, the day that Regan had proposed his job-swapping idea to Baker. The State Department had rebuffed previous efforts of Jenco family members to see the president. The meeting in the library gave the Jencos an opportunity that might never come again, and they made the most of it. Two of Father Jenco's brothers put Reagan on the spot. They wanted to know why he was willing to make a deal to release the Shiites held by the Israelis but not for their brother. Reagan was defensive and uncomfortable, saying, as he almost always did when pressed, that he was doing everything he could. After a half hour of this the son of one of the TWA hostages said sympathetically to Reagan, "Mr. President, I don't know how you can stand your job."[38] On that note, Regan finally pulled Reagan away. The president was so visibly shaken that Regan asked him if he needed to compose himself before his speech. Reagan shook his head and wobbled through a mostly tax reform speech on the high school steps that included a vow that "terrorists, and those who support them, must and will be held to account."

Even before this meeting, the TWA hijacking had drawn national attention to the seven Americans who had been kidnapped one by one in Lebanon in 1984 and early 1985. The White House and State Department usually had little to say about these hostages, to the frustration of their families, but in a June 26 speech in San Francisco, Secretary of State Shultz had declared, "We insist on release of our hostages, all forty-six of them, immediately." Shultz did not actually expect that the various Shiite groups holding the seven Americans would release them with the TWA passengers, but he thought it worthwhile to make the try. Nothing came of this demand, however, except to advertise the concern of the U.S. government for the well-being of its citizens held hostage in Lebanon—and the government's impotence to free them.

Reagan's personal feelings about freeing these hostages was the principal cause, though not the only one, for his enthusiastic pursuit of the Iran initiative. Reagan insisted to me in interviews for this book, as he has in public statements, that he favored the idea of establishing friendly relations with the successors to Khomeini "in that era when every other day the media was saying that the ayatollah wouldn't live out the week."[39] There is no reason to doubt this statement. Reagan, as much as Casey or McFarlane, was a veteran Cold Warrior who usually responded favorably to arguments based on denying the Soviets a strategic advantage. The arguments of Casey and McFarlane that easing the U.S. weapons ban against Iran might avert a Soviet-supported takeover after Khomeini's death were designed to appeal to Reagan's anticommunism, and they did. The view that the United States could block the spread of Soviet influence in the Middle East by dealing secretly with "moderates" in Iran and the view that supplying arms to Iran would end the hostage crisis were mutually reinforcing illusions.

But it was the plight of the hostages that was decisive in leading Reagan to approve an initiative that flatly contradicted his general policy of not negotiating with terrorists or kidnappers and his specific policy of not selling arms to Iran. "He wanted to get the hostages out," said George Shultz. "And his staff people who worked on him, I believe, did exactly what . . . staff people shouldn't do. They knew he had a soft spot for the hostages. And they exploited him."[40] Shultz opposed the policy but was ineffective in countering this exploitation. While he and Weinberger strongly opposed the strategic assumptions of the Iran initiative advanced by McFarlane and Casey, no one seems to have warned the president that any hostages who were freed as a result of a deal with Iran could be quickly replaced by other Americans. Certainly neither McFarlane nor Regan made this vital point. And both men, whose accounts of what happened in the summer of 1985 differ in other respects, agree that Reagan's principal motivation was to free the hostages. "It is just undeniable that Reagan's obsession with freeing the hostages overrode anything else," said McFarlane.[41]

Regan made the point more vividly. "He [Reagan] was the guy that knew the Iranians had rubbed Jimmy Carter's nose in it and waited until after his presidency ended to release those hostages and let them fly back," Regan said. "And Ronald Reagan made the first announcement on these hostages and got a big hand about it. Now all of a sudden he's got the same situation, and he's responsible for it and he's thinking to himself, 'What's history going to say about me?' And here are these poor people in jail, being browbeaten, tortured. He would see [hostage] Terry Anderson's sister, Peggy Say, constantly in the media. . . . He would see that captive. Come back to the actor. Remember, he puts himself into the part. All of a sudden he's envisioning himself as a captive alone in a dank, damp prison, and where's the president of the United States? What the hell is he doing to get me out of this fucking place? Nothing. . . . Ronald Reagan eats his heart out over this. It worries him. It's with him."[42]

The captivity of the hostages also gnawed at Regan. Behind the bluster and the displays of temper, Regan was a patriot as sentimental as the president he served. He had no use for the Iranian middlemen—"rug merchants," he would call them—and he seems to have accepted the strategic evaluations of McFarlane and Casey at face value. But the chief of staff definitely wanted the captive Americans back, and his own feelings made it difficult for him to step back and serve as a check on the president, even if he had been otherwise inclined to do so. The president wanted the hostages out. So, too, did Donald Regan.

On July 2, Reagan went to Arlington National Cemetery and placed a wreath on the grave of Petty Officer Stethem, the Navy diver murdered in the hijacking of TWA Flight 847. Then he went to Andrews Air Force Base to welcome home the freed passengers, saying, "I know you care deeply about Robbie Stethem and what was done to him. We will not forget what was done to him. There will be no forgetting. His murderers must be brought to justice. Nor will we forget the seven

Americans who were taken captive before you and who are captive still. They must be released. The homecoming won't be complete until all have come home."

McFarlane attended this emotional ceremony, at once solemn and joyful. The next day in his basement office in the White House he received David Kimche, the conspiratorial director general of the Israeli Foreign Ministry, who had suggestions on how to make the homecoming complete. McFarlane and Kimche, a former high-ranking spy for the Israeli intelligence agency Mossad, were friends who had worked together in attempting to define a U.S.-Israeli strategic relationship when McFarlane was at the State Department. McFarlane admired the Israelis for their success in counterterrorism, and he looked up to Kimche. He listened avidly as Kimche told him that the Israelis had connections with moderates in the Iranian ruling circle who wanted to avert chaos after Khomeini's death. (Khomeini, then eighty-five, did not die for another four years.) Their contact was an exiled Iranian merchant named Manucher Ghorbanifar. Kimche suggested that these Iranians could demonstrate their interest in improving relations with the West by obtaining release of the American hostage William Buckley and perhaps of other hostages as well. As a token of good faith, the United States could in turn permit a small quantity of U.S. antitank weapons to be shipped to Iran.

Kimche was vague about the details. But if McFarlane had told his Israeli visitor that his proposal was a clear violation of Reagan administration policy, as it was, the arms-for-hostages deal might have ended then and there. Instead, McFarlane embraced the plan, which fit perfectly with what he hoped could be accomplished in Iran. The possibility of getting Buckley back was an inducement that McFarlane knew would appeal to Casey, his principal ally in furthering a strategic initiative. Kimche insisted, however, that the CIA could not be involved in the project. Nor, he said, would the Israelis use Mossad, with whom Kimche was no longer on good terms. Instead, the Israeli operation would be conducted out of the prime minister's office and by private citizens. These conditions were no deterrent to McFarlane. He had confidence that the NSC staff could do what was necessary, providing the president approved.

The exclusion of the CIA was necessary because, as Kimche knew, Ghorbanifar was in disrepute with the agency. Suspected of serving as an informant for the shah's intelligence service SAVAK, Ghorbanifar had fled for his life after the Iranian revolution to Paris, where he made a shadowy living brokering deals and information between Western governments and the new Iranian regime. He had been a reporting source in the early 1980s for the CIA, which described him as a "rumormonger of occasional usefulness." [43] Early in 1984, Ghorbanifar had approached U.S. Army intelligence in West Germany, saying he had information on Iranian-sponsored terrorist activities and the kidnapping of Buckley. The CIA gave Ghorbanifar a polygraph test, which he failed. Three months later, when Ghorbanifar approached the CIA with more information, he was given another lie detector test. Again, he flunked it. On July 25, 1984, the CIA issued a rare "fabricator notice" warning U.S. intelligence agencies that Ghorbanifar "should be regarded as an intelligence fabricator and a nuisance." This known liar was the reed on which McFarlane and Kimche proposed to build the new U.S. relationship with Iran.

McFarlane would eventually tell the Tower Board that he mentioned his conversation with Kimche to Reagan before the president entered Bethesda Naval Hospital to undergo cancer surgery on July 13. (Surgeons the same day removed a five-centimeter cancerous growth in Reagan's intestine and a large section of the intestine itself.) It seems likely that McFarlane would have mentioned it, since the purpose of Kimche's request was to obtain presidential approval for the initiative and the weapons transfers. The matter of the hostages was so much on Reagan's mind that he asked Regan if there was any new information about them on the evening of July 13, soon after signing a letter in which he reclaimed the presidential powers he had delegated to Vice President Bush during surgery. When Regan returned to the hospital the next day, he said, the president "once again . . . raised the subject of the hostages, asking whether I thought Syria or Iran might be helpful." [44]

Reagan also wrote about the hostages in a July 17 diary entry that he would later say marked "the beginning of what became known as the Iran-Contra affair." [45] After praising the "miracle of miracles" of being able to drink a cup of tea and expressing the hope that his feeding tube would soon be removed, Reagan wrote: "Some strange soundings are coming from some Iranians. Bud M. will be here tomorrow to talk about it. It could be a breakthrough on getting our seven kidnap victims back. Evidently the Iranian economy is disintegrating fast under the strain of war." [46]

This diary entry makes it clear that it was the hostages rather than a strategic initiative with Iran that was on Reagan's mind when he met on

July 18 in the hospital with McFarlane, with Regan present. In the first of three interviews with the Tower Board, McFarlane concealed Reagan's single-mindedness by saying that the Israelis wanted to know the president's "attitude toward engaging with Iran in a political agenda, period." But in his third interview with the board on February 21, 1987, McFarlane admitted that it had been "misleading at least, and wrong at worst, for me to overly gild the president's motives . . . to portray them as mostly directed toward political outcomes." McFarlane went on to describe Reagan's emotional commitment to winning release of the hostages.

Regan told the Tower Board that McFarlane had informed the president at the hospital meeting "that we had had a contact from Iranians whom he had reason to believe had reasonably good connections within Iran but who were on the outside and this had come primarily as a result of Israeli connection with the Iranians." Reagan was interested. "The president after asking quite a few questions—and I would say the discussion lasted for perhaps 20, 25 minutes—assented and said yes, go ahead," Regan said. "Open it up." [47]

By the time Regan wrote For the Record, the discussion of the arms initiative in the hospital had shrunk to "no more than ten or twelve minutes," with the balance of McFarlane's time with the president consumed with discussions of the upcoming Geneva arms talks. Regan said he wondered if he would even have remembered the discussion except for his difficulties in securing Nancy Reagan's approval for McFarlane's visit to the hospital. But he also wrote in his memoirs that "my notes say 'Middle East/Hostage Release/problem,' then 'Soviet/ Geneva arms talks.' " [48] It is surprising that Regan thinks he might have forgotten a hospital room conversation where McFarlane proposed an initiative with Iran designed to free the American hostages, particularly when it concluded with Reagan saying, "Open it up." Apart from such disclaimers, there is little substantive difference between Regan's account and McFarlane's account in his third Tower Board interview of what happened in the hospital. Despite McFarlane's roundabout way of putting things and his own interest in the strategic aspects of the Iran relationship, he realized at all times after Reagan's confrontation with the Jenco family that the central issue for the president was the release of the American hostages. Regan realized this, too. At no time, as far as can be ascertained from records, testimony or my interviews with McFarlane and Regan, did either of them ever flatly describe the Iran initiative to the president as a trade of arms for hostages, although

Shultz would say to Reagan that the initiative would be perceived as such a trade. This refusal by McFarlane and Regan to call the initiative what it really was encouraged Reagan in his rationalization that he was not negotiating with kidnappers but with persons who might have an influence on the kidnappers. This remains Reagan's rationalization to this day. Because of his obsession with freeing the hostages, he allowed U.S. policy to become hostage to the seven Americans held captive in Lebanon.

The Israelis, however, were reluctant to proceed with the initiative without explicit U.S. approval. Israeli Defense Minister Yitzhak Rabin wanted assurances that the secretary of state knew of the plan and that Reagan unequivocally approved.[49] The Israelis insisted on a meeting with Ghorbanifar to secure a commitment for the release of the hostages in return for shipment of 100 TOW (tube-launched, optically tracked, wire-guided) antitank missiles. The meeting occurred in Israel on July 25, where Ghorbanifar also raised the question of Iran's need for antiaircraft missile spare parts. Ghorbanifar told the Israelis that some hostages would be released within two to three weeks of the delivery, although he also warned that the Iranians might want to keep some of the hostages for leverage. Three days later the Israelis briefed Ledeen on the meeting and told him they would not proceed with the arms shipment unless the U.S. government specifically authorized the transfer.

Kimche returned to Washington on August 2 to meet with McFarlane and obtain the U.S. decision on the sale. McFarlane agreed to present the issue to Reagan, which he did on August 6, making the strategic case for the initiative but also telling the president that four hostages would be released in return for the shipment of the 100 TOWs. White House records show that the August 6 meeting was attended by the president, Bush, Shultz, Weinberger, McFarlane and Regan. McFarlane made a pitch for the arms sale and said the U.S. government could deny any participation in it. Shultz warned that this would be risky. He called the proposal "a very bad idea" and discounted the supposed strategic objective of the initiative, saying that "we were just falling into the arms-for-hostages business and we shouldn't do it."[50] Weinberger also opposed the sale and pointed out that it would contradict the goals of Operation Staunch. No one can recall that Bush said anything at this meeting. The vice president lacked the close relationship with Regan that he had enjoyed with James Baker, and his practice in the second term during controversial White House meetings was usually to keep his opinions to himself and convey his views to Reagan privately. While Bush tended to distrust the Israelis, he was as cognizant as Regan and McFarlane of the president's obsession with the hostages and does not appear to have opposed the weapons sale. Regan's recollection of the meeting was that Reagan cautioned McFarlane to "go slow" and to "make sure we know who we are dealing with before we get too far into this."[51] All participants in the meeting agree that Reagan made no decision at the time.

According to McFarlane, Reagan telephoned him several days later and authorized approval of the Israeli sale to Iran of modest quantities of "TOW missiles or other military spares."[52] The United States would in turn replenish the Israeli weapons stocks. Regan has disputed McFarlane's assertion that Reagan gave prior authorization to the sale. He testified that Reagan appeared surprised when he was told in September that the missiles had been shipped. Reagan first told the Tower Board that he had approved the sale in advance. In a subsequent interview, after Regan had told the president that he seemed surprised when he learned of the sale, Reagan changed his story and told the board he had not approved of the shipment until after it was made. When the board sought to resolve the conflict between these two accounts, Reagan said he couldn't recall when he first gave approval to the arms shipments.

The Tower Board believed McFarlane's version of the story. McFarlane had been the subordinate of John Tower, the board chairman, and the colleague of Brent Scowcroft. But Muskie, who is notably independent in his assessments and barely knew McFarlane, told me he thought McFarlane had "made some mistakes" but was "trying to tell us the truth, even though sometimes he had to revise his testimony."[53] The congressional committees that investigated the Iran-contra affair also believed McFarlane, saying that "the evidence supports [the] conclusion" that Reagan gave prior approval to the sale.[54] Although the committees didn't say it, the "evidence" was based on more than McFarlane's testimony. Committee attorneys had examined Reagan diary entries that had been copied verbatim by attorney Arthur B. Culvahouse, who became White House counsel early in 1986. Under an agreement with Culvahouse, the attorneys for the congressional committees were able to use the information but were prohibited from citing or quoting the actual diary entries unless they were otherwise in the public record. The committees also had access to communications between Reagan and Israeli officials, which remain classified, and to an Israeli historical chronology. The accumulated evidence did indeed show that Reagan had given prior approval.

But the committees left the public impression that they were relying solely on McFarlane for their conclusion and incorrectly asserted that "McFarlane had no motive to approve a sale of missiles to Iran if the President had not authorized it." McFarlane had plenty of motivation, since he advocated a strategic opening to Iran and was also supportive of the effort to free the hostages. What McFarlane lacked was not motivation but the means to transfer U.S. weapons to Israel, or to Iran, without presidential approval. "I had no custody over weapons," McFarlane has observed in reference both to the Israeli arms replenishment and the later direct sale of U.S. weapons to Iran. "There was no way I could approve an operation that required furnishing of weapons to anyone in Iran, particularly when the weapons were under control of someone [Weinberger] who opposed the idea." [55]

The TOWs (96 of them rather than the 100 that had been discussed) were shipped by Israel to Iran on August 20. No American hostages were freed. Ghorbanifar's excuse was that the missile delivery was received by the commander of the Iranian Revolutionary Guards rather than the moderate faction for which it was intended. With McFarlane's agreement, Ledeen met again with Kimche in London to discuss ways to bring out the hostages and then flew to Santa Barbara to brief McFarlane on the discussions while Reagan was vacationing at his ranch. But while Ledeen continued to serve as a go-between with the Israelis, Oliver North now also became involved. At McFarlane's instruction the State Department issued North a passport under the name "William P. Goode" for use in "a sensitive operation in Europe in connection with our hostages in Lebanon." Poindexter set up a private interoffice channel for North on the NSC computer system, appropriately called "Operation Blank Check."

On September 3, Ledeen met in Paris with Ghorbanifar, Kimche and Israeli businessmen Al Schwimmer and Yaacov Nimrodi at the luxurious Prince de Galles Hotel, where Ghorbanifar "transmitted the [Iranian] regime's proposal" for another 400 TOW missiles in exchange for the hostages.[56] Ledeen and the Israelis were at last becoming suspicious of Ghorbanifar's claims. When they challenged him, according to Ledeen, Ghorbanifar picked up the telephone and called the Iranian prime minister's office. "Nimrodi [who was fluent in Farsi] listened in on the extension and confirmed that this was indeed the official position of the Iranian government," Ledeen subsequently wrote.[57]

In his book *Perilous Statecraft,* Ledeen compared the governmental decision-making process in Iran, where thousands had been summarily executed and international law flouted in the taking of the U.S. embassy, with the workings of cabinet government in the Reagan administration. Without offering evidence to support his view, Ledeen claims that the ayatollah functioned as a sort of Reaganesque leader of last resort who was brought in to deal with conflicts that competing factions within the government could not resolve. Such a conflict, he says, occurred over the Iranian promise to release the hostages in exchange for the 400 TOWs; Khomeini decided to accept the missiles and free a single hostage. By any standard, what the Iran regime was in fact doing was reneging on the deal it had agreed to in the Paris meeting. But the Reagan administration was given an opportunity to withdraw from this one-sided bargain, and McFarlane did not take it. After Ghorbanifar had told the Israelis of the Iranian regime's decision, Kimche asked McFarlane to choose an American hostage. McFarlane selected Buckley. Ghorbanifar said that Buckley was too ill to travel. (Actually, Buckley had died on June 3, 1985, from a pulmonary infection following medical neglect and mistreatment by his captors. The CIA had received reports of Buckley's death when McFarlane made his choice, but was not definitely able to confirm them until late in 1986.) Instead of Buckley, the American hostage Reverend Benjamin Weir was released on September 15 near the U.S. embassy in Beirut a day after a DC-8 had transported 408 additional TOW missiles to Iran.

There is no doubt that Reagan approved this deal in advance. "We are satisfied from our review of all the evidence that the president was informed and approved of the transactions in the hope that the hostages would be released," the report of the Iran-contra congressional committees declared. Although not stated in the report, the principal evidence for this conclusion was provided by the president's diary entries. Drawing upon the same entries, Reagan acknowledged that he had approved the deal with the understanding that "the transaction was to be solely between Israel and the Iranian moderates and would not involve our country, although we would have to waive for Israel our policy prohibiting any transfer of American-made weapons to Iran."[58]

Reagan did not raise the question of whether these "moderates" actually existed or display any skepticism about Israel's motives. Despite his unpleasant experience with Menachem Begin in 1983, Reagan naïvely tended to accept Israeli assessments as accurate. "We had great respect for Israel's intelligence abilities relating to matters in the Middle East, and, as a result, we gave their assertions a great deal of credence," Reagan said.[59] That Israel and the United States might have had divergent interests in Iran does not seem to have occurred to him. It was enough for Reagan to learn that Israeli Prime Minister Shimon Peres supported the arms transfer. "The truth is, once we had information from Israel that we could trust the people in Iran, I didn't have to think thirty seconds about saying yes to their proposal," Reagan said in his memoirs.[60] He wanted to free the hostages, and he took the Israelis at their word.

The Israeli sales of TOWs to Iran—in effect, U.S. sales since the Israeli weapons were being replenished by the United States—established the pattern for the Iran initiative, which was driven by Reagan's willingness to sacrifice his publicly proclaimed policies in the hope of freeing the hostages. The decision was indisputably Reagan's. It clearly undermined Operation Staunch and violated the president's avowed policy of denying weapons to terrorists. "Truth may be a rare commodity in Iran; it's alive and well in America," Reagan had said on January 27, 1981, in welcoming home the Americans who had been held captive in the U.S. embassy in Tehran. In his speech to them he had warned terrorists that "when the rules of international behavior are violated, our policy will be one of swift and effective retribution." But truth was not alive and well at the White House in 1985. Publicly, Reagan still described Iran as a major source of terrorism in Lebanon and Europe. Secretly, he was supplying missiles to Iran. "The lesson to Iran was unmistakable," the congressional report concluded. "All U.S. positions and principles were negotiable, and breaches by Iran went unpunished. Whatever Iran did, the U.S. could be brought back to the arms bargaining table by the promise of another hostage."

The pattern persisted in the next U.S.-guaranteed sale of Israeli arms to Iran, this time of HAWK (Homing All-the-Way Killer) antiaircraft missiles in November. Even Ledeen was by now having reservations. At a meeting with Ghorbanifar, Schwimmer and Nimrodi at the Old Executive Office Building across from the White House on October 3 he urged that the hostage question be abandoned on grounds that as long as "we continued to sell arms to the Iranians, we would never be able to evaluate their real intentions, since they would do almost anything in order to lay their hands on the weapons"[61]—anything, apparently, except keep their promise to release all the hostages. Ledeen believed that if U.S.-Iranian relations actually improved, freedom of the hostages would be a necessary by-product of the new relationship. When he made this point to Casey, the CIA director told him, "With this president we have to do the hostages first."[62]

Ledeen's account is obviously self-serving, but on this point it has the ring of truth. In his testimony to the Tower Board, McFarlane confirmed that Ledeen had indeed advocated that the United States should, in Ledeen's words, "shut down the hostage matter and pursue the political business." This did not prevent Ledeen from passing on Iran's new "blanket order"—150 HAWK missiles, 200 Sidewinder missiles and 30 to 50 Phoenix missiles. McFarlane was also having some doubts. He told the Tower Board in the second of his three interviews that, although the president had been "pleased" by Weir's release, the delivery of only one hostage "seemed to me a very clear evidence of bad faith." But McFarlane nevertheless proceeded to arrange for the next shipment of missiles, this time the HAWKs. And instead of taking Ledeen's suggestion to drop the hostage-dealings, the NSC staff dropped Ledeen and turned operations over to North.

North and Amiram Nir, Israeli Prime Minister Peres' counterterrorism adviser, met in Washington on November 14. "Although they apparently did not discuss arms sales to Iran, they did set the foundation for a variety of future Israeli-U.S. covert operations," the congressional inquiry concluded.[63] North's notes show that he anticipated operations that would require a million dollars a month. He and Nir discussed how they could raise the money, whether or not to use the Israelis as a conduit and how they could, in the words of the notes, "Set up joint/Israeli cover op."[64] On the same day McFarlane briefed Casey, his deputy John N. McMahon and Poindexter about the operation. Three days later, on November 17, with McFarlane preparing to leave for Geneva and Reagan's first summit with Soviet leader Mikhail Gorbachev, North was put in charge of the pending shipment of HAWK missiles to Iran. On the following day North arranged with Richard Secord, a retired U.S. Air Force major general who became the driving force in the web of covert financial undertakings known as The Enterprise, for the deposit of $1 million by Schwimmer into Lake Resources, the dummy corporation controlled by Secord in Switzerland. North and Secord testified to the congressional committees that the money was for chartering planes to transport the HAWK missiles to Iran. The committees, noting discrepancies in Secord's statement, suspected that the money had been used for bribes and concluded that "the purpose for this $1 million deposit is unclear."[65]

North now took control of the complicated scheme to remove the HAWKs from Israeli weapons stocks, transship them through Portugal to Iran and see to it that the weapons were replaced from U.S. stocks. The notes inadvertently left in the NSC computer system—called

"PROF," for Professional Office System, hence PROF notes—show that North informed Poindexter of what he was doing, including Secord's involvement and the weapons replenishment, well in advance of the HAWK shipment, which was supposed to occur on November 21.* But almost everything that could go wrong with the shipment did, starting with Portugal's refusal to allow landing rights to the El Al 747 that was transporting the HAWKs to Iran. In an effort to gain Portugal's permission, North turned to CIA and State Department officials, widening the circle of those who knew of the deal but without telling them the full story.

North lied to Robert Oakley, director of counterterrorism at the State Department, telling him that the HAWK missiles had been discovered in a warehouse in Portugal where "one of his people" was seeking arms for the contras "and learned that the Israelis had been obtaining arms from the same source for shipment to Iran."[66] Oakley was also told that one or more U.S. hostages would soon be released in Lebanon. Based on this information Oakley allowed North to tell the U.S. embassy in Portugal that State was "aware" of the operation and that the embassy "could request clearances" for the plane that was to transport the missiles to Iran.[67] Portugal nonetheless refused, and the missile-laden 747 was forced to return to Israel in mid-flight.

The president, Shultz and Regan were briefed on the operation by McFarlane on the afternoon of November 19 in Geneva, the first day of the summit. (Shultz testified he had been told about the missile shipment in Geneva, apparently before this briefing, in a call from McFarlane on a secure telephone line.) Regan has strong recollections of the meeting, which took place in his second-floor bedroom in the Villa Palmetta. He found McFarlane's account "difficult to follow because of the many bizarre elements involved," one of them the cover story that the missiles being shipped were oil-drilling equipment. "Even if the Iran-contra affair had never become a cause célèbre, I would remember this meeting vividly," Regan wrote in his memoir. "This was certainly the first time the President had heard the whole scenario. It was not in his character to be especially interested in the nuts and bolts,

---

* The PROF notes were the vital discovery of the Tower Board. The FBI and the independent counsel's staff had requested the notes stored in Poindexter's and North's desk computers, most of which had been destroyed. But Kenneth J. Kreig, then a twenty-six-year-old Pentagon intern working for the Tower Board, asked also if there were backup copies of the notes in the computer's mainframe. This search produced the thousands of memos and communications by Poindexter and North that undergirded the investigations by the congressional committees and the independent counsel. Kreig is the unsung hero of the entire Iran-contra inquiry.

and he asked no probing questions." Regan said the timing of the briefing "could not have been worse, from the point of view of capturing Reagan's full attention. He had just left Gorbachev; he had had no lunch; and many other items dealing with the summit, which was uppermost in his mind, remained to be discussed."[68]

But whether preoccupied with the summit or not, Reagan was clearly approving of the continuing effort to obtain release of American hostages through the currency of sending missiles to Iran. In his first meeting with the Tower Board on January 16, 1987, Reagan could not recall how the HAWK shipment came about, but said he had objected to it and that as a result of his objections the shipment was returned to Israel. This recollection is totally wrong. When I asked Regan if McFarlane had obtained the approval of the president for the arms sales, Regan said:

"Sure he got approval from him. There was no such thing as diversion at that point. There was no mention of contras in this at all. . . . Did Ronald Reagan approve shipment of HAWK missiles to Iran in 1985? Definitely yes."[69]

And when, I asked, did McFarlane get this approval?

"July of '85 in the hospital [Regan replied]. He said, 'Okay, proceed. Make the contact. Talk about it.' August: 'Yes.' A further talk after he'd returned and was upstairs in the family quarters. 'Yes, proceed with this.' September, the shipments are going to be made. 'Okay.' October, Geneva, the deed is being done as we sit here in this room. Definitely Ronald Reagan approved of that."[70]

After more delays, 18 of the 80 HAWKs finally reached Iran on November 25 on a charter operated by St. Lucia Airways, a CIA proprietary airline whose use had been suggested to North by Dewey Clarridge, his old CIA colleague from contra operations who was now chief of European operations for the agency. But despite the last-minute help from the CIA, the operation had been thoroughly bungled by North and the Israelis. After all the ruses and secrecy to conceal the origin of the weapons, they were found to still carry their Israeli markings and in some cases the Star of David. The missiles were also an older model of HAWK unsuitable for Iran's purpose of shooting down high-flying reconnaissance planes and Iraqi bombers. (Actually, even the newer HAWKs were designed for use against low- and medium-altitude aircraft, an important technical fact of which neither Ledeen, Ghorbanifar nor the Israeli intermediaries seem to have been aware.) The Iranians, who had reneged on their earlier promises to release the hostages, were now the ones to feel cheated. Iran insisted on getting its money back, and the Israelis returned more than $8 million of the $11 million, keeping the remainder for the 18 missiles and the costs of delivery.

If the TOW shipments and the release of Weir had set the pattern for the initiative, the first HAWK shipment confirmed its futility. The deal caused many recriminations among the Israelis and the Iranians and the middlemen. No hostages were released. CIA deputy McMahon was enraged that North had embroiled the agency in the operation without following authorized procedures. The only beneficiaries of the bungling were North and Secord, who kept the $1 million Schwimmer had put into the Lake Resources bank account, to help the contras and provide profits for The Enterprise.

McFarlane was particularly unhappy. He had confided to friends in the weeks leading up to the Geneva summit that he wanted out of the White House, mostly because of his problems with Regan. He returned from Geneva exhausted and depressed and became even more despondent when he learned what had happened to the HAWK shipment. On December 2 in Los Angeles, where Reagan had attended a celebrity fund-raiser the night before, McFarlane told the president he wanted to quit, citing family reasons. McFarlane was apt to act on impulse when tired or depressed, and I am convinced from subsequent conversations with him that he regretted resigning almost as soon as he had done so, but Reagan accepted the resignation. Although Reagan often resisted resignations, he had told McFarlane long before that he would never stand in the way of anyone who needed to leave because of family matters. McFarlane remembered this and couched his desire to resign in these terms. Two days later the president named McFarlane's deputy John Poindexter as his new national security adviser. Poindexter had the support of everyone that mattered—Shultz and Weinberger, as well as Regan and McFarlane. It was quite typical of Reagan to select a deputy under the circumstances, particularly for a position he did not value all that much. He may also have realized that the secrecy of the Iran initiative recommended staying within the inner NSC staff circle.

The proximate cause of McFarlane's resignation was his frustration with Don Regan. Although their differences were well known and had been widely reported, the president routinely lied in responding to reports of administration conflict and he did so again in appointing Poindexter. When a reporter asked Reagan to explain the role the Regan-McFarlane conflict had played in the resignation, he said, "You have all been misinformed about that."[71] In fact, McFarlane had been driven wild by rumors, which he blamed on Regan and his aides, that he had engaged in extramarital affairs. I was aware of the rumors, which Regan had raised at a meeting of reporters and editors, and had discussed them with McFarlane. McFarlane believed they were part of a deliberate campaign to harm his standing with the first lady and drive him out of the White House, a view that then seemed consistent to me with the Regan pattern of making life uncomfortable for any aide who was an independent force. Others also knew of the rumormongering: it has been reported in *Landslide: The Unmaking of the President 1984–1988,* by *Wall Street Journal* White House correspondent Jane Mayer and Doyle McManus of the *Los Angeles Times* and was cited by Ledeen in his book as the reason for McFarlane's resignation.

In retrospect, I am not certain that Regan was trying to force McFarlane out. Regan often gossiped; he gratuitously mentioned the private lives of two other well-known administration officials in an interview for this book. But whether Regan's action was deliberate or compulsive, there is no doubt that McFarlane was damaged by it. He is a family man of considerable scruple and extreme sensitivity, and he did not know how to deal with the rumors. He was also worn out by overwork, dissatisfied with his standing with the president and his battles with cabinet officers and—as none of us realized then—badly frustrated by the busted Iran initiative. It was clear to McFarlane's friends that he was under an emotional strain, although few knew the full extent of it. Ledeen, who did, talked to Kimche about McFarlane. "Some strong men are flexible, and bend in a hostile wind," Kimche told him. "Others are too rigid, try to stand against it, and break. Bud has broken."[72]

The Iran initiative might never have been conceived without McFarlane. It also might have ended if McFarlane had stayed on as national security adviser, for he would soon be convinced that Ghorbanifar was deserving of the "fabricator" label that the CIA had attached to him. John Marlan Poindexter did not trouble himself with such evaluations. He had got along with three quite different national security advisers by going along. Poindexter had grown up in the tiny town of Odon, Indiana, where his father was the president of the town's only bank. His interest was in science and mathematics, at which he excelled. At Annapolis he earned four years of straight A's and graduated first in his class. Subsequently, he attended Cal Tech on a scholarship and earned a doctorate in nuclear physics. After serving as an assistant to three secretaries of the Navy, he became commander of a guided missile cruiser. In the Reagan administration he had watched from the inside as three national security advisers were ground up by the president's indifference and "cabinet government." Poindexter thought he could avoid their fate. His view of his role was much the same as that of columnist William Safire, who wrote when Poindexter was appointed that the president preferred "a broker to a player."[73] Shultz and Weinberger also liked the idea of a broker. They were weary of being challenged from the White House, as Shultz had been by Clark and Weinberger by McFarlane.

Rarely has such an intelligent and unassuming man been so poorly suited for the high position he inherited as Poindexter was as Reagan's national security adviser. He lacked Clark's understanding of Reagan or McFarlane's political experience and knowledge of world affairs. Though he held one of the most political jobs in Washington, Poindexter disdained politics. Introverted and reclusive in his habits, he deliberately isolated himself from Congress, the media and the political cross currents of Reagan's White House. Unlike McFarlane, he never challenged Regan, who soon lost interest in him. Poindexter was a remote figure even within the NSC, where he set up a naval chain-of-command system, kept the door to his office closed and dealt with others through his deputies or by computer messages. His reading tended to the scientific and technical. When I mentioned to Poindexter during an interview that even some Republican congressmen had complained about his inaccessibility, he told me that he had no responsibility for dealing with Congress and gave the impression he also had no interest. On another occasion, at a dinner party in Santa Barbara, Poindexter confided to me that the African National Congress had an extremely small following in South Africa—an astonishing statement at a time when he was making recommendations to Reagan to oppose South African sanctions. Despite his reputed technical brilliance, his knowledge of public affairs was narrow and skimpy. And his problems were compounded by the untimely death from liver cancer in 1986 of his deputy Don Fortier, one of the few members of the NSC staff who had worked in Congress and appreciated the importance of executive-legislative relations. "John's a complex person—a very dedicated, extremely conservative man who had come through a peculiar military atmosphere," one of his friends and former subordinates told me. "He was a nuclear officer without much experience in commanding large units who was isolated from the real world, the political world. He had a much stronger aversion to political process than most military people."

This aversion would enable Poindexter to carry out what he believed to be the wishes of his commander in chief without troubling himself about the legality of his conduct. He would never become remorseful, as McFarlane would, about lying to Congress, nor does he seem to have fully shared the emotional hostility toward his critics characteristic of Secord and North. "Political process" simply did not pop up on Admiral Poindexter's mental radar screen. He was able with a clear conscience to ignore the Constitution and to violate the laws he was sworn to uphold.

Poindexter's withdrawn, antipolitical method of operation would enable the venturesome and temperamentally opposite Oliver North to gain lock-stock-and-barrel control over the many-sided Iran initiative. North was nearly forty-two years old when the Iran initiative was launched in 1985. Like McFarlane and Poindexter, North was a small-town boy (Philmont, New York, in his case), whose entry to the wider world had been through the U.S. Naval Academy. North's path had not been easy. As a passenger on a weekend trip while at the academy he had suffered severe knee and back injuries in a car accident. It was questionable whether he would ever walk again, let alone obtain his goal of winning a commission in the Marines. But North restored his mobility through intensive exercise and was readmitted to Annapolis as a plebe at the relatively advanced age of twenty in 1964. After graduation he served with distinction as a Marine in Vietnam, where he was wounded at least twice and won the Silver Star and Bronze Star for valor as well as two Purple Hearts. Those who served under him considered North an extraordinary Marine officer. Former corporal Ernie Tuten, a machine gunner in North's platoon, said North was "one in a million" when it came to leading troops into battle and was "extra cool under fire." [74]

Even in the Marines, however, the North legend was accompanied by ambiguities and seeming deceptions. In one celebrated story, to which Tuten said he was a witness, North led two fifteen-man "killer teams" into the demilitarized zone to capture a North Vietnamese Army soldier in an effort to demonstrate that the NVA was operating inside the DMZ. The NVA soldier was supposedly captured but died from wounds, and the story hushed up by North and his men. The story is disputed by a legendary Marine officer, Lieutenant General Victor H. (Brute) Krulak, who wrote of North: "His combat exploits in Vietnam are romanticized, like the Sunday-supplement tale of his valiant single-handed midnight forays across the DMZ to capture and bring back a North Vietnamese prisoner. It is an exciting story, but like many others, it never happened." [75] Five years after he returned from Vietnam, North checked into Bethesda Naval Hospital, where he spent twenty-two days. He was diagnosed as suffering from "delayed battle stress." [76]

Both North's leadership qualities and his talent for deception were observed by colleagues on the NSC staff. One of these colleagues, who was initially impressed with North, told me that North had long before the Iran initiative excitedly related the account of what he described as a private meeting with Reagan. The colleague subsequently learned that North had indeed been with the president, but as part of a large group. Constantine Menges relates several similar deceptions in his book *Inside the National Security Council,* including an occasion where North described the details of the conversation during a dinner with Jeane Kirkpatrick. When Menges later asked Kirkpatrick whether a particular subject had been discussed at this dinner, she told him, "I've never had dinner with Oliver North." [77]

The reclusive Poindexter and the outgoing North would form an odd team. Unlike Poindexter, North enjoyed dealing with people face to face, and possessed a salesman's gift for marketing his causes. While Poindexter preferred to work behind his closed door, alone with his computer, North was always out of the office, always in the field. Although his free-wheeling style worried professionals at State, the CIA and the Pentagon, even North's critics acknowledged that he had a knack for knowing what buttons to push in the bureaucracy. Bill Clark, who liked him, once told me that North was not the kind of person you would send out on the street. But McFarlane felt a kinship with North based on their experiences as Marine Corps officers in Vietnam and made of him a protégé. He turned North loose in a big way, and Poindexter had neither the skill nor the sense to rein him in.

On December 4, the same day Poindexter was announced as McFarlane's replacement, North sent the new national security adviser a long PROF note reviewing the story of the HAWK missile shipment and proposing a new arms sale to Iran. The tone of the message suggests that North now viewed himself as the conceptualizer as well as the chief operating officer of the Iran initiative. It also shows that North understood the extent to which the White House had become hostage to the hostages. North said that while he, Secord and the Israelis "all agree that there is a high degree of risk in pursuing the course we have started, we are now so far down the road that stopping what has been started could have even more serious repercussions." Later in the memo, he spelled out exactly what he meant. Since the Iranians had "a very unsophisticated view of things" and were especially distrustful of the United States and Israel, stopping the arms sales could "incur the greater likelihood of reprisals against us for 'leading them on.' These reprisals could take the form of additional hostage seizures, execution of some/all now held, or both." [78]

North's new plan was at once fantastic and precise. He proposed supplying Iran with 3,300 TOWs and 50 improved HAWK missiles, delivered in increments. The first "AMCIT," the NSC term for the American citizens held hostage, would be released after the delivery of the first 300 TOWs. Another hostage would be freed after the next delivery of 300 missiles. The sequence of weapons shipments and hostage releases would continue until, after delivery of 1,300 of the TOWs and all of the HAWK missiles, every one of the American hostages would be freed. North then proposed that the remaining 2,000 TOWs be delivered, and French hostages released in return.

While North and McFarlane discussed the new arms-for-hostages plan, Poindexter took to Reagan on the morning of December 5 a "finding" he had received from the CIA giving retroactive approval to the agency's participation in the November weapons transfers to Iran. A finding is a presidential authorization for covert action, normally delivered in writing. This particular finding had been drafted by CIA counsel Stanley Sporkin at the request of McMahon, who said that after he was informed about CIA involvement in the November missile shipment he "went through the overhead pointing out that there was no way we could become involved in any implementation of this mission without a finding." [79] The one-page finding was straightforward in its description of the mission as a trade of arms for hostages. But it was unusual in that it ratified "all prior actions taken by U.S. government officials in furtherance of this effort" [80] and that it instructed CIA Director Casey not to brief Congress on the operation. Casey sent it to the White House with a recommendation that Reagan sign it. Poindexter disliked the finding because it said nothing about the supposed larger purposes of the initiative, now little more than a cover story for the arms-for-hostages effort. When Poindexter was questioned by the congressional committees, he could not recall discussing the finding with anyone except Casey and McMahon, and neither Regan nor McFarlane remember having seen it. But Poindexter nevertheless presented it to Reagan, who dutifully signed it. No copies were made of the finding, which was stored in the safe of Poindexter's NSC counsel, Paul Thompson.[81] When the Iran-contra scandal became public nearly a year later, Poindexter took the finding out of the safe and tore it up. He said he realized the document could cause "significant political embarrassment"[82] to the president because it revealed that the initiative was really a trade of arms for hostages.

North was never one for wasting time. On December 6 he flew to New York to discuss with Israeli officials his new plan for supplying arms to Iran and freeing the hostages. According to Israeli records, this was the meeting where North first mentioned that the United States wanted to use profits from future arms sales to Iran to assist the Nicaraguan contras.[83] (North does not recall the subject having come up at this time, although he concedes the possibility.) From New York, North flew to London to meet with Secord, Ghorbanifar, Kimche, Schwimmer and Nimrodi and discuss the missile sale proposal he had forwarded to Poindexter.

While North acted, Reagan was burning the bridges that might have allowed him a safe retreat from the risky ground of the Iran initiative. On Saturday morning, December 7, he assembled his principal advisers in the White House family quarters in an informal discussion to consider his options. McFarlane for the last time chaired the meeting, which also was attended by Shultz, Weinberger, McMahon, Regan and Poindexter. McMahon was sitting in for Casey, who was traveling. Bush, who had been invited, instead decided to adhere to his planned schedule and attend the Army-Navy football game. By opting to miss the meeting, Bush avoided expressing himself on a critical issue on which he knew the president to have strong feelings. Shultz and Weinberger welcomed the chance to express themselves. While the Tower Board would later conclude that the two cabinet officers subsequently distanced themselves from information that the initiative was continuing despite their objections, they made their case most strongly on this day. Shultz said the initiative would "negate the whole policy" of not making "deals with terrorists." He predicted that the deal would become public and shake moderate Arabs when they learned that the United States was "breaking our commitment to them and helping the radicals in Tehran fight their fellow Arab Iraq."[84]

Weinberger had taken a lawyer's care in preparing for this meeting, and he used nearly a half hour, an unusually long time with Reagan, to make the case that the arms deal would violate the U.S. embargo on sending arms to Iran as well as the restrictions on third-country transfers contained in the Arms Export Control Act. The secretary of defense said he "raised every point that occurred to me, including the fact that we were at the same time asking other countries not to make sales of weapons to Iran, that there was no one of any reliability or, indeed, any sense with whom we could deal in Iran . . . that if we were trying to help get hostages released, why there would be a real worry that the matter would not be held in any way confidential, that we would be subjected to blackmail, so to speak, by people who did know it in Iran and elsewhere, and that we had no interest whatsoever in helping Iran in any military way, even a minor way, and that in every way it was a policy that we should not engage in and most likely would not be successful." [85]

Reagan knew before the December 7 meeting that Shultz and Weinberger opposed sending arms to Iran under any guise. But on this particular Saturday he also was advised to abandon the initiative by Chief of Staff Don Regan, who usually gave him automatic support. Regan had thought the initiative worth trying, and would swing back to this view, but he was impressed by the arguments of Shultz and Weinberger and possessed a stockbroker's sense that putting more resources in the arms-for-hostages market was a losing proposition. "Cut your losses," he advised the president. [86] In effect this was also the opinion of McMahon, who approached the issue from the perspective of an intelligence professional. While not empowered to make a formal CIA recommendation, the skeptical McMahon effectively demolished McFarlane's favorite argument that the arms sales were a useful device for establishing a relationship with "moderates" in Iran. "I said I was unaware of any moderates in Iran, that most of the moderates had been slaughtered by Khomeini, that whatever arms we give to these so-called moderates they will end up supporting the Khomeini regime, and they would go to the front and be used against the Iraqis and that would be bad," McMahon later testified. [87]

In response to this skepticism, Reagan demonstrated an awesome stubbornness. One side of Reagan's temperament was a passive disengagement from most of the many issues that passed before him. The other side was an intense, almost passionate commitment to causes he visualized in personal terms, as he did the plight of the American hostages. On this issue, McFarlane's observation that Reagan was overly impressed with successful and independently wealthy policy advisers such as Shultz, Weinberger and Regan did not apply. Reagan had both the courage and the ignorance to ignore the collective wisdom of his experts and follow his own counsel when he was convinced he was on the right course. More than three years later Reagan told me that he did not believe the warnings that the initiative would inevitably become public and cause his presidency great harm. Characteristically, he also credited those who had warned him. "I will tell you that both Cap and George Shultz thought of that and thought that if it ever became [public], it would look like we were trading arms for hostages, it would be made to look like that," Reagan said. "Well, they turned out to be right. I didn't at the time see how it possibly could, when we were dealing with some people who had to literally hide from their own government to save their lives. . . . I said to both those fellows [Shultz and Weinberger] when we were talking, 'Look, if I've got a child kidnapped for ransom, I don't believe in paying ransom. But if I suddenly discover there's somebody else who might be able to get that child back from the kidnapper and knows a way to get it back, yes, I'd reward that individual.' But I never convinced them. And now, as I say, they turned out to be right." [88]

Had Reagan been harboring second thoughts about the wisdom of continuing the Iran initiative, December 7, 1985, would have been the time for turning back. Never again would Reagan's advisers be as forceful and united in opposition as they were on this day. Never again would Don Regan side so completely with the opponents of the idea. Never again would Reagan receive such a blunt face-to-face appraisal from a high-ranking CIA official of the futility of finding "moderates" in Iran with whom it would be useful to conduct an arms-for-hostages relationship. Reagan ignored them all. He saw himself as the representative of the American people, and he was confident he knew the people's will. When Weinberger insisted that "there are legal problems here, Mr. President, in addition to all the policy problems," [89] Reagan replied bluntly that he didn't "feel we can leave any stone unturned in trying to get the hostages back." [90] "The American people will never forgive me if I fail to get these hostages out over this legal question," the president said, softening his remark with a Reaganesque quip that if laws were broken and people went to jail, "visiting hours are Thursday." [91]

Reagan's only specific decision at the December 7 meeting was to send McFarlane to London to join North, Secord, Ghorbanifar and the

Israelis in their discussions. While McFarlane then believed that the Iran initiative was hanging by a thread, this decision to send McFarlane as an emissary suggests that Reagan had not abandoned it. Considering what he had said to Shultz and Weinberger at the meeting and what he did afterward, it is likely that Reagan had already made a decision in his heart to continue with the effort to free the hostages even if that meant supplying Iran with arms. Poindexter's recollection of the meeting is that Reagan wanted to pursue every means to accomplish this purpose. Weinberger, who may have been more impressed with his arguments than with the president's response to them, was the only participant in the December 7 meeting who left the White House family quarters secure in the belief that the initiative was dead. He returned to the Pentagon and told an aide that "this baby had been strangled in its cradle, that it was finished." [92] Shultz did not share this opinion. He felt that Reagan "was somewhat on the fence but rather annoyed at me and Secretary Weinberger because I felt . . . he was very concerned about the hostages as well as very much interested in the Iran initiative." [93]

McFarlane flew to London the next day on what he assumed was his final mission for the Reagan administration. He had never met Ghorbanifar. McFarlane was imbued with a sense of regret that undoubtedly reflected his mixed feelings about leaving the White House as well as concern over the course of the Iran initiative. He saw his mission as a final opportunity to rescue a policy that he still regarded as a momentous strategic opening. Ghorbanifar had no such illusions. The practical Iranian merchant had received North's latest proposal, and he understood that the initiative now amounted to nothing more than a trade of arms for hostages. Ghorbanifar had gone to London not to engage in strategic abstractions but to bargain coldly over the value of each hostage, using TOW missiles as the principal currency. When McFarlane lectured him on strategic issues, Ghorbanifar responded by declaring that the United States had "cheated" him by sending Iran the wrong missiles in November. After listening to this diatribe for half an hour, McFarlane told Ghorbanifar to "go pound sand" [94] and walked out of the room in the West End apartment where they were meeting. The next day he flew back to Washington with North and Secord.

On the plane trip home McFarlane expressed his disappointment with Ghorbanifar, calling him "one of the most despicable characters he had ever met." [95] Despicable he may have been, but Ghorbanifar was at the time behaving more realistically than the troubled and idealistic

McFarlane. Based on his dealings with the Israelis and with Ledeen and North, the Iranian had every reason to believe that Reagan was more concerned with freeing hostages than with the pie-in-the-sky prospects of a U.S.-Iran strategic initiative. North understood this, even if Mc-Farlane did not. On their return, North wrote an "eyes only" memo called "Next Steps" that he sent to McFarlane and Poindexter. In this memo North reviewed the history of the arms deals and discussed five options he believed were available to the administration. The first option was the arms deal North had proposed to Poindexter and then to Ghorbanifar in London. The second was an Israeli delivery of 400 to 500 TOWs to Iran to restore "good faith." The third was a military raid to free the hostages, always a dubious proposition, since it was not known precisely where the hostages were held. The fourth was a "do nothing" option that North considered "very dangerous since U.S. has, in fact, pursued earlier presidential decision to play along with Gorban-ifahr's [*sic*] plan. U.S. reversal now in midstream could ignite Iranian fire—hostages would be our minimum losses." [96]

North's fifth option would become the new form of the Iran initiative. He proposed selling U.S. arms directly to Iran, acting on the basis of a new presidential finding, and using Secord and his Enterprise as the conduit. Funneling the money through Secord would enable North to accomplish his larger purpose of providing funds for the contras, the objective he had mentioned to the Israelis the previous week. North did not mention this purpose in the memo, although he would later specif-ically obtain Poindexter's approval for the diversion.

On December 10, McFarlane conveyed his misgivings about Ghor-banifar to the president in a meeting at the White House attended by Casey, North, Poindexter and Regan. But McFarlane also mentioned North's concern that the hostages would be killed if the initiative was halted—a surefire way of maintaining Reagan's interest in continuing it. Reagan suggested that the Israelis might be allowed to go on man-aging the program. While McFarlane would later say that he thought the Iran initiative was dead after December 10, the other participants in the meeting did not share this opinion. Recognizing how committed Reagan was to winning freedom for the hostages, Regan had begun to retreat from the "cut your losses" position he had taken three days earlier when Shultz and Weinberger were pressing their case against sending weapons to Iran. Poindexter, North and Casey still favored the initiative. A memo sent after the meeting from Casey to McMahon said that Reagan "had not entirely given up" on encouraging further deals between the Israelis and the Iranians. "I suspect he [Reagan] would be willing to run the risk and take the heat in the future if this will lead to springing the hostages. It appears that Bud [McFarlane] has the action."[97]

But the action was now Poindexter's, and he and North quickly plunged ahead. Poindexter told North to keep the initiative going by devising a new covert-action finding, recruiting a new team to conduct the transactions and devising a legal way in which the United States could sell arms to Iran. The latter point was critical because the Arms Export Control Act required congressional notification of any arms sale that exceeded $14 million. Poindexter asked North to work with "the appropriate people at CIA and in Ed Meese's office, if not Ed Meese himself." (Meese, having survived a stormy confirmation hearing, was by now attorney general.)

Israel's Amiram Nir, the adviser to Peres on terrorism, now reentered the scene. Nir's idea, which had the approval of his government, was that Iran might influence the Hezbollah to release the American hostages if Israel agreed to release Shiite prisoners held by the Israeli-backed Southern Lebanon Army—in effect an extension of the deal that had freed the American passengers on the hijacked TWA airliner the previous June. After discussing this plan with Ghorbanifar in London, Nir flew to Washington on January 2, 1986, to present it to Poindexter and North. Notes of the meeting taken by Poindexter show that Nir proposed shipping 4,000 "unimproved TOWs" to Iran. There were at the time, with Weir's release and Buckley's death, five American hostages in Lebanon. Nir said all would be released after the shipment of the first 500 TOWs had been received by Iran. Simultaneously, Israel would release twenty to thirty Hezbollah prisoners "who don't have blood on their hands."[98] Nir also discussed using some of the profits from the sale of the TOWs for "other cooperative activities."[99] North testified that he did not believe Nir specifically mentioned the contras at their meeting, but there would have been no need to do so. Nir already knew from what North had said to the Israelis early in December that it was the contras that the Americans had in mind.

Casey was incapacitated by the time the Tower Board conducted its inquiry, and he died soon after the joint congressional committees began forty days of public hearings on the Iran-contra affair in the spring of 1987. But the notes and letters he left behind show that Casey played a vital and supportive role in the process that led to Reagan's formal approval of the initiative. One aspect of Casey's role was keeping

Ghorbanifar involved in the initiative despite the negative evaluations of the Iranian by McFarlane and the CIA itself. Ledeen was the catalyst. Although he had lost direct access to the national security adviser when Poindexter replaced McFarlane, Ledeen continued to urge the CIA to establish an intelligence relationship with Ghorbanifar. With North's approval Ledeen met early in December with the CIA's Clarridge and Charles Allen, the agency's senior Iran analyst, to tell them of Ghorbanifar's contacts inside Iran and described him, according to a memo written afterward by Allen, as "a good fellow who is a lot of fun." [100] The CIA officials were unimpressed, but Casey instructed Clair George, deputy director of operations, to arrange for a new evaluation of Ghorbanifar. Two CIA officials interviewed Ghorbanifar at a meeting at Ledeen's home on December 22 attended by North, where Ledeen described the Iranian as "a wonderful man . . . almost too good to be true." [101] But when the CIA gave this "wonderful man" a third lie detector test, he managed to answer accurately only two of the fifteen questions put to him: his name and his nationality.[102] Even though no one else at the CIA wanted to have anything to do with Ghorbanifar, Casey obligingly passed him on to Reagan and the NSC staff team then engaged in planning the next stage of the Iran initiative. In an "eyes only" letter to the president on December 23, Casey said that one of the initiatives for freeing the hostages involved use of Ghorbanifar. "He has 3 or 4 scenarios he would like to play out," Casey wrote.[103] This letter demonstrates Casey's continuing support for the initiative despite the skepticism at the CIA. That he would send such a letter to Reagan shows he understood the president's unflagging interest in the various schemes to free the hostages by transferring weapons to Iran.

On January 6, Poindexter told Reagan of the Nir proposal at his morning national security briefing, which was attended by Regan and Bush. Reagan welcomed the idea and scheduled an NSC meeting the next day to discuss it. He also signed a new finding that authorized covert action to continue the Iran initiative, permit the sale of weapons to Iran and keep the initiative secret from Congress. CIA legal counsel Sporkin had insisted that reference to the hostages, which was omitted in the original draft, be included because it was "a very important element" that "ought to be in there." [104] North explained that the State Department did not want any reference to the hostages because this would create an appearance of a "hostage-for-arms shipment" and therefore not "look right." [105] Casey backed Sporkin, however, and Reagan's goal of freeing the hostages was described in the finding that was presented to him. Poindexter testified that he had not intended that Reagan sign it immediately because he considered it a proposal requiring further discussion. Reagan nonetheless almost casually signed it, putting his official stamp of approval on the initiative for a second time.

The next day, January 7, Poindexter convened a full National Security Council meeting to discuss Nir's proposal. Neither Poindexter nor Reagan mentioned that the finding authorizing continuation of the initiative had been signed by the president the day before. The cast for this meeting included Reagan, Bush, Shultz, Weinberger, Meese, Casey, Poindexter and Regan. While Weinberger found it to be "very much a rerun" of the meeting held exactly a month earlier in the family quarters, the substitution of Casey for McMahon and Regan's support of the new proposal changed the dynamics of the discussion. Casey, Poindexter and Regan supported the initiative. Meese, relying on a legal opinion prepared by Attorney General William French Smith in 1981, said it was lawful for the United States to replenish Israeli missile stocks. Bush seems to have said nothing. Weinberger and Shultz again objected. "I made the same points, George Shultz made the same points. Bill Casey felt there would be an intelligence gain, and there was also talk of the hostages as one of the motivating factors," Weinberger said, ". . . but the responses of the president seemed to me to indicate he had changed his view and had now decided he wanted to do this." [106] Shultz left the meeting "puzzled [and] distressed." [107] The lack of opposition to the proposal, he later said, "almost seemed unreal." [108]

During the next ten days Poindexter and North engaged in a complicated restructuring that converted the initiative into a direct U.S. sale of arms to Iran using Secord as the intermediary. While this restructuring would ease the task of aiding "Ollie's boys in Central America," [109] as Ghorbanifar called them, the change in the form of the initiative was inspired less by North's desire to help the contras than by the practical need of overcoming bureaucratic and legal objections within the administration against using Israel as a go-between. Israel saw Nir's proposal as an opportunity to upgrade its missile arsenal at no cost by shipping basic TOWs to Iran and replenishing its stocks with a more advanced and expensive U.S. version of the missile. This arrangement disturbed the CIA, and the transshipping of the weapons also posed a legal obstacle. After the January 7 meeting, Meese had learned that U.S. law required notification of Congress whenever U.S. weapons were transferred by a third country. This meant that if the TOWs were shipped by Israel, as proposed by Nir, Reagan could not legally keep the initiative a secret. But the principal obstacle to Nir's proposal was Weinberger, who raised objections to it and to every variant of the plan that North proposed. Weinberger was trying to accomplish through bureaucratic means what he had been unable to do in a direct appeal to the president, as North and Casey fully realized. In a PROF message to Poindexter on January 15, North wrote: "Casey believes that Cap will continue to create roadblocks until he is told by you that the President wants this to move NOW and that Cap will have to make it work. Casey points out that we have now gone through three different methodologies in an effort to satisfy Cap's concerns and that no matter what we do there is always a new objection." [110]

On January 16, Poindexter convened a meeting in his office in an effort to navigate the Weinberger roadblock. Weinberger, Meese, Casey and Sporkin attended. Meese said Israel should not ship weapons out of its stocks and recommended that the United States sell missiles directly to the Iranians to avoid the legal requirement of congressional notification. Weinberger objected again, saying he wanted Defense Department lawyers to examine the proposal. The next day Casey told Sporkin he had received a call from Weinberger, who said that "his people have looked it over and . . . signed off on the project." [111] Weinberger does not remember any such conversation. Nor does anyone at the Defense Department seem to have legally reviewed the plan.

It is too much to say that Casey preserved the Iran initiative. The prime mover of the initiative was Reagan himself, not North or Casey, and the president was determined to free the hostages by keeping the missiles flowing to Iran. But Casey's crucial assistance at this time enabled the hard-pressed NSC staff to prevail over the resistance of Weinberger. Casey was the only cabinet officer who took Reagan's side and provided a counterweight to Shultz and Weinberger. His position and his friendship with Reagan guaranteed him access to the White House, where Poindexter also helped to keep open the channels between the president and his director of central intelligence. Long after the congressional investigation had ended, Sporkin told me he believed that Reagan appreciated Casey for wanting to carry out his agenda on Iran. "Reagan was frustrated," Sporkin said. "Weinberger was Dr. No, and Shultz was Dr. I Don't Want to Know. Reagan wanted to get something done, and he had his two major bureaucracies, his secretaries of defense and state, who didn't want to do anything. I think Bill was willing to help and that the president had confidence in Bill." [112]

On January 17, Poindexter at his morning national security briefing presented a new finding to Reagan, virtually identical in wording to the January 6 finding. The restructuring was explained not in the finding itself but in a cover memorandum prepared by North and signed by Poindexter which said that the arms sales to Iran should be conducted by the United States rather than Israel for legal reasons. "The objectives of the Israeli plan could be met if the CIA, using an authorized agent as necessary, purchased arms from the Department of Defense under the Economy Act and then transferred them to Iran directly after receiving appropriate payment from Iran," the memo stated.[113] Secord, although not mentioned by name in the memorandum, was the "authorized agent." But even if Secord had been named, Reagan would not have known it, for he did not bother to read the cover memorandum. Instead, he simply signed the finding and Poindexter wrote "RR per JMP" on the line of the memorandum provided for the president's signature of approval. There is no doubt, however, that Reagan knew what he was approving. That day he wrote in his diary, "I agreed to sell TOWs to Iran."

The deed was now finally done. During a six-week period beginning on December 6, Reagan had signed three findings approving the covert U.S. arms sale to Iran in violation of his publicly stated policy and his promises never to negotiate with terrorists. He had held two full-dress discussions with his top national security officials and ignored and overrode the powerful and passionately argued recommendations of Weinberger and Shultz. The result, even apart from the illegal diversion to the contras, was one of the great debacles of U.S. foreign policy.

On January 17, Poindexter telephoned Weinberger and informed him of Reagan's action. This put an end to the secretary of defense's stalling. Weinberger directed his military aide, Major General Colin Powell, to arrange for the transfer of 3,504 TOW missiles to the CIA for transshipment to Iran through Secord. Before the deal exploded in the administration's face ten months later, 1,500 of these missiles would be delivered to Iran along with a quantity of spare parts for HAWK missiles. Israel received another 500 missiles to replace those it had shipped to Iran. At Casey's order and over the objections of the resident professionals at the CIA, Iran was provided with U.S. intelligence about Iraqi military deployments. The Enterprise accumulated millions of dollars from the arms sale in its Swiss bank accounts to aid the contras and line the pockets of Secord and Hakim. The United States became the laughingstock of the Middle East and eventually of the world.

And the hostages? Instead of accomplishing Reagan's goal of freeing the five Americans held captive in Lebanon, the arms initiative resulted in more hostages being captured than were freed. After Secord and North delivered the first 1,000 TOWs in two shipments on February 17 and 27, not a single American hostage was released. After McFarlane and North had transported HAWK spare parts on their bizarre mission to Tehran late in May, the hostage-holders had released Father Jenco on July 26. He had been replaced by three new hostages, Frank Reed, Joseph Cicippio and Edward Tracy, who were kidnapped in September and October. After 500 Israeli TOWs were delivered to Iran on October 30 and 31 and promptly replaced from CIA stocks, hostage David Jacobsen was freed on November 2. Three more Americans—Alann Steen, Jesse Turner and Robert Polhill—were taken hostage on January 24, 1987. (In addition, American hostage Peter Kilburn, the former librarian at the American University in Beirut, had been killed in captivity on April 14, 1986, apparently in retaliation for the U.S. raid on Libya.) Reagan had signed his third finding on January 17, 1986, in the hope of freeing the five Americans who were then suffering in captivity in Lebanon. Two of these hostages had been released and another murdered. As Weinberger and Shultz had warned, the Iranian-supported Hezbollah had replenished their hostage stocks. A year and a week after Reagan signed his third and final finding approving the covert arms deal, seven Americans were held captive in Lebanon. The Iran initiative had provided more of an incentive for kidnapping Americans than for releasing them.

Seen in this retrospective summary, the initiative was a catastrophe. Seen as the initiative unfolded, it sometimes resembled a comic opera with tragic overtones and an unhappy ending. In ignoring the CIA's well-documented reservations about Ghorbanifar, North and Secord had created the conditions where both the United States and Iran could be betrayed. This became evident late in February after the first 500 U.S. TOWs had been delivered to Iran without producing a hostage release. North and Secord flew to Frankfurt, West Germany, to discuss the situation with Ghorbanifar and Ahmed Kangarlou, the Iranian prime minister's aide for weapons procurement and the first representative of the Khomeini regime to meet directly with the Americans. CIA Near East Division chief Tom Twetten, Nir and Hakim also attended the February 25–26 meetings at the Frankfurt Sheraton airport hotel. Hakim, who wore a wig so he would not be recognized as a former retainer of the shah, had been brought along as a translator because of his fluency in both Farsi and English. He soon discovered that Ghorbanifar was making false translations in an effort to mislead the two sides into thinking they were in agreement. They were not. Kangarlou had been told by Ghorbanifar that the United States would send Iran sophisticated Phoenix missiles that had been on the shopping list Ghorbanifar had presented to Ledeen the previous October. Kangarlou said that once the Phoenix missiles were delivered, Iran could make a "start" in releasing the hostages. Twetten was convinced that Kangarlou was "on the low end of the scale of intelligence" for the job he held and that Ghorbanifar had promised him "hundreds of Phoenix missiles, howitzers, TOWs—just about anything else he wants."[114]

But intelligence was also a scarce commodity within the Reagan administration. It should have been obvious to North and Secord when no hostages were released after the first February shipment that the United States was being taken to the cleaner's, the phrase subsequently used by George Shultz to describe the entire operation. And it also should have been evident to them after the Frankfurt meeting, as it was to Twetten, that Ghorbanifar had duped both sides. By any rational standard, Ghorbanifar should have been dismissed as a middleman then and there. Instead, Secord and North sent the next shipment of 500 TOWs to Iran on February 27, again receiving no hostages in return. By now, including the Israeli deliveries of the previous summer and fall, the Iranians had received 1,504 missiles and released only Benjamin Weir. The judgment of North and Secord may have been affected by money. They were charging the Iranians far more for the weapons than had been paid the Defense Department, and the February shipments alone had created a $6.3 million surplus for Lake Resources. This meant arms for the contras and profits for Secord and Hakim. But Poindexter, whose academic record bespoke a brilliance rarely reflected in his operational conduct as national security adviser, certainly should have recognized by the time of the Frankfurt meeting that Ghorbanifar had been promising hostages he could not deliver. Though Poindexter was angry that the hostages had not been delivered, he approved sending the second February shipment of TOW missiles. So did Donald Regan. "How many times do we put up with this rug merchant type of stuff?"[115] he complained, but he never reviewed the transactions or sought to dissuade Reagan from continuing the initiative. He was preoccupied with the tax and budget bills, Regan said, so "I wasn't paying that much attention to it."[116] The man who thought of himself as White House CEO and a superb manager wasn't managing at all.

And what of Weinberger and Shultz, the only two high-ranking adversaries of the initiative within the administration? Both of them seem to have given up hope after January 1986 of stopping the initiative they had so strenuously opposed. "Secretary Shultz and Secretary Weinberger in particular distanced themselves from the march of events," concluded the Tower Board. "Secretary Shultz specifically requested to be informed only as necessary to perform his job. Secretary Weinberger had access through intelligence to details about the operation. Their obligation was to give the president their full support and continued advice with respect to the program, or, if they could not in conscience do that, to so inform the president. Instead they simply distanced themselves from the program." [117]

Weinberger and Shultz were stung by these statements, for they had opposed the initiative, and Weinberger, at least, thought they had stopped it in December 1985. Neither Weinberger nor Shultz was specifically informed of the January 17 finding. There is nonetheless strong evidence to support the Tower Board's conclusion. Weinberger clearly knew about the weapons transfers, for he had followed the president's orders transmitted to him by Poindexter on January 17 to release the TOW missiles to the CIA. He also knew the purpose for which the missiles were being transferred, for he had discussed (and opposed) the arms sale the day before in the discussion in Poindexter's office. While Weinberger imposed more obstacles to the arms sales than anyone else in the administration, he was well aware throughout 1986 that the United States was sending TOW missiles to Iran.

Shultz also went along, and for a longer period. After McFarlane told him in Geneva of the upcoming November HAWK shipment, Shultz strenuously objected—but to McFarlane, rather than Reagan. When McFarlane made his presentation to Reagan, Shultz and Regan in Geneva on November 19, 1985, "Shultz's facial expressions and body language strongly suggested that he believed he had more important things to discuss with the president, and he commented very sparingly," Regan said.[118] After Shultz and Weinberger had made their case against the initiative at the December 7 meeting, it was Shultz who sensed that Reagan was unhappy with what they had said. Shultz told me that he shared McFarlane's view at the time that the upcoming London meeting would "kill off" the initiative,[119] but his testimony to the congressional committees shows that he remained aware of Reagan's willingness to send arms to Iran if it meant the freedom of the hostages.

Shultz had also left the crucial January 7 National Security Council meeting knowing that he and Weinberger had lost their argument against the initiative. Instead of pushing the issue, Shultz avoided a confrontation with the president. "We had our meetings with Poindexter, Cap and I, and he told us he was trying to move things along, but it was hard and these people were elusive, and so on," Shultz told me. "So I don't know Cap's thinking but my thinking was, 'Well, I'll bide my time, but I haven't changed my opinion.' " [120]

A thousand TOW missiles were sent to Iran while Shultz was biding his time. Shultz claims not to have known further about what was going on until he was informed about an offshoot of the arms deal while attending the Tokyo economic summit in May 1986.* "And I raised hell about it," Shultz said. [121] He sought out Poindexter to make his complaint but instead ran into Don Regan, who promised to raise the matter with the president. According to Regan's later testimony, he never did. When Shultz eventually found Poindexter, the national security adviser told him that the operation he had heard about was being directed by the Israelis, saying, "We are not dealing with these people. This is not our deal." [122] Shultz did not pursue it. He did not seek a meeting with Reagan to discuss the matter nor make inquiries of Bush or Weinberger. Bush, often an ally of Shultz, knew about McFarlane's upcoming trip to Iran and had asked Poindexter to delay it until he had completed a trip to Saudi Arabia early in May. Word of the dealings with Iran was even getting around the State Department. When Peter Rodman went to the NSC from State in 1986, he was broadly acquainted with the outline of the initiative, on which he was promptly briefed and which he strongly opposed. The view within the NSC was that the secretary of state preferred not to know what was happening. And Poindexter, keenly aware of Shultz's opposition to the initiative, was more than willing to accommodate him.

The real failure of Shultz and Weinberger on the Iran initiative was their unwillingness to take concerted action to stop a proposal that both of them thought likely to prove ruinous to their country and their president and was certain to become public. Weinberger could have

---

* Early in May, Ghorbanifar, Nir and Saudi financier Adnan Khashoggi met with British entrepreneur Tiny Rowlands and sought to enlist him in a plan to sell large amounts of grain, military spare parts and weapons to Iran. According to the congressional committees, they told Rowlands that their plan had the endorsement of the U.S. government. Following this meeting, Rowlands informed the U.S. embassy of the plan. Charles Price, the U.S. ambassador to London, passed the information on to Undersecretary of State Michael Armacost, who informed Shultz. The same day Price discussed the information on a secure phone with Poindexter in Tokyo, who said there was a "shred of truth" in Nir's allegation of White House involvement but added that Nir was "up to his own games."

picked up the telephone at any time after January 17 and told Shultz that the NSC staff and Casey had prevailed in their efforts to convince the president to trade weapons to Iran for hostages. Or Shultz could have asked him, since he knew that on this issue he and Weinberger were in agreement. It seems astonishing, considering their strong feelings about the harm that could be caused by the initiative, that neither Weinberger nor Shultz made any effort to join forces. "Both Shultz and Weinberger were opposed to the deal," observed Robert Oakley, the State Department counterterrorism director. "Do you suppose for one moment that Reagan would have persisted in it if the two of them had got together, gone to Jim Baker and said, 'The three of us have to talk to you about that?' They could have convinced him, but they were never into that. There was too much feuding." [123] Weinberger made a joke of it after the initiative became public, saying to the secretary of state, "We must never again agree on anything, because look what happened." [124]

What Weinberger and Shultz also could have done, singly or in combination, was resign. The thought seems never to have occurred to Weinberger. It certainly occurred to Shultz, who told me he thought about quitting after getting word at the Tokyo economic summit that the United States was involved in sending arms to Iran. "And I was told [by Poindexter]," he said, " 'Look, it's not our thing. We have nothing to do with that. So don't worry. Nothing's happened.' So I said, 'Well, I don't have anything to resign about.' " [125] But Shultz had threatened to resign rather easily when he was personally offended, and would again. He first offered to quit in 1983 when he learned that Clark had sent McFarlane on a secret mission to the Middle East. He threatened to resign in 1985 when Clark and Meese induced Reagan to sign the order that would have permitted lie detector tests of cabinet officials. And he threatened again to quit in August 1986 when White House aide Jonathan Miller sought to limit his travel. All of these threatened resignations were over what amounted to points of personal privilege, and the White House backed down each time.

Whether Reagan would have changed course on a policy matter on which he felt strongly is an open question, but he also felt strongly, as he had told McFarlane after the 1984 election, about keeping both Shultz and Weinberger in his cabinet. Neither Weinberger nor Shultz was willing to put the president to the test. In declining to risk their positions to stop the Iran initiative, Shultz and Weinberger were following the custom that usually prevails in Washington. Only some thirty officials in the executive branch of the government with the rank of assistant secretary or above have resigned their positions in public protest during the entire twentieth century. The examples provided by Elliot Richardson in the Nixon administration and Cyrus Vance in the Carter administration are few and far between.*

The one official privy to the Iran initiative who had resigned, though scarcely in protest, never really left the Reagan administration. When Bud McFarlane went off the White House payroll at the end of 1985 he took with him to his Bethesda, Maryland, home a computer that kept him electronically linked with Poindexter and the NSC staff. Reagan told McFarlane in their farewell session that the White House would like to call on him if anything developed on the Iran initiative.[126] The computer was a symbol of Poindexter's reliance on the man he had replaced; it was also a showing of sympathy for a colleague who seemed under emotional strain at the time of his resignation. McFarlane said it was "kind of a half kindness, kind of a half wanting to keep in touch." [127] As the arms deals with Iran unfolded early in 1986, Poindexter and North consulted McFarlane. When the February shipments of TOWs failed to obtain the freedom of any hostages, they turned to McFarlane to help rescue the failing initiative that he had launched.

Ronald Reagan's subordinates often despaired of him because he seemed to inhabit a fantasy world where cinematic events competed for attention with reality. But in their different ways, McFarlane and North seem to have been as divorced from reality as Reagan. North's grasp of reality is reflected in the "notational time line" he submitted on January 24, 1986, to Poindexter. The time line was a projected chronology of the hostage recovery and the delivery and financing of the weapons sales to Iran. The majority report of the congressional committees that investigated the Iran-contra affair termed this chronology "sophisticated," but "bizarre" might have been a better description. One of its

* After President Nixon fired Watergate special prosecutor Archibald Cox on October 20, 1973, Attorney General Richardson, Deputy Attorney General William Ruckelshaus and members of their staffs resigned in public protest—the event known as the "Saturday Night Massacre." Vance resigned in April 1980 because he did not agree with President Carter's decision to rescue the American hostages in Tehran by force. He kept his resignation secret until after the failed raid, then stepped down. A 1975 study, *Resignation in Protest* by Edward Weisband and Thomas M. Franck, found that there had been only twenty-four such resignations in the executive branch in the first seven decades of the twentieth century. The only Reagan official with the rank of assistant secretary or above to resign was Bernard Kalb, the State Department spokesman, who quit on October 8, 1986, after a story by Bob Woodward in *The Washington Post* revealed a secret campaign of disinformation conducted by Poindexter against Libya.

projected entries, on February 11, the anniversary of the Islamic revolution in Iran, was "Khomeini steps down." Poindexter did not challenge this premise, which contradicted U.S. intelligence estimates on the actual situation in Iran. The PROF note correspondence between North and McFarlane also revealed some strange comments by McFarlane. McFarlane's note to North after the latter had returned from Frankfurt in February was particularly strange. Even though not a single hostage had been released following delivery of the 1,000 TOWs, North was convinced that the United States stood on the verge of "a major breakthrough" with Iran. He sent McFarlane a note telling him this. McFarlane replied with a message that began, "Roger, Ollie. Well done—if the world only knew how many times you have kept a semblance of integrity and gumption to US policy, they would make you Secretary of State. But they can't know and would complain if they did —such is the state of democracy in the late 20th century." [128] *

After the Frankfurt meetings, North advanced the idea of a secret mission to Tehran to negotiate directly with the Iranians. It was now becoming increasingly clear that the earlier negative assessment of Ghorbanifar by the CIA and McFarlane had been distressingly accurate. (McFarlane never deviated from the evaluation he had made of Ghorbanifar at the December meeting in London—in one PROF note to North he described him as "a self-serving mischief maker.") [130] As the idea for a direct U.S.-Iran meeting evolved over the two months, Poindexter expressed skepticism both about Ghorbanifar and the integrity of the Iranian regime itself. In an April 16 note to North, two days after the bombing of Libya, Poindexter said, "You may go ahead and go, but I want several points made clear to them. There are not to be any parts delivered until all the hostages are free in accordance with the plan that you layed [sic] out for me before. None of this half shipment before all are released crap. It is either all or nothing. Also you may tell them that the president is getting very annoyed at their continual stalling. He will not agree to any more changes in the plan." [131]

Despite the firmness of this instruction, North and Secord freely ignored it in their attempts to appease the Iranians in the months ahead. Secord denied in his testimony to the congressional committees that the Iranians had ever agreed to release all the hostages, a premise that was

* Looking back on what he calls the "false adulation" of this note, McFarlane said he was trying to cheer North up. "Ollie then, and for a long time, was given to mood swings and idiosyncratic behavior and occasionally deep depression. . . . And so without any justification for it except to lift him out of his depression, I wrote that stupid note." [129]

the basis for Reagan's agreement to send McFarlane and North to Iran in May. McFarlane was less cavalier. He can be faulted for his illusions about the prospects for a new strategic relationship with Iran as well as for his illusions about North, but McFarlane would not deviate from his instructions that all the hostages must be released as a condition for further arms deliveries. These instructions were conveyed to him by Poindexter, who said he had discussed them with the president. Poindexter had first raised the McFarlane mission with Reagan on May 12 and obtained his formal approval for the trip three days later. McFarlane knew from his own dealings with Reagan that the president's principal goal was to free the hostages. This was a precondition to any new U.S.-Iran relationship, and McFarlane would not retreat from it.

While Poindexter clearly conveyed Reagan's views about the priority of the hostages to McFarlane and North, he also shielded the president from an extended advance discussion of the mission, which was controversial even within the NSC staff. Three days before the trip Rodman sent a memo to Poindexter warning of the danger of basing the mission on the premise that the hostages would be freed. "We might be gearing our policy too much to the hostage issue rather than to the strategic menace that the [Iran] regime represents," Rodman said.[132] Poindexter did not trouble to reply. He had already dealt bluntly with North when North proposed that he and McFarlane meet with the president, Shultz and Weinberger before going to Iran—a note which suggests that North, at least, believed that the two dissenting cabinet secretaries were on board. Poindexter replied, "I don't want a meeting with RR, Shultz and Weinberger."[133] The day after he received this note North told Poindexter that he should at least discuss the risks of the mission with McFarlane. "While we all expect this thing to go peachy smooth, it may not," North said. "RCM is taking no small risk in this endeavor. . . . While I'm confident he'll be back next week, I could be wrong and it may be a very long time before anyone sees him again."[134]

Poindexter heeded North's advice and talked to McFarlane before the mission, repeating the instructions that the hostages were to be freed before any additional HAWK spare parts were sent to Iran. McFarlane knew the mission was potentially dangerous, and he was as fully prepared as North to take the risks. But both men were risking more than their own lives. As the congressional committees observed, "The Tehran trip was both an extraordinarily heroic and a very foolish mission for McFarlane and his companions. As the immediate predecessor of the national security adviser, McFarlane knew many of the nation's most sensitive secrets. North was privy to some of them as well, as was [NSC aide Howard] Teicher. Yet, the plan called for them to go to Tehran under false passports and pseudonyms without even safe conduct documents from the Iranian government." [135] As a precaution, McFarlane and North carried suicide pills.

Bearing fake Irish passports, McFarlane and North flew to Tehran from Tel Aviv on May 25, a Sunday morning, in an unmarked Israeli 707 loaded with one of the twelve pallets of HAWK spare parts that the U.S. side had agreed to supply in return for freedom of the hostages. The remaining eleven pallets had been loaded on another plane in Tel Aviv under Secord's control, waiting to be delivered as soon as the hostages were in U.S. custody. Also aboard the plane that landed in Tehran were Teicher, George Cave of the CIA, a CIA radioman who set up a coded satellite link with Washington and Israel's Amiram Nir, posing as an American. The CIA had never liked the idea of using Hakim as a translator and had insisted that he be replaced by Cave, a former Tehran station chief who spoke fluent Farsi. The visiting delegation brought gifts: two .357 pistols and a chocolate layer cake decorated with a brass key. They also brought maps for conducting eight hours of intelligence briefings on Iraq—part of the deal the Americans had agreed to on Casey's order despite the reservations of McMahon and Cave about sharing intelligence with the Iranians.

After eight years of U.S.-Iran estrangement, expectations were high. McFarlane anticipated conducting a dialogue with the three highest-ranking officials below Khomeini: President Mohammed Ali Khameni, Prime Minister Hussein Moussavi and the speaker of the Iranian parliament, Ali Akbar Hashemi Rafsanjani. But McFarlane's hopes sunk swiftly when no one met them at the airport. After the Americans had waited an hour, Ghorbanifar and the government's arms buyer Kangarlou showed up with a detachment of young Revolutionary Guards, who took the gifts and unloaded the spare parts from the plane. So much for a new "strategic initiative" resembling Kissinger's historic breakthrough to China. Months later, Rafsanjani would reveal that the guards had devoured the cake.

The Americans were taken to downtown Tehran and lodged in the entire top floor of the run-down Independence Hotel, formerly the Tehran Hilton. From their fifteenth-floor balconies they could see the skyline of Tehran, with half-built skyscrapers that had been abandoned after the fall of the shah. McFarlane was quickly disillusioned. In a gloomy cable to Poindexter summarizing the first day's events,

McFarlane said, "It may be best for us to try to picture what it would be like if, after nuclear attack, a surviving Tatar became Vice President; a recent grad student became Secretary of State; and a bookie became the interlocutor for all discourse with foreign countries. While the principals are a cut above this level of qualification the incompetence of the Iranian government to do business requires a rethinking on our part."[136]

But during the next four days the Iranians would actually prove quite competent in negotiating for their objectives, which once again differed radically from the promised agenda—or at least the agenda that McFarlane thought had been promised to the Americans. The Iranians began by making the Americans cool their heels at the hotel. When a delegation finally arrived to negotiate at 5:00 P.M., it included only Ghorbanifar, Kangarlou and a low-ranking deputy to the prime minister who used the pseudonym Ali Najavi. The Iranians were interested primarily in the delivery of the remaining spare parts. The two sides could not get beyond platitudinous agreement on U.S. acceptance of the Iranian revolution and mutual distrust of the Soviet Union. McFarlane kept trying to steer the discussion to the hostages, who, he had been told, would be released as soon as the U.S. delegation had arrived in Tehran. Finally, Najavi said that "as a humanitarian gesture, Iran will send a delegation to Beirut to solve that problem."[137] The comment suggested that efforts to free the hostages had not even begun, and McFarlane became angry. He told North they were negotiating with "nobodies" who could neither release the hostages nor begin a dialogue on behalf of Iran.

McFarlane withdrew from the discussions, informing the Iranians that "as a minister, I expect to meet with other decision-makers. Otherwise, you can work with my staff."[138] To underscore his point he remained in his room while North carried on the negotiations. By the evening of the second day in Tehran this tactic had prompted the Iranians to send in a higher-ranking negotiator, Hossein Najafabadi, a member of the parliament and an adviser to Rafsanjani. Najafabadi was suave and well-spoken. McFarlane, on North's assessment, would say in a cable late that night to Poindexter that he was "a considerable cut above the bush leaguers we have been dealing with."[139] Still, McFarlane remained in his room. North stated the U.S. position, saying that if the hostages were released the remaining HAWK spare parts would be delivered within ten hours and that two radar systems would subsequently be sold to Iran.

But Najafabadi, while conciliatory in manner, soon made it clear that he was operating from a different set of instructions than the U.S. team. In a four-hour-and-twenty-minute meeting that lasted until 1:50 A.M. on Tuesday, May 27, Najafabadi offered a sophisticated analysis of Soviet foreign policy intentions. "I am happy to hear you believe in an independent sovereign Iran," Najafabadi said. "We are hopeful that all American moves will be to support this dialogue. But we feel the whole world is trying to weaken us. We feel and see the Russian danger much more than you. You see the threat with high technology. We feel it, touch it, see it. It is not easy to sleep next to an elephant that you have wounded. To weaken Iran does not mean the Soviets want Iran. It means they want to reach the warm waters of the [Persian] Gulf. Our Gulf neighbors know this. We share thousands of kilometers of land and water border. If we are weakened, you can forecast what will happen."[140]

This lecture contested the premise on which McFarlane had constructed his fragile idea of a strategic opening to Iran. While Najafabadi's view of Soviet intentions was at least as harsh as McFarlane's or Casey's, he was also contending that it was in the interests of the United States to aid Iran regardless of what happened to the hostages. After demolishing the premise of the strategic initiative, Najafabadi flatly contradicted North's assertion that Iran had agreed to a ministerial-level meeting and suggested that it would be dangerous for Rafsanjani or other Iranian leaders to meet with McFarlane. Najafabadi pointed out that "the first revolutionary government" had been deposed after Prime Minister Mehdi Bazargan (later executed) had met with Carter's national security adviser, Zbigniew Brzezinski. "As a government we don't want to be crushed tomorrow," Najafabadi said. "We want to stay in power and solve these problems between us."[141] When North said that Ghorbanifar had told them that McFarlane would be able to meet with Rafsanjani and the Iranian prime minister and president, Najavi said that North had agreed to come to Iran in advance to set the agenda and had not come. "We did not mention McFarlane," he said. "The last phone call did not mention ministerial meetings."[142]

Both Iranians also disputed North's contention that Iran had agreed to free the hostages upon McFarlane's arrival, although Najafabadi said he hoped the man they had sent to Lebanon could "solve this problem." But he stressed that delivery of the remaining HAWK spare parts was crucial and said that Iran sought other weapons purchases amounting to a "$2.5 billion deal." Najafabadi said it was up to the United

States to "remove the obstacles," [143] by which he meant delivering the remaining spare parts. The U.S. side had continually referred to the hostages as "obstacles" to better relations. The Iranians were now using the same word to describe the weapons. But McFarlane stuck to his instructions that release of all the hostages was a precondition to any further weapons deliveries. After receiving North's report McFarlane sent Poindexter a cable saying that unless the hostages were released by the following evening the Iranians were "aware that we will leave and that the balance of the shipment will not be delivered." [144]

The next day the Iranians upped the ante. Najafabadi told North, Cave and Teicher that those holding the hostages in Lebanon had imposed new conditions for their release, including Israeli withdrawal from the Golan Heights and southern Lebanon and release of seventeen prisoners held by Kuwait since undertaking a terrorist bombing spree against six targets, including the U.S. embassy, on December 12, 1983. It was these prisoners (called the "Dawa prisoners" because fourteen of them belonged to an Iranian-backed group known as el Dawa) who had inspired the kidnapping of the Americans in Lebanon in the first place. The Reagan administration had consistently used the Kuwaiti action as an example of how nations should respond to terrorism—by refusing to bargain with terrorists and kidnappers. By abandoning this wise policy in pursuit of the Iran initiative, the U.S. team had opened itself to a renewed demand that these prisoners be freed in a trade for the hostages kidnapped to accomplish this purpose.

McFarlane now dropped his insistence on meeting a ranking Iranian official. It was clear that no one higher than Najafabadi would be sent to meet him, and the two men negotiated alone for three hours. Mc-Farlane insisted that all of the hostages were supposed to be released once the U.S. delegation arrived in Tehran. Najafabadi with some agitation wanted to know who had agreed to these terms. "Ghorbanifar and Kangarlou," McFarlane said. Najafabadi replied that Iran had been told that all the spare parts would be delivered before the hostages were released. McFarlane held firm. He told Najafabadi that the U.S. delegation would leave and that the other spare parts would not be sent. In a cable to Poindexter he said, "My judgment is that they are in a state of great upset, schizophrenic over their wish to get more from the deal but sobered to the fact that their interlocutors may have misled them." [145]

The threat to leave had its intended effect. Soon Najafabadi came back to him saying that the Hezbollah in Lebanon had dropped all demands except freedom of the Dawa prisoners. McFarlane said that

U.S. policy was to respect the judicial policy of other nations. Najafabadi then implored McFarlane to deliver the remaining spare parts. "Since the plane is loaded, why not let it come?" he said. "You would leave happy. The president would be happy. . . . If the plane arrives before tomorrow morning, the hostages will be freed by noon. We do not wish to see our agreement fail in the final stage." McFarlane would not budge. "We delivered hundreds of weapons," he said. "You can release the hostages, advise us and we will deliver the weapons." [146]

By now the Iranians must have realized that North was more flexible than McFarlane. Najafabadi made a suggestion that their aides try to work out a compromise. McFarlane consented with the proviso that "staff agreements must be approved by our leaders." [147] Later, Mc-Farlane would come to the conclusion that North had long realized that Ghorbanifar was a liar who had made different promises to the two sides but thought he could solve the problem by paying off Ghorbanifar and his Iranian accomplices. McFarlane believes that Poindexter had also been deceived by North. "It was a hostage bazaar," he said. "I think North knew when we went there that they hadn't agreed to release the hostages." [148]

Near midnight the two staffs reached what appeared to be an agreement. It provided that the second 707 carrying the remainder of the HAWK spare parts would depart within the hour. If the hostages had not been released by 4:00 A.M., the plane would turn back and the U.S. delegation would leave Tehran immediately. North was also flexible about the Dawa prisoners—in contradiction of U.S. policy. He proposed a statement saying that the United States would work through international and religious organizations and third parties in "a humanitarian effort" to secure their release. This statement was designed to give Iran leverage in persuading the Hezbollah to release the hostages. But Najafabadi said that Iran could not accomplish this by 4:00 A.M. and asked for more time. McFarlane, who held a final brief meeting with Najafabadi in an effort to find common ground, was convinced that the Iranians were simply stalling and said to North that they should leave. North told him that the plane had not completed refueling.

Najafabadi showed up again at 2:00 A.M. on Wednesday, May 28. He pleaded that the U.S. delegation give him until 6:00 A.M. to get an answer on the hostages. McFarlane gave him until 6:30. He told Najafabadi that if he gave him a time for the hostages' release, "we will launch the aircraft [with the spare parts] so that it will land here two hours after the hostages are in U.S. custody." He then went off to bed.

But North, Nir and Ghorbanifar stayed awake. They had money in mind as well as the American hostages. Ghorbanifar had borrowed $15 million from his friend Adnan Khashoggi to pay for the shipment. Secord had paid $6.5 million of that to the CIA. In cahoots with Ghorbanifar, North and Secord were vastly overcharging Iran for the HAWK spare parts. Cave had realized that something was amiss two days earlier when Ghorbanifar had drawn him aside and told him to say that the cost of the spare parts was $24.5 million if he was asked. Cave knew that this was about four times what they cost. Secord and North stood to make $18 million on the deal, to pay off themselves and Ghorbanifar and help the contras. Sometime during the early morning hours North sent Secord a message directing him to send the plane carrying the spare parts.

While McFarlane slept, Kangarlou arrived at the hotel with another proposal: two of the hostages would be released immediately, the spare parts would be sent and the remaining hostages would be freed. North accepted this proposal, but McFarlane would not. When he awakened and was told that the plane was en route, he angrily countermanded North and directed that the plane return to Israel. He also refused to accept the two-hostage deal. At the airport, Kangarlou tried again. Again McFarlane refused. He told Kangarlou to tell his superiors that "this was the fourth time they had failed to honor an agreement. The lack of trust will endure for a long time."[149] The U.S. delegation flew out of Tehran at 8:55 A.M. for Tel Aviv, its mission a failure. Reagan wrote in his diary, "It was a heartbreaking disappointment for all of us."[150]

It was during the layover at Tel Aviv that McFarlane learned that more than the freedom of the hostages and the strategic opening had been involved in the mission to Tehran. "Don't be too down-hearted," North said to McFarlane. "The one bright spot is that we're using part of the money in those transactions for Central America."[151]

The following day McFarlane briefed Reagan, Poindexter, Bush and Regan on what had happened in Iran. It was a short briefing, and McFarlane said he felt "kind of hurried along by Regan."[152] McFarlane reviewed the meetings in Iran. He told Reagan that "there were people there who wanted to change things, but they were too weak to move" and recommended that talks should be broken off with the Iranians.[153] Neither McFarlane nor anyone else mentioned the "bright spot"—that the arms deals had provided help for the contras. McFarlane testified that he assumed Poindexter had approved of the diversion and that he would not have made a decision of such magnitude on his own.

20

STRUGGLES
AT TWILIGHT

*A few months ago I told the American people I did not
trade arms for hostages. My heart and my best intentions
still tell me that's true, but the facts and the evidence tell
me it is not.*

RONALD REAGAN,
March 4, 1987[1]

Throughout the secret dealings with Iran and the flow of U.S.
missiles and military spare parts to the Iranian revolutionary government, Ronald Reagan masqueraded as a resolute foe of international
terrorism. And in 1986, for one of the few times in his presidency, he
went beyond denunciation. On April 14, U.S. Air Force and Navy
bombers based in England struck the Libyan cities of Tripoli and Benghazi in retaliation for the bombing of a West Berlin disco where an
American serviceman had been killed. The planes dropped more than
ninety 2,000-pound bombs, at least two of which hit Splendid Gate,
the barracks of Libyan strongman Moammar Qadaffi. The bombs killed
Qadaffi's adopted two-year-old daughter and wounded two of his sons,
but Qadaffi was sleeping in a tent outside the compound and escaped
injury. Scores of civilians died in the U.S. raid, which was widely criticized in Europe and the Third World. France, which had refused over-

flight permission for the U.S. bombers, led the critics. "I don't believe that you stop terrorism by killing 150 Libyans who have done nothing," said French President François Mitterrand.[2] The raid was nonetheless popular with a majority of Americans, who were pleased that Reagan had finally acted to discourage terrorism.

Reagan underscored his resolve on August 27 when he signed a new antiterrorism law that banned all military sales to nations, including Iran, designated as supporters of terrorism. "We can never legislate an end to terrorism," Reagan said in a statement issued after he signed the bill. "However, we must remain resolute in our commitment to confront this criminal behavior in every way—diplomatically, economically, legally and, when necessary, militarily."[3] This claim that the United States was confronting terrorism "in every way" became part of Reagan's boast that America was once more "standing tall." Campaigning to keep the Senate in Republican hands that fall, Reagan said repeatedly, "Every nickel-and-dime dictator the world over knows that if he tangles with the United States of America, he will pay a price."[4]

Reagan's presidential approval ratings were never higher than in the spring and summer of 1986. White House pollster Richard Wirthlin took a survey in May that gave the president a 70 percent favorable rating and an unheard-of 82 percent favorable rating among young voters. Reagan reached his all-time high in a Gallup Poll the following month, with a 68 percent approval rating. Reagan's soaring popularity helped contra aid supporters in the House push through an aid package for the rebels ($100 million, including $70 million in military aid) for the first time in three years despite the forceful resistance of House Speaker Tip O'Neill. The package passed the House by a 12-vote margin on June 25. Reagan hailed it as "a step forward in bipartisan consensus in American foreign policy."[5]

The American public's infatuation with its smiling and unquenchably optimistic president crested on Liberty Weekend, a July 3–6 extravaganza in New York harbor in honor of the centennial of the Statue of Liberty. As described by *The Washington Post*, "A mile-long laser beam leaped across New York Harbor and lit the Statue of Liberty tonight in a blaze of red and white as the nation celebrated the 100th birthday of its most visible freedom. On an unseasonably cold, windy platform on Governors Island, with the twinkling lights of tall ships piercing the sunset, President Reagan and French President François Mitterrand opened the four-day, $32 million party of song, dance, fireworks and patriotic speeches."[6] Three thousand corporate donors who had paid $5,000 apiece, a thousand journalists from forty nations and an estimated one billion television viewers watched as Reagan pressed a button that launched the laser beam and proclaimed, "We are the keepers of the flame of liberty; we hold it high tonight for the world to see." [7]

Liberty Medals, created for the occasion, were presented by Reagan to a dozen naturalized citizens, including Itzhak Perlman, Irving Berlin, Bob Hope, Henry Kissinger and Elie Wiesel. They were distributed during a variety show in which Gregory Peck, Elizabeth Taylor, Kenny Rogers, Andy Williams and Frank Sinatra participated. The show was interrupted by many awkward pauses for television commercials on ABC-TV, which had paid $10 million for exclusive domestic rights. Reagan was back in show business again. Liberty Weekend was a David Wolper production, with the Statue of Liberty serving as leading lady and Reagan cast as the male lead. *Time* magazine's cover that week depicted a jubilant Reagan, with fireworks bursting in air behind him. "Ronald Reagan has a genius for American occasions," said the cover story. "He is a Prospero of American memories, a magician who carries a bright, ideal America like a holograph in his mind and projects its image in the air. . . . Reagan, master illusionist, is himself a kind of American dream. Looking at his genial, crinkly face prompts a sense of wonder: How does he pull it off?" [8]

What Oliver North hoped to pull off on Liberty Weekend was a hostage release that he believed would make Reagan even more popular. Despite McFarlane's recommendation after the Tehran mission to end the secret shipment of U.S. weapons to Iran, Reagan had never abandoned the initiative. He had been typically uncommunicative when McFarlane briefed him, so much so that McFarlane would later say that the president didn't react to his evaluation. Reagan was disappointed that the mission had failed, but he never issued an order to discontinue the initiative. North continued to work with Ghorbanifar and the Israelis in an effort to arrange a trade of arms for hostages. Their political goal was to free a hostage so he could be on stage with Reagan during Liberty Weekend. If this happened, Ghorbanifar wrote his principal Iran contact Kangarlou, "we could exploit it and benefit from it a great deal; we could get the Americans to accept many of our demands." [9] Subsequently, Ghorbanifar told Amiram Nir that a hostage would be freed in time for the celebration. Nir passed this information on to North, who sent a team to Wiesbaden in anticipation of a hostage release. When nothing happened, Poindexter admonished North for falsely raising expectations and told him not to talk to the Israeli official for a while.

. . .

The record suggests that Reagan was determined to get the hostages out, by whatever means possible, and that Poindexter sought to accommodate him. In the heady days after the Libyan raid, military options had again been examined. Records kept by Poindexter's deputy Rodney McDaniel show that military alternatives were discussed by Reagan and Poindexter while McFarlane and North were still in Tehran. This discussion was reflected in a note sent by Poindexter to North soon after the Tehran mission which said, "I am beginning to think that we need to seriously think about a rescue effort for the hostages." [10] North replied that "we have not had much success with this kind of endeavor in the past" and proposed continuing in the "current effort" [11] (i.e., the effort to free the hostages by trading arms for them) instead. Poindexter did not discourage North from pursuing the "current effort," but he also explored the military option. On June 6, Reagan approved military planning to rescue the hostages, and Poindexter asked Casey to intensify the CIA's efforts to locate them. Nothing came of it. The CIA was able to obtain information on the probable location of only two of the hostages and was not optimistic about rescuing them. Even if these hostages survived a rescue effort, the others almost certainly would be killed. The military option lost by default. Instead of planning a military operation, North continued in his efforts to free the hostages through variations of the deal that McFarlane had rejected in Tehran.

Profit motives were now driving the U.S.-Iran initiative. Ghorbanifar, who had sought to make a financial killing, faced ruin or worse unless he could repay the $15 million he had borrowed from Adnan Khashoggi. To pay his debts he needed to deliver the remaining HAWK spare parts to Iran. Secord and Hakim also sought to complete the deal. When they decided to resell U.S. parts to Iran at vastly inflated prices and keep more than half the difference for themselves, they had become profiteers posing as patriots. North also wanted to complete the aborted spare parts delivery, although he sought the money for the contras rather than for himself. He was a zealot and an adventurer, fond of assigning himself such code names as "Blood and Guts" and "Steelhammer," but he was not a profiteer. North was subsequently convicted for accepting an illegal gratuity in the form of a $13,800 security system for his suburban Virginia home, but his action reflected a cloak-and-dagger mind-set rather than a desire to enrich himself from the Iran arms sales. His goals of freeing the hostages and helping the contras were also the president's objectives.

But the profiteering from the arms sales made these goals more contradictory than compatible. In overcharging Iran for U.S. weapons and spare parts, North and Secord generated funds to help the contras while undermining the effort to free the hostages. North should have recognized this, for he was aware that one of the principal barriers to obtaining freedom for the hostages was the view of the Iranians that they were being systematically cheated by the United States and Israel. After the bungled partial delivery of the HAWK missiles from Israel the previous November, North had warned Poindexter that the Iranians would be unlikely to free the hostages in a "single transaction" because of their sensitivity about being "scammed."[12] These justifiable suspicions increased in the wake of the Tehran mission. On June 30, Kangarlou told the CIA's George Cave in a telephone conversation that he had obtained a factory price list of HAWK spare parts which showed the Iranians were being overcharged 600 percent. The same day Ghorbanifar informed Charles Allen, the senior CIA analyst on the Iran project, that the Iranians had complained to him about overcharges. Cave bought time by asking for proof, but he did not alleviate Iranian suspicions. Whether the Iranians would have released additional hostages had they been dealt with honestly cannot be known. What is known is that the Iranians were cheated, in violation of U.S. policy and law and common sense. The only practical Iranian leverage for retaliating was to hold the hostages or to take new ones. Under the circumstances it is not surprising that the Iranians balked at hostage releases and never freed more than a single hostage at any one time.

The willingness of North, Secord and Hakim to systematically cheat the Iranians reflected an attitude of condescension that consistently prevailed in U.S. dealings with Iran. The original initiative had been inspired by a belief that the United States and Iran had common interests in opposing Soviet expansionism, but U.S. policymakers displayed little respect for Iranians and even less for their revolution. Reagan longed for the days of the shah. Weinberger and Shultz, who opposed the arms sales, were supportive of Iraq in the gulf war. Don Regan referred to the Iranians as "rug merchants," and McFarlane used the same phrase in one of the cables he sent to Poindexter from Tehran.[13] North said calmly that he had "lied every time I met the Iranians,"[14] as if this were a proper way for U.S. officials to conduct themselves. He never offered to refund any of the overcharges tucked away in The Enterprise's overflowing bank accounts. Neither those who organized the secret arms deals nor those who opposed them had much use for Iran. In this attitude, administration officials from Reagan on down perfectly mirrored the attitudes of their countrymen, who nourished grievances formed during the long ordeal of the Americans held hostage after the 1979 takeover of the U.S. embassy in Tehran. After the Iran initiative was disclosed, Richard Wirthlin told me that Reagan would have been damaged less in the court of public opinion if he had secretly sent weapons to the Soviet Union.

Working with the Israelis and North, the financially desperate Ghorbanifar now tried to force a hostage release and keep the initiative alive. On July 8 he sent a letter to Kangarlou suggesting that the United States would lose interest in the initiative unless an American hostage was freed. On July 26, Father Jenco was blindfolded, bundled into the trunk of a car and driven from Beirut to Damascus, where he was released on the side of a highway. On July 27 in Frankfurt, Ghorbanifar outlined a six-step plan to North and Cave for continuing the initiative on terms highly favorable to Iran. The first step was payment of $4 million to Ghorbanifar, ostensibly for the spare parts that had been delivered on the Tehran mission but actually for the release of Jenco. Ghorbanifar was paid on July 28. The rest of his proposal called for further deliveries of HAWK spare parts and radars, in return for the sequential release of hostages. Ghorbanifar had also told the Iranians that the United States would provide 1,000 additional TOW missiles free if they could prove that they had been overcharged for the HAWK spare parts. This plan, passed on to Poindexter by North, repudiated the firm stand McFarlane had taken in Tehran of refusing to deliver any additional spare parts until all the American hostages were released.

But North, though often described as an independent "cowboy," was not acting alone. North and Casey were working in concert to keep the arms-for-hostages deal going, with arguments carefully constructed to impress Reagan. The day of Jenco's release, North sent a memo to Poindexter describing the freeing of the priest as "a second and positive step in our protracted and difficult dialogue with the Iranians." [15] He included a Casey memo that said "the Ghorbanifar-Kangarlou connection has worked for the second time—and another American has been released." [16] The CIA director recommended strongly that the initiative be continued and urged that the United States meet Kangarlou's "minimum arguments that would lead to release of the rest of the hostages." [17] Unless this was done, Casey said, it was "entirely possible" that Iran or Hezbollah "could resort to the murder of one or more of the remaining hostages." [18] North made the same argument, saying that "if we want to prevent the death of one of the three remaining hostages, we are going to have to do something." [19]

Poindexter informed Reagan, who was at Camp David, of Jenco's release by telephone, using the North and Casey memos as the basis of his briefing. The view that the remaining hostages faced death if arms deliveries to Iran were halted undoubtedly would have been a clinching argument with Reagan, if any was needed. On July 29, after meeting in Germany with Jenco, North sent a memo to Poindexter urging him to brief Reagan "and obtain his approval for having the 240 HAWK missile parts shipped from Israel to Iran as soon as possible, followed by a meeting with the Iranians in Europe."[20] Poindexter made a note on the memorandum that Reagan approved the shipment on July 30. The HAWK parts were flown to Iran on August 4 in an Israeli plane with a crew provided by Secord. Iran had now received all of the spare parts for which it had offered two hostages in May. In return, Iran had released only Father Jenco.

And Iran was in no mood to release additional hostages or pressure Hezbollah to do so. Instead, the Iranians furnished the proof of the overcharges that Cave had asked for in the form of a factory price list dated November 1, 1985. The Iranians wanted compensation. They were also angered by the results of an inspection of the August 4 shipment, which included 177 spare parts they had not ordered and another 63 that were defective. Ghorbanifar, under pressure from Iran to make good on the shipment but still needing $10 million to repay Khashoggi, complained "hysterically"[21] to Charles Allen about the situation, to which North proposed a dishonest solution. Despite his warning to Poindexter the previous December about Iranian sensitivity to being "scammed," it seems never to have occurred to North that he was creating impediments to release of the hostages by cheating the Iranians. He had already instructed his deputy, Lieutenant Colonel Robert Earl, to use a 3.7 multiplier in calculating prices on future arms shipments, an overcharge of 270 percent. North's response to Iran's producing the factory price list was to ask the CIA to forge a phony price list, something the agency's Office of Technical Services was unable or unwilling to do. His response to Ghorbanifar's complaints was to seek another channel for selling arms to Iran.

Ghorbanifar had by now worn out his welcome with all the Americans. His price markups had contributed to the problems with the Iranians, to whom he had also lied repeatedly. The CIA had never wanted to use him in the first place and would not have done so except for Casey's certification of Ghorbanifar to North after he had flunked his third polygraph test. Now, Secord proposed finding a "second channel" for dealing with Iran, a task for which his associate Albert Hakim, an Iranian who had become a naturalized American citizen, was ideally suited. Working his way through two expatriate contacts, one of whom he promised a "good commission" for his work, Hakim soon established contact with Ali Hashemi Bahremani, a youthful nephew of Rafsanjani who had fought with the Iranian Revolutionary Guards on the Iraqi front. The combination of Bahremani's war record and his personal relationship with the supposedly moderate speaker of the Iranian parliament was impressive to Secord, who reported to North on August 26 that "we have opened up a new and probably much better channel into Iran."[22] North agreed, but he did not completely drop Ghorbanifar. His worry was that Ghorbanifar would destroy the initiative by going public if the Americans refused to deal with him.

By the summer of 1986 word of the secret arms deals with Iran was spreading rapidly throughout the Reagan administration. At North's request, Amiram Nir briefed George Bush when the vice president visited Jerusalem on June 29. Bush's chief of staff, Craig Fuller, who took extensive notes of the briefing that he subsequently turned over to the Tower Board, was amazed by the story. Bush, who already knew more than he was letting on, listened calmly and thanked Nir "for having pursued this effort despite doubts and reservations throughout the process."[23] A few days later Admiral William J. Crowe Jr., chairman of the Joint Chiefs of Staff, was informed of the U.S.-Iran arms deals by his special assistant, Lieutenant General John Moellering, who had been briefed by Assistant Secretary of Defense Richard Armitage. Crowe confronted Weinberger, asking him why the chiefs had been excluded from the decision-making process. Weinberger said this had been determined by Reagan, who as commander in chief "can do what he wants to do."[24] Shultz also was alerted, in a July 2 memo from Under Secretary of State Michael Armacost, who noted renewed conjecture "that the NSC-sponsored search for a U.S.-Iran deal for hostages will produce an early result."[25] Making the case that Shultz himself had made seven months earlier in opposing the Iran initiative, Armacost warned, "As this story surfaces, we are going to sow more and more confusion among our friends, who will recall our frequent lectures on no deals for hostages and no arms for Iran."[26] Shultz took no action. He did not raise the matter in his weekly meetings with Reagan, and he could not even remember seeing the memo when he testified before the Tower Board. As the initiative expanded, both the secretary of state and the secretary of defense continued to avert their gaze.

Meanwhile, the second channel prospered, running in congruence with the first. Bahremani told the Americans he had been informed about Ghorbanifar's activities and thought him to be a "crook" but said he would help him to win the release of additional hostages. On August 8, North, Nir and Cave negotiated a new and remarkably one-sided agreement with Ghorbanifar that provided for delivery of 500 TOW missiles to Iran and replacement of the incorrect items from the August 4 shipment. This would be followed by release of a single hostage, delivery of 500 TOWs and a radar, followed by another hostage release. Afterward, North proposed a repeat of the Tehran mission, in which he would bring 100 TOWs and another radar and return with the final hostage and the body of Buckley. North outlined this plan in a memo to Poindexter on September 2. On September 8, North added more details in another memo and the news, based on a telephone conversation between Kangarlou and Cave, that Iranian Prime Minister Mir Hussein Moussavi approved of the second channel. North saw this as "confirmation that Rafsanjani may be moving to take control of the entire process of the United States relationship and the hostages."[27] The next day this sanguine view was dashed by the kidnapping of Frank Reed in Beirut.

Even a "master illusionist," as *Time* had accurately described Reagan, might reasonably have been expected to discard illusion for reality after the kidnapping of Reed and the follow-up kidnapping of Joseph Cicippio three days later. It should now have been apparent to Reagan, as it had been to Shultz and Weinberger when the initiative began, that paying bribes to hostage-takers encourages additional hostage-taking. North, who wanted the initiative to continue because of its importance to The Enterprise and the contras, was worried that Reagan might draw this reasonable conclusion. The day of Reed's kidnapping, North confided to his notebook his concern that Reagan might cancel the initiative. But North need not have worried. Reagan was by now so stubbornly committed to the trade of arms for hostages that he was not dissuaded from his course even when the two new hostages were taken. Instead of cancelling the entire initiative, he again discussed with Poindexter on September 9 the possibility of a military initiative to free whatever hostages could be located. Once again, this course was rejected on the grounds that more hostages were likely to be killed than freed. Instead, Reagan gave his blessing to what North was already attempting—pursuing the second channel of Rafsanjani's nephew Bahremani "to develop links to the Iranian government."[28] North was instructed by Poindexter to raise $4 million to buy out Ghorbanifar and cut him out of further shipments, "if at all possible."[29] Even this belated restraint was conditional. "If there is no other channel for financing future arms shipments, then Ghorbanifar will be used as a last resort," Charles Allen reported in a September 10 memo to Bill Casey.[30] Despite the kidnapping of two more Americans by terrorists with ties to Iran, Reagan remained firmly committed to selling arms to Iran in an effort to win the freedom of the hostages.

Reagan's desire to free the hostages had inspired his original approval of the McFarlane proposal to endorse Israeli arms sales in 1985 and his subsequent endorsements of North's dealings. There is no doubt that he felt deeply about the captive Americans. But his failure to reexamine his course after it had become clear that the initiative was resulting in the capture of additional hostages remains one of the enduring mysteries of the affair. It is possible that Reagan persuaded himself that Reed and Cicippio were held by a rival group of kidnappers, a dubious rationalization for further dealings with Iran. The groups holding the hostages used different names, but the CIA always believed they had links with one another or were a single group with many aliases. (The latter suspicion would be confirmed in 1990 when Reed was released and told of being held with Terry Anderson.) It is also likely that Reagan was told that the second channel presented an opportunity to form the strategic anti-Soviet relationship with Iran that McFarlane had advocated. Secord, whose primary interest was the profits from the arms sales, told North that his first meeting with Bahremani in Brussels on August 25 was "a comprehensive tour de force"[31] and said that "all things [would be] negotiable if we can clear the hostage matter quickly."[32]

But at all stages of the initiative and in all channels, arms were the only currency for dealing with Iran. When Bahremani was brought by Secord to Washington on September 19 for two days of surreptitiously taped talks in the Old Executive Office Building, he carried with him an extensive list of weapons sought by the Khomeini regime as well as the information that Kangarlou had "played a role" in Reed's kidnapping to put "additional pressure on the United States to send the next shipment."[33] Though the January 17 finding signed by Reagan had envisioned providing a small amount of arms for defensive purposes, Bahremani sought an array of offensive weapons for use in the Iraq war. He also sought U.S. support to topple the Iraqi military ruler Saddam Hussein, to whom the United States had tilted in the gulf war. And

Bahremani was interested in the Dawa prisoners, a subject that North interjected into the discussion. North said the United States could not intervene to free them but expressed confidence Kuwait would take this action "if the government of Iran goes quietly to Kuwait and promises them no terrorism." [34]

After the first day of meetings North and Bahremani walked across the driveway that separates the Old Executive Office Building from the White House. It was a Friday, and Reagan was at Camp David. The day before, in Montgomery, the president had delivered a campaign speech for U.S. Senator Jeremiah Denton of Alabama, who had spent seven and one-half years in a North Vietnamese prison camp. Denton, then facing a political challenge he would not survive, was chairman of a Senate subcommittee on security and terrorism. With himself as president and Denton in the Senate, said Reagan, in a slight variation of his usual theme, "every nickel-and-dime fanatic and dictator knows that if he chooses to tangle with the United States of America, he'll have to pay a price." [35] What would the American people have thought (what might Denton have thought?) if they had known that on the day after this speech a Marine lieutenant colonel was giving an exclusive guided tour of the White House, including the Oval Office, to a member of the Iranian Revolutionary Guards? North was full of himself at this time. Pausing before a portrait of Theodore Roosevelt during the tour, North told Bahremani how Roosevelt had negotiated an end to the Russo-Japanese War in 1905 and won the Nobel Peace Prize for his efforts. In a memo to Poindexter the next day North asked, "Anybody for RR getting the same prize?" [36]

The talks in Washington ended with Bahremani proposing a joint U.S.-Iran commission to develop the relationship between the two countries. With Poindexter's approval, North appointed himself, Secord and Cave as the American representatives. Bahremani then proposed another meeting and said he would keep in touch through Secord and Hakim in the interim. Poindexter briefed Reagan on the discussions with Bahremani on September 23, and the president and his national security adviser subsequently approved a second round of meetings with Bahremani in Frankfurt, again at the airport Sheraton Hotel where North had in February negotiated a TOW shipment to Iran. This time North brought with him as a gift for Rafsanjani a bible inscribed by Reagan. The bible was intended to signify Reagan's approval of the initiative. At North's request, submitted through Poindexter, Reagan had hand-copied a verse from Paul's Epistle to the Galatians: "And the scripture, foreseeing that God would justify the Gentiles by faith, preached the gospel beforehand to Abraham, saying, 'All the nations shall be blessed in you.' " Reagan identified the verse as Galatians 3:8, signed it and dated it, "Oct. 3, 1986."[37]

North was now at apogee, quickly to descend. Bahremani had brought with him to the meeting Ali Samaii, an intelligence officer who had attended the first meeting with Ghorbanifar and Kangarlou in Frankfurt as well as some of the negotiations with McFarlane in Tehran. This should have been a tipoff, if any was needed, that the "first chan-nel" of Ghorbanifar and the "second channel" of Bahremani were running in the same course. While North and Cave had unpleasant memories of Samaii, whom they called "the monster," Hakim was happy to see him and viewed him as "the engine" of a definitive agree-ment with the Iranian regime. Samaii was insistent on U.S. concessions, and North was more than willing to oblige. North was a particularly inventive liar at the Frankfurt talks. In his efforts to placate the Iranians, North described Iraq as the problem and said Reagan had confided to him in a conversation at Camp David, "Saddam Hussein is a shit." Hakim, who was translating, balked at using the word, but North said, "Go ahead. That's his [Reagan's] word, not mine."[38] North, who had never been alone with Reagan and never would be, also invented a conversation in which the president returned to the White House after a weekend of prayer and dramatically instructed North to tell the Iran-ians that God had told him to accept the Islamic revolution in Iran.[39] In giving him the Bible as a gift for Rafsanjani, North said Reagan had declared, "This is a promise that God gave to Abraham. Who am I to say that we should not do this?"[40]

It is doubtful if such nonsense favorably impressed the Iranian ne-gotiators. Without inventing a conversation with Reagan, McFarlane had opened discussions in Tehran five months earlier by saying that the U.S. government accepted the Iranian revolution. This polite formality had led nowhere. The Iranians needed weapons and spare parts to survive, not private assurances that the "Great Satan" recognized the legitimacy of their regime. By the time of the Frankfurt talks, Samaii and Bahremani wanted much more from North than Najafabadi had asked of McFarlane in Tehran. Even North's opening offer went be-yond the Iranian demands in Tehran and beyond the concessions North had been willing to make at that time. In Frankfurt, North offered to deliver 2,000 TOWs, free medical supplies and additional intelligence information in return for a single hostage and the "promise" of two more hostages once the Dawa prisoners were freed. Hostages Reed and Cicippio were not included in the deal, even as a promise, although Bahremani had implicated Kangarlou in Reed's capture.

Favorable as these terms were to the Iranians, they were not enough for Samaii. He asked for artillery to attack Iraq, which North said the United States would be willing to provide on condition that the shells not be used against Baghdad. North's offer flatly violated the proviso in the January finding limiting sales to "defensive" weapons. When Samaii asked North to "show me the way" to win the confidence of his superiors and the Lebanese kidnappers of the American hostages, North mentioned the Dawa prisoners and said he understood the desire of the Lebanese Shiites to free their "brethren who are held in Kuwait as convicted terrorists."[41] North assured Samaii that the United States would not criticize Kuwait if the Dawa seventeen were freed and said that he and Poindexter had conveyed this view to the Kuwaiti foreign minister on October 3.* He said that all Kuwait would need was a promise from "somebody in authority"[43] that there would be no more attacks on the nation's ruling family.

North's concession was a repudiation of the antiterrorist policy long enunciated by Reagan, Shultz and other high-ranking U.S. officials, including Poindexter. U.S. officials had frequently praised Kuwait for its courage in refusing to release the convicted Dawa terrorists. A few days after the Frankfurt meeting, *Newsweek* learned of reports that the Dawa prisoners might be released and inquired if the Reagan administration was prepared to make concessions. The response was a White House "press guidance" that reiterated U.S. policy. "We will not negotiate the exchange of innocent Americans for the release from prison of tried and convicted murderers held in a third country," the statement said. "To make such concessions would jeopardize the safety of other American citizens and would only encourage more terrorism."[44] As a description of administration conduct, the statement was a lie. As a summary of the risks of the exchange of hostages, it was accurate and predictive. On October 21, American writer Edward Tracy was cap-

---

* Congressional investigators were unable to determine whether Poindexter actually made this offer to Kuwait in the October 3 meeting. But in view of Poindexter's subsequent willingness to make concessions on the issue of the Dawa prisoners, it seems likely that he did so. The difference between Poindexter and North on this matter seems to have been more of style than of substance. North believed the prisoners would be released eventually and testified that "the United States might as well get something for them."[42] Poindexter was willing to deal, but more circumspect in his approach; he was keenly aware that George Shultz was firmly opposed to using the Dawa prisoners as bargaining leverage.

tured in Lebanon, increasing the store of U.S. hostages held by Iran and its Shiite allies.

North did not stay for the wind-up of the Frankfurt talks. He returned to Washington after learning that a C-123 plane transporting arms and supplies to the contras had been downed by a Nicaraguan missile. A crew member, Eugene Hasenfus, had been captured. The timing of the incident could not have been worse from North's point of view. The first portion of the military aid Congress had approved in June was finally scheduled to reach the contras later in October. In the meantime the rebels had been held together by the CIA and a North venture known as Project Democracy, which funneled private contributions and some of the overcharges from the Iran arms sales to the contra forces. The capture of Hasenfus threatened to expose these covert efforts, about which North and Poindexter had lied to Congress, less than a month before the midterm elections. North had no choice but to give the Hasenfus affair his top priority.

Secord, who had business in Brussels, and Cave also departed, leaving Hakim in charge. The CIA had disliked relying on Hakim even for translation at the Frankfurt meeting. Now the Iranian-born businessman was running the show, armed only with the loose guidelines of North's negotiating proposal. The initiative that was supposed to chart the course of U.S.-Iranian relations had been put in the hands of a private citizen who had lived most of his life in Iran, lacked any background in diplomatic negotiation and stood, by his own estimate, to make "many millions" of dollars from the agreement he was negotiating. Hakim was not troubled with concerns about conflicts of interest. "What bothered me was that we didn't have the competence within the government to do what I could do," he testified more than eight months later. "That still bothers me." [45]

North had given both Hakim and the Iranians a deadline when he left. He had also told Hakim that the president wanted a hostage released by election day. North said that if no agreement was concluded by the time he returned to Washington he would report to Reagan that the meeting was unsuccessful and recommend that the second channel be closed. The effect of this deadline was to pressure Hakim to make additional concessions to the Iranians. The nine-point agreement that Hakim would refer to proudly as the "Hakim Accords" provided for delivery of 500 TOWs and presentation of a plan for freeing the Dawa prisoners before the release of any American hostage. Even then, only a single hostage would definitely be freed. The Iranians promised to make "all effective possible effort" to obtain release of a second hostage. Regardless of whether this effort succeeded, another 1,000 TOWs were to be sent to Iran, plus technical assistance to operate the HAWKs and additional intelligence information about Iraq. The agreement had been written in Farsi. When Secord returned from Brussels, he cabled a translation of it to North with his approval. North was jubilant, seeing the accords as a way to free two hostages for "nothing more than the two sets of 500 TOWs." [46]

The agreement in the secret talks that so delighted North and Hakim forfeited any remaining semblance of American honor, a word that seems not to have been mentioned during the negotiations. The Dawa prisoners aside, the agreement violated the principles that Poindexter had laid down as Reagan's policy at the time of the Tehran mission. Poindexter had specifically instructed McFarlane that all American hostages would have to be released as a condition of further arms deliveries to Iran, and McFarlane had aborted the mission when the Iranians would not comply with these terms. Even North, who had been willing to accept two hostages in Tehran, had taken the position at the Washington meeting with Bahremani that all the hostages must be freed. But the agreement reached in Frankfurt provided weapons, technical assistance, medicines and vital intelligence to Iran for the guarantee of only one hostage in return. The three Americans kidnapped in September and October to give the Iranians extra bargaining power were barely mentioned. The eighth point of the nine-point "Hakim Accords" said only that "Iran will continue its effort for creating the grounds for the release of the rest of the hostages" [47]—and this after 1,500 TOWs had been delivered and the Dawa prisoners freed. The return of Buckley's body was not mentioned at all.

Reagan, who prided himself on consistency, seems not to have noticed, then or later, that when he approved the "Hakim Accords" he was abandoning the administration's position on the Dawa prisoners and the principle that all the hostages be freed. He does not even mention these accords in his memoirs, and I have been told that his diary entries do not reveal any cognizance of how much he had conceded. Few of the details of the approval process are known, but Reagan did not waste any time in acting. Hakim testified that after the translation of the accords was submitted to Washington on October 8, he was informed by North that day of the president's approval. Reagan's unpublished diary entries apparently support this assertion and so does the fact that a draft of the agreement was sent the same day to the CIA. But Reagan did not realize, or at least did not accept, the fact that the agreement had been reached in negotiation with the Revolutionary Guards rather than the "moderate elements" described in the January finding. The notion that U.S. negotiators were dealing with "moderates" had become firmly implanted on Reagan's mental cassette, never to be dislodged. (Reagan continued to insist in an interview for this book that he had been dealing with moderates.) [48]

Poindexter deserves some of the blame for Reagan's lack of awareness. The congressional investigators who had access to the relevant diary entries concluded that the national security adviser never told Reagan that the "second channel" was the Revolutionary Guards. Poindexter may also have slid over the concessions the United States was offering on the Dawa prisoners. He later maintained that the accords had not compromised U.S. policy on the Dawa prisoners because Secord was a private citizen. Poindexter testified that he told the president about every point in the agreement, "and he approved the ones that applied to the U.S. government." [49] This rationalization may also have been embraced by Reagan. In fact, every one of the nine points in the accords involved the U.S. government. North, who represented the government, had made the original offer to help with the Dawa prisoners. And Secord was not functioning as a private citizen in Frankfurt. Poindexter had approved North's appointment of Secord to the commission to conduct the negotiations, and he had briefed Reagan on the negotiations and the composition of the U.S. team.

Surprises were in store for North, Secord, Hakim and Cave when they met with Bahremani and Samaii on October 29 at Mainz, south of Frankfurt, to implement the agreement. It was the Wednesday before the midterm elections, and rumors of hostage releases were circulating in the Middle East. Bahremani told the Americans that the deal was in danger of exposure because radical students in Iran opposed to the initiative had printed "five million" pamphlets describing McFarlane's visit to Tehran. An account of the mission also had been published by a small Hezbollah newspaper in Baalbek, the Revolutionary Guard center in Lebanon. The Americans were worried that the story would get out. When Bahremani said that Rafsanjani wanted to rebuild Phoenix missiles that the Iranians possessed but were unable to operate, North and Secord told him that the political risk of sending in U.S. technicians to accomplish this purpose was too great as long as the hostages were still held. If Iran could get the hostages out, Secord promised, "we'll go back in and rebuild the goddamn air force. I built it once, I'll go back in and build it again. That was my baby . . . I built that air force—four and a half years on it."[50]

Bahremani's other surprise, one that Cave said "really blew our minds,"[51] was the information that the second channel of which Secord was so proud had really been an offshoot of the first. Bahremani told the Americans that when Najafabadi had raised the issue of establishing relations with the United States, Rafsanjani had favored it "but for his own politics he decided to get all the groups involved and give them a role to play."[52] Thus was the "second channel" created. Rafsanjani's purpose, Bahremani explained, was to give "all parties" in Iran a stake in the initiative so that there would not be "an internal war" if it failed. The great conflict between "radicals" and "moderates" on which the Iran initiative had been premised was a U.S. delusion that the Iranians had exploited for their own purposes.

North and Secord were now desperate to win the freedom of at least one American hostage before election day. North argued that he had kept his end of the bargain and had "already met with the Kuwait foreign minister secretly in my spare time between blowing up Nicaragua."[53] The congressional committees would later determine that North "divulged to the Iranians classified material of particular sensitivity."[54] But the message that it was necessary to act before the election got through to the Iranians. After the Mainz meeting broke up, North reported through his deputy Robert Earl to Poindexter that Bahremani had assured him that two or three hostages held by Hezbollah would be released not later than Sunday, November 2. To insure that Reagan received political credit for the anticipated hostage releases, North proposed that the president himself make the announcement as soon as the "AMCITS" were in U.S. government hands but "before CNN knows it has happened."[55] The Americans thought it so urgent to complete the deal before the election that 500 TOWs were shipped to Iran from Israeli stocks on October 30 and 31, to be replaced the following week by an equivalent number of American missiles. North and Secord flew to Cyprus and then took a helicopter to Beirut to await the release of the hostages. They had cover for their actions in the person of Terry Waite, the special envoy for the Archbishop of Canterbury, who had extricated four British citizens from a Libyan jail and had been credited by the White House for the release in 1985 of American hostage Benjamin Weir, the first beneficiary of the arms-for-hostages dealings. Waite, who would later become a hostage himself, was accustomed to working with North and did so on this occasion. He made an appearance in Beirut on Friday, October 31, and called the Associated Press office. "Something might happen," Waite announced. "Nothing hard yet, but it's moving."[56] Then he flew to Cyprus in a U.S. Army helicopter.

The American hostages in Lebanon were not a political issue in the 1986 elections, and there is nothing to indicate that their release would have affected Senate campaigns then being waged on various domestic and personal issues. But North, Secord, Poindexter and Casey thought of politics in conspiratorial terms. When he served as Reagan's campaign manager during the 1980 campaign, Casey had worried that President Carter would spring "an October surprise" and try to win the election with a dramatic stroke that would free the Americans then held hostage in the Tehran embassy. The lack of such a surprise had benefited Reagan and the Republican Party, especially in Senate races. The idea that the 1980 election might have turned on the hostage issue, in itself questionable, stuck in the minds of the Americans conducting the 1986 negotiations. They simply assumed that freeing an American hostage would help the Republican Party keep control of the Senate.

That control of the Senate was critical for the Reagan administration there was no doubt, either then or later. In 1980 the Republicans had gained twelve seats, winning control of the Senate for the first time since 1952. Throughout the next six years the Senate had been Reagan's pillar on fiscal issues and foreign policy, usually by supporting him and sometimes (as in the imposition of sanctions against South Africa) by saving him from himself. Reagan was never a nuts-and-bolts politician, but he realized the importance of keeping the Senate in Republican hands. In an extraordinary midterm campaign effort, Reagan had traveled 24,000 miles and made fifty-four appearances in twenty-two states, raising $33 million for Republican candidates. Most of that effort had been directed at holding the Senate, which hung in the balance in October 1986. As Reagan campaigned in seven midwestern and western states the week before the election, Poindexter hoped that the announcement of a hostage release would tip the election in the GOP's favor. Riding in a car to a campaign event with Poindexter about ten days before the election, White House political director Mitch Daniels made an innocuous comment about the plight of the hostages in Lebanon. Poindexter surprised him by responding, "Look for some good news, and I think you'll have it in a timely fashion."[57] Daniels did not press the normally taciturn admiral for details, but he realized that Poindexter was suggesting that an American hostage would be released before election day. In 1986 it was the Reagan White House that was preparing its own "October surprise." *

Reagan spent the final weekend before the election at his mountain-top ranch northwest of Santa Barbara, exhausted from campaigning. Daniels, armed with the latest polling information in closely contested elections, was disconsolate about his party's prospects for holding on to the Senate. Even presidents reelected by landslides have found it difficult to transfer their popularity in midterm elections. Franklin Roosevelt had learned this the hard way in 1938, as had Dwight Eisenhower in 1958. It was apparent to Daniels that Reagan was about to learn the same lesson in 1986.

At nine minutes after midnight on the morning of Sunday, November 2, Reagan was awakened in his ranch house by a telephone call from Poindexter, calling on his secure line from the White House staff office at the Santa Barbara Biltmore. Poindexter told the president that American hostage David Jacobsen had just been released in Beirut and said he was hopeful that another hostage would soon be released. Jacobsen had been freed on the Beirut seafront, near the wreckage of the bombed-out U.S. embassy, and picked up by North's waiting helicopter. He was the second and last hostage to be released as a result of the 1986 arms shipments to Iran. The Americans had sold thousands of TOW missiles and hundreds of HAWK spare parts and donated valuable intelligence information to Iran in the effort to free Jenco and Jacobsen. The Iranians and Hezbollah had given nothing but money and two quickly replaced hostages in return. After the kidnapping of the three Americans in September and October, the Lebanese terrorists with whom Reagan had promised never to bargain held one more hostage in custody than when the bartering began.

Poindexter was under pressure on the day of Jacobsen's release, and with him the White House staff. He had optimistically composed a statement welcoming the release of two hostages and discussed it cryptically with White House spokesman Larry Speakes. When a second hostage was not released, Poindexter drafted a statement in Reagan's

---

* Daniels was surprised by Poindexter's remark but did not attach any significance to it until after the Iran initiative had been disclosed. When Daniels and I had dinner in Santa Barbara on the weekend before the election, we briefly discussed the rumors of a hostage release produced by Waite's return to Lebanon. Daniels thought then that the principal impact of a hostage release would be to distract public attention from the election. Since Republican Senate candidates in four closely contested western states, including California, were trailing but closing on their opponents, Daniels did not view any such distraction as necessarily helpful to the GOP goal of holding the Senate.

name expressing "personal appreciation to the various parties and intermediates who have been helpful" in arranging Jacobsen's release. "We have been working through a number of sensitive channels for a long time," the statement said. "Unfortunately, we cannot divulge any of the details of the release because the lives of other Americans and other Western hostages are still at risk." The statement said that "no political goals are or will be achieved by resorting to extortion and terrorism."[58] The Iranians and their Lebanese allies had, of course, achieved many of their goals by this method.

Those of us in the White House press corps who had accompanied Reagan to Santa Barbara had no hint of the reasons for Jacobsen's release, but we were being bombarded by calls from editors wanting to know more about the U.S. role. Speakes, who usually made himself scarce in Santa Barbara, worked overtime that weekend, pressing Poindexter for information with limited success. Mitch Daniels has a vivid memory of Speakes striding into the staff office at the Biltmore and asking Poindexter if any concessions had been made to obtain Jacobsen's release. Poindexter did not answer him, but instead retreated to his desk and composed a short statement for Speakes to give reporters. Daniels wondered why Poindexter had not simply told Speakes, "No."[59]

Speakes was also wondering. He had been skittish about information provided him by Poindexter ever since the admiral had lied to him in 1983 about the invasion of Grenada. When news reports had linked North to Hasenfus late in October, Speakes had ducked questions, telling reporters he didn't "know anything about it."[60] Speakes realized, however, that something more was expected of him on the morning of November 2. To those of us who reached Speakes early in the day, he emphasized that his information about Jacobsen had come from Poindexter, which we knew to be a thinly disguised warning to believe it at our risk. Later in the morning, when Speakes gave a formal briefing, he followed his instructions and gave much of the credit for Jacobsen's release to Terry Waite but protected himself by leaving the door open to other explanations. NBC's Andrea Mitchell noticed that Speakes was hedging and said he was "leaving the clear impression that someone else has been involved in this besides Terry Waite."[61] Speakes did not disagree. "The United States government has certainly been involved," he said. "We have had a very active program of securing the release of those held hostage for a period of time, and certainly the president's men have been involved in it."[62]

The White House spokesman was treading a fine line, trying to follow his instructions while also conveying his suspicion that there was more to Jacobsen's release than he had been told. But Speakes found it difficult to keep his temper under pressure. Late in the briefing, he was asked by Ira Allen of United Press International if Reagan would attempt to exploit the hostage release politically. This was exactly the purpose that North and Poindexter had in mind by insisting on a hostage release before the election. But Speakes disliked Allen, and he allowed his personal feelings to overcome his judgment. "Is the president going to play politics with this issue?" Speakes said in a cold fury. "No. You're in one inch of getting your head lopped off with a question like that." [63]

Jacobsen's release could not keep the Senate in Republican hands. Neither could Reagan's strenuous campaigning, which continued unabated on the morning of November 3 with speeches for Senate candidates in Nevada and California. These two races were a paradigm of the 1986 campaign. In Nevada, the Republican nominee was a former Democrat named James Santini, who had been pressed into running after popular incumbent Paul Laxalt had declined to seek reelection. The Reagans knew that Laxalt's retirement put an otherwise safe Senate seat at risk, and Nancy Reagan had pleaded on the phone with Laxalt to reconsider his decision to retire. Laxalt, displaying a stubbornness worthy of Reagan, had stuck to his decision and devoted his energies to electing Santini. But Laxalt's popularity was no more transferable than Reagan's. Santini was distrusted by Democrats as a turncoat and not fully accepted by Republicans. Reagan was highly popular in Nevada. Santini, who trailed throughout, surged in the polls after Reagan spoke on his behalf in Las Vegas on June 25, and again after a Reagan stop in Reno on October 30. The problem, as Daniels observed, was that the surges did not hold and that it was impossible for Reagan to take up residence in Nevada for the duration of the campaign. Daniels, supported by Don Regan, opposed a final Reagan trip to Nevada. But Reagan heeded Laxalt's urging and decided to make a final try. His speech in Las Vegas on the morning of November 3 stressed the importance of retaining a Republican Senate. "My name will never appear on a ballot again," he said. "But if you'd like to vote for me one more time, you can do so by voting for Jim Santini." He concluded with a variation of the theme: "When you go to the polls, win one for Jim Santini, win one for the future and for America's future, and, yes, win one for the Gipper." *

* Reagan used this message during the last three weeks of the campaign in states where there were Senate contests, even though Daniels always acknowledged the difficulty of transferring the presi-

Later that morning Reagan spoke in Costa Mesa, California, on behalf of Republican Senate candidate Ed Zschau, who was locked in a close race with California's veteran Democratic senator Alan Cranston. Reagan was on old home ground in Orange County, where he had launched his campaign for governor twenty years earlier. Overcome with sentiment, he seemed almost to have forgotten about Zschau. Reagan told a flag-waving and youthful audience that their children or grandchildren would someday ask them about "a November day a long time ago when a former sports announcer named Dutch Reagan came to town for the last campaign. And should that happen—and since I won't be able to myself—I hope you'll tell them for me that I said it wasn't true, that there are really no last, no final campaigns, that each generation must renew and win again for itself the precious gift of liberty, the sacred heritage of freedom. . . . Being an American also means that on certain special days, for a few precious moments, all of us—black or white, Jew or gentile, rich or poor—we are all equal, with an equal chance to decide our destiny, to determine our future, to cast our ballot. Tell them, too, of my fondest hope, my greatest dream for them: that they would always find here in America a land of hope, a light unto the nations, a shining city on a hill. . . . I'm proud to be an American, where at last I know I'm free. And I won't forget the men who died, who gave that right to me. And I'll gladly stand up next to you and defend her still today. 'Cause there ain't no doubt I love this land. God bless the U.S.A."[65] And the audience responded, in the Olympics chant of 1984 when all things seemed possible, "U.S.A.! U.S.A.! U.S.A.!"

Zschau lost. So did Santini and six of the dozen Republican senators who had been swept to victory in the 1980 electoral landslide. The Democrats recaptured the Senate, winning nine seats held by Republicans while losing only one of their own. Reagan, who in 1980 had been widely credited on what some thought scant evidence for the triumph of other Republicans, abruptly lost his reputation as a political magician. In fact, Reagan may actually have had a greater impact in the 1986 elections than in any of his previous campaigns, although this could not be demonstrated by the outcomes. Santini had trailed by 13 percentage

---

dent's popularity to GOP Senate candidates. The targets of the message were Republican-leaning independents who had voted for Reagan in 1984 but were indifferent to the Senate races. Reagan's presence and message was intended to get these voters to the polls. "We thought Reagan might be the tiebreaker," Daniels said. "It was the only thing we had left to do."[64]

points when Reagan campaigned for him in Reno on October 30. He was down by 8 points when Reagan returned to Las Vegas on November 3. He lost by only 6 points. Zschau, a businessman-congressman who resisted professional political advice, had frittered away his chances by vacationing while Cranston was waging a negative television campaign defining Zschau as a "flip-flop" candidate. Zschau lost by 2 points, closer than he had been in any poll. Nationally, Republican candidates for the Senate fared better in percentage terms (49 percent) in 1986 than when the same seats were up in 1980 (47 percent). But Republicans won nearly every close contest in 1980, while losing eleven of the fifteen closest races in 1986.

The Reagan administration had also run out of luck in its covert attempt to barter arms for hostages. On Monday, November 3, the Lebanese magazine *Al-Shiraa* had published the story of McFarlane's mission that had been related earlier in the radical student pamphlets and the Hezbollah newspaper in Baalbek. The same day, the Hezbollah faction known as Islamic Jihad (Holy War) claimed credit for the release of Jacobsen, saying it had acted in response to White House "overtures." On November 4, election day in the United States, Rafsanjani acknowledged McFarlane's mission in a speech to the Iranian parliament. Both *Al-Shiraa* and Rafsanjani repeated the erroneous version of the story contained in the student pamphlets, saying that McFarlane had visited Tehran in October. When reporters asked McFarlane about Rafsanjani's account, he denied he had gone to Iran in October without saying that he had been there in May.

McFarlane's evasion and some calculated stonewalling by Reagan and Poindexter succeeded in fending off an increasingly suspicious White House press corps until after the election. This was not entirely a matter of political duplicity, of which there would be plenty from the White House in the weeks ahead. Based on coded reports he had received from North, Poindexter still hoped a second hostage might be released. Keeping the lid on served the dual purpose of preserving this possibility and the political objective of concealing the initiative until after the election. Speakes was told not to comment. When he was asked on Air Force One en route from Las Vegas to Los Angeles whether Iran was involved in the negotiations to free Jacobsen, Speakes said, "I'm not going to get into any of that stuff."[66] Reagan also declined comment to shouted questions as he boarded Air Force One in Los Angeles en route to Washington. But the story was now circulating on the wire services, and Speakes knew that "No comment" was wearing thin. On the flight back to Washington he went to Poindexter, who after several tries wrote out a cryptic memo on a sheet of yellow paper in question-and-answer form. The answer to the question of whether the United States still maintained an arms embargo against Iran was: "As long as Iran advocates the use of terrorism, the U.S. embargo will continue." The answer to the question of whether the embargo was still in effect was "Yes."[67] Speakes became worried that Poindexter was pulling another Grenada. When he repeated the answers to reporters, he made a point of telling them that the information had been provided by Poindexter.

The story broke in U.S. newspapers on Wednesday morning, November 5, based largely on Rafsanjani's speech. Terry Waite, who had accompanied Jacobsen from Beirut to Cyprus and then to Wiesbaden, West Germany, held a news conference there, saying the situation was "very sensitive" and hinting of more hostage releases to come. "At the moment the two people specifically in my sights are Terry Anderson and Tom Sutherland," Waite said.[68] But Anderson and Sutherland were not released, and extensive accounts of the Iran initiative were reported in November 6 editions of *The Washington Post* and the *Los Angeles Times*. At a White House bill-signing ceremony the same day a reporter shouted to Reagan, "Mr. President, do we have a deal going with Iran of some sort?" Reagan denied it. "No comment," he said. "But could I suggest an appeal to all of you with regard to this: that the speculation, the commenting and all, on a story that has come out of the Middle East and that to us has no foundation—that all of that is making it more difficult for us in our effort to get the other hostages free."[69]

Congress was soon in an uproar over the disclosures. Senate Majority Leader Bob Dole expressed concern that the administration had rewarded terrorists, and Senate Minority Leader Robert Byrd demanded a full investigation. Instead of acknowledging the truth, Reagan tried to use David Jacobsen to deflect further inquiries. Reagan presented a tired and distraught Jacobsen to reporters in the White House Rose Garden on November 7, saying that "a great many prayers have been answered by his presence in our country."[70] Jacobsen, who had been badly treated in captivity, implored reporters not to speculate, saying he had been released through the humanitarian intervention of Terry Waite, who was "free of all governments and any types of deals."[71] Jacobsen was merely repeating what he had been told. Reagan, who knew that Waite was a cover story rather than the reason for Jacobsen's

release, relied on Jacobsen to make the case that discussion of the
initiative could harm the remaining hostages.

The safety of the hostages became Reagan's excuse for lying and
would remain his excuse long after it was evident that no additional
hostages would be released. But most of his lies were self-serving and
of no conceivable help to the hostages. It did not help the hostages for
Reagan to say that the initiative had "no foundation." And it did not
help, either, that Reagan, facing the clamorous reporters with Jacobsen
at his side, lied in saying that Shultz and Weinberger had supported the
initiative he denied even existed. Reagan may not have known that
North had told the Iranian negotiators at the Mainz meeting that the
two cabinet secretaries opposed the policy. But their opposition had
already been disclosed by the *Los Angeles Times* and *The Washington
Post* the previous day, and Reagan hurt only his own credibility by
denying it. Reagan may have been too distraught to recognize this.
When reporters asked him why he didn't dispel speculation by telling
what had happened, he said, "Because it has to happen again and again
and again until we have them all back." [72]

As Reagan and Jacobsen turned away from the podium, reporters
continued to shout questions. Jacobsen wheeled on them saying, "In
the name of God, would you please be responsible and back off." [73]
Don Regan later observed that Jacobsen's performance "had the flavor
of ventriloquism. Jacobsen was saying exactly what the president himself would have said if he had been able to afford the luxury of losing
his temper." [74]

North, meanwhile, was trying to keep the initiative alive. On November 8, North, Secord, Cave and Hakim met in Geneva with Samaii,
who by now suspected Ghorbanifar of being an Israeli agent and was
wary of further deals. North told Samaii he had come to Geneva "at
the order of the president" and declared that his objective was the same
as it had been in Washington and Frankfurt. Samaii said the Dawa
prisoners would have to be freed before the "other two hostages" could
be released.* The Americans responded that they had done everything
"humanly possible" to accomplish this and suggested that Iran send a
delegation to Kuwait. The meeting broke up without agreement, but
North remained optimistic. He wrote in his notebook for November 8

---

* By the "other two hostages," Samaii was referring to Terry Anderson and Thomas Sutherland,
who had been held hostage since the spring of 1985. The U.S. position in the negotiations had
eroded so badly that freeing the three hostages snatched in Lebanon in September and October
of 1986 does not seem even to have been discussed.

that Samaii had said that "something may be possible"[75] if some, rather than all, of the Dawa prisoners were released. On November 11, at Hakim's request, North drafted a statement for Rafsanjani, which proclaimed that "acts of terrorism are not acceptable to advance the aims of the Islamic Revolution."[76]

The Iran initiative was finished, though Reagan, Poindexter and North were slow to realize it. Reagan clung for days to the illusion of additional hostage releases, although even a superficial reading of the accords that had been reached at Frankfurt should have convinced him otherwise. The Iranians had done everything they had said they would do short of some movement by Kuwait on the Dawa prisoners. The problem was not Iranian duplicity but the one-sided nature of the deal that had been struck at Frankfurt. The Iranians had promised the definite release of only a single hostage and had delivered him in the person of Jacobsen. There would be no more hostage releases during the Reagan presidency, although four other Americans would be kidnapped in Lebanon.

Reagan, who prided himself on his negotiating skills, was unwilling to face the fact that he had agreed to a terrible bargain. Trading arms for hostages was a most dubious premise in the first place. But even if the premise is granted, it made no sense for the United States to deliver the arms first and hope for the hostage releases later. McFarlane, despite his enthusiasm for the Iran initiative, had recognized this in Tehran and had been told by Poindexter that this was the president's position. Reagan could never bring himself to admit that he had been outsmarted. He was angry with the press and the Iranians, when he should have been angry with Poindexter and North—and with himself.

Poindexter was by then so far in over his head that he seemed not to have any awareness of the depth of the water. His counsel almost until the day he was asked for his resignation was to keep the lid on and say as little as possible. Privately, he enlisted McFarlane and North in the preparation of a chronology of events that would turn out to be misleading in some respects and totally false in others. But Poindexter proceeded slowly and deliberately, puffing on his pipe as was his habit, and downplaying the importance of the clamor in Congress and the media. He loved secrecy, and he had secrets to conceal.

Don Regan was hardly the ideal chief of staff for such a crisis. Except at one meeting the previous December, he had supported the trade of arms for hostages, and he continued to support the deal after it was disclosed. At no time during the crisis did he recognize the depth of public and congressional feelings about covert dealings with Iran. Regan wanted Reagan to speak out—"I don't believe we can stonewall," he told the president[77]—but in defense of the covert dealings with Iran rather than his public position of refusing to deal with terrorists. The White House chief of staff had a thin grasp of history. He thought that sending thousands of missiles to Iran in return for two hostages was comparable to Nixon's secret 1972 decision to reestablish relations with China and to President Harry Truman's decision to accept West Germany "into the family of nations" after World War II[78] —as if this also were a secret decision. But Regan at least realized that Reagan's public credibility was at stake and that it was necessary for the president to defend himself. He warned the president that he would be "ripped apart" if he kept silent and persuaded him to call a meeting to devise a strategy for response. On Monday, November 10, a National Security Planning Group convened in the Situation Room with Reagan, Bush, Regan, Shultz, Weinberger, Casey, Meese, Poindexter and his deputy Alton Keel in attendance.

Shultz had been doing a slow burn that would eventually turn into a white heat. More than anyone else with access to the president, he recognized that the initiative totally undermined U.S. policy of discouraging other nations from sending arms to Iran or aiding terrorists. Shultz had been traveling in Europe when the story of the Iran initiative broke. Searching for an acceptable way to reassure U.S. allies, he had sent a cable to Poindexter suggesting a White House statement describing the Iran initiative as "a special, one-time operation based on humanitarian grounds and decided by the President within his Constitutional responsibility to act for the service of the national interest—and that our policies toward terrorism and toward the Iran/Iraq war stand."[79]

Such a statement would not have been wholly accurate, even on the basis of Shultz's limited knowledge of the 1985 HAWK shipment and the McFarlane mission to Tehran. But it was too much of an explanation for Poindexter, who nourished a hope of further hostage releases and rejected the idea of any White House statement. Poindexter had replied that he did not believe "that now is the time to give the facts to the public."[80] His grasp of reality can be adduced from his assurance to Shultz that "when we do lay out the facts, it will be well received since it is a good story."[81] Poindexter actually believed this. On November 7 he sent a PROF note to McFarlane assuring him that his nemesis Don Regan had "agreed that he would keep his mouth shut." Poindexter added that "we have a damned good story to tell when we are ready.

Right now would be an absolutely stupid time for the administration to say anything."[82]

By the time the NSPG convened on November 10, Shultz wanted the story out whether it was good or bad. But Reagan had already decided on a line of defense that was based on saying as little as possible. Knowing that his secretaries of state and defense were unsympathetic to the Iran initiative, Reagan had turned for guidance to Bill Casey, who before the meeting had exchanged with Poindexter drafts of a proposed presidential statement. Casey described Poindexter's draft as doing "little more than say we reviewed the matter and discovered we didn't break the law."[83] Casey said his draft "says a little more."[84] What it said was reflected in Reagan's opening comments to the NSPG meeting on the kind of statement he wanted: "We have not dealt directly with terrorists, no bargaining, no ransom. Some things we can't discuss because of long-term consideration of people with whom we have been talking about the future of Iran."[85]

After this brief declaration Poindexter gave an inaccurate and incomplete history of the Iran initiative, which he described as aimed at achieving a "long-term strategic relationship with Iran" with the subsidiary goals of strengthening Iranian moderates, halting terrorism and freeing the hostages. He did not mention that the "moderates" included some of the most radical members of the Khomeini regime. He described the January 17 finding, but omitted mention of the two earlier findings signed by Reagan. He said that the Iran initiative had begun when the United States accidentally came upon an Israeli warehouse in Portugal while attempting to discover whether the Israelis were shipping arms to Iran. (This was a repeat of the lie that North had told State Department counterterrorism chief Robert Oakley in November 1985 to enlist Oakley's aid in sending the first HAWK shipment to Iran.) Poindexter also claimed that the TOW missiles shipped by Israel to Iran had been sent without the president's permission. He said there had been three arms shipments to Iran, when there had in fact been five. He said that the total number of TOW missiles sold to Iran was 1,000, when it had been 2,004. He said that the last shipment of TOWs, shipped to Iran on October 30 and 31 to obtain Jacobsen's release, had been shipped by Israel. This was technically true, but totally misleading. Israel had sent the missiles at the NSC staff's request, and the CIA had replenished the Israeli stocks on November 7.

Shultz and Weinberger listened to this account with growing anger and amazement. They knew more than they subsequently acknowledged, since the weapons shipped to Iran had been provided to the CIA by the Department of Defense, and Shultz had been warned in June and July by Under Secretary Armacost of further arms-for-hostages dealings. But Shultz and Weinberger were busy men, and neither of them had fully grasped the scope of the initiative, even to the extent laid out to them this day by Poindexter. They had opposed the policy from the outset as risky and foolish, and now they vented their anger in comments they tried to direct at Poindexter rather than the president. Weinberger pointed out that "we had agreed there would be no more shipments after the first 500 TOWs unless we got back all the captives" —substantially the instructions McFarlane had followed in Tehran. Poindexter's reply gave the game away. "It just always came back to the president," he said. "He agreed to go forward. It seemed the only way to get the hostages out."*

This response set off Shultz, who warned against linking the weapons delivery to release of hostages in any statement. Reagan didn't see any such link. He said that terrorists "had not profited" and insisted once more that the United States was dealing with Iranian moderates who could influence the terrorists, rather than with the terrorists themselves. Shultz didn't buy it. "I'm not sure what's the difference," he said. Shultz acknowledged that the initiative had produced "more good contacts in Iran than I was aware of. We should pursue this, but we must not gild the lily. . . . We are paying a high price."[87]

Reagan now became irritated with Shultz. He insisted that the U.S. government had a responsibility to protect its citizens. Shultz agreed but said the direct connection of weapons sales and hostage releases made the initiative seem like a trade of arms for hostages. The secretary of state was still reluctant to make the case against the initiative as bluntly as he would a few days later, but he was rapidly emerging as the cabinet officer most openly skeptical of Reagan's rationalizations. In this meeting, however, Shultz blamed the Israelis more than Reagan, saying that "the Israelis suckered us so they could sell what they wanted."[88] Meese then leaped to Reagan's defense, arguing that the specific events in the initiative were unrelated and saying that there had

---

* It is a fair surmise that everyone in the November 10 meeting knew they were talking for history. Congress was then demanding an investigation and it was evident that many details of the initiative would be exposed. In contrast to many earlier meetings where only a laconic Poindexter notation or a Reagan diary entry survives as a record, there are many accounts of the November 10 meeting. Regan and Keel made notes, Weinberger wrote a memorandum afterward and Shultz dictated his recollections. The congressional committees concluded that "these records contain no material differences."[86]

been "no ransom" paid for the hostages. Regan insisted that a public statement was necessary that would be appreciated by "thinking people —not the press." [89] Only Poindexter was opposed to a statement. He had so little insight into what was happening that he thought Congress and the media would lose interest and the controversy would die out. On this point, at least, Reagan knew better. He had become convinced, as he put it, that he was "being held out to dry" and agreed that a statement was necessary. "Avoid specifics," he said. "Declare that whatever we've done is consistent with our policy." [90]

The statement was prepared that afternoon from the draft submitted by Casey, with editing by Poindexter and Meese. It was as misleading as Poindexter's account of the initiative had been at the NSPG meeting. The statement denied that the United States had sought "to reward hostage-takers by meeting their demands," and falsely asserted that there had been "unanimous support for the president's decisions." Weinberger, who knew better, signed off on this version. Shultz, who had left on a trip, received the draft by cable and quibbled with the wording. He replied to Poindexter that he supported the president but opposed the policy. Poindexter made a slight change in the wording— a distinction Shultz chose to see as a difference—and the statement was issued late in the day by Speakes. "As has been the case in similar meetings with the president and his senior advisers on this matter, there was unanimous support for the President," the statement said. "While specific decisions discussed at the meeting cannot be divulged, the President did ask that it be reemphasized that no U.S. laws have been or will be violated and that our policy of not making concessions to terrorists remains intact." [91]

The statement raised more questions than it answered. This was also true of a two-hour briefing that Reagan, Shultz and Poindexter conducted for congressional leaders at the White House on November 12. Answering questions from reporters in the White House driveway after this session, the congressional leaders, especially Senator Byrd, made it clear that they did not accept Reagan's explanations. Regan, who did not have much respect for Congress anyway, was convinced that the president could prevail only by taking his case to the people. This was also the view of White House communications director Patrick Buchanan, who warned Regan in a memo that the secret Iran initiative had the potential to "do deep and permanent damage to the president's standing." [92] This damage was accumulating day by day, and Buchanan, with bitter memories of Richard Nixon's fall, had a sense of urgency about regaining the political offensive. Regan agreed. During his tenure as chief of staff he had acquired the dualistic view common to those who served Reagan at close quarters for any extended period of time. While Regan held a low opinion of Reagan's intellect, he had an almost mystical faith in the president's ability to persuade the American people. Regan prevailed on Reagan to make a speech that the president himself was reluctant to deliver.

Reagan's reluctance may have been intuitive. He had been shaken by the storm of criticism in Congress and the media and the increasing opposition of Shultz, who told the congressional leaders on November 12 that the State Department had nothing to do with the initiative. Reagan was in no mood to give a speech on television. He may have known far too little about Iran, but he understood the hazards of going to the people with a case that was fundamentally unbelievable. Reagan treasured the bond he had forged with the American people and understood that his success on television was a principal source of his power and popularity. He believed that television was a powerful mirror that reflected a performer's intentions and detected evidence of insincerity and untruthfulness. Reagan tended to invest himself in his role in any performance, but he gave special weight to the credibility of his televised speeches. Once he told a story on television, he could rarely be convinced that it wasn't true.

Unfortunately for Reagan, his November 13 speech to the nation was neither accurate nor believable. This was not the fault of Buchanan, who crafted it largely from information that North supplied to him. Buchanan and Speakes were at a constant disadvantage in their efforts to construct a comprehensible defense because much of their information was based on the misrepresentations of Poindexter and North. Though Poindexter was subsequently convicted of lying to Congress, it is arguable that he did far more damage to the Reagan presidency by lying to administration officials who were trying to make a credible case for Reagan's actions. The November 13 speech is a case in point. Although it forcefully presented the rationale for a U.S.-Iran relationship, complete with the argument that Iran was a strategic bulwark against the Soviets and the analogy of Nixon's secret initiative with China, the speech was peppered with factual inaccuracies. The most glaring of these, which was promptly pounced upon by Reagan's critics in Congress and the media, was the claim that all the "defensive" weapons and spare parts supplied to Iran "could easily fit into a single cargo plane." This false information had been provided by Poindexter.

Watching the speech on television, I was struck by the validity of Reagan's long-held view about the revealing quality of the medium. All of the practiced confidence that one associates with a scripted Reagan performance was missing. Instead of the self-assured "Great Communicator" whom America had applauded on Liberty Weekend and after many of his other speeches, Reagan was on this night a carping, angry and defensive politician who blamed the media for his troubles much like any other cornered politician. Some of this edge was in the text, for Buchanan had not forgiven the national media for their role in the demise of Richard Nixon and frequently reflected this attitude in the words he wrote for others. But Reagan usually criticized the media in an abstract rather than a personal way, even though he had never trusted the press institutionally since the embarrassing stories after the breakup of his marriage with Jane Wyman. Now, as he confided to his friends and his diary, Reagan thought the media had turned on him without reason. He could not admit to himself or to the country that the initiative had been both bungled and ill-conceived. In crises this adult child of an alcoholic found it as difficult as his father to accept responsibility for his own actions. Others were always to blame when something went wrong.

"Since the welcome return of former hostage David Jacobsen, there has been unprecedented speculation and countless reports that have not only been wrong but have been potentially dangerous to the hostages and destructive of the opportunity before us," Reagan said. "The efforts of courageous people like Terry Waite have been jeopardized. So extensive have been the false rumors and erroneous reports that the risks of remaining silent now exceed the risks of speaking out." Later in the speech he said, "Our government has a firm policy not to capitulate to terrorist demands. That no-concessions policy remains in force, in spite of the wildly speculative and false stories about arms for hostages and alleged ransom payments. We did not—repeat, did not—trade weapons or anything else for hostages, nor will we." This became Reagan's official version of the truth and the one he would always believe.

But the public, for once, did not believe Reagan. An ABC poll of 510 adults taken after the speech showed that 79 percent opposed delivering arms to Iran to win freedom of the hostages and that 72 percent disapproved of "shipping arms to Iran as a way of improving relations with moderate elements in that country." By 56 to 35 percent, those polled said that Reagan had abandoned his previous policies and "has been negotiating with terrorists by supplying Iran with arms." A *Los Angeles Times* survey found that only 14 percent of Americans accepted Reagan's version as accurate. Richard Wirthlin's reliable surveys produced a similar finding. These polls were a signal that Reagan had forfeited the vital asset of his credibility, which had usually been high even when people disagreed with him. Reagan had used his ultimate weapon of taking his case to the people, and he had failed.

Shultz now became increasingly assertive—and increasingly isolated within the administration. The day after Reagan's speech Shultz pointedly distanced himself from the president through State Department spokesman Charles Redman, who said the secretary of state "was not directly involved, although he was sporadically informed of some details"[93] of the Iran initiative. The same day, in his weekly meeting with Reagan, Shultz pressed him to make a definitive statement that the United States would not sell additional arms to Iran. Reagan and Poindexter, still nourishing the hope of further hostage releases, would not agree to it. On November 15, Shultz made the same point in a memorandum. On November 16, he laid out his case against the Iran arms sales in a dramatic interview on the CBS program *Face the Nation,* where he told Lesley Stahl that he could no longer speak for the administration on the issue. *Washington Post* television critic Tom Shales called the program "Gipperdämmerung,"[94] and conservatives were incensed. Shultz had long been unpopular with the administration's right wing, which viewed him as too accommodating to the Soviet Union and insufficiently enthusiastic about the contras. Now he was also seen as disloyal to the president.

Casey and Poindexter, who had much to conceal, feared Shultz's growing independence. So, in his own way, did Don Regan, who was the target of much criticism from Republicans in Congress and Nancy Reagan. Regan had backed the Iran initiative without knowing very much about it. He was becoming increasingly suspicious of Poindexter, but his instincts were to rally behind the president in his moment of crisis. Regan thought Shultz was engaged in a power play instead of operating as a loyal member of the team. White House officials spread stories that Nancy Reagan was unhappy with Shultz's performance on *Face the Nation* and wanted him fired. The first lady was never delighted with criticism of her husband and she was indeed temporarily annoyed with Shultz, but the people she really wanted replaced were Regan and Poindexter. Shultz may have had a sense of this, for he kept in touch with Deaver, but he had no one that he could turn to at the White

House. He was a voice of integrity within the government, but he was very much alone.

Shultz's isolation was really Reagan's loss. Instead of turning to his secretary of state, Reagan was getting his information from those who had led him astray in the first place—chiefly Poindexter, North and McFarlane. He was also depending for political advice on Regan, who ignored the signals from the polls and his own deepening reservations about Poindexter and launched the White House "spin patrol" in defense of the covert dealings with Iran. Regan meant well. In time, he would come to the view that the president had forfeited his precious credibility because "he was not telling the whole truth" and that no one had told him the truth.[95] But this was hindsight. In the crisis of November 1986, Regan passed up the opportunity to make common cause with Shultz and force the truth out of the NSC staff. Instead, he bulled ahead in a campaign that unthinkingly undermined Reagan's claim that he had not traded arms for hostages. On November 14, the day after Reagan's disastrous television speech, Regan told reporters that the president had asked him "every single morning" if efforts to free the hostages had been successful. When he was asked if Reagan had been preoccupied with the hostages, Regan said, "Yes, and that's a damn good thing that we have a president like that. . . . You can rest assured tonight that if you were ever taken hostage, your government's behind you." *

This campaign continued throughout the next critical week, with Regan strongly defending Reagan without concern for the consistency of his arguments. The White House chief of staff thought of himself as a supersalesman, and he expressed confidence that he could turn public opinion around. He may have been misled by the success of the White House efforts after the October 11–12 meeting in Reykjavik, Iceland, between Reagan and Soviet leader Mikhail Gorbachev, when a media blitz persuaded a majority of Americans that a summit Shultz had first described as a failure was really a success. "Some of us are like a shovel brigade that follows a parade down Main Street cleaning up," Regan told *The New York Times'* Bernard Weinraub on November 14. "We took Reykjavik and turned what was really a sour situation into some-

---

* Poindexter was still saying, as he did to *The Washington Post* on November 14, that "those who are familiar with the details of the operation are still optimistic" that it would prove successful. Inexplicably, in contradiction to Reagan's assertion in his television speech, Poindexter also said the unexpected revelation of the arms sales might "expedite" the process of improving U.S.-Iranian relations and lead to release of more hostages.[96] He made a similar statement November 16 on NBC's *Meet the Press.*

thing that turned out pretty well."⁹⁷ But the circumstances were vastly different after the Iran initiative disclosures than after Reykjavik. For one thing, the post-Reykjavik "spin patrol" had the active participation of Shultz, whose assessment of the summit had brightened after he reflected on it. Shultz aside, Americans were in any event more inclined to rally behind a president who had stood up to a Soviet leader than a president who was contradicting his principles by secretly selling arms to Iran. Regan could not grasp this difference, and he compounded Reagan's problems by patronizing the president. "Does a bank president know whether a bank teller is fiddling around with the books?" he asked rhetorically. "No."⁹⁸ When David Hoffman and I asked Regan whether he should accept some responsibility for the Iran decisions, he said he was willing to do so but added: "The president as a very manly CEO said the ultimate decision was mine to make; I'll take the responsibility for that decision. It was a courageous thing for the president to do. We allowed him to do it."⁹⁹

Regan also allowed Reagan to dig an even deeper hole for himself at a prime-time news conference on November 19. News conferences were under the best of circumstances a far dicier proposition for Reagan than any scripted television speech. But Reagan, following his usual practice of avoiding the press during election campaigns, had not held a news conference since August 12 in Chicago. Regan and Speakes had promised that Reagan would hold a news conference in November, and the White House chief of staff scheduled it after receiving an astrologically approved date from Nancy Reagan. Favorable signs or not, the first lady was flatly opposed to a news conference. She believed that her husband was emotionally unprepared to face a barrage of questions at a time when his confidence had been shaken by the loss of public credibility.

Even a more intellectually confident or better informed president might have been confused by the reconstruction of events supplied to Reagan. Poindexter's guide was a seventeen-page NSC "maximum chronology" that McFarlane later said had a "primary objective" of distancing the president from the approval of the arms sales. McFarlane contributed a November 18 memorandum to this chronology, which he would later acknowledge to the Tower Board "was not a full and completely accurate account."¹⁰⁰ The memorandum and the chronology were used to prepare Reagan's opening statement at the news conference.

McFarlane had been invited by Poindexter soon after the initiative became public to assist North in preparing the chronological account.

Over a two-week period between November 5 and November 20 the chronology went through at least a dozen versions, none of them fully accurate. But the chronology did contain vital information that alerted the Justice Department to probable violations of the Arms Export Control Act. At Meese's request, Assistant Attorney General Charles Cooper had been attempting to determine if the secret arms sales were legal. Cooper, who knew nothing of the 1985 arms shipments, filed a memo on November 12 saying that the sales complied with the law as long as there was a presidential finding before they occurred. On November 17, Cooper received a draft version of the chronology describing the 1985 shipments. He informed Meese, who said he was unaware of any shipments before the finding.

Cooper's concern led to a meeting on the morning of November 18 among the principal lawyers for the White House, the Justice and State departments, the NSC and the CIA in the office of White House counsel Peter Wallison. But Paul Thompson, the NSC counsel, refused to disclose information about the 1985 shipments, saying he was acting on Poindexter's instructions. Abraham Sofaer, the experienced State Department legal adviser, exploded in anger. He suspected a conspiracy, and he told Wallison that it was "extremely serious" for the NSC to withhold information from the president's counsel. Wallison agreed. When Sofaer returned to the State Department, he complained to Shultz, who backed him. At the insistence of Wallison and the State Department, Poindexter briefed Sofaer and Michael Armacost early that evening, telling them of the August and September 1985 shipments of TOWs by Israel but withholding the fact of Reagan's prior authorization. Most important, Poindexter omitted any mention of the November 1985 HAWK spare parts shipment. Sofaer left the meeting convinced he did not yet have the full story.

Sofaer was not alone. Earlier that same day Poindexter had conducted the foreign policy portion of the rehearsal for the next evening's news conference. The rehearsal followed a time-honored format, with Reagan fielding questions from staff members who played the role of reporters. Regan, despite his insistence on the news conference, now smelled a disaster. "The president kept making mistakes," Regan said. "He could not keep the sequence of events straight or remember exactly what he had approved or what he had been told. This was because he was being told that he had been told things that he had not in fact been told. Poindexter was withholding the whole story from him." [101]

Reagan was also making mistakes because the story of the Iran initiative he had related to the American people simply did not fit with the facts, even to the extent the president knew them. But there is no doubt that Poindexter was withholding information. While Reagan was struggling in preparation for the Wednesday news conference, Poindexter was worrying about testimony that he and Casey were scheduled to give to the Senate and House intelligence committees that Friday, November 21. On the busy day of November 18, Poindexter took time to place a telephone call to Casey. Since Casey was traveling in Central America, the CIA taped the conversation and a record of it survived for the various investigations. Poindexter told Casey that the NSC had finished preparation of its chronology and urged him to return by Thursday afternoon so they could coordinate their testimony. Casey asked pointedly whether "State" or "Defense" would be at the meeting. "I'd like to spend some time—just the two of us," Poindexter replied. He added that Meese said he wanted to be helpful and would meet with them Thursday. Casey told Poindexter to set a time for any meetings he wanted and assured him that he would be there.

The news conference of November 19 was an even worse disaster than Regan had anticipated. The president opened with a statement reiterating the multiple purposes of the initiative, listing release of the hostages as the last of four objectives. Without mentioning Shultz or Weinberger by name, Reagan acknowledged that "several top advisers opposed the sale of even a modest shipment of defensive weapons and spare parts to Iran." Reagan said he had "weighed their views" before deciding to proceed. "And the responsibility for the decision and the operation is mine and mine alone," he said. Reagan seemed more composed in reading this opening statement in the East Room than he had been in delivering his speech from the Oval Office. He knew he faced a difficult half hour and that it was necessary for him to keep his temper under control.

But if Reagan was more effective in this performance than he had been six days earlier, the content of his news conference answers was even more damaging than his television speech had been. Almost every answer that dealt with a question about the Iran initiative was at variance with the facts. The most serious misstatement, and one Reagan certainly knew was false, was his response to a question from Charles Bierbauer of CNN, who asked if the United States had been involved with Israel in supplying weapons to Iran. "We, as I say, have had nothing to do with other countries or their shipment of arms or doing what they're doing," Reagan said. When NBC's Andrea Mitchell pointed out that

Don Regan had told reporters that the U.S. government had condoned an Israeli weapons shipment to Iran just before the release of American hostage Benjamin Weir, Reagan went deeper into the hole, saying, "Well, no, I've never heard Mr. Regan say that, and I'll ask him about that." But he did not have to ask. Within twenty minutes of the news conference the White House chief of staff directed the press office to issue a correction acknowledging that "there was a third country involved in our secret project with Iran." Regan later blamed Reagan's lie about third countries on Poindexter, saying that the national security adviser had given the president the impression that Israel's role must not be mentioned.

In addition to denying Israel's role and repeating as truth Poindexter's howler that all the weapons shipped to Iran could be fitted into "a single cargo plane," Reagan tried to play down the hostage aspect of the Iran initiative while taking credit for the hostage releases. When NBC's Chris Wallace asked Reagan if he hadn't been sending a message to terrorist-minded nations that they could gain from holding hostages, Reagan said, "No, I don't see where the kidnappers or the hostage-holders gained anything. They didn't get anything. They let the hostages go. Now, whatever is the pressure that brought that about, I'm just grateful for the fact that we got them." He failed to mention that three Americans had been kidnapped to replace the three hostages that had been released. And even though the October agreement in Frankfurt had guaranteed the release of only a single hostage, the president said, "And as a matter of fact, I believe and have reason to believe that we would have had all five of them by this last weekend had it not been for the attendant confusion that arose here in the reporting room."

For Reagan, the truth had now become clear. The media were to blame for wrecking the initiative by disclosing it. He was not to blame and never would be. When Jeremiah O'Leary of *The Washington Times* asked Reagan why he simply wouldn't admit a mistake "so that you can get on with the next two years," the president replied, "Because I don't think a mistake was made. It was a high-risk gamble, and it was a gamble that, as I've said, I believe the circumstances warranted." To ABC's Sam Donaldson, who wanted to know what Reagan could do to repair his credibility, he said, "Well, I imagine I'm the only one around who wants to repair it, and I didn't have anything to do with damaging it."

Two of the administration officials who had done the most harm to Reagan's credibility were about to inflict some additional damage.

Casey and Poindexter met on the morning of November 20, the day after the news conference, to plan the testimony they would give the following day before the House and Senate intelligence committees. Meese attended the meeting along with North, Cooper, Thompson and Deputy CIA Director Robert Gates. Shultz and Weinberger, as Casey had requested, were excluded. So were Regan and White House counsel Peter Wallison, who subsequently complained to the Justice and NSC attorneys about not being allowed to attend. Casey proposed an insert in the testimony saying that the CIA believed the 1985 HAWK shipment to have been "oil-drilling equipment," the cover story McFarlane had outlined to Reagan, Regan and Shultz at the Geneva summit. North suggested changing the statement to say that "no one in the U.S. government"[102] knew that the 1985 HAWK shipment contained arms. North's version was accepted. Meese left before the meeting was over to give a speech at West Point.

After this meeting Wallison received a call from State Department counsel Abraham Sofaer, who told him that Shultz remembered being told by McFarlane about the HAWK shipment in November 1985. Wallison passed this information on to Cooper and Thompson, urging that they get the facts straight. This was not an easy task. McFarlane and North told Thompson they did not know that the November 1985 shipment contained missiles. Cooper talked by phone with Sofaer, who insisted that Shultz was certain of his recollection. Sofaer said that he would "leave the government" unless Casey changed his testimony. "We may all have to," Cooper replied.[103]

Shultz had watched the president's news conference in dismay. He was convinced that Reagan was destroying himself by parroting false information that had been provided to him by the NSC staff or Casey. At this critical moment Shultz acted boldly to save the Reagan presidency. Even though he had repeatedly been rebuffed by the president and the White House staff, he called Don Regan and said he wanted to tell Reagan of serious errors in his answers at the news conference. Regan set up a meeting for 5:00 P.M. on November 20 in the family quarters, where an angry secretary of state confronted Reagan in what Shultz later described as "a long, tough discussion, not the kind of discussion I ever thought I would have with the president of the United States."[104] With Regan and Poindexter looking on, Shultz bluntly told the president he had erred in denying that the initiative was a trade for hostages, in denying Israel's role and in claiming that Iran no longer practiced terrorism. "You have to look at these facts," Shultz said.[105]

Don Regan would later say that the president was "puzzled" by Shultz's "heated" presentation. "As far as he [Reagan] knew, he had stated the facts exactly as they were," Regan recalled. "Poindexter defended the information he had provided to the president and offered no new data." [106]

Shultz also warned Reagan that Casey was preparing to testify falsely before the congressional intelligence committees about the November 1985 HAWK shipment, saying that no one in the U.S. government had known about it beforehand. In fact, the president himself had known of the shipment, although he may have forgotten it. McFarlane had briefed Reagan, Regan and Shultz on the impending HAWK shipment at the Geneva summit, also relating the cover story that the cargo was oil-drilling equipment. While Regan omitted mention of any contribution to this discussion in *For the Record,* he told me long afterward that he had sided with Shultz. [107] What Regan also did, as he did relate in his memoirs, was suggest that Attorney General Meese gather all the facts about what had happened. [108]

Nonetheless, Casey and Poindexter proceeded to lie about the U.S. role in the HAWK shipment and other 1985 arms shipments to Iran when they testified to the House and Senate intelligence committees on November 21. Poindexter told the Senate Intelligence Committee that Reagan had not learned of the August and September TOW shipments to Israel until after the fact and had then expressed his displeasure at the action. He said the U.S. government had not learned until January 1986 that the November 1985 flight to Iran had carried HAWK missiles and had subsequently persuaded Iran to return the missiles to Israel. (The Iranians had actually returned the missiles because they had no capability against high-flying planes.) Poindexter promised he would make additional checks of his records and report back to the committees. Instead, he returned to his office and destroyed the December 5, 1985, presidential finding in which Reagan had given retroactive approval to the U.S. delivery of the HAWKs and which described the operation as an arms-for-hostages trade.

Casey testified next. Heeding the objections of Shultz and Sofaer, he had deleted from his opening statement the phrase that "no one in the U.S. government found out that our airline had landed HAWK missiles into Iran until mid-January." [109] Still, Casey stuck essentially to the cover story that the CIA had been asked by the NSC staff to transport oil-drilling equipment and did not know "until later on" that it was shipping missiles. Poindexter's story was that he hadn't known about the

CIA flight at the time; Casey's story was that the CIA staff had acted at the NSC's request and hadn't known the nature of the plane's cargo. Senator Patrick Leahy wondered if the two stories fit together into a single story creating "plausible deniability" for administration knowledge of the missile shipment. "Hadn't thought about it," Casey told Leahy. "I hadn't thought about it." [110] Later, Casey recited his cover story on the HAWK shipment to the House Intelligence Committee, but also volunteered and twice repeated the tidbit that the NSC staff was "guiding and active in the private provision of weapons to the contras." [111]

While Casey was trying to protect himself by suggesting that the NSC staff was to blame for whatever had gone wrong, Meese was moving to take control of the administration response. He saw himself as Reagan's protector in time of need. Despite his public adulation of the president, Meese knew from long experience that Reagan rarely understood the operational aspects of policies he had approved. He also knew that Reagan tended to retreat when faced with conflict in his official family. In Sacramento, when Governor Reagan's political future had been threatened by a "homosexual scandal" involving two of his aides, Meese had been a key member of the team that had quietly eased the aides out of government without disclosing the reason for their departure. Even though he had been warned by Cooper that the 1985 arms sales to Iran raised possible violations of the Arms Export Control Act, Meese saw the problem in political terms. After a meeting with top advisers at the Justice Department on Friday morning, November 21, which included a briefing by Cooper on the discrepancies in the various recollections of the HAWK shipment, Meese decided to propose that he gather the facts so that the administration could speak with a single voice. Meese called Poindexter and asked him to set up a meeting with Reagan. As Meese saw it, he was now acting as "legal adviser to the president." [112]

Meese met later that morning with Reagan, Regan and Poindexter. Even though Poindexter had provided much of the information upon which Reagan had made the contradictory statements in his speech and news conference, neither Meese nor Regan objected to his presence in the meeting. But Regan had already suggested that Meese make an inquiry, and Reagan accepted Meese's proposal with his usual lack of discussion. Meese returned to the Justice Department and calmly told his team that Reagan had authorized him to "get his arms around the Iranian initiative." [113] Poindexter meanwhile was informing Oliver North of the inquiry and telling him that Meese would be sending investigators to review documents. North hopped a cab to Michael Ledeen's suburban Maryland home, where Ledeen was meeting with McFarlane. North warned them both that Meese was now looking into the arms sales transactions. McFarlane gave North a ride back to the White House in his car. During the drive North said he was going to have a "shredding party" that weekend. "Ollie, look, you have acted under instruction at all times and I'm confident that you have nothing to worry about," McFarlane told him. "Let it all happen, and I'll back you up."[114]

North moved quickly, but Meese did not. Meeting with FBI Director William Webster on an unrelated matter that afternoon, Meese told him that Reagan had authorized him to gather information on the arms sales. Webster asked if he needed FBI help. Meese declined, saying there was no reason to believe that any crime had been committed. Webster agreed, but he did not have the benefit of Meese's warning from Cooper that the 1985 arms sales may have violated the Arms Export Control Act. Had the FBI been called in at this time and the records sealed, most of the material that was destroyed during the next two days could have been preserved. Instead, North, assisted by his deputy Robert Earl and his secretary Fawn Hall, began a systematic destruction and alteration of documents relating to the Iran covert action and the still-undiscovered diversion of the proceeds to the contras. Most of the altered documents were memoranda North had written to McFarlane. They were clumsily changed to eliminate references showing the NSC staff's role in arranging for military aid to the contras during the period it was prohibited by Congress. The changes were easily detected in the subsequent congressional and criminal investigations. The destroyed documents were another matter. Only one of the five memoranda that North said he wrote about the diversion of arms sales profits to the contras was ever found.* Assisted by Earl and Hall, North assembled a foot and a half of documents, including his note-

---

* Whether or not such memoranda existed is a matter of dispute. North testified to the congressional committees that he had sent Poindexter "diversion" memos for five transactions and said, "The three transactions that I supervised, coordinated, managed were all approved by Admiral Poindexter. I assumed that [Admiral Poindexter] had solicited and obtained the consent of the President."[115] Poindexter could not at first recall seeing any such memos, although he said after North had testified that "it appears it is possible" he saw one such memo. Poindexter said earlier in his deposition to the congressional committees that he had "told Colonel North repeatedly not to put anything in writing on the transfer of funds to the contras and not to talk to anybody about it."[116] He testified that he had been told by North about the diversion in early February 1986 and verbally approved of it. Poindexter acknowledged that he had led North to believe that Reagan had approved the diversion.

books and telephone logs, to feed into his shredding machine. So much was shredded that the machine jammed, and Hall had to call a technician from the White House Crisis Management Center to fix it. Once the machine was fixed, North and Hall resumed shredding. But there were so many documents to destroy that many remained unshredded when North quit late that night after the machine jammed again.

While North shredded and Meese unhurriedly began his inquiry, Reagan spent a leisurely weekend at Camp David. His only public activity was his weekly Saturday radio speech, devoted on this occasion to the merits of volunteerism. As Reagan began his speech shortly after noon, Assistant Attorney General William Bradford Reynolds and John Richardson, the attorney general's chief of staff, were searching through documents in North's office in the Old Executive Office Building. North was not there. Reynolds and Richardson were met by Earl, who gave them a pile of documents and then telephoned North to inform him of the search. Reynolds and Richardson were looking for information on the November 1985 HAWK shipment and trying to determine if the arms deal had been a trade for hostages. But in a white folder stamped with a red White House label Reynolds came across a document headed "Release of American Hostages in Beirut." It was a highly detailed April 4, 1986, memo from North to Poindexter. Reynolds thumbed through it quickly. Under a heading labeled "Discussion," he found these two paragraphs:

> $2 million will be used to purchase replacement TOWs for the original 508 sold by Israel to Iran for the release of Benjamin Weir. This is the only way that we have found to meet our commitment to replenish these stocks.
>
> $12 million will be used to purchase critically needed supplies for the Nicaraguan Democratic Resistance Forces. This material is essential to cover shortages in resistance inventories resulting from their current offensives and Sandinista counter-attacks and to "bridge" the period between now and when Congressionally-approved lethal assistance (beyond the $25 million in "defensive" arms) can be delivered. [117]

Reynolds was shocked. "Holy Jesus," he said, and showed the memo to Richardson, who also realized the document's significance. Reynolds was by now suspicious enough of North to slip the memo back into its folder rather than place it on a nearby table with a stack of documents he had marked with paper clips for copying. But Reynolds was not a prosecutor. He did not think in terms of sealing the office or wonder if North might destroy implicating documents. When Reynolds and Richardson left for lunch with Meese and Cooper, they met North coming back into his office. At lunch at the Old Ebbitt Grill across from the Treasury Department, Reynolds revealed his find to Meese, who had that morning been alerted by George Shultz to the possibility of a connection between the arms sales and the contras. The attorney general had begun his day by interviewing Shultz and his assistant Charles Hill at the State Department. Hill's notes show that Shultz told Meese: "Another angle worries me. Could get mixed up with help for freedom fighters in Nicaragua. One thing may be overlapping with another. May be a connection." [118] Meese responded by telling Shultz this was "a political connection that enemies of the administration would love to wrap together." [119]

While Reynolds was reporting to Meese, North was selecting more documents to be shredded, this time in the White House Situation Room because his own shredder had again jammed. As on Friday, Meese might have preserved valuable information had he called in the FBI and sealed North's office that Saturday afternoon. But no member of the Justice Department team conducting the inquiry seems even to have raised the possibility that documents might be destroyed over the weekend. McFarlane, who had been told by North about the "shredding party," had not volunteered this information to Meese and Cooper when they interviewed him Friday afternoon, November 21, soon after the document destruction had begun. With his own shredder again repaired, North would continue that evening to destroy documents in his office until at least 4:30 A.M. on Sunday, November 23. When North was asked at the congressional hearings why he continued the process of document destruction while Reynolds and Richardson were conducting an official investigation, he said, "They were working on their projects; I was working on mine."

Meese continued with his inquiry, again without a sense of urgency. He had planned to interview North on Sunday morning, but he postponed the interview at North's request until Sunday afternoon. In the meantime, Meese had received a telephone call from Bill Casey, who asked him to come by his house on Saturday evening. Meese obliged. Even though questions about Casey's testimony on the HAWK shipment had prompted the inquiry in the first place, Meese saw Casey alone and took no notes. According to Meese, Casey told him that a former business associate named Roy Furmark had called on him on October 6 and told him that some Canadians who had helped finance the Iran arms sales were threatening to expose the deal because they had not been repaid. They said they were owed $10 million of the money put up for Ghorbanifar by Adnan Khashoggi. Casey said the Canadians would claim that the proceeds had been used for "Israeli or United States Government projects." Meese testified that he did not mention the diversion memo to Casey in their discussion. "I felt it was not appropriate to discuss this with anyone, even as good a friend as Mr. Casey, until I found out what it was all about," he said.[120]

But Casey knew considerably more than Meese did about what the diversion document was "all about." Events were closing in on both the CIA director and North, and Casey wanted to remove the man he considered the principal obstacle. Casey's villain was George Shultz. Earlier that day Casey had asked Mike Deaver to come to his home for a meeting. Deaver had been out of the White House for six months, but Casey knew that he remained influential with the president and on close terms with Nancy Reagan. Casey asked Deaver what he thought about the scandal. "I don't know anything about it, but the only way it will go away is if some heads roll," Deaver responded. "Someone high up" would have to be fired, he told Casey. "Shultz," said Casey. Deaver asked who could replace Shultz. "[Jeane] Kirkpatrick," Casey said. "You'd have a hard time doing that," warned Deaver.[121] Casey was undeterred. That evening, after Meese had left, Casey wrote Reagan a letter urging him to fire his secretary of state.

At 2:00 P.M. on Sunday, Meese conducted his interview of North, with Reynolds and Richardson taking notes. Meese began by asking North what he knew about the November 1985 HAWK shipment. North said he had organized and directed the operation, but lied in saying that he had not known the nature of the cargo. And he again lied in telling Meese that he had called someone at the CIA, possibly Casey, and informed him when he learned that the plane was carrying missiles. (North would later acknowledge that these statements were untrue when he testified before Congress under a grant of limited immunity.)[122] North also gave Meese a false account of what had been done with the money from the Iran arms sales, saying that it passed from the Iranians to the Israelis, who put it into a CIA account. He said nothing about Lake Resources, the dummy account set up by Secord to fund the contras and the other projects of The Enterprise.

But North told more of the truth than Reagan had—or ever would

—when Meese asked him if the August 1985 TOW shipments were really a trade of arms for hostages. "It always came back to the hostages," North said,[123] adding that it would be a terrible mistake to say that Reagan had been seeking a strategic relationship with Iran.

Meese then showed North a copy of the diversion memo. North, who later said he believed that all the incriminating documents had been destroyed, was, in Meese's words, "visibly surprised."[124] North asked if a cover memo had been found with the document. Reynolds volunteered that none had been found, and Meese asked North if they should have found one. "No," North said.[125] Cover memos were often used to describe the routing of documents and might have revealed if Reagan had approved the diversion. When Meese asked North if he had discussed the diversion with the president, North replied that he had reported through Poindexter.

Even though Poindexter had now been directly implicated, Meese did not rush off to interview him. He would not meet with Poindexter for another twenty-four hours, but he interviewed McFarlane again on Monday morning, November 24. As in his meeting with Casey, Meese met with McFarlane alone and took no notes. McFarlane testified that Meese had only two questions for him: Did he know of the diversion, and had he told anyone else about it? McFarlane's answer to the first question was that North had told him about the diversion after the failure of the mission in Tehran. The answer to the second question was no.[126]

Meese had promised Don Regan he would try to wrap up his inquiry in time for a National Security Planning Group meeting on the Iran initiative scheduled for Monday afternoon. That morning he called Regan and said he wanted to talk to him and then to the president. Meese showed up in the chief of staff's office at 11:00 A.M., told him about the diversion memo and said someone had been "cooking the accounts."[127] Regan was horrified. "Based upon my experience on Wall Street, my experience as secretary of the treasury, I know you don't screw around with federal funds," he said later. "And this is government money."[128]

But Meese was not ready to inform the president. As Reagan's chief of staff in Sacramento and as his counsellor in the White House, Meese had rarely burdened Reagan with progress reports. He preferred giving him a summation once he had defined the options and made an assessment. For now, Meese told the president that he had uncovered "a terrible mess" relating to the Iran arms sales and would report back to him later in the day. No one kept notes of this meeting either, but

Regan subsequently recalled that Meese said to Reagan, "I have got a few last-minute things to button up before I can give you the details." [129] Reagan expressed no curiosity about the nature of the "terrible mess." Regan's explanation for this was that Reagan, never one to keep foreign visitors waiting, was in a hurry to attend his next meeting, with Zulu chief Mongosuthu Gatsha Buthelezi. In the picture-taking session before this meeting, reporters asked Reagan if it had been wrong of him to approve arms sales to Iran. "I'm not going to lie about that," Reagan said. "I didn't make a mistake." [130]

At two o'clock that afternoon Reagan presided over the NSPG meeting in the Situation Room. Bush, Poindexter, Casey, Meese, Weinberger, Shultz, Regan and George Cave of the CIA attended. The Iran initiative was the sole topic of discussion. When the president asked if the problem of the 1985 HAWK shipment had been resolved, Poindexter blamed McFarlane for not having informed others. Reagan said nothing—even though he had been briefed about the shipment by McFarlane before it occurred, approved the retroactive finding and had been reminded of his actions five days earlier by Shultz and Regan. The discussion then turned to the issue of continuing covert meetings with the Iranians, which Casey and Poindexter favored and Shultz opposed. Reagan again said little, but he gave the impression he wanted to keep the initiative going.

The NSPG meeting had lasted for an hour and forty-five minutes and been conducted in a vacuum. Of those attending the meeting, at least Meese, Regan, Poindexter and Casey knew of the diversion and Reagan knew at least of some sort of "terrible mess" of which Meese had warned. The diversion nonetheless went unmentioned, even though its discovery had rendered continuation of the Iran initiative politically impossible, even if everyone in the room had favored it.

After the NSPG meeting Meese met with Poindexter for five minutes to discuss the diversion. As in his meeting with Casey and his second meeting with McFarlane, Meese was alone and took no notes. Poindexter told Meese that North had given him hints about the contra funding and that he had not inquired further. The specificity of the diversion memo suggested that Poindexter knew more than he was telling, but Meese did not press him or even ask the obvious question of whether Reagan had approved the diversion. Poindexter understandably considered Meese an ally and seems to have entertained the hope he might be spared. "I have talked to Ed twice today on this and he is still figuring out what to do," said Poindexter in a message to North that evening. "I have told him that I am prepared to resign. I told him I would take the cue from him. . . . If we don't leave, what would you think about going out to CIA and being a special assistant to Bill? That would put you in the operational world officially." [131]

Meese now finally told the president about the nature of the "terrible mess." He arrived in the Oval Office at 4:22 P.M.—"late," observed Regan—and laid out the story. The Iranians had been charged $30 million for $12 million worth of missiles. No one could account for the missing $18 million, but North had admitted diverting some of these funds to the contras. Meese did not ask the president if he had known about the diversion or approved it. "I think he said something like 'I can't believe it,'" Meese recalled afterward. "It was clear from the reaction from both him and Don Regan that neither one of them knew anything about it." [132] But Regan's recollection is that Meese had told him about the diversion that morning. He agreed that Reagan seemed shocked at the information. "He blanched when he heard Meese's words," wrote Regan. "The color drained from his face, leaving his skin pasty white. . . . Nobody who saw the president's reaction that afternoon could believe for a moment that he knew about the diversion of funds before Meese told him about it." [133]

But this would not be the last word about Reagan's knowledge of the diversion, even from Regan, as we shall soon see. At the time, however, Regan and Meese were concerned less with what Reagan knew and when he had known it than with the formidable task of saving the Reagan presidency. The question of Reagan's knowledge was not even addressed. Meese said later that he had feared Reagan would be impeached. So did Regan, who was then struggling to save his own job in the face of increasing criticism of his performance from many members of Congress, Republican officials, the media and Nancy Reagan. Much of this criticism was justified, but Regan tried to respond with strength and purpose in the hour of Reagan's need.

The morning meeting with Meese had given Regan a head start in developing a political strategy for dealing with the diversion. The essence of this strategy was to portray Reagan as a president who was outraged to learn that money from the arms sales had been sent covertly to the contras and determined to uncover the facts. Whether or not he was outraged, Reagan was certainly stunned and defensive. He does not seem to have been particularly coherent. By Regan's account the president spent only sixteen minutes discussing the situation with him and Meese when he learned of the diversion, a time that also included Meese's report. Regan proposed informing the leaders of Congress and the press the following morning. He called for setting up a bipartisan board of inquiry—a proposal that within two days would result in appointment of the President's Special Review Board (Tower Board), whose members were selected and asked to serve by Regan. Meese, although he subsequently seems to have toyed with the idea of naming a "special counsel" who would be under his control, told Reagan that appointment of an independent counsel might be necessary. Regan also said, and Meese agreed, that Poindexter and North would have to go. The president said nothing, a silence his aides interpreted as giving assent. Meese left and Reagan was left alone with his chief of staff. Though it was not yet 5:00 P.M., Regan could see that Reagan was shaken and he gently suggested to the president that he retire to the family quarters and leave everything to him.

Casey made a last attempt to stop the news from coming out. Responding to a call from Casey, Regan stopped at agency headquarters in Langley, Virginia, on his way home that evening. The CIA director warned him that disclosure would be ruinous. The Iranians would be angry at having been overcharged, the Israelis would be exposed, the contra cause would be damaged, communism would continue to spread throughout Central America. Regan agreed that disclosure was damaging but said the story had to come out. By the time Meese stopped on his way to work next morning to see Casey at his home, the CIA director was also saying that it was necessary to go public with the story. The reader will no longer be surprised that there are no notes of this meeting with Casey, either. Meese left Richardson in the car while he visited Casey. The attorney general then went to the White House and told Poindexter he would have to resign.

Poindexter heard the bad news again from Regan. Unaware that Meese had spoken to Poindexter, Regan set out to track him down and tell him he was finished as national security adviser. Regan was almost never calm in such circumstances, but Poindexter was his usual imperturbable self when Regan came upon him eating a breakfast of ham and eggs in his office. When Regan, in his blunt way, asked why he had done nothing to stop North, Poindexter said, "I felt sorry for the contras. I was so damned mad at Tip O'Neill for the way he was dragging the contras around that I didn't want to know what, if anything, was going on. I should have, but I didn't." [134]

As he had promised Meese and Regan, Poindexter brought his letter of resignation when he came to see Reagan that morning for what normally would have been the daily national security briefing. Reagan accepted the letter without opening it and said he was "sorry." Poindexter and Regan would also remember that Reagan said that, in resigning, the admiral was following a tradition of accepting responsibility for what had happened to his ship.[135] Reagan, not Poindexter, was in fact the captain of this particular "ship," although the president does not seem to have recognized it. But Reagan was sympathetic to Poindexter, and to North as well. Later that day, after North had been fired and his office finally sealed, Reagan had the White House operator track him down in Secord's office. North stood at attention while Reagan talked to him on the telephone. "Ollie, you're a national hero," Reagan said. According to North, the president also told him that the story of his exploits would one day make a great movie.[136]

Reagan announced the resignation of Poindexter and the firing of North in the White House briefing room at 12:05 P.M., Tuesday, November 25, saying that he was "deeply troubled that the implementation of a policy aimed at resolving a truly tragic situation in the Middle East has resulted in such controversy." After declaring that he believed "our policy goals to be well founded," Reagan added that "information brought to my attention yesterday convinced me that in one aspect implementation of that policy was seriously flawed." As soon as he had finished his statement, Reagan was almost drowned out by shouted questions from reporters. He responded to only one question before he turned the briefing over to Meese, the question that reporters had learned was the one most likely to get Reagan's goat. "Did you make a mistake in sending arms to Tehran?" a reporter asked. "No, and I'm not taking any more questions," Reagan said.[137] Meese then announced the findings of his weekend inquiry, repeating as fact the lies that North had told him about the routing of the Iran arms sales proceeds. It is no wonder that North, watching on television as Meese continued his briefing, decided that he needed legal assistance. Meese's strategy for protecting Reagan was to say that Oliver North was responsible for everything. Only North knew "precisely," said Meese. "Admiral Poindexter did know that something of this nature was occurring, but he did not look into it further." Meese claimed that Bill Casey, his old friend from the 1980 campaign, had not known anything at all.*

Of course, Casey knew far more about what was going on in Central America than Meese did. If he had been the least bit suspicious or even

---

* Meese was categorically protective of Casey, who was an instant target of media suspicion once the diversion was announced. At the November 25 briefing Meese responded to a question about Casey's knowledge by saying, "CIA Director Casey, Secretary of State Shultz, Secretary of Defense Weinberger, myself, the other members of the NSC, none of us knew." No one had asked if Shultz, Weinberger or Meese had known anything.

careful, Meese might have surmised from the scrap of conversation Casey had related to him about his meeting with Roy Furmark that profits from the arms sales to Iran were floating around somewhere. The overcharges for the weapons and spare parts that were delivered to Iran were a sensitive issue within the CIA, where Iran analyst Charles Allen had complained on October 1 to Deputy Director Robert Gates that he suspected some of the proceeds were going to the contras. Gates didn't want to get involved, and Allen repeated his suspicions to Casey a week later. This happened to be the day after Furmark called on Casey to tell him that some of the financiers of the arms deal wanted to be repaid. Furmark had also told Casey about Lake Resources and identified the account as belonging to North. Casey did not let on to Furmark that he already knew. The CIA director had encouraged North and quietly promoted Project Democracy. He had been one of the earliest sponsors of the Iran initiative itself. But the White House strategy was to put the blame on North, not Casey. The CIA director had on several occasions talked to the president alone, which North had never done. Anything that was pinned on Casey might also be pinned on Reagan.

Reagan, however, was charitable to his deposed subordinates and angry only at the media, whom he continued to blame for the failure of the Iran initiative. He did not, as he confided to *Time* columnist Hugh Sidey on November 26, feel in the least "betrayed" by North. "He has a fine record," Reagan said. "He is a national hero. My only criticism is that I wasn't told everything." As Reagan saw it, "this whole thing boils down to a great irresponsibility on the part of the press," which had refused to heed his pleas not to pursue the scandal. "I have to say that there is bitter bile in my throat these days," he told Sidey. "I've never seen the sharks circling like they are now with blood in the water. What is driving me up the wall is that this wasn't a failure until the press got a tip from that rag in Beirut and began to play it up. I told them that publicity could destroy this, that it could get people killed. They then went right on."[138]

What *did* the president know and when did he know it? This had been the central issue in the Watergate scandal and it became and remains a principal unanswered question of the Iran-contra affair. When a White House tape demonstrated beyond doubt that President Nixon had known of Attorney General John Mitchell's involvement in the Watergate burglary six days after it occurred and had for two years directed a coverup of this crime, Nixon was forced to resign to avoid impeachment. Twelve years later the memory of Watergate and of Nixon's resignation remained vivid in Washington, but there were now no secret White House tapes to aid the investigation, and many presumably vital documents had been destroyed. Still, impeachment was a possibility. "Yes, that was a concern," Meese said under cross-examination by North's attorney Brendan Sullivan during North's trial. Meese said he may have avoided the word in speaking to Reagan about the "tremendous consequences" of the diversion but was sure he had mentioned it to Regan and to others.[139]

By November 1986 the cracks in the Reagan façade were beginning to show. The results of the 1986 elections, after a campaign that Reagan had made a test of his personal prestige, demonstrated that he had become politically vulnerable even in advance of the Iran-contra disclosures. And these disclosures did more damage to Reagan than the initial reports of the Watergate coverup had caused Nixon. This was partly because Reagan's reputation for integrity and his credibility were vastly higher than Nixon's, or for that matter, than most other politicians'. He had farther to fall, and he fell faster.

On December 2 the *New York Times*/CBS Poll recorded a drop in Reagan's approval rating from 67 to 46 percent, a figure that the Gallup Organization said was the sharpest one-month drop in presidential approval rating recorded in any survey since such polling began in 1936. Meese was right to worry about the possibility of impeachment. When Nixon resigned, no president had been impeached in more than a century, and none has ever been removed by this method. The idea of taking such action seemed in the early 1970s a drastic adventure into uncharted territory. But in 1986 impeachment no longer seemed an unthinkable remedy for presidential excess. The Democrats, encouraged by the election, were then in an increasingly rebellious mood. They were anxious to seize the initiative from a president who had frustrated them for six years. The liberals in the House, led by Tip O'Neill, were as fervently opposed to the contras as Reagan was supportive of them. They believed, with good reason, that the administration had deceived them about what was going on in Central America. But Reagan had nonetheless managed to keep the contras going, although their cause was never popular with a majority of the American people. Ironically, disclosure of the diversion came at a time when Reagan had finally succeeded in persuading Congress to grant a limited amount of U.S. military aid to the Nicaraguan rebels. The diversion provided an enormous opportunity for the anti-contra forces to reverse this decision. "It's going to be a cold day in Washington before any more money goes to Nicaragua," said Republican Senator David Durenberger of Minnesota, a reluctant contra supporter. "Ollie may have killed off his Nicaraguan program." [140]

Reagan's loyalists, Stu Spencer and Deaver as well as Meese, were concerned that the diversion disclosure might also spell the end of Reagan's political career. Spencer was being consulted with increasing frequency at Nancy Reagan's insistence, partly to help her rid the White House of Don Regan but also to calm and steady the shaken president. Spencer was not sanguine. "What I saw was a big black pit opening, and I don't know how many people are going to fall into it," Spencer told me. [141] The Californians who rallied to Reagan's side knew how little he customarily knew about what was done in his name. They worried that in his enthusiasm for the contras he might have signed off on a program to aid them without bothering to inquire about the legality of his actions. Spencer knew that Reagan often did not grasp the implications of his directives. As recounted earlier, Deaver had come upon Reagan in 1983 as he was signing a clearly unconstitutional order that would have permitted the attorney general, then William French Smith, to accept the vice president's resignation if he refused to take a lie detector test. Meese, who had urged Reagan to sign that order, knew that the president asked few questions of trusted advisers when they brought documents to him for his signature. Everyone who knew Reagan well believed that he would have decided to obey the law—*if anyone had bothered to point out to him that an action he was contemplating or been asked to approve was illegal.*

This is a huge "if." The view that Reagan needed protection from himself was an axiom among the veteran Reaganites, whatever their ideological persuasion. This may have been why Meese did not even ask the president if he had approved of what North had done. Meese would have realized, as Spencer and Deaver did, that much depended on how North's actions had been described to him. Those familiar with the way both Reagan and Poindexter operated, as Bud McFarlane was, thought it would have been out of character for Poindexter not to mention the diversion to Reagan. Poindexter had, after all, obtained Reagan's approval for the December 5, 1985, covert finding on Iran— the one that clearly identified the deal as an arms-for-hostages trade without the camouflage of the strategic initiative—even though Poindexter strongly disapproved of the way the finding was formulated.

McFarlane would be forever convinced that Poindexter, "integrity personified as the military defines it," would also have considered it his duty to tell the president about the diversion. "Even though he had run a considerable risk, he would have told the commander in chief about it, probably told him he had acted without authority. And the commander in chief would have said, 'Well, I'll be darned, John, that's great,' and promptly forgot about it." [142] McFarlane knew from experience how little Reagan remembered.

But it was difficult for reporters or official investigators to operate on the premise that the president of the United States could take such a casual approach to policy, particularly a policy that was probably illegal. We were all children of Watergate. My editors at *The Washington Post* and most of my colleagues in the press corps were from beginning to end more tantalized by the Nixon question—what did he know and when did he know it?—than by any other issue. We were reluctant to entertain the idea that Reagan might have casually nodded agreement to some laconic report of Poindexter's without knowing, or remembering, that he had done so. And yet it was commonplace for Reagan's principal policy advisers to find the president inattentive, unfocused and incurious and to depart from meetings not knowing what, if anything, had been decided. Reagan's hearing problems, especially when there was outside noise or if several people talked at once, added an extra dimension of distraction. Communicating with Reagan was an art form in which few excelled and that no one, with the possible exception of Nancy Reagan, had totally mastered.

As matters turned out, the investigative focus on the unresolvable question of whether Reagan had approved the diversion soon obscured the folly of the Iran initiative itself, which may have been fortunate for Reagan. Wirthlin's surveys demonstrated that most Americans, particularly in the critical period following the disclosures, were angrier about the arms sales to Iran than about the funneling of money to the contras. This was not because Americans cared about the contras, who never at any time in their existence attracted majority support in the United States. It was because they had trusted Reagan, who had promised that he would never deal with terrorists and instead sold arms to the nation that Americans then most resented and identified with terrorism. Americans were divided on the question of whether Reagan had known about the diversion, but they could see plainly that he had traded arms for hostages. The more he lied about this, the deeper his credibility problem became.

Eventually, however, the preoccupation with the contra diversion and the various exploits of North's Project Democracy and Secord's Enterprise created its own diversion away from the Iran initiative. What Reagan knew about the contra diversion and when he knew it became the sole issue on which his political survival turned. This preoccupation had a curious and largely exculpatory impact on the examination of the Iran part of the Iran-contra affair, even though the initiative had been undertaken in defiance of Reagan's declared policies and cast the United States as a hypocrite in the eyes of allies it was asking to embargo arms to Iran. Once the initiative became a secondary issue, the burden of defense for Reagan was minimal. All he had to do was say over and over again that he never knew what North had been doing. After Poindexter testified that he had not told the president of the diversion ("The buck stops here with me"), Reagan could have been brought down only by a signed document that showed his approval of the diversion. Watergate had taught presidents never to make tapes. And if any incriminating document had existed, Poindexter or North had been given ample opportunity to destroy it while Meese conducted his leisurely inquiry without sealing their offices.

Meese was reluctant to appoint a special prosecutor, but agreed to this necessary step as pressure on the administration mounted early in December. Independent counsel Lawrence Walsh, an Oklahoma attorney who had held several positions in the Eisenhower and Nixon administrations, was appointed on December 19. While the Tower Board was examining the Iran-contra affair and Walsh was organizing his investigation team in mid-December, the whispered explanation at the White House of Reagan's shaky performances in his November speech and news conference was that the president, then nearly seventy-six, was showing signs of age. Speaking under ground rules of anonymity, several people who had known Reagan for many years suggested to me that he was slipping. Presumably, this was intended as an excuse for Reagan's conduct but it seemed to me a worrisome suggestion, for two years remained in Reagan's second term. It was also a defense, if defense it can be called, that does not withstand historical scrutiny.

The fact is that Reagan's memory had never been good when he faced investigation. This had been demonstrated in 1962 when the Justice Department investigated Reagan's old employer, the Music Corporation of America (MCA), for its control over show business and alleged conflicts of interest in simultaneously representing clients, studios and networks. Reagan testified to a grand jury on February 5, 1962, the day before his fifty-first birthday. At issue was his action as president of the Screen Actors Guild in 1952 in signing an unprecedented and secret waiver allowing MCA to produce an unlimited number of television shows. Reagan remembered almost nothing about it, or about a follow-up waiver signed in 1954. The two points of which he was certain—that other agencies had been given the same kind of waiver and that no financial consideration had been given for granting the waiver to MCA—were wrong. When Reagan was pressed on these and other points, his strategy, as Garry Wills has observed, "was to retreat toward constantly expanding areas of forgetfulness. At first, he thought he could not remember anything from the summer of 1952 because he was married in March of that year, and was on a kind of extended honeymoon. Later, he thought of another reason for his amnesia: 'You keep saying in the summer. I think maybe one of the reasons I don't recall was because I feel that in the summer of 1952, I was up in Glacier National Park making a cowboy picture for RKO . . . so it's very possible there were some things going on that I would not participate in but I have no recollection of this particularly.' "[143] The picture to which Reagan was referring, *Cattle Queen of Montana,* was made two years later.

After Reagan became governor, his aides noticed that he often did not remember what he had done and sometimes not even what he had said. He was easily distracted, and even more easily carried away. While there are many examples, the one that lingers is a remark in a 1970 speech given by Reagan about the campus turmoil in California. Speaking without text, Reagan abruptly declared that "if it takes a bloodbath" to end the rioting, "let's get it over with." When aides told him afterward that the remark could be politically damaging, Reagan denied that he had used the word "bloodbath." The aides had to play a tape recording of the speech to convince him that he had used the offending phrase.[144]

Reagan's recollections of how the Iran initiative had come about were put to a troublesome test by the Tower Board. In his first meeting with the board on January 26, 1987, Reagan astonished Regan and White House counsel Peter Wallison by saying that he had approved the first TOW shipments by Israel to Iran sometime in August 1985 and also agreed to replenish Israeli weapons from U.S. stocks. Reagan brought with him a copy of McFarlane's testimony to the Senate Foreign Relations Committee of January 16, 1987, highlighting a portion in which McFarlane testified that Reagan had given prior approval to the Israeli sale. The president said McFarlane had laid out events quite nicely.

Reagan's testimony was damaging to Don Regan, who had testified to the board on January 7 that Reagan had not given prior approval to the August shipment of Israeli TOW missiles. In fact, said Regan, the president had been "upset" when McFarlane told him of the shipment. As Regan remembered it, McFarlane had explained to the president after the event that the Israelis "had simply taken it upon themselves to do this." [145] Regan was dismayed that Reagan had sided with McFarlane and not with him—and he was convinced that he was right and they were wrong. The issue was important to the White House chief of staff, who was then fighting to save his job. David Abshire, the former NATO ambassador brought in by Regan as special counsellor on the Iran-contra affair, believes Regan had two motivations: he "strongly felt" that his recollection was correct, and he was also "anti-McFarlane." [146] After Reagan's testimony, Abshire joined Vice President Bush, Wallison and Regan in going through the calendar with Reagan and trying to help him refresh his recollection.

"Were you surprised?" Wallison asked Reagan.

"Yes, I guess I was surprised," Reagan said.

"That's what I remember," said Regan. "I remember you being angry and saying something like, 'Well, what's done is done.' "

"You know, I think he's right," Reagan said to Wallison. [147]

But on February 10, the day before Reagan was to testify to the Tower Board a second time, it was obvious to Regan and Wallison that the president was still shaky in his recollections. Wallison drew up what Abshire called an "aide-mémoire" [148] to help the president recall what he had told them. At the top Wallison wrote, "On the issue of the TOW shipment in August, in discussing this matter with me and David Abshire, you said you were surprised to learn that the Israelis had shipped the arms. If that is your recollection, and if the question comes up at the Tower Board meeting, you might want to say that you were surprised." [149]

The question, of course, came up. It was raised by chairman John Tower when the board interviewed Reagan a second time on February 11 in the Oval Office. After a preliminary discussion about presidents and their NSC staffs, Tower asked Reagan about the discrepancy between his statement and Regan's on the question of whether he had given prior approval to the Israeli arms shipment. Reagan rose from his chair, walked around his desk and said to Wallison, "Peter, where is that piece of paper you had that you gave me this morning?" Then he picked up the paper and began to read, "If the question comes up at the Tower Board meeting, you might want to say that you were surprised."[150]

Tower's jaw went slack. It was, as Abshire put it, "a low moment."[151] Tower suspected that Reagan was being manipulated by his counsel, and the Tower Board's chief of staff, Rhett Dawson, asked Wallison for a "copy of the script" when the board departed.[152] But Wallison was even more amazed than the Tower Board by Reagan's response. "I was horrified, just horrified," Wallison recalled later. "I didn't expect him to go and get the paper. The purpose of it was just to recall to his mind before he goes into the meeting that on something that he had been all over the lot on for so long, he had seemed to have come to some conclusions. . . . God, it was just terrible."[153]

The Tower Board had been exposed to the real Reagan, as he was seen at close range every day by the handful of aides with personal access to him. And neither Tower nor his colleagues Brent Scowcroft and Edmund Muskie knew what to make of Reagan's performance. They had not imagined that he would be devoid of any independent recollection or so mentally confused, and they thought it useless to question him further. Instead, Tower concluded the meeting and the board members retreated to their offices, where, as Dawson remembers it, "Ed and Tower and Brent slumped on the couch or in their chairs just thunderstruck by what [had] happened."[154] Reagan's recollections were worthless. "My conclusion is that he was influenced by the last person he talked to," said Wallison later. "He had no recollection of his own."[155]

Muskie was particularly appalled. As a former senator and former secretary of state, he understood that presidents are busy people who cannot remember everything. But he had never seen such forgetful performances as the ones Reagan had given in his two appearances before the board. "All the testimony we got from everybody was that the president was preoccupied with this goddamn problem every day," Muskie said. "Every day in someone's presence he said, 'What's new on the hostages?' . . . And this was certainly a high priority item with him, and yet he had so little to tell us about [it]. I mean, the Israelis sent special emissaries to ask if they could be of help in getting the hostages released. They thought that they could. They had contact with the Iranians and they thought that if they could transfer some of their weapons—U.S. weapons—to the Iranians, this could be used as a quid pro quo. This comes to a president who is agonizing over this thing every day, and yet he can't remember anything about it. My God!" [156]

Muskie might have been even more appalled if he had known of a conversation between Don Regan and the president about the contra diversion after Reagan's first Tower Board interview. Regan had assumed from the president's shocked reaction to Meese's revelation of the diversion that he was hearing about it for the first time. But Reagan was really as uncertain about whether he had been told about the diversion as he was of the timing of his approval of Israeli weapons shipments to Iran. Here is what Regan told me:

> Now I was not present at the first [Tower Board] interview with Ronald Reagan. But in preparation for his interview the president went over some facts—I think George Bush was there. This was one morning when just the three of us were sitting there. I don't want to swear to George Bush being there, but I think he was. And as we always did whenever there was a reporter coming in to interview Reagan or he was going to a press conference or anyone coming in, we went over the subject with him. And I said to him, "What is your recollection? Do you remember Bud [McFarlane] or John Poindexter ever telling you anything about the contras?" He said, "No." So I said, "Well, that's the story you've got to tell."
>
> Well, after the interview he [Reagan] was sitting there and he said, "Well, it seems to me that maybe I did." I said, "Now wait a minute, Mr. President, are you absolutely sure of this, because a lot hinges on this. You've got to check your diaries carefully and check your memory carefully." And he said, "No, I don't [remember them telling him about the diversion]." [157]

The extent of Reagan's forgetfulness and his tendency to change his story about two issues of such importance to him—arms sales to Iran to free the hostages and aid to the contras—are suspicious. The board was not questioning Reagan about "details," as White House spokesmen often described the process, but about the central events relating to the Iran arms sales and, later, the extracurricular assistance to the contras. "The key to the whole thing is he can remember," observed Stu Spencer, who came to the conclusion that Reagan had been "used" in the Iran-contra affair by Bill Casey and the NSC staff. "There are some things he remembers very poorly, but I think he wants to remember them very poorly. He really has a good memory." [158]

This good memory was little in evidence during Reagan's Tower Board interviews. After his dismal performance in the second interview the board was not eager to interview him again. Tower, after conferring with his board, told Abshire that if Reagan wanted to say anything else on the subject he should do it by written note. The board was running out of time to deliver its report, and Reagan agreed on the day of his second interview to extend its reporting deadline for a week, until February 26. The extension had nothing to do with the interview; it was granted because the board had on February 9 discovered the computer-stored backup PROF notes that North and Poindexter believed they had destroyed. The board wanted time to examine these notes. In the meantime, press reports contributed to an increased sense of pressure and uncertainty within the White House. Meese's earlier fears of impeachment now had new credence. Abshire was concerned that Reagan's remaining credibility would be shattered when his contradictory accounts about the birth of the Iran initiative became known after issuance of the Tower Report. "I felt Don Regan had to be cut out of the process," Abshire said. "I went in to see Reagan with Wallison and told him we had a real crisis of credibility." [159]

Reagan responded by criticizing himself for the inadequacy of his diary entries in August and September of 1985 (when he was recovering from his cancer operation). Abshire was struck by the degree to which Reagan blamed himself and told him that he thought McFarlane and Regan should have taken accurate notes. But this was water over the dam. There were no notes to prove what Reagan had done, and the president finally said he simply could not remember which of the accounts he had given was correct. Abshire told him that if he had anything more to say on the subject to the Tower Board he should put it in writing, as Tower had requested. On a yellow sheet of paper dated February 20, Reagan then wrote, "I'm trying to recall events that happened eighteen months ago, I'm afraid that I let myself be influenced by others' recollections, not my own. . . . I have no personal notes or records to help my recollection on this matter. The only honest answer is to state that try as I might, I cannot recall anything whatsoever about whether I approved an Israeli sale in advance or whether I approved replenishment of Israeli stocks around August of 1985. My answer therefore and the simple truth is, 'I don't remember, period.' " [160] When Abshire asked Reagan who had refreshed his recollection, the president said, "Regan." [161] Abshire had the letter typed and took it to Tower, bringing with him the handwritten original to show that the words were actually the president's.

It is possible that both McFarlane and Regan had testified accurately. McFarlane distrusted Regan and might have made it a point to inform the president of the impending Israeli TOW shipments when Regan was not present. If Reagan had been inattentive, or McFarlane had been unclear, the president might have expressed surprise when he was subsequently informed of the Israeli shipment, although it is unlikely he was disturbed to learn of it. It is indisputable that Reagan's view of the arms shipments to Iran was that they were a means to accomplish the result of freeing the American hostages. The Tower Board interviewed McFarlane three times on this issue, once in Bethesda Naval Hospital after he had attempted suicide on February 9 by taking an overdose of Valium. The board essentially accepted McFarlane's account and concluded that it was "most likely" that Reagan had given McFarlane verbal approval beforehand of the Israeli shipment and approved replenishment of the TOW missiles from U.S. stocks. The congressional committees, which had the advantage of access to Reagan's diary entries and a detailed Israeli chronology, reached a similar conclusion. But neither the board nor the committees had sufficient evidence to determine if Reagan had also approved the contra diversion. The Tower Board said backhandedly that "no evidence has come to light" to contradict Reagan's claim.[162] "I guess we couldn't bring ourselves to believe that he [Reagan] would be lying about that sort of thing," Muskie said. "I don't like to think that he was."[163]

Brent Scowcroft was as reluctant as Muskie to accuse Reagan of lying, but he continues to suspect that Reagan might have been informed of the diversion and then forgotten about it. Scowcroft, a retired Air Force general, had the most staff experience of the Tower Board members as well as the most experience in national security affairs. He had served as Henry Kissinger's assistant in the Nixon and Ford presidencies and then as Ford's national security adviser. He had also worked with Reagan on the Scowcroft Commission, where he had been exposed to the president's limited knowledge of strategic nuclear issues. Scowcroft's considerable insights into the workings of the Reagan national security process were enhanced by his friendships with Bush and McFarlane. He knew Poindexter fairly well. And he concluded that Reagan may have unknowingly approved the diversion. "Poindexter may have found a way in briefing him to say, 'By the way, we've found a way to help the contras from this, too,' " Scowcroft said. "It may have been done in a casual way that didn't raise the legalities of the issue."[164]

It is difficult to express such suspicions in formal reports, even a report as extraordinary and valuable as the one produced by the Tower

Board. The board operated under severe limitations. It lacked sub-poena power and was therefore unable to compel the testimony of North and Poindexter. It was thrown off stride by the unexpected contradictions in Reagan's testimony. Nonetheless, the board con-ducted sixty interviews in its ninety days of existence and found the PROF notes that had eluded the FBI and the independent counsel. Despite difficult deadline pressures, the board assembled an authorita-tive account that became the basis of the later legislative and criminal investigations. "The arms transfers to Iran and the activities of the NSC staff in support of the contras are case studies in the perils of policy pursued outside the constraints of orderly process," the board reported. "The Iran initiative ran directly counter to the administration's own policies on terrorism, the Iran/Iraq war, and military support to Iran. This inconsistency was never resolved. . . . The result taken as a whole was a U.S. policy that worked against itself." [165]

But despite their conscientiousness in describing what went wrong, the Tower Board members avoided harsh personal criticism of Reagan. They were trying to describe the flaws of the process, not bring down the president. While the Tower Report blamed Reagan for failing to make proper use of the NSC staff system, it phrased its larger concern most diplomatically: "President Reagan's personal management style places an especially heavy responsibility on his key advisors." [166] In fact, Muskie and Scowcroft wondered if this "management style" did not place an impossible burden on these advisers, but the report stopped short of saying this. No matter how confused or ineffective he may have been, Reagan was the president of the United States. And even after Watergate and Vietnam, the American presidency is guarded by a cer-tain mystique and reverence. Neither the Tower Board nor the congres-sional committees after it were collectively willing to express disrespect for the presidency, even though many of their members were dismayed by Reagan's conduct.*

John Tower was particularly diplomatic in his assessment. He con-sidered Reagan "a very, very honest man" but also believed that the president had rationalized his conduct because he could not accept what he had done. "If the president had been put on a polygraph test

---

* The glimpse of Reagan's deficiencies displayed in his second interview with the board and in many of his diary entries was unnerving to board members and congressmen alike. Late in 1987, Repub-lican Senator William Cohen of Maine, one of the most observant members of the congressional committees, confided to an interviewer that it would be a "waste of time" to talk to Reagan because "with Ronald Reagan, no one is there. The sad fact is we don't have a president." [167]

and had been asked the question whether or not he exchanged arms for hostages, he would have answered in the negative and would have passed the polygraph test because he was genuinely convinced that he had not traded arms for hostages," Tower said.[168] His words had a historical echo. After listening to the June 23, 1972, tape recording that incriminated Nixon in the Watergate coverup and cost him his presidency, his special counsel Fred Buzhardt said in 1974, "[Nixon] really believed what he was saying. It was pathetic . . . he could have passed a lie-detector test."[169]

And Reagan no doubt could also have passed a lie detector test on the question of the contra diversion. Following past practice, he again retreated into "constantly expanding areas of forgetfulness" whenever he was questioned about the issue. The record nonetheless suggests that Reagan knew more about the covert efforts to help the contras than he acknowledged in his public statements or his testimony to the Tower Board, even if he had conveniently forgotten what he knew. He had played an active role in the discussions to solicit funds for the contras from third countries, and he was aware of contributions for the contras from Saudi Arabia, Taiwan and the Sultan of Brunei. As noted in Chapter 14, the president had on June 25, 1984, concluded a crucial NSPG meeting where the legality of such third-country contributions was debated by saying, "If such a story gets out, we'll all be hanging by our thumbs in front of the White House until we find out who did it."[170]

At the time of this meeting Reagan had been informed by McFarlane that Prince Bandar, the Saudi ambassador to Washington, had agreed to contribute funds for the contras. Beginning in July 1984 the Saudis began secret payments of $1 million a month, deposited into an account controlled by contra leader Adolfo Calero in the Cayman Islands. Saudi King Fahd offered Reagan another $24 million for the contras during a state visit to Washington in February 1985. (The Saudis contributed a total of $32 million for the contras between July 1984 and March 1985.) When Bob Woodward learned of this in 1987, he asked me to find out what the White House had to say about the Saudi contributions. I talked to National Security Adviser Frank Carlucci, who said there had been "no solicitation of Fahd for the contras by the president."[171]

Carlucci, who had been out of government at the time of the Reagan-Fahd meeting, based his statement on an interview of most of the participants in the meeting, including an interview of the president conducted in the presence of then-White House Chief of Staff Howard

Baker. Reagan's credibility hinged on the definition of the word "solicitation." McFarlane had pointed out the problems of obtaining congressional aid for the contras to Bandar, and the highly intelligent Saudi ambassador had then "volunteered"[172] the contributions. And Fahd had similarly volunteered to increase the Saudi contribution to the contras. After McFarlane testified to the congressional committees about the Saudi donations, Reagan finally came forward to acknowledge that he had discussed the matter with Fahd. Reagan said he had not solicited the money but had "expressed pleasure"[173] when Fahd told him that the contribution to the contras was being increased.

Reagan also helped with the domestic fund-raising for the contras. This arm of the operation was conducted by Carl (Spitz) Channell under the auspices of the impressive-sounding National Endowment for the Preservation of Liberty and the American Conservative Trust. Channell subsequently pleaded guilty to conspiring to defraud the government by soliciting contributions for military aid to the contras under the cover of a tax-exempt charitable foundation. On January 30, 1986, Reagan spoke to nineteen of Channell's wealthiest donors in the Roosevelt Room of the White House, telling them that their contributions would help prevent the Soviets from consolidating their "client state" in Nicaragua. North and Elliott Abrams also addressed the assembled donors with speeches on the military and political situation in Central America that emphasized the dangers of Marxist-Leninist expansion in the hemisphere and the plight of the contras.

Ostensibly, Channell was seeking funds to wage a public relations campaign in behalf of contra aid. Actually, about $3 million of the $4 million he raised was used for North's military resupply of the contras. It is unlikely this disappointed the donors, most of whom ardently supported the effort of the contras to overthrow the Sandinistas. John Ramsey of Wichita Falls, Texas, one of the donors who attended the meeting with Reagan in the Roosevelt Room, contributed $100,000 and said, "If they could have given the money for weapons legally, that would have suited me fine."[174] Reagan attended at least half a dozen "photo opportunities" organized by Channell for his donors. The arrangements were made by David Fischer, Reagan's former personal aide, who dealt with Don Regan and the White House schedulers and was paid $662,000 for his services over a two-year period. Unlike James Baker and Mike Deaver, Regan made no effort to keep Reagan from posing with the contras or their supporters. Regan had no particular illusions about the contras, but he knew that the president wanted to help them in any way he could.

And Reagan did more than simply appear at photo opportunities or thank foreign and domestic contributors. Documents released at the North trial show that the president in February 1985 approved a plan designed to "entice" Honduras to continue arms deliveries to the contras by speeding up U.S. economic and military aid to Honduras. When a Honduran military commander seized a contra military shipment in early 1985, Reagan called the Honduran president to get him to release it.[175] Poindexter, even while insisting he had never told Reagan of the diversion itself, testified that he had briefed him on a clandestine Costa Rican airstrip built by North's network to aid the contras at a time when U.S. aid to the rebels was prohibited. Poindexter also said that Reagan knew North was "the chief staff officer . . . carrying out his charter to keep the contras alive"[176] during the two-year ban on most U.S. military aid.

Reagan would have a difficult time keeping his story straight. This was partly because of his mental confusion and partly because he seems to have wanted to claim credit for helping the contras even while distancing himself from the diversion. After Senator Daniel Inouye of Hawaii, a co-chairman of the congressional investigation, observed that Reagan had known about "outside funding" for the contras, Reagan at first denied it, then said, "With regard to whether private individuals were giving money to support the contras, yes, I was aware that people were doing that. But there was nothing in the nature of a solicitation by the administration, to my knowledge, of anyone to do that."[177] He made this statement on May 3, during a brief exchange with reporters in which he acknowledged the contribution of King Fahd. In a longer exchange on May 15, Reagan objected to being portrayed as "uninformed about everything."[178] After giving a rambling account of the Iran initiative in which he once more asserted that arms had not been sent to the Iranian regime, Reagan said with some pride that he was regularly briefed on the various efforts to help the contras. "As a matter of fact, I was very definitely involved in decisions about support to the freedom fighters," Reagan said. "It was my idea to begin with."[179]

These were the words Reagan had used to me when he claimed credit for originating the Strategic Defense Initiative. Saying that a particular proposal was "my idea to begin with" was Reagan's way of responding to critics who portrayed him as ignorant or distanced from crucial decisions. And there was often a grain of truth to Reagan's assertions when he claimed credit for the ideas that motivated his policies. SDI had been developed as a political proposal by McFarlane and Chief of Naval Operations James Watkins, with scientific encouragement from

Edward Teller and others, but Reagan had been interested in the notion of antimissile defense since the days when he was a science-fiction enthusiast. The contras were sponsored by Casey and promoted by North and Elliott Abrams, with propaganda supplied by Patrick Buchanan and the White House speechwriters. But Reagan had long favored using the Marxist-Leninist idea of armies of "national liberation" against Communist regimes. He had from the first embraced the proposal to use supposedly indigenous "freedom fighters" rather than U.S. military forces against the Sandinistas. The political problem for Reagan after the diversion was disclosed on November 25, 1986, was that his desire to take credit for the contras conflicted with the effort to keep him distanced from the diversion.

Reagan, who knew little about how any federal program operated and was largely uninterested in matters of process, may not have known specifically that proceeds from the Iran arms sales were being placed into accounts for the contras. He may have known it and forgotten it. Or, as Scowcroft and McFarlane suggested, he may have been informed in a way that never really registered. But what Reagan certainly knew and consistently conveyed to his subordinates was that the contras needed far more help than Congress was willing to give them. Because of this knowledge and belief, Reagan encouraged Americans and friendly foreign leaders to help the contra cause. Oliver North may have gone beyond his instructions, but he was carrying out missions that Reagan wanted accomplished, both in his efforts to free the hostages and to help the Nicaraguan rebels. It is no wonder that Reagan considered North a national hero.

Reagan was able to avert the impeachment that Meese and others had considered a serious possibility because the contra diversion could not be pinned on him. But in the last two months of 1986 and the first two months of 1987 he was overwhelmed by the realization that he had lost the trust of the American people. "He never had his integrity questioned before," said Nancy Reagan. "And that really, really bothered him." [180] Emotionally, Reagan was at the ebb tide of his presidency. More than any policy or personal friendship, he cherished his bond with the American people. Wirthlin's polls and almost every news account he read or watched on television reminded Reagan that the people thought he was lying. Reagan could neither face the audience he thought had turned against him nor bring himself to ask forgiveness for selling arms to Iran. In his heart of hearts he believed he had done the right thing, no matter what the evidence showed. While the polls suggested that Reagan still possessed deep reserves of popularity (people thought he was lying about the Iran-contra affair but was generally honest), his advisers found him stubborn and prideful when they suggested he could make amends by admitting mistakes. Regan and his aides tried out various formulations on Reagan that would, as Wallison put it, "enable him to say that he had made a mistake without actually saying that he had made a mistake, but he refused to say it." [181] The most Reagan would do while Regan was in the White House was to say in his weekly radio speech of December 6 "that the execution of these [Iran initiative] policies were flawed and mistakes were made"—a declaration similar to the one that Bush had used three days earlier after clearing his speech with the White House. But Reagan's admission was overshadowed by still another unrealistic defense of the initiative, which he claimed had failed only because his "effort to establish a relationship with responsible moderates in Iran" had been leaked to the press. He just could not bring himself to say he had been wrong.

If the president was stubborn, Nancy Reagan was frightened. She had been the lone holdout against the assumption that Reagan should seek a second term. What was happening to the Reagan presidency in 1986 seemed to her the fulfillment of a terrible premonition. More politically astute than her husband, Nancy Reagan took the threat of impeachment seriously. She also realized that Reagan could not survive without his credibility. But "Ronnie" would never be the villain in her eyes. Her first remedy for repairing the damage to his presidency was a top-to-bottom housecleaning in the White House, starting with the chief of staff.

The first lady was not alone in wanting Don Regan to depart. Regan's portrayal of what happened to him is that he was run out of the White House by Nancy Reagan, with assistance from Deaver and Spencer. But this gives the first lady too much credit—or too much blame. What is largely missing from Regan's harrowing tale in *For the Record* is the leading role played in his demise by the accumulated hostility of Republican congressional leaders, who had long resented his nonconsultative style, his disdain for politics and his displays of ego. The Republican establishment, with few exceptions, wanted Regan out. "It took this crisis for me to realize, 'Oh, Jesus, I don't have a friend in town here,' " Regan told me much later. " 'Why don't I have a friend?' " [182]

The answer of White House political director Mitch Daniels to Regan's lament was that the chief of staff had not cultivated any friends except the president. "Washington is a place where if you don't build an inventory of friends and allies no one will come to your aid in time of trouble," [183] observed Daniels, who got along with Regan but was never really valued by him. The quiet, diminutive Daniels kept his distance from any organized campaign to oust Regan, but he had reached the conclusion that the chief of staff was a burden on the Reagan presidency. Under Daniels and his predecessors the White House political office had accumulated a voluminous list of key local officeholders, Republican Party officials and old-line Reaganites. When Daniels and his aides sampled this list for suggestions on how the White House should respond to the crisis, they found an overwhelming demand for Regan's removal. "We consulted well over a hundred people," Daniels said. "The view was unanimous that he [Regan] should leave." [184] Daniels prided himself on giving professional political recommendations. He went to Regan on his own in mid-December to tell him about the consensus of Republican opinion that he should resign. "I told Don what they thought," Daniels said. "It was what I thought, too, and I told him so. He disagreed and said it wouldn't do any good. He thought he needed to stay to preserve stability." [185]

Regan also thought he needed to stay to preserve his own reputation. He had mentioned to Reagan in October that he might want to retire after the elections or early in 1987, but he wanted to leave at a time of his choosing rather than under pressure. Unlike Poindexter and North he had no reason to be concerned about criminal prosecution, but he was unprepared to take the political fall for a scandal he believed he had done nothing to cause. "I knew that if I walked the plank, there goes my reputation forever," Regan said.[186]

From the point of view of Spencer and Deaver, as well as Nancy Reagan, Regan was too much a part of the political problem to become part of the solution. Regan was now haunted by his frequent boasts of the managerial control he had exercised as "chief operating officer" of the White House. His critics turned a deaf ear to his claim that he had no control over Poindexter and the NSC staff largely because, as Scowcroft put it, "He kept saying he did. One of the reasons McFarlane quit was because Regan wanted McFarlane to report through him." [187] As previously recounted, Regan had dressed down McFarlane early in 1985 for not telling him first before he awakened the president to inform him that the Soviets had killed a U.S. Army officer in East Germany. He told the Tower Board that he usually attended the national security briefings given by McFarlane and, after him, by Poindexter. Regan was stuck with the perception he had created. When David Hoffman and I interviewed Regan on November 21, the occasion on which he described the president as a "manly CEO," he opened the session by lecturing us about his lack of control over the national security adviser and his staff. Regan wanted it both ways. While it may indeed have been true that Regan had paid insufficient attention to Poindexter's activities, it was too late for him to undo the impression that he and his aides had tried so assiduously to convey.

Stu Spencer was uninterested in Regan's excuses. Spencer saw himself as a modern version of the western gunslinger who shows up in times of trouble and drives the bad guys out of town. He arrived in Washington in November 1986 at Nancy Reagan's bidding, cast in his familiar role as Reagan's troubleshooter in time of need. Spencer talked tough, but he had acquired an affectionate regard for the Reagans. He was also personally disgusted by the performance of Regan, whom he had defended to Nancy Reagan and others during the Bitburg controversy and later to his friends in Republican circles when they were accusing Regan of wrecking budget negotiations with Congress. "I thought the guy had some potential for growth, and I was wrong," Spencer said. "[He] became a prime minister, he became a guy that was in every photo op, he wasn't watching the shop. And he surrounded himself with yes people. Those were all signs of weakness to me." [188]

Spencer knew so little about the background of the Iran-contra affair that he had never even heard Oliver North's name until he was fired. But Spencer knew and distrusted Bill Casey and assumed as a matter of course that the CIA director had "played to Reagan's dark side." [189] Spencer saw the issue in practical, political terms. The Reagan presidency was falling into "a black hole" of undetermined depth.* Someone would have to be sacrificed to save the president. "The old safe position is to hang three sons of bitches and get it over with," said Spencer. "Throw them to the wolves." [191] Poindexter was already gone. Spencer now believed that it was necessary for Reagan also to rid himself of Casey and Regan.

Natural causes removed Casey from the scene. He suffered a seizure in his office on December 15, as he was preparing to testify before the

---

* Spencer was almost as appalled by Shultz and Weinberger, who had opposed the Iran initiative but distanced themselves from it, as he was by Casey and Regan, who had promoted it. "If they [Shultz and Weinberger] really thought it was a black hole they would have fought, and they didn't fight," Spencer said. "It was almost like, 'I'm going to get my ass off the hook on this one by saying you shouldn't do this.' You can always sit in a meeting in Washington and get your ass off a hook, because that's the way they play the whole game in Washington." [190]

Senate Intelligence Committee. Three days later doctors removed a cancerous tumor from his brain. Nancy Reagan and Spencer pressed for a quick resignation, but Regan thought it was unfair to dismiss the CIA director when he was incapacitated. Besides, there was no one immediately available to replace Casey. CIA Deputy Director Robert Gates proposed three former Republican senators, John Tower, Paul Laxalt and Howard Baker, but none of them wanted the job under the circumstances. On January 28, while Gates was reporting to him in the hospital, Casey abruptly announced that it was time for him to "get out of the way." [192] The next day Meese and Regan went to Georgetown Hospital and accepted Casey's resignation.

But Regan was in good health and full of fight. Reagan did not want to fire him, and the more that congressional Republicans and Nancy Reagan shoved, the more Reagan resisted. Neither Spencer nor Deaver could get anywhere with the president. Deaver made the most determined effort. He saw the president three times in November and December, twice with Spencer. Originally, Reagan brushed aside Deaver's entreaty to get on top of the situation, saying he had staff to deal with the political response. When Deaver, with Spencer at his side, argued that Regan had to go, the president became angry.

"This is difficult, but you're not the first president to face difficult decisions," Deaver said.

"I'll be goddamned if I'll throw somebody else out to save my own ass," Reagan responded.

"It's not your ass I'm talking about," said Deaver. "You stood up on the steps of the Capitol and took an oath to defend the Constitution and this office. You've got to think of the country first."

"I've always thought of the country," Reagan said, throwing his pen so hard it bounced off the carpet. [193]

Spencer, realizing that Reagan was too angry to back down, said nothing. "Thanks for backing me up," Deaver said sardonically to Spencer after they had left the White House. [194]

Deaver and Spencer called for reinforcements in the persons of Washington power attorney Robert Strauss and William Rogers, who had served as Nixon's secretary of state. Deaver organized a private meeting at the White House residence with Strauss, Rogers, the Reagans and himself. Don Regan, who was not invited, later said he thought it was "ridiculous" [195] for the Reagans to consult with Strauss because he was a former Democratic national chairman. But Strauss did not come to the White House as a Democrat. While he had worked hard to reelect Jimmy Carter and defeat Reagan, Strauss enjoyed being a power broker and he had an old-fashioned, patriotic appreciation of the presidency. He did not want to see Reagan driven from office. When Deaver called and asked him to come to the White House on the evening of December 4, Strauss replied that he would come only if the Reagans wanted to hear the truth as he saw it.

Strauss had a score to settle with his conscience. During the Johnson administration he had been invited to the White House by the president and asked to give his opinion of the Vietnam War. "I told Johnson in front of a witness everything I thought Johnson wanted to hear," said Strauss. "He didn't want to hear any criticism and I didn't give him any. And I didn't believe what I said at the time and I was ashamed of myself when I left, and I told [Reagan] this. I think I even went so far as to use the expression 'I felt like a common prostitute' or 'a three-dollar prostitute' or something." [196]

Strauss, Rogers and Deaver walked to the White House through an underground tunnel running from the Treasury. It had been used as an air-raid shelter during World War II, and Strauss was fascinated to find it still stocked with hospital beds and medical equipment. They went upstairs to the residence, where they were greeted by the Reagans. Strauss talked frankly, telling Reagan of how he had lied to Johnson and learned from his experience and told the truth to Carter. He credited Reagan with restoring national confidence but said this confidence was being eroded by the Iran-contra scandal. He received no backing from Rogers, who tried to comfort the president by mentioning an ABC poll that he said showed a slight rebound in Reagan's popularity. Alluding to this poll, Strauss said that Reagan would still carry his home state of Texas by a 2-1 margin. "But this won't continue forever in my judgment, Mr. President," Strauss said. "And it's like a cancer and it will eat away. And if it gets very far before it's treated, there will be no way to turn it around." [197]

Strauss delivered a blunt and critical assessment of how the White House had responded to the crisis. He told Reagan he thought it was being badly managed. He told him that his press conference had been a mistake, "because you didn't have your facts right and you looked bad and you got bad advice." He advised against further press conferences until Reagan knew more about what had happened. And he told Reagan that it was necessary for him to get "personally on top of the problem," [198] saying that it didn't appear to him or others in Washington that he had done this. The problem, Strauss said, was not what

Reagan knew about the Iran-contra affair but what he didn't know. This struck a chord with Nancy Reagan.

"Bob is just saying to you, Ronnie, that he thinks you're telling the truth as you see it and, number two, it's inaccurate," she said.[199] "And he's saying to you that that's the worst of all worlds. If you're telling the truth and know it isn't the truth, that's bad enough. But when you tell what you believe is the truth and it's inaccurate, then you're really in trouble."[200]

"And I know you don't like to hear it," Reagan said to his wife.[201]

But Nancy Reagan was not done. She turned to Strauss and said, "You're the first person who's said that to Ronnie clearly and strongly besides me."[202] Then she asked Strauss what he would do. He thought that Reagan desperately needed changes in the White House. "You've got a managerial problem and you've got a press and congressional problem and they're not any of them being handled well," he said.[203] Strauss said that Reagan's personal feelings about Don Regan were not what mattered in the crisis he faced. "It doesn't make any difference whether he's a saint or a sinner [or] whether he's your closest, most cherished friend," said Strauss. He suggested that Secretary of Labor Bill Brock or Howard Baker or former transportation secretary Drew Lewis would be a good replacement for Regan. "They all have good press relations, they all have good [Capitol] Hill relations," said Strauss, suggesting that any of them could enable Reagan to make "a fresh start."[204]

Reagan appreciated that Strauss had spoken frankly to him, but he was unmoved by his arguments. The president said he had not traded arms for hostages, had not known about the diversion and had acted to find the truth by appointing the Tower Board. He expressed great confidence in Ed Meese, saying that he was on top of the situation. He repeated what he had said to Deaver about not throwing Regan to the wolves. He praised Regan for working out differences between Senate Majority Leader Bob Dole and Senate Minority Leader Robert Byrd on the structure and timing of the congressional investigations of the Iran-contra affair. Dole had been pushing for a special congressional session. The White House opposed a special session and also preferred a single investigation by joint committees rather than separate inquiries by each house of Congress. The White House got its way, in part because Strauss also favored this approach and had quietly served as a mediator. When Reagan credited Regan for this effort, Strauss told the president that he had spent three hours on the telephone on Thanksgiving Day with Dole and Byrd in a successful effort to resolve their differences.[205]

"Well, I didn't know that it had come about that way or everyone's role in it, but I want to thank you," Reagan said.

"I didn't do it for thanks," Strauss said.[206]

The meeting ended cordially, but it was obvious to Strauss that Reagan agreed with Bill Rogers that the Iran-contra affair would blow over. He was angry at Rogers for leaving him to make his case alone. Strauss went home, drank two vodkas, had a bowl of soup and climbed into bed. Just as he was falling asleep, the phone rang. Nancy Reagan was on the line, thanking him for what he had said.

"Ronnie was upset," she said. "It upset him because he was troubled by what you said. He heard what you said, even though you felt tonight it was just a waste of your time. Ronnie hears and he heard everything you said tonight. And he was troubled during dinner. He didn't eat his dinner. He was terribly troubled."

"I'm so sorry," Strauss said.

"No. I'm not," she said. "He needed to be troubled. He has to have his mind opened and his eyes open on this and see what's happening to him."[207]

But as troubled as he was, it was difficult for Reagan to get a grip on what was happening to him. He was now besieged within the White House, where his wife and chief of staff were engaged in open warfare. After one furious disagreement, Regan and Nancy Reagan hung up on each other, so angry that neither knew who had slammed the phone down first. But Reagan was, as he put it in his memoirs, "troubled by this kind of temperamental outburst [of Regan's], especially toward Nancy, who has always had only my best interests at heart."[208]

Reagan became listless and dispirited. He brightened slightly when he went to California for his annual New Year's vacation in Palm Springs, where he could tell old stories to old friends and play golf with George Shultz. Since Regan had decided to spend the vacation away from Nancy Reagan in Florida, it was a peaceful interlude. But when Reagan returned to Washington, the battles started again. Regan would later say that Reagan "dislikes confrontations more than any man that I have ever known."[209] It was an accurate assessment. Since childhood, his response to conflict had always been withdrawal, but he could now find no haven either in the White House family quarters or the Oval Office. His wife and chief of staff were no longer speaking to each other except through Bill Henkel and David Abshire, and their enmity could

not be avoided by Reagan. On January 5, 1987, the president underwent prostate surgery, from which he was slow to recover. He did not
want to discuss Don Regan or the Iran-contra affair. In the first weeks
of the new year, Stu Spencer began to wonder if Reagan's presidency
would survive.

Regan had his own plan for preserving the Reagan presidency and
salvaging his own reputation, not necessarily in that order. He wanted
Reagan to change the subject—"create a diversion" was the way Regan
put it[210]—and give speeches around the country on such issues as U.S.-
Soviet relations, the Strategic Defense Initiative and the necessity for a
balanced budget. As Regan saw it, Reagan could duck the inevitable
Iran-contra questions at photo opportunities by smiling sweetly and
saying, "Look, it's in the hands of the Tower Commission."[211] In time,
Iran-contra would simply go away.

This simpleminded strategy was more revealing of the deficiency of
Regan's political judgment than were the harsh criticisms of those who
were trying to force him out of the White House. The Congress, the
media and the public were clamoring for explanations about the Iran-
contra affair. Reagan needed desperately to deal with the issue and
believe in himself again, which is what Nancy Reagan had in mind when
she said it was good that Strauss had troubled him. It should have been
evident to Regan that Reagan was too confused and emotionally
strained to launch a speaking tour or hold another news conference, as
it was evident to Paul Laxalt and David Abshire, as well as Deaver,
Spencer and dozens of Republicans with whom I discussed the situation
at the time. But Regan's judgment was clouded by his effort to save his
own job and reputation.

Regan would subsequently claim that his strategy was frustrated by
the refusal of Nancy Reagan and her astrologer to permit the president
to travel or take questions from the press. This was a sensational charge
that vastly overrated Joan Quigley's importance. According to Mitch
Daniels, scheduling had been no problem in the 1986 campaign, when
he had often added political events on short notice. Regan's strategy of
dealing with the scandal by trying to change the subject was frustrated
by common sense, not astrology. As Abshire and others have attested,
Nancy Reagan opposed public appearances by her husband even on
astrologically favorable dates because she did not think he should risk
further misstatements until the Tower Board had completed its report.
Her only opposition came from Regan and those aides who depended
on him for their White House employment.

Those with independent judgment were dismayed by the conduct of

Regan, not of the first lady. Chief among these was Abshire, who had been brought into the White House as special counsellor by Regan just after Christmas. Abshire barely knew Nancy Reagan, but he sought her out on February 3 at the suggestion of Charles Wick and Robert Strauss after she had made a remark on television that reflected a misconception of his role. "She had apparently assumed that I would produce and judge the facts and put the case to rest," Abshire said.[212] He had no such illusions about his task, which he said was "not to reach judgment but to see that the independent investigating bodies were able to make the judgments, to see that the flawed process which got us into the Iran-contra mess was now met and matched with due process."[213] He found that Nancy Reagan "quickly understood this important difference."[214] She urged that he meet privately with Reagan, which had been one of Abshire's conditions for accepting the assignment as special counsellor. "Nancy Reagan, far from being the meddlesome and overly protective person" described by Regan, "was anxious mainly that the facts be aired, the crisis passed and the broader business of government resumed as soon as possible," Abshire would conclude. In contrast, he found that Regan "often seemed more concerned with his own welfare . . . than with the president's."[215]

The irony of Regan's demise was that he was ultimately forced out because of the way he dealt with the people he had brought into the White House to solve the crisis—principally Abshire and the three members of the Tower Board. Tall and soft-spoken with a scholarly manner, Abshire was a respected figure in Washington conservative circles. He had served as a front-line company commander in Korea and as assistant secretary of state in the Nixon and Ford administrations. The author of seven books on foreign policy, he was the founder and president of the Center for Strategic and International Studies. He met with Reagan privately twelve times in the first two months of 1987, more than anyone else in this period except for Nancy Reagan and Regan. Abshire liked Reagan immensely but found him naïve. He thought Reagan was "an Eagle Scout" who found it difficult to believe "that down below there is anybody but other Eagle Scouts."[216] And like other thoughtful people who dealt with Reagan, Abshire also wondered if the president had been told about the contra diversion by Poindexter without realizing it. Once he suggested this to Reagan as a possibility, saying that Poindexter might have quietly included Iran on a list of countries that had been helpful to the contras. "No, that never happened," Reagan said. "I would remember it."[217]

But it was the problem of Reagan's faulty memory at the second

Tower Board interview that led Abshire and Regan into conflict. Abshire and Regan had worked together at the outset, with friction arising only when Abshire insisted on meeting alone with the president. This seemed a particularly necessary condition after the second interview, when the Tower Board blamed Regan for influencing the president's recollection of when he had first approved the arms sales. Abshire had not shown Regan the president's handwritten letter saying that he had allowed his memory to be influenced by the recollections of others. "I knew Don could be hurt by that language, but that had to be done," said Abshire. "This had to be the president, the way he wrote it with no editing or anything else."[218]

It was the president's version of events, rather than any action of Nancy Reagan, that effectively ended Regan's White House career. Once Reagan had decided that it was Regan who had influenced him to contradict himself, the chief of staff's days were abruptly numbered, though the president could never bring himself to confront Regan directly. Abshire could see that a collision was approaching and he called on Regan, with the approval of Vice President Bush and the first lady, to suggest that he resign for the good of the presidency. The meeting was friendly, but Regan, as he had done with Daniels in December, dismissed the suggestion by saying that Abshire should write him a memo about it. It was too late for memos. Within two days of the February 20 letter to the Tower Board in which Reagan disclaimed any recollection of when he had first authorized the arms sales, John Tower called Abshire and said the board wanted to brief Regan personally on the report on February 25, the day before it would be publicly issued. What the board wanted to do, Tower said, was to explain to Reagan privately the reasons for its conclusions without giving Regan another chance to influence the president's recollections about the history of the arms sales.

Abshire called Regan and told him about Tower's request. Regan was furious. "Go back and tell them we can't do that," he said.[219] By now, Regan had an intimation that the board had accepted McFarlane's version instead of his own about the Israeli arms sales. Abshire returned to Tower and told him what Regan had said. Tower was adamant. Short of a direct order from the president to do otherwise, the board insisted on giving the report directly to Reagan without risking the chance that Regan would influence his reaction to it. Abshire called Regan again and told him what Tower had said. "He was livid," said Abshire.[220]

"You haven't been around these things enough. You never put the president in that kind of position. And the chief of staff goes over things in advance . . . and we brief him," Regan said.[221]

"We've already had this credibility problem," Abshire replied. "We've pinned our total comeback on the credibility of the Tower Board report and if we jeopardize it now everything we've been doing will fall apart."[222]

Then they started shouting at each other. Abshire told Regan that he was "his own worst enemy" and so close to the situation that he had lost his judgment. Regan fired back that Abshire wasn't close enough. But he was defeated, and knew it. "All right," Regan said. "It's your show. You go ahead and have it your way but you'll accept the responsibility."[223]

At three o'clock the following afternoon, February 25, the board briefed Reagan. In contrast to his earlier appearances, the president seemed unusually alert as the board members went through the report with him. Tower had undertaken the burden of much of the questioning of Reagan, but it was Scowcroft who now led the way in explaining why the board had concluded that Reagan had traded arms for hostages. Carefully, Scowcroft led Reagan through the expedition of McFarlane and North to Tehran in May 1986, when Secord's plane had been on an airport runway in Israel waiting to deliver its cargo of missiles once word had been given that the hostages were released. "Yes, if the plane was waiting there to receive word on the hostages, the arms are loaded up, then it was arms for hostages," Reagan said.[224] Tower and Scowcroft were convinced they had persuaded the president. Abshire was also pleased with the "good meeting." He thought that Reagan would repeat what he had said in a nationally televised speech the following Wednesday, March 4, finally describing the Iran initiative as it was seen by others.

The Tower Report finished Regan's tenure as chief of staff in a single paragraph. "More than almost any chief of staff of recent memory, he asserted personal control over the White House staff and sought to extend his control to the national security advisor," the report said. "He was personally active in national security affairs and attended almost all of the relevant meetings regarding the Iran initiative. He, as much as anyone, should have insisted that an orderly process be observed. In addition, he especially should have ensured that plans were made for handling any public disclosure of the initiative. He must bear primary responsibility for the chaos that descended upon the White House when such disclosure did occur."[225]

This assessment, although resented by Regan, made it clear even to him that he would have to leave before the president gave his nationally televised speech on March 4. Reagan had already gently asked for his resignation, suggesting in a conversation on February 23 that he ought to leave before the Tower Report was issued. Regan had responded heatedly, in words Reagan had often used to defend him. "You can't do that to me, Mr. President," he said. "If I go before that report is out, you throw me to the wolves. I deserve better treatment than that."[226] Reagan was shaken. It was difficult for him to ask for anyone's resignation under the best of circumstances, and he had now done so and been rebuffed. He asked Regan when he wanted to leave, and the chief of staff replied, "The first part of next week." Regan says that Reagan "agreed to this timetable"[227] for what the chief of staff still hoped would be a dignified exit.

But Regan had waited too long. On Thursday, February 26, Vice President Bush had lunch with Regan and asked him when he would be leaving. Again, Regan's temper flared. He was particularly upset that Reagan had delegated the assignment of dismissing him to Bush, although Regan had followed this practice himself when he used Buchanan as his messenger to fire White House chief speechwriter Bently Elliott. Bush said he would go back to the president with Regan's message that he wanted to leave the following week. According to Reagan, Bush told him he had seen a side of Regan he had never seen before—"an outburst of temper." But later in the afternoon, Regan talked to Bush again and said his resignation would be on the president's desk the first thing Monday morning. In his diary the president wrote, "My prayers have really been answered."[228]

Reagan had already placed a call to Howard Baker in Florida with the intention of asking him to become his new chief of staff. Baker was out, taking his grandchildren to the Miami Metrozoo. "Well, tell him I need him because we've got a zoo up here," Reagan said to Baker's wife, Joy.[229] Baker called back, accepted the job and agreed to fly to Washington the following morning. On the flight he fell into conversation with a *Miami Herald* editor, talking freely about his prospects in the 1988 presidential campaign but making no mention of the assignment he was being asked to undertake. In discussing the Tower Report and the Reagans, however, Baker spoke more freely. Referring to the feud between Don Regan and Nancy Reagan, Baker said that "when she gets her hackles up, she can be a dragon."[230]

Baker went to the White House through the Treasury underground route with his old Senate colleague and Reagan's friend, Paul Laxalt. Baker had been Laxalt's choice to replace Regan. When stories began circulating that Regan would not survive the Tower Report, Laxalt had been mentioned as a possible replacement. The former Nevada senator still entertained presidential aspirations, and had no interest in becoming the White House chief of staff. He went to Reagan and took his name out of consideration. "Howard Baker is the person you need now," Laxalt said. "Well, hell, he's going to run for president," said Reagan. Laxalt said he wasn't sure that Baker wanted to run, "and this may be a good reason for him to have a graceful exit."[231] As Reagan put it in his diary, "Paul was right."[232]

Baker later told me that he had decided on the Miami–Washington flight that he didn't want to become White House chief of staff. His unguarded remark about Nancy Reagan to a newspaper editor would certainly suggest that he had no intention of working in the White House. But if Baker was having second thoughts, he proved unable to resist the appeal for help from a "badly shaken" president. "Howard, we've got a bad situation on our hands here, and I need you to be my chief of staff," Reagan said. Baker said he "heard himself say, all right, I will."[233] To Reagan, Baker's acceptance seemed another answered prayer.

Despite the secrecy of Baker's meeting with the president, word soon circulated that he would be replacing Regan. It was reported by CNN late that afternoon. National Security Adviser Frank Carlucci was told about the report and went to Regan's office, where the chief of staff was completing an interview with reporters from *Time*. Carlucci waited. When the reporters had finished, Carlucci went into Regan's office and told him about the CNN report. Regan exploded in a typical rage and dictated a one-sentence letter to his secretary addressed to the president: "I hereby resign as chief of staff to the president of the United States." But Carlucci insisted that Regan talk to the president before he left and, when Regan wouldn't place the call, Carlucci did it himself. The president called back immediately, saying he was sorry that the news about Baker had become public but that he hoped Regan would stay until Monday, to allow him to make a formal announcement of his resignation and consult with Baker. "I'm sorry, but I won't be in anymore," Regan said, with great emotion.[234] He had served Reagan for six years, and told the president that he "deserved better treatment than this."[235] Again, Reagan asked him to stay and make the transfer smoothly, but Regan felt too humiliated. He said goodbye. The two men never talked again. When I asked Regan two years later about his departure, he said that he was "very hurt" that Reagan had never called him since.[236]

A new cast was now in place at the White House. The energetic Frank Carlucci, who had thirty years' experience as foreign service officer, bureaucrat, diplomat, and deputy director of the CIA and the Pentagon, had been named to replace Poindexter on December 2 and taken over as national security adviser in January. He had immediately abolished the political-military affairs unit that had served as North's launching pad within the NSC staff. "I could never figure out what it did," Carlucci said months later. "In any case, it made no sense to me because almost everything we do involves political and military affairs. The way it was set up simply invited trouble, and, of course, trouble came along."[237] Carlucci brought in his own trusted team, including Army Lieutenant General Colin L. Powell, who became his successor a year later when Carlucci became secretary of defense. Carlucci also fired several people and transferred others and, in a symbolic act, left the door to his office open, which Poindexter had always kept closed.

"We set out to restore the credibility of the institution, to restore it to its proper role as an interagency body," Carlucci said. "That is its honest broker role, and we set out to reestablish it. We took the NSC out of operations."[238] He also restored a mood of professional normalcy to a workaholic staff that often seemed driven by an almost frantic sense of mission. Soon after arriving at the NSC, Carlucci asked Colin Powell why the NSC had so many secretaries. Powell checked and told him it was because the staff was accustomed to working eighteen hours a day, seven days a week. "Colin, get rid of half of them," said Carlucci, who sent out the word that "henceforth we go home at six at night and we don't work weekends."[239] Carlucci set the example by walking out of his office at 6:00 P.M. his first day on the job with a tennis racket under his arm.[240] He also shut down his desk computer, on which members of the staff had been used to communicating with Poindexter. "People began to realize that the quickest way to get me was either by telephone or to walk in the door," Carlucci said. "And that also contributed to a change in the atmosphere. We weren't working through machines, we were working with each other as human beings."[241]

Under Howard Baker a similar sense of normalcy soon returned to the White House, aided by a new supporting cast. After Larry Speakes left on February 1, he was replaced as White House spokesman by Marlin Fitzwater, who proved more popular and trusted than his predecessor with the White House press corps. The confrontational Patrick Buchanan resigned on March 1 and was replaced by a longtime Baker aide, Thomas Griscom. Baker also brought in his confidant Arthur B. Culvahouse to replace Wallison as White House counsel. He hired Rhett Dawson, the Tower Board chief of staff, as White House administrative officer. And in an echo of the administration's halcyon first-term days, Ken Duberstein came to the White House as Baker's deputy, bringing a valuable set of relationships with politicians and reporters. At Baker's behest, Duberstein accepted the responsibility of dealing with Nancy Reagan, who was once more openly welcomed as a political adviser. In 1988, when Baker resigned because of his wife's illness, Duberstein succeeded him as chief of staff.

This group had its share of conflicts, differences and ups and downs. But the besieged mood at the White House vanished with Regan's departure. Baker had known Reagan for many years. He was an experienced attorney and had served as vice chairman of the Senate committee that investigated Watergate and set in motion the disintegration of the Nixon presidency. Because of this experience, Baker took the idea of impeachment seriously, and he would subsequently warn Reagan that he and Culvahouse would tell him if any evidence that came to light during the Iran-contra investigations required him to hire his own counsel. It helped that Baker had no illusion that he was president. "I believe you know since we know each other well, but that I should tell you for the sake of saying it, [that] I understand that you are president and I am not," Baker said to Reagan at their first morning staff meeting on March 2.[242] Reagan would remind him of this statement from time to time when they disagreed, but their relationship was relaxed and respectful. Baker did not seek to be a "yes man" to the president or to act in his name and tell him later. At the same time Baker managed to convey a sense of urgency to his team—"a realization that [Reagan] was on the ropes and we had to somehow get our shit together," said Dawson.[243] More than any other single person, it was Howard Baker who brought Reagan back.

In the critical first days of March, however, there still remained the task of persuading Reagan to admit to the American people that he had actually traded arms for hostages. "Dave, everybody in the United States might believe that it's arms for hostages, but I'm stubborn," he had told Abshire early in the final week of February. "I don't."[244] Reagan appeared to have accepted the reality of the arms-for-hostages trade in his February 25 meeting with the Tower Board. After the meeting, however, Abshire found that Reagan had "reverted back" to his original view.[245]

The task of persuading Reagan to make a public admission fell to the team of speechwriter Landon Parvin, Stu Spencer and John Tower, with the usual orchestration by Nancy Reagan. Tower's role has deliberately been kept secret, largely because Spencer thought it was unwise to advertise that the chairman of the board that had just passed judgment on Reagan's activities was now assisting him in his response to the Tower Report. But Tower's presence was necessary because none of the others knew enough of the facts. "The only guy who knew what the hell was going on that I trusted was John Tower," said Spencer.[246]

Reagan's personal secretary, Kathy Osborne, had called Parvin early in the last week of February and told him that the president wanted him to work on the March 4 speech. Parvin, who had heard reports that Nancy Reagan wanted him to work on the speech, called the first lady and asked her whom he could trust. "Abshire," she told him, but also said that it would be necessary for him to talk to the president before he had finished the speech.[247] Parvin talked to Abshire, Fitzwater, Colin Powell, James Baker, Wirthlin, Wallison, Regan aide Dennis Thomas and Congressman Richard Cheney, whose judgment he highly valued. All of them had suggestions for the speech, but Parvin did not know how far he could go in writing that Reagan had traded arms for hostages. On February 27, the day of Don Regan's angry departure, Parvin placed another call to Nancy Reagan. Come to the White House at five thirty, she said, for a meeting with the president.[248]

Parvin went to the White House, half expecting that Howard Baker would be there. But Baker had returned to Florida to tell his wife about his new job. When the elevator doors to the residence opened, disgorging Parvin and Spencer, John Tower was there to meet them. He had been brought in a back way. Reagan was wearing a jogging suit. Parvin thought he looked "shaken." They gathered in the sitting room, where Nancy Reagan came and went during the meeting, participating only occasionally in the discussions. Reagan and Tower talked sympathetically about McFarlane, then recovering from his suicide attempt. Both of them expressed the view that McFarlane, for all his troubles, was a decent and conscientious man. Then they began discussing the speech, and Reagan launched into the familiar analogy he used to rationalize that the Iran initiative had not been a trade of arms for hostages. "If you had a child who had been kidnapped and you knew someone who knew them, wouldn't you deal with the intermediaries?" Reagan said.

"You wouldn't be dealing with the kidnappers, you'd be dealing with the intermediaries who are not involved in the kidnapping."[249] He also wondered aloud if the entire initiative had not been a setup by the Iranians. Tower said that was possible.[250]

But it was Tower, more than anyone, who forced Reagan to face the reality of what he had done, or at least what had been done in his name. "John leveled," said Spencer.[251] Parvin found Tower "very candid."[252] Tower reminded Reagan of the board's findings and the revelations contained in the notes discovered on the NSC computers. He was worried about the future of the Reagan presidency, so much so that at one point he advised Reagan to hire his own counsel. The implication that Reagan could face impeachment was unmistakable. Reagan realized that Tower was trying to help him. When he thanked him for his services to his country, Tower was moved to tears. Even Spencer, who fancied himself as unemotional, was moved. "God, I was as hard-nosed as anybody in the meeting," he said. "I got a little tear in my eye when I saw John crying. I thought, 'Jesus Christ, what am I into now?' Then I look at the old man and he didn't cry—because he can cry too, you know. . . . He's sitting there. He handled it very well."[253]

This may have been the moment when Reagan realized that it would be necessary for him, at least in an indirect way, to acknowledge that he had traded arms for hostages and to accept responsibility for what he had done. But Reagan wasn't ready to say it. How to phrase it was critical to Parvin. "I needed to know how far the president would go and basically what I could say," Parvin said afterward. "I had no idea until then what his thinking was. I knew what others thought he should say, but that didn't tell me what he wanted to say and, more importantly, what he was prepared to say. When I left, I thought he was still grappling with it."[254]

Parvin went to the White House on Saturday morning, February 28, to meet Baker's transition team of Griscom and James Cannon, a Washington attorney and politician who was a longtime Baker associate. Then Parvin went home to work on the speech. Wirthlin had urged him to use the active voice, to advance constructive suggestions and to declare that Reagan would meet with the NSC staff and say, "You're not going to do this anymore."[255] Colin Powell agreed, and directed that the meeting be set up. Parvin was still not sure of what to say about arms for hostages. He remembered that Nancy Reagan had said to him in a phone conversation before the Tower Report that the president had not intended such a trade "but in the execution this is what happened."[256] Parvin would think afterward that this may have been the unconscious inspiration for the words that he wrote and that Reagan would deliver to the nation: "A few months ago I told the American people I did not trade arms for hostages. My heart and my best intentions still tell me that's true, but the facts and the evidence tell me it is not. As the Tower Board reported, what began as a strategic opening to Iran deteriorated, in its implementation, into trading arms for hostages. This runs counter to my own beliefs, to administration policy, and to the original strategy we had in mind. There are reasons why it happened, but no excuses. It was a mistake."

Parvin still needed to run the speech by Reagan. He handed it out on Monday morning, March 2, in the Oval Office to the president, Abshire, Baker and the president's son Ron, who had come to Washington to give his father moral support. Baker and Abshire read it and said they liked it. Parvin asked Reagan if there was anything in the speech he didn't like. "No," said Reagan, "but I want to look at it some more."[257]

On Tuesday morning Reagan met in the Oval Office to discuss the speech with Baker, Bush, Carlucci and Powell, who had brought a proposed insert from Weinberger clearing himself and Shultz of any responsibility for what had gone wrong. While he did not press the matter as strongly as Weinberger did, Shultz had made it known to Powell that he also wanted absolution for his role. The proposed passage said, "As a matter of simple fairness, however, I must say that I believe the commission's comments about George Shultz and Cap Weinberger are incorrect. Both of them vigorously opposed the arms sales to Iran and they so advised me several times. The commission's statements that the two secretaries did not support the president are also wrong. They did support me despite their known opposition to the program. I now find that both secretaries were excluded from meetings on the subject by the same people and process used to deny me vital information about this whole matter."[258]

Baker and Bush opposed the insert. They believed, as did Spencer and Nancy Reagan, that Reagan should accept the Tower Report without quibble. They liked what Parvin had written: "I've studied the board's report. Its findings are honest, convincing, and highly critical; and I accept them." Baker and Bush thought that Weinberger's proposed passage detracted from unqualified acceptance of the report. They argued the point, but Reagan wanted to be fair to "Cap and George," and he accepted the insert. Baker showed it after lunch to

Parvin, who thought it "absolutely horrible."[259] Baker suggested substituting a couple of innocuous sentences and talking to the president
about it. Parvin wrote out something vague and went to Reagan with it.
Reagan said the substitution wouldn't meet Weinberger's objections
but that the defense secretary was in the Cabinet Room, where a cabinet
meeting had just concluded. Why not try it on him, suggested Reagan.
Parvin did, but Weinberger would not listen. Parvin thought he was
being stubborn and selfish. Later he told me, "If Weinberger had
fought as hard against the arms deal as he did to get this in, I'd think
better of him."[260]

Parvin went back to Baker. "He's the most stubborn man I ever
met," he said of Weinberger.[261] Baker laughed. "You should try to deal
with him on appropriations," he said.[262] Parvin had still not put the
insert in the speech, and Reagan took it back to the residence without
the passage.

On Wednesday, the morning of the speech, the insert was still not in
the speech. Parvin suggested to Baker that he leave it out and then
blame him for it when Weinberger complained. "No, because I'm the
one who will be blamed for it," Baker replied.[263] But Baker wasn't
finished. This was his third day as White House chief of staff, and he
was already willing to stand up to the president.

Spencer, who had been briefly out of town on business, had returned
to Washington. Baker knew that Spencer would be his ally. So was
Dick Wirthlin, who had been shown the insert by Parvin and thought
it "disastrous."[264] Baker assembled another meeting that morning with
Reagan, Spencer, Wirthlin and Parvin to talk the president out of de-
tracting from his speech by exculpating Weinberger and Shultz. Baker,
Spencer, Wirthlin and Parvin all spoke and all made the same point.
Parvin thought that Spencer was particularly effective. "You've got one
shot to make an impression," Spencer said to the president. "Don't
screw it up."[265] Reagan agreed to call Weinberger and say that he was
not going to use the insert.*

The March 4 speech was a turning point for Reagan. He still faced
many difficult days during the Iran-contra hearings and he would subsequently "revert," to use Abshire's word, to his original contention

---

* Reagan gave Weinberger and Shultz a mild version of the exculpatory comments they sought in
his weekly radio speech on March 14, saying that "both Secretary Shultz and Secretary Weinberger
advised me strongly not to pursue the initiative." But Reagan took no issue with the Tower Report,
and his remarks in the radio speech received far less public attention than Weinberger's passage
would have aroused had it been included in the March 4 speech.

that he had not traded arms for hostages. Reagan would never be able to accept completely his complicity in the affair—in his memoirs he would say that "it was as if Americans were forgiving me for something I hadn't done."[266] Parvin, whose speech had brought Reagan as close as he would ever come to an outright admission of trading arms for hostages, concluded that what Reagan had really wanted to say was "I didn't do it, and I'll never do it again."[267] But on March 5, an overnight CBS News poll showed a 9-point jump in Reagan's approval ratings. (Respondents approved of his job performance by a 51-42 percent margin.) He did even better in Wirthlin's polls, and worried House Minority Leader Robert Michel was so relieved that he said, "Reagan isn't altogether out of the woods, but he's certainly gotten to the fire-break."[268] *The Washington Post,* which had been sharply critical of Reagan, gave the speech its editorial blessing. "President Reagan gave the right speech last night," said the lead editorial. "That he did not rend his garments, tear his hair or otherwise engage in the rituals of mortification that had been prescribed here and there is neither surprising nor especially to the point. For the president did what he had to: he admitted plenty, and he pledged to redeem the damage in his final two years in office."[269]

Reagan would never again bask in the unquestioned trust of the American people as he had done in the rocket's red glare of Liberty Weekend. He was no longer the magical sun king, no longer the Prospero of American memories who towered above ordinary politicians and could expect always to be believed. But he had regained his political footing and his trust in himself. By acknowledging, even backhandedly, that the Iran initiative had been wrong, he had made it possible to get on with the real foreign policy business of his presidency—on to a constructive relationship with the Soviet Union and to a nuclear arms treaty that pointed the path to the future. Stu Spencer would summarize it in words less elegant but more telling than any editorial: "The Iran-contra thing went away awful fast. The people all thought he was guilty. He made a goddamn mistake, that's all. They gave him the benefit of the doubt—he made a goddamn mistake, now let's go on."[270]

21

THE NEW ERA

*The only reason I'd never met with General Secretary
Gorbachev's predecessors was because they kept dying on
me. . . . Then along came Gorbachev. He was different
in style [and] in substance . . . from previous Soviet
leaders. He is a man who takes chances and that's what
you need for progress. He is a remarkable force for
change in that country.*

RONALD REAGAN,
February 1, 1989[1]

Ronald Reagan's second term in office nearly coincided with the
first four years of Mikhail Gorbachev's leadership, the period when the
United States and the Soviet Union abandoned four decades of confrontation and turned to what Reagan called "a new era" of cooperation. Overcoming their own suspicions and the deeper reservations of
conservative forces in both societies, Gorbachev and Reagan walked
together down the path that led to the end of the Cold War. It was
a hesitant walk, with many pauses along the way, and it would remain
for President Bush to complete the journey with Gorbachev. But in
1987, after significant Soviet concessions, Reagan and Gorbachev signed

the first treaty in history to reduce the nuclear arsenals of the super-powers.

Historically, each leader served the other's purpose. Gorbachev arrived on the scene when the failure of the Communist experiment could no longer be concealed from the Soviet people. He opened up Soviet society ("glasnost") and attempted to restructure its economy ("perestroika"). To attain these goals, he sought a reduction in Soviet military spending and international tensions. He needed Western economic credits and a breathing spell. He had much to gain and little to lose by dealing realistically with the popular president of the United States.

Reagan had reasons of his own for reaching out to Gorbachev. Even though he had been reelected in a landslide, he had nothing to show for his first four years in U.S.-Soviet relations and not much in foreign policy accomplishment of any kind. He had always argued that the U.S. military buildup he had nurtured was a means to the end of constructive negotiation with the Soviets, and he had now convinced himself that the United States could bargain from strength. Reagan knew that he was freer to deal with the Soviets than any American president of the Cold War. He could not be savaged for being "soft on communism." He could not be associated even with Richard Nixon's policy of détente, which Reagan had criticized as a Republican presidential candidate opposing Gerald Ford in 1976. No conservative criticism of Reagan for accommodating the Soviets would ever have resonance with the American public. As Richard Wirthlin's polls showed, the public concern about Reagan, even after his landslide reelection, was that he was too inflexible in his dealings with the Soviet Union. This was also a concern of U.S. allies. By dealing with Gorbachev, Reagan enhanced his political standing at home and in Europe.

Both leaders were driven by considerations more profound than their own political positions. Gorbachev wanted to salvage his country economically, as Reagan's first political hero, Franklin Roosevelt, had done a half century earlier in the United States. Reagan sought to rid the world of nuclear weapons. His principal advisers did not share this radical goal, which was in any case incapable of accomplishment through U.S.-Soviet negotiations, since at least Britain, France, China, India and Israel also possessed nuclear capability. But Reagan, for all his managerial limitations, was a visionary president. While he needed more assistance than any other modern U.S. president in the day-to-day operations of the presidency, Reagan held firm to a core of unshakable opinions. His advisers would never convince him that he had gone overboard in his passion for decreasing income taxes or that he had violated his own policies in attempting to free the American hostages. Nor would they ever convert him to the conventional wisdom of nuclear deterrence.

As we saw in Chapter 13, Reagan was awed by the biblical prophecy of Armageddon, which he translated into a vision of nuclear hell on earth. He proposed to avert Armageddon in two ways: development of an antimissile defense system through the Strategic Defense Initiative (SDI) and reduction of nuclear arsenals through negotiations with the Soviets. He often repeated the words he had spoken to the Japanese Diet on November 11, 1983: "A nuclear war can never be won and must never be fought." Since nuclear war "would certainly mean the end of civilization as we knew it," and since there would always be a risk of nuclear war as long as there were nuclear weapons, it seemed logical to Reagan that all such weapons must be eliminated. As he put it in his memoirs:

> My dream, then, became a world free of nuclear weapons.
>
> Some of my advisors, including a number at the Pentagon, did not share this dream. They couldn't conceive of it. They said a nuclear-free world was unattainable and it would be dangerous for us even if it were possible; some even claimed nuclear war was "inevitable" and we had to prepare for this reality. They tossed around macabre jargon about "throw weights" and "kill ratios" as if they were talking about baseball scores. But for the eight years I was president I never let my dream of a nuclear-free world fade from my mind.
>
> Since I knew it would be a long and difficult task to rid the world of nuclear weapons, I had this second dream: the creation of a defense against nuclear missiles, so we could change from a policy of assured destruction to one of assured survival.[2]

Ultimately, Reagan's desire to reduce the threat of nuclear war proved inspirational and productive—in large measure because Gorbachev showed himself willing to take the risks of reducing nuclear arsenals, withdrawing Soviet troops from Afghanistan and restructuring Soviet society. But in U.S.-Soviet dealings during Reagan's presidency, his two dreams were often in collision. Because the Soviets were frightened by the prospect of competing with the United States in the multiple and open-ended technologies of an antimissile system, the Strategic Defense Initiative was useful in prodding them to return to the arms-control bargaining table. But the Soviet purpose once the bargaining was joined was always to get rid of SDI or, failing that, to limit it to a bare-bones research program. Reagan envisioned an anti-missile defense system as an umbrella that would protect the population in event of a nuclear attack. The Soviets saw it as a shield behind which an aggressor nation could launch a nuclear attack of its own. Reagan's dream of a U.S. antimissile defense system was a nightmare to Soviet leaders. They were far more alarmed by Reagan's commitment to SDI than they were encouraged by his proclaimed passion for reducing nuclear arsenals.

That the Soviets responded this way was partly Reagan's fault. He had underestimated the damage done to U.S.-Soviet dialogue by his description of the Soviet Union as "the evil empire" and "the focus of evil." And he was tardy in recognizing that the unnamed advisers he criticizes in his memoirs for accepting the inevitability of confrontation —notably Caspar Weinberger and Richard Perle at the Pentagon and National Security Adviser William Clark—did not share his desire to achieve a nuclear arms reduction treaty with the Soviet Union.

Clark's suspicions of the Soviets were demonstrated by his counsel in the tense summer of 1983. In March, Reagan had delivered his "evil empire" and "Star Wars" speeches. The Soviets had responded in Tass by comparing Reagan to Hitler. But on July 4, 1983, Soviet leader Yuri Andropov wrote Reagan a private letter in which he said the two leaders should focus on "the elimination of the nuclear threat."[3] Reagan sent a cordial reply, suggesting that U.S.-Soviet negotiators pursue this goal in Geneva. But Clark persuaded Reagan to delete a paragraph from his letter that included these words: "If we can agree on mutual, verifiable reductions in the number of nuclear weapons we both hold could this not be a first step toward the elimination of all such weapons? What a blessing this would be for the people we both represent."[4]

Although Andropov responded positively to Reagan's letter, nothing came of the exchange. Instead, U.S.-Soviet relations reached a low point after the downing of a Korean Air Lines passenger jet on September 1, 1983, with 269 people aboard, including sixty-one U.S. citizens. This was followed by harsh exchanges of rhetoric between U.S. and Soviet spokesmen.* After the West German Bundestag voted in November to

---

* It is notable, however, that even the downing of KAL 007 did not discourage Reagan in his view that U.S.-Soviet negotiations were necessary and desirable. He was at his ranch when the airliner was shot down. After returning to Washington he met in the Situation Room with his advisers to discuss the crisis. Clark, Weinberger and Casey made the point that the incident showed the brutal

accept deployment of U.S. Pershing II and cruise missiles, the Soviets walked out of the arms control talks in Geneva. Andropov, suffering from kidney ailments, was by then too ill to appear in public. He died on February 9, 1984, and was succeeded by Konstantin Chernenko.

Though it was Gorbachev who would lead the Soviets out of the Cold War, it was the transitional Chernenko who turned away from confrontation with the United States. Chernenko, who had served for three decades as Leonid Brezhnev's most intimate aide, was the last of the reactionary, old-guard Soviet leaders. He was suffering from pulmonary emphysema and other ailments when he assumed office and would live for little more than a year. Even in his first months in office, Chernenko rarely appeared in public and, as Reagan expertly noted, "seldom said anything without a script."[6] During his brief tenure he halted the modest economic reforms begun by Andropov and tried to rehabilitate Stalin's reputation. But in the summer of 1984, according to Gorbachev biographers Dusko Doder and Louise Branson, "Chernenko reached two critical conclusions that opened the way for the resumption of the Geneva talks. First was his assessment that Reagan would be reelected . . . second was his decision to abandon Andropov's insistence on the removal of Pershings and cruise missiles as a precondition for talks."[7]

Reagan welcomed the change in Soviet attitudes, for several reasons. After Robert McFarlane replaced Clark, Reagan no longer was receiving divided counsel from his national security adviser and his secretary of state on the merits of U.S.-Soviet negotiation. And Reagan's political advisers wanted him to demonstrate his readiness to negotiate with the Soviets. The opportunity came on September 28 when veteran Soviet Foreign Minister Andrei Gromyko, after addressing the United Nations and meeting with Shultz, called on Reagan at the White House. Reagan and Gromyko talked for three and a half hours, making little progress but giving Reagan an opportunity to stress that U.S.-Soviet relations had his personal attention and high priority. Though Gromyko issued a typically tough-worded statement after the meeting, *The Washington Post* on October 18 published an interview with Chernenko in which he avoided mentioning Soviet preconditions for resumption of the suspended nuclear arms control talks. On November 17, eleven days after

---

nature of the Soviets. Shultz argued that it was important not to overreact, and Reagan agreed. "The world will react to this," he said. "It's important that we not do anything that jeopardizes the long-term relationship with the Soviet Union."[5]

Reagan's landslide reelection, the Soviets agreed to resume the negotiations. On January 7–8, 1985, Shultz and Gromyko met in Geneva to discuss the agenda.

The structure of the new talks demonstrated the importance both sides attached to the Strategic Defense Initiative. Reagan did not want to yield on SDI and would have preferred that it not even be a subject of negotiation. The Soviets, who wanted SDI discarded, were insistent that what they called "space weapons" be discussed. What Shultz and Gromyko agreed to was a tripartite set of negotiations in Geneva. One team of negotiators would focus on strategic nuclear weapons—the various long-range missiles that the Soviet Union and the United States had aimed at each other. Another team would deal with space weapons, or, as the United States viewed the issue, antimissile defense. The third set of negotiations would focus on the intermediate-range and shorter-range missiles based in Europe and by the Soviets in Asia. All these questions, however, were supposed to be "examined and resolved in their interrelationship."

On the evening of March 10, the day the U.S. and Soviet delegations arrived in Geneva, Chernenko died and was replaced by Gorbachev. According to subsequent accounts, the crucial role in his selection seems to have been played by Gromyko, at seventy-six the senior member of the Politburo. Gorbachev was then just fifty-four, twelve years younger than the average age of the members of the Communist Party Central Committee. Gromyko, in an emotional speech, contended that Gorbachev was decisive, intelligent and capable in foreign affairs despite his relative youth. "Comrades, this man has a nice smile but he's got iron teeth," Gromyko said.[8] *

Gorbachev was born to a family of peasants in the Stavropol district in the northern foothills of the Caucasus region on March 2, 1931, at a time when Reagan, then twenty, was completing his junior year at Eureka College. Reagan knew the relatively mild hardships caused by the Depression in small-town Illinois. Gorbachev was touched by the horrors of Stalin's ruthless effort to drive farmers off their private land onto collective farms. The farmers revolted and killed their cattle. Agricultural output collapsed and millions died in the resulting famine. Other

* This comment was omitted from the official Soviet account of the March 11 plenum of the Central Committee where Gorbachev was chosen as Chernenko's replacement but was later reported by a member of the Central Committee. In a photo session at the first Reagan-Gorbachev meeting in Geneva on November 19, 1985, Sam Donaldson repeated Gromyko's words to Gorbachev and asked him for his reaction. "It hasn't yet been confirmed," Gorbachev said good-naturedly. "As of now, I'm still using my own teeth."[9]

millions were herded into the Soviet prison camps of the Gulag, among them one of Gorbachev's grandfathers. New hardships arrived when Gorbachev was ten and Nazi armies invaded the Soviet Union. His older brother was drafted into the Red Army and killed in battle and his father, also drafted, was wounded in Poland. The Germans occupied the Stavropol district for eight months, although the area in which Gorbachev lived escaped major destruction.

Mikhail Gorbachev prospered in this turmoil. A scholar has noted that he "was a beneficiary of the Stalin era and its rapid social mobility, though he has since been critical of the arbitrary abuse of power which accompanied collectivization of agriculture and high-speed industrialization."[10] At the age of fourteen Gorbachev distinguished himself as a combine operator. His skills and hard work as a farm worker won him an award and a coveted invitation to attend Moscow State University, where he studied law and became a member of the legal faculty. He rose slowly but surely in Communist ranks, becoming the protégé of Andropov, the former head of the Soviet secret police, the KGB. While most of Gorbachev's experience was in managing the morass that is Soviet agriculture, he was widely exposed to foreign leaders in the two years before he replaced Chernenko. On a brief visit to London in 1984, Gorbachev particularly impressed Margaret Thatcher, who conveyed her high impression of him to her friend the president of the United States.

As this thumbnail biography suggests, Gorbachev differed from Reagan in the rigors of his personal experiences and in his analytical skills. But the leaders shared some personal traits. Gorbachev was known for his magnetic personality. In high school he had displayed an interest in dramatics and was considered "a very good actor." Like Reagan, he possessed "an almost blind faith in himself" and especially valued personal experience. "He had grasped that any hardship could be endured if one had resources of one's own; he was stubborn to a fault, once he had made up his mind," wrote Gorbachev's biographers.[11] They could have said the same about Reagan.

Reagan was awakened by McFarlane at 4:00 A.M. on March 11 and told of Chernenko's death. He said in his diary that he thought about attending the funeral and decided against it. "My gut instinct said no," Reagan wrote. "Got to the office at 9. George Shultz had some arguments that I should. He lost. I don't think his heart was really in it."[12] If true, this may have been because Shultz, after having lost a similar argument with Reagan after the death of Brezhnev, realized that the president had little interest in attending the funeral of a Soviet leader. (For all his travels, Reagan still disliked flying when he didn't think it was necessary. He also disliked going to funerals, any funeral.) Instead, Reagan sent Shultz and Vice President Bush, who carried a letter from the president inviting Gorbachev to a summit. "You can be assured of my personal commitment to working with you and the rest of the Soviet leadership in serious negotiations," the letter said. "In that spirit I would like you to visit me in Washington at your earliest convenient opportunity." [13]

Gorbachev was interested, although not yet ready to commit to a summit, much less a summit in Washington. He replied on March 24 with a letter pledging "peaceful competition" instead of confrontation with the United States and stressing that the Soviet leadership was committed to avoiding the "catastrophic consequences" of a nuclear war. "I think that it is also clear from my letter that we attach great importance to contacts at the highest level," Gorbachev wrote. "For this reason I have a positive attitude to the idea you expressed about holding a personal meeting between us." [14]

And so began a correspondence that continued through the Reagan presidency and beyond. The two leaders exchanged more than a score of letters while Reagan was in office, usually using them to explore various foreign policy positions. The letters were a useful device because they bore the imprimatur of the two leaders and therefore helped avoid misunderstandings. But most of Reagan's letters lacked the spontaneity he had displayed in writing Brezhnev in 1981 or the easy candor he would express to Gorbachev in their personal meetings.

In fact, Reagan did not even write most of the letters sent to Gorbachev over his name. According to McFarlane, the early letters were usually suggested by Shultz, "sometimes by me and occasionally by the president." [15] These letters were drafted by Mark Palmer, a Soviet affairs expert at the State Department, in consultation with Jack Matlock, the principal Soviet expert on the NSC staff and later the U.S. ambassador to Moscow. Matlock's specialty was cranking in points or anecdotes that would demonstrate knowledge of Russian culture. The letters were reviewed by Shultz and McFarlane, who usually made few changes. McFarlane recalled that "on one or two occasions I asked him [Reagan] to write a letter by hand, as an affectation to demonstrate his personal involvement. Once or twice he contributed." [16]

While the atmosphere of the U.S.-Soviet relationship improved almost immediately, it took eight months of back-and-forth discussion before Reagan and Gorbachev held their first summit in Geneva. Though Reagan was now dealing directly with a Soviet leader, he had not resolved the differences within his own administration on the goals of these negotiations. In mid-1985 these differences focused on the question of whether the United States should continue to abide by the limits on strategic weapons set by the SALT II treaty signed in 1979 by Carter and Brezhnev.

Reagan had campaigned against the treaty in 1980, calling it "fatally flawed" because it regulated an increase in strategic missile arsenals rather than reducing them. Under prodding from Congress, he had continued to abide by the SALT II limits even though the treaty had never been ratified. On Memorial Day 1982, Reagan had announced that the United States would abide by the limits "as long as the Soviet Union showed equal restraint." The limits were so high that they then imposed no practical restriction on the U.S. military buildup. But by 1985 the administration was bumping up against the limits, which were scheduled to be exceeded when a new Trident submarine was deployed that fall. Shultz and the Joint Chiefs proposed scrapping an older Poseidon submarine to stay within the SALT II limits. They contended that the Soviets had abided by the weapons ceilings in the treaty and that it was therefore militarily unwise for the United States to disavow them and permit an unrestricted nuclear arms race. Weinberger and Perle, supported by Arms Control and Disarmament Agency director Kenneth Adelman, wanted Reagan to renounce the treaty on grounds the Soviets were cheating on SALT II.*

Tugged back and forth between Shultz and Weinberger, Reagan typically tried to appease them both. He decided on June 6 and announced four days later that the United States would take no action "to undercut existing arms control agreements" but also rapped the Soviets. "They have failed to comply with several provisions of SALT II, and we have serious concerns regarding their compliance with the provisions of other accords," Reagan said. The decision pleased Shultz,

---

* There is no doubt that the Soviets were at the minimum exploiting ambiguities in the treaty. SALT II permitted each side to develop one additional "new type" of land-based ICBM. The Soviets began testing one, called the SS-24, in 1982 and in 1983 began testing another weapon, the SS-25, which they claimed was a variation of the first missile and which the United States said was an entirely new missile. The Soviets were also alleged to have violated restrictions on the encoding of electronic missile testing data, known as telemetry. In addition, Soviet construction of a gigantic radar station at Krasnoyarsk in Siberia seems to have been a clear violation of the ABM treaty. The Soviets acknowledged this after Reagan was no longer in office and dismantled the Krasnoyarsk station.

while the language encouraged the conservatives to continue their battle against SALT II. Reagan was typically happy that he had mollified both factions. "Apparently my decision was right—at least I'm being called a statesman by both the left and the right," he wrote in his diary.[17]

The Reagan-Gorbachev summit in Geneva was announced early in July 1985. It came as no surprise. When David Hoffman and I had interviewed Reagan on April 1, he made a point of saying that the killing of a U.S. Army major by Soviet soldiers in East Germany on March 25 had not discouraged him from having a summit with Gorbachev. ("I want a meeting even more . . . to sit down and look someone in the eye and talk to him about what we can do to make sure nothing of this kind ever happens again," Reagan said.)[18] Shultz and McFarlane were already preparing another invitation to Gorbachev for a summit, which Reagan extended in an April 4 letter. The letter objected to the killing of the U.S. officer (which Shultz and McFarlane viewed as an unfortunate affair but not an expression of Gorbachev's policy), criticized Soviet policy in Afghanistan and observed that the Soviets were engaged in missile defense even while mounting a public relations campaign against the Strategic Defense Initiative. The missile defense system that the Soviets were building around Moscow was permitted by the 1972 Anti-Ballistic Missile (ABM) treaty, as Gorbachev noted in a ten-page reply to Reagan's letter in early June. Gorbachev said that comparing the limited Soviet missile-defense effort to SDI was an example in which "apples are confused with oranges."[19] But Gorbachev agreed that their differences on this issue were a good reason for a summit.

Reagan probably prepared with greater care for the Geneva summit than for any other event of his presidency. He managed to impress even McFarlane, who was often discouraged by the president's inattentiveness and thin grasp of issues. Well before the summit date was decided, McFarlane had begun a series of what he called "tutorials" to equip Reagan with the information needed to deal with Gorbachev. Matlock was commissioned to prepare twenty-five papers explaining Soviet objectives, strategy and negotiating tactics as well as Russian culture and history. Matlock was ideally suited for the task. In addition to his knowledge of Russian culture he also understood that Reagan learned by relating information to his own experiences. By playing on Reagan's own insights and prejudices, Matlock's papers engrossed the president in a way rarely accomplished by any briefing paper. The opening passage of the paper on Soviet psychology demonstrates Matlock's method. "Yes, they lie and cheat," it began. "And they can stonewall in negotiations when it seems in their interest to strike a deal. They have a sense of pride and 'face' that makes the proverbial Oriental variety pale in comparison. Yet, in private, with people he trusts, the Russian can be candid to a fault—groveling in his nation's inadequacies—and so scrupulously honest that it can be irritating, as when he makes a big deal over having forgotten to return a borrowed pencil."[20]

McFarlane doled these papers out to Reagan one a week for six months before the Geneva summit. Reagan became so enthusiastic about them that he urged Bush and Don Regan to read them, and McFarlane saw to it that they received duplicate sets of the papers. Reagan also prepared by consulting his old adviser Richard Nixon, who told him not to try to back Gorbachev into a corner. "You have to leave them maneuvering room," Nixon said. "They have to save face back home."[21] And on November 7, Reagan brought into the White House a group of experts to advise him on Soviet conditions and Gorbachev's probable strategy. White House spokesman Larry Speakes said the most useful advice came from William Hyland, the editor of *Foreign Affairs,* who believed the timing of the summit was good for the United States because "our own economy is resurgent, while the Soviet economy is in shambles."[22]

While Reagan was preparing for his performance in Geneva, Gorbachev was demonstrating the diplomacy that would in later years captivate Europe. In April, Gorbachev had announced a moratorium on the deployment of the SS-20 missiles that had prompted the United States to deploy its Pershing and cruise missiles. By itself, this statement had limited propaganda value since it was widely known that the Soviets had deployed sufficient SS-20s to hit every vital target in Western Europe. But in Paris on October 2, Gorbachev announced that the number of SS-20s fixed on European targets would be reduced to 243, the level of June 1984. This missile diplomacy was accompanied by a bid for Western European economic support and the beginning of Gorbachev's campaign to demonstrate a commonality of interests between Europe and the Soviet Union. An editorial in *Pravda* on November 13, less than a week before the Geneva summit, was titled "Europe —Our Common Home."

Reagan arrived in Geneva on November 16, to give him time to overcome the fatigue of his transatlantic flight before the summit. His arrival was marred by one of those periodic reminders of the painful divisions within the Reagan official family. Weinberger had not been included in the U.S. delegation, but a letter he had written to Reagan warning of the continued dangers of U.S. adherence to the SALT II limits had been leaked to *The New York Times* and *The Washington Post.* On Air Force One, heading for Geneva, McFarlane said the letter was "a blatant attempt to undermine the president just before the summit."²³ Reagan was angry about it, but Weinberger denied that the Pentagon was the source of the leak, and Perle suggested to me that it was the work of Weinberger's opponents to discredit him. The president took everyone at his word. When Reagan was asked at a photo session if he would fire Weinberger, he replied, "Hell, no."²⁴

Reagan was in a confident mood when the summit opened at 10:00 A.M. on November 19. He felt "up" for Gorbachev, as accomplished actors do when they have mastered a script and are ready for a big performance. And he took the initiative immediately when Gorbachev arrived at Fleur d'Eau, a nineteenth-century lakeside château that was the site of the formal summit sessions. Removing his overcoat, Reagan stepped out into the cold and waited at the top of the steps for Gorbachev, who was wearing a heavy topcoat and a black fedora, which he doffed theatrically. "As we shook hands for the first time, I had to admit—as Margaret Thatcher and Prime Minister Brian Mulroney predicted I would—that there was something likeable about Gorbachev," Reagan would say later. "There was warmth in his face and his style, not the coldness bordering on hatred I'd seen in most senior Soviet officials I'd met until then."²⁵

First impressions have always been important to Reagan, and his discovery that he liked Gorbachev was crucial. From the moment they shook hands, Reagan would always see Gorbachev in human terms even when they disagreed most profoundly. At this first meeting Reagan steered Gorbachev into a pale-blue sitting room where they talked with only their interpreters present and decided they should review the full range of their differences. Gorbachev would later say they had decided at the start "not to tell each other banalities,"²⁶ and both leaders seem to have appreciated the other's frankness. A meeting that had been scheduled for fifteen minutes lasted for sixty-four minutes before Gorbachev and Reagan joined their foreign ministers and other experts in the first plenary session in the château's ornate salon.

In the plenary session, the two leaders expressed the basic ideological convictions of the Cold War. Gorbachev said the United States was run by a military-industrial complex that promoted paranoia about the Soviet Union, which had peaceful intentions. Though Reagan had expected this, he was surprised when Gorbachev added that conservative think tanks such as the Heritage Foundation and the Hoover Institution (which Shultz was associated with) had given the president plans for ruining the Soviet economy. Reagan said he usually opposed government manipulation of the economy, in the United States or elsewhere. He responded to Gorbachev's speech about the militaristic designs of the military-industrial complex and the U.S. ruling class with his own litany about Soviet imperialism and the Soviet Union's attempts to undermine democracies. Reagan argued that the Soviets had given the West good reason to build up its military strength.

When they broke for lunch, Reagan's advisers were confident that he had held his own. McFarlane felt then, and throughout the summit, that Reagan proved "almost unique in his ability to sustain a conversation for more than five minutes." [27] At lunch with his advisers at Maison de Sasussure, the home of Prince Karim Aga Khan that the Reagans used during their stay in Geneva, the president was in a joking mood. Reagan said the long translations that morning had reminded him of foreign films where someone talked endlessly and the words "That's fine" [28] were flashed as a subtitle on the screen. Playing off a comment by Ken Adelman, who said that the Soviet Union was the only nation in the world surrounded by hostile Communist states, Reagan said, "No wonder they feel so nervous! With all those commies around them, who wouldn't feel bad?" [29]

But the lightheartedness vanished quickly in the afternoon session. During a discussion of arms control issues, Reagan fervently defended the Strategic Defense Initiative and attacked the reliance of the superpowers on "mutual assured destruction." Reagan argued, as he often had with his own advisers, that this was an immoral policy. He said he realized that the Soviets thought SDI would make it easier for the United States to launch a first strike against the Soviet Union. But he said that the United States had no such intention and was willing to prove it by sharing the SDI technology with the Soviet Union once it had been developed.

Gorbachev was disdainful. "It's not convincing," he said. "It's emotional. It's a dream. Who can control it? Who can monitor it? It opens up an arms race in space."

"As I said to you, I have a right to think you want to use your missiles against us," Reagan replied. "With mere words we cannot abolish the threat." [30]

Gorbachev became angry, wanting to know why Reagan did not believe him when he said the Soviets had no aggressive intentions. "I cannot say to the American people that I could take you at your word if *you* don't believe *us,*" Reagan said.[31] Gorbachev continued to denounce SDI, then subsided. Reagan suggested they get a breath of fresh air, and the two leaders, bundled up against the cold, walked together to a pool house near the shore of Lake Geneva.

Their meeting at the pool house before a roaring fire would give the Geneva meeting its name: "the fireside summit."[32] It was a triumph more of planning than of spontaneity, for the White House team had realized that there would come a moment when Reagan and Gorbachev should break away from the formal discussion and have a meeting of their own. Reagan was equipped with a manila folder of arms-control guidelines prepared by his advisers. Reagan showed them to Gorbachev, who rejected them all. But the Soviet leader did not want their discussion to break up because of their disagreement on space missiles, and he said they should continue to talk.

It was on their walk back to the château after this meeting in the pool house that Reagan proposed what would later be considered the most substantive achievement of the Geneva summit—an agreement to hold future summits. Pausing in a parking lot before they reached the château, Reagan invited Gorbachev to come to Washington for a summit. Gorbachev accepted and quickly proposed a follow-up summit in Moscow, to which Reagan readily agreed. Reagan's advisers were pleasantly surprised that he had taken it upon himself to nail down the next summit, although the president was, as McFarlane later said, "a little shaky on the dates of what Gorbachev had agreed to."[33] As it turned out, Reagan and Gorbachev would keep their promises to each other after a year's delay; another summit would intervene before the two leaders visited each other's country.

Reagan and Gorbachev met again on Wednesday, November 20, this time at the Soviet mission in Geneva. First they held a private session with only interpreters present and then a plenary session with the foreign ministers and advisers. They were no closer than they had been the day before on SDI, and they also predictably differed on Afghanistan, Nicaragua and other regional conflicts of the Cold War and on human rights conditions in the Soviet Union. But Gorbachev had some surprises in store for the Americans. Instead of giving the stock Soviet reply that human rights issues in the USSR were an internal matter, Gorbachev took the offensive by raising the plight of unemployed workers in the United States. "The most basic human right is everyone's right to a job," he said, to which Reagan responded by explaining how unemployment insurance works.[34] Gorbachev also "quoted statements by some of our more extreme feminists who claimed American women were downtrodden and argued that we treated blacks like slaves." Reagan told Gorbachev his information was out of date. "Things have changed," he said.[35]

It was on Afghanistan that Gorbachev proved most revealing. Shultz was particularly struck by Gorbachev's low-key, emotionless defense of Soviet policy in Afghanistan. Gorbachev said he had learned of the Afghanistan invasion in a radio broadcast, which Reagan thought suggested that Gorbachev was saying he had "no responsibility and little enthusiasm" for the war.[36] In contrast to Gorbachev, Reagan was highly emotional in his denunciation of Soviet conduct in Afghanistan. He had met with Afghan leaders and seen pictures of children disfigured by Soviet bombs, some of which had been disguised to resemble toys. At his best, Reagan shared with the blind Earl of Gloucester in *King Lear* the capacity to "see feelingly" the plight of war's victims. On January 24, 1986, after a visit to the Oval Office of five Afghan children, Reagan wrote in his diary: "They were mere babies. But all victims of Soviet bombings. One little girl with her face virtually destroyed. Three with one arm each and one without one leg. I'd like to send the photos to Gen. Secretary Gorbachev."[37]

But even without the photos, Gorbachev surely understood that Reagan felt deeply about Afghanistan. Shultz was impressed by the president's passionate denunciation of the Afghan war, and Adelman thought he was seeing Reagan at his best.[38] Much to Adelman's dismay, however, Reagan was far more timid on human rights. He had presented to Gorbachev at their private meeting a list of Soviet citizens, most of them Jews, who were being denied permission to leave the Soviet Union, but he did not press him on this issue in the plenary session. "Reagan was not being Reagan; he was being messenger," Adelman wrote in retrospect. ". . . Richard Nixon had convinced him that the only way to help Soviet dissidents was through 'quiet diplomacy.' He should take Gorbachev aside, tell what a problem this thing was back home and hope for the best. . . . So he followed Nixon in tone and technique. So he mouthed the briefing material—all this stuff about hurting 'the relationship' if human rights weren't improved and so on. This was the President's worst hour in Geneva; it was to become his best in Moscow."[39]

By late Wednesday afternoon it was apparent to both delegations that there would be no breakthroughs on strategic defense. The teams of specialists on both sides had worked through most of the previous night trying to draft a statement that agreed on the principle of 50 percent reductions in strategic nuclear arsenals and sidestepped the fundamental difference on space issues. The negotiators were exhausted. They had agreed only to a statement of cooperation on air safety designed to prevent a repetition of the KAL 007 disaster and on a new agreement reestablishing educational, scientific, cultural and athletic exchanges that had been dropped by Carter after the invasion of Afghanistan. This was not enough for anyone to portray the summit as a success. Members of the U.S. team had already discussed among themselves the strategy they might use to put a positive "spin" on an unsuccessful summit, but neither Reagan nor Gorbachev wanted this outcome.

So the two negotiating teams went off to try again on a joint statement while Reagan and Gorbachev once more met in private, and Reagan told stories about his days in Hollywood. At dinner that night, hosted by the Reagans at Fleur d'Eau, Shultz and members of the Soviet team came in to tell the leaders that they were at loggerheads over the language of the statement. Singling out Soviet official Georgi Korniyenko, Shultz said angrily that he was not following Gorbachev's instructions. Gorbachev turned to Korniyenko and said, "Do it the way we discussed." This confident display of leadership was evidence to Reagan that Gorbachev was "a man who was sure of himself and his power."[40]

Knowing they had to come up with something, the weary negotiators finally reached a compromise at 4:45 A.M. on Thursday morning, November 21. The statement pledged the two superpowers to seek a 50 percent reduction in nuclear arms "appropriately applied." No one knew for sure what "appropriately applied" meant, either then or now, since the two sides count nuclear arsenals differently. But it was enough for the leaders to proclaim the summit a qualified success. The statement also included a pledge to accelerate progress toward "an interim agreement on medium-range missiles in Europe." Later that morning Reagan and Gorbachev appeared at the international press center in Geneva to express a joint determination to curb the arms race and "improve U.S.-Soviet relations and the international situation as a whole." Just before they read their statements, Reagan turned to Gorbachev and whispered, "I bet the hard-liners in both our countries are bleeding when we shake hands."[41] Gorbachev nodded in agreement.

The Reagan-Gorbachev exchanges at Geneva were more memorable than the statement they signed. For two leaders who loved to talk, both had proved pretty good listeners. Despite their differences, Reagan had been impressed by what Gorbachev had to say—and what he hadn't said. What Gorbachev had not said, observed Reagan later, was "that he was dedicated to the Marxian philosophy of a one-world Communist state. And every other Russian leader had pledged that was their goal."[42] Reagan had also discovered that he shared "a kind of chemistry"[43] with Gorbachev. "Yes, we argued and we'd go nose to nose," Reagan said. "But when the argument was over, it was like it is with us. He wasn't stalking out of there and [saying] 'down with the lousy Americans' or anything. We fought it out and maybe knew we were going to fight it out again, but when the meeting was over we were normal."[44] Dealing with Gorbachev reminded Reagan of his after-hours relationship with Tip O'Neill. Gorbachev "could tell jokes about himself and even about his country, and I grew to like him more."[45]

While the two leaders had established the foundations of a personal relationship, the summit had made no progress toward Gorbachev's principal goal of halting "Star Wars," and its promises of nuclear arms reduction were vague. In Geneva's aftermath, Gorbachev sought to claim the initiative with additional arms control proposals, including a sweeping January 15, 1986, plan to reduce by half the U.S. and Soviet strategic nuclear arsenals within a period of five to eight years and to eliminate all superpower arsenals by the year 2000. At the same time he discarded long-term Soviet insistence that British and French nuclear weapons be included in the count of Western medium-range missiles capable of striking Soviet targets. Gorbachev's new goal was to prevent these aging arsenals from being modernized. As part of the agreement he proposed, the United States would not be permitted to transfer its nuclear technology to Western Europe.

These were important proposals, designed politically to exploit differences within Britain and France and to accentuate differences within NATO. "The Soviet offer . . . reawakened fears in Western Europe that the Russians were once again trying to decouple U.S. and Western European security arrangements," wrote a British student of nuclear affairs.[46] The British government's view was that the Soviets were trying to divide NATO and stir up antinuclear sentiment in Europe as it had done before the deployment of the Pershing II and cruise missiles in 1983. After consulting with the allies, Shultz and his leading arms negotiator, Paul Nitze, on February 23 rejected the Soviet attempt to prevent the British and French missiles from being modernized and offered a counterproposal that would eliminate U.S. and Soviet intermediate-range weapons over a three-year period. Thatcher followed up with a letter of her own to Gorbachev on March 10, firmly expressing her objections. Her positive view of Gorbachev had not swept away the suspicion that the Soviets had changed tactics rather than goals.[47]

Then came a catastrophe that transformed Europe's lingering skepticism about Soviet intentions into anger and fear. In the early morning hours of April 26, 1986, an explosion destroyed Reactor No. 4 at the Chernobyl nuclear power station in the Ukraine. Firefighters rushed from Kiev, eighty miles away, to prevent the blaze from spreading to Reactor No. 3. Ultimately, thirty people died and as many as 100,000 received varying degrees of radiation. The fire inside Reactor No. 4 raged for days, and scientists expressed fears that it would lead to an uncontrollable nuclear meltdown.

Gorbachev was the exponent of glasnost, but his first reaction to the worst disaster in the history of nuclear power was to stonewall. Although abnormal levels of radiation were quickly detected in Sweden, the Soviets refused to provide any information. Not until the evening of April 28, nearly sixty-seven hours after the Chernobyl explosion, did the Soviets give a terse account of the accident, and only then because Sweden was about to issue a radiation alert. As a radiation cloud spread across Europe and the world, European officials expressed anger at the paucity of information provided by the Soviets. By May 3, with the industrialized democracies gathering in Tokyo for their annual economic summit, the radioactive cloud had reached Japan. From Tokyo, Reagan denounced the Soviets for their "stubborn refusal" to provide a full account of the Chernobyl accident.[48] This did not happen until May 14, when a haggard Gorbachev gave a television address that coupled a report on the disaster with attacks on the West for conducting an "unrestrained anti-Soviet propaganda campaign." U.S. officials noted that Gorbachev offered neither regrets nor apologies in his speech, but Reagan nonetheless sent a sympathetic letter to Gorbachev.

Chernobyl was an epochal event that damaged Gorbachev's leadership at home and abroad. Soviet citizens had learned more about what was happening in the critical days after the Chernobyl explosion from the Voice of America and the BBC than from their own government. Europeans were scathing in their criticism of Soviet unconcern for how they had treated their neighbors in their supposed "common home." The disaster appears to have had a profound impact on Gorbachev. "Although he would not apologize for his handling of Chernobyl, he was changed by it," wrote Gorbachev biographers Doder and Branson.

"From that point on, natural disasters and man-made calamities would be reported promptly in the Soviet media."[49]

Chernobyl also had an impact on Reagan. "Chernobyl showed again what an abyss will open if nuclear war befalls mankind," Gorbachev had said in his television speech. Reagan agreed. The calamity at Chernobyl seemed to Reagan a sign that the world was threatened by the cataclysmic disaster of Armageddon, the biblical story in which his antinuclear vision is rooted. Reagan knew the passage in the Book of Revelation (8:10) that told of how "a great star fell from heaven, blazing like a torch, and it fell on a third of the rivers and on the fountains of water. The name of the star is Wormwood. A third of the waters became wormwood, and many men died of the water, because it was made bitter." When Reagan learned that "Chernobyl" is the Ukrainian word for "wormwood," he was certain that the disaster at Reactor No. 4 was indeed a portent of Armageddon.*

In retrospect, Reagan was convinced that the explosion at Reactor No. 4 had made Gorbachev more receptive to the need for nuclear arms reduction. Soon after leaving office, Reagan told Landon Parvin, "Thirty-five thousand people still can't go home. Chernobyl was less than one warhead, and look what happened."[51] He expanded on this idea in his memoirs, written a year and a half later. "Seventy years of Communism had bankrupted the Soviet Union economically and spiritually," Reagan wrote. "Gorbachev must have realized it could no longer support or control Stalin's totalitarian colonial empire; the survival of the Soviet Union was more important to him. He must have looked at the economic disaster his country was facing and concluded that it couldn't continue spending so much of its wealth on weapons and an arms race that—as I told him at Geneva—we would never let his country win. I'm convinced the tragedy at Chernobyl a year after Gorbachev took office also affected him and made him try harder to resolve Soviet differences with the West."[52]

While Gorbachev was trying to recover the political initiative after the damage inflicted by Chernobyl, the Reagan administration was once

---

* Reagan was circumspect about his views at the time, perhaps mindful of the problem the Armageddon issue had caused him in the 1984 campaign. But on March 28, 1987, at the Gridiron Dinner in Washington, Reagan related his conviction that Chernobyl had been biblically foretold in a conversation with James McCartney of Knight-Ridder Newspapers, then the president of the Gridiron Club. After quoting from the Book of Revelation, Reagan said, "So there you have it. The Chernobyl disaster was predicted in the Bible two thousand years ago." In telling the story, however, Reagan misremembered the name of the star. He told McCartney that "Chernobyl" was the Ukrainian word for "wedgwood."[50]

more torn apart by an internecine struggle over the symbolic and emotional issue of SALT II. Early in 1986 administration conservatives, led by Weinberger, Adelman and Casey, launched a campaign intended to dispose of SALT II once and for all. Shultz and Admiral William J. Crowe, chairman of the Joint Chiefs of Staff, resisted. Crowe feared that a presidential decision to abandon the SALT II limits would encourage the Soviet Union to accelerate a buildup of its strategic missile forces before the United States had completed its own strategic modernization program. Shultz warned that the allies and Congress would object to any scrapping of SALT II. Reagan's heart was with the conservatives: he had campaigned against the treaty in 1980, he was convinced that the Soviets had violated its provisions and he disliked any treaty that provided for nuclear arms increases rather than reductions. But his head warned him not to antagonize the Soviets at a time when he had restored a dialogue with them and was looking forward to another summit with Gorbachev.

On May 27, 1986, Reagan finally scrapped U.S. adherence to SALT II, but did so in a way that created confusion about what he actually intended. In a White House statement Reagan announced that the United States would no longer base its decisions "on standards contained in the SALT structure, which has been undermined by Soviet noncompliance, and especially in a flawed SALT II treaty, which was never ratified, would have expired if it had been ratified and has been violated by the Soviet Union." But the statement also said that the United States would remain in technical compliance with the treaty for several months by retiring two outmoded twenty-year-old Poseidon submarines for budgetary reasons. If the Soviet Union took "constructive steps" before the United States actually exceeded the SALT II limits, said Reagan, "we will certainly take this into account." *

Adelman believes that Reagan may have decided finally to repudiate SALT II because of a comment made by Senator Dan Quayle of Indiana, a member of a group of anti-SALT senators who visited the White House at the urging of Weinberger and Adelman. Quayle said continued adherence to SALT II would establish a "Reagan precedent" that

---

* The national media, including *The Washington Post,* was confused by the dual signal sent by Reagan. The *Post* story, written by Walter Pincus and me, carried the headline "Compliance with SALT Continued" and focused largely on how the United States would remain in technical compliance with the treaty. ABC News opened its report on the evening of May 27 by saying that Reagan had decided to continue in compliance, unwisely adding that "the message from the White House is very clear." *The New York Times* changed its message between editions, emphasizing compliance in its first story and the break with SALT II in its second.

would associate the treaty with him rather than with Carter. "When Quayle said this, Reagan sat up and ground his teeth, a telltale sign of aggravation," Adelman observed.[53] Shultz said it "became clear to me" that Reagan had simply decided to follow his gut instincts.[54] In his memoirs Reagan said, "Frankly, I was just tired of living by the rules and having the other side violate them."[55]

While Reagan's SALT II decision had little immediate practical effect, it bothered the Soviets, who announced on June 1 that they would not consider themselves bound by any provisions of the treaty once the United States exceeded the weapons ceiling limits. And the Soviets were even more disturbed by the Reagan administration's creative interpretation of the 1972 ABM treaty. The treaty had been traditionally interpreted to forbid the development of antimissile systems, especially space-based systems, such as those envisioned by Reagan when he unveiled SDI in 1983. Laboratory research was permitted, but the Pentagon wanted a broader interpretation that would permit actual testing of components in a missile-defense system. Late in 1985, Richard Perle found an unexpected ally in the person of State Department legal adviser Abraham Sofaer, who delighted the Pentagon and dismayed Shultz and Nitze by agreeing that the ABM treaty had been too narrowly interpreted.

Sofaer presented his memorandum permitting the broad interpretation on October 3, 1985. The next day, at the urging of Weinberger, this interpretation was secretly adopted as administration policy at a White House meeting of the president's principal arms control advisers. The meeting was chaired by National Security Adviser Robert McFarlane, who viewed the new interpretation as helpful to his "sting" campaign to convince Reagan to trade away SDI deployment for reductions in Soviet strategic missile forces. No matter how the ABM treaty was interpreted, deployment of an antimissile system would not be technologically feasible until well after the Reagan presidency had ended. McFarlane reasoned that Reagan would be more likely to trade away SDI deployment if the ABM treaty was interpreted to allow testing and development of SDI components.*

* But McFarlane gave the game away on October 6, when he was questioned on NBC's *Meet the Press* by Robert Kaiser, a *Washington Post* editor and former Moscow correspondent. When Kaiser pressed McFarlane about the incompatibility of SDI and the ABM treaty, McFarlane acknowledged that the administration's interpretation of the treaty prohibited only deployment of a missile-defense system.[56] McFarlane told me that Shultz called him and dressed him down after the program. It was one of the few times on U.S.-Soviet issues that McFarlane pleased Weinberger and displeased the secretary of state.

The new interpretation appealed to Reagan, who held a romantic notion of SDI's feasibility and had little interest in the fine points. Reagan was not capable of resolving the differences between his advisers, and rarely said anything at the NSPG meetings where the ABM treaty was discussed. When he did comment, he usually limited himself to such generalizations as saying that "SDI is not a bargaining chip" or proclaiming his interest in ridding the world of nuclear weapons. But Reagan's diary entries show that he embraced the broad interpretation of the ABM treaty. This is not surprising. Basically, Reagan wanted to be told how a missile-defense system could be constructed, not of technological or legal barriers to its deployment. He was never receptive to the McFarlane "sting" because he did not want to abandon his dream of a missile-proof system that would protect Americans from nuclear annihilation.

Nonetheless, Reagan realized that Shultz was right in saying that the broad interpretation of the ABM treaty would cause problems with the Congress and U.S. allies, even with Margaret Thatcher, who wanted SDI to be limited to a research program. Following his usual pattern, Reagan tried to split the difference between his advisers. On October 11, 1985, Shultz persuaded Reagan to accept a compromise that was a masterpiece of double-talk. The compromise, worked out by Shultz and Nitze, proclaimed the legality of the broad interpretation while saying that the administration would abide by the traditional interpretation as a matter of policy. This straddle failed to satisfy either the Soviet Union or the U.S. Congress. Marshal Sergei Akhromeyev, chief of the Soviet General Staff, denounced the broad interpretation of the ABM treaty as "a deliberate deceit." The former U.S. officials who had negotiated the ABM treaty rejected the new interpretation, and Congress eventually insisted that the administration accept the traditional, strict interpretation as the legal one.[57]

By the summer of 1986 the promises of strategic nuclear arms reductions that Gorbachev and Reagan had made to each other at Geneva seemed incapable of fulfillment. Gorbachev wanted confinement of SDI to the laboratory as the price of any agreement to reduce Soviet missile arsenals. Reagan wanted reductions and an unconstrained SDI as well. And Reagan's advisers were, as usual, divided in their counsel and in their objectives. Shultz and Nitze wanted a strategic arms agreement, even if this required concessions on SDI. Weinberger and Perle were skeptical of the value of arms control agreements with the Soviet Union and saw SDI as a means to prevent one. McFarlane was gone from the government, and his replacement, John Poindexter, though not a major player on arms control issues, tilted to the Pentagon view. But the arms control specialist on the NSC staff, Colonel Robert Linhard, recognized that the administration was at least as hampered by its own internal conflicts as by Soviet intransigence.

These conflicts slowed down a process that was moving none too swiftly in the first place. Every new proposal to the Soviets, every Reagan letter to Gorbachev, every speech on U.S.-Soviet relations became a tortuous exercise in reconciling conflicting State Department and Pentagon drafts. Linhard helped cobble together and reconcile the conflicting views as best he could, but Reagan himself was committed both to a strategic agreement and to SDI and refused to view these goals as incompatible. Reagan wanted the Soviets to make a 50 percent reduction in their offensive nuclear capability while simultaneously accepting U.S. deployment of a defensive system that would make the Soviet Union more vulnerable to surprise attack. On June 19, 1986, before a high school class in Glassboro, New Jersey, where President Lyndon Johnson and Soviet Premier Alexei Kosygin had begun the SALT process in 1967, Reagan urged Gorbachev to join him in taking "action in the name of peace" to reduce nuclear arsenals. But Reagan also said that SDI "might one day enable us to put in space a shield that missiles could not penetrate, a shield that could protect us from nuclear missiles just as a roof protects a family from rain."

The Glassboro speech, while also an exercise in public relations, was an accurate reflection of Reagan's views. Meanwhile, Poindexter and Linhard were struggling behind the scenes to reconcile conflicting versions of a new letter that was to be sent to Gorbachev in an effort to spur the lagging arms control negotiations. The letter went through many drafts. As finally approved at an NSPG meeting on July 17, it leaned heavily on a version originally suggested by Weinberger and Perle. The letter proposed that the United States and the Soviet Union abide by the ABM treaty for a period of five years. There would then be a two-year period during which each side would inform the other of its proposals to eliminate ballistic missiles, deploy a missile defense system and share the research of its strategic defense efforts. Either side could then withdraw from the ABM treaty on six months' notice. In effect, this provided for a seven-and-one-half-year period of continued compliance with the ABM treaty, although Reagan always referred to it as a five-year plan.

This "zero ballistics missile" plan appealed to Reagan's vision of a world free of nuclear weapons. The concession to Shultz and Nitze of seven and one-half years of compliance with the ABM treaty did not give away much from the Pentagon point of view, since it was unlikely that an antimissile system could be deployed within this time period. Shultz went along with the letter, realizing how much the zero ballistics missile idea appealed to Reagan. On July 18, Reagan wrote in his diary: "Well, we finally came up with a letter to Gorbachev that I can sign. In fact, it's a good one and should open the door to some real arms negotiations if he is really serious." [58] On July 25 the letter was sent to Gorbachev over Reagan's signature. Reminding Gorbachev of the promise he had made in the parking lot in Geneva, Reagan invited him to come to Washington to discuss the proposal and whatever other matters were on his mind.

Gorbachev did not respond to this letter until mid-September. In the interval U.S.-Soviet relations were dampened by the arrest of Gennady Zakharov, a Soviet physicist working at the United Nations. Zakharov was arrested by the FBI on a New York City subway platform on August 23 while exchanging money for classified documents. A week later the KGB arrested Nicholas Daniloff, the Moscow correspondent for *U.S. News & World Report,* and accused him of being a spy. It was a classic Cold War gambit that in Washington raised new doubts about whether Gorbachev was really different from his predecessors. In December 1984, Daniloff had delivered to the U.S. embassy in Moscow a letter from a KGB agent posing as a dissident Orthodox priest. Though Daniloff never saw the "priest" again, the incident became the pretext for using the journalist as a hostage to trade for Zakharov.

On September 5, Reagan sent a personal message to Gorbachev assuring him of Daniloff's innocence. He followed this up by denouncing Daniloff's arrest as an "outrage," and the United States expelled twenty-five members of the Soviet mission to the United Nations on the grounds they had been involved in spying. The Soviets denounced the action as illegal, and Gorbachev said publicly on September 18 that Daniloff was "a spy who was caught in the act." The real spy was Zakharov, and the Soviets were determined to get him back. Gorbachev had also accurately calculated that Reagan was more interested in another summit than in holding firm on Daniloff. On September 19, Soviet Foreign Minister Eduard Shevardnadze visited the White House to deliver a letter Gorbachev had written on September 15. Replying to Reagan's proposals of July 25 as well as to his demand that Daniloff be freed, the letter chided Reagan for using the Daniloff affair to launch a "massive hostile campaign" against the Soviet Union.[59] It also upbraided the president for refusing to go along with the Soviet extension of a moratorium on nuclear testing. Adelman thought the letter "longer-than-usual" and "nastier-than-ever," [60] and Poindexter found the tone of the message insulting.

The substance of the letter was no more encouraging than the tone. Gorbachev said that Reagan's proposal to observe the ABM treaty for five years while work proceeded on a missile defense system "complicates even what has been achieved." Reminding Reagan that he had warned him at Geneva that the Soviet Union would not assist the United States to "rush with weapons in space," Gorbachev pledged continued resistance to SDI. "We favor the strengthening of the ABM treaty regime," he said. "This is precisely the reason for our position that [SDI] work should be confined to laboratories and that the treaty should be observed strictly for a period of up to fifteen years." [61]

But the letter also offered Reagan the opportunity he had been seeking for a second summit. Gorbachev said that since there had been no major movement since Geneva, "I have come to the conclusion that the negotiations need a major impulse; otherwise, they would continue to mark time while creating only the appearance of preparations for our meeting on American soil." [62] He proposed a preparatory meeting with Reagan in Iceland or London to see if they could make progress on the unresolved issues before a Washington summit. Reagan did not hesitate. As he put it in his diary, he "opted for Iceland," making it clear to Shevardnadze that he would take up Gorbachev's offer.[63] Formal acceptance was delayed until Shultz and Shevardnadze worked out a Zakharov-Daniloff swap on September 29. As part of the deal, the Soviets agreed to allow dissidents Yuri Orlov and his wife, Irina Valitova, to emigrate to the United States. Nonetheless, the swap was on balance a victory for Gorbachev. As Serge Schmemann put it in *The New York Times,* "He got his man home, he set a precedent that would make Western governments think twice about arresting Soviet spy suspects, and he could take credit for arranging a superpower meeting and so salvaging the East-West dialogue." [64] Gorbachev may have been encouraged to think that Reagan was an easy mark.

Reagan, however, was eager to go to Reykjavik. He had the utmost faith in his ability to negotiate with Gorbachev, and he believed that the Soviet leader would not have written the letter unless he wanted to make a deal. He was encouraged in this view by Shultz, who shared Gorbachev's view that the stalled negotiations at Geneva needed a "major impulse" from the leaders. But the agreement to attend a snap summit in Iceland, even for preparatory purposes, flew in the face of previous U.S. declarations that any superpower summit should be carefully prepared with an agenda worked out well in advance. Reagan, who would be jolted by the twin blows of the Iran-contra disclosures and loss of the Senate in November, was brimming with confidence in September. Don Regan and Poindexter raised no caution flags. The mood in the White House was so secure that no one even bothered to prepare a fallback position that could be cited should the Reykjavik summit prove a bust.

In contrast to the tutorials in which he had immersed himself before Geneva, Reagan made no special preparations for Reykjavik. As he saw it, he had put his proposals on the table in the July 25 letter, and he envisioned the Iceland meeting as an agenda-setter for a Washington summit. Reagan never lost sight of his grand goal of ridding the world of nuclear weapons and his other goal of constructing a missile defense that would shield the American people as a roof "protects a family from rain." But he was bored, as many are, by the arcane substance of arms control. Ken Adelman has shudderingly described the final meeting in advance of Reykjavik as one in which Reagan could not follow Poindexter's convoluted summary of the positions that had been taken by the two superpowers.[65]

The one point on which Reagan was clear and persistent in the final pre-Reykjavik meeting with his advisers was that he wanted to eliminate all intermediate-range (INF) missiles in Europe. This was the "zero option" that Reagan had proposed in 1981. The zero option had not, however, been the U.S. position since March 1985, when U.S. negotiators in Geneva proposed equal limits of INF forces at any level set by the Soviets. But Gorbachev had said in his September 15 letter that the Soviets wanted "complete elimination of U.S. and Soviet missiles in Europe," and Reagan proposed to take him up on it. This left unsolved the problem of Soviet intermediate-range missiles in Asia. Reagan brushed aside this concern by declaring that the United States could put comparable missiles in Alaska, far away from targets in European Russia. "The more the President talked like this, the more nervous our INF negotiator, Mike Glitman, became," said Adelman.[66] But Reagan said that agreeing to a zero option in Europe might help persuade Gorbachev to get rid of all nuclear weapons. At the minimum he believed it could lead to an INF agreement that would at least closely approach his original zero-option proposal.

Reagan flew to Reykjavik, the Icelandic capital, on Thursday, October 9, to assure he would be well rested for his weekend meetings. Watching on television as Gorbachev arrived on Friday evening, Reagan quipped, "When you stop trying to take over the world, then maybe we can do some business." [67] * But Gorbachev had plenty of business he wanted to do in Iceland. The two leaders opened their summit on Saturday morning, October 11, at Hofdi House, a reputedly haunted former ambassadorial residence overlooking the sea that was often used for official receptions. As soon as they were seated together at a wooden rectangular table with their interpreters and note-takers, Gorbachev pulled a set of notes from his briefcase and proceeded to present what he called his "bold, unorthodox" proposals to limit strategic weapons, intermediate-range missiles and missiles in space. The proposals included what Gorbachev called "substantial" cuts in the mammoth, long-range ICBMs that were the most dangerous element of the Soviet nuclear arsenal and the one the Americans most wanted to reduce.

The conversation continued for fifty-one minutes, most of it dominated by the voluble Gorbachev. Then they were joined by Shultz and Shevardnadze, and Gorbachev read aloud his proposals from a three-page paper. The proposals were in the form of a directive to be issued on Sunday afternoon by the two leaders to their foreign ministers outlining the "principles" for them to follow in drawing up agreements to be signed at a Washington summit. Gorbachev proposed a 50 percent cut in strategic nuclear forces. He reiterated the idea he had expressed in his letter to Reagan of eliminating U.S. and Soviet intermediate-range missiles in Europe while permitting British and French missiles to remain. This, Gorbachev told Reagan, was "your own zero option." Gorbachev also said that a way might be found to deal with the remaining Soviet SS-20s in Asia. And he proposed that both sides abide by the strict interpretation of the ABM treaty for ten years, during which SDI research would be confined to the laboratory. This was a concession, since the Soviets had previously insisted on fifteen years of compliance with the ABM treaty.

When the meeting broke up, Reagan had difficulty reconstructing many of the specifics for his advisers. But he had no doubt of Gorba-

---

* This crack was vintage Reagan. But he also showed a respect for the Soviets, at least publicly, that had been conspicuously absent in the pre-Gorbachev days. As Reagan arrived at Hofdi House on October 11 for his first meeting with Gorbachev, CBS correspondent Bill Plante shouted at him from among a group of reporters, "Are you going to give away the store?" Reagan replied, "Don't own the store." [68]

chev's main objective. "He's brought a whole lot of proposals, but I'm afraid he's going after SDI," Reagan said to Shultz.[69] The president, Shultz and other members of the American team then retired to the "bubble"—a tiny room of transparent plastic made secure from electronic eavesdropping—to devise a strategy for dealing with Gorbachev.

That afternoon Reagan and Gorbachev met again, this time with Shultz and Shevardnadze present from the start. Reagan reiterated his view, as he had at Geneva, that SDI did not have offensive capabilities. He compared SDI to gas masks that had been used during World War I to protect soldiers and to an insurance policy for both sides. Reagan proposed a new treaty to replace the ABM treaty. Gorbachev replied that the ABM treaty should be strengthened, not discarded. To resolve their differences, Shultz proposed setting up two working groups of experts, one to deal with arms control and the other with human rights and regional issues. Paul Nitze was named to head the U.S. arms control working group, facing off against a Soviet team of experts headed by Marshal Akhromeyev.[70] The presence of the plainspoken Soviet military leader signified to the Americans that the Soviet military establishment would be a party to any agreement.

The experts worked from 8:00 P.M. until 2:00 A.M., creating what at times seemed to some of the American participants to be a brave new world of arms control. Akhromeyev's bluff, direct way of speaking impressed the Americans, and the Soviets gave ground on several technical issues that had long been a matter of contention. The most important of these concessions, Shultz said afterward, was Soviet agreement to count U.S. long-range bombers in a way that would permit the United States to maintain its advantage in this category. But the Soviets balked at establishing a separate limit of 3,000 warheads on heavy ICBMs. Akhromeyev, like his U.S. military counterparts, wanted as much flexibility as possible in determining the composition of the Soviet strategic force.

At 2:00 A.M. Akhromeyev requested a recess. He and Nitze reported back to Shevardnadze and Shultz. When the two working groups returned to the table an hour later, the Soviets made more concessions. The negotiations continued for another five hours. When they broke up, the two sides were close to agreement on the cuts to be made in offensive weapons. On Sunday morning, October 12, Reagan and Gorbachev met for what was supposed to be their last meeting in Reykjavik. They accepted the results of the working groups on offensive cuts, but were still far apart on strategic defense. The two leaders agreed that

Shultz and Shevardnadze should make a last attempt to reach a compromise and to meet again that afternoon. When this meeting was over, Shultz summoned the arms control working group and Poindexter. "We're at a very serious impasse on SDI," he said.[71]

The seriousness of the impasse was evident when Shevardnadze and his team arrived after lunch to continue the discussion. The Soviet foreign minister did not want to talk about the progress on offensive nuclear weapons. Instead, he demanded to know if Reagan would accept the ten-year period of strict compliance with the ABM treaty. "That's got to be settled," Shevardnadze said. "If it's not, nothing else is agreed. We're prepared to come down to ten years, but no lower. If it's not, let's go home."[72] Turning to Max Kampelman, he said, "You are a creative person—can't you think of something?" And to Nitze he said, "You are so experienced—can't you come up with something?"[73]

While this conversation was going on, Perle and Linhard were busily writing down a counterproposal on a sheet of legal-sized yellow paper. They passed a note to Shultz, who said to Shevardnadze, "You've seen some writing at that end of the table. This is an effort by some of us here to see if we can't break the impasse."[74] Shultz read the proposal aloud, then said that when he gave it to Reagan "the sound you hear may be the president banging my head against the wall."[75]

The new proposal broke into two parts the ten-year period of compliance with the ABM treaty that Gorbachev had proposed. During the first five years strategic nuclear arsenals would be reduced 50 percent, as the negotiators had agreed in their all-night session. Both sides would abide by the treaty for another five years if all ballistic missiles were eliminated during that time. After ten years each side would be free to deploy a strategic defense system. Shevardnadze said this would require the Soviets to deploy a defensive system and might be rejected by Gorbachev.

Despite Shultz's jocular remark about having his head banged against the wall, Reagan thought the proposal drawn up by Perle and Linhard was "imaginative." When Shultz presented it to him shortly after 2:00 P.M., Reagan said, "He gets his precious ABM treaty, and we get all his ballistic missiles. And after that we deploy SDI in space. Then it's a whole new ball game."[76] Reagan's only concern was whether it was practical for the United States to eliminate all its ballistic missiles within ten years. Perle told him this could be done and alluded to new "Stealth" technology that would enable the United States to maintain an effective nuclear deterrence force of bombers and cruise missiles.

When Reagan and Gorbachev met again just before 3:00 P.M., Gorbachev took the U.S. proposal and expanded on it. The Soviet leader had, after all, advanced his own plan ten months earlier for eliminating nuclear weapons by the year 2000. Now he proposed to do away with all nuclear weapons in ten years. This would include bombers and cruise missiles, in which the United States had an advantage, as well as ballistic missiles, in which the Soviets were ahead. Gorbachev said that the U.S. proposal was imprecise, referring to "offensive ballistic missiles" in one section and to "strategic arms" in another. Why not get rid of all nuclear weapons? he wanted to know. "It would be fine with me if we eliminated all nuclear weapons," Reagan said.[77]

And it would have been "fine" with the president, for that is what he wanted to do. What was not fine was Gorbachev's insistence on confining SDI to the laboratory. After Gorbachev reiterated this position, Reagan became angry. "I've said again and again that SDI wasn't a bargaining chip," he said. "I've told you, if we find out that SDI is practical and feasible, we'll make that information known to you and everyone else so that nuclear weapons can be made obsolete. Now, with all that we have accomplished here, you do this and throw in this roadblock and everything is out the window. There is no way we are going to give up research to find a defense weapon against nuclear missiles."[78]

Both men stood their ground. As Gorbachev saw it, Reagan's refusal to confine SDI to a laboratory research program would create irresistible momentum toward deployment of space weapons. Gorbachev said he would be regarded as "the village idiot" in Moscow if he agreed to cuts in Soviet offensive weapons while no restrictions were placed on SDI. Reagan clung to his competing dreams of a world without nuclear weapons and a world in which people would be protected from nuclear war by an antimissile defense. He was impervious to the argument that a defensive shield might encourage delusions of invulnerability and enhance the risk of nuclear war because he did not accept the idea that the United States would ever initiate a nuclear attack. As Reagan saw it, an antimissile system was simply a good insurance policy for both sides. Repeatedly he insisted that it was only the single word "laboratory," to which Gorbachev proposed to confine SDI research, that stood in the way of an agreement. Reagan said he had made a promise to the American people to develop SDI and would not go back on his word. Noting how close they were to an agreement, he asked Gorbachev to "give me this one thing."[79]

Finally, they could get no further. Gorbachev said he didn't believe

Reagan when he said the United States would share the fruits of its SDI research with other nations. Reagan became intensely angry. "I realized he had brought me to Iceland with one purpose: to kill the Strategic Defense Initiative," Reagan said later.[80] He would not do it.

The two leaders had by now met for nearly four hours on Sunday afternoon, including a recess during which Perle and Linhard made cosmetic revisions in their plan in an unsuccessful attempt to placate Gorbachev on the ABM treaty.[81] Night was falling. Gorbachev would not agree to SDI research beyond the laboratory, and Reagan would not give up on SDI. After Gorbachev refused his request to "give me this one thing," Reagan closed his briefing book and stood up, ending the summit. "The meeting is over," he said. "Let's go, George, we're leaving."[82]

Gorbachev was stunned. The Soviets had already made it known they were willing to spend another day in Reykjavik. Gorbachev had more to say. As Reagan put his coat on, Gorbachev said to him, "Can't we do something about this?" Reagan had had enough. "It's too late," he said.[83] *

Journalists from many nations had crowded into the summit press center in a downtown Reykjavik hotel, awaiting word on the deliberations. Rumors and expectations of agreement had grown steadily. But these expectations receded when the waiting reporters saw the television picture of Reagan and Gorbachev departing grimly from Hofdi House. And they were dashed even more at the sight of Shultz, who arrived at 7:20 P.M. at the press center in a mournful mood. Shultz briefings were often tedious, but the thirty-minute report he gave after the collapse of the Reykjavik summit was riveting and emotional. Summarizing the progress that had been made and the ultimate collapse of the talks, Shultz said, "And so in the end, with great reluctance, the president . . . simply had to refuse to compromise the security of the U.S., of our allies and freedom by abandoning the shield that has held in front of freedom." With a weary Max Kampelman looking on in tears, Shultz made no effort to hide his own "great sense of disappointment." They had made a "tremendous amount of headway" at Reykjavik, he said, "but in the end we couldn't quite make it."[85]

The world initially shared Shultz's disappointment. "Reagan-

---

* Anatoly Dobrynin subsequently told William Hyland that Gorbachev wasn't finished talking when Reagan "walked away out of exasperation." Hyland believes that Reagan's walkout was fortuitous, enabling him to get credit "for being tough" and probably to avoid a joint communiqué in which the two leaders would have declared a goal of abolishing ballistic missiles as a step toward ridding the world of all nuclear weapons. This would certainly have unnerved U.S. allies. "I think Gorbachev would have done a great deal of damage in a communiqué," Hyland said.[84]

Gorbachev Summit Talks Collapse as Deadlock on SDI Wipes Out Other Gains," read the two-line banner headline in *The Washington Post* the next morning. *Time*'s cover proclaimed, "No Deal: Star Wars Sinks the Summit." Reagan and his team were widely criticized for going to Reykjavik unprepared to deal with Gorbachev. U.S. allies complained that Reagan had walked to the brink of a deal to eliminate nuclear weapons without any advance consultation. Republican politicians worried that Reykjavik would become a negative symbol in the fall election campaign.

But the negative fallout was short-lived. This had less to do with the happy face that the White House "spin patrol" tried to put on the summit than with Reagan's own performance in a televised speech to the nation the day after he returned from Iceland. While Reagan gave himself the best lines in his exchange with Gorbachev, he told the truth as he saw it. "I told him I had pledged to the American people that I would not trade away SDI—there was no way I could tell our people their government would not protect them against nuclear destruction," Reagan said. "I went to Reykjavik determined that everything was negotiable except two things: our freedom and our future."

Reagan claimed in his speech that "we made progress in Iceland." And Gorbachev also took this view, although this assessment was overshadowed by his criticisms of Reagan at a post-summit news conference that was even bleaker in tone than the one given by Shultz. Gorbachev accused the Americans of coming to Iceland "empty-handed," and said "it would have taken a madman to accept" Reagan's SDI proposal. But Gorbachev also said, "We have reached agreement on many things. We have traveled a long road."

The American people made a similar evaluation. A *New York Times*–CBS poll taken the week after Reykjavik showed an 11-point jump (to 72 percent) in the percentage of Americans who thought that Reagan was successfully handling relations with the Soviet Union. And for the first time, a majority of Americans believed that the meetings between Reagan and Gorbachev would lead to nuclear arms control agreements.

The American people were right, although it would require nearly a year for this hopefulness to be translated into any kind of treaty. Reagan and Gorbachev had taken each other's measure in their Reykjavik weekend, and neither was in doubt where the other stood. Both were stubborn men. After Reykjavik it was evident to Gorbachev that Reagan would not permit SDI to be limited to the laboratory in return for nuclear arms reductions. And it was equally clear to Reagan that Gorbachev would not allow deep reductions in Soviet strategic nuclear forces unless SDI was restrained. This conflict proved an insurmountable barrier to negotiating a Strategic Arms Reduction Treaty (START) and to the euphoric idea of a world without nuclear missiles.* But it did not close the door on an INF treaty, which in time would prove the lonely child of Reykjavik.

At Reykjavik the two sides had narrowed their differences on the provisions of a prospective INF treaty. In his successful effort to get Reagan to say yes to what had been his own proposal, Gorbachev had proposed elimination of all intermediate-range U.S. and Soviet missiles in Europe, with the Soviets retaining 100 missiles in Asia offset by the same number of U.S. missiles based in the United States. This was progress. At the same time, however, the Soviets had taken a step away from a separate treaty on intermediate-range missiles. At Geneva the two sides had agreed to work for a separate, "interim" treaty on these missiles. At Reykjavik the Soviets had linked any INF treaty to constraints on SDI that Reagan refused to accept.

On February 28, 1987, however, Gorbachev unlinked the INF treaty from other agreements. A report from the Soviet news agency Tass, issued in Gorbachev's name, said, "The Soviet Union suggests that the problem of medium-range missiles in Europe be singled out from the package of issues, and that a separate agreement on it be concluded, and without delay." A multitude of motives seems to have guided this decision. Judging from the statements of Deputy Foreign Minister Yuli Vorontsov, who had taken over direction of the Soviet delegation in the Geneva talks, Gorbachev hoped that this unlinking of the INF treaty would give "positive impetus" [87] to the full range of arms control negotiations. But the Soviets also did not want to lose the opportunity to get rid of the fast-flying U.S. Pershing II missiles that could, from their bases in West Germany, reach targets within the Soviet Union in a few minutes. Political considerations also were involved. As a British analyst noted, "The Russians needed to give the whole disarmament process another lease of life before the campaign for the presidential election in 1988 paralyzed the presidency." [88] And Reagan did not want his term

---

* The inability of Reagan and Gorbachev to reach agreement on a plan to eliminate all ballistic missiles within ten years came as an immense relief to the Joint Chiefs of Staff. The chiefs believed such a commitment would undermine congressional support for such controversial and costly ballistic missiles as the MX and the Trident II. On October 27, Admiral William Crowe, chairman of the Joint Chiefs, advised Reagan not to submit a zero ballistics proposal to the Soviets at the Geneva arms talks. Margaret Thatcher, almost always influential with Reagan, "discreetly and confidentially" [86] expressed a similar view to the president.

to end without concluding a nuclear arms reduction treaty with Gorbachev.

Reagan quickly took up the Soviet offer. He said on March 3 that Gorbachev's statement of February 28 "removes a serious obstacle to progress toward INF reductions," while also stressing that any INF agreement "must be effectively verifiable." On March 4, U.S. negotiators submitted a draft INF treaty to the Soviets at Geneva, using the Reykjavik formula of removing all intermediate-range missiles from Europe while permitting 100 Soviet missiles to remain in Asia. Nonetheless, Reagan's preference for his original "zero option" was clear. In presenting the draft, the U.S. team said it would prefer elimination of all intermediate-range missiles.

Problems remained on both sides. For the Soviet Union, the 100 missiles that would be retained in Asia promised tensions with Japan and China. But the principal problem was West Germany, which wanted to retain seventy-two aging Pershing I-A missiles armed with U.S. nuclear warheads. The Germans saw these missiles as an offset against shorter-range nuclear missiles (SS-12s and SS-23s) that the Soviets would retain in East Germany and Czechoslovakia.

On April 12–15 in Moscow, where Shultz conducted three days of meetings with Gorbachev and Shevardnadze, the Soviets threw the German ball into the American court. Gorbachev told Shultz that upon completion of the INF treaty the Soviet Union would destroy its shorter-range missiles in East Germany and Czechoslovakia. In effect, this left it up to the Americans to persuade the West Germans that the Pershing I-As would also have to go. But Gorbachev's willingness to take this extra step removed any lingering U.S. doubts that the Soviets were serious about wanting an INF treaty. On April 15, Shultz announced that the two sides had agreed that intermediate-range missiles would be destroyed within a period of four to five years and that an INF treaty must contain provisions "for very strict and intrusive verification." The Soviets presented their version of a draft treaty in the Geneva negotiations on April 27.

Events now moved swiftly. On June 12, appropriately enough in Reykjavik, NATO foreign ministers called for "global and effectively verifiable" elimination of all intermediate-range and shorter-range missiles. On July 23, Gorbachev announced that the Soviets had accepted this concept, known as "double global zero," and would destroy their intermediate-range and shorter-range missiles if the United States would do the same. On August 26, Chancellor Helmut Kohl announced that West Germany would dismantle its Pershing I-As.

"Double global zero" was welcomed by U.S. intelligence agencies, which opposed intrusive verification of an INF treaty. "Verification" had long been a battle cry of U.S. arms control opponents, who knew from experience that the Soviets inevitably rejected proposals requiring inspections on their territory. Soviet refusal to allow on-site inspections to determine treaty compliance had often been cited by American conservatives, including Reagan, as a sign that the Soviets would cheat at every chance. But Gorbachev had changed the rules and forced U.S. officials to contemplate the consequences of the verification policies they had routinely advocated. The "intrusive verification" plan announced by Shultz in Moscow would have placed U.S. and Soviet inspectors at each other's factories to count the missiles as they came off the production lines. Faced with this prospect, it was the CIA and the National Security Agency rather than the KGB that blinked. The U.S. intelligence agencies made it clear to the White House that the Soviets might glean valuable information from the intrusive verification agreement. "Double global zero" solved much of this problem. Factory inspectors would not be needed because there would be no new missiles to count. On the same day that Kohl announced the plan to destroy the Pershing I-As, U.S. negotiators at Geneva presented a revised verification proposal doing away with factory inspection.

Soviet acceptance of the "double global zero" formula led swiftly to resolution of the remaining issues. On September 18, Shevardnadze and Shultz met in Washington and announced they had agreed in principle on an INF treaty. Officials of the two governments cleared away remaining technical obstacles in three days of meetings in Moscow in late October. On October 30, Shevardnadze arrived again in Washington for another meeting with Shultz and announced that Gorbachev would come to Washington for a summit, at which he and Reagan would sign the INF treaty.

Reagan was particularly pleased by the announcement of agreement on an INF treaty and a summit in Washington. He had been discouraged and on the political defensive through much of the spring and summer of 1987, when domestic attention was focused on the prolonged congressional investigation of the Iran-contra affair. Like other presidents dogged by domestic scandal, he sought solace by playing the role of statesman abroad. In June he made a ten-day tour of Europe that included participation in the economic summit in Venice. The trip was capped by a visit to West Berlin, where Reagan gave one of the most celebrated speeches of his presidency. Standing before the Brandenburg Gate, then the symbol of Europe's division, Reagan challenged

Gorbachev to create a new era of freedom in Europe. He raised the question of whether the stirrings of "reform and openness" that had begun in the Soviet Union signaled "profound changes" in Soviet policy or were simply "token gestures." And then he said:

> There is one sign the Soviets can make that would be unmistakable, that would advance dramatically the cause of freedom and peace.
> General Secretary Gorbachev, if you seek peace, if you seek prosperity for the Soviet Union and Eastern Europe, if you seek liberalization: Come here to this gate! Mr. Gorbachev, open this gate! Mr. Gorbachev, tear down this wall! [89]

Later, Reagan would tell me that he could hear the anger in his voice as he spoke those lines, which had been drafted by White House speechwriter Peter Robinson.[90] He was angry not at Gorbachev but at the East German police, who just before his speech had herded people away from loudspeakers near the Brandenburg Gate to prevent them from hearing what Reagan had to say. But the old performer need not have worried that he would not be heard, at least on this day. His words resonated throughout Europe and were heard as far away as Moscow. And after Gorbachev had agreed to the Washington summit, Reagan sent him the message again. In a speech televised to Europe on November 4 he said, "Wouldn't it be a wonderful sight for the world to see, if someday General Secretary Gorbachev and I could meet in Berlin and together take down the first bricks of that wall, and could continue taking down walls until the distrust between our peoples and the scars of the past are forgotten?"

But at the Washington summit, it was Gorbachev who was the star performer. The capital city, which usually takes visitors in stride, was gripped with what *Washington Post* columnist Tom Shales called "Gorby fever." [91] On December 7, soon after arriving in Washington, Gorbachev addressed an eclectic group of celebrities (the guest list included Billy Graham, Henry Kissinger and Yoko Ono) at the Soviet embassy. "Something very serious is afoot, something very profound . . . ," he said. "[There is] an awareness that we cannot go on as we are, that we cannot leave our relations as they are." [92] By December 10, departure day, Gorbachev was conducting himself as if he were an American politician, much to the consternation of the Secret Service and the KGB. Wherever he went, crowds lined the street to applaud

him. On busy Connecticut Avenue he brought traffic to a halt by ordering his limousine to stop so he could get out and shake hands with well-
wishers.

The serious business of the summit was done in the East Room of
the White House on the afternoon of December 8. Sitting side by side
at a table once used by Abraham Lincoln, Reagan and Gorbachev
signed the document formally known as the "Treaty Between the
United States of America and the Union of Soviet Socialist Republics
on the Elimination of Their Intermediate-Range and Shorter-Range
Missiles." Their action would lead, over a three-year period, to the
destruction of 859 U.S. nuclear missiles and 1,836 Soviet nuclear missiles with a range of 300 to 3,400 miles. But the treaty's importance, as
Reagan said at the signing ceremony, transcended numbers. While only
about 4 percent of the nuclear arsenals of the superpowers were eliminated by the INF treaty, it was the first U.S.-Soviet treaty of any kind
to provide for destruction of nuclear weapons and the first to provide
for on-site monitoring of this destruction by the two nations.

In signing the INF treaty, Reagan and Gorbachev demonstrated a
comfortable familiarity with each other that was the by-product of their
meetings in Geneva and Reykjavik.

"We have listened to the wisdom of an old Russian maxim," said
Reagan, using a phrase that he had repeated scores of times. "The
maxim is *doverey, no proverey*—trust but verify."

"You repeat that at every meeting," Gorbachev said good-
humoredly.

"I like it," Reagan said.[93]

But the private meetings did not go as well as the public ones. After
the signing ceremony ended at 2:00 P.M., Reagan and Gorbachev
walked together to the State Dining Room, where they delivered separate televised statements to worldwide audiences. Next on the agenda
was a plenary session, where the two leaders were joined by their senior
advisers for what was supposed to be a discussion of arms control
issues. Shultz had moved the meeting from the Oval Office to the larger
Cabinet Room so that more officials from both sides could attend.*
Reagan seemed disconcerted by the change. After starring in his big

---

* This was the second Reagan-Gorbachev meeting of the summit. They had met one-on-one that
morning in the Oval Office at a ceremonial meeting where Reagan had given Gorbachev a pair of
cuff links on which swords were being beaten into plowshares. Gorbachev wasn't particularly
interested in the cuff links. "I had been trying to tell Reagan that the Russians don't wear French
cuffs," Colin Powell said.[94]

scene, the treaty-signing ritual, the president was now behaving as if he had been taken to the wrong set and asked to perform without a script. Reagan did not know what to say to Gorbachev, who began the meeting by giving a progress report on perestroika. It was apparent to Shultz and National Security Adviser Colin Powell that Reagan, who often faded in midafternoon, was disoriented. "Since he didn't know what he should talk about, Reagan told stories," Powell said later.[95]

By the Washington summit Gorbachev was quite used to Reagan's collection of anti-Soviet anecdotes. The Soviet leader usually laughed politely at Reagan's stories, and he occasionally contributed his own jokes about the backwardness of the Soviet bureaucracy. But Gorbachev took pride in the political changes in the Soviet system, which was the point of his opening remarks to Reagan in their session that afternoon. He found nothing funny when Reagan responded to his account with an old story about a Russian-speaking American scholar who had taken a taxi to the airport for a flight to the Soviet Union. The cab driver was a young man who had not completed college, and the scholar asked him what he intended to do when he had finished his education. "I haven't decided yet," the driver told him. When the scholar arrived in Moscow, his cab driver was also a young man who had not completed his education. In response to the scholar's question about what he wanted to do when he finished his schooling, the driver replied, "They haven't told me yet."[96]

Gorbachev was clearly offended that his glowing description of the changes in the Soviet Union had been answered by this shopworn anecdote. "It *was* offensive," Powell said. "The meeting was a disaster."[97] As soon as it was over, Shultz, Powell and White House Chief of Staff Howard Baker took Reagan aside and expressed their concern. "I guess I shouldn't have told that joke," Reagan said.[98] But it was not the joke alone that had distressed Shultz, who called the entire meeting "a bad show."[99] Reagan had simply paid no attention to what was happening and been unable to carry on a conversation with Gorbachev. It was an embarrassing performance, and one that Reagan agreed should not be repeated. That night Powell wrote some formal talking points and took them to Shultz, who edited them. Baker and Powell gave them to Reagan the next morning, directing him to stick to the script and tell no jokes. Meeting with Gorbachev in the Oval Office on December 9, Reagan was alert and businesslike.

But while there were no more embarrassments, there was also no progress toward a strategic arms treaty, and for the same reason as at

Reykjavik. Reagan was still wedded to an antimissile system. Gorbachev was still determined to confine SDI to the laboratory. By now, each man knew the other's position by heart. "We are going forward with the research and development necessary to see if this is a workable concept, and if it is, we are going to deploy it," said Reagan.[100] "Mr. President, you do what you have to do," said Gorbachev. "And if in the end you think you have a system you want to deploy, go ahead and deploy it. Who am I to tell you what to do? I think you're wasting money."[101]

Reagan and Gorbachev also discussed their differences on Nicaragua while the two of them were walking to lunch at the White House on the last day of the summit. Reagan told him that he could "go a long way toward improving U.S.-Soviet relations" by ending the shipment of Soviet weapons to the Sandinista government.[102] Gorbachev responded by suggesting that both sides end shipments of arms to Central America, including U.S. weapons to El Salvador. This, Reagan was unprepared to do. While Reagan claims in his memoirs that Gorbachev responded positively to him and halted Soviet weapons shipments to Nicaragua, they actually continued into 1989, when the Bush administration concluded an agreement to end the Nicaraguan war.

Judged in political terms, the Washington summit was a "clear success," as Reagan called it in a rainswept exchange of remarks on the South Lawn on December 10. Gorbachev said at the farewell ceremony that "a good deal has been accomplished," although the major accomplishments—the signing of the treaty and an agreement to meet in Moscow in 1988—had been decided before the summit. Reagan and Gorbachev had played well together on television, and Reagan's fumbling performance in the meeting after the treaty-signing had been concealed from the media and the American people. In their public appearances both leaders had conveyed an impression of confidence and good will that signaled that their nations were moving away from the perils of the Cold War and the specter of nuclear confrontation. Their political fortunes had been bolstered in the process. Reagan continued his climb in public approval after the dark days of the Iran-contra inquiries. Gorbachev's biographers said that "the Russians were startled" by the Soviet leader's popularity in the United States.[103]

But while the Washington summit was hailed as a step toward peace by the populations of the United States and the Soviet Union, and by much of the rest of the world, the end of the Cold War was a gloomy prospect for many American conservatives. The conservative movement was immune to "Gorby fever" and distrusted U.S.-Soviet arms control treaties as a matter of principle, even treaties in which two-thirds of the missiles to be destroyed were Soviet missiles. The conservatives longed for the bad old days after the Soviet invasion of Afghanistan when they had been able to mobilize public opinion against the SALT II treaty and forced President Carter to withdraw it from Senate consideration rather than face a humiliating defeat on ratification. But the conservatives were now on the defensive. Reagan, who had been one of their most effective spokesmen in opposing SALT II, was one of the architects of the INF treaty. Ignoring the fact that Reagan had favored a "zero option" INF treaty since 1981, conservatives claimed that the vicissitudes of the Iran-contra inquiries had caused him to become overly accommodating to Gorbachev. New Right leader Paul Weyrich summed up the concerns of the right wing shortly before the Washington summit by saying, "Reagan is a weakened president, weakened in spirit as well as clout, and not in a position to make judgments about Gorbachev at this time." [104]

The principal concern of conservatives was that the INF treaty would lead inevitably to other U.S.-Soviet treaties and a reduction of U.S. influence in Europe. Soon after Reagan and Gorbachev signed the INF treaty, Senator Quayle told Peter Jennings of ABC that he was "not ready to consent [to it] right now." Pressed by Jennings on what worried him, Quayle said, "The thing that worries me most about it is that we now have in momentum a potentially [*sic*] denuclearization of Western Europe, and therefore war would in fact be more of a possibility than now." [105]

This was not an isolated view, nor one limited to the far right of the political spectrum. Henry Kissinger, while expressing support for the treaty, said he had "grave reservations" about its effect on the East-West balance of power. [106] Reagan avoided a public quarrel with Kissinger, but the president and his arms control advisers were angered at the ammunition his testimony to the Senate Foreign Relations Committee provided to conservative critics of the treaty. They suspected that Kissinger's skepticism was at least partly ego-driven, and that he was being critical because he had played no role in the negotiations. But other advocates of traditional deterrence expressed similar views. The knowledgeable William Hyland, editor of *Foreign Affairs,* shared the view that denuclearization was "dangerous for Europe." [107] Even Paul Nitze, the premier U.S. arms control negotiator, would have preferred a token deployment of U.S. and Soviet intermediate-range missiles in Europe to the zero option on the grounds that it would have preserved a U.S. nuclear stake in the defense of Europe. Richard Perle, author of the original zero-option idea in 1981, thought that the entire INF process was a diversion. "I didn't like the INF program from the beginning," said Perle, who in 1987 had resigned from the administration so he could speak freely. "But we were stuck with it, because the U.S. and its allies had invested a lot of political capital in launching that program and it was politically important for the alliance that we not fail to bring it to a conclusion."[108]

This logic led Perle to profess reluctant support for the INF treaty, while warning of the dire consequences of any future strategic arms treaty that would sacrifice SDI. But Reagan's ideological mentor and frequent ally William F. Buckley led a campaign in *National Review* against Senate ratification of the treaty. "He [Reagan] disappointed me on the INF treaty," Buckley said. "I simply couldn't understand his enthusiasm for a treaty that minimized the number of weapons but wasn't tied into the larger question of whether Europe was really more safe or less safe than before."[109] Reagan looked up to Buckley and was distressed at his opposition. He called Buckley to the White House for a friendly conversation, but failed to convince him that the INF treaty was in the best interests of the United States.

Even with Buckley in opposition, the conservative movement was no match for the president in the public debate over the INF treaty. Reagan may have been at a loss for words when left to his own devices in a meeting with Gorbachev, but he had a shrewd understanding of the mind-set of conservatives and realized that many of them were unreconciled to an end to the Cold War. Unlike many of his ideological soulmates, Reagan genuinely feared a conflict with the Soviet Union. He literally viewed the INF treaty as a step away from Armageddon. On this issue, he was a servant of peace who performed effectively without a script. On December 3, in an Oval Office interview with network anchormen, Reagan said that some conservatives who were opposed to the treaty were "ignorant of the advances that had been made in verification" and that others accepted the inevitability of war. "I think that some of the people who are objecting the most and just refusing even to accede to the idea of ever getting any understanding, whether they realize it or not, those people basically down in their deepest thoughts have accepted that war is inevitable and that there must come to be a war between the superpowers."

Reagan's record of anticommunism was his strong suit in the INF treaty ratification debate that followed the summit. It was an article of faith both in Washington and Moscow that this record gave Reagan a unique advantage in deflecting the inevitable conservative opposition to any U.S.-Soviet arms control treaty. And such proved to be the case. A voter survey conducted during the second week of January 1988 found that six out of ten Americans (59 percent) believed that an INF treaty must be in the national interest if Reagan believed it to be "a good deal." The poll found a near consensus for the INF treaty, which was supported by 79 percent of Americans and opposed by only 17 percent.[110]*

Even so, ratification of the INF treaty was no cakewalk. A few days after this survey was taken, Hedrick Smith wrote in *The New York Times Magazine* that "right-wing groups—using sophisticated techniques deployed so successfully by the left-liberal coalition in its battle against the [Supreme Court] confirmation of Judge Robert H. Bork—have mounted a strong campaign against the INF treaty."[111] The techniques included 300,000 letters, 5,000 cassette recordings of an attack on the treaty by General Bernard Rogers, the former supreme commander of NATO, and newspaper advertising comparing Reagan to Neville Chamberlain, the gullible British prime minister who signed an accord with Hitler and predicted "peace in our time."[112] In the Senate, where the treaty underwent hundreds of hours of review by three committees, Republican conservatives led by Jesse Helms of North Carolina and Steven Symms of Idaho introduced amendments that would have required Soviet compliance with other treaties as a condition of the INF treaty becoming operable. They were known as "killer amendments" because they were unacceptable to the Soviets.

Meanwhile, liberal Democrats led by Joseph Biden of Delaware hoisted the administration on the petard of its own loose interpretation of the ABM treaty of 1972. Biden sought a treaty reservation that would have, in effect, written into law what Democrats regarded as the Senate's historic powers in treaty-making. He settled, after much negotiation with Shultz and Senate Republicans, for a condition banning future administrations from reinterpreting the INF treaty. It was the only major condition attached to the treaty.

While Shultz mollified the Senate and worked with Shevardnadze to

---

* The survey, conducted by Market Opinion Research as part of a series of polls on security issues done by a bipartisan consortium of polling firms, also found that 56 percent of Americans favored a nuclear-free world, compared to 41 percent who wanted the United States to maintain a nuclear deterrent.

resolve last-minute technical issues involving Soviet compliance, Reagan defused the opposition from the right. Helms disputed Reagan's claim that the treaty contained strong safeguards to assure compliance, saying instead that it was "an engraved invitation to cheat." Helms's most sensational accusation, which was supported by Perle, was that various drafting errors and loopholes would permit the Soviets to maintain a "secret force" of SS-20 missiles after the treaty was ratified. This was the sort of charge that might have rallied Republicans to oppose a treaty submitted by a Democratic president, but Reagan had far more standing with rank-and-file conservatives than either Helms or the New Right activists opposing the treaty. In the end, all of the "killer amendments" were rejected, with none of them receiving more than fifteen votes. The impending Moscow summit late in May 1988 gave a sense of urgency to the process. Reagan did not want the embarrassment of arriving in Moscow with the treaty unratified, and Senate leaders agreed with him. After choking off a Helms-led filibuster, the Senate approved the INF treaty by a 93-5 vote on May 27, two days before Reagan began his fourth summit with Gorbachev.

By this time, Gorbachev had become even more popular in the United States than he had been during the Washington summit. He had reinforced the good impression he had made in the West with a bold decision to withdraw Soviet forces from Afghanistan, a bloody quagmire that increasingly seemed the Soviet analogue of Vietnam. The decision had been a long time in the making. At the Geneva summit in 1985, Gorbachev had given a hint of his thinking when he made the point that the invasion had been undertaken by his predecessors. In December 1986 an aide to Gorbachev told a visiting delegation from a Dartmouth U.S.-Soviet discussion group, "We know we have to get out, but we don't know how to get out. Please help us." [113] On February 8, 1988, Gorbachev announced he would withdraw Soviet troops if agreement was reached in U.N.-sponsored peace talks between Afghanistan and Pakistan. On April 14 representatives of these two nations, the Soviet Union and the United States signed an accord in Geneva in which the Soviets agreed to begin pulling out their forces by May 15 and to complete the withdrawal by February 15, 1989.

While the progress on Afghanistan made the Soviets seem less threatening and gave a boost to the INF ratification campaign, it was a blow to U.S. conservatives who wanted to topple the Communist government of Afghanistan. On April 12, New Right leader Paul Weyrich visited the White House as head of a delegation of eight conservatives who were worried that Gorbachev was tricking Reagan into an accommodation beneficial only to the Soviets. Constantine Menges lectured Reagan on past Soviet perfidies, suggesting that the Afghan freedom fighters were being "set up as the intransigent forces" so that the Soviets could reenter the country.[114] Reagan would have none of it. The president, said Weyrich, "insisted that he simply knew more about what was going on" than the conservatives did.[115]

But despite the INF treaty and the progress on Afghanistan, plenty of differences remained between the superpowers, and it was evident well before the Moscow summit that there would be no strategic arms treaty for Reagan and Gorbachev to sign. Although Nitze and his Soviet counterparts in the arms talks at Geneva put forth a number of innovative ideas, the fundamental differences between Reagan and Gorbachev over SDI were too great to bridge. Reagan realized this early in 1988. He told me in a February 25 interview (in which he also said that he took Gorbachev at his word about withdrawing from Afghanistan) that "the time is too limited" for U.S. and Soviet negotiators to complete work on a strategic arms treaty before the Moscow summit.[116] While Reagan still expressed hope that a strategic arms treaty could be signed before he left office, he must have realized by then that his differences with Gorbachev on this issue were insurmountable. In any case, he used the interview as an occasion to repeat his vow that he would not use SDI as "a bargaining chip." Without concessions from Reagan on restricting SDI, there would be none from Gorbachev on reducing the Soviet ICBM force. A U.S.-Soviet strategic arms accord would remain unfinished business when Reagan left office.

Gorbachev and Reagan signed two modest arms control agreements in Moscow, providing for advance notice of ballistic missile tests and establishing a technical procedure for verification. Neither side pretended that these accords were particularly important. What was important was that Reagan was for the first time visiting the land he had called "the evil empire" and doing business with Gorbachev, whom he now referred to as "my friend."[117] No one understood this better than Gorbachev. "I would like to say that realism is an important quality in President Reagan as a politician," Gorbachev said on the eve of Reagan's arrival in Moscow. "Who would have thought in the early eighties that it would be President Reagan who would sign with us the first nuclear-arms reduction agreement in history?"[118]

Who indeed? The Moscow summit symbolized that the United States and the Soviet Union were finally emerging from the Cold War. As *The*

Washington Post expressed it editorially on the day the summit opened, Reagan's visit meant that "there will be few Americans left who refuse to lend Moscow at least some legitimacy, some psychological parity in their minds. Probably no one else—no, not Richard Nixon, who was himself in Moscow 14 years ago—could carry this sort of heavy symbolic baggage. No one else so well represents the American temper, with its provincial tinge and its ingrained skepticism but also with its hope and openness. The latter quality is, moreover, not the new and little-tried Soviet glasnost but the old authentic American openness— the right stuff." [119]

Reagan had more in mind in Moscow, however, than simply showing up. He saw a summit on Soviet soil as a unique opportunity to make the case for democracy and freedom. On human rights, Reagan had traveled as far as the Nixon policy of "quiet diplomacy" could take him. He wanted to do more. He had muted his human rights appeal at Geneva, but at Reykjavik had brought Gorbachev a list of 1,200 Soviet Jews who sought to emigrate. In Washington he had given Gorbachev other lists of Soviet dissidents and members of separated families who wanted to rejoin their relatives in the United States. In Moscow he presented Gorbachev with a list of fourteen specific human rights cases on which the United States sought action. Gorbachev became testy about it. When asked if he would act on the U.S. requests, Gorbachev replied, "There are too many lists." [120]

Reagan served notice even before he arrived that he intended to make human rights issues a focus of the Moscow summit. Speaking in Helsinki on May 27, Reagan praised the human rights accords signed there thirteen years earlier by thirty-five nations, including the Soviet Union and the United States. Reagan had been a critic of the accords when President Ford signed them. Now, however, he said that the accords had succeeded in setting "new standards of conduct" in human rights. Reagan's speech in Finlandia Hall was carefully and deliberately balanced: he praised Gorbachev for extending human rights in the Soviet Union while also saying that much more needed to be done.

Reagan particularly wanted to dramatize the plight of Soviet Jews. At the suggestion of Nancy Reagan he proposed to begin the summit by visiting the home of a well-known "refusenik" family, Yuri and Tanya Zieman. Their twelve-year-old daughter Vera was a talented pianist known as "Moscow's Orphan Annie" because of her red hair. In a letter to Reagan she had written, "Unlike Annie I have a family, and it is about its fate that I want to tell you." [121] The Reagans hoped to get the Ziemans out, and Nancy Reagan thought the event would "spice up" the summit. But it was too much spice for the Soviets. Shevardnadze's deputy, Alexander Bessmertnykh, warned Colin Powell the Ziemans would never be allowed to emigrate if Reagan insisted on visiting them.[122] Powell passed this message to the Reagans, who reluctantly abandoned the idea. Overriding the concern of the Secret Service, they opted instead for a walk on the Arbat, a famous Moscow pedestrian mall lined with artisans' shops and small cafés.

On May 29, 1988, the Arbat was packed with a friendly crowd of Sunday strollers. When word passed that the Reagans were in their midst, the crowd surged forward, wanting to get a glimpse of the president. Suddenly, the Arbat was transformed into a panicked scene in which the KGB formed a flying wedge and charged the crowd, hurling people aside and pounding on them with their fists. U.S. reporters (including me) and cameramen, who had sometimes complained about the far milder tactics of the Secret Service, were astounded by the rough-handed treatment. So was Reagan, who muttered that the Soviet Union "is still a police state." [123] That night he wrote in his diary: "It was amazing how quickly the street was jammed curb to curb with people—warm friendly people who couldn't have been more affectionate. In addition to our Secret Service, the KGB was on hand, and I've never seen such brutal manhandling as they did on their own people who were in no way getting out of hand." [124]

When Gorbachev was in Washington, the Russians had been surprised at his popularity in the U.S. capital. Now they were surprised at the welcome given Reagan in Moscow. Everywhere his motorcade went, crowds lined the streets to cheer him. "The speeches he [Reagan] delivered to the students . . . and to the Soviet writers and intellectuals were perhaps his most spectacular performances and touched the deepest chords of the Russian psyche," wrote Gorbachev's biographers. "The Russians loved him." [125] They quoted a Muscovite as saying, "I'm not religious, but I was delighted to hear him end his speeches by saying 'God bless you.' We never heard it said before on television." [126]

Few moments of Reagan's Moscow performances had been left to chance. Except for the melee on the Arbat, an impromptu visit to Gorbachev's dacha and the last of the four Reagan-Gorbachev meetings, every scene of the summit had been carefully choreographed. The principal producers were White House communications director Thomas Griscom and Colin Powell, who headed a summit planning group that three months in advance reviewed the themes and purposes of every speech Reagan would give in Moscow. Their aim was a production that Moscow and the world would find "coherent and convincing." [127] To this end, the Reagan script was crafted by Tony Dolan, the veteran Cold Warrior who headed the White House speechwriters, and dotted with Russian literary allusions supplied by U.S. Ambassador Jack Matlock and James Billington, the librarian of Congress and a historian of Russian culture. Reagan rehearsed his message in a series of domestic speeches. The themes of these speeches were tested for their acceptance by Americans in an out-of-town tryout of Reagan's before a "focus group" assembled by pollster Richard Wirthlin in Philadelphia.

For Reagan, it was the role of a lifetime. "In the movie business, actors often get what we call typecast," he told artistic and cultural leaders in Moscow in an address composed by White House speechwriter Clark Judge. "The studios come to think of you as playing certain kinds of roles . . . and no matter how hard you try, you just can't get them to think of you in any other way. Well, politics is a little like that, too. So I've had a lot of time and reason to think about my role." He then quoted from the famous Soviet filmmaker Sergei Eisenstein: "The most important thing is to have the vision. The next is to grasp and hold it. You must see and feel what you are thinking. You must see it and grasp it." [128] What Reagan grasped, at least as a performer, was that he voiced the aspirations of Russians yearning to be free with as much conviction as he had voiced the aspirations of Americans. "Pretty soon, at least for me, it becomes harder and harder to force any member of humanity into a straitjacket, into some rigid form in which you all expect to fit," Reagan said. "As I see it, political leadership in a democracy requires seeing past the abstractions and embracing the vast diversity of humanity and doing it with humility, listening as best you can not just to those with high positions but to the cacophonous voices of ordinary people and trusting those millions of people, keeping out of their way. . . . And the word we have for this is freedom." [129]

Looking back on the Moscow odyssey after he returned home, Reagan would compare it to an epic film produced by Cecil B. DeMille and say he felt as though he had "dropped into a grand historical moment." [130] It was an epic framed in photo opportunities in the Kremlin and in Red Square, where Reagan and Gorbachev walked together and answered planted questions that were more carefully scripted than any Reagan speech. But these ceremonial appearances were overshadowed by Reagan's scenes with political and religious dissidents, artists, intellectuals and students. On May 30, Reagan visited the Danilov Monastery, a spiritual oasis of Orthodox religious in the heart of Moscow, and proclaimed his "hope for a new age of religious freedom in the Soviet Union." Then he spoke at Spaso House to ninety-six dissidents who had come from all corners of the Soviet empire to meet the American president.* The group included Yuri and Tanya Zieman. It also included Abe Stolar, who was born in Chicago and brought to the Soviet Union as a child by leftist parents in the 1930s and had been stuck there ever since. Stolar wanted to come home. When Reagan saw him, he stuck out his hand and said, "I've just spoken to Mikhail Gorbachev about you. I told him we came from the same state and were born at the same time." [131]

In his speech to the dissidents, Reagan declared that his human rights agenda in Moscow was freedom of religion, freedom of speech and freedom of travel for the Soviet people. "I've come to Moscow with this human rights agenda because . . . it is our belief that this is a moment of hope," Reagan said. "The new Soviet leaders appear to grasp the connection between certain freedoms and economic growth. The freedom to keep the fruits of one's own labor, for example, is a freedom that the present reforms seem to be enlarging. We hope that one freedom will lead to another and another; that the Soviet government will understand that it is the individual who is always the source of economic creativity, the inquiring mind that produces a technical breakthrough, the imagination that conceives of new products and markets; and that in order for the individual to create, he must have a sense of just that—his own individuality, his own self-worth. He must sense that others respect him and, yes, that his nation respects him—respects him enough to grant him all his human rights." Near the conclusion of his speech, Reagan quoted the poet Aleksander Pushkin: "It's time, my friend, it's time."

The premier performance of Reagan in his role as freedom's advocate occurred on May 31 when he stood beneath a gigantic white bust of Lenin at Moscow State University and addressed the students on the values of a free society. The speech, composed by White House speechwriter Josh Gilder and drawing on themes Reagan had used since his GE days, was a compelling defense of "the riot of experiment that is

---

* Spaso House, where the Reagans stayed on the visit to Moscow, is the U.S. ambassador's residence and therefore sovereign American territory. The Soviets, after delicate negotiations, agreed to draw a distinction between Reagan's meeting with dissidents at Spaso House and his proposed visit to the Ziemans'. But Reagan did not muzzle his human rights views in any of his meetings—he freely expressed them in his speeches everywhere and in his meetings with Gorbachev.

the free market" and the virtues of political and economic competition. "Freedom is the right to question and change the established way of doing things," Reagan said. "It is the continuing revolution of the marketplace. It is the understanding that allows us to recognize short-comings and seek solutions. It is the right to put forth an idea, scoffed at by the experts, and watch it catch fire among the people. It is the right to dream—to follow your dream or stick to your conscience, even if you're the only one in a sea of doubters." Then, as the students listened raptly, Reagan shared with them an idealized view of U.S. history, explaining that "Americans seek always to make friends of old antagonists," as they had done with the British after the Revolutionary War, with themselves after the Civil War and with the Germans and Japanese after World War II. Now, he suggested, it was time for Americans and the citizens of the Soviet Union to become friends:

> Your generation is living in one of the most exciting, hopeful times in Soviet history. It is a time when the first breath of freedom stirs the air and the heart beats to the accelerated rhythm of hope, when the accumulated spiritual energies of a long silence yearn to break free. . . .
> We do not know what the conclusion will be of this journey, but we're hopeful that the promise of reform will be fulfilled. In this Moscow spring, this May 1988, we may be allowed that hope: that freedom, like the fresh green sapling planted over Tolstoy's grave, will blossom forth at last in the rich fertile soil of your people and culture. We may be allowed to hope that the marvelous sound of a new openness will keep rising, ringing through, leading to a new world of reconciliation, friendship and peace.

Compared to these speeches, three of Reagan's four meetings with Gorbachev were pale and largely ceremonial exchanges. Reagan was more selective in the jokes he told than he had been in Washington and generally careful to stay within the boundaries of his script. Gorbachev, in turn, was more patient and relaxed than at previous summits, treating Reagan as if he were a respected and near-retired elder statesman. When a tired Reagan seemed bewildered by the questions of reporters at one photo opportunity, Gorbachev protectively ended the questioning. And Gorbachev also listened carefully to the message of peace that Reagan had brought with him to Moscow. "Somebody asked the president whether he still considered the Soviet Union to be an evil empire," Gorbachev said at a dinner speech. "He said no, and he said that within the walls of the Kremlin, next to the czar's gun, right in the heart of the evil empire. We take note of that. As the ancient Greeks said, 'Everything flows, everything changes. Everything is in a state of flux.' "[132]

But at their final business meeting of the summit on June 1, Gorbachev finally challenged Reagan as he had done at each of their previous three summits. The challenge was over the text of a joint communiqué that the leaders were to issue later in the day reviewing their exchanges on various issues. Gorbachev wanted it to include a statement he had given to Reagan at their first private meeting in Moscow three days earlier. The Gorbachev statement began by saying that the two leaders believed that no problem in the world should be resolved by military means and went on to describe "peaceful coexistence" as "a universal principle of international relations." It said that other mandatory standards for international relations were "equality of all states, noninterference in internal affairs and freedom of sociopolitical choice."

Reagan liked the tone of the statement and told this to Gorbachev. He added, however, that he wanted to see how it sounded to his advisers. They didn't like it. To George Shultz and Defense Secretary Frank Carlucci, the words "peaceful coexistence" smacked of Soviet propaganda campaigns during the heyday of the Cold War. The other points of Gorbachev's proposal seemed aimed at undermining the U.S. commitment to anticommunist guerrilla movements as well as the campaign for human rights. Powell thought Gorbachev's aim was to "trick him [Reagan] into a backdoor commitment" to halt assistance to rebel forces in Afghanistan.[133]

In place of the Gorbachev statement, Reagan's diplomatic team worked out a watered-down and inoffensive declaration that spoke of resolving conflicts on the basis of "mutual interest and concern." The Soviets had accepted the wording, and the joint communiqué had been printed and was ready for distribution when Reagan and his advisers sat down at a long table in the ornate St. Catherine's Hall in the Kremlin for the final session with Gorbachev. Midway through the meeting, Gorbachev's tone abruptly changed. He moved forward in his chair, reminding a U.S. participant of a prizefighter getting ready for a punch.

"Why is 'peaceful coexistence' a bad term?" Gorbachev asked. "Why are you against it? What are you against here?" he said, handing Reagan a single sheet of paper with the statement he had proposed three days earlier.[134] Then Gorbachev turned to Shultz and Carlucci across the table. "What about you, George? Frank? Why not this language?"[135]

Reagan was taken aback. He had typically paid little attention to the language of the joint statement, assuming that his advisers had settled any differences. Shultz thought the differences were settled. The meeting was already running overtime and an audience was waiting in another room for a ceremony where Reagan and Gorbachev would sign the ratification documents carrying out the INF accord. "This is no time to start writing the joint statement," Shultz said.[136] He and Powell suggested a short recess to talk with Reagan.

The president huddled with Shultz, Powell and Carlucci in a corner of the room, where his advisers repeated their objections. Reagan did not want to disappoint Gorbachev but said he would follow their advice. He then walked across the room and told Gorbachev, "No, we can't do it."[137]

"Well, Mr. President, I don't understand why you're not for peace," said Gorbachev.[138]

Reagan did not take the bait. Instead, he quietly repeated that he couldn't accept Gorbachev's language. Gorbachev fell silent for a moment, then brightened. "Mr. President, we had a great time," he said, and put his arm around Reagan.[139] Gorbachev's gambit had failed, but he had become used to Reagan's matching stubbornness. Without rancor, the two men then turned and walked together to the treaty ceremony, the final business of the summit.

Reagan departed for London on June 2 after a news conference at Spaso House in which he blamed human rights abuses in the Soviet Union on the "bureaucracy" and said there had been "a sizable improvement" under Gorbachev. Some of us who were there wondered if Reagan was backing away from the strong human rights stand he had taken. But he believed that Gorbachev had heard his message and would respond to it. Gorbachev had already freed more than three hundred persons on the lists that Reagan had given him. Within a few months, another one hundred dissidents would be allowed to emigrate, including many who had heard Reagan speak at Spaso House. The Ziemans and the Stolar family would be among those who got out. And tens of thousands of Jews would leave in the years to come in a mighty exodus to the United States and Israel after the Gorbachev government relaxed restrictions on emigration.

Speaking in Guildhall in London on June 3, Reagan celebrated the

Moscow summit as a turning point in East-West relations and declared that a "worldwide movement toward democracy" was ushering in "the hope of a new era in human history, and, hopefully, an era of peace and freedom for all." The speech echoed Reagan's prediction at Westminster six years earlier that "the tides of history were running in the cause of liberty." It also echoed the prediction of his friend Margaret Thatcher, whom Reagan described as "a voice that never sacrificed its anticommunist credentials" but had first sized up Gorbachev in 1984 as someone with whom the West could "do business." Thatcher responded admiringly, saying that the Moscow summit would "encourage the course of history for years to come." Reagan deserved much credit for his leadership of the alliance, she said, and for his confident attempt "to enlarge freedom the world over."

"God bless America," she concluded with quiet emotion, as if these familiar words had just occurred to her. The Guildhall audience burst into applause.

From uncertain beginnings, Reagan and Gorbachev had walked their long road together out of the darkness of the Cold War. After the summits in Geneva, Reykjavik, Washington and Moscow, they could glimpse the dawn of a restored relationship in which the United States and the Soviet Union would once again cooperate in international affairs. While both sides still possessed terrifying nuclear power, Gorbachev and Reagan had set back the doomsday clock. Their meetings marked the beginnings of an even brighter period in U.S.-Soviet relations that would be ushered in during the Bush administration when Gorbachev released the Soviet grip on Eastern Europe and allowed the Germans to tear down the Berlin Wall.

Reagan and Gorbachev never lost their appreciation of each other. They knew their nations had passed a turning point from which they could not turn back except at their mutual peril. On September 20, 1988, Gorbachev expressed his feelings in a long letter to Reagan and said in the concluding paragraph, "Our relationship is a dynamic stream and you and I are working together to widen it. A stream cannot be slowed down, it can only be blocked or diverted. But that would not be in our interests." [140]

They would exchange many more letters and meet again, although their formal summitry was at an end. They held one more meeting during the Reagan presidency, on Governors Island in New York on December 7, 1988, the day before Gorbachev told the United Nations that he would reduce Soviet military forces by half a million troops.* They met again on June 4, 1990, in San Francisco, where the United Nations was born. Gorbachev gave Reagan a bear hug, and they went off to talk together with their wives. The next day Gorbachev called upon George Shultz, who said he understood that the Soviet leader's meetings had gone well with President Bush in Washington. "Yes," Gorbachev said, "but Reagan was there when times were really tough."

Gorbachev and Reagan met for a seventh time on September 17, 1990, in Moscow. By this time Gorbachev was an embattled leader who was trying to cope with food shortages and challenges to his rule. Reagan was by now a fading celebrity, whose popularity had declined since leaving office. But neither of them would ever forget what they had done together.

"Who would have thought that the warmth of that fireplace in Geneva would melt the ice of the Cold War?" Reagan said.[143]

Toasting him, Gorbachev welcomed Reagan to the Soviet Union "as a man who did a lot to make relations with our country the way they are now."[144]

It may well have been Reagan's most important contribution of his presidency.

---

* During this meeting Gorbachev remarked on Reagan's love for horses, saying that he rode only in automobiles and didn't even know from which side to mount a horse. "The left, the left," said Reagan, and Gorbachev was convulsed with laughter.[141] But the meeting turned serious when George Bush, then the president-elect, broke in to say that he and the American people wanted to know if perestroika would succeed. "Jesus Christ himself could not tell you that," Gorbachev replied soberly.[142]

22

VISIONS
AND LEGACIES

We meant to change a nation, and instead we changed a world.

RONALD REAGAN,
January 11, 1989[1]

One of Ronald Reagan's fantasies as president was that he would take Mikhail Gorbachev on a tour of the United States so the Soviet leader could see how ordinary Americans lived. Reagan often talked about it. He imagined that he and Gorbachev would fly by helicopter over a working-class community, viewing a factory and its parking lot filled with cars and then circling over the pleasant neighborhood where the factory workers lived in homes "with lawns and backyards, perhaps with a second car or a boat in the driveway, not the concrete rabbit warrens I'd seen in Moscow." The helicopter would descend, and Reagan would invite Gorbachev to knock on doors and ask the residents "what they think of our system."[2] The workers would tell him how wonderful it was to live in America.

Reagan never ceased to marvel at his own country, which experience had taught him was a land of opportunity in which neither inherited wealth nor a prestigious education was prerequisite for success. Reagan's own parents had been too poor to own a home, let alone a second car or a boat, and Reagan believed himself to be a most typical American. He had the advantage over other politicians of never thinking himself special, despite all the special things that he had done. He accepted the presidency as his destiny, not his due, and viewed his extraordinary career as vindicating the promise of America. In his own eyes, Reagan was Everyman, or at least every American. He credited his success to a system in which "everyone can rise as high and as far as his ability will take him." [3]

Reagan held an innocent and unshakable belief in the myth of American exceptionalism. "Someone once said that the difference between an American and any other kind of person is that an American lives in anticipation of the future because he knows it will be a great place," Reagan said. [4] And so it was for Reagan. He welcomed the future, but it did not change him. He possessed, as George Will put it, a "talent for happiness." [5] He clung to his core beliefs, dressed and ate plainly, never put on airs and treated those around him with quiet courtesy. When he left the White House, he was as cheerful and unassuming as when he had arrived at Eureka College from Dixon nearly six decades earlier.

Reagan's naturalness was appreciated by ordinary Americans, and he knew it. That was what he had meant when he confided almost shyly on the eve of the 1980 election that Americans thought of him as "one of them" and said he had "never been able to detach myself or think that I, somehow, am apart from them." [6] This feeling of oneness was reflected in his sentimental vision of America. "To me our country is a living, breathing presence, unimpressed by what others say is impossible, proud of its own success, generous, yes, and naïve, sometimes wrong, never mean and always impatient to provide a better life for its people in a framework of a basic fairness and freedom," Reagan had said in announcing his presidential candidacy. [7] What George Bush dismissed as "the vision thing" was for Reagan the central purpose of the presidency. "With Reagan, the perfection of the pretense lies in the fact that he does not know he is pretending," Garry Wills has observed. "He believes the individualist myths that help him play his communal role. He is the sincerest claimant to a heritage that never existed, a perfect blend of an authentic America he grew up in and of that America's own fables about its past." [8]

Of all the myths in which Reagan believed, none was more fundamental to his vision and his message than the notion that Americans had taken control of their destiny without assistance from the central government. He imagined that the American nation had been carved from wilderness by pioneers unrestrained by the forces of nature or the power of the state. The tales he loved most as boy and man were stories of individualist heroes. Reagan never noticed that it was the government that had protected these frontier heroes, set aside land for homes and schools, built telegraph lines and underwritten construction of an intercontinental railway system. The individualist myths that formed the core of the Reagan vision ignored government's role in the building of the West, as Reagan ignored the beneficial role of the federal government in his own life. Reagan had been taught to be thankful, and he remained forever grateful to Franklin Roosevelt for rescuing his parents from poverty in the dark days of the Depression. But FDR, like the pioneers of old, was to Reagan a personal hero rather than the creator of the limited welfare state that was called the New Deal. He thought always in terms of individual deeds and individual leadership. America was "we" to Ronald Reagan, a "we" of heroic individuals, while government was always "they." He was one with the people but not with the remarkable system by which Americans govern themselves. Because he loved his country deeply without caring enough for its government, Reagan's vision was flawed and inevitably conflicted. And from his conflicted vision would flow a highly conflicted presidential legacy.

This conflicted vision was at the root of the ethical problems that plagued the Reagan presidency. Reagan thought so little of government that he did not think enough about it. When he was struggling to win the Republican presidential nomination in 1976, his supporters published a book of quotations listing Reagan's opinions on 155 topics. It contained thirteen entries on "government," including one of Reagan's favorite cliches: "Government does not solve problems; it subsidizes them." Ethics in government was not mentioned in any of the entries. When Reagan's campaign staff in 1980 issued a list of his positions on seventy issues from "agricultural subsidies" to "Taiwan," Reagan again had nothing to say about ethics in government. And he also had practically nothing to say on the subject while in the White House or afterward in his memoirs.

Reagan wrongly assumed that those who followed his banner necessarily had higher ethical standards than those who spent their lives in government service, which he viewed as remote from the lives of the people. Reagan did not think of government as his career even after serving eight years as governor of California and eight years as president, not to mention another six years devoted primarily to the pursuit of the presidency. Reagan was a salesman who could convince himself of almost anything. His most remarkable self-deception was his belief that he was not really a politician at all, but simply an actor on loan from Hollywood who had entered politics because he wanted to restrain the power of an increasingly intrusive government. "I was a citizen-politician, and it seemed the right thing for a citizen to do," he said in his farewell address.[9] While he valued the presidency, he emphasized that it was "an institution of which presidents are granted only temporary custody."[10]

Had Reagan cared more about governance, instead of simply setting the agenda for the government he led, he might have instructed his appointees in the famous maxim of Grover Cleveland that "a public office is a public trust." Had he seen government service as a noble calling, he might have been more sensitive to the damage that could be caused to it by those who used their office to advance or to enrich themselves. But since Reagan viewed government as an institution necessarily riddled with waste, fraud and abuse, it never occurred to him that some of his own appointees might be especially wasteful or fraudulent. Ethics in government, said James Baker, was not "a big thing" to Reagan. "I don't think it was something in the big picture," he said.[11]

The principal consequence of ethics in government not being "a big thing" was that ethical standards within the Reagan administration too often depended upon the personal standards of the officeholder. Except when under pressure from Congress or the media, and sometimes even then, Reagan allowed his appointees to make the determination of what was ethically appropriate. During Reagan's first term, White House Chief of Staff James Baker routinely recused himself from discussion of any oil or gas issue because of his own energy holdings and kept an arm's-length relationship with those seeking White House favors. Ed Meese, serving alongside Baker as presidential counsellor, was a sounding board for friends and Reagan supporters seeking government favors. Early in the administration Meese set a tone of favoritism by helping longtime personal friend E. Robert Wallach to obtain a government contract for a firm later known as Wedtech Corporation. As former Justice Department spokesman Terry Eastland subsequently observed of Meese, "He left his shirttail hanging out at such length that it was easy for those who wished him ill to try to pull him down."[12] Throughout his four years as White House counsellor and three as attorney general, Meese was blind to the impact of his carelessness on his reputation and the reputation of the administration that he served.

Because of his position as the nation's chief law enforcement official,

Meese was the Reagan administration's most visible symbol of ethical insensitivity. But there were many others. The Environmental Protection Agency under Anne Gorsuch Burford was rocked by charges of political favoritism and mismanagement. Rita Lavelle, head of EPA's waste management program, was convicted of lying to Congress and obstructing a congressional inquiry into the agency's handling of a toxic waste dump. She served three months of a six-month sentence. Deputy Secretary of Defense Paul Thayer resigned one day before the Securities and Exchange Commission charged him with passing insider trader information to friends, from which they made $3 million in profits. Thayer pled guilty to obstruction of justice and served nineteen months in prison. Thomas Reed, who had served in Reagan's gubernatorial cabinet and managed his reelection campaign in 1970, resigned from a key post on the National Security Council staff in 1983 after he too was accused of insider trading. Reed was acquitted and returned to private life.

What was probably the biggest domestic scandal of the Reagan administration occurred in the Department of Housing and Urban Development under Secretary Samuel Pierce, the only cabinet member to head a department throughout both Reagan terms. "During much of the 1980s, HUD was enveloped by influence peddling, favoritism, abuse, greed, fraud, embezzlement and theft," the House Government Operations Committee concluded unanimously after a protracted investigation. "In many housing programs, objective criteria gave way to political preference and cronyism, and favoritism supplanted fairness."[13] Two years after the end of the Reagan presidency, Pierce and other former HUD officials remain under investigation by independent counsel Arlin Adams. Reagan never once during his presidency visited the Department of Housing and Urban Development, an agency he considered a notorious example of unneeded government.

For each well-publicized scandal, there were many other less-noticed ones that reflected an ethical unconcern all too common in the Reagan administration. Guy Fiske resigned as deputy secretary of commerce after charges that he was discussing taking a job at the Communications Satellite Corporation while he was in charge of negotiating the sale of the department's weather satellites to the same company. Robert Nimmo, a former California legislator and friend of Meese, resigned as head of the Veterans Administration after a General Services Administration report accused him of misusing government transportation. C. McClain Haddow, the chief of staff of the Health and Human Services Department, resigned and pled guilty to conflict-of-interest charges after a federal grand jury indicted him for diverting $33,500 to his credit union account from a foundation that received $300,000 annually from HHS. These incidents were small in comparison to the Iran-contra diversion or the scandals at HUD. Taken together, however, they reflected a disturbing pattern that mocked Reagan's pledge to rid the government of waste, fraud and abuse.

Democrats largely failed in their periodic attempts to hold Reagan accountable for the ethical insensitivity so common in his administration. Partly, this was because Reagan's personal honesty could not be seriously questioned. And partly, it was because the critics overstated their case and often did not approach what they called the "sleaze" issue with clean hands. Congressman Tony Coelho of California, chairman of the Democratic congressional campaign committee in 1984 and a principal exponent of the "sleaze" theme, compiled fifty cases of misconduct by administration officials that lumped unproven charges of ethical misconduct with Meese's conflicts of interest and the EPA scandals. Coelho rose to the position of Democratic whip but resigned from Congress in 1989 after published reports of an unusual $100,000 junk bond investment arranged for him by a major Democratic contributor. His departure followed the resignation of House Speaker James Wright, an even less credible critic of Reagan administration ethical practices. Wright was forced to quit after a House ethics subcommittee reported that he had repeatedly broken House rules by accepting $145,000 in "gifts" from a business associate with direct interest in legislation. Reagan was by then out of office, but public concern about the probity and hypocrisy of Congress had long preceded the demise of Wright and Coelho. Because a majority of Americans trusted Reagan more than they trusted Congress, the Democrats lacked political credibility in propounding the sleaze issue. Reagan also curiously benefited from the perception that he was not minding the executive store and therefore was not responsible for the ethical lapses of his subordinates. The message of the polls during the Reagan years was that few Americans blamed the president for ethical embarrassments within his administration, except when Meese was involved. And even Americans who found the administration's ethical standards deficient were apt to be more suspicious of corruption in Congress than in the executive branch.

Terry Eastland, a thoughtful conservative who served from 1983 to 1988 in the Justice Department, contends persuasively that the Reagan administration never mastered the "new ethics environment" created by a combination of post-Watergate distrust of the presidency, media aggressiveness and the Ethics in Government Act of 1978.* This law was the offshoot of an attempt by President Carter to "restore the confidence of the American people in their own government." [16] To accomplish this goal Carter laid down rigorous conflict-of-interest guidelines for the top two thousand political appointees in government, most of which were incorporated in the 1978 law that Congress passed at his request. The Ethics in Government Act revolutionized the rules of public service in Washington by requiring extensive financial disclosure, divestiture of assets that could create conflicts of interest and restrictions on post-government employment.

It was because of this law that Attorney General William French Smith returned a $50,000 severance payment he had received from a steel company in which he had served as a member of the board of directors. It was because of this law that Michael Deaver and Lyn Nofziger were investigated and prosecuted by independent counsels (special prosecutors) for lobbying their former employers after they left the White House. And it was because of this law that reporters and public interest groups had at their disposal extensive financial disclosure information that enabled them to pursue their investigations.

Critics of the Ethics in Government Act sometimes argued that it was too strict and deprived the government of competent people who could not afford to put their assets into a blind trust or were, for perfectly good reasons, unwilling to make total disclosure of their financial affairs. But the law had been in effect for more than two years when Reagan took office, and the Reagan team should have been aware of the difficulties it had caused its principal sponsor, Jimmy Carter. Although Carter, like Reagan, was widely viewed as incorruptible, several of his prominent appointees found the "new ethics environment" inhospitable. Carter's longtime friend and political bankroller Bert Lance had been forced to resign as management and budget director following a congressional investigation into his finances. Carter's chief of staff,

---

* Eastland, who had served as William French Smith's chief speechwriter before becoming Justice Department spokesman, was fired by Meese on May 13, 1988, apparently because Meese believed he needed a more aggressive defense of his conduct in the wake of the resignations of top department officials. Eastland, who was respected by both the conservative community and the media, disclosed the firing in a letter in which he said he had defended Meese "to the best of my ability." [14] Meese told me later he had no question about Eastland's loyalty but had decided his spokesman was "burned out," [15] a description that applied to many people at Justice in those days and perhaps to Meese himself. My own view is that Meese had become uncomfortable with Eastland because he knew that Eastland was disturbed by the attorney general's favoritism to Wallach.

Hamilton Jordan, and a top campaign aide, Tim Kraft, had been investigated and cleared by special prosecutors of charges they had used cocaine. These were not charges that would have been pursued by the Justice Department in the pre-Watergate years. But they were a sign of the times that Reagan ignored. As Eastland observed, Reagan had "no strategy for coping with the new environment."[17]

Because Reagan lacked a strategy, his vaunted White House public relations machinery functioned ineffectively in responding to allegations of misconduct. Since Reagan had never followed Carter's example of promulgating a standard of what he expected from his appointees, White House officials were forced to deal with charges of wrongdoing on a case-by-case basis. They were often defensive, which had the effect of making the administration's ethics-in-government record seem even worse than it was. In fact, a majority of those accused of ethical misconduct in the Reagan administration were cleared of any legal wrongdoing. On May 25, 1987, more than two years after he was indicted and resigned his post as labor secretary, Raymond Donovan and seven other executives in his New Jersey construction company were acquitted of charges of fraud and grand larceny after an eight-month trial. (Turning to the chief prosecutor, Donovan asked angrily, "Which office do I go to to get my reputation back?")[18] Nofziger was convicted of illegal lobbying, but his conviction was reversed on appeal. The investigation into Deaver's activities resulted in a conviction, but for perjury, lying to a congressional committee, rather than for illegal lobbying. He did not receive a jail sentence. The allegations against Deaver and Nofziger involved activities in which they had engaged after leaving the White House, not while working for the Reagan administration.

The acquittal of Donovan inspired Reagan to issue a statement describing his former labor secretary as "a man of integrity"[19] in whom he had never lost confidence. It also reconfirmed Reagan's belief that accusations of ethical impropriety raised against his appointees were largely the product of partisanship. In this view Reagan much resembled Harry Truman, the last Democrat for whom he had voted in a presidential election. Even after prominent members of his administration had been convicted, Truman dismissed Republican accusations of corruption as "phony." Truman biographer Robert Donovan observed that "Truman angrily regarded attacks on any of his subordinates as attacks upon himself, which may have been true as far as it went, yet such a response was not a satisfactory one to allegations raised against individual officials."[20]

Robert Donovan's comment would apply with equal validity to Reagan. When I asked Reagan in 1988 about the multiplicity of scandals in his administration, he responded, "I have a feeling that there's a certain amount of politics involved in all of this and I have a feeling that I'm really the target they would like to get at, and they are doing it by going after these other people."[21] Or as Truman put it more colorfully, his critics had made a "fraudulent build-up of flyspecks on our Washington window into a big blot or mess."[22]

Reagan's belief that attacks on his subordinates were really disguised attacks on him did not cause him to deal with all scandals equally. He was, to borrow Martin Anderson's phrase, "warmly ruthless" in allowing his White House staff to oust Burford at EPA. He also often acquiesced when any of his four chiefs of staff recommended the dismissal of a secondary official suspected of ethical irregularities. But he resisted all suggestions that he rid himself of Meese, who had been his chief of staff for six of the eight years Reagan was governor of California. Despite the worries of Vice President Bush that Meese's conduct would become a 1988 campaign issue and a call for Meese's resignation from his conservative hometown newspaper in San Diego, Reagan stood by his embattled attorney general until Meese was ready to leave.

Meese was under investigation during much of his seven and one-half years in the White House and Justice Department. In 1984 he was investigated for failing to report reimbursements on more than thirty trips as White House counsellor. In 1985 the Office of Government Ethics concluded he had violated conflict-of-interest rules. In 1987 Meese acknowledged that he had intervened in behalf of Wedtech in its efforts to win a defense contract but said that no wrongdoing was involved. Later that year independent prosecutor James C. McKay investigated Meese's efforts to help his friend Wallach secure U.S. government backing for an oil pipeline from Iraq to Jordan. Morale at Justice plummeted. Graffiti appeared on walls denouncing Meese as a "pig" and a "crook." On March 29, 1988, the Justice Department was rocked by the resignation of Deputy Attorney General Arnold Burns and William Weld, the assistant attorney general who headed the criminal division.

Burns and Weld did not fit the mold of the partisan critics who had long disparaged Meese. By early 1988 many Democrats had muted their criticisms of the attorney general, perhaps in the hope that Meese would cling to office and become a campaign issue later in the year. Burns was a conservative Republican and a respected former prosecutor. Weld was a patrician Republican, who in 1990 would be elected the governor of Massachusetts. Both of them quit in disgust at the extent of Meese's involvement with Wallach in the proposed Iraq-Jordan pipeline, although Burns agreed to stay on for another four weeks while a search was conducted for a replacement. On April 22, the day before Burns formally left Justice, he and Weld went to the White House at the request of Howard Baker to explain their reasons for leaving to Reagan and Bush.

Their forty-minute meeting with the president and vice president, also attended by Baker and White House counsel A. B. Culvahouse, was one of the most revealing in the Reagan presidency. Burns was both blunt and theatrical, saying that he remained a Reagan supporter and would do anything the president wanted him to do "including going up and down the halls of the White House with a broom in my behind"[23]—anything, that is, except remain at the Justice Department. Burns had warned Meese a year earlier that his relationship with Wallach gave the impression of a conflict of interest. Meese had ignored him, and the conflicts had grown worse. Burns said he liked Meese but thought that he had been "hornswoggled and bamboozled" by Wallach (who would later be convicted for his role in the Wedtech scandal). Burns added solemnly that "the temple of justice" had been besmirched by Meese's conduct.[24]

Reagan laughed when Burns made his crack about putting a broom up his behind, but said little as Burns explained his reasons for leaving. The president's face was ashen. Bush twice interrupted to ask questions of Burns. When he inquired about morale at the Justice Department, Burns told him it was at its nadir, the lowest "probably since the founding of the republic."[25]

By the time Weld spoke, in a less animated presentation, Reagan was fading. Two of the participants in the meeting told me that the president nodded off while Weld was speaking to him. And what Weld had to say was important. He told Reagan that if it were left to him he would seek an indictment of Meese, probably the first time in history that a political appointee who headed the Justice Department's criminal division told a president that his attorney general should be prosecuted. Reagan did not respond. Immediately after his meeting with Burns and Weld, he met with Meese, who blandly denied that his effectiveness had been impaired in any way by the continuing investigation and said he had done nothing wrong. Reagan believed him. The following day he gave Meese a vote of confidence and made it clear to Howard Baker that, short of an indictment, he would not ask Meese to resign. There was no indictment. After fourteen months of investigation, McKay concluded on July 5, 1988, that Meese had "probably violated the criminal law" on four occasions but said he had decided against prosecuting him because "there is no evidence that Mr. Meese acted from motivation for personal gain."[26] Meese responded to this news on the same day by declaring himself "completely vindicated."[27] Much to the relief of Bush, the attorney general also resigned. In 1989, a report by the Justice Department's Office of Professional Responsibility said that Meese had engaged in "conduct which should not be tolerated of any government employee, especially not the attorney general."[28]

Meese's ethical problems aside, the Justice Department in the Reagan years succeeded in carrying out Reagan's mandate of changing the federal judiciary in a direction that would "more heavily weigh society's interest in the punishment of criminals"[29] and "interpret the laws, not make them."[30] Much of this was the work of Reagan's first attorney general, William French Smith, although it continued largely unabated under Meese. If Reagan is judged by the standard of his campaign promises, he was more successful in judicial selection than in any other area of domestic governance. While he lost a stormy battle to put Judge Robert H. Bork on the Supreme Court, Reagan won the war to remake the federal judiciary and, to a large degree, the high court itself.

Because Reagan served two terms in an era of one-term presidencies, he was able to appoint more federal judges than any president in history and a higher percentage of the judiciary than any president except Franklin Roosevelt. Overall, Reagan named 78 appeals court judges and 290 district court judges who were confirmed by the Senate, slightly more than half of the federal judiciary. But most conservatives would probably agree with Terry Eastland that "Reagan's success lies not simply in quantity but quality" and that Reagan attained his goal of selecting judges who favor "judicial restraint."[31] Despite some well-publicized exceptions, including five judicial nominations rejected by the Senate and several others that were withdrawn, Reagan also tended to appoint highly qualified judges. Political scientist Sheldon Goldman, a leading authority on Reagan's judicial appointments, has noted that the qualifications of Reagan's federal judges as measured by the American Bar Association (ABA) stand up well when compared to the qualifications of judges appointed by his four presidential predecessors.*

* The ABA's highest rating is "exceptionally well qualified," a rating reserved for only a handful of judges. Reagan's record in naming judges in this category ranked slightly ahead of Carter's and slightly below Nixon's. But if judges in the second category, "well qualified," are included, Reagan ranked above Carter, Ford, Nixon and Johnson. All told, 157 Reagan judges (54 percent) received

Reagan may have fallen asleep when Weld was telling him about Meese's misdeeds, but he was alert to his opportunity to change the composition of the federal judiciary. In this, he resembled his onetime hero FDR more than any other president. "Like Franklin Roosevelt, Ronald Reagan saw the federal judiciary as crucial to achieving a major part of his presidential agenda," Goldman observed.[32] One reason for this may have been that Reagan, like Roosevelt but unlike any of the six presidents who served between them, had a big-state governor's background. While Reagan overall had a good record in naming qualified judges as governor, several of his appointments had been controversial. Reagan himself had been bitterly disappointed when the judge he had named to head the California Supreme Court wrote the decision striking down the state's capital punishment statute after Reagan had left the governor's office.[33] Smith and Meese were keenly aware of Reagan's feelings about judicial selection and shared his determination to find judges who would take a conservative view of the law.

Their instrument for accomplishing this purpose was the new Office of Legal Policy (OLP) that Smith established in the Justice Department to organize judicial selection. Eastland has described how it worked. "OLP cast its net far and wide, past the country club lawyers that populate the Republican Party to include law professors and others who have actually thought about the law. OLP began at the beginning, with a candidate's name and résumé, and then went to work, collecting every piece of published writing by the person as well as interviewing by telephone those who know the candidate both professionally and personally."[34] In a break with precedent, leading judicial candidates were brought to Washington for detailed interviews designed to elicit their judicial philosophy. According to both Goldman and Eastland, however, these interviews stopped short of "litmus test" questions; prospective judges were not asked their personal or political views on abortion, the death penalty or anything else. But the process produced conservative judges. Smith also saw to it that the Reagan administration had more control of the political selection process by asking senators to provide three to five names for every homestate judicial vacancy instead

---

the ABA's two highest ratings. Reagan also named a higher percentage of women and Hispanics to the bench than any president except Carter and a higher percentage of Catholics than any president except Johnson, but a lower percentage of blacks than any of these presidents. Reagan also created diversity of another kind, by naming fewer judges from Ivy League backgrounds than any president and more who came from public educational institutions than any president except Carter.

of the one they had previously submitted. Powerful senators could still influence the process, but it was much more under executive control than in previous administrations.

While public attention was focused on Reagan's Supreme Court appointments, his Justice Department was systematically changing the face of the federal judiciary. It was for this reason, more than any other, that Goldman concluded that Reagan will be seen as having had the greatest influence on the American judiciary and law since Franklin Roosevelt, leaving "a judicial legacy [that] will be with us well into the next century." [35]

Reagan also changed the Supreme Court, although not as much as the fervent activists of the New Right would have liked. He appointed the first woman to the high court, Sandra Day O'Connor, fulfilling a pledge he had made during a low point of his 1980 presidential campaign. Reagan's campaign had gone "flat," as Stu Spencer put it in mid-October.[36] On October 14, for the only time in the campaign, pollster Richard Wirthlin's trackings showed Carter marginally ahead. So Reagan's campaign strategists rummaged about for a new issue and came up with the idea of putting a woman on the Supreme Court. At a news conference in Los Angeles on October 14, Reagan promised that he would name a woman to "one of the first Supreme Court vacancies in my administration."

This promise gave Reagan a lot of running room, but he chose not to take advantage of it. In February 1981, Justice Potter Stewart told his old friend George Bush that he intended to leave at the end of the term. When Smith, Meese and Mike Deaver discussed Stewart's impending retirement with Reagan, the president reminded them of his campaign promise. As Deaver remembers it, his instruction was to "find a woman who was qualified and come back and discuss it if that wasn't possible." [37] Reagan's desire to appoint a woman to the first high court vacancy rather than to "one of the first" openings effectively ruled out Antonin Scalia and Bork, the favorite choices at Justice and of conservative intellectuals. They were nonetheless on the first list of twenty names, twelve of them women, that Smith compiled for the prospective Stewart vacancy. When it became clear to Smith that Reagan was intent on putting a woman on the court, he narrowed the list to four women, including O'Connor, an Arizona appeals court judge and former state senator.

O'Connor had other things going for her besides gender. At fifty-one, she was young enough to have many years of service on the court.

She also had the support of Smith, of two influential fellow Stanford Law School alumni—Justice William Rehnquist and William Baxter, then head of the Justice Department's antitrust section—and of Senators Barry Goldwater and Paul Laxalt. And she made a good impression on Reagan, who was "charmed" by her and quickly convinced that she was the right person for the job.[38] He never interviewed anyone else. Reagan nominated O'Connor on July 7, 1981, six days after the interview. She was quickly confirmed by the Senate over the opposition of Moral Majority president Jerry Falwell, New Right leader Richard Viguerie and the National Right to Life Committee, which objected to O'Connor's co-sponsorship as state senator of legislation that made "all medically acceptable family-planning methods and information" available to anyone.*

Reagan also exploited his opportunity to remake the court when Chief Justice Warren Burger resigned in 1986. On Meese's advice, he elevated the court's most conservative member, Justice William Rehnquist, to chief justice and named Scalia to the vacancy. Long before Burger stepped down, Meese had directed Assistant Attorney General William Bradford Reynolds to prepare a list of potential nominees in case another high court vacancy occurred. Reynolds had assigned a score of Justice Department officials to research the backgrounds of prospective appointees. (Eastland was given the task of researching Scalia.) All of the candidates' writings were assembled and studied, with Bork and Scalia emerging as the top two of twenty candidates. "Neither was given top billing, for the simple reason that everyone was agreed both would make excellent judges," Eastland said.[40]

Age and politics resolved the issue in favor of Scalia. At fifty, he was eight years younger than Bork. He was also an Italian-American, and no one of Italian ancestry had ever been appointed to the court. This was an obvious advantage in an election year, and it freed the Justice Department to focus on the more difficult task of defending Rehnquist's record. Senate liberals led by Ted Kennedy mounted a strong campaign to discredit the conservative Rehnquist. Though his nomination was never seriously in doubt, the thirty-three votes against Rehnquist in the Senate were the most votes cast against any justice or chief justice confirmed in this century. Scalia, whose legal views were considered indistinguishable from Bork's by the militant conservatives at Justice, was confirmed unanimously.

---

* Falwell said that all "good Christians" should be concerned about the O'Connor appointment. Goldwater responded, "Every good Christian ought to kick Falwell right in the ass."[39]

But the Reagan administration paid the price for the easy confirmation of Scalia after Justice Lewis Powell's resignation on June 26, 1987, gave Reagan the opportunity to fill a third vacancy on the court. Democratic recapture of the Senate in 1986 had changed the political balance of power, and the Democrats were in control of the confirmation process. And Powell's resignation came at a time when the White House was struggling to control the damage being inflicted by congressional hearings into the Iran-contra affair and Meese was being investigated by independent prosecutor McKay. Despite these liabilities, it is likely that the administration could have won approval for the conservative justice of its choice if Bork had been named to the court in 1986 and Scalia had been available to fill the Powell vacancy. Italian-Americans are a potent political constituency in Ted Kennedy's home state of Massachusetts and many other states. It is doubtful if Kennedy, who had praised Scalia and voted for him, would have mounted a campaign against his confirmation or succeeded in such an effort if he had tried. Bork, however, was a vulnerable political target.

No one disputed Bork's brilliance or legal qualifications, which included an "exceptionally well qualified" rating from the ABA. But Bork's provocative writings over nearly a quarter century and his decisions as a judge on the U.S. Court of Appeals for the District of Columbia (of which Scalia had also been a member) since 1982 had made him a lightning rod for liberal opposition. Civil rights groups saw Bork as the symbol of an administration and a Justice Department that were trying to turn the clock back on affirmative action. And Bork's repeated criticisms of *Griswold v. Connecticut,* a 1965 decision in which the Supreme Court had struck down a law prohibiting use of contraceptives and declared that Americans enjoy a right of privacy "unenumerated" in the Constitution, raised fears that he would tip the balance on the court against the 1973 Supreme Court decision in *Roe v. Wade,* which legalized abortion. Bork, reflecting a view held by Scalia and many other conservatives, considered *Roe* "an unconstitutional decision, a serious and wholly unjustifiable judicial usurpation of state legislative authority." [41]

Neither Reagan nor Meese anticipated the effective public relations campaign that would be waged to block Bork's confirmation. Neither did the usually politically astute White House Chief of Staff Howard Baker, although Baker typically would have preferred a less controversial nominee. Only one other justice in this century—a southern Republican nominated by President Herbert Hoover during the Depression

—had been rejected solely on political grounds.[42] In announcing the nomination of Bork on July 1, Reagan stressed Bork's formidable legal and scholarly credentials and said he "shares my view that judges' personal preferences and values should not be part of their constitutional interpretation." But Senator Kennedy, not Reagan, framed the context of the confirmation debate with a statement the same day contending that "Robert Bork's America is a land in which women would be forced into back alley abortions, blacks would sit at segregated lunch counters, rogue police could break down citizens' doors in midnight raids, school children could not be taught about evolution, writers and artists could be censored at the whim of government, and the doors of the federal courts would be shut on the fingers of millions of citizens for whom the judiciary is—and is often the only—protector of the individual rights that are the heart of democracy."[43]

Kennedy's statement, as Ethan Bronner observed in his authoritative and troubling account of the Bork confirmation battle, "shamelessly twisted Bork's world view"[44] and shattered the long-held belief that a Supreme Court nomination was above politics.* Ideology had played a role in the rejection of two Nixon appointees to the high court, but one of these nominees had been accused of conflicts of interest and the other possessed an undistinguished legal record and a segregationist background. The battle over Bork was different because it challenged his opinions, not his legal qualifications or personal integrity. In opposing his confirmation, Kennedy and Senate Judiciary Committee Chairman Joseph Biden of Delaware openly asserted the Senate's right to reject a nominee simply because it disagreed with him. This is a defensible position, but Bork's foes, as Bronner and others have observed, distorted his positions in order to assert it. Some of those engaged in the demonizing of Bork even maintained that he favored a return to the era of "separate but equal" treatment of the races, even though Bork had long defended the 1954 Supreme Court ruling striking down this segregationist doctrine.

Viewed in cold political terms, the campaign against Bork was masterful and the one waged in his behalf inept. Reagan had often succeeded as a politician by going over the heads of his opposition and appealing directly to the people. But in the battle for Bork's confirmation, it was the liberal opposition groups, led by the umbrella organi-

---

* Bronner, the Supreme Court correspondent for *The Boston Globe*, wrote a balanced and detailed book about the Bork confirmation fight, *Battle for Justice: How the Bork Nomination Shook America*, that accurately represents the views of the various combatants.

zation known as the Leadership Conference on Civil Rights, that made
the popular case. Bork was beaten in the court of public opinion long
before he was rejected by the Senate. By portraying Bork as a foe of
civil rights, his adversaries cost him the support of southern Democrats
crucial to his confirmation. The more accurate depiction of Bork as a
foe of abortion rights cost him support among women. And the skillful
use of television advertising by the liberal lobbying group known as
People for the American Way cast Bork as a right-wing ideologue opposed even to free speech. Particularly effective was an American Way
commercial narrated by Gregory Peck that asked Americans to urge
their senators to vote against the nomination "because if Robert Bork
wins a seat on the Supreme Court, it will be for life—his life and
yours." [45] Bronner concluded that Reagan's liberal adversaries
triumphed by using the sort of symbolism and simplicities at which
Reagan had long excelled. "They took Bork's own words and decisions
and pared away subtleties, complications and shadings," he wrote.
"What remained was neither lie nor truth. It was half-truth. Like the
half-truths of the Reagan years, it played well." [46]

And it played even better because administration officials lacked a
coherent strategy for obtaining Bork's confirmation. The White House
staff and Reagan described Bork as a moderate conservative who was a
facsimile of Lewis Powell. The Justice Department, which knew better,
openly advertised Bork's conservatism. Neither the White House nor
Justice sufficiently appreciated the degree to which the public was being
persuaded that Bork was a right-wing extremist. While Bork's foes were
launching their public relations campaign, Reagan took an unusually
long vacation of twenty-four days from mid-August through the first
week of September at his California ranch. He did not make any telephone calls to senators on behalf of Bork until September 30, when
most of them had made up their minds, and he did not call most
southern senators at all.

Finally, Bork proved unimpressive when he testified before the Senate Judiciary Committee for five days in mid-September. Bork was principled: he said at one point that he would be "disgraced in history" if
he answered questions one way and voted otherwise on the court—a
scruple that has not troubled some court appointees who have survived
the confirmation process. [47] But he came across as aloof and distant on
television, especially when a pro-Bork senator, Alan Simpson of Wyoming, asked him why he wanted to be a justice. Bork said it would be
"an intellectual feast just to be there and to read the briefs and discuss

things with counsel and discuss things with my colleagues." [48] A *Washington Post*–ABC News poll taken during and after Bork's five days of testimony showed that public opinion shifted against his nomination while he was appearing before the Judiciary Committee. The campaign on both sides continued for another month, but Bork was beyond rescue. On October 23, after three days of debate, the Senate rejected him by a vote of 58-42.

Conservatives viewed Bork's defeat as a tragedy, but the next attempt to fill the Powell vacancy had overtones of comic opera. After Bork went down, Reagan nominated Douglas H. Ginsburg, a forty-one-year-old former Harvard law professor who had served only a year on the U.S. Court of Appeals for the District of Columbia. Ginsburg had been assistant attorney general of the antitrust division at the Justice Department, where he was close to William Bradford Reynolds and shared his militant conservatism. Ginsburg was Reynolds' choice to fill the vacancy. Meese complied, and submitted Ginsburg's name to the White House, along with that of Anthony Kennedy, an appointee of President Ford to the Ninth Circuit Court of Appeals in California. Meese, officially neutral, told me at the time and afterward that he considered both judges to be acceptable, but it is clear that his real preference was Ginsburg.

Kennedy, however, was the preference of White House Chief of Staff Howard Baker and White House counsel A. B. Culvahouse, who realized that he was less controversial, possessed more judicial experience and would be far easier to confirm than Ginsburg. Ken Duberstein, then second in command on the White House staff, also wanted Kennedy because he knew that a prolonged Ginsburg confirmation battle which ended in defeat might give the Senate an excuse to deprive Reagan of filling the vacancy, leaving the decision to his successor. But administration conservatives were pro-Ginsburg, in part because of their belief that Kennedy was "a Ford man" while Ginsburg was one of their own. At Meese's urging, his predecessor William French Smith weighed in with a recommendation for Ginsburg. This may have been decisive, for Smith's views carried weight with Reagan.

Had Howard Baker operated in the directive style of his predecessors, Kennedy might have been the nominee. James Baker and Don Regan typically reviewed controversial appointments in private with Reagan before his decisions. Howard Baker operated in the more consultative style of the Senate, and he had promised Meese that he would be present for the final decision. He was a man of his word. Baker recommended Kennedy while Meese, although saying that Kennedy would also be acceptable, favored Ginsburg. Reagan decided on Ginsburg, apparently influenced by the fact that he was ten years younger and might have longer service on the court.

But the Ginsburg nomination quickly collapsed. The pro-life Right cooled to his nomination when it was learned that his wife, an obstetrician, had once performed abortions. Then it turned out that Ginsburg, during a period when he participated in developing the Justice Department's position on a Supreme Court case involving the First Amendment rights of cable television, had been an investor in a cable company. The Justice Department began a preliminary investigation into whether he had violated the law, an inquiry that was a prerequisite to appointment of an independent prosecutor. The decisive blow came when it was reported that Ginsburg had used marijuana, not only as a student but when he was a law professor at Harvard. Conservatives in the administration and the Senate were outraged. Ginsburg acknowledged the use of marijuana but said it had been a youthful mistake. William J. Bennett, the education secretary, after obtaining tacit approval from Reagan and Howard Baker, called Ginsburg and told him that he had no choice except to withdraw.[49] Ginsburg then quit. The fiasco of his nomination had lasted ten days and reflected badly on Meese and Reynolds, who had neglected the careful research that had typified the Justice Department's earlier judicial selections. The process also reflected poorly on the FBI. "Something was wrong with an FBI process unable to find what journalists said they were routinely told when making inquiries in and around Harvard," Eastland observed.[50] After Ginsburg withdrew, FBI Director William Sessions announced that the FBI would be more careful in investigating future presidential nominees.

But the quick collapse of the Ginsburg nomination was actually a blessing in disguise for Reagan. It left him with the straight-arrow Kennedy, whose mainstream conservative views much resembled those of Lewis Powell. Kennedy was a Roman Catholic who had never expressed his personal views on abortion in his writings. The 1987 *Almanac of the Federal Judiciary,* in describing the way lawyers viewed Judge Kennedy, said: "Courteous, stern on the bench, somewhat conservative, bright, well prepared, filled with nervous energy, asks many questions, good analytical mind, not afraid to break new ground, open minded good business lawyer, hard to peg, an enigma, tends to agonize over opinions."[51] The FBI inquiries in Kennedy's hometown of Sacramento, where he was the son of one of the state capital's best-known lobbyists, found he was widely admired. Senate liberals were overjoyed, figuring that Kennedy was the best Supreme Court appointment they were ever likely to get from the Reagan administration. Kennedy was nominated by Reagan on November 11 and unanimously confirmed by the Senate on February 3, 1988.

Reagan was pleased. While he always hated to lose any battle with Congress, he had taken the rejection of Bork and the embarrassment of Ginsburg in stride, in part because he had little personal connection with either man.[52] What Reagan had wanted to do was move the court in the direction of a more conservative construction of the Constitution, and he had certainly accomplished that. Kennedy proved more of a First Amendment civil libertarian than Bork would have been, as he demonstrated by his concurring opinion when the court ruled on June 21, 1989, that a Texas statute prohibiting flag desecration was unconstitutional and struck down similar laws in forty-eight states. The vote was 5-4, with Scalia joining in Justice William Brennan's majority opinion and O'Connor joining the dissent of Chief Justice Rehnquist. "It is poignant but fundamental that the flag protects those who hold it in contempt," Kennedy wrote.[53] Bork said subsequently that he thought that laws prohibiting flag desecration were constitutional. Had he been a member of the high court, the 5-4 split would have gone the other way.

Otherwise, Kennedy was as dependably conservative as Bork would have been. He took a dim view of abortion rights and the court, at least for the two years after Reagan's presidency, weakened *Roe* while stopping short of overturning it. This was not because of Kennedy but because of O'Connor, who was reluctant to provide the swing vote that would sweep away this abortion-rights precedent. If this bothered Reagan, he did not show it. He had asked O'Connor how she felt about abortion when he interviewed her in July 1981. She had replied that abortion was abhorrent to her but said she would not allow her personal views to influence her judicial decisions. This answer had been satisfactory to Reagan. He had an Everyman's view of the law and the Constitution and did not spend time reflecting on the proposition that personal views must inevitably influence judicial opinions. Reagan had meant what he said when he proclaimed his intention to choose justices who would interpret the laws, not make them. He did not share the view of those militant intellectuals, some of them ensconced at Justice, who sought to replace judicial activism of the Left with judicial activism of the Right.

Nor was Reagan as obsessive about anti-abortion legislation as he often seemed. Again his legacy on this issue was conflicted. Early in his California governorship he had signed a permissive abortion bill that has resulted in more than a million abortions. Afterward, he inaccurately blamed this outcome on doctors, saying that they had deliberately misinterpreted the law.* When Reagan subsequently ran for president, he won backing from pro-life forces by advocating a constitutional amendment that would have prohibited all abortions except when necessary to save the life of the mother. Reagan's stand was partly a product of political calculation, as was his tactic after he was elected of addressing the annual pro-life rally held in Washington by telephone so that he would not be seen with the leaders of the movement on the evening news. Pro-life activists attributed this to Deaver's image-consciousness, but Reagan continued the practice after Deaver had left the White House.

While I do not doubt Reagan's sincerity in advocating an anti-abortion amendment, he invested few political resources toward obtaining this goal and it was not a high priority of those close to him. None of his White House chiefs of staff wanted Reagan to become involved in the issue, and many of the Californians he brought with him to Washington also lacked pro-life zeal. Eastland remembers that Meese while at Justice expressed personal and policy views on abortion that would be regarded as "middle of the road." That is also my own recollection from California, where Meese's experience as a deputy district attorney had led him to believe that restrictive abortion laws encouraged the birth of unwanted children who were often abused and neglected. Lyn Nofziger, who had urged Reagan to sign the permissive abortion legislation in California, believed in a woman's right to have an abortion. Nancy Reagan avoided any comment on the issue but was widely believed to be sympathetic to the abortion-rights view. Reagan managed to keep the pro-life forces in his corner, but he was not an especially avid crusader for their cause.

---

* When the bill was being debated in the legislature, its opponents said that a provision allowing an abortion if a doctor determined that the mental health would be endangered by completion of a pregnancy would permit unrestricted abortions. This point was made directly to Reagan by the bill's opponents, including Roman Catholic Cardinal Francis McIntyre. But under pressure from Republican state legislators, Reagan signed the Therapeutic Abortion Act of 1967. When it soon became evident that the opponents had been right in saying that the new law would permit abortions for nearly every woman who sought one, Reagan blamed doctors, often singling out psychiatrists, for utilizing the "loophole" that authorized abortions to preserve the mother's mental health. A more extensive account of Reagan's role in dealing with this legislation appears in *Reagan*, pages 128–32.

Nor did Reagan devote much of his energies to other aspects of what was often called his "social agenda." Some of the items on this agenda, such as his call for a constitutional amendment to restore prayer in schools, were never more than throwaway lines intended to comfort the so-called Religious Right or some other element of the conservative constituency. Reagan was serious about reducing the scourge of drugs, and the efforts of his administration went well beyond Nancy Reagan's "just say no" campaign. The Justice Department under William French Smith involved the FBI in the fight against drugs, added five hundred Drug Enforcement Administration agents, established thirteen regional antidrug task forces and chalked up record numbers of drug seizures and convictions.* But the magnitude of the drug problem, especially in the inner cities of America, was at least as great when Reagan left office as when he entered it.

Meanwhile, the great social concerns of education and public health became back-burner issues for the Reagan administration. Reagan's antigovernment vision had no room for a federal Department of Education, which he had pledged to abolish if elected president. It was one of his silliest promises, and no serious attempt was made to keep it. (Instead of doing away with Education and the Department of Energy, as he also promised, Reagan eventually added another cabinet-level department by heeding the pleas of veterans groups and creating the Department of Veterans Affairs.) Under the guidance of Terrel H. Bell, a professional educator who was repeatedly badgered by administration conservatives, a commission named by the Department of Education did produce one of the most thoughtful documents to emerge from any government agency during the Reagan presidency, the 1983 report *A Nation at Risk: The Imperative for National Reform.* The report sparked a national drive for educational excellence and led to a ranking of states in various categories of educational achievement that provided a yardstick for improvement. Though Reagan praised the report, his interest in it was largely rhetorical.

On health issues, Reagan's presidency coincided with the emergence

---

* Except for Reagan, Smith had few fans at the White House or among Reagan's cadre of outside political advisers. He was widely viewed as a country-club lawyer who couldn't wait to return to Los Angeles. But the liberal legal analyst Steven Brill concluded in 1982 that "Smith has in his own quiet way become the most effective attorney general to serve since an equally unprepared Robert Kennedy was named to the post in 1960." [54] Brill rated Smith highly for his management of the Justice Department's "mega-bureaucracy," his independence from the White House when independence was required and the quality of his legal product. He also said that Smith's otherwise good record in judicial selection had been "marred by a wholesale neglect of black America." [55] Both the positive and negative evaluations have stood the test of time.

of the epidemic of acquired immune deficiency syndrome (AIDS). The AIDS virus was sexually transmitted, and transmitted also by transfusions of contaminated blood and by contaminated needles shared by IV drug abusers. The disease was inevitably fatal. Its victims, usually young adults, wasted away and died slow, painful deaths. By the end of Reagan's first term the Centers for Disease Control (CDC) had confirmed 3,700 AIDS deaths, most of them homosexual men in San Francisco, Los Angeles and New York. By the time Reagan left office, the CDC had confirmed 82,764 AIDS cases and 46,344 AIDS deaths.[56] The CDC physicians estimated that ten Americans were infected with the virus for every case that had been reported.

Reagan's response to this epidemic was halting and ineffective. In the critical years of 1984 and 1985, according to his White House physician, Brigadier General John Hutton, Reagan thought of AIDS as though "it was measles and it would go away."[57] What changed Reagan's view was the death on October 2, 1985, of his friend Rock Hudson. The actor had been a guest at a White House state dinner the previous August and Nancy Reagan had noticed that he had lost weight. When she inquired about his health, Hudson told her, "I caught some flu bug when I was visiting Israel. I'm feeling fine now."[58] But Hudson was not fine. His death focused the attention of Americans on AIDS and shook the Reagans. The president issued a statement of sympathy and praise for Hudson, saying that he would be remembered for his "dynamic impact on the film industry." The statement made no mention of AIDS, but Reagan went to Dr. Hutton and questioned him about the disease. Hutton gave a lengthy explanation. "I always thought the world would end in a flash, but this sounds like it's worse," Reagan said.[59]

Even with his new knowledge, however, Reagan was slow to join the battle against AIDS. Two weeks earlier, when a reporter noted that AIDS researchers at the National Cancer Institute were calling for a huge increase in research money to combat the new epidemic, Reagan had said that AIDS research was "a top priority."[60] But he did not mention AIDS in public again until February 5, 1986, when he told employees at the Department of Health and Human Services that "One of our highest public-health priorities is going to continue to be finding a cure for AIDS."[61] The same day, however, the Reagan budget proposed spending levels that would have cut funds for AIDS research. The Office of Management and Budget called the cut an "increase" because it was more than OMB had previously requested. But Congress appropriated more funds than the Reagan administration had requested, as it would again.

On February 5, Reagan also announced that he was asking the sur-geon general to prepare a major report on AIDS, saying, "We're going to focus on prevention."[62] The surgeon general was Dr. C. Everett Koop, a stern-visaged evangelical Christian who wore a Dutch sea cap-tain's beard and the traditional braided surgeon general's uniform. His appointment had been a small but sweet victory for the New Right and Senator Jesse Helms of North Carolina, who valued Koop less because he was a gifted and famous pediatric surgeon at Children's Hospital in Philadelphia than because he had in 1979 on his own initiative con-ducted a twenty-city lecture tour in which he equated abortion with euthanasia and compared it to the morality of the Nazi death camps. Koop had been opposed by liberals. Senator Ted Kennedy, fore-shadowing the sledgehammer rhetoric he would employ against Bork, deplored Koop's "cruel, outdated, and patronizing stereotypes" of women in society.[63] *The New York Times* in an editorial called Koop "Dr. Unqualified."[64] But Koop was confirmed by the Senate on a 68-24 vote and gradually won the respect of many who had opposed him. He faced the AIDS epidemic with the uncompromising honesty that was characteristic of his career.

The report that Koop issued on October 22, 1986, did not confuse AIDS with measles or other lesser diseases. Instead, Koop estimated that by the end of 1991, 179,000 Americans would die from AIDS and another 145,000 would require hospitalization. He warned Americans that AIDS could be controlled only by changes in personal behavior. At a press conference he described his remedy: "One, abstinence; two, monogamy; three, condoms." He also stressed that AIDS could not be contracted through casual contact and emphasized the need for educa-tion in the schools "at the lowest grade possible."[65]

Koop's report divided Reagan's conservative constituency. Those as-sociated with the Religious Right were generally accepting of it and with Koop's sympathetic attitude to AIDS victims. The first speech Koop gave after issuing his report was at Liberty University in Lynchburg, Virginia, at the invitation of its founder, Jerry Falwell. The more secular elements of the New Right, hostile to sex education and often to ho-mosexuals, were angered by Koop's report. Phyllis Schlafly, opposing Koop's suggestion to teach teenagers the dangers of unsafe sex, said his proposal amounted to "incredible, multimillion-dollar free publicity" for condom manufacturers, who "want to go into the schools and teach children how to engage in safe sodomy and safe fornication by the use of these contraceptives." This attitude found resonance within the Rea-gan administration, where Koop's critics included William Bennett,

Bell's successor as secretary of education; Gary Bauer, a Bennett aide who became the White House domestic policy adviser; and Patrick Buchanan, the White House director of communications. Buchanan had expressed a characteristic view in a sarcastic 1983 column he wrote before joining the White House staff: "The poor homosexuals. They have declared war on nature and now nature is exacting an awful retribution." [66]

These conservatives were comfortable with abstinence, but not with condoms. Their opposition frustrated Koop, who on a trip to San Francisco in early March of 1987 called upon Reagan to assume a role of leadership in dealing with the epidemic. Later that month a *Washington Post*–ABC News poll showed that two-thirds of Americans called AIDS the greatest health threat facing the nation. Reagan finally agreed, declaring on April 1 that AIDS was "public health enemy Number One." [67] But he remained reluctant to use his presidential bully pulpit to send a clear public message about the AIDS epidemic. The reluctance reflected Reagan's own old-fashionedness, reinforced by Bennett and Bauer. The president was sympathetic to AIDS victims and hopeful that medical science would find a cure, but he found it distasteful to make a speech advocating the use of condoms. He moved slowly on the issue, prodded by Nancy Reagan's pleas to speak out more forcefully against AIDS. At her request he finally agreed to deliver a speech at a fund-raising dinner for the American Foundation for AIDS Research. She thought the White House speechwriting department too reactionary for this task and brought in her own favorite speechwriter, Landon Parvin, to draft the address.

Parvin had left the White House at the end of 1983 to go into business for himself. When he was called in by Nancy Reagan to write the AIDS speech, he was surprised to find that the president had never discussed the subject with Koop. The surgeon general had been effectively walled off from the president by HHS assistant secretary Edward Brand and other conservatives, and neither Reagan nor Koop had scaled the wall. At Parvin's behest Nancy Reagan arranged for Koop to be present at a cabinet meeting attended by his superiors at HHS. Koop made what Parvin considered a "simple, forthright" [68] appeal to denounce the fears engendered by AIDS. But neither Bennett nor Bauer wanted the president to even mention contraceptives. And Bauer displayed an attitude toward AIDS victims that repelled Parvin. "Would you want to get into a hot tub [with people] with open sores over their bodies?" he said to Parvin when they were discussing what Reagan should say at the AIDS fund-raiser. [69]

Parvin nonetheless tried to write a straightforward speech that incorporated many of Koop's remarks about AIDS prevention. Almost every passage involved a struggle with the conservatives. "The speech was watered down," he said afterward. "Every time you'd say something strong, someone would have an objection to it." [70] Parvin's proposal to say that AIDS was not spread by food handling was struck. [71] Finally, in an attempt to say something specific and useful opposing prejudice against AIDS victims, Parvin invoked Nancy Reagan's name. "Look, this is the way she wants it," he said. [72] This tactic helped, but the final product was not satisfying to either the speechwriter or the conservatives who opposed candid talk by the president. Throughout the drafting process Reagan remained largely a bystander, who, as far as anyone could tell, preferred a platitudinous middle ground.

And that is the way the speech turned out. If Reagan had delivered it two or three years earlier, it would have been seen as forward-looking and might have had significant impact. By mid-1987, however, Reagan was only repeating public knowledge when he declared that "AIDS affects all of us." [73] Still, Parvin's invocation of Nancy Reagan had enabled him to retain a softened but still significant passage that stressed the unlikelihood of casual transmission of AIDS. "There's no reason for those who carry the AIDS virus to wear a scarlet A," Reagan said. "We're still learning about how AIDS is transmitted, but experts tell us you don't get it from telephones or swimming pools or drinking fountains. You don't get it from shaking hands or sitting on a bus . . . and most important, you don't get AIDS by donating blood." [74] This was as far as Reagan was willing to go. The speech said almost nothing about how people *did* get AIDS and mentioned neither condoms nor Bennett's favorite remedy, abstinence. Instead of Koop's frank talk, Reagan said that "education is critical to clearing up the fears." [75]

By the time Reagan gave his speech on May 31, 1987, a Sunday evening, it is likely that anything he might have said would have been regarded as too little and too late by many in the audience who crowded into a hot, steamy tent along the Potomac River. Many in the crowd of contributors to AIDS research booed when Reagan said he had added AIDS to the list of contagious diseases for which immigrants and aliens seeking permanent residence could be denied entry to the United States. They booed again when Reagan proposed mandatory testing of federal prisoners for AIDS and said he had ordered a review to see if required testing could be used in other federal facilities, such as veterans hospitals. Public health officials and civil liberties groups opposed compulsory mass screening for AIDS, which they thought violated rights of privacy without being particularly productive in detecting the disease. The federal courts later determined that mandatory testing was unconstitutional.

The boos might have been even louder if the audience had known what had been deleted from the speech. Parvin had included in his draft a specific reference to the courageous struggle of Ryan White, an Indiana teenager who had been ostracized in his hometown of Kokomo after he contracted AIDS from a blood-clotting agent that was being used to treat his hemophilia. Ryan White became a national spokesman for AIDS victims and, as one account described it, "a sane and compassionate voice for education about and treatment of the illness."[76] He said he had come "face-to-face with death" as a thirteen-year-old but decided "to live a normal life."[77] But Reagan did not call attention to White's struggle. The reference to White had been dropped in the speech-drafting process during Parvin's struggle with the conservatives and replaced by a mention of three unnamed Florida children who had been victims of AIDS discrimination. By the time Reagan got around to using Ryan White as a dramatic example of prejudice against AIDS victims, he no longer possessed the presidential pulpit and White was in his final weeks of life. In March 1990, Reagan and White met in Los Angeles and announced formation of a national AIDS education program by athletes and entertainers.[78]

Ryan White died in an Indianapolis hospital on April 8, 1990, less than a month after his meeting with Reagan. He was eighteen years old. Reagan had been moved by White's courage, and he wrote a tribute to him for *The Washington Post,* saying that "we owe it to Ryan to make sure that the fear and ignorance that chased him from his home and school will be eliminated." In the op ed page article Reagan said, "How Nancy and I wish there had been a magic wand we could have waved that would have made it all go away."[79] Parvin thought that Reagan's sentiments would have meant more if he had bothered to pay tribute to White when he was alive and Reagan was president. And Parvin was not alone. A *Post* reader named David Robinson, who said he was a gay man who had suffered from AIDS for three years, wrote a letter to the editor after Reagan's article appeared. "He [Reagan] may not have had a wand, but he had the next best thing: the presidency of the United States during the first eight years of the AIDS epidemic," Robinson wrote. "Reagan could have improved the survival chances of Ryan White and other people with AIDS by speaking out often and forcefully on AIDS."[80]

This he never did. Reagan's principal legacy in dealing with AIDS was one of missed opportunity. Reagan thought homosexuality "a sad thing" but he had no antipathy toward gays and lesbians. He was capable of compassion for AIDS victims, and he did not share the bigoted belief that the disease was a wrathful God's punishment for homosexual conduct. In 1978, as a private citizen, Reagan had surprised many conservatives by opposing a California ballot proposition sponsored by a demagogic Republican state legislator that would have prohibited gay people from teaching in public schools. His opposition was crucial in defeating the measure. Because Reagan exemplified traditional values and had enormous credibility, especially with conservatives, he could also have led the way in dispelling the fears and prejudices aroused by AIDS.

But Reagan was more distanced in the White House than he had been in California from such awful realities as the AIDS epidemic, and his presidential leadership on this issue was largely limited to isolated displays of conflicting symbolism. In July 1987, on the same day he visited the National Institutes of Health and held an AIDS-stricken baby in his arms, Reagan appointed an AIDS commission that included opponents of AIDS education and was devoid of physicians who had treated AIDS patients or scientists who had engaged in AIDS research. The commission appointments reflected the influence of conservatives who feared not only AIDS but homosexuals. In naming this body, Reagan sent an unfortunate message to the public that he did not care enough about the AIDS problem to muster the best scientific information available. After he left the White House and returned to Los Angeles, Reagan may have sensed that he should have done more about AIDS, although he did not say so directly. "It wasn't easy," he told me in 1990. "Here suddenly was a brand-new disease and you didn't have the facts or figures."[81] But Reagan had not sought the facts and figures from Koop, who knew them. He had hesitated in speaking out. When he finally spoke, he had failed to issue a clarion call. On an issue on which he might have demonstrated great leadership, Reagan was content to play the role of an exceptionally passive president.

Reagan's principal mission in the presidency, or so he thought, was to rein in a government he considered an obstacle to economic opportunity and human liberty. His complaint that the federal government had "overspent, overestimated and overregulated"[82] changed little over the years, but the audience for this message grew steadily larger during the 1970s. Many Americans believed, as Theodore White put it, that "their government was choking them, wasting their money, forcing up prices, poking its nose into local affairs." [83] This view was not a figment of a Reagan stump speech. Between 1970 and 1980 the social regulatory agencies of the federal government grew from twelve to eighteen and their budgets increased from $1.4 billion to $7.5 billion. During the same decade the *Code of Federal Regulations* almost doubled, from 54,000 pages to nearly 100,000 pages. [84]

The belief that regulatory reform was needed had the status of consensus by the time Reagan took office. According to a 1978 estimate of economist Murray Weidenbaum, who became Reagan's first chairman of the Council of Economic Advisers, government regulations were costing U.S. businesses as much as $100 billion annually, slowing economic growth and pushing up the costs of goods and services. [85] Economists of otherwise conflicting views agreed that government too often collaborated with the businesses it supposedly regulated, fixing prices and protecting inefficient corporations from the risks of the marketplace.

Congress had not waited for the Reagan presidency to begin deregulation. The most significant economic deregulation took place during the Carter administration, when Congress deregulated the airline, trucking, railroad and financial industries. Most of the new laws were the product of cooperation between President Carter and a coalition of liberals and conservatives in Congress. Senator Kennedy had been a leader in the battle for airline and trucking deregulation. These deregulatory laws had wide popular support, and the Reagan team hoped that additional deregulation would help revive the economy and restore business confidence. In his famous "Dunkirk" memo written a month before he took over as director of the Office of Management and Budget, David Stockman said that "a dramatic, substantial rescission of the regulatory burden is needed for the short term cash flow relief it will provide to business firms and [for] the long term signal it will provide to corporate investment planners." [86] As Weidenbaum explained the philosophy of deregulation, it reflected the Reagan administration's "fundamental view . . . that the people who make up the economy—workers, managers, savers, investors, buyers and sellers—do not need government to make their decisions for them on how to run their lives. As we see it, the most appropriate role for government economic policy is to provide a stable framework in which private individuals and business firms can plan confidently and make their own decisions." [87]

But the Reagan administration never provided such a stable framework. Reagan was not interested in the complexities of regulatory reform, and he drew no distinction between regulations restraining economic competition and regulations designed to enforce laws protecting the environment or the health and safety of Americans. Congress and the Carter administration had recognized this distinction and adopted new measures to protect Americans from the hazards of toxic wastes, polluted air and water and unsafe or unhealthy working conditions. Because Reagan did not realize that such "social regulation," as it was sometimes called, had popular support, he quickly shattered the consensus he had inherited.

OMB led the deregulatory charge, seeking to accomplish through executive action what another administration might have attempted through the legislative process. Under Stockman and an office headed by his eventual successor James Miller, OMB became a clearinghouse in which all federal regulations were subject to a strict cost-benefit analysis. Working with OMB, a task force headed by Vice President Bush recommended that hundreds of federal regulations be discarded or modified. The Commerce Department drew up a list of what the U.S. Chamber of Commerce called the "terrible twenty" regulations most offensive to U.S. businesses.[88] This hit list included some of the regulations most critical to the health and safety of Americans: regulations for classifying hazardous waste, lowering air pollutants, licensing nuclear plants and classifying and restricting possible carcinogens.

This pro-industry approach produced an inevitable backlash. Consumer activist Ralph Nader charged that Weidenbaum's claim of substantial economic savings from deregulation was "ideological arithmetic"[89] that ignored the costs in lives, injuries and illnesses caused by reduced safety standards in factories, mills and mines and on the highways. Public interest groups and labor unions sued federal agencies in the federal courts and won some important cases. One court ruled that the Occupational Safety and Health Administration (OSHA), a favorite target of ridicule in Reagan's campaign speeches, had an obligation to protect workers from toxic substances without weighing the balance between costs and benefits.[90] But OMB continued arbitrarily to remove regulations that offended businesses, usually after closed hearings at which consumers had no say. Typical of OMB actions that supposedly carried out Reagan's mission of getting government "off the backs of the people" was a decision, at the request of pharmaceutical manufacturers, to eliminate a label on aspirin bottles warning of the risk of Reye's syndrome to children who took aspirin for influenza or chicken pox. A group known as Public Citizen successfully sued to require that the label be restored.

Because of the courts, Congress and the public interest groups, the Reagan administration had limited success in discarding many of the social regulations that had accumulated during the Nixon, Ford, and especially the Carter years. But Reagan succeeded in heading off proposals for new social regulations. At the urging of automobile manufacturers, for instance, the administration first delayed and then discarded a deadline that would have required all automobiles to have air bags or automatic seat belts by 1983. Such actions won praise from industry but by no means satisfied the demands of conservatives who had anticipated a massive reduction of government regulations already in force. Delivering the verdict of pro-deregulation economists, William Niskanen concluded in *Reaganomics* that "little deregulation" had occurred during the Reagan years.[91]

Reagan might have been able to do more if his approach to deregulation had been less overtly pro-business. Instead, he aroused the hostility of liberals with appointments that critics likened to naming a fox to guard a chicken coop. John Shad, the vice president of E. F. Hutton, was named to head the Securities and Exchange Commission. Thorne Auchter, vice president of his family's Florida construction firm, was selected to direct the businessman's bête noire, the Occupational Safety and Health Administration. OSHA had cited the Auchter firm for forty-nine violations during the 1970s, and it was no surprise that Auchter sought to restrict OSHA's authority. Nonetheless, an authoritative Urban Institute study concluded that the leadership of Auchter, Shad and other administration officials drawn from business ranks was more successful and fair-minded than the leadership provided by politicians such as the EPA officials who were "friendly to industry."[92] * Over time, it was the ideologues and not the businessmen who discredited regulatory reform.

The hope of the conservatives had been that successful administrative deregulation would make the case for new laws easing federal regulations. Instead, the arbitrary behavior of OMB and other agencies aroused congressional hostility. "The various elements of the Reagan

---

* The Urban Institute, as part of its extensive analysis of changing domestic priorities during the Reagan years, undertook a comprehensive examination of the administration's deregulatory efforts. Particularly useful is the 1984 book published by the institute, *Relief or Reform? Reagan's Regulatory Dilemma*, by George C. Eads and Michael Fix.

regulatory strategy that played so well politically during the first few months of the administration—the freeze on effective dates for rules, the regulatory hit lists, the appointment of politically attuned rather than professional competent administrators, the targeted budget cuts and personnel actions, the meetings with business groups to the virtual exclusion of any other interested parties—all tended to undermine the perception that the Reagan administration could be counted on to use in a responsible way any additional discretion it might be granted," the Urban Institute study found. "Indeed, the opposite impression was created. Congress was put in a mood to tighten, not loosen, the 'regulatory ratchet' and to scrutinize every action of administration regulatory officials." [93]

Ultimately, the EPA scandals crystallized public and congressional opposition to deregulation. Burford's sorry performance created among environmental organizations what Weidenbaum called "a solid phalanx of opposition to virtually every regulatory change proposed by the Reagan administration." [94] This opposition was telling. After the downfall of Burford at EPA and subsequently of James Watt at Interior, deregulation fell into disrepute among the administration pragmatists—the James Bakers and William Ruckelshauses. Deregulation was put on the back burner, becoming more of an attitude than a policy. It was also another of the administration's bungled opportunities. The Reagan administration gave a bad name to all deregulation at the very time economic deregulation was producing positive results. The Staggers Act, which deregulated the railroad and trucking industries, has resulted (as of 1990) in savings on rail rates of 22 percent since it was passed in 1980 as well as an improvement in train reliability. Energy decontrol was also economically successful, although few of the benefits were put to good use. When Reagan took office, he immediately removed controls on oil prices that were scheduled to lapse nine months later. The result was lower gasoline and oil prices and, for a time, an oil glut. Had Reagan taken advantage of this to fill the nation's strategic reserves with cheap oil or to reduce U.S. dependency on foreign oil by imposing an oil import fee, or to encourage conservation through a gasoline tax, he would have left his successor less a prisoner of events in the Middle East. But Reagan abhorred taxes, and he did not accept the necessity of oil conservation. His trust was in the magic of the marketplace.

Overall, Reagan left a ruinous regulatory legacy. Deregulation of oil prices led to the waste of irreplaceable energy resources. The early laxity of regulatory enforcement at EPA increased the hazardous waste problem. And relaxation of regulatory restraints on thrift institutions contributed to the savings-and-loan scandal. The combined effect of these policies was to destroy public confidence in deregulation. "If you thought about deregulation in 1979, it seemed a brave new world," said Urban Institute analyst Michael Fix. "Now the very idea seems disreputable. People at the outset of the Reagan administration thought we were drowning in government red tape. Now they think we're not being protected." [95]

This lack of protection was most dramatically demonstrated in the collapse, at taxpayer expense, of a huge segment of the savings-and-loan industry. The S&L scandal is the most expensive government-caused scandal in history, but its magnitude was not fully recognized until Reagan was safely back in California and Bush was in the White House. By late 1990 it was estimated that the cost to taxpayers of the S&L bailout might reach $500 billion over a thirty-year period, and there were those who thought that even this staggering sum was conservative. The actual cost will depend on the fate of the remaining S&Ls, some of which remain in shaky condition. By the late summer of 1990, after some 600 S&L failures, fewer than half of the surviving 2,500 thrift institutions were in top fiscal health. Many commercial banks were also in serious financial trouble.

Accountability for the scandal rests at many doors. Bert Ely, a Washington financial consultant and recognized authority on the S&L crisis, believes that what happened to the thrifts was inherent in the system of depositor insurance passed in the grim days of the Depression.[96] Though Franklin Roosevelt ultimately signed the bill creating federal deposit insurance, he had warned at his first news conference on March 8, 1933, that such insurance had the effect of guaranteeing "bad banks as well as good banks."* But thrift institutions became enormously popular during the 1930s as the means for millions of American families to realize their dream of owning a home. The thrifts loaned money over periods of twenty and thirty years without being able to increase the low fixed interest rates agreed to at the time of the loan. Depositors, meanwhile, were free to withdraw their money and often did so whenever it became possible to earn a higher interest rate elsewhere.

---

* As Ely put it, "The drunk drivers of the banking world pay no more for their deposit insurance than do their sober siblings."[97] In testimony before the House Budget Committee on January 26, 1989, Ely detailed fifteen causes of the S&L crisis, beginning with the system of deposit insurance and ending with federal tax and regulatory policies during the Reagan years that contributed to the "mess."

The defect of this "maturity mismatch," as it was called, was hidden as long as interest rates remained relatively stable. But as inflation rose in the 1970s, depositors withdrew their money from S&Ls and put it in money-market accounts established by banks and brokerage houses at higher rates than the thrifts were allowed to pay. The S&Ls were on the ropes, but they were a potent source of political campaign contributions. Congress in 1980 came to their rescue and removed ceilings on the interest rates S&Ls could pay depositors. Within two years the reserves of the thrifts, which were paying interest rates as high as 18 percent to depositors while collecting 8 percent mortgages, dropped from $31 billion to $4 billion. But the 1980 legislation had also allowed federal officials to lower the requirement for capital reserves, keeping marginal S&Ls in business. At the insistence of Senator Alan Cranston of California and House Banking chairman Fernand St Germain of Rhode Island, two Democrats who had been heavy beneficiaries of S&L contributions, the bill also raised the amount of federal insurance for each depositor from $40,000 to $100,000. This encouraged brokerage houses such as Merrill Lynch to package sums in $100,000 chunks and parcel them around to various savings-and-loan institutions. By paying slightly more than its competitors, even a debt-ridden S&L could attract these brokered deposits, which were backed with the full faith and credit of the federal government at no risk to the brokers and their wealthy customers.

The Reagan administration soon made a bad situation worse, again with the cooperation of a Congress that rarely asked hard questions of major campaign contributors. In 1982 new legislation co-authored by St Germain and Republican Senator Jake Garn of Utah allowed the S&Ls to expand beyond home loans into a wide variety of investments. The Garn–St Germain Act opened the door to unsavory and underworld entrepreneurs who pilfered thrifts, bought luxury automobiles and airplanes and invested deposits in worthless land and unneeded office buildings and condominiums. Texas Democrat James Wright, a recipient of thrift contributions, had supported the bill as House majority leader but would say in retrospect that the legislation was "a grotesque error." [98]

And it was an error compounded by the Reagan administration.*

---

* But not by the Reagan administration alone. The Garn–St Germain Act allowed thrift institutions to choose whether they wanted to be chartered under federal or state regulations. In California, where state regulators had been closely monitoring state-chartered thrifts, many of these institutions switched to federal charters in the early 1980s. State legislators then became concerned that

Even before the bill was passed, Richard Pratt, the deregulation-minded head of the Federal Home Loan Bank Board, had engineered a series of accounting changes that allowed the thrifts to conceal their insolvency. His policies were strongly backed by Secretary of the Treasury Donald Regan, who saw the rule changes as a way of helping "a sick industry." [101] But the Reagan administration was unwilling to treat the cause of the illness. "This was a failure of government," said William Seidman, head of the Federal Deposit Insurance Corporation. "The Reagan administration turned these [S&L] people loose. Frankly, I thought it was crazy." [102]

Reagan knew little about what was going on in the savings-and-loan industry except that the administration was trying to salvage the thrifts through his favorite remedy of deregulation. He did not raise the issue with anyone, and no one raised it with him. Reagan had been an independently wealthy man for nearly three decades before he became president, and his financial affairs were handled by attorneys and accountants. His idea of a savings-and-loan president was George Bailey, the altruistic president of a thrift institution in the mythical town of Bedford Falls in the 1946 Frank Capra movie *It's a Wonderful Life*. Bailey had been portrayed by Reagan's friend Jimmy Stewart (of whom the president could do an acceptable impersonation). But times had changed since 1946, the year that Reagan renewed his movie career, and the thrift industry had changed even more.

After passage of the Garn–St Germain Act, only vigorous regulation could have prevented vast fraud. Instead, Pratt and the Federal Home Loan Bank Board in April 1982 abolished a regulation that required thrifts to have at least four hundred stockholders, most of them drawn from the local community. This allowed a single operator to take over a thrift and run it into the ground. *U.S. News & World Report* gave a vivid summary of what happened next: "Scores of investors like Charles Keating moved in swiftly, turning the thrift industry into a huge casino where only taxpayers could lose. The most unscrupulous operators traded worthless land parcels back and forth, each time raising the value on their books and creating nothing of value. Many S&L kingpins lived

---

they would lose S&L campaign contributions if all the thrifts became federally chartered. On the last day of the 1982 legislative session, shortly before the Garn–St Germain Act was passed, the California legislature with only a single dissenting vote dropped almost all regulations on state-chartered thrifts.[99] This action enticed hordes of unscrupulous operators to open new state-chartered thrifts. Under such circumstances it is not surprising that state-chartered thrifts accounted for two-thirds of the total S&L losses.[100]

like royalty, buying opulent homes, yachts and political influence. Cronies and insiders obtained huge loans with little collateral. In 'cash for trash' schemes some borrowers used the funds to buy real estate owned by an S&L at inflated prices. And many of those who weren't deliberately pillaging their S&L's were simply lousy business operators, investing in everything from bull-sperm banks to shopping centers in the desert." [103]

In 1983 Pratt quit the Reagan administration to join Don Regan's former firm of Merrill Lynch. His replacement as chairman of the Federal Home Loan Bank Board was Edwin Gray, an undistinguished Ed Meese protégé who had served as an assistant press secretary for Reagan in Sacramento and in the White House as deputy director of the Office of Policy Development. In 1982 he had returned to his hometown of San Diego, where he worked at a local S&L run by a longtime Reagan contributor. Gray was then recruited by the thrift industry to replace Pratt. "I was appointed because it was thought that I would be a patsy for the industry," Gray said later. [104] The industry had every reason to make this evaluation. Gray was a Reagan loyalist who believed in deregulation and was widely viewed as earnest, hardworking and not especially bright. "The S&L industry wanted me, so I was automatic," Gray said. "But they really didn't know me, because I didn't know myself. I didn't know who I was." [105]

Gray learned a lot about himself in the next two years. At first he was the "patsy" the industry expected him to be. But when Gray was informed by his examiners in August 1983 that S&Ls were raking in unlimited amounts of money through brokered deposits and making bad loans, he proposed a regulation to prohibit money brokers from sending funds to thrifts. The proposed ruling sent a signal to the White House as well as to unscrupulous thrifts that Gray was wandering off the reservation, even though his independence was slow to produce results. While the regulation he proposed was eventually adopted over the opposition of Treasury, it failed to survive a court challenge. Nor could Gray obtain action by Congress, where restrictions on brokered deposits were opposed by the money brokers who were cleaning up under the new rules. And in the process of pushing for changes, Gray earned the enmity of former Wall Streeter Don Regan, who complained that Gray was not a team player. By 1985, with Regan in the White House as chief of staff and Gray waging a battle with OMB for more bank examiners, the word was sent to Gray by two Californians in the White House that Regan wanted him out. [106] Gray refused to quit. He wanted to take his case to the president but was told that Reagan accepted Regan's advice on financial matters. When Gray appealed to OMB for more examiners, David Stockman passed the request on to his deputy Constance Horner, who turned Gray down and called him a "re-regulator." [107] Bill Seidman, surprised and impressed by the fight Gray was making, urged him to continue the battle. But Seidman too was accused of having re-regulatory impulses.[108] In the Reagan administration, this was one of the ultimate insults.

Over time, Gray learned he had the capacity to resist the industry and the administration that had been his patrons. He became convinced that in their fervor for deregulation Reagan and Regan simply refused to distinguish between an industry in which the risks were borne by investors and one in which the risks were passed on to the taxpayers in the form of federal insurance. "The administration was so ideologically blinded that it couldn't understand the difference between thrift deregulation and airline deregulation," Gray said. "I'm not a rocket scientist, but I understand that." [109]

In fact, it is an axiom among authorities on regulatory reform that deregulation requires supervision. If a financial institution is given freedom to determine its loan portfolio and its interest rates, more stringent inspections are necessary to protect those who take the risks of underwriting the deposits. Because the Reagan administration ignored this axiom, U.S. taxpayers will be paying for the S&L bailout at least until the year 2020. The costs could have been substantially reduced if the administration had heeded the growing signs of scandal and changed course. Financial expert Bert Ely, who believes Gray waited too long to blow the whistle, estimates that the S&L bailout would have cost taxpayers $25 billion if the administration had acted in 1983 and still less than $100 billion by 1986.[110] But admitting the dimension of the S&L scandal also would have required acknowledging that the administration's budget deficit estimates were shockingly low. No high official, including Treasury Secretary James Baker, was willing to take the political risk of such a confession. When Ely went up to a senior Treasury official at a 1986 congressional hearing and asked him when he was going to admit the size of the S&L problem, the official replied, "Not on my watch." [111]

This reply could serve as the epitaph for the administration's economic policy in the twilight years of the Reagan presidency. On the surface, all was well. The economic expansion rolled along, unaccompanied by the high inflation rates that had turned past booms into busts.

While some economists warned that the vaunted Reagan prosperity had been purchased by a national credit card that had transformed the United States from international creditor into one of the world's great debtor nations, most Americans accepted the boom at face value. Wall Street shuddered on October 19, 1987, when the stock market dropped 500 points, stirring memories among those of Reagan's generation of the fabled crash of 1929. But the market soon resumed its march to historic highs. Few Americans questioned the basis of their record prosperity.

Beneath the surface, as financial writer John Berry observed, the powerful U.S. economic machine was "powered by consumer spending and fueled by debt, tuned to gratify today's desires rather than to meet tomorrow's needs." [112] The nation's private wealth, adjusted for inflation, grew only 8 percent in the last five Reagan years compared to 31 percent in the period between 1975 and 1980, years that Reagan had derided as inflation-prone and unproductive. "Reagan was enthusiastic about financing defense and foreign aid, and Congress was enthusiastic about financing domestic spending," said Republican Congressman Willis Gradison of Ohio, a fiscal expert who had served as an assistant secretary of the treasury in the Eisenhower administration. "They reached compromises that only a politician could love." [113]

These compromises steadily increased the national debt at the same time that private debt was also mounting. Other industrialized democracies also struggled with deficits, but most of them had higher rates of saving to finance their debt. America was a spender, not a saver, during the Reagan years, and the president's only response to the problem was to blame Congress. While Reagan would say at the end of his presidency that the deficit was one of his "regrets," [114] he never seemed to understand the role he had played in accumulating it by submitting eight consecutive unbalanced budgets. "For the average American the eighties was a better decade than the seventies, but that's not the real question," said Gradison. "The legacy in both the public and private sectors was a reliance on debt and foreign lending that led to less control over our economic destiny." [115] As Reagan's friend George Will sadly observed at the conclusion of the Reagan presidency, "Much happened in the way of silent rot as we mortgaged much of our future vitality." [116]

The source of this rot was Reagan's inability to gain fiscal control of the government he had so often promised to cut down to size. Total federal spending measured in constant 1990 dollars was $1.9 trillion more from 1981 to 1990 than it would have been had spending levels remained the same as they had been in 1980. Had Reagan called a halt to the built-in growth of the welfare state, he would have been forced to forgo the military buildup and tax cuts he had also promised or to ask the American people for sacrifices in their standard of living. Reagan must have known by his second term that sacrifices were necessary and that the federal budget could not be balanced simply by eliminating "waste, fraud and abuse." But Reagan's public image was his prized possession, and he knew that not even his popularity could survive a substantial cutback in Social Security or other social programs valued by wage-earning Americans. Reagan knew that the New Deal was here to stay. He never had any intention of asking for sacrifices.

Like Franklin Roosevelt, however, Reagan understood the value of inspirational leadership. He resembled FDR in recognizing that Americans respond to assertions of optimism even when solutions are not in easy sight. When Reagan took office, public confidence in government was at its lowest ebb since the Depression. President Carter, trying to cope with the loss of confidence, had made the political mistake of blaming the American people for the nation's problems, saying in 1979 that Americans suffered from "a crisis of confidence . . . that strikes at the very heart and soul and spirit of our national will." [117] Reagan did not believe this, then or ever. "I find no national malaise," he said. "I find nothing wrong with the American people." [118]

Nor did Reagan find anything wrong with himself. His self-assurance was a tonic for a nation that longed for new leadership, and even Americans who had not voted for him put their trust in Reagan. In a *New York Times*–CBS Poll taken soon after Reagan took office, nine out of ten respondents said that Reagan would see to it that the United States was again respected by other nations. But his greatest service was in restoring the respect of Americans for themselves and their own government after the traumas of Vietnam and Watergate, the frustration of the Iran hostage crisis and a succession of seemingly failed presidencies. Reagan's critics sometimes derided him as a "Dr. Feelgood," but Reagan took this as a compliment. He recognized, as he said at the end of his presidency, that the restoration of American morale had been one of the "great triumphs" of his presidency.[119] Since the view that Americans hold of their government is strongly linked to what they think of their president, Reagan's success in making Americans feel better about themselves also had the unintended consequence of making Americans feel better about the government he had so often denounced.

. . .

Since the turn of the century, no president save FDR defined a decade as strikingly as Ronald Reagan defined the 1980s. Dwight Eisenhower, the president of the 1950s, had been the nation's most popular general in its most popular war. He had found partisan politics distasteful. Reagan was more passive and less analytical than Eisenhower but more attuned to his party and the people. While a puzzle to those who had known him for many years, he was never a remote figure to the American public. Reagan's geniality, his stubborn individualism and anti-intellectualism, his self-deprecating wit and his passionate opposition to taxes set the tone for a decade that was at once a period of national renewal and national excess. The Reagan recession, the worst since the Depression, was followed by the Reagan recovery, which became the longest peacetime boom in history. It was marked by the creation of 18.4 million new jobs and an uneven distribution of prosperity. It is often said that the rich became richer during the Reagan years while the poor became poorer, but this is not quite right. The real income of every strata of Americans increased during the 1980s after declining during the 1970s.[120] What distinguished Reagan's America was that the very rich became much richer while the differences between those who prospered and those who didn't—differences reflecting region, race, occupation, age, marital status and personal circumstances—became demonstrably wider. For many Americans the economic experience of the decade was summarized in the words of Michigan autoworker Ed Schmitt, who told David Broder he was doing worse "but doing well."[121] A poll taken by Peter Hart in 1989 found that three-fourths of all Americans said they had fulfilled most or all of their material needs.* And for many Americans, satisfaction went beyond material needs. T. R. Reid of *The Washington Post* has observed that for the nation as a whole the eighties were a period of creed, not greed, in which the number of Americans who volunteered their time for church, charity, civic and educational causes increased far faster than the population.[123] On Main Street, the 1980s were more often than not a "we decade."

This was not true on Wall Street, where the decade was one of merger mania and what may have been the last stand of unrestrained free

---

* The high index of economic satisfaction recorded in Hart's survey may reflect the upward mobility that was a significant feature of the Reagan years. Only 20 percent of Americans had incomes above $29,070 in 1980. By 1988 this group (measured in constant 1988 dollars) comprised 38 percent, a phenomenal increase.[122] But the least-educated workers in the bottom quintile of wage earners and a disproportionate number of black and Hispanic workers did not share in this prosperity even though the real income of the bottom fifth increased as a whole.

enterprise. The administration cheered from the sidelines as corporate America engaged in a record wave of 25,000 mergers, takeovers and restructurings. Antitrust enforcement did not disappear, but it focused largely on price-fixing and other criminal activities. Size itself or market domination was no longer an antitrust criterion. Robert Bork hailed this approach as a departure from heavy-handed, "government knows best" interference in the marketplace and noted approvingly that the Supreme Court had endorsed it.[124] But others saw government's unconcern with mergers as leading to reduced competition, higher prices and fewer product choices for consumers. "Many of these massive combinations—in oil, steel, airline and other basic industries—would never have passed muster under any other administration, be it Democratic or Republican," contended New York Attorney General Robert Abrams.[125] But Reagan's belief was that government should get out of the way, and government did. In 1987 junk bond salesman Michael Milken earned $550 million, or more than $1.5 million a day. While wages of American workers were declining, the average compensation of the highest-paid chief executive officers of the nation's corporations was rising (in constant 1980 dollars) from $3 million a year in 1980 to more than $12 million in 1988. "Greed is healthy," Wall Street financier Ivan Boesky had proclaimed before his fall. There were many others on Wall Street and in Washington who agreed with him.

Reagan was personally closer to Main Street than to Wall Street. He remained a secure, old-fashioned man who fed the White House squirrels, related anecdotes to aides whose names he often could not remember and reminisced about his life in the movie business. He also remained a visionary and a dreamer. One of his dreams was that the nations of North America would collaborate in an economic alliance that would be the most productive in the world. He had called this notion "the North American accord" when he announced his candidacy in 1979, and it had largely been dismissed as a campaign gimmick. Reagan took it seriously. Once in office, he avidly promoted a free trade agreement between the United States and Canada to wipe away all trade barriers. Such an idea had been discussed for decades without becoming more than talk, but Reagan and Canadian Prime Minister Brian Mulroney overcame protectionist objections on both sides of the border as well as the concerns of some Canadians that they would be culturally subjugated by the United States.* Reagan also took the next step toward

* After many delays the Canada-U.S. Free Trade Agreement was approved by Congress and the Canadian Parliament and signed by Reagan while on vacation in Palm Springs on January 2, 1988.

what could become a North American common market by approving a "framework agreement" with Mexico. These accords may prove among the most valuable of his legacies.

Reagan's other legacies are a study in contradictions. A strong case can be made that he accomplished least in the domestic arena, where most was expected of him, and most in foreign affairs, in which expectations were low and Reagan's experience practically nonexistent. Princeton professor Fred Greenstein, an authority on the Eisenhower presidency, found the Reagan presidency "an interesting mix of brilliance and inadequacy."[127] Greenstein said that Eisenhower operated with a "hidden hand" and Reagan with "no hands"[128] but believed Reagan was nonetheless curiously effective. "Despite the belief that he is a passive president, he is a powerhouse—especially when he has a good team behind him," Greenstein said shortly before Reagan left office.[129]

And a powerhouse Reagan often was, even though his hands were not on the throttle much of the time. There is no gainsaying that his success was often a reflection of the prowess of his White House staff, which was of overall high quality through his first term, ineffective in the first two years of his second term and strong again in the last two years after Donald Regan was succeeded by Howard Baker and then by Ken Duberstein and John Poindexter was replaced by Frank Carlucci and then by Colin Powell. But it was Reagan, not his staff, who set the agenda and established the priorities for the major accomplishments and debacles of his presidency. It was Reagan who wanted the tax cuts and the military buildup. It was Reagan, although not Reagan alone, who wanted to negotiate with Mikhail Gorbachev. And it was Reagan, again not alone, who advocated the sale of U.S. arms to Iran in exchange for American hostages.

Reagan had no difficulty in setting priorities when he could consult his mental script. His core agenda was well known to everyone who worked for him. On issues where his script provided little guidance, however, Reagan tended to rely on the advice provided by the career professionals who were members of the federal bureaucracy so often scorned in his political speeches. He was often well served by this tendency. One of the best examples of where Reagan acted wisely on

---

The White House had planned to celebrate the new closeness between the two nations with a telephone call between Reagan and Mulroney in Canada. When it was discovered that Mulroney was vacationing in Florida, White House Chief of Staff Ken Duberstein arranged for the call to be placed through the prime minister's office in Ottawa to give the event an international flavor.[126]

the basis of professional advice was in his response to events in the Philippines, where analysts in the CIA, the State Department and the Navy had concluded that Ferdinand Marcos was an impediment to U.S. interests. Their views were forcefully represented within the administration by Paul Wolfowitz at the State Department, Richard Armitage at the Pentagon and especially by Admiral William Crowe, the chairman of the Joint Chiefs of Staff, who had served as Navy commander in the Pacific.*

Reagan liked Marcos, whom he had first met in September 1969 while representing President Nixon on a trip to the Philippines. He knew Marcos had won a medal of valor for his role in the defense of Bataan, and he accepted without skepticism the legend that Marcos had led a group of Filipino guerrillas in harassing the Japanese and providing intelligence information to U.S. forces. The story was a Marcos invention. In fact, the U.S. military had distrusted Marcos so much during World War II that they had refused him supplies on the grounds that he was not actually involved in anti-Japanese activity.[131] The full extent of the fraud was not known until an American scholar documented it from reports in the National Archives in 1986,[132] but Reagan did not accept it even then. Long after Marcos had been deposed, Reagan told National Security Adviser Colin Powell that Marcos had been "a hero with the Philippine scouts, who had come out of the hills to help Americans in World War II."[133]

But Reagan did not stand in the way when Crowe and Secretary of State George Shultz insisted that it was necessary to find a democratic alternative in the Philippines. Under Shultz's prodding, Reagan sent Senator Paul Laxalt as an emissary to Marcos. Laxalt's mission had the dual purpose of demonstrating to Marcos that the concerns of the State Department had reached the White House and of giving Reagan a firsthand appraisal of the situation. Laxalt realized that Marcos was sinking, but Reagan was being urged by Don Regan to stick by him. Both Regan and Reagan worried about the example of Iran, when the United States by abandoning the shah had encouraged the forces of

---

* Crowe, who visited the Philippines before returning to Washington in 1984, was concerned that growing resentment against Marcos would result in a successful Communist rebellion that would deprive the United States of its bases in the Philippines. He wrote a letter to Marcos proposing various reforms and sent a report to Reagan urging a U.S. campaign to persuade Marcos to resign. "Things had to change," Crowe later said. "Marcos was not making the decisions that had to be made, primarily because of personal vanity. His health was a serious problem. He was concerned about his survival, his affluence and his well-being, and the country was sliding downhill. So I felt he had to go."[130]

fundamentalist revolution. The professionals at State urged Reagan to support Corazon Aquino, who won the election of February 7, 1986, only to find it stolen from her by Marcos. Reagan hesitated, saying there had been fraud "on both sides." [134] But as the prospects for a bloody battle in the streets of Manila increased, Reagan accepted the advice of Shultz and the professionals. On February 24 he issued a public plea for Marcos to resign. The next afternoon Laxalt received a call from Marcos wanting to know if the statement represented Reagan's view. Laxalt returned the call from the White House and offered him asylum in America if he peacefully abdicated. "I think you should cut, and cut cleanly," Laxalt said. "I think the time has come." Marcos said he was "very, very disappointed" but accepted exile in Hawaii. [135]

Two years later Reagan again put aside his personal feelings and gave the green light to the Justice Department to press an investigation of Marcos and his wife Imelda for allegedly conspiring with Adnan Khashoggi, the Saudi financier who had helped bankroll the Iran arms deal, to embezzle more than $100 million of Philippine funds and invest them in Manhattan real estate. [136] (All three were indicted, but the dying Marcos was too ill to stand trial, and Imelda Marcos and Khashoggi were acquitted.) [137] Reagan had not wanted Marcos indicted. He still believed him to be a hero, albeit one who had been corrupted by power, and he was concerned that prosecution of Marcos might discourage other unpopular rulers from peacefully abdicating. Again, however, he listened to professional advice, this time from the Justice Department, Duberstein and Powell, who argued that a grant of asylum should not be allowed to protect anyone from prosecution for crimes committed after they had been given refuge. [138] Reagan agreed. His action came as an immense relief to George Bush, who on a 1981 visit to Manila had extravagantly praised Marcos for "adherence to democratic principles and to the democratic process" [139] and was worried that his comments would become an issue in the presidential campaign.

Reagan was unstinting in his support for Bush in 1988, campaigning in remote areas of the South and West where his popularity with conservative Democrats and independents was especially high. Even though some Reagan loyalists considered Bush an uncertain champion of Reaganism and would have preferred that the president keep a lower profile, Reagan rooted for Bush to win the nomination and did everything he could to help him win the election. In 1980 he had been reluctant to put Bush on the ticket because he thought he lacked "spunk." [140] But Reagan had grown to like his vice president during their eight years together in the White House and to appreciate his consistent loyalty. He also knew that the 1988 election would inevitably be seen as a referendum on the policies of Reaganism.

And it was policies that mattered to Reagan. He was not overimpressed by his own reputation as the "Great Communicator," which he realized was often used to suggest that Americans liked the way he said things but disagreed with what he was saying. Reagan knew better. "I never thought it was my style or the words I used that made a difference: it was the content," Reagan said in his farewell address. "I wasn't a great communicator, but I communicated great things, and they didn't spring full bloom from my brow, they came from the heart of a great nation—from our experience, our wisdom, and our belief in the principles that have guided us for two centuries. They called it the Reagan revolution. Well, I'll accept that, but for me it always seemed more like the great rediscovery, a rediscovery of our values and our common sense."

There may have been more to it than that. Walter Lippmann once said of Charles de Gaulle that his greatness was not because de Gaulle was in France but because France was in de Gaulle. Similarly, the greatness of Reagan was that he carried a shining vision of America inside him. He had brought that vision with him from Dixon and learned in Hollywood and on the GE circuit to play the role of the wholesome American who would set things right. It was a most natural role. Reagan may not have been a great president, but he was a great American who held a compelling vision of his country. "They say the United States has had its day in the sun; that our nation has passed its zenith," he had said in his 1980 campaign. "They expect you to tell your children . . . that the future will be one of sacrifice and few opportunities. My fellow Americans, I utterly reject that view." [141]

In rejecting an era of limits, Reagan expressed a core conviction of the nation. One of the reasons that he so easily and unwisely brushed aside dire predictions of scientists and environmentalists about acid rain or global warming was that he never accepted—indeed, could not accept—that there are limitations imposed by nature on all people, even Americans. Reagan believed with an unshakable faith that some invention or technological breakthrough would inevitably provide new answers to problems that today seem insoluble. "If there is one thing we are sure of, it is . . . that nothing is impossible, and that man is capable of improving his circumstances beyond what we are told is fact," he said.[142]

Nothing is impossible. This is what Reagan believed, and what made him so appealing to his fellow Americans and in time to others in the world as well. "It must be admitted that quite frequently we all not only underestimated Reagan but greatly oversimplified him," wrote Gennady Vasilyev in an assessment in *Pravda*. "We took his external simplicity for simplemindedness, his rhetoric for his essence, his shows of toughness for an inability to be flexible." [143] Vasilyev, who understood that Reagan remained an actor at heart, believed that the presidency had turned out to be Reagan's "best role." So did Reagan, who in his final days in office often remarked that his career as an actor had prepared him for the presidency. It was a role in which he had played himself and which he performed consistently with style and with grace.

No other president ever reached the White House by the road that Ronald Reagan traveled, and the path he followed is no longer there. When Reagan was a movie actor, pursuing what he then believed was the career of his dreams, Hollywood seemed a romantic extension of the world he had known in Dixon and Des Moines. The world of illusion suited Reagan, and it was easy for him to portray the good guy in films that were usually sentimental celebrations of America. Portraying a citizen president should have been more demanding, but Reagan also performed this role too effortlessly. Because of his ability to reflect and give voice to the aspirations of his fellow citizens, Reagan succeeded in reviving national confidence at a time when there was a great need for inspiration. This was his great contribution as president. But because he believed in happy endings obtained with too little sacrifice, this revived confidence became an end in itself that Reagan rarely sought to focus on higher goals. He aged little in the presidency and took his role too lightly. In the end, it proved too big for his talents.

On January 20, 1989, after 2,923 days in the presidency, Reagan flew off without regrets into the California sunset. He left office with a higher public approval rating than any other modern president.[144] Americans felt comfortable with him, if sometimes puzzled by the inconsistencies and paradoxes of the man and his administration. After he was gone, even Americans who had ardently supported Reagan began to wonder if they had understood him as well as they believed. As the Cold War ended and domestic prosperity faded, a debate began about Reagan's conflicting legacies. It is also a debate about the essence and direction of America.

NOTES

Confidential sources are immensely valuable to Washington reporters and contemporary biographers. They are also dangerous. People allowed the protection of anonymity may be willing to say what they are unwilling to say on the record or what they have been forbidden to disclose. But such confidences impose a burden on the confidant, as well as on the reader. The reporter or biographer privy to confidential material should examine every available source or record of the information given him, holding anonymous information to a higher standard of verification than information that is a matter of record. I have followed this practice to the best of my ability and have relied on confidential sources only when vital information could not be obtained by other means.

Since first writing about Ronald Reagan in 1965, I have interviewed him on more than forty occasions. Much of the source material in this book is based on these interviews, on my experience as a White House correspondent for *The Washington Post* during the Reagan presidency, on earlier assignments covering Reagan campaigns and the first term of his governorship for the *San Jose Mercury-News,* on 250 interviews conducted specifically for this book (including three with Reagan and two with Nancy Reagan), on hundreds of other interviews for two earlier books on Reagan or for newspaper articles, on various books written about Reagan and on Reagan's 1965 autobiography *Where's the Rest of Me?* and his 1990 memoirs *An American Life.*

Where's the Rest of Me? is cited in these notes as WTROM. The citations to *Reagan* refer to my 1982 biography of Reagan. The citations to *Ronnie and Jesse* refer to my 1969 dual biography of Reagan and Jesse Unruh, *Ronnie and Jesse: A Political Odyssey.* Where a Reagan speech, comment, statement or document is cited, it appears in *The Public Papers of the Presidents* for that date, unless otherwise noted.

All interviews were conducted by me, unless otherwise noted. Gwen Rubinstein worked for me as a researcher when she conducted the interviews cited in these notes.

The historical material on James Watt in Chapter 17 is drawn from research prepared for me by Tom Kizzia in 1981.

The notes were prepared by Mary Shinkwin Cannon, who is my wife and was the principal researcher on this book. We have followed the practice of not identifying the source of material in the chapter notes if it is identified in the text.

CHAPTER 1—*Back to the Future*

1. Interview with George Shultz, February 13, 1989.
2. Interview with Kenneth Duberstein, March 30, 1989.
3. Lee May and Laurie Becklund, "Citizen Reagans Are Home After Bittersweet Farewell," *Los Angeles Times,* January 21, 1989.
4. Interview with Kathy Osborne, September 19, 1989.
5. Ronald Reagan, *Speaking My Mind,* p. 404.
6. May and Becklund, "Citizen Reagans Are Home After Bittersweet Farewell."
7. Tom Shales, "The Gaffes, the Glories and a Short Goodbye," *The Washington Post,* January 21, 1989.
8. Interview with James Baker, May 23, 1989.
9. Interview with James Kuhn, June 9, 1989. In his epilogue in *An American Life,* Reagan uses the word "shack" instead of "bungalow."
10. Judith Havemann, "Adding Up the Reagan Renovations," *The Washington Post,* September 7, 1988.
11. Ibid.
12. *Time,* December 22, 1980.
13. Prime rate figures from the Federal Reserve Board; inflation figures from Mark Memmott, "Inflation Runs at Even 4.4% Through 1988," *USA Today,* January 20, 1989; civilian unemployment figures from the Bureau of Labor Statistics.
14. *Economic Report of the President, February 1988,* U.S. Government Printing Office, Washington, D.C., p. 248.
15. Bureau of Economic Analysis.
16. Michael R. Kagay, "Satisfaction on Rise in U.S., Gallup Poll Finds," *The New York Times,* December 25, 1988.
17. Interview with Landon Parvin, June 7, 1989.
18. *Ronnie and Jesse,* p. 70.
19. Department of Commerce.
20. Ibid.
21. John D. McClain, "Foreign Direct Investments in U.S. Rise 61 Pct.," *The Washington Post,* May 31, 1989.
22. George Will, "How Reagan Changed America," *Newsweek,* January 9, 1989.
23. Doyle McManus and Douglas Jehl, "Reagan Era: What Will History Say?" *Los Angeles Times,* August 21, 1988.
24. Interview with Peter Hart, June 16, 1989.
25. Inaugural Address, January 20, 1981.
26. Peter Behr, "Wave of Mergers, Takeovers Is a Part of Reagan Legacy," *The Washington Post,* October 30, 1988.
27. New Statistics Information Office, Internal Revenue Service.

28. Cindy Skrzycki, "Poll Finds Less Worker Emphasis on Materialism," *The Washington Post,* January 10, 1989.

29. Reagan press conference, June 16, 1981.

30. Louis Harris, *Inside America,* p. 25.

31. Linda Hallberg, Association of Home Appliance Manufacturers, Chicago.

32. Paul Farhi, "Consumers Hit Pause Button on Sales of Video Recorders," *The Washington Post,* January 14, 1989.

33. Robert J. Samuelson, "The Binge Is Over," *The Washington Post,* July 5, 1989.

34. "Goodbye to the Gipper," *Newsweek,* January 9, 1989.

35. Ronald Reagan and David Brinkley: A Farewell Interview, ABC News, December 22, 1988.

36. *Statistical Abstract of the United States 1989,* Department of Commerce, Table 177.

37. *HIV/AIDS Surveillance,* Centers for Disease Control, June 1989 issue, Table 7.

38. *Statistical Abstract of the United States 1989,* Table 548.

39. "Children and Families: Key Trends in the 1980s," staff report of the Select Committee on Children, Youth and Families, U.S. House of Representatives, December 1988, p. 12. Also "The Poverty Figures," Editorial, *The Washington Post,* September 1, 1988.

40. "Children and Families," p. 11.

41. *Crime in the United States,* Uniform Crime Reports 1988, Federal Bureau of Investigation, p. 47. There were 22,520 murders in 1981 and 20,680 in 1988.

42. There were 27,596 suicides in 1981 and 26,560 in 1988. National Center for Health Statistics. There were 1,361,820 violent crimes in 1981 and 1,566,220 in 1988. *Crime in the United States,* p. 47.

43. Philip J. Hilts, "Blacks' Life Expectancy Drops," *The Washington Post,* December 15, 1988.

44. Patrice Gaines-Carter, "Warren Burns, 22; 'Disrespect Somebody, and You're Dead,' " *The Washington Post,* January 1, 1989.

45. Lynne Duke, "Death Cast Long Shadow Over '88," *The Washington Post,* January 1, 1989. The official figure reported to the FBI was 369 murders during 1988. FBI counts do not include justifiable homicides, and the D.C. police said in October 1989 that three of the homicides in 1988 were justified. For more information on this, see "District's Homicide Count May Not Have Tied Record," *The Washington Post,* October 31, 1989.

46. Public Information Branch, D.C. Police Department.

47. Richard Morin, "Demographic Line Between Slain, Slayer Indistinguishable," *The Washington Post,* January 1, 1989.

48. Amy Pyle and Laurie Becklund, "Nancy Reagan Withdraws Support for Drug Facility," *Los Angeles Times,* May 27, 1989.

49. "Goodbye to the Gipper."

50. 1988 data: *Digest of Education Statistics,* National Center for Education Statistics, U.S. Department of Education, p. 117. 1980 data: Richard L. Berke, "Student Survey Detects Decline in Use of Crack," *The New York Times,* March 1, 1989.

51. In his second annual message to Congress on December 1, 1862, Abraham Lincoln said, "We know how to save the Union. . . . We shall nobly save or meanly lose the last, best hope of earth. Other means may succeed; this could not fail.

The way is plain, peaceful, generous, just—a way which if followed the world will forever applaud and God must forever bless." Reagan may have been borrowing this secondhand, for the reference to the United States as "the last best hope" had also been used by Franklin Roosevelt—and also without attribution.

52. David Gergen, "Ronald Reagan's Most Important Legacy," *U.S. News & World Report,* January 9, 1989.
53. Remarks to American troops at Camp Liberty Bell, South Korea, November 13, 1983.
54. Veterans of Foreign Wars Convention, Chicago, August 18, 1980.
55. Remarks at the Armed Forces farewell salute in Camp Springs, Maryland, January 12, 1989.
56. Ibid.
57. Lou Cannon, "Bittersweet Trip for the Reagans," *The Washington Post,* January 21, 1989.
58. Interview with reporters aboard SAM 27000, January 20, 1989.
59. Lou Cannon, "A Sentimental Journey," *The Washington Post,* January 23, 1989.
60. Cannon, "Bittersweet Trip for the Reagans."
61. Ibid.
62. Ibid.
63. Ibid.
64. May and Becklund, "Citizen Reagans Are Home After Bittersweet Farewell."
65. Interview with James Kuhn, June 9, 1989.
66. Ibid.
67. Ibid.
68. Interviews with James Kuhn, June 9, 1989, and Kenneth Duberstein, March 30, 1989.

CHAPTER 2—*A Reagan Portrait*

1. Interview with Nancy Reagan, May 5, 1989.
2. William Faulkner, "On Privacy," *Harper's,* July 1955.
3. Remarks and a question-and-answer session on the program for economic recovery with newspaper editors and radio and television directors, White House, February 19, 1982.
4. Lou Cannon, "Speaker Calls President Insensitive," *The Washington Post,* January 29, 1986.
5. Reagan started wearing a hearing aid in his right ear in 1983. He began wearing a second hearing aid in March 1985. Susanne M. Schafer, "Reagan Now Experimenting with Hearing Aid in Each Ear," Associated Press, March 20, 1985.
6. Thomas Jefferson letter to Elbridge Gerry, May 13, 1797: "The second office of this government is honorable & easy, the first is but a splendid misery." Quoted in *The Splendid Misery,* by Jack Bell.
7. Interview with Nancy Reagan, May 5, 1989.

CHAPTER 3—*The Acting Politician*

1. Remarks to the Dothan–Houston County Chamber of Commerce, Dothan, Alabama, June 10, 1986.

2. *Reagan,* p. 20.
3. Ronald Reagan, *Speaking My Mind,* p. 14.
4. McDowell, a columnist for the *Richmond Times-Dispatch,* was being installed as president of the Gridiron Club.
5. Interview with Charles McDowell, March 2, 1989.
6. Ibid.
7. Garry Wills, *Reagan's America,* p. 29.
8. *WTROM,* p. 37.
9. *Ronnie and Jesse,* p. 14.
10. *Reagan,* p. 319.
11. *Ronnie and Jesse,* p. 82.
12. Ibid., p. 86.
13. Remarks at the 84th annual dinner of the Irish American Historical Society, New York, November 6, 1981.
14. Wills, *Reagan's America,* p. 179.
15. *Ronnie and Jesse,* p. 29.
16. Ibid., pp. 130–31.
17. Ibid., p. 142.
18. Ibid., p. 131.
19. As Reagan described the strike in his autobiography, it was a noble cause designed to prevent financially strapped Eureka College from dropping classes that upperclassmen needed for graduation. The actual reasons for the strike, more complex than Reagan remembers, are discussed by Garry Wills in *Reagan's America,* Chap. 5.
20. *Ronnie and Jesse,* p. 251.
21. Ibid., p. 148.

CHAPTER 4—*The Acting President*

1. Remarks at Republican Party fund-raising dinner, Los Angeles, May 25, 1982.
2. Ronald Reagan and David Brinkley: A Farewell Interview, ABC News, December 22, 1988.
3. George Will, "How Reagan Changed America," *Newsweek,* January 9, 1989.
4. Reagan had memorized this Cobb column and quoted it in public on rare occasions, always with slight variations. It is quoted here from an interview he held with six newspaper reporters, including me, on January 18, 1989, two days before he left the White House. Reagan also used substantially the same quotation in remarks at the opening of the Bob Hope Cultural Center in Palm Springs, California, on January 2, 1988, and in remarks at a gala at Ford's Theatre, Washington, D.C., on June 24, 1988.
5. Interview with Ronald Reagan, May 5, 1989.
6. Tom Shales, " 'White House:' A Star Is Gone," *The Washington Post,* July 5, 1989.
7. Interview with Ronald Reagan, May 5, 1989.
8. Interview with Fred De Cordova, June 7, 1989.
9. Interview with James Kuhn, June 9, 1989.
10. Interview with Rhett Dawson, March 15, 1989.

11. Interview with Kenneth Duberstein, April 27, 1989.
12. Ibid.
13. Remarks at the annual convention of the National Association of Evangelicals, Orlando, Florida, March 8, 1983.
14. Lou Cannon, "President Goes to the Movies, Skips New Hampshire for Now," *The Washington Post,* June 13, 1983.
15. Lars-Erik Nelson, "Ron's War—And the Real War," *New York Daily News,* December 16, 1983.
16. *Reader's Digest,* April 1944.
17. "Ron Flies by Seat of Pants?" *New York Daily News,* December 18, 1983.
18. Ibid.
19. Ronald Reagan, *Speaking My Mind,* p. 127.
20. *WTROM,* pp. 52–53.
21. Interview with Ronald Reagan, February 10, 1989.
22. Fallston High School, Fallston, Maryland, December 4, 1985.

CHAPTER 5—*Offstage Influences*

1. *Reagan,* p. 307n.
2. Interview with Paul Laxalt, May 27, 1980.
3. *Reagan,* p. 253.
4. Casey served as S.E.C. chairman from 1973–74.
5. *Reagan,* p. 274
6. Ibid.
7. Interview with Stuart Spencer, May 2, 1989.
8. When Ed Meese was asked about his new title, he spelled it with two l's rather than with one, which is the more common spelling of the word.
9. Helene von Damm, *At Reagan's Side,* p. 126.
10. Stephen E. Ambrose, *Nixon,* p. 546.
11. Interview with Michael Deaver, November 20, 1989.
12. *Reagan,* p. 179.
13. Barry M. Goldwater, *Goldwater,* p. 256.
14. *Reagan,* p. 187.
15. Reagan press conference, August 27, 1974.
16. Interview with Ken Khachigian, August 7, 1989.
17. Interview with Richard Wirthlin, August 10, 1988.
18. Theodore H. White, *Breach of Faith,* p. 316.
19. Interview with Alexander Haig, June 6, 1989.
20. Alexander M. Haig Jr., *Caveat,* p. 7.
21. Interview with Michael Deaver, May 23, 1989.
22. *Reagan,* p. 308.
23. Interview with George Shultz, February 13, 1989.
24. Michael K. Deaver, *Behind the Scenes,* p. 173.
25. Interview with George Shultz, February 13, 1989.
26. von Damm, *At Reagan's Side,* p. 127.
27. Interview with Stuart Spencer, May 2, 1989.
28. Bob Woodward, *Veil,* p. 42.

29. von Damm, *At Reagan's Side,* p. 137.
30. Interview with Stuart Spencer, December 8, 1988.
31. Laurence I. Barrett, *Gambling with History,* p. 67.
32. Jeane J. Kirkpatrick, "Dictatorships and Double Standards," *Commentary,* November 1979.
33. Interview with David Stockman, November 14, 1981.
34. Interview with John Block, August 30, 1989.
35. von Damm, *At Reagan's Side,* p. 130.
36. *Reagan,* p. 312
37. Ibid., pp. 311–12.
38. Terrel H. Bell, *The Thirteenth Man,* p. 2.

CHAPTER 6—*Heroic Dreams*

1. Remarks to the American Society of Newspaper Editors, Washington, D.C., April 9, 1986.
2. After Reagan left the White House, he told Landon Parvin, "I had an agenda I wanted to get done. I came with a script." Interview with Landon Parvin, March 7, 1989.
3. Garry Wills, *Reagan's America,* p. 267.
4. Ronald Reagan, *Speaking My Mind,* p. 419.
5. This is from a speech Reagan gave on October 15, 1974. It is in *Quotable Ronald Reagan,* published by JRH & Associates, Inc., 1975.
6. Inaugural Address, January 5, 1967.
7. Interview with William F. Buckley, May 16, 1989.
8. David A. Stockman, *The Triumph of Politics,* p. 10.
9. Wills, *Reagan's America,* pp. 173–79.
10. Interview with Ronald Reagan, July 30, 1981.
11. Wills, *Reagan's America,* p. 268.
12. *Reagan,* p. 324.
13. This is from a speech Reagan gave on June 22, 1972, *Quotable Ronald Reagan.*
14. Interview with Alan Greenspan, May 11, 1989.
15. Ronald Reagan, *Speaking My Mind,* p. 59.
16. Interview with Nancy Reagan, May 5, 1989.
17. Interview with Ronald Reagan, February 10, 1989.
18. Ken Khachigian.
19. David Gergen.
20. James Baker.
21. Richard Darman.
22. Edwin Meese.
23. Richard Wirthlin.
24. Michael Deaver.
25. Interview with Ronald Reagan, July 30, 1981.
26. Interview with Ken Khachigian, May 3, 1989.
27. Ibid.
28. Interview with Ken Khachigian, August 7, 1989.
29. Interview with Ken Khachigian, May 3, 1989.

30. Interview with Ken Khachigian, August 7, 1989.
31. William Safire, "The Land Is Bright," *The New York Times,* January 22, 1981.
32. Inaugural Address, January 20, 1981. Without using Treptow's name, Reagan also quoted the words from Treptow's diary in remarks at a White House briefing for supporters and presidents of historically black colleges, September 19, 1986; in this meeting he said the author of the diary was a young American soldier who died in the First World War and was buried in a field in France.
33. Ibid.
34. This information was provided by Kathy Osborne, Reagan's personal secretary, who searched his files in 1989.
35. Interview with Ken Khachigian, August 7, 1989.
36. Interview with Ken Khachigian, August 7, 1989.
37. Inaugural Address, January 20, 1981.

CHAPTER 7—*Halcyon Days*

1. Final report of the Initial Actions Project, p. 1.
2. *Reagan,* p. 205.
3. For an extended discussion of Reagan's role as "company man" in Hollywood, see Garry Wills, *Reagan's America,* pp. 261–324.
4. Elisabeth Bumiller, "The Reagans' Hello Party," *The Washington Post,* November 19, 1980.
5. Ibid.
6. Michael K. Deaver, *Behind the Scenes,* p. 100. Deaver said that Reagan "was referring to the mullahs, and to the ayatollah, but also, I think, to the American voters who had turned with such a meanness of spirit against Jimmy Carter." Reagan, of course, had encouraged the voters to turn on Carter. He also often used the pronoun "they" in an amorphous way that referred to everyone in general and no one in particular.
7. Alexander M. Haig Jr., *Caveat,* pp. 78–79.
8. Jimmy Carter, *Keeping Faith,* p. 577.
9. Ibid., p. 578.
10. Ibid.
11. Interview with Stuart Eizenstat, August 4, 1989.
12. Interview with Edwin Meese, August 2, 1989.
13. James L. Rowe Jr., "Interest Level at Historic High," *The Washington Post,* December 11, 1980.
14. "The Biggest Challenge," *Time,* January 19, 1981.
15. Final report of the Initial Actions Project, p. 2.
16. Interview with David Gergen, March 6, 1989.
17. Final report of the Initial Actions Project, p. 9.
18. Ibid., p. 18.
19. Reagan often told the story, notably in his autobiography and in the speech announcing his presidential candidacy on November 13, 1979, about how his father Jack was fired from his job as store manager for a "cheap shoe chain outfit" on Christmas Eve in 1931. Garry Wills, in *Reagan's America,* pp. 60–61, makes a convincing case that Reagan has his chronology confused and that the event he describes actually occurred a year later. Wills points out that Reagan always credits

the New Deal for putting his father to work as a relief administrator but neglects to mention that Jack Reagan used his influence to secure Neil Reagan a job in the Federal Emergency Relief Administration at a time when local politicians opposed governmental hiring of men from the same family because so many heads of families were still unemployed.

20. David A. Stockman, *The Triumph of Politics,* p. 9.
21. Arthur M. Schlesinger Jr., *The Coming of the New Deal,* p. 567.
22. Thomas Cronin, *The State of the Presidency,* p. 84.
23. Final report of the Initial Actions Project, p. 6 in the Summary.
24. Dick Kirschten, "The Reagan Team Comes to Washington, Ready to Get Off to a Running Start," *National Journal,* November 15, 1980.
25. Interview with David Gergen, March 6, 1989.
26. Interview with Stuart Eisenstat, August 4, 1989.
27. Laurence I. Barrett, *Gambling with History,* p. 392.
28. Interview with Ronald Reagan, March 27, 1981.
29. Interview with Willis Gradison, August 2, 1989.
30. Tony Kornheiser, "Tip O'Neill's Toughest Inning: The Sermon on the Mound," *The Washington Post,* May 31, 1981.
31. Haynes Johnson, " 'High-Risk' President Reassessed," *The Washington Post,* November 8, 1981.
32. Interview with Stuart Spencer, January 6, 1988.
33. Interview of Ronald Reagan by Dan Blackburn, NBC Radio, October 31, 1980.
34. Interview with Ronald Reagan, February 10, 1989.
35. Address to the nation on the economy, February 5, 1981.
36. *Time,* February 2, 1981.
37. Lou Cannon, "Now the Real St. Ronald vs. the Rhetorical Dragon," *The Washington Post,* February 18, 1981.
38. John B. Anderson in the Iowa forum of six Republican presidential candidates, Des Moines, January 6, 1980.
39. Exchange with reporters on the program for economic recovery, February 19, 1981.
40. Lou Cannon and Lee Lescaze, "The Relaxed Approach," *The Washington Post,* February 9, 1981.
41. Ibid.

CHAPTER 8—*Kidding on the Square*

1. Gridiron Dinner, March 28, 1987.
2. Interview with Bob Orben, September 13, 1989.
3. Owen Ullmann, "Mr. Everyman," *The Philadelphia Inquirer,* August 17, 1986.
4. Interview with John F. W. Rogers, February 22, 1989.
5. Interview with Bob Orben, September 13, 1989.
6. E. B. White, *Essays of E. B. White,* p. 245.
7. Interview with Alan Greenspan, May 11, 1989.
8. Executive Forum, Washington, D.C., March 30, 1987.
9. Remarks at the annual meeting of the National Association of Manufacturers, May 29, 1986.
10. *Reagan,* p. 329.

11. *Ronnie and Jesse,* p. 226.
12. Interview with Margaret Tutwiler, May 23, 1989.
13. *Reagan,* p. 253.
14. Interview with Glenn Campbell, April 5, 1989.
15. Ibid.
16. Interview with Alan Greenspan, May 11, 1989.
17. Interview with Arthur B. Culvahouse, March 27, 1989.
18. *Reagan,* p. 258.
19. Remarks at the swearing-in ceremony for Susan M. Phillips as chairman of the Commodity Futures Trading Commission, The White House, November 17, 1983.
    20. Reagan offered this analysis during a break in a 1968 interview for my first book, *Ronnie and Jesse.* The ground rules for these sessions were that I would not take notes or tape-record except during the formal interviews, so my comments here are from memory.
21. *Reagan,* p. 378n.
22. Marianne Moore, *The Pangolin.*
23. "Charlie Rose Show," KXAS, Fort Worth, Texas, May 1, 1980.
24. Ullmann, "Mr. Everyman."
25. This anecdote was related to me by Lloyd Cutler, Fred Barnes and Bill Plante, who had been told it on separate occasions by Reagan. Owen Ullmann used a version of this story in "Mr. Everyman."
26. Phil McCombs, "Regan's Jest Desserts," *The Washington Post,* February 1, 1988.
27. Remarks at a Republican Party fund-raising dinner, Los Angeles, August 22, 1985.
28. *Reagan,* p. 250. Michael Reagan says in his book, *On the Outside Looking In,* that he told his father this joke on Thanksgiving in 1979 (p. 170).
29. *Reagan,* p. 250.
30. Ibid., pp. 250–51.
31. Interview with Glenn Campbell, April 5, 1989.
32. *Reagan,* p. 260.
33. Douglas E. Kneeland, "Challenges to Statements Putting Reagan on the Defensive," *The New York Times,* April 13, 1980.
34. Laurence I. Barrett, *Gambling with History,* p. 25.
35. Interview with Karna Small, July 26, 1989. For further information on the butter surplus, see Robert G. Kaiser and Lee Lescaze, "White House Stalling on Butter Sales in World Market," *The Washington Post,* May 29, 1981.
36. Remarks at the welcoming ceremony for Prime Minister Lee Kuan Yew of Singapore, October 8, 1985.
37. Remarks at the Los Angeles County Board of Supervisors town meeting, March 3, 1982.
38. Reagan tells of his childhood experience with poor eyesight and the first time he tried on his mother's glasses in *WTROM,* pp. 24–25.
39. Remarks and a question-and-answer session via satellite to Republican campaign events, October 18, 1982.
40. Remarks at a White House briefing for supporters, February 9, 1987.
41. Interview of Ronald Reagan by Burl Osborne and Carl Leubsdorf of the *Dallas Morning News,* January 8, 1985.
42. Remarks to private-sector leaders during a White House briefing on the MX missile, March 6, 1985.

43. Remarks to People to People high school student ambassadors, June 24, 1987. Reagan gave a similar formulation in responding to questions from students at Moscow State University, May 31, 1988.

44. Remarks at the Western Hemisphere legislative leaders forum, Old Executive Office Building, January 24, 1985.

45. James M. Perry, "For the Democrats, Pam's Is the Place for the Elite to Meet," *The Wall Street Journal,* October 8, 1981.

46. David A. Stockman, *The Triumph of Politics,* p. 345.

47. Ibid.

48. Interview with Richard Perle, March 9, 1989.

49. Interview with George Will, January 31, 1989.

50. Ibid.

51. Interview with Martin Anderson, February 13, 1989.

52. Interview with Annelise Anderson, April 6, 1989.

53. Interview with Richard Wirthlin, March 3, 1989.

54. Interview with George Shultz, February 13, 1989.

55. Interview with William F. Buckley, May 10, 1989.

56. Interview with Annelise Anderson, April 6, 1989.

57. Interview with Robert Kaiser, July 11, 1989.

58. Interview with Annelise Anderson, April 6, 1989.

59. Interview with Ed Yoder, March 23, 1989.

60. Interview with George Will, January 31, 1989.

61. Presidential news conference, January 29, 1981.

62. Interview with Ronald Reagan, February 25, 1988.

63. Interview with William F. Buckley, May 16, 1989.

64. Interview with Howard Gardner, July 21, 1989.

65. Conversation with Stuart Spencer, September 12, 1989.

66. *Ronnie and Jesse,* p. 8.

67. Letter from Howard Gardner, dated November 16, 1989.

68. Interview with Richard Allen, April 29, 1989.

69. Interview with Martin Anderson, April 4, 1989.

70. Interview with Edwin Meese, August 2, 1989.

71. *Ronnie and Jesse,* p. 166.

72. Harry Farrell, "People and Politics: Spencer Williams Off to Washington," *San Jose Mercury-News,* January 2, 1969.

73. *Reagan,* p. 297n.

74. Ibid., p. 297.

75. Elizabeth Kastor and Barbara Feinman, "The Gridiron and the Fond Farewell," *The Washington Post,* March 28, 1988.

76. *Time,* April 13, 1981.

77. Ibid.

CHAPTER 9—*Hail to the Chief*

1. Interview with Ronald Reagan, May 5, 1989.

2. Henry Adams, *The Education of Henry Adams,* p. 418.

3. Ibid.

4. *Reagan,* p. 304.

5. James Gerstenzang, "President Will 'Be More Alert' In Future Outings," Associated Press, April 23, 1981. This was less than a month after the assassination attempt, a period during which Reagan did his work in the family quarters rather than the Oval Office. Throughout his presidency Reagan often changed to pajamas and robe when he worked, read or relaxed in the residence, even on those rare occasions when he received aides or congressmen in crisis situations. He always dressed in suit and tie when working in the Oval Office.

6. Elisabeth Bumiller, "Psssst! Mr. President!; What to Do When the Chief Nods Off," *The Washington Post*, August 16, 1984. Steven R. Weisman, "Western White House; How Reagan Spent His Vacation, Really Spent It," *The New York Times*, August 15, 1984.

7. Interview with Anne Higgins, April 19, 1989.

8. Harold J. Laski, *The American Presidency*, p. 26.

9. George E. Reedy, "Discovering the Presidency," *The New York Times*, January 20, 1985.

10. Interview with Robert McFarlane, February 21, 1989.

11. Lou Cannon, *Reporting: An Inside View*, p. 235.

12. Kenneth L. Adelman, *The Great Universal Embrace*, p. 46.

13. Interview with John F. W. Rogers, February 22, 1989.

14. Ibid.

15. Interview with Robert McFarlane, February 21, 1989.

16. Ibid.

17. Interview with Alexander Haig, June 6, 1989.

18. David A. Stockman, *The Triumph of Politics*, p. 129.

19. Interview with Alexander Haig, June 6, 1989.

20. Interview with William Clark, March 20, 1989.

21. Stockman, *The Triumph of Politics*, p. 290.

22. Ibid., p. 291.

23. Ibid., p. 356.

24. Interview with Annelise Anderson, April 6, 1989.

25. Interview with Kenneth Duberstein, August 30, 1989.

26. Interview with Annelise Anderson, April 6, 1989.

27. David Hoffman and Lou Cannon, "Stockman, on the Mend, Reeducates Reagan," *The Washington Post*, February 6, 1983.

28. February 16, 1981.

29. Interview with William Clark, March 20, 1989.

30. William Safire, "Those Upraised Hands," *The New York Times*, June 18, 1981.

31. Pool report, lunch in the Oval Office with George Bush, by Bruce Drake, *New York Daily News*, November 9, 1982.

32. March 28, 1981.

33. Lou Cannon and Lee Lescaze, "Presidential Performance Improves as Rust Rubs Off," *The Washington Post*, June 28, 1981.

34. Stockman, *The Triumph of Politics*, p. 360.

35. *Reagan*, p. 386.

36. Stansfield Turner, "MX Is a Serious Mistake," *The Washington Star*, March 29, 1981, reprinted from *The New York Times Magazine*.

37. Report of Secretary of Defense Harold Brown to the Congress on the FY 1982

Budget, FY 1983 Authorization Request and FY 1982–86 Defense Programs, January 19, 1981.

38. *Reagan,* p. 388.
39. Interview with John Tower, November 7, 1989.
40. Interview with William Dickinson, November 3, 1981.
41. Interview with Caspar Weinberger, March 17, 1989.
42. Reagan news conference, March 14, 1967.
43. Kenneth L. Adelman, *Great Universal Embrace,* p. 172.
44. Ibid.

CHAPTER 10—*Passive President*

1. Interview with Nancy Reagan, May 5, 1989.
2. Interview with Lyn Nofziger, June 13, 1989.
3. Interview with Frank Fahrenkopf, March 6, 1989.
4. Interview of Tom Clancy by Gwen Rubinstein, May 30, 1989.
5. Interview with James Kuhn, March 6, 1989.
6. *Reagan,* p. 306.
7. Interview with Margaret Tutwiler, May 23, 1989.
8. Peggy Noonan, "Confessions of a White House Speechwriter," *The New York Times Magazine,* October 15, 1989.
9. Interview with Anne Higgins, April 19, 1989.
10. Martin Anderson, *Revolution,* p. 290.
11. Interview with Martin Anderson, April 4, 1989.
12. Interview with George Steffes, April 25, 1989.
13. Interview with Bill Plante, October 5, 1989.
14. Interview with Bob Sims, March 20, 1989.
15. Interview with Martin Anderson, April 4, 1989.
16. Annelise Anderson and Dennis L. Bark, eds, *Thinking About America,* p. 129.
17. Terrel H. Bell, *The Thirteenth Man,* p. 39.
18. Interview with David Gergen, March 6, 1989.
19. Anne M. Burford, *Are You Tough Enough?,* p. 213.
20. Interview with Bently Elliott, October 6, 1989.
21. Interview with Peggy Noonan, September 30, 1989.
22. Sara Fritz, "Hello, This Is Ronald Reagan—Yes, Really," *U.S. News & World Report,* March 21, 1983.
23. Interview with Anne Higgins, April 19, 1989.
24. Arthur M. Schlesinger Jr., *The Coming of the New Deal,* p. 586.
25. David A. Stockman, *The Triumph of Politics,* p. 355.
26. Interview with A. C. Lyles, January 3, 1989.
27. Interview with Richard Helms, June 12, 1989.
28. Barry M. Goldwater, *Goldwater,* p. 393.
29. Interview with Caspar Weinberger, March 17, 1989.
30. Interview with Arthur B. Culvahouse, March 27, 1989.
31. Interview with Martin Anderson, April 4, 1989.
32. Interview with Colin Powell, February 23, 1989.
33. Anderson, *Revolution,* p. 291.

34. Interview with Ronald Reagan, February 10, 1989.
35. Ibid.
36. Ann Reilly Dowd, "What Managers Can Learn from Manager Reagan," *Fortune,* September 15, 1986.
37. Bradley H. Patterson Jr., *The Ring of Power,* p. 17.
38. Ibid., p. 23.
39. Clyde V. Prestowitz Jr., *Trading Places,* p. 18.
40. Anderson, *Revolution,* p. 226.
41. Interview with Ed Rollins, January 30, 1989.
42. Interview with Robert Carleson, September 21, 1989.
43. Interview with Craig Fuller, May 9, 1989.
44. Interview with Nancy Reagan, May 5, 1989.
45. Ralph Robinson, "Reagan Keeps His Advice in Mind," *The Boston Globe,* July 31, 1981.
46. Interview with Richard Allen, April 29, 1989.
47. Ibid.
48. Interview with Alexander Haig, June 6, 1989.
49. Laurence I. Barrett, *Gambling with History,* p. 231.
50. *Reagan,* p. 398.
51. Ibid.
52. Ibid., p. 398n.
53. Don Oberdorfer and Martin Schram, "Haig Believes a Reagan Aide Is Campaigning Against Him," *The Washington Post,* November 4, 1981.
54. Lee Lescaze, "Reagan Talks to Haig, Allen on Ending Feud," *The Washington Post,* November 6, 1981.
55. *Reagan,* p. 400.
56. Interview with Alexander Haig, June 6, 1989.
57. Ibid.
58. Ibid.
59. Alexander M. Haig Jr., *Caveat,* p. 76.
60. Ibid., p. 85.
61. Interview with Alexander Haig, June 6, 1989.
62. Ibid.
63. Interview with David Gergen, March 6, 1989.
64. Interview with Michael Deaver, November 15, 1988. In his presidential memoirs, Reagan does not mention this incident, but says that "others told me he [Haig] had shocked some congressmen by giving them the impression that if it were up to him, he'd deal with some of our problems in Central America and Cuba with a bombing run or an invasion" (*An American Life,* p. 361).
65. Interview with Michael Deaver, November 15, 1988.
66. Ibid.
67. Ronnie Dugger, *On Reagan,* p. 344.
68. Michael K. Deaver, *Behind the Scenes,* p. 168.
69. *Reagan,* p. 395.
70. Ibid.
71. Ibid.
72. Barrett, *Gambling with History,* p. 117.

73. Haig, *Caveat,* p. 160.

74. Haig insisted in *Caveat* that he knew the correct order of succession and had merely misspoken, saying "constitutionally" when he ought to have said "administratively." However, White House counsel Fielding says that Haig, after returning to the Situation Room, continued to argue that he had accurately described the process of presidential succession. "That's right, isn't it, Fred," Fielding remembers him saying. "No, that's not right, Al," he replied. Presidential succession, as established in 3 U.S. Code 19, is: president, vice president, speaker of the House, president pro tempore of the Senate, secretaries of the following departments—State, Treasury, Defense, Justice, (Attorney General), Interior, Agriculture, Commerce, Labor, Health and Human Services, Housing and Urban Development, Transportation, Energy and Education. The military command authority passes directly from the president to the secretary of defense. The Situation Room is considered a military command post; therefore, technically the defense secretary can be considered to be in charge there.

75. *Reagan,* p. 396.

76. Barrett, *Gambling with History,* pp. 239–40.

77. Interview with Robert McFarlane, October 11, 1989.

78. Haig, *Caveat,* p. 335.

79. Ibid., p. 311.

80. Ibid.

81. Ibid., p. 312.

82. Ibid.

83. Interview with Robert McFarlane, October 11, 1989.

84. Ibid.

85. Haig, *Caveat,* p. 313.

86. Interview with Robert McFarlane, October 11, 1989.

87. Haig, *Caveat,* p. 313.

88. Barrett, *Gambling with History,* p. 247.

89. Ronald Reagan, *An American Life,* p. 361.

90. Ibid., p. 270.

91. Barrett, *Gambling with History,* p. 248.

92. Interview with George Shultz, February 13, 1989.

93. Ibid.

CHAPTER 11—*The Loner*

1. Interview with George Will, January 31, 1989.

2. *WTROM,* p. 12.

3. Ibid., p. 64.

4. Publication of *WTROM* contributed to the underestimation of Reagan as a political candidate. Several members of the Brown administration were convinced, or so they told me late in 1965, that the book would prove an embarrassment to Reagan because of his acknowledgment that he had belonged to organizations influenced or dominated by the Communist Party.

5. *WTROM,* p. 12.

6. Ibid., p. 14.

7. Ibid., pp. 12–13.
8. Ibid., p. 18.
9. Ibid., p. 14.
10. Interview with Neil Reagan, June 19, 1989.
11. Ibid.
12. Interview with Ronald Reagan, May 5, 1989.
13. Ibid.
14. Ibid.
15. *WTROM*, p. 113.
16. Ibid.
17. Ibid., p. 115.
18. Herbert L. Gravitz and Julie D. Bowden, *Recovery: A Guide for Adult Children of Alcoholics*, p. 17.
19. Ibid., p. 24.
20. Emmy E. Werner, "Resilient Offspring of Alcoholics: A Longitudinal Study from Birth to Age 18," *Journal of Studies on Alcohol*, January 1986.
21. Ibid.
22. Ibid.
23. Ibid.
24. Interview with Ronald Reagan, February 10, 1989.
25. See Dr. James R. Milam and Katherine Ketcham, *Under the Influence*.
26. Interview with Ronald Reagan, May 5, 1989.
27. Interview of Roberta Meyer by Gwen Rubinstein, April 19, 1989.
28. Garry Wills, *Reagan's America*, p. 24.
29. Ibid., p. 25.
30. *WTROM*, p. 20.
31. Ibid., p. 17.
32. Nancy Reagan, *My Turn*, p. 107.
33. Maureen Reagan, *First Father, First Daughter*, p. 64.
34. Nancy Reagan, *My Turn*, p. 108.
35. Judith Brimberg, "Denver Woman Cherishes Note from a 'Stranger,' " *The Denver Post*, January 22, 1981.
36. Interview with Nancy Reagan, May 5, 1989.
37. Ibid.
38. Wills, *Reagan's America*, p. 15.
39. *Ronnie and Jesse*, p. 5.
40. *WTROM*, p. 16.
41. Ibid., p. 25.
42. Interview with Patti Davis, October 19, 1989.
43. Interview with Peggy Noonan, September 30, 1989.
44. Wills, *Reagan's America*, p. 27.
45. *WTROM*, p. 21.
46. Mark Shields, "President Reagan's Wide World of Sports," *Inside Sports*, March 31, 1981.
47. Wills, *Reagan's America*, p. 31.
48. Interview with Ronald Reagan, July 30, 1981.
49. *WTROM*, p. 54.

50. Ibid., p. 27.
51. Ibid.
52. Ibid., p. 85.
53. Wills, *Reagan's America,* p. 278.
54. Interview with Stuart Spencer, January 20, 1989.
55. Gerald R. Ford, *A Time to Heal,* p. 294.
56. Spencer told me after the campaign that he was convinced that Reagan would in all probability have developed unstoppable momentum if he had won the New Hampshire primary. Ford's strategy was therefore based on winning early and often in the primaries, which the president and Spencer believed would dry up Reagan's campaign financing and drive him from the race.
57. Interview with Paul Laxalt, May 22, 1989.
58. "Interview: Ron Reagan," *fathers,* July-August 1986.
59. *Reagan,* p. 41.
60. Interview with Paul Laxalt, May 22, 1989.
61. Reagan recounts in *WTROM* (p. 7) that when he was born his "face was blue from screaming, my bottom was red from whacking, and my father . . . said shakily, 'For such a little bit of a fat Dutchman, he makes a hell of a lot of noise, doesn't he?' " From his birth, his nickname was "Dutch."
62. Interview with Michael Deaver, May 23, 1989.
63. Gene Raffensperger, "Reagan Saved Woman in '33 from Robber," *Des Moines Register,* January 28, 1984.
64. Remarks at an Iowa caucus rally, Des Moines, February 20, 1984.
65. Bill Boyarsky, *The Rise of Ronald Reagan,* p. 60.
66. *Reagan,* p. 36n.
67. Myron S. Waldman, "Growing Up in the Midwest," *Newsday,* January 18, 1981.
68. Carey McWilliams, *Southern California: An Island on the Land,* p. 170.
69. Wills, *Reagan's America,* p. 152.
70. Boyarsky, *The Rise of Ronald Reagan,* p. 63.
71. Interview with Edward Anhalt, October 25, 1989.
72. *Reagan,* pp. 135–38
73. "The President-Elect Talks About His Health, His Children and His Divorce," *People,* January 5, 1981.
74. This is a familiar Reagan line. It was recalled by him in a 1968 interview.
75. Interview with Nancy Reagan, May 5, 1989.
76. Ibid.
77. *Reagan,* p. 64.
78. Interview with Ronald Reagan, July 30, 1981.
79. *Reagan,* p. 66.
80. Interview with Nancy Reagan, May 5, 1989.
81. Ibid.
82. "Interview: Ron Reagan."
83. Maureen Reagan, *First Father, First Daughter,* p. 69.
84. Michael Reagan, *On the Outside Looking In,* p. 96.
85. Interview with Patti Davis, October 19, 1989.
86. "Interview: Ron Reagan."
87. Michael Reagan, *On the Outside Looking In,* p. 52.

88. Maureen Reagan, *First Father, First Daughter,* Chap. 6.
89. Interview with Maureen Reagan, August 31, 1981.
90. Michael Reagan, *On the Outside Looking In,* p. 10.
91. Interview with Patti Davis, October 19, 1989.
92. Peggy Noonan, "Who Was That Masked Man?" *Mirabella,* December 1989.
93. Interview with Nancy Reagan, May 5, 1989.
94. Nancy Reagan, *My Turn,* p. 106.
95. Interview with Landon Parvin, October 18, 1989
96. Interview with Paul Laxalt, May 22, 1989.
97. A Spanish proverb quoted by Samuel Johnson.
98. Interview with Landon Parvin, October 18, 1989.
99. Interview with Paul Laxalt, May 22, 1989.
100. Michael Reagan, *On the Outside Looking In,* p. 33.

CHAPTER 12—*Staying the Course*

1. Bureau of Labor Statistics.
2. "Paying More for Money," *Time,* March 8, 1982.
3. "Booms, Busts and Birth of a Rust Bowl," *Time,* December 27, 1982.
4. "Tales of Ten Cities," *Time,* January 31, 1983.
5. These are the figures of the Gallup Organization, used here because they provide a base of historical comparison with other presidencies. The surveys taken by Richard Wirthlin's polling group, Decision Making Information, for the benefit of the president and Republican candidates showed a similar pattern, with slightly different percentages.
6. Ronald Reagan, *Speaking My Mind,* pp. 74–75.
7. My authority for this is William Safire, who shares credit for the coinage of "Nixonomics" with columnists Robert Novak and Rowland Evans. Safire believes that both phrases caught on because they are euphonious, while "Bushonomics," for instance, is not. "Reaganomics" was used journalistically as a description of Reagan's economic program as early as the 1980 campaign, most often in reference to his tax plan.
8. Remarks at a fund-raising dinner for Senator Charles H. Percy, Chicago, January 19, 1983.
9. William A. Niskanen, *Reaganomics,* p. 4.
10. William Safire in his *Political Dictionary* traces the origins of "trickle-down" to the famous "Cross of Gold" speech delivered in 1896 by the populist orator William Jennings Bryan. "There are those who believe that, if you will only legislate to make the well-to-do prosperous, their prosperity will leak on through to those below," Bryan said.
11. Laurence I. Barrett, *Gambling with History,* p. 194.
12. Ibid., p. 195.
13. Interview with William Niskanen, December 8, 1989.
14. Martin Anderson, *Revolution,* p. 164.
15. Interview with George Shultz, February 13, 1989.
16. Raymond Moley, *After Seven Years,* p. 48.
17. Niskanen, *Reaganomics,* p. 24.

18. "Challenge to Change," *Time,* March 2, 1981.
19. Ibid.
20. "Big Labor Cries 'Foul,' " *Time,* March 2, 1981.
21. William Greider, "The Education of David Stockman," *The Atlantic,* December 1981.
22. Arthur M. Schlesinger Jr., *The Coming of the New Deal,* pp. 309–10.
23. "A Debt-Threatened Deam," *Time,* May 24, 1982.
24. Niskanen, *Reaganomics,* p. 40. In 1903 Charles Ponzi settled in Boston's Italian North End. He ran a pyramid scam that bilked $14 million from some 20,000 Bostonians. He was deported to Italy in 1934 and died a pauper.
25. "A Debt-Threatened Dream."
26. Richard Bergholz, "Latest Debate: What Did Reagan Say About a Voluntary Social Security?" *Los Angeles Times.*
27. Ibid.
28. David A. Stockman, *The Triumph of Politics,* p. 161.
29. Ibid.
30. William Greider, *The Education of David Stockman and Other Americans,* p. 33.
31. Ibid.
32. Stockman, *The Triumph of Politics,* p. 168.
33. Ibid., p. 160.
34. Ibid., p. 162.
35. Interview with Stephen Bell, November 20, 1989.
36. Ibid.
37. Ibid.
38. Ibid.
39. Ibid.
40. Ibid.
41. Ibid.
42. Stockman, *The Triumph of Politics,* p. 162.
43. Ibid., p. 182.
44. Interview with David Stockman, November 14, 1981.
45. Stockman, *The Triumph of Politics,* p. 187.
46. Niskanen, *Reaganomics,* p. 38.
47. Stockman, *The Triumph of Politics,* p. 187.
48. Ibid.
49. Ibid., p. 188.
50. David S. Broder, "Reagan Proposes 10% Cut in Social Security Costs," *The Washington Post,* May 13, 1981.
51. Niskanen, *Reaganomics,* p. 38.
52. Stockman, *The Triumph of Politics,* p. 396.
53. Ibid., pp. 396–97.
54. John M. Berry, "Rosy Scenario for Reagan Sees Inflation Rate Plummeting," *The Washington Post,* February 7, 1981.
55. Stockman, *The Triumph of Politics,* p. 93.
56. Ibid., p. 111.
57. Ibid., p. 95.
58. Ibid., p. 96.

59. Ibid.
60. Ibid., p. 97.
61. "Challenge to Change."
62. Ibid.
63. Stockman, *The Triumph of Politics*, p. 99.
64. Barrett, *Gambling with History*, p. 188.
65. Greider, *The Education of David Stockman and Other Americans*, p. xxi.
66. *Reagan,* p. 334n.
67. Lou Cannon, " 'A New Coalition,' " *The Washington Post,* June 26, 1981.
68. Stockman, *The Triumph of Politics,* p. 223.
69. Exchange with reporters on economic and foreign policy issues, October 18, 1981; see also Stockman, *The Triumph of Politics,* p. 340.
70. Exchange with reporters about extension of the Voting Rights Act, November 6, 1981.
71. Stockman, *The Triumph of Politics,* p. 81.
72. Ibid.
73. John M. Berry, " 'Trickle-Down' Theory Suffers from Its Name," *The Washington Post,* January 10, 1982.
74. Jim Baker's first wife, Mary Stuart McHenry Baker, died of breast cancer in February 1970 when she was thirty-eight years old. He was just under forty years old and had four sons, ranging from eight to fifteen years old. In 1973 he married Susan Garrett Winston, who was divorced and had three children. In 1977, Mary Bonner was born to Jim and Susan Baker.
75. Interview with David Gergen, December 1, 1989.
76. Stockman, *The Triumph of Politics,* p. 5.
77. Ibid., p. 3.
78. Interview with David Gergen, December 1, 1989.
79. Ibid.
80. Tom Shales, "Through the Safety Net; The Victims of Reagan's Administration," *The Washington Post,* April 21, 1982.
81. Interview with David Gergen, December 1, 1989.
82. "The Dismal Science Hits a Nerve," *Time,* January 24, 1983.
83. Interview with David Gergen, December 1, 1989.
84. William Greider, *Secrets of the Temple,* p. 449.
85. Niskanen, *Reaganomics,* p. 162.
86. Ibid., p. 156.
87. "Paying More for Money."
88. Anderson, *Revolution,* pp. 250–51.
89. Ibid., p. 251.
90. Ibid.
91. Ibid., p. 252.
92. Interview with William Niskanen, December 8, 1989.
93. Interview with Michael Deaver, November 20, 1989.
94. Anderson, *Revolution,* p. 252.
95. Greider, *Secrets of the Temple,* p. 420.
96. Ibid., pp. 419–20.
97. Ibid., p. 426.

98. Niskanen, *Reaganomics,* pp. 168–69.
99. Interview with Martin Anderson, November 16, 1989.
100. Greider, *Secrets of the Temple,* p. 505.
101. Ibid., p. 422.
102. "Opinion Roundup," *Public Opinion,* April/May 1983.
103. Remarks and a question-and-answer session with regional editors and broadcasters on domestic and foreign policy issues, White House, February 9, 1983.
104. Question-and-answer session with high school students, Old Executive Office Building, March 25, 1983.
105. Interview with Bently Elliott, October 6, 1989.
106. John M. Berry, "Underlying Flaws in Economy Mar Legacy of Reagan Years," *The Washington Post,* November 6, 1988.
107. Ibid.
108. Testimony before the Senate Committee on Banking, Housing, and Urban Affairs by Prof. Benjamin M. Friedman of Harvard University, November 14, 1989.
109. Niskanen, *Reaganomics,* p. 314.
110. Interview with William Niskanen, December 8, 1989.
111. Interview with Peter Domenici, December 12, 1989.
112. Alan S. Blinder, "The Economic Myths That the 1980s Exploded," *Business Week,* November 27, 1989.

CHAPTER 13—*Focus of Evil*

1. Interview with Ronald Reagan, February 10, 1989.
2. Interview with Ronald Reagan, February 25, 1988.
3. "On Soviet Morality," *Time,* February 16, 1981.
4. Ibid.
5. "Sizing Up the Kremlin," Editorial, *The Washington Post,* February 1, 1981.
6. "A Message for Moscow," *Time,* February 9, 1981.
7. Reagan often gave this defense in public in later years. When David Hoffman and I interviewed him on January 16, 1984, for *The Washington Post,* he said: "Ever since the first press conference, there has been a distortion of an answer of mine to a question . . . that I called the Soviets a lot of names . . . everyone seems to have forgotten that I was quoting them with regard to lying, cheating and so forth. I didn't say that that was my opinion of them. I made it very plain that they themselves, in their writing and their speaking over the years, have said that anything of this kind that furthers socialism is moral. . . . Lenin's famous line that 'Treaties are like pie crusts. They're made to be broken.'" In a May 5, 1989, interview with me for this book, he was still repeating the same thoughts: "The Soviet Union, and I can't say this with the present leader, but every leader before him of the Soviet Union has gone before the great Soviet Congress and so forth and the party and said that their goal must be the Marxian belief in a one world Communist state. So, in other words, they were expansionist. They were trying to carry their system to the world."
8. Larry Ceplair and Steven Englund, *Inquisition in Hollywood,* p. 68.
9. *WTROM,* p. 160.
10. *Ronnie and Jesse,* p. 37.

11. *WTROM,* p. 162.
12. *Reagan,* p. 81.
13. Ibid., pp. 83–84.
14. Philip Dunne, *Take Two,* p. 206. See also *Reagan,* p. 84.
15. *WTROM,* p. 199.
16. Conversation with Frank Mankiewicz, January 1990.
17. *Ronnie and Jesse,* p. 39.
18. Laurence I. Barrett, *Gambling with History,* p. 57.
19. Garry Wills, *Reagan's America,* p. 197.
20. Maureen Reagan, *First Father, First Daughter,* p. 61.
21. Wills, *Reagan's America,* p. 197.
22. Bob Slosser, *Reagan Inside Out,* p. 16.
23. Daniel Schorr, "Reagan Recants; His Path from Armageddon to Détente," *Los Angeles Times,* January 3, 1988.
24. Ibid.
25. Interview with Ronald Reagan, May 5, 1989.
26. Interview with Stuart Spencer, May 2, 1989.
27. "People-American-Way; Study Warns of Impact of Armageddon Theology on U.S. Policy," *Business Wire,* April 1, 1985.
28. Kenneth L. Woodward, "Arguing Armageddon," *Newsweek,* November 5, 1984.
29. Interview with Robert McFarlane, December 23, 1989.
30. Ibid.
31. Conversation with Frank Carlucci, December 31, 1989.
32. Strobe Talbott, *Deadly Gambits,* p. 263n.
33. Ibid., p. 273n.
34. Ronald Reagan, "How to Make Yourself Important," *Photoplay,* August 1942.
35. Interview with Viktor Belenko, June 14, 1989.
36. Martin Anderson, *Revolution,* pp. 72–74.
37. Lou Cannon, "Arms Boost Seen as Strain on Soviets," *The Washington Post,* June 19, 1980.
38. Interview with John Block, August 30, 1989.
39. Ronald Reagan, *An American Life,* p. 270.
40. Michael K. Deaver, *Behind the Scenes,* p. 263.
41. Ibid.
42. Ibid.
43. Ronald Reagan, *An American Life,* p. 272.
44. Barrett, *Gambling with History,* p. 32.
45. Remarks and question-and-answer session with regional editors and broadcasters, White House, September 16, 1985.
46. Dusko Doder, *Shadows and Whispers,* p. 31.
47. Interview with Alexander Haig, June 6, 1989.
48. Ibid.
49. Talbott, *Deadly Gambits,* p. 17.
50. Interview with Richard Perle, March 9, 1989.
51. Barrett, *Gambling with History,* p. 312.
52. Interview with Stuart Spencer, May 2, 1989.
53. Interview with Robert McFarlane, January 16, 1990.
54. Interview with George Shultz, April 6, 1989.

55. Don Oberdorfer, "Reagan and the World: Foreign Policy; Part I," *The Washington Post,* November 20, 1983.
56. Interview with George Shultz, April 6, 1989.
57. Interview with Richard Perle, March 9, 1989.
58. Conversation with George Shultz, April 6, 1989.
59. Interview with Michael Deaver, January 1990.
60. Interview with George Shultz, February 13, 1989.
61. "Men of the Year," *Time,* January 2, 1984.
62. Interview with George Shultz, April 6, 1989.
63. Helene von Damm, *At Reagan's Side,* pp. 291–92.
64. Interview with William Clark, March 20, 1989.
65. Interview with George Shultz, February 13, 1989.
66. Barrett, *Gambling with History,* p. 291.
67. William Safire, "Essay; Touching a Nerve," *The New York Times,* October 18, 1982.
68. Helen Thomas, "Reagan Forecasts Summit in '84," United Press International, May 19, 1983.
69. Murrey Marder, "The U.S.-Soviet War of Words Escalates," *The Washington Post,* November 21, 1983.
70. Doder, *Shadows and Whispers,* p. 39.
71. "Ronald Reagan's Flower Power," Editorial, *The New York Times,* June 9, 1982.
72. Ronald Reagan, *Speaking My Mind,* p. 108.
73. Interview with David Gergen, March 6, 1989.
74. Interview with Anthony Dolan, May 18, 1989.
75. Interview with Robert McFarlane, January 16, 1990.
76. Ibid.
77. Strobe Talbott, *The Russians and Reagan,* p. 122.
78. Oberdorfer, "Reagan and the World: Foreign Policy; Part I."
79. Anderson, *Revolution,* p. 83.
80. Conversation with Edward Teller, January 17, 1990.
81. Interview with Ronald Reagan, February 10, 1989.
82. Ibid.
83. Anderson, *Revolution,* p. 85.
84. Ibid., p. 94.
85. Ibid., p. 96.
86. Ibid.
87. Interview with Ronald Reagan, February 10, 1989.
88. Kenneth Adelman, *The Great Universal Embrace,* p. 306.
89. Strobe Talbott, *The Master of the Game,* p. 111.
90. Conversation with Strobe Talbott, January 1990.
91. Interview with Robert McFarlane, October 11, 1989.
92. Ibid.
93. Conversation with Strobe Talbott, January 1990.
94. Interview with Robert McFarlane, October 11, 1989.
95. Ibid.
96. Gregg Easterbrook, "James Watkins and the Morality of Nukes," *The Washington Post Magazine,* February 18, 1990.
97. Interview with James Watkins, February 3, 1990.

98. Frederick H. Hartmann, *Naval Renaissance: The U.S. Navy in the 1980s,* p. 253.
99. Interview with John Vessey, January 26, 1990.
100. Ibid.
101. Hartmann, *Naval Renaissance,* p. 254.
102. Conversation with James Watkins, February 3, 1990.
103. Interview with James Watkins, February 3, 1990.
104. Hartmann, *Naval Renaissance,* p. 255.
105. Ibid.
106. Interview with James Watkins, February 3, 1990.
107. Interview with Robert McFarlane, October 11, 1989.
108. Ibid.
109. Hartmann, *Naval Renaissance,* p. 256.
110. Interview with Robert McFarlane, October 11, 1989.
111. Hartmann, *Naval Renaissance,* p. 256.
112. Interview with Ronald Reagan, February 10, 1989.
113. Hartmann, *Naval Renaissance,* p. 258.
114. Interview with James Watkins, February 3, 1990.
115. Interview with Robert McFarlane, February 3, 1990.
116. Ibid.
117. Hartmann, *Naval Renaissance,* p. 258.
118. Interview with John Vessey, January 26, 1990.
119. Talbott, *The Master of the Game,* p. 193.
120. Interview with William Clark, March 20, 1989.
121. Ibid.
122. The costs of SDI have been variously calculated, partly because much more money has been authorized for the program than has been actually spent on it. The figure used here is based on the calculation of John E. Pike, associate director of the Federation of American Scientists, through fiscal year 1990. Interview with John Pike, January 28, 1990.

CHAPTER 14—*Freedom Fighters*

1. Remarks to elected officials during a White House briefing on U.S. assistance for the Nicaraguan democratic resistance, March 14, 1986.
2. *Reagan,* p. 217.
3. Lou Cannon, "Reagan Says U.S. Owes 'Contras' Help," *The Washington Post,* March 2, 1985.
4. Interview with Ronald Reagan, May 5, 1989.
5. Conversation with Kenneth Duberstein, October 19, 1989.
6. David Hoffman, "Reagan Sees Limited Help for Hostages," *The Washington Post,* January 27, 1987.
7. Interview with Richard Perle, March 9, 1989.
8. Interview with Donald Regan, February 2, 1990.
9. *Reagan,* p. 215.
10. William F. Buckley Jr., *On the Firing Line,* p. 364. When Buckley suggested to Reagan in a telephone conversation that he debate the treaty in a two-hour special, Reagan said, "Why should I want to debate with you?" He subsequently changed his mind and agreed to appear.

11. Ibid., p. 381.
12. Interview with Michael Deaver, November 15, 1988.
13. Lou Cannon and Lee Lescaze, " 'The Main Accomplishment Has Been . . . Our Economic Program,' " excerpts from an interview with President Reagan, *The Washington Post,* March 29, 1981.
14. Interview with Robert McFarlane, January 5, 1990.
15. Ibid.
16. Ibid.
17. Laurence I. Barrett, *Gambling with History,* p. 209.
18. Ibid.
19. Martin Schram, "Caspar One-Note's Military March," *The Washington Post,* April 18, 1982.
20. This was a frequent observation about Weinberger, first made in print to the best of my knowledge on p. 96 of *Best Laid Plans: The Inside Story of America's War Against Terrorism* by David C. Martin and John Walcot. Weinberger often joked about his height. When he posed for pictures with the rotating military guard in front of his office, he would quip that he needed a box to stand on.
21. Saul Friedman, "Four-Star Warrior," *Newsday Magazine,* February 11, 1990.
22. "The Uses of Military Power," remarks by Caspar Weinberger to the National Press Club, November 28, 1984.
23. Ibid.
24. Roy Gutman, *Banana Diplomacy,* p. 174.
25. Bob Woodward, *Veil,* p. 36.
26. Interview with Michael Deaver, February 1, 1990.
27. Interview with Ronald Reagan, February 26, 1990.
28. Ibid.
29. Gutman, *Banana Diplomacy,* pp. 46–49.
30. Ibid., p. 57.
31. Ibid.
32. Ibid., p. 55.
33. Woodward, *Veil,* p. 173.
34. Ibid., p. 455n.
35. *Report of the Congressional Committees Investigating the Iran-Contra Affair,* p. 29.
36. Lou Cannon, "Reagan Defends Nicaraguan Role," *The Washington Post,* May 5, 1983.
37. Ibid.
38. Interview with Rodney McDaniel, March 13, 1989.
39. Ibid.
40. Constantine Menges, *Inside the National Security Council,* p. 386.
41. Interview with Jeane Kirkpatrick, March 7, 1990.
42. Interview with Rodney McDaniel, March 13, 1989.
43. Address to the nation on U.S. policy in Central America, May 9, 1984.
44. Interview with Bently Elliott, March 7, 1990.
45. Robert J. Donovan, *Conflict and Crisis,* p. 283.
46. Ibid., p. 284.
47. Ibid., p. 286.
48. Charles Krauthammer, "Nicaraguan Nettle," *New Republic,* May 9, 1983.
49. Charles Krauthammer letter to Lou Cannon, March 8, 1990.

50. Charles Krauthammer, "The Reagan Doctrine," *Time,* April 1, 1985.
51. Interview with Fred Iklé, March 6, 1990.
52. Gorbachev described Afghanistan as a "bleeding wound" in his speech to the Twenty-seventh Communist Party Congress in Moscow on February 25, 1986. See Dusko Doder and Louise Branson, *Gorbachev: Heretic in the Kremlin,* p. 291.
53. Conversation with Rodney McDaniel, April 1990.
54. Interview with Robert McFarlane, January 5, 1990.
55. "Message to Congress on Freedom, Regional Security and Global Peace," March 14, 1986.
56. Interview with Robert McFarlane, March 14, 1990.
57. Interview with Jeane Kirkpatrick, March 7, 1990.
58. Interview with George Bush, March 7, 1990.
59. Interview with Jeane Kirkpatrick, March 7, 1990.
60. Ibid.
61. Gutman, *Banana Diplomacy,* p. 126.
62. Ibid., p. 124.
63. Interview with Jeane Kirkpatrick, March 7, 1990.
64. Gutman, *Banana Diplomacy,* p. 133.
65. Ibid., p. 181.
66. Interview with Jeane Kirkpatrick, March 7, 1990.
67. Gutman, *Banana Diplomacy,* p. 197.
68. Lou Cannon, "Hang the Polls, Conviction Is What Counts on Latin Policy," *The Washington Post,* May 14, 1984.
69. Gutman, *Banana Diplomacy,* p. 335.
70. Ibid., p. 211.
71. Ibid.
72. Interview with Jeane Kirkpatrick, March 7, 1990.
73. Interview with Bently Elliott, March 7, 1990.
74. Menges, *Inside the National Security Council,* p. 94.
75. Interview with Michael Deaver, February 1, 1990.
76. Interview with James Baker, March 7, 1990.
77. Menges, *Inside the National Security Council,* p. 107.
78. Gutman, *Banana Diplomacy,* p. 243.
79. Ibid., pp. 254–55.
80. *Report of the Congressional Committees Investigating the Iran-Contra Affair,* p. 38.
81. Interview with Robert McFarlane, March 14, 1990.
82. *Report of the Congressional Committees Investigating the Iran-Contra Affair,* p. 39.
83. George Lardner Jr., "Reagan Urged Aid Secrecy," *The Washington Post,* March 11, 1989.
84. Interview with Robert McFarlane, January 5, 1990.
85. Ibid.
86. Ibid.

CHAPTER 15—*Lost in Lebanon*

1. Remarks and a question-and-answer session with regional editors and broadcasters on the situation in Lebanon, White House, October 24, 1983.

2. *Report of the Department of Defense Commission on Beirut International Airport Terrorist Act,* October 23, 1983, report dated December 20, 1983, p. 24; hereinafter referred to as the Long Report.

3. Jack Sirica of the *San Jose Mercury* obtained this copy of the FBI dossier through the Freedom of Information Act.

4. Laurence I. Barrett, *Gambling with History,* p. 272.

5. Ibid., p. 275.

6. Alexander M. Haig Jr., *Caveat,* p. 325.

7. William B. Quandt, "Reagan's Lebanon Policy: Trial and Error," *Middle East Journal,* Spring 1984.

8. Haig, *Caveat,* p. 328.

9. "Prime Minister Issues Harsh Criticism of U.S.," Associated Press, December, 20, 1981.

10. Barrett, *Gambling with History,* p. 271.

11. Haig, *Caveat,* p. 337.

12. Ibid., p. 341.

13. Ibid., p. 344.

14. Ibid., p. 346.

15. Remarks and a question-and-answer session at a meeting with editors and broadcasters from western states, Los Angeles, July 1, 1982.

16. David C. Martin and John Walcott, *Best Laid Plans: The Inside Story of America's War Against Terrorism,* p. 93.

17. Ibid., p. 92.

18. Don Oberdorfer and John M. Goshko, "U.S. Set to Send Troops to Lebanon," *The Washington Post,* July 7, 1982.

19. Interview with Howard Teicher, March 28, 1990.

20. Remarks and a question-and-answer session at a briefing on federalism for state and local officials, Los Angeles, July 6, 1982.

21. Haig, *Caveat,* p. 351.

22. "American Troops in Beirut," Editorial, *The Washington Post,* July 7, 1982.

23. Oberdorfer and Goshko, "U.S. Set to Send Troops to Lebanon."

24. Michael K. Deaver, *Behind the Scenes,* p. 166.

25. Interview with Geoffrey Kemp, February 1, 1990.

26. Ibid.

27. Deaver, *Behind the Scenes,* p. 166.

28. Ibid.

29. Interview with Geoffrey Kemp, February 1, 1990.

30. Interview with Fred Iklé, March 6, 1990.

31. Interview with Richard Perle, March 9, 1989.

32. Interview with Kenneth Adelman, September 20, 1989.

33. Ibid.

34. Interview with Frank Carlucci, March 22, 1989.

35. Ibid.

36. Interview with Colin Powell, February 23, 1989.

37. Ibid.

38. Interview with Caspar Weinberger, March 17, 1989.

39. Interview with Colin Powell, February 23, 1989.

40. Quandt, "Reagan's Lebanon Policy: Trial and Error."
41. Remarks to reporters on Lebanon and the Middle East, September 8, 1982.
42. "A Growing Sense of Betrayal," *Time,* October 24, 1982.
43. Martin and Walcott, *Best Laid Plans,* p. 95.
44. Ibid.
45. Interview with Caspar Weinberger, March 29, 1990.
46. Conversation with Howard Teicher, March 28, 1990.
47. Interview with Caspar Weinberger, March 29, 1990.
48. Ibid.
49. Martin and Walcott, *Best Laid Plans,* p. 98.
50. Geoffrey Kemp, "Lessons of Lebanon: A Guideline for Future U.S. Policy," *Middle East Insight,* Summer 1988.
51. Ibid.
52. Interview with Caspar Weinberger, March 29, 1990.
53. Bob Woodward, *Veil,* pp. 219–20.
54. Quandt, "Reagan's Lebanon Policy: Trial and Error."
55. Martin and Walcott, *Best Laid Plans,* p. 111.
56. Interview with Geoffrey Kemp, February 1, 1990.
57. Ibid.
58. Interview with George Shultz, April 6, 1989.
59. Interview with Caspar Weinberger, March 29, 1990.
60. Ibid.
61. Kemp, "Lessons of Lebanon."
62. Ibid.
63. Ibid.
64. Martin and Walcott, *Best Laid Plans,* p. 113.
65. Interview with Geoffrey Kemp, February 1, 1990.
66. Lou Cannon, "President's Strong Man Stretches South," *The Washington Post,* August 3, 1983.
67. Roy Gutman, *Banana Diplomacy,* p. 148.
68. Interview with George Shultz, February 13, 1989.
69. Ibid.
70. Interview with William Clark, February 20, 1990.
71. Interview with Robert McFarlane, April 2, 1990.
72. Ibid.
73. Don Oberdorfer, " 'Disgrace'; Shultz's Roar on Policy-Making Got Results," *The Washington Post,* October 23, 1983.
74. Interview with Caspar Weinberger, March 17, 1989.
75. Martin and Walcott, *Best Laid Plans,* p. 115.
76. Ibid.
77. On October 19, 1966, Senator George Aiken of Vermont said that the United States should proclaim victory in Vietnam by reaching the limited objective of containing the aggression by the North Vietnamese and should withdraw the troops to the major population centers. If there were no further attacks, the U.S. should bring its troops home. These statements were capsulized by the media into "The U.S. should declare victory and get out," although he never said these exact words.

78. Martin and Walcott, *Best Laid Plans,* p. 117.
79. Ibid., p. 120.
80. Interview with William Clark, March 20, 1989.
81. Ibid.
82. Martin and Walcott, *Best Laid Plans,* p. 122.
83. Lou Cannon and George Wilson, "Reagan Authorized Marines to Call In Beirut Air Strikes," *The Washington Post,* September 13, 1983.
84. Deaver, *Behind the Scenes,* p. 170.
85. Hedrick Smith, "Reagan Upgrading Lebanon Presence," *The New York Times,* September 13, 1983.
86. Interview with William Clark, March 20, 1989.
87. Hedrick Smith, *The Power Game: How Washington Works,* p. 445.
88. Interview with William Clark, March 20, 1989.
89. This section is based on interviews with Clark, Baker, Deaver, Meese, Weinberger and others conducted under ground rules that allowed me to use the material without direct attribution to the individual participants.
90. Smith, *The Power Game,* p. 323.
91. Ibid., p. 324.
92. Interview with Michael Deaver, April 17, 1990.
93. Ronald Reagan, *An American Life,* p. 448.
94. Accounts of this incident appear in Deaver, *Behind the Scenes,* pp. 85–88, and in *Reagan,* pp. 238–40.
95. Interview with Michael Deaver, April 10, 1990.
96. Ronald Reagan, *An American Life,* p. 448.
97. Interview with Jeane Kirkpatrick, March 7, 1990.
98. Clark spoke highly to me and others of McFarlane's "bravery" after he dictated his cable requesting a change in the rules of engagement. Deaver believes that he may have talked in the same vein to Reagan.
99. Ronald Reagan, *An American Life,* p. 448.
100. Deaver, *Behind the Scenes,* p. 130.
101. In *Behind the Scenes,* Deaver wrote that if Baker had been appointed national security adviser, "almost assuredly there would have been no arms sold to Iran, no Swiss bank accounts or secret funds diverted to the Contras, no foreign policy seemingly created by Rube Goldberg" (p. 130).
102. Interview with Stuart Spencer, April 11, 1990.
103. Lou Cannon, "Reagan Appoints McFarlane Adviser on U.S. Security," *The Washington Post,* October 18, 1983.
104. Long Report, pp. 3, 63.
105. Long Report, pp. 61–62.
106. Martin and Walcott, *Best Laid Plans,* p. 124.
107. Ibid., p. 147.
108. Ibid.
109. Long Report, pp. 32–33.
110. "The Decision to Assist Grenada," statement by Langhorne A. Motley, assistant secretary for inter-American affairs, before the House Armed Services Committee, January 24, 1984.
111. Interview with Robert McFarlane, April 16, 1990.

112. "D-Day in Grenada," *Time,* November 7, 1983.
113. Interview with Robert McFarlane, April 16, 1990.
114. Ronald Reagan, *An American Life,* p. 437.
115. Interview with Ronald Reagan, May 5, 1989.
116. Interview with Robert McFarlane, April 2, 1990.
117. Conversation with Colin Powell, April 17, 1990. When I interviewed Caspar Weinberger on March 17, 1989, he stated these same feelings to me twice during the interview: "And it's a source of enormous pain and unhappiness to me that I was not persuasive enough to have the force withdrawn before that tragedy happened"; and "I was just very unhappy with myself that I hadn't been able to be more persuasive."
118. Lou Cannon and Juan Williams, "161 Marines Killed in Beirut," *The Washington Post,* October 24, 1983.
119. *The Washington Post,* Editorial, October 24, 1983.
120. *New York Daily News,* Editorial, October 24, 1983.
121. *USA Today,* Editorial, October 24, 1983.
122. Interview with Richard Wirthlin, April 18, 1990.
123. Tip O'Neill, *Man of the House,* p. 366.
124. Interview with Caspar Weinberger, March 29, 1990.
125. Lou Cannon, "Strategic Airport, Hostage Fears Led to Move," *The Washington Post,* October 26, 1983.
126. "D-Day in Grenada."
127. Interview with Michael Deaver, October 24, 1983.
128. "The Decision to Assist Grenada."
129. Richard Harwood, "Tidy U.S. War Ends: 'We Blew Them Away,' " *The Washington Post,* November 6, 1983.
130. Interview with Robert McFarlane, February 21, 1989.
131. Lou Cannon and David Hoffman, "There Is a New Feeling on the Part of the American People," *The Washington Post,* January 22, 1984. Excerpts from an interview with President Reagan on January 16, 1984.
132. Martin and Walcott, *Best Laid Plans,* p. 147.
133. Conversation with Stuart Spencer, January 5, 1988.
134. Martin and Walcott, *Best Laid Plans,* p. 137.
135. Long Report, pp. 39, 44.
136. Helen Dewar and Margaret Shapiro, "Hill Leaders Split Over Pulling Out Troops in Beirut," *The Washington Post,* January 24, 1984.
137. Interview with Robert McFarlane, February 21, 1989.
138. Ibid.
139. Martin and Walcott, *Best Laid Plans,* p. 148.
140. "Excerpts from the *Journal's* Interview with the President," *The Wall Street Journal,* February 3, 1984.
141. Martin and Walcott, *Best Laid Plans,* p. 149.
142. Interview with Robert McFarlane, April 20, 1990.
143. Ibid.
144. Background briefing by senior administration official on the situation in Lebanon, Point Mugu NAS, California, Office of the Press Secretary, February 7, 1984.

CHAPTER 16—*An Actor Abroad*

1. Remarks and a question-and-answer session with students at Fudan University, Shanghai, April 30, 1984.
2. Interview with Marybel Batjer, March 30, 1989.
3. Remarks and a question-and-answer session with students at Fudan University, Shanghai, April 30, 1984.
4. Reagan made this observation when we were chatting on a domestic trip during the early days of his California governorship.
5. Reagan often told this story during the later years of his presidency. It is quoted here from his remarks to students at Moscow State University on May 31, 1988.
6. Remarks and a question-and-answer session with students at Fudan University, Shanghai, April 30, 1984.
7. The White House usually corrected Reagan misstatements by putting an asterisk after the misstatement in the transcript of his remarks and noting at the bottom of the page what Reagan had meant to say. In this case, however, the misstatement was omitted in the transcript issued at the time. What Reagan said is accurately reproduced in the 1982 *Public Papers of the Presidents* (p. 1542), with the notation that "Bogotá" was a "White House correction."
8. Question-and-answer session with reporters on the president's trip to Latin America, December 4, 1982.
9. Ibid.
10. "Reagan's Related to Royalty—Back a Millennium or So," Associated Press, *Los Angeles Times,* November 11, 1980.
11. Remarks to the citizens of Ballyporeen, Ireland, June 3, 1984.
12. Pool report by Bob Rowley, *Chicago Tribune,* and Eleanor Clift, *Newsweek,* June 3, 1984.
13. Reagan's feelings about this play, *Journey's End,* are recounted on p. 37 of *WTROM* and in Chap. 3 of this book.
14. Ronald Reagan, "Margaret Thatcher and the Revival of the West," *National Review,* May 19, 1989. Reagan also recounted this exchange in his "Farewell Interview" with David Brinkley on ABC News, December 22, 1988.
15. Remarks at the welcoming ceremony for Prime Minister Margaret Thatcher, February 26, 1981.
16. Toasts of President Reagan and Prime Minister Thatcher at a luncheon honoring the president, London, June 8, 1982.
17. Margaret Thatcher, "Reagan's Leadership, America's Recovery," *National Review,* December 30, 1988.
18. Hedrick Smith, "Reagan, Reflecting on Ottawa Parley, Praises Mitterrand," *The New York Times,* July 23, 1981.
19. Press briefing by Edwin Meese, Ottawa, July 19, 1981.
20. Smith, "Reagan, Reflecting on Ottawa Parley, Praises Mitterrand."
21. Lou Cannon, "Reagan Describes Summit Meeting as 'Worth Its Weight in Gold,' " *The Washington Post,* July 23, 1981.
22. Ibid.
23. James Reston, "Notes from the Cellar," *The New York Times,* July 22, 1981.
24. Ibid.

25. Lee Lescaze and Hobart Rowan, "Reagan Praises Cancún 'Success,' " *The Washington Post,* October 24, 1981.
26. Lee Lescaze, "Reagan Uses Hotel Like White House," *The Washington Post,* October 24, 1981.
27. Ibid.
28. Karen Elliott House and Alan L. Otten, "White House Hopes Summits Will Enhance the President's Stature," *The Wall Street Journal,* May 28, 1982.
29. Lou Cannon, "Soviets Assail Reagan's European Trip," *The Washington Post,* June 13, 1982.
30. William Safire, "Dissareagan," *The New York Times,* June 7, 1982.
31. Cannon, "Soviets Assail Reagan's European Trip."
32. Remarks on arrival in Berlin, June 11, 1982.
33. Ibid.
34. Pool report by Susan Page, *Newsday,* and Sara Fritz, *U.S. News & World Report,* June 11, 1982.
35. Lou Cannon, "On the Continent, Nodding Off and Fending Off the Press," *The Washington Post,* June 14, 1982.
36. Ibid.
37. Ibid.
38. Pool report by Vic Ostrowidzki, Hearst Newspapers, November 11, 1983.
39. Press briefing by Secretary of State George Shultz, Seoul, November 13, 1983.
40. Lou Cannon, "Reagan's Asian Takes Are in the Can," *The Washington Post,* November 15, 1983.
41. Francis X. Clines, "A Reporter's Notebook: Reagan's Visit Is a Tour de Force for the Image Makers," *The New York Times,* November 14, 1983.
42. Cannon, "Reagan's Asian Takes Are in the Can."
43. Ibid.
44. Question-and-answer session with high school students on domestic and foreign policy issues, Old Executive Office Building, December 2, 1983.
45. Informal exchange with employees at the Weyerhaeuser Industries–Port of Tacoma Log Export Shipping Facility, Tacoma, Washington, April 19, 1984.
46. Ibid.
47. Steven R. Weisman, "Reagan Ends Trip as Thousands Jam Shanghai Streets," *The New York Times,* May 1, 1984.
48. "The Making of a New China Hand," *Newsweek,* May 7, 1984.
49. Lou Cannon, "Finding Capitalism in China Provides an Out on Old Stances," *The Washington Post,* May 7, 1984.
50. Lou Cannon, "Reagan, Pope Urge Renewed Peace Efforts," *The Washington Post,* May 3, 1984.
51. Remarks at the welcoming ceremony for Pope John Paul II, Fairbanks, Alaska, May 2, 1984.
52. John Vinocur, "D-Day + 40 Years," *The New York Times,* May 13, 1984.
53. Hugh Sidey, "Remembering the Sacrifices of D-Day," *Time,* June 11, 1984.
54. *WTROM,* p. 137.
55. Ibid.
56. Garry Wills, *Reagan's America,* p. 164.
57. Ibid., p. 167.

58. *WTROM,* p. 159.
59. Pool report by Bob Rowley, *Chicago Tribune,* June 6, 1984.
60. Ronald Reagan, *Speaking My Mind,* p. 127. See also an earlier reference to this in Chap. 4 of this book.
61. From the notes of Joanne Omang of *The Washington Post,* and Lou Cannon, "Dramatic Account About Film of Nazi Death Camps Questioned," *The Washington Post,* March 5, 1984.
62. Cannon, "Dramatic Account About Film of Nazi Death Camps Questioned."
63. Wills, *Reagan's America,* p. 167.
64. Interview with foreign journalists, April 29, 1985.
65. Robert H. Abzug, *Inside the Vicious Heart: Americans and the Liberation of Nazi Concentration Camps,* p. 30.
66. These newsreels are available for inspection at the Motion Picture Branch of the National Archives, Washington, D.C. I also viewed unedited Army Air Corps stock footage taken of Orhdruf in March 1945 before U.S. troops reached the camp. Reagan conceivably might have seen this footage, which in one reel shows a pile of human bones. Because of the distance from which it was shot, however, this footage is much less graphic than the films shown on the newsreels after the camp was liberated.
67. Pool report by Bob Timberg, Baltimore *Sun,* May 5, 1985.
68. Lou Cannon, "President Welcomed in Grenada," *The Washington Post,* February 21, 1986. Sam Donaldson asked the question, although I did not identify him in my story.

CHAPTER 17—*Morning Again in America*

1. Remarks at a Reagan-Bush rally, Chicago, November 4, 1984.
2. Jeffrey D. Alderman, ABC News poll, Yearend Wrapup 1984.
3. Peter Goldman and Tony Fuller, *The Quest for the Presidency 1984,* p. 30.
4. Remarks at a Reagan-Bush rally, Cupertino, California, September 3, 1984.
5. "Every Region, Every Age Group, Almost Every Voting Bloc," *Time,* November 19, 1984.
6. Radio address to the nation on the Summer Olympic Games, July 28, 1984.
7. Amitai Etzioni, "The Democrats Need a Unifying Theme," *The New York Times,* October 5, 1984.
8. Alderman, ABC News poll.
9. Warren Brown, "U.S. Begins Firing Striking Air Controllers; Five Jailed," *The Washington Post,* August 6, 1981.
10. Interview with Donald Rumsfeld, May 14, 1990.
11. Ronald Reagan, *An American Life,* p. 283.
12. Interview of Jim Jones by Gwen Rubinstein, April 24, 1989.
13. Ibid.
14. Lou Cannon, "Speaker Calls President Insensitive," *The Washington Post,* January 29, 1986.
15. Tip O'Neill, *Man of the House,* p. 362.
16. Ibid.
17. Ibid.

18. Ibid., p. 363.
19. The president's news conference, June 14, 1984.
20. Lou Cannon, "Reagan's Presidency: Past and Prospect," *The Washington Post,* January 22, 1984.
21. Michael K. Deaver, *Behind the Scenes,* p. 39.
22. "Co-Starring at the White House," *Time,* January 14, 1985.
23. *Ronnie and Jesse,* pp. 177–78.
24. Interview with Paul Laxalt, May 22, 1989.
25. Interview with Stuart Spencer, May 2, 1989.
26. Nancy Reagan, *My Turn,* p. 264.
27. Ibid., p. 23.
28. Interview with Nancy Reagan, May 5, 1989.
29. Deaver, *Behind the Scenes,* p. 39.
30. Ibid.
31. Interview with Nancy Reagan, February 10, 1989.
32. Ibid.
33. Nancy Reagan, *My Turn,* p. 264.
34. Interview with Ed Rollins, May 14, 1990.
35. Michael Barone, *Our Country: The Shaping of America from Roosevelt to Reagan,* p. 640.
36. Jack W. Germond and Jules Witcover, *Wake Us When It's Over,* p. 413.
37. David S. Broder, "Overriding the Issues; Mondale Finds Message Obscured," *The Washington Post,* September 23, 1984.
38. Ibid.
39. Republican pollster Robert Teeter told me this story during the 1984 campaign. Similar versions of the line are quoted in Germond and Witcover, *Wake Us When It's Over,* p. 339 and Goldman and Fuller, *The Quest for the Presidency 1984,* p. 265.
40. Interview with Ed Rollins, May 14, 1990.
41. Marilyn Moon and Isabel V. Sawhill, "Family Incomes: Gainers and Losers," in *The Reagan Record,* edited by John L. Palmer and Isabel V. Sawhill, pp. 319–320.
42. Ibid., p. 336.
43. William Greider, "The Education of David Stockman," *The Atlantic,* December 1981.
44. Interview of Gary Bauer by Carl Cannon, c. May 1990.
45. Interview with Michael Deaver, May 22, 1990.
46. Interview of Gary Bauer by Carl Cannon, c. May 1990.
47. " 'Welfare Queen' Becomes Issue in Reagan Campaign," *The New York Times,* February 15, 1976; reprinted from *The Washington Star.*
48. David S. Broder, "Still Learning To Be the Opposition,"*The Washington Post,* February 15, 1981.
49. Henry Allen, "The Saga of Burky and Dutch," *The Washington Post,* March 7, 1981. See also *Reagan,* p. 38.
50. Interview with Michael Deaver, May 22, 1990.
51. Laurence I. Barrett, *Gambling with History,* p. 426.
52. Ibid., p. 419.

53. Remarks and a question-and-answer session with the student body of Providence–St. Mel High School, Chicago, May 10, 1982.

54. See "Ronald Reagan and Tax Exemptions for Racist Schools," a case study prepared by David Whitman for use at the Center for Press, Politics and Public Policy at the Kennedy School of Government, Harvard University. Released November 7, 1984. Copyright 1984 by the President and Fellows of Harvard College.

55. This story was recounted to me by Mike Deaver on May 22, 1990. It is also related in Barrett, *Gambling with History,* p. 416.

56. "Ronald Reagan and Tax Exemptions for Racist Schools," p. 73.

57. Paul Taylor, "Defeat for Religious Right, Vindication for Civil Rights Groups," *The Washington Post,* May 25, 1983.

58. Interview with David Gergen, March 6, 1989.

59. Interview with Ronald Reagan, February 26, 1990.

60. "A New Round of Musical Chairs Claims Mike Deaver, the Last of Reagan's California Cronies," *People,* April 15, 1985.

61. Lou Cannon and Joel Kotkin, "Old Frontier Sees Bright New Frontier," *The Washington Post,* June 7, 1979.

62. *Reagan,* p. 351.

63. Ibid., pp. 351–52.

64. Ibid., p. 349. For a more detailed account of this controversy, see *Ronnie and Jesse,* pp. 213–27.

65. *Reagan,* p. 369.

66. Ibid., p. 358.

67. Interview with Ronald Reagan, February 26, 1990.

68. *Reagan,* p. 363.

69. Paul R. Portney, "Natural Resources and the Environment," in *The Reagan Record,* p. 173.

70. "A Problem That Cannot Be Buried," *Time,* October 14, 1985.

71. Jules Witcover, *The Resurrection of Richard Nixon,* p. 463.

72. *Reagan,* p. 113.

73. Lou Cannon, "Overzealous Aides Misuse Secret Service, Media and the Boss," *The Washington Post,* September 3, 1984.

74. Ibid.

75. Ibid.

76. Goldman and Fuller, *The Quest for the Presidency 1984,* pp. 310–11.

77. Meg Greenfield, "Advantage, Mr. Mondale," *The Washington Post,* October 10, 1984.

78. Germond and Witcover, *Wake Us When It's Over,* p. 496.

79. Ibid.

80. Ibid.

81. Conversation with Stuart Spencer, May 17, 1990.

82. David S. Broder, "Mondale Tries Kennedy Style," *The Washington Post,* October 8, 1984.

83. Ibid.

84. Martin Schram, "Group of Viewers Shifts Opinions But Not Its Votes," *The Washington Post,* October 9, 1984.

85. Rich Jaroslovsky and James M. Perry, "Fitness Issue; New Question in Race: Is

Oldest U.S. President Now Showing His Age?" *The Wall Street Journal,* October 9, 1984.

86. Lou Cannon, "Reagan, After Debate, Incumbent Struggles to Regain Stride," *The Washington Post,* October 9, 1984.

87. Informal exchange with reporters on the presidential campaign, October 12, 1984.

88. Susanne M. Schafer, "Laxalt Says Reagan Brutalized by Debate Briefings," Associated Press, October 11, 1984.

89. In *"What Does Joan Say?"* Joan Quigley acknowledges she picked October 7 as the day for the debate but also asserts, "It was the only time I failed the Reagans or gave them less than excellent advice" (p. 92).

90. Conversation with Stuart Spencer, May 17, 1990.

91. Goldman and Fuller, *The Quest for the Presidency 1984,* p. 339.

92. Garry Wills, *Reagan's America,* p. 195.

93. Germond and Witcover, *Wake Us When It's Over,* p. 533.

94. At the president's news conference on May 13, 1982, Reagan said in response to a question on nuclear arms reduction, "That is the missile sitting there in its silo in which there could be the possibility of miscalculation. That is the one that people know that once that button is pushed, there is no defense; there is no recall. And it's a matter of minutes, and the missiles reach the other country. Those that are carried in bombers, those that are carried in ships of one kind or another, or submersibles, you are dealing there with a conventional type of weapon or instrument, and those instruments can be intercepted. They can be recalled if there has been a miscalculation. And so they don't have the same, I think, psychological effect that the presence of those other ones that, once launched, that's it; they're on their way, and there's no preventing, no stopping them."

95. David S. Broder, "Encounter Leaves Reagan on Course," *The Washington Post,* October 22, 1984.

CHAPTER 18—*Turning Point*

1. Ronald Reagan, *An American Life,* p. 536.

2. Jeffrey H. Birnbaum and Alan S. Murray, *Showdown at Gucci Gulch,* p. 44.

3. Donald T. Regan, *For the Record,* p. 219.

4. Lou Cannon, "President Wants to Keep His 'Winning Team' Intact, Aide Says," *The Washington Post,* November 8, 1984.

5. Interview with Richard Darman, April 10, 1987.

6. Interview with Ronald Reagan, February 10, 1989.

7. Michael K. Deaver, *Behind the Scenes,* p. 134.

8. Regan, *For the Record,* p. 227.

9. Ibid., p. 228.

10. Ibid., p. 108.

11. Ibid., p. 124.

12. Myra MacPherson, "Regan," *The Washington Post,* February 13, 1985.

13. Jane Mayer and Doyle McManus, *Landslide,* p. 36.

14. MacPherson, "Regan."

15. Regan, *For the Record,* pp. 212–13.
16. Birnbaum and Murray, *Showdown at Gucci Gulch,* pp. 286–87.
17. Nancy Reagan, *My Turn,* p. 313.
18. Interview with Donald Regan, May 17, 1989.
19. Deaver, *Behind the Scenes,* p. 173.
20. Regan, *For the Record,* p. 257, and interview with Donald Regan, April 6, 1989.
21. Informal exchange with reporters concerning Secretary of Health and Human Services Margaret M. Heckler, September 30, 1985.
22. Remarks announcing the nomination of Margaret M. Heckler as ambassador to Ireland and a question-and-answer session with reporters, October 1, 1985.
23. Peggy Noonan, *What I Saw at the Revolution,* pp. 203–4.
24. Larry Speakes, *Speaking Out,* p. 136.
25. James R. Dickenson, "Media Boxer in Reagan Corner," *The Washington Post,* February 6, 1985.
26. Lou Cannon, "Out of Step with Reagan," *The Washington Post,* February 11, 1985.
27. Deaver, *Behind the Scenes,* p. 182.
28. James S. Kunen, "Patrick Buchanan," *People,* August 29, 1988.
29. Lou Cannon, "Regan in Debut, Meets the Press," *The Washington Post,* February 6, 1985.
30. Patrick J. Buchanan, "The Contras Need Our Help," *The Washington Post,* March 5, 1986.
31. Martin Schram, "White House Officials, Sen. Jepsen Reach Uneasy Truce on AWACS Flap," *The Washington Post,* February 12, 1982.
32. The president's news conference, March 21, 1985.
33. Interview with Lou Cannon, Dave Hoffman and Len Downie, *The Washington Post,* April 1, 1985.
34. Remarks and a question-and-answer session with regional editors and broadcasters, White House, April 18, 1985.
35. Hedrick Smith, *The Power Game,* p. 376.
36. David Hoffman, "President Defends Tour Plans," *The Washington Post,* April 13, 1985.
37. Ibid.
38. Interview with Ed Rollins, January 30, 1989.
39. Ibid.
40. Deaver, *Behind the Scenes,* p. 182.
41. Ronald Reagan, *Speaking My Mind,* p. 257.
42. Interview with Richard Wirthlin, March 3, 1989.
43. Interview with Donald Regan, May 17, 1989.
44. Remarks at a conference on religious liberty, Old Executive Office Building, April 16, 1985.
45. Interview with Ed Rollins, January 30, 1989.
46. Interview with Richard Fox by Gwen Rubinstein, May 8, 1989.
47. Interview with Ed Rollins, January 30, 1989.
48. Smith, *Power Game,* p. 377.
49. Interview with Richard Fox by Gwen Rubinstein, May 8, 1989.
50. Interview with Ed Rollins, January 30, 1989.

51. Ibid.
52. David Hoffman, "Aides in Two Capitals Said to Share Blame for Bitburg Blunder," *The Washington Post,* May 1, 1985.
53. Remarks on presenting the Congressional Gold Medal to Elie Wiesel and on signing the Jewish Heritage Week Proclamation, White House, April 19, 1985.
54. Ibid.
55. Regan, *For the Record,* p. 261.
56. Chuck Conconi, "Personalities," *The Washington Post,* March 21, 1990.
57. Lou Cannon, "Dole, Wick Join Critics of Trip," *The Washington Post,* April 25, 1985.
58. Ibid.
59. Interview with Rev. Billy Graham, April 23, 1985.
60. Interview with Robert McFarlane, July 5, 1990.
61. Nancy Reagan, *My Turn,* p. 46.
62. *WTROM,* p. 283.
63. Nancy Reagan, *My Turn,* p. 47.
64. Joan Quigley, *"What Does Joan Say?"* p. 120.
65. Conversation with Michael Deaver, November 20, 1989.
66. Conversation with Michael Deaver, June 9, 1988.
67. Ibid.
68. Christoph Bertram, "Bitburg: A Lack of Historical Understanding," *The Washington Post,* April 12, 1985.

CHAPTER 19—*Darkness at Noon*

1. *Report of the President's Special Review Board,* February 26, 1987, p. III–12: hereinafter referred to as *Tower Report.*
2. Congressional Quarterly, Inc., *The Iran-Contra Puzzle,* p. C–100.
3. Larry Speakes, *Speaking Out,* p. 152.
4. *Tower Report,* p. IV–13.
5. *Report of the Congressional Committees Investigating the Iran-Contra Affair,* November 1987, p. 331; hereinafter referred to as *Iran-Contra Affair.*
6. Interview with Stuart Spencer, January 6, 1988.
7. Robert Timberg, "Ex-Marine Nobody Knows Becomes National Security 'Mover, Shaker,'" Baltimore *Sun,* June 13, 1983.
8. Jane Mayer, "Vietnam Service Isn't on the Résumés of Some Vocal, Middle-Aged Hawks," *The Wall Street Journal,* February 11, 1985.
9. Lou Cannon, "McFarlane's Hidden Hand Helps Shape U.S. Foreign Policy," *The Washington Post,* February 15, 1985.
10. Robert Timberg, "McFarlane Tightens Foreign Policy Grip," Baltimore *Sun,* February 6, 1985.
11. Interview with Richard Armitage, April 11, 1989.
12. Interview with Donald Regan, May 17, 1989.
13. William Safire, "Ten Myths About the Reagan Debacle," *The New York Times Magazine,* March 22, 1987.
14. Interview with Robert McFarlane, January 5, 1990.
15. Ibid.

16. *Iran-Contra Affair,* p. 157.
17. Sixty-six hostages were taken at the embassy. Fourteen were subsequently released and the remaining fifty-two were held the entire 444 days.
18. Interview with Robert McFarlane, July 5, 1990.
19. Caspar Weinberger, *Fighting for Peace,* p. 358.
20. *Tower Report,* p. B-3.
21. Weinberger, *Fighting for Peace,* p. 362.
22. *Tower Report,* pp. B-7–B-8.
23. Bob Woodward, *Veil,* p. 407.
24. *Tower Report,* p. B-4.
25. Ibid.
26. *Iran-Contra Affair,* p. 165.
27. Michael A. Ledeen, *Perilous Statecraft,* p. 97.
28. Interview with Peter Rodman, July 10, 1990.
29. *Tower Report,* p. B-9.
30. Weinberger, *Fighting for Peace,* p. 363.
31. Ibid., pp. 363–64.
32. David C. Martin and John Walcott, *Best Laid Plans,* p. 146.
33. Ibid., p. 177.
34. Interview with Patrick Buchanan, June 1985.
35. Martin and Walcott, *Best Laid Plans,* p. 185.
36. Lou Cannon, "What Happened to Reagan the Gunslinger," *The Washington Post,* July 7, 1985.
37. Jane Mayer and Doyle McManus, *Landslide,* p. 96.
38. Ibid., p. 102.
39. Interview with Ronald Reagan, February 10, 1989.
40. Interview with George Shultz, February 13, 1989.
41. Interview with Robert McFarlane, July 5, 1990.
42. Interview with Donald Regan, February 2, 1990.
43. *Iran-Contra Affair,* p. 164.
44. Donald T. Regan, *For the Record,* p. 17.
45. Ronald Reagan, *An American Life,* p. 501.
46. Ibid., pp. 501–2.
47. *Tower Report,* p. B-16.
48. Regan, *For the Record,* p. 20.
49. *Iran-Contra Affair,* p. 167.
50. Ibid.
51. Ibid.
52. Ibid.
53. Interview with Edmund Muskie, November 27, 1989.
54. *Iran-Contra Affair,* p. 168.
55. Interview with Robert McFarlane, July 5, 1990.
56. Ledeen, *Perilous Statecraft,* p. 134.
57. Ibid.
58. Ronald Reagan, *An American Life,* p. 505.
59. Ibid., p. 506.
60. Ibid.

61. Ledeen, *Perilous Statecraft,* p. 137.
62. Ibid., p. 138.
63. *Iran-Contra Affair,* pp. 175–76.
64. Ibid.
65. Ibid., p. 179.
66. Ibid., p. 181.
67. Ibid.
68. Regan, *For the Record,* pp. 320–21.
69. Interview with Donald Regan, February 2, 1990.
70. Ibid.
71. Remarks announcing the resignation of Robert C. McFarlane as assistant to the president for national security affairs and the appointment of John M. Poindexter, December 4, 1985.
72. Ledeen, *Perilous Statecraft,* p. 150.
73. William Safire, "Mr. Option Three," *The New York Times,* December 5, 1985.
74. *U.S. News & World Report, The Story of Lieutenant Colonel Oliver North,* p. 12.
75. Ibid.
76. Ibid., p. 14.
77. Constantine Menges, *Inside the National Security Council,* p. 193.
78. PROF note from North to Poindexter. See *Tower Report,* pp. B-40–B-42, and *Iran-Contra Affair,* pp. 194–95.
79. *Tower Report,* p. B-39.
80. Ibid., p. B-40.
81. *Iran-Contra Affair,* p. 197.
82. Ibid.
83. Ibid.
84. Ibid., p. 198.
85. Ibid.
86. Congressional Quarterly, Inc., *Iran-Contra Puzzle,* p. 138.
87. *Iran-Contra Affair,* p. 198.
88. Interview with Ronald Reagan, February 10, 1989.
89. Congressional Quarterly, Inc., *Iran-Contra Puzzle,* p. C–114.
90. Ibid., p. C–99.
91. Ibid., p. C–114. See also *Iran-Contra Affair,* p. 198.
92. *Iran-Contra Affair,* p. 199. See also Weinberger, *Fighting for Peace,* p. 373.
93. *Iran-Contra Affair,* p. 198.
94. Ibid., p. 199.
95. Ibid.
96. Ibid.
97. Ibid., p. 200.
98. Ibid., p. 201.
99. Ibid., pp. 201–2.
100. Ibid., p. 200.
101. Ibid.
102. Ibid., p. 205.
103. Ibid., p. 201.

104. Ibid., p. 203.
105. Ibid.
106. Ibid.
107. Ibid.
108. Ibid.
109. Ibid., p. 205.
110. Ibid., p. 206.
111. Ibid., p. 208.
112. Interview with Stanley Sporkin, February 12, 1990.
113. *Iran-Contra Affair,* p. 208.
114. *Tower Report,* p. B-77.
115. Congressional Quarterly, Inc., *Iran-Contra Puzzle,* p. C–127.
116. Ibid.
117. *Tower Report,* p. IV–11.
118. Regan, *For the Record,* p. 320.
119. Interview with George Shultz, February 13, 1989.
120. Ibid.
121. Ibid.
122. *Iran-Contra Affair,* p. 229.
123. Conversation with Robert Oakley, January 30, 1989.
124. Interview with Caspar Weinberger, March 17, 1989.
125. Interview with George Shultz, February 13, 1989.
126. Interview with Robert McFarlane, July 30, 1990.
127. Ibid.
128. *Iran-Contra Affair,* p. 220.
129. Interview with Robert McFarlane, January 5, 1990.
130. *Iran-Contra Affair,* p. 223.
131. *Tower Report,* p. B-91. See also *Iran-Contra Affair,* p. 242.
132. *Tower Report,* p. B-100.
133. Ibid., p. B-96.
134. Ibid., p. B-99.
135. *Iran-Contra Affair,* p. 237.
136. *Tower Report,* p. B-101.
137. Ibid., p. B-105.
138. Ibid., p. B-107.
139. *Iran-Contra Affair,* p. 239.
140. *Tower Report,* p. B-109.
141. Ibid.
142. Ibid., p. B-110.
143. Ibid., pp. B-110–B-111.
144. *Iran-Contra Affair,* p. 239.
145. *Tower Report,* p. B-114.
146. *Iran-Contra Affair,* p. 240. See also *Tower Report,* p. B-115.
147. *Tower Report,* p. B-116.
148. Interview with Robert McFarlane, July 30, 1990.
149. *Tower Report,* p. B-117.
150. Ronald Reagan, *An American Life,* p. 521.

151. See *Tower Report,* p. B-121, and Congressional Quarterly, Inc., *Iran-Contra Puzzle,* p. C–25.
152. Interview with Robert McFarlane, July 30, 1990.
153. Ibid.

CHAPTER 20—*Struggles at Twilight*

1. Address to the nation on the Iran arms and contra aid controversy, March 4, 1987.
2. Jim Hoagland, "Mitterrand: U.S., France Are United on Essentials," *The Washington Post,* June 29, 1986.
3. Statement on signing the Omnibus Diplomatic Security and Antiterrorism Act of 1986, August 27, 1986.
4. Remarks at a campaign rally for Senator Mark N. Andrews, Grand Forks, North Dakota, October 17, 1986.
5. Statement on House of Representatives approval of assistance for the Nicaraguan democratic resistance, June 25, 1986.
6. Margot Hornblower, "Liberty's Flame Relit as Gala Begins," *The Washington Post,* July 4, 1986.
7. Remarks on the lighting of the torch of the Statue of Liberty, New York, July 3, 1986.
8. Lance Morrow, "Yankee Doodle Magic," *Time,* July 7, 1986.
9. *Report of the President's Special Review Board,* February 26, 1987, p. B-132; hereinafter referred to as *Tower Report.*
10. Ibid., B-128.
11. Ibid.
12. *Report of the Congressional Committees Investigating the Iran-Contra Affair,* November 1987, p. 245; hereinafter referred to as *Iran-Contra Affair.*
13. *Tower Report,* p. B-102.
14. *Iran-Contra Affair,* p. 260.
15. *Tower Report,* pp. B-139–B-140.
16. Ibid., p. B-141.
17. Ibid.
18. Ibid.
19. Ibid. p. B-142.
20. *Iran-Contra Affair,* p. 247.
21. Ibid., p. 248.
22. Ibid., p. 249.
23. Ibid., p. 248.
24. Ibid., p. 247.
25. *Tower Report,* p. B-136.
26. Jane Mayer and Doyle McManus, *Landslide,* p. 257.
27. *Iran-Contra Affair,* p. 250. See also *Tower Report,* p. B-152.
28. *Tower Report,* p. B-153.
29. Ibid., p. B-152. See also *Iran-Contra Affair,* p. 250.
30. *Tower Report,* p. B-153.
31. *Iran-Contra Affair,* p. 249.
32. *Tower Report,* p. B-149.

33. *Iran-Contra Affair,* p. 252.
34. Ibid.
35. Remarks at a campaign rally for Senator Jeremiah A. Denton, Montgomery, Alabama, September 18, 1986.
36. *Iran-Contra Affair,* p. 253.
37. Ibid. See also Mayer and McManus, *Landslide,* p. 266.
38. *Iran-Contra Affair,* p. 255.
39. Ibid.
40. Ibid.
41. Ibid.
42. Ibid., p. 258.
43. Ibid., p. 255.
44. Ibid., p. 258.
45. Ibid., p. 256.
46. Ibid., p. 258.
47. Ibid., p. 257.
48. Interview with Ronald Reagan, February 10, 1989.
49. *Iran-Contra Affair,* p. 258.
50. Ibid., p. 260.
51. Ibid., p. 261.
52. Ibid.
53. Ibid.
54. Ibid., p. 260.
55. *Tower Report,* p. B-171. See also *Iran-Contra Affair,* p. 261.
56. "Waite Travels to Beirut, Reports Progress in Effort to Free U.S. Hostages," Associated Press, November 1, 1986.
57. Interview with Mitchell Daniels, August 6, 1990.
58. Statement by the president, November 2, 1986.
59. Interview with Mitchell Daniels, August 6, 1990.
60. Press briefing by Larry Speakes, October 27, 1986.
61. Press briefing by Larry Speakes, November 2, 1986.
62. Ibid.
63. Ibid.
64. Interview with Mitchell Daniels, August 6, 1990.
65. Remarks at a Republican Party rally, Costa Mesa, California, November 3, 1986.
66. Pool report, Air Force One, Las Vegas to Los Angeles, by Dennis Mullin, *U.S. News & World Report,* and George DeLama, *Chicago Tribune,* November 3, 1986.
67. David Hoffman, "White House Resisted Arms Sales Revelations," *The Washington Post,* January 31, 1987.
68. Robert J. McCartney, "Iran Says McFarlane, Others Came on Secret Mission to Tehran," *The Washington Post,* November 5, 1986.
69. Remarks on signing the Immigration Reform and Control Act of 1986, November 6, 1986.
70. Remarks and an informal exchange with reporters prior to a meeting with David Jacobsen, November 7, 1986.
71. Ibid.
72. Ibid.

73. Ibid.
74. Donald T. Regan, *For the Record,* p. 27.
75. *Iran-Contra Affair,* p. 262.
76. Ibid.
77. Regan, *For the Record,* p. 26.
78. Lou Cannon and David Hoffman, "Regan Says Jury Out on Iran Deal," *The Washington Post,* November 22, 1986.
79. *Iran-Contra Affair,* p. 293.
80. Ibid.
81. Ibid.
82. Ibid., p. 294.
83. Ibid., p. 295n.
84. Ibid.
85. Ibid., p. 295.
86. Ibid., p. 294.
87. Mayer and McManus, *Landslide,* p. 298. See also *Iran-Contra Affair,* p. 295.
88. Mayer and McManus, *Landslide,* p. 298.
89. Ibid.
90. Ibid.
91. Ibid., p. 299.
92. Ibid., p. 300.
93. Walter Pincus, "Reagan Ordered Casey to Keep Iran Mission from Congress," *The Washington Post,* November 15, 1986.
94. Tom Shales, "Shultz, His Medium and His Message; The Secretary Sends His Boss a Nationwide Signal," *The Washington Post,* November 18, 1986.
95. Regan, *For the Record,* p. 32.
96. Pincus, "Reagan Ordered Casey to Keep Iran Mission from Congress."
97. Bernard Weinraub, "Criticism on Iran and Other Issues Put Reagan's Aides on Defensive," *The New York Times,* November 16, 1986.
98. "Who Knew What and When Did They Know It?" *Time,* December 8, 1986.
99. Cannon and Hoffman, "Regan Says Jury Out on Iran Deal."
100. *Tower Report,* p. D-5.
101. Regan, *For the Record,* p. 35.
102. *Iran-Contra Affair,* p. 301.
103. Ibid.
104. Ibid., p. 298.
105. Ibid.
106. Regan, *For the Record,* p. 37.
107. Interview with Donald Regan, August 18, 1990.
108. Regan, *For the Record,* p. 37.
109. *Iran-Contra Affair,* p. 302.
110. Ibid., p. 303.
111. Ibid.
112. Ibid., p. 305.
113. Ibid.
114. Ibid.
115. "The Iran-Contra Hearings," excerpts of testimony, *The Washington Post,* July 8, 1987. See also *Iran-Contra Affair,* p. 226.

116. *Iran-Contra Affair,* p. 272.
117. Ibid., p. 225.
118. Ibid., p. 309.
119. Ibid.
120. Ibid., p. 311.
121. Interview with Michael Deaver, February 1990.
122. *Iran-Contra Affair,* p. 312.
123. Ibid.
124. Ibid.
125. Ibid.
126. Ibid., p. 314.
127. Interview with Donald Regan, August 19, 1990.
128. Interview with Donald Regan, May 17, 1989.
129. *Iran-Contra Affair,* p. 314.
130. Exchange with reporters at a photo opportunity on November 24, 1986, not recorded in *Public Papers of the Presidents.* See also Mayer and McManus, *Landslide,* p. 341.
131. Mayer and McManus, *Landslide,* p. 343. See also *Iran-Contra Affair,* p. 315.
132. Interview with Edwin Meese, April 11, 1989.
133. Regan, *For the Record,* p. 38.
134. Ibid., p. 42.
135. *Iran-Contra Affair,* pp. 316, 317.
136. Hugh Sidey, "An Interview with the President," *Time,* December 8, 1986, and David E. Rosenbaum, "Secord Recounts Being Told Reagan Knew of His Work," *The New York Times,* May 7, 1987.
137. Remarks announcing the review of the National Security Council's role in the Iran arms and contra aid controversy, November 25, 1986.
138. Sidey, "An Interview with the President."
139. George Lardner Jr., "Meese Details White House Crisis," *The Washington Post,* March 29, 1989.
140. George J. Church, "Who Was Betrayed?" *Time,* December 8, 1986.
141. Interview with Stuart Spencer, May 2, 1989.
142. Interview with Robert McFarlane, July 30, 1990.
143. Garry Wills, *Reagan's America,* p. 273.
144. "Reagan Calls 'Bloodbath' Wrong," Associated Press, April 17, 1970.
145. Congressional Quarterly, Inc., *The Iran-Contra Puzzle,* p. 75.
146. Interview with David Abshire, December 20, 1989.
147. Interview with Peter Wallison, July 5, 1989.
148. Ibid.
149. Ibid.
150. Interview with Rhett Dawson, March 14, 1989.
151. Interview with David Abshire, December 20, 1989.
152. Interview with Peter Wallison, July 5, 1989.
153. Ibid.
154. Interview with Rhett Dawson, March 14, 1989.
155. Interview with Peter Wallison, July 5, 1989.
156. Interview with Edmund Muskie, November 27, 1989.
157. Interview with Donald Regan, May 17, 1989.

158. Interview with Stuart Spencer, May 2, 1989.
159. Interview with David Abshire, September 8, 1990.
160. *Tower Report,* pp. B-19–B-20.
161. Interview with David Abshire, September 8, 1990.
162. *Tower Report,* p. III-21.
163. Interview with Edmund Muskie, November 27, 1989.
164. Interview with Brent Scowcroft, July 28, 1990.
165. *Tower Report,* p. IV-1.
166. Ibid., p. IV-10.
167. Confidential interview, 1987.
168. Interview with John Tower, November 7, 1989.
169. Theodore H. White, *Breach of Faith,* p. 10.
170. George Lardner Jr., "Reagan Urged Aid Secrecy," *The Washington Post,* March 11, 1989.
171. Bob Woodward and Lou Cannon, "McFarlane Note Told of Saudi Cash," *The Washington Post,* March 19, 1987.
172. David Hoffman and Bob Woodward, "McFarlane Said to Solicit Contra Aid from Saudis," *The Washington Post,* May 14, 1987.
173. Ibid.
174. Thomas B. Edsall and Ted Gup, "The Crisis of the Reagan Presidency," *The Washington Post,* March 7, 1987.
175. George Lardner Jr., "Trial Told of Reagan's Contra Role," *The Washington Post,* March 16, 1989.
176. Joe Pichirallo, "Hearings Suggest Reagan Had Wider Contra Role," *The Washington Post,* July 19, 1987.
177. Informal exchange with reporters on the Iran arms and contra aid controversy, New York, May 3, 1987.
178. Remarks and a question-and-answer session with Southeast regional editors and broadcasters, May 15, 1987.
179. Pichirallo, "Hearings Suggest Reagan Had Wider Contra Role,"
180. Interview with Nancy Reagan, May 5, 1989.
181. Interview with Peter Wallison, July 5, 1989.
182. Interview with Donald Regan, February 2, 1990.
183. Interview with Mitchell Daniels, August 6, 1990.
184. Ibid.
185. Ibid.
186. Interview with Donald Regan, February 2, 1990.
187. Interview with Brent Scowcroft, July 28, 1990.
188. Interview with Stuart Spencer, May 2, 1989.
189. Ibid.
190. Ibid.
191. Ibid.
192. Bob Woodward, *Veil,* p. 504. On March 3, Reagan replaced him with FBI director William Webster.
193. Interview with Michael Deaver, August 1987.
194. Ibid.
195. Interview with Donald Regan, May 17, 1989.

196. Interview with Robert Strauss, March 31, 1989.
197. Ibid.
198. Ibid.
199. Ibid.
200. Ibid.
201. Ibid.
202. Ibid.
203. Ibid.
204. Ibid.
205. Ibid.
206. Ibid.
207. Ibid.
208. Ronald Reagan, *An American Life,* p. 537.
209. Regan, *For the Record,* p. 98.
210. Interview with Donald Regan, May 17, 1989.
211. Ibid.
212. David M. Abshire, "Don Regan's Real 'Record': Looking Out for Number 1," *The Washington Post,* May 15, 1988.
213. Ibid.
214. Ibid.
215. Ibid.
216. Interview with David Abshire, December 18, 1989.
217. Interview with David Abshire, December 20, 1989.
218. Ibid.
219. Interview with David Abshire, December 18, 1989.
220. Ibid.
221. Ibid.
222. Ibid.
223. Ibid.
224. Interview with David Abshire, December 20, 1989.
225. *Tower Report,* p. IV-11.
226. Regan, *For the Record,* p. 97.
227. Ibid., p. 98.
228. Ronald Reagan, *An American Life,* p. 538.
229. Lou Cannon, "Howard Baker a 'Solution' Now Viewed as Problem," *The Washington Post,* November 8, 1987.
230. Heath Merriwether, "Story Was in Next Seat, but Baker Kept It to Himself," *Miami Herald,* March 1, 1987.
231. Interview with Paul Laxalt, May 22, 1989.
232. Ronald Reagan, *An American Life,* p. 539.
233. Interview with Howard Baker, May 22, 1989.
234. Regan, *For the Record,* p. 373.
235. Ibid.
236. Interview with Donald Regan, May 17, 1989.
237. Lou Cannon, "Trouble-Shooting with Carlucci," *The Washington Post,* November 30, 1987.
238. Ibid.

239. Interview with Frank Carlucci, March 22, 1989.
240. Ibid.
241. Ibid.
242. Interview with Howard Baker, May 22, 1989.
243. Interview with Rhett Dawson, March 14, 1989.
244. Interview with David Abshire, December 20, 1989.
245. Ibid.
246. Interview with Stuart Spencer, May 2, 1989.
247. Interview with Landon Parvin, March 9, 1989.
248. Interview with Landon Parvin, April 17, 1989.
249. Ibid.
250. Ibid.
251. Interview with Stuart Spencer, May 2, 1989.
252. Interview with Landon Parvin, April 17, 1989.
253. Interview with Stuart Spencer, May 2, 1989.
254. Interview with Landon Parvin, April 17, 1989.
255. Ibid.
256. Ibid.
257. Ibid.
258. Ibid.
259. Ibid.
260. Ibid.
261. Ibid.
262. Ibid.
263. Ibid.
264. Interview with Landon Parvin, March 9, 1989.
265. Interview with Landon Parvin, April 17, 1989.
266. Ronald Reagan, *An American Life,* p. 541.
267. Conversation with Landon Parvin, March 7, 1990.
268. Gerald M. Boyd, "President Asserts He Is Moving Away from Iran Affair," *The New York Times,* March 6, 1987.
269. "The President's Speech," Editorial, *The Washington Post,* March 5, 1987.
270. Interview with Stuart Spencer, May 2, 1989.

CHAPTER 21—*The New Era*

1. Ronald Reagan, *Speaking My Mind,* p. 247. Landon Parvin, to whom Reagan said these words, believes they occurred in a conversation on February 1, 1989.
2. Ronald Reagan, *An American Life,* p. 550.
3. Martin Anderson, *Revolution: The Reagan Legacy,* p. xxxviii.
4. Ibid., p. xxxix.
5. Interview with Michael Deaver, January 11, 1990.
6. Ronald Reagan, *An American Life,* p. 602.
7. Dusko Doder and Louise Branson, *Gorbachev: Heretic in the Kremlin,* pp.111–112.
8. Ibid., p. 64.
9. Pool report by David Hoffman, *The Washington Post,* and Morton Kondracke, *Newsweek,* November 19, 1985.

10. Jonathan Haslam, *The Soviet Union and the Politics of Nuclear Weapons in Europe, 1967–87,* p. 142.
11. Doder and Branson, *Gorbachev,* p. 9.
12. Ronald Reagan, *An American Life,* p. 611.
13. Ibid., p. 612.
14. Ibid., pp. 613–14.
15. Interview with Robert McFarlane, September 11, 1990.
16. Ibid.
17. Ronald Reagan, *An American Life,* p. 621.
18. Lou Cannon and David Hoffman, "Gorbachev Endorses Idea of Summit Meeting," *The Washington Post,* April 2, 1985.
19. Ronald Reagan, *An American Life,* p. 618.
20. Interview with Robert McFarlane, September 11, 1990.
21. Larry Speakes, *Speaking Out,* p. 125.
22. Ibid., p. 124.
23. Lou Cannon, "Reagan Voices Summit Hopes," *The Washington Post,* November 17, 1985.
24. Pool report by Barry Seaman, *Time,* and Bruce Drake, *New York Daily News,* November 17, 1985.
25. Ronald Reagan, *An American Life,* p. 635.
26. Doder and Branson, *Gorbachev,* p. 113.
27. Interview with Robert McFarlane, September 11, 1990.
28. Kenneth L. Adelman, *The Great Universal Embrace,* pp. 122–23.
29. Ibid., p. 127.
30. Evan Thomas, "Fencing at the Fireside Summit," *Time,* December 2, 1985.
31. Ibid.
32. The phrase "fireside summit" was the coinage of White House spokesman Larry Speakes.
33. Interview with Robert McFarlane, September 11, 1990.
34. Ronald Reagan, *An American Life,* p. 638.
35. Ibid.
36. Ibid., p. 639.
37. Ibid., p. 651.
38. Adelman, *The Great Universal Embrace,* p. 140.
39. Ibid., p. 144.
40. Ronald Reagan, *An American Life,* p. 640.
41. Lou Cannon, "Reagan Tells Aides of Geneva's Promise," *The Washington Post,* November 23, 1985.
42. Interview with Ronald Reagan, February 26, 1990.
43. Ibid.
44. Ibid.
45. Ronald Reagan, *An American Life,* p. 639.
46. Haslam, *The Soviet Union and the Politics of Nuclear Weapons in Europe, 1967–1987,* p. 161.
47. Ibid., pp. 161–62.
48. Lou Cannon and Hobart Rowan, "Chernobyl in Spotlight at Summit," *The Washington Post,* May 4, 1986.
49. Doder and Branson, *Gorbachev,* p. 134.

50. Interview with James McCartney by Gwen Rubinstein, January 20, 1989.
51. Conversation with Landon Parvin, September 12, 1990.
52. Ronald Reagan, *An American Life,* p. 708.
53. Adelman, *The Great Universal Embrace,* p. 279.
54. Interview with George Shultz, February 13, 1989.
55. Ronald Reagan, *An American Life,* p. 665.
56. Strobe Talbott, *The Master of the Game,* p. 246.
57. For a detailed discussion of this episode, see ibid., pp. 237–50.
58. Ronald Reagan, *An American Life,* p. 666.
59. Ibid., p. 669. Reagan said in his memoirs that Shevardnadze actually forgot to bring the Gorbachev letter with him and had to send a KGB agent to fetch it from the Soviet embassy but that they discussed Gorbachev's proposals while waiting for the letter to arrive.
60. Adelman, *The Great Universal Embrace,* p. 25.
61. Ronald Reagan, *An American Life,* pp. 670–71.
62. Ibid., p. 672.
63. Ibid., p. 669.
64. Serge Schmemann, "A Success, to a Point, for Gorbachev," *The New York Times,* October 1, 1986.
65. Adelman, *The Great Universal Embrace,* pp. 36–39.
66. Ibid., pp. 37–38.
67. Ibid., p. 44.
68. Pool report by Bob Timberg, Baltimore *Sun;* Lou Cannon, *The Washington Post;* Jerry O'Leary, *The Washington Times;* Bob Toth, *Los Angeles Times;* Owen Ullmann, Knight-Ridder; Ed Hodges, *Durham Morning Herald;* and Steve Kurkjian, *The Boston Globe,* October 11, 1986.
69. Don Oberdorfer, "At Reykjavik, Soviets Were Prepared and U.S. Improvised," *The Washington Post,* February 16, 1987.
70. In addition to Nitze, the U.S. members of the arms control working group were Max Kampelman, the head of the U.S. negotiating team in Geneva, and veteran arms negotiator Ed Rowney plus Adelman, Perle and Linhard.
71. Oberdorfer, "At Reykjavik, Soviets Were Prepared and U.S. Improvised."
72. Ibid.
73. Ibid.
74. Ibid.
75. Talbott, *The Master of the Game,* p. 323.
76. Ibid., p. 324.
77. Conversation with Don Oberdorfer, September 8, 1990.
78. Ronald Reagan, *An American Life,* p. 677.
79. Oberdorfer, "At Reykjavik, Soviets Were Prepared and U.S. Improvised."
80. Ronald Reagan, *An American Life,* p. 679.
81. Oberdorfer, "At Reykjavik, Soviets Were Prepared and U.S. Improvised."
82. Ronald Reagan, *An American Life,* p. 679.
83. Interview with William Hyland, March 28, 1989.
84. Ibid.
85. Press briefing by Secretary of State George P. Shultz, Reykjavik, October 12, 1986.

86. Talbott, *The Master of the Game,* p. 328.
87. Haslam, *The Soviet Union and the Politics of Nuclear Weapons in Europe, 1967–1987,* p. 169.
88. Ibid.
89. Remarks at the Brandenburg Gate, June 12, 1987.
90. Interview with Ronald Reagan, February 26, 1990.
91. Tom Shales, "Gorbachev, Up Close and Affable," *The Washington Post,* December 1, 1987.
92. David Espo, "Soviet Leader Takes Case for 'New Relationship' to Prominent Americans," Associated Press, December 8, 1987.
93. "Remarks Before Signing the Treaty," United Press International, *The Washington Post,* December 9, 1987.
94. Interview with Colin Powell, February 13, 1990.
95. Ibid.
96. Remarks at Independence Day celebration, July 3, 1987. This is one of Reagan's favorite stories. On May 10, 1987, he related it in his remarks at the Tuskegee University commencement, Tuskegee, Alabama, and the "scholar" was a diplomat; on December 1, 1987, it was a college professor when he spoke at Duval County High School in Jacksonville, Florida. He also included it in *An American Life* (p. 715).
97. Interview with Colin Powell, February 13, 1990.
98. Ibid.
99. Conversation with Don Oberdorfer, September 8, 1990.
100. Talbott, *The Master of the Game,* p. 363.
101. Ibid.
102. Ronald Reagan, *An American Life,* p. 701.
103. Doder and Branson, *Gorbachev,* p. 286.
104. Lou Cannon, "More Than Teflon and Tinsel," *The Washington Post,* December 7, 1987.
105. Interview of Senator Dan Quayle by Peter Jennings, ABC News, December 8, 1987.
106. Helen Dewar, "Kissinger Backs Pact, with Misgivings," *The Washington Post,* February 24, 1988.
107. Interview with William Hyland, March 28, 1989.
108. Interview with Richard Perle, March 9, 1989.
109. Interview with William F. Buckley, May 10, 1989.
110. "Americans Talk Security," Second Survey, conducted by Market Opinion Research of Detroit.
111. Hedrick Smith, "The Right Against Reagan," *The New York Times Magazine,* January 17, 1988.
112. Ibid.
113. Doder and Branson, *Gorbachev,* p. 225.
114. Telephone interview with Paul Weyrich, April 12, 1988.
115. Ibid.
116. Interview of the president by Lou Cannon, *The Washington Post,* February 25, 1988.
117. Doder and Branson, *Gorbachev,* p. 319.

118. Ibid.

119. "Ronald Reagan's Summit," Editorial, *The Washington Post,* May 29, 1988.

120. Pool report by George Condon, Copley Newspapers, and Hugh Sidey, *Time,* May 30, 1988.

121. Jacob V. LaMar, "The Lonely World of a Refusenik," *Time,* June 6, 1988.

122. Conversation with Colin Powell, March 18, 1989.

123. George J. Church, "A Gentle Battle of Images," *Time,* June 13, 1988.

124. Ronald Reagan, *An American Life,* p. 709.

125. Doder and Branson, *Gorbachev,* p. 320.

126. Ibid.

127. Lou Cannon and Don Oberdorfer, "The Scripting of the Moscow Summit," *The Washington Post,* June 9, 1988.

128. Remarks at a luncheon hosted by leaders of the cultural and art community, Moscow, May 31, 1988.

129. Ibid.

130. Cannon and Oberdorfer, "The Scripting of the Moscow Summit."

131. Felicity Barringer, "President Meets with Dissidents, and Tea and Empathy Are Served," *The New York Times,* May 31, 1988.

132. Doder and Branson, *Gorbachev,* p. 320.

133. Conversation with Colin Powell, March 18, 1989.

134. Lou Cannon and Don Oberdorfer, "The Superpowers' Struggle Over 'Peaceful Coexistence,' " *The Washington Post,* June 3, 1988.

135. Church, "A Gentle Battle of Images."

136. Cannon and Oberdorfer, "The Superpowers' Struggle Over 'Peaceful Coexistence.' "

137. Ibid.

138. Ibid.

139. Ibid.

140. Ronald Reagan, *An American Life,* p. 719.

141. Interview with Kenneth Duberstein, December 8, 1988. See also Doder and Branson, *Gorbachev,* p. 18.

142. Interview with Kenneth Duberstein, December 8, 1988.

143. "Ron and Gorby Remember the Good Old Days," Reuters, September 18, 1990.

144. Ibid.

CHAPTER 22—*Visions and Legacies*

1. Farewell address to the nation, January 11, 1989.

2. Ronald Reagan, *An American Life,* p. 715.

3. Address to students, June 21, 1974, quoted in *Quotable Ronald Reagan,* by JRH Associates.

4. Reagan announcement speech, New York, November 13, 1979.

5. George Will, "How Reagan Changed America," *Newsweek,* January 9, 1989.

6. Interview of Ronald Reagan by Dan Blackburn, NBC Radio, October 31, 1980.

7. Reagan announcement speech.

8. Garry Wills, *Reagan's America,* p. 94.

9. Farewell address.

10. Ronald Reagan, *An American Life,* p. 721.

11. Interview with James Baker, March 7, 1990.
12. Interview with Terry Eastland, October 1, 1990. See also his forthcoming book on the Reagan and Bush presidencies, to be published by The Free Press.
13. Ronald J. Ostrow, "Panel Charges Pierce Steered Funds to Friends," *Los Angeles Times,* November 2, 1990.
14. Ruth Marcus, "Meese Fires His Chief Spokesman," *The Washington Post,* May 17, 1988.
15. Interview with Edwin Meese, April 11, 1989.
16. Associated Press, October 26, 1978.
17. Interview with Terry Eastland, October 1, 1990.
18. George Lardner Jr., "Bronx Jury Acquits Donovan," *The Washington Post,* May 26, 1987.
19. Ibid.
20. Robert J. Donovan, *Tumultuous Years,* p. 114.
21. Interview of the president by Lou Cannon of *The Washington Post,* February 25, 1988.
22. Harry S. Truman, *Memoirs: Years of Trial and Hope,* p. 498. See also Lou Cannon, "The Buck Stops Where?" *The Washington Post,* February 29, 1988.
23. Interview with Arnold Burns, October 16, 1989.
24. Ibid.
25. Ibid.
26. George Lardner Jr., "McKay Reports Four 'Probable' Meese Offenses," *The Washington Post,* July 19, 1988.
27. Ruth Marcus, "Attorney General Meese to Resign, 'Vindicated' by Special Counsel Probe," *The Washington Post,* July 6, 1988.
28. Ruth Marcus, "Justice Dept. Report Sharply Criticizes Meese," *The Washington Post,* January 17, 1989.
29. "Ronald Reagan Speaks Out on the Issues," prepared by the Research and Policy Division of the Reagan for President Office, January 31, 1980.
30. Interview with Terry Eastland, October 1, 1990.
31. Ibid.
32. Sheldon Goldman, "Reagan's Judicial Legacy: Completing the Puzzle and Summing Up," *Judicature,* April–May 1989.
33. California's capital punishment law, since reinstated in a more restrictive form, was struck down on December 7, 1976, in a decision written by Chief Justice Donald Wright.
34. Interview with Terry Eastland, October 1, 1990.
35. Goldman, "Reagan's Judicial Legacy."
36. *Reagan,* p. 290.
37. Interview with Michael Deaver, December 3, 1981.
38. Ibid.
39. *Reagan,* p. 315.
40. Interview with Terry Eastland, October 1, 1990.
41. Ethan Bronner, *Battle for Justice,* p. 92.
42. Ibid., p. 113.
43. Ibid., p. 98. See also Terry Eastland, "Bork Revisited," *Commentary,* February 1990.
44. Bronner, *Battle for Justice,* p. 99.

45. Ibid., p. 155.
46. Ibid., p. 160.
47. Linda Greenhouse, "Bork Sets Forth Spirited Defense of His Integrity," *The New York Times,* September 19, 1987.
48. Bronner, *Battle for Justice,* p. 275.
49. Ibid., p. 335.
50. Interview with Terry Eastland, October 1, 1990.
51. Robert Reinhold, "Man in the News: Restrained Pragmatist Anthony M. Kennedy," *The New York Times,* November 12, 1987.
52. Reagan gives Bork only a single mention in his memoirs and does not even refer to his defeat. He does not mention Ginsburg at all.
53. Al Kamen, "Court Nullifies Flag-Desecration Laws," *The Washington Post,* June 22. 1989.
54. Steven Brill, "Report Card on William French Smith," *The American Lawyer,* July 1982.
55. Ibid.
56. This was the CDC figure through December 1988 at the time Reagan left office. But the statistics for AIDS have lagged behind the actual total. According to CDC spokesman Kent Taylor in a November 5, 1990, interview, subsequent updatings show that the actual number of cases by the end of 1988 was 98,935 and the number of deaths 57, 542.
57. Warren King, "Reagan Regarded AIDS 'Like It Was Measles,'" *Seattle Times,* August 31, 1989. In a letter to the *Seattle Times* on September 14, 1989, Hutton said that comparing AIDS to measles was an "unfortunate analogy" and asserted that Reagan "was by no means uninformed or unconcerned about AIDS."
58. Randy Shilts, *And the Band Played On,* p. 476.
59. King, "Reagan Regarded AIDS 'Like It Was Measles.'"
60. The president's news conference, September 17, 1985.
61. Remarks to employees of the Department of Health and Human Services, February 5, 1986.
62. Ibid.
63. "Senate Confirms Koop, 68–24," United Press International, November 17, 1981.
64. "Dr. Unqualified," Editorial, *The New York Times,* April 9, 1981.
65. Cristine Russell, "AIDS Report Calls for Sex Education," *The Washington Post,* October 23, 1986.
66. Shilts, *And the Band Played On,* p. 311.
67. Remarks at the College of Physicians, Philadelphia, April 1, 1987.
68. Interview with Landon Parvin, May 15, 1990.
69. Ibid.
70. Ibid.
71. Ibid.
72. Ibid.
73. Remarks at the American Foundation for AIDS Research awards dinner, May 31, 1987.
74. Ibid.
75. Ibid.
76. Richard Pearson, "AIDS Patient Ryan White Dies," *The Washington Post,* April 9, 1990.

77. Ibid.
78. Ibid.
79. Ronald Reagan, " 'We Owe It to Ryan,' " *The Washington Post,* April 11, 1990.
80. Letter to the editor, *The Washington Post,* April 14, 1990.
81. Interview with Ronald Reagan, February 26, 1990.
82. Lou Cannon, "Reagan Announces, Urges Strength at Home, Abroad," *The Washington Post,* November 14, 1979.
83. Theodore H. White, "Summing Up," *The New York Times Magazine,* April 25, 1982.
84. Ibid.
85. For a discussion of how Weidenbaum arrived at his admittedly rough estimate, see George C. Eads and Michael Fix, *Relief or Reform? Reagan's Regulatory Dilemma,* pp. 28–31.
86. Dave Stockman, "The Stockman Manifesto," excerpts from his "Avoiding a GOP Economic Dunkirk," *The Washington Post,* December 14, 1980.
87. Eads and Fix, *Relief or Reform?,* p. 2.
88. "The 'Terrible 20' Regulations," *The Washington Post,* August 4, 1981.
89. Felicity Barringer, "Nader to Stockman: U.S. Rules Saved Economy $5.7 Billion," *The Washington Post,* August 11, 1981.
90. Linda Greenhouse, "Justices Decide U.S. Must Protect Workers' Safety Despite High Cost," *The New York Times,* June 16, 1981.
91. William Niskanen, *Reaganomics,* p. 315.
92. Eads and Fix, *Relief or Reform?,* p. 144.
93. Ibid., p. 256.
94. George C. Eads and Michael Fix, eds., *The Reagan Regulatory Strategy: An Assessment,* p. 19.
95. Interview with Michael Fix, October 8, 1990.
96. Testimony by Bert Ely to House Budget Committee, January 26, 1989.
97. Bert Ely, "Comment: Federal Deposit Insurance Is Beyond Any Fix or Reform," *American Banker,* August 27, 1990.
98. Steven V. Roberts with Gary Cohen, "Villains of the S&L Crisis," *U.S. News & World Report,* October 1, 1990.
99. Ibid. See also Stephen Pizzo, Mary Fricker and Paul Muolo, *In$ide Job: The Looting of America's Savings and Loans,* p. 21.
100. Roberts, "Villains of the S&L Crisis."
101. Ibid.
102. Interview with William Seidman, July 15, 1990.
103. Roberts, "Villains of the S&L Crisis."
104. Interview with Edwin Gray, September 12, 1990.
105. Ibid.
106. Ibid.
107. Pizzo, Fricker and Muolo, *In$ide Job,* p. 263.
108. Interview with William Seidman, July 15, 1990.
109. Interview with Edwin Gray, September 12, 1990.
110. Interview with Bert Ely, October 8, 1990.
111. Roberts, "Villains of the S&L Crisis."
112. John M. Berry, "Underlying Flaws in Economy Mar Legacy of Reagan Years," *The Washington Post,* November 6, 1988.

113. Interview with Willis Gradison, November 1, 1990.
114. Farewell address.
115. Interview with Willis Gradison, November 1, 1990.
116. Will, "How Reagan Changed America."
117. *Reagan,* p. 301n.
118. Ibid., p. 301.
119. Farewell address.
120. Michael Novak, "People Are Moving Up, the American Way," *Los Angeles Times,* October 18, 1990.
121. David S. Broder, "The Decade of Patchy Prosperity," *The Washington Post,* December 10, 1989.
122. Novak, "People Are Moving Up, the American Way."
123. T.R. Reid, "A Flirtation with Greed, But Bedrock Beliefs Stay Solid," *The Washington Post,* December 14, 1989.
124. Peter Behr, "Wave of Mergers, Takeovers Is a Part of Reagan Legacy," *The Washington Post,* October 30, 1988.
125. Ibid.
126. Conversation with Stuart Auerbach, July 17, 1990.
127. Lou Cannon, "Reagan Leaving Legacy of Surprises," *The Washington Post,* January 15, 1989.
128. Fred I. Greenstein, "Reagan Was No Eisenhower," *The New York Times,* July 26, 1989.
129. Interview with Fred I. Greenstein, January 1989.
130. Stanley Karnow, *In Our Image,* p. 407.
131. Ibid., p. 369.
132. Ibid. See also Jeff Gerth, "Marcos' Wartime Role Discredited in U.S. Files," *The New York Times,* January 23, 1986.
133. Interview with Colin Powell, February 13, 1990.
134. The president's news conference, February 11, 1986.
135. David Hoffman and Lou Cannon, "In Crucial Call, Laxalt Told Marcos: 'Cut Cleanly,' " *The Washington Post,* February 26, 1986.
136. Ruth Marcus, "U.S. Indicts Marcoses in $100 Million Plot," *The Washington Post,* October 22, 1988.
137. Howard Kurtz, "U.S. Jury Clears Marcos in Fraud Case," *The Washington Post,* July 3, 1990.
138. Lou Cannon and Ruth Marcus, "Indictment of Marcos Due Today," *The Washington Post,* October 21, 1988.
139. Keith B. Richburg and William Branigin, "Ferdinand Marcos Dies in Hawaii at 72," *The Washington Post,* September 29, 1989.
140. *Reagan,* p. 263.
141. "The Republicans in Detroit," text of Reagan's speech accepting the Republican nomination, *The Washington Post,* July 18, 1980.
142. Reagan announcement speech.
143. Gennady Vasilyev, "A Political Portrait: Reagan's Best Role," *Pravda,* January 20, 1989, quoted in *Current Digest of the Soviet Press,* February 15, 1989.
144. Reagan's final approval rating in the Gallup poll was 63 percent, the highest of any president since Franklin Roosevelt. His final approval rating in *The New York Times*–CBS Poll was 68 percent.

BIBLIOGRAPHY

BOOKS AND MANUSCRIPTS

Abzug, Robert H. *Inside the Vicious Heart; Americans and the Liberation of Nazi Concentration Camps.* New York: Oxford University Press, 1985.

Adams, Henry. *The Education of Henry Adams, An Autobiography.* Boston: Houghton Mifflin, 1918.

Adelman, Kenneth L. *The Great Universal Embrace, Arms Summitry—A Skeptic's Account.* New York: Simon & Schuster, 1989.

Ambrose, Stephen E. *Nixon, The Education of a Politician 1913–1962.* New York: Simon & Schuster, 1987.

Anderson, Annelise, and Dennis L. Bark, Editors. *Thinking About America, The United States in the 1990s.* Stanford, California: Hoover Institution Press, 1988.

Anderson, Martin. *Revolution.* New York: Harcourt Brace Jovanovich, 1988.

———. *Revolution: The Reagan Legacy.* Stanford, California: Hoover Institution Press, 1990.

Barone, Michael. *Our Country; The Shaping of America from Roosevelt to Reagan.* New York: The Free Press, 1990.

Barrett, Laurence I. *Gambling with History, Ronald Reagan in the White House.* Garden City, New York: Doubleday, 1983

Barron, John, *MiG Pilot, The Final Escape of Lieutenant Belenko.* New York: McGraw-Hill, 1980.

Behlmer, Rudy. *Inside Warner Bros. (1935–1951).* New York: Viking, 1985.

Beilenson, Laurence W. *The Treaty Trap, A History of the Performance of Political Treaties by the United States and European Nations.* Washington, D.C.: Public Affairs Press, 1969.

Bell, Jack. *The Splendid Misery.* Garden City, New York: Doubleday, 1960.

Bell, Terrel H. *The Thirteenth Man: A Reagan Cabinet Memoir.* New York: The Free Press, 1988.

Birnbaum, Jeffrey H., and Alan S. Murray. *Showdown at Gucci Gulch: Lawmakers, Lobbyists, and the Unlikely Triumph of Tax Reform.* New York: Random House, 1987.

Boyarsky, Bill. *The Rise of Ronald Reagan.* New York: Random House, 1968.

Bronner, Ethan. *Battle For Justice; How The Bork Nomination Shook America.* New York: W. W. Norton, 1989.

Brook-Shepherd, Gordon. *The Storm Birds; Soviet Postwar Defectors.* New York: Weidenfeld & Nicholson, 1989.

Buckley, William F. Jr. *On the Firing Line, The Public Life of Our Public Figures.* New York: Random House, 1989.

Bureau of the Census, Department of Commerce. *Statistical Abstract of the United States 1989.* Washington, D.C.: U.S. Government Printing Office, 1989.

Burford, Anne M., with John Greenya. *Are You Tough Enough?* New York: McGraw-Hill, 1986.

Cannon, Lou. *Reagan.* New York: G. P. Putnam's Sons, 1982.

———. *Reporting: An Inside View.* Sacramento, California: California Journal Press, 1977.

———. *Ronnie and Jesse: A Political Odyssey.* Garden City, New York: Doubleday, 1969.

Carter, Jimmy. *Keeping Faith, Memoirs of a President.* New York: Bantam, 1982.

Ceplair, Larry, and Steven Englund. *The Inquisition in Hollywood, Politics in the Film Community 1930–1960.* Garden City, New York: Anchor Press/Doubleday, 1980.

Congressional Quarterly, Inc. *The Iran-Contra Puzzle,* Washington D.C.: Congressional Quarterly, Inc., 1987.

Cronin, Thomas. *The State of the Presidency.* Boston: Little, Brown, 1980.

Davis, Patti, with Maureen Strange Foster. *Home Front.* New York: Crown, 1986.

Davis, Peter. *Where Is Nicaragua?* New York: Simon & Schuster, 1987.

De Cordova, Fred. *Johnny Came Lately.* New York: Simon & Schuster, 1988.

Deaver, Michael K., with Mickey Herskowitz. *Behind the Scenes.* New York: William Morrow, 1987.

Doder, Dusko. *Shadows and Whispers, Power Politics Inside the Kremlin from Brezhnev to Gorbachev.* New York: Penguin, 1988.

Doder, Dusko, and Louise Branson. *Gorbachev: Heretic in the Kremlin.* New York: Viking Penguin, 1990.

Donovan, Robert J. *Conflict and Crisis, The Presidency of Harry S Truman 1945–1948.* New York: W. W. Norton, 1977.

———. *Tumultuous Years; The Presidency of Harry S Truman.* New York: W. W. Norton, 1982.

Dugger, Ronnie. *On Reagan, The Man & His Presidency.* New York: McGraw-Hill, 1983.

Dunne, Philip. *Take Two.* New York: McGraw-Hill, 1980.

Eads, George C., and Michael Fix. *Relief or Reform? Reagan's Regulatory Dilemma.* Washington, D. C.: The Urban Institute Press, 1984.

Eads, George C., and Michael Fix, Editors. *The Reagan Regulatory Strategy, An Assessment.* Washington, D. C.: The Urban Institute Press, 1984.

Edwards, Anne. *Early Reagan, The Rise to Power.* New York: William Morrow, 1987.

Ford, Gerald R. *A Time To Heal, The Autobiography of Gerald R. Ford.* New York: Harper & Row, 1979.

Gardner, Howard. *Frames of Mind, The Theory of Multiple Intelligences.* New York: Basic Books, Inc., 1985.

Germond, Jack W., and Jules Witcover. *Wake Us When It's Over; Presidential Politics of 1984.* New York: Macmillan, 1985.

Gilbert, Martin. *Final Journey, The Fate of the Jews in Nazi Germany.* New York: Mayflower Books, 1979.

Goldman, Peter, and Tony Fuller. *The Quest for the Presidency 1984.* New York: Bantam, 1985.

Goldwater, Barry M., with Jack Casserly. *Goldwater.* New York: Doubleday, 1988.

Gorbachev, Mikhail. *At the Summit.* New York: Richardson, Steirman & Black, 1988.

Gravitz, Herbert L., and Julie D. Bowden. *Recovery: A Guide for Adult Children of Alcoholics.* New York: Simon & Schuster, 1985.

Greider, William. *Secrets of the Temple, How the Federal Reserve Runs the Country.* New York: A Touchstone Book, 1987.

———. *The Education of David Stockman and Other Americans.* New York: A Signet Book, 1986.

Gutman, Roy. *Banana Diplomacy, The Making of American Policy in Nicaragua 1981–1987.* New York: Simon & Schuster, 1988.

Haig, Alexander M., Jr. *Caveat: Realism, Reagan, and Foreign Policy.* New York: Macmillan, 1984.

Halsell, Grace. *Prophecy and Politics, Militant Evangelists on the Road to Nuclear War.* Westport, Connecticut: Lawrence Hill & Company, 1986.

Harris, Louis. *Inside America.* New York: Vintage, 1987.

Haslam, Jonathan. *The Soviet Union and the Politics of Nuclear Weapons in Europe, 1969–87.* Ithaca: Cornell University Press, 1990.

Higham, Charles. *Warner Brothers.* New York: Charles Scribner's Sons, 1975.

Jones, Charles O., Editor. *The Reagan Legacy, Promise and Performance.* Chatham, New Jersey: Chatham House Publishers, Inc., 1988.

JRH & Associates, Inc. *Quotable Ronald Reagan.* San Diego: JRH & Associates, Inc., 1975.

Karnow, Stanley. *In Our Image, America's Empire in the Philippines.* New York: Random House, 1989.

Laski, Harold J. *The American Presidency, an Interpretation.* New York: Harper & Brothers, 1940.

Ledeen, Michael A. *Perilous Statecraft: An Insider's Account of the Iran-Contra Affair.* New York: Charles Scribner's Sons, 1988.

Lekachman, Robert. *Greed Is Not Enough: Reaganomics.* New York: Pantheon, 1982.

Lindsey, Hal, with C. C. Carlson. *The Late Great Planet Earth.* New York: Bantam, 1973.

Martin, David C., and John Walcott. *Best Laid Plans, The Inside Story of America's War Against Terrorism.* New York: A Touchstone Book, 1988.

Mayer, Jane, and Doyle McManus. *Landslide: The Unmaking of the President 1984–1988.* Boston: Houghton Mifflin, 1988.

McWilliams, Carey. *Southern California: An Island on the Land.* Santa Barbara: Peregrine Smith, Inc., 1973.

Menges, Constantine C. *Inside the National Security Council: The True Story of the Making and Unmaking of Reagan's Foreign Policy.* New York: Simon & Schuster, 1988.

Milam, Dr. James R., and Katherine Ketcham. *Under the Influence.* New York: Bantam, 1983.

Moley, Raymond. *After Seven Years.* New York: Harper & Brothers, 1939.

Neustadt, Richard E. *Presidential Power, the Politics of Leadership from FDR to Carter.* New York: Macmillan, 1980.

Niskanen, William A. *Reaganomics: An Insider's Account of the Policies and the People.* New York: Oxford University Press, 1988.

Nixon, Richard M. *The Memoirs of Richard Nixon.* New York: Grosset & Dunlap, 1978.

Noonan, Peggy. *What I Saw at the Revolution: A Political Life in the Reagan Era.* New York: Random House, 1990.

O'Neill, Tip, with William Novak. *Man of the House: The Life and Political Memoirs of Speaker Tip O'Neill.* New York: Random House, 1987.

Palmer, John L., and Isabel V. Sawhill, Editors. *The Reagan Record.* Cambridge, Massachusetts: Ballinger Publishing Co., 1984.

Patterson, Bradley H., Jr. *The Ring of Power: The White House Staff and Its Expanding Role in Government.* New York: Basic Books, 1988.

Pizzo, Stephen, Mary Fricker, and Paul Muolo. *In$ide Job; The Looting of America's Savings and Loans.* New York: McGraw-Hill, 1989.

President's Special Review Board. *Report of the President's Special Review Board.* Washington, D.C.: U.S. Government Printing Office, 1987.

Prestowitz, Clyde V., Jr. *Trading Places: How We Allowed Japan to Take the Lead.* New York: Basic Books, 1988.

Quigley, Joan. *"What Does Joan Say?" My Seven Years as White House Astrologer to Nancy and Ronald Reagan.* New York: Birch Lane Press, 1990.

Reagan, Maureen. *First Father, First Daughter, A Memoir.* Boston: Little, Brown, 1989.

Reagan, Michael, with Joe Hyams. *On the Outside Looking In.* New York: Zebra Books, 1988.

Reagan, Nancy, with William Novak. *My Turn, the Memoirs of Nancy Reagan.* New York: Random House, 1989.

Reagan, Ronald. *An American Life.* New York: Simon & Schuster, 1990.

———. *Speaking My Mind.* New York: Simon & Schuster, 1989.

Reagan, Ronald, and Richard C. Hubler. *Where's the Rest of Me? Ronald Reagan Tells His Own Story.* New York: Dell, 1965.

Regan, Donald T. *For the Record, From Wall Street to Washington.* New York: Harcourt Brace Jovanovich, 1988.

Rogin, Michael. *Ronald Reagan, the Movie and Other Episodes in Political Demonology.* Berkeley: University of California Press, 1987.

Safire, William. *Before the Fall: An Inside View of the Pre-Watergate White House.* New York: Doubleday, 1975.

Schlesinger, Arthur M., Jr. *The Coming of the New Deal*. Boston: Houghton Mifflin, 1959.

———. *The Imperial Presidency*. Boston: Houghton Mifflin, 1973.

Shilts, Randy. *And the Band Played On: Politics, People and the AIDS Epidemic*. New York: St. Martin's Press, 1987.

Slosser, Bob. *Reagan Inside Out*. Waco, Texas: Word Books, 1984.

Smith, Hedrick. *The Power Game: How Washington Works*. New York: Random House, 1988.

Sontag, Susan. *On Photography*. New York: Farrar, Straus and Giroux, 1973.

Speakes, Larry, with Robert Pack. *Speaking Out: The Reagan Presidency from Inside the White House*. New York: Charles Scribner's Sons, 1988.

Stockman, David A. *The Triumph of Politics: How the Reagan Revolution Failed*. New York: Harper & Row, 1986.

Sulzberger, C. L., and the Editors of American Heritage. *The American Heritage Picture History of World War II*. New York: American Heritage/Bonanza Books, 1966.

Talbott, Strobe. *Deadly Gambits: The Reagan Administration and the Stalemate in Nuclear Arms Control*. New York: Knopf, 1984.

———. *The Master of the Game: Paul Nitze and the Nuclear Peace*. New York: Knopf, 1988.

———. *The Russians and Reagan*. New York: Vintage, 1984.

Time, Editors. *The Winning of the White House 1988*. New York: Time, Inc., 1988.

Truman, Harry S. *Memoirs: Years of Trial and Hope*. Garden City, New York: Doubleday, 1956.

U.S. House of Representatives Select Committee to Investigate Covert Arms Transactions with Iran and U.S. Senate Select Committee on Secret Military Assistance to Iran and the Nicaraguan Opposition. *Report of the Congressional Committees Investigating the Iran-Contra Affair*. Washington, D.C.: U.S. Government Printing Office, 1987.

U.S. News & World Report, Editors. *The Story of Lieutenant Colonel Oliver North*. Washington, D.C.: *U.S. News & World Report*, 1987.

von Damm, Helene. *At Reagan's Side; Twenty Years in the Political Mainstream*. New York: Doubleday, 1989.

Watt, James, with Doug Wead. *The Courage of a Conservative*. New York: Simon & Schuster, 1985.

Weinberger, Caspar. *Fighting for Peace; Seven Critical Years in the Pentagon*. New York: Warner Books, 1990.

Weisband, Edward, and Thomas M. Franck. *Resignation in Protest*. New York: Grossman Publishers, 1975.

White, E. B. *Essays of E. B. White*. New York: Harper & Row, 1977.

White, Theodore H. *Breach of Faith, The Fall of Richard Nixon*. New York: Atheneum, 1975.

Wills, Garry. *Reagan's America*. Garden City, New York: Doubleday, 1985.

Witcover, Jules. *The Resurrection of Richard Nixon*. New York: G. P. Putnam's Sons, 1970.

Woodward, Bob. *Veil: The Secret Wars of the CIA 1981–1987*. New York: Simon & Schuster, 1987.

ARTICLES AND DOCUMENTS

Abshire, David M. "Don Regan's Real 'Record'; Looking Out for Number 1," *The Washington Post,* May 15, 1988.

Alderman, Jeffrey D. ABC News poll, Yearend Wrapup 1984.

Allen, Henry. "The Saga of Burky and Dutch," *The Washington Post,* March 7, 1981.

Associated Press. "Prime Minister Issues Harsh Criticism of U.S.," December 20, 1981.

———. "Reagan's Related to Royalty—Back a Millennium or So," *Los Angeles Times,* November 11, 1980.

———. "Reagan Calls 'Bloodbath' Wrong," April 17, 1970.

———. "Waite Travels to Beirut, Reports Progress in Effort to Free U.S. Hostages," November 1, 1986.

Barringer, Felicity. "Nader to Stockman: U.S. Rules Saved Economy $5.7 Billion," *The Washington Post,* August 11, 1981.

———. "President Meets with Dissidents, and Tea and Empathy Are Served," *The New York Times,* May 31, 1988.

Behr, Peter. "Wave of Mergers, Takeovers Is a Part of Reagan Legacy," *The Washington Post,* October 30, 1988.

Bergholz, Richard. "Latest Debate: What Did Reagan Say About a Voluntary Social Security?" *Los Angeles Times.*

Berke, Richard L. "Student Survey Detects Decline in Use of Crack," *The New York Times,* March 1, 1989.

Berry, John M. "Rosy Scenario for Reagan Sees Inflation Rate Plummeting," *The Washington Post,* February 7, 1981.

———. "Underlying Flaws in Economy Mar Legacy of Reagan Years," *The Washington Post,* November 6, 1988.

———. " 'Trickle-Down' Theory Suffers From Its Name," *The Washington Post,* January 10, 1982.

Bertram, Christoph. "Bitburg: A Lack of Historical Understanding," *The Washington Post,* April 12, 1985.

Blinder, Alan S. "The Economic Myths That the 1980s Exploded," *Business Week,* November 27, 1989.

Boyd, Gerald M. "President Asserts He Is Moving Away from Iran Affair," *The New York Times,* March 6, 1987.

Brill, Steven. "Report Card on William French Smith," *The American Lawyer,* July 1982.

Brimberg, Judith. "Denver Woman Cherishes Note from a 'Stranger,' " *The Denver Post,* January 22, 1981.

Broder, David S. "Encounter Leaves Reagan on Course," *The Washington Post,* October 22, 1984.

———. "Mondale Tries Kennedy Style," *The Washington Post,* October 8, 1984.

———. "Overriding the Issues; Mondale Finds Message Obscured," *The Washington Post,* September 23, 1984.

———. "Reagan Proposes 10% Cut in Social Security Costs; President Faces Potentially Divisive Battle; Battle Likely Over Cuts in Social Security," *The Washington Post,* May 13, 1981.

———. "Still Learning To Be the Opposition," *The Washington Post,* February 15, 1981.

————. "The Decade of Patchy Prosperity," *The Washington Post,* December 10, 1989.

Brown, Warren. "U.S. Begins Firing Striking Air Controllers," *The Washington Post,* August 6, 1981.

Buchanan, Patrick J. "The Contras Need Our Help," *The Washington Post,* March 5, 1986.

Bumiller, Elisabeth. "Pssst! Mr. President!; What to Do When the Chief Nods Off," *The Washington Post,* August 16, 1984.

————. "The Reagans' Hello Party," *The Washington Post,* November 19, 1980.

Business Wire. "People-American-Way; Study Warns of Impact of Armageddon Theology on U.S. Policy," April 1, 1985.

Cannon, Lou. "A Buoyant Farewell For Reagan," *The Washington Post,* June 22, 1988.

————. "A Sentimental Journey," *The Washington Post,* January 23, 1989.

————. "Arms Boost Seen as Strain on Soviets," *The Washington Post,* June 19, 1980.

————. "Bittersweet Trip for the Reagans," *The Washington Post,* January 21, 1989.

————. "Dole, Wick Join Critics of Trip," *The Washington Post,* April 25, 1985.

————. "Dramatic Account About Film of Nazi Death Camps Questioned," *The Washington Post,* March 5, 1984.

————. "Finding Capitalism in China Provides an Out on Old Stances," *The Washington Post,* May 7, 1984.

————. "Hang the Polls, Conviction Is What Counts on Latin Policy. *The Washington Post,* May 14, 1984.

————. "Howard Baker a 'Solution' Now Viewed as Problem," *The Washington Post,* November 8, 1987.

————. "McFarlane's Hidden Hand Helps Shape U.S. Foreign Policy," *The Washington Post,* February 15, 1985.

————. "More Than Teflon and Tinsel," *The Washington Post,* December 7, 1987.

————. "Now the Real St. Ronald vs. the Rhetorical Dragon," *The Washington Post,* February 18, 1981.

————. "On the Continent, Nodding Off and Fending Off the Press," *The Washington Post,* June 14, 1982.

————. "Out of Step with Reagan," *The Washington Post,* February 11, 1985.

————. "Overzealous Aides Misuse Secret Service, Media and the Boss," *The Washington Post,* September 3, 1984.

————. "President Goes to the Movies, Skips New Hampshire for Now," *The Washington Post,* June 13, 1983.

————. "President Wants to Keep His 'Winning Team' Intact, Aide Says," *The Washington Post,* November 8, 1984.

————. "President Welcomed in Grenada," *The Washington Post,* February 21, 1986.

————. "President's Strong Man Stretches South," *The Washington Post,* August 3, 1983.

————. "Reagan Announces, Urges Strength at Home, Abroad," *The Washington Post,* November 14, 1979.

————. "Reagan Appoints McFarlane Adviser on U.S. Security," *The Washington Post,* October 18, 1983.

————. "Reagan Defends Nicaraguan Role," *The Washington Post,* May 5, 1983.

————. "Reagan Describes Summit Meeting as 'Worth Its Weight in Gold,' " *The Washington Post,* July 23, 1981.

————. "Reagan Leaving Legacy of Surprises," *The Washington Post,* January 15, 1989.

————. "Reagan Says U.S. Owes 'Contras' Help; Conservative Gathering Hears Emotionally Charged Speech," *The Washington Post,* March 2, 1985.

————. "Reagan Tells Aides of Geneva's Promise," *The Washington Post,* November 23, 1985.

————. "Reagan Voices Summit Hopes," *The Washington Post,* November 17, 1985.

————. "Reagan's Asian Takes Are in the Can," *The Washington Post,* November 15, 1983.

————. "Reagan's Presidency: Past and Prospect," *The Washington Post,* January 22, 1984.

————. "Reagan, After Debate, Incumbent Struggles to Regain Stride," *The Washington Post,* October 9, 1984.

————. "Reagan, Pope Urge Renewed Peace Efforts," *The Washington Post,* May 3, 1984.

————. "Regan in Debut, Meets the Press; New Staff Chief Finds Buchanan Holding the Limelight," *The Washington Post,* February 6, 1985.

————. "Soviets Assail Reagan's European Trip; President Gained His Major Goal," *The Washington Post,* June 13, 1982.

————. "Speaker Calls President Insensitive," *The Washington Post,* January 29, 1986.

————. "Staying On Track," *The Washington Post,* March 7, 1988.

————. "Strategic Airport, Hostage Fears Led to Move," *The Washington Post,* October 26, 1983.

————. "Trouble Shooting with Carlucci," *The Washington Post,* November 30, 1987.

————. "What Happened to Reagan the Gunslinger," *The Washington Post,* July 7, 1985.

————. " 'A New Coalition,' " *The Washington Post,* June 26, 1981.

Cannon, Lou, and David Hoffman. "Gorbachev Endorses Idea of Summit Meeting," *The Washington Post,* April 2, 1985.

————"Regan Says Jury Out on Iran Deal," *The Washington Post,* November 22, 1986.

————. "There Is a New Feeling on the Part of the American People," excerpts from an interview with President Reagan, *The Washington Post,* January 16, 1984.

Cannon, Lou, and Joel Kotkin. "Old Frontier Sees Bright New Frontier," *The Washington Post,* June 7, 1979.

Cannon, Lou, and Lee Lescaze. "Presidential Performance Improves as Rust Rubs Off," *The Washington Post,* June 28, 1981.

————. "The Relaxed Approach," *The Washington Post,* February 9, 1981.

————. " 'The Main Accomplishment Has Been . . . Our Economic Program,' " excerpts from an interview with President Reagan, *The Washington Post,* March 29, 1981.

Cannon, Lou, and Ruth Marcus. "Indictment of Marcos Due Today," *The Washington Post,* October 21, 1988.

Cannon, Lou, and Don Oberdorfer. "The Scripting of the Moscow Summit," *The Washington Post,* June 9, 1988.

————. "The Superpowers' Struggle over 'Peaceful Coexistence,' " *The Washington Post,* June 3, 1988.

Cannon, Lou, and Hobart Rowan. "Chernobyl in Spotlight at Summit," *The Washington Post,* May 4, 1986.

Cannon, Lou, and Juan Williams. "161 Marines Killed in Beirut; U.S. May Station Many Offshore," *The Washington Post,* October 24, 1983.

Cannon, Lou, and George Wilson. "Reagan Authorized Marines to Call in Beirut Air Strikes; Opposed to Invoking War Powers Measure," *The Washington Post,* September 13, 1983.

Centers for Disease Control. *HIV/AIDS Surveillance,* June 1989.

Church, George J. "A Gentle Battle of Images," *Time,* June 13, 1988.

———. "Who Was Betrayed?" *Time,* December 8, 1986.

Clines, Francis X. "A Reporter's Notebook: Reagan's Visit Is a Tour de Force for the Image Makers," *The New York Times,* November 14, 1983.

CNN. "A Farewell Conversation with President Ronald Reagan and Mrs. Reagan," January 16, 1989.

Conconi, Chuck. "Personalities," *The Washington Post,* March 21, 1990.

Dewar, Helen. "Kissinger Backs Pact, with Misgivings; Rejecting INF Treaty Would 'Magnify All Difficulties,' Senate Told," *The Washington Post,* February 24, 1988.

Dewar, Helen, and Margaret Shapiro. "Hill Leaders Split Over Pulling Out Troops in Beirut," *The Washington Post,* January 24, 1984.

Dickenson, James R. "Media Boxer in Reagan Corner," *The Washington Post,* February 6, 1985.

Dowd, Ann Reilly. "What Managers Can Learn From Manager Reagan," *Fortune,* September 15, 1986.

Duke, Lynne. "Death Cast Long Shadow Over '88," *The Washington Post,* January 1, 1989.

Easterbrook, Gregg. "James Watkins and the Morality of Nukes," *The Washington Post Magazine,* February 18, 1990.

Edsall, Thomas B., and Ted Gup. "The Crisis of the Reagan Presidency; The Lake Resources Inc. Account; $1.7 Million Funneled to Swiss Account Used by NSC Aide," *The Washington Post,* March 7, 1987.

Ely, Bert. "Comment: Federal Deposit Insurance Is Beyond Any Fix or Reform," *American Banker,* August 27, 1990.

Espo, David. "Soviet Leader Takes Case for 'New Relationship' to Prominent Americans," Associated Press, December 8, 1987.

Etzioni, Amitai. "The Democrats Need a Unifying Theme," *The New York Times,* October 5, 1984.

Farhi, Paul. "Consumers Hit Pause Button on Sales of Video Recorders," *The Washington Post,* January 14, 1989.

Farrell, Harry. "People and Politics: Spencer Williams Off to Washington," *San Jose Mercury News,* January 2, 1969.

fathers. "Interview: Ron Reagan," July–August 1986.

Faulkner, William. "On Privacy," *Harper's,* July 1955.

Federal Bureau of Investigation, Department of Justice. *Crime in the United States,* Uniform Crime Reports 1988, Released August 6, 1989.

Fritz, Sara. "Hello, This Is Ronald Reagan—Yes, Really," *U.S. News & World Report,* March 21, 1983.

Gaines-Carter, Patrice. "Warren Burns, 22; 'Disrespect Somebody, and You're Dead,' " *The Washington Post,* January 1, 1989.

Gergen, David. "Ronald Reagan's Most Important Legacy," *U.S. News & World Report,* January 9, 1989.

Gerstenzang, James. "President Will 'Be More Alert' in Future Outings," Associated Press, April 23, 1981.

Gerth, Jeff. "Marcos' Wartime Role Discredited in U.S. Files," *The New York Times,* January 23, 1986.

Goldman, Sheldon. "Reagan's Judicial Legacy: Completing the Puzzle and Summing Up," *Judicature,* April–May 1989.

Greenfield, Meg. "Advantage, Mr. Mondale," *The Washington Post,* October 10, 1984.

Greenhouse, Linda. "Bork Sets Forth Spirited Defense of His Integrity," *The New York Times,* September 19, 1987.

———. "Justices Decide U.S. Must Protect Workers," *The New York Times,* June 16, 1981.

Greenstein, Fred I. "Reagan Was No Eisenhower," *The New York Times,* July 26, 1989.

Greider, William. "The Education of David Stockman," *The Atlantic,* December 1981.

Harwood, Richard. "Tidy U.S. War Ends: 'We Blew Them Away'," *The Washington Post,* November 6, 1983.

Havemann, Judith. "Adding up the Reagan Renovations," *The Washington Post,* September 7, 1988.

Hilts, Philip J. "Blacks' Life Expectancy Drops," *The Washington Post,* December 15, 1988.

Hoagland, Jim. "Mitterrand: U.S., France Are United on Essentials," *The Washington Post,* June 29, 1986.

Hoffman, David. "Reagan Sees Limited Help for Hostages; U.S. Had Advised Americans of Danger," *The Washington Post,* January 27, 1987.

———. "Aides in 2 Capitals Said to Share Blame for Bitburg Blunder," *The Washington Post,* May 1, 1985.

———. "President Defends Tour Plans," *The Washington Post,* April 13, 1985.

———. "White House Resisted Arms Sales Revelations," *The Washington Post,* January 31, 1987.

Hoffman, David, and Lou Cannon. "In Crucial Call, Laxalt told Marcos: 'Cut Cleanly,' " *The Washington Post,* February 26, 1986.

———. "Stockman, on the Mend, Reeducates Reagan," *The Washington Post,* February 6, 1983.

Hoffman, David, and Bob Woodward. "McFarlane Said to Solicit Contra Aid from Saudis; Source Contradicts Administration Account," *The Washington Post,* May 14, 1987.

Hornblower, Margot. "Liberty's Flame Relit as Gala Begins," *The Washington Post,* July 4, 1986.

House, Karen Elliott, and Alan L. Otten. "White House Hopes Summits Will Enhance the President's Stature," *The Wall Street Journal,* May 28, 1982.

Jaroslovsky, Rich, and James M. Perry. "Fitness Issue; New Question in Race; Is Oldest U.S. President Now Showing His Age?" *The Wall Street Journal,* October 9, 1984.

Johnson, Haynes. " 'High Risk' President Reassessed," *The Washington Post,* November 8, 1981.

Kagay, Michael R. "Satisfaction on Rise in U.S., Gallup Poll Finds," *The New York Times,* December 25, 1988.

Kaiser, Robert G., and Lee Lescaze. "White House Stalling on Butter Sales in World Market," *The Washington Post,* May 29, 1981.

Kamen, Al. "Court Nullifies Flag-Desecration Laws," *The Washington Post,* June 22, 1989.

Kastor, Elizabeth, and Barbara Feinman. "The Gridiron and the Fond Farewell," *The Washington Post,* March 28, 1988.

Kemp, Geoffrey. "Lessons of Lebanon: A Guideline for Future U.S. Policy," *Middle East Insight,* Summer 1988.

King, Warren. "Reagan Regarded AIDS 'Like It Was Measles'—His Doctor Found President Slow to Grasp Epidemic," *Seattle Times,* August 31, 1989.

Kirkpatrick, Jeane J. "Dictatorships and Double Standards," *Commentary,* November 1979.

Kirschten, Dick. "The Reagan Team Comes to Washington, Ready to Get Off to a Running Start," *National Journal,* November 15, 1980.

Kneeland, Douglas E. "Challenges to Statements Putting Reagan on the Defensive," *The New York Times,* April 13, 1980.

Kornheiser, Tony. "Tip O'Neill's Toughest Inning: The Sermon on the Mound," *The Washington Post,* May 31, 1981.

Krauthammer, Charles. "Nicaraguan Nettle," *The New Republic,* May 9, 1983.

———. "The Reagan Doctrine," *Time,* April 1, 1985.

Kunen, James S. "Patrick Buchanan," *People,* August 29, 1988.

Kurtz, Howard. "U.S. Jury Clears Marcos in Fraud Case; Khashoggi Also Acquitted," *The Washington Post,* July 3, 1990.

LaMar, Jacob V. "The Lonely World of a Refusenik," *Time,* June 6, 1988.

Lardner, George, Jr. "Bronx Jury Acquits Donovan," *The Washington Post,* May 26, 1987.

———. "McKay Reports 4 'Probable' Meese Offenses," *The Washington Post,* July 19, 1988.

———. "Meese Details White House Crisis; Fear of Impeachment Gripped Staff in Late '86, North Trial Told," *The Washington Post,* March 29, 1989.

———. "Reagan Urged Secrecy: North Trial Hears a Plan to Give Contras Third-Country Help," *The Washington Post,* March 11, 1989.

———. "Trial Told of Reagan's Contra Role," *The Washington Post,* March 16, 1989.

Lescaze, Lee. "Reagan Talks to Haig, Allen, on Ending Feud," *The Washington Post,* November 6, 1981.

———. "Reagan Uses Hotel Like White House; Reagan Wins Gamble, Emerges Unhurt," *The Washington Post,* October 24, 1981.

Lescaze, Lee, and Hobart Rowan. "Reagan Praises Cancun 'Success'; Leaders Give Upbeat Appraisal of Results of Cancun Summit," *The Washington Post,* October 24, 1981.

Letters to the Editors. *Time,* December 22, 1980.

MacPherson, Myra. "Regan," *The Washington Post,* February 13, 1985.

Marcus, Ruth. "Justice Dept. Report Sharply Criticizes Meese," *The Washington Post,* January 17, 1989.

———. "Meese Fires his Chief Spokesman," *The Washington Post,* May 17, 1988.

———. "U.S. Indicts Marcoses in $100 Million Plot," *The Washington Post,* October 22, 1988.

Marder, Murrey. "The U.S.-Soviet War of Words Escalates," *The Washington Post,* November 21, 1983.

May, Lee, and Laurie Becklund. "Citizen Reagans Are Home After Bittersweet Farewell," *Los Angeles Times,* January 21, 1989.

Mayer, Jane. "Vietnam Service Isn't on the Resumés of Some Vocal, Middle-Aged Hawks," *The Wall Street Journal,* February 11, 1985.

McCartney, Robert J. "Iran Says McFarlane, Others Came on Secret Mission to Tehran; Waite: Release Prospects 'Reasonably Strong'," *The Washington Post,* November 5, 1986.

McClain, John D. "Foreign Direct Investments in U.S. Rise 61 Pct.," *The Washington Post,* May 31, 1989.

McCombs, Phil. "Regan's Jest Desserts," *The Washington Post,* February 1, 1988.

McManus, Doyle, and Douglas Jehl. "Reagan Era: What Will History Say?" *Los Angeles Times,* August 21, 1988.

Merriwether, Heath. "Story was in next seat, but Baker kept it to himself," *The Miami Herald,* March 1, 1987.

Morin, Richard. "Demographic Line Between Slain, Slayer Indistinguishable," *The Washington Post,* January 1, 1989.

Morrow, Lance. "Yankee Doodle Magic," *Time,* July 7, 1986.

Motley, Langhorne A. "The Decision To Assist Grenada," statement before the House Armed Services Committee, January 24, 1984.

Nelson, Lars-Erik. "Ron's War—And the Real War," *New York Daily News,* December 16, 1983.

New York Daily News. Editorial, October 24, 1983.

———. "Ron Flies by Seat of Pants?" December 18, 1983.

Newsweek. "A Truly Open Mind," February 16, 1981.

———. "Goodbye to the Gipper," January 9, 1989.

———. "The Making of a New China Hand," May 7, 1984.

Noonan, Peggy. "Confessions of a White House Speechwriter," *The New York Times Magazine,* October 15, 1989.

———. "Who Was That Masked Man?," *Mirabella,* December 1989.

Novak, Michael. "People Are Moving Up, the American Way," *Los Angeles Times,* October 18, 1990.

Oberdorfer, Don. "At Reykjavik, Soviets Were Prepared and the U.S. Improvised," *The Washington Post,* February 16, 1987.

———. "Reagan & The World: Foreign Policy; Part I," *The Washington Post,* November 20, 1983.

———. " 'Disgrace'; Shultz's Roar on Policy-Making Got Results," *The Washington Post,* October 23, 1983.

Oberdorfer, Don, and John M. Goshko. "U.S. Set to Send Troops to Lebanon; Peace-Keeping Force," *The Washington Post,* July 7, 1982.

Oberdorfer, Don, and Martin Schram. "Haig Believes a Reagan Aide Is Campaigning

Against Him; Haig Believes a Reagan Aide Is Behind 'Guerrilla Campaign,' " *The Washington Post,* November 4, 1981.

Ostrow, Ronald J. "Panel Charges Pierce Steered Funds to Friends," *Los Angeles Times,* November 2, 1990.

Pearson, Richard. "AIDS Patient Ryan White Dies," *The Washington Post,* April 9, 1990.
People. "A New Round of Musical Chairs Claims Mike Deaver, the Last of Reagan's California Cronies," April 15, 1985.

————. "The President-Elect Talks About His Health, His Children and His Divorce," January 5, 1981.

Perry, James M. "For the Democrats, Pam's Is the Place for the Elite to Meet," *The Wall Street Journal,* October 8, 1981.

Pichirallo, Joe. "Hearings Suggest Reagan Had Wider Contra Role; Briefings During Ban Outlined by Admiral," *The Washington Post,* July 19, 1987.

Pincus, Walter. "Reagan Ordered Casey to Keep Iran Mission from Congress; White House Fails to Calm Concerns on Secret Deals," *The Washington Post,* November 15, 1986.

Public Opinion. "Opinion Roundup," April/May 1983.

Pyle, Amy, and Laurie Becklund. "Nancy Reagan Withdraws Support for Drug Facility," *Los Angeles Times,* May 27, 1989.

Quandt, William B. "Reagan's Lebanon Policy: Trial and Error," *Middle East Journal,* Spring 1984.

Raffensperger, Gene. "Reagan Saved Woman in '33 from Robber," *Des Moines Register,* January 28, 1984.

Reader's Digest, April 1944.

Reagan for President Research and Policy Division. "Ronald Reagan Speaks Out on the Issues," January 31, 1980.

Reagan, Ronald. "How to Make Yourself Important," *Photoplay,* August 1942.

————. "Margaret Thatcher and the Revival of the West," *National Review,* May 19, 1989.

————. " 'We Owe It to Ryan,' " *The Washington Post,* April 11, 1990.

Reedy, George E. "Discovering the Presidency," *The New York Times,* January 20, 1985.

Reid, T.R. "A Flirtation With Greed, but Bedrock Beliefs Stay Solid," *The Washington Post,* December 14, 1989.

Reinhold, Robert. "Man in the News; Restrained Pragmatist Anthony M. Kennedy," *The New York Times,* November 12, 1987.

Report of Secretary of Defense Harold Brown to the Congress on the FY 1982 Budget, FY 1983 Authorization Request and FY 1982–86 Defense Programs, January 19, 1981.

Report of the Department of Defense Commission on Beirut International Airport Terrorist Act, October 23, 1983. Released December 20, 1983.

Reston, James. "Notes from the Cellar," *The New York Times,* July 22, 1981.

Reuters. "Ron and Gorby Remember the Good Old Days," September 18, 1990.

Richburg, Keith B., and William Branigin. "Ferdinand Marcos Dies in Hawaii at 72," *The Washington Post,* September 29, 1989.

Roberts, Steven V., with Gary Cohen. "Villains of the S&L crisis," *U.S. News & World Report,* October 1, 1990.

Robinson, David. "He Should Have Spoken Sooner," letter to the editor, *The Washington Post,* April 14, 1990.

Robinson, Ralph. "Reagan keeps his advice in mind," *The Boston Globe,* July 31, 1981.

Rosenbaum, David. "Secord Recounts Being Told Reagan Knew of His Work," *The New York Times,* May 7, 1987.

Rowe, James L. Jr. "Interest Level at Historic High," *The Washington Post,* December 11, 1980.

Russell, Cristine. "AIDS Report Calls for Sex Education," *The Washington Post,* October 23, 1986.

Safire, William. "Dissareagan," *The New York Times,* June 7, 1982.

———. "Essay; Touching a Nerve," *The New York Times,* October 18, 1982.

———. "Mr. Option Three," *The New York Times,* December 5, 1985.

———. "Ten Myths About the Reagan Debacle," *The New York Times Magazine,* March 22, 1987.

———. "The Land Is Bright," *The New York Times,* January 22, 1981.

———. "Those Upraised Hands," *The New York Times,* June 18, 1981.

Samuelson, Robert J. "The Binge Is Over," *The Washington Post,* July 5, 1989.

Schafer, Susanne M. "Laxalt Says Reagan Brutalized by Debate Briefings," Associated Press, October 11, 1984.

———. "Reagan Now Experimenting With Hearing Aid in Each Ear," Associated Press, March 20, 1985.

Schmemann, Serge. "A Success, to a Point, for Gorbachev," *The New York Times,* October 1, 1986.

Schorr, Daniel. "Reagan Recants; His Path from Armageddon to Detente," *Los Angeles Times,* January 3, 1988.

Schram, Martin. "Caspar One-Note's Military March," *The Washington Post,* April 18, 1982.

———. "Group of Viewers Shifts Opinions but Not Its Votes," *The Washington Post,* October 9, 1984.

———. "White House Officials, Sen. Jepsen Reach Uneasy Truce on AWACS Flap," *The Washington Post,* February 12, 1982.

Shales, Tom. "Gorbachev, Up Close and Affable," *The Washington Post,* December 1, 1987.

———. "Shultz, His Medium and His Message; The Secretary Sends His Boss a Nationwide Signal," *The Washington Post,* November 18, 1986.

———. "The Gaffes, The Glories and a Short Goodbye," *The Washington Post,* January 21, 1989.

———. "Through the Safety Net; The Victims of Reagan's Administration," *The Washington Post,* April 21, 1982.

———. " 'White House:' A Star is Gone," *The Washington Post,* July 5, 1989.

Shields, Mark. "President Reagan's Wide World of Sports," *Inside Sports,* March 31, 1981.

Sidey, Hugh. "An Interview with the President," *Time,* December 8, 1986.

———. "Remembering the Sacrifices of D-Day," *Time,* June 11, 1984.

Skrzycki, Cindy. "Poll Finds Less Worker Emphasis on Materialism," *The Washington Post,* January 10, 1989.

Smith, Hedrick. "Reagan Upgrading Lebanon Presence," *The New York Times,* September 13, 1983.

———. "Reagan, Reflecting on Ottawa Parley, Praises Mitterrand," *The New York Times,* July 23, 1981.

———. "The Right Against Reagan," *The New York Times Magazine,* January 17, 1988.

Stockman, Dave. "The Stockman Manifesto," excerpts from his "Avoiding a GOP Economic Dunkirk," *The Washington Post,* December 14, 1980.

Taylor, Paul. "Defeat for Religious Right, Vindication for Civil Rights Groups; Issue of Racially Biased Schools Seen as Administration Fiasco," *The Washington Post,* May 25, 1983.

Thatcher, Margaret. "Reagan's Leadership, America's Recovery," *National Review,* December 30, 1988.

The New York Times. "Ronald Reagan's Flower Power," Editorial, June 9, 1982.

The Wall Street Journal. "Excerpts from the *Journal*'s Interview with the President," February 3, 1984.

The Washington Post. "American Troops in Beirut," Editorial, July 7, 1982.

———. "District's Homicide Count May Not Have Tied Record," October 31, 1989.

———. "Ronald Reagan's Summit," Editorial, May 29, 1988.

———. "Sizing Up the Kremlin," Editorial, February 1, 1981.

———. "The Poverty Figures," Editorial, September 1, 1988.

———. "The President's Speech," Editorial, March 5, 1987.

———. "The Republicans in Detroit; 'The Time Is Now . . . to Recapture our Destiny,' " text of Reagan's speech accepting the Republican nomination, July 18, 1980.

———. "The 'Terrible 20' Regulations," August 4, 1981.

———. Editorial, October 24, 1983.

The Washington Star. " 'Welfare Queen' Becomes Issue in Reagan Campaign," reprinted in *The New York Times,* February 15, 1976.

Thomas, Evan. "Fencing at the Fireside Summit," *Time,* December 2, 1985.

Thomas, Helen. "Reagan Forecasts Summit in '84," United Press International, May 19, 1983.

Timberg, Robert. "Ex-marine nobody knows becomes national security 'mover, shaker,' " Baltimore *Sun,* June 13, 1983.

———. "McFarlane tightens foreign policy grip," Baltimore *Sun,* February 6, 1985.

Time. April 13, 1981.

———. February 2, 1981.

———. "A Debt-Threatened Dream," May 24, 1982.

———. "A Growing Sense of Betrayal," October 4, 1982.

———. "A Message for Moscow," February 9, 1981.

———. "A Problem that Cannot Be Buried," October 14, 1985.

———. "Big Labor Cries 'Foul,' " March 2, 1981.

———. "Booms, Busts and Birth of a Rust Bowl," December 27, 1982.

———. "Challenge to Change," March 2, 1981.

———. "Co-Starring at the White House," January 14, 1985.

———. "D-Day in Grenada," November 7, 1983.

———. "Every Region, Every Age Group, Almost Every Voting Bloc," November 19, 1984.

———. "Men of the Year," January 2, 1984.

———. "On Soviet Morality," February 16, 1981.

———. "Paying More for Money," March 8, 1982.

———. "Tales of Ten Cities," January 31, 1983.

———. "The Biggest Challenge," January 19, 1981.

———. "The Dismal Science Hits a Nerve," January 24, 1983.

———. "Who Knew What And When Did They Know It?" December 8, 1986.

Turner, Stansfield. "MX Is a Serious Mistake," *The Washington Star,* March 29, 1981, reprinted from *The New York Times Magazine.*

U.S. Government Printing Office. *Economic Report of the President,* February 1988.

U.S. House of Representatives Select Committee on Children, Youth and Families. *Children and Families: Key Trends in the 1980s,* December 1988.

Ullmann, Owen. "Mr. Everyman," *The Philadelphia Inquirer,* August 17, 1986.

United Press International. "Remarks Before Signing the Treaty," *The Washington Post,* December 9, 1987.

———. "Senate Confirms Koop, 68–24," November 17, 1981.

USA Today. Editorial, October 24, 1983.

Vasilyev, Gennady. "A Political Portrait: Reagan's Best Role," *Pravda,* January 20, 1989, quoted in *The Current Digest of the Soviet Press,* February 15, 1989.

Waldman, Myron S. "Growing Up in the Midwest," *Newsday,* January 18, 1981.

Weinberger, Caspar. "The Uses of Military Power," remarks to the National Press Club, November 28, 1984.

Weinraub, Bernard. "Criticism on Iran and Other Issues Put Reagan's Aides on Defensive," *The New York Times,* November 16, 1986.

Weisman, Steven R. "Reagan Ends Trip as Thousands Jam Shanghai Streets," *The New York Times,* May 1, 1984.

———. "Western White House; How Reagan Spent His Vacation, Really Spent It," *The New York Times,* August 15, 1984.

Werner Emmy E. "Resilient Offspring of Alcoholics: A Longitudinal Study from Birth to Age 18," *Journal of Studies on Alcohol,* January 1986.

White, Theodore H. "Summing Up," *The New York Times Magazine,* April 25, 1982.

Whitman, David. "Ronald Reagan and Tax Exemptions for Racist Schools," case study prepared for use at the Center for Press, Politics and Public Policy at the Kennedy School of Government, Harvard University, November 7, 1984.

Will, George. "How Reagan Changed America," *Newsweek,* January 9, 1989.

Woodward, Bob, and Lou Cannon. "McFarlane Note Told of Saudi Cash; Iran-Contra Probers Look for Covert Action 'Slush' Fund," *The Washington Post,* March 19, 1987.

Woodward, Kenneth L. "Arguing Armageddon," *Newsweek,* November 5, 1984.

INDEX